A History of Western Society

Eighth Edition

A History of Western Society

Volume I
From Antiquity to the Enlightenment

John P. McKay
University of Illinois at Urbana-Champaign

Bennett D. Hill
Georgetown University

John Buckler
University of Illinois at Urbana-Champaign

HOUGHTON MIFFLIN COMPANY
Boston   New York

Publisher: Charles Hartford
Senior Sponsoring Editor: Nancy Blaine
Senior Development Editor: Julie Swasey
Editorial Associate: Annette Fantasia
Senior Project Editor: Christina Horn
Editorial Assistant: Michelle O'Berg
Senior Art and Design Coordinator: Jill Haber
Senior Photo Editor: Jennifer Meyer Dare
Senior Composition Buyer: Sarah Ambrose
Manufacturing Coordinator: Chuck Dutton
Senior Marketing Manager: Sandra McGuire
Marketing Assistant: Molly Parke

Text credits:
Page 558: Poem by Joost van den Vondel, quoted in *Europe in the Seventeenth Century,* by David Ogg. Copyright © 1967 by A & C Black, Ltd.

Volume I cover image: Hans Holbein the Younger (1497–1543), *Portrait of a Young Merchant,* probably the Nuremberg patrician Hans von Muffel, age 28, painted 1541. Kunsthistorisches Museum, Vienna, Austria/Erich Lessing/Art Resource, NY.

Printed in the U.S.A.

Library of Congress Control Number: 2004116682

ISBN: 0-618-52267-0

1 2 3 4 5 6 7 8 9-VH-09 08 07 06 05

About the Authors

John P. McKay Born in St. Louis, Missouri, John P. McKay received his B.A. from Wesleyan University (1961), his M.A. from the Fletcher School of Law and Diplomacy (1962), and his Ph.D. from the University of California, Berkeley (1968). He began teaching history at the University of Illinois in 1966 and became a professor there in 1976. John won the Herbert Baxter Adams Prize for his book *Pioneers for Profit: Foreign Entrepreneurship and Russian Industrialization, 1885–1913* (1970). He has also written *Tramways and Trolleys: The Rise of Urban Mass Transport in Europe* (1976) and has translated Jules Michelet's *The People* (1973). His research has been supported by fellowships from the Ford Foundation, the Guggenheim Foundation, the National Endowment for the Humanities, and IREX. He has written well over a hundred articles, book chapters, and reviews, which have appeared in numerous publications, including *The American Historical Review, Business History Review, The Journal of Economic History,* and *Slavic Review.* He contributed extensively to C. Stewart and P. Fritzsche, eds., *Imagining the Twentieth Century* (1997).

Bennett D. Hill A native of Philadelphia, Bennett D. Hill earned an A.B. from Princeton (1956) and advanced degrees from Harvard (A.M., 1958) and Princeton (Ph.D., 1963). He taught history at the University of Illinois at Urbana, where he was department chairman from 1978 to 1981. He has published *English Cistercian Monasteries and Their Patrons in the Twelfth Century* (1968), *Church and State in the Middle Ages* (1970), and articles in *Analecta Cisterciensia, The New Catholic Encyclopaedia, The American Benedictine Review,* and *The Dictionary of the Middle Ages.* His reviews have appeared in *The American Historical Review, Speculum, The Historian,* the *Journal of World History,* and *Library Journal.* He is one of the contributing editors to *The Encyclopedia of World History* (2001). He has been a Fellow of the American Council of Learned Societies and served on the editorial board of *The American Benedictine Review,* on committees of the National Endowment for the Humanities, and as Vice President of the American Catholic Historical Association (1995–1996). A Benedictine monk of St. Anselm's Abbey in Washington, D.C., he is also a Visiting Professor at Georgetown University.

John Buckler Born in Louisville, Kentucky, John Buckler received his B.A. (summa cum laude) from the University of Louisville in 1967. Harvard University awarded him the Ph.D. in 1973. From 1984 to 1986 he was an Alexander von Humboldt Fellow at the Institut für Alte Geschichte, University of Munich. He has lectured at the Fondation Hardt at the University of Geneva and at the University of Freiburg. He is currently a professor of Greek history at the University of Illinois. In 1980 Harvard University Press published his *Theban Hegemony, 371–362 B.C.* He has also published *Philip II and the Sacred War* (Leiden 1989) and co-edited *BOIOTIKA: Vorträge vom 5. Internationalen Böotien-Kolloquium* (Munich 1989). In 2003 he published *Aegean Greece in the Fourth Century B.C.* In the following year appeared his editions of W. M. Leake, *Travels in the Morea* (three volumes), and Leake's *Peloponnesiaca.* He has also published numerous articles in various international journals.

Brief Contents

Contents

Chapter 1

Chapter 2

Chapter 6

Chapter 7

Chapter 8

Chapter 9

Chapter 10

Chapter 11

The Creativity and Vitality of the High Middle Ages   331

Chapter 12

The Crisis of the Later Middle Ages   379

Chapter 13

European Society in the Age of the Renaissance 413

Chapter 14

Reform and Renewal in the Christian Church 453

Maps

Listening to the Past

Preface

A **History of Western Society** grew out of the authors' desire to infuse new life into the study of Western civilization. We knew that historians were using imaginative questions and innovative research to open up vast new areas of historical interest and knowledge. We also recognized that these advances had dramatically affected the subject of European economic, intellectual, and, especially, social history, while new research and fresh interpretations were also revitalizing the study of the traditional mainstream of political, diplomatic, and religious development. Despite history's vitality as a discipline, however, it seemed to us that both the broad public and the intelligentsia were generally losing interest in the past. That, fortunately for us all, has not proven the case.

It was our conviction, based on considerable experience introducing large numbers of students to the broad sweep of Western civilization, that a book reflecting current trends could excite readers and inspire a renewed interest in history and our Western heritage. Our strategy was twofold. First, we made social history a core element of our work. We not only incorporated recent research by social historians but also sought to recreate the life of ordinary people in appealing human terms. At the same time we were determined to give great economic, political, cultural, and intellectual developments the attention they unquestionably deserve. We wanted to give individual readers and instructors a balanced, integrated perspective so that they could pursue—on their own or in the classroom—those themes and questions that they found particularly exciting and significant. In an effort to realize fully the potential of our fresh yet balanced approach, we made many changes, large and small, in the editions that followed.

Changes in the Eighth Edition

In preparing the Eighth Edition we have worked hard to keep our book up-to-date by including as much valuable and relevant scholarship as possible. We have also strengthened our distinctive yet balanced approach to a wide range of topics. Several main lines of revision have guided our many changes.

"Images in Society" Feature

A photo essay, "Images in Society," represents a distinctive feature of this Eighth Edition. The complete text now contains seven essays (three new to this edition), each consisting of a short narrative with questions, accompanied by several pictures. The goal of the feature is to encourage students to think critically: to view and compare visual illustrations and draw conclusions about the societies and cultures that produced those objects. Thus, in Chapter 1 appears the discovery of the "Iceman," the frozen remains of an unknown herdsman. "The Roman Villa at Chedworth" in Britain mirrors Roman provincial culture (Chapter 6). The essay "From Romanesque to Gothic" treats the architectural shift in medieval church building, and aims to show how the Gothic cathedral reflected the ideals and values of medieval society (Chapter 11). Chapter 14 presents "From Reformation to Baroque," which examines both the Protestant and Catholic views of religious art. Moving to modern times, the focus in Chapter 19 changes to "London: The Remaking of a Great City," which depicts how Londoners rebuilt their city after a great catastrophe. "Class and Gender Boundaries in Women's Fashion, 1850–1914" studies women's clothing in relationship to women's evolving position in society and gender relations (Chapter 24). "Pablo Picasso and Modern Art" looks at some of Picasso's greatest paintings to gain insight into his principles and the modernist revolution in art (Chapter 28).

"Individuals in Society" Feature

Included in each chapter is the feature "Individuals in Society," which offers a brief study of a woman, man, or group, informing us about the societies in which they lived. Each study or biographical sketch has been carefully integrated into the body of the text. The "Individuals in Society" feature grew out of our long-standing focus on people's lives and the varieties of historical experience, and we believe that readers will empathize with these human beings as they themselves seek to define their own identities. The spotlighting of individuals, both famous and obscure, perpetuates the greater attention to cultural and intellectual developments that we used to invigorate our social history in earlier editions, and it reflects changing interests within the historical profession as well as the development of "micro-history."

The range of men and women we consider is broad. For this edition, and sometimes at readers' suggestion, we have dropped some individuals and replaced them with others who add their own contributions to history. They include such fascinating people as Quintus Sertorius, who tried to create a Roman-style state in Spain (Chapter 5); Ebo of Reims, the son of a serf whom Charlemagne liberated, who rose to become archbishop under Louis the Pious (Chapter 8); Vera Brittain, an English writer and nurse during World War I who contributed a famous autobiographical work entitled *Testament of Youth* (1933) (Chapter 27); Primo Levi, an Italian Jew who wrote of his experiences in a Nazi concentration camp (Chapter 29); and Kofi Annan, the present secretary-general of the United Nations (Chapter 31).

Expanded Ethnic and Geographic Scope

In the Eighth Edition we have added significantly more discussion of groups and regions that are frequently shortchanged in the general histories of Europe and Western civilization. This expanded scope reflects the renewed awareness within the profession of Europe's enormous historical diversity, as well as the efforts of contemporary Europeans to understand the ambivalent and contested meanings of their national, regional, ethnic, and pan-European identities. Examples of this enlarged scope include a new discussion of the Sea Peoples (Chapter 3); slavery in eastern Europe (Chapter 10); expanded coverage of the peasant revolts to include revolts in Flanders (Chapter 12); the Reformation in eastern Europe (Chapter 14); the Columbian Exchange (Chapter 15); an examination of the contribution of slaves to the Atlantic economy (Chapter 19); railroad construction in Africa, Asia, and Latin America and a discussion of British women and their role in imperial India (Chapter 26); and the Armenian genocide (Chapter 27). We have devoted special attention in the Eighth Edition to increasing the treatment of the Islamic world. Examples include an updated discussion of the basic tenets of Islam (Chapter 7); the slave trade between Europe and the Muslim world (Chapter 8);

Moorish Spain (Chapter 9); the Arab influence in Sicily (Chapter 11); revised material on the Ottoman Empire (Chapter 17); the French conquest of Algeria (Chapter 23); the Ottomans and the war in Asia and Africa and peace treaties affecting Arab nations and the creation of Israel (Chapter 27); and the debate over Islamic headscarves in France, Islamic fundamentalists, and the wars in Afghanistan and Iraq (Chapter 31).

Incorporation of Recent Scholarship

This edition includes the best of previous scholarship, while blending in the most important recent findings. Learning is fortunately never static. We have also strived to include new material on women and gender relations. The process has led to some organization changes, as can be seen below. In Chapter 1 the whole concept of "What Is History and Why" now explores the very concept of what we mean by the "West." Without Eurocentricism, the discussion simply points to the many contributions of Western societies to the full realm of human progress. This new edition, as previous ones, highlights human contacts. Thus, in Chapter 2 updated material on the siege of Jerusalem includes both Jewish and Assyrian accounts of the episode. In so doing, readers understand how historians understand their sources. Chapter 3 gives expanded discussion of life in the countryside and revises material on Spartan and Athenian women. Cultural aspects include recent findings on religion, especially on local and domestic cults. Chapter 4 contains a new "Listening to the Past" that confronts the controversial notion that Alexander the Great wanted to create a "Brotherhood of Man" and includes new material on Antiochus II and his treatment of the Jews. Chapter 5 includes expanded discussion of clientage, of Roman women and child rearing, and of those client kingdoms that subsequently form part of the Roman Empire. Chapter 6 features a new discussion of the Lost Gospels, early Christian writings that were not included in the New Testament. There is also a fully updated section on the movement from the classical world to late antiquity.

In Chapter 7 readers can find an updated discussion of Islam and its tenets, including reference to the "Five Pillars of Islam." Chapter 8 continues the theme of contacts between the European and Islam worlds by including a new section on the slave trade between Europe and the Muslim world. Chapter 9 furthers the link between Europe and its Eastern neighbors, covering the Crusades and the role of women in them and adding a section on Moorish Spain. An important feature of Chapter 10 is the treatment of slavery in eastern

Europe and new material on medieval rural economy. Chapter 11 incorporates a new discussion of the Arab influence in Sicily and offers a thoughtful appreciation of the rising commercial class. Chapter 14 inspects the somewhat neglected topic of the Reformation in eastern Europe, linking it to the changes occurring in western Europe. Chapter 15 examines not only the religious views of the period but also the debates among religious writers about the role of women in society, as well as scholarly debates over witch-hunts. A new section on the Columbian Exchange has also been added to this chapter. Chapter 16 is particularly important because it explores the evolution of the state and defines its relations with religious elements of society. Much of this chapter has been revised and new material on the Edict of Nantes added.

Chapters 17–20 present such topics as recent material on the Ottoman Empire, a discussion of slaves and the Atlantic economy, and treatment of abandoned children and the creation of foundling homes. Chapter 19 also contains a new "Images in Society" feature on "London: The Remaking of a Great City." Chapter 22 contributes attention to the consequences of industrialization for the working class of England. There is a new discussion of the French conquest of Algeria after 1830 in Chapter 23. Chapter 26 examines recent studies on railroad construction in Africa, Asia, and Latin America, as well as on British women and their role in imperial India. This chapter also includes a new "Listening to the Past" feature on British women in India. Chapter 27 has been fully revised to incorporate more material on the Middle East. There is expanded coverage of the breakup of the Ottoman Empire, the creation of Israel, and the effects of the peace treaties on Arab nations, as well as a new discussion of the Armenian genocide of 1915.

Chapter 30 includes a rewritten section on decolonization that stresses the agency of former colonies and new material on the development of the German Green political movement. Chapter 31 addresses such current topics as the challenges of globalization, the uncertainty of the effects of Russian president Putin's administration, and the entry of former communist states into the European Union. Also pertinent are the new sections on the al-Qaeda attack of September 11, 2001, and the wars in Afghanistan and Iraq and their effects on European-American relations.

Revised Full-Color Art and Map Programs

Finally, the illustrative component of our work has been carefully revised. We have added many new illustrations

to our extensive art program, which includes more than four hundred color reproductions, letting great art and important events come alive. As in earlier editions, all illustrations have been carefully selected to complement the text, and all carry informative captions, based on thorough research, that enhance their value. Artwork remains an integral part of our book; the past can speak in pictures as well as in words. The use of full color serves to clarify the maps and graphs and to enrich the textual material. The maps and map captions have been updated to correlate directly to the text, and new maps have been added in Chapters 8, 10, and 27.

Distinctive Features

In addition to the "Images in Society" and "Individuals in Society" essays, distinctive features from earlier editions guide the reader in the process of historical understanding. Many of these features also show how historians sift through and evaluate evidence. Our goal is to suggest how historians actually work and think. We want the reader to think critically and to realize that history is neither a list of cut-and-dried facts nor a senseless jumble of conflicting opinions. To help students and instructors realize this goal, we have significantly expanded the discussion of "what is history" in Chapter 1 of this edition.

Primary Sources

A two-page feature, entitled "Listening to the Past," extends and illuminates a major historical issue considered in each of the text's chapters. In the new edition we have reviewed our selections and made judicious substitutions. For example, in Chapter 4 comes a discussion of the much-debated topic of "Alexander and the Brotherhood of Man." Chapter 10 introduces the reader to the fascinating "Pilgrim's Guide to Santiago de Compostela." Chapter 11 provides a selection dealing with early Islamic views on trade, again based on recent scholarship. Chapter 26 treats the privileges and tribulations of British women in India. The feature in Chapter 29, "Stalin Justifies the Five-Year Plan," explores the controversies surrounding Stalin's attempt to turn the Soviet Union into one unified and modern government. Chapter 31 takes a contemporary examination of "The West in World Affairs" by including two contrasting documents on American foreign policy.

Each primary source opens with a problem-setting introduction and closes with "Questions for Analysis" that invite students to evaluate the evidence as historians would. Drawn from a range of writings addressing a variety of social, cultural, political, and intellectual issues, these sources promote active involvement and critical interpretation. Selected for their interest and importance and carefully fitted into their historical context, these sources do indeed allow the student to "listen to the past" and to observe how history has been shaped by individual men and women, some of them great aristocrats, others ordinary folk.

Problems of Historical Interpretation

We believe that including examples of problems of historical interpretations in our text helps our readers develop the critical-thinking skills that are among the most precious benefits of studying history. Examples of this more open-ended, interpretative approach include the debate over the concept of history itself and our notion of "the West" (Chapter 1), an examination of the transition from antiquity to the early Middle Ages and a discussion of the importance of the Lost Gospels (Chapter 6), the question of European racism in the Middle Ages (Chapter 12), the issue of gender in the Italian cities of the Renaissance (Chapter 13), the renewed debate on personal and collective responsibility for the Holocaust (Chapter 29), the dynamics of the great purges in the Soviet Union (Chapter 29), the process of reconstruction in eastern Europe, the debate over globalization, and the issue of American unilateralism in the world today (Chapter 31).

Improved Chapter Features

Other distinctive features from earlier editions have been reviewed and improved in this Eighth Edition. To help guide the reader toward historical understanding, we pose specific historical questions at the beginning of each chapter. These questions are then answered in the course of each chapter, and each chapter concludes with a concise summary of its findings. All of the questions and summaries have been re-examined and frequently revised in order to maximize the usefulness of this popular feature.

Comparative timelines begin each chapter and organize historical events into three categories: political/military, social/economic, and intellectual/religious. In addition, topic-specific timelines appear at key points throughout the book. Once again we provide a unified timeline at the end of the text. Comprehensive and easy to locate, this useful timeline allows students to compare simultaneous political, economic, social, cultural, intellectual, and scientific developments over the centuries.

A list of Key Terms concludes each chapter. These terms are highlighted in boldface in the text. The student may use these terms to test his or her understanding of the chapter's material.

In addition to posing chapter-opening questions and presenting more problems in historical interpretation, we have quoted extensively from a wide variety of primary sources in the narrative, demonstrating in our use of these quotations how historians evaluate evidence. Thus primary sources are examined as an integral part of the narrative as well as presented in extended form in the "Listening to the Past" chapter feature. We believe that such an extensive program of both integrated and separate primary source excerpts will help readers learn to interpret and think critically.

Each chapter concludes with carefully selected suggestions for further reading. These suggestions are briefly described to help readers know where to turn to continue thinking and learning about the Western world. Also, chapter bibliographies have been thoroughly revised and updated to keep them current with the vast amount of new work being done in many fields.

Flexible Format

Western civilization courses differ widely in chronological structure from one campus to another. To accommodate the various divisions of historical time into intervals that fit a two-quarter, three-quarter, or two-semester period, A History of Western Society is published in four versions, three of which embrace the complete work:

- One-volume hardcover edition: A HISTORY OF WESTERN SOCIETY
- Two-volume paperback: A HISTORY OF WESTERN SOCIETY, *Volume I: From Antiquity to the Enlightenment* (Chapters 1–17); *Volume II: From Absolutism to the Present* (Chapters 16–31)
- Three-volume paperback: A HISTORY OF WESTERN SOCIETY, *Volume A: From Antiquity to 1500* (Chapters 1–13); *Volume B: From the Renaissance to 1815* (Chapters 12–21); *Volume C: From the Revolutionary Era to the Present* (Chapters 21–31)
- A HISTORY OF WESTERN SOCIETY, *Since 1300* (Chapters 12–31), for courses on Europe since the Renaissance

Note that overlapping chapters in both the two- and the three-volume sets permit still wider flexibility in matching the appropriate volume with the opening and closing dates of a course term.

Ancillaries

Learning and teaching ancillaries also contribute to the usefulness of the text. The new *Houghton Mifflin History Companion* is a collection of resources designed to complement the use of this edition. It is organized according to the chapters in the text and has three parts—the *Instructor Companion,* the *Student Research Companion,* and the *Student Study Companion.* First, the *Instructor Companion* is a free, searchable CD-ROM featuring hundreds of historical images and maps in PowerPoint format. Each image is accompanied by notes that place it in its proper historical context. The maps and images are correlated to the text's table of contents and are also searchable by other criteria. They are formatted for easy presentation in the classroom. The CD-ROM also includes the *HM Testing* program, a computerized version of the *Test Items* to enable instructors to alter, replace, or add questions, as well as resources from the *Instructor's Resource Manual.*

Second, the *Student Research Companion* is a free web-based tool with one hundred interactive maps and hundreds of primary sources. The primary sources include headnotes that provide pertinent background information and questions that students can answer and e-mail to their instructors. This website also provides students and teachers with additional information for the documents that are featured in the text. It has lengthy, searchable bibliographies that permit students to launch research assignments or pursue personal interests while giving teachers an outstanding opportunity to get directed guidance to the best historical literature in fields outside their own areas of expertise.

Third, the *Student Study Companion* is a free online study guide to accompany our text. It incorporates aspects of the last edition's print study guide and student website, as well as a variety of new interactive resources created by Laura Trauth of the Community College of Baltimore Country, Essex, and Carol Bresnahan Menning of the University of Toledo. The *Student Study Companion* contains a wealth of tutorial resources, including self-tests (ACE questions) with feedback, chronological ordering exercises, review questions, web activities, and interactive exercises on the "Individuals in Society" and "Images in Society" features. There are also a variety of review materials on the site, such as learning objectives, chapter summaries, outlines, a glossary of key terms, a searchable bibliography, links to web resources, and even general material on good study techniques. Finally, visitors to the site can also access some of the older "Individuals in Society" features that did not make it into the Eighth Edition.

The print *Instructor's Resource Manual and Test Items,* thoroughly revised by John Reisbord of Vassar College, includes instructional objectives, annotated chapter outlines, suggestions for lectures and discussion, term paper and class activity topics, further information on the "Images in Society" features, primary source exercises, map activities, and lists of Internet and audiovisual resources. The test items section offers identification, multiple-choice, map, and essay questions for a total of approximately two thousand test items.

For institutions using either the Blackboard™ or WebCT™ platforms, we have designed course cartridges that include *HM Testing,* learning objectives, chapter summaries, study outlines, quizzes, and other study resources.

Finally, a set of full-color Map Transparencies of all the maps in the text is available on adoption.

Acknowledgments

It is a pleasure to thank the many instructors who read and critiqued the manuscript through its development:

Janice Amos
Florida Community College–Jacksonville

Jay Bergman
Central Connecticut State University

Margaret M. Bostwick
John Jay College of Criminal Justice

Allan Christelow
Idaho State University

James B. Collins
Georgetown University

Melissa Barden Dowling
Southern Methodist University

Joanne M. Ferraro
San Diego State University

Dennis Frey, Jr.
Mercer County Community College

Alison Futrell
University of Arizona

Elizabeth Heineman
University of Iowa

Blair T. Hinson
Tri-County Technical College

Thomas Kuehn
Clemson University

Lawrence Langer
University of Connecticut

Paul Douglas Lockhart
Wright State University

Elizabeth Makowski
Texas State University at San Marcos

Brent Maner
Kansas State University

Sarah Miller
Lourdes College

Jo Ann H. Moran Cruz
Georgetown University

Joe Perry
Georgia State University

Laura L. Phillips
Eastern Washington University

Anna Marie Roos
University of Minnesota-Duluth

Gavriel Rosenfeld
Fairfield University

Paul Teverow
Missouri Southern State University–Joplin

Leslie Tuttle
University of Kansas

It is also a pleasure to thank our many editors at Houghton Mifflin for their efforts over many years. To Christina Horn, who guided production in the ever-more intensive electronic age, and to Julie Swasey, our development editor, we express our special appreciation. And we thank Carole Frohlich for her contributions in photo research and selection.

Many of our colleagues at the University of Illinois and at Georgetown University continued to provide information and stimulation, often without even knowing it. We thank them for it. Bennett Hill wishes to express his appreciation to Donald Franklin for his support and encouragement in the preparation of this Eighth Edition. John Buckler thanks Professor Jack Cargill for his advice on topics in Chapter 2. And he wishes to thank Professor Nicholas Yalouris, former General Inspector of Antiquities, for his kind permission to publish the mosaic from Elis, Greece, in Chapter 3. He also wishes to thank Dr. Amy C. Smith, Curator of the Ure Museum of Archaeology of the University of Reading for her kind permission to publish the vase on page 63. John McKay expresses his deep appreciation to Jo Ann McKay for her sharp-eyed editorial support and unfailing encouragement.

Each of us has benefited from the criticism of his co-authors, although each of us assumes responsibility for what he has written. John Buckler has written the first six chapters; Bennett Hill has continued the narrative through Chapter 16; and John McKay has written Chapters 17 through 31. Finally, we continue to welcome the many comments and suggestions that have come from our readers, for they have helped us greatly in this ongoing endeavor.

J. P. M.   B. D. H.   J. B.

A History of Western Society

Peace Panel, Standard of Ur. This scene depicts the royal family on the upper band and various conquered peoples, bringing the king tribute, on the lower bands. *(Courtesy of the Trustees of the British Museum)*

chapter

1 Origins

*T*he civilization and cultures of the modern Western world, like great rivers, have many sources. These sources have flowed from many places and directions. Peoples in western Europe developed numerous communities uniquely their own but also sharing some common features. They mastered such diverse subjects as astronomy, mathematics, geometry, trigonometry, engineering, religious practices, and social organization. Yet the earliest of these peoples did not record their learning and lore in systems of writing. Their lives and customs are consequently largely lost to us.

In the East, however, other early peoples confronted many of the same basic challenges as those in the West. They also made progress, but they took the important step of recording their experiences in writing. The most enduring innovations occurred in the ancient Near East, a region that includes the lands bordering the Mediterranean's eastern shore, the Arabian peninsula, parts of northeastern Africa, and perhaps above all Mesopotamia, the area of modern Iraq. Fundamental to the development of Western civilization and culture was the invention of writing by the Sumerians, which allowed knowledge of the past to be preserved. It also facilitated the spread and accumulation of learning, science, and literature. Ancient Near Eastern civilizations also produced the first written law codes, as well as religious concepts that still permeate daily life. Writing is the primary reason modern people look to the East as the richest sources of their origins.

But how do we know and understand these things? Before embarking on the study of history, it is necessary to ask, "What is it?" Only then can the peoples and events of tens of thousands of years be placed into a coherent whole. Once the nature of history is understood, further questions can be asked and reasonably answered. Specifically for this chapter,

- What were the fundamental Neolithic contributions to the rise of Western civilization?
- What caused Mesopotamian culture to become predominate in most of the ancient Near East?
- How did the Egyptians contribute to this vast story?

- What did the arrival of the Hittites on the frontiers of Mesopotamia and Egypt mean to the more advanced cultures of their new neighbors?

These are the questions we will explore in this chapter.

What Is History and Why?

The term "history" comes from the Greek word *historie,* coined by Herodotus in the fifth century B.C. For him it meant the record of his investigations and inquiries into the past, which he published for future generations. Since his initial venture, history has remained the effort to reconstruct the past to discover what people thought, what they did, and how their beliefs and actions continue to influence human life. To appreciate the past fully, we must put it into perspective so that we can understand the factors that have helped to shape us as individuals, the society in which we live, and the nature of other people's societies. Why else should we study civilizations as separated from ours through time, distance, and culture as classical Greece, medieval Germany, and modern Russia? Although most of the people involved in these epochs are long dead, what they did has touched everyone alive today.

To answer the questions mentioned above, historians examine a variety of evidence. They usually begin with primary sources, firsthand accounts by people who lived through the events, people in the best position to know what happened, who was responsible for it, why it happened, and what it meant. Individuals left numerous narratives and many other types of literary documents recording their experiences; the human tendency to keep the past alive produces a huge collection of writings. In addition to detailed narratives, there are chronicles, in which people noted events in their chronological order (therefore the name) and sometimes offered brief explanations of what occurred. A unique literary source for the record of antiquity is papyrology, the study of documents written on manuscripts made from papyrus, a plant that grows abundantly in Egypt. Ancient peoples ranging from inhabitants of the Old Kingdom of Egypt to those living during the Roman period recorded not only literature but also deeds, contracts, and descriptions of local customs. In the medieval period scribes produced thousands of documents giving detailed accounts of agricultural life on manors—how they were run, what the local customs were, and how society actually functioned. These scribes, generally Christian monks, also left a record of religious thinking and political affairs. Whether written thousands of years ago or reported in the morning newspapers, these records constitute the primary sources upon which history is built.

Inscriptions are another literary source of information about the past. An inscription is anything written on imperishable material such as stone. Societies have often carved their messages in stone for several important reasons. First, any literate person could understand them. They also served as public records erected in open places for all to see. Documents ranging from ancient treaties that have survived the ravages of time, to religious proclamations of faith and honorific decrees issued during the medieval period, to the Vietnam memorial in Washington can all be considered inscriptions. Even the simple dog tag worn by members of our armed forces is a historical inscription. Coins, too, often bear inscriptions. During the Roman Empire the emperors recorded their regnal dates on their currency, thus giving a public record of their reign. In the United States today, many recent quarters proclaim when various states entered the Union, some pertinent symbol, and the date of issue. No matter what their form, these are all written records.

Further evidence of the importance of literary sources, especially in the contemporary world, comes from official statistics covering almost everything from the annual number of deaths in automobile accidents to the daily results of the stock market. Even e-mail ensures the quick and wide dispersal of information throughout the world. All of these written materials provide historians with intriguing raw resources.

Historians also receive help from nonliterary sources such as archaeology. Excavations of various sites have revealed much information from all periods that is not present in the written record. So-called museum archaeologists make sense of what field archaeologists have found. New explorations of long lost sites have in many cases literally uncovered the physical remains of earlier cultures. Archaeology has thus proven invaluable in providing a unique, visible picture of how people actually lived, and comparisons of these findings document how cultures developed. Many travelers today walk the streets of Ephesus, where Paul the Apostle preached. Current excavations at Old Sarum in England vividly reveal how its prehistoric society gave way to the new Christianity: the old pagan mound still rises above the newly excavated early but sophisticated Christian cathedral. In the United States itself archaeology has shed light on the first years of European habitation in New York City and on the lives of Native Americans in the West.

In the face of this remarkable body of literary and nonliterary evidence, historians must try to distinguish the accurate from the false and biased. They do so by focusing on the earliest information first. They compare various versions of particular events or large trends with one another. Some people who have left evidence of the past

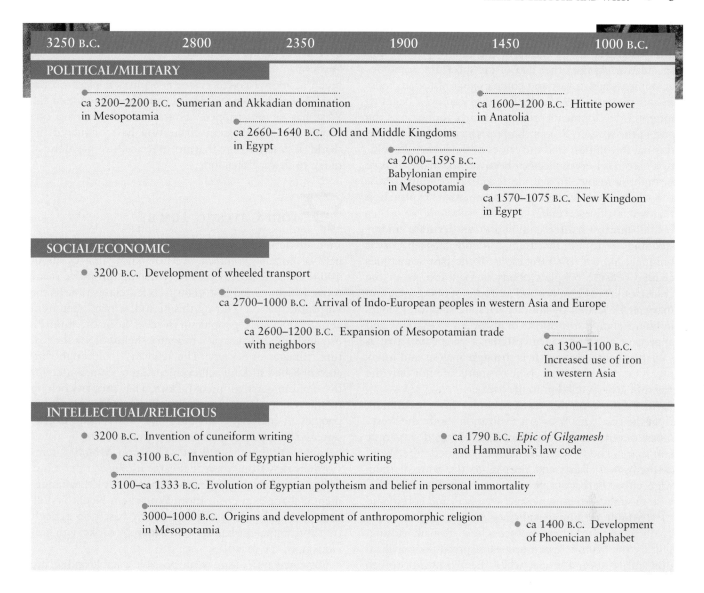

3250 B.C.	2800	2350	1900	1450	1000 B.C.

POLITICAL/MILITARY

● ca 3200–2200 B.C. Sumerian and Akkadian domination in Mesopotamia

● ca 2660–1640 B.C. Old and Middle Kingdoms in Egypt

● ca 1600–1200 B.C. Hittite power in Anatolia

● ca 2000–1595 B.C. Babylonian empire in Mesopotamia

● ca 1570–1075 B.C. New Kingdom in Egypt

SOCIAL/ECONOMIC

● 3200 B.C. Development of wheeled transport

● ca 2700–1000 B.C. Arrival of Indo-European peoples in western Asia and Europe

● ca 2600–1200 B.C. Expansion of Mesopotamian trade with neighbors

● ca 1300–1100 B.C. Increased use of iron in western Asia

INTELLECTUAL/RELIGIOUS

● 3200 B.C. Invention of cuneiform writing

● ca 3100 B.C. Invention of Egyptian hieroglyphic writing

● ca 1790 B.C. *Epic of Gilgamesh* and Hammurabi's law code

● 3100–ca 1333 B.C. Evolution of Egyptian polytheism and belief in personal immortality

● 3000–1000 B.C. Origins and development of anthropomorphic religion in Mesopotamia

● ca 1400 B.C. Development of Phoenician alphabet

were more intelligent or better informed than others, and their testimony is preferred by historians and indeed strengthened by other writers who independently reported the same things. When two or more dependable sources record the same thing in the same way, historians conclude that they present an accurate account of events.

Once historians decide which sources are reliable, they use this information to establish facts or to explain the meaning of their findings. Their conclusions, when published, are considered secondary sources, scholarly interpretations of what they and others discovered. For instance, a scholar who finds an undiscovered manuscript reads it to understand its contribution to existing historical knowledge. The next question becomes how to fit it into what is already known. The problem then becomes

whether the manuscript is accurate and whether it agrees with known sources. If it does, it strengthens their value. If, however, it does not, scholars must reopen the whole question of what actually happened. In short, history must be rethought on the very basis of every new piece of evidence.

Understanding of the past does not necessarily come easily—that is one of the joys and frustrations of history. Unlike chemists, historians cannot reproduce experiments under controlled conditions. No two historical events are precisely alike. People cannot be put into test tubes, and they are not as predictable as atoms or hydrocarbons. History is about people, the most complex organisms on this planet. To complicate matters, for many epochs of history only the broad outlines are known, so interpretation is especially difficult. For example, historians know that the

Hittite Empire collapsed at the height of its power, but interpretations of the causes of the catastrophe are still speculative. At the other end of the spectrum, some developments are so vast and complex that historians must master mountains of data before they can even begin to interpret developments properly. Events as diverse as the end of the western Roman Empire, the origins of the Industrial Revolution, and the causes of the French Revolution are very complicated because so many people brought so many different forces to bear for so many reasons. In such cases, there is never one simple explanation that will satisfy everyone.

Still another matter complicates an accurate understanding of the past: the attempt to understand history is uniquely human. Interpretations of the past sometimes change because people's points of view change in the course of life. The values and attitudes of one generation may not be shared by another. Despite such differences in interpretation, the efforts of historians to examine and appreciate the past can give them a perspective that is valuable to the present. It is through analysis and interpretation that historians come to appreciate not only the past but also its relation to life today.

An example of this process comes from examining what the concepts "Western civilization" and "the West" mean. Interpretations of them have changed over time and space. The Greeks, for instance, defined "the West" as themselves; lands and peoples to the west of them were either barbarians or unknown. The Romans likewise thought of themselves as "Western" and considered their neighbors in modern France, Greece, and Germany as outsiders until they adopted Greco-Roman culture. During the Middle Ages Europeans spread their civilization into eastern Europe, while the Byzantines spread classical and medieval culture into Russia. This intermingling changed the concept of "the West." Social practices and traditional Mediterranean ideas resulted in a civilization that could reasonably be called "European."

In the early modern period, during the age of exploration, Europeans discovered the New World, the Americas, and ventured farther into the Pacific. By geographical expansion and emigration they gradually so Europeanized the peoples there that they also entered the intellectual world of the West. West met East in social, economic, intellectual, and cultural contexts. During the nineteenth and twentieth centuries, modern technology significantly reinforced earlier Western values of individualism and private enterprise. The Chinese and Japanese willingly adopted certain aspects of Western culture, such as commercial connections and Western-style armed forces, and some learned Western languages. Yet they also clung to

very many of their native ways. Today people the world over use computers, cellular telephones, and e-mail—all Western inventions. Therefore, the West is obviously as much a cultural concept as it is a physical place on the map. Local differences remain, but the influence of the West has far outstripped geography. Although no one should say that Western civilization has conquered the world, it is safe to say that no other culture has done as much to shape global life.

From Caves to Towns

Virtually every day brings startling news about the path of human evolution. We now know that by about 400,000 B.C. early peoples were making primitive stone tools, which has led historians to refer to this time as the Paleolithic period. During this period, which lasted until about 7000 B.C., people survived as nomadic hunters, usually living in caves or temporary shelters. (See the feature "Images in Society: The Iceman.") Although they accomplished striking achievements, they contributed little to our understanding of history. They properly belong to the realm of anthropology, which studies prehistoric peoples. A reasonable dividing line between anthropology and history is the **Neolithic period,** usually dated between 7000 and 3000 B.C. The term *Neolithic* stems from the new stone tools that came into use at that time. The ways in which peoples used these tools led to fundamental changes in civilization. With them Neolithic folk built a life primarily and permanently based on agriculture and animal husbandry. They thereby broke with previous nomadic practices.

Sustained agriculture made possible a stable and secure life. Neolithic farmers developed the primary economic activity of the ancient world and one still vital today. With this settled routine came the evolution of towns and eventually of cities. Neolithic farmers usually raised more food than they could consume, so their surpluses permitted larger, healthier populations. Population growth in turn created an even greater reliance on settled farming, as only systematic agriculture could sustain the increased numbers of people. Since surpluses of food could also be bartered for other commodities, the Neolithic era witnessed the beginnings of the large-scale exchange of goods. Neolithic farmers also improved their tools and agricultural techniques. They domesticated bigger, stronger animals to work for them, invented the plow, and developed new mutations of seeds. By 3000 B.C. they had invented the wheel. Agricultural surpluses also made possible the division of labor. It freed some people to become craftsmen and artisans, who made tools, pottery vessels, woven baskets, clothing, and jewelry. In short, these advances resulted in a wealthier, more comfortable, and more complex life.

These developments generally led to the further evolution of towns and a whole new way of life. People not necessarily related to one another created rudimentary governments that transcended the family. These governments, led by a recognized central authority, made decisions that channeled the shared wisdom, physical energy, and resources of the whole population toward a common goal. These societies made their decisions according to custom, the generally accepted norms of traditional conduct. Here was the beginning of law. Towns also meant life in individual houses or groups of them, which led to greater personal independence. Growing wealth and the need for communal cooperation prompted people to erect public buildings and religious monuments. These groups also protected their possessions and themselves by raising walls.

Many scholars consider walled towns the basic feature of Neolithic society. Yet numerous examples prove that some Neolithic towns existed without stone or mud-brick walls. For instance, at Stonehenge in England the natives erected wooden palisades for safety. At Unteruhldingen in Germany the community established its unwalled town just offshore on a lake. They let nature defend them. The most concentrated collection of walled towns is found in Mesopotamia. This fact presents a historical problem. Since generations of archaeologists and historians have concentrated their attention on this region, they have considered it typical. Yet they have failed to appreciate properly circumstances elsewhere. The fundamental points about this period are that these folk created stable communities based on agriculture. They defended their towns in various ways by common consent and effort. This organized communal effort is far more important than the types of defenses they built.

The simplest way to support these conclusions is to examine briefly Stonehenge now and Mesopotamia afterward, each in its own unique context. A mute but engaging glimpse of a particular Neolithic society can readily be seen today in industrial England. Between 4700 and 2000 B.C. arose the Stonehenge people, named after the

Stonehenge   Seen in regal isolation, Stonehenge sits among the stars and in April 1997 was along the path of the comet Hale-Bopp. Long before Druids existed, a Neolithic society laboriously built this circle to mark the passing of the seasons. *(Jim Burgess)*

Images in Society

The Iceman

On September 19, 1991, two German vacationers climbing in the Italian Alps came upon one of the most remarkable finds in European history: a corpse lying face-down and covered in ice (Image 1). They stumbled upon a mystery that still intrigues archaeologists and many others in the scientific world. After chiseling the body out of the ice, various specialists examined the man. Having died 5,300 years ago, he is the earliest and best-preserved corpse from the Neolithic period (Image 2).

The skin of most corpses found in glaciers appears white and waxy, but the skin of the Iceman, as he is generally known, was brown and dry. Forces of nature had so desiccated the body that it became mummified: the body, including the internal organs, was perfectly preserved. The Iceman's less perishable possessions also survived, so scientists were able to examine him almost as though he had died recently.

The Iceman was quite fit, was between twenty-five and thirty-five years of age, and stood about five feet two inches tall. The bluish tinge of his teeth showed that he had enjoyed a diet of milled grain, perhaps millet—and also showed that he came from an environment where crops were grown. He wore an unlined robe of animal skins that he had stitched together with careful needlework, using thread made of grass, which he probably had made for himself. Over his robe he wore a cape of grass, very much like capes worn by shepherds in this region as late as the early twentieth century (even as late as the Second World War German soldiers stuffed straw into their boots to withstand the fierce Russian cold). The Iceman also wore a furry cap.

The equipment discovered with the Iceman demonstrates his mastery of several technologies. He carried a hefty copper ax (a sign of stoneworking), but he seems to have relied chiefly on archery. In his quiver were numerous wooden arrow shafts and two finished arrows, all indicating a great deal of knowledge and ingenuity (Image 3). The arrows had flint heads (another sign of stoneworking), and feathers were attached with a resin-like glue to the ends of the shafts. These simple facts convey much information

Image 1 The Discovery of the Iceman *(Paul Hanny/Liaison/ Getty Images)*

Image 2 The Face of the Iceman *(Keystone Press Agency Ltd./Rex Features)*

Image 4 X-ray of the Iceman's Shoulder *(South Tyrol Museum of Archaeology/AP/Wide World Photos)*

Image 3 The Iceman's Quiver *(S.N.S./Sipa Press)*

about the technological knowledge of this mysterious man. He knew how to work stone, he knew the value of feathers to direct the arrows, and he was fully aware of the basics of ballistics. He chose for his bow the wood of the yew, some of the best wood in central Europe. Yet yew trees do not grow everywhere, so the use of yew wood proves that the Iceman had thoroughly explored his environment. He carried his necessary supplies in a primitive rucksack that he had made.

One last mystery surrounds the Iceman. When his body was first discovered, scholars assumed that he was a hapless traveler overtaken by a fierce snowstorm. But a recent autopsy found an arrowhead lodged under his left shoulder (Image 4). The Iceman was not alone on his last day. Someone accompanied him,

someone who shot him from below and behind. The Iceman is the victim in the first murder mystery of Western history.

Given this information, can you picture the circumstances of the Iceman's discovery (Image 1)? What was he doing there? From Image 2 can you imagine how nature preserved his remains? From the picture of his arrows (Image 3) can you conclude anything about the Iceman's self-reliance? From Image 4 comes the evidence for the cause of his death. Does it necessarily prove that Neolithic society was as violent as ours?

The **history companion** *features additional information and activities related to this topic.* **history.college.hmco.com/students**

famous stone circle on Salisbury Plain. Though named after a single spot, this culture spread throughout Great Britain, Ireland, and Brittany in France. Circles like Stonehenge sometimes contained the houses of permanent settlers. Some were fortified enclosures, in which the inhabitants established a safe haven for themselves. Both were proto-urban centers. Some of these sites have yielded burial remains. Others were dedicated to religious rituals. They provided magical, not military, protection. They all served diverse social functions, another testimony to Neolithic creativity. Stonehenge and neighboring sites reveal the existence of prosperous, well-organized, and centrally led communities. They also provide evidence for cooperation among similarly constituted societies. None of them individually could have built the circle. By pooling their resources, human and material, they raised it. Thus Stonehenge itself testifies to contact and cohesion among stable groups that cooperated toward a common goal. These factors alone prove the widening horizon of these Neolithic peoples.

Stonehenge offers another insight into this Neolithic culture. It indicates an intellectual world that encompassed astronomy, the environment, and religion. The circle is oriented toward the midwinter sunset and the midsummer sunrise. Stonehenge thus marked the clocklike celestial change of the seasons. This silent evidence proves the existence of a society prosperous enough to endure over long periods during which lore about heaven and earth could be preserved and passed along to successive generations. It also demonstrates that these communities considered themselves members of a wider world that they amiably shared with the deities of nature and the broader universe. Even the magnificent Stonehenge, however, cannot lead to history. The Stonehenge people achieved wonders, but they lacked the literacy to spread their legacy to others beyond their own culture. That breakthrough came in Mesopotamia.

*M*esopotamian Civilization

In the East peoples faced many challenges similar to those of their Western contemporaries. In western Asia this process can easily be seen in Mesopotamia, the Greek name for the land between the Euphrates and Tigris Rivers. There the arid climate confronted the peoples with the hard problem of farming with scant water supplies. In the East farmers learned to irrigate their land and later to drain it to prevent the buildup of salt in the soil. **Irrigation** on a large scale, like building stone circles in the West, demanded organized group effort. That in

turn underscored the need for strong central authority to direct it. In the East, as in the West, this corporate spirit led to governments in which individuals participated in the whole community while subordinating some of their particular concerns to its broader interests. These factors made urban life possible in a demanding environment. By about 3000 B.C. the Sumerians, whose origins are mysterious, established a number of cities in the southernmost part of Mesopotamia, which became known as Sumer. The Sumerians soon turned the region into what generations have called the "cradle of civilization" (see Map 1.1). Some might argue that this phrase should be honorably retired, for civilization was advancing by various degrees from England to Mesopotamia. No one, however, can deny that the fundamental innovation of the Sumerians was the creation of writing, which helped unify this society culturally and opened it to the broader world that we still share today.

The Invention of Writing and the First Schools

The origins of writing probably go back to the ninth millennium B.C., when Near Eastern peoples used clay tokens as counters for record keeping. By the fourth millennium people had realized that drawing pictures of the tokens on clay was simpler than making tokens. This breakthrough in turn suggested that more information could be conveyed by adding pictures of still other objects. The result was a complex system of pictographs, in which each sign pictured an object. These pictographs were the forerunners of a Sumerian form of writing known as **cuneiform,** from the Latin term for "wedge-shaped," used to describe the strokes of the stylus.

How did this pictographic system work, and how did it evolve into cuneiform writing? At first, if a scribe wanted to indicate a star, he simply drew a picture of it (line A of Figure 1.1) on a wet clay tablet, which became rock-hard when baked. Anyone looking at the picture would know what it meant and would think of the word for star. This complicated and laborious system had serious limitations. It could not represent abstract ideas or combinations of ideas. For instance, how could it depict a slave woman?

The solution appeared when the scribe discovered that signs could be combined to express meaning. To refer to a slave woman the scribe used the sign for woman (line B) and the sign for mountain (line C)—literally, "mountain woman" (line D). Because the Sumerians regularly obtained their slave women from the mountains, this combination of signs was easily understandable.

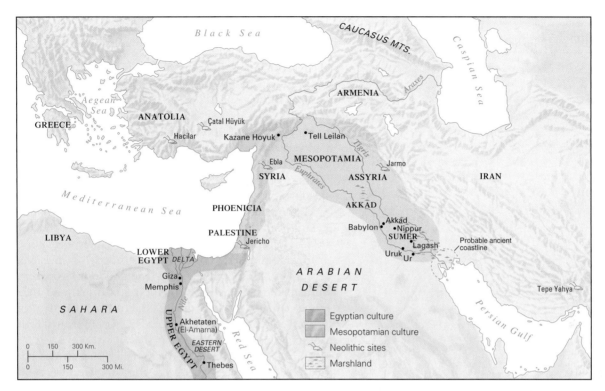

MAP 1.1 Spread of Cultures in the Ancient Near East This map illustrates the spread of the Mesopotamian and Egyptian cultures through a semicircular stretch of land often called the Fertile Crescent. From this area knowledge and use of agriculture spread throughout the western part of Asia Minor.

The next step was to simplify the system. Instead of drawing pictures, the scribe made conventionalized signs that were generally understood to represent ideas. Thus the signs became *ideograms:* they symbolized ideas. The sign for star could also be used to indicate heaven, sky, or even god.

The real breakthrough came when the scribe learned to use signs to represent sounds. For instance, the scribe drew two parallel wavy lines to indicate the word *a* or "water" (line E). Besides water, the word *a* in Sumerian also meant "in." The word *in* expresses a relationship that is very difficult to represent pictorially. Instead of trying to invent a sign to mean "in," some clever scribe used the sign for water because the two words sounded alike. This phonetic use of signs made possible the combining of signs to convey abstract ideas.

The Sumerian system of writing was so complicated that only professional scribes mastered it, and even they had to study it for many years. By 2500 B.C. scribal schools flourished throughout Sumer. Most students came from wealthy families and were male. Each school had a master, teachers, and monitors. Discipline was strict, and students were caned for sloppy work and misbehavior. One graduate of a scribal school had few fond memories of the joy of learning:

My headmaster read my tablet, said:
"There is something missing," caned me.

. . . .

The fellow in charge of silence said:
"Why did you talk without permission," caned me.
The fellow in charge of the assembly said:
"Why did you stand at ease without permission," caned me.[1]

The Sumerian system of schooling set the educational standards for Mesopotamian culture, and the Akkadians and, later, the Babylonians adopted its practices and techniques. Mesopotamian education always had a practical side because of the economic and administrative importance of scribes. Most scribes took administrative positions in the temple or palace, where they kept records of business transactions, accounts, and inventories. But scribal schools did not limit their curriculum to business affairs. They were also centers of culture and scholarship. Topics of study included mathematics,

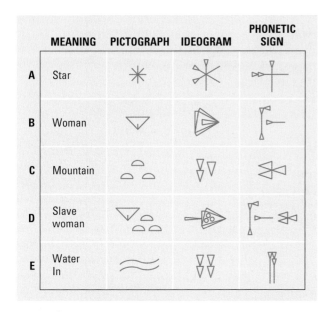

	MEANING	PICTOGRAPH	IDEOGRAM	PHONETIC SIGN
A	Star			
B	Woman			
C	Mountain			
D	Slave woman			
E	Water In			

FIGURE 1.1 Sumerian Writing   (*Source: Excerpted from S. N. Kramer,* The Sumerians: Their History, Culture and Character, *University of Chicago Press, Chicago, 1963. Copyright © 1963 by The University of Chicago Press. Reprinted by permission.*)

botany, and linguistics. Advanced students copied and studied the classics of Sumerian literature. Talented students and learned scribes wrote compositions of their own. As a result, many literary, mathematical, and religious texts survive today, giving a full picture of Mesopotamian intellectual and spiritual life.

Mesopotamian Thought and Religion

The Mesopotamians made significant and sophisticated advances in mathematics using a numerical system based on units of sixty, ten, and six. They developed the concept of place value—that the value of a number depends on where it stands in relation to other numbers. The Mesopotamians did not consider mathematics a purely theoretical science. The building of cities, palaces, temples, and canals demanded practical knowledge of geometry and trigonometry.

Mesopotamian medicine was a combination of magic, prescriptions, and surgery. Mesopotamians believed that demons and evil spirits caused sickness and that magic spells could drive them out. Or, they believed, the physician could force the demon out by giving the patient a foul-tasting prescription. As medical knowledge grew, some prescriptions were found to work and thus were true medicines. In this slow but empirical fashion medicine grew from superstition to an early form of rational treatment.

Mesopotamian thought had a profound impact in theology and religion. The Sumerians originated many beliefs, and their successors added to them. The Mesopotamians believed that many gods run the world, but they did not consider all gods and goddesses equal. Some deities had very important jobs, taking care of music, law, sex, and victory, while others had lesser tasks, overseeing leatherworking and basketweaving. The god in charge of metalworking was hardly the equal of the god of wisdom.

Mesopotamian gods lived their lives much as human beings lived theirs. The gods were anthropomorphic, or human in form. Unlike men and women, they were powerful and immortal and could make themselves invisible. Otherwise, Mesopotamian gods and goddesses were very human: they celebrated with food and drink, and they raised families. They enjoyed their own "Garden of Eden," a green and fertile place. They could be irritable, vindictive, and irresponsible.

The Mesopotamians did not worship their deities because the gods were benevolent. Human beings were too insignificant to pass judgment on the conduct of the gods, and the gods were too superior to honor human morals. Rather, the Mesopotamians worshiped the gods because they were mighty. Likewise, it was not the place of men and women to understand the gods. The Sumerian equivalent to the biblical Job once complained to his god:

The man of deceit has conspired against me,
And you, my god, do not thwart him,
You carry off my understanding.[2]

The motives of the gods were not always clear. In times of affliction one could only pray and offer sacrifices to appease them.

The Mesopotamians had many myths to account for the creation of the universe. According to one Sumerian myth (echoed in Genesis, the first book of the Bible), only the primeval sea existed at first. The sea produced heaven and earth, which were united. Heaven and earth gave birth to Enlil, who separated them and made possible the creation of the other gods. Babylonian beliefs were similar. In the beginning was the primeval sea, the goddess Tiamat, who gave birth to the gods. When Tiamat tried to destroy the gods, Marduk, the chief god of the Babylonians, proceeded to kill her and divide her body and thus created the sky and earth. These myths are the earliest known attempts to answer the question, "How did it all begin?" The Mesopotamians obviously thought about these matters, as about the gods, in human terms. They never organized their beliefs into a philosophy, but their myths offered understandable explanations of natural phenomena. The myths were emotionally satisfying, and that was their greatest appeal.

In addition to myths, the Sumerians produced the first epic poem, the *Epic of Gilgamesh,* which evolved as a reworking of at least five earlier myths. An epic poem is a narration of the achievements, labors, and sometimes the failures of heroes that embodies a people's or a nation's conception of its own past. Historians can use epic poems to learn about various aspects of a society, and to that extent epics can be used as historical sources. The Sumerian epic recounts the wanderings of Gilgamesh—the semihistorical king of Uruk—and his companion Enkidu, their fatal meeting with the goddess Ishtar, after which Enkidu dies, and Gilgamesh's subsequent search for eternal life. During his search Gilgamesh learns that life after death is so dreary that he returns to Uruk, where he becomes a good king and ends his life happily. The *Epic of Gilgamesh* is not only an excellent piece of literature but also an intellectual triumph. It shows the Sumerians grappling with such enduring questions as life and death, humankind and deity, and immortality. Despite its great antiquity, it addresses questions of importance to people today. (See the feature "Listening to the Past: A Quest for Immortality" on pages 30–31.)

Sumerian Society

Their harsh environment fostered a grim, even pessimistic, spirit among the Mesopotamians. The Sumerians sought to please and calm the gods, especially the patron deity of the city. Encouraged and directed by the traditional priesthood, which was dedicated to understanding the ways of the gods, the people erected shrines in the center of each city and then built their houses around them. The best way to honor the gods was to make the shrine as grand and as impressive as possible, for gods who had a splendid temple might think twice about sending floods to destroy the city.

Sumerian society was a complex arrangement of freedom and dependence, and its members were divided into four categories: nobles, free clients of the nobility, commoners, and slaves. **Nobles** consisted of the king and his family, the chief priests, and high palace officials. Generally, the king rose to power as a war leader, elected by the citizenry, who established a regular army, trained it, and led it into battle. The might of the king and the frequency of warfare quickly made him the supreme figure in the city, and kingship soon became hereditary. The symbol of royal status was the palace, which rivaled the temple in grandeur.

The king and the lesser nobility held extensive tracts of land that were, like the estates of the temple, worked by slaves and clients. **Clients** were free men and women who were dependent on the nobility. In return for their labor, the clients received small plots of land to work for themselves. Although this arrangement assured the clients of a livelihood, the land they worked remained the possession of the nobility or the temple. Thus not only did the nobility control most—and doubtless the best—land, they also commanded the obedience of a huge segment of society. They were the dominant force in Mesopotamian society.

Commoners were free citizens. They were independent of the nobility; however, they could not rival the nobility in social status and political power. Commoners belonged to large patriarchal families who owned land in their own right. Commoners could sell their land, if the family approved, but even the king could not legally take their land without their approval. Commoners had a voice in the political affairs of the city and full protection under the law.

Until comparatively recent times, slavery has been a fact of life throughout the history of Western society. Some Sumerian slaves were foreigners and prisoners of war. Some were criminals who had lost their freedom as punishment for their crimes. Still others served as slaves to repay debts. These were more fortunate than the others, because the law required that they be freed after three years. But all slaves were subject to whatever treatment their owners might mete out. They could be beaten and even branded. Yet they were not considered dumb beasts. Slaves engaged in trade and made profits. Indeed, many slaves were able to buy their freedom. They could borrow money and received at least some legal protection.

*T*he Spread of Mesopotamian Culture

The Sumerians established the basic social, economic, and intellectual patterns of Mesopotamia, but the Semites played a large part in spreading Sumerian culture far beyond the boundaries of Mesopotamia. The interaction of the Sumerians and Semites, in fact, gives one of the very first glimpses of a phenomenon that can still be seen today. History provides abundant evidence of peoples of different origins coming together, usually on the borders of an established culture. The result was usually cultural change, outweighing any hostility, for each side learned from the other. The outcome in these instances was the evolution of a new culture that consisted of two or more

Sargon of Akkad This bronze head, with elaborately worked hair and beard, portrays the great conqueror Sargon of Akkad. The eyes were originally inlaid with precious jewels, which have since been gouged out. This head was found in the ruins of the Assyrian capital of Ninevah, where it had been taken as loot. (*Claus Hansmann, Munich*)

and venerated culture. It also provided an easy means of communication among people on a broad scale. The Eblaites (a Semitic people) could efficiently deal with the Mesopotamians and others who embraced this culture in ways that all could understand. Culture ignores borders. Despite local variations, so much common ground existed that similar political and economic institutions, exchange of ideas and religious beliefs, methods of writing, and a shared etiquette served as links among all who embraced Mesopotamian culture.

The Triumph of Babylon

Although the empire of Sargon was extensive, it was short-lived. The Akkadians, too, failed to solve the problems posed by Mesopotamia's geography and population pattern. It was left to the Babylonians to unite Mesopotamia politically and culturally. The Babylonians were Amorites, a Semitic people who had migrated from Arabia and settled on the site of Babylon along the middle Euphrates, where that river runs close to the Tigris. Babylon enjoyed an excellent geographical position and was ideally suited to be the capital of Mesopotamia. It dominated trade on the Tigris and Euphrates Rivers: all commerce to and from Sumer and Akkad had to pass by its walls. It also looked beyond Mesopotamia. Babylonian merchants followed the Tigris north to Assyria and Anatolia. The Euphrates led merchants to Syria, Palestine, and the Mediterranean. The city grew great because of its commercial importance and soundly based power.

Babylon was also fortunate to have a farseeing and able king, Hammurabi (r. 1792–1750 B.C.). Hammurabi set out to do three things: make Babylon secure, unify Mesopotamia, and win for the Babylonians a place in Mesopotamian civilization. The first two he accomplished by conquering Assyria in the north and Sumer and Akkad in the south. Then he turned to his third goal.

Politically, Hammurabi joined in his kingship the Semitic concept of the tribal chieftain and the Sumerian idea of urban kingship. Culturally, he encouraged the spread of myths that explained how Marduk, the god of Babylon, had been elected king of the gods by the other Mesopotamian deities. Hammurabi's success in making Marduk the god of all Mesopotamians made Babylon the religious center of Mesopotamia. Through Hammurabi's genius the Babylonians made their own contribution to Mesopotamian culture—a culture vibrant enough to maintain its identity while assimilating new influences. Hammurabi's conquests and the activity of Babylonian merchants spread this enriched culture north to Anatolia and west to Syria and Palestine.

old parts. Although the older culture almost invariably looked on the newcomers as inferior, the new just as invariably contributed something valuable to the old. So it was in 2331 B.C. The Semitic chieftain Sargon conquered Sumer and created a new empire. The symbol of his triumph was a new capital, the city of Akkad. Sargon, the first "world conqueror," led his armies to the Mediterranean Sea. Although his empire lasted only a few generations, it spread Mesopotamian culture throughout the Fertile Crescent, the belt of rich farmland that extends from Mesopotamia in the east up through Syria in the north and down to Egypt in the west (see Map 1.1).

The question to answer is why Mesopotamian culture had such an immediate and wide appeal. In the first place it was successful and enjoyed the prestige of its success. Newcomers wanted to find a respectable place in this old

Law Code of Hammurabi Hammurabi ordered his code to be inscribed on a stone pillar and set up in public. At the top of the pillar Hammurabi is depicted receiving the scepter of authority from the god Shamash. *(Hirmer Verlag München)*

Life Under Hammurabi

One of Hammurabi's most memorable accomplishments was the proclamation of a **law code** that offers a wealth of information about daily life in Mesopotamia. Hammurabi's was not the first law code in Mesopotamia; indeed, the earliest goes back to about 2100 B.C. Like earlier lawgivers, Hammurabi proclaimed that he issued his laws on divine authority "to establish law and justice in the language of the land, thereby promoting the welfare of the people." Hammurabi's code inflicted such penalties as mutilation, whipping, and burning. Despite its severity, a spirit of justice and a sense of responsibility pervade the code. Hammurabi genuinely felt that his duty was to govern the Mesopotamians as righteously as possible. He tried to regulate the relations of his people so that they could live together in harmony.

The practical impact of Hammurabi's code is much debated. There is much disagreement about whether it recorded laws already established, promulgated new laws, or simply proclaimed what was just and proper. It is also unknown whether Hammurabi's proclamation, like others before it, was legally binding on the courts. At the very least, Hammurabi pronounced to the world what principles of justice he encouraged, while giving everyone visible evidence of his intentions as ruler of Babylonia.

The Code of Hammurabi has two striking characteristics. First, the law differed according to the social status of the offender. Aristocrats were not punished as harshly as commoners, nor commoners as harshly as slaves. Second, the code demanded that the punishment fit the crime. It called for "an eye for an eye, and a tooth for a tooth," at least among equals. However, an aristocrat who destroyed the eye of a commoner or slave could pay a fine instead of losing his own eye. Otherwise, as long as criminal and victim shared the same social status, the victim could demand exact vengeance.

Hammurabi's code began with legal procedure. There were no public prosecutors or district attorneys, so individuals brought their own complaints before the court. Each side had to produce written documents or witnesses to support its case. In cases of murder, the accuser had to prove the defendant guilty; any accuser who failed to do so was put to death. This strict law was designed to prevent people from lodging groundless charges. The Mesopotamians were very worried about witchcraft and sorcery. Anyone accused of witchcraft, even if the charges were not proved, underwent an ordeal by water. The gods themselves would decide the case. The defendant was thrown into the Euphrates, which was considered the instrument of the gods. A defendant who sank was guilty; a defendant who floated was innocent. Another procedural regulation covered the conduct of judges. Once a judge had rendered a verdict, he could not change it. Any judge who did so was fined heavily and deposed. In short, the code tried to guarantee a fair trial and a just verdict.

Consumer protection is not a modern idea; it goes back to Hammurabi's day. Merchants and businessmen had to guarantee the quality of their goods and services.

A boat builder who did sloppy work had to repair the boat at his own expense. A boatman who lost the owner's boat or sank someone else's boat replaced it and its cargo. House builders guaranteed their work with their lives. Careless work could result in the collapse of a house and the death of its inhabitants. If that happened, the builder was put to death. A merchant who tried to increase the interest rate on a loan forfeited the entire amount. Hammurabi's laws tried to ensure that consumers got what they paid for and paid a just price.

Because farming was essential to Mesopotamian life, Hammurabi's code dealt extensively with agriculture. Tenant farming was widespread, and tenants rented land on a yearly basis. Instead of money they paid a portion of their crops as rent. Unless the land was carefully cultivated, it quickly reverted to wasteland. Therefore, tenants faced severe penalties for neglecting the land or not working it at all. Since irrigation was essential to grow crops, tenants had to keep the canals and ditches in good repair. Otherwise the land would be subject to floods and farmers would face crippling losses. Anyone whose neglect of the canals resulted in damaged crops had to bear all the expense of the lost crops. Those tenants who could not pay the costs were forced into slavery.

Hammurabi gave careful attention to marriage and the family. As elsewhere in the Near East, marriage had aspects of a business agreement. The prospective groom and the father of the future bride arranged everything. The man offered the father a bridal gift, usually money. If the man and his bridal gift were acceptable, the father provided his daughter with a dowry. After marriage the dowry belonged to the woman (although the husband normally administered it) and was a means of protecting her rights and status. Once the two men agreed on financial matters, they drew up a contract; no marriage was considered legal without one. Either party could break off the marriage, but not without paying a stiff penalty. Fathers often contracted marriages while their children were still young. The girl either continued to live in her father's house until she reached maturity or went to live in the house of her father-in-law. During this time she was legally considered a wife. Once she and her husband came of age, they set up their own house.

The wife was expected to be rigorously faithful. The penalty for adultery was death. According to Hammurabi's code: "If the wife of a man has been caught while lying with another man, they shall bind them and throw them into the water."[3] The husband had the power to spare his wife by obtaining a pardon for her from the king. He could, however, accuse his wife of adultery even if he had not caught her in the act. In such a case she could try to clear herself before the city council that investigated the charge. If she was found innocent, she could take her dowry and leave her husband. If a woman decided to take the direct approach and kill her husband, she was impaled.

The husband had virtually absolute power over his household. He could even sell his wife and children into slavery to pay debts. Sons did not lightly oppose their fathers, and any son who struck his father could have his hand cut off. A father was free to adopt children and include them in his will. Artisans sometimes adopted children to teach them the family trade. Although the father's power was great, he could not disinherit a son without just cause. Cases of disinheritance became matters for the city to decide, and the code ordered the courts to forgive a son for his first offense. Only if a son wronged his father a second time could he be disinherited.

Law codes, preoccupied as they are with the problems of society, provide a bleak view of things. Other Mesopotamian documents give a happier glimpse of life. Although Hammurabi's code dealt with marriage in a hard-fisted fashion, a Mesopotamian poem tells of two people meeting secretly in the city. Their parting is delightfully romantic:

Come now, set me free, I must go home,
Kuli-Enlil . . . set me free, I must go home.
What can I say to deceive my mother?[4]

Countless wills and testaments show that husbands habitually left their estates to their wives, who in turn willed the property to their children. All this suggests happy family life. Hammurabi's code restricted married women from commercial pursuits, but financial documents prove that many women engaged in business without hindrance. Some carried on the family business, while others became wealthy landowners in their own right. Mesopotamians found their lives lightened by holidays and religious festivals. Traveling merchants brought news of the outside world and swapped marvelous tales. Despite their pessimism, the Mesopotamians enjoyed a vibrant and creative culture, a culture that left its mark on the entire Near East.

Egypt, the Land of the Pharaohs (3100–1200 B.C.)

The Greek historian and traveler Herodotus in the fifth century B.C. called Egypt the "gift of the Nile." No other single geographical factor had such a fundamental and profound impact on the shaping of Egyptian life, society, and history as the Nile (see Map 1.2). Unlike the rivers of

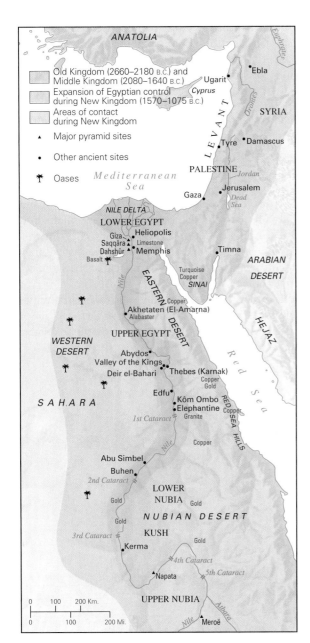

MAP 1.2 Ancient Egypt Geography and natural resources provided Egypt with centuries of peace and abundance.

He that waters the meadows which Re [Ra] created,
He that makes to drink the desert . . .
He who makes barley and brings emmer [wheat] into
  being . . .
He who brings grass into being for the cattle . . .
He who makes every beloved tree to grow . . .
O Nile, verdant art thou, who makest man and cattle to
  live.[5]

In the mind of the Egyptians, the Nile was the supreme fertilizer and renewer of the land. Each September the Nile floods its valley, transforming it into a huge area of marsh or lagoon. By the end of November the water retreats, leaving behind a thin covering of fertile mud ready to be planted with crops.

The annual flood made the growing of abundant crops almost effortless, especially in southern Egypt. Herodotus, used to the rigors of Greek agriculture, was amazed by the ease with which the Egyptians raised crops:

For indeed without trouble they obtain crops from the land more easily than all other men. . . . They do not labor to dig furrows with the plough or hoe or do the work which other men do to raise grain. But when the river by itself inundates the fields and the water recedes, then each man, having sown his field, sends pigs into it. When the pigs trample down the seed, he waits for the harvest. Then when the pigs thresh the grain, he gets his crop.[6]

The extraordinary fertility of the Nile Valley made it easy to produce an annual agricultural surplus, which in turn sustained a growing and prosperous population. The Nile also unified Egypt. The river was the region's principal highway, promoting easy communication throughout the valley.

Egypt was fortunate in that it was nearly self-sufficient. Besides the fertility of its soil, Egypt possessed enormous quantities of stone, which served as the raw material of architecture and sculpture. Abundant clay was available for pottery, as was gold for jewelry and ornaments. The raw materials that Egypt lacked were close at hand. The Egyptians could obtain copper from Sinai and timber from Lebanon. They had little cause to look to the outside world for their essential needs, a fact that helps to explain the insular quality of Egyptian life.

The God-King of Egypt

Geographical unity quickly gave rise to political unification of the country under the authority of a king whom the Egyptians called "pharaoh." The precise details of this process have been lost. The Egyptians themselves

Mesopotamia, it rarely brought death and destruction by devastating entire cities. The river was primarily a creative force. The Egyptians never feared the relatively tame Nile in the way the Mesopotamians feared the Tigris. Instead, they sang its praises:

Hail to thee, O Nile, that issues from the earth and comes to
  keep Egypt alive! . . .

told of a great king, Menes, who united Upper and Lower Egypt into a single kingdom around 3100 B.C. Thereafter the Egyptians divided their history into dynasties, or families of kings. For modern historical purposes, however, it is more useful to divide Egyptian history into periods (see page 19). The political unification of Egypt ushered in the period known as the Old Kingdom (2660–2180 B.C.), an era remarkable for prosperity, artistic flowering, and the evolution of religious beliefs.

In religion, the Egyptians developed complex, often contradictory, ideas of their gods. They were polytheistic in that they worshiped many gods, some mightier than others. Their beliefs were all rooted in the environment and human ecology. The most powerful of these gods was Amon, a primeval sky-god, and Ra, the sun-god. Amon created the entire cosmos by his thoughts. He caused the Nile to make its annual inundations and the northern wind to blow. He brought life to the land and its people, and he sustained both. The Egyptians cher-

ished Amon because he championed fairness and honesty, especially for the common people. The Egyptians called him the "vizier of the humble" and the "voice of the poor." He was also a magician and physician who cured ills, protected people from natural dangers, and protected travelers. The Egyptians considered Ra the creator of life. He commanded the sky, earth, and underworld. This giver of life could also take it without warning. Ra was associated with the falcon-god Horus, the "lord of the sky," who served as the symbol of divine kingship. Horus united Egypt and bestowed divinity on the pharaoh. The obvious similarities between Amon and Ra eventually led the Egyptians to combine them into one god, **Amon-Ra.** Yet the Egyptians never fashioned a formal theology to resolve these differences. Instead they worshiped these gods as different aspects of the same celestial phenomena.

The Egyptians likewise developed views of an afterlife that reflected the world around them. The dry air of Egypt preserves much that would decay in other climates.

Ra and Horus The god Ra appears on the left in a form associated with Horus, the falcon-god. The red circle over Ra's head identifies him as the sun-god. In this scene Ra also assumes characteristics of Osiris, god of the underworld. He stands in judgment of the dead woman on the right. She meets the god with respect but without fear, as he will guide her safely to a celestial heaven. (*Egyptian Museum, Cairo*)

Periods of Egyptian History

Period	Dates	Significant Events
Archaic	3100–2660 B.C.	Unification of Egypt
Old Kingdom	2660–2180 B.C.	Construction of the pyramids
First Intermediate	2180–2080 B.C.	Political chaos
Middle Kingdom	2080–1640 B.C.	Recovery and political stability
Second Intermediate	1640–1570 B.C.	Hyksos "invasion"
New Kingdom	1570–1075 B.C.	Creation of an Egyptian empire; Akhenaten's religious policy

Thus there was a sense of permanence about Egypt: the past was never far from the present. The dependable rhythm of the seasons also shaped the fate of the dead. According to the Egyptians, Osiris, a fertility god associated with the Nile, died each year, and each year his wife, Isis, brought him back to life. Osiris eventually became king of the dead, and he weighed human beings' hearts to determine whether they had lived justly enough to deserve everlasting life. Osiris's care of the dead was shared by Anubis, the jackal-headed god who annually helped Isis to resuscitate Osiris. Anubis was the god of mummification, so essential to Egyptian funerary rites. The Egyptians preserved these ideas in the ***Book of the Dead,*** which explained that after death the soul left the body to become part of the divine. It entered gladly through the gate of heaven and remained in the presence of Aton (a sun-god) and the stars. Thus the Egyptians did not draw a firm boundary between the human and the divine, and life did not end with death.

The focal point of religious and political life in the Old Kingdom was the **pharaoh,** who commanded the wealth, resources, and people of all Egypt. The pharaoh's power was such that the Egyptians considered him to be Horus in human form. The link between the pharaoh and Horus was doubly important. In Egyptian religion Horus was the son of Osiris, which meant that the pharaoh, a living god on earth, became one with Osiris after death. The pharaoh was not simply the mediator between the gods and the Egyptian people. Above all, he was the power that achieved the integration between gods and human beings, between nature and society, that ensured peace and prosperity for the land of the Nile. The pharaoh was thus a guarantee to his people, a pledge that the gods of Egypt (strikingly unlike those of Mesopotamia) cared for their people.

The king's surroundings had to be worthy of a god. Only a magnificent palace was suitable for his home; in fact, the very word *pharaoh* means "great house." Only later, in the Eighteenth Dynasty (see page 23), did it come to mean "king." Just as the pharaoh occupied a great house in life, so he reposed in a great **pyramid** after death. The massive tomb contained all the things

Anubis and the Underworld   In this scene from a coffin, Anubis embalms a body. The jars containing the corpse's internal organs are lined up beneath the bier. The heads on the jars represent the sons of Horus, who like their father tended the dead. The remains will all be buried together for eternity. *(Egyptian Museum, Cairo)*

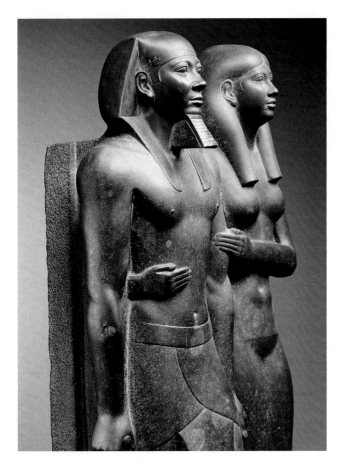

King Menkaure and Queen The pharaoh and his wife represent all the magnificence, serenity, and grandeur of Egypt. *(Old Kingdom, Dynasty 4, reign of Mycerinus, 2532–2510 B.C.; Greywacke; H × W × D: 54¹¹/₁₆ × 22³/₈ × 21⁵/₁₆ in. (139 × 57 × 54 cm). Harvard University—Museum of Fine Arts Expedition, 11.1738. Museum of Fine Arts, Boston.)*

needed by the pharaoh in his afterlife. The walls of the burial chamber were inscribed with religious texts and spells relating to the king's journeys after death. Contrary to common belief, no curses for violation of the pyramid have been found. The pyramid also symbolized the king's power and his connection with the sun-god. After burial the entrance was blocked and concealed to ensure the pharaoh's undisturbed peace. To this day the great pyramids at Giza near Cairo bear silent but magnificent testimony to the god-kings of Egypt.

The Pharaoh's People

Because the common folk stood at the bottom of the social and economic scale, they were always at the mercy of grasping officials. The arrival of the tax collector was never a happy occasion. One Egyptian scribe described the worst that could happen:

And now the scribe lands on the river-bank and is about to register the harvest-tax. The janitors carry staves and the Nubians rods of palm, and they say, Hand over the corn, though there is none. The cultivator is beaten all over, he is bound and thrown into a well, soused and dipped head downwards. His wife has been bound in his presence and his children are in fetters.[7]

That was an extreme situation. Nonetheless, taxes might amount to 20 percent of the harvest, and tax collection could be brutal.

The regularity of the climate meant that the agricultural year was also routine and dependable. For the Egyptian peasants who formed the bulk of the population, the agricultural year normally began in July, when the mud of the Nile covered the land. The waters receded four months later, and then the land was plowed and sowed. This was a particularly busy time, for the crop had to be planted before the land dried. The next period, from mid-March to July, saw the harvesting of crops. Farmers also nurtured a large variety of fruit trees, vegetables, and vines. They tended cattle and poultry, and when time permitted, they hunted and fished in the marshlands of the Nile. People could routinely depend on these aspects of life. This very regularity gave a sense of calm and order to Egypt that was not found in Mesopotamia or later in Greece.

Egyptian society seems to have been a curious mixture of freedom and constraint. Slavery did not become widespread until the New Kingdom (1570–1075 B.C.). There was neither a caste system nor a color bar, and humble people could rise to the highest positions if they possessed talent. On the other hand, most ordinary folk were probably little more than serfs who could not easily leave the land of their own free will. Peasants were also subject to forced labor, including work on the pyramids and canals. Young men were drafted into the pharaoh's army, which served both as a fighting force and as a labor corps.

The vision of thousands of people straining to build the pyramids and countless artists adorning the pharaoh's tomb brings to the modern mind a distasteful picture of oriental despotism. Indeed, the Egyptian view of life and society is alien to those raised on the Western concepts of individual freedom and human rights. To ancient Egyptians the pharaoh embodied justice and order—harmony among human beings, nature, and the divine. If

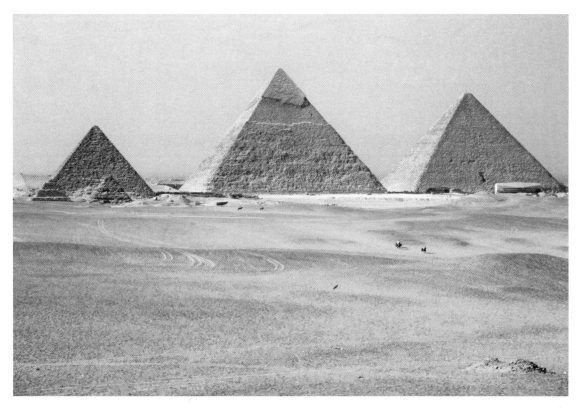

Pyramids of Giza Giza was the burial place of the pharaohs of the Old Kingdom and of their aristocracy, whose smaller rectangular tombs surround the two foremost pyramids. The small pyramid probably belonged to a pharaoh's wife. *(Barry Iverson / Woodfin Camp & Associates)*

the pharaoh was weak or allowed anyone to challenge his unique position, he opened the way to chaos. Twice in Egyptian history the pharaoh failed to maintain rigid centralization. During those two eras, known as the First and Second Intermediate Periods, Egypt was exposed to civil war and invasion. Yet the monarchy survived, and in each period a strong pharaoh arose to crush the rebels or expel the invaders and restore order.

The Hyksos in Egypt (1640–1570 B.C.)

While Egyptian civilization flourished behind its bulwark of sand and sea, momentous changes were taking place in the ancient Near East, changes that would leave their mark even on rich, insular Egypt. These changes involved enormous and remarkable movements, especially of peoples who spoke Semitic tongues.

The original home of the Semites was perhaps the Arabian peninsula. Some tribes moved into northern Meso-

potamia, others into Syria and Palestine, and still others into Egypt. Shortly after 1800 B.C. people whom the Egyptians called **Hyksos,** which means "Rulers of the Uplands," began to settle in the Nile Delta. The movements of the Hyksos were part of a larger pattern of migration of peoples during this period. The history of Mesopotamia records many such wanderings of people in search of better homes for themselves. Such nomads normally settled in and accommodated themselves with the native cultures. The process was mutual, for each group had something to give and to learn from the other.

So it was in Egypt, but Egyptian tradition, as later recorded by the priest Manetho in the third century B.C., depicted the coming of the Hyksos as a brutal invasion:

In the reign of Toutimaios—I do not know why—the wind of god blew against us. Unexpectedly from the regions of the east men of obscure race, looking forward confidently to victory, invaded our land, and without a battle easily seized

Egyptian Fisherman   Here two fishing boats on the Nile, operating together, use a net to catch abundant and various fish. The artist has also included some specimens of foliage among which the men worked. *(Egyptian Expedition of The Metropolitan Museum of Art, Rogers Fund, 1930 [30.4.120]. Photograph © 1977 The Metropolitan Museum of Art)*

Shabti Figurines   The Egyptians believed in an afterlife in which earthly work must go on. They made Shabti figurines that could be called magically to life to do that work for them. The figurines fulfilled in death the tasks that ordinary human beings did in life. *(Courtesy of the Trustees of the British Museum)*

it all by sheer force. Having subdued those in authority in the land, they then barbarously burned our cities and razed to the ground the temples of the gods. They fell upon all the natives in an entirely hateful fashion, slaughtering them and leading both their children and wives into slavery. At last they made one of their people king, whose name was Salitis. This man resided at Memphis, leaving in Upper and Lower Egypt tax collectors and garrisons in strategic places.[8]

The Hyksos created a capital city at Avaris, located in the northeastern Nile Delta, but they probably exerted direct rule no farther south.

Although the Egyptians portrayed the Hyksos as a conquering horde, they were probably no more than nomads looking for good land. Their entry into the delta was probably gradual and generally peaceful. The Hyksos brought with them the method of making bronze and casting it into tools and weapons that became standard in Egypt. They thereby brought Egypt fully into the **Bronze Age** culture of the Mediterranean world, a culture in which the production and use of bronze implements became basic to society. Bronze tools made farming more efficient than ever before because they were sharper and more durable than the copper tools they replaced. The Hyksos' use of bronze armor and weapons as well as horse-drawn chariots and the composite bow, made of laminated wood and horn and far more powerful than the simple wooden bow, revolutionized Egyptian warfare. However much the Egyptians learned from the Hyksos, Egyptian culture eventually absorbed the newcomers. The Hyksos came to worship Egyptian gods and modeled their monarchy on the pharaonic system.

The New Kingdom: Revival and Empire (1570–1075 B.C.)

Politically, Egypt was only in eclipse. The Egyptian sun shone again when a remarkable line of kings, the pharaohs of the Eighteenth Dynasty, arose to challenge the Hyksos. These pharaohs pushed the Hyksos out of the delta, subdued Nubia in the south, and conquered Palestine and parts of Syria in the northeast. In this way, Egyptian warrior-pharaohs inaugurated the New Kingdom—a period in Egyptian history characterized by enormous wealth and conscious imperialism. During this period, probably for the first time, widespread slavery became a feature of Egyptian life. The pharaoh's armies returned home leading hordes of slaves, who constituted a new labor force for imperial building projects.

The kings of the Eighteenth Dynasty created the first Egyptian empire. They ruled Palestine and Syria through their officers and incorporated into the kingdom of Egypt the neighboring region of Nubia. Egyptian religion and customs flourished in Nubia, making a huge impact on African culture there and in neighboring areas. The warrior-kings celebrated their success with monuments on a scale unparalleled since the pharaohs of the Old Kingdom had built the pyramids. Even today the colossal granite statues of these pharaohs and the rich tomb objects of Tutankhamon ("King Tut") testify to the might and splendor of the New Kingdom.

One of the most extraordinary of this unusual line of kings was Akhenaten (r. 1367–1350 B.C.), a pharaoh more concerned with religion than with conquest. Nefertiti, his wife and queen, encouraged his religious bent. (See the feature "Individuals in Society: Nefertiti, the 'Great Wife.'") The precise nature of Akhenaten's religious beliefs remains debatable. The problem began during his own lifetime. His religion was often unpopular

Tutankhamon as Pharaoh   This painted casket depicts the pharaoh as the defender of the kingdom repulsing its invaders. Tutankhamon rides into battle under the signs of the sun-disk and the vulture-goddess, indicating that he and Egypt enjoy the protection of the gods. *(Egyptian Museum, Cairo)*

MAP 1.3 Balance of Power in the Near East   This map shows the regions controlled by the Hittites and Egyptians at the height of their power. The striped area represents the part of Mesopotamia conquered by the Hittites during their expansion eastward.

among the people and the traditional priesthood, and its practice declined in the later years of his reign. After his death, it was condemned and denounced; consequently, not much is known about it. Most historians, however, agree that Akhenaten and Nefertiti were monotheists; that is, they believed that the sun-god Aton, whom they worshiped, was universal, the only god. They considered all other Egyptian gods and goddesses frauds and disregarded their worship. Yet their belief suffered from an obvious flaw. The pharaoh himself was considered the son of god, and monotheism obviously cannot have two gods. What Akhenaten meant by **monotheism** is that only Aton among the traditional Egyptian deities was god.

Akhenaten's monotheism, imposed from above, failed to find a place among the people. The prime reason for Akhenaten's failure is that his god had no connection with the past of the Egyptian people, who trusted the old gods and felt comfortable praying to them. Average Egyptians were no doubt distressed and disheartened when their familiar gods were outlawed, for those gods

were the heavenly powers that had made Egypt powerful and unique. The fanaticism and persecution that accompanied the new monotheism were in complete defiance of the Egyptian tradition of tolerant **polytheism,** or worship of several gods. Thus, when Akhenaten died, his religion died with him.

The Hittites

About the time the Hyksos entered the Nile Delta, the Hittites, who had long been settled in Anatolia (modern Turkey), became a major power in that region and began to expand eastward (see Map 1.3). The Hittites were an Indo-European people. The term **Indo-European** refers to a large family of languages that includes English, most of the languages of modern Europe, Greek, Latin, Persian, and Sanskrit, the sacred tongue of ancient India. During the eighteenth and nineteenth centuries European scholars learned that peoples who spoke related languages had spread as far west as Ireland and as far

Nefertiti, the "Great Wife"

The Egyptians always named the pharaoh's wife the "great wife," somewhat in the way that Americans refer to the president's wife as the "first lady." The great wife legitimized her husband's exercise of power through religious beliefs. The Egyptians believed that she was divinely born and that Amon took the human form of her husband, impregnated her, oversaw the development of the child in her womb, and ensured a healthy delivery. Thus the child was the offspring of both the god and the pharaoh. The great wife could not legally be pharaoh, for only a male could exercise that power. Yet only she could make legitimate a man's right to power. The Egyptians literally and formally considered hers the throne of power, although her power was passive rather than active. Egyptian artists usually depicted the great wife with as much care and dignity as they did the pharaoh. They stylized her body as that of the ideal woman, and her portrait was more idealized than realistic.

So stood things until Nefertiti, who was an exceptional great wife. Unlike her predecessors, she was not content to play a passive role in Egyptian life. Like her husband, Akhenaten, she passionately embraced the worship of Aton. She used her position to support her husband's zeal to spread the god's worship. Together they built a new palace at Akhetaten, the present Amarna, away from the old centers of power. There they developed and promulgated the cult of Aton to the exclusion of the traditional deities. Nearly the only literary survival of their religious belief is the "Hymn to Aton," which declares Aton to be the only god. It also mentions Nefertiti as "the great royal consort whom he !Akhenaten! loves, the mistress of the Two Lands !Upper and Lower Egypt!"

Yet something mysterious and unexplained later occurred at the royal court. Akhenaten stripped Nefertiti of her crown name, which was the equivalent of divorce, and exiled her to a palace in the northernmost part of Amarna. It is quite possible, but beyond proof, that Akhenaten wanted a reconciliation with the old gods and their priests. The cult of Aton was so unpopular among the Egyptians that many considered it sacrilegious. Unwilling to alienate the Egyptian people and their religious leaders any longer, Akhenaten may have dropped or at least softened his insistence on Aton's divine position. Nefertiti in that case may have held true to her religious faith and been punished accordingly. At the death of Akhenaten his memory and that of Nefertiti were cursed, and their palace at

Amarna was abandoned. This abandonment (and the fact that Amarna was recovered only in the twentieth century) accounts for the little that is now known of the royal couple. Nonetheless, no queen before Nefertiti had played such an active part in Egyptian religious life.

Nefertiti, queen of Egypt. (Bildarchiv Preussischer Kulturbesitz/Art Resource, NY)

Nefertiti likewise played a novel role in Egyptian art. In funerary and temple art she is usually depicted with Akhenaten and their daughters. This practice went against the tradition of presenting the royal couple as austere and aloof. Instead, Nefertiti and Akhenaten were portrayed as an ordinary family. Their daughters often appear playing on their parents' laps or with one another. Even Nefertiti's own appearance in Egyptian art was a departure from tradition. As the illustration here shows, the famous bust of her is a realistic, not an idealized, portrait. The face is one of grace, beauty, and dignity. It is the portrait of an individual, not a type.

Nefertiti's bust has its own story. When Akhenaten's successor abandoned the palace at Amarna, the site was ignored, except as a source for building materials. Nefertiti's bust remained in the sculptor's workroom, which eventually caved in. There it lay, undamaged, for more than three thousand years. On December 6, 1912, a German archaeological team discovered it intact and sent it to Germany. After World War II, the bust was moved to its current home outside Berlin, where Nefertiti can still be admired today.

Questions for Analysis

1. Did Nefertiti's individualism have any effect on Egyptian society?
2. Did she have a more profound and philosophical concept of divinity, or were her beliefs purely personal?

The **history companion** *features additional information and activities related to this topic.* history.college.hmco.com/students

east as Central Asia. Archaeologists were able to date the migrations roughly and put them into their historical context.

The rise of the Hittites to prominence in Anatolia is reasonably clear. During the nineteenth century B.C. the native kingdoms in the area engaged in suicidal warfare that left most of Anatolia's once-flourishing towns in ashes and rubble. In this climate of exhaustion the Hittite king Hattusilis I built a hill citadel at Hattusas, the modern Boghazköy, from which he led his Hittites against neighboring kingdoms. Hattusilis's grandson and successor, Mursilis I (ca 1595 B.C.), extended the Hittite conquests as far as Babylon. Upon his return home, the victorious Mursilis was assassinated by members of his own family, an act that plunged the kingdom into confusion and opened the door to foreign invasion. Mursilis's career is representative of the success and weakness of the Hittites. They were extremely vulnerable to attack by vigilant and tenacious enemies. Yet once they were united behind a strong king, the Hittites were a power to be reckoned with.

The Hittites, like the Egyptians of the New Kingdom, produced an energetic and able line of kings who built a powerful empire. Perhaps their major contribution was the introduction of iron into war and agriculture in the form of weapons and tools. Around 1300 B.C. the Hittites stopped the Egyptian army of Rameses II at the Battle of Kadesh in Syria. Having fought each other to a standstill, the Hittites and Egyptians first made peace, then an alliance. Alliance was followed by friendship, and friendship by active cooperation. The two greatest powers of the early Near East tried to make war between them impossible.

They next included the Babylonians in their diplomacy. All three empires developed an official etiquette in which they treated one another as "brothers." They made alliances for offensive and defensive protection, and swore to uphold one another's authority. These contacts facilitated the exchange of ideas throughout the Near East. Furthermore, the Hittites passed much knowledge and lore from the Near East to the newly arrived Greeks in Europe. The details of Hittite contact with the Greeks are unknown, but enough literary themes and physical objects exist to prove the connection.

Hittite Solar Disc This cult standard represents Hittite concepts of fertility and prosperity. The circle surrounding the animals is the sun, beneath which stands a stag flanked by two bulls. Stylized bull's horns spread from the base of the disc. The symbol is also one of might and protection from outside harm. (*Museum of Anatolian Civilizations, Ankara*)

The Fall of Empires and the Survival of Cultures (ca 1200 B.C.)

The height of Hittite and Egyptian power came to a tumultuous end, but the achievements of these peoples lasted long after their governments had been overthrown or diminished in power. New political alignments appeared, but to some degree they all adopted and adapted the examples of their predecessors. They likewise embraced the cultures of those whom they had replaced on the political map.

Political Chaos

Like the Hittite kings, Rameses II (ca 1290–1224 B.C.) used the peace after the Battle of Kadesh to promote the prosperity of his own kingdom. Free from the expense and waste of warfare, he concentrated the income from the natural wealth and the foreign trade of Egypt on internal affairs. In many ways, he was the last great pharaoh of Egypt.

This stable and generally peaceful situation endured until the late thirteenth century B.C., when both the Hittite and the Egyptian empires were destroyed by invaders. The most famous of these marauders, called the **Sea Peoples** by the Egyptians, remain one of the puzzles of ancient history. Despite much new work, modern archaeology is still unable to identify the Sea Peoples satisfactorily. The reason for this uncertainty is that the Sea Peoples were a collection of peoples who went their own, individual ways after their attacks on the Hittites and Egyptians. It is known, however, that their incursions were part of a larger movement of peoples. Although there is serious doubt about whether the Sea Peoples alone overthrew the Hittites, they did deal both the Hittites and the Egyptians a hard blow, making the Hittites vulnerable to overland invasion from the north and driving the Egyptians back to the Nile Delta. The Hittites fell under the external blows, but the Egyptians, shaken and battered, retreated to the delta and held on.

Cultural Endurance and Dissemination

The Egyptians and Mesopotamians established basic social, economic, and cultural patterns in the ancient Near East. Moreover, they spread them far beyond their homelands. Egypt exerted vast influence in Palestine and Syria, while Mesopotamia was influential in southern Anatolia (modern Turkey). Yet it is a mistake to think that these older civilizations moved into a cultural vacuum.

In Palestine and southern Syria the Egyptians found Semitic peoples living in small walled towns. Municipal life was quite advanced, with towns that included urban centers and small outlying hamlets. Although these societies were primarily based on agriculture, there is ample evidence of international trade. In short, both Palestine and Syria possessed an extensive political, social, and religious organization even before the arrival of the Egyptians. Contact had begun as early as the Bronze Age, when the Egyptians had moved along the eastern Mediterranean coast. The contact immediately led to trade. The Egyptians exploited the turquoise and copper trade in the area, and exported local pottery and other goods. Sometimes the Egyptians traded peacefully, but at other times they resorted to military invasion.

Farther north the Egyptians made maritime contact with the Phoenicians, most clearly seen from the excavations at Byblos. The two peoples exchanged not only goods but also technological knowledge. The Egyptians learned many shipbuilding techniques, their own boats being better designed for the Nile than the open sea. The Phoenicians in turn adopted aspects of Egyptian technology. Yet the cultural exchange between the two peoples was by far more important. The Phoenicians honored some Egyptian gods and adopted Egyptian artistic motifs. They learned the Egyptian script and became acquainted with some Egyptian myths. At the same time some deities of Byblos made their appearance in Egypt. Despite armed conflict, trade, not warfare, generally characterized relations in the area.

The situation in northern Syria was similar to that in southern Syria and Palestine. Cities were common, normally ruled by royal families. The families usually shared power and dealt jointly with foreign affairs. They often left the internal administration of the cities to local elders. The cities were primarily mercantile centers but also rich in agricultural produce, timber, and metal deposits. The need for record keeping soon led to the development of writing. These northern Semites adopted Sumerian writing in order to understand their neighbors to the east, but they also adapted it to write their own northern Semitic language. Their texts provide a wealth of information about the life of northern Syria. In the process, northern Syrians gained a solid knowledge of Mesopotamian literature, mathematics, and culture. Both local and Sumerian deities were honored. Despite Mesopotamian influence, northern Syria maintained its native traditions. The cultural exchange was a mixture of adoption, adaptation, contrast, and finally balance, as the two cultures came to understand each other.

Southern Anatolia presented a somewhat similar picture. Human settlement there consisted of trading colonies and small agricultural communities. Thousands of cuneiform tablets testify to commercial and cultural exchanges with Mesopotamia. In Anatolia kingship and temple were closely allied, but the government was not a **theocracy** (rule by a priestly order). A city assembly worked together with the king, and provincial cities were administered by a prince. The political and social organization was one of a firmly established native culture that gladly received foreign ideas while keeping its own identity.

A pattern emerged in Palestine, Syria, and Anatolia. In these areas native cultures established themselves during the prehistoric period. Upon coming into contact with the Egyptian and Mesopotamian civilizations, they adopted many aspects of these cultures, adapting them to their own traditional customs. Yet they also contributed to the advance of Egyptian and Mesopotamian cultures by introducing new technologies and religious ideas. The result was the emergence of a huge group of communities stretching from Egypt in the south to Anatolia in the north and from the Levant in the west to Mesopotamia in the east. Each enjoyed its own individual character, while at the same time sharing many common features with its neighbors.

Summary

For thousands of years Paleolithic peoples roamed this planet seeking game. Only in the Neolithic era—with the invention of new stone tools, a reliance on sustained agriculture, and the domestication of animals—did people begin to live in permanent locations. These villages evolved into towns, where people began to create new social bonds and political organizations. The result was economic prosperity.

The earliest area where these developments led to genuine urban societies is Mesopotamia. Here the Sumerians and then other Mesopotamians developed writing, which enabled their culture to be passed on to others. The wealth of the Mesopotamians made it possible for them to devote time to history, astronomy, urban planning, medicine, and other arts and sciences. Mesopotamian culture was so rich and advanced that neighboring peoples eagerly adopted it, thereby spreading it through much of the Near East.

Nor were the Mesopotamians alone in advancing the civilization of the day. In Egypt another strong culture developed, one that made an impact in Africa, the Near East, and, later, in Greece. The Egyptians too enjoyed such prosperity that they developed writing of their own, mathematical skills, and religious beliefs that influenced the lives of their neighbors. Into this world came the Hittites, an Indo-European people who were culturally less advanced than the Mesopotamians and Egyptians. The Hittites learned from their neighbors and rivals, but they also introduced their own sophisticated political system for administering their empire, a system that in some ways influenced both their contemporaries and later peoples.

Key Terms

Neolithic period	pyramid
irrigation	Hyksos
cuneiform	Bronze Age
nobles	monotheism
clients	polytheism
law code	Indo-European
Amon-Ra	Sea Peoples
Book of the Dead	theocracy
pharaoh	

Notes

1. Quoted in S. N. Kramer, *The Sumerians* (Chicago: University of Chicago Press, 1963), p. 238. John Buckler is the translator of all uncited quotations from a foreign language in Chapters 1–6.
2. J. B. Pritchard, ed., *Ancient Near Eastern Texts,* 3d ed. (Princeton, N.J.: Princeton University Press, 1969), p. 590. Hereafter called ANET.
3. Ibid., p. 171.
4. Kramer, p. 251.
5. ANET, p. 372.
6. Herodotus, *The Histories* 2.14.
7. Quoted in A. H. Gardiner, "Ramesside Texts Relating to the Taxation and Transport of Corn," *Journal of Egyptian Archaeology* 27 (1941): 19–20.
8. Manetho, *History of Egypt,* frag. 42.75–77.

Suggested Reading

Some very illuminating general studies of Near Eastern developments have been published. A broad-ranging work, A. Kuhrt, *The Ancient Near East,* 2 vols. (1995), covers the region from the earliest time to Alexander's conquest. Most welcome is D. Schmandt-Besserat's two-volume work on the origins of writing, *Before Writing,* vol. 1 (1992), which explores the origins of writing, and vol. 2 (1992), which provides actual evidence on the topic. G. Visicato, *The Power of Writing* (2000), studies the practical importance of early Mesopotamian scribes. For the Stonehenge people A. Burl, the leading expert on the topic, provides *The Stone-*

henge People (1987) and *Great Stone Circles* (1999), which examine the people and their monuments.

P. Charvat, *Mesopotamia Before History* (2002), examines the economic, social, and spiritual aspects of the people from about 10,000 to 2334 B.C. H. W. F. Saggs, *The Babylonians* (2000), treats all the eras of Mesopotamian history. G. Stein and M. S. Rothman, *Chiefdoms and Early States in the Near East* (1994), provides a clear view of the political evolution of the region. An ambitious work is M. Hudson and B. Levine, *Privatization in the Ancient Near East and the Classical World* (1996), which treats the concept of private property. A. R. George, *The Babylonian Gilgamesh Epic,* 2 vols. (2003), is a useful resource. G. Leick, *The Babylonians* (2002), provides an introduction to all aspects of Babylonian life and culture.

M. Rice, *Egypt's Making* (2004), treats the origins of Egyptian history. D. P. Silverman, *Ancient Egypt* (1997), also gives a good general account of the region. S. Donadoni, ed., *The Egyptians* (1997), treats various aspects of Egyptian history and life. A. G. McDowell, *Village Life in Ancient Egypt* (1999), is a readable study of the basic social and economic factors of the entire period. D. Meeks and C. Favard-Meeks, *Daily Life of the Egyptian Gods* (1996), with a learned and original point of view, discusses how the Egyptian gods are sometimes treated in literature as an ethnic group not so very different from human beings. A. R. David, *Pyramid Builders of Ancient Egypt,* 2d ed. (1996), studies the lives of the people who actually labored to build the pyramids for their pharaohs. A. Blackman, *Gods, Priests and Men* (1993), is a series of studies in the religion of pharaonic Egypt. Z. Hawass, *Silent Images: Women in Pharaonic Egypt* (2000), blends text and pictures to draw a history of ancient Egyptian women. T. Bryce, *Letters of the Great Kings of the Ancient Near East* (2004), covers the literary correspondence among the major monarchs of the Late Bronze Age. E. D. Oren, *The Hyksos* (1997), concentrates on the archaeological evidence for them.

The coming of the Indo-Europeans receives the attention of M. R. Dexter and K. Jones-Bley, eds., *The Kurgan Culture and the Indo-Europeanization of Europe* (1997), a controversial work that explores the homeland of the Indo-Europeans and the nature of their movements. Less challenging but perhaps more useful is A. Harding, *European Societies in the Bronze Age* (2000), a comprehensive survey of developments in Europe. Often and unfortunately neglected, the Hittites have received relatively little new attention. Dated but solid is O. R. Gurney, *The Hittites,* 2d ed. (1954), a fine introduction by an eminent scholar. Good also is J. G. MacQueen, *The Hittites and Their Contemporaries in Asia Minor,* 2d ed. (1986). The Sea Peoples have been studied by T. and M. Dothan, *People of the Sea* (1992), who concentrate their work on the Philistines.

A truly excellent study of ancient religions, from Sumer to the late Roman Empire, is M. Eliade, ed., *Religions of Antiquity* (1989), which treats concisely but amply all of the religions mentioned in Chapters 1–6.

Listening to the Past

A Quest for Immortality

*T*he human desire to escape the grip of *death, to achieve immortality, is one of the oldest wishes of all peoples. The Sumerian* Epic of Gilgamesh *is the earliest recorded treatment of this topic. The oldest elements of the epic go back at least to the third millennium* B.C. *According to tradition, Gilgamesh was a king of Uruk whom the Sumerians, Babylonians, and Assyrians considered a hero-king and a god. In the story Gilgamesh and his friend Enkidu set out to attain immortality and join the ranks of the gods. They attempt to do so by performing wondrous feats against fearsome agents of the gods, who are determined to thwart them.*

During their quest Enkidu dies. Gilgamesh, more determined than ever to become immortal, begins seeking anyone who might tell him how to do so. His journey involves the effort not only to escape from death but also to reach an understanding of the meaning of life.

The passage begins with Enkidu speaking of a dream that foretells his own death.

Listen, my friend [Gilgamesh], this is the dream I dreamed last night. The heavens roared, and earth rumbled back an answer; between them I stood before an awful being, the sombre-faced man-bird; he had directed on me his purpose. His was a vampire face, his foot was a lion's foot, his hand was an eagle's talon. He fell on me and his claws were in my hair, he held me fast and I smothered; then he transformed me so that my arms became wings covered with feathers. He turned his stare towards me, and he led me away to the palace of Irkalla, the Queen of Darkness [the goddess of the underworld; in other words, an agent of death], to the house from which none who enters ever returns, down the road from which there is no coming back.

At this point Enkidu dies, whereupon Gilgamesh sets off on his quest for the secret of immortality. During his travels he meets with Siduri, the wise and good-natured goddess of wine, who gives him the following advice.

Gilgamesh, where are you hurrying to? You will never find that life for which you are looking. When the gods created man they allotted to him death, but life they retained in their own keeping. As for you, Gilgamesh, fill your belly with good things; day and night, night and day, dance and be merry, feast and rejoice. Let your clothes be fresh, bathe yourself in water, cherish the little child that holds your hand, and make your wife happy in your embrace; for this too is the lot of man.

Ignoring Siduri's advice, Gilgamesh continues his journey, until he finds Utnapishtim. Meeting Utnapishtim is especially important because, like Gilgamesh, he was once a mortal, but the gods so favored him that they put him in an eternal paradise. Gilgamesh puts to Utnapishtim the question that is the reason for his quest.

Oh, father Utnapishtim, you who have entered the assembly of the gods, I wish to question you concerning the living and the dead, how shall I find the life for which I am searching?

Utnapishtim said, "There is no permanence. Do we build a house to stand forever, do we seal a contract to hold for all time? Do brothers divide an inheritance to keep forever, does the flood-time of rivers endure? . . . What is there between the master and the servant when both have fulfilled their doom? When the Anunnaki [the gods of the underworld], the judges, come together, and Mammetun [the goddess of fate] the mother of destinies, together they decree the fates of men. Life and death they allot but the day of death they do not disclose.

Then Gilgamesh said to Utnapishtim the Faraway, "I look at you now, Utnapishtim, and your appearance is no different from mine; there is nothing strange in your features. I thought I should find you like a hero prepared for battle, but you lie here taking your ease on your back. Tell me truly, how was it that you came to enter the company of the gods and to possess everlasting life?" Utnapishtim said to Gilgamesh, "I shall reveal to you a mystery, I shall tell you a secret of the gods."

Utnapishtim then tells Gilgamesh of a time when the great god Enlil had become angered with the Sumerians and encouraged the other gods to wipe out humanity. The god Ea, however, warned Utnapishtim about the gods' decision to send a great flood to destroy the Sumerians. He commanded Utnapishtim to build a boat big enough to hold his family, various artisans, and all animals in order to survive the flood that was to come. Although Enlil was infuriated by the Sumerians' survival, Ea rebuked him. Then Enlil relented and blessed Utnapishtim with eternal paradise. After telling the story, Utnapishtim foretells Gilgamesh's fate.

Utnapishtim said, ". . . The destiny was fulfilled which the father of the gods, Enlil of the mountain, had decreed for Gilgamesh: In nether-earth the darkness will show him a light: of mankind, all that are known, none will leave a monument for generations to compare with his. The heroes, the wise men, like the new moon have their waxing and waning. Men will say, Who has ever ruled with might and power like his? As in the dark month, the month of shadows, so without him there is no light. O Gilgamesh, this was the meaning of your dream [of immortality]. You were given the kingship, such was your destiny, everlasting life was not your destiny. Because of this do not be sad at heart, do not be grieved or oppressed; he [Enlil] has given you power to bind and to loose, to be the darkness and the light of mankind. He has given unexampled supremacy over the people, victory in

Gilgamesh, from decorative panel of a lyre unearthed at Ur. *(The University Museum, University of Pennsylvania, neg. T4-108)*

battle from which no fugitive returns, in forays and assaults from which there is no going back. But do not abuse this power, deal justly with your servants in the palace, deal justly before the face of the Sun."

Questions for Analysis

1. What does the *Epic of Gilgamesh* reveal about Sumerian attitudes toward the gods and human beings?

2. At the end of his quest, did Gilgamesh achieve immortality? If so, what was the nature of that immortality?

3. What does the epic tell us about Sumerian views of the nature of human life? Where do human beings fit into the cosmic world?

Source: The Epic of Gilgamesh, translated by N. K. Sanders. Penguin Classics 1960, Second revised edition, 1972, pp. 91–119. Copyright © N. K. Sanders, 1960, 1964, 1972. Reproduced by permission of Penguin Books Ltd.

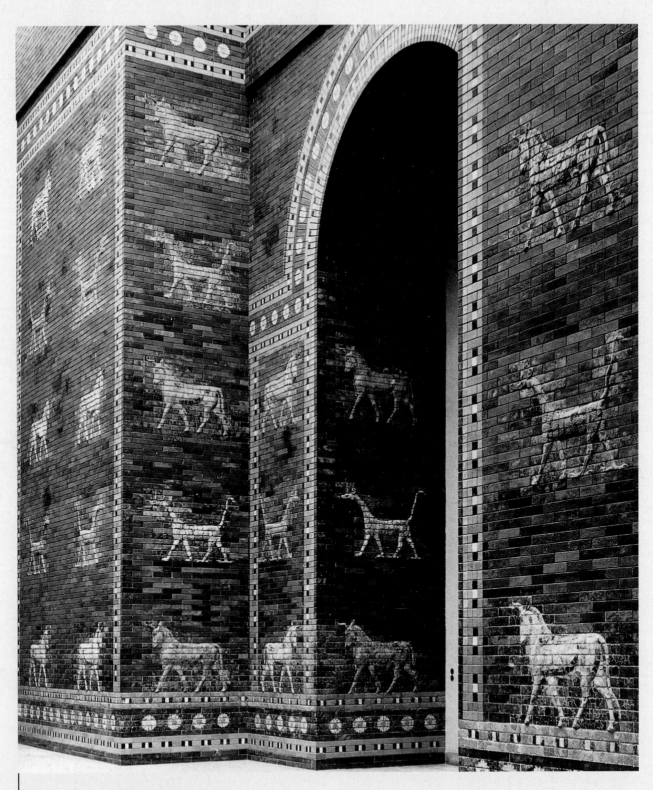

Reconstruction of the "Ishtar Gate," Babylon, early sixth century B.C. Located in the Berlin Museum. *(Bildarchiv Preussischer Kulturbesitz/Art Resource, NY)*

Small Kingdoms and Mighty Empires in the Near East

*T*he migratory invasions that brought down the Hittites and stunned the Egyptians in the late thirteenth century B.C. ushered in an era of confusion and weakness. Although much was lost in the chaos, the old cultures of the ancient Near East survived to nurture new societies. In the absence of powerful empires, the Phoenicians, Hebrews, and many other peoples carved out small independent kingdoms, until the Near East was a patchwork of them. During this period Hebrew culture and religion evolved under the influence of urbanism, kings, and prophets.

In the ninth century B.C. this jumble of small states gave way to an empire that for the first time embraced the entire Near East. Yet the very ferocity of the Assyrian Empire led to its downfall only two hundred years later. In 550 B.C. the Persians and Medes, who had migrated into Iran, created a "world empire" stretching from Anatolia in the west to the Indus Valley in the east. For over two hundred years the Persians gave the ancient Near East peace and stability.

- How did Egypt, its political greatness behind it, pass on its cultural heritage to its African neighbors?
- How did the Hebrew state evolve, and what was daily life like in Hebrew society?
- What forces helped to shape Hebrew religious thought, still powerfully influential in today's world?
- What enabled the Assyrians to overrun their neighbors, and how did their cruelty finally cause their undoing?
- Last, how did Iranian nomads create the Persian Empire?

This chapter will look at these questions.

*R*ecovery and Diffusion

If the fall of empires was a time of massive political disruption, it also ushered in a period of cultural diffusion, an expansion of what had already blossomed in the broad region. Even though empires expired, many small kingdoms survived, along with a largely shared culture. These small states and local societies

MAP 2.1 Small Kingdoms of the Near East   This map illustrates the political fragmentation of the Near East after the great wave of invasions that occurred during the thirteenth century B.C.

had learned much from the great powers, but they nonetheless retained their own lore and native traditions, which they passed on to their neighbors, thus diffusing a Near Eastern culture that was slowly becoming common in nature. The best-known examples can be found along the coast of the eastern Mediterranean, where various peoples—some of them newcomers—created homes and petty kingdoms in Phoenicia and Palestine. After the Sea Peoples raided Egypt, a branch of them, known in the Bible as Philistines, settled along the coast of Palestine (see Map 2.1). Establishing themselves in five cities somewhat inland from the sea, the Philistines set about farming and raising flocks.

A Shattered Egypt and a Rising Phoenicia

The invasions of the Sea Peoples brought the great days of Egyptian power to an end. The long wars against invaders weakened and impoverished Egypt, causing polit-

ical upheaval and economic chaos. One scribe left behind a somber portrait of Egypt stunned and leaderless:

The land of Egypt was abandoned and every man was a law to himself. During many years there was no leader who could speak for others. Central government lapsed, small officials and headmen took over the whole land. Any man, great or small, might kill his neighbor. In the distress and vacuum that followed . . . men banded together to plunder one another. They treated the gods no better than men, and cut off the temple revenues.[1]

No longer able to dream of foreign conquests, Egypt looked to its own security from foreign invasion. Egyptians suffered a four-hundred-year period of political fragmentation, a new dark age known to Egyptian specialists as the Third Intermediate Period (eleventh–seventh centuries B.C.). (See the feature "Individuals in Society: Wen-Amon.")

In southern Egypt, meanwhile, the pharaoh's decline opened the way to the energetic Nubians, who extended their authority northward throughout the Nile Valley. Since the imperial days of the Eighteenth Dynasty (see pages 23–24), the Nubians, too, had adopted many features of Egyptian culture. Now Nubian kings and aristocrats embraced Egyptian culture wholesale. Thus the Nubians and the Libyans repeated an old Near Eastern phenomenon: new peoples conquered old centers of political and military power but were assimilated into the older culture.

The reunification of Egypt occurred late and unexpectedly. With Egypt distracted and disorganized by foreign invasions, an independent African state, the kingdom of Kush, grew up in the region of modern Sudan with its capital at Nepata. Like the Libyans, the Kushites worshiped Egyptian gods and used Egyptian hieroglyphs. In the eighth century B.C. their king, Piankhy, swept through the entire Nile Valley from Nepata in the south to the delta in the north. United once again, Egypt enjoyed a brief period of peace during which Egyptians continued to assimilate their conquerors. Nonetheless, reunification of the realm did not lead to a new Egyptian empire.

Yet Egypt's legacy to its African neighbors remained vibrant and rich. By trading and exploring southward along the coast of the Red Sea, the Egyptians introduced their goods and ideas as far south as the land of Punt, probably a region on the Somali coast. Egypt was the primary civilizing force in Nubia, which became another version of the pharaoh's realm, complete with royal pyramids and Egyptian deities. Egyptian religion penetrated as far south as Ethiopia.

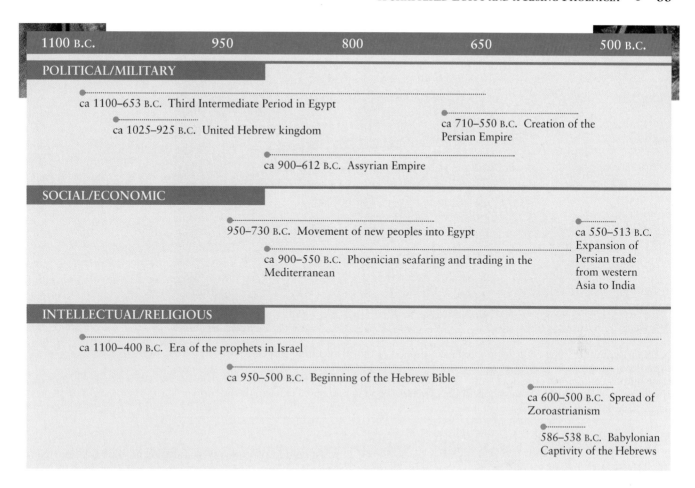

1100 B.C.	950	800	650	500 B.C.

POLITICAL/MILITARY

ca 1100–653 B.C. Third Intermediate Period in Egypt

ca 1025–925 B.C. United Hebrew kingdom

ca 710–550 B.C. Creation of the Persian Empire

ca 900–612 B.C. Assyrian Empire

SOCIAL/ECONOMIC

950–730 B.C. Movement of new peoples into Egypt

ca 550–513 B.C. Expansion of Persian trade from western Asia to India

ca 900–550 B.C. Phoenician seafaring and trading in the Mediterranean

INTELLECTUAL/RELIGIOUS

ca 1100–400 B.C. Era of the prophets in Israel

ca 950–500 B.C. Beginning of the Hebrew Bible

ca 600–500 B.C. Spread of Zoroastrianism

586–538 B.C. Babylonian Captivity of the Hebrews

One of the sturdy peoples who rose to prominence were the Phoenicians, a Semitic-speaking people who had long inhabited several cities along the coast of modern Lebanon. They had lived under the shadow of the Hittites and Egyptians, but in this period the Phoenicians enjoyed full independence. Unlike the Philistine newcomers, who turned from seafaring to farming, the Phoenicians took to the sea and became outstanding merchants and explorers. They played a predominate role in international trade, manufacturing many goods. The

Life Goes On Although the Egyptians suffered political defeat, much of their society continued without interruption. Here a farmer and two oxen still plow their field as usual. In many instances, a change of rule did not greatly affect the lives of ordinary people. *(Erich Lessing/Art Resource, NY)*

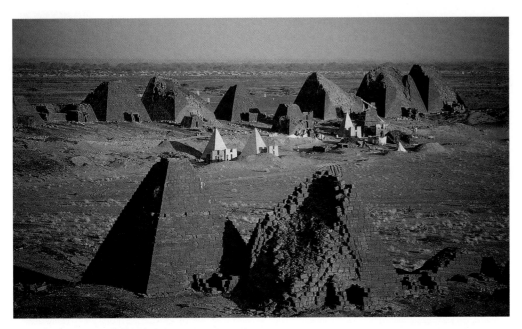

Nubian Pyramids   The Nubians adopted many aspects of Egyptian culture and customs. The pyramids shown here are not as magnificent as their Egyptian predecessors, but they served the same purpose of honoring the dead king. Their core was constructed of bricks, which were then covered with stone blocks. At the doors of the pyramids stood monumental gates to the interiors of the tombs. *(Michael Yamashita)*

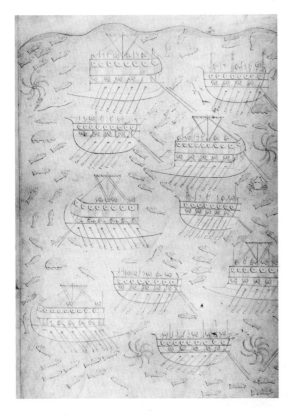

most valued products were purple and blue textiles, from which originated their Greek name, Phoenicians, meaning **"Purple People."** They also worked metals, which they shipped processed or as ore. They imported rare goods and materials from Persia in the East and from their neighbors to the south. Their exported wares went to Egypt, as far west as North Africa and Spain, and even into the Atlantic. The variety and quality of their exports generally made them welcome visitors. Although their goal was trade, not colonization, they nevertheless founded Carthage in 813 B.C., a city that would one day struggle with Rome for domination of the western Mediterranean. Their voyages naturally brought them into contact with the Greeks, to whom they introduced the older cultures of the Near East. Indeed, their enduring significance lay in their spreading the experiences of the East throughout the western Mediterranean.

Phoenician culture was urban, based on the prosperous commercial centers of Tyre, Sidon, and Byblos. The

Phoenician Biremes   This Assyrian artist has caught the savor of a Phoenician fleet at sea. The ships are biremes, meaning ships with two banks of oars, capable of carrying cargo and fighting as warships. *(Courtesy of the Trustees of the British Museum)*

Wen-Amon

Surprising as it may sound, the life of a bureaucrat is not always easy. Wen-Amon, an official of the temple of Amon-Ra at Karnak in Egypt, learned that on an authorized mission to Phoenicia. He left his own narrative of his travels, which date to sometime in the eleventh century B.C. Egypt, the shattered kingdom, could no longer exert the authority that it had enjoyed under the pharaohs of the New Kingdom. Despite this political disruption, Egyptian officials continued to expect the traditional respect of the people whom they called "Asiatics." These Asiatics, however, had begun to doubt the power of Egypt and expressed their independence by openly opposing its authority.

Wen-Amon personally experienced this changed atmosphere when he was sent to Byblos in Phoenicia to obtain lumber for Amon-Ra's ceremonial barge. Wen-Amon's detailed account of his experiences comes in the form of an official report to the chief priest of the temple.

Entrusted with ample funds in silver to pay for the lumber, Wen-Amon set out on his voyage. He docked at Dor, in modern Israel, which was independent of the pharaoh, but the local prince received him graciously. While his ship was at anchor, one of Wen-Amon's own sailors vanished with the silver. Wen-Amon immediately reported the robbery to the prince and demanded that he investigate the theft. Wen-Amon pointed out that the silver belonged to Amon-Ra and the great men of Egypt. The prince flatly told Wen-Amon that he did not care whether Wen-Amon and the others were important men. He pointed out that an Egyptian, one of Wen-Amon's own men, had stolen the silver. It was not the prince's problem. No earlier Asian prince would have dared speak to a high Egyptian official in such terms.

Although rebuffed, Wen-Amon found a ship from Byblos and robbed it of an equivalent amount of silver. When he left Dor and entered the harbor of Byblos, the prince there, who had learned of the theft, ordered him to leave. For twenty-nine days there was an impasse. Each day that Wen-Amon remained, the prince told him to get out, but respect both for the great days of Egypt and for Amon-Ra kept the prince from laying hands on Wen-Amon. Finally, the prince sent for Wen-Amon and asked for his papers. A heated argument ensued, with the prince shouting, "I am not your servant. I am not the servant of him who sent you either." Then he asked Wen-Amon what silly voyage he was making. By this time the Egyptian was greatly annoyed,

Pillars of the great temple of Amon at Karnak, New Kingdom. (Marc Bernheim/Woodfin Camp & Associates)

and he reminded the prince of the greatness of Amon-Ra. He flatly stated that unless the prince honored the great god, he and his land would have neither health nor prosperity. When the two calmed down, the prince agreed to send the timber to Egypt.

After the timber was loaded aboard his ship, Wen-Amon saw eleven enemy ships entering the harbor. They anchored, and those in charge reported to the prince of Byblos that they had come for the Egyptians. He refused to hand them over, saying that he would never arrest a messenger of Amon-Ra. He agreed, however, to send Wen-Amon away first and allow the enemy ships to pursue the Egyptians. Stormy seas blew the Egyptian ship into Hittite territory. When Wen-Amon landed there, Queen Heteb granted him protection and asylum.

The papyrus breaks off at this point, but it is obvious that Wen-Amon weathered his various storms to return safely to Egypt. The document illustrates the presumption of power by Wen-Amon and his bluster at the lack of respect shown him. It also shows how Egypt's neighbors no longer feared Egyptian power. Finally, it illustrates the impact of Egyptian culture and religion on the peoples living along the coast of the Levant. Although Egyptian political power was in eclipse, its cultural legacy endured.

Questions for Analysis

1. What do Wen-Amon's experiences tell us about political conditions in the eastern Mediterranean?
2. Since Wen-Amon could no longer depend upon the majesty of Egypt for respect, how did he fulfill his duty?

The **history companion** *features additional information and activities related to this topic.* history.college.hmco.com/students

HIEROGLYPHIC	REPRESENTS	UGARITIC	PHOENICIAN	GREEK	ROMAN
	Throw stick			Γ	G
	Man with raised arms			E	E
	Basket with handle			K	K
	Water			M	M
	Snake			N	N
	Eye			O	O
	Mouth			Π	P
	Head			P	R
	Pool with lotus flowers		W	Σ	S
	House			B	B
	Ox-head			A	A

FIGURE 2.1 Origins of the Alphabet   List of Roman, hieroglyphic, Ugaritic, Phoenician, and Greek sign forms. *(Source: A. B. Knapp,* The History and Culture of Ancient Western Asia and Egypt, *Dorsey Press, Chicago, 1988, p. 191. Reprinted by permission of Wadsworth, a division of Thomson Learning, www.thomsonrights.com.)*

Phoenicians' overwhelming cultural achievement was the development of an alphabet (see Figure 2.1): they, unlike other literate peoples, used one letter to designate one sound, a system that vastly simplified writing and reading. The Greeks modified this alphabet and then used it to write their own language.

The Children of Israel

The fall of the Hittite Empire and Egypt's collapse created a vacuum of power in the western Near East that allowed for the rise of numerous small states. South of Phoenicia arose a small kingdom, the land of the ancient Jews or Hebrews. It is difficult to say precisely who the Hebrews were and what brought them to this area, because virtually the only source for much of their history is the Bible, which is essentially a religious document. Even though it contains much historical material, it also contains many Hebrew myths and legends. Moreover, it was compiled at different times, with the earliest parts dating to between about 950 and 800 B.C.

Earlier Mesopotamian and Egyptian sources refer to people called the **Hapiru,** which seems to mean homeless, independent **nomads.** These nomads led roaming lives, always in search of pasturage for their flocks. According to Hebrew tradition, the followers of Abraham migrated from Mesopotamia, but Egyptian documents record Hapiru already in Syria and Palestine in the second millennium B.C. The Hebrews were probably a part of them. Together with other seminomadic peoples, they probably migrated into the Nile Delta seeking good land. According to the Bible the Egyptians enslaved them. One group, however, under the leadership of Moses, perhaps a semimythical figure, left Egypt in what the Hebrews remembered as the Exodus. From Egypt they wandered in the Sinai Peninsula, until they settled in Palestine in the thirteenth century B.C.

In Palestine the Hebrews encountered the Philistines; the Amorites, relatives of Hammurabi's Babylonians; and the Semitic-speaking Canaanites. Despite numerous wars, contact between the Hebrews and their new neighbors was not always hostile. The Hebrews freely mingled with the Canaanites, and some went so far as to worship **Baal,** an ancient Semitic fertility god represented as a golden calf. Archaeological research supports the biblical account of these developments. In 1990 an expedition sponsored by Harvard University discovered a statue of a golden calf in its excavations of Ashkelon in modern Israel. Despite the anger expressed in the Bible over Hebrew worship of

The Golden Calf According to the Hebrew Bible, Moses descended from Mount Sinai, where he had received the Ten Commandments, to find the Hebrews worshiping a golden calf, which was against Yahweh's laws. In July 1990 an American archaeological team found this model of a gilded calf inside a pot. The figurine, which dates to about 1550 B.C., is strong evidence for the existence of the cult represented by the calf in Palestine. *(Courtesy of the Leon Levy Expedition to Ashkelon. Photo: Carl Andrews)*

Baal, there is nothing surprising about the phenomenon. Once again, newcomers adapted themselves to the culture of an older, well-established people.

The greatest danger to the Hebrews came from the Philistines, whose superior technology and military organization at first made them invincible. In Saul (ca 1000 B.C.), a farmer of the tribe of Benjamin, the Hebrews found a champion and a spirited leader. In the biblical account Saul carried the war to the Philistines, often without success. Yet in the meantime he established a monarchy over the twelve Hebrew tribes.

Saul's work was carried on by David of Bethlehem, who in his youth had followed Saul into battle against the Philistines. Through courage and cunning, David pushed

back the Philistines and waged war against his other neighbors. To give his kingdom a capital, he captured the city of Jerusalem, which he enlarged, fortified, and made the religious and political center of his realm. David's military successes won the Hebrews unprecedented security, and his forty-year reign was a period of vitality and political consolidation. His work in consolidating the monarchy and enlarging the kingdom paved the way for his son Solomon.

Solomon (ca 965–925 B.C.) applied his energies to creating a nation out of a collection of tribes ruled by a king. He divided the kingdom into twelve territorial districts cutting across the old tribal borders. To bring his kingdom up to the level of its more sophisticated neighbors, he set about a building program to make Israel a respectable Near Eastern state. Work was begun on a magnificent temple in Jerusalem and on cities, palaces, fortresses, and roads. Solomon dedicated the temple in grand style and made it the home of the Ark of the Covenant, the cherished chest that contained the holiest of Hebrew religious articles. The temple in Jerusalem was intended to be the religious heart of the kingdom and the symbol of Hebrew unity. Solomon turned a rude kingdom into a state with broad commercial horizons and greater knowledge of the outside world. At his death, the Hebrews broke into two political halves (see Map 2.1). The northern part of the kingdom of David and Solomon became Israel, with its capital at Samaria. The southern half was Judah, and Jerusalem remained its center. With political division went a religious rift: Israel, the northern kingdom, established rival sanctuaries for gods other than Yahweh. The Hebrew nation was divided, but at least it was divided into two far more sophisticated political units than before the time of Solomon. Nonetheless, war soon broke out between them, as recorded in the Bible. Unexpected and independent evidence of this warfare came to light in August 1993, when an Israeli archaeologist found an inscription that refers to the "House of David," the royal line of Israel. The stone celebrates an Israelite victory from the early ninth century B.C. This discovery is the first mention of King David's royal family outside the Bible and helps to confirm the biblical account of the fighting between the two kingdoms.

Eventually, the northern kingdom of Israel was wiped out by the Assyrians, but the southern kingdom of Judah survived numerous calamities until the Babylonians crushed it in 587 B.C. The survivors were sent into exile in Babylonia, a period commonly known as the **Babylonian Captivity.** In 538 B.C. the Persians, under their king Cyrus the Great, permitted some forty thousand exiles to return to Jerusalem. During and especially after the Babylonian Captivity, the exiles redefined their beliefs and practices, and thus established what they believed was the law of Yahweh. Those who lived by these precepts can be called *Jews.*

The Evolution of Jewish Religion

Hand in hand with their political evolution from fierce nomads to urban dwellers, the Hebrews were evolving spiritual ideas that still permeate Western society. Their chief literary product, the Hebrew Bible, has fundamentally influenced both Christianity and Islam and still exerts a compelling force on the modern world.

Fundamental to an understanding of Jewish religion is the concept of the **Covenant,** a formal agreement between Yahweh and the Hebrew people. According to the Bible, the god **Yahweh,** who in medieval Latin became "Jehovah," appeared to Moses on Mount Sinai. There Yahweh made a covenant with the Hebrews that was in fact a contract: if the Hebrews worshiped Yahweh as their only god, he would consider them his chosen people and protect them from their enemies. The Hebrews believed that Yahweh had led them out of bondage in Egypt and had helped them to conquer their new land, the Promised Land. In return, the Hebrews worshiped Yahweh alone and obeyed his Ten Commandments, an ethical code of conduct revealed to them by Moses.

Unlike Akhenaten's monotheism, Hebrew monotheism became the religion of a whole people, deeply felt and cherished. Some might fall away from Yahweh's worship, and various holy men had to exhort the Hebrews to honor the Covenant, but on the whole the people clung to Yahweh. Yet the Hebrews did not consider it their duty to spread the belief in the one god, as later Christians did. As the chosen people, their chief duty was to maintain the worship of Yahweh as he demanded. That worship was embodied in the Ten Commandments, which forbade the Hebrews to steal, murder, lie, or commit adultery. The Covenant was a constant force in Hebrew life (see the feature "Listening to the Past: The Covenant Between Yahweh and the Hebrews" on pages 52–53).

From the Ten Commandments evolved Hebrew law, a code of law and custom originating with Moses and built on by priests and prophets. The earliest part of this code, the **Torah** or Mosaic law, was often as harsh as Hammurabi's code, which had a powerful impact on it. Later tradition, largely the work of prophets who lived from the eleventh to the fifth centuries B.C., was more humanitarian. The work of the prophet Jeremiah (ca 626 B.C.) exemplifies this gentler spirit. According to Jeremiah,

Yahweh demanded righteousness from his people and protection for the weak and helpless.

The uniqueness of this phenomenon can be seen by comparing the essence of Hebrew monotheism with the religious outlook of the Mesopotamians. Whereas the Mesopotamians considered their gods capricious, the Hebrews knew what Yahweh expected. The Hebrews believed that their god would protect them and make them prosper if they obeyed his commandments. The Mesopotamians thought human beings insignificant compared to the gods, so insignificant that the gods might even be indifferent to them. The Hebrews, too, considered themselves puny in comparison to Yahweh. Yet they were Yahweh's chosen people, whom he had promised never to abandon. Finally, though the Mesopotamians believed that the gods generally preferred good to evil, their religion did not demand ethical conduct. The Hebrews could please their god only by living up to high moral standards as well as worshiping him.

Daily Life in Israel

The nomadic Hebrews first entered modern Palestine as tribes, numerous families who thought of themselves as all related to one another. At first, good farmland, pastureland, and water spots were held in common by the tribe. Common use of land was—and still is—characteristic of nomadic peoples. Typically each family or group of families in the tribe drew lots every year to determine who worked which fields. But as formerly nomadic peoples turned increasingly to settled agriculture, communal use of land gave way to family ownership. In this respect the experience of the ancient Hebrews seems typical of that of many early peoples. Slowly the shift from nomad to farmer affected far more than just how people fed themselves. Family relationships reflected evolving circumstances. With the transition to settled agriculture, the tribe gradually became less important than the extended family. With the advent of village life and finally full-blown urban life, the extended family in turn gave way to the nuclear family.

For women, however, the evolution of Jewish society led to less freedom of action, especially in religious life. At first women served as priestesses in festivals and religious cults. Some were considered prophetesses of Yahweh, although they never conducted his official rituals. In the course of time, however, the worship of Yahweh became more male-oriented and male-dominated. Increasingly, he also became the god of holiness, and to worship him people must be pure in mind and body. Women were seen as ritually impure because of menstruation and childbirth.

Because of these "impurities," women now played a much reduced role in religion. Even when they did participate in religious rites, they were segregated from the men. For the most part, women were largely confined to the home and the care of the family.

Marriage was one of the most important and joyous events in Hebrew family life. The typical marriage in ancient Israel was monogamous, and a virtuous wife was revered and honored.

As in most other societies, in ancient Israel the early education of children was in the mother's hands. She taught her children right from wrong and gave them their first instruction in the moral values of society. As boys grew older, they received education from their fathers in religion and the history of their people. Many children were taught to read and write, and the head of each family was probably able to write. Fathers also taught sons the family craft or trade. Boys soon learned that inattention could be painful, for Jewish custom advised fathers to be strict: "He that spareth his rod hateth his son: but he that loveth him chasteneth him betimes."[2]

The development of urban life among the Jews created new economic opportunities, especially in crafts and trades. People specialized in certain occupations, such as milling flour, baking bread, making pottery, weaving, and carpentry. All these crafts were family trades. Sons worked with their father, daughters with their mother. If the business prospered, the family might be assisted by a few paid workers or slaves. The practitioners of a craft usually lived in a particular section of town, a custom still prevalent in the Middle East today. Commerce and trade developed later than crafts. Trade with neighboring countries was handled by foreigners, usually Phoenicians. Jews dealt mainly in local trade, and in most instances craftsmen and farmers sold directly to their customers.

These social and economic developments also left their mark on daily life by prompting the compilation of two significant works, the Torah and the Talmud. The Torah is basically the Mosaic law, or the first five books of the Bible. The Talmud is a later work composed during the period between the Roman destruction of the second temple in A.D. 70 and the Arab conquest of A.D. 636. The **Talmud** records civil and ceremonial law and Jewish legend. The dietary rules of the Jews provide an excellent example of both the relationship between the Torah and the Talmud and their effect on ordinary life and culture. According to the Torah, people were not to eat meat that they found in the field. This very sensible prohibition protected them from eating dangerous food. Yet if meat from the countryside could not be eaten, some rules were needed for meat in the city. The solution found in the Talmud was a set of regulations for the proper way to conduct ritual slaughter. Together these two works regulated and codified Jewish dietary customs.

Assyria, the Military Monarchy

Small kingdoms like those of the Phoenicians and the Hebrews could exist only in the absence of a major power. The beginning of the ninth century B.C. saw the rise of such a power: the Assyrians of northern Mesopotamia, whose chief capital was at Nineveh on the Tigris River. The Assyrians were a Semitic-speaking people heavily influenced, like so many other peoples of the Near East, by the Mesopotamian culture of Babylon to the south. They were also one of the most warlike peoples in history, largely because throughout their history they were threatened by neighboring folk. Living in an open, exposed land, the Assyrians experienced frequent and devastating attacks by the wild, war-loving tribes to their north and east and by the Babylonians to the south. The constant threat to survival experienced by the Assyrians promoted political cohesion and military might. Yet they were also a mercantile people who had long pursued commerce with both the Babylonians in the south and other peoples in the north.

The Power of Assyria

For over two hundred years the Assyrians labored to dominate the Near East. In 859 B.C. the new Assyrian king, Shalmaneser, unleashed the first of a long series of attacks on the peoples of Syria and Palestine. Year after relentless year, Assyrian armies hammered at the peoples of the West. These ominous events inaugurated two turbulent centuries marked by Assyrian military campaigns, constant efforts by Syria and the two Jewish kingdoms to maintain or recover their independence, and eventual Assyrian conquest of Babylonia and northern Egypt. In addition, periodic political instability occurred in Assyria itself, which prompted stirrings of freedom throughout the Near East.

Under the Assyrian kings Tiglath-pileser III (774–727 B.C.) and Sargon II (r. 721–705 B.C.), both mighty warriors, the Near East trembled as never before under the blows of Assyrian armies. The Assyrians stepped up their attacks on Anatolia, Syria, and Palestine. The kingdom of Israel and many other states fell; others, like the kingdom of Judah, became subservient to the warriors from the Tigris. In 717 to 716 B.C., Sargon led his army in a sweeping attack along the Philistine coast, where he

Surrender of the Jews   The Jewish king Jahu finally surrendered to the Assyrians. Here his envoy kneels before the Assyrian king Shalmaneser III in total defeat. Although the Assyrian king treated Jahu well, his people were led off into slavery. *(British Museum/Michael Holford)*

defeated the pharaoh. Sargon also lashed out at Assyria's traditional enemies to the north and then turned south against a renewed threat in Babylonia. By means of almost constant warfare, Tiglath-pileser III and Sargon carved out an Assyrian empire that stretched from east and north of the Tigris River to central Egypt (see Map 2.2). Revolt against the Assyrians inevitably promised the rebels bloody battles and cruel sieges.

Though atrocity and terrorism struck unspeakable fear into Assyria's subjects, Assyria's success was actually due to sophisticated, farsighted, and effective military organization. By Sargon's time the Assyrians had invented the mightiest military machine the ancient Near East had ever seen. The mainstay of the Assyrian army was the infantryman armed with spear and sword and protected by helmet and armor. The Assyrian army also featured archers, some on foot, others on horseback, still others in chariots—the latter ready to wield lances once they had expended their supply of arrows. Some infantry archers wore heavy armor. These soldiers served as a primitive field artillery, whose job was to sweep the enemy's walls of defenders so that others could storm the defenses. Slingers also served as artillery in pitched battles. For mobility on the battlefield, the Assyrians organized a corps of chariots.

Assyrian military genius was remarkable for the development of a wide variety of siege machinery and techniques, including excavation to undermine city walls and battering rams to knock down walls and gates. Never before in the Near East had anyone applied such technical knowledge to warfare. The Assyrians even invented the concept of a corps of engineers, who bridged rivers with

pontoons or provided soldiers with inflatable skins for swimming. And the Assyrians knew how to coordinate their efforts, both in open battle and in siege warfare. King Sennacherib's account of his siege of Jerusalem in 701 B.C. is a vivid portrait of the Assyrian war machine:

As to Hezekiah, the Jew, he did not submit to my yoke, I laid siege to 46 of his strong cities, walled forts and to the countless small villages in their vicinity, and conquered them by means of well-stamped earth-ramps, and battering rams brought thus near to the walls combined with the attack by foot soldiers, using mines, breaches as well as sapper work. . . . Himself I made prisoner in Jerusalem, his royal residence, like a bird in a cage. I surrounded him with earthwork in order to molest those who were leaving his city's gate.[3]

The Jews recorded this same incident, and historians find it interesting to see how two different peoples interpreted the same event. The Jews ignored political and military events and insisted that the siege of Jerusalem resulted from Hezekiah's disbelief that Yahweh could repel the Assyrian invasion. For the Assyrians the conquest was proof of their military superiority. For the Jews it stood as a symbol of the fate of those who mistrusted their god.

Assyrian Rule and Culture

Not only did the Assyrians know how to win battles, but they also knew how to use their victories. As early as the reign of Tiglath-pileser III, the Assyrian kings began to organize their conquered territories into an empire. The lands closest to Assyria became provinces governed by

MAP 2.2 The Assyrian and Persian Empires   The Assyrian Empire at its height (ca 650 B.C.) included almost all of the old centers of power in the ancient Near East. By 513 B.C., however, the Persian Empire not only included more of that area but also extended as far east as western India. With the rise of the Medes and Persians, the balance of power in the Near East shifted east of Mesopotamia for the first time.

Assyrian officials. Kingdoms beyond the provinces were not annexed but became dependent states that followed Assyria's lead. The Assyrian king chose their rulers either by regulating the succession of native kings or by supporting native kings who appealed to him. Against more distant states the Assyrian kings waged frequent war in order to conquer them outright or make the dependent states secure.

In the seventh century B.C. Assyrian power seemed firmly established. Yet the downfall of Assyria was swift and complete. Babylon finally won its independence in 626 B.C. and joined forces with a newly aggressive people, the Medes, an Indo-European-speaking folk from Iran. Together the Babylonians and the Medes destroyed the Assyrian Empire in 612 B.C., paving the way for the rise of the Persians. The Hebrew prophet Nahum spoke for many when he asked: "Nineveh is laid waste: who will bemoan her?"[4] Their cities destroyed and their power shattered, the Assyrians disappeared from history, remembered only as a cruel people of the Old Testament

who oppressed the Hebrews. Two hundred years later, when the Greek adventurer and historian Xenophon passed by the ruins of Nineveh, he marveled at the extent of the former city but knew nothing of the Assyrians. The glory of their empire was forgotten.

Yet modern archaeology has brought the Assyrians out of obscurity. In 1839 the intrepid English archaeologist and traveler A. H. Layard began the most noteworthy excavations of Nineveh, then a mound of debris beside the Tigris. His findings electrified the world. Layard's workers unearthed masterpieces, including monumental sculpted figures—huge winged bulls, human-headed lions, and sphinxes—as well as brilliantly sculpted friezes. Equally valuable were the numerous Assyrian cuneiform documents, which ranged from royal accounts of mighty military campaigns to simple letters by common people.

Among the most renowned of Layard's finds were the Assyrian palace reliefs, whose number has been increased by the discoveries of twentieth-century archaeologists. Assyrian kings delighted in scenes of war, which their

Royal Lion Hunt   This wall painting from the seventh century B.C. depicts the Assyrian king frightening a lion, a typical representation of the energy and artistic brilliance of Assyrian artists. The lion hunt signified the king as the protector of society, not simply as a sportsman. *(Louvre/ Réunion des Musées Nationaux/Art Resource, NY)*

artists depicted in graphic detail. By the time of Ashurbanipal (r. 668–633 B.C.), Assyrian artists had hit on the idea of portraying a series of episodes—in fact, a visual narrative of events that had actually taken place. Scene followed scene in a continuous frieze, so that the viewer could follow the progress of a military campaign from the time the army marched out until the enemy was conquered.

Assyrian art fared better than Assyrian military power. The techniques of Assyrian artists influenced the Persians, who adapted them to gentler scenes. In fact, many Assyrian innovations, military and political as well as artistic, were taken over wholesale by the Persians. Although the memory of Assyria was hateful throughout the Near East, the fruits of Assyrian organizational genius helped enable the Persians to bring peace and stability to the same regions where Assyrian armies had spread terror.

The Empire of the Persian Kings

Like the Hittites before them, the Iranians were Indo-Europeans from central Europe and southern Russia. They migrated into the land to which they have given their name, the area between the Caspian Sea and the Persian Gulf. Like the Hittites, they then fell under the spell of the more sophisticated cultures of their Mesopotamian neighbors. Yet the Iranians went on to create one of the greatest empires of antiquity, one

that encompassed scores of peoples and cultures. The Persians, the most important of the Iranian peoples, had a farsighted conception of empire. Though as conquerors they willingly used force to accomplish their ends, they normally preferred to depend on diplomacy to rule. They usually respected their subjects and allowed them to practice their native customs and religions. Thus the Persians gave the Near East both political unity and cultural diversity. Never before had Near Eastern people viewed empire in such intelligent and humane terms.

The Land of Mountains and Plateau

Persia—the modern country of Iran—is a stark land of towering mountains and flaming deserts, with a broad central plateau in the heart of the country (see Map 2.2). Iran stretches from the Caspian Sea in the north to the Persian Gulf in the south. Between the Tigris-Euphrates Valley in the west and the Indus Valley in the east rises an immense plateau, surrounded on all sides by lofty mountains that cut off the interior from the sea.

Iran's geographical position and topography explain its traditional role as the highway between East and West. Throughout history wild, nomadic peoples migrating from the broad steppes of Russia and Central Asia have streamed into Iran. The very harshness of the geography urged them to continue in search of new and more hospitable lands. Confronting the uncrossable salt deserts, most have turned either eastward or westward, moving on until they reached the advanced and wealthy urban centers of Mesopotamia and India. When cities emerged along the natural lines of East-West communication, Iran became the area where nomads met urban dwellers, a meeting ground of unique significance for the civilizations of both East and West.

The Coming of the Medes and Persians

The Iranians entered this land around 1000 B.C. They were part of the vast movement of Indo-European-speaking peoples whose wanderings led them into Europe, the Near East, and India in many successive waves (see page 24). These Iranians were nomads who migrated with their flocks and herds. Like their kinsmen the Aryans, who moved into India, they were also horse breeders, and the horse gave them a decisive military advantage over the prehistoric peoples of Iran. The Iranians rode into battle in horse-drawn chariots or on horseback and easily swept the natives before them. Yet, because the influx of Iranians went on for centuries, there continued to be constant cultural interchange between conquering newcomers and conquered natives.

The Iranians initially created a patchwork of tiny kingdoms, of which Siyalk was one. The chieftain or petty king was basically a warlord who depended on fellow warriors for aid and support. This band of noble warriors formed the fighting strength of the army. The king owned estates that supported him and his nobles; for additional income the king levied taxes, which were paid in kind and not in cash. He also demanded labor services from the peasants. Below the king and his warrior-nobles were free people who held land and others who owned nothing. Artisans produced the various goods needed to keep society running. At the bottom of the social scale were slaves—probably both natives and newcomers—to whom fell the drudgery of hard labor and household service to king and nobles.

Gradually two groups of Iranians began coalescing into larger units. The Persians had settled in Persia, the modern region of Fars, in southern Iran. Their kinsmen the Medes occupied Media in the north, with their capital at Ecbatana, the modern Hamadan. The Medes were exposed to attack by nomads from the north, but their greatest threat was the frequent raids of the Assyrian army. Even though distracted by grave pressures from their neighbors, the Medes united under one king around 710 B.C. and extended their control over the Persians in the south. In 612 B.C. the Medes were strong enough to join the Babylonians in overthrowing the Assyrian Empire. With the rise of the Medes, the balance of power in the Near East shifted for the first time east of Mesopotamia.

The Creation of the Persian Empire

In 550 B.C. Cyrus the Great (r. 559–530 B.C.), king of the Persians and one of the most remarkable statesmen of antiquity, threw off the yoke of the Medes by conquering them and turning their country into his first *satrapy,* or province. In the space of a single lifetime, Cyrus created one of the greatest empires of antiquity. Two characteristics lift Cyrus above the common level of warrior-kings. First, he thought of Iran, not just Persia and Media, as a state. His concept has survived a long, complex, and often turbulent history to play its part in the contemporary world.

Second, Cyrus held an enlightened view of empire. Many of the civilizations and cultures that fell to his armies were, he realized, far older, more advanced, and more sophisticated than his. Free of the narrow-minded snobbery of the Egyptians, the religious exclusiveness of the Hebrews, and the calculated cruelty of the Assyrians, Cyrus gave Near Eastern peoples and their cultures his respect, toleration, and protection. Conquered peoples continued to enjoy their institutions, religions, languages, and ways of life under the Persians. The Persian Empire, which Cyrus created, became a political organization sheltering many different civilizations. To rule such a vast area and so many diverse peoples demanded talent, intelligence, sensitivity, and a cosmopolitan view of the world. These qualities Cyrus and many of his successors possessed in abundance. Though the Persians were sometimes harsh, especially with those who rebelled against them, they were for the most part enlightened rulers. Consequently, the Persians gave the ancient Near East over two hundred years of peace, prosperity, and security.

Cyrus showed his magnanimity at the outset of his career. Once the Medes had fallen to him, Cyrus united them with his Persians. Persepolis became a Persian seat of power. Medes were honored with important military and political posts and thenceforth helped the Persians to rule the expanding empire. Cyrus's conquest of the Medes resulted not in slavery and slaughter but in the union of Iranian peoples.

With Iran united, Cyrus looked at the broader world. He set out to achieve two goals. First, he wanted to win control of the west and thus of the terminal ports of the great trade routes that crossed Iran and Anatolia. Second, Cyrus strove to secure eastern Iran from the pressure of

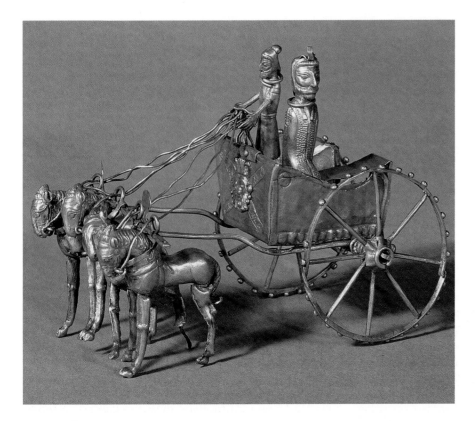

Persian Charioteers   Here are two Persians riding in a chariot pulled by four horses. The chariot is simple in construction but elegant in ornamentation. The harness of the horses is worked in elaborate and accurate detail. This chariot was used for ceremonial purposes, not for warfare. *(Courtesy of the Trustees of the British Museum)*

nomadic invaders. In 550 B.C. neither goal was easy to accomplish. To the northwest was the young kingdom of Lydia in Anatolia, whose king Croesus was proverbial for his wealth. To the west was Babylonia, enjoying a new period of power now that the Assyrian Empire had been crushed. To the southwest was Egypt, still weak but sheltered behind its bulwark of sand and sea. To the east ranged tough, mobile nomads, capable of massive and destructive incursions deep into Iranian territory.

Cyrus turned first to Croesus's Lydian kingdom, which fell to him around 546 B.C. He established a garrison at Sardis, the capital of Lydia, and ordered his gener-

Persian Saddle-Cloth   This elaborately painted piece of leather, dating from the fourth or third centuries B.C., served a ceremonial rather than a practical function. *(The State Hermitage Museum)*

Funeral Pyre of Croesus This scene, an excellent example of the precision and charm of ancient Greek vase painting, depicts the Lydian king Croesus on his funeral pyre. He pours a libation to the gods, while his slave lights the fire. Herodotus has a happier ending, when he says that Cyrus the Great set fire to the pyre, but that Apollo sent rain to put it out. *(Louvre/Réunion des Musées Nationaux/Art Resource, NY)*

als to subdue the Greek cities along the coast of Anatolia. Cyrus had thus gained the important ports that looked out to the Mediterranean world. In addition, for the first time the Persians came into direct contact with the Greeks, a people with whom their later history was to be intimately connected.

From Lydia, Cyrus next marched to the far eastern corners of Iran. In a brilliant campaign he conquered the regions of Parthia and Bactria. All of Iran was now Persian, from Mesopotamia in the west to the western slopes of the Hindu Kush in the east. In 540 B.C. Cyrus moved against Babylonia, now isolated from outside help. When Persian soldiers marched quietly into Babylon the next year, the Babylonians welcomed Cyrus as a liberator. Cyrus won the hearts of the Babylonians with humane treatment, toleration of their religion, and support of their efforts to refurbish their capital.

Cyrus was equally generous toward the Jews. He allowed them to return to Palestine, from which they had been deported by the Babylonians. He protected them, gave them back the sacred items they used in worship, and rebuilt the temple of Yahweh in Jerusalem. The Old Testament sings the praises of Cyrus, whom the Jews considered the shepherd of Yahweh, the lord's anointed. Rarely have conquered peoples shown such gratitude to their conquerors. Cyrus's benevolent policy created a Persian Empire in which the cultures and religions of its members were respected and honored. Seldom have conquerors been as wise, sensitive, and farsighted as Cyrus and his Persians.

Thus Spake Zarathustra

Iranian religion was originally simple and primitive. **Ahuramazda,** the chief god, was the creator and benefactor of all living creatures. Yet, unlike Yahweh, he was not a lone god. The Iranians were polytheistic. Mithra, the sun-god, whose cult would later spread throughout the Roman Empire, saw to justice and redemption. Other Iranian deities personified the natural elements: moon, earth, water, and wind. As in ancient India, fire was a particularly important god. The sacred fire consumed the blood sacrifices that the early Iranians offered to all of their deities.

Early Iranian religion was close to nature and unencumbered by ponderous theological beliefs. A priestly class, the **Magi,** developed among the Medes to officiate at sacrifices, chant prayers to the gods, and tend the sacred flame. In time the Iranians built fire temples for these sacrifices. As late as the nineteenth century, fire was still worshiped in Baku, a major city on the Russian-Iranian border.

Around 600 B.C. the religious thinking of Zarathustra—Zoroaster, as he is better known—breathed new meaning into Iranian religion. So little is known of Zoroaster that even the date of his birth is unknown, but it cannot be earlier than around 1100 B.C. The most reliable information about Zoroaster comes from the *Zend Avesta,* a collection of hymns and poems, the earliest part of which treats Zoroaster and primitive Persian religion. Zoroaster preached a novel concept of divinity and human life. Life,

The Impact of Zoroastrianism   The Persian kings embraced Zoroastrianism as the religion of the realm. This rock carving at Behistun records the bond. King Darius I is seen trampling on one rebel with others behind him. Above is the sign of Ahuramazda, the god of truth and guardian of the Persian king. *(Robert Harding Picture Library)*

he taught, is a constant battleground for two opposing forces, good and evil. Ahuramazda embodied good and truth but was opposed by Ahriman, a hateful spirit who stood for evil and falsehood. Ahuramazda and Ahriman were locked together in a cosmic battle for the human race, a battle that stretched over thousands of years.

Zoroaster emphasized the individual's responsibility to choose between good and evil. He taught that people possessed the free will to decide between Ahuramazda and Ahriman and that they must rely on their own conscience to guide them through life. Their decisions were crucial, Zoroaster warned, for there would be a time of reckoning. He promised that Ahuramazda would eventually triumph over evil and lies, and that at death each person would stand before the tribunal of good. Ahuramazda, like the Egyptian god Osiris, would judge whether the dead had lived righteously and on that basis would weigh their lives in the balance. In short, Zoroaster taught the concept of a Last Judgment at which Ahuramazda would decide each person's eternal fate.

In Zoroaster's thought the Last Judgment was linked to the notion of a divine kingdom after death for those who had lived according to good and truth. Liars and the wicked, denied this blessed immortality, would be condemned to eternal pain, darkness, and punishment. Thus Zoroaster preached a Last Judgment that led to a heaven or a hell.

Though tradition has it that Zoroaster's teachings originally met with opposition and coldness, his thought converted Darius (r. 521–486 B.C.), one of the most energetic men ever to sit on the Persian throne. The Persian royal family adopted **Zoroastrianism** but did not try to impose it on others. Under the protection of the Persian kings, Zoroastrianism swept through Iran, winning converts and sinking roots that sustained healthy growth for centuries. Zoroastrianism survived the fall of the Persian Empire to influence liberal Judaism, Christianity, and early Islam, largely because of its belief in an afterlife that satisfied the longings of most people. Good behavior in the world, even though unrecognized at the time, would be amply rewarded in the hereafter. Evil, no matter how powerful in life, would be punished after death. Zoroastrianism presented the ideal of a fair god who would honor the good with a happy life in heaven. It had a profound impact on Manichaeism, a religion that was to pose a significant challenge to Christianity and to spread through the Byzantine Empire. In some form or another Zoroastrian concepts still pervade the major religions of the West and every part of the world touched by Islam. A handful of the faithful still follow the teachings of

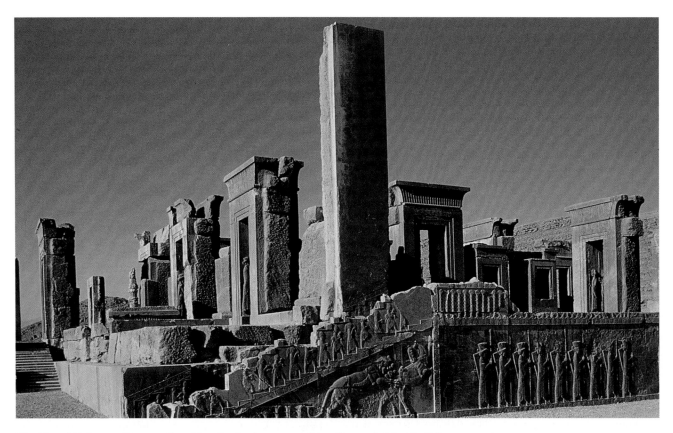

The Royal Palace at Persepolis   King Darius began and King Xerxes finished building a grand palace worthy of the glory of the Persian Empire. Pictured here is the monumental audience hall, where the king dealt with ministers of state and foreign envoys. *(George Holton/Photo Researchers)*

Zoroaster, whose vision of divinity and human life has long outlived him.

Persia's World Empire

Cyrus's successors rounded out the Persian conquest of the ancient Near East. In 525 B.C. Cyrus's son Cambyses (r. 530–522 B.C.) subdued Egypt. Darius (r. 521–486 B.C.) and his son Xerxes (r. 486–464 B.C.) invaded Greece but were forced to retreat (see pages 70–71); the Persians never won a permanent foothold in Europe. Yet Darius carried Persian arms into India. Around 513 B.C. western India became the Persian satrapy of Hindush, which included the valley of the Indus River. Thus within thirty-seven years (550–513 B.C.) the Persians transformed themselves from a subject people to the rulers of an empire that included Anatolia, Egypt, Mesopotamia, Iran, and western India. They had created a **world empire** encompassing all of the oldest and most honored kingdoms

and peoples of the ancient Near East. Never before had the Near East been united in one such vast political organization (see Map 2.2).

The Persians knew how to use the peace they had won on the battlefield. Unlike the Assyrians, they did not resort to royal terrorism to keep order. Like the Assyrians, however, they employed a number of bureaucratic techniques to bind the empire together. The sheer size of the empire made it impossible for one man to rule it effectively. Consequently, the Persians divided the empire into some twenty huge satrapies measuring hundreds of square miles apiece, many of them kingdoms in themselves. Each satrapy had a governor, usually drawn from the Median and Persian nobility and often a relative of the king; the governor, or **satrap,** was directly responsible to the king. Others were local dynasts subject to the Persian king. An army officer, also responsible to the king, commanded the military forces stationed in the satrapy. Still another official collected the taxes. Moreover, the king sent out royal inspectors to watch the satraps and other officials, a method of surveillance later used by the medieval king Charlemagne.

Effective rule of the empire demanded good communications. To meet this need the Persians established a network of roads. The main highway, known as the **Royal Road,** spanned some 1,677 miles from the Greek city of Ephesus on the coast of Asia Minor to Susa in western Iran. The distance was broken into 111 post stations, each equipped with fresh horses for the king's messengers. Other roads branched out to link all parts of the empire from the coast of Asia Minor to the valley of the Indus River. This system of communications enabled the Persian king to keep in intimate touch with his subjects and officials. He was able to rule efficiently, keep his ministers in line, and protect the rights of the peoples under his control.

Summary

During the centuries following the Sea Peoples' invasions, Egypt was overrun by its African neighbors, but its long and rich traditions and culture, its firmly established religion, and its administrative techniques became the heritage of these conquerors. The defeat of Egypt also led to conditions that allowed the Hebrews to create their own state. A series of strong leaders fighting hard wars won the Hebrews independence and security. In this atmosphere Hebrew religion evolved and flourished, thanks to priests, prophets, and common piety among the people. Daily life involved the transition from nomad to farmer, and people's lives revolved around the religious and agricultural year.

In the eighth century B.C. the Hebrews and others in the ancient Near East fell to the onslaught of Assyria, a powerful Mesopotamian kingdom. The Assyrians combined administrative skills, economic acumen, and wealth with military organization to create an aggressive military state. Yet the Assyrians' military ruthlessness and cruelty raised powerful enemies against them. The most important of these enemies were the Iranians, who created the Persian Empire. The Persians had migrated into Iran, settled the land, and entered the cultural orbit of the Near East. The result was rapid progress in culture, economic prosperity, and increase in population, which enabled them to create the largest empire yet seen in the Near East. Unlike the Assyrians, however, they ruled mildly and gave the Near East a long period of peace.

Key Terms

"Purple People"	Talmud
Hapiru	Ahuramazda
nomads	Magi
Baal	Zoroastrianism
Babylonian Captivity	world empire
Covenant	satrap
Yahweh	Royal Road
Torah	

Notes

1. James H. Breasted, *Ancient Records of Egypt,* vol. 4 (Chicago: University of Chicago Press, 1907), para. 398.
2. Proverbs 13:24.
3. J. B. Pritchard, ed., *Ancient Near Eastern Texts,* 3d ed. (Princeton, N.J.: Princeton University Press, 1969), p. 288.
4. Nahum 3:7.

Suggested Reading

C. Gates, *The Archaeology of Urban Life in the Ancient Near East and Egypt, Greece, and Rome* (2003), provides a comprehensive survey of ancient life primarily from an archaeological point of view, but one that includes cultural and social interests. D. B. Redford, *Egypt, Canaan, and Israel in Ancient Times* (1992), is an excellent study of relations among the three states. D. O'Connor, *Ancient Nubia* (1994), which is well illustrated, gives the freshest treatment of that region and points to its importance in African developments.

R. G. Morkot, *The Black Pharaohs* (2000), examines the growth of the Kushite kingdom and its rule over pharaonic Egypt in the eighth century B.C. S. T. Smith, *Wretched Kush* (2003), examines Nubia to understand its native culture and the Egyptian influence on it. G. Herm, *The Phoenicians* (1975), treats Phoenician seafaring and commercial enterprises, as does the more recent G. E. Markoe, *The Phoenicians* (2000), a fresh investigation of these sailors at home and abroad in the western Mediterranean. Similarly, M. Gil, *A History of Palestine* (1997), provides the most recent treatment of that region.

The Jews have been one of the best-studied people in the ancient world, so the reader can easily find many good treatments of Jewish history and society. A rewarding approach is J. Bartlett, ed., *Archaeology and Biblical Interpretation* (1997). Similar is R. S. Zwi Werblowsky and G. Wigoder, eds., *The Oxford Dictionary of the Jewish Religion* (1997). For the Jews in Egypt, two good studies have appeared: J. K. Hoffmeier, *Israel in Egypt* (1997), which discusses the evidence for the authenticity of the tradition concerning the Exodus; and J. Assmann, *Moses the Egyptian* (1997), which is a study in monotheism. B. N. Porter, ed., *One God or Many?* (2000), explores the concept of monotheism in Assyrian and Jewish religion. A broader interpretation of Jewish religious developments can be found in S. Niditch, *Ancient Israelite Religion* (1997). G. Alon, *The Jews in Their Land* (1989), covers the Talmudic age. J. Pastor, *Land and Economy in Ancient Palestine* (1997), discusses the basics of economic life of the period. S. Niditch, *War in the Hebrew Bible* (1992), addresses the ethics of violence in the Bible. H. W. Attridge, ed., *Of Scribes and Scrolls* (1990), gives a fascinating study of the Hebrew Bible and of Christian origins. Turning to politics, M. Smith, *Palestinian Parties and Politics That Shaped the Old Testament,* 2d ed. (1987), takes a practical look at events. W. D. Davis et al., *The Cambridge History of Judaism,* vol. 1 (1984), begins an important synthesis with work on Judaism in the Persian period. R. Hachlili, *Ancient Jewish Art and Archaeology in the Land of Israel* (1988), attempts to trace the development and meaning of Jewish art in its archaeological context.

The Assyrians, despite their achievements, have not attracted the scholarly attention that other Near Eastern peoples have. Even though woefully outdated, A. T. Olmstead, *History of Assyria* (1928), has the merit of being soundly based in the original sources. H. W. F. Saggs, *Everyday Life in Babylonia and Assyria,* rev. ed. (1987), offers a general and well-illustrated survey of Mesopotamian history from 3000 to 300 B.C. M. T. Larsen, *The Conquest of Assyria* (1996), gives a fascinating account of the modern discovery of the Assyrians. Those who appreciate the vitality of Assyrian art should start with the masterful work of R. D. Barnett and W. Forman, *Assyrian Palace Reliefs,* 2d ed. (1970), an exemplary combination of fine photographs and learned, but not difficult, discussion.

A comprehensive survey of Persian history is given by one of the leading scholars in the field, R. N. Frye, *History of Ancient Iran* (1984). I. Gershevitch, ed., *The Cambridge History of Iran,* vol. 2 (1985), provides the reader with a full account of ancient Persian history, but many of the chapters are out-of-date. E. Herzfeld, *Iran in the Ancient East* (1987), puts Persian history in a broad context. Most welcome is M. A. Dandamaev, *A Political History of the Achaemenid Empire* (1989), which discusses in depth the history of the Persians and the organization of their empire. Finally, M. Boyce, a leading scholar in the field, provides a sound and readable treatment of the essence of Zoroastrianism in her *Zoroastrianism* (1979).

Listening to the Past

The Covenant Between Yahweh and the Hebrews

*T*hese passages from the Hebrew Bible address two themes important to Hebraic thinking. The first is the meaning of kingship; the second is the nature of the Covenant between the Hebrews and the Lord, Yahweh. The selection also raises the difficult question of how much of the Hebrew Bible can be accepted historically. As we discussed in this chapter, the Hebrew Bible is not a document that we may accept as literal truth, but it does tell us a great deal about the people who created it. From the following passages we may discern what the Hebrews thought about their own past and religion.

The background of the excerpt is a political crisis that has some archaeological support. The war with the Philistines put a huge strain on Hebrew society. The passage below describes one such incident when Nahash, the king of the Ammonites, threatens to destroy the Hebrews. A new and effective political and military leadership was needed to meet the situation. The elders of the tribes had previously chosen judges to lead the community only in times of crisis. The Hebrews, however, demanded that a kingship be established, even though Yahweh was their king. They turned to Samuel, the last of the judges, who anointed Saul as the first Hebrew king. In this excerpt Samuel reviews the political, military, and religious situation confronting the Hebrews, reminding them of their obligation to honor the Covenant and expressing hesitation in naming a king.

Then Nahash the Ammonite came up and encamped against Jabeshgilead: and all the men of Jabesh said unto Nahash, Make a covenant with us, and we will serve thee. And Nahash the Ammonite answered them, On this condition will I make a covenant with you, that I may thrust out all your right eyes, and lay it for a reproach upon all Israel. And the elders of Jabesh said unto him, Give us

seven days' respite, that we may send messengers unto all the coasts of Israel: and then, if there be no man to save us, we will come out to thee.

Then came the messengers to Gibeah of Saul, and told the tidings in the ears of the people: and all the people lifted up their voices, and wept. And, behold, Saul came after the herd out of the field; and Saul said, What aileth the people that they weep? And they told him the tidings of the men of Jabesh. And the Spirit of God came upon Saul when he heard those tidings, and his anger was kindled greatly. And he took a yoke of oxen, and hewed them in pieces, and sent them throughout all the coasts of Israel by the hands of messengers, saying, Whosoever cometh not forth after Saul and after Samuel, so shall it be done unto his oxen. And the fear of the Lord fell on the people, and they came out with one consent. And when he numbered them in Bezek, the children of Israel were three hundred thousand, and the men of Judah thirty thousand. And they said unto the messengers that came, Thus shall ye say unto the men of Jabeshgilead, To morrow, by that time the sun be hot, ye shall have help. And the messengers came and shewed it to the men of Jabesh; and they were glad. Therefore the men of Jabesh said, To morrow we will come out unto you, and ye shall do with us all that seemeth good unto you. And it was so on the morrow, that Saul put the people in three companies; and they came into the midst of the host in the morning watch, and slew the Ammonites until the heat of the day: and it came to pass, that they which remained were scattered, so that two of them were not left together.

And the people said unto Samuel, Who is he that said, Shall Saul reign over us? bring the men, that we may put them to death. And Saul said, There shall not a man be put to death this day: for to day the Lord hath wrought salvation in Israel. Then said Samuel to the people, Come, and let us go to Gilgal, and renew the kingdom there. And all the people went to Gilgal; and there they made Saul king before the Lord in Gilgal; and there they sacrificed sacrifices of peace offerings before the Lord; and there Saul and all the men of Israel rejoiced greatly.

And Samuel said unto all Israel, Behold, I have hearkened unto your voice in all that you said to me, and have made a king over you. And now, behold, the king walks before you; and I am old and gray-headed; and behold, my sons are with you: and I have walked before you from my childhood until this day. Behold, here I am: witness against me before the Lord, and before his anointed: whose ox have I taken? or whose ass have I taken? or whom have I defrauded? whom have I oppressed? or of whose hand have I received any bribe to blind my eyes with it? and I will restore it to you.

And they said, You have not defrauded us, nor oppressed us, neither have you taken anything from any man's hand. And he said to them, the Lord is witness against you, and his anointed is witness this day, that you have not found anything in my hand. And they answered, he is witness. And Samuel said unto the people, It is the Lord that advanced Moses and Aaron, and that brought your fathers up out of the land of Egypt. Now therefore stand still, that I may reason with you before the Lord of all the righteous acts of the Lord, which he did to you and your fathers.

At this point Samuel reminds the Hebrews of their Covenant with Yahweh. He lists the times when they had broken that Covenant, the times when they had served other gods. He also reminds them of Yahweh's punishment for their backsliding. He tells them frankly that they are wrong to demand a king to rule over them, for Yahweh was their lord, god, and king. Nonetheless, Samuel gives way to their demands.

Now therefore behold the king whom you have chosen, and whom you have desired! and behold, the Lord has set a king over you. If you will fear the Lord, and serve him, and obey his voice, and not rebel against the commandment of the Lord, then shall both you and also the king who reigns over you continue following the Lord your God: But if you will not obey the voice of the Lord, but rebel against the commandment of the Lord, then shall the hand of the Lord be against you, as it was against your fathers. Now therefore stand and see this great thing, which the Lord will do before your eyes. Is it not wheat harvest today? I will call to the Lord, and he shall send thunder and rain; that you may perceive and see that your wickedness is great,

Ark of the Covenant, depicted in a relief from Capernaum Synagogue, second century A.D. *(Ancient Art & Architecture Collection)*

which you have done in the sight of the Lord, in asking you a king. So Samuel called to the Lord; and the Lord sent thunder and rain that day: and all the people greatly feared the Lord and Samuel. And all the people said to Samuel, pray for your servants to the Lord your God, so that we will not die: for we have added to all of our sins this evil, to ask us for a king. And Samuel said to the people, Fear not: you have done all this wickedness; yet turn not aside from following the Lord, but serve the Lord with all your heart; And do not turn aside; for then should you go after vain things, which cannot profit nor deliver; for they are vain. For the Lord will not forsake his people for his great name's sake: because it pleases the Lord to make you his people. Moreover, as for me, God forbid that I should sin against the Lord in ceasing to pray for you: but I will teach you the good and the right way: Only fear the Lord, and serve him in truth with all your heart: for consider how great things he has done for you. But if you shall still act wickedly, you will be consumed, both you and your king.

Questions for Analysis

1. How did Samuel explain his anointment of a king?

2. What was Samuel's attitude toward kingship?

3. What were the duties of the Hebrews toward Yahweh?

4. Might those duties conflict with those toward the secular king? If so, in what ways, and how might the Hebrews avoid the conflict?

Source: 1 Samuel 11:1–15; 12:1–7, 13–25. Abridged and adapted from *The Holy Bible,* King James Version.

Dionysos at sea. Dionysos here symbolizes the Greek sense
of exploration, independence, and love of life. *(Bildarchiv
Preussischer Kulturbesitz/Art Resource, NY)*

chapter

3

The Legacy of Greece

*T*he rocky peninsula of Greece was the home of the civilization that fundamentally shaped Western civilization. The Greeks were the first to explore most of the questions that continue to concern Western thinkers to this day. Going beyond mythmaking and religion, the Greeks strove to understand, in logical, rational terms, both the universe and the position of people in it. The result was the birth of philosophy and science—subjects that were as important to most Greek thinkers as religion. The Greeks speculated on human beings and society and created the very concept of politics.

While the scribes of the ancient Near East produced king lists, the Greeks invented history to record, and understand, how people and states functioned in time and space. In poetry the Greeks spoke as individuals. In drama they dealt with the grandeur and weakness of humanity and with the demands of society on the individual. The greatest monuments of the Greeks were not temples, statues, or tombs, but profound thoughts set down in terms as fresh and immediate today as they were some 2,400 years ago.

The history of the Greeks is divided into two broad periods: the Hellenic period (the subject of this chapter), roughly the time between the arrival of the Greeks (approximately 2000 B.C.) and the victory over Greece in 338 B.C. by Philip of Macedon; and the Hellenistic period (the subject of Chapter 4), the age beginning with the remarkable reign of Philip's son, Alexander the Great (336–323 B.C.) and ending with the Roman conquest of the Hellenistic East (200–146 B.C.).

- What geographical factors helped to mold the evolution of the city-state and to shape the course of the Greek experience?
- What was the nature of the early Greek experience, and how did the impact of the Minoans and Mycenaeans lead to the concept of a heroic past?
- How did the Greeks develop basic political forms, forms as different as democracy and tyranny, that have influenced all of later Western history?
- What did the Greek intellectual triumph entail, and what were its effects?
- Last, how and why did the Greeks eventually fail?

These profound questions, which can never be fully answered, are the themes of this chapter.

MAP 3.1 Ancient Greece In antiquity the home of the Greeks included the islands of the Aegean and the western shore of Turkey as well as the Greek peninsula itself.

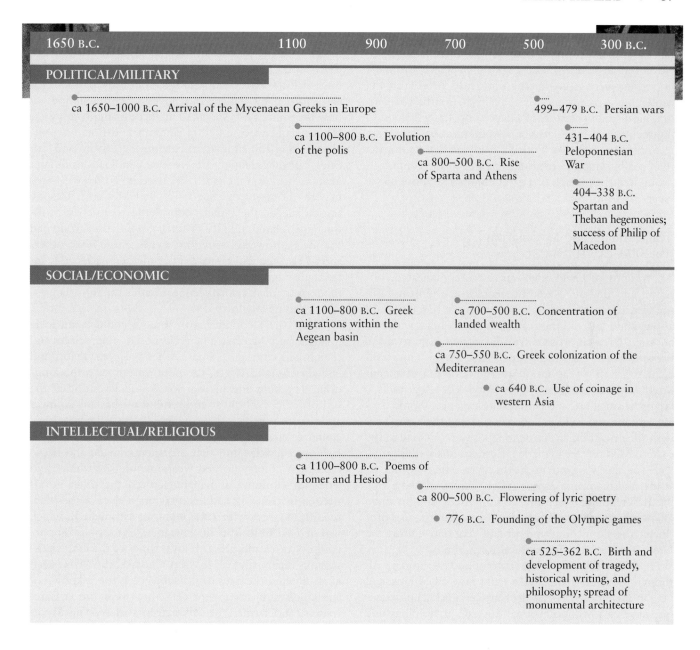

1650 B.C.			1100	900	700	500	300 B.C.

POLITICAL/MILITARY

ca 1650–1000 B.C. Arrival of the Mycenaean Greeks in Europe

499–479 B.C. Persian wars

ca 1100–800 B.C. Evolution of the polis

431–404 B.C. Peloponnesian War

ca 800–500 B.C. Rise of Sparta and Athens

404–338 B.C. Spartan and Theban hegemonies; success of Philip of Macedon

SOCIAL/ECONOMIC

ca 1100–800 B.C. Greek migrations within the Aegean basin

ca 700–500 B.C. Concentration of landed wealth

ca 750–550 B.C. Greek colonization of the Mediterranean

ca 640 B.C. Use of coinage in western Asia

INTELLECTUAL/RELIGIOUS

ca 1100–800 B.C. Poems of Homer and Hesiod

ca 800–500 B.C. Flowering of lyric poetry

776 B.C. Founding of the Olympic games

ca 525–362 B.C. Birth and development of tragedy, historical writing, and philosophy; spread of monumental architecture

Hellas: The Land

Hellas, as the ancient Greeks still call their land, encompassed the Aegean Sea as well as the Greek peninsula (see Map 3.1). Mountains divide the land, leaving few plains and rivers that are generally no more than creeks, most of which go dry in the summer. Greece is, however, blessed with good harbors, the most important of which look to the east. The islands of the Aegean serve as stepping-stones to Asia Minor, usually defined as the region from the modern Turkish coast to the Euphrates River. Thus Greece proper and the **Aegean basin** formed an intimate realm for a common Greek culture. The major regions of Greece were Thessaly and Boeotia in the north and center, lands marked by fertile plains and small rivers that flowed even in summer. Good and abundant land provided the wealth to maintain a strong population capable of fielding good cavalry and infantry. Immediately to the south of Boeotia is Attica, an area of thin soil but home to the olive and the vine. Its harbors looked to the Aegean, which invited its inhabitants, the Athenians, to concentrate on maritime commerce. Still farther south in the

Peloponnesus the land is a patchwork of high mountains and small plains. These geographical features divided the area into several regions, of which the most important were Argos in the northeast, Arcadia in the center, and Laconia and Messenia in the south. The geographical fragmentation of Greece encouraged political fragmentation. Furthermore, communications were extraordinarily poor. Rocky tracks were far more common than roads, which were seldom paved. These conditions prohibited the growth of a great empire like those of the Near East.

The Minoans and Mycenaeans (ca 2000–ca 1100 B.C.)

The origins of Greek civilization are complicated, obscure, and diverse. Neolithic peoples had already built prosperous communities in the Aegean, but not until about 2000 B.C. did they establish firm contact with one another. By then artisans had discovered how to make bronze, which gave these Stone Age groups more efficient tools and weapons. With the adoption of metallurgy came even greater prosperity. The Aegean is a relatively small sea, and land is seldom far off. Some Cretan farmers and fishermen began to trade their surpluses with their neighbors. The central position of Crete in the eastern Mediterranean made it a crucial link in this trade. The Cretans voyaged to Egypt, Asia Minor, other islands, and mainland Greece. They thereby played a vital part in creating an Aegean economy that brought them all into close contact. These favorable circumstances produced the flourishing and vibrant **Minoan** culture on Crete, named after the mythical King Minos.

As seen earlier, only literacy can lead to history. Although the Minoans created a script now called Linear A, very little of it can be read with any certainty. Thus it cannot serve as a historical source. Instead, archaeology and art offer some glimpses of life on the island. The symbol of Minoan culture was the palace and its outlying buildings. About 1650 B.C. Crete was dotted with them, such as those at Mallia on the northern coast and Kato Zakro on the eastern tip of the island. Towering above all others in importance was the palace at Cnossus. It was the political and economic center of its society, but its relations with the other palaces are still disputed. Each palace was the political and economic center of its society. Few specifics are known about Minoan life except that at its head stood a king and his nobles, who governed the lives of their farmers, sailors, shepherds, and artisans. Minoan society, at Cnossus and elsewhere, was wealthy and, to judge by the absence of fortifications on the island, peaceful.

This pleasant situation continued until the arrival of Greek-speaking peoples in the Balkans around 2000 B.C. They came gradually as individual groups who spoke various dialects of the same language. Study of these dialects, aided by archaeology, gives a reasonable idea of how the immigrants spread. The three main groups were the Aeolians, who settled in Thessaly and Boeotia. Others speaking Ionian made their homes in Attica and Euboea, but they claimed that they were indigenous. A later group whose tongue was Dorian occupied Argos, Laconia (the home of the Spartans), and Messenia. Despite these dialects, the Greeks considered themselves a distinct and related folk. By about 1650 B.C. one group had founded a powerful kingdom at Mycenae, while others spread elsewhere in Greece. They merged with native inhabitants, and from that union emerged the society that modern scholars call **Mycenaean,** after the most famous site of this new culture.

Under these conditions of foreign contact and local growth, early Mycenaean Greeks raised other palaces and established cities at Thebes, Athens, Tiryns, Pylos, and elsewhere. As in Crete, the political unit was the kingdom. The king and his warrior aristocracy stood at the top of society. The seat and symbol of the king's power and wealth was his palace, which was also the economic center of the kingdom. Within its walls royal craftsmen fashioned jewelry and rich ornaments, made and decorated fine pottery, forged weapons, prepared hides and wool for clothing, and manufactured the other goods needed by the king and his retainers. Palace scribes kept records in Greek with a script known as **Linear B,** which was derived from Minoan Linear A. The scribes kept account of taxes and drew up inventories of the king's possessions. From the palace, as at Cnossus, the Mycenaean king directed the lives of his subjects. Little is known of the king's subjects except that they were the artisans, traders, and farmers of Mycenaean society. The Mycenaean economy was marked by an extensive division of labor, all tightly controlled from the palace. At the bottom of the social scale were the slaves, who were normally owned by the king and aristocrats but who also worked for ordinary craftsmen.

The Linear B tablets also held a surprise for those interested in Greek religion. Some of them recorded offerings to deities such as Zeus, Apollo, and Athena, the traditional Olympian gods. As late as 1995 Greek archaeologists in Thebes discovered over two hundred new Linear B tablets that are as yet unpublished. These tablets, as well as those already known, prove that the Greeks brought their traditional deities with them on their journey to Greece.

Mycenaean Lion Hunt The Mycenaeans were a robust, warlike people who enjoyed the thrill and the danger of hunting. This scene on the blade of a dagger depicts hunters armed with spears and protected by shields defending themselves against charging lions. *(National Archaeological Museum/Archaeological Receipts Fund)*

Contacts between the Minoans and Mycenaeans were originally peaceful, and Minoan culture flooded the Greek mainland. But around 1450 B.C. the Mycenaeans attacked Crete, destroying many Minoan palaces and taking possession of the grand palace at Cnossus. For about the next fifty years the Mycenaeans ruled much of the island until a further wave of violence left Cnossus in ashes.

Whatever the explanation of these events, Mycenaean kingdoms in Greece benefited from the fall of Cnossus and the collapse of its trade. Mycenaean commerce quickly expanded throughout the Aegean, reaching as far abroad as Anatolia, Cyprus, and Egypt. Throughout central and southern Greece Mycenaean culture flourished as never before. Palaces became grander, and citadels were often protected by mammoth stone walls. Prosperity, however, did not bring peace, and between 1300 and 1000 B.C. kingdom after kingdom suffered attack and destruction. Some modern scholars have attributed these events to the Sea Peoples, who wreaked such havoc in the eastern Mediterranean (see page 27). The best argument for absolving them from blame lies in the lack of any alien artifacts in Greece and the Aegean. If invaders, they proved remarkably tidy. Although later Greeks accused the Dorians of overthrowing the Mycenaean kingdoms, these centers undoubtedly fell because of mutual discord, just as their descendants would commit political suicide in the Peloponnesian War (see pages 73–74).

The fall of the Mycenaean kingdoms ushered in a period of such poverty, disruption, and backwardness that historians usually call it the "Dark Age" of Greece (ca 1100–800 B.C.). Even literacy, which was not widespread

in any case, was a casualty of the chaos. Nonetheless, the Greeks survived the storm to preserve their culture and civilization. Greece remained Greek; nothing essential was swept away. Greek religious cults remained vital to the people, and basic elements of social organization continued to function effectively. It was a time of change and challenge, but not of utter collapse.

This period also saw a development of enormous importance for the course of Western civilization. The disruption of Mycenaean societies caused the widespread and prolonged movement of Greek peoples. They dispersed beyond mainland Greece farther south to Crete and in greater strength across the Aegean to the shores of Asia Minor. They arrived during a time when traditional states and empires had collapsed. Economic hardship was common, and various groups wandered for years. Yet by the end of the Dark Age the Greeks had spread their culture throughout the Aegean basin.

Homer, Hesiod, Gods, and Heroes (1100–800 B.C.)

The Greeks, unlike the Hebrews, had no sacred book that chronicled their past. Instead they had Homer's *Iliad* and *Odyssey* to describe a time when gods still walked the earth. And they learned the origin and descent of the gods from the *Theogony,* an epic poem by Hesiod. Instead of authentic history, the poems of Homer and Hesiod offered the Greeks an ideal past, a largely legendary Heroic Age. These literary works deserve reading for their own sakes, but they are not reliable historical documents.

Nor were they meant to be. In terms of pure history they contain scraps of information about the Bronze Age, much about the early Dark Age, and some about the poets' own era. Chronologically, then, the Heroic Age falls mainly in the period between the collapse of the Mycenaean world and the rebirth of literacy.

The *Iliad* recounts an expedition of Mycenaeans, whom Homer called "Achaeans," to besiege the city of Troy in Asia Minor. The heart of the *Iliad,* however, concerns the quarrel between Agamemnon, the king of Mycenae, and Achilles, the tragic hero of the poem, and how their quarrel brought suffering to the Achaeans. Only when Achilles put away his anger and pride did he consent to come forward, face, and kill the Trojan hero Hector. The *Odyssey,* probably composed later than the *Iliad,* narrates the adventures of Odysseus, one of the Achaean heroes who fought at Troy, during his voyage home from the fighting.

The splendor of these poems does not lie in their plots, although the *Odyssey* is a marvelous adventure story. Rather, both poems portray engaging but often flawed characters who are larger than life and yet typically human. Homer was also strikingly successful in depicting the great gods, who generally sit on Mount Olympus and watch the fighting at Troy like spectators at a baseball game, although they sometimes participate in the action. Homer's deities are reminiscent of Mesopotamian gods and goddesses. Hardly a decorous lot, the Olympians are raucous, petty, deceitful, and splendid. In short, they are human.

Homer at times portrayed the gods in a serious vein, but he never treated them in a systematic fashion, as did Hesiod, who lived somewhat later than Homer. Hesiod's epic poem the *Theogony* traces the descent of Zeus. Hesiod was influenced by Mesopotamian myths, which the Hittites had adopted and spread to the Aegean. Like the Hebrews, Hesiod envisaged his cosmogony—his account of the way the universe developed—in moral terms. Zeus, the son of Cronus, defeated his evil father and took his place as king of the gods. He then sired Lawfulness, Right, Peace, and other powers of light and beauty. Thus, in Hesiod's conception, Zeus was the god of righteousness, who loved justice and hated wrongdoing.

*T*he Polis

After the upheavals that ended the Mycenaean period and the slow recovery of prosperity during the Dark Age, the

Polis of Argos   This view of modern Argos remarkably illustrates the structure of an ancient polis. Atop the hill in the background are the remains of the ancient acropolis. At its foot to the right are foundations of ancient public and private buildings, spreading beyond which are modern houses, situated where ancient houses were located. The trees and cut grain in the foreground were also major features of the *chora,* the agricultural basis of the polis. *(John Buckler)*

Greeks developed their basic political and institutional unit, the **polis.** The term *polis* is generally interpreted as "city-state," one of the worst possible translations of a word that is basically untranslatable. Despite its defects, however, *city-state* is at least a term generally understood and accepted. Two problems arise in an attempt to understand the polis. The first is how it developed, and the second is what it was. Even the Greeks took the polis for granted. Although they remembered a time when kings ruled over many parts of Greece, they did not know how the polis evolved from those legendary kingdoms. In his *Politics* (1.1.9) Aristotle describes the growth of the polis in terms that are as biological as they are political. For example, he states that "man is by nature a being of the polis." He means that people developed the polis as naturally as plants and animals themselves develop. The biological analogy is wrong, but the concept of political evolution is largely correct.

Recent archaeological expeditions and careful study have done much to clarify the origins of the polis. Even during the late Mycenaean period, towns had grown up around palaces. These towns and even smaller villages performed basically local functions. The first was to administer the ordinary political affairs of the community. The village also served a religious purpose in that no matter how small, each had its local cult to its own deity. The exchange of daily goods made these towns and villages economically important, if only on a small scale. These settlements also developed a social system that was particularly their own. They likewise had their own views of the social worth and status of their inhabitants and the nature of their public responsibilities. In short, they relied on custom and mutual agreement to direct their ordinary affairs.

The coming of the Dorians did not significantly change this political evolution, but it had two effects. In some cases it disrupted the task of rebuilding and consolidating some of these developing communities. The Dorians at times carved out territory for themselves at the expense of the natives, but they also assimilated the culture around them. This process actually strengthened the sense of identity among the local people. The situation could have been cataclysmic, but for the most part it was not. The native inhabitants acknowledged their differences with the newcomers. They maintained their traditional religion, albeit sometimes in altered form, but they also accepted the religious validity of new cults. In addition, they looked upon the Dorians as fellow Greeks. Recent archaeological and historical studies reveal a picture of continuity and assimilation.

When fully developed, each polis normally shared a surprisingly large number of features with other poleis. Physically a polis was a society of people who lived in a city *(asty)* and cultivated the surrounding countryside *(chora)*. The city's water supply came from public fountains, springs, and cisterns. By the fifth century B.C. the city was generally surrounded by a wall. The city contained a point, usually elevated, called the **acropolis** and a public square or marketplace called the *agora*. On the acropolis, which in the early period was a place of refuge, stood the temples, altars, public monuments, and various dedications to the gods of the polis. The agora was originally the place where the warrior assembly met, but it became the political center of the polis. In the agora were porticoes, shops, and public buildings and courts.

Until quite recently most scholars have concentrated their attention on the city. The city provides a wealth of evidence on urban planning and daily life, and often yields public documents that illustrate the actual functioning of the polis. Nevertheless, the countryside was vital to the city and to the polis in general for a variety of reasons. Previous pictures of life there depict a scene that is dull and backward: not much happening in the country. Reality was very different. The traditional view overlooks the vitality and the basic importance of the village. The essential significance of the land is that it fed the city. Agriculture in most Greek communities indeed proved basic and far more important than local trade and urban economic dealings. Life in the polis demanded the integration of the chora and the city.

Since the Neolithic period, agriculture had provided the basis for Greek society. Farmers learned how to tame and nurture wild strains of trees and other plants. They discovered the value of irrigation to intensify their agricultural yields. The agricultural significance of the farmers on the chora and the regularity of the seasons bred a stable society. Farmers innately formed a rough agrarian egalitarianism that made itself felt throughout the polis. While mostly content to leave daily politics to the men of the city, farmers always made their opinions known to their fellow citizens. Although they spent most of their days tending their fields and remained the economic basis of the polis, they never ignored the larger political issues confronting their community.

A previously unappreciated aspect of the countryside was its religious significance. Today people normally think first of the great religious festivals celebrated in the city. Although they were indeed important, most Greek religious practices were rooted in the country. The sanctuaries there were a reflection of the cults of the deities that nurtured the polis. The sanctuaries themselves and

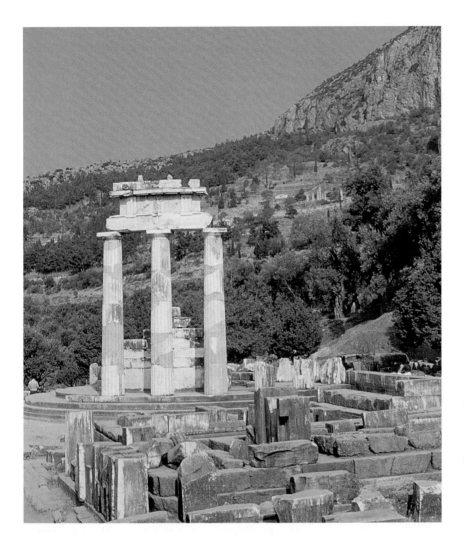

The Delphic Oracle The Marmaria, the sanctuary of Athena, is seen here against the backdrop of the mountains that surround the sanctuary of Apollo. Around the oracle clustered many temples to various deities, shrines, and other sacred buildings, all of them in a remote mountainous area especially chosen by Apollo to be his home and the place where he answered the supplications of the faithful. *(John Buckler)*

the religious rites connected with them were means of appealing to the gods to protect the crops, animals, and people who depended on the earth for survival. The sanctuaries and other religious sites on the borders of the polis linked country and city dwellers in one religious unit. They also served as sources of identification of the polis in that sacred buildings, shrines, and altars were the physical symbols of a particular people, no matter where in the polis they lived. The religious dedications in them were the possessions not only of the gods but also of the polis itself. The permanent dedications made to the gods reflected the power and prestige of the polis.

The average polis did not have a standing army. Instead it relied on its citizens for protection. Very rich citizens often served as cavalry, which was, however, never as important as the heavily armed infantry, or **hoplites.** These were the backbone of the army. They wore metal helmets and body armor, carried heavy, round shields,

and armed themselves with spears and swords. They provided their own equipment and were basically amateurs. In the classical period (ca 500–338 B.C.) they were generally wealthy landowners who were accustomed to outdoor labor. When in battle, they stood in several dense lines, in which cohesion and order became as valuable as courage. This effort also gave them a sense of comradeship and pride. Poor men made up the lightly armed infantry. Usually wielding only a javelin or two, they used their mobility in rough areas to harass hoplites. In some instances the citizens of a polis hired mercenaries to fight their battles. Mercenaries were expensive, untrustworthy, and willing to defect to a higher bidder. Even worse they sometimes seized control over the polis that had hired them.

Regardless of its size or wealth, the polis was fundamental to Greek life. The polis was far more than a political institution. Above all it was a community of citizens,

Early Greek Warfare   Before the hoplites became the backbone of the army, wealthy warriors rode into battle in a chariot, dismounted, and engaged the enemy. This scene, almost a photograph, shows on the left the warrior protecting the chariot before it returns to the rear. The painter has caught the lead horses already beginning the turn. *(Courtesy of the Ure Museum of Greek Archaeology, University of Reading)*

and the affairs of the community were the concern of all. The customs of the community were at the same time the laws of the polis. Even though the physical, religious, and political form of the polis varied from place to place, it was the very badge of Greekness.

The polis could be governed in any of several ways. First, it could be a **monarchy,** a term derived from the Greek for "the rule of one man." A king could represent the community, reigning according to law and respecting the rights of the citizens. Second, the **aristocracy** could govern the state. A literal political translation of this term means "power in the hands of the best." It signifies that only the very cream of society exercised authority. Third, the running of the polis could be the duty and prerogative of an **oligarchy,** which literally means "the rule of a few"—in this case a small group of wealthy citizens not necessarily of aristocratic birth. Or the polis could be governed as a **democracy,** the power of the people, a concept that in Greece meant that all citizens, without respect to birth or wealth, administered the workings of government. How a polis was governed depended on who had the upper hand. When the wealthy held power, they usually instituted oligarchies; when the people could break the hold of the rich, they established democracies. In any case no polis ever had an ironclad, unchangeable constitution. Still another form of Greek government was **tyranny.** Under tyranny the polis was ruled by a tyrant, a man who had seized power by unconstitutional means, generally by using his wealth to gain a political following that could topple the existing government.

The most popular of these political ideals were democracy and oligarchy. Athens presents the best example of democracy in action, but other democracies give a more complete view of its nature. Greek democracies were in fact little more than expanded oligarchies. None of them reflect the modern concept that "all men are created equal." All democracies, Athens included, jealously guarded political rights that they refused to share even with other members of their polis. Some free men and all women were often not active citizens of a democracy. Resident foreigners, though themselves free, and slaves were excluded from citizen rights, except for protection under the law. The attraction of democracy was that at least it permitted more citizens—not more people in general—to direct the political, diplomatic, and military programs of the polis. Even though others lived in a democratic polis, only the citizens were sovereign.

Many Greeks rejected democracy because they thought it unstable and violent. Indeed, many considered it mob rule, governed by the least desirable elements of society. Although these suspicions were somewhat unfair, some democracies sometimes went beyond their own laws and customs to impose their will on an unwilling majority of the population, many of whom had no voice in government. Despite its several failings, democracy at least gave the broadest opportunity for all citizens to express their views and put them into action. Successful democracies generally kept the needs and the opinions of the disenfranchised in consideration so that all could work for the common good.

Many Greeks, perhaps even the majority, preferred oligarchic constitutions. Oligarchy has not received much recent attention and is widely misunderstood. It was the government of the prosperous but left the door open to political and social advancement. Oligarchy was not generally oppressive, and it surprisingly possessed a democratic aspect. All members of an oligarchic government had a passive citizenship in which they enjoyed civil rights. If members of the polis could meet property or money qualifications, they could enter the governing circle. Thus oligarchy also provided an avenue for political and social advancement. Members of the oligarchy had the wealth and knowledge to devote their time to public affairs and work toward the common good. The best example is Corinth, where landowners, merchants, artisans, and working people stood solidly behind a government that prospered for well over 350 years. At Corinth the wealthy governed according to the ideal called **isonomia,** which means limited political equality under the law. Although the wealthy governed the city, they officially endorsed social mobility. Furthermore, Corinthian oligarchs listened to the will of the people, a major factor in their long success. Oligarchy was often popular in Greece because it provided political stability.

Whatever its constitution, the very integration of the polis proved to be one of its weaknesses. Although each polis was normally jealous of its independence, some Greeks banded together to create leagues of city-states. Here was the birth of Greek federalism, a political system in which several states formed a central government while remaining independent in their internal affairs. United in a league, a confederation of city-states was far stronger than any of its individual members and better able to withstand external attack.

Yet even federalism could not overcome the passionate individualism of the polis, which proved to be a serious weakness. The citizens of each polis were determined to remain free and autonomous. Rarely were the Greeks willing to unite in larger political bodies. The political result in Greece, as in Sumer, was almost constant warfare. The polis could dominate, but unlike Rome it could not incorporate.

𝒯he Archaic Age (800–500 B.C.)

Generally known as Archaic primarily because of its art and literature, this period can be seen as a time when the Greeks recovered from the downfall of the Mycenaean kingdoms and continued the advances made during the Dark Age. These years ushered in one of the most vibrant periods of Greek history, an era of extraordinary expansion geographically, artistically, and politically. Greeks ventured as far east as the Black Sea and as far west as Spain (see Map 3.2). With the rebirth of literacy, this period also witnessed a tremendous literary flowering as poets broke away from the heroic tradition and wrote about their own lives. Politically these were the years when Sparta and Athens—the two poles of the Greek experience—rose to prominence.

Overseas Expansion

During the years 1100–800 B.C. the Greeks not only recovered from the breakdown of the Mycenaean world but also grew in wealth and numbers. This new prosperity brought with it new problems. The increase in population meant that many men and their families had very little land or none at all. Land hunger and the resulting social and political tensions drove many Greeks to seek new homes outside of Greece. Other factors, largely intangible, played their part as well: the desire for a new start, a love of excitement and adventure, and natural curiosity about what lay beyond the horizon.

From about 750 to 550 B.C., Greeks from the mainland and Asia Minor traveled throughout the Mediterranean and even into the Atlantic Ocean in their quest for new land. They sailed in the greatest numbers to Sicily and southern Italy, where there was ample space for expansion. They also sailed farther west to Sardinia, southern France and Spain, and even the Canary Islands. In Sicily they found the Sicels, who had already adopted many Carthaginian customs, including a nascent urban culture. Fiercely independent, they greeted the coming of the Greeks just as they had the arrival of the Carthaginians. They welcomed Greek culture but not Greek demands for their land. Nonetheless, the two peoples made a somewhat uneasy accommodation. There was enough land in Sicily for Greeks and Sicels alike, so both flourished, albeit not always peacefully.

In southern Italy the Greeks encountered a number of Indo-European peoples. They were for the most part rural and enjoyed few material comforts. Some of their villages were evolving into towns, but in the mountains looser tribal units prevailed. They both welcomed Greek culture, and the Greeks found it easy to establish prosperous cities without facing significant local hostility.

Some adventurous Greeks sailed to Sardinia and the southern coast of modern France. In Sardinia they established outposts that were originally trading stations, meant primarily for bartering with the natives. Commerce was so successful that some Greeks established

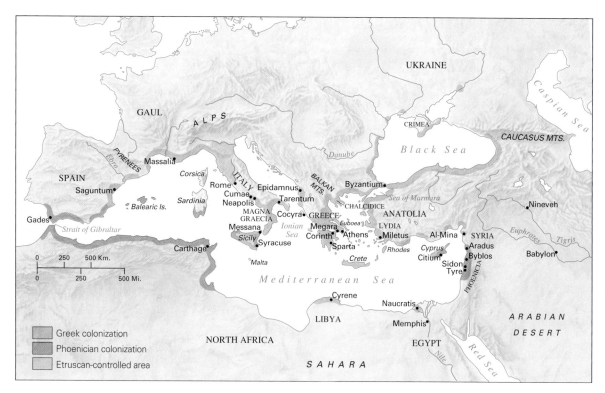

MAP 3.2 Colonization of the Mediterranean Though the Greeks and Phoenicians colonized the Mediterranean basin at about the same time, the Greeks spread much farther.

permanent towns there. Greek influence, in terms of physical remains and the ideas that they reflect, was far stronger on the island than was recognized even a few years ago. From these new outposts Greek influence extended to southern France. The modern city of Marseilles began as a Greek colony and later sent settlers to southern Spain.

Colonization changed the entire Greek world, both at home and abroad. In economic terms the expansion of the Greeks created a much larger market for agricultural and manufactured goods. From the east, especially from the northern coast of the Black Sea, came wheat in a volume beyond the capacity of Greek soil. In return flowed Greek wine and olive oil, which could not be produced in the harsher climate of the north. Greek-manufactured goods, notably rich jewelry and fine pottery, circulated from southern Russia to Spain. During this same period the Greeks adopted the custom of minting coins, which they apparently imported from Lydia. At first coinage was of little economic importance, and only later did it replace the common practice of barter. In the barter system one person simply exchanges one good for another without the use of money. Each person decides the value of the

goods traded. Even today, especially in the backcountry of Greece, a surprisingly large number of economic transactions are done by barter. Thus Greek culture and economics, fertilized by the influences of other societies, spread throughout the Mediterranean basin.

Colonization presented the polis with a huge challenge, for it required organization and planning on an unprecedented scale. The colonizing city, called the *metropolis,* or mother city, first decided where to establish the colony, how to transport colonists to the site, and who would sail. Then the metropolis collected and stored the supplies that the colonists would need both to feed themselves and to plant their first crop. The metropolis also had to provide adequate shipping for the voyage. All preparations ready, a leader, called an **oikist,** ordered the colonists to sail. The oikist was then in full command of the band until the colony was established in its new site and capable of running its own affairs. A significant aspect of colonizing ventures was that colonists sailed as equals, and as equals they set about building a new life together.

Once the colonists landed, the oikist laid out the new polis, selected the sites of temples and public buildings,

Periods of Greek History

Period	Significant Events	Major Writers
Bronze Age 2000–1100 B.C.	Arrival of the Greeks in Greece Rise and fall of the Mycenaean kingdoms	
Dark Age 1100–800 B.C.	Greek migrations within the Aegean basin Social and political recovery Evolution of the polis Rebirth of literacy	Homer Hesiod
Archaic Age 800–500 B.C.	Rise of Sparta and Athens Colonization of the Mediterranean basin Flowering of lyric poetry Development of philosophy and science in Ionia	Archilochus Sappho Tyrtaeus Solon Anaximander Heraclitus
Classical Period 500–338 B.C.	Persian wars Growth of the Athenian Empire Peloponnesian War Rise of drama and historical writing Flowering of Greek philosophy Spartan and Theban hegemonies Conquest of Greece by Philip of Macedon	Herodotus Thucydides Aeschylus Sophocles Euripides Aristophanes Plato Aristotle

and established the government. Then he surrendered power to the new leaders. The colony was thereafter independent of the metropolis. For the Greeks, colonization had two important aspects. First, it demanded that the polis assume a much greater public function than ever before, thus strengthening the city-state's institutional position. Second, colonization spread the polis and its values far beyond the shores of Greece. Even more important, colonization on this scale had a profound impact on the course of Western civilization. It meant that the prevailing culture of the Mediterranean basin would be Greek, the heritage to which Rome would later fall heir.

One man can in many ways stand as the symbol of the vital and robust era of colonization. Archilochus, the bastard son of an aristocrat, was born on the island of Paros. He knew that because of his illegitimacy he would never inherit his father's land, and this knowledge seems to have made him self-reliant. He was also a poet of genius, the first of the lyric poets who left an indelible mark on this age. Unlike the epic poets, who portrayed the deeds of heroes, Archilochus sang of himself. He knew the sea, the dangers of sailing, and the price that the sea often exacted.

He spoke of one shipwreck in grim terms and even treated the god of the sea with irony: "Of fifty men gentle Poseidon left one, Koiranos, to be saved from shipwreck."

Together with others from Paros he took part in the colonization of Thasos in the northern Aegean. He described the island in less than glowing terms: "Like the spine of an ass it stands, crowned to the brim with a wild forest." His opinion of his fellow colonists was hardly kinder: "So the misery of all Greece came together in Thasos." Yet at Thasos he fell in love with a woman named Neoboule. They did not marry because her father opposed the match. In revenge, Archilochus seduced Neoboule's younger sister, railed at the entire family, and left Thasos to live the life of a mercenary.

His hired lance took him to Euboea, and he left a striking picture of the fighting there:

Not many bows will be strung, nor slings be slung
When Ares begins battle in the plain.
There will be the mournful work of the sword:
For in this kind of battle are the spear-famed
Lords of Euboea experienced.[1]

Archilochus exemplifies the energy, restlessness, self-reliance, and sense of adventure that characterized this epoch. People like him broke old ties, faced homelessness and danger, and built new homes for themselves. They made the Mediterranean Greek.

Lyric Poets

Archilochus the colonist and adventurer is not nearly as important as Archilochus the lyric poet, whose individualism set a new tone in Greek literature. For the first time in Western civilization, men and women began to write of their own experiences. Their poetry reflected their belief that they had something precious to say about themselves. To them poetry did not belong only to the gods or to the great heroes on the plain of Troy. Some lyric poets used their literary talents for the good of their city-states. They stood forth as individuals and in their poetry urged their countrymen to be patriotic and just.

One of the most unforgettable of these writers is the poet Sappho. Unlike Archilochus, she neither braved the wilds nor pushed into the unknown, yet she was no less individual than he. Sappho was born in the seventh century B.C. on the island of Lesbos, a place of sun, sea, and rustic beauty. Her marriage produced a daughter, to whom she wrote some of her poems. Sappho's poetry is personal and intense. She delighted in her surroundings, which were those of aristocratic women, and celebrated the little things around her. Hers was a world of natural beauty, sacred groves, religious festivals, wedding celebrations, and noble companions. Sappho fondly remembers walks with a woman friend:

How we went to every hill, brook,
And holy place, and when early spring
Filled the woods with noises of birds
And a choir of nightingales—we two
In solitude were wandering there.[2]

Sappho is best known for erotic poetry, for she expressed her love frankly and without shame. She was bisexual, and much of her poetry deals with her homosexual love affairs. In one of her poems she remembers the words of her lover:

Sappho, if you do not come out,
I swear, I will love you no more.
O rise and free your lovely strength
From the bed and shine upon us.
Lifting off your Chian nightgown, and
Like a pure lily by a spring,
Bathe in the water.[3]

Mosaic Portrait of Sappho The Greek letters in the upper left corner identify this idealized portrait as that of Sappho. The mosaic, which was found in Sparta, dates to the Roman Empire and testifies to Sappho's popularity in antiquity. *(Museum of Sparta/Archaeological Receipts Fund)*

In antiquity Sappho's name became linked with female homosexual love. Today the English word *lesbian* is derived from Sappho's island home. The Greeks accepted bisexuality—that men and women could enjoy both homosexual and heterosexual lovemaking. Homosexual relationships normally carried no social stigma.

In their poetry Archilochus and Sappho reveal two sides of Greek life in this period. Archilochus exemplifies the energy and adventure of the age, while Sappho expresses the intensely personal side of life. The link connecting the two poets is their individualism, their faith in themselves, and their desire to reach out to other men and women in order to share their experiences, thoughts, and wisdom.

The Growth of Sparta

During the Archaic period the Spartans expanded the boundaries of their polis and made it the leading power in Greece. Like other Greeks, the Spartans faced the problems of overpopulation and land hunger. Unlike other Greeks, the Spartans solved these problems by conquest, not by colonization. To gain more land the

Spartans set out in about 735 B.C. to conquer Messenia, a rich, fertile region in the southwestern Peloponnesus. This conflict, the First Messenian War, lasted for twenty years and ended in a Spartan triumph. The Spartans appropriated Messenian land and turned the Messenians into *helots,* or state serfs.

In about 650 B.C. Spartan exploitation and oppression of the Messenian helots led to a helot revolt so massive and stubborn that it became known as the Second Messenian War. The Spartan poet Tyrtaeus, a contemporary of these events, vividly portrays the ferocity of the fighting:

For it is a shameful thing indeed
When with the foremost fighters
An elder falling in front of the young men
Lies outstretched,
Having white hair and grey beard,
Breathing forth his stout soul in the dust,
Holding in his hands his genitals
stained with blood.[4]

Confronted with such horrors, Spartan enthusiasm for the war waned. Finally, after some thirty years of fighting, the Spartans put down the revolt. Nevertheless, the political and social strain it caused led to a transformation of the Spartan polis.

It took the full might of the Spartan people, aristocrat and commoner alike, to win the Second Messenian War. After the victory the non-nobles, who had done much of the fighting, demanded rights equal to those of the nobility. They had taken their place in the battle line next to their aristocratic neighbors but lacked the social prestige and political rights of their noble companions. The agitation of these non-nobles disrupted society until the aristocrats agreed to remodel the state.

The "Lycurgan regimen," as these reforms were called after a legendary lawgiver, was a new political, economic, and social system. Political distinctions among the Spartans were eliminated, and all citizens became legally equal. Actual governance of the polis was in the hands of two kings, who were primarily military leaders. The kings and twenty-eight elders made up a council that deliberated on foreign and domestic matters and prepared legislation for the assembly, which consisted of all Spartan citizens. The real executive power of the polis was in the hands of five *ephors,* or overseers, elected from and by all the people. In effect the Lycurgan regime did nothing more than broaden the aristocracy, while at the same time setting limits on its size. Social mobility was for the most part abolished, and instead an aristocratic warrior class governed the polis.

To provide for their economic needs the Spartans divided the land of Messenia among all citizens. Helots worked the land, raised the crops, provided the Spartans with their living, and occasionally served in the army. The Spartans kept the helots in line by means of systematic terrorism, hoping to beat them down and keep them quiet. Spartan citizens were supposed to devote their time exclusively to military training.

In the Lycurgan system every citizen owed primary allegiance to Sparta. Suppression of the individual together with emphasis on military prowess led to a barracks state. Family life itself was sacrificed to the polis. Once Spartan boys reached the age of seven, they were enrolled in separate companies with other boys their age. They slept outside on reed mats and underwent rugged physical and military training until age twenty-four, when they became frontline soldiers. For the rest of their lives, Spartan men kept themselves prepared for combat. Their military training never ceased, and the older men were expected to be models of endurance, frugality, and sturdiness to the younger men. In battle Spartans were supposed to stand and die rather than retreat. An anecdote about one Spartan mother sums up Spartan military values. As her son was setting off to battle, the mother handed him his shield and advised him to come back either victorious, carrying the shield, or dead, being carried on it. In the Lycurgan regimen Spartan men were expected to train vigorously, disdain luxury and wealth, do with little, and like it.

Similar rigorous requirements applied to Spartan women, who may have been unique in all of Greek society. They were prohibited from wearing jewelry or ornate clothes. They too exercised strenuously in the belief that hard physical training promoted the birth of healthy children. Yet they were hardly oppressed. They enjoyed a more active and open public life than most other Greek women, even though they could neither vote nor hold office. They were far more emancipated than many other Greek women in part because Spartan society felt that mothers and wives had to be as hardy as their sons and husbands. Sparta was not a place for weaklings, male or female. Spartan women saw it as their privilege to be the wives and mothers of victorious warriors, and on several occasions their own courage became legendary. They had a reputation for an independent spirit and self-assertion. This position stemmed from their genuine patriotism, but also from their title to much Spartan land. Though nominally under the guidance of a male guardian, they often managed their own financial affairs. Aristotle testifies that at one point they owned two-fifths of the land in Sparta. For all of these reasons, they shared a footing with Spartan men that most other Greek women lacked in their own societies.

Along with the emphasis on military values for both sexes, the Lycurgan regimen had another purpose as well: it served to instill in society the civic virtues of dedication to the state and a code of moral conduct. These aspects of the Spartan system were generally admired throughout the Greek world.

The Evolution of Athens

Like Sparta, Athens faced pressing social and economic problems during the Archaic period, but the Athenian response was far different from that of the Spartans. Instead of creating an oligarchy, the Athenians extended to all citizens the right and duty of governing the polis. Indeed, the Athenian democracy was one of the most thoroughgoing in Greece.

The late seventh century B.C. was for Athens a time of turmoil, the causes for which are virtually unknown. In 621 B.C. Draco, an Athenian aristocrat, doubtless under pressure from the peasants, published the first law code of the Athenian polis. His code was thought harsh, but it nonetheless embodied the ideal that the law belonged to the citizens. Nevertheless, peasant unrest continued.

By the early sixth century B.C. social and economic conditions led to another explosive situation. The aristocracy still governed Athens oppressively. The aristocrats owned the best land, met in an assembly to govern the polis, and interpreted the law. Noble landowners were forcing small farmers into economic dependence. Many families were sold into slavery; others were exiled and their land was pledged to the rich. Poor farmers who had borrowed from their wealthy neighbors had to put up their land as collateral. If a farmer was unable to repay the loan, his creditor put a stone on the borrower's field to signify his indebtedness and thereafter took one-sixth of the annual yield until the debt was paid. If the farmer had to borrow again, he pledged himself and sometimes his family. If he was again unable to repay the loan, he became the slave of his creditor. Because the harvests of the poor farmer were generally small, he could usually raise enough crops to live on but not enough to repay his loan.

In many other city-states conditions like those in Athens led to the rise of tyrants. One person who recognized these problems clearly was Solon, himself an aristocrat and poet, and a man opposed to tyrants. He was also the one man in Athens who enjoyed the respect of both aristocrats and peasants. Like Hesiod, Solon used his poetry to condemn the aristocrats for their greed and dishonesty. Solon recited his poems in the Athenian agora, where everyone could hear his relentless call for justice and fairness. The aristocrats realized that Solon was no crazed revolutionary, and the common people trusted him. Around 594 B.C. the nobles elected him *archon,* chief magistrate of the Athenian polis, and gave him extraordinary power to reform the state.

Solon immediately freed all people enslaved for debt, recalled all exiles, canceled all debts on land, and made enslavement for debt illegal. He also divided society into four legal groups on the basis of wealth. In the most influential group were the wealthiest citizens, but even the poorest and least powerful group enjoyed certain rights. Solon allowed them into the old aristocratic assembly, where they could take part in the election of magistrates.

In all his work Solon gave thought to the rights of the poor as well as the rich. He gave the commoners a place in government and a voice in the political affairs of Athens. Although Solon's reforms solved some immediate problems, they did not bring peace to Athens. Some aristocrats attempted to make themselves tyrants, while others banded together to oppose them. In 546 B.C. Pisistratus, an exiled aristocrat, returned to Athens, defeated his opponents, and became tyrant. Pisistratus reduced the power of the aristocracy while supporting the common people. Under his rule Athens prospered, and his building program began to transform the city into one of the splendors of Greece. His reign as tyrant promoted the growth of democratic ideas by arousing in the Athenians rudimentary feelings of equality.

Athenian acceptance of tyranny did not long outlive Pisistratus, for his son Hippias ruled harshly, committing excesses that led to his overthrow. After a brief period of turmoil between factions of the nobility, Cleisthenes, a wealthy and prominent aristocrat, emerged triumphant in 508 B.C., largely because he won the support of the people. Cleisthenes created the Athenian democracy with the full knowledge and approval of the Athenian people. He reorganized the state completely but presented every innovation to the assembly for discussion and ratification. All Athenian citizens had a voice in Cleisthenes' work.

Cleisthenes created the **deme,** a local unit, to serve as the basis of his political system. Citizenship was tightly linked to the deme, for each deme kept the roll of those within its jurisdiction who were admitted to citizenship. Cleisthenes also created ten new tribes as administrative units. All the demes were grouped in tribes, which thus formed the link between the demes and the central government. The central government included an assembly of all citizens and a new council of five hundred members. Cleisthenes is often credited with the institution of *ostracism,* a vote of the Athenian people by which the man receiving the most votes went into exile. The goal of ostracism was to rid the state peacefully of a difficult or potentially dangerous politician.

The democracy functioned on the idea that all full citizens, the *demos,* were sovereign. Yet not all citizens could take time from work to participate in government. Therefore, they delegated their power to other citizens by creating various offices meant to run the democracy. The most prestigious of them was the board of ten archons, who were charged with handling legal and military matters. Six of them oversaw the Athenian legal system. They presided over courts, fixed dates for trials, and ensured that the laws of Athens were consistent. They were all elected for one year. After leaving office they entered the *Areopagus,* a select council of ex-archons who handled cases involving homicide, wounding, and arson.

Legislation was in the hands of two bodies, the **boule,** or council, composed of five hundred members, and the **ecclesia,** the assembly of all citizens. The boule, separate from the Areopagus, was perhaps the major institution of the democracy. By supervising the various committees of government and proposing bills to the assembly, it guided Athenian political life. It received foreign envoys and forwarded treaties to the assembly for ratification. It oversaw the granting of state contracts and was responsible for receiving many revenues. It held the democracy together. Nonetheless, the assembly had the final word. Open to all male citizens over eighteen years of age, it met at a specific place to vote on matters presented to it. The assembly could either accept, amend, or reject bills put before it. Every member could express his opinion on any subject on the agenda, and a simple majority vote was needed to pass or reject a bill.

Athenian democracy was to prove an inspiring ideal in Western civilization. It demonstrated that a large group of people, not just a few, could efficiently run the affairs of state. By heeding the opinions, suggestions, and wisdom of all its citizens, the polis enjoyed the maximum amount of good counsel. Because all citizens could speak their minds, they did not have to resort to rebellion or conspiracy to express their desires.

The Classical Period (500–338 B.C.)

In the years 500 to 338 B.C., Greek civilization reached its highest peak in politics, thought, and art. In this period the Greeks beat back the armies of the Persian Empire. Then, turning their spears against one another,

they destroyed their own political system in a century of warfare. Some thoughtful Greeks felt prompted to record and analyze these momentous events. Herodotus (ca 485–425 B.C.), from Asia Minor, traveled the Greek world to piece together the course of the Persian wars. Although he consulted documents when he could find them, he relied largely on the memories of the participants. Not only is he the "father of history," he is also the first oral historian. Next came Thucydides (ca 460–ca 399 B.C.), whose account of the Peloponnesian War remains a classic of Western literature. Unlike Herodotus, he was often a participant in the events that he described.

This era also saw the flowering of philosophy, as thinkers in Ionia and on the Greek mainland began to ponder the nature and meaning of the universe and human experience; they used their intellects to explain the world around them and to determine humanity's place in it. The Greeks invented drama, and the Athenian tragedians Aeschylus, Sophocles, and Euripides explored themes that still inspire audiences today. Greek architects reached the zenith of their art and created buildings whose very ruins still inspire awe. Because Greek intellectual and artistic efforts attained their fullest and finest expression in these years, this age is called the "classical period." Few periods in the history of Western society can match it in sheer dynamism and achievement.

The Persian Wars (499–479 B.C.)

One of the hallmarks of the classical period was warfare. In 499 B.C. the Ionian Greeks, with the feeble help of Athens, rebelled against the Persian Empire. In 490 B.C. the Persians struck back at Athens but were beaten off at the Battle of Marathon, a small plain in Attica (see Map 3.3). This victory taught the Greeks that they could defeat the Persians and successfully defend their homeland. It prompted the Persians to try again. In 480 B.C. the Persian king Xerxes led a mighty invasion force into Greece. In the face of this emergency, many of the Greeks united and pooled their resources to resist the invaders. The Spartans provided the overall leadership and commanded the Greek armies. The Athenians, led by the wily Themistocles, provided the heart of the naval forces.

The first confrontations between the Persians and the Greeks occurred at the pass of Thermopylae and in the waters off Artemisium, the northern tip of Euboea. At Thermopylae the Greek hoplites, heavily armed foot soldiers, showed their mettle. Before the fighting began, a report came in that when the Persian archers shot their bows the arrows darkened the sky. One gruff Spartan

MAP 3.3 The Peloponnesian War   This map, which shows the alignment of states during the Peloponnesian War, vividly illustrates the large scale of the war and its divisive impact.

replied merely, "Fine, then we'll fight in the shade." The Greeks at Thermopylae fought heroically, but the Persians took the position. In 480 B.C. the Greek fleet, inspired by the energetic Themistocles, met the Persian armada at Salamis, an island just south of Athens. Though outnumbered by the Persians, the Greek navy won an overwhelming victory. The remnants of the Persian fleet retired, and with them went all hope of Persian victory. In the following year, a coalition of Greek forces, commanded by the Spartan Pausanias with assistance from the Athenian Aristides, smashed the last Persian army at Plataea, a small polis in Boeotia. Greece remained free.

The significance of these Greek victories is nearly incalculable. By defeating the Persians, the Greeks ensured that oriental monarchy would not stifle the Greek achievement. Even the term "oriental monarchy" offers an insight to Greek thinking. For them monarchy was un-Greek. The Persian king symbolized lack of freedom and submission to one man. Monarchy had become a threat to the very concept of individual Greek freedom. The Greeks were thus able to develop their particular genius in freedom. These decisive victories meant that Greek political forms and intellectual concepts would be the heritage of the West.

Growth of the Athenian Empire (478–431 B.C.)

For the Greeks, who had just won the Persian wars, that conflict was a beginning, not an end. Before them was a novel situation: the defeat of the Persians had created a power vacuum in the Aegean. The state with the strongest navy could turn the Aegean into its lake. In 478 B.C., to take advantage of this situation, the Athenians

Thermopylae   At a spot on Colonus Hill, the Greeks tried to hold the flank of the Athenian fleet that failed to defeat the Persian navy at nearby Artemisium. Here at Thermopylae the Greeks withstood superior numbers only to face the ultimate defeat at the small Colonus Hill at the middle bottom of the heights. *(Courtesy of the Estate of R. V. Schoder)*

and their allies, again led by Aristides, formed the **Delian League,** a grand naval alliance aimed at liberating Ionia from Persian rule. The league took its name from the small island of Delos, on which stood a religious center sacred to all parties. The Delian League was intended as a free alliance under the leadership of Athens. Athenians provided most of the warships and crews and determined how many ships or how much money each member of the league should contribute to the allied effort.

The Athenians, supported by the Delian League and led by the young aristocrat Cimon, carried the war against Persia. But Athenian success had a sinister side. While the Athenians drove the Persians out of the Aegean, they also became increasingly imperialistic, even to the point of turning the Delian League into an Athenian empire. Athens began reducing its allies to the status of subjects. The Athenians sternly put down dissident or rebellious governments, replacing them with trustworthy puppets. Tribute was often collected by force, and the Athenians placed the economic resources of the Delian League under tighter and tighter control.

Athens justified its conduct by its successful leadership. In about 467 B.C. Cimon defeated a new and huge Persian force at the Battle of the Eurymedon River in Asia Minor, once again removing the shadow of Persia from the Aegean. But as the threat from Persia waned and the Athenians treated their allies more harshly, major allies such as Thasos revolted (ca 465 B.C.), requiring the Delian League to use its forces against its own members. The expansion of Athenian power and the aggressiveness of Athenian rule also alarmed Sparta and its allies. While relations between Athens and Sparta cooled, Pericles (ca 494–429 B.C.) became the leading statesman in Athens. Like the democracy he led, Pericles, an aristocrat of solid intellectual ability, was aggressive and imperialistic. At last, in 459 B.C. Sparta and Athens went to war over conflicts between Athens and some of Sparta's allies. Though the Athenians conquered Boeotia, Megara, and Aegina in the early stages of the war, they met defeat in Egypt and later in Boeotia. The war ended in 445 B.C. with no serious damage to either side and nothing settled. But this war divided the Greek world between the two great powers.

During the 440s and 430s Athens continued its severe policies toward its subject allies and came into conflict with Corinth, one of Sparta's leading supporters (see Map 3.3). In 433 B.C. Athens sided with Corcyra against Corinth in a dispute between the two. Together with the Corcyraean fleet, an Athenian squadron defeated the Corinthian navy in open combat. The next year Corinth and Athens collided again, this time over the Corinthian colony of Potidaea, in a conflict the Athenians also won. In this climate of anger and escalation, Pericles took the next step. To punish Megara for alleged sacrilege, Pericles in 432 B.C. persuaded the Athenians to pass a law, the Megarian Decree, which excluded Megarians from trading with Athens and its empire. In response the Spartans convened a meeting of their allies, whose complaints of Athenian aggression ended with a demand that Athens be stopped. Reluctantly the Spartans agreed to declare war. The real reason for war, according to the Athenian historian Thucydides, was very simple: "The truest explanation, though the one least mentioned, was the great growth of Athenian power and the fear it caused the Lacedaemonians [Spartans], which drove them to war."[5]

The Peloponnesian War (431–404 B.C.)

At the outbreak of this conflict, the Peloponnesian War, the Spartan ambassador Melesippus warned the Athenians: "This day will be the beginning of great evil for the Greeks." Few men have ever prophesied more accurately. The Peloponnesian War lasted a generation and brought in its wake fearful plagues, famine, civil wars, widespread destruction, and huge loss of life.

After a Theban attack on the nearby polis of Plataea, the Peloponnesian War began in earnest. In the next seven years, the army of Sparta and its Peloponnesian allies invaded Attica five times. The Athenians stood behind their walls, but in 430 B.C. the cramped conditions nurtured a dreadful plague, which killed huge numbers, eventually claiming Pericles himself. (See the feature "Listening to the Past: The Great Plague at Athens, 430 B.C." on pages 92–93.) The death of Pericles opened the door to a new breed of politicians, men who were rash, ambitious, and more dedicated to themselves than to Athens. One such was Cleon, a very daring and in some ways a very capable man. To divert the constant Spartan invasions of Attica, Cleon proposed a counterattack at Pylos, a rocky peninsula in Messenia immediately opposite the Spartan-occupied island of Sphacteria. Spartan forces were defeated, yet the outcome failed to bring peace. Instead, the energetic Spartan commander Brasidas widened the war in 424 B.C. by capturing Amphipolis on the

northern coast of the Aegean, one of Athens's most valuable subject states. Two years later, both Cleon and Brasidas were killed in a battle to recapture the city. Recognizing that ten years of war had resulted only in death, destruction, and stalemate, Sparta and Athens concluded the Peace of Nicias in 421 B.C.

The Peace of Nicias resulted in a cold war. But even cold war can bring horror and misery. Such was the case when in 416 B.C. the Athenians sent a fleet to the neutral island of Melos with an ultimatum: the Melians could surrender or perish. The motives of the Athenians were frankly and brutally imperialistic. The Melians resisted. The Athenians conquered them, killed the men of military age, and sold the women and children into slavery.

The cold war grew hotter, thanks to the ambitions of Alcibiades (ca 450–404 B.C.), an aristocrat, a kinsman of Pericles, and a student of the philosopher Socrates. A shameless opportunist, Alcibiades widened the war to further his own career and to increase the power of Athens. He convinced the Athenians to attack Syracuse, the leading polis in Sicily. His only valid reason lay in the argument that such an operation would cut the grain supply from Sicily to the Peloponnesus. The undertaking was vast, requiring an enormous fleet and thousands of sailors and soldiers. Trouble began at the outset. Alcibiades' political enemies indicted him, whereupon he fled to Sparta rather than stand trial. Meanwhile, in 414 B.C. the Athenians laid siege to Syracuse. The Syracusans fought back bravely, and even a huge Athenian relief force failed to conquer the city. Finally, in 413 B.C. the Syracusans counterattacked, completely crushing the Athenians. Thucydides wrote the epitaph for the Athenians: "infantry, fleet, and everything else were utterly destroyed, and out of many few returned home."[6]

The disaster in Sicily ushered in the final phase of the war, which was marked by three major developments: the renewal of war between Athens and Sparta, Persia's intervention in the war, and the revolt of many Athenian subjects. The year 413 B.C. saw Sparta's declaration of war against Athens and widespread revolt within the Athenian Empire. Yet Sparta still lacked a navy, the only instrument that could take advantage of the unrest of Athens's subjects, most of whom lived either on islands or in Ionia. The sly Alcibiades, now working for Sparta, provided a solution: he engineered an alliance between Sparta and Persia. The Persians agreed to build a fleet for Sparta. In return, the Spartans promised to give Ionia back to Persia. Now equipped with a fleet, the Spartans challenged the Athenians in the Aegean, the result being a long roll of inconclusive naval battles.

The strain of war prompted the Athenians in 407 B.C. to recall Alcibiades from exile. He cheerfully double-crossed the Spartans and Persians, but even he could not restore Athenian fortunes. In 405 B.C. Athens met its match in the Spartan commander Lysander, a man whose grasp of strategy, politics, and diplomacy easily rivaled Alcibiades'. Lysander destroyed the last Athenian fleet at the Battle of Aegospotami, after which the Spartans blockaded Athens until it was starved into submission. After twenty-seven years the Peloponnesian War was over, and the evils prophesied by the Spartan ambassador Melesippus in 431 B.C. had come true.

Athenian Arts in the Age of Pericles

In the last half of the fifth century B.C., Pericles turned Athens into the showplace of Greece. He appropriated Delian League funds to pay for a huge building program, planning temples and other buildings to honor Athena, the patron goddess of the city, and to display to all Greeks the glory of the Athenian polis. Pericles also pointed out that his program would employ many Athenians and bring economic prosperity to the city.

Thus began the undertaking that turned the Acropolis into a monument for all time. Construction of the Parthenon began in 447 B.C., followed by the Propylaea, the temple of Athena Nike (Athena the Victorious), and the Erechtheum (see Map 3.4). Even the pollution of modern Athens, although it is destroying the ancient buildings, cannot rob them of their splendor and charm.

The planning of the architects and the skill of the workmen who erected these buildings were both very sophisticated. Visitors approaching the Acropolis first see the Propylaea, the ceremonial gateway, a building of complicated layout and grand design whose Doric columns seem to hold up the sky. On the right is the small temple

The Acropolis of Athens These buildings embody the noblest spirit of Greek architecture. At the right rises the Parthenon, the temple that honored Athena and Athens alike. The Erechtheum stands next to it and to its left the Propylaea and the small temple of Athena Nike. Despite the ravages of time, they abide today in their silent grandeur. *(Courtesy, Sotiris Toumbis Editions)*

MAP 3.4 Ancient Athens By modern standards the city of Athens was hardly more than a town, not much larger in size than one square mile. Yet this small area reflects the concentration of ancient Greek life in the polis.

of Athena Nike, whose dimensions harmonize with those of the Propylaea. The temple was built to commemorate the victory over the Persians, and the Ionic frieze above its columns depicts the struggle between the Greeks and the Persians. Here for all the world to see is a tribute to Athenian and Greek valor—and a reminder of Athens's part in the victory.

To the left of the visitors, as they pass through the Propylaea, stands the Erechtheum, an Ionic temple that housed several ancient shrines. On its southern side is the famous Portico of the Caryatids, a porch whose roof is supported by statues of Athenian maidens. The graceful Ionic columns of the Erechtheum provide a delicate relief from the prevailing Doric order of the massive Propylaea and Parthenon.

As visitors walk on, they obtain a full view of the Parthenon, thought by many to be the perfect Doric temple. The Parthenon is the chief monument to Athena and her city. The sculptures that adorn the temple portray the greatness of Athens and its goddess. The figures on the eastern pediment depict Athena's birth, those on the west the victory of Athena over the god Poseidon in their struggle for the possession of Attica. Inside the Parthenon stood a huge statue of Athena, the masterpiece of the great sculptor Phidias.

In many ways the Athenian Acropolis is the epitome of Greek art and its spirit. Although the buildings were dedicated to the gods and most of the sculptures portray gods, these works nonetheless express the Greek fascination with the human and the rational. Greek deities were anthropomorphic, and Greek artists portrayed them as human beings. While honoring the gods, Greek artists were thus celebrating human beings. In the Parthenon sculptures it is visually impossible to distinguish the men and women from the gods and goddesses. The Acropolis also exhibits the rational side of Greek art. Greek artists portrayed action in a balanced, restrained, and sometimes even serene fashion, capturing the noblest aspects of human beings: their reason, dignity, and promise.

Other aspects of Athenian cultural life were as rooted in the life of the polis as were the architecture and sculpture of the Acropolis. The development of drama was tied to the religious festivals of the city. The polis sponsored the production of plays and required that wealthy citizens pay the expenses of their production. At the beginning of the year, dramatists submitted their plays to the archon. He chose those he considered best and assigned a theatrical troupe to each playwright. Although most Athenian drama has perished, enough has survived to prove that the archons had superb taste. Many plays were highly controversial, but the archons neither suppressed nor censored them.

The Athenian dramatists were the first artists in Western society to examine such basic questions as the rights of the individual, the demands of society on the individual, and the nature of good and evil. Conflict is a constant element in Athenian drama. The dramatists used their art to portray, understand, and resolve life's basic conflicts.

Aeschylus (525–456 B.C.), the first of the great Athenian dramatists, was also the first to express the agony of the individual caught in conflict. In his trilogy of plays, *The Oresteia*, Aeschylus deals with the themes of betrayal, murder, and reconciliation, urging that reason and justice be applied to reconcile fundamental conflicts. The final play concludes with a prayer that civil dissension never

be allowed to destroy the city and that the life of the city be one of harmony and grace.

Sophocles (496–406 B.C.) also dealt with matters personal and political. In *Antigone* he expresses the precedence of divine law over human defects and touches on the need for recognition of the law and adherence to it as a prerequisite for a tranquil state.

Sophocles' masterpieces have inspired generations of playwrights. Perhaps his most famous plays are *Oedipus the King* and its sequel, *Oedipus at Colonus. Oedipus the King* is the ironic story of a man doomed by the gods to kill his father and marry his mother. Try as he might to avoid his fate, Oedipus's every action brings him closer to its fulfillment. When at last he realizes that he has carried out the decree of the gods, Oedipus blinds himself and flees into exile. In *Oedipus at Colonus* Sophocles dramatizes the last days of the broken king, whose patient suffering and uncomplaining piety win him an exalted position. In the end the gods honor him for his virtue. The interpretation of these two plays has been hotly debated, but Sophocles seems to be saying that human beings should obey the will of the gods, even without fully understanding it, for the gods stand for justice and order.

Euripides (ca 480–406 B.C.), the last of the three great Greek tragic dramatists, also explored the theme of personal conflict within the polis and sounded the depths of the individual. With Euripides drama entered a new, in many ways more personal, phase. To him the gods were

Mosaic of the Muses   Not found in a great or famous urban center, this mosaic nonetheless testifies to the wide dissemination of culture and art throughout Greece. The figures of the mosaic represent the nine Muses, goddesses of the arts. The lyre of Apollo occupies the center, and Clio, the goddess of history, is represented by the scroll in the upper right of the lyre. *(Professor Nicolas Yalouris, Former General Inspector of Antiquities, Athens)*

far less important than human beings. The essence of Euripides' tragedy is the flawed character—men and women who bring disaster on themselves and their loved ones because their passions overwhelm reason. Although Euripides' plays were less popular in his lifetime than were those of Aeschylus and Sophocles, Euripides was a dramatist of genius whose work later had a significant impact on Roman drama.

Writers of comedy treated the affairs of the polis bawdily and often coarsely. Even so, their plays also were performed at religious festivals. The comic playwrights dealt primarily with the political affairs of the polis and the conduct of its leading politicians. Best known are the comedies of Aristophanes (ca 445–386 B.C.), an ardent lover of his city and a merciless critic of cranks and quacks. He lampooned eminent generals, at times depicting them as morons. He commented snidely on Pericles, poked fun at Socrates, and hooted at Euripides. Like Aeschylus, Sophocles, and Euripides, Aristophanes used his art to dramatize his ideas on the right conduct of the citizen and the value of the polis.

Despite the undeniable achievements of the Athenians, many modern historians have exaggerated their importance. They have created the notion of Athenocentricism, the mistaken opinion that Athens stood solely at the center of classical Greek life. This idea fails to do justice to the other Greeks who also shaped society, culture, and history. Athenocentricism actually distorts and denies the richness of the Greek experience. Greece, like the United States, profited by incorporating many different ideas into one enduring culture.

Daily Life in Periclean Athens

In sharp contrast with the rich intellectual and cultural life of Periclean Athens stands the simplicity of its material life. The Athenians—and in this respect they were typical of Greeks in general—lived very happily with comparatively few material possessions. In the first place, there were very few material goods to own. The thousands of machines, tools, and gadgets considered essential for modern life had no counterparts in Athenian life.

The Athenian house was rather simple. Whether large or small, the typical house consisted of a series of rooms built around a central courtyard, with doors opening onto the courtyard. Many houses had bedrooms on an upper floor. Artisans and craftsmen often set aside a room to use as a shop or work area. The two principal rooms were the men's dining room and the room where the women worked wool. Other rooms included the kitchen and bathroom. By modern standards there was not much

furniture. In the men's dining room were couches, a sideboard, and small tables. Cups and other pottery were often hung on the wall from pegs.

In the courtyard were the well, a small altar, and a washbasin. If the family lived in the country, the stalls of the animals faced the courtyard. Country dwellers kept oxen for plowing, pigs for slaughtering, sheep for wool, goats for cheese, and mules and donkeys for transportation. Even in the city chickens and perhaps a goat or two roamed the courtyard together with dogs and cats.

Cooking, done over a hearth in the house, provided welcome warmth in the winter. Baking and roasting were done in ovens. Food consisted primarily of various grains, especially wheat and barley, as well as lentils, olives, figs, and grapes. Garlic and onion were popular garnishes, and wine was always on hand. These foods were stored at home in large jars; with them the Greek family sometimes ate fish, chicken, and vegetables. Women ground wheat into flour, baked it into bread, and on special occasions made honey or sesame cakes. The Greeks used olive oil for cooking, as families still do in modern Greece; they also used it as an unguent and as lamp fuel.

By American standards the Greeks did not eat much meat. On special occasions, such as important religious festivals, the family ate the animal sacrificed to the god and gave the god the exquisite delicacy of the thighbone wrapped in fat. The only Greeks who consistently ate meat were the Spartan warriors. They received a small portion of meat each day, together with the infamous Spartan black broth, a ghastly concoction of pork cooked in blood, vinegar, and salt. One Greek, after tasting the broth, commented that he could easily understand why the Spartans were so willing to die.

In the city a man might support himself as a craftsman—a potter, bronzesmith, sailmaker, or tanner—or he could contract with the polis to work on public buildings, such as the Parthenon and Erechtheum. Men without skills worked as paid laborers but competed with slaves for work. Slaves were usually foreigners and often barbarians. By "barbarians" the Greeks meant people whose native language was not Greek. Citizens, slaves, and barbarians were paid the same amount for their work.

Slavery was commonplace in Greece, as it was throughout the ancient world. In its essentials Greek slavery resembled Mesopotamian slavery. Slaves received some protection under the law and could buy their freedom. On the other hand, masters could mistreat or neglect their slaves, although killing them was illegal. Most slaves in Athens served as domestics and performed light labor around the house. Nurses for children, teachers of reading and writing, and guardians for young men were often

Priestess   The bronze figurine captures all of the dignity, charm, and skill of the bronzesmith. The priestess holds the simple cult vessels, but the most striking aspect of the piece is her elaborately decorated gown. *(Réunion des Musées Nationaux/Art Resource, NY)*

slaves. The lives of these slaves were much like those of their owners. Other slaves were skilled workers, who could be found working on public buildings or in small workshops.

The importance of slavery in Athens must not be exaggerated. Athenians did not own huge gangs of slaves as did Roman owners of large estates. Slave labor competed with free labor and kept wages down, but it never replaced the free labor that was the mainstay of the Athenian economy.

Most Athenians supported themselves by agriculture, but unless the family was fortunate enough to possess holdings in a plain more fertile than most of the land, they found it difficult to reap a good crop from the soil. Many people must have consumed nearly everything they raised. Attic farmers were free and, though hardly prosperous, by no means destitute. They could usually expect yields of five bushels of wheat and ten of barley per acre for every bushel of grain sown. A bad harvest meant a lean year. In many places farmers grew more barley than wheat because of the nature of the soil. Wherever possible farmers also cultivated vines and olive trees.

The social condition of Athenian women has been the subject of much debate and little agreement. One of the difficulties is the fragmentary nature of the evidence. Women appear frequently in literature and art, often in idealized roles, but seldom in historical contexts of a wider and more realistic nature. This is due in part to the fact that most Greek historians of the time recounted primarily the political, diplomatic, and military events of the day, events in which women seldom played a notable part. Yet that does not mean that women were totally invisible in the life of the polis. It indicates instead that ancient sources provide only a glimpse of how women affected the society in which they lived. Greek wives, for example, played an important economic and social role by their management of the household. Perhaps the best way to describe the position of the free woman in Greek society is to use the anthropologist's term *liminal,* which means in this case that although women lacked official power, they nonetheless played a vital role in shaping the society in which they lived. The same situation had existed in Hammurabi's Babylonia, and it would later recur in the Hellenistic period. The mere fact that Athenian and other Greek women did not sit in the assembly does not mean that they did not influence public affairs.

The status of a free woman of the citizen class was strictly protected by law. Only her children, not those of foreigners or slaves, could be citizens. Only she was in charge of the household and the family's possessions. Yet the law protected her primarily to protect her husband's interests. Raping a free woman was a lesser crime than seducing her, because seduction involved the winning of her affections. This law was concerned not with the husband's feelings but with ensuring that he need not doubt the legitimacy of his children.

Woman Grinding Grain Here a woman takes the grain raised on the family farm and grinds it by hand in a mill. She needed few tools to turn the grain into flour. *(National Archaeological Museum, Athens/Archaeological Receipts Fund)*

Women in Athens and elsewhere in Greece received a certain amount of social and legal protection from their dowries. Upon marriage, the bride's father gave the couple a gift of land or money, which the husband administered. However, it was never his; and in the rare cases of divorce, it returned to the wife's domain. The same is often true in Greece today among the upper class.

Ideally, respectable women lived a secluded life in which the only men they saw were relatives. How far this ideal was actually put into practice is impossible to say. At least Athenian women seem to have enjoyed a social circle of other women of their own class. They also attended public festivals, sacrifices, and funerals. Nonetheless, prosperous and respectable women probably spent much of their time in the house. A white complexion—a sign that a woman did not have to work in the fields—was valued highly. Yet the demands of survival required some ordinary women to work in honest, if somewhat humble, jobs. Chief among them were such ordinary occupations as shopkeepers, which obviously included a public economic importance. In the house, cooks and wet nurses helped to keep the family running efficiently.

Courtesans lived the freest lives of all Athenian women. Although some courtesans were simply prostitutes, others added intellectual accomplishments to physical beauty. In constant demand, cultured courtesans moved freely in male society. Their artistic talents and intellectual abilities appealed to men who wanted more than sex. The most famous of all courtesans was Aspasia, mistress of Pericles and supposedly a friend of Socrates. (See the feature "Individuals in Society: Aspasia.")

A woman's main functions were to raise the children, oversee the domestic slaves and hired labor, and together with her maids work wool into cloth. The women washed the wool in the courtyard and then brought it into the women's room, where the loom stood. They spun the wool into thread and wove the thread into cloth. They also dyed wool at home and decorated the cloth by weaving in colors and designs. The woman of the household either did the cooking herself or directed her maids. In a sense, poor women lived freer lives than did wealthier women. They performed manual labor in the fields or sold goods in the agora, going about their affairs much as men did.

A distinctive feature of Athenian life and of Greek life in general was acceptance of homosexuality. The Greeks accepted the belief that both homosexual and heterosexual practices were normal parts of life. They did not think that these practices created any particular problems for those who engaged in them.

No one has satisfactorily explained how the Greek attitude toward homosexual love developed or determined how common homosexual behavior was. Homosexuality was probably far more common among the aristocracy than among the lower classes. Even among the aristocracy attitudes toward homosexuality were complex and sometimes conflicting. Most people saw homosexual love affairs among the young as a stage in the development of a mature heterosexual life. Warrior aristocracies generally emphasized the physical side of the relationship in the belief that warriors who were also lovers would fight all the harder to impress and to protect each other. Whatever their intellectual content, homosexual love affairs were also overtly sexual.

Greek Religion

Greek religion is extremely difficult for modern people to understand, largely because of the great differences between Greek and modern cultures. In the first place, it is not even easy to talk about "Greek religion," since the Greeks had no uniform faith or creed. Although the Greeks usually worshiped the same deities—Zeus, Hera,

Apollo, Athena, and others—the cults of these gods and goddesses varied from polis to polis. The Greeks had no sacred books such as the Bible, and Greek religion was often a matter more of ritual than of belief. Nor did cults impose an ethical code of conduct. Greeks did not have to follow any particular rule of life, practice certain virtues, or even live decent lives in order to participate. Unlike the Egyptians and Hebrews, the Greeks lacked a priesthood as the modern world understands the term. In Greece priests and priestesses existed to care for temples and sacred property and to conduct the proper rituals, but not to make religious rules or doctrines, much less to enforce them. In short, there existed in Greece no central ecclesiastical authority and no organized creed.

Although temples to the gods were common, they were unlike modern churches or synagogues in that they were not normally places where a congregation met to worship as a spiritual community. Instead, the individual Greek either visited the temple occasionally on matters of private concern or walked in a procession to a particular temple to celebrate a particular festival. In Greek religion the altar, which stood outside the temple, was important; when the Greeks sought the favor of the gods, they offered them sacrifices. Greek religious observances were generally cheerful. Festivals and sacrifices were frequently times for people to meet together socially, times of high spirits and conviviality rather than of pious gloom. By offering the gods parts of the sacrifice while consuming the rest themselves, worshipers forged a bond with the gods.

The most important members of the Greek pantheon were Zeus, the king of the gods, and his consort, Hera. Although they were the mightiest and most honored of the deities who lived on Mount Olympus, their divine children were closer to ordinary people. Apollo was especially popular. He represented the epitome of youth, beauty, benevolence, and athletic skill. He was also the god of music and culture and in many ways symbolized the best of Greek culture. His sister Athena, who patron-

Temple at Bassae   The temple at Bassae stands in wild splendor in the mountains of Arcadia. It is an almost perfect Dorian temple, with its massive columns surrounding the cella, the inner room that contained the statue of Apollo. In such elevated, lonely places many Greeks felt that they entered a region dear to the gods. (*John Buckler*)

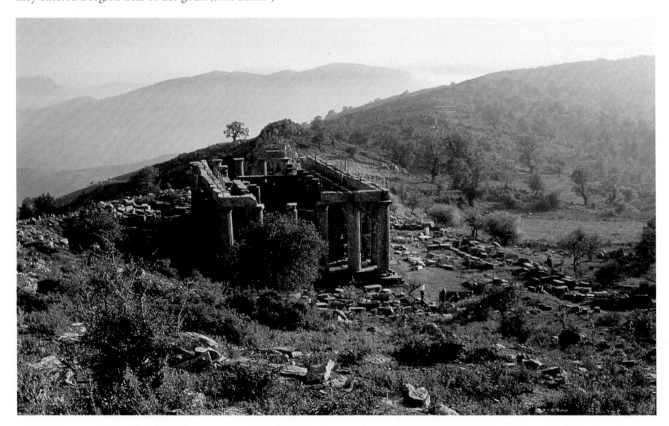

Individuals in Society

Aspasia

Idealized portrait of Aspasia. (Alinari/Art Resource, NY)

"If it is necessary for me indeed to speak of female virtues, to those of you who have now become widows, I shall explain the entire situation briefly. It is in your hands whether you will not fall below your nature. The greatest glory to you is to be least talked about by men, either for excellence or blame" (Thucydides 2.46). These warm-hearted words were reportedly uttered by Pericles to the widows at a public funeral honoring those killed during the first year of the Peloponnesian War. At the same time he was enjoying a long-standing affair with Aspasia, who was very much talked about by men and women. Whether Pericles actually said these words is for the most part irrelevant. Their significance is in their expression of the Athenian ideal of the role of the proper Athenian lady. In short, she should stay at home and limit her talents to her household. The broader world was beyond her.

Aspasia was born in the Greek city of Miletus and came to Athens in about 445 B.C. She is easily one of the most intriguing women of ancient history. Little is known about her life, but she played a role in Athenian society that was far more renowned than, and far different from, that allegedly proposed by Pericles. The irony of her life is that she became his mistress and enjoyed a very public career, exactly the opposite of the opinions attributed to Pericles in the Funeral Oration.

Once in Athens, Aspasia became a *hetaira*, which literally means "companion." The duties of a hetaira varied. She could be someone who accompanied men at dinners and drinking parties, but she could also be a prostitute. The comic poet Aristophanes specifically calls Aspasia a madam. The major attractions of a successful hetaira included beauty, intelligent conversation, and proper etiquette. In return she was paid for her charms. She also enjoyed the opportunity to become the mistress of a wealthy man. Although some have made much of the hetaira as a sexual partner of her client, she also filled an intellectual role not usually expected of a proper wife.

Aspasia fits into the category of a lovely and very intelligent companion. Ancient legend reports that she taught rhetoric, an essential tool for Athenian politicians. That meant that her pupils were necessarily men. She thus enjoyed a rare opportunity for a woman to influence the men who shaped the political life of Athens. Plutarch reports that Aspasia enjoyed the company of the foremost men in Athens. Their conversa-

tions included philosophy, and she is reputed to have taught Socrates the art of public speaking. The claim is probably false, but it at least points to her reputation as a very accomplished woman.

The great change in Aspasia's life came with her introduction to Pericles, who was reportedly taken with her rare political wisdom. More can be imagined. After Pericles divorced his wife, he took Aspasia as his mistress. She and Pericles produced a son, also named Pericles. Although it was illegal for the son of a foreign parent to be granted Athenian citizenship, the laws were waived in this case. That remarkable fact is testimony to the respect that a number of Athenians felt not only for the great statesman but also for Aspasia. Others ridiculed the connection and felt that Pericles was making a fool of himself. The majority thought otherwise, or the son would not have been granted citizenship.

Aspasia's achievements are clear. She lifted herself from a vulnerable to a respected position in Athenian society. It is not enough to ascribe this to her beauty. Her intelligence and her sense of culture were equally, if not more, important. Social mobility in classical Athens was rare, but Aspasia proves that it was possible.

Questions for Analysis

1. What talents enabled Aspasia to rise from companion or courtesan to a generally respected person in society?
2. What made Aspasia's position in Athens precarious despite her obvious talents?

The **history companion** *features additional information and activities related to this topic.* history.college.hmco.com/students

Sacrificial Scene   Much of Greek religion was simple and festive, as this scene demonstrates. The participants have dressed in their finest clothes and crowned themselves with garlands. Musicians add to the festivities. Only the sheep will not enjoy the ceremony. *(National Archaeological Museum, Athens/Archaeological Receipts Fund)*

ized women's crafts such as weaving, was also a warrior-goddess. Best known for her cult at Athens, to which she gave her name, she was highly revered throughout Greece, even in Sparta, which eventually became a fierce enemy of Athens. Artemis was Apollo's elder sister. A virgin and a huntress, she oversaw women's passage from virginity to marriage. Paradoxically, though a huntress, she also

A Greek God   Few pieces of Greek art better illustrate the conception of the gods as greatly superior forms of human beings than this magnificent statue, over six feet ten inches in height. Here the god, who may be either Poseidon or Zeus, is portrayed as powerful and perfect but human in form. *(National Archaeological Museum, Athens/Archaeological Receipts Fund)*

protected wildlife. There was something wild and free about her. Other divinities watched over every aspect of human life.

The Greeks also honored some heroes. A hero was born of a union of a god and a mortal and was an intermediate between the divine and the human. A hero displayed his divine origins by performing deeds beyond the ability of human beings. Herakles (or Hercules) was easily the greatest of them. He successfully fulfilled twelve labors, all of which pitted him against mythical opponents or tasks. Like other heroes, he protected mortals from supernatural dangers. The Greeks created other divinities with various purposes and powers, but in the hero, they believed, human beings could partake of divinity.

Besides the Olympian gods, each polis had its own minor deities, each with his or her own local cult. In many instances Greek religion involved the official gods and goddesses of the polis and their cults. The polis administered the cults and festivals, and all were expected to participate in this civic religion, regardless of whether they even believed in the deities being worshiped. Participating unbelievers, who seem to have been a small minority, were not considered hypocrites. Rather, they were seen as patriotic, loyal citizens who in honoring the gods also honored the polis. If this attitude seems contradictory, an analogy may help. Before baseball games Americans stand at the playing of the national anthem, whether they are Democrats, Republicans, or neither, and whether they agree or disagree with the policies of the current administration. They honor their nation as represented by its flag, in somewhat the same way an ancient Greek honored the polis and demonstrated solidarity with it by participating in the state cults.

Some Greeks turned to mystery religions like those of the Eleusinian mysteries in Attica and of Trophonios in Boeotia. These mystery religions in some ways foreshadowed aspects of early Christian practices by their rites of initiation, their acceptance of certain doctrines, and generally their promise of life after death. The basic concept of these cults was to unite individuals in an exclusive religious society with particular deities. Those who joined them went through a period of preparation in which they learned the essential beliefs of the cult and its necessary rituals. Once they had successfully undergone initiation, they were forbidden to reveal the secrets of the cult. Consequently, modern scholars know comparatively little about their tenets.

For most Greeks religion was quite simple and close to nature. They believed in the supernatural and the primitive. The religion of the common people was a rich combination of myth, ritual, folklore, and cult. So much of popular religion was taken for granted that comparatively little of it is now known. Much religion was local and indeed domestic. Each village possessed its own cults and rituals, and individual families honored various deities privately in their homes. These native rites often remained unknown far beyond their own communities. Women generally played an important part in these celebrations, which in general included all elements of society, slaves included.

Though Greek religion in general was individual or related to the polis, the Greeks also shared some Pan-Hellenic festivals, the chief of which were held at Olympia in honor of Zeus and at Delphi in honor of Apollo. The festivities at Olympia included the famous games, athletic contests that have inspired the modern Olympic games. Held every four years, these games were for the glory of Zeus. They attracted visitors from all over the Greek world and lasted well into Christian times. The Pythian games at Delphi were also held every four years, but these contests differed from the Olympic games by including musical and literary contests. Both the Olympic and the Pythian games were unifying factors in Greek life, bringing Greeks together culturally as well as religiously.

The Flowering of Philosophy

The myths and epics of the Mesopotamians are ample testimony that speculation about the origin of the universe and of mankind did not begin with the Greeks. The signal achievement of the Greeks was the willingness of some to treat these questions in rational rather than mythological terms. Although Greek philosophy did not fully flower until the classical period, Ionian thinkers had already begun in the Archaic period to ask what the universe was made of. These men are called the Pre-Socratics, for their

work preceded the philosophical revolution begun by the Athenian Socrates. Though they were keen observers, the Pre-Socratics rarely undertook deliberate experimentation. Instead, they took individual facts and wove them into general theories. Despite appearances, they believed, the universe was actually simple and subject to natural laws. Drawing on their observations, they speculated about the basic building blocks of the universe.

The first of the Pre-Socratics, Thales (ca 600 B.C.), learned mathematics and astronomy from the Babylonians and geometry from the Egyptians. Yet there was an immense and fundamental difference between Near Eastern thought and the philosophy of Thales. The Near Eastern peoples considered such events as eclipses to be evil omens. Thales viewed them as natural phenomena that could be explained in natural terms. In short, he asked why things happened. He believed the basic element of the universe to be water. Although he was wrong, the way in which he had asked the question was momentous: it was the beginning of the scientific method.

Thales' follower Anaximander continued his work. Anaximander was the first of the Pre-Socratics to use general concepts, which are essential to abstract thought. One of the most brilliant of the Pre-Socratics, a man of striking originality, Anaximander theorized that the basic element of the universe is the "boundless" or "endless"—something infinite and indestructible. In his view the earth floats in a void, held in balance by its distance from everything else in the universe. Anaximander even concluded that mankind had evolved naturally from lower organisms: "In water the first animal arose covered with spiny skin, and with the lapse of time some crawled onto dry land and breaking off their skins in a short time they survived."[7] This remarkable speculation corresponds crudely to Darwin's theory of the evolution of species, although it predates Darwin by two and a half millennia.

An Ionian, Heraclitus (ca 500 B.C.), declared the primal element to be fire. He also declared that the world had neither beginning nor end: "This world, the world of all things, neither any god nor man made, but it always was and it is and it will be: an everlasting fire, measures kindling and measures going out."[8] Although the universe was eternal, according to Heraclitus, it changed constantly. An outgrowth of this line of speculation was the theory of Democritus that the universe was made of invisible, indestructible atoms. The culmination of Pre-Socratic thought was the theory that four simple substances made up the universe: fire, air, earth, and water.

Not all of these early philosophers devoted their attention to pure philosophy or natural science. Aesop (d. 564 B.C.)

devoted his attention to ethics, the treatment of moral behavior. A slave endowed with a keen mind, Aesop made his points by using fables, which were as popular in antiquity as they are today. Fables make their points metaphorically, often using animals instead of people as the main characters. His tales spread throughout Greece, survived in medieval and modern Europe, and not only can still be enjoyed in books today but also sometimes even form the plot line of Bugs Bunny cartoons. They are a reservoir of good sense and simple patterns of behavior. An example will illustrate Aesop's method of conveying his message. In one of his fables Aesop tells of a hungry fox who encounters sun-ripened grapes in a vineyard. Try as he might, he cannot reach them. In disgust he leaves, muttering that they are probably sour and wormy anyway, whence comes our expression "sour grapes." The moral is that all fools can criticize what they cannot get. Many people who never read the writings of philosophers learned from such fables as Aesop's something about life and ethics.

With this impressive heritage behind them, the philosophers of the classical period ventured into new areas of speculation. This development was partly due to the work of Hippocrates (second half of the fifth century B.C.), the father of medicine. Like Thales, Hippocrates sought natural explanations for natural phenomena. Basing his opinions on empirical knowledge, not on religion or magic, he taught that natural means could be employed to fight disease. In his treatise *On Airs, Waters, and Places,* he noted the influence of climate and environment on health. Hippocrates and his followers put forward a theory that was to prevail in medical circles until the eighteenth century. The human body, they declared, contained four humors, or fluids: blood, phlegm, black bile, and yellow bile. In a healthy body the four humors were in perfect balance; too much or too little of any particular humor caused illness. But Hippocrates broke away from the mainstream of Ionian speculation by declaring that medicine was a separate craft—just as ironworking was—that had its own set of principles.

The distinction between natural science and philosophy on which Hippocrates insisted was also promoted by the Sophists, who traveled the Greek world teaching young men. Despite differences of opinion on philosophical matters, the Sophists all agreed that human beings were the proper subject of study. They also believed that excellence could be taught, and they used philosophy and rhetoric to prepare young men for life in the polis. The Sophists put great emphasis on logic and the meanings of words. They criticized traditional beliefs, religion, rituals,

and myths and even questioned the laws of the polis. In essence they argued that nothing is absolute, that everything is relative. Hence more traditional Greeks considered them wanton and harmful, men who were interested in "making the worse seem the better cause."

One of those who was thought to be a Sophist was Socrates (ca 470–399 B.C.). He was not strictly a Sophist, because he never formally taught or collected fees from anyone. He nonetheless shared the Sophists' belief that human beings and their environment were the essential subjects of philosophical inquiry. Like the Sophists, Socrates thought that excellence could be learned and passed on to others. His approach when posing ethical questions and defining concepts was to start with a general topic or problem and to narrow the matter to its essentials. He did so by continuous questioning, a running dialogue. Never did he lecture. Socrates thought that by constantly pursuing excellence, an essential part of which was knowledge, human beings could approach the supreme good and thus find true happiness. Yet in 399 B.C. Socrates was brought to trial, convicted, and executed on charges of corrupting the youth of the city and introducing new gods.

Socrates' student Plato (427–347 B.C.) carried on his master's search for truth. Unlike Socrates, Plato wrote down his thoughts and theories and founded a philosophical school, the Academy. Most people rightly think of Plato as a philosopher. Yet his writings are also literary essays of great charm. They draw out characters, locales, and scenes from ordinary life that would otherwise be lost. In addition, Plato used satire, irony, and comedy to relay his thoughts. Despite all the reverence that people normally pay to Plato, they can also read him for the sheer fun of it. Behind the elegance of his literary style, however, stand the profound thoughts of a brilliant mind that grappled with the problems of his own day and the eternal realities of life. The destruction and chaos of the Peloponnesian War prompted him to ask new and different questions about the nature of human society. He pondered where, why, and how the polis had gone wrong. Thus he gave serious thought to the very nature of the polis and what was the best form that it should take. In these considerations Plato was not only a philosopher but a political scientist and a utopian, a man who genuinely thought that he could create a form of government that would give people the most ethical and satisfying way of life possible. He spent his entire life trying to determine the ideal polis.

The ideal polis could exist only when its citizens were well educated. Plato tried to show that a life of ignorance was wretched. From education came the possibility of determining an all-comprising unity of virtues that would lead to an intelligent, moral, and ethical life. Yet can virtue be taught? Plato never satisfactorily answered his own question. He concluded that only divine providence could guide people to virtue. In his opinion divine providence was one intelligible and individualistic being. In short, he equated god with the concept of good. Plato's tool was mathematics as the servant of education. Human life is transitory, but ideas are permanent. If people could master the essential ideas, guided by mathematics, their souls would become immortal. Here is where the state helped people to reach this goal. It was the highest duty of true statesmen to educate their people in this regard.

Plato developed the theory that all visible, tangible things are unreal and temporary, copies of "forms" or "ideas" that are constant and indestructible. Only the mind, not the senses, can perceive eternal forms. In Plato's view the highest form is the idea of good. He discussed these ideas in two works. In *The Republic* Plato applied his theory of forms to politics in an effort to describe the ideal polis. His perfect polis was utopian; it aimed at providing the greatest good and happiness to all its members. Plato thought that the ideal polis could exist only if its rulers were philosophers. He divided society into rulers, guardians of the polis, and workers. The role of people in each category would be decided by the education, wisdom, and ability of the individual. In Plato's republic men and women would be equal to one another, and women could become rulers. The utopian polis would be a balance, with each individual doing what he or she could to support the state and with each receiving from the state his or her just due. In *The Laws,* however, he drew a more authoritarian picture of government and society, one not so very different from that of twentieth-century dictatorship. If Plato ultimately failed to realize his utopia, he at least introduced to others the concept that they could strive to shape an ideal society.

Aristotle (384–322 B.C.) carried on the philosophical tradition of Socrates and Plato. A student of Plato, Aristotle went far beyond him in striving to understand the universe. The range of Aristotle's thought is staggering. Everything in human experience was a fit subject for his inquiry. In *Politics* Aristotle followed Plato's lead by writing about the ideal polis. Yet Aristotle approached the question more realistically than Plato and criticized *The Republic* and Plato's other writings on many points. In his *Politics* and elsewhere, Aristotle stressed moderation, concluding that the balance of his ideal state depended on people of talent and education who could avoid extremes.

Aristotle also tried to understand the changes of nature—what caused them and where they led. Hence he was both a philosopher and a scientist. He became increasingly interested in the observation and explanation of natural phenomena. The range of his interests was stunning, embracing logic, dialectic, ethics, natural sciences, politics, poetry, and art. He used logic as his method of scientific discussion. His method was the syllogism, whereby he reasoned from a general statement to a particular conclusion. His thinking was so different from Plato's that he established his own school. He held lectures in a gymnasium and afterward discussed topics with students while walking under the eaves of the building. From the colonnade around which they walked, his students gained the name Peripatetics.

Aristotle also attempted to bridge the gap that Plato had created between abstract truth and concrete perception. He argued that the universe is finite, spherical, and eternal. Here he discusses an immaterial being that is his conception of god. Yet his god neither created the universe nor guided it. The inconsistencies of Aristotle on these matters are obvious. His god is without purpose. Yet for him scientific endeavor, the highest attainable form of living, reaches the divine.

Aristotle expressed the heart of his philosophy in two masterful works, *Physics* and *Metaphysics*. In them he combined empiricism, or observation, and speculative method. In *Physics* he tried to explain all of nature by describing how natural physical phenomena work on one another and how these actions lead to the results that people actually see around them daily. He postulated the four principles of matter, form, movement, and goal. A good analogy is a seed. It possesses both matter and an encoded form. Form determines whether the plant will be a rose or poison ivy. Growth represents movement, and the mature plant the goal of the seed. Although Aristotle considered nature impersonal, he also felt that it had its own purposes. In a sense, this is a rudimentary ancestor of the concept of evolution.

In *On the Heaven* Aristotle took up the thread of Ionian speculation. His theory of cosmology added ether to air, fire, water, and earth as building blocks of the universe. He concluded that the universe revolves and that it is spherical and eternal. He wrongly thought that the earth was the center of the universe, with the stars and planets revolving around it. The Hellenistic scientist Aristarchus of Samos later realized that the earth revolves around the sun, but Aristotle's view was accepted until the time of the sixteenth-century astronomer Nicolaus Copernicus.

Statue of Eirene   The Athenians erected this statue of Eirene (Peace) holding Ploutos (Wealth) in her left arm. Athens had seen only war for some fifty-six years, and the statue celebrated the Common Peace of 375 B.C. The bitter irony of this poignant scene is that the treaty lasted scarcely a year. *(Glyptothek, Munich/Studio Koppermann)*

Aristotle possessed one of the keenest and most curious philosophical minds of Western civilization. While rethinking the old topics explored by the Pre-Socratics, he also created whole new areas of study. In short, he tried to learn everything possible about the universe and everything in it. He did so in the belief that all knowledge could be synthesized to produce a simple explanation of the universe and of humanity. Because he was such a popular and prolific writer, his works circulated widely throughout the Greek world. The Ptolemies, a line of Hellenistic kings (see pages 107–108), accumulated as many of them as possible in their famous library at Alexandria. The mere fact that he put his thoughts into writing ensured their preservation.

The Final Act (404–338 B.C.)

The turbulent period from 404 to 338 B.C. is sometimes mistakenly seen as a period of failure and decline. It was instead a vibrant era in which Plato and Aristotle thought and wrote, one in which literature, oratory, and historical writing flourished. The architects of the fourth century B.C. designed and built some of the finest buildings of the classical period, and engineering made great strides. If the fourth century was a period of decline, this was so only in politics. The Peloponnesian War and its aftermath proved that the polis had reached the limits of its success as an effective political institution. The attempts of various city-states to dominate the others led only to incessant warfare. The polis system was committing suicide.

The Greeks of the fourth century B.C. experimented seriously with two political concepts in the hope of preventing war. First was the **Common Peace,** the idea that the states of Greece, whether large or small, should live together in peace and freedom, each enjoying its own laws and customs. In 386 B.C. this concept was a vital part of a peace treaty with the Persian Empire, in which the Greeks and Persians pledged themselves to live in harmony.

Federalism, the second concept to become prominent, already had a long history in some parts of Greece (see page 64). Strictly speaking, the new impetus toward federalism was intended more to gain security through numbers than to prevent war. Greek leagues had usually grown up in regions where geography shaped a well-defined area and where people shared a broad kinship. By banding together, the people of these leagues could marshal their resources, both human and material, to defend themselves from outside interference. In the fourth century B.C. at least ten other federations of states either

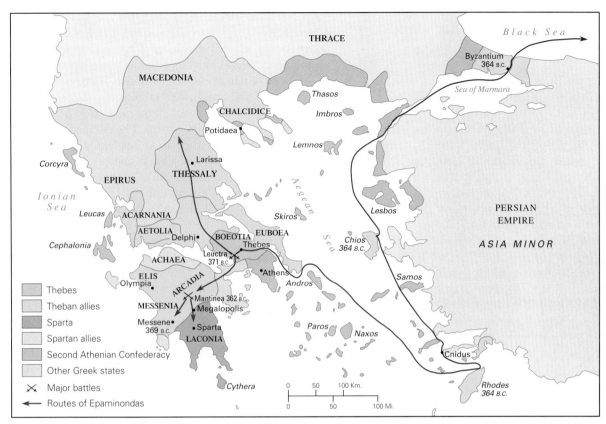

MAP 3.5 Greece in 362 B.C. The fourth century B.C. witnessed the rapid growth of Greek federalism as states sought allies to gain security from rival powers.

came into being or were revitalized (see Map 3.5). Federalism never led to a United States of Greece, but the concept held great importance not only for fourth-century Greeks but also for the Hellenistic period and beyond. In 1787, when the Founding Fathers met in Philadelphia to frame the Constitution of the United States, they studied Greek federalism very seriously in the hope that the Greek past could help guide the American future.

The Struggle for Hegemony

If neither the Common Peace nor federalism put an end to interstate rivalry, the main reason was the stubborn desire of the principal states to dominate the others. The chief states, Sparta, Athens, and Thebes, each tried to create a **hegemony,** that is, a political ascendancy over other states, even though they sometimes paid lip service to the ideals of the Common Peace. In every instance, the ambition, jealousy, pride, and fear of the major powers doomed the effort to achieve genuine peace. In short, each major power

wanted to be the leader, or *hegemon,* and refused to bow to the others who aspired to the same position.

When the Spartan commander Lysander defeated Athens in 404 B.C., the Spartans used their victory to build an empire instead of ensuring the freedom of all Greeks. Their decision quickly brought the Spartans into conflict with Persia, which now demanded the return of Ionia to its control (see page 70), and also with their own allies. The Spartan king Agesilaos, an impetuous man of mediocre ability, waged a fruitless war against the Persians in Ionia. From 400 to 386 B.C. that war eventually engulfed Greece itself. After years of stalemate the Spartans made peace with Persia and their Greek enemies. The result was the first formal Common Peace, the King's Peace of 386 B.C., which cost Sparta its empire but not its position of ascendancy in Greece.

Not content with Sparta's hegemony of Greece, Agesilaos betrayed the very concept of the Common Peace to punish cities that had opposed Sparta during the war. He treacherously ordered Thebes to be seized and even

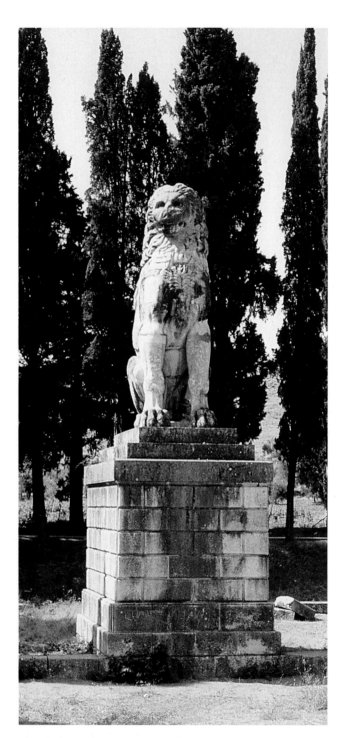

The Lion of Chaeronea   This stylized lion marks the mass grave of nearly three hundred elite Theban soldiers who valiantly died fighting the Macedonians at the Battle of Chaeronea. After the battle, when Philip viewed the bodies of these brave troops, he said: "May those who suppose that these men did or suffered anything dishonorable perish wretchedly." *(Caroline Buckler)*

condoned an unwarranted and unsuccessful attack on Athens. Agesilaos had gone too far. Even though it appeared that his naked use of force had made Sparta supreme in Greece, his imperialism was soon to lead to Sparta's downfall at the hands of the Thebans, the very people whom he sought to tyrannize.

The first sign of Spartan failure came in 378 B.C. after an unprovoked attack on Athens. The enraged Athenians created the Second Athenian Confederacy, a federation of states to guarantee the Greeks their rights under the Common Peace (see Map 3.5). Thebes joined Athens, and the two fought Sparta until 371 B.C. Owing to its growing fear of Theban might, Athens made a separate peace with Sparta. Left alone, Thebes defended itself until later that year, when the brilliant Theban general Epaminondas routed the Spartan army on the small plain of Leuctra.

The defeat of the once-invincible Spartans stunned the Greeks, who wondered how Thebes would use its victory. Epaminondas, also a gifted statesman, immediately grappled with the problem of how to translate military success into political reality. First, in a series of invasions he eliminated Sparta as a major power and liberated Messenia. He concluded alliances with many Peloponnesian states but made no effort to dominate them. Steadfastly refusing to create a Theban empire, he instead sponsored federalism in Greece. He also threw his support behind the Common Peace. Although he made Thebes the leader of Greece from 371 to 362 B.C., other city-states and leagues were bound to Thebes only by voluntary alliances. By his insistence on the liberty of the Greeks, Epaminondas, more than any other person in Greek history, successfully blended the three concepts of hegemony, federalism, and the Common Peace. His premature death at the Battle of Mantinea in 362 B.C. put an end to his efforts, but not to these three political ideals. The question was whether anyone or any state could realize them all.

Philip and the Macedonian Ascendancy

While the Greek states exhausted one another in endless conflicts, a new and unlikely power rose in the north. In 359 B.C. Philip II, one of the most remarkable men in history, became king of Macedonia. Macedonia was by nature potentially strong. The land, extensive and generally fertile, bordered on the east by the Aegean Sea, nurtured a numerous and hardy population. Yet Macedonia was often distracted by foreign opportunists, the Athenians among them, and divided by internal dissension. Nevertheless, under a strong king Macedonia was a power to be reckoned with. Although the Greeks considered the Macedonians backward, Philip was a brilliant, cultured, and sometimes charming man. As a youth he spent several years in Thebes, when Epaminondas was at the height of his power. In Thebes Philip learned about Greek politics and observed the military innovations of Epaminondas. He also fully understood the strengths and needs of the Macedonians, whose devotion he won virtually on the day that he ascended the throne.

The young Philip, already a master of diplomacy and warfare, quickly saw Athens as the principal threat to Macedonia. Once he had secured the borders of Macedonia against barbarian invaders, he launched a series of military operations in the northwestern Aegean. Not only did he win rich territory, but he also slowly pushed the Athenians out of the region. Yet the Greeks themselves opened to him the road to ultimate victory in Greece. The opportunity came from still another internecine Greek conflict, the Sacred War of 356 to 346 B.C. The war broke out when the Phocians seized and plundered the sanctuary of Apollo at Delphi. Their sacrilege was openly condoned by Athens and Sparta. When the Thebans and other Greeks failed to liberate Delphi, they invited Philip to intervene. He quickly crushed the Phocians in 346 B.C. and intimidated Athens and Sparta. Athens immediately made peace with him, and he returned to his ambitions in the northern Aegean.

One man in Athens, the orator and politician Demosthenes, concluded that Philip wanted not peace but the rule of all of Greece. He accused Philip of a war of aggression, against which he warned his countrymen and the rest of Greece. Conventional wisdom holds that Demosthenes was right, but careful examination of the treaty and subsequent events prove that Athens, not Philip, broke the peace. Others also saw Philip as a threat. A comic playwright used graveyard humor to depict one of Philip's ambassadors warning the Athenians:

Do you know that your battle will be with men
Who dine on sharpened swords,
And gulp burning firebrands for wine?
Then immediately after dinner the slave
Brings us dessert—Cretan arrows
Or pieces of broken spears.
We have shields and breastplates for
Cushions and at our feet slings and arrows,
And we are crowned with catapults.[9]

These dire predictions and the progress of Philip's military operations at last had their effect. Demosthenes persuaded the Athenians to make an alliance with Thebes, which also saw the Macedonian threat. In 338 B.C. the armies of Thebes and Athens met Philip's veterans at the Boeotian city of Chaeronea. There on one summer's day Philip's army won a hard-fought victory that gave him command of Greece and put an end to classical Greek freedom. Because the Greeks could not put aside their quarrels, they fell to an invader. Yet Philip was wise enough to retain much of what the fourth-century Greeks had achieved. Not opposed to the concepts of peace and federalism, he sponsored a new Common Peace in which all of Greece, except Sparta, was united in one political body under his leadership. Philip thus used the concepts of hegemony, the Common Peace, and federalism as tools of Macedonian domination. The ironic result was the end of the age of classical Greece.

Summary

The mountainous geography of Greece divides the land into small pockets, so that at first small settlements were the natural pattern of human inhabitation. Never cut off from one another, these settlements evolved a common political and social institution, the polis. Although the causes for this common development are still unknown, the polis proved basic to Greek life. It was far different from the political institutions of the earlier Minoan and Mycenaean kingdoms, which did, however, leave all Greeks the heritage of a heroic past. Through the poetry of Homer and the monumental ruins of the Bronze Age, later Greeks remembered a time when great kings ruled the land. The polis, however, was a dramatic break with this past, and in this atmosphere the Greeks developed basic political forms that are still alive in the contemporary world. The Greeks gave serious thought to the relationship between society and the polis and the nature of political rights. From these thoughts, which they put into practice, developed concepts such as democracy and tyranny. The polis was, however, never by any means utopian. It did not reflect the modern ideas of equality and universal citizenship, but its emphasis on the various and compatible roles that different people filled in the polis made for a harmonious society. The Greek passion for open debate and exchange of ideas was also important to the intellectual explosion of Greek philosophy. Not bound to religion, Greek philosophy considered the human mind to be a sufficient tool to understand the cosmos. This line of thinking underlies modern scientific thought. In view of all their great achievements, it seems incomprehensible that the Greeks and their polis could fail. Yet the desire of several powerful city-states to dominate the others led to years of warfare that eventually weakened them all and left them vulnerable to the successful intervention of the Macedonian king, Philip II.

Key Terms

Aegean basin	tyranny
Minoan	isonomia
Mycenaean	oikist
Linear B	deme
polis	boule
acropolis	ecclesia
hoplites	Delian League
monarchy	Common Peace
aristocracy	federalism
oligarchy	hegemony
democracy	

Notes

1. F. Lasserre, *Archiloque* (Paris: Société d'Edition "Les Belles Let-tres," 1958), frag. 9, p. 4. John Buckler is the translator of all uncited quotations from a foreign language in Chapters 1–6.
2. W. Barnstable, *Sappho* (Garden City, N.Y.: Doubleday, 1965), frag. 24, p. 22.
3. Ibid., frag. 132, p. 106.
4. J. M. Edmonds, *Greek Elegy and Iambus* (Cambridge, Mass.: Harvard University Press, 1931), I.70, frag. 10.
5. Thucydides, *History of the Peloponnesian War* 1.23.
6. Ibid., 7.87.6.
7. E. Diels and W. Krantz, *Fragmente der Vorsokratiker*, 8th ed. (Berlin: Weidmannsche Verlagsbuchhandlung, 1960), Anaximan-der frag. A30.
8. Ibid., Heraclitus frag. B30.
9. J. M. Edmonds, *The Fragments of Attic Comedy* (Leiden: E. J. Brill, 1971), 2.366–369, Mnesimachos frag. 7.

Suggested Reading

Translations of the most important writings of the Greeks and Romans can be found in the volumes of the Loeb Classical Library published by Harvard University Press. Paperback editions of the major Greek and Latin authors are available in the Penguin Classics. Translations of documents include C. Fornara, *Translated Documents of Greece and Rome,* vol. 1 (1977), and P. Harding, vol. 2 (1985).

Among the many general treatments of Greek history is H. Bengtson, *History of Greece* (English trans., 1988). J. Boardman et al. produced between 1982 and 1994 the second edition of the *Cambridge Ancient History,* vols. 3 to 6, which covers all of classical Greek history. Although the work is written by many distinguished classical scholars, the delays in publication unfortunately make some of the contributions out-of-date. On the whole, however, the work is solid.

A number of books on early Greece are available in addition to those cited in the Notes. C. G. Thomas, *Myth Be-comes History* (1993), is an excellent treatment of early Greece and modern historical attitudes toward it, as is R. Drews, *The End of the Bronze Age* (1993). R. Osborne, *Greece in the Making* (1996), is a general survey of developments from 1200 to 479 B.C. J. Boardman, *The Greeks Overseas* (2001), provides a masterful examination of Greek expansion into the Mediterranean. J. N. Coldstream, *Geometric Greece,* 2d ed. (2003), studies the evolution of Greek society from 900 to 700 B.C. I. Malkin, ed., *Ancient Perceptions of Greek Ethnicity* (2001), deals with how the Greeks and their neighbors defined themselves as a people. C. Morgan, *Early Greek States Beyond the Polis* (2003), demonstrates that Greek states went far beyond the concept of the polis. Her study is important for its exploration of conditions in central Greece and the northern Peloponnesus.

Some of the most original and substantial twentieth-century work on the development of the polis appears in M. H. Hansen and K. Raaflaub, eds., *Studies in the Ancient Greek Polis* (1995) and *More Studies in the Ancient Polis* (1996). Related in topic are A. Burford, *Land and Labor in the Greek World* (1993), which covers the entire topic of agriculture, from tools to practices of land use; and M. D. and R. Higgins, *A Geological Companion to Greece* (1996), the first modern study to link geology, archaeology, and patterns of ancient settlement.

R. Gotshalk, *Homer and Hesiod, Myth and Philosophy* (2000), provides a good account of these authors' poetry and their purpose. A. T. Edwards, *Hesiod's Ascra* (2004), studies Hesiod's home and environment in west-central Boeotia and his broader intellectual world. J. M. Snyder, *Lesbian Desire in the Lyrics of Sappho* (1997), explores female eroticism. C. Roebuck, *Economy and Society in the Early Greek World* (1984), is still a reliable, though somewhat dated, treatment of the topic. R. A. Tomlinson, *From Mycenae to Constantinople* (1992), is a broad study of the evolution of the city in the Greco-Roman world.

W. Burkert, *The Orientalizing Revolution* (1992), is a masterful discussion of Near Eastern influence on early Greek culture. A good survey of work on Sparta is P. Cartledge, *Sparta and Lakonia* (1979), and his *The Spartans* (2002) presents a general survey of Sparta's role in Greek history. S. Hodkinson, *Property and Wealth in Classical Sparta* (2000), discusses the basic aspects of Spartan life. The Athenian democracy and the society that produced it continue to attract scholarly attention. Interesting and important are M. Ostwald, *From Popular Sovereignty to the Sovereignty of Law* (1986); M. H. Hansen, *The Athenian Assembly* (1987); and J. Ober, *Mass and Elite in Democratic Athens* (1989). M. Ostwald, *Oligarchia* (2000), is the first new treatment of oligarchy in decades.

The history of the fifth century B.C. and the outbreak of the Peloponnesian War are treated in M. McGregor, *The Athenians and Their Empire* (1987); G. E. M. de Ste. Crois, *The Origins of the Peloponnesian War* (1972), despite its defects; A. Ferrill, *The Origins of War* (1985), chap. 4; and

E. Badian, *From Plataea to Potidaea* (1993), a collection of essays on major aspects of the period.

The fourth century was one of the most fertile fields of late-twentieth-century research. P. Cartledge, *Agesilaos and the Crisis of Sparta* (1987), treats Spartan government and society in its period of greatness and collapse. J. Buckler, *The Theban Hegemony, 371–362 B.C.* (1980), examines the period of Theban ascendancy, and his *Philip II and the Sacred War* (1989) studies the ways in which Philip of Macedonia used Greek politics to his own ends. His broader study, *Aegean Greece in the Fourth Century B.C.* (2003), covers a previously unexplored period. Similarly, H. Beck and J. Buckler, *Central Greece and the Politics of Power in the Fourth Century B.C.* (2005), not only questions the value of Athenocentrism but also emphasizes the significance of states elsewhere in Greece. J. Cargill, *The Second Athenian League* (1981), a significant study, traces Athenian policy during the fourth century. G. Cawkwell, *Philip of Macedon* (1978), analyzes the career of the great conqueror, and R. M. Errington, *A History of Macedonia* (English trans., 1990), is the best general treatment of the topic published in recent years. Last, see L. A. Tritle, ed., *The Greek World in the Fourth Century* (1997), a comprehensive but somewhat uneven collection of essays on the period, and P. Georges, *Barbarian Asia and the Greek Experience* (1994), which explores Greek responses to the native peoples of Asia Minor in the fifth and fourth centuries B.C.

Greek social life has received a great deal of attention, constituting a theme of continuing interest among classical scholars. J. T. Roberts, *Athens on Trial* (1996), discusses how Athens, the pristine democracy, nurtured its own antidemocratic thought. C. B. Patterson, *The Family in Greek History* (2001), treats the public and private relations of the family, which were interconnected. S. B. Pomeroy's *Spartan Women* (2002) is an imperfect but nonetheless useful study of women. M. Golden, *Children and Childhood in Ancient Athens* (1993), studies a neglected topic. D. Cohen, *Law, Sexuality, and Society* (1992), discusses what the Athenians thought was proper moral behavior and how they tried to enforce it. J. J. Winkler, *The Constraints of Desire* (1989), examines the anthropology of sex and gender in ancient Greece. S. Isager and J. E. Skydsgaard, *Ancient Greek Agriculture* (1992), endorses the theory that agriculture was the main source of wealth in ancient Greece. D. Sansone, *Greek Athletics and the Genesis of Sport* (1988), which is well illustrated, provides a good and far-ranging treatment of what athletics meant to the classical Greek world. The topic of slavery is addressed in Y. Garlan, *Slavery in Ancient Greece* (1988), and in the more adventurous E. M. Wood, *Peasant-Citizen and Slave* (1988), which links the two groups to the founding of Athenian democracy.

For Greek literature, culture, and science, see A. Lesky's classic *History of Greek Literature* (English trans., 1963), and for drama, H. C. Baldry, *The Greek Tragic Theater* (1971). Still unsurpassed in Greek philosophy is J. Burnet, *Greek Philosophy* (1914). M. Clagett, *Greek Science in Antiquity* (1971), is the best place to start on this somewhat neglected topic. Relatively new work on Greek philosophy comes from P. Kingsley, *Ancient Philosophy* (1996), which studies the effects of myth and magic on the development of Greek philosophy. A novel approach to the topic is J. K. Ward, ed., *Feminism in Ancient Philosophy* (1996). M. Ferejohn, *The Origins of Aristotelian Science* (1991), discusses earlier Greek scientific thought and Artistotle's response to it. Two works explore medicine: M. D. Grmek, *Diseases in the Ancient Greek World* (1991), and J. Longrigg, *Greek Rational Medicine* (1993), which emphasizes the importance of Greek physicians who concentrated on natural causes of illness and their cure rather than on magic and religion.

Studies of Greek religions and myth include J. D. Mikalson, *Athenian Popular Religion* (reprint, 1987), which opens a valuable avenue to the understanding of Greek popular religion in general. P. N. Hunt, ed., *Encyclopedia of Classical Mystery Religions* (1993), provides more than a thousand entries on mystery religions. It also discusses the later competition between them and Christianity. The classic book E. R. Dodds, *The Greeks and the Irrational* (1951), discusses a hitherto neglected side of intellectual history. In general, W. Burkert, *Greek Religion* (1987), gives a masterful survey of ancient religious beliefs. More recently he has explored the effects of biology on the evolution of Greek religion in *Creation of the Sacred* (1996). Last, K. Dowden, *The Uses of Greek Mythology* (1992), is a systematic study of the importance of mythology to Greek history, which explores its originality and its relation to Greek culture in general.

Listening to the Past

The Great Plague at Athens, 430 B.C.

In 430 B.C. many of the people of Attica sought refuge in Athens to escape the Spartan invasion. The overcrowding of people, the lack of proper sanitation, and the scarcity of clean water exposed the huddled population to virulent disease. Under these conditions, a severe plague attacked the crowded masses. The great historian Thucydides lived in Athens at the time and contracted the disease himself. He was one of the fortunate ones who survived the ordeal. For most people, however, the disease proved fatal. Thucydides left a vivid description of the nature of the plague and of people's reaction to it.

People in perfect health suddenly began to have burning feelings in the head; their eyes became red and inflamed; inside their mouths there was bleeding from the throat and tongue, and the breath became unnatural and unpleasant. The next symptoms were sneezing and hoarseness of voice, and before long the pain settled on the chest and was accompanied by coughing. Next the stomach was affected with stomach-aches and with vomitings of every kind of bile that has been given a name by the medical profession, all this being accompanied by great pain and difficulty. In most cases there were attacks of ineffectual retching, producing violent spasms; this sometimes ended with this stage of the disease, but sometimes continued long afterwards. Externally the body was not very hot to the touch, nor was there any pallor: the skin was rather reddish and livid, breaking out into small pustules and ulcers. But inside there was a feeling of burning, so that people could not bear the touch even of the lightest linen clothing, but wanted to be completely naked, and indeed most of all would have liked to plunge into cold water. Many of the sick who were uncared for actually did so, plunging into the water-tanks in an effort to relieve a thirst which was unquenchable; for it was just the same

with them whether they drank much or little. Then all the time they were afflicted with insomnia and the desperate feeling of not being able to keep still.

In the period when the disease was at its height, the body, so far from wasting away, showed surprising powers of resistance to all the agony, so that there was still some strength left on the seventh or eighth day, which was the time when, in most cases, death came from the internal fever. But if people survived this critical period, then the disease descended to the bowels, producing violent ulceration and uncontrollable diarrhoea, so that most of them died later as a result of the weakness caused by this. For the disease, first settling in the head, went on to affect every part of the body in turn, and even when people escaped its worst effects, it still left its traces on them by fastening upon the extremities of the body. It affected the genitals, the fingers, and the toes, and many of those who recovered lost the use of these members; some, too, went blind. There were some also who, when they first began to get better, suffered from a total loss of memory, not knowing who they were themselves and being unable to recognize their friends.

Words indeed fail one when one tries to give a general picture of this disease; and as for the suffering of individuals, they seemed almost beyond the capacity of human nature to endure. Here in particular is a point where the plague showed itself to be something quite different from ordinary diseases: though there were many dead bodies lying about unburied, the birds and animals that eat human flesh either did not come near them or, if they did taste the flesh, died of it afterwards. Evidence for this may be found in the fact that there was a complete disappearance of all birds of prey: they were not to be seen either around the bodies or anywhere else. But dogs, being domestic animals, provided the best opportunity of observing this effect of the plague.

These, then, were the general features of the disease, though I have omitted all kinds of peculiarities which occurred in various individual cases. Meanwhile, during all this time there was no serious outbreak of any of the usual kinds of illness; if any such cases did occur, they ended in the plague. Some died in neglect, some in spite of every possible care being taken of them. As for a recognized method of treatment, it would be true to say that no such thing existed; what did good in some cases did harm in others. Those with naturally strong constitutions were no better able than the weak to resist the disease, which carried away all alike, even those who were treated and dieted with the greatest care. The most terrible thing of all was the despair into which people fell when they realized that they had caught the plague. Terrible, too, was the sight of people dying like sheep through having caught the disease as a result of nursing others. This indeed caused more deaths than anything else. For when people were afraid to visit the sick, then they died with no one to look after them. Indeed, there were many houses in which all the inhabitants perished through lack of attention. When, on the other hand, they did visit the sick, they lost their own lives, and this was particularly true of those who made it a point of honor to act properly. Such people felt ashamed to think of their own safety and went into their friends' houses at times when even the members of the household were so overwhelmed by the weight of their calamities that they had actually given up the usual practice of making laments for the dead. Yet still the ones who felt most pity for the sick and the dying were those who had had the plague themselves and had recovered from it. They knew what it was like and at the same time felt themselves to be safe, for no one caught the disease twice, or, if he did, the second attack was never fatal. . . .

A factor that made matters much worse than they were already was the removal of people from the country into the city, and this particularly affected the newcomers. There were no houses for them, and, living as they did during the hot season in badly ventilated huts, they died like flies. The bodies of the dying were heaped one on top of the other, and half-dead creatures could be seen staggering about in the streets or flocking around the fountains in their desire for water.

The catastrophe was so overwhelming that people, not knowing what would happen next to them, became indifferent to every rule of religion and law. Athens owed to the plague the beginnings of a state of unprecedented lawlessness. People now began openly to venture on acts of self-indulgence which before then they used to keep in the dark.

Coin depicting the god Asclepius, represented by a snake, putting an end to urban plague. *(Bibliothèque nationale de France)*

Thus they resolved to spend their money quickly and to spend it on pleasure, since money and life alike seemed equally ephemeral. As for what is called honor, no one showed himself willing to abide by its laws, so doubtful was it whether one would survive to enjoy the name for it. It was generally agreed that what was both honorable and valuable was the pleasure of the moment and everything that might conceivably contribute to that pleasure. No fear of god or law of man had a restraining influence. As for the gods, it seemed to be the same thing whether one worshiped them or not, when one saw the good and the bad dying indiscriminately. As for offenses against human law, no one expected to be punished. Instead, everyone felt that already a far heavier sentence had been passed on him and was hanging over him, and that before the time for its execution arrived, it was only natural to get some pleasure out of life.

This, then, was the calamity that fell upon Athens, and the times were hard indeed, with people dying inside the city and the land outside being laid waste.

Questions for Analysis

1. What does this account of the plague say about human nature when put in an extreme crisis?

2. Does popular religion offer any solace during such a catastrophe?

3. How did public laws and customs cope with such a disaster?

Source: R. Warner, trans., *Thucydides, History of the Peloponnesian War* (Penguin Classics, 1954), pp. 152–156. Translation copyright © Rex Warner, 1954. Reproduced by permission of Penguin Books Ltd.

Portrait of a girl, Pompeii, ca A.D. 75. Her stylus, pad, and pensive expression suggest the broad and personal intellectual horizons of the Hellenistic world. *(Werner Forman Archives/Art Resource, NY)*

chapter

4

Hellenistic Diffusion

*T*wo years after his conquest of Greece, Philip of Macedon fell victim to an assassin's dagger. Philip's twenty-year-old son, historically known as Alexander the Great (r. 336–323 B.C.), assumed the Macedonian throne. This young man, one of the most remarkable personalities of Western civilization, was to have a profound impact on history. By overthrowing the Persian Empire and by spreading *Hellenism*—Greek culture, language, thought, and way of life—as far as India, Alexander was instrumental in creating a new era, traditionally called **Hellenistic** to distinguish it from the Hellenic. As a result of Alexander's exploits, the individualistic and energetic culture of the Greeks came into intimate contact with the venerable older cultures of the Near East.

The impact of Philip and Alexander was so enormous that the great German historian Hermann Bengtson has commented:

Philip and his son Alexander were the ones who opened the door of the world to the Macedonians and Greeks. With Macedonian imperialism was joined the diffusion of the Greek spirit, which permeated the entire ancient world. Without the achievement of these two kings, neither the Roman Empire nor the diffusion of Christianity would have been conceivable.[1]

- Is this estimation correct, or is it mere rhetoric?

- What did the spread of Hellenism mean to the Greeks and the peoples of the Near East?

- What did the meeting of West and East hold for the development of economics, religion, philosophy, women's concerns, science, and medicine?

These are the questions we will explore in this chapter.

Alexander and the Great Crusade

In 336 B.C. Alexander inherited not only Philip's crown but also his policies. After his victory at Chaeronea, Philip had organized the states of Greece into a huge league under his leadership and announced to the Greeks his plan to lead them and his Macedonians against the Persian Empire. Fully intending to carry out Philip's designs, Alexander proclaimed to the Greek world that the

MAP 4.1 Alexander's Conquests   This map shows the course of Alexander's invasion of the Persian Empire and the speed of his progress. More important than the great success of his military campaigns was his founding of Hellenistic cities in the East.

invasion of Persia was to be a great crusade, a mighty act of revenge for the Persian invasion of Greece in 480 B.C. It would also be the means by which Alexander would create an empire of his own in the East.

Despite his youth, Alexander was well prepared to lead the attack. Philip had groomed his son to become king and given him the best education possible. In 334 B.C. Alexander led an army of Macedonians and Greeks into Asia Minor. With him went a staff of philosophers and poets, scientists whose job it was to map the country and study strange animals and plants, and the historian Callisthenes, who was to write an account of the campaign. Alexander intended not only a military campaign but also an expedition of discovery.

In the next three years Alexander won three major battles at the Granicus River, Issus, and Gaugamela. As Map 4.1 shows, these battle sites stand almost as road signs marking his march to the East. When Alexander

reached Egypt, he quickly seized the land, honored the priestly class, and was proclaimed pharaoh, the legitimate ruler of the country. He next marched to the oasis of Siwah, west of the Nile Valley, to consult the famous oracle of Zeus-Amon. No one will ever know what the priest told him, but henceforth Alexander considered himself the son of Zeus. Next he marched into western Asia, where at Gaugamela he defeated the Persian army. After this victory the principal Persian capital of Persepolis easily fell to him. There he performed a symbolic act of retribution by burning the buildings of Xerxes, the invader of Greece. In 330 B.C. he took Ecbatana, the last Persian capital, and pursued the Persian king to his death.

The Persian Empire had fallen, and the war of revenge was over, but Alexander had no intention of stopping. He dismissed his Greek troops but permitted many of them to serve on as mercenaries. Alexander then began his personal odyssey. With his Macedonian soldiers and

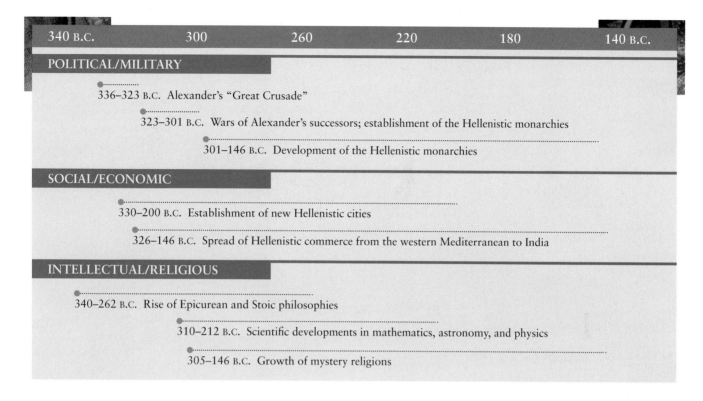

340 B.C.	300	260	220	180	140 B.C.

POLITICAL/MILITARY

336–323 B.C. Alexander's "Great Crusade"

323–301 B.C. Wars of Alexander's successors; establishment of the Hellenistic monarchies

301–146 B.C. Development of the Hellenistic monarchies

SOCIAL/ECONOMIC

330–200 B.C. Establishment of new Hellenistic cities

326–146 B.C. Spread of Hellenistic commerce from the western Mediterranean to India

INTELLECTUAL/RELIGIOUS

340–262 B.C. Rise of Epicurean and Stoic philosophies

310–212 B.C. Scientific developments in mathematics, astronomy, and physics

305–146 B.C. Growth of mystery religions

Greek mercenaries, he set out to conquer the rest of Asia. He plunged deeper into the East, into lands completely unknown to the Greek world. It took his soldiers four additional years to conquer Bactria and the easternmost parts of the now-defunct Persian Empire, but still Alexander was determined to continue his march.

In 326 B.C. Alexander crossed the Indus River and entered India. There, too, he saw hard fighting, and finally at the Hyphasis River his troops refused to go farther. Alexander was enraged by the mutiny, for he believed he was near the end of the world. Nonetheless, the army stood firm, and Alexander relented. Still eager to explore the limits of the world, Alexander turned south to the Arabian Sea. Though the tribes in the area did not oppose him, he waged a bloody, ruthless, and unnecessary war against them. After reaching the Arabian Sea and turning west, he led his army through the grim Gedrosian Desert. The army suffered fearfully, and many soldiers died along the way; nonetheless, in 324 B.C. Alexander reached his camp at Susa. The great crusade was over, and Alexander himself died the next year in Babylon.

*A*lexander's Legacy

Alexander so quickly became a legend during his lifetime that he still seems superhuman. That alone makes a rea-soned interpretation of him very difficult. Some historians have seen him as a high-minded philosopher, and none can deny that he possessed genuine intellectual gifts. Others, however, have portrayed him as a bloody-minded autocrat, more interested in his own ambition than in any philosophical concept of the common good. Alexander is the perfect example of the need for the historian carefully to interpret the known facts.

The historical record shows that Alexander in a drunken brawl murdered the friend who had saved his life at the Battle of the Granicus River. Alexander also used his power to have several other trusted officials, who had done nothing to offend him, assassinated. Other uglier and grimmer facts argue against the view that Alexander was a humane and tolerant man. In eastern Iran and India he savagely and unnecessarily slaughtered peoples whose only crime was their desire to be left in peace.

The only rationale to support those who see Alexander as a philosopher-king comes from a banquet held in 324 B.C. at the end of his career of carnage. This event is very important for a variety of reasons. It came immediately on the heels of a major Macedonian mutiny. The veteran and otherwise loyal Macedonians resented Alexander's new policy of giving high offices to Persians, people whom they had conquered after great suffering. Alexander realized that his Macedonians were too few to

Alexander at the Battle of Issus   At left, Alexander the Great, bareheaded and wearing a breastplate, charges King Darius, who is standing in a chariot. The moment marks the turning point of the battle, as Darius turns to flee from the attack. *(National Museum, Naples/Alinari/Art Resource, NY)*

administer his new empire and that he needed the ability and experience of the Persians. As a gesture of reconciliation and to end the mutiny, Alexander named the entire Macedonian army his kinsmen and held a vast banquet to heal wounds. He reserved the place of honor for the Macedonians, giving the Persians and others positions of lesser status. At the banquet Alexander offered a public prayer for harmony and partnership between the Macedonians and the Persians, and this prayer has been interpreted as an expression of deep philosophical views. (See the feature "Listening to the Past: Alexander and the Brotherhood of Man" on pages 122–123.) But far from representing an ideal desire for the brotherhood of man, the gesture was a blatant call for Macedonians and Persians to form a superior union for the purpose of ruling his new empire. It is undeniably true that the concepts of universal harmony and the brotherhood of man became common during the Hellenistic period, but they were the creations of talented philosophers, not the battle-hardened king of Macedonia.

Alexander was instrumental in changing the face of politics in the eastern Mediterranean. His campaign swept away the Persian Empire, which had ruled the East for over two hundred years. In its place he established a Macedonian monarchy.

More important in the long run was his founding of new cities and military colonies, which scattered Greeks and Macedonians throughout the East. Thus the practical result of Alexander's campaign was to open the East to the tide of Hellenism.

The Political Legacy

In 323 B.C. Alexander the Great died at the age of thirty-two. The main question at his death was whether his vast empire could be held together. A major part of his legacy is what he had not done. Although he fathered a successor while in Bactria, his son was an infant at Alexander's death. The child was too young to assume the duties of kingship and was cruelly murdered. That meant that

MAP 4.2 The Hellenistic World   After Alexander's death, no single commander could hold his vast conquests together, resulting in the empire's breakup into several kingdoms and leagues.

Alexander's empire was a prize for the taking by the strongest of his generals. Within a week of Alexander's death a round of fighting began that was to continue for forty years. No single Macedonian general was able to replace Alexander as emperor of his entire domain. In effect, the strongest divided it among themselves. By 263 B.C. three officers had split the empire into large monarchies (see Map 4.2). Antigonus Gonatas became king of Macedonia and established the Antigonid dynasty, which ruled until the Roman conquest in 168 B.C. Ptolemy, son of Lagus, made himself king of Egypt, and his descendants, the Ptolemies, assumed the powers and position of pharaohs. Seleucus, founder of the Seleucid dynasty, carved out a kingdom that stretched from the coast of Asia Minor to India. In 263 B.C. Eumenes, the Greek ruler of Pergamum, a city in western Asia Minor, won his independence from the Seleucids and created the Pergamene monarchy. Though the Seleucid kings soon lost control of their

easternmost provinces, Greek influence in this area did not wane. In modern Turkestan and Afghanistan another line of Greek kings established the kingdom of Bactria and even managed to spread their power and culture into northern India.

The political face of Greece itself changed during the Hellenistic period. The day of the polis was over; in its place rose leagues of city-states. The two most powerful and extensive were the Aetolian League in western and central Greece and the Achaean League in the Peloponnesus. Once-powerful city-states like Athens and Sparta sank to the level of third-rate powers.

The political history of the Hellenistic period was dominated by the great monarchies and the Greek leagues. The political fragmentation and incessant warfare that marked the Hellenic period continued on an even wider and larger scale during the Hellenistic period. Never did the Hellenistic world achieve political stability or lasting peace. Hellenistic kings never forgot the vision of Alexander's empire, spanning Europe and Asia, secure under the rule of one man. Try though they did, they were never able to re-create it. In this respect Alexander's legacy fell not to his generals but to the Romans of a later era.

The Cultural Legacy

As Alexander waded ever deeper into the East, distance alone presented him with a serious problem: how was he to retain contact with the Greek world behind him? Communications were vital, for he drew supplies and reinforcements from Greece and Macedonia. Alexander had to be sure that he was never cut off and stranded far from the Mediterranean world. His solution was to plant cities and military colonies in strategic places. In these settlements Alexander left Greek mercenaries and Macedonian veterans who were no longer up to active campaigning. Besides keeping the road open to the West, these settlements served the purpose of dominating the countryside around them.

Their military significance apart, Alexander's cities and colonies became powerful instruments in the spread of Hellenism throughout the East. Plutarch described Alexander's achievement in glowing terms: "Having founded over 70 cities among barbarian peoples and having planted Greek magistracies in Asia, Alexander overcame its wild and savage way of life."[2] Alexander had indeed opened the East to an enormous wave of immigration, and his successors continued his policy by inviting Greek colonists to settle in their realms. For seventy-five years after Alexander's death, Greek immigrants poured into the East. At least 250 new Hellenistic colonies were established. The Mediterranean world had seen no comparable movement of peoples since the days of Archilochus (see page 66), when wave after wave of Greeks had turned the Mediterranean basin into a Greek-speaking region.

Street Musicians This mosaic portrays a scene from New Comedy, which specialized in light humor. The men to the right play the tympanum and cymbals. The woman plays the flute, and the boy may just be enjoying the show. Such musicians were common in the Hellenistic period, and in their own humble way enlivened the daily grind. *(Museo Nazionale, Naples/Archaeological Receipts Fund)*

One concrete and almost exotic example of these trends comes from the newly discovered Hellenistic city of Ay Khanoum. Situated on the borders of Russia and Afghanistan and not far from China, the city was predominately Greek. It had the typical Greek trappings of a gymnasium, various temples, and administration buildings. It was not, however, purely Greek. It also contained an oriental temple and artistic remains that prove that the Greeks and the natives had already embraced aspects of each other's religions. One of the most curious discoveries was a long inscription written in Greek verse by Clearchus, a pupil of Aristotle. The inscription, carved in stone, was set up in a public place for all to see. Clearchus had simply copied the precepts of famous Greeks. The inscription was philosophy for the common people, a contribution to popular culture. It provided the Greeks with a link to their faraway homeland. It was also an easy way to make at least some of Greek culture available to natives.

The overall result of Alexander's settlements and those of his successors was the spread of Hellenism as far east as India. Throughout the Hellenistic period, Greeks and Easterners became familiar with and adapted themselves to each other's customs, religions, and ways of life. Although Greek culture did not completely conquer the East, it gave the East a vehicle of expression that linked it to the West. Hellenism became a common bond among the East, peninsular Greece, and the western Mediterranean. This pre-existing cultural bond was later to prove supremely valuable to Rome—itself heavily influenced by Hellenism—in its efforts to impose a comparable political unity on the known world.

The Spread of Hellenism

When the Greeks and Macedonians entered Asia Minor, Egypt, and the more remote East, they encountered civilizations older than their own. In some ways the Eastern cultures were more advanced than the Greek, in others less so. Thus this third great tide of Greek migration differed from preceding waves, which had spread over land that was uninhabited or inhabited by less-developed peoples.

What did the Hellenistic monarchies offer Greek immigrants politically and materially? More broadly, how did Hellenism and the cultures of the East affect one another? What did the meeting of East and West entail for the history of the world?

Cities and Kingdoms

One of the major developments of these new kingdoms was the resurgence of monarchy, which had many reper-

cussions. For most Greeks monarchs were something out of the heroic past, something found in Homer's *Iliad* but not in daily life. Furthermore, most Hellenistic kingdoms embraced numerous different peoples who had little in common. Hellenistic kings thus needed a new political concept to unite them. One solution was the creation of a ruler cult that linked the king's authority with that of the gods. Thus, royal power had divine approval and was meant to create a political and religious bond between the kings and their subjects. These deified kings were not considered gods as mighty as Zeus or Apollo, and the new ruler cults probably made little religious impact on those ruled. Nonetheless, the ruler cult was an easily understandable symbol of unity within the kingdom.

Monarchy also included royal women, who began to play an active part in political and diplomatic life. Some of them did so in their own right, others by manipulating their husbands. For the most part they served as examples that women too were capable of shouldering vast responsibilities and performing them successfully. (See the feature "Individuals in Society: Queen Cratesicleia's Sacrifice.")

Although Alexander's generals created huge kingdoms, the concept of monarchy, even when combined with the ruler cult, never replaced the ideal of the polis. Consequently, the monarchies never won the deep emotional loyalty that Greeks had once felt for the polis. Hellenistic kings needed large numbers of Greeks to run their kingdoms. Otherwise royal business would grind to a halt, and the conquerors would soon be swallowed up by the far more numerous conquered population. Obviously, then, the kings had to encourage Greeks to immigrate and build new homes. The Hellenistic kings thus confronted the problem of making life in the new monarchies resemble the traditional Greek way of life. Since Greek civilization was urban, the kings continued Alexander's policy of establishing cities throughout their kingdoms in order to entice Greeks to immigrate. Yet the creation of these cities posed a serious political problem that the Hellenistic kings failed to solve.

To the Greeks civilized life was unthinkable without the polis, which was far more than a mere city. The Greek polis was by definition **sovereign**—an independent, autonomous state run by its citizens, free of any outside power or restraint. Hellenistic kings, however, refused to grant sovereignty to their cities. In effect, these kings willingly built cities but refused to build a polis.

Hellenistic monarchs gave their cities all the external trappings of a polis. Each had an assembly of citizens, a council to prepare legislation, and a board of magistrates to conduct the city's political business. Yet, however similar to the Greek polis they appeared, these cities could not engage in diplomatic dealings, make treaties, pursue their own foreign policy, or wage their own wars. None could govern its own affairs without interference from the king, who, even if he stood in the background, was the real sovereign. In the eyes of the king the cities were important parts of the kingdom, but the welfare of the whole kingdom came first. The cities had to follow royal orders, and the king often placed his own officials in the cities to see that his decrees were followed.

A new Hellenistic city differed from a Greek polis in other ways as well. The Greek polis had enjoyed political and social unity even though it was normally composed of citizens, slaves, and resident aliens. The polis had one body of law and one set of customs. In the Hellenistic city Greeks represented an elite citizen class. Natives and non-Greek foreigners who lived in Hellenistic cities usually possessed lesser rights than Greeks and often had their own laws. In some instances this disparity spurred natives to assimilate Greek culture in order to rise politically and socially. The Hellenistic city was not homogeneous and could not spark the intensity of feeling that marked the polis.

An excellent example of this process comes from the city of Pergamum in northwestern Anatolia. Previously an important strategic site, its new Greek rulers turned it into a magnificent city complete with all the typical buildings of the polis. They built the usual government buildings, gymnasia, and baths. They founded a library second only to that in Alexandria. They erected temples to the traditional deities, but they also built an imposing temple to the Egyptian gods. Furthermore, Jews established a synagogue in the city. Especially in the agora Greeks and Easterners met to conduct business and to learn about each other. Greeks felt as though they were at home, and Easterners made their contributions to the evolving culture.

The old Greek cities of Asia Minor actually, if unintentionally, aided this development by maintaining and spreading traditions that went back for centuries. They served as models for the new foundations by providing a rich legacy of culture and tradition. They shone with such physical beauty in buildings and arts that through their very charm they made Hellenism attractive. They also represented a gracious style of civilized life. In their very

The Main Street of Pergamum No matter where in old Greece they had come from, all Greeks would immediately feel at home walking along this main street in Pergamum. They would all see familiar sights. To the left is the top of the theater where they could watch the plays of the great dramatists, climb farther to the temple, and admire the fortifications on the right. *(Faith Cimok, Turkey)*

Individuals in Society

Queen Cratesicleia's Sacrifice

Hellenistic queens were hardly ordinary women, but they were women nonetheless. The Spartan Cratesicleia combined in herself the duties of queen mother to her homeland and mother of her own family. Her finest hour came in 225 B.C., when Sparta tried to reassert itself as a major power. As was seen in Chapter 3, Epaminondas and the Thebans had shattered Spartan might. Yet in the late third century B.C., Cratesicleia's son, King Cleomenes, made a valiant effort to restore Sparta's fortunes. He tried to win control of the Peloponnesus and stoutly opposed King Antigonus of Macedonia, who drove him back to Sparta. At this point Ptolemy, son of the Macedonian Lagus and king of Egypt, offered to help, but at a high and humiliating price.

Now, Ptolemy the king of Egypt promised Cleomenes aid and assistance, but demanded his mother [Cratesicleia] and his children as hostages. For a long time, therefore, he was ashamed to tell his mother, and though he often went to her and was at the very point of letting her know, he held his peace, so that she on her part became suspicious and enquired of his friends whether there was not something that he wished to tell her but hesitated to do so. Finally, when Cleomenes plucked up courage to speak to the matter, his mother burst into a hearty laugh and said: "Was this the thing that you often had a mind to tell me but lost your courage? Hurry, put me on board a ship, and send this frail body wheresoever you think it will be of most use to Sparta, before old age destroys it sitting idly here."

Accordingly, when all things were ready, they came to Taenarus [a harbor in Laconia] by land, while the army escorted them under arms. And as Cratesicleia was about to embark, she drew Cleomenes aside by himself into the temple of Poseidon, and after embracing and kissing him in his anguish and deep trouble, said: "Come, king of the Spartans, when we go forth let no one see us weeping or doing anything unworthy of Sparta. For this lies in our power, and this alone; but as for the issues of Tyche [Fortune], we shall have what the deity may grant." After saying this, she composed herself and proceeded to the ship with her little grandson, and bade the captain to put to sea with all speed. And when she arrived in Egypt, and learned that Ptolemy was receiving embassies and proposals from Antigonus, and heard that although the Achaeans invited Cleomenes to make peace with them, he was afraid on her account to end the war without the consent of

Ptolemy, she sent word to him that he must do what was fitting and advantageous for Sparta, and not, because of one old woman and a little boy, be ever in fear of Ptolemy.

With the time and the military support bought in large part by Cratesicleia's sacrifice, Cleomenes renewed the war against the Macedonians. Yet at the Battle of Sellasia in 222 B.C., Antigonus defeated him, forcing him to flee to Ptolemy in Egypt. There in defeat and disgrace, he died the victim of a palace plot. Plutarch recounts Ptolemy's response:

From Corone (shown here in an 1829 sketch) Cratesicleia did her duty by sailing as a hostage to Egypt. (Boccuet in *Expédition scientifique de Moree*)

When Ptolemy learned of these events, he gave orders that the body of Cleomenes should be flayed and hung up, and that his children, his mother, and the women who were with her, should be killed. . . . And Cratesicleia herself was not one bit dismayed at death, but asked only one favor, that she might die before the children died. However, when they arrived at the place of execution, first the children were murdered before her eyes, and then Cratesicleia herself was killed, making only this one cry at sorrows so great: "O children, where have you gone?"

Though horrified, she nonetheless met her death with dignity and without fear. Plutarch ends the story by observing: "Virtue cannot be outraged by the might of Tyche," or, it can be said, by human barbarity.

Questions for Analysis

1. Was Cratesicleia's valor any greater or less than that of Spartan soldiers who defended the state on the battlefield?
2. What does this episode tell us about the tradition of Spartan patriotism?
3. Was Cleomenes justified in putting his family in such jeopardy?

Source: Quotations reprinted by permission of the publishers and Trustees of the Loeb Classical Library from *Plutarch: Vol. X— Plutarch Lives,* trans. B. Perrin (Cambridge, Mass.: Harvard University Press, 1921). The Loeb Classical Library® is a registered trademark of the President and Fellows of Harvard College.

The **history companion** *features additional information and activities related to this topic.* history.college.hmco.com/students

Ladies Chatting In the Hellenistic period, art gracefully embraced the ordinary. This terra-cotta group has captured two well-dressed ladies in intimate conversation. This small piece is realistic in depicting the women, the styles of their clothes, and even their varied colors. *(British Museum/Michael Holford)*

combination of refinement, sophistication, and elegance they inspired imitation of the best in Greek culture. All new cities saw in them a link between the past and the blossoming future.

In many respects the Hellenistic city resembled a modern city. It was a cultural center with theaters, temples, and libraries. It was a seat of learning, home of poets, writers, teachers, and artists. It was a place where people could find amusement. The Hellenistic city was also an economic center that provided a ready market for grain and produce raised in the surrounding countryside. The city was an emporium, scene of trade and manufacturing. In short, the Hellenistic city offered cultural and economic opportunities but did not foster a sense of united, integrated enterprise.

There were no constitutional links between city and king. The city was simply his possession. Hellenistic kings tried to make the kingdom the political focus of citizens' allegiance. If the king could secure the frontiers of his kingdom, he could give it a geographical identity. He could then hope that his subjects would direct their primary loyalty to the kingdom rather than to a particular city. However, the kings' efforts to fix their borders led only to sustained warfare. Boundaries were determined by military power, and rule by force became the chief political principle of the Hellenistic world.

Though Hellenistic kings never built a true polis, that does not mean that their urban policy failed. Rather, the Hellenistic city was to remain the basic social and political unit in the Hellenistic East until the sixth century A.D. Cities were the chief agents of Hellenization, and their influence spread far beyond their walls. These cities formed a broader cultural network in which Greek language, customs, and values flourished. Roman rule in the Hellenistic East would later be based on this urban culture, which facilitated the rise and spread of Christianity. In broad terms, Hellenistic cities were remarkably successful.

The Greeks and the Opening of the East

If the Hellenistic kings failed to satisfy the Greeks' political yearnings, they nonetheless succeeded in giving them unequaled economic and social opportunities. The ruling dynasties of the Hellenistic world were Macedonian, and Greeks filled all important political, military, and diplomatic positions. They constituted an upper class that sustained Hellenism in the barbarian East. Besides building Greek cities, Hellenistic kings offered Greeks land and money as lures to further immigration.

The opening of the East offered ambitious Greeks opportunities for well-paying jobs and economic success.

Theater of Stratos   Excavation of this theater in Stratos, a major city in northwestern Greece, began only in 1994. Not a city in the mainstream of Greek affairs, Stratos nevertheless shared the love and appreciation of the arts that stamped all of Greek culture. Even in its partially excavated state, the theater boasts the remains of a stone building in the foreground, the orchestra, and behind it the seats. Beyond its many architectural refinements, the theater is of interest because most Greek plays were staged in small theaters such as this. *(John Buckler)*

The Hellenistic monarchy, unlike the Greek polis, did not depend solely on its citizens to fulfill its political needs. Talented Greeks could expect to rise quickly in the governmental bureaucracy. Appointed by the king, these administrators did not have to stand for election each year, as had many officials of a Greek polis. Since they held their jobs year after year, they had ample time to evolve new administrative techniques. Naturally they became more efficient than the amateur officials common in Hellenic Greek city-states. The needs of the Hellenistic monarchy and the opportunities it offered thus gave rise to a professional corps of Greek administrators.

Greeks and Macedonians also found ready employment in the armies and navies of the Hellenistic monarchies. Alexander had proved the Greco-Macedonian style of warfare to be far superior to that of the Easterners, and Alexander's successors, themselves experienced officers, realized the importance of trained Greek and Macedonian soldiers. Moreover, Hellenistic kings were extremely reluctant to arm the native populations or to allow them to serve in the army, fearing military rebellions among their conquered subjects. The result was the emergence of professional armies and navies consisting entirely of Greeks and Macedonians.

Greeks were able to dominate other professions as well. The kingdoms and cities recruited Greek writers and artists to create Greek literature, art, and culture on Asian soil. Architects, engineers, and skilled craftsmen found their services in great demand because of the building policies of the Hellenistic monarchs. If Hellenistic kingdoms were to have Greek cities, those cities needed Greek buildings—temples, porticoes, gymnasia, theaters, fountains, and houses. Architects and engineers were sometimes commissioned to design and build whole cities, which they laid out in checkerboard fashion and filled with typical Greek buildings. An enormous wave of construction took place during the Hellenistic period.

The Great Altar of Pergamum   A new Hellenistic city needed splendid art and architecture to prove its worth in Greek eyes. The king of Pergamum ordered the construction of this monumental altar, now in Berlin. The scenes depict the mythical victory of the Greek gods over the Giants, who symbolize barbarism. The altar served the propaganda purpose of celebrating the victory of Hellenism over the East. *(Bildarchiv Preussischer Kulturbesitz/Art Resource, NY)*

New opportunities opened for women as well, owing in part to the examples of the queens. Especially in social and economic pursuits women played an expanded role. More women than ever before received educations that enabled them to enter medicine and other professions. Literacy among women increased dramatically, and their options expanded accordingly. Some won fame as poets, while others studied with philosophers and contributed to the intellectual life of the age. As a rule, however, these developments touched only wealthier women, and not all of them. Although some poor women were literate, most were not.

The major reason for the new prominence of women was their increased participation in economic affairs. During the Hellenistic period some women took part in commercial transactions. They still lived under legal handicaps; in Egypt, for example, a Greek woman needed a male guardian to buy, sell, or lease land, to borrow money, and to represent her in other transactions. Yet often such a guardian was present only to fulfill the letter of the law. The woman was the real agent and handled the business being transacted. In Hellenistic Sparta, women accumulated large fortunes and vast amounts of land. As early as

the beginning of the Hellenistic period, women owned two-fifths of the land of Laconia. Spartan women, however, were exceptional. In most other areas even women who were wealthy in their own right were formally under the protection of their male relatives.

Women also began to participate in politics on a limited basis. They served in civil capacities, for which they often received public acknowledgment. Women sometimes received honorary citizenship from foreign cities because of aid given in times of crisis. Few women achieved these honors, however, and those who did were from the upper classes.

Despite the opportunities they offered, the Hellenistic monarchies were hampered by their artificial origins. Their failure to win the political loyalty of their Greek subjects and their policy of wooing Greeks with lucrative positions encouraged a feeling of uprootedness and self-serving individualism among Greek immigrants. Once a Greek had left home to take service with, for instance, the army or the bureaucracy of the Ptolemies, he had no incentive beyond his pay and the comforts of life in Egypt to keep him there. If the Seleucid king offered him more money or a promotion, he might well accept it and take his talents to Asia Minor. Why not? In the realm of the Seleucids he, a Greek, would find the same sort of life and environment that the kingdom of the Ptolemies had provided him. Thus professional Greek soldiers and administrators were very mobile and apt to look to their own interests, not their kingdom's.

One result of these developments was that the nature of warfare changed. Except in the areas of Greece and to some extent Macedonia, Hellenistic soldiers were professionals. Unlike the citizen hoplites of classical Greece, these men were regular soldiers capable of intricate maneuvers. Hellenistic kings paid them well, often giving them land as an incentive to remain loyal. Only in Macedonia among the kingdoms was there a national army that was devoted to its land, homes, and monarchy. The loyalty, skill, and bravery of Macedonian soldiers made them the most formidable in the Hellenistic world.

As long as Greeks continued to replenish their professional ranks, the kingdoms remained strong. In the process they drew an immense amount of talent from the Greek peninsula, draining the vitality of the Greek homeland. However, the Hellenistic monarchies could not keep recruiting Greeks forever, in spite of their wealth and willingness to spend lavishly. In time the huge surge of immigration slowed greatly. Even then the Hellenistic monarchs were reluctant to recruit Easterners to fill posts normally held by Greeks. The result was at first the stagnation of the Hellenistic world and finally, after 202 B.C., its collapse in the face of the young and vigorous Roman republic.

Greeks and Easterners

The Greeks in the East were a minority, and Hellenistic cities were islands of Greek culture in an Eastern sea. But Hellenistic monarchies were remarkably successful in at least partially Hellenizing Easterners and spreading a uniform culture throughout the East, a culture to which Rome eventually fell heir. The prevailing institutions, laws, and language of the East became Greek. Indeed, the Near East had seen nothing comparable since the days when Mesopotamian culture had spread throughout the area.

Yet the spread of Greek culture was wider than it was deep. At best it was a veneer, thicker in some places than in others. Hellenistic kingdoms were never entirely unified in language, customs, and thought. Greek culture took firmest hold along the shores of the Mediterranean, but in the Far East, in Persia and Bactria, it eventually gave way to Eastern cultures. The principal reason for this curious phenomenon is that Greek culture generally did not extend far beyond the reaches of the cities. Many

East Meets West Ptolemy V, a Macedonian by birth and the Hellenistic king of Egypt, dedicated this stone to the Egyptian sacred bull of the Egyptian god Ptah. Nothing here is Greek or Macedonian, a sign that the conquered had, in some religious and ceremonial ways, won over their conquerors. *(Egyptian Museum, Cairo)*

Easterners adopted the aspects of Hellenism that they found useful, but others in the countryside generally did not embrace it wholly.

The Ptolemies in Egypt provide an excellent example of this situation. They made little effort to spread Greek culture, and unlike other Hellenistic kings they were not city builders. Indeed, they founded only the city of Ptolemais near Thebes. At first the native Egyptian population, the descendants of the pharaoh's people, retained their traditional language, outlook, religion, and way of life. Initially untouched by Hellenism, the natives continued to be the foundation of the state: they fed it by their labor in the fields and financed its operations with their taxes.

Under the pharaohs talented Egyptians had been able to rise to high office, but during the third century B.C. the Ptolemies cut off this avenue of advancement. Instead of converting the natives to Hellenism, the Ptolemies tied them to the land even more tightly, making it nearly impossible for them to leave their villages. The bureaucracy of the Ptolemies was ruthlessly efficient, and the native population was viciously and cruelly exploited. Even in times of hardship the king's taxes came first, although payment might mean starvation for the natives. Their desperation was summed up by one Egyptian, who scrawled the warning: "We are worn out; we will run away."[3] To many Egyptians revolt or a life of brigandage was certainly preferable to working the land under the harsh Ptolemies.

Throughout the third century B.C. the Greek upper class in Egypt had little to do with the native population. Many Greek bureaucrats established homes in Alexandria and Ptolemais, where they managed finances, served as magistrates, and administered the law. Other Greeks settled in military colonies and supplied the monarchy with fighting men. But in the second century B.C. Greeks and native Egyptians began to intermarry and mingle their cultures. The language of the native population influenced Greek, and many Greeks adopted Egyptian religion and ways of life. Simultaneously, natives adopted Greek customs and language and began to play a role in the administration of the kingdom and even to serve in the army. While many Greeks and Egyptians remained aloof from each other, the overall result was the evolution of a widespread Greco-Egyptian culture.

Meanwhile the Seleucid kings established many cities and military colonies in western Asia Minor and along the banks of the Tigris and Euphrates Rivers in order to nurture a vigorous and large Greek population. Especially important to the Seleucids were the military colonies, for they needed Greeks to defend the kingdom. The Seleucids had no elaborate plan for Hellenizing the native population, but the arrival of so many Greeks was bound to have an impact. Seleucid military colonies were generally founded near native villages, thus exposing Easterners to all aspects of Greek life. Many Easterners found Greek political and cultural forms attractive and imitated them. In Asia Minor and Syria, for instance, numerous native villages and towns developed along Greek lines, and some of them became Hellenized cities. Farther east, the Greek kings who replaced the Seleucids in the third century B.C. spread Greek culture to their neighbors, even into the Indian subcontinent.

For Easterners the prime advantage of Greek culture was its very pervasiveness. The Greek language became the common speech of the East. A common dialect called **koine** even influenced the speech of peninsular Greece itself. Greek became the speech of the royal court, bureaucracy, and army. It was also the speech of commerce: any Easterner who wanted to compete in business had to learn it. As early as the third century B.C. some Greek cities were giving citizenship to Hellenized natives.

The vast majority of Hellenized Easterners, however, took only the externals of Greek culture while retaining the essentials of their own ways of life. Though Greeks and Easterners adapted to each other's ways, there was never a true fusion of cultures. Nonetheless, each found useful things in the civilization of the other, and the two fertilized each other. This fertilization, this mingling of Greek and Eastern elements, is what makes Hellenistic culture unique and distinctive.

Hellenism and the Jews

A prime illustration of how the East took what it wanted from Hellenism while remaining true to itself is the impact of Greek culture on the Jews. At first, Jews in Hellenistic cities were treated as resident aliens. As they grew more numerous, they received permission to form a political corporation, a **politeuma,** which gave them a great deal of autonomy. The Jewish politeuma, like the Hellenistic city, obeyed the king's commands, but there was virtually no royal interference with the Jewish religion. Indeed, the Greeks were always reluctant to tamper with anyone's religion. Antiochus III (ca 242–187 B.C.), for instance, recognized that most Jews had become loyal subjects, and he treated them with great kindness and dignity. In his efforts to solidify his empire he endorsed their religious customs and ensured their political rights. He went so far as to deny any uninvited foreigner permission to enter the temple at Jerusalem. As a result, Hellenism and Judaism usually met on friendly terms. Only the Seleucid king Antiochus Epiphanes (175–ca 164 B.C.) tried to suppress the Jewish religion in Judaea. He did so not because he hated the Jews (who were a small part of his kingdom), but because he was trying to unify his realm culturally to meet the threat of Rome. To the Jews he extended the same policy that he applied to all subjects. Apart from this instance, Hellenistic Jews suffered no official religious persecution. Some Jews were given the right to become full citizens of Hellenistic cities, but few exercised that right. Citizenship would have allowed them to vote in the assembly and serve as magistrates, but it would also have obliged them to worship the gods of the city—a practice few Jews chose to follow.

Jews living in Hellenistic cities often embraced a good deal of Hellenism. So many Jews learned Greek, especially in Alexandria, that the Old Testament was translated into Greek, and services in the synagogue came to be conducted in Greek. Jews often took Greek names, used Greek political forms, adopted Greek practice by forming their own trade associations, put inscriptions on graves as the Greeks did, and much else. Yet no matter how much of Greek culture or its externals Jews borrowed, they normally remained attached to their religion. Thus, in spite of Hellenistic trappings, Hellenized Jews remained Jews at heart.

The Economic Scope of the Hellenistic World

Alexander's conquest of the Persian Empire not only changed the political face of the ancient world but also brought the East fully into the sphere of Greek economics. Yet the Hellenistic period did not see a revolution in the way people lived and worked. The material demands of Hellenistic society remained as simple as those of Athenian society in the fifth century B.C. Clothes and furniture were essentially unchanged, as were household goods, tools, and jewelry. The real achievement of Alexander and his successors was linking East and West in a broad commercial network. The spread of Greeks throughout the East created new markets and stimulated trade. The economic unity of the Hellenistic world, like its cultural bonds, would later prove valuable to the Romans.

Commerce

Alexander's conquest of the Persian Empire had immediate effects on trade. In the Persian capitals Alexander had found vast sums of gold, silver, and other treasure. This wealth financed the creation of new cities, the building of roads, and the development of harbors. Most of the great monarchies coined their money on the Attic standard, which meant that much of the money used in Hellenistic kingdoms had the same value. Traders were less in need of moneychangers than in the days when each major power coined money on a different standard. As a result of Alexander's conquests, geographical knowledge of the East increased dramatically, making the East far better known to the Greeks than previously. The Greeks spread their law and methods of transacting business throughout the East. Whole new fields lay open to Greek merchants, who eagerly took advantage of the new opportunities. Commerce itself was a leading area where Greeks and Easterners met on grounds of common interest. In bazaars, ports, and trading centers Greeks learned of Eastern customs and traditions while spreading knowledge of their own culture.

The Seleucid and Ptolemaic dynasties traded as far afield as India, Arabia, and sub-Saharan Africa. Overland trade with India and Arabia was conducted by caravan and was largely in the hands of Easterners. The caravan trade never dealt in bulk items or essential commodities; only luxury goods could be transported in this very expensive fashion. Once the goods reached the Hellenistic monarchies, Greek merchants took a hand in the trade.

Essential to the caravan trade from the Mediterranean to Afghanistan and India were the northern route to Dura on the Euphrates River and the southern route through Arabia. The desert of Arabia may seem at first unlikely and inhospitable terrain for a line of commerce, but to the east of it lies the plateau of Iran, from which trade routes stretched to the south and still farther east to China. Commerce from the East arrived at Egypt and the excellent harbors of Palestine, Phoenicia, and Syria. From these ports goods flowed to Greece, Italy, and Spain. The backbone of this caravan trade was the camel—shaggy, ill-tempered, but durable. Only its mother could consider it beautiful, but the camel is a splendid beast of burden, and few other animals could have endured the harsh heat and aridity of the caravan routes.

Over the caravan routes traveled luxury goods that were light, rare, and expensive. In time these luxury items became more of a necessity than a luxury. In part this development was the result of an increased volume of trade. In the prosperity of the period more people could afford to buy gold, silver, ivory, precious stones, spices, and a host of other easily transportable goods. Perhaps the most prominent goods in terms of volume were tea and silk. Indeed, the trade in silk gave the major route the name the **Great Silk Road,** for not only was this route prominent in antiquity, but it also was used in early modern times. In return the Greeks and Macedonians sent east manufactured goods, especially metal weapons, cloth, wine, and olive oil. Although these caravan routes can trace their origins to earlier times, they became far more prominent in the Hellenistic period. Business customs developed and became standardized, so that merchants from different nationalities communicated in a way understandable to all of them.

The durability and economic importance of these caravan routes are amply demonstrated by the fact that the death of Alexander, the ensuing wars of his successors, and the triumph of the Parthians in Iran had little effect

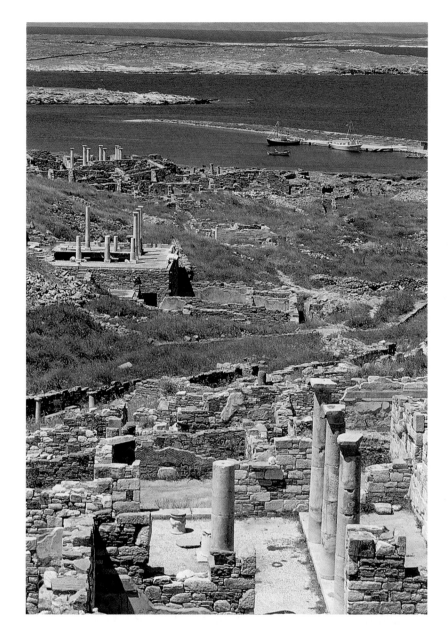

Harbor and Warehouse at Delos   During the Hellenistic period Delos became a thriving trading center. Shown here is the row of warehouses at water's edge. From Delos cargoes were shipped to virtually every part of the Mediterranean. *(Adam Woolfit/Woodfin Camp & Associates)*

on the trade. Numerous mercantile cities grew up along these distant tracks, places where native cultures combined with both Greco-Macedonian and Eastern cultures to create local but nonetheless cosmopolitan societies that were neither entirely Western nor entirely Eastern. The commercial contacts brought people together, even if sometimes indirectly. The merchants and the caravan cities were links in a chain that reached from the Mediterranean Sea at least to Afghanistan and Iran. Ideas passed along these routes as easily as, and probably more comfortably than, gold and ivory.

The Ptolemies discovered how to use monsoon winds to establish direct contact with India. One hardy merchant has left a firsthand account of sailing this important maritime route:

Hippalos, the pilot, observing the position of the ports and the conditions of the sea, first discovered how to sail across the ocean. Concerning the winds of the ocean in this region, when with us the Etesian winds begin, in India a wind between southwest and south, named for Hippalos, sets in from the open sea. From then until now some mariners set forth from Kanes and some from the Cape of Spices. Those sailing to Dimurikes [in southern India] throw the bow of the ship farther out to sea. Those bound for Barygaza and the realm of the Sakas [in northern India] hold to the land no more than three days; and if the wind remains favorable, they hold the same course through the outer sea, and they sail along past the previously mentioned gulfs.[4]

Although this sea route never replaced overland caravan traffic, it kept direct relations between East and West alive, stimulating the exchange of ideas as well as goods.

More economically important than this exotic trade were commercial dealings in essential commodities like raw materials, grain, and industrial products. The Hellenistic monarchies usually raised enough grain for their own needs as well as a surplus for export. For the cities of Greece and the Aegean this trade in grain was essential, because many of them could not grow enough. Fortunately for them, abundant wheat supplies were available nearby in Egypt and in the Crimea in southern Russia.

Most trade in bulk commodities was seaborne, and the Hellenistic merchant ship was the workhorse of the day. The merchant ship had a broad beam and relied on sails for propulsion. It was far more seaworthy than the contemporary warship, which was long, narrow, and built for speed. A small crew of experienced sailors could handle the merchant vessel easily. Maritime trade provided opportunities for workers in other industries and trades: sailors, shipbuilders, dockworkers, accountants, teamsters, and pirates. Piracy was always a factor in the Hellenistic world and remained so until Rome extended its power throughout the East.

The Greek cities paid for their grain by exporting olive oil and wine. When agriculture and oil production developed in Syria, Greek products began to encounter competition from the Seleucid monarchy. Later in the Hellenistic period, Greek oil and wine found a lucrative market in Italy. Another significant commodity was fish, which for export was either salted, pickled, or dried. This trade was doubly important because fish provided poor people with an essential element of their diet. Salt too was often imported, and there was some very slight trade in salted meat, which was a luxury item. Far more important was the trade in honey, dried fruit, nuts, and vegetables. Of raw materials, wood was high in demand, but little trade occurred in manufactured goods.

Slaves were a staple of Hellenistic trade. The wars provided prisoners for the slave market; to a lesser extent, so did kidnapping and capture by pirates. The number of slaves involved cannot be estimated, but there is no doubt that slavery flourished. Both old Greek states and new Hellenistic kingdoms were ready slave markets, as was Rome when it emerged triumphant from the Second Punic War (see pages 134–135).

Throughout the Mediterranean world slaves were almost always in demand. Only the Ptolemies discouraged both the trade and slavery itself, and they did so only for economic reasons. Their system had no room for slaves, who would only have competed with free labor. Otherwise slave labor was to be found in the cities and temples of the Hellenistic world, in the factories and fields, and in the homes of wealthier people. In Italy and some parts of the East, slaves performed manual labor for large estates and worked the mines. They were vitally important to the Hellenistic economy.

Industry

Although demand for goods increased during the Hellenistic period, no new techniques of production appear to have developed. The discoveries of Hellenistic mathematicians and thinkers failed to produce any significant corresponding technological development. Manual labor, not machinery, continued to turn out the raw materials and few manufactured goods the Hellenistic world used. Human labor was so cheap and so abundant that kings had no incentive to encourage the invention and manufacture of laborsaving machinery.

The Ptolemies ran their gold mines along the same harsh lines. One historian gives a grim picture of the miners' lives:

The kings of Egypt condemn [to the mines] those found guilty of wrong-doing and those taken prisoner in war, those who were victims of false accusations and were put into jail because of royal anger. . . . The condemned—and they are very many—all of them are put in chains, and they work persistently and continually, both by day and throughout the night, getting no rest, and carefully cut off from escape.[5]

The Ptolemies even condemned women and children to work in the mines. All of them—men, women, and boys—worked until they died.

Apart from gold and silver, which were used primarily for coins and jewelry, iron was the most important metal and saw the most varied use. Even so, the method of its production never became very sophisticated. The Hellenistic Greeks did manage to produce a low-grade steel by adding carbon to iron.

Pottery remained an important commodity, and most of it was made locally. The pottery used in the kitchen, the coarse ware, did not change at all. Fancier pots and bowls, decorated with a shiny black glaze, came into use during the Hellenistic period. This ware originated in Athens, but potters in other places began to imitate its style, heavily cutting into the Athenian market. In the second century B.C. a red-glazed ware, often called Samian, burst on the market and soon dominated it. Athens still held its own, however, in the production of fine pottery. Despite the change in pottery styles, the method of production of all pottery, whether plain or fine, remained essentially unchanged.

Agriculture

Hellenistic kings paid special attention to agriculture. Much of their revenue was derived from the produce of royal land, rents paid by the tenants of royal land, and taxation of agricultural land. Some Hellenistic kings even sought out and supported agricultural experts. The Ptolemies, for instance, sponsored experiments on seed grain, selecting seeds that seemed hardy and productive and trying to improve their characteristics. Indeed, the Ptolemies made the greatest strides in agriculture, and the reason for their success was largely political. Egypt had a strong tradition of central authority dating back to the pharaohs, which the Ptolemies inherited and tightened. They could decree what crops Egyptian farmers would plant and what animals would be raised, and they had the power to carry out their commands. The Ptolemies recognized the need for well-planned and constant irrigation, and much native labor went into the digging and maintenance of canals and ditches. The Ptolemies also reclaimed a great deal of land from the desert, including the Fayum, a dried lake bed near the Nile.

The centralized authority of the Ptolemies explains how agricultural advances occurred at the local level in Egypt. But such progress was not possible in any other Hellenistic monarchy. Despite royal interest in agriculture and a more studied approach to it in the Hellenistic period, there is no evidence that agricultural productivity increased. Whether Hellenistic agricultural methods had any influence on Eastern practices is unknown.

*H*ellenistic Intellectual Advances

Although it was once fashionable to criticize the intellectual achievements of the Hellenistic period in contrast to those of the classical period, the critics themselves deserve the criticism. The peoples of the Hellenistic era took the ideas and ideals of the classical Greeks and advanced them to new heights. Their achievements created the intellectual and religious atmosphere that deeply influenced Roman thinking and eventually the religious thought of liberal Judaism and early Christianity. Far from being stagnant, this was a period of vigorous growth. Its achievements included new religious ideas, startling innovations in philosophy, and remarkable advances in science and medicine.

Religion in the Hellenistic World

In religion Hellenism gave Easterners far less than the East gave the Greeks. At first the Hellenistic period saw the spread of Greek religious cults throughout the East. When Hellenistic kings founded cities, they also built temples and established new cults and priesthoods for the old Olympian gods. The new cults enjoyed the prestige of being the religion of the conquerors, and they were supported by public money. The most attractive aspects of the Greek cults, at least to the Greeks, were their rituals and festivities, as they were at least familiar. Greek cults sponsored literary, musical, and athletic contests, which were staged in beautiful surroundings among impressive Greek buildings. In short, the cults offered bright and lively entertainment, both intellectual and physical. They fostered Greek culture and traditional sports and thus were a splendid means of displaying Greek civilization in the East.

Despite various advantages, Greek cults suffered from some severe shortcomings. They were primarily concerned with ritual. Participation in the civic cults did not even require belief (see pages 79–83). On the whole, the civic cults neither appealed to religious emotions nor embraced matters such as sin and redemption. Greek mystery religions helped fill this gap, but the centers of these religions were in old Greece. Although the new civic cults were lavish in pomp and display, they could not satisfy deep religious feelings or spiritual yearnings.

Even though the Greeks participated in the new cults for cultural reasons, they felt little genuine religious attachment to them. In comparison with the emotional and sometimes passionate religions of the East, the Greek cults seemed sterile. Greeks increasingly sought solace from other sources. Educated and thoughtful people turned to philosophy as a guide to life, while others turned to superstition, magic, or astrology. Still others might shrug and speak of **Tyche,** which meant "Fate" or "Chance" or "Doom"—a capricious and sometimes malevolent force.

In view of the spiritual decline of Greek religion, it is surprising that Eastern religions did not make more

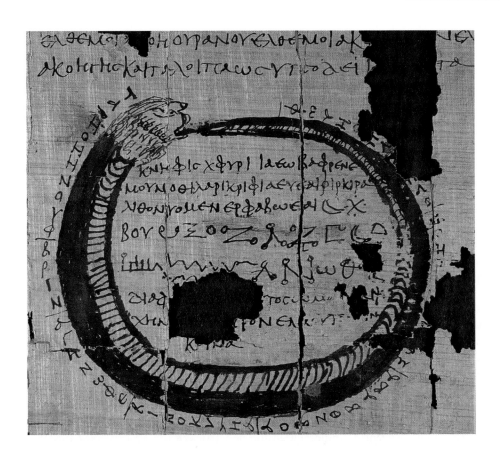

Hellenistic Magic This magical text, written in Greek and Egyptian, displays a snake surrounding the magical incantation. The text is intentionally obscure. *(British Library)*

immediate headway among the Greeks. Although Hellenistic Greeks clung to their own cults as expressions of their Greekness rather than for any ethical principles, they did not rush to embrace native religions. Only in the second century B.C., after a century of exposure to Eastern religions, did Greeks begin to adopt them.

Nor did Hellenistic kings make any effort to spread Greek religion among their Eastern subjects. The Greeks always considered religion a matter best left to the individual. Greek cults were attractive only to those socially aspiring Easterners who adopted Greek culture for personal advancement. Otherwise Easterners were little affected by Greek religion. Nor did native religions suffer from the arrival of the Greeks. Some Hellenistic kings limited the power of native priesthoods, but they also subsidized some Eastern cults with public money. Alexander the Great actually reinstated several Eastern cults that the Persians had suppressed.

The only significant junction of Greek and Eastern religious traditions was the growth and spread of new **mystery religions,** so called because they featured a body of ritual not to be divulged to anyone not initiated into the cult. These new mystery cults incorporated aspects of both Greek and Eastern religions and had broad appeal for both Greeks and Easterners who yearned for personal immortality. Since the Greeks were already familiar with old mystery cults, such as the Eleusinian mysteries in Attica, the new cults did not strike them as alien or barbarian. Familiar, too, was the concept of preparation for an initiation. Devotees of the Eleusinian mysteries and other such cults had to prepare themselves mentally and physically before entering the gods' presence. Thus the mystery cults fit well with Greek usage.

The new religions enjoyed one tremendous advantage over the old Greek mystery cults. Whereas old Greek mysteries were tied to particular places, such as Eleusis, the new religions spread throughout the Hellenistic world. People did not have to undertake long and expensive pilgrimages just to become members of the religion. In that sense the mystery religions came to the people, for temples of the new deities sprang up wherever Greeks lived.

The mystery religions all claimed to save their adherents from the worst that fate could do and promised life for the soul after death. They all had a single concept in common: the belief that by the rites of initiation devotees became united with the god, who had himself died and risen from the dead. The sacrifice of the god and his victory over death saved the devotee from eternal death. Similarly, all mystery religions demanded a period of preparation in which the convert strove to become holy, that is, to live by the religion's precepts. Once aspirants had prepared themselves, they went through an initiation in which they learned the secrets of the religion. The initiation was usually a ritual of great emotional intensity, symbolizing the entry into a new life.

The Eastern mystery religions that took the Hellenistic world by storm were the Egyptian cults of Serapis and Isis. Serapis, who was invented by King Ptolemy, combined elements of the Egyptian god Osiris with aspects of the Greek gods Zeus, Pluto (the prince of the underworld), and Asclepius. Serapis was believed to be the judge of souls, who rewarded virtuous and righteous people with eternal life. Like Asclepius, he was a god of healing. Serapis became an international god, and many Hellenistic Greeks thought of him as Zeus. Associated with Isis and Serapis was Anubis, the old Egyptian god who, like Charon in the Greek pantheon, guided the souls of initiates to the realm of eternal life.

The cult of Isis enjoyed even wider appeal than that of Serapis. Isis, wife of Osiris, claimed to have conquered Tyche and promised to save any mortal who came to her. She became the most important goddess of the Hellenistic world, and her worship was very popular among women. Her priests claimed that she had bestowed on humanity the gift of civilization and founded law and literature. She was the goddess of marriage, conception, and childbirth, and like Serapis she promised to save the souls of her believers.

There was neither conflict between Greek and Eastern religions nor wholesale acceptance of one or the other. Nonetheless, Greeks and Easterners noticed similarities among their respective deities and assumed that they were worshiping the same gods in different garb. These tendencies toward religious universalism and the desire for personal immortality would prove significant when the Hellenistic world came under the sway of Rome, for Hellenistic developments paved the way for the spread of Christianity.

Philosophy and the People

Philosophy during the Hellenic period was the exclusive province of the wealthy, for only they had leisure enough to pursue philosophical studies. During the Hellenistic period, however, philosophy reached out to touch the lives of more men and women than ever before. The reasons for this development were several. Since the ideal of the polis had declined, politics no longer offered people an intellectual outlet. Moreover, much of Hellenistic life, especially in the new cities of the East, seemed unstable and without venerable traditions. Greeks were far more

A Happy Fisherman   Hellenistic art delighted in the ordinary. Here a comfortable young man is about to catch a fish for dinner. Above him is a more fortunate bird, which remains idly indifferent. *(Archaeological Receipts Fund)*

Tyche This statue depicts Tyche as the bringer of bounty to people. Some Hellenistic Greeks worshiped Tyche in the hope that she would be kind to them. Philosophers tried to free people from her whimsies. Others tried to placate her. *(Faith Cimok, Turkey)*

mobile than they had ever been before, but their very mobility left them feeling uprooted. Many people in search of something permanent, something unchanging in a changing world, turned to philosophy. Another reason for the increased influence of philosophy was the decline of traditional religion and a growing belief in Tyche. To protect against the worst that Tyche could do, many Greeks looked to philosophy.

Philosophers themselves became much more numerous, and several new schools of philosophical thought emerged. In spite of their many differences, the major branches of philosophy agreed on the necessity of making people self-sufficient. They all recognized the need to equip men and women to deal successfully with Tyche. The major schools of Hellenistic philosophy all taught that people could be truly happy only when they had turned their backs on the world and focused full attention on one enduring thing. They differed chiefly on what that enduring thing was.

Two significant philosophies caught the minds and hearts of contemporary Greeks and some Easterners, as well as some later Romans. The first was **Epicureanism,** a practical philosophy of serenity in an often tumultuous world. Epicurus (340–270 B.C.) founded this school of philosophy based on scientific theories. Accepting Democritus's idea that the universe is composed of indestructible particles, Epicurus put forward a naturalistic theory of the universe. Although he did not deny the existence of the gods, he taught that they had no effect on human life. The essence of Epicurus's belief was that the principal good of human life is pleasure, which he defined as the absence of pain. He was not advocating drunken revels or sexual dissipation, which he thought actually caused pain. Instead, Epicurus concluded that any violent emotion is undesirable and advocated mild self-discipline. Even poverty he considered good, as long as people had enough food, clothing, and shelter. Epicurus also taught that individuals can most easily attain peace and serenity by ignoring the outside world and looking into their personal feelings and reactions. Thus Epicureanism led to quietism.

Epicureanism taught its followers to ignore politics and issues, for politics led to tumult, which would disturb the soul. Although the Epicureans thought that the state originated through a social contract among individuals, they did not care about the political structure of the state. They were content to live in a democracy, oligarchy, monarchy, or any other form of government, and they never speculated about the ideal state. Their ideals stood outside all political forms.

Opposed to the passivity of the Epicureans, Zeno (335–262 B.C.), a philosopher from Citium in Cyprus, advanced a different concept of human beings and the universe. Zeno first came to Athens to form his own school, the Stoa, named after the building where he preferred to teach. **Stoicism** became the most popular Hellenistic philosophy and the one that later captured the mind of Rome. Zeno and his followers considered nature an expression of divine will; in their view, people could be happy only when living in accordance with nature. They stressed the unity of man and the universe, stating that all men were brothers and obliged to help one another. Stoicism's science was derived from Heraclitus, but its broad and warm humanity was the work of Zeno and his followers.

Unlike the Epicureans, the Stoics taught that people should participate in politics and worldly affairs. Yet this idea never led to the belief that individuals should try to change the order of things. Time and again the Stoics used the image of an actor in a play: the Stoic plays an assigned part but never tries to change the play. To the Stoics the important question was not whether they achieved anything, but whether they lived virtuous lives. In that way they could triumph over Tyche, for Tyche could destroy achievements but not the nobility of their lives.

Though the Stoics evolved the concept of a world order, they thought of it strictly in terms of the individual. Like the Epicureans, they were indifferent to specific political forms. They believed that people should do their duty to the state in which they found themselves. The universal state they preached about was ethical, not political. The Stoics' most significant practical achievement was the creation of the concept of **natural law.** The Stoics concluded that as all men were brothers, partook of divine reason, and were in harmony with the universe, one law—a part of the natural order of life—governed them all.

The Stoic concept of a universal state governed by natural law is one of the finest heirlooms the Hellenistic world passed on to Rome. The Stoic concept of natural law, of one law for all people, became a valuable tool when the Romans began to deal with many different peoples with different laws. The ideal of the universal state gave the Romans a rationale for extending their empire to the farthest reaches of the world. The duty of individuals to their fellows served the citizens of the Roman Empire as the philosophical justification for doing their duty. In this respect, too, the real fruit of Hellenism was to ripen only under the cultivation of Rome.

Hellenistic Science

The area in which Hellenistic culture achieved its greatest triumphs was science. The most notable of the Hellenistic astronomers was Aristarchus of Samos (ca 310–230 B.C.),

who was educated in Aristotle's school. Aristarchus concluded that the sun is far larger than the earth and that the stars are enormously distant from the earth. He argued against Aristotle's view that the earth was the center of the universe. Instead, Aristarchus propounded the **heliocentric theory**—that the earth and planets revolve around the sun. His work is all the more impressive because he lacked even a rudimentary telescope. Aristarchus had only the human eye and brain, but they were more than enough.

Unfortunately, Aristarchus's theories did not persuade the ancient world. In the second century A.D. Claudius Ptolemy, a mathematician and astronomer in Alexandria, accepted Aristotle's theory of the earth as the center of the universe, and this view prevailed for fourteen hundred years. Aristarchus's heliocentric theory lay dormant until resurrected in the sixteenth century by the brilliant Polish astronomer Nicolaus Copernicus.

In geometry Hellenistic thinkers discovered little that was new, but Euclid (ca 300 B.C.), a mathematician who lived in Alexandria, compiled a valuable textbook of existing knowledge. His book *The Elements of Geometry* has exerted immense influence on Western civilization, for it rapidly became the standard introduction to geometry. Generations of students, from the Hellenistic period to the present, have learned the essentials of geometry from it.

The greatest thinker of the Hellenistic period was Archimedes (ca 287–212 B.C.), who was a clever inventor as well. He lived in Syracuse in Sicily and watched Rome emerge as a power in the Mediterranean. When the Romans laid siege to Syracuse in the Second Punic War, Archimedes invented a number of machines to thwart the armed forces. His catapults threw rocks large enough to sink ships and disrupt battle lines. His grappling devices lifted ships out of the water. Archimedes built such machines out of necessity, but they were of little real interest to him. In a more peaceful vein he invented the **Archimedean screw** (a pump to irrigate fields) and the compound pulley. Plutarch described Archimedes' dramatic demonstration of how easily his pulley could move huge weights with little effort:

A three-masted merchant ship of the royal fleet had been hauled on land by hard work and many hands. Archimedes put aboard her many men and the usual freight. He sat far away from her; without haste, but gently working a compound pulley with his hand, he drew her towards him smoothly and without faltering, just as though she were running on the surface of the sea.[6]

Archimedes was far more interested in pure mathematics than in practical inventions. His mathematical re-

Tower of the Four Winds This remarkable building, which still stands in Athens, was built by an astronomer to serve as a sundial, water-clock, and weather vane. It is one of the few examples of the application of Hellenistic science to daily life. *(Ronald Sheridan/Ancient Art & Architecture Collection Ltd.)*

search, covering many fields, was his greatest contribution to Western thought. In his book *On Plane Equilibriums* Archimedes dealt for the first time with the basic principles of mechanics, including the principle of the lever. He once said that if he were given a lever and a suitable place to stand, he could move the world. With his treatise *On Floating Bodies* Archimedes founded the science of hydrostatics. He concluded that whenever a solid floats in a liquid, the weight of the solid is equal to the weight of liquid displaced. The way he made his discovery has become famous:

When he was devoting his attention to this problem, he happened to go to a public bath. When he climbed down into the bathtub there, he noticed that water in the tub equal to the bulk of his body flowed out. Thus, when he observed this method of solving the problem, he did not wait. Instead, moved with joy, he sprang out of the tub, and rushing home naked he kept indicating in a loud voice that he had indeed discovered what he was seeking. For while running he was shouting repeatedly in Greek, "eureka, eureka" ("I have found it, I have found it.").[7]

Archimedes was willing to share his work with others, among them Eratosthenes (285–ca 204 B.C.), a man of almost universal interests. From his native Cyrene in North Africa, Eratosthenes traveled to Athens, where he studied philosophy and mathematics. He refused to join any of the philosophical schools, for he was interested in too many things to follow any particular dogma. Around

245 B.C. King Ptolemy invited Eratosthenes to Alexandria. The Ptolemies had done much to make Alexandria an intellectual, cultural, and scientific center. Eratosthenes came to Alexandria to become librarian of the royal library, a position of great prestige. The library was a huge collection of Greek writings, including such classic works as the poems of Homer, the histories of Herodotus and Thucydides, and the philosophical works of Plato and Aristotle. The library became one of the foremost intellectual centers of the ancient world. Eratosthenes had the honor of becoming its head. While there he continued his mathematical work and by letter struck up a friendship with Archimedes.

Unlike Archimedes, Eratosthenes did not devote his life entirely to mathematics, although he never lost interest in it. He used mathematics to further the geographical studies for which he is most famous. He calculated the circumference of the earth geometrically, estimating it as about 24,675 miles. He was not wrong by much: the earth is actually 24,860 miles in circumference. Eratosthenes also concluded that the earth was a spherical globe, that the landmass was roughly four-sided, and that the land was surrounded by ocean. He discussed the shapes and sizes of land and ocean and the irregularities of the earth's surface. He drew a map of the earth and used his own system of explaining the divisions of the earth's landmass.

Using geographical information gained by Alexander the Great's scientists, Eratosthenes tried to fit the East into Greek geographical knowledge. Although for some reason he ignored the western Mediterranean and Europe, he declared that a ship could sail from Spain either around Africa to India or directly westward to India. Not until the great days of Western exploration did sailors such as Vasco da Gama and Magellan actually prove Eratosthenes' theories. Like Eratosthenes, other Greek geographers also turned their attention southward to Africa. During this period the people of the Mediterranean learned of the climate and customs of Ethiopia and gleaned some scant information about equatorial Africa.

In the Hellenistic period the scientific study of botany had its origin. Aristotle's pupil Theophrastus (ca 372–288 B.C.), who became head of the Lyceum, the school established by Aristotle, studied the botanical information made available by Alexander's penetration of the East. Aristotle had devoted a good deal of his attention to zoology, and Theophrastus extended his work to plants. He wrote two books on the subject, *History of Plants* and *Causes of Plants*. He carefully observed phe-nomena and based his conclusions on what he had actually seen. Theophrastus classified plants and accurately described their parts. He detected the process of germination and realized the importance of climate and soil to plants. Some of Theophrastus's work found its way into agricultural handbooks, but for the most part Hellenistic science did not carry the study of botany further.

Despite its undeniable brilliance, Hellenistic science suffered from a remarkable weakness almost impossible for practical-minded Americans to understand. Although scientists of this period invented such machines as the air gun, the water organ, and even the steam engine, they never used their discoveries as laborsaving devices. No one has satisfactorily explained why these scientists were so impractical, but one answer is quite possible: they and the rest of society saw no real need for machines. Slave labor was especially abundant, a fact that made the use of laborsaving machinery superfluous. Science was applied only to war. Even though Hellenistic science did not lead the ancient world to an industrial revolution, later Hellenistic thinkers preserved the knowledge of machines and the principles behind them. In so doing they saved the discoveries of Hellenistic science for the modern age.

Hellenistic Medicine

The study of medicine flourished during the Hellenistic period, and Hellenistic physicians carried the work of Hippocrates into new areas. Herophilus, who lived in the first half of the third century B.C., worked at Alexandria and studied the writings of Hippocrates. He accepted Hippocrates' theory of the four humors and approached the study of medicine in a systematic, scientific fashion. He dissected dead bodies and measured what he observed. He discovered the nervous system and concluded that two types of nerves, motor and sensory, existed.

Herophilus also studied the brain, which he considered the center of intelligence, and discerned the cerebrum and cerebellum. His other work dealt with the liver, lungs, and uterus. His younger contemporary Erasistratus also conducted research on the brain and nervous system and improved on Herophilus's work. Erasistratus too followed in the tradition of Hippocrates and preferred to let the body heal itself by means of diet and air.

Both Herophilus and Erasistratus were members of the **Dogmatic school** of medicine at Alexandria. In this school speculation played an important part in research. So, too, did the study of anatomy. To learn more about human anatomy, Herophilus and Erasistratus dissected corpses and even vivisected criminals whom King Ptolemy contributed

An Unsuccessful Delivery This funeral stele depicts a mother who has perhaps lost her own life as well as her baby's. Maternal and infant mortality were quite common in antiquity. A similar stele elsewhere bears the heartbreaking words attributed to the mother by her grieving family: "All my labor could not bring the child forth; he lies in my womb, among the dead." *(National Archaeological Museum, Athens/Archaeological Receipts Fund)*

dria. Claiming that the Dogmatists' emphasis on anatomy and physiology was misplaced, they concentrated instead on the observation and cure of illnesses. They also laid heavier stress on the use of drugs and medicine to treat illnesses. Heraclides of Tarentum (perhaps first century B.C.) carried on the Empirical tradition and dedicated himself to observation and use of medicines. He discovered the benefits of opium and worked with other drugs that relieved pain. He also steadfastly rejected the relevance of magic to drugs and medicines.

The Hellenistic world was also plagued by people who claimed to cure illnesses through incantations and magic. Their potions included such concoctions as blood from the ear of an ass mixed with water to cure fever, or the liver of a cat killed when the moon was waning and preserved in salt. Broken bones could be cured by applying the ashes of a pig's jawbone to the break. The dung of a goat mixed with old wine was good for healing broken ribs. One charlatan claimed that he could cure epilepsy by making the patient drink spring water, drawn at night, from the skull of a man who had been killed but not cremated. These quacks even claimed that they could cure mental illness. The treatment for a person suffering from melancholy was calf dung boiled in wine. No doubt the patient became too sick to be depressed.

Quacks who prescribed such treatments were very popular but did untold harm to the sick and injured. They and greedy physicians also damaged the reputation of dedicated doctors who honestly and intelligently tried to heal and alleviate pain. The medical abuses that arose in the Hellenistic period were so flagrant that the Romans, who later entered the Hellenistic world, developed an intense dislike and distrust of physicians. The Romans considered the study of Hellenistic medicine beneath the dignity of a Roman, and even as late as the time of the Roman Empire, few Romans undertook the study of Greek medicine. Nonetheless, the work of men like Herophilus and Serapion made valuable contributions to the knowledge of medicine, and the fruits of their work were preserved and handed on to the West.

Summary

It can safely be said that Philip and Alexander broadened Greek and Macedonian horizons, but not in ways that they had intended. Although Alexander established Macedonian and Greek colonies across western and central Asia for military reasons, they resulted in the spread of Hellenism as a side effect. In the Aegean and Near East the fusion of Greek and Eastern cultures laid the social,

for the purpose. The practice of vivisection seems to have been short-lived, although dissection continued. Better knowledge of anatomy led to improvements in surgery. These advances enabled the Dogmatists to invent new surgical instruments and techniques.

In about 280 B.C. Philinus and Serapion, pupils of Herophilus, led a reaction against the Dogmatists. Believing that the Dogmatists had become too speculative, they founded the **Empiric school** of medicine at Alexanintellectual, and cultural foundations on which the Romans would later build. In the heart of the old Persian Empire, Hellenism was only another new influence that was absorbed by older ways of thought and life. Yet overall, in the exchange of ideas and the opportunity for different cultures to learn about one another, a new cosmopolitan society evolved. That society in turn made possible such diverse advances as a wider extent of trade and agriculture, the creation of religious and philosophical ideas that paved the way for Christianity, and greater freedom for women. People of the Hellenistic period also made remarkable advances in science and medicine. They not only built on the achievements of their predecessors, but also produced one of the most creative intellectual eras of classical antiquity.

Key Terms

Hellenistic
sovereign
koine
politeuma
Great Silk Road
Tyche
mystery religions
Epicureanism
Stoicism

natural law
heliocentric theory
Archimedean screw
Dogmatic school
Empiric school

Notes

1. H. Bengtson, *Philipp und Alexander der Grosse* (Munich: Callwey, 1985), p. 7. John Buckler is the translator of all uncited quotations from a foreign language in Chapters 1–6.
2. Plutarch, *Moralia* 328E.
3. Quoted in W. W. Tarn and G. T. Griffith, *Hellenistic Civilizations*, 3d ed. (Cleveland and New York: Meridian Books, 1961), p. 199.
4. *Periplous of the Erythraian Sea* 57.
5. Diodorus 3.12.2–3.
6. Plutarch, *Marcellus* 14.13.
7. Vitruvius, *On Architecture* 9 Preface, 10.

Suggested Reading

General treatments of Hellenistic political, social, and economic history can be found in F. W. Walbank et al., *The Cambridge Ancient History,* 2d ed., vol. 7, pt. 1 (1984). Shorter is F. W. Walbank, *The Hellenistic World,* rev. ed. (1993), a fresh appraisal by one of the foremost scholars in the field. The undisputed classic in this area is M. Rostovtzeff, *The Social and Economic History of the Hellenistic World,* 3 vols. (1941). More recently Z. H. Archibald et al.,

Hellenistic Economics (2001), has reopened the topic with fresh results. R. M. Errington, *A History of Macedonia* (English trans., 1990), places Macedonia clearly within a much broader Hellenistic context. A new examination of significant aspects of the period comes from R. W. Wallace and E. M. Harris, eds., *Transitions to Empire,* pt. 2 (1996). Good selections of primary sources in accurate and readable translation can be found in M. M. Austin, *The Hellenistic World from Alexander to the Roman Conquest* (1981), and S. M. Burstein, *The Hellenistic Age from the Battle of Ipsos to the Death of Kleopatra III* (1985).

Each year brings a new crop of biographies of Alexander the Great. Still the best is J. R. Hamilton, *Alexander the Great* (1973). Although many historians have idealized Alexander the Great, recent scholarship has provided a more realistic and unflattering view of him. Political studies of the Hellenistic period include A. B. Bosworth, *Conquest and Empire* (1988), which sets Alexander's career in a broad context, and F. L. Holt, *Alexander the Great and Bactria* (1988), which discusses the formation of a Greco-Macedonian frontier in central Asia. Several works deal with the Hellenization of much of the Mediterranean world: P. M. Frazer, *Cities of Alexander the Great* (1996), and, more broadly, G. M. Cohen, *The Hellenistic Settlements in Europe, the Islands, and Asia Minor* (1996), a welcome contribution to the understanding of the impact of the Greeks on the world around them. Among the studies of those who shaped these developments, J. J. Gabbert, *Antigonus II Gonatas* (1997), treats one of the most influential of Alexander's successors. J. Ma, *Antiochus III and the Cities of Western Asia Minor* (2000), makes an important contribution to the spread and significance of Hellenism throughout this rich area.

A. K. Bowman, *Egypt After the Pharaohs* (1986), is a readable account of the impact of the Greeks and Macedonians on Egyptian society. The same topic is treated by N. Lewis, a major scholar in the field, in his *Greeks in Ptolemaic Egypt* (1986). A brief study comes from the pen of another major scholar, A. E. Samuel, *The Shifting Sands of History: Interpretations of Ptolemaic Egypt* (1989), which deals with history and historiography. W. Heckel, *The Marshals of Alexander's Empire* (1992), treats the careers of the more than 130 men who were not actually Alexander's chief officers but nonetheless substantially shaped Hellenistic political history. S. Sherwin-White and A. Kuhrt, *From Samarkand to Sardis* (1992), offer a study of the Seleucid monarchy that puts it in an Asian rather than a Greek perspective. J. D. Grainger, *Seleukos Nikator* (1990), examines how the Hellenistic king created his empire. R. A. Billows, *Antigone the One-Eyed and the Creation of the Hellenistic State* (1990), examines the career of the one man who most nearly reunited Alexander's empire. E. V. Hansen, *The Attalids of Pergamon,* 2d ed. (1971), though dated, is still the best treatment of that kingdom. B. Bar-Kochva, *Judas Maccabaeus* (1988), treats the Jewish struggle against the Seleucids and Hellenistic influences. A good portrait of one of the busiest ports in the Hellenistic world can be found in R. Garland, *Piraeus* (1987).

Much work has focused on the spread of Hellenism throughout the Near East. Very extensive is A. Kuhrt and S. Sherwin-White, eds., *Hellenism in the East* (1988), which touches on a broad range of topics, including biblical studies, Christianity, and Islam. A. E. Samuel, *The Promise of the West* (1988), studies the connections among Greek, Roman, and Jewish culture and thought and their significance for Western history. P. McKechnie, *Outsiders in the Greek Cities of the Fourth Century* (1989), provides an interesting study of the social dislocation of the Greeks in the time of Philip II and Alexander the Great. N. L. Collins, *The Library in Alexandria and the Bible in Greek* (2000), demonstrates that King Ptolemy ordered the translation of the Bible into Greek to increase his famous library and attract foreign scholars.

No specific treatment of women in the Hellenistic world yet exists, but two studies shed light on certain aspects of the topic. N. L. Goodrich, *Priestesses* (1989), examines the importance of priestesses in cults from the Near East to Ireland. S. B. Pomeroy, *Women in Hellenistic Egypt* (1984), studies women in the kingdom from which the most ancient evidence has survived.

Two general studies of religion in the Hellenistic world are F. Grant, *Hellenistic Religion: The Age of Syncretism* (1953), and H. J. Rose, *Religion in Greece and Rome* (1959). L. H. Feldman, *Jew and Gentile in the Ancient World* (1993), argues that the pagan response to Judaism within the Greco-Roman period was not as negative as often thought. R. van den Broek et al., eds., *Knowledge of God in the Graeco-Roman World* (1988), is a difficult but rewarding collection of essays that

points out how similarly pagans, Hellenistic Jews, and Christians thought about human attempts to know God. R. E. Witt, *Isis in the Graeco-Roman World* (1971), an illustrated volume, studies the origins and growth of the Isis cult. More specifically, S. K. Heyob, *The Cult of Isis Among Women in the Graeco-Roman World* (1975), explores its popularity among women. The cult of Isis's consort Osiris is the subject of J. G. Griffiths, *The Origins of Osiris and His Cult* (1980). For the mystery cults in general, see W. Burkert, *Ancient Mystery Cults* (1987), written by one of the finest scholars in the field.

Hellenistic philosophy and science have attracted the attention of a number of scholars, and the various philosophical schools are especially well covered. A general treatment can be recommended because it deals with the broader question of the role of the intellectual in the classical and Hellenistic worlds: F. L. Vatai, *Intellectuals in Politics in the Greek World from Early Times to the Hellenistic Age* (1984). Broader is S. Blundell, *The Origin of Civilization in Greek and Roman Thought* (1986), a survey of classical political and social theories through a period of ten centuries, from Aristotle to the Stoics and their Roman successors. A. W. Bulloch et al., *Images and Ideologies* (1993), is a broad-ranging work that studies all the important intellectual aspects of Hellenistic history. Newer and also comprehensive is R. W. Sharples, *Stoics, Epicureans, Sceptics* (1996), which provides a good synthesis of these three major branches of Hellenistic philosophy. A good survey of Hellenistic science is G. E. R. Lloyd, *Greek Science After Aristotle* (1963), and specific studies of major figures can be found in T. L. Heath's solid work, *Aristarchos of Samos* (1920), still unsurpassed, and E. J. Dijksterhuis, *Archimedes*, rev. ed. (1987).

Listening to the Past

Alexander and the Brotherhood of Man

One historical problem challenged historians throughout the twentieth century and has yet to be solved to everyone's satisfaction. After returning to Opis, north of Babylon in modern Iraq, Alexander found himself confronted with a huge and unexpected mutiny by his Macedonian veterans. He held a banquet to pacify them, and he included in the festivities some Persians and other Asian followers, some nine thousand in all. During the festivities he offered a public prayer for harmony and partnership in rule between the Macedonians and Persians. Many modern scholars have interpreted this prayer as an expression of his desire to establish a "brotherhood of man." The following passage provides the evidence for this view. From it all readers can determine for themselves whether Alexander attempted to introduce a new philosophical ideal or whether he harbored his own political motives for political cooperation.

8. When [Alexander] arrived at Opis, he collected the Macedonians and announced that he intended to discharge from the army those who were useless for military service either from age or from being maimed in the limbs; and he said he would send them back to their own abodes. He also promised to give those who went back as much extra reward as would make them special objects of envy to those at home and arouse in the other Macedonians the wish to share similar dangers and labours. Alexander said this, no doubt, for the purpose of pleasing the Macedonians; but on the contrary they were, not without reason, offended by the speech which he delivered, thinking that now they were despised by him and deemed to be quite useless for military service. Indeed, throughout the whole of this expedition they had been offended at many other things; for his adoption of the Persian dress, thereby exhibiting

his contempt for their opinion often caused them grief, as did also his accoutring the foreign soldiers called Epigoni in the Macedonian style, and the mixing of the alien horsemen among the ranks of the Companions. Therefore they could not remain silent and control themselves, but urged him to dismiss all of them from his army; and they advised him to prosecute the war in company with his father, deriding Ammon by this remark. When Alexander heard this . . . , he ordered the most conspicuous of the men who had tried to stir up the multitude to sedition to be arrested. He himself pointed out with his hand to the shield-bearing guards those whom they were to arrest, to the number of thirteen; and he ordered these to be led away to execution. When the rest, stricken with terror, became silent, he mounted the platform again, and spoke as follows:

9. "The speech which I am about to deliver will not be for the purpose of checking your start homeward, for, so far as I am concerned, you may depart wherever you wish; but for the purpose of making you understand when you take yourselves off, what kind of men you have been to us who have conferred such benefits upon you. . . .

10. . . . Most of you have golden crowns, the eternal memorials of your valour and of the honour you receive from me. Whoever has been killed has met with a glorious end and has been honoured with a splendid burial. Brazen statues of most of the slain have been erected at home, and their parents are held in honour, being released from all public service and from taxation. But no one of you has ever been killed in flight under my leadership. And now I was intending to send back those of you who are unfit for service, objects of envy to those at home; but since you all wish to depart, depart all of you! Go back and report at home that your king Alexander, the conqueror of the Persians, Medes, Bactrians, and Sacians; the man who has subjugated the Uxians, Arachotians,

and Drangians; who has also acquired the rule of the Parthians, Chorasmians, and Hyrcanians, as far as the Caspian Sea . . . —report that when you returned to Susa you deserted him and went away, handing him over to the protection of conquered foreigners. Perhaps this report of yours will be both glorious to you in the eyes of men and devout I ween in the eyes of the gods. Depart!"

11. Having thus spoken, he leaped down quickly from the platform, and entered the palace, where he paid no attention to the decoration of his person, nor was any of his Companions admitted to see him. Not even on the morrow was any one of them admitted to an audience; but on the third day he summoned the select Persians within, and among them he distributed the commands of the brigades, and made the rule that only those whom he proclaimed his kinsmen should have the honour of saluting him with a kiss. But the Macedonians who heard the speech were thoroughly astonished at the moment, and remained there in silence near the platform; nor when he retired did any of them accompany the king, except his personal Companions and the confidential body-guards. Though they remained most of them had nothing to do or say; and yet they were unwilling to retire. But when the news was reported to them . . . they were no longer able to restrain themselves; but running in a body to the palace, they cast their weapons there in front of the gates as signs of supplication to the king. Standing in front of the gates, they shouted, beseeching to be allowed to enter, and saying that they were willing to surrender the men who had been the instigators of the disturbance on that occasion, and those who had begun the clamour. They also declared they would not retire from the gates either day or night, unless Alexander would take some pity upon them. When he was informed of this, he came out without delay; and seeing them lying on the ground in humble guise, and hearing most of them lamenting with loud voice, tears began to flow also from his own eyes. He made an effort to say something to them, but they continued their importunate entreaties. At length one of them, Callines by name, a man conspicuous both for his age and because he was a captain of the Companion cavalry, spoke as follows, "O king, what grieves the Macedonians is that you have already made some of the Persians kinsmen to yourself, and that Persians are called Alexander's kinsmen, and have the honour of

This gilded case for a bow and arrows indicates that Alexander's success came at the price of blood. These vigorous scenes portray more military conflict than philosophical compassion. *(Archaeological Museum Salonica/Dagli Orti/The Art Archive)*

saluting you with a kiss; whereas none of the Macedonians have as yet enjoyed this honour." Then Alexander interrupting him, said, "But all of you without exception I consider my kinsmen, and so from this time I shall call you." When he had said this, Callines advanced and saluted him with a kiss, and so did all those who wished to salute him. Then they took up their weapons and returned to the camp, shouting and singing a song of thanksgiving. After this Alexander offered sacrifice to the gods to whom it was his custom to sacrifice, and gave a public banquet, over which he himself presided, with the Macedonians sitting around him; and next to them the Persians; after whom came the men of the other nations, preferred in honour for their personal rank or for some meritorious action. The king and his guests drew wine from the same bowl and poured out the same libations, both the Grecian prophets and the Magians commencing the ceremony. He prayed for other blessings, and especially that harmony and community of rule might exist between the Macedonians and Persians.

Questions for Analysis

1. What was the purpose of the banquet at Opis?

2. Were all of the guests treated equally?

3. What did Alexander gain from bringing together the Macedonians and Persians?

Source: F. R. B. Goldophin, ed., *The Greek Historians,* vol. 2. Copyright 1942 and renewed 1970 by Random House, Inc. Used by permission of Random House, Inc.

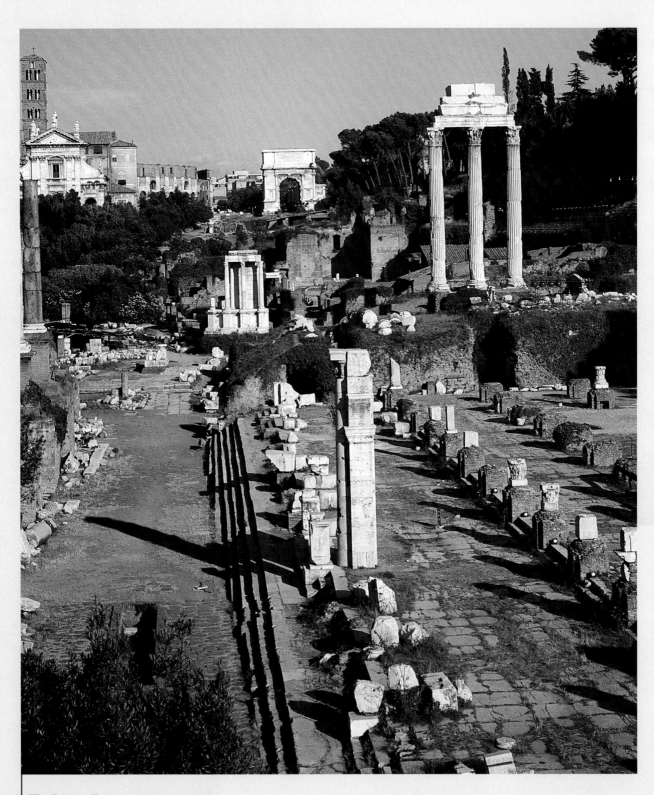

The Roman Forum. *(Josephine Powell)*

chapter

5

The Rise of Rome

*W*ho is so thoughtless and lazy that he does not want to know in what way and with what kind of government the Romans in less than 53 years conquered nearly the entire inhabited world and brought it under their rule—an achievement previously unheard of?"[1] This question was first asked by Polybius, a Greek historian who lived in the second century B.C. With keen awareness Polybius realized that the Romans were achieving something unique in world history.

What was that achievement? Was it simply the creation of a huge empire? Hardly. The Persians had done the same thing. For that matter, Alexander the Great had conquered vast territories in a shorter time. Was it the creation of a superior culture? Even the Romans admitted that in matters of art, literature, philosophy, and culture they learned from the Greeks. Rome's achievement lay in the ability of the Romans not only to conquer peoples but to incorporate them into the Roman system. Rome succeeded where the Greek polis had failed. Unlike the Greeks, who refused to share citizenship, the Romans extended their citizenship first to the Italians and later to the peoples of the provinces. With that citizenship went Roman government and law. Rome created a world state that embraced the entire Mediterranean area and extended northward.

Nor was Rome's achievement limited to the ancient world. Rome's law, language, and administrative practices were a precious heritage to medieval and modern Europe. London, Paris, Vienna, and many other modern European cities began as Roman colonies or military camps. When the Founding Fathers created the American republic, they looked to Rome as a model. On the darker side, Napoleon and Mussolini paid their own tribute to Rome by aping its forms. Whether Founding Father or modern autocrat, all were acknowledging admiration for the Roman achievement.

Roman history is usually divided into two periods: the republic, the age in which Rome grew from a small city-state to ruler of an empire, and the empire, the period when the republican constitution gave way to constitutional monarchy.

- How did Rome rise to greatness?
- What effects did the conquest of the Mediterranean have on the Romans themselves and on the conquered peoples?
- Finally, why did the republic collapse?

These are the questions we will explore in this chapter.

The Land and the Sea

To the west of Greece the boot-shaped peninsula of Italy, with Sicily at its toe, occupies the center of the Mediterranean basin. As Map 5.1 shows, Italy and Sicily thrust southward toward Africa: the distance between southwestern Sicily and the northern African coast is at one point only about a hundred miles. Italy and Sicily literally divide the Mediterranean into two basins and form the focal point between the halves.

Like Greece and other Mediterranean lands, Italy enjoys a genial, almost subtropical climate. The winters are rainy, but the summer months are dry. Because of the climate the rivers of Italy usually carry little water during the summer, and some go entirely dry. The low water level of the Arno, one of the principal rivers of Italy, once led Mark Twain to describe it as "a great historical creek with four feet in the channel and some scows floating around. It would be a very plausible river if they would pump some water into it."[2] The Arno at least is navigable. Most of Italy's other rivers are not. Clearly these small rivers were unsuitable for regular, large-scale shipping. Italian rivers, unlike Twain's beloved Mississippi, never became major thoroughfares for commerce and communication.

Geography encouraged Italy to look to the Mediterranean. In the north Italy is protected by the Apennine Mountains, which break off from the Alps and form a natural barrier. The Apennines hindered but did not prevent peoples from penetrating Italy from the north. Throughout history, in modern times as well as ancient, various invaders have entered Italy by this route. North of the Apennines lies the Po Valley, an important part of modern Italy. In antiquity this valley did not become Roman territory until late in the history of the republic. From the north the Apennines run southward the entire length of the Italian boot; they virtually cut off access to the Adriatic Sea, a feature that further induced Italy to look west to Spain and Carthage rather than east to Greece.

Even though most of the land is mountainous, the hill country is not as inhospitable as are the Greek highlands. In antiquity the general fertility of the soil provided the basis for a large population. Nor did the mountains of Italy so carve up the land as to prevent the development of political unity. Geography proved kinder to Italy than to Greece.

In their southward course the Apennines leave two broad and fertile plains, those of Latium and Campania. These plains attracted settlers and invaders from the time when peoples began to move into Italy. Among these peoples were the Romans, who established their city on the Tiber River in Latium.

This site enjoyed several advantages. The Tiber provided Rome with a constant source of water. Located at an easy crossing point on the Tiber, Rome stood astride the main avenue of communication between northern and southern Italy. The famous seven hills of Rome were defensible and safe from the floods of the Tiber. Rome was in an excellent position to develop the resources of Latium and maintain contact with the rest of Italy.

The Etruscans and Rome (750–509 B.C.)

In recent years archaeologists have found traces of numerous early peoples in Italy. The origins of these cultures and their precise relations with one another are not completely understood. In fact no totally coherent account of the prehistory of Italy is yet possible, but certain elements of this period are yearly coming into sharper focus. One fundamental fact is, however, indisputable: from about 1000 to 875 B.C. many peoples speaking Indo-European languages were moving into Italy from the north, probably in small groups.

Only with the coming of the Greeks does Italy enter into the light of history. Yet Italy had a long prehistory before the Greeks arrived. Old legends preserved a faint memory of past events, and modern archaeology has brought much of this distant past to light. The Greeks encountered the Etruscans, Celts, and Italians, all scattered along the peninsula and each independent of the other.

The Etruscans

Despite much uncertainty, a generally reliable outline of events can be sketched. Among the various peoples in Italy were the Etruscans, one of the most mysterious peoples of antiquity. Who they were and where they came from are topics still being argued.

Of greater importance than the question of the origins of the Etruscans is an understanding of their accomplishments. Once established as a major player in Italian life,

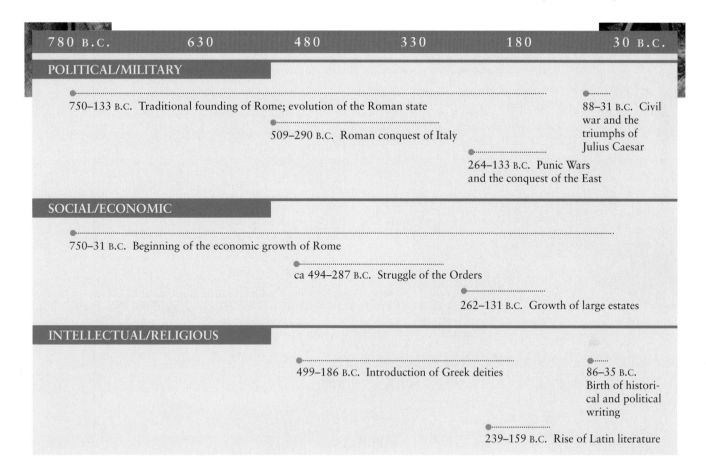

780 B.C.	630	480	330	180	30 B.C.

POLITICAL/MILITARY

750–133 B.C. Traditional founding of Rome; evolution of the Roman state

509–290 B.C. Roman conquest of Italy

264–133 B.C. Punic Wars and the conquest of the East

88–31 B.C. Civil war and the triumphs of Julius Caesar

SOCIAL/ECONOMIC

750–31 B.C. Beginning of the economic growth of Rome

ca 494–287 B.C. Struggle of the Orders

262–131 B.C. Growth of large estates

INTELLECTUAL/RELIGIOUS

499–186 B.C. Introduction of Greek deities

86–35 B.C. Birth of historical and political writing

239–159 B.C. Rise of Latin literature

they exported their rich mineral resources to pay for luxury goods imported from the eastern Mediterranean. They also played an important role in the wider Mediterranean world because of their contacts with their neighbors. In addition, they created an export market in olive oil and wine. Their society evolved cities that resembled Greek city-states, and their wealth, along with their political and military institutions, enabled them to form a loosely organized league of cities whose domination extended as far north as the Po Valley and as far south as Latium and Campania (see Map 5.1). In Latium they founded cities and took control of a small collection of villages subsequently called Rome. By the seventh century B.C. they had fully entered the cosmopolitan life of the Mediterranean world.

The Romans

The Romans, as they have been called from antiquity to today, were part of the larger movements of Italic peoples. Archaeology places them on the site of modern Rome in the eighth century B.C. The Etruscans found

them settled on three of Rome's seven hills. According to Roman legend, Romulus and Remus founded Rome in 753 B.C. Romulus built his settlement on the Palatine Hill, while Remus chose the Aventine (see inset, Map 5.1). Jealous of his brother's work, Remus ridiculed it by jumping over Romulus's unfinished wall. In a rage Romulus killed his brother and vowed, "So will die whoever else shall leap over my walls." In this instance legend preserves some facts. Archaeological investigation has confirmed that the earliest settlement at Rome was situated on the Palatine Hill and that it dates to the first half of the eighth century B.C. The legend also shows traces of Etruscan influence on Roman customs. The inviolability of Romulus's walls recalls the Etruscan concept of the **pomerium,** a sacred boundary intended to keep out anything evil or unclean.

During the years 753 to 509 B.C., the Romans embraced many Etruscan customs. They adopted the Etruscan alphabet, which the Etruscans themselves had adopted from the Greeks. The Romans later handed on this alphabet to medieval Europe and thence to the modern Western world. The Romans also adopted symbols of

Rome

0   500   1000 M.
0   1500   3000 Ft.

FIELD OF MARS

QUIRINAL HILL

VIMINAL HILL

Tiber

CAPITOLINE MT.

ESQUILINE MT.

Senate House

Forum

Regia

Temple of
Jupiter

JANICULUM

PALATINE
MT.

CAELIAN MT.

Circus
Maximus

AVENTINE MT.

ALPS

APENNINES

Po

Arno

UMBRIA

PICENUM

ETRURIA

Tiber

SABINI

AEQUI

VESTINI

Veii

Rome

SAMNIUM

LATIUM

APULIA

CAMPANIA

CALABRIA

Tarentum

LUCANIA

CORSICA

Adriatic Sea

SARDINIA

Tyrrhenian Sea

BRUTTIUM

Messana

Mediterranean Sea

SICILY

Syracuse

Carthage

Cape
Bon

NORTH AFRICA

0   50   100 Km.
0   50   100 Mi.

━━━ Roman boundary before the Punic Wars

━━━ Roman boundary before Augustus

──── Roman internal regional divisions

──── Major road

Sarcophagus of Lartie Seianti
The woman portrayed on this lavish sarcophagus is the noble Etruscan Lartie Seianti. Although the sarcophagus is her place of burial, she is portrayed as in life, comfortable and at rest. The influence of Greek art on Etruscan is apparent in almost every feature of the sarcophagus. (*Archaeological Museum, Florence/Nimatallah/Art Resource, NY*)

political authority from the Etruscans. The symbol of the Etruscan king's right to execute or scourge his subjects was a bundle of rods and an ax, called in Latin the **fasces,** which the king's retainer carried before him on official occasions. When the Romans expelled the Etruscan kings, they created special attendants called "lictors" to carry the fasces before their new magistrates, the consuls. Even the *toga,* the white woolen robe worn by the citizens, came from the Etruscans. In engineering and architecture the Romans adopted from the Etruscans the vault and the arch. Above all, it was thanks to the Etruscans that the Romans truly became urban dwellers.

Etruscan power and influence at Rome were so strong that Roman traditions preserved the memory of Etruscan kings who ruled the city. Under the Etruscans, Rome enjoyed contacts with the larger Mediterranean world, and the city began to grow. In the years 575 to 550 B.C. temples and public buildings began to grace the city. The Capitoline Hill became the religious center of the city when the temple of Jupiter Optimus Maximus (Jupiter the Best and Greatest) was built there. The **Forum** ceased to be a cemetery and began its history as a public meeting place, a development parallel to that of the Greek agora. Trade in metalwork became common, and the wealthier Roman classes began to import large numbers of fine Greek vases. The Etruscans had found Rome a collection of villages and made it a city.

The Roman Conquest of Italy (509–290 B.C.)

Early Roman history is an uneven mixture of fact and legend. Roman traditions often contain an important kernel of truth, but that does not make them history. In many cases they are significant because they illustrate the ethics, morals, and ideals that Roman society considered valuable.

According to Roman tradition, the Romans expelled the Etruscan king Tarquin the Proud from Rome in 509 B.C. and founded the republic. In the years that followed, the Romans fought numerous wars with their neighbors on the Italian peninsula. They became soldiers, and the grim fighting bred tenacity, a prominent Roman trait. At an early date the Romans also learned the value of alliances and how to provide leadership for their allies. Alliances with the Latin towns around them provided them with a large reservoir of manpower. These alliances involved the Romans in still other wars and took them farther afield in the Italian peninsula.

The growth of Roman power was slow but steady. Not until roughly a century after the founding of the republic

MAP 5.1 Italy and the City of Rome The geographical configuration of the Italian peninsula shows how Rome stood astride north-south communication routes and how the state that united Italy stood poised to move into Sicily and northern Africa.

Personification of Summer   Nothing better illustrates the coming of summer than this painting. Summer appears as a winged goddess, elegant and serene. She also brings with her the fruits of the season and a sense of plenty. *(Antiquarium Castellemare di Stabia/Dagli Orti/The Art Archive)*

in the end. Although Rome had yet to subdue the whole peninsula, for the first time in history the city stood unchallenged in Italy.

Sometimes unappreciated is the way the Romans spread their culture through religious cults, mythology, and drama. They, like other pagans, liberally shared their religious beliefs with others, which in turn furthered the Romanization of Italy. They welcomed their neighbors to religious places of assembly, thereby including them in specifically Roman cults. The Italians thus learned of particular Roman deities and their religious traditions. The Romans and Italians grew closer together by the mutual understanding of and participation in the religious rites of Roman cults. The Romans did not force their religion on the Italians; instead they invited them to participate. The process also enabled the Italians to understand the Romans better and to see them as fellow members of a broad Italian political and social family.

Roman religion opened a unique way to the appreciation of Roman law. Seen at its ideal, religion was virtually inseparable from law. Yet the spread of Roman culture

Beware of the Dog   The mosaic set at the entrance of a villa at Pompeii serves as a humorous warning to unwanted guests. Behind it was in reality a very live dog that served as a protector of the house. *(Museo Archeologico Nazionale Naples/Erich Lessing/Art Resource, NY)*

did the Romans drive the Etruscans entirely out of Latium. Around 390 B.C. the Romans suffered a major setback when a new people, the Celts—or **Gauls,** as the Romans called them—swept aside a Roman army and sacked Rome. More intent on loot than on land, they agreed to abandon Rome in return for a thousand pounds of gold.

From 390 to 290 B.C. the Romans rebuilt their city and recouped their losses. They also reorganized their army to create the mobile legion, a flexible unit capable of fighting on either broken or open terrain. The Romans finally brought Latium and their Latin allies fully under their control and conquered Etruria (see Map 5.1). In 343 B.C. they grappled with the Samnites in a series of bitter wars for the possession of Campania and southern Italy. The Samnites were a formidable enemy and inflicted serious losses on the Romans. But the superior organization, institutions, and manpower of the Romans won out was not part of a planned ideological onslaught by the Romans. Nor was it very different from the ways in which the Romans extended their political, military, and legal systems. Even so, the process eventually created a common ground for all the peoples living in Italy and made Italy Roman. In later years the Romans continued this process until all these influences spread throughout the Mediterranean basin.

Rome's success in diplomacy and politics was as important as its military victories. With many of their oldest allies, such as the Latin cities, they shared full Roman citizenship. In other instances they granted citizenship without the **franchise** (*civitas sine suffragio*). Allies who held this status enjoyed all the rights of Roman citizenship except that they could not vote or hold Roman offices. They were subject to Roman taxes and calls for military service but ran their own local affairs. The Latin allies were able to acquire full Roman citizenship by moving to Rome. A perhaps humble but very efficient means of keeping the Romans and their colonies together were the Roman roads, many of which were in use as late as the medieval period. These roads provided an easy route of communication between the capital and outlying areas, allowed for the quick movement of armies, and offered an efficient means of trade. They were the tangible sinews of unity.

By their willingness to extend their citizenship, the Romans took Italy into partnership. Here the political genius of Rome triumphed where Greece had failed. Rome proved itself superior to the Greek polis because it both conquered and shared the fruits of conquest with the conquered. Rome could consolidate where Greece could only dominate. The unwillingness of the Greek polis to share its citizenship condemned it to a limited horizon. Not so with Rome. The extension of Roman citizenship strengthened the state, gave it additional manpower and wealth, and laid the foundation of the Roman Empire.

The Roman State

The Romans summed up their political existence in a single phrase: *senatus populusque Romanus,* "the Roman senate and the people." The real genius of the Romans lay in the fields of politics and law. Unlike the Greeks, they did not often speculate on the ideal state or on political forms. Instead, they realistically met actual challenges and created institutions, magistracies, and legal concepts to deal with practical problems. Change was consequently commonplace in Roman political life, and

the constitution of 509 B.C. was far simpler than that of 27 B.C. Moreover, the Roman constitution, unlike the American, was not a single written document. Rather, it was a set of traditional beliefs, customs, and laws.

In the early republic social divisions determined the shape of politics. Political power was in the hands of the aristocracy—the **patricians,** who were wealthy landowners. Patrician families formed clans, as did aristocrats in early Greece. They dominated the affairs of state, provided military leadership in time of war, and monopolized knowledge of law and legal procedure. The common people of Rome, the **plebeians,** had few of the patricians' advantages. Some plebeians formed their own clans and rivaled the patricians in wealth. Many plebeian merchants increased their wealth in the course of Roman expansion, but most plebeians were poor. They were the artisans, small farmers, and landless urban dwellers. The plebeians, rich and poor alike, were free citizens with a voice in politics. Nonetheless, they were overshadowed by the patricians.

Perhaps the greatest institution of the republic was the **senate,** which had originated under the Etruscans as a council of noble elders who advised the king. During the republic the senate advised the consuls and other magistrates. Because the senate sat year after year, while magistrates changed annually, it provided stability and continuity. It also served as a reservoir of experience and knowledge. Technically, the senate could not pass legislation; it could only offer its advice. But increasingly, because of the senate's prestige, its advice came to have the force of law.

The Romans created several assemblies through which the people elected magistrates and passed legislation. The earliest was the *comitia curiata,* which had religious, political, and military functions. According to Roman tradition, King Servius Tullius (578–535 B.C.), who reorganized the state into 193 *centuries* for military purposes, created the *comitia centuriata* as a political body to decide Roman policy. The comitia centuriata voted in centuries, which in this instance means political blocs. The patricians possessed the majority of centuries because they shouldered most of the burden of defense. Thus they could easily outvote the plebeians. In 471 B.C. the plebeians won the right to meet in an assembly of their own, the *concilium plebis,* and to pass ordinances. In 287 B.C. the bills passed in the concilium plebis were recognized as binding on the entire population.

The chief magistrates of the republic were the two consuls, elected for one-year terms. At first the consulship was open only to patricians. The consuls commanded the army in battle, administered state business, convened the comitia centuriata, and supervised financial affairs. In effect, they and the senate ran the state. The consuls appointed *quaestors* to assist them in their duties, and in 421 B.C. the quaestorship became an elective office open to plebeians. The quaestors took charge of the public treasury and prosecuted criminals in the popular courts.

In 366 B.C. the Romans created a new office, that of **praetor,** and in 227 B.C. the number of praetors was increased to four. When the consuls were away from Rome, the praetors could act in their place. The praetors dealt primarily with the administration of justice. When he took office, a praetor issued a proclamation declaring the principles by which he would interpret the law. These proclamations became very important because they usually covered areas where the law was vague and thus helped clarify the law.

Other officials included the powerful *censors,* created in 443 B.C., who had many responsibilities, the most important being supervision of public morals, the power to determine who lawfully could sit in the senate, the registration of citizens, and the leasing of public contracts. Later officials were the *aediles,* four in number, who supervised the streets and markets and presided over public festivals.

After the age of overseas conquest, the Romans divided the Mediterranean area into provinces governed by ex-consuls and ex-praetors. Because of their experience in Roman politics, they were well suited to administer the affairs of the provincials and to fit Roman law and custom into new contexts.

One of the most splendid achievements of the Romans was their development of law. Roman law began as a set of rules that regulated the lives and relations of citizens. This civil law, or **ius civile,** consisted of statutes, customs, and forms of procedure. Roman assemblies added to the body of law, and praetors interpreted it. The spirit of the law aimed at protecting the property, lives, and reputations of citizens, redressing wrongs, and giving satisfaction to victims of injustice.

As the Romans came into more frequent contact with foreigners, they had to devise laws to deal with disputes between Romans and foreigners and between foreigners under Roman jurisdiction. In these instances, where there was no precedent to guide the Romans, the legal decisions of the praetors proved of immense importance. The praetors adopted aspects of other legal systems and resorted to the law of equity—what they thought was right and just to all parties. Free, in effect, to determine law, the praetors enjoyed a great deal of flexibility. This situation illustrates the practicality and the genius of the Romans. By addressing specific, actual circumstances the praetors developed a body of law, the *ius gentium,* "the law of peoples," that applied to Romans and foreigners and that laid the foundation for a universal conception of law. By the time of the late republic, Roman jurists were reaching decisions on the basis of the Stoic concept of **ius naturale,** "natural law," a universal law that could be applied to all societies.

Social Conflict in Rome

Another important aspect of early Roman history was a great social conflict, usually known as the **Struggle of the Orders,** that developed between patricians and plebeians. The plebeians wanted real political representation and safeguards against patrician domination. The plebeians' efforts to obtain recognition of their rights is the crux of the Struggle of the Orders.

Rome's early wars gave the plebeians the leverage they needed: Rome's survival depended on the army, and the army needed the plebeians. The first showdown between plebeians and patricians came, according to tradition, in 494 B.C. To force the patricians to grant concessions, the plebeians seceded from the state; they literally walked out of Rome and refused to serve in the army. The plebeians' general strike worked. Because of it the patricians made important concessions. One of these was social. In 445 B.C. the patricians passed a law, the *lex Canuleia,* which for the first time allowed patricians and plebeians to marry one another. Furthermore, the patricians recognized the right of plebeians to elect their own officials, the **tribunes.** The tribunes in turn had the right to protect the plebeians from the arbitrary conduct of patrician magistrates. The tribunes brought plebeian grievances to the senate for resolution. The plebeians were not bent on undermining the state. Rather, they used their gains only to win full equality under the law.

The law itself was the plebeians' primary target. Only the patricians knew what the law was, and only they could argue cases in court. All too often they had used the law for their own benefit. The plebeians wanted the law codified and published. The result of their agitation was the Law of the Twelve Tables, so called because the laws, which covered civil and criminal matters, were inscribed on twelve large bronze plaques. Later still, the plebeians forced the patricians to publish legal procedures as well. The plebeians had broken the patricians' legal monopoly and henceforth enjoyed full protection under the law.

The decisive plebeian victory came with the passage of the Licinian-Sextian rogations (or laws) in 367 B.C. Licinius and Sextus were plebeian tribunes who led a ten-year fight for further reform. Rich plebeians, such as Licinius and Sextus themselves, joined the poor to mount a sweeping assault on patrician privilege. Wealthy plebeians wanted the opportunity to provide political leadership for the state. They demanded that the patricians allow them access to all the magistracies of the state. If they could hold the consulship, they could also sit in the senate and advise the senate on policy. The two tribunes won approval from the senate for a law that stipulated that one of the two annual consuls must be a plebeian. Though decisive, the Licinian-Sextian rogations did not automatically end the Struggle of the Orders. That happened only in 287 B.C. with the passage of a law, the *lex Hortensia,* that gave the resolutions of the concilium plebis the force of law for patricians and plebeians alike.

The results of the compromise between the patricians and the plebeians were far-reaching. They secured economic reform and defined the access of all citizens to public land. The principal result was the definition of political leadership. Plebeians could now hold the consulship, which brought with it the consular title, places of honor in the senate, and such cosmetic privileges as wearing the purple toga, the symbol of aristocracy. Far more important, the compromise established a new nobility shared by the plebeians and the patricians. They were both groups of wealthy aristocrats who had simply agreed to share the great offices of power within the republic. This would lead not to major political reform but to an extension of aristocratic rule. Nevertheless, the patricians were wise enough to give the plebeians wider political rights than they had previously enjoyed. The compromise was typically Roman.

The Struggle of the Orders resulted in a Rome stronger and better united than before. It could have led to anarchy, but again certain Roman traits triumphed. The values fostered by their social structure predisposed the Romans to compromise, especially in the face of common danger. Resistance and confrontation in Rome never exploded into class warfare. Instead, both sides resorted to compromises to hammer out a realistic solution. Important, too, were Roman patience, tenacity, and a healthy sense of the practical. These qualities enabled both sides to keep working until they had resolved the crisis. The Struggle of the Orders ended in 287 B.C. with a new concept of Roman citizenship. All citizens shared equally under the law. Theoretically, all could aspire to the highest political offices. Patrician or plebeian, rich or poor, Roman citizenship was equal for all.

Roman Expansion

Once the Romans had settled their internal affairs, they were free to turn their attention to the larger world around them. As seen earlier, they had already come to terms with the Italic peoples in Latium. Only later did Rome achieve primacy over its Latin allies, partly because of successful diplomacy and partly because of overwhelming military power. In 282 B.C. Rome expanded even farther in Italy and extended its power across the sea to Sicily, Corsica, and Sardinia.

Italy Becomes Roman

In only twenty years, from 282 to 262 B.C., the Romans dramatically built on their earlier successes. Just as they had spread their religion through cult, mythology, and drama, now they expanded politically throughout Italy. Their energy was remarkable, and the results they achieved were not always due to warfare. They established a string of colonies throughout Italy, some of them populated by Romans and others by Latins. The genius of the Romans lay in bringing these various peoples into one political system. First the Romans divided the Italians into two broad classes. Those living closest to Rome were incorporated into the Roman state. They enjoyed the full franchise and citizenship that the Romans themselves possessed. The other class comprised those Italians who lived farther afield. They were bound by treaty with the Romans and were considered allies. Although they received lesser rights of active citizenship, the allies retained their right of local self-government. The link between the allies and Rome was as much social as political, as both were ruled by aristocrats.

These contacts—social, political, and legal—with their neighbors led the Romans to a better acquaintance with the heritage, customs, and laws of their fellow Italians. Rome and the rest of Italy began to share similar views of their common welfare. By including others in the Roman political and social system, Rome was making Italy Roman.

Overseas Conquest (282–146 B.C.)

In 282 B.C., when the Romans had reached southern Italy, they embarked upon a series of wars that left them the rulers of the Mediterranean world. The nature of these wars demands attention. Unlike the Italians or even the Etruscans, the Romans felt that they were dealing with foreigners, people not akin to them. They were also moving into areas largely unfamiliar to them. These wars became fiercer and were fought on a larger scale than those in Italy. Yet there was nothing ideological about them. Unlike Napoleon or Hitler, the Romans did not map out grandiose strategies for world conquest. They had no idea of what lay before them. If they could have looked into the future, they would have stood amazed. In many instances the Romans did not even initiate action; they simply responded to situations as they arose. Nineteenth-century Englishmen were fond of saying, "We got our empire in a fit of absence of mind." The Romans could not go quite that far. Though they sometimes declared war reluctantly, they nonetheless felt the need to dominate, to eliminate any state that could threaten them.

The Samnite wars had drawn the Romans into the political world of southern Italy. In 282 B.C., alarmed by the powerful newcomer, the Greek city of Tarentum in southern Italy called for help from Pyrrhus, king of Epirus in western Greece. A relative of Alexander the Great and an excellent general, Pyrrhus won two furious battles but suffered heavy casualties—thus the phrase **Pyrrhic victory** for a victory involving severe losses. Roman bravery and tenacity led him to comment: "If we win one more battle with the Romans, we'll be completely washed up." Against Pyrrhus's army the Romans threw new legions, and in the end manpower proved decisive. In 275 B.C. the Romans drove Pyrrhus from Italy and extended their sway over southern Italy. Once they did, the island of Sicily became a key for them to block Carthaginian expansion northward.

The Punic Wars and Beyond (264–133 B.C.)

By 264 B.C. Carthage (see Map 5.2) was the unrivaled power of the western Mediterranean. Since the second half of the eighth century B.C. it had built its wealth on trade in tin and precious metals. It commanded one of the best harbors on the northern African coast and was supported by a fertile hinterland. The Carthaginians were for the most part merchants, not soldiers, and they made contributions to geographical knowledge by exploring as far west as the Atlantic coasts of northern Africa and Spain. They soon dominated the commerce of the western Mediterranean. By the fourth century B.C. they were fully integrated into the Hellenistic economy, which now spread from Gibraltar to the Parthian empire.

Commercial ambitions led to political conflict. Expansion led to war with the Etruscans and Greeks, but the Carthaginians won control of parts of Sardinia, Spain, and Sicily. At the end of a long string of wars, the Carthaginians held control of only the western tip of Sicily but retained considerable influence farther to the west. In fact, the Carthaginians had created and defended a mercantile empire that stretched from western Sicily to beyond Gibraltar.

This in essence is the background of the **First Punic War** between Rome and Carthage, two powers expanding into the same area. The First Punic War lasted for twenty-three years (264–241 B.C.). The Romans quickly learned that they could not conquer Sicily unless they controlled the sea. Although they lacked a fleet and hated the sea as fervently as cats hate water, with grim resolution the Romans built a navy. They fought seven major naval battles with the Carthaginians, won six, and finally wore them down. In 241 B.C. the Romans took possession of Sicily, which became their first real province. Once again Rome's resources, manpower, and determination proved decisive.

The peace treaty between the two powers brought no peace, in part because in 238 B.C. the Romans took advantage of Carthaginian weakness to seize Sardinia and Corsica. Although unable to resist, many Carthaginians concluded that genuine peace between Carthage and Rome was impossible. One such man was Hamilcar Barca, a Carthaginian commander who had come close to victory in Sicily. The only way Carthage could recoup its fortune was by success in Spain, where the Carthaginians already enjoyed a firm foothold. In 237 B.C. Hamilcar led an army to Spain in order to turn it into Carthaginian territory. With him he took his nineteen-year-old son, Hannibal, but not before he had led Hannibal to an altar and made him swear ever to be an enemy to Rome. In the following years Hamilcar and his son-in-law Hasdrubal subjugated much of southern Spain and in the process rebuilt Carthaginian power. Rome responded in two ways: first, the Romans made a treaty with Hasdrubal in which the Ebro River formed the boundary between Carthaginian and Roman interests, and second, the Romans began to extend their own influence in Spain.

In 221 B.C. the young Hannibal became Carthaginian commander in Spain, and soon Roman and Carthaginian policies clashed at the city of Saguntum. When Hannibal laid siege to Saguntum, which lay within the sphere of Carthaginian interest, the Romans declared war, claiming that Carthage had attacked a friendly city. So began the Second Punic War, one of the most desperate wars

Triumphal Column of Caius Duilius   This curious monument celebrates Rome's first naval victory in the First Punic War. In the battle Caius Duilius destroyed fifty Carthaginian ships. He then celebrated his success by erecting this column that portrays the prows of the enemy ships projecting from the column. *(Alinari/Art Resource, NY)*

ever fought by Rome. In 218 B.C. Hannibal struck first by marching more than a thousand miles over the Alps into Italy. Once there, he defeated one Roman army at the Battle of Trebia and later another at the Battle of Lake Trasimene in 217 B.C. In the following year, Hannibal won his greatest victory at the Battle of Cannae, in which he inflicted some forty thousand casualties on the Romans. He then spread devastation throughout Italy, and a number of cities in central and southern Italy rebelled against Rome. Syracuse, Rome's ally during the First Punic War, also went over to the Carthaginians. Yet

Hannibal failed to crush Rome's iron circle of Latium, Etruria, and Samnium. The wisdom of Rome's political policy of extending rights and citizenship to its allies showed itself in these dark hours. And Rome fought back.

In 210 B.C. Rome found its answer to Hannibal in the young commander Scipio, later better known as Scipio Africanus. Scipio copied Hannibal's methods of mobile warfare, streamlining the legions by making their components capable of independent action and introducing new weapons. In the following years, Scipio operated in Spain, which in 207 B.C. he wrested from the Carthaginians. Also in 207 B.C. the Romans sealed Hannibal's fate in Italy. At the Battle of Metaurus, the Romans destroyed a major Carthaginian army coming to reinforce Hannibal. With Hannibal now bottled up in southern Italy, Scipio in 204 B.C. struck directly at Carthage itself. A Roman fleet landed his legions in North Africa, which prompted the Carthaginians to recall Hannibal from Italy to defend the homeland.

In 202 B.C., near the town of Zama (see Map 5.2), Scipio defeated Hannibal in one of the world's truly decisive battles. Scipio's victory meant that the world of the western Mediterranean would henceforth be Roman. Roman language, law, and culture, fertilized by Greek influences, would in time permeate this entire region. The victory at Zama meant that Rome's heritage would be passed on to the Western world.

The **Second Punic War** contained the seeds of still other wars. Unabated fear of Carthage led to the Third Punic War, a needless, unjust, and savage conflict that ended in 146 B.C. when Scipio Aemilianus, grandson of Scipio Africanus, destroyed the old hated rival. As the Roman conqueror watched the death pangs of that great city, he turned to his friend Polybius with the words: "I fear and foresee that someday someone will give the same order about my fatherland." It would, however, be centuries before an invader would stand before the gates of Rome.

During the war with Hannibal, the Romans had invaded Spain, a peninsula rich in material resources and the home of fierce warriors. When the Roman legions tried to reduce the Spanish tribes, they met with bloody and determined resistance. Not until 133 B.C., after years of brutal and ruthless warfare, did Scipio Aemilianus finally conquer Spain.

Rome Turns East (211–133 B.C.)

During the dark days of the Second Punic War, King Philip V of Macedonia made an alliance with Hannibal against Rome. Despite the mortal struggle in the West,

MAP 5.2 Roman Expansion During the Republic The main spurt of Roman expansion occurred between 264 and 133 B.C., when most of the Mediterranean fell to Rome, followed by the conquest of Gaul and the eastern Mediterranean by 44 B.C.

the Romans found the strength to turn eastward to settle accounts. Their first significant victory came over the Macedonians in 197 B.C. The Roman general Titus Flamininus demanded that the Macedonians agree to give full liberty to the Greeks. (See the feature "Listening to the Past: Titus Flamininus and the Liberty of the Greeks" on pages 150–151.) Two years later he defeated the Spartans. In 189 B.C. the Seleucid kingdom fell to the Romans, but decisive victory came in 146 B.C., when the Romans conquered the Achaean League, sacked Corinth, and finally defeated Macedonia, which they made a Roman province. In 133 B.C. Attalus III, the last king of Pergamum, bequeathed his kingdom to the Romans. The Ptolemies of Egypt meekly obeyed Roman wishes.

The Romans had used the discord and disunity of the Hellenistic world to divide and conquer it. Once they had done so, they faced the formidable challenge of governing it without further warfare, which they met by establishing the first Roman provinces in the East. They ultimately succeeded in fusing the honored culture and civilization of the Hellenistic East with the new and vibrant Roman civilization of the West. As seen earlier, Greek cultural influence had already fertilized Roman life, but now Rome began to create the political and administrative machinery to hold the Mediterranean together under a mutually shared cultural and political system. The Romans, nonetheless, were as usual practical as well as somewhat altruistic. They declared that the Mediterranean had become *mare nostrum,* "our sea."

Old Values and Greek Culture

Rome had conquered the Mediterranean world, but some Romans considered that victory a misfortune. The historian Sallust (86–34 B.C.), writing from hindsight, complained that the acquisition of an empire was the beginning of Rome's troubles:

But when through labor and justice our Republic grew powerful, great kings defeated in war, fierce nations and mighty peoples subdued by force, when Carthage the rival of the Roman people was wiped out root and branch, all the seas and lands lay open, then fortune began to be harsh and to throw everything into confusion. The Romans had easily borne labor, danger, uncertainty, and hardship. To them leisure, riches—otherwise desirable—proved to be burdens and torments. So at first money, then desire for power grew great. These things were a sort of cause of all evils.[3]

Sallust was not alone in his feelings. At the time some senators had opposed the destruction of Carthage on the grounds that fear of their old rival would keep the Romans in check. In the second century B.C. the Romans learned that they could not return to what they fondly considered a simple life. They were world rulers. The responsibilities they faced were complex and awesome. They had to change their institutions, social patterns, and way of thinking to meet the new era. They were in fact building the foundations of a great imperial system. It was a daunting challenge, and there were failures along the way. Roman generals and politicians would destroy each other. Even the republican constitution would eventually be discarded. But in the end Rome triumphed here just as it had on the battlefield, for out of the turmoil would come the *pax Romana*—"Roman peace."

How did the Romans of the day meet these challenges? How did they lead their lives and cope with these momentous changes? Obviously there are as many answers to these questions as there were Romans. Yet two men represent the major trends of the second century B.C. Cato the Elder shared the mentality of those who longed for the good old days and idealized the traditional agrarian way of life. Scipio Aemilianus led those who embraced the new urban life, with its eager acceptance of Greek culture. Forty-nine years older than Scipio, Cato was a product of an earlier generation, one that confronted a rapidly changing world. Cato and Scipio were both aristocrats, and neither of them was typical, even of the aristocracy. But they do exemplify opposing sets of attitudes that marked Roman society and politics in the age of conquest.

Cato and the Traditional Ideal

Marcus Cato (234–149 B.C.) was born a plebeian, but his talent and energy carried him to Rome's highest offices. He cherished the old virtues and consistently imitated the old ways. In Roman society ties within the family were very strong. In this sense Cato and his family were typical. Cato was **paterfamilias,** a term that meant far more than merely "father." The paterfamilias was the oldest dominant male of the family. He held nearly absolute power over the lives of his wife and children as long as he lived. He could legally kill his wife for adultery or divorce her at will. He could kill his children or sell them into slavery. He could force them to marry against their will. Until the paterfamilias died, his sons could not legally own property. At his death the wife and children of the paterfamilias inherited his property.

Like most Romans, Cato and his family began the day early in the morning. The Romans divided the period of daylight into twelve hours and the darkness into another

A Fashionable Roman Room This elaborate wall painting decorated a bedroom of a villa near Pompeii. The scene depicts a sacred precinct. Upon awakening, the owners looked upon a small round temple set in the middle of a larger, more stately temple. The vista is one of regal splendor. *(The Metropolitan Museum of Art, Rogers Fund, 1903 [03.14.13a–g]. Photograph © 1986 The Metropolitan Museum of Art)*

twelve. The day might begin as early as half past four in summer, as late as half past seven in winter. Because Mediterranean summers are invariably hot, the farmer and his wife liked to take every advantage of the cool mornings. Cato and his family, like modern Italians, ordinarily started the morning with a light breakfast, usually nothing more than some bread and cheese. After breakfast the family went about its work.

Because of his political aspirations, Cato often used the mornings to plead law cases. He walked to the marketplace of the nearby town and defended anyone who wished his help. He received no fees for these services but did put his neighbors in his debt. In matters of law and politics Roman custom was very strong. It demanded that Cato's clients give him their political support or their votes in repayment whenever he asked for them. These clients knew and accepted their obligations to Cato for his help. The notion of clientage was a particularly Roman social and political custom: free men entrusted their lives to a more powerful man, and in exchange they gained from their patron some social entertainment and his protection. Custom, not law, gov-

erned this relationship. In return for his generosity toward his clients, the patron expected their support in public life and private matters. The bond thus proved reciprocal. Clientage helped people of lower social status to advance themselves and to advance the careers of their patrons.

Cato's wife (whose name is unknown) was the matron of the family, a position of authority and respect. The virtues of a Roman matron were fidelity, chastity, modesty, and dedication to the family. Cato's wife also followed the old ways. While he was in town, she ran the household. She spent the morning spinning and weaving wool for the clothes that the family wore. She supervised the domestic slaves, planned the meals, and devoted a good deal of attention to her son.

Though always legally under the authority and protection of their fathers, husbands, and other male members of the family, Roman women inherited wealth in their own names, which they generally bequeathed to their children. They managed their own finances and property, albeit under the guardianship of a male relative. They brought to their marriage a dowry that remained theirs, both as a means of contributing to the welfare of the family and as personal insurance for themselves. Upon divorce, a woman retained her dowry, although once again some male relative formally administered it for her.

Women's essential duty was the initial rearing of their children. Yet a warning demands attention. Most of the information from classical sources about women and child rearing comes from aristocratic sources that cannot reasonably be applied to the lower orders of society. Nonetheless, enough information remains to indicate that the lives of these children were pleasantly ordinary. Very young children played with the same sort of simple toys that entertain children today. The high mortality rate among infants meant that their parents did not necessarily invest much affection in them, a situation that changed as the republic gave way to the more stable and comfortable times of the empire. Levels of affection cannot be measured, but probability suggests that the lower classes enjoyed their children as much as most people have done from time immemorial.

Both Romans and Greeks felt that children should be raised in the lap of their mother, a woman who kept her house in good order and personally saw to the welfare of her children. In wealthy homes during the period, the matron had begun to employ a slave as a wet nurse. Cato's wife refused to delegate her maternal duties. Like most ordinary Roman women, she nursed her son herself and bathed and swaddled him daily. Later, in addition to playing with toys and dolls, children kept dogs and cats as pets. Dogs were also popular and valuable as house guards. Children played all sorts of games; games of chance were very popular. Until the age of seven children were under their mother's care. During this time the matron began to educate her daughters in the management of the household. After the age of seven, sons—and in many wealthy households daughters too—began to receive formal education.

In the country Romans like Cato continued to take their main meal at midday. This meal included either coarse bread made from the entire husk of wheat or porridge made with milk or water; it also included turnips, cabbage, olives, and beans. With the midday meal the family drank ordinary wine mixed with water. Afterward any Roman who could took a nap. This was especially true in the summer, when the Mediterranean heat can be fierce. Slaves, artisans, and hired laborers, however, continued their work. In the evening Romans ate a light meal and went to bed at nightfall.

The agricultural year followed the sun and the stars—the farmer's calendar. Like Hesiod in Boeotia, the Roman farmer looked to the sky to determine when to

plant, weed, shear sheep, and perform other chores. Spring was the season for plowing. Roman farmers plowed their land at least twice and preferably three times. The third plowing was to cover the sown seed in ridges and to use the furrows to drain off excess water. Farmers used oxen and donkeys to pull the plow, collecting the dung of the animals for fertilizer. Besides spreading manure, some farmers fertilized their fields by planting lupines and beans; when they began to pod, the farmers plowed them under. The main money crops, at least for rich soils, were wheat and flax. Forage crops included clover, vetch, and alfalfa. Prosperous farmers like Cato raised olive trees chiefly for the oil. They also raised grapevines for the production of wine. Cato and his neighbors harvested their cereal crops in summer and their grapes in autumn. Harvests varied depending on the soil, but farmers could usually expect yields of 5½ bushels of wheat or 10½ bushels of barley per acre.

An influx of slaves resulted from Rome's wars and conquests. The Roman attitude toward slaves and slavery had little in common with modern views. To the Romans slavery was a misfortune that befell some people, but it did not entail any racial theories. Races were not enslaved because the Romans thought them inferior. The black African slave was treated no worse—and no better—than the Spaniard. Indeed, some slaves were valued because of their physical distinctiveness: black Africans and blond Germans were particular favorites. For the talented slave the Romans always held out the hope of eventual freedom. **Manumission**—the freeing of individual slaves by their masters—became so common that it had to be limited by law. Not even Christians questioned the institution of slavery. It was just a fact of life.

For Cato and most other Romans, religion played an important part in life. Originally the Romans thought of the gods as invisible, shapeless natural forces. Only through Etruscan and Greek influence did Roman deities take on human form. Jupiter, the sky-god, and his wife, Juno, became equivalent to the Greek Zeus and Hera. Mars was the god of war but also guaranteed the fertility of the farm and protected it from danger. The gods of the Romans were not loving and personal. They were stern, powerful, and aloof. But as long as the Romans honored the cults of their gods, they could expect divine favor.

Along with the great gods the Romans believed in spirits who haunted fields, forests, crossroads, and even the home itself. Some of these deities were hostile; only magic could ward them off. The spirits of the dead, like ghosts in modern horror films, frequented places where they had lived. They too had to be placated but were ordinarily benign. As the poet Ovid (43 B.C.–A.D. 17) put it:

The spirits of the dead ask for little.
They are more grateful for piety than for an expensive
*   gift—*
Not greedy are the gods who haunt the Styx below.
A rooftile covered with a sacrificial crown,
Scattered kernels, a few grains of salt,
Bread dipped in wine, and loose violets—
These are enough.
Put them in a potsherd and leave them in the middle of the
*   road.*[4]

A good deal of Roman religion consisted of rituals such as those Ovid describes. These practices lived on long after the Romans had lost interest in the great gods. Even Christianity could not entirely wipe them out. Instead, Christianity was to incorporate many of these rituals into its own style of worship.

Scipio Aemilianus: Greek Culture and Urban Life

The old-fashioned ideals that Cato represented came into conflict with a new spirit of wealth and leisure. The conquest of the Mediterranean world and the spoils of war made Rome a great city. Roman life, especially in the cities, was changing and becoming less austere. The spoils of war went to build baths, theaters, and other places of amusement. Romans and Italian townspeople began to spend more of their time in leisure pursuits. Simultaneously, the new responsibilities of governing the world produced in Rome a sophisticated society. Romans developed new tastes and a liking for Greek culture and literature. They began to learn the Greek language. It became common for an educated Roman to speak both Latin and Greek. Hellenism dominated the cultural life of Rome. Even die-hards like Cato found a knowledge of Greek essential for political and diplomatic affairs. The poet Horace (64–8 B.C.) summed it up well: "Captive Greece captured her rough conqueror and introduced the arts into rustic Latium."

One of the most avid devotees of Hellenism and the new was Scipio Aemilianus, the destroyer of Carthage. Scipio realized that broad and worldly views had to replace the old Roman narrowness. The new situation called for new ways. Rome was no longer a small city on the Tiber; it was the capital of the world, and Romans had to adapt themselves to that fact. Scipio was ready to become an innovator in both politics and culture. He broke with the past in the conduct of his political career,

African Acrobat   Conquest and prosperity brought exotic pleasure to Rome. Every feature of this sculpture is exotic. The young African woman and her daring gymnastic pose would catch anyone's attention. And to add to the spice of her act, she performs using a live crocodile as her platform. Americans would have loved it. *(Courtesy of the Trustees of the British Museum)*

choosing a more personal style of politics, one that reflected his own views and looked unflinchingly at the broader problems that the success of Rome brought to its people. He embraced Hellenism wholeheartedly. Perhaps more than anyone else of his day, Scipio represented the new Roman—imperial, cultured, and independent.

In his education and interests, too, Scipio broke with the past. As a boy he had received the traditional Roman training, learning to read and write Latin and becoming acquainted with the law. He mastered the fundamentals of rhetoric and learned how to throw the javelin, fight in armor, and ride a horse. But later Scipio also learned Greek and became a fervent Hellenist. As a young man he formed a lasting friendship with the historian Polybius, who actively encouraged him in his study of Greek culture and in his intellectual pursuits. In later life Scipio's love of Greek learning, rhetoric, and philosophy became legendary. Scipio also promoted the spread of Hellenism in Roman society. He became the center of the Scipionic Circle, a small group of Greek and Roman artists, philosophers, historians, and poets. Conservatives like Cato tried to stem the rising tide of Hellenism, but men like Scipio carried the day and helped make the heritage of Greece an abiding factor in Roman life.

The new Hellenism profoundly stimulated the growth and development of Roman art and literature. The Roman conquest of the Hellenistic East resulted in wholesale confiscation of Greek paintings and sculpture to grace Roman temples, public buildings, and private homes. Roman artists copied many aspects of Greek art, but their emphasis on realistic portraiture carried on a native tradition.

Fabius Pictor (second half of the third century B.C.), a senator, wrote the first *History of Rome* in Greek. Other Romans translated Greek classics into Latin. Still others, such as the poet Ennius (239–169 B.C.), the father of Latin poetry, studied Greek philosophy, wrote comedies in Latin, and adapted many of Euripides' tragedies for the Roman stage. Plautus (ca 254–184 B.C.) specialized in rough humor. He too decked out Greek plays in Roman dress but was no mere imitator. The Roman dramatist Terence (ca 195–159 B.C.), a member of the Scipionic Circle, wrote comedies of refinement and grace that owed their essentials to Greek models. His plays lacked the energy and the slapstick of Plautus's rowdy plays. All of early Roman literature was derived from the Greeks, but it managed in time to speak in its own voice and to flourish because it had something of its own to say.

The conquest of the Mediterranean world brought the Romans leisure, and Hellenism influenced how they spent their free time. Many rich urban dwellers changed their eating habits by consuming elaborate meals of exotic dishes. A whole suckling pig stuffed with sausages was a favorite treat, and a lucky guest might even dine on peacocks, ostriches, and rare fish, all washed down with vintage wines.

During the second century B.C. the Greek custom of bathing also became a Roman passion and an important part of the day. In the early republic Romans had bathed infrequently, especially in the winter. Now large buildings

Roman Table Manners   This mosaic is a floor that can never be swept clean. It whimsically suggests what a dining room floor looked like after a lavish dinner and also tells something about the menu: a chicken head, a wishbone, and remains of various seafood, vegetables, and fruit are easily recognizable. *(Museo Gregoriano Profano, Vatican Museums/Scala/Art Resource, NY)*

Dressing of the Bride Preparing for the wedding was an occasion for fun and ceremony. On the night before the event, the bride tried on her wedding dress for a favorable omen. The next morning her mother fastidiously dressed her or supervised a maid to do so. Last, the bride was crowned with a veil of flowers she had picked herself. *(Vatican Museums/Scala/Art Resource, NY)*

containing pools and exercise rooms went up in great numbers, and the baths became an essential part of the Roman city. Architects built intricate systems of aqueducts to supply the bathing establishments with water. Conservatives railed at this Greek custom, calling it a waste of time and an encouragement to idleness. They were correct in that bathing establishments were more than just places to take a bath. They included gymnasia, where men exercised and played ball. Women had places of their own to bathe, generally sections of the same baths used by men; for some reason, women's facilities lacked gymnasia. The baths contained hot-air rooms to induce a good sweat and pools of hot and cold water to finish the actual bathing. They also contained snack bars and halls where people chatted and read. The baths were socially important places where men and women went to see and be seen. Social climbers tried to talk to the right people and wangle invitations to dinner; politicians took advantage of the occasion to discuss the affairs of the day. Despite the protests of conservatives and moralists, the baths at least provided people—rich and poor—with places for clean and healthy relaxation.

Did Hellenism and new social customs corrupt the Romans? Perhaps the best answer is this: the Roman state and the empire it ruled continued to exist for six more centuries. Rome did not collapse; the state continued to prosper. The golden age of literature was still before it. The high tide of its prosperity still lay in the future. The Romans did not like change but took it in stride. That was part of their practical turn of mind and their strength.

The Late Republic (133–31 B.C.)

The wars of conquest created serious problems for the Romans, some of the most pressing of which were political. The republican constitution had suited the needs of a simple city-state but was inadequate to meet the requirements of Rome's new position in international affairs (see Map 5.2). Sweeping changes and reforms were necessary to make it serve the demands of a state holding vast territory. A system of provincial administration had to be established. Officials had to be appointed to govern the provinces and administer the law. These officials and administrative organs had to find places in the constitution. Armies had to be provided for defense, and a system of tax collection had to be created.

Other political problems were equally serious. During the wars Roman generals commanded huge numbers of troops for long periods of time. These men of great power and prestige were on the point of becoming too mighty for the state to control. Although Rome's Italian allies had borne much of the burden of the fighting, they received fewer rewards than did Roman officers and soldiers. Italians began to agitate for full Roman citizenship, including the right to vote.

Unrest in Rome and Italy

There were serious economic problems, too. Hannibal's operations and the warfare in Italy had left the countryside a shambles. The movements of numerous armies had disrupted agriculture. The prolonged fighting had also drawn untold numbers of Roman and Italian men away from their farms for long periods. The families of these soldiers could not keep the land under full cultivation. The people who defended Rome and conquered the world for Rome became impoverished for having done their duty.

These problems, complex and explosive, largely account for the turmoil of the closing years of the republic. The late republic was one of the most dramatic eras in Roman history. It produced some of Rome's most famous figures: the Gracchi, Marius, Sulla, Cicero, Pompey, and Julius Caesar, among others. In one way or another, each of these men attempted to solve Rome's problems. Yet they were also striving for the glory and honor that were the supreme goals of the senatorial aristocracy. Personal ambition often clashed with patriotism to create political tension throughout the period.

When the legionaries returned to their farms in Italy, they encountered an appalling situation. All too often their farms looked like the farms of people they had conquered. Two courses of action were open to them. They could rebuild as their forefathers had done, or they could take advantage of an alternative not open to their ancestors and sell their holdings. The wars of conquest had made some men astoundingly rich. These men wanted to invest their wealth in land. They bought up small farms to create huge estates, which the Romans called **latifundia.**

The purchase offers of the rich landowners appealed to the veterans for a variety of reasons. Many veterans had seen service in the East, where they had tasted the rich city life of the Hellenistic states. They were reluctant to return home and settle down to a dull life on the farm. Often their farms were so badly damaged that rebuilding hardly seemed worthwhile. Besides, it was hard to make big profits from small farms. Nor could the veterans sup-

plement their income by working on the latifundia. Although the owners of the latifundia occasionally hired free men as day laborers, they preferred to use slaves. Slaves could not strike or be drafted into the army. Confronted by these conditions, veterans and their families opted to sell their land. They took what they could get for their broken farms and tried their luck elsewhere.

Most veterans migrated to the cities, especially to Rome. Although some found work, most did not. Industry and small manufacturing were generally in the hands of slaves. Even when work was available, slave labor kept the wages of free men low. Instead of a new start, veterans and their families encountered slum conditions that matched those of many modern American cities.

This trend held ominous consequences for the strength of Rome's armies. The Romans had always believed that only landowners should serve in the army, for only they had something to fight for. Landless men, even if they were Romans and lived in Rome, could not be conscripted into the army. These landless men may have been veterans of major battles and numerous campaigns; they may have won distinction on the battlefield. But once they sold their land, they became ineligible for further military service. A large pool of experienced manpower was going to waste. The landless ex-legionaries wanted a new start, and they were willing to support any leader who would provide it.

One man who recognized the plight of Rome's peasant farmers and urban poor was an aristocrat, Tiberius Gracchus (163–133 B.C.). Appalled by what he saw, Tiberius warned his countrymen that the legionaries were losing their land while fighting Rome's wars:

The wild beasts that roam over Italy have every one of them a cave or lair to lurk in. But the men who fight and die for Italy enjoy the common air and light, indeed, but nothing else. Houseless and homeless they wander about with their wives and children. And it is with lying lips that their generals exhort the soldiers in their battles to defend sepulchres and shrines from the enemy, for not a man of them has an hereditary altar, not one of all these many Romans an ancestral tomb, but they fight and die to support others in luxury, and though they are styled masters of the world, they have not a single clod of earth that is their own.[5]

Until his death Tiberius Gracchus sought a solution to the problems of the veterans and the urban poor.

After his election as tribune of the people in 133 B.C., Tiberius proposed that public land be given to the poor in small lots. Although his reform enjoyed the support of some very distinguished and popular aristocrats, he immediately ran into trouble for a number of reasons. First,

Pompeii The eruption of Mt. Vesuvius that buried this Italian city in A.D. 79 preserved a singular view of Roman life. The huge temple of Jupiter in the near foreground dominated the city. Other temples and sacred places surround it. Next to it lie the marketplace and various public buildings. *(Guido Alberto Rossi/Altitude)*

his reform bill angered many wealthy aristocrats who had usurped large tracts of public land for their own use. They had no desire to give any of it back, so they bitterly resisted Tiberius's efforts. This was to be expected, yet he unquestionably made additional problems for himself. He introduced his land bill in the concilium plebis without consulting the senate. When King Attalus III left the kingdom of Pergamum to the Romans in his will, Tiberius had the money appropriated to finance his reforms—another slap at the senate. As tribune he acted totally within his rights. Yet the way in which he proceeded was unprecedented. Many powerful Romans became suspicious of Tiberius's growing influence with the people, some even thinking that he aimed at tyranny. Others opposed him because of his unparalleled methods. After all, there were proper ways to do things in Rome, and he had not followed them. As a result, violence broke out when a large body of senators, led by the *pontifex maximus* (the chief priest), killed Tiberius in cold blood. It was a black day in Roman history. The very people who directed the

affairs of state and administered the law had taken the law into their own hands. The death of Tiberius was the beginning of an era of political violence. In the end that violence would bring down the republic.

Although Tiberius was dead, his land bill became law. Furthermore, Tiberius's brother Gaius Gracchus (153–121 B.C.) took up the cause of reform. Gaius was a veteran soldier with an enviable record, but this fiery orator made his mark in the political arena. Gaius also became tribune and demanded even more extensive reform than his brother. To help the urban poor Gaius pushed legislation to provide them with cheap grain for bread. He defended his brother's land law and suggested other measures for helping the landless. He proposed that Rome send many of its poor and propertyless people out to form colonies in southern Italy. The poor would have a new start and lead productive lives. The city would immediately benefit because excess, nonproductive families would leave for new opportunities abroad. Rome would be less crowded, sordid, and dangerous.

Gaius went a step further and urged that all Italians be granted full rights of Roman citizenship. This measure provoked a storm of opposition, and it was not passed in Gaius's lifetime. Yet in the long run he proved wiser than his opponents. In 91 B.C. many Italians revolted against Rome over the issue of full citizenship, thus triggering the Social War, so named from the Latin word *socium*, or "ally." After a brief but hard-fought war (91–88 B.C.), the senate gave Roman citizenship to all Italians. Had the senate listened to Gaius earlier, it could have prevented a great deal of bloodshed. Yet Gaius himself was also at fault. Like his brother Tiberius, Gaius aroused a great deal of personal and factional opposition. To many he seemed too radical and too hasty to change things. Many political opponents considered him belligerent and headstrong. When Gaius failed in 121 B.C. to win the tribunate for the third time, he feared for his life. In desperation he armed his staunchest supporters, whereupon the senate ordered the consul Opimius to restore order. He did so by having Gaius killed, along with three thousand of Gaius's supporters who opposed the senate's order. Once again the cause of reform had met with violence.

The death of Gaius brought little peace, and trouble came from two sources: the outbreak of new wars in the Mediterranean basin and further political unrest in Rome. In 112 B.C. Rome declared war against the rebellious Jugurtha, king of Numidia in North Africa. Numidia had been one of Rome's **client kingdoms,** kingdoms still ruled by their own kings but subject to Rome. These kingdoms entered into a political relationship with Rome that was usually friendly but was not a relationship between equals: Rome always remained the senior partner. The kingdoms followed Rome's lead in foreign affairs but conducted their own internal business according to their own laws and customs. Client kingdoms generally lay on the outskirts of Roman control, which gave them an additional measure of local control. The benefits of these relations were mutual, for the client kingdoms enjoyed the protection of Rome while defending Rome's borders. In time many of these states became provinces of the Roman Empire.

Meanwhile, the Roman legions made little headway against Jugurtha until 107 B.C., when Gaius Marius, an Italian *new man* (a politician not from the traditional Roman aristocracy), became consul. Marius's values were those of the military camp. A man of fierce vigor and courage, Marius saw the army as the tool of his ambition. He took the unusual but not wholly unprecedented step of recruiting an army by permitting landless men to serve in the legions. Marius thus tapped Rome's vast reservoir of idle manpower. His volunteer army was a professional force, not a body of draftees. In 106 B.C. Marius and his new army handily defeated Jugurtha.

An unexpected war broke out in the following year when two German peoples, the Cimbri and Teutones, moved into Gaul and later into northern Italy. After the Germans had defeated Roman armies sent to repel them, Marius was again elected consul, even though he was legally ineligible. From 104 to 100 B.C. Marius annually held the consulship. Despite the military necessity, Marius's many consulships meant that a Roman commander repeatedly held unprecedented military power in his hands. This would later translate into a political problem that the Roman republic never solved.

Before engaging the Cimbri and Teutones, Marius reformed the Roman army. There was, however, a disturbing side to his reforms, one that would henceforth haunt the republic. To encourage enlistments, Marius promised land to his volunteers after the war. Poor and landless veterans flocked to him, and together they conquered the Germans by 101 B.C. When Marius proposed a bill to grant land to his veterans, the senate refused to act, in effect turning its back on the soldiers of Rome. It was a disastrous mistake. Henceforth the legionaries expected the commanders—not the senate or the state—to protect their interests. Through Marius's reforms the Roman army became a professional force, but it owed little allegiance to the state. By failing to reward the loyalty of Rome's troops, the senate set the stage for military rebellion and political anarchy.

The Social War brought Marius into conflict with Sulla, who was consul in 88 B.C. First Marius and later Sulla defeated the Italian rebels. In the final stages of the war, while putting down the last of the rebels, Sulla was deposed from his consulship because of factional chaos in Rome. He immediately marched on Rome and restored order, but it was an ominous sign of the deterioration of Roman politics and political ideals. With some semblance of order restored, Sulla in 88 B.C. led an army to the East, where King Mithridates of Pontus in Asia Minor challenged Roman rule. In Sulla's absence, rioting and political violence again exploded in Rome. Marius and his supporters marched on Rome and launched a reign of terror.

Although Marius died peacefully in 86 B.C., his supporters continued to hold Rome. Once Sulla had defeated Mithridates, he once again, this time in 82 B.C., marched on Rome. After a brief but intense civil war, Sulla entered Rome and ordered a ruthless butchery of his opponents. He also proclaimed himself dictator. He launched many political and judicial reforms, including strengthening the senate while weakening the tribunate, increasing the number of magistrates in order to administer Rome's provinces better, and restoring the courts.

In 79 B.C. Sulla voluntarily abdicated his dictatorship and permitted the republican constitution to function normally once again. Yet his dictatorship cast a long shadow over the late republic. Sulla the political reformer proved far less influential than Sulla the successful general and dictator. Civil war was to be the constant lot of Rome for the next fifty years, until the republican constitution gave way to the empire of Augustus in 27 B.C. The history of the late republic is the story of the power struggles of some of Rome's most famous figures: Julius Caesar and Pompey, Augustus and Marc Antony. One figure who stands apart is Cicero (106–43 B.C.), a practical politician whose greatest legacy to the Roman world and to Western civilization is his mass of political and oratorical writings. Yet Cicero commanded no legions, and only legions commanded respect.

Civil War

In the late republic many other Romans were grappling with the simple and inescapable fact that their old city-state constitution was unequal to the demands of overseas possessions and the governing of provinces. (See the feature "Individuals in Society: Quintus Sertorius.") Thus even Sulla's efforts to put the constitution back together proved hollow. Once the senate and other institutions of the Roman state had failed to come to grips with the needs of empire, once the authorities had lost control of their own generals and soldiers, and once the armies put their faith in commanders instead of in Rome, the republic was doomed.

Sulla's real political heirs were Pompey and Julius Caesar, with at least Caesar realizing that the days of the old republican constitution were numbered. Pompey, a man of boundless ambition, began his career as one of Sulla's lieutenants. After his army put down a rebellion in Spain, he himself threatened to rebel unless the senate allowed him to run for consul. He and another ambitious politician, Crassus, pooled political resources, and both won the consulship. They dominated Roman politics until the rise of Julius Caesar, who became consul in 59 B.C. Together the three concluded a political alliance, the **First Triumvirate,** in which they agreed to advance one another's interests.

The man who cast the longest shadow over these troubled years was Julius Caesar (100–44 B.C.). More than a mere soldier, Caesar was a cultivated man. Born of a noble family, he received an excellent education, which he

Julius Caesar This realistic bust of Caesar captures all of the power, intensity, and brilliance of the man. It is a study of determination and an excellent example of Roman portraiture. *(Museo Archeologico Nazionale Naples/Scala/Art Resource, NY)*

furthered by studying in Greece with some of the most eminent teachers of the day. He had serious intellectual interests, and his literary ability was immense. Caesar was a superb orator, and his affable personality and wit made him popular. He was also a shrewd politician of unbridled ambition. Since military service was an effective steppingstone to politics, Caesar launched his military career in Spain, where his courage won the respect and affection of his troops. Personally brave and tireless, Caesar was a military genius who knew how to win battles and turn victories into permanent gains.

In 58 B.C. Caesar became governor of Cisalpine Gaul, or modern northern Italy. By 50 B.C. he had conquered all of Gaul, or modern France. Caesar's account of his operations, his *Commentaries* on the Gallic wars, became a classic in Western literature and most schoolchildren's introduction to Latin. By 49 B.C. the First Triumvirate had fallen apart. Crassus had died in battle, and Caesar and Pompey, each suspecting the other of treachery, came to blows. The result was a long and bloody civil war that raged from Spain across northern Africa to Egypt.

Individuals in Society

Quintus Sertorius

Quintus Sertorius, son of a prominent Italian family, stands as a prime example of the transition of the Roman republic from local power to master of the Mediterranean world. Born not in Rome itself but in nearby Nurisa (modern Norcia) in 126 B.C., he became a Roman citizen. Like many of his contemporaries, he rose to high office and took part in the political and military upheavals of the day. He became a rebel against Rome and helped to shape the new Mediterranean community.

Sertorius launched his public career in Rome, where he mastered Roman law and became a gifted military officer. When two barbarian tribes invaded Gaul in 105 B.C., he fought so effectively there that his ability and valor brought him to the attention of senior Roman military commanders. These events honed his martial skills and acquainted him with the new peoples gradually entering western Europe.

Sertorius's success in Gaul led him in 97 B.C. to higher command in Spain. From that time until his death his destiny and Spain's would be intertwined. He, like Marius, Sulla, and other notable men, was swept up in this vast and chaotic episode in republican history. He chose the wrong side and upon defeat fled to Spain, where he worked to establish his own independent authority.

A surprising accident put another tool of authority into Sertorius's hands. As the story goes, one of his soldiers, while hunting, encountered a white fawn. Instead of killing the doe, he presented it to Sertorius, who made a pet of it. Sertorius declared that the animal was the gift of Diana, whose attributes included the gifts of wisdom and prophecy. The superstitious Spaniards, who had long believed in Diana's cult of the stag, believed that Diana had blessed Sertorius. This divine endorsement made him seem more Spanish and enhanced his authority among the Spaniards.

The Roman civil war soon reached Spain. Sertorius's reputation and exploits persuaded many Spaniards to invite him to lead them against the Romans. He agreed, even though he always remained a Roman at heart. He began to organize these supporters along Roman military lines. He taught them Roman principles of military command and tactics so that they could meet the greatly feared Roman army in successful, organized bodies.

These things done, Sertorius led the Spaniards against the Romans. Instead of meeting the Roman legions face-to-face, he resorted to ambushes, flanking movements, and quick marches to isolate the enemy. He also struck at Roman supply lines. His success prompted many

Romans to switch sides. Even some senators left Rome to join him. Welcoming them with honor, he got them involved in the civil government that he introduced. Sertorius modeled his Spanish state along Roman civil lines but under his leadership. Spain had never seen so many military, cultural, and civil developments in such a short time.

Many Greeks and Romans joined Sertorius because of his success and generosity. This flattering response seemed to bolster his plans but led to his failure and death. The Romans to whom he had bestowed a home began to insult, punish, and abuse the Spaniards while doing everything possible to thwart Sertorius's plans. Then they rebelled against him, hoping either to topple him and reign in his place or to return the province to Roman rule. Finally, with a treachery that matched that of the conspirators against Caesar, some Romans who were still considered loyal assassinated Sertorius at a banquet in 73 B.C. Roman generals from the East easily took control of Spain and ultimately reaped Sertorius's harvest.

Death and defeat did not erase Sertorius's achievements in Spain. He above any of his predecessors introduced the region to Greco-Roman culture. He gave the land and its peoples a civil government that united them. He turned their tribal hordes into an army along Roman lines. He paved the way for peaceful Spanish inclusion into the quickly evolving Roman Empire.

Coin attributed to Q. Sertorius, reflecting his attempt to unite Romano-Spanish traditional themes. (From Jean Mazard, Corpus Numorum Mumidiae Mauritaniaque, 1955. Photo: Caroline Buckler)

Questions for Analysis

1. How did Sertorius create a state in Spain?
2. What was his legacy to Spain, Rome, and Western civilization in general?

The *features additional information and activities related to this topic.*
history.college.hmco.com/students

Although Pompey enjoyed the official support of the government, Caesar finally defeated Pompey's forces in 45 B.C. He had overthrown the republic and made himself dictator.

Julius Caesar was not merely another victorious general. Politically brilliant, he was determined to make basic reforms, even at the expense of the old constitution. He took the first long step to break down the barriers between Italy and the provinces, extending citizenship to many of the provincials who had supported him. Caesar also took measures to cope with Rome's burgeoning population. By Caesar's day perhaps 750,000 people lived in Rome. Caesar drew up plans to send his veterans and some 80,000 of the poor and unemployed to colonies throughout the Mediterranean. He founded at least twenty colonies, most of which were located in Gaul, Spain, and North Africa. These colonies were important agents in spreading Roman culture in the western Mediterranean. A Roman empire composed of citizens, not subjects, was the result.

In 44 B.C. a group of conspirators assassinated Caesar and set off another round of civil war. Caesar had named his eighteen-year-old grandnephew, Octavian—or Augustus, as he is better known to history—as his heir. Augustus joined forces with two of Caesar's lieutenants, Marc Antony and Lepidus, in a pact known as the Second Triumvirate, and together they hunted down and defeated Caesar's murderers. In the process, however, Augustus and Antony came into conflict. Antony, "boastful, arrogant, and full of empty exultation and capricious ambition," proved to be the major threat to Augustus's designs.[6] In 33 B.C. Augustus branded Antony a traitor and rebel. Augustus painted lurid pictures of Antony lingering in the eastern Mediterranean, a romantic and foolish captive of the seductive Cleopatra, queen of Egypt and bitter enemy of Rome. In 31 B.C., with the might of Rome at his back, Augustus encountered and defeated the army and navy of Antony and Cleopatra at the Battle of Actium in Greece. Augustus's victory put an end to an age of civil war that had lasted since the days of Sulla.

Summary

The rise of Rome to greatness resulted from many factors. At the outset the geographical position of Rome put it on good, natural lines of communication within Italy. The Italian peninsula itself was generally fertile, and the mountains did not prevent political unification. The Etruscans transformed the Roman settlements into a city. Once free of the Etruscans, the Romans used their political organization, their prosperity, and their population to

conquer their neighbors. Yet instead of enslaving them, the Romans extended citizenship to the conquered. Having united Italy under them, the Romans became a major power that looked to the broader Mediterranean world. In a succession of wars with Carthage, in Spain, and in the Hellenistic East, Rome won an empire. These conquests not only prompted the Romans to invent a system to administer the empire but also brought them into the mainstream of Hellenistic civilization. The wealth derived from the empire meant that life for many Romans became richer. But there was also a dark side to these developments. Personal ambition, as well as defects in the Roman system of government, led some ambitious leaders to seize unprecedented power. Others resisted, throwing the republic into a series of civil wars. Finally, Caesar and his grandnephew Octavian restored order, but in the process the Roman republic had become a monarchy.

Key Terms

pomerium	Struggle of the Orders
fasces	tribunes
Forum	Pyrrhic victory
Gauls	First Punic War
franchise	Second Punic War
patricians	paterfamilias
plebeians	manumission
senate	latifundia
praetor	client kingdoms
ius civile (civil law)	First Triumvirate
ius naturale (natural law)	

Notes

1. Polybius, *The Histories* 1.1.5. John Buckler is the translator of all uncited quotations from a foreign language in Chapters 1–6.
2. Mark Twain, *The Innocents Abroad* (New York: Signet Classics, 1966), p. 176.
3. Sallust, *War with Catiline* 10.1–3.
4. Ovid, *Fasti* 2.535–539.
5. Plutarch, *Life of Tiberius Gracchus* 9.5–6.
6. Plutarch, *Life of Antony* 2.8.

Suggested Reading

H. H. Scullard gives a broad account of Roman history in *A History of the Roman World, 753–146 B.C.,* 4th ed. (1993), to which should be added T. Cornell, *The Beginnings of Rome* (1995), which covers the history of Rome from the Bronze Age to the Punic Wars. The Etruscans have inspired a great deal of work. The best treatment is H. Barker and

T. Rasmussen, *The Etruscans* (1997). E. Gabba, *Dionysius and the History of Archaic Rome* (1991), is the study of the origins of Rome by an eminent scholar who also looks at how the Greeks perceived it. A great deal of work has been done on the importance of the Gauls and Celts, notably D. Rankin, *Celts and the Classical World* (1996).

Roman expansion continues to attract attention. Easily available is C. J. Smith, *Early Rome and Latium: Economy and Society, c. 1000 to 500 B.C.* (1996). Many studies deal with Roman expansion throughout the Mediterranean. In Italy itself D. J. Gargola, *Lands, Laws, and Gods* (1995), examines how the Roman magistrates regulated the public lands of Rome. Similar is N. Morley, *Metropolis and Hinterland* (1996), a study of how Romans and Italians integrated their economies between 200 B.C. and A.D. 200. J. Lazenby addresses Rome's conflict with Carthage in two books: *First Punic War* (1996) and *Hannibal's War* (1978), dealing with the Second Punic War. R. Kallet-Marx, *Hegemony to Empire* (1995), examines how Rome's power in the eastern Mediterranean became established between 148 and 62 B.C. S. L. Dyson, *The Creation of the Roman Frontier* (1985), deals with the process by which the Romans established their frontiers, and K. R. Bradley, *Slavery and Rebellion in the Roman World* (1989), analyzes the slave revolts of Spartacus and others. C. Bruun, ed., *The Roman Middle Republic, ca. 400–133 B.C.* (2000), examines anew many central issues of the period; unfortunately, many of the chapters are in foreign languages.

One of the best studies of Rome's political evolution is A. N. Sherwin-White, *Roman Citizenship*, 2d ed. (1973), a classic work of enduring value. J. F. Gardner, *Being a Roman Citizen* (1993), is a broad work that includes material on ex-slaves, the lower classes, and much else. E. S. Gruen explores the effects of the introduction of Greek ideas, literature, and learning into central aspects of Roman life in two books: *Culture and National Identity in Republican Rome* (1992) and *Studies in Greek Culture and Roman Policy* (1996). The topic of Roman intellectual and cultural growth is one of the most studied aspects of republican history. G. B. Conte, *Latin Literature* (1994), is a comprehensive work that begins with the origins of Latin literature and continues into the early medieval period. E. Fantham, *Roman Literary Culture* (1996), answers the question of who in Rome read the books that helped shape Roman culture. T. N. Habesich, *The Politics of Latin Literature* (1998), studies the intimate relationship between the literature and politics of ancient Rome.

The great figures and events of the late republic have been the object of much work. E. S. Gruen, *The Last Generation of the Roman Republic* (1974), treats the period as a whole. Very important are the studies of E. Badian, *Roman Imperialism in the Late Republic* (1968) and *Publicans and Sinners* (1972). R. Syme, *The Roman Revolution,* rev. ed. (1952), is a classic. Valuable also are P. A. Brunt, *Social Conflicts in the Roman Republic* (1971); A. W. Lintott, *Violence in the Roman Republic* (1968); and J. K. Evans, *War, Women and Children in Ancient Rome* (1991).

Many works deal with individual Romans who left their mark on this period. H. C. Boren, *The Gracchi* (1968), treats the work of the two brothers, and A. M. Eckstein's *Senate and Generals* (1987) discusses how the decisions of individual generals affected both the senate and Roman foreign relations. A. Keaveney, *Sulla: The Last Republican* (1983), is a study of a man who thought of himself as a reformer. A. E. Astin has produced two works that are far more extensive than their titles indicate: *Scipio Aemilianus* (1967) and *Cato the Censor* (1978). J. Leach, *Pompey the Great* (1978), surveys the career of this politician, and B. Rawson, *The Politics of Friendship: Pompey and Cicero* (1978), treats both figures in their political environment. M. Gelzer, *Caesar, Politician and Statesman* (English trans., 1968), is easily the best study of one of history's most significant figures. N. Wood, *Cicero's Social and Political Thought* (1991), is an original study of Cicero's thought about the Rome of his day. E. G. Huzar, *Marc Antony* (1987), offers a new assessment of the career of the man who challenged Octavian for control of the Roman world. Caesar's onetime colleague Marcus Crassus is studied in B. A. Marshall, *Crassus: A Political Biography* (1976), and A. Ward, *Marcus Crassus and the Late Roman Republic* (1977). R. S. Weigel, *Lepidus* (1992), covers the career of the third member of the Second Triumvirate.

K. D. White, *Roman Farming* (1970), deals with agriculture. Greek cultural influence on Roman life is the subject of A. Wardman, *Rome's Debt to Greece* (1976). H. H. Scullard, *Festivals and Ceremonies of the Roman Republic* (1981), gives a fresh look at religious practices. R. Turcam, *The Gods of Ancient Rome* (2000), provides a concise survey of the Roman pantheon. Work on Roman social history has advanced in several areas. G. Alfoeldy, a major scholar, has written *The Social History of Rome* (1985), an ambitious undertaking. G. G. Fagan, *Bathing in Public in the Roman World* (1998), carefully explains the social significance of the Roman bath. S. Dixon, *The Roman Mother* (1988), focuses on women's role as mothers within the Roman family. Two works concentrate on the family and women's domestic and religious roles in society: J. K. Evans, *War, Women, and Children in Ancient Rome* (1991), and A. Fraschetti, *Roman Women* (1993), which is devoted primarily to aristocratic women. A wealth of other research on the Roman family and related topics has appeared, including K. R. Bradley, *Discovering the Roman Family* (1990), a series of essays on Roman social history; S. Dixon, *The Roman Family* (1992); S. Treggiari, *Roman Marriage* (1991); and R. A. Baumann, *Women and Politics in Ancient Rome* (1992). A novel work is E. Eyben, *Restless Youth in Ancient Rome* (1993), which explores the mores of youth of the upper class. C. A. Williams, *Roman Homosexuality* (1999), argues that the stigma for the practice was placed not so much on the physical act as on the social status of the participants.

Listening to the Past

Titus Flamininus and the Liberty of the Greeks

After his arrival in Greece in 197 B.C., Titus Flamininus defeated the Macedonians in Thessaly. He next sent his recommendations to the Roman senate on the terms of the peace agreement. The following year the senate sent him ten commissioners, who agreed with his ideas. The year 196 B.C. was also the occasion when the great Pan-Hellenic Isthmian games were regularly celebrated near Corinth. Many of the dignitaries and the most prominent people of the Hellenistic world were present. Among them was Flamininus, who came neither as a participant in the games nor solely as a spectator of them. Instead, he took the occasion to make a formal announcement about Roman policy. There in Isthmia he officially announced that Rome granted freedom to the Greeks. He assured his audience that Rome had not come as a conqueror. The eminent Greek biographer Plutarch has left a vivid account of the general response to this pronouncement.

Accordingly, at the Isthmian games, where a great throng of people were sitting in the stadium and watching the athletic contests (since, indeed, after many years Greece had at last ceased from wars waged in hopes of freedom, and was now holding festival in time of assured peace), the trumpet signalled a general silence, and the herald, coming forward into the midst of the spectators, made proclamation that the Roman senate and Titus Quintius Flamininus proconsular general, having conquered King Philip and the Macedonians, restored to freedom, without garrisons and without imposts, and to the enjoyment of their ancient laws, the Corinthians, the Locrians, the Phocians, the Euboeans, the Achaeans of Phthiotis, the Magnesians, the Thessalians, and the Perrhaebians. At first, then, the proclamation was by no means

generally or distinctly heard, but there was a confused and tumultuous movement in the stadium of people who wondered what had been said, and asked one another questions about it, and called out to have the proclamation made again; but when silence had been restored, and the herald in tones that were louder than before and reached the ears of all, had recited the proclamation, a shout of joy arose, so incredibly loud that it reached the sea. The whole audience rose to their feet, and no heed was paid to the contending athletes, but all were eager to spring forward and greet and hail the saviour and champion of Greece.

And that which is often said of the volume and power of the human voice was then apparent to the eye. For ravens which chanced to be flying overhead fell down into the stadium. The cause of this was the rupture of the air; for when the voice is borne aloft loud and strong, the air is rent asunder by it and will not support flying creatures, but lets them fall, as if they were over a vacuum, unless, indeed, they are transfixed by a sort of blow, as of a weapon, and fall down dead. It is possible, too, that in such cases there is a whirling motion of the air, which becomes like a waterspout at sea with a refluent flow of the surges caused by their very volume.

Be that as it may, had not Titus, now that the spectacle was given up, at once foreseen the rush and press of the throng and taken himself away, it would seem that he could hardly have survived the concourse of so many people about him at once and from all sides. But when they were tired of shouting about his tent, and night was already come, then, with greetings and embraces for any friends and fellow citizens whom they saw, they betook themselves to banqueting and carousing with one another. And here, their pleasure naturally increasing, they moved to reason and discourse about Greece, saying that although she had waged many wars for the sake of her freedom, she had not yet obtained a more secure or more delightful exercise of it than now, when others had striven in her behalf, and she herself, almost without a drop of blood or a pang of grief, had borne away the fairest and most enviable of prizes. Verily, they would say, valour and wisdom are rare things among men, but the rarest of all blessings is the just man. For men like Agesilaüs, or Lysander, or Nicias, or Alcibiades could indeed conduct wars well, and understood how to be victorious commanders in battles by land and sea, but they would not use their successes so as to win legitimate favour and promote the right. Indeed, if one excepts the action at Marathon, the sea-fight at Salamis, Plataea, Thermopylae, and the achievements of Cimon at the Eurymedon and about Cyprus, Greece has fought all her battles to bring servitude upon herself, and every one of her trophies stands as a memorial of her own calamity and disgrace, since she owed her overthrow chiefly to the baseness and contentiousness of her leaders. Whereas men of another race, who were thought to have only slight sparks and insignificant traces of a common remote ancestry, from whom it was astonishing that any helpful word or purpose should be vouchsafed to Greece—these men underwent the greatest perils and hardships in order to rescue Greece and set her free from cruel despots and tyrants.

So ran the thoughts of the Greeks; and the acts of Titus were consonant with his proclamations. For at once he sent Lentulus to Asia to set Bargylia free, and Stertinius to Thrace to deliver the cities and islands there from Philip's garrisons. Moreover, Publius Villius sailed to have a conference with Antiochus concerning the freedom of the Greeks who were under his sway. Titus himself also paid a visit to Chalcis, and then sailed from there to Magnesia, removing their garrisons and restoring to the peoples their constitutions. He was also appointed master of ceremonies for the Nemeian games at Argos, where he conducted the festival in the best possible manner, and once more publicly proclaimed freedom to the Greeks. Then he visited the different cities, establishing among them law and order, abundant justice, concord, and mutual friendliness. He quieted their factions and restored their exiles, and plumed himself on his persuading and reconciling the Greeks more than on his conquest of the Macedonians, so that their freedom presently seemed to them the least of his benefactions. . . .

This coin provides a contemporary profile of Titus Flamininus, which also illustrates Roman realism in portraiture. *(Courtesy of the Trustees of the British Museum)*

. . . In the case of Titus and the Romans, . . . gratitude for their benefactions to the Greeks brought them, not merely praises, but also confidence among all men and power, and justly too. For men not only received the officers appointed by them, but actually sent for them and invited them and put themselves in their hands. And this was true not only of peoples and cities, nay, even kings who had been wronged by other kings fled for refuge into the hands of Roman officials, so that in a short time—and perhaps there was also divine guidance in this—everything became subject to them. But Titus himself took most pride in his liberation of Greece.

Questions for Analysis

1. Did Titus Flamininus really want peace for the Greeks, or was this a cynical propaganda gesture?

2. What caused Greek political difficulties in the first place?

3. Was the Greek response to Titus Flamininus's proclamation genuine and realistic?

Source: Reprinted by permission of the publishers and the Trustees of the Loeb Classical Library from *Plutarch: Volume X—Parallel Lives.* Loeb Classical Library Volume L 102, trans. B. Perrin (Cambridge, Mass.: Harvard University Press, 1921). The Loeb Classical Library® is a registered trademark of the President and Fellows of Harvard College.

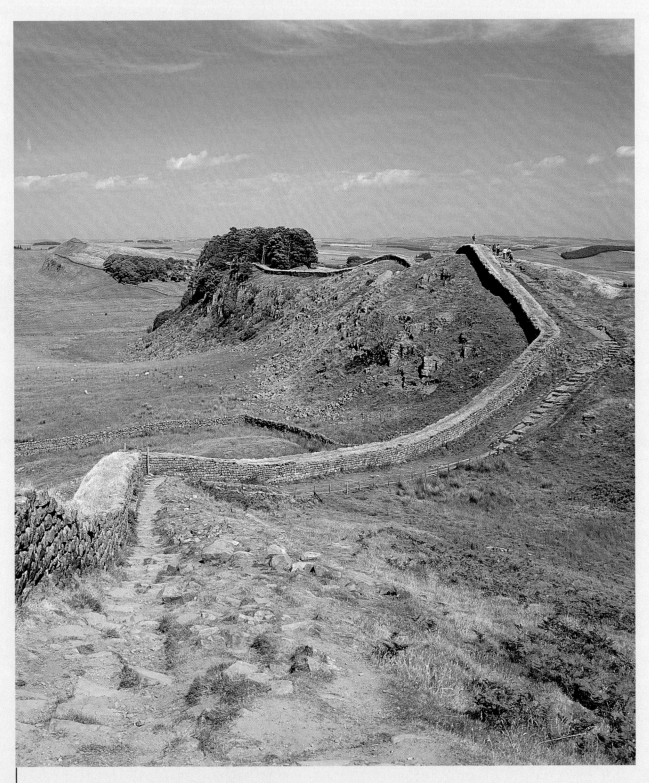

Hadrian's Wall. *(D. J. Ball/Tony Stone Images/Getty Images)*

chapter

6

The Pax Romana

*H*ad the Romans conquered the entire Mediterranean world only to turn it into their battlefield? Would they, like the Greeks before them, become their own worst enemies, destroying one another and wasting their strength until they perished? At Julius Caesar's death in 44 B.C. it must have seemed so to many. Yet finally, in 31 B.C., Augustus restored peace to a tortured world, and with peace came prosperity, new hope, and a new vision of Rome's destiny. The Roman poet Virgil expressed this vision most nobly:

You, Roman, remember—these are your arts:
To rule nations, and to impose the ways of peace,
To spare the humble and to war down the proud.[1]

In place of the republic, Augustus established what can be called a constitutional monarchy. He attempted to achieve lasting cooperation in government and balance among the people, magistrates, senate, and army. His efforts were not always successful. His settlement of Roman affairs did not permanently end civil war. Yet he carried on Caesar's work. It was Augustus who created the structure that the modern world calls the "Roman Empire." He did his work so well and his successors so capably added to it that Rome realized Virgil's hope. For the first and second centuries A.D. the lot of the Mediterranean world was the Roman peace—the **pax Romana,** a period of security, order, harmony, flourishing culture, and expanding economy. It was a period that saw the wilds of Gaul, Spain, Germany, eastern Europe, and western Africa introduced to Greco-Roman culture. By the third century A.D., when the empire began to give way to the medieval world, the greatness of Rome and its culture had left an indelible mark on the ages to come.

- How did the Roman emperors govern the empire, and how did they spread Roman influence into northern Europe?
- What were the fruits of the pax Romana?
- Why did Christianity, originally a minor local religion, sweep across the Roman world to change it fundamentally?
- Finally, how did the Roman Empire meet the grim challenge of barbarian invasion and subsequent economic decline?

These are the main questions we will consider in this chapter.

Augustus's Settlement (31 B.C.–A.D. 14)

When Augustus put an end to the civil wars that had raged since 88 B.C., he faced monumental problems of reconstruction. Sole ruler of the entire Mediterranean world as no Roman had ever been before, he had a rare opportunity to shape the future. But how?

Augustus could easily have declared himself dictator, as Caesar had, but the thought was repugnant to him. Augustus was neither an autocrat nor a revolutionary. His solution, as he put it, was to restore the republic. But was that possible? Some eighteen years of anarchy and civil war had shattered the republican constitution. In stark reality, by Augustus's day no one alive had even lived under the ancestral constitution. The events of the middle republic, the aftermath of the Punic Wars, and the upheavals of the civil wars had dramatically and irreversibly changed it. Nor could it be rebuilt. Augustus recognized these problems but did not let them stop him. From 29 to 23 B.C. he toiled to heal Rome's wounds. The first problem facing him was to rebuild the constitution and the organs of government. Next he had to demobilize much of the army yet maintain enough soldiers in the provinces of the empire to meet the danger of barbarians at Rome's European frontiers. Augustus was highly successful in meeting these challenges. His gift of peace to a war-torn world sowed the seeds of a literary flowering that produced some of the finest fruits of the Roman mind.

The Principate and the Restored Republic

Augustus claimed that in restoring constitutional government he was also restoring the republic. Typically Roman, he preferred not to create anything new; he intended instead to modify republican forms and offices to meet new circumstances. Augustus planned for the senate to take on a serious burden of duty and responsibility. He expected it to administer some of the provinces, continue to be the chief deliberative body of the state, and act as a court of law. Yet he did not give the senate enough power to become his partner in government. As a result, the senate could not live up to the responsibilities that Augustus assigned. Many of its prerogatives shifted to Augustus and his successors by default.

Augustus's own position in the restored republic was something of an anomaly. He could not simply surrender the reins of power, for someone else would only have seized them. But how was he to fit into a republican constitution? Again Augustus had his own answer. He became *princeps civitatis,* "First Citizen of the State." This prestigious title carried no power; it indicated only that Augustus was the most distinguished of all Roman citizens. In effect, it designated Augustus as the first among equals, a little "more equal" than anyone else in the state. Clearly, much of the *principate,* as the period of First Citizen is known, was a legal fiction. Yet that need not imply that Augustus, like a modern dictator, tried to clothe himself with constitutional legitimacy. In an inscription known as *Res Gestae* (The Deeds of Augustus), Augustus described his constitutional position:

In my sixth and seventh consulships [28–27 B.C.], I had ended the civil war, having obtained through universal consent total control of affairs. I transferred the Republic from my power to the authority of the Roman people and the senate. . . . After that time I stood before all in rank, but I had power no greater than those who were my colleagues in any magistracy.[2]

What is to be made of Augustus's constitutional settlement? Despite his claims to the contrary, Augustus had not restored the republic. Augustus had created a **constitutional monarchy,** something completely new in Roman history. The title **princeps,** First Citizen, came to mean in Rome, as it does today, "prince" in the sense of a sovereign ruler.

Augustus was not exactly being a hypocrite, but he carefully kept his real military power in the background. As consul he had no more constitutional and legal power than his fellow consul. Yet in addition to the consulship Augustus had many other magistracies, which his fellow consul did not. Constitutionally, his ascendancy within the state stemmed from the number of magistracies he held and the power granted him by the senate. At first he held the consulship annually; then the senate voted him proconsular power on a regular basis. The senate also voted him *tribunicia potestas*—the "full power of the tribunes." Tribunician power gave Augustus the right to call the senate into session, present legislation to the people, and defend their rights. He held either high office or the powers of chief magistrate year in and year out. No other magistrate could do the same. In 12 B.C. he became *pontifex maximus,* the chief priest of the state. By assuming this position of great honor, Augustus also became chief religious official. Without specifically saying so, he had created the office of emperor, which included many traditional powers separated from their traditional offices.

The main source of Augustus's power was his position as commander of the Roman army. His title **imperator,**

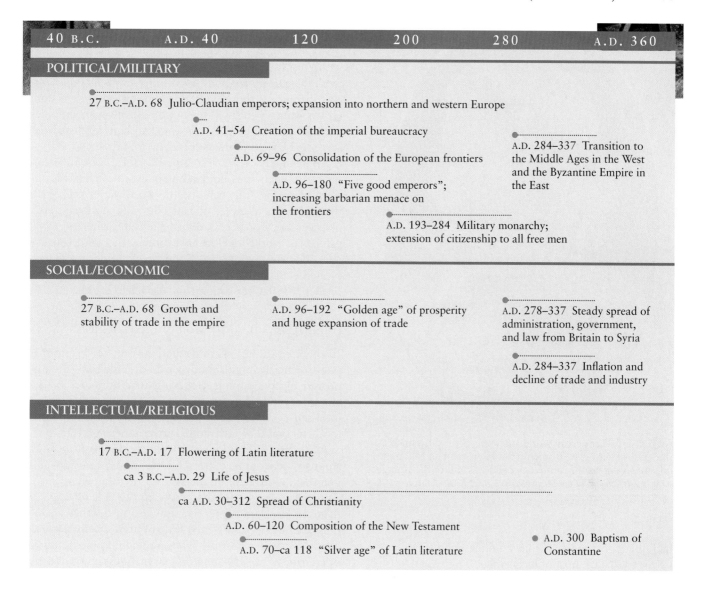

40 B.C.	A.D. 40	120	200	280	A.D. 360

POLITICAL/MILITARY

27 B.C.–A.D. 68 Julio-Claudian emperors; expansion into northern and western Europe

A.D. 41–54 Creation of the imperial bureaucracy

A.D. 69–96 Consolidation of the European frontiers

A.D. 284–337 Transition to the Middle Ages in the West and the Byzantine Empire in the East

A.D. 96–180 "Five good emperors"; increasing barbarian menace on the frontiers

A.D. 193–284 Military monarchy; extension of citizenship to all free men

SOCIAL/ECONOMIC

27 B.C.–A.D. 68 Growth and stability of trade in the empire

A.D. 96–192 "Golden age" of prosperity and huge expansion of trade

A.D. 278–337 Steady spread of administration, government, and law from Britain to Syria

A.D. 284–337 Inflation and decline of trade and industry

INTELLECTUAL/RELIGIOUS

17 B.C.–A.D. 17 Flowering of Latin literature

ca 3 B.C.–A.D. 29 Life of Jesus

ca A.D. 30–312 Spread of Christianity

A.D. 60–120 Composition of the New Testament

A.D. 70–ca 118 "Silver age" of Latin literature

A.D. 300 Baptism of Constantine

with which Rome customarily honored a general after a major victory, came to mean "emperor" in the modern sense of the term. Augustus governed the provinces where troops were needed for defense. The frontiers were his special concern. There Roman legionaries held the German barbarians at arm's length. The frontiers were also areas where fighting could be expected to break out. Augustus made sure that Rome went to war only at his command. He controlled deployment of the Roman army and paid its wages. He granted it bonuses and gave veterans retirement benefits. Thus he avoided the problems with the army that the old senate had created for itself. Augustus never shared control of the army, and no Roman found it easy to defy him militarily.

Augustus made a momentous change in the army by making it a permanent, professional force. This was Rome's first standing army. Soldiers received regular and standard training under career officers who advanced in rank according to experience, ability, valor, and length of service. Legions were transferred from place to place, as the need arose. They had no regular barracks. In later years of the empire soldiers could live with their families in the camps themselves. By making the army professional, Augustus forged a reliable tool for the defense of the empire. The army could also act against the central authority, much as Marius's army had earlier. Yet the mere fact that men could make a career of the army meant that it became a recognized institution of government and that its soldiers

Augustus as Emperor   Augustus appears on this cameo as the ideal leader of the Roman state. He is calm and thoughtful. He also epitomizes the dignity and wealth of the Roman Empire. *(Courtesy of the Trustees of the British Museum)*

had the opportunity to achieve a military effectiveness superior to that of most of its enemies.

The very size of the army was a special problem for Augustus. Rome's legions numbered thousands of men, far more than were necessary to maintain peace. What was Augustus to do with so many soldiers? This sort of problem had constantly plagued the late republic, whose leaders never found a solution. Augustus gave his own answer in the *Res Gestae:* "I founded colonies of soldiers in Africa, Sicily, Macedonia, Spain, Achaea, Gaul, and Pisidia. Moreover, Italy has 28 colonies under my auspices."[3] At least forty new colonies arose, most of them in the western Mediterranean. Augustus's veterans took abroad with them their Latin language and culture. His colonies, like Julius Caesar's, were a significant tool in the spread of Roman culture throughout the West.

Roman colonies were very different from earlier Greek colonies. Greek colonies were independent. Once founded, they went their own way. Roman colonies were part of a system—the Roman Empire—that linked East with West in a mighty political, social, and economic network. The glory of the Roman Empire was its great success in uniting the Mediterranean world and spreading Greco-Roman culture throughout it. Roman colonies played a crucial part in that process, and Augustus deservedly boasted of the colonies he founded.

Augustus, however, also failed to solve a momentous problem. He never found a way to institutionalize his position with the army. The ties between the princeps and the army were always personal. The army was loyal to the princeps but not necessarily to the state. The Augustan principate worked well at first, but by the third century A.D. the army would make and break emperors at will. Nonetheless, it is a measure of Augustus's success that his settlement survived as long and as well as it did.

Augustus's Administration of the Provinces

In the areas under his immediate jurisdiction, Augustus put provincial administration on an ordered basis and improved its functioning. Believing that the cities of the empire should look after their own affairs, he encouraged local self-government and urbanism. Augustus respected local customs and ordered his governors to do the same.

As a spiritual bond between the provinces and Rome, Augustus encouraged the cult of Roma, goddess and guardian of the state. In the Hellenistic East, where kingworship was an established custom, the cult of *Roma et Augustus* grew and spread rapidly. Augustus then introduced it in the West. By the time of his death in A.D. 14, nearly every province in the empire could boast an altar or a shrine to *Roma et Augustus*. In the West it was not the person of the emperor who was worshiped but his *genius*—his guardian spirit. In praying for the good health and welfare of the emperor, Romans and provincials were praying for the empire itself. The cult became a symbol of Roman unity.

Roman Expansion into Northern and Western Europe

For the history of Western civilization one of the most momentous aspects of Augustus's reign was Roman expansion into the wilderness of northern and western Europe (see Map 6.1). In this respect Augustus was following in Julius Caesar's footsteps. Carrying on Caesar's work, Augustus pushed Rome's frontier into the region of modern Germany.

Boscoreale Cup   The central scene lavishly depicted on the side of a silver cup shows Augustus seated in majesty. In his right hand he holds an orb that represents his position as master of the world. The scroll in his left hand symbolizes his authority as lawgiver. On his right is a group of divinities who support his efforts, on his left a group of barbarians who have submitted to Rome. (© Musée du Louvre)

Augustus began his work in the west and north by completing the conquest of Spain. In Gaul, apart from minor campaigns, most of his work was peaceful. He founded twelve new towns, and the Roman road system linked new settlements with one another and with Italy. But the German frontier, along the Rhine River, was the scene of hard fighting. In 12 B.C. Augustus ordered a major invasion of Germany beyond the Rhine. Roman legions advanced to the Elbe River, and a Roman fleet explored the North Sea and Jutland. The area north of the Main River and west of the Elbe was on the point of becoming Roman. But in A.D. 9 Augustus's general Varus lost some twenty thousand troops at the Battle of the Teutoburger Forest. Thereafter the Rhine remained the Roman frontier.

Meanwhile more successful generals extended the Roman standards as far as the Danube. Roman legions penetrated the area of modern Austria, southern Bavaria, and western Hungary. The regions of modern Serbia, Bulgaria, and Romania fell. Within this area the legionaries built fortified camps. Roads linked these camps with one another, and settlements grew up around the camps. Traders began to frequent the frontier and to traffic with the barbarians. Thus Roman culture—the rough-and-ready kind found in military camps—gradually spread into the northern wilderness.

Although this process is most clearly seen in the provincial towns and cities, people in the countryside likewise adopted the aspects of Roman culture that appealed to them. Roman culture was adaptable and convenient, and the Romans did not force it on others. All over the empire native peoples adopted those aspects that fit in with their own ways of life. That much said, ambitious people throughout the empire knew that the surest path to political advancement lay in embracing Roman civilization and culture.

One excellent example of this process comes from the modern French city of Lyons. The site was originally the capital of a native tribe, and after his conquest of Gaul, Caesar made it a Roman military settlement. Augustus took an important step toward Romanization and conciliation in 12 B.C., when he made it a political and religious center, with responsibilities for administering the area and for honoring the gods of the Romans and Gauls. Physical symbols of this fusion of two cultures can still be seen today. For instance, the extensive remains of the amphitheater and other buildings at Lyons testify to the fact that the Gallo-Roman city was prosperous enough to afford expensive Roman buildings and the style of life that

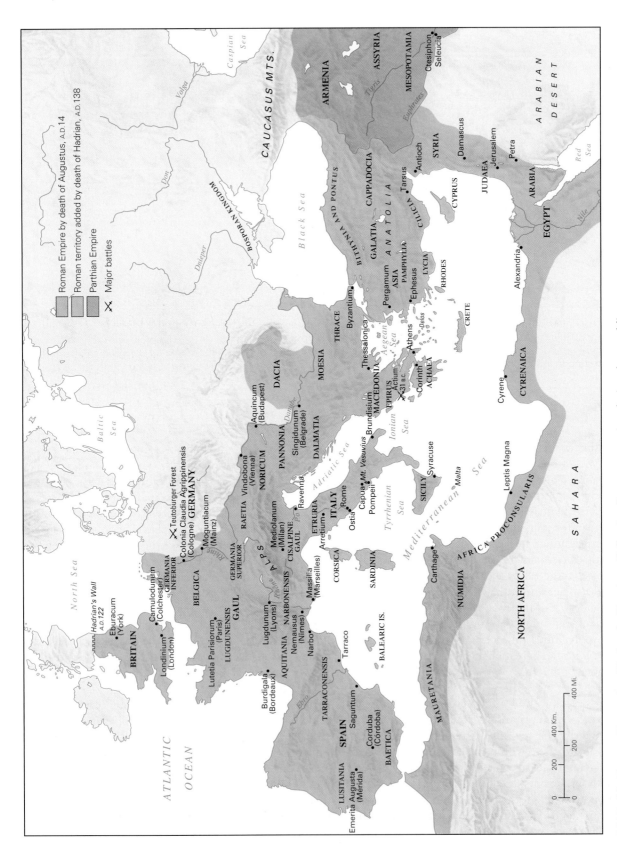

MAP 6.1 Roman Expansion Under the Empire Following Roman expansion during the republic, Augustus added vast tracts of Europe to the Roman Empire, which the emperor Hadrian later enlarged by assuming control over parts of central Europe, the Near East, and North Africa.

they represented. Second, the buildings show that the local population appreciated Roman culture and did not find it alien. At Lyons, as at many other of these new cities, there emerged a culture that was both Roman and native. Many such towns were soon granted Roman citizenship for their embrace of Roman culture and government and their importance to the Roman economy. (See the feature "Listening to the Past: Rome Extends Its Citizenship" on pages 188–189.)

Although Lyons is typical of the success of Romanization in new areas, the arrival of the Romans often provoked resistance from **barbarians,** tribes of peoples who were not Greco-Roman and who simply wanted to be left alone. In other cases the prosperity and wealth of the new Roman towns lured barbarians eager for plunder. The Romans maintained peaceful relations with the barbarians whenever possible, but Roman legions remained on the frontier to repel hostile barbarians. The result was the evolution of a consistent, systematic frontier policy.

Literary Flowering

The Augustan settlement's gift of peace inspired a literary flowering unparalleled in Roman history. With good reason this period is known as the golden age of Latin literature. Augustus and many of his friends actively encouraged poets and writers. Horace, one of Rome's finest poets, offered his own opinion of Augustus and his era:

With Caesar [Augustus] the guardian of the state
Not civil rage nor violence shall drive out peace,
Nor wrath which forges swords
And turns unhappy cities against each other.[4]

These lines are not empty flattery, despite Augustus's support of many contemporary Latin writers. To a generation that had known only vicious civil war, Augustus's settlement was an unbelievable blessing.

The tone and ideal of Roman literature, like that of the Greeks, was humanistic and worldly. Roman poets and prose writers celebrated the dignity of humanity and the range of its accomplishments. They stressed the physical and emotional joys of a comfortable, peaceful life. Their works were highly polished, elegant in style, and intellectual in conception. Roman poets referred to the gods often and treated mythological themes, but always the core of their work was human, not divine.

Virgil (70–19 B.C.), Rome's greatest poet, celebrated the new age in the *Georgics,* a poetic work on agriculture in four books. Virgil delighted in his own farm, and his poems sing of the pleasures of peaceful farm life. The poet also tells how to keep bees, grow grapes and olives, plow, and manage a farm. Throughout the *Georgics* Virgil writes about things he himself has seen, rather than drawing from the writings of others. Virgil could be vivid and graphic as well as pastoral. Even a small event could be a drama for him. The death of a bull while plowing is hardly epic material, yet Virgil captures the sadness of the event in the image of the farmer unyoking the remaining animal:

Look, the bull, shining under the rough plough,
falls to the ground
and vomits from his mouth blood mixed with foam,
and releases his dying groan.
Sadly moves the ploughman, unharnessing the
young steer grieving for the death of his brother
and leaves in the middle of the job
the plough stuck fast.[5]

Virgil's poetry is robust yet graceful. A sensitive man who delighted in simple things, Virgil left in his *Georgics* a charming picture of life in the Italian countryside during a period of peace.

Virgil's masterpiece is the *Aeneid,* an epic poem that is the Latin equivalent of the Greek *Iliad* and *Odyssey.* In the *Aeneid* Virgil expressed his admiration for Augustus's work by celebrating the shining ideal of a world blessed by the pax Romana. Virgil's account of the founding of Rome and the early years of the city gave final form to the legend of Aeneas, the Trojan hero who escaped to Italy at the fall of Troy. The principal Roman tradition held that Romulus was the founder of Rome, but the legend of Aeneas was known as early as the fifth century B.C. Virgil linked the legends of Aeneas and Romulus and preserved them both; in so doing he connected Rome with Greece's heroic past. He also mythologized later aspects of Roman history. Recounting the story of Aeneas and Dido, the queen of Carthage, Virgil made their ill-fated love affair the cause of the Punic Wars. But above all the *Aeneid* is the expression of Virgil's passionate belief in Rome's greatness. It is a vision of Rome as the protector of the good and noble against the forces of darkness and disruption.

The poet Ovid shared Virgil's views of the simple pleasures of life and also celebrated the popular culture of the day. In his *Fasti* (ca A.D. 8) he takes a personal approach to discuss and explain the ordinary festivals of the Roman year, festivals that most Romans took for granted. Without his work the modern world would be much the poorer in its knowledge of the popular religion of imperial Rome. For instance, he tells his readers that on a journey to Rome he encountered a white-robed crowd in the middle of the road. A priest and farmers were performing an annual festival. Ovid stopped to ask the priest

Virgil and the *Aeneid* Virgil's great epic poem, the *Aeneid,* became a literary classic immediately on its appearance and has lost none of its power since. The Roman world honored Virgil for his poetic genius not only by treasuring his work but also by portraying him in art. Here two Muses, who inspired artists, flank the poet while he writes his epic poem. *(C. M. Dixon)*

what was happening. The priest explained that they were sacrificing to Mildew, not a farmer's favorite goddess. By burning the offerings the priest and his friends asked the goddess to be so content with them that she would not attack the crops. He further asked her not to attack the farmers' tools but to be satisfied with swords and other weapons of iron. He reminded her that "there is no need for them; the world lives in peace."[6] In his poetry Ovid, like Virgil, celebrates the pax Romana, while giving a rare glimpse of ordinary Roman life.

In its own way Livy's history of Rome, titled simply *Ab Urbe Condita* (From the Founding of the City), is the prose counterpart of the *Aeneid*. Livy (59 B.C.–A.D. 17) received training in Greek and Latin literature, rhetoric, and philosophy. He even urged the future emperor Claudius to write history. Livy loved and admired the heroes and great deeds of the republic, but he was also a friend of Augustus and a supporter of the principate. He especially approved of Augustus's efforts to restore republican virtues. Livy's history began with the legend of Aeneas and ended with the reign of Augustus. His theme of the republic's greatness fitted admirably with Augustus's program of restoring the republic. Livy's history was colossal, consisting of 142 books, and only a quarter of it still exists. Livy was a sensitive writer and something of a moralist. Like Thucydides, he felt that history should be applied to the present. His history later became one of Rome's legacies to the modern world. During the Renaissance *Ab Urbe Condita* found a warm admirer in the poet Petrarch and left its mark on Machiavelli, who read it avidly.

The poet Horace (65–8 B.C.) rose from humble beginnings to friendship with Augustus. The son of an ex-slave and tax collector, Horace nonetheless received an excellent education. He loved Greek literature and finished his education in Athens. After Augustus's victory he returned to Rome and became Virgil's friend. Horace happily turned his pen to celebrating Rome's newly won

Ara Pacis This scene from the Ara Pacis, the Altar of Peace, celebrates Augustus's restoration of peace and the fruits of peace. Here Mother Earth is depicted with her children. The cow and the sheep under the goddess represent the prosperity brought by peace, especially the agricultural prosperity so highly cherished by Virgil. *(Art Resource, NY)*

peace and prosperity. One of his finest odes commemorates Augustus's victory over Cleopatra at Actium in 31 B.C. Cleopatra is depicted as a frenzied queen, drunk with desire to destroy Rome. Horace saw in Augustus's victory the triumph of West over East, of simplicity over oriental excess. One of the truly moving aspects of Horace's poetry, like Virgil's and Ovid's, is his deep and abiding gratitude for the pax Romana.

The solidity of Augustus's work became obvious at his death in A.D. 14. Since the principate was not technically an office, Augustus could not legally hand it to a successor. Augustus recognized this problem and long before his death had found a way to solve it. He shared his consular and tribunician powers with his adopted son, Tiberius, thus grooming him for the principate. In his will Augustus left most of his vast fortune to Tiberius, and the senate formally requested Tiberius to assume the burdens of the principate. Formalities apart, Augustus had succeeded in creating a dynasty.

The Coming of Christianity

During the reign of the emperor Tiberius (A.D. 14–37), perhaps in A.D. 29, Pontius Pilate, prefect of Judaea, the Roman province created out of the Jewish kingdom of Judah, condemned Jesus of Nazareth to death. At the time a minor event, this has become one of the best-known moments in history. How did these two men come to their historic meeting? The question is not idle, nor the answer simple. The Hellenistic world and Rome were as important as Judaism to Christianity. As seen in Chapter 4, the Hellenistic Greeks provided the entire East with a common language, widely shared literary forms, and a pervasive culture that had for years embraced Judaea. Rome contributed political administration to Hellenistic culture. The mixture was not always harmonious. Some Jews embraced aspects of Greco-Roman culture, while others shunned it. It was a situation common to other parts of the Roman Empire, where people addressed these novel developments in their own ways. In Judaea Roman rule aroused hatred and unrest among some Jews. This climate of hostility affected the lives of all who lived there. It formed the backdrop of Jesus' life, and it had a fundamental impact on his ministry. These factors also ultimately paved the way for Christianity to spread far from its native land to the broader world of the Roman Empire. Without an understanding of this age of anxiety in Judaea, one cannot fully appreciate Jesus and his followers.

Unrest in Judaea

The entry of Rome into Jewish affairs was anything but peaceful. The civil wars that destroyed the republic wasted the prosperity of Judaea and the entire eastern Mediterranean world. Jewish leaders took sides in the fighting, and Judaea suffered its share of ravages and military confiscations. Peace brought little satisfaction to the Jews. Although Augustus treated Judaea generously, the Romans won no popularity by making Herod king of Judaea (ca 37–4 B.C.). King Herod gave Judaea prosperity and security, but the Jews hated his acceptance of Greek culture. He was also a bloodthirsty prince who murdered his own wife and sons. At his death the Jews in Judaea broke out in revolt. For the next ten years Herod's successor waged almost constant war against the rebels. Added to the horrors of civil war were years of crop failure, which caused famine and plague. Men calling themselves prophets proclaimed the end of the world and the coming of the **Messiah,** the savior of Israel.

At length the Romans intervened to restore order. Augustus put Judaea under the charge of a prefect answerable directly to the emperor. Religious matters and local affairs became the responsibility of the *Sanhedrin,* the highest Jewish judicial body. Although many prefects tried to perform their duties scrupulously and conscientiously, many others were rapacious and indifferent to Jewish culture. Often acting from fear rather than cruelty, some prefects fiercely stamped out any signs of popular discontent. Pontius Pilate, prefect from A.D. 26 to 36, is typical of such incompetent officials. Especially hated were the Roman tax collectors, called "publicans," many of whom pitilessly gouged the Jews. *Publicans* and *sinners*—the words became synonymous. Clashes between Roman troops and Jewish guerrillas inflamed the anger of both sides.

Among the Jews two movements spread. First was the rise of the Zealots, extremists who worked and fought to rid Judaea of the Romans. Resolute in their worship of Yahweh, they refused to pay any but the tax levied by the Jewish temple. Their battles with the Roman legionaries were marked by savagery on both sides. As usual the innocent caught in the middle suffered grievously. As Roman policy grew tougher, even moderate Jews began to hate the conquerors. Judaea came more and more to resemble a tinderbox, ready to burst into flames at a single spark.

The second movement was the growth of militant **apocalypticism**—the belief that the coming of the Messiah was near. This belief was an old one among the Jews. But by the first century A.D. it had become more widespread and fervent than ever before. Typical was the Apocalypse of Baruch, which foretold the destruction of the Roman Empire. First would come a period of great tribulation, misery, and injustice. At the worst of the suffering, the Messiah would appear. The Messiah would destroy the Roman legions and all the kingdoms that had ruled Israel. Then the Messiah would inaugurate a period of happiness and plenty for the Jews.

This was no abstract notion among the Jews. As the ravages of war became widespread and conditions worsened, more and more people prophesied the imminent coming of the Messiah. One such was John the Baptist, "the voice of one crying in the wilderness, Prepare ye the way of the lord."[7] Many Jews did just that. The sect described in the Dead Sea Scrolls readied itself for the end of the world. Its members were probably Essenes, and their social organization closely resembled that of early Christians. Members of this group shared possessions, precisely as John the Baptist urged people to do. Yet this sect, unlike the Christians, also made military preparations for the day of the Messiah.

Jewish religious aspirations were only one part of the story. What can be said of the pagan world of Rome and its empire, into which Christianity was shortly to be born? To answer that question one must first explore the spiritual environment of the pagans, many of whom would soon be caught up in the new Christian religion. The term **pagans** refers to all those who believed in the Greco-Roman gods. Paganism at the time of Jesus' birth can be broadly divided into three spheres: the official state religion of Rome, the traditional Roman cults of hearth and countryside, and the new mystery religions that flowed from the Hellenistic East. The official state religion and its cults honored the traditional deities: Jupiter, Juno, Mars, and such newcomers as Isis (see page 114). This very formal religion was conducted on an official level by socially prominent state priests. It was above all a religion of ritual and grand spectacle, but it provided little emotional or spiritual comfort for the people. The state cults were a bond between the gods and the people, a religious contract to ensure the well-being of Rome. Most Romans felt that the official cults must be maintained, despite their lack of spiritual content, simply for the welfare of the state. After all, observance of the traditional official religion had brought Rome victory, empire, security, and wealth.

For emotional and spiritual satisfaction, many Romans observed the old cults of home and countryside, the same cults that had earlier delighted Cato the Elder (see page 137). These traditional cults brought the Romans back in touch with nature and with something elemental to Roman life. Particularly popular was the rustic shrine—often a small building or a sacred tree in an enclosure—to honor the native spirit of the locality. Though familiar and simple, even this traditional religion was not enough for many. They wanted something more personal and immediate. Many common people believed in a supernatural world seen dimly through dreams, magic, miracles, and spells. They wanted some sort of revelation about this supernatural world and security in it after death. Some people turned to astrology in the belief that they could read their destiny in the stars. But that was cold comfort, since they could not change what the stars foretold.

Many people in the Roman Empire found the answer to their need for emotionally satisfying religion and spiritual security in the various Hellenistic mystery cults. Such cults generally provided their adherents with an emotional outlet. For example, the cult of Bacchus was marked by wine drinking and often by drunken frenzy. The cult of the Great Mother, Cybele, was celebrated with emotional and even overwrought processions, and it offered its worshipers the promise of immortality. The appeal of the mystery religions was not simply that they provided emotional release. They gave their adherents what neither the traditional cults nor philosophy could—above all, security. Yet the mystery religions were by nature exclusive, and none was truly international, open to everyone.

The Life and Teachings of Jesus

Into this climate of Roman religious yearning, political severity, fanatical Zealotry, and Messianic hope came Jesus of Nazareth (ca 3 B.C.–A.D. 29). He was raised in Galilee, stronghold of the Zealots. Galilee had been influenced by Hellenism, and most people in the southern part spoke Greek as well as their native language. Through Galilee passed major trade routes, which means that it was hardly a backwater or isolated region. Ideas moved as easily as merchandise along these routes.

Much contemporary scholarship has attempted to understand who Jesus was and what he meant by his teachings. Views vary widely. Some see him as a visionary and a teacher, others as a magician and a prophet, and still others as a rebel and a revolutionary. The search for the historical Jesus is complicated by many factors. One is the difference between history and faith. History relies on proof for its conclusions; faith depends on belief. The burden of history is not only to establish the facts whenever possible but also to interpret them properly. Whether or not historians believe in Jesus' divinity is irrelevant in purely scholarly terms. Their duty is to understand him in his religious, cultural, social, and historical context.

To sort out these various, but not necessarily conflicting, interpretations historians must begin with the sources. The principal evidence for the life and deeds of Jesus is the four Gospels of the New Testament. They are called the canonical Gospels because early Christians accepted them as authentic. These Gospels are neither biographies of Jesus nor histories of his life. They are records of his teachings and religious doctrines with certain details of his life. The aim was to build a community of faith that believed that Jesus represented the culmination of the Messianic tradition. The Gospels were written some seventy-five years after his death, and modern biblical scholars have used literary analysis to detect a number of discrepancies among the four. For that matter, so did ancient writers, both pagan and Christian. These discrepancies are not the result of the authors having had different memories of the events of Jesus' life and mission. Instead, the writers all gave their own theological interpretations of them. As if the topic needs further complication, more gospels existed in antiquity than are now found in the New Testament.

For example, the so-called Lost Gospels contain a huge amount of material on Jesus' life and teachings not found elsewhere. Literary remains of these writings have survived under the names of the apostles Peter and Thomas and Jesus' mother Mary. The discoveries of papyri in Egypt have brought to light many other writings. Early Christian communities cultivated many versions of Jesus' life, many of them contradictory. These are the marks not of heresy but rather of the differences of beliefs among scattered groups of early Christians. They all prove the diversity of early Christian religious thought.

There is no simple solution to this complex historical problem. Perhaps the wisest perspective is that of Helmut Koester, who masterfully evaluates the matter: "In the first century and early second century the number of gospels in circulation must have been much larger, at least

Pontius Pilate and Jesus   This Byzantine mosaic from Ravenna illustrates a dramatic moment in Jesus' trial and crucifixion. Jesus stands accused before Pilate, but Pilate symbolically washes his hands of the whole affair. *(Scala/Art Resource, NY)*

a good dozen of which we at least have some pieces, and everybody could and did rewrite, edit, revise, and combine however he saw fit."[8] That point is at the heart of the textual problems of the tradition of Jesus' life.

What can reasonably be said of Jesus, based on the evidence, is that he preached a heavenly kingdom, one of eternal happiness in a life after death. His teachings were essentially Jewish. His orthodoxy enabled him to preach in the synagogue and the temple. His major deviation from orthodoxy was his insistence that he taught in his own name, not in the name of Yahweh. Was he then the Messiah? A small band of followers thought so, and Jesus claimed that he was. Yet Jesus had his own conception of the Messiah. Unlike the Messiah of the Apocalypse of

Baruch, Jesus would not destroy the Roman Empire. He told his disciples flatly that they were to "render unto Caesar the things that are Caesar's." Jesus would establish a spiritual kingdom, not an earthly one. He told his disciples that his kingdom was "not of this world."

Of Jesus' life and teachings the prefect Pontius Pilate knew little and cared even less. All that concerned him was the maintenance of peace and order. The crowds following Jesus at the time of the Passover, a highly emotional time in the Jewish year, alarmed Pilate, who faced a volatile situation. Some Jews believed that Jesus was the long-awaited Messiah. Others were disappointed because he refused to preach rebellion against Rome. Still others who hated and feared Jesus wanted to be rid of him. The last thing Pilate wanted was a riot on his hands. To avert riot and bloodshed, Pilate condemned Jesus to death. It is a bitter historical irony that such a gentle man died such a cruel death. After being scourged, he was hung from a cross until he died in the sight of family, friends, enemies, and the merely curious.

Once Pilate's soldiers had carried out the sentence, the entire matter seemed to be closed. Yet on the third day after Jesus' crucifixion, an odd rumor began to circulate in Jerusalem. Some of Jesus' followers were saying he had risen from the dead, while others accused them of having stolen his body. For the earliest Christians and for generations to come, the resurrection of Jesus became a central element of faith—and more than that, a promise: Jesus had triumphed over death, and his resurrection promised all Christians immortality. In Jerusalem, meanwhile, the tumult subsided. Jesus' followers lived quietly and peacefully, unmolested by Roman or Jew. Pilate had no quarrel with them, and Judaism already had many minor sects.

The Spread of Christianity

The memory of Jesus and his teachings sturdily survived. Believers in his divinity met in small assemblies or congregations, often in one another's homes, to discuss the meaning of Jesus' message. These meetings always took place outside the synagogue. They included such orthodox Jews as the Pharisees. These earliest Christians were clearly defining their faith to fit the life of Jesus into an orthodox Jewish context. Only later did these congregations evolve into what can be called a church with a formal organization and set of beliefs. One of the first significant events occurred in Jerusalem on the Jewish festival of Pentecost, when Jesus' followers assembled. They were joined by Jews from many parts of the world, including some from as far away as Parthia to the east, Crete to the west, Rome, and Ethiopia. These early followers were Hellenized Jews, many of them rich merchants. They were in an excellent position to spread the word throughout the known world.

The catalyst in the spread of Jesus' teachings and the formation of the Christian church was Paul of Tarsus, a Hellenized Jew who was comfortable in both the Roman and Jewish worlds. He had begun by persecuting the new sect, but on the road to Damascus he was converted to belief in Jesus. He was the single most important figure responsible for changing Christianity from a Jewish sect into a separate religion. Paul was familiar with Greek philosophy, and he had actually discussed the tenets of the new religion with Epicurean and Stoic philosophers in Athens.

Indeed, one of his seminal ideas may have stemmed from the Stoic concept of the unity of mankind. He proclaimed that the mission of Christianity was "to make one of all the folk of men."[9] His vision was to include all the kindred of the earth. That concept meant that he urged the Jews to include non-Jews in the faith. He was the first to voice a universal message of Christianity.

Paul's vision was both bold and successful. When he traveled abroad, he first met with the leaders of the local synagogue, then went among the people. He applied himself especially to the Greco-Romans, whom he did not consider common or unclean because they were not Jews. He went so far as to say that there were no differences between Jews and **Gentiles** (non-Jews), which in orthodox Jewish thought was not only revolutionary but also heresy. Paul found a ready audience among the Gentiles, who converted to the new religion with surprising enthusiasm. A significant part of this process was the acceptance of Gentile women into the faith. The reasons for this were several. First, intermarriage between Greeks and Jews was common. More important, Christianity gave women more rights than they could expect from either paganism or Judaism. For women Christianity was a source of liberation.

Surprisingly the Gentile response pleased the Jews in Jerusalem. The inclusion of Gentiles led to a growing distinction between Christians and Jews. Paul went so far as to say that Christian baptism was different from the Jewish baptism practiced by John the Baptist. The break came when Paul told the Jews that because they would not believe in Jesus' mission to them, he would teach that the salvation of God was sent to the Gentiles, who would listen to the Word. Christianity was no longer a Jewish sect.

Christianity might have remained just another oriental sect until it reached Rome, the capital of the Western world. Contrary to modern notions, the early Christians were generally tolerated. Paganism had room for many religions. Rome proved to be a dramatic step in the spread of Christianity for different reasons. First, Jesus had told his followers to spread his word throughout the world, thus making his teachings universal. The pagan Romans also considered their secular empire universal, and early Christians there combined the two concepts of **universalism.** Nonetheless, Christians always held religion in higher esteem than politics and government, a problem that would relentlessly plague medieval Europe. Secular Rome provided another advantage to Christianity. If all roads led to Rome, they also led outward to the provinces of central and western Europe. The very stability and extent of the Roman Empire enabled early Christians easily

The Catacombs of Rome The early Christians used underground crypts and rock chambers to bury their dead. The bodies were placed in these galleries and then sealed up. The catacombs became places of pilgrimage, and in this way the dead continued to be united with the living. *(Catacombe di Priscilla, Rome/ Scala/Art Resource, NY)*

to spread their faith. Paul himself said of the Christians in Rome (1 Romans 8): "First I thank my God through Jesus Christ for you all, that your faith is spoken of throughout the whole world." The **catacombs** just outside of Rome testify to the vitality of the new religion and pagan toleration of it. Although many people today think of the catacombs, which were large cemeteries, as secret meeting places of oppressed Christians, they were actually huge public underground cemeteries along the famous Via Appia, one of Rome's proudest lanes. From Rome Christianity spread southward to Africa and northward into Europe and across the Channel to Britain.

The catacombs and other archaeological sites provide a concrete idea of how Christianity spread in the West. At first pagan and Christian artistic motifs were common, and in some cases pagan influence proved stronger than Christian. Later tombs, however, were decorated more with biblical scenes. The catacombs eventually became the honored resting places of the early popes and

sites of pilgrimage. Although at first the religious community in Rome was a very important one among many, in the course of time it would become the center of Western Christendom.

The Appeal of Christianity

Christianity appealed to common people and to the poor. Its communal celebration of the Lord's Supper gave men and women a sense of belonging. Christianity also offered its adherents the promise of salvation. Christians believed that Jesus on the cross had defeated evil and that he would reward his followers with eternal life after death. Christianity also offered the possibility of forgiveness. Human nature was weak, and even the best Christians would fall into sin. But Jesus loved sinners and forgave those who repented. In its doctrine of salvation and forgiveness alone, Christianity had a powerful ability to give solace and strength to believers.

Christianity was attractive to many because it gave the Roman world a cause. Instead of passivity, Christianity stressed the ideal of striving for a goal. Every Christian, no matter how poor or humble, supposedly worked to realize the triumph of Christianity on earth. This was God's will, a sacred duty for every Christian. By spreading the word of Christ, Christians played their part in God's plan. No matter how small, the part each Christian played was important. Since this duty was God's will, Christians believed that the goal would be achieved. The Christian was not discouraged by temporary setbacks, believing Christianity to be invincible.

Christianity gave its devotees a sense of community. No Christian was alone. All members of the Christian community strove toward the same goal of fulfilling God's plan. Each individual community was in turn a member of a greater community. And that community, the Church General, was indestructible. After all, Jesus himself had reportedly promised, "Thou art Peter, and upon this rock I will build my church; and the gates of hell shall not prevail against it."[10]

The Julio-Clauians and the Flavians (27 B.C.–A.D. 96)

For fifty years after Augustus's death the dynasty that he established—known as the **Julio-Claudians** because they were all members of the Julian and Claudian clans—provided the emperors of Rome. Some of the Julio-Claudians, such as Tiberius and Claudius, were sound rulers and able administrators. Others, including Caligula and Nero, were weak and frivolous men who exercised their power stupidly and brought misery to the empire. Nonetheless, the Julio-Claudians were responsible for some notable achievements. During their reigns the empire largely prospered.

One of the most momentous achievements of the Julio-Claudians was Claudius's creation of an imperial bureaucracy composed of professional administrators. Even the most energetic emperor could not run the empire alone. The numerous duties and immense responsibilities of the emperor prompted Claudius to delegate power. He began by giving the freedmen of his household official duties, especially in finances. It was a simple, workable system. Claudius knew his ex-slaves well and could discipline them at will. The effect of Claudius's innovations was to enable the emperor to rule the empire more easily and efficiently.

One of the worst defects of Augustus's settlement—the army's ability to interfere in politics—became obvious during the Julio-Claudian period. Augustus had created a special standing force, the Praetorian Guard, as an imperial bodyguard. In A.D. 41 one of the Praetorians murdered Caligula while others hailed Claudius as the emperor. Under the threat of violence, the senate ratified the Praetorians' choice. It was a story repeated frequently. During the first three centuries of the empire, the Praetorian Guard all too often murdered emperors they were supposed to protect and saluted emperors of their own choosing.

In A.D. 68 Nero's inept rule led to military rebellion and his death, thus opening the way to widespread disruption. In A.D. 69, the "Year of the Four Emperors," four men claimed the position of emperor. Roman armies in Gaul, on the Rhine, and in the East marched on Rome to make their commanders emperor. The man who emerged triumphant was Vespasian, commander of the eastern armies, who entered Rome in 70 and restored order. Nonetheless, the Year of the Four Emperors proved that the Augustan settlement had failed to end civil war.

Not a brilliant politician, Vespasian did not institute sweeping reforms, as had Augustus, or solve the problem of the army in politics. To prevent usurpers from claiming the throne, Vespasian designated his sons Titus and Domitian as his successors. By establishing the Flavian dynasty (named after his clan), Vespasian turned the principate into an open and admitted monarchy. He also expanded the emperor's power by increasing the size of the budding bureaucracy Claudius had created.

One of Vespasian's first tasks was to suppress rebellions that had erupted at the end of Nero's reign. The most famous had taken place in Judaea, which still seethed long after Jesus' crucifixion. Long-standing popular unrest and atrocities committed by Jews and Romans alike sparked a massive revolt in A.D. 66. Four years later a Roman army reconquered Judaea and reduced Jerusalem by siege. The Jewish survivors were enslaved, their state destroyed. The mismanagement of Judaea was one of the few—and worst—failures of Roman imperial administration.

The Flavians carried on Augustus's work on the frontiers. Domitian, the last of the Flavians, won additional territory in Germany and consolidated it in two new provinces. He defeated barbarian tribes on the Danube frontier and strengthened that area as well. Even so, Domitian was one of the most hated of Roman emperors because of his cruelty, and he fell victim to an assassin's dagger. Nevertheless, the Flavians had given the Roman world peace and had kept the legions in line. Their work paved the way for the era of the "five good emperors," the golden age of the empire.

Roman History After Augustus

Period	Important Emperors	Significant Events
Julio-Claudians 27 B.C.–A.D. 68	Augustus, 27 B.C.–A.D. 14 Tiberius, 14–37 Caligula, 37–41 Claudius, 41–54 Nero, 54–68	Augustan settlement Beginning of the principate Birth and death of Jesus Expansion into northern and western Europe Creation of the imperial bureaucracy
Year of the Four Emperors 69	Nero Galba Otho Vitellius	Civil war Major breakdown of the concept of the principate
Flavians 69–96	Vespasian, 69–79 Titus, 79–81 Domitian, 81–96	Growing trend toward the concept of monarchy Defense and further consolidation of the European frontiers
Antonines 96–180	Nerva, 96–98 Trajan, 98–117 Hadrian, 117–138 Antoninus Pius, 138–161 Marcus Aurelius, 161–180 Commodus, 180–192	The "golden age"—the era of the "five good emperors" Economic prosperity Trade and growth of cities in northern Europe Beginning of barbarian menace on the frontiers
Severi 193–235	Septimius Severus, 193–211 Caracalla, 198–217 Elagabalus, 218–222 Severus Alexander, 222–235	Military monarchy All free men within the empire given Roman citizenship
"Barracks Emperors" 235–284	Twenty-two emperors in forty-nine years	Civil war Breakdown of the empire Barbarian invasions Severe economic decline
Tetrarchy 284–337	Diocletian, 284–305 Constantine, 306–337	Political recovery Autocracy Legalization of Christianity Transition to the Middle Ages in the West Birth of the Byzantine Empire in the East

The Age of the "Five Good Emperors" (A.D. 96–180)

The Flavians gave way to a remarkable line of emperors, generally known as the **five good emperors,** who ruled the empire wisely, fairly, and humanely. They created an almost unparalleled period of prosperity and peace. Their generally victorious wars were confined to the frontiers, and even the serenity of Augustus's day seemed to pale in comparison. These emperors were among the noblest, most dedicated, and ablest men in Roman history. Yet fundamental political and military changes had taken place since the time of Augustus's rule.

The Antonine Monarchy

Augustus had claimed that his influence arose from the collection of offices the senate had bestowed on him.

The Emperor Marcus Aurelius This equestrian statue, with the emperor greeting his people, represents both the majesty and the peaceful intentions of this emperor and philosopher—one of the five good emperors.
(Erich Lessing/Art Resource, NY)

pire. The easiest and most efficient way to run the Roman Empire was to invest the emperor with vast powers. Furthermore, Roman emperors on the whole proved to be effective rulers and administrators. As capable and efficient emperors took on new tasks and functions, the emperor's hand was felt in more areas of life and government. Increasingly the emperors became the source of all authority and guidance in the empire. The five good emperors were benevolent and exercised their power intelligently, but they were absolute kings all the same. Lesser men would later throw off the façade of constitutionality and use this same power in a despotic fashion.

Typical of the five good emperors is the career of Hadrian, who became emperor in A.D. 117. He was born in Spain, a fact that illustrates the importance of the provinces in Roman politics. Hadrian received his education at Rome and became an ardent admirer of Greek culture. He caught the attention of his elder cousin Trajan, the future emperor, who started him on a military career. At age nineteen Hadrian served on the Danube frontier, where he learned the details of how the Roman army lived and fought and saw for himself the problems of defending the frontiers. When Trajan became emperor in A.D. 98, Hadrian was given important positions in which he learned how to defend and run the empire. At Trajan's death in 117 Hadrian assumed power.

Roman government had changed since Augustus's day. One of the most significant changes was the enormous growth of the imperial bureaucracy created by Claudius. Hadrian reformed this system by putting the bureaucracy on an organized, official basis. He established imperial administrative departments to handle the work formerly done by imperial freedmen. Hadrian also separated civil service from military service. Men with little talent or taste for the army could instead serve the state as administrators. Hadrian's bureaucracy demanded professionalism from its members. Administrators made a career of the civil service. These innovations made for more efficient running of the empire and increased the authority of the emperor—the ruling power of the bureaucracy.

Changes in the Army

The Roman army had also changed since Augustus's time. The Roman legion had once been a mobile unit, but its duties under the empire no longer called for mobility. The successors of Augustus generally called a halt to further conquests. The army was expected to defend what had already been won. Under the Flavian emperors

However, there was in law no such office as emperor. Augustus was merely the First Citizen. Under the Flavians the principate became a full-blown monarchy, and by the time of the Antonines the principate was an office with definite rights, powers, and prerogatives. In the years between Augustus and the Antonines, the emperor had become an indispensable part of the imperial machinery. In short, without the emperor the empire would quickly fall to pieces. Augustus had been monarch in fact but not in theory; during their reigns, the Antonines were monarchs in both.

The five good emperors were not power-hungry autocrats. The concentration of power was the result of em-

MAP 6.2 Roman Britain Though the modern state of Great Britain plays a major role in international affairs, it was a peripheral part of the Roman Empire, a valuable area but nonetheless definitely on the frontier.

(A.D. 69–96) the frontiers became firmly fixed, except for a brief period under Trajan, who attempted to expand the empire. Forts and watch stations guarded the borders. Behind the forts the Romans built a system of roads that allowed the forts to be quickly supplied and reinforced in times of trouble. The army had evolved into a garrison force, with legions guarding specific areas for long periods.

The personnel of the legions was changing, too. Italy could no longer supply all the recruits needed for the army. Increasingly only the officers came from Italy and from the more Romanized provinces. The legionaries were mostly drawn from the less civilized provinces, especially the ones closest to the frontiers. A major trend was already obvious in Hadrian's day: fewer and fewer Roman soldiers were really Roman. In the third century A.D. the barbarization

of the army would result in an army indifferent to Rome and its traditions. In the age of the five good emperors, however, the army was still a source of economic stability and a Romanizing agent (see Map 6.2). Men from the provinces and even barbarians joined the army to learn a trade and to gain Roman citizenship. Even so, the signs were ominous. Veterans from Julius Caesar's campaigns would hardly have recognized Hadrian's troops as Roman legionaries. (See the feature "Individuals in Society: Bithus, a Typical Roman Soldier.")

Life in the "Golden Age"

Many people, both ancient and modern, have considered these years one of the happiest epochs in Western history. But popular accounts have also portrayed Rome as already decadent by the time of the five good emperors. If Rome was decadent, who kept the empire running? For that matter, can life in Rome itself be taken as representative of life in other parts of the empire? Rome was unique and must be seen as such. Surely Rome no more resembled a provincial city like Cologne than New York could possibly resemble Watseka, Illinois. Only when the uniqueness of Rome is understood in its own right can one turn to the provinces to obtain a full and reasonable picture of the empire under the Antonines.

Imperial Rome

Rome was truly an extraordinary city, especially by ancient standards. It was also enormous, with a population somewhere between 500,000 and 750,000. Although it could boast of stately palaces, noble buildings, and beautiful residential areas, most people lived in jerrybuilt apartment houses. Fire and crime were perennial problems, even after Augustus created fire and urban police forces. Streets were narrow and drainage was inadequate. During the republic sanitation had been a common problem. Numerous inscriptions record prohibitions against dumping human refuse and even cadavers on the grounds of sanctuaries and cemeteries. Under the empire this situation improved. By comparison with medieval and early modern European cities, Rome was a healthy enough place to live.

Rome was such a huge city that the surrounding countryside could not feed it. Because of the danger of starvation, the emperor, following republican practice, provided the citizen population with free grain for bread and, later, oil and wine. By feeding the citizenry the emperor prevented

Bithus, a Typical Roman Soldier

Few people think of soldiers as missionaries of culture, but they often are. The culture that they spread is seldom of high intellectual or artistic merit, but they expose others to their own traditions, habits, and ways of thinking. A simple modern example may suffice. In World War II American GIs in Italy taught children there how to play baseball. From their very presence the young Americans taught their Italian friends many other things about the United States and themselves learned a great deal about Italian life and values. Even today a stranger can wander around an Italian town and see the results of this meeting of two cultures.

The same was true of the armies of the Roman Empire. The empire was so vast even by modern standards that soldiers were recruited from all parts of it to serve in distant places. A soldier from Syria might find himself keeping watch on Hadrian's Wall in Britain. He brought with him the ideas and habits of his birthplace and soon realized that others lived life differently. Yet they all lived in the same empire. Despite their ethnic differences, they were united by many commonly shared beliefs and opinions. Although the Roman Empire never became totally Romanized, soldiers, like officials and merchants, played their part in disseminating Roman ideas of government, religion, and way of life.

One such person was the infantryman Bithus, who was a native of Thrace, the modern region of northeastern Greece. His career was eventful but not particularly distinguished. He is, however, typical of many others who also served in the legions. Bithus's military life took him far from his native Thrace. He was stationed largely in Syria, where he mingled with other soldiers from throughout the empire. He came into contact with people from as far west as Gaul and Spain, from western Africa, and from the modern Middle East. Unlike many other cohorts that were shifted periodically, he saw service in one theater. After twenty-five years of duty, he received his reward on November 7, 88. Upon his mustering out of the army, he received the grant of Roman citizenship for himself and his family. In his civilian life the veteran enjoyed a social status that granted him honor and privileges accorded only to Romans. From his military record, there is no reason to conclude that Bithus had even seen Rome, but because of his service to it, he became as much a Roman as anyone born near the Tiber.

The example of Bithus is important because it is typical of thousands of other people who voluntarily

Idealized statue of a Roman soldier.
(Deutsches Archaeologisches Institut, Rome)

supported the empire. One of the rewards of their service was that in the process they learned about the nature of the empire, and they exchanged experiences with other soldiers and the local population that helped shape a sense that the empire was a human as well as a political unit.

Questions for Analysis

1. What did Bithus gain from his twenty-five years of service in the Roman army?
2. What effect did soldiers such as Bithus have on the various parts of the Roman Empire where they served, both in their way of seeing new cultures and in their way of sharing new experiences?

Source: Corpus Inscriptionum Latinarum, vol. 16 (Berlin: G. Reimer, 1882), no. 35.

The **history companion** *features additional information and activities related to this topic.* history.college.hmco.com/students

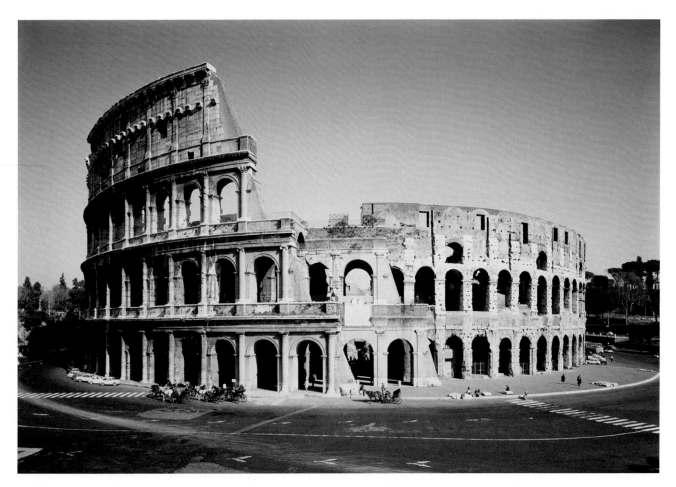

The Coliseum   This splendid building was the site of some of Rome's bloodiest games. In it thousands of spectators viewed gladiatorial games between men, sometimes women, and animals. Yet it stands as a monument to the Roman sense of beauty and architectural skill. *(Scala/Art Resource, NY)*

bread riots caused by shortages and high prices. For the rest of the urban population who did not enjoy the rights of citizenship, the emperor provided grain at low prices. This measure was designed to prevent speculators from forcing up grain prices in times of crisis. By maintaining the grain supply the emperor kept the favor of the people and ensured that Rome's poor and idle did not starve.

The emperor also entertained the Roman populace, often at vast expense. The most popular forms of public entertainment were gladiatorial contests and chariot racing. Gladiatorial fighting was originally an Etruscan funerary custom, a blood sacrifice for the dead. Even a humane man like Hadrian staged extravagant contests. In A.D. 126 he sponsored six days of such combats, during which

1,835 pairs of gladiators dueled, usually with swords and shields. Many **gladiators** were criminals, some of whom were sentenced to be slaughtered in the arena. These convicts were given no defensive weapons and stood little real chance of survival. Other criminals were sentenced to fight in the arena as fully armed gladiators. Some gladiators were the slaves of gladiatorial trainers; others were prisoners of war. Still others were free men who volunteered for the arena. Even women at times engaged in gladiatorial combat. What drove these men and women? Some obviously had no other choice. For a criminal condemned to die, the arena was preferable to the imperial mines, where convicts worked digging ore and died under wretched conditions. At least in the arena the gladiator

Gladiatorial Games Though hardly games, these contests were vastly popular among the Romans. Here two terra cotta figurines forever fight it out to the death. *(Scala/Art Resource, NY)*

might fight well enough to win freedom. Others no doubt fought for the love of danger or for fame. Although some Romans protested gladiatorial fighting, most delighted in it—one of their least attractive sides. Not until the fifth century did Christianity put a stop to it.

The Romans were even more addicted to chariot racing than to gladiatorial shows. Under the empire four permanent teams competed against one another. Each had its own color—red, white, green, or blue. Some Romans claimed that people cared more about their favorite team than about the race itself. Two-horse and four-horse chariots ran a course of seven laps, about five miles. A successful driver could be the hero of the hour. One charioteer, Gaius Appuleius Diocles, raced for twenty-four years. During that time he drove 4,257 starts and won 1,462 of them. His admirers honored him with an inscription that proclaimed him champion of all charioteers.

But people like the charioteer Diocles were not typical of the common Roman. Ordinary Romans were proud of their work and accomplishments, affectionate toward their families and friends, and eager to be remembered after death. They did not spend their lives in idleness, watching gladiators or chariot races; instead, they had to make a living. They dealt with everyday problems and rejoiced over small pleasures.

Rome and the Provinces

The question of how much Roman civilization influenced life in the **provinces** is impossible to answer, but enough evidence survives to indicate a complex development. The problem, as usual, depends primarily on the surviving sources. The rural population throughout the empire left few records, yet the inscriptions that remain point to a melding of cultures. A growing number of inscriptions prove that indigenous peoples and newcomers alike learned at least a smattering of Latin in the West and Greek in the East. They used the official imperial languages largely for legal and state religious purposes. Moreover, knowledge of them enhanced the social and political status of their speakers. They were no longer outsiders. Language provided these people with the tool to take their place in the actual running of the empire. They became bilingual—they spoke their native language and either Latin or Greek. The provincial peoples of the Roman Empire were not linguists, but those in the West were unintentionally creating the Romance family of languages, which includes Spanish, Italian, French, Portuguese, and Romanian. This process was at first more urban than rural, but the importance of cities and towns to the life of the wider countryside ensured that its effects

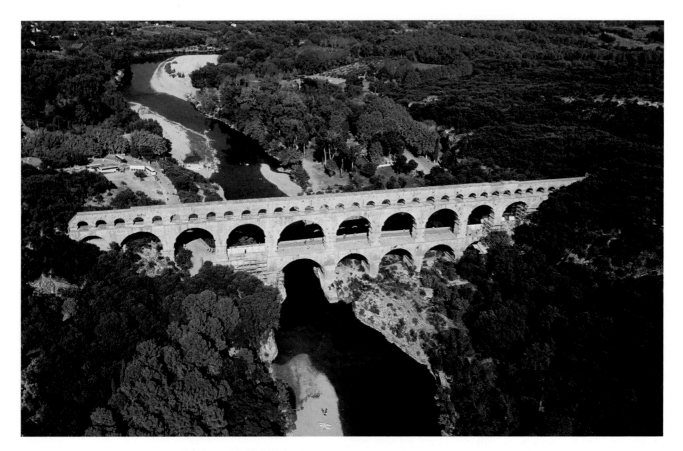

Pont du Gard   Long after the Roman Empire gave way to the medieval world, this aqueduct still stands in France, where until recently it still carried water to Nîmes. The aqueduct is not only a splendid feat of Roman engineering but also a work of art. *(Yann Arthus-Bertrand/Altitude)*

spread far afield. Rather than think in terms of one language and culture dominating another, it is far more accurate to observe the evolution of a new culture, with each existing culture fertilizing others.

A brief survey of the provinces proves the point. For instance, in Gaul country people retained their ancestral gods, and there was not much difference in many parts of the province between the original Celtic villages and their Roman successors. Life along the Rhine River is likewise illustrative of the interaction between natives and newcomers. The distinction came with the growth of Roman military colonies along the river, which fostered a life quite different from that of the countryside around them. On the western bank the villages remained largely Celtic in cultural, social, and political organization. Roman influence in this region lay more in methods of production than in cultural innovations. Yet the very success of Roman merchants transformed the economy of the area.

This region provides an excellent illustration of how Romanization of the provinces actually worked. The Romans provided the capital for commerce, agricultural development of the land, and large-scale building. Roman merchants also became early bankers, who loaned money to the natives and often brought them under financial control. The native inhabitants formed the labor force. They normally lived in villages and huts near the villas of successful merchants. Thus contact between the two groups was generally as much economic as social and cultural. Although Roman ideas spread and there was a good deal of cultural blending, native customs and religions continued to thrive. The Romans also learned about and began to respect native gods. Worship of them became popular among the Romans and the Greeks, which encouraged local peoples to preserve their religions.

The situation on the eastern bank of the Rhine was also typical of life on the borders, but it demonstrates the rawer features of frontier life. To this troubled land the

Romans brought peace and stability, first by building forts and roads and then by opening the rivers to navigation. Around the forts grew native villages, and peace encouraged more intensive cultivation of the soil. The region became more prosperous than ever before, and prosperity attracted Roman settlers. In this rough and often unforeseen manner there developed a pattern of farms and agricultural estates, where Roman veterans mingled with the Celtic aristocracy. The **villa,** a country estate, not the city, was the primary unit of organized political life. This pattern of life differed from that of the Mediterranean, but it prefigured that of the early Middle Ages. The same was true in Britain, where the normal social and economic structures were farms and agricultural villages. (See the feature "Images in Society: The Roman Villa at Chedworth" on pages 176–177.) Very few cities were to be found, and many native Britons were largely ignorant of Greco-Roman culture.

Across eastern Europe the pattern was much the same. In the Alpine provinces north of Italy, Romans and native Celts came into contact in the cities, but native cultures flourished in the countryside. In Illyria and Dalmatia, the regions of modern Albania and the former Yugoslavia, the native population never widely embraced either Roman culture or urban life. Similarly, the Roman soldiers who increasingly settled parts of these lands made little effort to absorb the natives or to Romanize them. To a certain extent Romanization occurred simply because these peoples lived in such close proximity.

The same situation existed in Asia Minor and Africa. The Romans built on earlier Greek achievements, but they apparently never tried to change the lives of the peoples who lived there. They concentrated their attention on the cities, which were the administrative, political, and economic centers of the countryside surrounding them. This was especially true of Syria, Judaea, and Egypt, where life outside the cities proceeded in traditional ways. The Romans, like the Greeks before them, largely ignored Nubia, the homeland of the Ethiopians. The destruction of Ethiopia at the end of the third century was due to its African neighbors, not the Romans.

In western Africa the Romans made a lasting impression on both urban and rural societies. There the large number of colonies of Roman veterans spread their culture over a wider spectrum than elsewhere. Nonetheless, this pattern was largely limited to the new cities established in the region. If western Africa was more Romanized than many other provinces, it was simply because there were more Romans there. The local populace learned to read and write a little Greek and Latin, and probably spoke more, but they never abandoned their traditional ways.

Obviously the Romans went to no great lengths to spread their culture. Their chief aim was political stability. As long as the empire prospered and the revenues reached the imperial coffers, the Romans were willing to live and let live. As a result, Europe fully entered into the economic and cultural life of the Mediterranean world (see Map 6.3).

The age of the five good emperors was generally one of peace, progress, and prosperity. The work of the Romans in northern and western Europe was a permanent contribution to the history of Western society. This period was also one of consolidation. Roads and secure sea-lanes linked the empire in one vast web. The empire had become a commonwealth of cities, and urban life was its hallmark.

Civil Wars and Invasions in the Third Century

The age of the five good emperors gave way to a period of chaos and stress. During the third century A.D. the empire was stunned by civil wars and barbarian invasions. By the time peace was restored, the economy was shattered, cities had shrunk in size, and agriculture was becoming manorial (see page 183). In the disruption of the third century and the reconstruction of the fourth, the medieval world had its origins.

After the death of Marcus Aurelius, the last of the five good emperors, his son Commodus, a man totally unsuited to govern the empire, came to the throne. His misrule led to his murder and a renewal of civil war. After a brief but intense spasm of fighting, the African general Septimius Severus defeated other rival commanders and established the Severan dynasty (A.D. 193–235). Although Septimius Severus was able to stabilize the empire, his successors proved incapable of disciplining the legions. When the last of the Severi was killed by one of his own soldiers, the empire plunged into still another grim, destructive, and this time prolonged round of civil wars.

Over twenty different emperors ascended the throne in the forty-nine years between 235 and 284, and many rebels died in the attempts to seize power. At various times parts of the empire were lost to rebel generals, one of whom, Postumus, set up his own empire in Gaul for about ten years (A.D. 259–269). Yet other men, like the iron-willed Aurelian (A.D. 270–275), dedicated their energies to restoring order. So many military commanders ruled that the middle of the third century has become known as the age of the **barracks emperors.** The Augustan principate had become a military monarchy, and that monarchy was nakedly autocratic.

Images in Society

The Roman Villa at Chedworth

On the European borders of the Roman Empire, the villa was often as important as the town. Indeed, villas sometimes assumed many of the functions of towns. They were economic and social centers from which landlords directed the life of the surrounding countryside. The villa at Chedworth in Roman Britain provides an excellent example of them. The ordinary villa included a large courtyard with barns, gardens, storehouses, and buildings for processing agricultural products and manufacturing goods. The villa also included the comfortable living quarters of the owner. These structures included the usual bedrooms and baths. A small temple or shrine often provided a center for religious devotions. Quarters for servants and slaves were nearby but set apart from the great houses. Equally important were the other buildings that served domestic and light industrial needs. The villa, then, was essentially a small, self-contained community. Yet it was not necessarily isolated. The villa at Chedworth was connected by roads and rivers to other similar neighboring villas. The whole picture depicts a society that, though rural, was nonetheless cultured, comfortable, and in touch with the wider world. A good analogy is the American southern plantation before the Civil War. Like many of these villas, Chedworth survived the demise of the Roman Empire. They all remained to play a crucial role in preserving Greco-Roman civilization in northern Europe.

What did a Roman villa look like, and how can archaeological remains define and explain its functioning? Since few ancient structures remain intact, many must obviously be reconstructed from excavations. Image 1 is the archaeological ground plan of Chedworth. At first it seems to show only a series of foundations. Yet a closer look reveals its design. The large buildings marked 3, 5a, and 5 are the remains of the manorial houses. Rooms 10 through 25a are the bath structures. Number 17 is a small temple. Buildings on the northern side, numbers 26–32, were domestic quarters.

Two questions immediately arise. How do we know what these buildings looked like, and how do we know how they functioned? By analyzing the physical remains and the building techniques of the site, archaeologists and architects have made a patient

Image 1 Ground Plan of the Roman Villa at Chedworth (*From R. Goodburn, The Roman Villa, Chedworth. Reproduced with permission.*)

reconstruction of the entire villa (see Image 2). Artifacts found in the structures reveal their functions. The most obvious example is the elaborate bath complex of numbers 19–25a. Image 3 gives an aerial view of the villa, and Image 4 provides an excellent cameo of the western wing of the villa.

From this information can you determine from the ground plan (Image 1) and the reconstruction (Image 2) what the villa actually looked like? From Image 3, an aerial view of Chedworth, together with

Images 1 and 2, can you locate the landlord's houses, the temple, and the domestic buildings? Now using these three images, can you identify the buildings in Image 4? Lastly, from this material can you imagine the functions of the villa in its environmental and cultural context?

The **history companion** *features additional information and activities related to this topic.* **history.college.hmco.com/students**

178

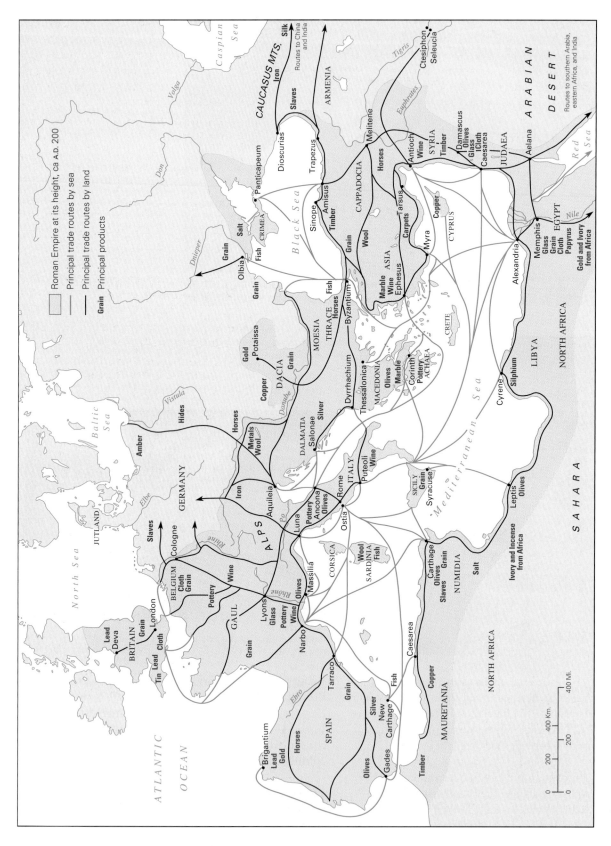

MAP 6.3 The Economic Aspect of the Pax Romana The Roman Empire was not merely a political and military organization but also an intricate economic network through which goods from Armenia and Syria were traded for Western products from as far away as Spain and Britain.

Barbarians on the Frontiers

The first and most disastrous result of the civil wars was trouble on the frontiers. It was Rome's misfortune that this era of anarchy coincided with immense movements of barbarian peoples. Historians still dispute the precise reason for these migrations, though their immediate cause was pressure from tribes moving westward across Asia. In the sixth century A.D. Jordanes, a Christianized Goth, preserved the memory of innumerable wars among the barbarians in his *History of the Goths*. Goths fought Vandals; Huns fought Goths. Steadily the defeated and displaced tribes moved toward the Roman frontiers.

When the barbarians reached the Rhine and Danube frontiers, they often found huge gaps in the Roman defenses. Typical is the case of Decius, a general who guarded the Danube frontier in Dacia (modern Romania). In A.D. 249 he revolted and invaded Italy in an effort to become emperor. Decius left the frontier deserted, and the Goths easily poured through, looking for new homes. During much of the third century A.D., bands of Goths devastated the Balkans as far south as Greece. They even penetrated Asia Minor. The Alamanni, a Germanic people, swept across the Danube. At one point they entered Italy and reached Milan before they were beaten back. Meanwhile the Franks, still another Germanic folk, hit the Rhine frontier. The Franks then invaded eastern and central Gaul and northeastern Spain. Saxons from Scandinavia sailed into the English Channel in search of loot. In the East the Sasanids overran Mesopotamia. If the army had been guarding the borders instead of creating and destroying emperors, none of these invasions would have been possible. The barracks emperors should be credited with one accomplishment, however: they fought barbarians when they were not fighting each other. Only that kept the empire from total ruin.

Turmoil in Farm and Village Life

How did the ordinary people cope with this period of iron and blood? What did it mean to the lives of men and women on farms and in villages? How did local officials continue to serve their emperor and neighbors? Some people became outlaws. Others lived more prosaically. Some voiced their grievances to the emperor, thereby leaving a record of the problems they faced.

In a surprising number of cases barbarians were less of a problem than lawless soldiers, imperial officials, and local agents. For many ordinary people official corruption was the tangible and immediate result of the breakdown of central authority. In one instance some tenant farmers in Lydia (modern Turkey) complained to the emperor about arbitrary arrest and the killing of prisoners. They claimed that police agents had threatened them and prevented them from cultivating the land. Tenant farmers in Phrygia (also in modern Turkey) voiced similar complaints. They suffered extortion at the hands of public officials. Military commanders, soldiers, and imperial agents requisitioned their livestock and compelled the farmers to forced labor. The farmers were becoming impoverished, and many people deserted the land to seek safety elsewhere. The inhabitants of an entire village in Thrace (modern Bulgaria) complained that they were being driven from their homes. From imperial and local officials they suffered insolence and violence. Soldiers demanded to be quartered and given supplies. Many villagers had already abandoned their homes to escape. The remaining villagers warned the emperor that, unless order was restored, they too would flee.

Local officials were sometimes unsympathetic or violent toward farmers and villagers because of their own plight. They were responsible for the collection of imperial revenues. If their area could not meet its tax quota, they paid the deficit from their own pockets. Because the local officials were themselves so hard-pressed, they squeezed whatever they could from the villagers and farmers.

Reconstruction Under Diocletian and Constantine (A.D. 284–337)

At the close of the third century A.D. the emperor Diocletian (r. 284–305) put an end to the period of turmoil. Repairing the damage done in the third century was the major work of the emperor Constantine (r. 306–337) in the fourth. But the price was high.

Under Diocletian, Augustus's polite fiction of the emperor as first among equals gave way to the emperor as absolute autocrat. The princeps became *dominus*—"lord." The emperor claimed that he was "the elect of god"— that he ruled because of divine favor. Constantine even claimed to be the equal of Jesus' first twelve followers. To underline the emperor's exalted position, Diocletian and Constantine adopted the gaudy court ceremonies and trappings of the Persian Empire. People entering the emperor's presence prostrated themselves before him and kissed the hem of his robes. Constantine went so far as to import Persian eunuchs to run the palace. The Roman emperor had become an oriental monarch.

No mere soldier, but rather an adroit administrator, Diocletian gave serious thought to the empire's ailments.

He recognized that the empire and its difficulties had become too great for one man to handle. To solve these problems, Diocletian divided the empire into a western and an eastern half (see Map 6.4). Diocletian assumed direct control of the eastern part; he gave the rule of the western part to a colleague, along with the title **augustus,** which had become synonymous with emperor. Diocletian and his fellow augustus further delegated power by appointing two men to assist them. Each man was given the title of *caesar* to indicate his exalted rank. Although this system is known as the **Tetrarchy** because four men ruled the empire, Diocletian was clearly the senior partner and final source of authority.

Each half of the empire was further split into two prefectures, each governed by a prefect responsible to an augustus. Diocletian reduced the power of the old provincial governors by dividing provinces into smaller units. He organized the prefectures into small administrative units called **dioceses,** which were in turn subdivided into small provinces. Provincial governors were also deprived of their military power, leaving them only civil and administrative duties.

Diocletian's political reforms were a momentous step. The Tetrarchy soon failed, but Diocletian's division of the empire into two parts became permanent. Constantine and later emperors tried hard but unsuccessfully to keep the empire together. Throughout the fourth century A.D. the eastern and the western sections drifted apart. In later centuries the western part witnessed the fall of Roman government and the rise of barbarian kingdoms, while the eastern empire evolved into the majestic Byzantine Empire.

The most serious immediate matters confronting Diocletian and Constantine were economic, social, and

Diocletian's Tetrarchy   The emperor Diocletian's attempt to reform the Roman Empire by dividing rule among four men is represented in this piece of sculpture, which in many features illustrates the transition from ancient to medieval art. Here the four tetrarchs demonstrate their solidarity by clasping one another on the shoulder. Nonetheless each man has his other hand on his sword—a gesture that proved prophetic when Diocletian's reign ended and another struggle for power began. *(Alinari/Art Resource, NY)*

The Arch of Constantine   To celebrate the victory that made him emperor, Constantine built his triumphal arch in Rome. Rather than decorate the arch with the inferior work of his own day, Constantine plundered other Roman monuments, including those of Trajan and Marcus Aurelius. *(C. M. Dixon)*

religious. They needed additional revenues to support the army and the imperial court. Yet the wars and the barbarian invasions had caused widespread destruction and poverty. The fighting had struck a serious blow to Roman agriculture, which the emperors tried to revive. Christianity had become too strong either to ignore or to crush. The responses to these problems by Diocletian, Constantine, and their successors helped create the economic and social patterns that medieval Europe inherited.

Inflation and Taxes

The barracks emperors had dealt with economic hardship by depreciating the currency, cutting the silver content of coins until money was virtually worthless. As a result, the entire monetary system fell into ruin. In Egypt governors had to order bankers to accept imperial money. The immediate result was crippling inflation throughout the empire.

The empire was less capable of recovery than in earlier times. Wars and invasions had disrupted normal commerce and the means of production. Mines were exhausted in the attempt to supply much-needed ores, especially gold and silver. The turmoil had hit the cities especially hard. Markets were disrupted, and travel became dangerous. Craftsmen, artisans, and traders rapidly left devastated regions. The prosperous industry and commerce of Gaul and the Rhineland declined markedly. Those who owed their prosperity to commerce and the needs of urban life likewise suffered. Cities were no longer places where trade and industry thrived. The devastation of the countryside increased the difficulty of feeding and supplying the cities. The destruction was so

MAP 6.4 The Roman World Divided Under Diocletian, the Roman Empire was first divided into a western and an eastern half, a development that foreshadowed the medieval division between the Latin West and the Byzantine East.

extensive that many wondered whether the ravages could be repaired at all.

The response of Diocletian and Constantine to these problems was marked by compulsion, rigidity, and loss of individual freedom. Diocletian's attempt to curb inflation illustrates the methods of absolute monarchy. In a move unprecedented in Roman history, he issued an edict that fixed maximum prices and wages throughout the empire.

The emperors dealt with the tax system just as strictly and inflexibly. As in the past, local officials bore the responsibility of collecting imperial taxes. Constantine made these officials into a hereditary class; son followed father whether he wanted to or not. In this period of severe depression many localities could not pay their taxes. In such cases these local officials had to make up the difference from their own funds. This system soon wiped out a whole class of moderately wealthy people. It was a bad policy for everyone involved.

With the monetary system in ruins, most imperial taxes became payable in kind—that is, in goods or produce instead of money. The major drawback of payment in kind is its demands on transportation. Goods have to be moved from where they are grown or manufactured to where they are needed. Accordingly, the emperors locked into their occupations all those involved in the growing, preparation, and transportation of food and essential commodities. A baker or shipper could not go into any other business, and his son took up the trade at his death. The late Roman Empire had a place for everyone, and everyone had a place.

The Decline of Small Farms

The late Roman heritage to the medieval world is most obvious in agriculture. Because of worsening conditions, free tenant farmers were reduced to serfdom. During the third century A.D. many were killed, fled the land to escape the barbarians, or abandoned farms ravaged in the fighting. Consequently, large tracts of land lay deserted. Great landlords with ample resources began at once to reclaim as much of this land as they could. The huge estates that resulted were the forerunners of medieval manors. Like manors, these villas were self-sufficient. Because they often produced more than they consumed, they successfully competed with the declining cities by selling their surplus in the countryside. They became islands of stability in an unsettled world.

While the villas were growing, the small farmers who remained on the land barely held their own. They were too poor and powerless to stand against the tide of chaos.

They were exposed to the raids of barbarians or brigands and to the tyranny of imperial officials. For relief they turned to the great landlords. After all, the landowners were men of considerable resources, lords in their own right. They were wealthy and had many people working their land. They were independent and capable of defending themselves. If need be, they could—and at times did—field a small force of their own. Already influential, the landowning class united in protest against the demands of imperial officials.

In return for the protection and security landlords could offer, the small landholders gave over their lands. Free men and their families became clients of the landlords and lost much of their freedom. To guarantee a steady supply of labor, the landlords bound them to the soil. They could no longer decide to move elsewhere. Henceforth they and their families worked their patrons' land, not their own. Free men and women were in effect becoming serfs.

The Acceptance of Christianity

In religious affairs Constantine took the decisive step of recognizing Christianity as a legitimate religion. No longer would Christians suffer persecution for their beliefs as they had occasionally experienced earlier. Constantine himself died a Christian in 337. Why had the pagans persecuted Christians in the first place? Polytheism is by nature tolerant of new gods and accommodating in religious matters. Why was Christianity singled out for violence? Such questions as these are still matters of scholarly debate to which some broad answers can be given.

A splendid approach to these problems has come from the eminent Italian scholar Marta Sordi.[11] Confronting a very complicated topic, she distinguishes among many different phases in the relationship between Christianity and official Roman acceptance of it. The Christians exaggerated the degree of pagan hostility to them, and most of the gory stories about the martyrs are fictitious. There were indeed some cases of pagan persecution of the Christians, but with few exceptions they were local and sporadic in nature. Even Nero's notorious persecution was temporary and limited to Rome. No constant persecution of Christians occurred. Instead, pagans and Christians alike enjoyed long periods of tolerance and even friendship. Nonetheless, some pagans thought that Christians were atheists because they scorned the traditional pagan gods. Christians in fact either denied the existence of pagan gods or called them evil spirits. They went so far as to urge people not to worship pagan gods.

Martyrion at Aphrodisias   This trefoil building in Asia Minor is probably the remains of a *martyrion,* or martyrium, a church dedicated to a martyr. Martyrs were people killed for their belief in Jesus' divinity. There were not as many martyrs as Christians claimed, but the Christians considered them all heroes. This church probably honors a martyr now unidentified. *(M. Ali Dogenci, Turkey)*

In turn pagans, who believed in their gods as fervently as the Christians theirs, feared that the gods would withdraw their favor from the Roman Empire because of Christian blasphemy.

At first many pagans genuinely misunderstood Christian practices and rites. Even educated and cultured people like the historian Tacitus opposed Christianity because they saw it as a bizarre new sect. Tacitus believed that Christians hated the whole human race. As a rule early Christians kept to themselves. Romans distrusted and feared their exclusiveness, which seemed unsociable and even subversive. They thought that such secret rites as the Lord's Supper, at which Christians said that they ate and drank the body and blood of Jesus, were acts of

cannibalism. Pagans also thought that Christians indulged in immoral and indecent rituals. They considered Christianity one of the worst of the oriental mystery cults, for one of the hallmarks of many of those cults was disgusting rituals.

Another source of misunderstanding was that the pagans did not demand that Christians *believe* in pagan gods. Greek and Roman religion was never a matter of belief or ethics. It was purely a religion of ritual. Yet Roman religion was inseparable from the state. An attack on one was an attack on the other. The Romans were being no more fanatical or intolerant than the eighteenth-century English judge who declared the Christian religion part of the law of the land. All the pagans expected was performance of the ritual act, a small token of sacrifice. Those Christians who sacrificed went free, no matter what they personally believed.

As time went on, pagan hostility decreased. Pagans realized that Christians were not working to overthrow the state and that Jesus was no rival of Caesar. The emperor Trajan forbade his governors to hunt down Christians. Trajan admitted that he thought Christianity an abomination, but he preferred to leave Christians in peace.

The stress of the third century, however, seemed to some emperors the punishment of the gods. What else could account for such anarchy? With the empire threatened on every side, a few emperors thought that one way to appease the gods was by offering them the proper sacrifices. Such sacrifices would be a sign of loyalty to the empire, a show of Roman solidarity and religious piety. Consequently, a new wave of persecutions began out of desperation. Although the Christians depicted the emperor Diocletian as a fiend, he persecuted them in the hope that gods would restore their blessings on Rome. Yet even these persecutions were never very widespread or long-lived; most pagans were not greatly sympathetic to the new round of persecutions. By the late third century, pagans had become used to Christianity. Constantine's acceptance of Christianity can be seen as the pagans' alliance with the strongest god of them all. Pagan and Christian alike must have been relieved when Constantine legalized the Christian religion.

In time the Christian triumph would be complete. In 380 the emperor Theodosius made Christianity the official religion of the Roman Empire. At that point Christians began to persecute the pagans for their beliefs. History had come full circle.

The Construction of Constantinople

The triumph of Christianity was not the only event that made Constantine's reign a turning point in Roman history. Constantine took the bold step of building a new capital for the empire. Constantinople, the New Rome, was constructed on the site of Byzantium, an old Greek city on the Bosporus. Throughout the third century emperors had found Rome and the West hard to defend. The eastern part of the empire was more easily defensible and escaped the worst of the barbarian devastation. It was wealthy and its urban life still vibrant. Moreover Christianity was more widespread in the East than in the West, and the city of Constantinople was intended to be a Christian center.

From the Classical World to Late Antiquity (ca A.D. 200–700)

Great historical movements always remain the subject of interpretation, controversy, and speculation. One of the most dramatic questions in this regard is whether the Roman Empire ever really fell. Nearly all historians today agree that history, like a river, constantly flows and that all divisions of time are artificial. Historians now realize that the years dividing classical antiquity from the medieval world deserve attention in their own right. This period is justly called "late antiquity," a period not entirely classical yet not quite medieval. It was simultaneously a time of continuity and change.

By about A.D. 500 the Mediterannean was split between the Greek East and the Latin West. Although energetic emperors tried to reunite the old empire, that effort lay beyond their strength. The Roman emperor in Byzantium, renamed Constantinople, ruled the East, and increasingly the Latin West became divided into various small kingdoms. The imperial system of Rome ceased to function efficiently as a unit. The Christian church as a result assumed various secular duties there. Bishops and other church officials in Rome fulfilled their new duties so ably that they enhanced their authority and raised the prestige of their god. As a result, actual power flowed from imperial officials to Christian prelates.

The situation in Roman Gaul can be taken as typical of the new situation in the West. Barbarians held military and political power but lacked the means and knowledge to administer their new domains effectively. They needed well-educated Romans, especially aristocrats, for that. These aristocrats not only possessed the experience to direct society but also held the respect of the native population. The barbarians realized that they needed to acquire the cultural and literary skills that would help them adjust to their new situation. They learned to respect the old society because they saw that destroying it would gain them nothing.

As so often happens in world history, the victors' logical and sensible decision was to adopt the culture of the conquered. The Christian church provided an excellent avenue to advance this goal, for by now many Roman aristocrats were church officials. Many barbarians converted to Christianity and as members of the clergy gained the social prestige and the practical knowledge they needed to win the allegiance of the people and to administer their lives. Western Europe thereby retained Christianity and the barbarians were brought into the fold of

Greco-Roman culture. Although progress in these developments was neither swift nor uniform, they eventually created a Christian Europe led by peoples whose cultural and political connections with the conquered produced a new society. Each side learned from the other, and both sides created a new culture. Late antiquity was a period of transition. The many forces that shaped it gave rise to a vibrant intellectual, spiritual, and political life that forever changed the face of Western civilization.

Summary

The Roman emperors expanded the provincial system established during the republic. They gave it more definite organization, both militarily to defend it and bureaucratically to administer it. The result was the pax Romana, a period of peace and prosperity for the empire. Into this climate came Christianity, which was able to spread throughout the Roman world because peace and security made communication within the empire safe and easy. Christianity satisfied people's emotional and spiritual needs in ways that traditional pagan religions did not. Although other mystery religions existed, they were normally exclusive in one way or another. Christianity was open to all, rich and poor, men and women. Paul of Tarsus was the first of many talented Christians to spread the new religion throughout the receptive world. But that world was disrupted in the third century by a combination of barbarian invasions, civil wars, and economic decline. The bonds that held the empire together weakened, and only the herculean efforts of the emperors Diocletian and Constantine restored order. Those emperors repulsed the barbarians, defeated rebellious generals, and reformed the economy in a restrictive way. The result was an empire very changed from the time of the Augustan peace, but one that left an enduring legacy for later generations.

Key Terms

pax Romana	catacombs
constitutional monarchy	Julio-Claudians
princeps	five good emperors
imperator	gladiators
barbarians	provinces
Messiah	villa
apocalypticism	barracks emperors
pagans	augustus
Gentiles	Tetrarchy
universalism	dioceses

Notes

1. Virgil, *Aeneid* 6.851–853. John Buckler is the translator of all uncited quotations from a foreign language in Chapters 1–6.
2. Augustus, *Res Gestae* 6.34.
3. Ibid., 5.28.
4. Horace, *Odes* 4.15.
5. Virgil, *Georgics* 3.515–519.
6. Ovid, *Fasti* 4.925.
7. Matthew 3:3.
8. Helmut Koester, in *Colloquy on New Testament Studies,* ed. B. Corley (Macon, Ga.: Mercer University Press, 1983), p. 77.
9. Acts 17:26.
10. Matthew 16:18.
11. See Marta Sordi, *The Christians and the Roman Empire* (London: Croom Helm, 1986).

Suggested Reading

Some good general treatments of the empire include J. Wacher, ed., *The Roman World,* 2 vols. (1987), which attempts a comprehensive survey of the Roman Empire, and M. Goodman, *The Roman World, 44 B.C.–A.D. 180* (1997). R. MacMullen, a leading scholar in the field, analyzes how Augustus Romanized the empire in his *Romanization in the Time of Augustus* (2000). Especially welcome is P. S. Wells, *The Barbarians Speak* (1999), which shows that indigenous peoples also helped shape the face of the Roman Empire. D. Noy, *Foreigners at Rome* (2000), studies the minglings of visitors and natives in the city and how tourists and locals affected each other's lives. Through all of these developments stood the Roman aristocracy, the subject of R. Syme, *The Augustan Aristocracy* (1985), which studies the new order that Augustus created to help him administer the empire. Rather than study the Augustan poets individually, see D. A. West and A. J. Woodman, *Poetry and Politics in the Age of Augustus* (1984).

Even though Augustus himself still remains an enigma, F. Millar and E. Segal, eds., *Caesar Augustus: Seven Aspects* (1984), is an interesting volume of essays that attempts, not always successfully, to penetrate the official façade of the emperor. Several books examine the reigns of some supposedly unpopular emperors. D. Shotter, *Tiberius Caesar* (1993), presents the most recent biography of this controversial emperor. Shotter continues his work on the emperors in *Nero* (1997). A. Ferrill does the same for his subject in *Caligula, Emperor of Rome* (1992). B. W. Jones, *The Emperor Domitian* (1992), is an attempt to understand this often hated emperor.

Work on the Roman army remains vibrant. A. Goldsworthy, *Roman Warfare* (2000), provides a concise treatment of warfare from republican to imperial times. D. J. Breeze and B. Dobson, *Roman Officers and Frontiers* (1993), analyzes the careers of officers and how they defended the frontiers.

The commercial life of the empire is the subject of K. Greene, *The Archaeology of the Roman Economy* (1986), which offers an intriguing way to picture the Roman economy through physical remains. The classic treatment, which ranges across the empire, is M. Rostovtzeff, *The Economic and Social History of the Roman Empire* (1957). J. Rich, *The City in Late Antiquity* (1992), traces the influence of late Roman cities on their medieval successors.

Social aspects of the empire are the subject of R. Mac-Mullen, *Roman Social Relations, 50 B.C. to A.D. 284* (1981). Two newer studies shed further light on social history: B. J. Brooten, *Love Between Women* (1996), examines early Christian responses to lesbianism; J. M. C. Toynbee, *Death and Burial in the Roman World* (1996), comprehensively examines all aspects of Roman religious practices and beliefs in an afterlife. D. G. Kyle, *Spectacles of Death in Ancient Rome* (1998), deals in grim detail with the ritualized violence of the gladiatorial games. K. R. Bradley, *Slaves and Masters in the Roman Empire* (1988), discusses the social controls in a slaveholding society. B. Cunliffe, *Greeks, Romans and Barbarians* (1988), uses archaeological and literary evidence to discuss the introduction of Greco-Roman culture into western Europe, while N. Pollard, *Soldiers, Cities, and Civilians in Roman Syria* (2000), gives a good case study of a part of the Eastern world.

A veritable explosion has taken place in the related topics of the identity of Jesus, the history of Christianity, its relationship to contemporary Judaism, and the role that paganism played in these developments. J. Meier, *A Marginal Jew* (1992), and P. Fredriksen, *From Jesus to Christ* (1988), study the images of Jesus in the New Testament. B. W. Winter, *After Paul Left Corinth* (2001), treats Paul's missionary work in the Roman world. M. Humphries, *Communities of the Blessed* (2000), covers the social environment and growth of Christianity in northern Italy from A.D. 200 to 400—a good case study. Two new studies examine the world of the catacombs: I. D. Portella, *Subterranean Rome* (1999), deals with a host of underground monuments; L. V. Rutgers, *Subterranean Rome* (2000), serves as a guide to the catacombs. Both are richly illustrated. Social history of early Christianity includes H. Y. Gamble, *Books and Readers in the Early Christian Church* (1995), and K. Haines-Eitzen, *Guardians of Letters* (2000), which demonstrate the power of the pen in the transmission of early Christian literature. All of the following works study how Roman aristocrats influenced both the barbarians and the development of Christianity in the West: G. W. Bowersock et al., eds., *Late Antiquity* (1999); M. R. Salzman, *The Making of a Christian Aristocracy* (2002); and T. S. Burns, *Rome and the Barbarians, 100 B.C.–A.D. 400* (2003). New approaches to early Christian society include H. Moxnes, ed., *Constructing Early Christian Families* (1997), and D. F. Sawyer, *Women and Religion in the First Christian Centuries* (1996).

Listening to the Past

Rome Extends Its Citizenship

One of the most dramatic achievements of the pax Romana was the extension of citizenship throughout the Roman Empire. People who had never visited Rome, and perhaps had never even seen a provincial governor, became members, not subjects, of their government. By granting citizenship to most people in the empire, the Roman government in effect took them into partnership.

Yet various emperors went even further by viewing Rome not only as a territorial but also as a political concept. In their eyes Rome was a place and an idea. Not every Roman agreed with these cosmopolitan views. The emperor Claudius (41–54) took the first major step in this direction by allowing Romanized Gauls to sit in the senate. He was roundly criticized by some Romans, but in the damaged stone inscription that follows, he presents his own defense.

Surely both my great-uncle, the deified Augustus, and my uncle, Tiberius Caesar, were following a new practice when they desired that all the flower of the colonies and the municipalities every-where—that is, the better class and the wealthy men—should sit in this senate house. You ask me: Is not an Italian senator preferable to a provincial? I shall reveal to you in detail my views on this matter when I come to obtain approval for this part of my censorship [a magistracy that determined who was eligible for citizenship and public offices]. But I think that not even provincials ought to be excluded, provided that they can add distinction to this senate house.

Look at that most distinguished and most flourishing colony of Vienna [the modern Vienne in France], how long a time already it is that it has furnished senators to this house! From that colony comes that ornament of the equestrian

order—and there are few to equal him—Lucius Vestinus, whom I cherish most intimately and whom at this very time I employ in my affairs. And it is my desire that his children may enjoy the first step in the priesthoods, so as to advance afterwards, as they grow older, to further honors in their rank. . . . I can say the same of his brother, who because of this wretched and most shameful circumstance cannot be a useful senator for you.

The time has now come, Tiberius Caesar Germanicus [Claudius himself], now that you have reached the farthest boundaries of Narbonese Gaul, for you to unveil to the members of the senate the import of your address. All these distinguished youths whom I gaze upon will no more give us cause for regret if they become senators than does my friend Persicus, a man of most noble ancestry, have cause for regret when he reads among the portraits of his ancestors the name Allobrogicus. But if you agree that these things are so, what more do you want, when I point out to you this single fact, that the territory beyond the boundaries of Narbonese Gaul already sends you senators, since we have men of our order from Lyons and have no cause for regret. It is indeed with hesitation, members of the senate, that I have gone outside the borders of the provinces with which you are accustomed and familiar, but I must now plead openly the cause of Gallia Comata [a region in modern France]. And if anyone, in this connection, has in mind that these people engaged the deified Julius in war for ten years, let him set against that the unshakable loyalty and obedience of a hundred years, tested to the full in many of our crises. When my father Drusus was subduing Germany, it was they who by their tranquility afforded him a safe and securely peaceful rear, even at a time when he had been summoned away to the war from the task of organizing the census which was still new and unaccustomed to the Gauls. How difficult such an operation is for us at this precise moment we are learning all too well from experience, even though the survey is aimed at nothing more than an official record of our resources. [The rest of the inscription is lost.]

Only later, in A.D. 212, did the emperor Caracalla (198–217) extend Roman citizenship to all freeborn men with the exception of those called dediticii, *whose identity remains a source of controversy. Caracalla claimed that he made this proclamation because the gods had saved him from a plot on his life. Some modern scholars, however, have suggested that he wanted more citizens to tax. Whatever the truth, Caracalla continued the work of Augustus (27 B.C.–A.D. 14) and Claudius. The Romans succeeded where the Greeks had failed: they built an empire of citizens. The following is a damaged copy of Caracalla's edict.*

The Emperor Caesar Marcus Aurelius Serverus Antoninus Augustus [Caracalla] declares: . . . I may show my gratitude to the immortal gods for preserving me in such [circumstances?]. Therefore I consider that in this way I can . . . rend proper service to their majesty . . . by bringing with me to the worship [?] of the gods all who enter into the number of my people. Accordingly, I grant Roman citizenship to all aliens, throughout the world, with no one remaining outside the citizen bodies except the *dediticii*. For it is proper that the multitude should not only help carry [?] all the burdens but should also now be included in my victory.

Citizenship was often granted to soldiers who had fought in the Roman army. The usual reasons were conspicuous bravery or wounds suffered in the course of duty. The emperor Trajan (98–117) made such a grant of citizenship in 106 to British soldiers who had served in the campaign in Dacia, a southern region of the former Yugoslavia. These men were also honored for their valor with an early discharge.

The Emperor Trajan . . . has granted Roman citizenship before completion of military service to the infantrymen and cavalrymen whose names appear below, serving in the First British

Provocatio, the right of appeal, was considered a fundamental element of Roman citizenship. (*Courtesy of the Trustees of the British Museum*)

Thousand-Man Ulpian Decorated Loyal Fortunate Cohort composed of Roman citizens, which is on duty in Dacia under Decimus Terentius Scaurianus, for having dutifully and faithfully discharged the Dacian campaign.

Questions for Analysis

1. What was the basic justification underlying Claudius's decision to allow Gallic nobles to sit in the senate? Did he see them as debasing the quality of the senate?

2. What do his words tell us about the changing nature of the Roman Empire?

3. What was the significance of Caracalla's extension of Roman citizenship to all freeborn men?

4. Notice that the Roman government did not extend citizenship to women. Speculate about the practical and ideological reasons for women's exclusion from political power.

Source: Slightly adapted and abbreviated from N. Lewis and M. Reinhold, *Roman Civilization*, 2 vols. Copyright © 1966 by Columbia University Press, New York. Reprinted with permission of the publisher.

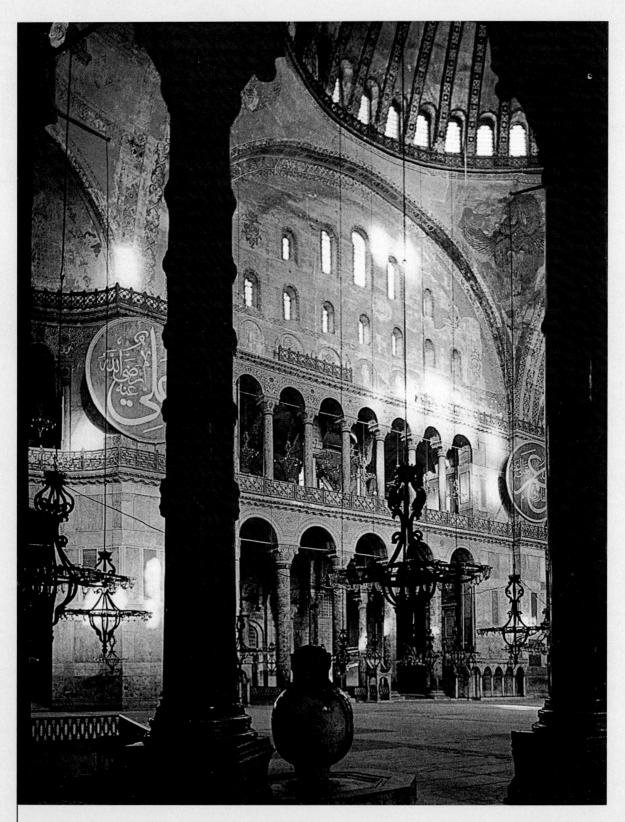

Sancta Sophia ("Holy Wisdom") remains Emperor Justinian's great masterpiece. After the Ottoman conquest in 1453, the Turks replaced Christian symbols with imperial Islamic insignia. *(Sadea Editore)*

chapter

7

The Making of Europe

*T*he centuries between approximately 400 and 900 present a paradox. On the one hand, they witnessed the disintegration of the western Roman Empire, which had been one of humanity's great political and cultural achievements. On the other hand, these five centuries were a creative and seminal period, during which Europeans laid the foundations for medieval and modern Europe. It is not too much to say that this period saw the making of Europe.

The idea of Europe—with the geographical and cultural implications that we in the early twenty-first century attach to the word—is actually a fairly recent notion. Classical geographers used the term *Europe* to distinguish it from Africa and Asia, the only other landmasses they knew, and medieval scholars imitated and followed the ancients. Only in the sixteenth century did the word *Europe* enter the common language of educated peoples living in the western parts of the European landmass and did the continent we call Europe gain a map-based frame of reference.[1] The vision of almost everyone else was provincial, limited by the boundaries of their province or even village. While the peoples living there did not define themselves as European for centuries, a European identity began to be forged in late antiquity and the early medieval period.

The basic ingredients that went into the making of a distinctly European civilization were the cultural legacy of Greece and Rome, the customs and traditions of the Germanic peoples, and the Christian faith. The most important of these was Christianity, because it absorbed and assimilated the other two. It reinterpreted the classics in a Christian sense. It instructed the Germanic peoples and gave them new ideals of living and social behavior. Christianity became the cement that held European society together. One of the burdens of this chapter is to explore how people's understanding of themselves shifted from a social or political one (Germanic or Celtic tribal, Roman citizen) to a religious one.

During this period, the Byzantine Empire, centered at Constantinople, served as a protective buffer between Europe and peoples to the east. The Byzantine Greeks preserved the philosophical and scientific texts of the ancient world, which later formed the basis for study in science and medicine, and produced a great synthesis of Roman law, the Justinian *Code*. In the urbane and sophisticated life led at Constantinople, the Greeks set a standard far above the primitive existence of the West.

In the seventh and eighth centuries, Arabic culture spread around the southern fringes of Europe—to Spain, Sicily, and North Africa, and to Syria, Palestine, and Egypt. The Arabs translated the works of such Greek thinkers as Euclid, Hippocrates, and Galen and made important contributions in mathematics, astronomy, and physics. In Arabic translation, Greek texts trickled to the West, and most later European scientific study rested on the Arabic work.

The civilization later described as European resulted from the fusion of the Greco-Roman heritage, Germanic traditions, the Christian faith, and significant elements of Islamic culture.

- How did these components act on one another?
- How did they lead to the making of Europe?
- What influence did the Byzantine and Islamic cultures have on the making of Europe?

These are some of the questions that will be explored in this chapter.

The Growth of the Christian Church

Although Christianity had explicit requirements and preached a kind of egalitarianism, in doctrine Christianity was a **syncretic faith**—that is, it absorbed and adopted many of the religious ideas of the eastern Mediterranean world. From Judaism came the concept, unique in the ancient world, of monotheism, belief in one God, together with the rich ethical and moral precepts of the Old Testament Scriptures. From Orphism, a set of sixth-century B.C. religious ideas, came the belief that the body is the prison of the soul. From Hellenistic thought derived the notion of the superiority of spirit over matter. Likewise, scholars have noticed the similarity between the career of Jesus and that of the gods of Eastern mystery cults such as Mithra, who died and rose from the dead and whose followers had a ceremony of communion in which the god's flesh was symbolically eaten. All of these ideas played a part in the formulation of Christian doctrine and in attracting people to it.

While many elements of the Roman Empire disintegrated, the Christian church survived and grew. What is the church? Scriptural scholars tell us that the earliest use of the word *church,* meaning assembly or congregation (in Greek, *ekklesia*), in the New Testament appears in Saint Paul's Letter to the Christians of Thessalonica in northern Greece, written about A.D. 51. By *ekklesia* Paul meant the local community of Christian believers. In Paul's later letters, the term *church* refers to the entire Mediterranean-wide assembly of Jesus' followers. After the legalization of Christianity by the emperor Constantine (see page 183) and the growth of institutional offices and officials, the word *church* was sometimes applied to those officials—much as we use the terms *the college* or *the university* when referring to academic administrators.

In early Christian communities, the local people elected their leaders, or bishops. Bishops were men with reputations for having a special spiritual charisma or with acknowledged administrative ability, learning, or preaching skills. Bishops had responsibility for the community's goods and oversaw the distribution of those goods to the poor. They also were responsible for maintaining orthodox (established or correct) doctrine within the community and for preaching. Bishops alone could confirm believers in their faith and ordain men as priests.

The bishops of Rome used the text known as the Petrine Doctrine (see page 194) to support their assertions of authority over the bishops in the church. Thus the popes maintained that they represented "the church." The word *church,* therefore, has several connotations. Although modern Catholic theology frequently defines the church as "the people of God" and identifies it with local and international Christian communities, in the Middle Ages the institutional and monarchical interpretations tended to be stressed.

Having gained the support of the fourth-century emperors, the church gradually adopted the Roman system of organization. Christianity had a dynamic missionary policy, and the church slowly succeeded in assimilating—that is, adapting—pagan peoples, both Germans and Romans, to Christian teaching. Moreover, the church possessed able administrators and leaders and highly literate and creative thinkers. These factors help to explain the survival and growth of the Christian church in the face of repeated Germanic invasions.

The Church and the Roman Emperors

The church benefited considerably from the emperors' support. In return, the emperors expected the support of the Christian church in maintaining order and unity. Constantine had legalized the practice of Christianity within the empire in 312 and encouraged it throughout his reign. He freed the clergy from imperial taxation. At churchmen's request, he helped settle theological disputes and thus preserved doctrinal unity within the church. Constantine generously endowed the building of

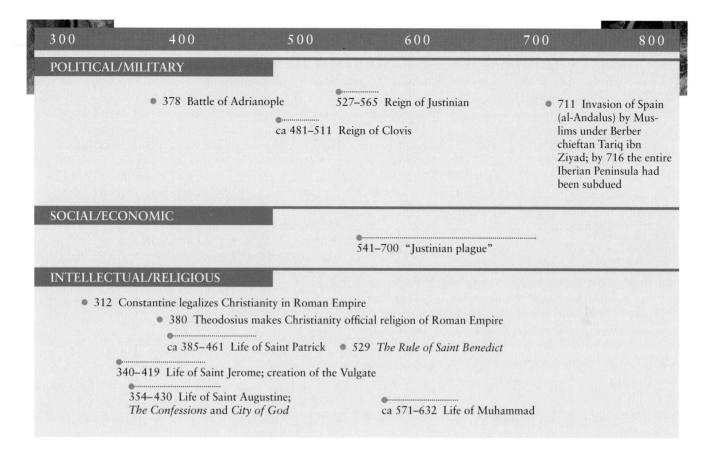

300	400	500	600	700	800

POLITICAL/MILITARY

- 378 Battle of Adrianople
- 527–565 Reign of Justinian
- ca 481–511 Reign of Clovis
- 711 Invasion of Spain (al-Andalus) by Muslims under Berber chieftan Tariq ibn Ziyad; by 716 the entire Iberian Peninsula had been subdued

SOCIAL/ECONOMIC

- 541–700 "Justinian plague"

INTELLECTUAL/RELIGIOUS

- 312 Constantine legalizes Christianity in Roman Empire
- 380 Theodosius makes Christianity official religion of Roman Empire
- ca 385–461 Life of Saint Patrick
- 529 *The Rule of Saint Benedict*
- 340–419 Life of Saint Jerome; creation of the Vulgate
- 354–430 Life of Saint Augustine; *The Confessions* and *City of God*
- ca 571–632 Life of Muhammad

Christian churches, and one of his gifts—the Lateran Palace in Rome—remained the official residence of the popes until the fourteenth century. Constantine also declared Sunday a public holiday, a day of rest for the service of God. As the result of its favored position in the empire, Christianity slowly became the leading religion.

In 380 the emperor Theodosius made Christianity the official religion of the empire. Theodosius stripped Roman pagan temples of statues, made the practice of the old Roman state religion a treasonable offense, and persecuted Christians who dissented from orthodox doctrine. Most significant, he allowed the church to establish its own courts with their own body of law, called "canon law." These courts, not the Roman government, had jurisdiction over the clergy and ecclesiastical disputes. At the death of Theodosius, the Christian church was considerably independent of the Roman state. The foundation for the medieval church's power had been laid.

What was to be the church's relationship to secular powers? How was the Christian to render unto Caesar the things that were Caesar's while returning to God what was due to God? This problem had troubled the earliest disciples of Christ. The toleration of Christianity

and the coming to power of Christian emperors in the fourth century did not make it any easier.

In the fourth century, theological disputes frequently and sharply divided the Christian community. Some disagreements had to do with the nature of Christ. For example, **Arianism,** which originated with Arius (ca 250–336), a priest of Alexandria, denied that Christ was divine and co-eternal with God the Father—two propositions of orthodox Christian belief. Arius held that God the Father was by definition uncreated and unchangeable. Jesus, however, was born of Mary, grew in wisdom, and suffered punishment and death. Therefore, Arius reasoned, Jesus the Son must be less or inferior to the Unbegotten Father, who was incapable of suffering and did not die. Jesus was created by the will of the Father and thus was not co-eternal with the Father. Orthodox theologians branded Arius's position a heresy—the denial of a basic doctrine of faith.

Arianism enjoyed such popularity and provoked such controversy that Constantine, to whom religious disagreement meant civil disorder, interceded. He summoned a council of church leaders to Nicaea in Asia Minor and presided over it personally. The council produced the

Nicene Creed, which defined the orthodox position that Christ is "eternally begotten of the Father" and of the same substance as the Father. Arius and those who refused to accept the creed were banished, the first case of civil punishment for heresy. This participation of the emperor in a theological dispute within the church paved the way for later emperors to do the same.

So active was the emperor Theodosius's participation in church matters that he was eventually at loggerheads with Bishop Ambrose of Milan (339–397). Theodosius ordered Ambrose to hand over his cathedral church to the emperor. Ambrose's response had important consequences for the future:

At length came the command, "Deliver up the Basilica"; I reply, "It is not lawful for us to deliver it up, nor for your Majesty to receive it. By no law can you violate the house of a private man, and do you think that the house of God may be taken away? . . . But do not burden your conscience with the thought that you have any right as Emperor over sacred things. . . . It is written, God's to God and Caesar's to Caesar. The palace is the Emperor's, the churches are the Bishop's. To you is committed jurisdiction over public, not over sacred buildings."[2]

Ambrose's statement was to serve as the cornerstone of the Christian theory of civil-ecclesiastical relations throughout the Middle Ages. Ambrose insisted that the church was independent of the state's jurisdiction and that, in matters relating to the faith or the church, the bishops were to be the judges of emperors, not the other way around. In a Christian society, harmony and peace depended on agreement between the bishop and the secular ruler. But if disagreement developed, the church was ultimately the superior power because the church was responsible for the salvation of all (including the emperor). In a letter to the emperor Anastasius I, Pope Gelasius I (492–496) put this idea another way. Gelasius stated that both authorities, the civil and the religious, were created by God and essential to a well-ordered Christian society. Each was supreme in its own domain—the church in the spiritual, the civil in the secular—and cooperation in building a Christian society was their mutual responsibility. In later centuries, theologians, canonists, and propagandists repeatedly cited Ambrose's and Gelasius's position as the basis of relations between the two powers.

Inspired Leadership

The early Christian church benefited from the brilliant administrative abilities of some church leaders and from identification of the authority and dignity of the bishop of Rome with the imperial traditions of the city. With the empire in decay, educated people joined and worked for the church in the belief that it was the one institution able to provide leadership. Bishop Ambrose, for example, the son of the Roman prefect of Gaul, was a trained lawyer and governor of a province. He is typical of those Roman aristocrats who held high public office, were converted to Christianity, and subsequently became bishops. Such men later provided social continuity from Roman to Germanic rule. As bishop of Milan, Ambrose himself exercised responsibility in the temporal as well as the ecclesiastical affairs of northern Italy.

During the reign of Diocletian (284–305), the Roman Empire had been divided for administrative purposes into geographical units called dioceses. Gradually the church made use of this organizational structure. Christian bishops established their headquarters, or sees, in the urban centers of the old Roman dioceses. Their jurisdiction extended throughout the diocese. The center of the bishop's authority was his cathedral (from the Latin *cathedra*, meaning "chair"). Thus church leaders capitalized on the Roman imperial method of organization and adapted it to ecclesiastical purposes. The bishops of Rome—known as "popes," from the Latin word *papa*, meaning "father"—claimed to speak and act as the source of unity for all Christians. The popes claimed to be the successors of Saint Peter and heirs to his authority as chief of the apostles, on the basis of Jesus' words:

You are Peter, and on this rock I will build my church, and the jaws of death shall not prevail against it. I will entrust to you the keys of the kingdom of heaven. Whatever you declare bound on earth shall be bound in heaven; whatever you declare loosed on earth shall be loosed in heaven.[3]

Theologians call this statement the **Petrine Doctrine**.

After the removal of the capital and the emperor to Constantinople (see page 185), the bishop of Rome exercised considerable influence in the West because he had no real competitor there. The bishops of Rome stressed that Rome had been the capital of a worldwide empire and emphasized the special importance of Rome in the framework of that empire. Successive bishops of Rome reminded Christians in other parts of the world that Rome was the burial place of Saint Peter and Saint Paul. Moreover, according to tradition, Saint Peter, the chief of Christ's first twelve followers, had lived and been executed in Rome. No other city in the world could make such claims. Hence the bishop of Rome was called "Patriarch of the West." In the East, the bishops of Antioch, Alexandria, Jerusalem, and Constantinople, because of the special dignity of their sees, also gained the title of patriarch. Their jurisdictions extended over lands adjoining their sees; they consecrated bishops, investigated heresy, and heard judicial appeals.

In the fifth century, the bishops of Rome began to stress their supremacy over other Christian communities and to urge other churches to appeal to Rome for the resolution of disputed doctrinal issues. Thus Pope Innocent I (401–417) wrote to the bishops of Africa:

We approve your action in following the principle that nothing which was done even in the most remote and distant provinces should be taken as finally settled unless it came to the notice of this See, that any just pronouncement might be confirmed by all the authority of this See.[4]

The prestige of Rome and the church as a whole was also enhanced by the courage and leadership of the Roman bishops. As described in Chapter 6 (see page 185), church officials played important roles in addressing civil problems previously handled by Roman imperial authorities. The fact that it was Christian leaders, rather than imperial administrators, who responded to dire urban needs could not help but increase the prestige and influence of the church.

Although Popes Innocent I and Leo I (440–461) strongly asserted the primacy of the Roman papacy, local Christian communities and their leaders often exercised authority over their churches. Particular social and political situations determined the actual power of the bishop of Rome in a given circumstance. The importance of arguments for the Roman primacy rests in the fact that they served as precedents for later appeals.

Missionary Activity

The word *catholic* derives from a Greek word meaning "general," "universal," or "worldwide." Christ had said that his teaching was for all peoples, and Christians sought to make their faith catholic—that is, believed everywhere. This could be accomplished only through missionary activity. As Saint Paul had written to the Christian community at Colossae in Asia Minor, "there is no room for distinction between Greek and Jew, between the circumcised or the uncircumcised, or between barbarian or Scythian, slave and free man. There is only Christ; he is everything and he is in everything."[5] Paul urged Christians to bring the "good news" of Christ to all peoples. The Mediterranean served as the highway over which Christianity spread to the cities of the empire.

During the Roman occupation, Christian communities were scattered throughout Gaul and Britain. The effective beginnings of Christianity in Gaul can be traced to Saint Martin of Tours (ca 316–397), a Roman soldier who, after giving away half his cloak to a naked beggar,

Ardagh Silver Chalice This chalice (ca 800) formed part of the treasure of Ardagh Cathedral in County Limerick, Ireland. It has been called "one of the most sumptuous pieces of ecclesiastical metalwork to survive from early medieval Europe." The circular filigree decoration resembles that of Irish manuscript illumination. *(National Museum of Ireland)*

had a vision of Christ and was baptized. Martin founded the monastery of Ligugé, the first in Gaul, which became a center for the evangelization of the country districts. In 372 he became bishop of Tours and introduced a rudimentary parish system. The Christianization of rural areas followed a different pattern from that of the cities.

Religion was not a private or individual matter; it was a social affair, and the religion of the chieftain or king determined the religion of the people. Thus missionaries concentrated their initial efforts not on the people, but on kings or tribal chieftains. According to custom, kings negotiated with all foreign powers, including the gods. Because Christian missionaries represented a "foreign" power (the Christian God), the king dealt with them. Germanic kings accepted Christianity because they believed the Christian God was more powerful than pagan ones and the Christian God would deliver victory in battle; or because Christianity taught obedience to (kingly) authority; or because Christian priests possessed knowledge and a charisma that could be associated with kingly power. Kings who converted, such as Ethelbert of Kent and the Frankish chieftain Clovis, sometimes had Christian wives. Conversion may also have indicated that barbarian kings wanted to enjoy the cultural advantages that Christianity brought, such as literate assistants and an ideological basis for their rule.

Tradition identifies the conversion of Ireland with Saint Patrick (ca 385–461). Born in western England to

Pope Gregory I (590–604) and Scribes   One of the four "Doctors" (or Learned Fathers) of the Latin church, Gregory is shown in this tenth-century ivory book cover writing at his desk while the Holy Spirit, in the form of a dove, whispers in his ear. Below, scribes copy Gregory's works. *(Kunsthistorisches Museum, Vienna/Art Resource, NY)*

MAP 7.1 Anglo-Saxon England   The seven kingdoms of the Heptarchy—Northumbria, Mercia, East Anglia, Essex, Kent, Sussex, and Wessex—dominated but did not subsume Britain. Scotland remained a Pict stronghold, while the Celts resisted invasion of their native Wales by Germanic tribes.

a Christian family of Roman citizenship, Patrick was captured and enslaved by Irish raiders and taken to Ireland, where he worked for six years as a herdsman. He escaped and returned to England, where a vision urged him to Christianize Ireland. In preparation, Patrick studied in Gaul and in 432 was consecrated a bishop. He landed in Ireland, where he converted the Irish tribe by tribe, first baptizing the king. In 445, with the approval of Pope Leo I, Patrick established his see in Armagh. The ecclesiastical organization that Patrick set up, however, differed in a fundamental way from church structure on the continent: Armagh was a monastery, and the monastery, rather than

the diocese, served as the center of ecclesiastical organization. Local tribes and the monastery were interdependent, with the clan supporting the monastery economically and the monastery providing religious and educational services for the tribe. By the time of Patrick's death, the majority of the Irish people had received Christian baptism. In his missionary work, Patrick had the strong support of Bridget of Kildare (ca 450–ca 528), daughter of a wealthy chieftain and one of the chieftain's concubines. Bridget defied parental pressure to marry and became a nun. She and the nuns at Kildare instructed relatives and friends in basic Christian doctrine, made religious vestments for churches, copied books, taught children, and above all set a religious example by their lives of prayer. In Ireland and later in continental Europe, women shared in the process of conversion.

MAP 7.2 The Spread of Christianity   Originating in Judaea, the southern part of modern Israel and Jordan, Christianity spread throughout the Roman world. Roman sea-lanes and roads facilitated the expansion.

A strong missionary fervor characterized Irish Christianity. Perhaps the best representative of Irish-Celtic zeal was Saint Columba (ca 521–597), who established the monastery of Iona on an island in the Inner Hebrides off the west coast of Scotland (see Map 7.1). Iona served as a base for converting the pagan Picts of Scotland. Columba's proselytizing efforts won him the title "Apostle of Scotland," and his disciples carried the Christian Gospel to the European continent.

The Christianization of the English really began in 597, when Pope Gregory I (590–604) sent a delegation of monks under the Roman Augustine to Britain. Augustine's approach, like Patrick's, was to concentrate on converting the king. When he succeeded in converting Ethelbert, king of Kent, the baptism of Ethelbert's people took place as a matter of course. Augustine established his headquarters, or see, at Canterbury, the capital of Kent.

In the course of the seventh century, two Christian forces competed for the conversion of the pagan Anglo-Saxons: Roman-oriented missionaries traveling north from Canterbury and Celtic monks from Ireland and northwestern Britain. Monasteries were established at Iona, Lindisfarne, Jarrow, and Whitby.

The Roman and Celtic traditions differed completely in their forms of church organization, types of monastic life, and methods of arriving at the date of the central feast of the Christian calendar, Easter. Through the influence of King Oswiu of Northumbria, the Synod (ecclesiastical council) of Whitby in 664 opted to follow the Roman practices. The conversion of the English and the close attachment of the English church to Rome had far-reaching consequences because Britain later served as a base for the Christianization of the continent (see Map 7.2).

Between the fifth and tenth centuries, the great majority of peoples living on the European continent and the nearby islands were baptized as Christians. Once a ruler had marched his people to the waters of baptism, though, the work of Christianization had only begun. Baptism meant either sprinkling the head or immersing the body in water. Conversion meant mental and heartfelt acceptance of the beliefs of Christianity. What does it mean to be a Christian? This question has troubled sincere people from the time of Saint Paul to the present. The problem rests in part in the basic teaching of Jesus in the Gospel:

Then fixing his eyes on his disciples he said: . . . "Happy are you when people hate you, drive you out, abuse you, denounce your name as criminal, on account of the Son of Man. . . .

"But I say this to you who are listening: Love your enemies, do good to those who hate you, bless those who curse you, pray for those who treat you badly. . . . Treat others as you would like them to treat you."[6]

If believed and accepted as a code of behavior, these are very radical and revolutionary ideas.

The German people were warriors who idealized the military virtues of physical strength, ferocity in battle, and loyalty to the leader. Thus the Germans had trouble accepting the Christian precepts of "love your enemies" and "turn the other cheek." The Germanic tribes found the Christian notions of sin and repentance virtually incomprehensible. Sin in Christian thought meant disobedience to the will of God as revealed in the Ten Commandments and the teaching of Christ. "Moral" behavior to the barbarians meant the observance of tribal customs and practices. Dishonorable behavior caused social ostracism. The inculcation of Christian ideals took a very long time.

Conversion and Assimilation

In Christian theology, conversion involves a turning toward God—that is, a conscious effort to live according to the Gospel message. How did missionaries and priests get masses of pagan and illiterate peoples to understand and live by Christian ideals and teachings? Through preaching, assimilation, and the penitential system. Preaching aimed at instruction and edification. Instruction presented the basic teachings of Christianity. Edification was intended to strengthen the newly baptized in their faith through stories about the lives of Christ and the saints. But deeply ingrained pagan customs and practices could not be stamped out by words alone or even by imperial edicts. Christian missionaries often pursued a

Germanic Bracteate (Gold Leaf) Pendant   This late-fifth-century piece, with the head of Rome above a wolf suckling Romulus and Remus, reflects Germanic assimilation of Roman legend and artistic design. *(Courtesy of the Trustees of the British Museum)*

policy of assimilation, easing the conversion of pagan men and women by stressing similarities between their customs and beliefs and those of Christianity. A letter from Pope Gregory I beautifully illustrates this policy. Sent to Augustine of Canterbury in Britain in 601, it expresses the pope's intention that pagan buildings and practices be given a Christian significance:

Therefore, when by God's help you reach our most reverent brother, Bishop Augustine, we wish you to inform him that we have been giving careful thought to the affairs of the English, and have come to the conclusion that the temples of the idols among that people should on no account be destroyed. The idols are to be destroyed, but the temples themselves are to be aspersed with holy water, altars set up in them, and relics deposited there. For if these temples are well-built, they must be purified from the worship of demons and dedicated to the service of the true God. In this way we hope that the people, seeing that their temples are not destroyed, may abandon their error and, flocking more readily to their accustomed resorts, may come to know and adore the true God.[7]

How assimilation works is perhaps best appreciated through the example of a festival familiar to all Americans, Saint Valentine's Day. There were two Romans named Valentine. Both were Christian priests, and both were martyred for their beliefs around the middle of February in the third century. Since about 150 B.C., the Romans had celebrated the festival of Lupercalia, at which they asked the gods for fertility for themselves, their fields, and their flocks. This celebration occurred in mid-February, shortly before the Roman New Year and the arrival of spring. Thus the early church "converted" the old festival of Lupercalia into Saint Valentine's Day. (Nothing in the lives of the two Christian martyrs connects them with lovers or the exchange of messages and gifts. That practice began in the later Middle Ages.) The fourteenth of February was still celebrated as a festival, but it had taken on Christian meaning.

A process that had an equally profound, if gradual, impact on the conversion of the pagan masses was the rite of reconciliation in which the sinner revealed his or her sins in order to receive God's forgiveness. In the early church, "confession" meant that the sinner publicly acknowledged charges laid against him or her and publicly carried out the penitential works prescribed by the priest or bishop. For example, the adulterer might have to stand outside the church before services wearing a sign naming his or her sin and asking the prayers of everyone who entered.

Beginning in the late sixth century, however, Irish and English missionaries brought the more private penitential system to continental Europe. **Penitentials** were manuals for the examination of conscience. The penitent knelt before the priest, who questioned the penitent about the sins he or she might have committed. A penance such as fasting for a period of time on bread and water was imposed as a medicine for the soul. Here is a section of the penitential prepared by Archbishop Theodore of Canterbury (668–690), which circulated widely at the time:

If anyone commits fornication with a virgin he shall do penance for one year. If with a married woman, he shall do penance for four years.

A male who commits fornication with a male shall do penance for three years.

If a woman practices vice with a woman, she shall do penance for three years.

Whoever has often committed theft, seven years is his penance, or such a sentence as his priest shall determine. . . .

Ivory Carving (sixth century)   At the end of a procession two men in a wagon carry a relic casket to the emperor (Theodosius?) at the doorway of a church under construction. Workmen are putting tiles on the church roof. The emperor hands the patriarch (holding a cross) a candle. The carving illustrates the adapting of Roman narrative style to Christian subject matter and thus the fusion of Roman and Christian cultures. *(Cathedral Treasury, Trier)*

Women who commit abortion before [the fetus] has life, shall do penance for one year or for the three forty-day periods or for forty days, according to the nature of the offense; and if later, that is, more than forty days after conception, they shall do penance as murderesses.

If a poor woman slays her child, she shall do penance for seven years. In the canon it is said that if it is a case of homicide, she shall do penance for ten years.[8]

Penitentials provide considerable information about the ascetic ideals of early Christianity and about the crime-ridden realities of Celtic and Germanic societies. Penitentials also reveal the ecclesiastical foundations of some modern attitudes toward sex, birth control, and abortion. The penitential system contributed to the gradual growth of a different attitude toward religion: formerly public, corporate, and social, religious observances slowly became private, personal, and individual.[9]

Christian Attitudes Toward Classical Culture

Probably the major dilemma the early Christian church faced concerned Greco-Roman culture. The Roman Empire as a social, political, and economic force gradually disintegrated. Its culture, however, survived. In Greek philosophy, art, and architecture, in Roman law, literature, education, and engineering, the legacy of a great civilization continued. The Christian religion had begun and spread within this intellectual and psychological milieu. What was to be the attitude of Christians to the Greco-Roman world of ideas?

Adjustment

Christians in the first and second centuries believed that the end of the world was near. They expected to witness the return of Christ, and therefore they considered knowledge useless and learning a waste of time. The important duty of the Christian was to prepare for the Second Coming of the Lord. Good Christians who sought the Kingdom of Heaven through the imitation of Christ believed they had to disassociate themselves from the "filth" that Roman culture embodied.

As Saint Paul wrote, "The wisdom of the world is foolishness, we preach Christ crucified." Tertullian (ca 160–220), an influential African church father and writer, condemned all secular literature as foolishness in the eyes of God. He called the Greek philosophers, such as Aristotle, "hucksters of eloquence" and compared them to "animals of self-glorification." "What has Athens to do with Jerusalem," he demanded, "the Academy with the Church? We have no need for curiosity since Jesus Christ, nor for inquiry since the gospel." Tertullian insisted that Christians would find in the Bible all the wisdom they needed.

On the other hand, Christianity encouraged adjustment to the ideas and institutions of the Roman world. Some biblical texts urged Christians to accept the existing social, economic, and political establishment. Specifically addressing Christians living among non-Christians in the hostile environment of Rome, the author of the First Letter of Peter had written about the obligations of Christians:

Always behave honorably among pagans, so that they can see your good works for themselves and, when the day of reckoning comes, give thanks to God for the things which now make them denounce you as criminals. . . .

For the sake of the Lord, accept the authority of every social institution: the emperor, as the supreme authority, and the governors as commissioned by him to punish criminals and praise good citizenship. God wants you to be good citizens. . . . Have respect for everyone and love for your community; fear God and honour the emperor.[10]

Even had early Christians wanted to give up Greco-Roman ideas and patterns of thought, they would have had great difficulty doing so. Therefore, they had to adapt their Roman education to their Christian beliefs. Saint Paul himself believed there was a good deal of truth in pagan thought, as long as it was correctly interpreted and understood.

The result was a compromise. Christians gradually came to terms with Greco-Roman culture. Saint Jerome (340–419), a distinguished theologian and linguist, remains famous for his translation of the Old and New Testaments from Hebrew and Greek into vernacular Latin. Called the "Vulgate," his edition of the Bible served as the official translation until the sixteenth century; even today, scholars rely on it. Familiar with the writings of classical authors, Saint Jerome also believed that Christians should study the best of ancient thought because it would direct their minds to God. Jerome maintained that the best ancient literature should be interpreted in light of the Christian faith.

Christian attitudes toward women and toward homosexuality illustrate the ways early Christians adopted the views of their contemporary world. Jesus, whom Christians accept as the Messiah, considered women the equal of men in his plan of salvation. He attributed no disreputable qualities to women, made no comment on the wiles of women, no reference to them as inferior creatures. On the contrary, women were among his earliest and most faithful converts. He discussed his mission with them (John 4:21–25); he accepted the ministrations of a reformed prostitute; and women were the first persons to whom he revealed himself after his resurrection (Matthew 28:9–10). Jewish and Christian writers, however, not Jesus, had a greater influence on the formation of medieval (and modern) attitudes toward women.

Jesus' message emphasized love for God and one's fellow human beings; later writers tended to stress Christianity as a religion of renunciation and self-denial. Their views derive from Platonic-Hellenistic ideas of the contemporary Mediterranean world. The Hellenistic Jewish philosopher Philo of Alexandria (ca 20 B.C.–ca A.D. 50), for example, held that since the female represented sense perception and the male the higher, rational soul, the female was inferior to the male. Philo accepted the biblical command to increase and multiply but argued that the only good of marriage was the production of children for the continuation of the race. Female beauty may come from God, who created everything, the African church father Tertullian wrote, but it should be feared. Women should wear veils, or men will be endangered by the sight of them. Perhaps the most revolting image of women comes from Saint John Chrysostom (347–407), patriarch of Constantinople and a ruthless critic of contemporary morals. Commenting on female beauty, he wrote that

if a man consider what is stored up inside those beautiful eyes and that straight nose, and the mouth and the cheeks, you will affirm the well-shaped body to be nothing else than a white sepulchre; the parts within are full of so much uncleanliness. Moreover, when you see a rag with any of these things on it, such as phlegm or spittle, you cannot bear to touch it, with even the tips of your fingers, nay you cannot even endure looking at it; yet you are in a flutter of excitement about the storehouses and depositories [women] of these things.[11]

The church fathers acknowledged that God had established marriage for the generation of children, but they believed it was a concession to weak souls who could not bear celibacy. God had clearly sanctioned marriage, and coitus was theoretically good since it was created by God. But in daily life, every act of intercourse was evil; the child was conceived by a sinful act and came into the world tainted with "original sin" (see page 203). Celibacy was the highest good, intercourse little more than animal lust.

The Marys at the Sepulcher This late-fourth-century ivory panel tells the story (Matthew 28:1–6) of Mary Magdalene and another Mary (*lower*), who went to Jesus' tomb to discover the stone at the entrance rolled away; that an angel had descended from heaven; and in shock the guards assigned (*upper*) to watch the tomb "trembled and became like dead men." The angel told the women that Jesus had risen. The blend of Roman artistic style—in spacing, drapery, men's hair fashion—and Christian subject matter shows the assimilation of classical form and Christian teaching. (*Castello Sforzesco/Scala/Art Resource, NY*)

Because women were considered incapable of writing on the subject, we have none of their views. The church fathers, by definition, were all males. Since many of them became aware of their physical desires when in the presence of women, misogyny (hatred of women) entered Christian thought. Although early Christian writers believed women the spiritual equals of men, and although some women, such as Saints Melania and Scholastica, exercised influence as teachers and charismatic leaders, Christianity became a male-centered and sex-negative religion.[12] Until perhaps very recently, this attitude dominated Western thinking on human sexuality.

Toward homosexuality, according to some scholars, Christians of the first three or four centuries imbibed the attitude of the world in which they lived. Like the Greeks, many Romans indulged in homosexual activity, and contemporaries did not consider such behavior (or inclinations to it) any more immoral, bizarre, or harmful than heterosexual behavior. Several emperors were openly homosexual, and homosexuals participated freely in all aspects of Roman life and culture. Early Christians, too, considered homosexuality a conventional expression of physical desire and were no more susceptible to antihomosexual prejudices than pagans were. What eventually led to a change in public and Christian attitudes toward homosexual behavior was the shift from the sophisticated urban culture of the Greco-Roman world to the rural culture of medieval Europe.[13]

Synthesis: Saint Augustine

The finest representative of the blending of classical and Christian ideas, and indeed one of the most brilliant thinkers in the history of the Western world, was Saint Augustine of Hippo (354–430). Saint Augustine was born into an urban family in what is now Algeria in North Africa. His father was a pagan; his mother, Monica, a devout Christian. Because his family was poor—his father was a minor civil servant—the only avenue to success in a highly competitive world was a classical education.

Augustine's mother believed that a good classical education, though pagan, would make her son a better Christian, so the child received his basic education in the local school. By modern and even medieval standards, that education was extremely narrow: textual study of the writings of the poet Virgil, the orator-politician Cicero, the historian Sallust, and the playwright Terence. At that time, learning meant memorization. Education in the late Roman world aimed at appreciation of words, particularly those of renowned and eloquent orators.

At the age of seventeen, Augustine went to nearby Carthage to continue his education. At Carthage Augustine entered a difficult psychological phase and began an intellectual and spiritual pilgrimage that led him through experiments with several philosophies and heretical Christian sects. In 383 he traveled to Rome, where he endured not only illness but also disappointment in his teaching: his students fled when their bills were due.

Finally, in Milan in 387, through the insights he gained from reading Saint Paul's Letter to the Romans, Augustine received Christian baptism. He later became bishop of the seacoast city of Hippo Regius in his native North Africa. He was a renowned preacher to Christians there, a vigorous defender of orthodox Christianity, and the author of over ninety-three books and treatises.

Augustine's autobiography, *The Confessions,* is a literary masterpiece and one of the most influential books in the history of Europe. Written in the form of a prayer, *The Confessions* describes Augustine's moral struggle, the conflict between his spiritual and intellectual aspirations and his sensual and material self.

Great are thou, O Lord, and exceedingly to be praised: great is thy power and of thy wisdom there is no reckoning. And man, indeed, one part of thy creation, has the will to praise thee: yea, man, though he bears his mortality about with him . . . even man, a small portion of thy creation, has the will to praise thee. Thou dost stir him up, that it may delight him to praise thee, for thou hast made us for thyself and our hearts are restless till they find repose in thee.[14]

The Confessions reveals the change and development of a human mind and personality steeped in the philosophy and culture of the ancient world. Many Greek and Roman philosophers had taught that knowledge and virtue are the same: a person who really knows what is right will do what is right. Augustine rejected this idea. He believed that a person may know what is right but fail to act righteously because of the innate weakness of the human will. People do not always act on the basis of rational knowledge. Here Augustine made a profound contribution to the understanding of human nature: he demonstrated that a learned person can also be corrupt and evil. *The Confessions,* written in the rhetorical style and language of late Roman antiquity, marks the synthesis of Greco-Roman forms and Christian thought.

Augustine's ideas on sin, grace, and redemption became the foundation of all subsequent Christian theology, Protestant as well as Catholic. He wrote that the basic or dynamic force in any individual is the will, which he defined as "the power of the soul to hold on to or to obtain an object without constraint." The end or goal of the will determines the moral character of the individual. When Adam ate the fruit forbidden by God in the Garden of Eden (Genesis 3:6), he committed the "original sin" and corrupted the will; by concupiscence, or sexual desire, which all humans have, Adam's sin was passed on by hereditary transmission through the flesh to all humanity. Original sin thus became a common social stain. Because Adam disobeyed God and fell, so all human beings have an innate tendency to sin: their will is weak. But according to Augustine, God restores the strength of the will through grace, which is transmitted through the sacraments.

Augustine also argued against the Donatist heretical movement promoted by the North African bishop of Carthage, Donatus (313–347). Donatism denied the value of sacraments administered by priests or bishops who had denied their faith under persecution or had committed grave sin. For the Donatists, the holiness of the minister was as important as the sacred rites he performed. Donatists viewed the true church, therefore, as a small spiritual elite that was an alternative to society. Augustine responded that, through God's action, the rites of the church have an objective and permanent validity, regardless of the priest's spiritual condition. The notion of the church as a special spiritual elite recurred many times in the Middle Ages. Each time it was branded a heresy, and Augustine's arguments were marshaled against it.

When the Visigothic chieftain Alaric conquered Rome in 410, horrified pagans blamed the disaster on the Christians. In response, Augustine wrote *City of God*. This profoundly original work contrasts Christianity with the secular society in which it existed. Filled with references to ancient history and mythology, it remained for centuries the standard statement of the Christian philosophy of history.

According to Augustine, history is the account of God acting in time. Human history reveals that there are two kinds of people: those who live according to the flesh in the City of Babylon and those who live according to the spirit in the City of God. The former will endure eternal hellfire; the latter enjoy eternal bliss.

Augustine maintained that states came into existence as the result of Adam's fall and people's inclination to sin. The state is a necessary evil, but it can work for the good by providing the peace, justice, and order that Christians need in order to pursue their pilgrimage to the City of God. The particular form of government—whether monarchy, aristocracy, or democracy—is basically irrelevant. Any civil government that fails to provide justice is no more than a band of gangsters.

Although the state results from moral lapse—from sin—neither is the church (the Christian community) entirely free from sin. The church is certainly not equivalent to the City of God. But the church, which is concerned with salvation, is responsible for everyone, including Christian rulers. Churches in the Middle Ages used Augustine's theory to defend their belief in the ultimate superiority of the spiritual power over the temporal. This remained the dominant political theory until the late thirteenth century.

Christian Monasticism

Christianity began and spread as a city religion. Since the first century, however, some especially pious Christians had felt that the only alternative to the decadence of urban life was complete separation from the world. All-consuming pursuit of material things, gross sexual promiscuity, and general political corruption disgusted them. They believed that the Christian life as set forth in the Gospel could not be lived in the midst of such immorality. They rejected the values of Roman society and were the first real nonconformists in the church.

The fourth century witnessed a significant change in the relationship of Christianity and the broader society. Until Constantine's legalization of Christianity, Christians were a persecuted minority. People were tortured and killed for their faith. Christians greatly revered these martyrs, the men and women who, like Jesus, suffered and died for their faith. When Christianity was legalized and the persecutions ended, a new problem arose. Whereas Christians had been a suffering minority, now they came to be identified with the state: non-Christians could not advance in the imperial service. And if Christianity had triumphed, so had "the world," since secular attitudes and values pervaded the church. The church of martyrs no longer existed, and some scholars believe the monasteries provided a way of life for those Christians who wanted to make a total response to Christ's teachings. The monks became the new martyrs. Saint Anthony of Egypt (251?–356), the earliest monk for whom there is concrete evidence and the person later considered the father of monasticism, went to Alexandria during the last persecution in the hope of gaining martyrdom. Christians believed that monks, like the martyrs before them, could speak to God and that their prayers had special influence with him.

Western Monasticism

Monasticism began in Egypt in the third century. At first individuals and small groups withdrew from cities and organized society to seek God through prayer in caves and shelters in the desert or mountains. Gradually large colonies of monks emerged in the deserts of Upper Egypt. They were called hermits, from the Greek word *eremos,* meaning "desert." Many devout women also were attracted to this **eremitical** life. We have no way of knowing how many hermits there were in the fourth and fifth centuries because their conscious aim was a hidden life known only to God. Although monks (and nuns) led isolated lives and the monastic movement represented the antithesis of the ancient ideal of an urban social existence, ordinary people soon recognized the monks and nuns as holy people and sought them as spiritual guides.

When monasticism spread to western Europe, several factors worked against the continuation of the eremitical form. The harsh weather of northern Europe for many months of the year discouraged isolated living. Dense forests filled with wild animals and wandering Germanic tribes presented obvious dangers. Also, church leaders did not really approve of eremitical life. Hermits sometimes claimed to have mystical experiences, direct communications with God. If hermits could communicate directly with the Lord, what need had they for the priest and the institutional church? Saint Basil (329?–379), the scholarly bishop of Caesarea in Cappadocia in Asia Minor, opposed the eremitical life on other grounds: the impossibility of material self-sufficiency; the danger of excessive concern with the self; and the fact that the eremitical life did not provide the opportunity for the exercise of charity, the first virtue of any Christian. The Egyptian ascetic Pachomius (290–346?) had organized communities of men and women at his coenobitic monastery at Tabennisi on the Upper Nile drawing thousands of recruits. Saint Basil and the church hierarchy encouraged **coenobitic monasticism,** communal living in monasteries. Communal living, they felt, provided an environment for training the aspirant in the virtues of charity, poverty, and freedom from self-deception.

In the fourth, fifth, and sixth centuries, Bishop Athanasius of Alexandria's *Life of St. Anthony,* the monk John Cassian's *Conferences,* which is based on his conversations with Egyptian monks, and other information about Egyptian monasticism came to the West. The literature of the Egyptian monastic experience led to a flood of converts. Many experiments in communal monasticism were made in Gaul, Italy, Spain, England, and Ireland. While at Rome, Saint Jerome attracted a group of aristocratic women, whom he instructed in the Scriptures and the ideals of ascetic life. After studying both eremitical and coenobitic monasticism in Egypt and Syria, John

Cassian established two monasteries near Marseilles in Gaul around 415. The abbey of Lérins on the Mediterranean Sea near Cannes (ca 410) also had significant contacts with monastic centers in western Asia and North Africa. Lérins encouraged the severely penitential and extremely ascetic behavior common in the East, such as long hours of prayer, fasting, and self-flagellation. It was this tradition of harsh self-mortification that the Roman-British monk Saint Patrick carried from Lérins to Ireland in the fifth century.

Around 540 the Roman senator Cassiodorus retired from public service and established a monastery, the Vivarium, on his estate in Italy. Cassiodorus wanted the Vivarium to become an educational and cultural center and enlisted highly educated and sophisticated men for it. He set the monks to copying both sacred and secular manuscripts, intending this to be their sole occupation. Cassiodorus started the association of monasticism with scholarship and learning. That developed into a great tradition in the medieval and modern worlds. But Cassiodorus's experiment did not become the most influential form of monasticism in European society. The fifth and sixth centuries witnessed the appearance of many other monastic lifestyles.

The Rule of Saint Benedict

In 529 Benedict of Nursia (480–543), who had experimented with both the eremitical and the communal forms of monastic life, wrote a brief set of regulations for the monks who had gathered around him at Monte Cassino between Rome and Naples. Recent research has shown that Benedict's *Rule* derives from a longer, repetitious, and sometimes turgid document called *The Rule of the Master.* Benedict's guide for monastic life proved more adaptable and slowly replaced all others. *The Rule of Saint Benedict* has influenced all forms of organized religious life in the Roman church.

Saint Benedict conceived of his *Rule* as a simple code for ordinary men. It outlined a monastic life of regularity, discipline, and moderation in an atmosphere of silence. Each monk had ample food and adequate sleep. The monk spent part of each day in formal prayer, which Benedict called the *Opus Dei* (Work of God) and Christians later termed the divine office, the public prayer of the church. This consisted of chanting psalms and other prayers from the Bible in that part of the monastery church called the "choir." The rest of the day was passed in manual labor, study, and private prayer. After a year of testing or probation, the novice (newcomer) made three vows.

Cum dombus misos plures parer accipe ly bfos.

Saint Benedict   Holding his *Rule* in his left hand, the seated and cowled patriarch of Western monasticism blesses a monk with his right hand. His monastery, Monte Cassino, is in the background. *(Biblioteca Apostolica Vaticana)*

First, he vowed stability: he promised to live his entire life in the monastery of his profession. The vow of stability was Saint Benedict's major contribution to Western monasticism; his object was to prevent the wandering so common in his day. Second, the monk vowed conversion of manners—that is, to strive to improve himself and to come closer to God. Third, he promised obedience, the most difficult vow because it meant the complete surrender of his will to the abbot, or head of the monastery.

The Rule of Saint Benedict expresses the assimilation of the Roman spirit into Western monasticism. It reveals the logical mind of its creator and the Roman concern for order, organization, and respect for law. Its spirit of moderation and flexibility is reflected in the patience, wisdom, and understanding with which the abbot is to govern and, indeed, with which life is to be led. The *Rule* was quickly adapted for women, and many convents of nuns were established in the early Middle Ages.

Saint Benedict's *Rule* implies that a person who wants to become a monk or nun need have no previous ascetic experience or even a particularly strong bent toward the religious life. Thus it allowed for the admission of newcomers with different backgrounds and personalities. From Chapter 59, "The Offering of Sons by Nobles or by the Poor," and from Benedict's advice to the abbot—"The abbot should avoid all favoritism in the monastery. . . . A man born free is not to be given higher rank than a slave who becomes a monk" (Chapter 2)— we know that men of different social classes belonged to his monastery. This flexibility helps to explain the attractiveness of Benedictine monasticism throughout the centuries.

At the same time, the *Rule* no more provides a picture of actual life in a Benedictine abbey of the seventh or eighth (or twenty-first) century than the American Constitution of 1789 describes living conditions in the United States today. A code of laws cannot do that. Monasteries are composed of individuals, and human beings defy strict classification according to rules, laws, or statistics. *The Rule of Saint Benedict* had one fundamental purpose: the exercises of the monastic life were designed to draw the individual slowly but steadily away from attachment to the world and love of self and toward the love of God.

Why did the Benedictine form of monasticism eventually replace other forms of Western monasticism? The answer lies partly in its spirit of flexibility and moderation and partly in the balanced life it provided. Early Benedictine monks and nuns spent part of the day in prayer, part in study or some other form of intellectual activity, and part in manual labor. The monastic life as conceived by Saint Benedict struck a balance between asceticism and activity. It thus provided opportunities for persons of entirely different abilities and talents—from mechanics to gardeners to literary scholars. Benedict's *Rule* contrasts sharply with Cassiodorus's narrow concept of the monastery as a place for aristocratic scholars and bibliophiles.

Benedictine monasticism suited the social circumstances of early medieval society. The German invasions had fragmented European life: the self-sufficient rural estate replaced the city as the basic unit of civilization. A monastery, too, had to be economically self-sufficient. It was supposed to produce from its lands and properties all that was needed for food, clothing, shelter, and liturgical service of the altar. The monastery fitted in—indeed, represented—the trend toward localism. The Benedictine form of religious life also proved congenial to women. Five miles from Monte Cassino at Plombariola, Benedict's twin sister Scholastica (480–543) adapted the *Rule* for the use of her community of nuns. The adoption of Benedict's *Rule* by houses of women paralleled that in houses of men.

Benedictine monasticism also succeeded partly because it was so materially successful. In the seventh and eighth centuries, monasteries pushed back forests and wastelands, drained swamps, and experimented with crop rotation. For example, the abbey of Saint Wandrille, founded in 645 near Rouen in northwestern Gaul, sent squads of monks to clear the forests that surrounded it. Within seventy-five years, the abbey was immensely wealthy. Such Benedictine houses made a significant contribution to the agricultural development of Europe. The communal nature of their organization, whereby property was held in common and profits were pooled and reinvested, made this contribution possible.

Finally, monasteries conducted schools for local young people. Some learned about prescriptions and herbal remedies and went on to provide medical treatment for their localities. A few copied manuscripts and wrote books. Local and royal governments drew on the services of the literate men and able administrators the monasteries produced. This was not what Saint Benedict had intended, but the effectiveness of the institution he designed made it perhaps inevitable.

Eastern Monasticism

From Egypt, Christian monasticism also spread to the Greek provinces of Syria and Palestine and to Constantinople itself. Saint Basil (see page 204) composed a set of regulations called the *Long Rules* that recommended communities of economically self-sufficient monks (or nuns) who lived lives of moderation. Basil discouraged the severe asceticism that was so common in Egypt and also supported the establishment of urban monasteries.

With financial assistance from the emperor Justinian I (527–565) and from wealthy nobles, monasteries soon spread throughout the empire, with seventy abbeys erected in Constantinople alone. Justinian granted the monks the right to inherit property from private citizens and the right to receive **solemnia,** or annual gifts, from the imperial treasury or from the taxes of certain provinces, and he prohibited lay confiscation of monastic estates. Beginning in the tenth century, the monasteries acquired fields, pastures, livestock, mills, saltworks, and urban rental properties, as well as cash and precious liturgical vessels. The exemption of Byzantine monasteries from state taxes also served to increase monastic wealth.

Monasticism in the Greek Orthodox world differed in fundamental ways from the monasticism that evolved in western Europe. First, while *The Rule of Saint Benedict* gradually became the universal guide for all western European monasteries, each individual house in the Byzantine world developed its own *typikon,* or set of rules for organization and behavior. The *typika* contain regulations about novitiate, diet, clothing, liturgical functions, commemorative services for benefactors, and the election of officials, such as the *hegoumenos,* or superior of the house. Second, while stability in the monastery eventually characterized Western monasticism, many Orthodox monks "moved frequently from one monastery to another or alternated between a coenobitic monastery and a hermit's kellion [cell]."[15] Finally, unlike the West, where monasteries often established schools for the education of the youth of the neighborhood, education never became a central feature of the Greek houses. Monks and nuns had to be literate to perform the services of the choir, and children destined for the monastic life were taught to read and write. In the monasteries where monks or nuns devoted themselves to study and writing, their communities sometimes played important roles in the development of theology and in the intellectual life of the empire. But those houses were very few, and no monastery assumed responsibility for the general training of the local young. Since bishops and patriarchs of the Greek church were recruited only from the monasteries, Greek houses did, however, exercise a cultural influence.

The Migration of the Germanic Peoples

The migration of peoples from one area to another has been a dominant and continuing feature of Western history. Mass movements of Europeans occurred in the fourth through sixth centuries, in the ninth and tenth centuries, and in the twelfth and thirteenth centuries. From the sixteenth century to the present, such movements have been almost continuous, involving not just the European continent but the entire world. The causes of early migrations varied and are not thoroughly understood by scholars. But there is no question that they profoundly affected both the regions to which peoples moved and the ones they left behind.

The Idea of the Barbarian

The Greeks and Romans invented the idea of the **barbarian.** The Romans labeled all peoples living outside the frontiers of the Roman Empire (except the Persians) as barbarians. Geography, rather than ethnic background, determined a people's classification. The Romans also held that peoples outside the empire had no history and were touched by history only when they entered the Roman Empire.

The modern study of ethnography (writing about the formation of ethnic groups) involves the systematic recording of the major characteristics of different human cultures. Scholars today identify three models of ethnic formation among the Germanic peoples who came in contact with the Romans and whom the Romans called barbarians.

First, there were those Germanic peoples whose identity was shaped by a militarily successful or "royal" family. For example, the Salian Franks, Lombards, and Goths attracted and controlled followers from other peoples by getting them to adhere to the cultural traditions of the leading family. Followers assimilated the "kernel family's" legendary traditions and myths, which traced their origins to a family or individual of divine ancestry. The kernel family led these followers from their original territory, won significant victories over other peoples, and settled someplace within the Roman world.

A second model of ethnic formation derives from Central Asian steppe peoples such as the Huns, Avars, and Alans. These were polyethnic, seminomadic, and sedentary groups led by a small body of steppe commanders.

(The term *steppe* refers to the vast semiarid plain in Russian Siberia.) These peoples constituted large confederations, whose success depended on constant expansion by military victory or the use of terror. Defeat in battle or the death of a leader could lead to the disintegration of the confederation.

The Alamanni and the Slavs represent a third model of barbarian ethnic formation. Because no evidence of

King Lhodari of the Alamanni The Alamanni occupied territory in southwestern Germany and Switzerland in the fifth century but didn't accept Christianity until the late seventh or early eighth century. King Lhodari had Alamanni law (hitherto transmitted orally) written down in Latin. (In French speech the name Allemands came to signify all Germans.) Here the ninth-century artist portrays Lhodari (*upper left*) in Roman military garb. (*Bibliothèque nationale de France*)

collective legends, genealogies, or traditions among these peoples survives, we do not know whether they had a consciousness of collective identity. They were loosely organized, short-lived bands of peoples who lacked centralized leadership. Because the Slavs intermingled with Turko-Tartar, Finnic, Germanic, and Mongol peoples, the early Slavs possessed no ethnic identity.

One fundamental trait characterizes all barbarian peoples: the formation of ethnic groups did not represent a single historical event. Rather, the formation of such peoples was a continuous and changing process extending over long periods of time.[16]

Celts and Germans

As Julius Caesar advanced through Gaul between 58 and 50 B.C. (see page 146), he encountered Celts and Germans. Modern historians have tended to use the terms *German* and *Celt* in a racial sense, but recent research stresses that *Celt* and *German* are linguistic terms, a Celt being one who spoke a Celtic language and a German one who spoke German. Celts and Germans displayed many similarities. Both were Indo-European peoples. In the first century A.D., the Celts lived east of the Rhine River in an area bounded by the Main Valley and extending westward to the Somme River. Germans were more numerous along the North and Baltic Seas. Both Germans and Celts used a wheeled plow and a three-field system of crop rotation. The Celts had developed iron manufacturing, using shaft furnaces as sophisticated as those of the Romans. The Celts' use of iron swords and spears suggests that they were not the "peaceful" people historians have long described them to be. There were probably many Celtic peoples with differing cultural traditions. By the fourth century B.C., under pressure from the Germans, the Celts had moved westward, settling in Brittany (modern northwestern France) and throughout the British Isles (England, Wales, Scotland, and Ireland). By the third century A.D., the Picts of Scotland, as well as the Welsh, Britons, and Irish, were peoples of Celtic descent.

The migrations of the Germanic peoples were important in the decline of the western Roman Empire and in the making of European civilization. Many modern scholars have tried to explain who the Germans were and why they migrated. The present consensus, based on the study of linguistic and archaeological evidence, is that there were not one but many Germanic peoples with very different cultural traditions. The largest Germanic tribe was a polyethnic group consisting of perhaps 15,000 to 20,000 warriors, which with women and children amounted to 100,000 people. It was supplemented by slaves, *coloni,* peoples who, because of their desperate situation under Roman rule, joined the Goths during their migrations.[17] Archaeological remains—bone fossils, cooking utensils, jewelry, weapons of war, and other artifacts—combined with linguistic data suggest three broad groupings of Germanic peoples. One group lived along the North and Baltic Seas in the regions of present-day northern Germany, southern Sweden, and Denmark. A second band inhabited the area between the Elbe and Oder Rivers. A third group lived along the Rhine and Weser Rivers, closest to the Roman frontier. Although these groupings sometimes showed cultural affiliation, they were very fluid and did not possess political, social, or ethnic solidarity.

Since about 150, Germanic tribes had pressed along the Rhine-Danube frontier of the Roman Empire. Some tribes, such as the Visigoths and Ostrogoths, led a settled existence, engaged in agriculture and trade, and accepted Arian Christianity. Tribes such as the Angles, Saxons, and Huns led a nomadic life unaffected by Roman influences. Scholars do not know exactly when the Mongolian tribe called the Huns began to move westward from China, but about 376 they pressured the Goths along the Rhine-Danube frontier.

Why did the Germans migrate? Recent scholarship suggests that their movements were *not* due to overpopulation, as scholars have long believed. Rather, movements may have occurred because barbarian societies were in a constant state of war. Or possibly "the primary stimulus for this gradual migration was the Roman frontier, which increasingly offered service in the (Roman) army and work for pay around the camps."[18]

Romanization and Barbarization

The Roman Empire, it should be remembered, centered on the Mediterranean. Italy, Spain, and North Africa were the areas most vital to it. Aside from Rome, obviously, Alexandria, Antioch, Ephesus, and later Constantinople represented the great economic, cultural, and population centers. North of Italy, in Gaul, Germany, and Britain, Celtic and Germanic peoples had long predominated. The Roman army had spread a veneer of Roman culture in the territories it controlled, but from the third to the sixth century, as Roman influence declined, native Germanic traditions reasserted themselves.

The Roman army had been the chief means of Romanization throughout the empire (see Chapter 6). But from the third century, the army became the chief agent of barbarization. How? In the third and fourth centuries, increasing pressures on the frontiers from the east and north placed greater demands on military manpower, which plague and a declining birthrate had reduced. Therefore, Roman generals recruited barbarians to fill the ranks. They bribed Germanic chiefs with treaties and gold, the masses with grain. By the late third century, a large percentage of military recruits came from the Germanic peoples.

Laeti, Foederati, Gentes

Besides army recruits, several types of barbarian peoples entered the empire and became affiliated with Roman government. The *laeti,* refugees or prisoners of war, were settled with their families in areas of Gaul and Italy under the supervision of Roman prefects and landowners. Generally isolated from the local Roman population, the laeti farmed regions depopulated by plague. The men had to serve in the Roman army. Free barbarian units called **foederati,** stationed near major provincial cities, represented a second type of affiliated barbarian group. Research has suggested that rather than giving them land, the Romans assigned the foederati shares of the tax revenues from the region.[19] Living in close proximity to Roman communities, the foederati quickly assimilated into Roman culture. In fact, in the fourth century, some foederati rose to the highest ranks of the army and moved in the most cultured and aristocratic circles. Third, the arrival of the Huns in the west in 376 precipitated the entry of entire peoples, the *gentes,* into the Roman Empire. Pressured by defeat in battle, starvation, or the movement of other peoples, tribes such as the Ostrogoths and Visigoths entered in large numbers.[20] Under the pro-Roman general Fritigern, the Visigoths petitioned the emperor Valens to admit them to the empire. Seeing in the hordes of warriors the solution to his manpower problem, Valens agreed. Once the Visigoths were inside the empire, Roman authorities exploited their hunger by forcing them to sell their own people as slaves in exchange for dog flesh: "the going rate was one dog for one Goth." Still, the Visigoths sought peace. Fritigern offered himself as a friend and ally of Rome, if Rome would grant his people the province of Thrace—land, crops, and livestock. With a Roman army of between thirty thousand and forty thousand men, against about ten thousand Goths, Valens did not take the offer seriously, and his council voted for battle. When the two armies met on August 9, 378, near Adrianople, the Visigoths slashed down the Roman army, including

thirty-five high-ranking officers and the emperor Valens himself. But the Goths had neither the equipment nor the tactical skill to take the city of Adrianople. The Battle of Adrianople marks no notable change in the military or political history of the Roman Empire. As the Visigoths migrated into Thrace and the Balkans, however, they forced the Romans to change imperial policy toward the barbarians. That policy alternated between official recognition by treaty and enmity. Alaric I's invasion of Italy and sack of Rome in 410 represents the culmination of hostility between the Visigoths and the Romans, but a year later Alaric died, and his successor led his people into Gaul.[21]

Except for the Lombards, whose conquests of Italy persisted into the mid-eighth century, the movements of Germanic peoples on the continent ended about 600 (see Map 7.3). Between 450 and 565, the Germans established a number of kingdoms, but none except the Frankish kingdom lasted very long. Since the German kingdoms did not have definite geographical boundaries, their locations are approximate. The Visigoths overran much of southwestern Gaul. Establishing their headquarters at Toulouse, they exercised a weak domination over Spain until a Muslim victory at Guadalete in 711 ended Visigothic rule. The Vandals, whose destructive ways are commemorated in the word *vandal,* settled in North Africa. In northern and western Europe in the sixth century, the Burgundians ruled over lands roughly circumscribed by the old Roman army camps at Lyons, Besançon, Geneva, and Autun.

In northern Italy, the Ostrogothic king Theodoric (r. 471–526) established his residence at Ravenna and gradually won control of all Italy, Sicily, and the territory north and east of the upper Adriatic. Although attached to the customs of his people, Theodoric pursued a policy of assimilation between Germans and Romans. He maintained close relations with the emperor at Constantinople and attracted to his administration able scholars such as Cassiodorus (see page 204). Theodoric's accomplishments were significant, but after his death his administration fell apart.

The kingdom established by the Franks in the sixth century, in spite of later civil wars, proved to be the most powerful and enduring of all the barbarian kingdoms. The Franks were a confederation of peoples who originated in the marshy lowlands north and east of the northernmost part of the Rhine frontier of the Roman Empire. They spoke a Germanic language. In the fourth and fifth centuries, they settled within the empire and allied with the Romans, some attaining high military and civil positions. In the sixth century one group, the Salian

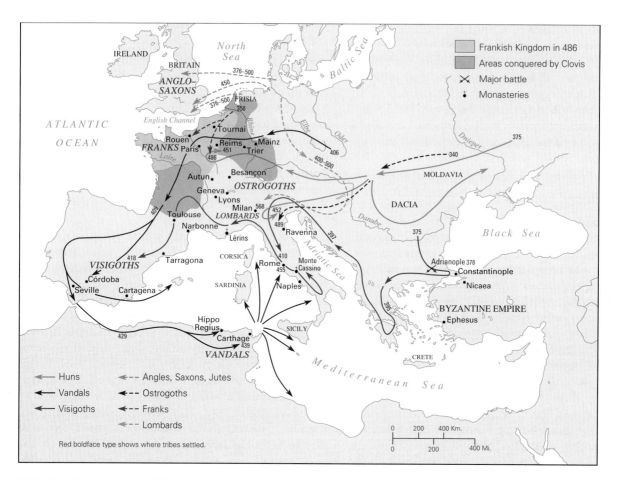

MAP 7.3 The Germanic Migrations   The Germanic tribes infiltrated and settled in all parts of western Europe. The Huns, who were not German ethnically, originated in Central Asia. The Huns' victory over the Ostrogoths led the emperor to allow the Visigoths to settle within the empire, a decision that proved disastrous for Rome.

Franks, issued a law code called the **Salic Law,** the earliest description of Germanic customs. Chlodio (fifth century) is the first member of the Frankish dynasty for whom evidence survives. According to legend, Chlodio's wife went swimming, encountered a sea monster, and conceived Merovech. The Franks believed that Merovech, a man of supernatural origins, founded the Merovingian dynasty.

The reign of Clovis (ca 481–511) marks the decisive period of the development of the Franks as a unified people. Through military campaigns, Clovis acquired the central provinces of Roman Gaul. The next two centuries witnessed the steady assimilation of Franks and Gallo-Romans, as many Franks adopted the Latin language and Roman ways, and Gallo-Romans copied Frankish customs and Frankish personal names. These centuries also

saw Frankish acquisition of the Burgundian kingdom and of territory held by the Goths in Provence.[22]

Many writers have debated the issue of Clovis's conversion from Arian to Roman Christianity. His near-contemporary Gregory, bishop of Tours, attributed Clovis's conversion to the influence of his Catholic wife, Chlotilde. Another contemporary writer holds that in his war with the Alamanni (ca 496), Clovis prayed to the Christian god; in thanksgiving for his victory, he accepted baptism. A third contemporary witness believed that the conversion was "the personal choice of an intelligent monarch." One student of the Franks argues that Clovis was baptized in 508 (not in 496, as has been traditionally believed), at the time he was at war in southwestern Gaul with the Visigothic king Alaric II, and that there was propaganda value to be gained by appearing as the defender of Catholicism against Arianism.[23] Certainly conversion brought Clovis the crucial support of the papacy and of the bishops of Gaul. (See the feature "Listening to the Past: The Conversion of Clovis" on pages 232–233.)

Germanic Society

Germanic society had originated with Iron Age peoples (800–500 B.C.) in the northern parts of central Europe and the southern regions of Scandinavia. After the Germans replaced the Romans, re-establishing their rule over most of the European continent, German customs and traditions formed the basis of European society for centuries. What patterns of social, political, and economic life characterized the Germans?

Scholars are hampered in answering such questions because the Germans did not write and thus kept no written records before their conversion to Christianity. The earliest information about them comes from moralistic accounts by such Romans as the historian Tacitus, who was acquainted only with the tribes living closest to the borders of the empire. Furthermore, Tacitus imposed Greco-Roman categories of tribes and nations on the German peoples he described, ethnographic classifications that have dominated scholarly writing until very recently. Only in the past few decades have anthropologists begun to study early German society on its own terms.

Kinship, Custom, and Class

The Germans had no notion of the state as we use the term today; they thought in social, not political, terms. The basic Germanic social unit was the tribe, or *folk.* Members of the folk believed that they were all descended from a common ancestor. Blood united them. Kinship protected them. Law was custom—unwritten, preserved in the minds of the elders of the tribe, and handed down by word of mouth from generation to generation. Every tribe had its customs, and every member of the tribe knew what they were. Members were subject to their tribe's customary law wherever they went, and friendly tribes respected one another's laws.

In the second and third centuries, Germanic peoples experienced continued stress and pressures from other peoples. A radical restructuring of tribes occurred as tribal groups splintered, some disappeared, and new tribes were formed.

Germanic tribes were led by kings, or tribal chieftains. The chief was that member of the folk recognized as the strongest and bravest in battle, elected from among the male members of the strongest family. He led the tribe in war, settled disputes among its members, conducted negotiations with outside powers, and offered sacrifices to the gods. The period of migrations and conquests of the western Roman Empire witnessed the strengthening of kingship among the Germanic tribes. Tribes that did not migrate did not develop kings.

Closely associated with the king in some southern tribes was the **comitatus,** or "war band." Writing at the end of the first century, Tacitus described the war band as the bravest young men in the tribe. They swore loyalty to the chief, fought with him in battle, and were not supposed to leave the battlefield without him; to do so implied cowardice, disloyalty, and social disgrace. A social egalitarianism existed among members of the war band. The comitatus had importance for the later development of feudalism.

During the migrations of the third and fourth centuries, however, and as a result of constant warfare, the war band was transformed into a system of stratified ranks. For example, among the Ostrogoths a warrior nobility and several other nobilities evolved. Contact with the Romans, who produced such goods as armbands for trade with the barbarians, stimulated demand for armbands. Thus armbands, especially the gold ones reserved for the "royal families," promoted the development of hierarchical ranks within war bands. During the Ostrogothic conquest of Italy under Theodoric, warrior-nobles also sought to acquire land, both as a mark of prestige and as a means to power. As land and wealth came into the hands of a small elite class, social inequalities emerged and gradually grew stronger.[24] These inequalities help to explain the origins of the European noble class (see pages 253–254).

Law

As long as custom determined all behavior, the early Germans had no need for written laws. Beginning in the late sixth century, however, German tribal chieftains began to collect, write, and publish lists of their customs. Why then? The Christian missionaries who were slowly converting the Germans to Christianity wanted to know the tribal customs and encouraged German rulers to set down their customs in written form. Churchmen wanted to read about German ways in order to assimilate the tribes to Christianity. Augustine of Canterbury, for example, persuaded King Ethelbert of Kent to have his folk laws written down: these *Dooms of Ethelbert* date from between 601 and 604, roughly five years after Augustine's arrival in Britain. Moreover, by the sixth century the German kings needed regulations for the Romans under their jurisdiction as well as for their own people.

According to the code of the Salian Franks, every person had a particular monetary value to the tribe. This value was called the **wergeld,** which literally means "man-money" or "money to buy off the spear." Men of fighting age had the highest wergeld, then women of childbearing age, children, and finally the aged. Everyone's value reflected his or her potential military worthiness. If a person accused of a crime agreed to pay the wergeld and if the victim and his or her family accepted the payment, there was peace (hence the expression "money to buy off the spear"). If the accused refused to pay the wergeld or if the victim's family refused to accept it, a blood feud ensued. Individuals depended on their kin for protection, and kinship served as a force of social control.

Historians and sociologists have difficulty interpreting the early law codes, partly because they are patchwork affairs studded with additions made in later centuries. Yet much historical information can be gleaned from these codes. For example, the Salic Law (see page 210) offers a general picture of Germanic life and problems in the early Middle Ages and is typical of the law codes of other tribes, such as the Visigoths, Burgundians, Lombards, and Anglo-Saxons.

The Salic Law lists the money fines to be paid to the victim or the family for such injuries as theft, rape, assault, arson, and murder:

If any person strike another on the head so that the brain appears, and the three bones which lie above the brain shall project, he shall be sentenced to 1200 denars, which make 300 shillings. . . .

If any one have killed a free woman after she has begun bearing children, he shall be sentenced to 2400 denars, which make 600 shillings. . . .

If any one shall have drawn a harrow through another's harvest after it has sprouted, or shall have gone through it with a wagon where there was no road, he shall be sentenced to 120 denars, which make 30 shillings.[25]

This is not a systematic statement of a body of law, but a list of fines for particular offenses. German law aimed at the prevention or reduction of violence. It was not concerned with abstract justice.

At first, Romans had been subject to Roman law and Germans to Germanic custom. As German kings accepted Christianity and as Romans and Germans increasingly intermarried, the distinction between the two laws blurred and, in the course of the seventh and eighth centuries, disappeared. The result would be the new feudal law, to which Romans and Germans were subject alike.

German Life

The Germans usually resided in small villages where climate and geography determined the basic patterns of agricultural and pastoral life. In the flat or open coastal regions, German males engaged in animal husbandry, especially cattle raising. Many tribes lived in small settlements on the edges of clearings where they raised barley, wheat, oats, peas, and beans. They tilled their fields with a simple wooden scratch plow and harvested their grains with a small iron sickle. The kernels of grain were ground up for flour or fermented into a strong, thick beer. Women performed the heavy work of raising, grinding, and preserving cereals, a mark, some scholars believe, of their low status in a male-dominated society. Women also had responsibility for weaving and spinning the thread that went into the manufacture of clothing and all textiles.

Within the small villages, there were great differences in wealth and status. Free men constituted the largest class. The number of cattle a man possessed indicated his wealth and determined his social status. "Cattle were so much the quintessential indicator of wealth in traditional society that the modern English term 'fee' (meaning cost of goods or services), which developed from the medieval term 'fief,' had its origin in the Germanic term *fihu* . . . , meaning cattle, chattels, and hence, in general, wealth."[26] Free men also shared in tribal warfare. Slaves (prisoners of war) worked as farm laborers, herdsmen, or household servants.

German society was patriarchal: within each household the father had authority over his wives, children, and slaves. The Germans practiced polygamy, and men who could afford them had more than one wife.

Did the Germans produce goods for trade and exchange? Ironworking represented the most advanced craft of the Germanic peoples. Much of northern Europe had iron deposits, and the dense forests provided wood for charcoal. Most villages had an oven and smiths who produced agricultural tools and instruments of war—one-edged swords, arrowheads, and shields. In the first two centuries A.D., the quantity and quality of German goods increased dramatically, and the first steel swords were superior to the weapons of Roman troops. But German goods were produced for war and the subsistence economy, not for trade. Goods were also used for gift giving, a major social custom. Gift giving conferred status on the giver, who, in giving, showed his higher (economic) status, cemented friendship, and placed the receiver in the giver's debt.[27] Goods that could not be produced in the village were acquired by raiding and warfare rather than by commercial exchanges. Raids between tribes brought the victors booty; the cattle and

Vandal Landowner   The adoption of Roman dress—short tunic, cloak, and sandals—reflects the way the Germanic tribes accepted Roman lifestyles. Likewise both the mosaic art form and the man's stylized appearance show the Germans' assimilation of Roman influences. (Notice that the rider has a saddle but no stirrups.) *(Courtesy of the Trustees of the British Museum)*

slaves captured were traded or given as gifts. Warfare determined the economy and the individual's status within the Germanic society.

What was the position of women in Germanic society? The law codes provide the best evidence. The codes show societies that regarded women as family property. A marriageable daughter went to the highest bidder. A woman of childbearing years had a very high wergeld. The codes also protected the virtue of women. For example, the Salic Law of the Franks fined a man the large amount of 15 solidi (from *solidus,* a coin originally minted by Constantine and later the basis of much European currency, such as the English shilling) if he pressed the hand of a woman,

35 if he touched her above the elbow. On the other hand, widows were sometimes seized on the battlefields where their dead husbands lay and forced to marry the victors. The sixth-century queen Radegund was forced to marry Chlotar I, the murderer of several of her relatives. Radegund later escaped her polygamous union and lived out her life in a convent. Still, the very high fine of 600 solidi for the murder of a woman of childbearing years—the same value attached to military officers of the king, priests, and boys preparing to become warriors—suggests the considerable status of women in Frankish society.

The authority of a father over his daughter or of a husband over his wife was almost absolute: he managed her property and represented her in court. However, once a widow (and there must have been many widows in such a violent, warring society), a woman assumed her husband's rights. She completely controlled their property and held the guardianship of their children. Religious writers and prelates doubted the spiritual equality of women with men. For those writers, women demonstrated their spiritual worth by converting their husbands, raising pious children, endowing churches and monasteries, and dispensing charity to the poor.

A few slaves and peasant women used their beauty and their intelligence to advance their positions. The slave Fredegunda, for whom King Chilperic murdered his Visigothic wife, became a queen and held her position after her husband's death.[28]

In monasteries and convents, women found outlets for their talents as writers, copyists, artists, embroiderers, and teachers. Some houses of religious women, such as Mauberge in northern Francia under Abbess Aldegund (ca 661), produced important scholarship. Women also used their economic abilities as managers of abbatial estates.[29] The dowry required for entrance to convents restricted admission to upper-class women.

Anglo-Saxon England

The island of Britain, conquered by Rome during the reign of Claudius, shared fully in the life of the Roman Empire during the first four centuries of the Christian era. A military aristocracy governed, and the official religion was the cult of the emperor. Towns were planned in the Roman fashion, with temples, public baths, theaters, and amphitheaters. In the countryside, large manors controlled the surrounding lands. Roman merchants brought Eastern luxury goods and Eastern religions—including Christianity—into Britain. The Celts with their iron spears had posed the greatest threat to Roman rule, and the Romans had suppressed the Celtic chieftains. In the course of the second and third centuries, the Celts assimilated to Roman culture.

The Roman army in Britain, as elsewhere, consisted largely of barbarian troops allowed to settle there as foederati (see page 209), in return for the responsibility of military defense. In 407 the emperor Honorius (r. 395–423), faced with the Visigothic army under Alaric, was forced to withdraw imperial troops from Britain. The Picts from Scotland continued to harass the north. According to the eighth-century historian Bede (see page 247), the Celtic king Vortigern invited the Saxons from Denmark to help him against his rivals in Britain. Teutonic tribes from modern-day Norway, Sweden, and

Denmark—the Angles, Saxons, and Jutes—stepped up their assaults, attacking in a hit-and-run fashion. Their goal was plunder, and at first their invasions led to no permanent settlements. As more Germans arrived, however, they took over the best lands and humbled the Britons. Increasingly, the Britons fled to Wales in the west and across the English Channel to Brittany. The sporadic raids continued for over a century and led to Germanic control of most of Britain. Historians have labeled the period 500 to 1066, the year of the Norman Conquest, "Anglo-Saxon."

Except for the Jutes, who probably came from Jutland (modern Denmark), the Teutonic tribes came from the least Romanized and least civilized parts of Europe. The Germans destroyed Roman culture in Britain. Tribal custom superseded Roman law.

The Anglo-Saxon invasion gave rise to a rich body of Celtic mythology, based on the writings of the ninth-century Welsh scholar Nennius; the mythology became known as the Arthurian legends. When Arthur, the illegitimate son of the king of Britain, successfully drew a sword from a stone, Merlin, the court magician, revealed Arthur's royal parentage. Arthur won recognition as king, and the mysterious Lady of the Lake gave him the invincible sword Excalibur, with which he fought many battles against the Saxon invaders. Arthur held his court at Camelot, with his knights seated at the Round Table (to avoid quarrels over precedence). Those knights—including Sir Tristan, Sir Lancelot, Sir Galahad, and Sir Percival (Parsifal), who came to represent the ideal of medieval knightly chivalry—played a large role in later medieval and modern literature.

The Arthurian legends represent Celtic hostility to the Anglo-Saxon invaders. The beginnings of the Germanic kingdoms in Britain are very obscure, but scholars suspect they came into being in the seventh and eighth centuries. The scholar Bede described seven kingdoms: the Jutish kingdom of Kent; the Saxon kingdoms of the East Saxons (Essex), South Saxons (Sussex), and West Saxons (Wessex); and the kingdoms of the Angles, Mercians, and Northumbrians (see Map 7.1). The names imply that these peoples thought of themselves in tribal rather than geographical terms. Because of Bede's categorization, scholars often refer to the Heptarchy, or seven kingdoms, of Anglo-Saxon Britain. The suggestion of total Anglo-Saxon domination, however, is not entirely accurate. Germanic tribes never subdued Scotland, where the Picts remained strong, or Wales, where the Celts and native Britons continued to put up stubborn resistance.

Thus Anglo-Saxon England was divided along ethnic and political lines. The Teutonic kingdoms in the south, east, and center were opposed by the Britons in the west, who wanted to get rid of the invaders. The Anglo-Saxon kingdoms also fought among themselves, causing boundaries to shift constantly. Finally, in the ninth century, under pressure of the Danish, or Viking, invasions, the Britons and the Germanic peoples were molded together under the leadership of King Alfred of Wessex (r. 871–899).

The Byzantine East (ca 400–788)

Constantine had tried to maintain the unity of the Roman Empire, but during the fifth and sixth centuries the western and eastern halves drifted apart. Later emperors worked to hold the empire together. Justinian (r. 527–565) waged long and hard-fought wars against the Ostrogoths and temporarily regained Italy and North Africa. But his conquests had disastrous consequences. Justinian's wars exhausted the resources of the Byzantine state, destroyed Italy's economy, and killed a large part of Italy's population. The wars paved the way for the easy conquest of Italy by another Germanic tribe, the Lombards, shortly after Justinian's death. In the late sixth century, the territory of the western Roman Empire came under Germanic sway, while in the East the Byzantine Empire (see Map 7.4) continued the traditions and institutions of the caesars.

While the western parts of the Roman Empire gradually succumbed to Germanic invaders, the eastern or Roman-Byzantine Empire survived Germanic, Persian, and Arab attacks. In 540 the Huns and Bulgars crossed the Danube and raided the Balkans as far south as the Isthmus of Corinth. In 559 a force of Huns and Slavs reached the gates of Constantinople. In 583 the Avars, a mounted Mongol people who had swept across Russia and southeastern Europe, seized Byzantine forts along the Danube and reached the walls of Constantinople. Between 572 and 630, the Sasanid Persians posed a formidable threat, and the Greeks were repeatedly at war with them. Beginning in 632, the Arabs pressured the Greek empire (see below). Why didn't one or a combination of these enemies capture Constantinople, as the Germans had taken Rome?

The answer lies in the strong military leadership the Greeks possessed, and even more in the city's location and its excellent fortifications. Under the skillful leadership of General Priskos (d. 612), Byzantine armies inflicted a severe defeat on the Avars in 601. Then, after a long war, the emperor Heraclius I (r. 610–641), helped by dynastic disputes among the Persians and Muslim pressures on them, crushed the Persians at Nineveh in Iraq. The Muslim Arabs now posed the greatest threat to the Byzantines. Why didn't they conquer the city? As one scholar explains, "If in the fourth century Constantine had chosen Antioch, Alexandria or Palestinian Caesarea as a capital there can be little doubt that the Roman empire would have gone as swiftly (to the Muslims) as the Persian."[30] The site of Constantinople was not absolutely impregnable—as the Venetians demonstrated in 1204 (see pages 279 and 353) and as the Ottoman Turks did in 1453. But it was almost so. By land, the 750-mile distance between Damascus, the Muslim capital, and Constantinople, some of it mountainous terrain, posed greater geographical and logistical problems than a seventh- or eighth-century government could solve. Massive triple walls, built by Constantine and Theodosius II (408–450) and kept in good repair, protected the city from sea invasion. Within the walls huge cisterns provided water, and vast gardens and grazing areas supplied vegetables and meat. Such strong fortifications and provisions meant that if attacked by sea, a defending people could hold out far longer than a besieging army.[31]

The Byzantine Empire maintained a high standard of living, and for centuries the Greeks were the most civilized people in the Western world. Most important, however, is the role of Byzantium as preserver of the wisdom of the ancient world. Byzantium protected and then handed on to the West the intellectual heritage of Greco-Roman civilization.

Byzantine East and Germanic West

As imperial authority disintegrated in the West during the fifth century, civic functions were performed first by church leaders and then by German chieftains. Meanwhile, in the East, the Byzantines preserved the forms and traditions of the old Roman Empire and even called themselves Romans. Byzantine emperors traced their lines back past Constantine to Augustus. The senate that sat in Constantinople carried on the traditions and preserved the glory of the old Roman senate. The army that defended the empire was the direct descendant of the old Roman legions. Even the chariot factions of the Roman Empire lived on under the Byzantines, who cheered their favorites as enthusiastically as had the Romans of Hadrian's day.

The position of the church differed considerably in the Byzantine East and the Germanic West. The fourth-century emperors Constantine and Theodosius I had wanted the church to act as a unifying force within the empire, but the Germanic invasions made that impossible. The bishops of Rome repeatedly called on the emperors at Constantinople for military support against the invaders, but rarely could the emperors send it. The church in the West steadily grew away from the empire

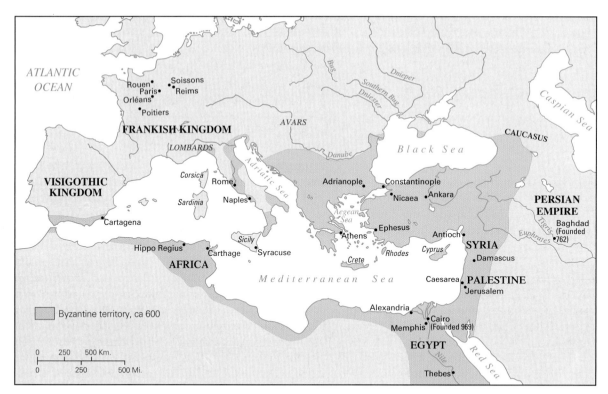

MAP 7.4 The Byzantine Empire, ca 600 The western territories acquired by Justinian's sixth-century wars proved a valuable source of Germanic warriors for use in the Balkans and enabled Byzantine emperors to influence the papacy, but their priorities were in the East.

and became involved in the social and political affairs of Italy and the West. Nevertheless, until the eighth century, the popes, who were often selected by the clergy of Rome, continued to send announcements of their elections to the emperors at Constantinople—a sign that the Roman popes long thought of themselves as bishops of the Roman Empire. Most church theology in the West came from the East.

Tensions occasionally developed between church officials and secular authorities in the West. The dispute between Bishop Ambrose of Milan and the emperor Theodosius (see page 194) is a good example. A century later, Pope Gelasius I (492–496) insisted that bishops, not civil authorities, were responsible for the administration of the church. Gelasius maintained that two powers governed the world: the sacred authority of popes and the royal power of kings. Because priests had to answer to God even for the actions of kings, the sacred power was the greater.

Students traditionally used the term **caesaropapism** to describe the supposedly unlimited power the emperor

had over the church, even in doctrinal matters. According to this theory, the **Orthodox church,** in contrast to the Western church, lost its independence and was a branch of the Byzantine state. Recent scholars reject this idea as too simple. On the one hand, emperors appointed the highest officials of the church hierarchy, including the patriarchs; the emperors or their representatives presided at ecumenical councils; and the emperors controlled some of the material resources of the church—land, rents, dependent peasantry. On the other hand, the emperors performed few liturgical functions and rarely tried to impose their views in theological disputes; Greek churchmen vigorously defended the church's independence, and some even asserted the superiority of the bishop's authority over the emperor; and the church possessed such enormous economic wealth and influence over the population that it could block governmental decisions.[32] Caesaropapism, therefore, exaggerates the degree of control the emperors had over the church.

The steady separation of the Byzantine East and the Germanic West rests partly on the ways Christianity and classical culture were received in the two parts of the Roman Empire. In the West, Christians initially constituted a small, alien minority within the broad Roman culture; they kept apart from the rest of society. In Byzantium, by contrast, most Greeks were Christian. *Apologists,* or defenders, of Christianity insisted on harmony between Christianity and classical culture: they used Greek philosophy to buttress Christian tenets. Politically, as we have seen, emperors beginning with Constantine worked for the unanimity of church and state.

The expansion of the Arabs in the Mediterranean in the seventh and eighth centuries furthered the separation of the Western and Eastern churches by dividing the two parts of Christendom. Separation bred isolation. Isolation, combined with prejudice on both sides, bred hostility. Finally, in 1054, a theological disagreement led the bishop of Rome and the patriarch of Constantinople to excommunicate each other. The outcome was a permanent *schism,* or split, between the Roman Catholic and Greek Orthodox churches. The Byzantine church claimed to be *orthodox,* that is, that it always possessed right doctrine.

Despite religious differences, the Byzantine Empire served as a bulwark for the West, protecting it against invasions from the East. The Greeks stopped the Persians in the seventh century. They blunted but could not stop Arab attacks in the seventh and eighth centuries, and they fought courageously against Turkish invaders until the fifteenth century, when they were finally overwhelmed. Byzantine Greeks slowed the impetus of Slavic incursions in the Balkans and held the Russians at arm's length.

Turning from war to peace, the Byzantines set about civilizing the Slavs, in Central Europe, in the Balkans and in Russia. In 863 the emperor Michael III sent the brothers Cyril (826–869) and Methodius (815–885) to preach Christianity in Moravia (the region of modern central Czech Republic). Other missionaries succeeded in converting the Russians in the tenth century. Cyril invented a Slavic alphabet using Greek characters, and this script (called the "Cyrillic alphabet") is still in use today. Cyrillic script made possible the birth of Russian literature. Similarly, Byzantine art and architecture became the basis and inspiration of Russian forms. The Byzantines were so successful that the Russians claimed to be the successors of the Byzantine Empire. For a time, Moscow was even known as the "Third Rome" (the second Rome being Constantinople).

The Law Code of Justinian

One of the most splendid achievements of the Byzantine emperors was the preservation of Roman law for the medieval and modern worlds. Roman law had developed from many sources—decisions by judges, edicts of the emperors, legislation passed by the senate, and the opinions of jurists expert in the theory and practice of law. By the fourth century, Roman law had become a huge, bewildering mass. Its sheer bulk made it almost unusable. Some laws had become outdated; some repeated or contradicted others.

Sweeping and systematic codification took place under the emperor Justinian. He appointed a committee of eminent jurists to sort through and organize the laws. The result was the *Code,* which distilled the legal genius of the Romans into a coherent whole, eliminated outmoded laws and contradictions, and clarified the law itself. Not content with the *Code,* Justinian set about bringing order to the equally huge body of Roman *jurisprudence,* the science or philosophy of law.

During the second and third centuries, the foremost Roman jurists had expressed varied learned opinions on complex legal problems. To harmonize this body of knowledge, Justinian directed his jurists to clear up disputed points and to issue definitive rulings. Accordingly, in 533 his lawyers published the *Digest,* which codified Roman legal thought. Finally, Justinian's lawyers compiled a handbook of civil law, the *Institutes.* These three works—the *Code, Digest,* and *Institutes*—are the backbone of the *corpus juris civilis,* the "body of civil law," which is the foundation of law for nearly every modern European nation.

The following excerpts on marriage and adultery from the corpus juris civilis provide valuable information on the status of women in Roman and Byzantine law:

—*Roman citizens unite in legal marriage when they are joined according to the precepts of the law, and males have attained the age of puberty and the females are capable of childbirth . . . [they must] if the latter have also the consent of the relatives under whose authority they may be, for this should be obtained and both civil and natural law require that it should be secured.*
—*The lex Julia ["Julian law," dating from 18 B.C.] declares that wives have no right to bring criminal accusations for adultery against their husbands, even though they may desire to complain of the violation of the marriage vow, for while the law grants this privilege to men it does not concede it to women.*[33]

Byzantine Intellectual Life

Among the Byzantines, education was highly prized, and because of them many masterpieces of ancient Greek literature survived to influence the intellectual life of the

Justinian and His Attendants This mosaic detail is composed of thousands of tiny cubes of colored glass or stone called *tessarae,* which are set in plaster against a blazing golden background. Some attempt has been made at naturalistic portraiture. *(Scala/Art Resource, NY)*

modern world. The literature of the Byzantine Empire was predominately Greek, although Latin was long spoken among top politicians, scholars, and lawyers. Indeed, Justinian's *Code* was first written in Latin. Among the large reading public, history was a favorite subject. Generations of Byzantines read the historical works of Herodotus, Thucydides, and others. Some Byzantine historians abbreviated long histories, such as those of Polybius, while others wrote detailed narratives of their own days.

The most remarkable Byzantine historian was Procopius (ca 500–ca 562), who left a rousing account praising Justinian's reconquest of North Africa and Italy. Proof that the wit and venom of ancient writers such as Archilochus and Aristophanes lived on in the Byzantine era can be found in Procopius's *Secret History,* a vicious and uproarious attack on Justinian and his wife, the empress Theodora. (See the feature "Individuals in Society: Theodora of Constantinople.") Witness the following description of Justinian's character by Procopius.

For he was at once villainous and amenable; as people say colloquially, a moron. He was never truthful with anyone, but always guileful in what he said and did, yet easily hoodwinked by any who wanted to deceive him. His nature was an unnatural mixture of folly and wickedness.[34]

How much of this is true, how much the hostility of a sanctimonious hypocrite relishing the gossip he spreads, we will never know. Certainly *The Secret History* is robust reading.

In mathematics and geometry, the Byzantines discovered little that was new. Yet they passed Greco-Roman

Individuals in Society

Theodora of Constantinople

The most notorious woman in Byzantine history, daughter of a circus bear trainer in the hippodrome, Theodora (ca 497–548) grew up in what contemporaries considered a morally corrupt atmosphere. Heredity gave her intelligence, wit, charm, and beauty, which she put to use as a striptease artist and actress. Modern scholars question the tales spread by the historian Procopius's *Secret History* (ca 550) about Theodora's insatiable sexual appetite, but the legend of her sensuality has often influenced interpretations of her.

Theodora gave up her stage career and passed her time spinning wool and discussing theological issues. When Justinian first saw her, he was so impressed by her beauty and wit, he brought her to the court, raised her to the *patriciate* (high nobility), and in 525 married her. When he was proclaimed co-emperor with his uncle Justin on April 1, 527, Theodora received the rare title of *augusta*, empress. Thereafter her name was always linked with Justinian's in the exercise of imperial power.

We know a fair amount about Theodora's public life. With four thousand attendants, she processed through the streets of Constantinople to attend Mass and celebrations thanking God for deliverance from the plague. She presided at imperial receptions for Arab sheiks, Persian ambassadors, Gothic princesses from the West, and barbarian chieftains from southern Russia. Her endowment of hospitals, orphanages, houses for the rehabilitation of prostitutes, and Monophysite churches gave her a reputation for piety and charity. But her private life remains hidden. She spent her days in the silken luxury of the *gynaceum* (women's quarters) among her female attendants and eunuch guards. She took the waters at the sulfur springs in Bithynia, and spent the hot summer months at her palace at Hieron, a small town on the Asiatic shore of the Bosporus. Justinian is reputed to have consulted her every day about all aspects of state policy.

One conciliar occasion stands out. In 532 various elements combined to provoke a massive revolt against the emperor. Shouting N-I-K-A (Victory), rioters swept through the city burning and looting. Justinian's counselors urged flight, but Theodora rose and declared:

For one who has reigned, it is intolerable to be an exile. . . . If you wish, O Emperor, to save yourself, there is no difficulty: we have ample funds and there are the ships. Yet reflect whether, when you have once escaped to a place of security, you will not prefer death to

safety. I agree with an old saying that the purple is a fair winding sheet.

The empress Theodora, with a halo—symbolic of power in Eastern art.
(Scala/Art Resource, NY)

Justinian rallied, had the rioters driven into the hippodrome, and ordered between thirty-five thousand and forty thousand men and women executed. The revolt was crushed. When the bubonic plague hit Justinian in 532, Theodora took over his duties. Her influence over her husband and her power in the Byzantine state continued until she died of cancer.

How do we assess this highly complicated woman who played so many roles, who could be ruthless and merciless, political realist and yet visionary, totally loyal to those she loved? As striptease artist? Actress? Politician? Pious philanthropist? Did she learn survival in the brutal world of the hippodrome? To jump from striptease artist and the stage all the way to the imperial throne suggests enormous intelligence. Is Theodora a symbol of that manipulation of beauty and cleverness by which some women (and men) in every age have attained position and power? Were her many charitable works, especially the houses for the rehabilitation of prostitutes, the result of compassion for a profession she knew well? Or were those benefactions only what her culture expected of the rich and famous? With twenty years service to Justinian and the state, is it fair to brand her as "notorious" for what may only have been youthful indiscretions?

Questions for Analysis

1. How would you assess the importance of ceremony in Byzantine life?
2. Since Theodora's name was always linked with Justinian's, was she a co-ruler?

The **history companion** *features additional information and activities related to this topic.* history.college.hmco.com/students

learning on to the Arabs, who assimilated it and made remarkable advances with it. The Byzantines were equally uncreative in astronomy and natural science, but at least they faithfully learned what the ancients had to teach. Only when science could be put to military use did the Byzantines make advances. For example, the best-known Byzantine scientific discovery was chemical—"Greek fire" or "liquid fire," an explosive compound made of crude oil mixed with resin and sulfur, which was heated and propelled by a pump through a bronze tube. As the liquid jet left the tube, it was ignited—somewhat like a modern flamethrower. "Greek fire" saved Constantinople from Arab assault in 678. In mechanics the Byzantines continued the work of Hellenistic and Roman inventors of artillery and siege machinery. Just as Archimedes had devised machines to stop the Romans, so Byzantine scientists improved and modified devices for defending their empire.

The Byzantines devoted a great deal of attention to medicine, and the general level of medical competence was far higher in the Byzantine Empire than it was in the medieval West. The Byzantines assimilated the discoveries of Hellenic and Hellenistic medicine but added very few of their own. The basis of their medical theory was Hippocrates' concept of the four humors (see page 84). Byzantine physicians emphasized the importance of diet and rest and relied heavily on herbal medicines. Perhaps their chief weakness was excessive use of bleeding and burning, which often succeeded only in further weakening an already feeble patient.

Greek medical science could not, however, cope with the terrible disease, often called the "Justinian plague," that swept through the Byzantine Empire, Italy, southern France, Iberia, and the Rhine Valley between 541 and about 700. Probably originating in northwestern India and carried to the Mediterranean region by ships, the disease followed the syndrome of modern forms of the bubonic plague. Characterized by high fevers, chills, delirium, and enlarged lymph nodes (the buboes that gave the disease its name), or by inflammation of the lungs that caused hemorrhages of black blood, the "Justinian plague" carried off tens of thousands of people.

Anicia Juliana (462?–528?)   Daughter of a Byzantine emperor and great benefactor of the church and of the arts, Anicia Juliana commissioned a manuscript of the works of the physician Dioscorides (fl. first century) on herbal medicines, which remained the standard reference work on the subject for centuries. She is shown here seated between two Virtues, Magnanimity and Patience. *(Osterreichische Nationalbibliothek)*

The epidemic had profound political as well as social consequences. It weakened Justinian's military resources, thus hampering his efforts to restore unity to the Mediterranean world. Demographic disasters resulting from the plague also prevented the Byzantine and Persian forces from offering more than token opposition to the Muslim armies when the Arabs swarmed out of Arabia in 634 (see page 224).[35]

Still, by the ninth or tenth century, most major Greek cities had hospitals for the care of the sick. The hospital operated by the Pantokrator monastery in Constantinople possessed fifty beds divided into five wards for different illnesses; a female gynecologist practiced in the women's ward. The hospital staff also included an ophthalmologist (specialist in the functions and diseases of the eye), a surgeon who performed hernia repairs, two general practitioners, two surgeons who worked an outpatient clinic, and an attendant responsible for keeping instruments clean. The imperial Byzantine government bore the costs of this and other hospitals.

The Arabs and Islam

In the seventh century A.D., two empires dominated the area today called the Middle East: the Byzantine-Greek-Christian empire and the Sasanian-Persian-Zoroastrian empire. The Arabian peninsula lay between the two. The Sasanian dynasty, which descended from Persian-speaking people of present-day southern Iran, maintained political control over very diverse peoples through government officials and by requiring loyalty to the ancient religion of Iraq, Zoroastrianism (see pages 47–48). The Sasanian capital of Ctesiphon in what is now central Iraq had become a center for Jewish religious learning and a refuge for pagan philosophers and medical scientists from the Greek cities after Justinian forbade the teaching of pagan philosophy and law in 529. The cosmopolitan culture thus created became the source for much classical Greek philosophical and medical knowledge that later came to the European world through the channel of Arabic translations.

Around 610, in the commercial city of Mecca in what is now Saudi Arabia, a merchant called Muhammad began to have religious visions. By the time he died in 632, all Arabia had accepted his creed. A century later, his followers controlled Syria, Palestine, Egypt, North Africa, Spain, and part of France. This Arabic expansion profoundly affected the development of Western civilization. Through centers at Salerno in southern Italy and Toledo in central Spain, Arabic and Greek learning reached the West.

The Arabs

In Muhammad's time, Arabia was inhabited by various tribes, most of them Bedouins. These nomadic peoples grazed goats and sheep on the sparse patches of grass that dotted the vast, semiarid peninsula. Other Arabs lived in the southern valleys and coastal towns along the Red Sea—in Yemen, Mecca, Medina, and the northwestern region called "Hejaz." The Hejazi led a more sophisticated life and supported themselves by agriculture and trade. Their caravan routes crisscrossed Arabia and carried goods to Byzantium, Persia, and Syria. The Hejazi had wide commercial dealings but avoided cultural contacts with their Jewish, Christian, and Persian neighbors. The wealth produced by their business transactions led to luxurious and extravagant living in the towns.

Although the nomadic Bedouins condemned the urbanized lifestyle of the Hejazi as immoral and corrupt, Arabs of both types respected one another's local tribal customs. They had no political unity beyond their tribal bonds. Custom demanded the rigid observance of family obligations and the performance of religious rituals. Custom insisted that an Arab be proud, generous, and swift to take revenge. Custom required courage in public and avoidance of behavior that could bring social disgrace.

Although the various tribes differed markedly, they did have certain religious rules in common. For example, all Arabs kept three months of the year as sacred; during that time, fighting stopped so that everyone could attend holy ceremonies in peace. The city of Mecca was the religious center of the Arab world, and fighting was never tolerated there. All Arabs prayed at the Kaaba, the sanctuary in Mecca. Within the Kaaba was a sacred black stone that Arabs revered because they believed it had fallen from heaven.

What eventually molded the diverse Arab tribes into a powerful political and social unity was the religion reformed by Muhammad.

Muhammad and the Faith of Islam

Except for a few vague remarks in the **Qur'an,** the sacred book of Islam, Muhammad (ca 571–632) left no account of his life. Arab tradition accepts as historically true some of the sacred legends that developed about him, but those legends were not written down until about a century after his death. (Similarly, the earliest accounts of the life of Jesus, the Christian Gospels, were not written until forty or sixty years after his death.) Orphaned at the age of six, Muhammad was brought up by his grandfather. As a young man, he became a merchant in the caravan trade. Later he entered the service of a wealthy widow, and their subsequent marriage brought him financial independence. The Qur'an reveals him as an extremely devout man, ascetic, self-disciplined, and literate, but not educated.

Since childhood Muhammad had been subject to seizures during which he completely lost consciousness and had visions. After 610 these attacks and the accompanying visions apparently became more frequent. Unsure for a time what he should do, Muhammad discovered his mission after a vision in which the angel Gabriel instructed him to preach. Muhammad described his visions in a stylized and often rhyming prose and used this literary medium as his *Qur'an,* or "prayer recitation." After Muhammad's death, scribes organized the revelations into chapters, and in 651 Muhammad's third successor as religious leader, Othman, arranged to have an official version of them published.

Like the Hebrew prophets of the Old Testament, Muhammad came as a reformer; he "was not the founder of Islam; he did not start a new religion."[36] The religion he reformed is called **Islam,** which means "submission to God," and Muslim means "one who submits." Muhammad's religion eventually attracted great numbers of people, partly because of the straightforward nature of its doctrines, unlike the subtle and complex reasoning of Christianity.

The strictly monotheistic theology outlined in the Qur'an has only a few tenets. Allah, the Arabic word for God, is all-powerful and all-knowing. Muhammad, Allah's prophet, preached his word and carried his message. Muhammad described himself as the successor both of the Jewish patriarch Abraham and of Christ, and he claimed that his teachings replaced theirs. Muhammad invited and won converts from Judaism and Christianity.

Because Allah is all-powerful, believers must submit themselves to him. This Islamic belief is closely related to the central feature of Muslim doctrine, the coming Day of Judgment. Muslims need not be concerned about *when* judgment will occur, but they must believe with absolute and total conviction that the Day of Judgment *will* come. Consequently, all of a Muslim's thoughts and actions should be oriented toward the Last Judgment and the rewards of Heaven. The Muslim vision of paradise features lush green gardens surrounded by refreshing streams. There the saved, clothed in rich silks, lounge on brocade couches, nibbling ripe fruits, sipping delicious beverages, and enjoying the companionship of physically attractive people.

In order for a person to merit the rewards of heaven, Muhammad prescribed a strict code of moral behavior. The Muslim must recite a profession of faith in God and in Muhammad as God's prophet: "There is no god but God and Muhammad is his prophet." The believer must pray five times a day, fast and pray during the sacred month of Ramadan, and make a pilgrimage to the holy city of Mecca once during his or her lifetime if practical. The believer must also contribute alms to the poor and needy. According to the Muslim *shari'a,* or sacred law, these constitute the **Five Pillars of Islam,** the basic tenets of the faith. In Muslim tradition, the Kaaba predates the creation of the world and represents the earthly counterpart of God's heavenly throne, to which "pilgrims come dishevelled and dusty on every kind of camel."[37] The Qur'an forbids alcoholic beverages and gambling. It condemns business *usury*—that is, lending money at interest rates or taking advantage of market demand for products by charging high prices for them. A number of foods, such as pork, are also forbidden, a dietary regulation adopted from the Mosaic law of the Hebrews.

By earlier Arab standards, the Qur'an sets forth an austere sexual morality. Muslim jurisprudence condemned licentious behavior on the part of men as well as women, which enhanced the status of women in Muslim society. So, too, did Muhammad's opposition to female infanticide. About marriage, illicit intercourse, and inheritance, the Qur'an states:

[Of] women who seem good in your eyes, marry but two, three, or four; and if ye still fear that ye shall not act equitably then only one. . . . The whore and the fornicator: whip each of them a hundred times. . . .

The fornicator shall not marry other than a whore; and the whore shall not marry other than a fornicator. . . .

Men who die and leave wives behind shall bequeath to them a year's maintenance.

And your wives shall have a fourth part of what you leave, if you have no issue [offspring]; but if you have issue, then they shall have an eighth part. . . .

With regard to your children, God commands you to give the male the portion of two females.

Polygyny, the practice of men having more than one wife, was common in Arab society before Muhammad, though for economic reasons the custom was obviously limited to the well-to-do. Nevertheless, some commentators hold that in limiting the number of wives to four—or even one if the man could not treat all fairly—Muhammad was being revolutionary.

Muhammad and the Earlier Prophets   Islamic tradition holds that Judaism, Christianity, and Islam all derive from the pure religion of Abraham, but humankind has strayed from that faith. Therefore, Muhammad, as "the seal (last) of the prophets," had to transmit God's revelations to humankind. Here Muhammad, with his head surrounded by fire representing religious fervor, leads Abraham, Moses, and Jesus in prayer. *(Bibliothèque nationale de France)*

Westerners tend to think polygyny degrading to women, but in a military society where there were apt to be many widows, polygyny provided women a measure of security. With respect to matters of property, Muslim women were more emancipated than Western women. For example, a Muslim woman retained complete jurisdiction over one-third of her property when she married and could dispose of it in any way she wished. Most women in the Germanic West lacked such power in the early Middle Ages.[38]

The Muslim who faithfully observed the laws of the Qur'an could hope for salvation. According to the Qur'an, salvation is by God's grace and choice alone. Because God is all-knowing and all-powerful, he knows from the moment of a person's conception whether or not that person will be saved. Although later Muslim

scholars have held a number of positions on the topic of predestination, from complete fatalism to a strong belief in human free will, Muhammad maintained that predestination gave believers the will and courage to try to achieve the impossible. Devout Muslims came to believe that the performance of the faith's basic rules would automatically gain them salvation. Moreover, the believer who suffered and died for his faith in battle was immediately ensured the rewards of the Muslim heaven.

What did early Muslims think of Jesus? Jesus is mentioned in ninety-three verses of the Qur'an, which affirms that he was born of Mary the Virgin. He is described as a righteous prophet who performed miracles and continued the work of Abraham and Moses, and he was a sign of the coming Day of Judgment. But Muslims held that

Jesus was only an apostle, not God, and that those (that is, Christians) who called Jesus divine committed blasphemy (showing contempt for God). Muslims esteemed the Judeo-Christian Scriptures as part of God's revelation, although they believed that Christian communities had corrupted the Scriptures and that the Qur'an superseded them. The Christian doctrine of the Trinity—that there is one God in three persons (Father, Son, and Holy Spirit)—posed a powerful obstacle to Muslim-Christian understanding because of Islam's total and uncompromising monotheism.[39]

There are many similarities among Islam, Christianity, and Judaism. All three religions are monotheistic; all worship the same God. Like Jews, Muslims customarily worship together at sundown on Fridays, and no assembly or organized church is essential. Muslims call Jews and Christians *dhimmis,* or "protected people," because they were people of the book, the Hebrew Scriptures.

Islam transcended the geographical and public aspects of Arabic tribal religion represented by Bedouin and Hejazi societies (see page 221). Every Muslim hoped that by following the requirements of Islam, he or she could achieve salvation. For the believer, the petty disputes and conflicts of tribal society paled before the simple teachings of Allah. On this basis, Muhammad united the nomads of the desert and the merchants of the cities. The doctrines of Islam, instead of the ties of local custom, bound all Arabs.

Nevertheless, a schism soon developed within the Islamic faith. In 661 the caliph Ali was assassinated. The title *caliph,* which meant "successor" to the Prophet (Muhammad), combined the ideas of spiritual and political leader of the *umma,* or Muslim community. Ali had claimed the caliphate on the basis of family ties: he was Muhammad's cousin and son-in-law. When Ali was murdered, his followers argued that he had been the Prophet's prescribed successor. These supporters of Ali were called *Shi'ites* or *Shi'a,* Arabic terms meaning "supporters" or "partisans" of Ali. In succeeding generations, Shi'ites emphasized the blood descent from Ali and claimed that their *imams* (whom other Muslims called caliphs) possessed divine knowledge that Muhammad had given to them as his heirs. Sunni Muslims stressed the *Sunna,* the account of the Prophet's sayings and conduct in particular situations. When an issue arose for which the Qur'an offered no solution, Muslim scholars searched the Sunna, which gained an authority comparable to the Qur'an itself. The term *Sunna* also means traditional beliefs and practices of the community. Both Shi'ites and Sunnites claimed to follow the Prophet's ex-

ample, but only the Sunnites appropriated the name. In a society that acknowledged no separation between religious and political authority, political opposition expressed itself in religious terms. Over the centuries, many different kinds of Shi'ites appeared. Sunnites identified themselves with religious orthodoxy; they considered the Shi'ites, who claimed special religious knowledge deriving from Ali, heretical. The Shi'ites were always a minority within Islam, potentially a dangerous one.

The Expansion of Islam

Despite this division within Islam, faith in Allah united the Arabs sufficiently to redirect their energies. Hostilities were directed outward. By the time Muhammad died in 632, he had welded together all the Bedouin tribes. The crescent of Islam, the Muslim symbol, prevailed throughout the Arabian peninsula. During the next century, between 632 and the Battle of Poitiers in 732, one rich province of the old Roman Empire after another came under Muslim domination—first Syria, then Egypt, and then all of North Africa (see Map 7.5). Long and bitter wars (572–591, 606–630) between the Byzantine and Persian Empires left both so weak and exhausted that they easily fell to Muslim attack. The governmental headquarters of this vast new empire was established at Damascus in Syria by the ruling Umayyad family. By the early tenth century, a Muslim proverb spoke of the Mediterranean Sea as a Muslim lake, though the Greeks at Constantinople contested that notion.

In 711 a Muslim force crossed the Strait of Gibraltar and at Guadalete in southern Spain easily defeated the weak Visigothic kingdom. A few Christian princes supported by the Frankish rulers held out in northern mountain fortresses, but the Muslims controlled most of Spain until the twelfth century. Between the tenth and fourteenth centuries, these northern Christian kingdoms, propelled by population growth, land hunger, nobles' demands for estates, advances in military technology, and the appetites of sheep moving from one grazing ground to another, pushed southward.

From the Arabian peninsula, Muslims carried their faith deep into Africa and across Asia all the way to India. In the West, however, Arab political influence was felt most heavily in Spain. A member of the Umayyad dynasty, Abd al-Rahman (r. 756–788), established a kingdom in Spain with its capital at Córdoba. In the eleventh century, the Umayyad caliphate splintered into a number of small kingdoms. With Muslim rule thus divided, the small northern Christian kingdoms expanded southward.

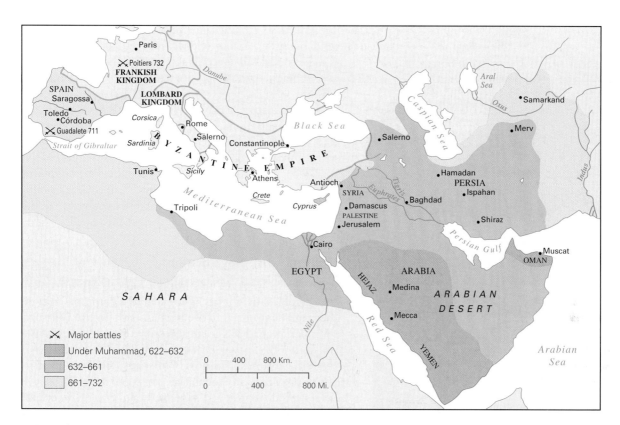

MAP 7.5 The Expansion of Islam to 732 Political weaknesses in the territories the Muslims conquered, as well as superior fighting skills, help explain the speed with which Islam expanded.

In the meantime, Jews in Muslim Spain were generally treated well and Christians tolerated so long as they paid a small tax.

In Spain, as elsewhere in the Arab world, the Muslims had an enormous impact on agricultural development. They began the cultivation of rice, sugar cane, citrus fruits, dates, figs, eggplants, carrots, and, after the eleventh century, cotton. These crops, together with new methods of field irrigation, led to what one scholar has called "a green revolution." Andalusian (southern) Spain developed

a complex and varied agricultural system, whereby a greater variety of soil types were put to efficient use; where fields that had been yielding one crop at most prior to the Islamic invasion were now capable of yielding three or more crops, in rotation; and where agricultural production responded to the demands of an increasingly sophisticated and cosmopolitan urban population by providing the towns with a variety of products unknown in northern Europe.[40]

In urban areas, Muslims made significant advances in thought. Toledo, for example, became an important center of learning, through which Arab intellectual achievements entered and influenced western Europe. Arabic knowledge of science and mathematics, derived from the Chinese, Greeks, and Hindus, was highly sophisticated. The Muslim mathematician al-Khwarizmi (d. 830) wrote the important treatise *Algebra,* the first work in which the word *algebra* is used mathematically. Al-Khwarizmi adopted the Hindu system of numbers (1, 2, 3, 4, etc.), used it in his *Algebra,* and applied mathematics to problems of physics and astronomy. Scholars at Baghdad translated Euclid's *Elements,* the basic text for plane and solid geometry. Muslims also instructed westerners in the use of the zero, which permitted the execution of complicated problems of multiplication and long division. Use of the zero represented an enormous advance over clumsy Roman numerals. (Since our system of numbers is actually Hindu in origin, the term *Arabic numerals* is a misnomer, coined about 1847.)

Harvesting Dates   This detail from an ivory casket given to a Córdoban prince reflects the importance of fruit cultivation in the Muslim-inspired agricultural expansion in southern Europe in the ninth and tenth centuries. (*Louvre/Réunion des Musées Nationaux/Art Resource, NY*)

Muslim medical knowledge far surpassed that of the West. By the ninth century, Arab physicians had translated most of the treatises of Hippocrates. The Baghdad physician al-Razi (865–925) produced an encyclopedic treatise on medicine that was translated into Latin and circulated widely in the West. Al-Razi was the first physician to make the clinical distinction between measles and smallpox. The great surgeon of Córdoba, al-Zahrawi (d. 1013), produced an important work in which he discussed the cauterization of wounds (searing with a branding iron) and the crushing of stones in the bladder. In ibn-Sina of Bukhara (980–1037), known in the West

as Avicenna, a physician, philologist, philosopher, poet, and scientist, Arabic science reached its peak. His *al-Qanun* codified all Greco-Arabic medical thought, described the contagious nature of tuberculosis and the spreading of diseases, and listed 760 pharmaceutical drugs.

Unfortunately, many of these treatises came to the West as translations from Greek to Arabic to Latin and inevitably lost a great deal in translation. Nevertheless, in the ninth and tenth centuries, Arabic knowledge and experience in anatomy and pharmaceutical prescriptions much enriched Western knowledge. Later, Greek philosophical thought passed to the West by way of Arabic translation.

Muslim-Christian Relations

Christian Europeans and Middle Eastern Muslims were geographical neighbors. They shared a common cultural heritage from the Judeo-Christian past. In the Christian West, Islam had the greatest cultural impact in Andalusia in southern Spain. Between roughly the eighth and twelfth centuries, Muslims, Christians, and Jews lived in close proximity in Andalusia, and some scholars believe the period represents a remarkable era of interfaith harmony. Many Christians adopted Arabic patterns of speech and dress, gave up the practice of eating pork, and developed a special appreciation for Arabic music and poetry. Some Christian women of elite status chose the Muslim practice of going in public with their faces veiled. Records describe Muslim and Christian youths joining in celebrations and merrymaking. These assimilated Christians, called **Mozarabs,** did not attach much importance to the doctrinal differences between the two religions.

Mozarabs soon faced the strong criticism of both Muslim scholars and Christian clerics. Muslim teachers feared that close contact between the two peoples would lead to Muslim contamination and become a threat to the Islamic faith. Christian bishops worried that a knowledge of Islam would lead to ignorance of essential Christian doctrines. Both Muslim scholars and Christian theologians argued that assimilation led to sensuality and that sensuality was ruining their particular cultures.

Thus, beginning in the late tenth century, Muslim regulations closely defined what Christians and Muslims could do. A Christian, however much assimilated, remained an **infidel.** An infidel was an unbeliever, and the word carried a pejorative or disparaging connotation. Mozarabs had to live in special sections of cities; could not learn the Qur'an, employ Muslim workers or ser-

Shroud Fragment Rich and powerful people were often buried in precious fabrics. This Islamic silk cloth brocaded with gold thread was produced in Almería, a Muslim city in southern Spain, around 1100. It bears false Arabic inscription for commercial purposes: "This was made in Baghdad, may God protect it." Made for a Christian bishop, the shroud is a fine example of cross-cultural influences. *(Silk and metallic yarns; compound weave; L × W: 16⅞ × 19¹¹⁄₁₆ in. [43 × 50 cm.]. Museum of Fine Arts, Boston, Ellen Page Hall Fund, 33.371)*

vants, or build new churches; and had to be buried in their own cemeteries. A Muslim who converted to Christianity immediately incurred a sentence of death. By about 1250, the **reconquista,** the Christian reconquest of Muslim Spain (see pages 287–289), had brought most of the Iberian Peninsula under Christian control. Christian kings set up schools that taught both Arabic and Latin, but these schools were intended to produce missionaries.

Beyond Andalusian Spain, mutual animosity restricted contact between the two peoples.[41] The Muslim assault on Christian Europe in the eighth and ninth centuries—

with villages burned, monasteries sacked, and Christians sold into slavery—left a legacy of bitter hostility. Christians felt threatened by a faith that acknowledged God as creator of the universe but denied the doctrine of the Trinity; that accepted Jesus as a prophet but denied his divinity; that believed in the Last Judgment but seemed to make sensuality Heaven's greatest reward. Europeans' perception of Islam as a menace helped to inspire the Crusades of the eleventh through thirteenth centuries (see pages 277–283).

In their understanding of the nature and purpose of the state, Muslims and Christians revealed an important similarity and a very real difference. Just as for Christians the state existed to provide the peace, order, and justice wherein the Christian could pursue his or her pilgrimage to the City of God (see page 203), so for Muslims the function of the Islamic state was "to assure that all Muslims could lead a life in keeping with the mandates of the Qur'an and discharge their obligations to Allah."[42] Thus both peoples viewed the state from a theological perspective. In the central Middle Ages, European rulers reinvigorated the concept of the state, in part an organized territory with definite geographical boundaries recognized by other states. Muslims, however, did not conceive of their states as territorial entities, as limited by distinct boundaries. A recent study of more than twenty Muslim geographers writing between 820 and 1320 shows that they paid little attention to, or entirely ignored, territorial boundaries.[43] Rather, what distinguished one region from another was whether most inhabitants were Muslims or nonbelievers. Those territories where the preponderance of the people were Muslims belonged to the *Dar-al-Islam,* the House of Islam; regions where most were Christians or of some other non-Muslim faith constituted the *Dar-al-Harb,* the House of War. All Muslims had the obligation of the *jihad* (literally "self-exertion"), to strive or struggle to lead a virtuous life and to spread God's rule and law. This expansion of Islam could be achieved by teaching, preaching, and, where necessary, armed conflict. A basic theme of the Qur'an was "striving in the path of God."[44] In some cases, "striving" was individual against sin; in others it was social and communal—a "holy war" in the literal sense of armed conflict. Some Muslim scholars consider war in the path of God "the sixth pillar of Islam."[45] With such conflicting views on so basic an institution, conflict seems almost inevitable. Modern notions of tolerance or religious pluralism were foreign to both Muslims and Christians.

By the thirteenth century, Western literature sometimes displayed a sympathetic view of Islam. The Bavarian knight Wolfram von Eschenbach's *Parzival* and the Englishman William Langland's *Piers the Plowman*—two poems that survive in scores of manuscripts, suggesting that they circulated widely—reveal some broad-mindedness and tolerance toward Muslims. Some travelers in the Middle East were impressed by the kindness and generosity of Muslims and with the strictness and devotion with which Muslims observed their faith.[46] More frequently, however, Christian literature portrayed Muslims as the most dreadful of Europe's enemies, guilty of every kind of crime. In his *Inferno,* the great Florentine poet Dante placed the Muslim philosophers Avicenna and Averroes with other virtuous "heathens," among them Socrates and Aristotle, in the first circle of hell, where they endured only moderate punishment. Muhammad, however, Dante consigned to the ninth circle, near Satan himself, where he was condemned as a spreader of discord and scandal. His punishment was to be continually torn apart from his chin to his anus.

Muslims had a strong aversion to travel in Europe. Medieval Europe had no resident Muslim communities where a traveler could find the mosques, foods, or other things desirable for the Muslim way of life. Muslims generally had a horror of going among those they perceived as infidels, and when compelled to make diplomatic or business contacts, they preferred to send Jewish or Christian intermediaries, or dhimmis. Commercially, from the Muslim perspective, Europe had very little to offer. Apart from woolens from the Frisian Islands in the North Sea, which the Muslims admired, there was a sizable trickle of slaves from central and southeastern Europe. Muslims felt that the only thing Europeans had to sell was their own people.

Did Western culture have any impact on Islam—which could be expected, given the geographical proximity of Europe and the Middle East? Muslims looked on Christianity as a flawed religion that Islam had superseded. One historian has written, "For the Muslim, Christ was a precursor, for the Christian Muhammad was an impostor. For the Muslim, Christianity was an early, incomplete, and obsolete form of the true religion." Religion dominated the Islamic perception of Europe. Muslims understood Europe not as Western or European or white, but as Christian. And the fact that European culture was Christian immediately discredited it in Muslim eyes. Christians were presumed to be hostile to Islam and thought to be culturally inferior. Therefore, Muslims had little interest in them or in European culture. For example, an enormous quantity of Muslim historical writing survives from the period between about 800 and 1600. Although the material reflects some knowledge of European geography, it shows an almost total lack of interest among Muslim scholars in European languages, life, and culture. Before the nineteenth century, not a single grammar book or dictionary of any Western language existed in the Muslim world. By contrast, Western scholarship on the Islamic world steadily advanced. By the early seventeenth century, curious European students could find an extensive literature on the history, religion, and culture of the Muslim peoples.[47]

Summary

The civilization that emerged in eighth-century Europe represented a fusion of classical, Christian, and Germanic elements. Latin was the language of educated people, and through the medium of Latin, Christian thinkers expressed both their own ideals and religious doctrines and the laws and customs of the Germanic peoples. Christian missionaries preached the Gospel to the Germanic peoples, instructed them in the basic tenets of the Christian faith, and used penitentials to give them a sense of right moral behavior. Monasteries provided a model of Christian living, a pattern of agricultural development, and a place for education and learning. Christianity, because it energetically and creatively fashioned the Germanic and classical legacies, proved the most powerful agent in the making of Europe.

Islam and Byzantium also made contributions. As the ancient world declined, religious faith, rather than imperial rule, became the core of social identity. Each area came to define its world in religious terms. Christians called their world *ecumenical,* meaning universal. Muslims divided the world into two fundamental sections: the House of Islam, which consisted of all those regions where the law of Islam prevailed, and the House of War, which was the rest of the world. By the logic of Islamic law, no political entity outside of Islam could exist permanently: "As there is one God in heaven, so there can be only one ruler on earth." Islam and Christianity thus each fused the social and political aspects of culture into a self-contained system.

Byzantium could not confine Islam to Arabia, but it thwarted the Muslim challenge to Christianity by restricting Arab expansion. This Byzantine check permitted a separate medieval Christendom to rise in the West. In the eighth century, spiritual loyalty to Rome enabled the papacy to develop into a supranational authority virtually independent of a secular power. The goals and energy of the bishops of Rome, combined with the military strength of the Frankish rulers, built a strong Christian faith in the Latin West.[48]

Key Terms

syncretic faith	eremitical
Arianism	coenobitic monasticism
Petrine Doctrine	solemnia
penitentials	barbarian
foederati	Qur'an
Salic Law	Islam
comitatus	Five Pillars of Islam
wergeld	Mozarabs
caesaropapism	infidel
Orthodox church	reconquista

Notes

1. See J. Hale, *The Civilization of Western Europe in the Renaissance* (New York: Atheneum, 1994), pp. xix, 3–5.
2. R. C. Petry, ed., *A History of Christianity: Readings in the History of Early and Medieval Christianity* (Englewood Cliffs, N.J.: Prentice-Hall, 1962), p. 70.
3. Matthew 16:18–19.
4. H. Bettenson, ed., *Documents of the Christian Church* (Oxford: Oxford University Press, 1947), p. 113.
5. Colossians 3:9–11.
6. Luke 6:20–31.
7. L. Sherley-Price, trans., *Bede: A History of the English Church and People* (Baltimore: Penguin Books, 1962), pp. 86–87.
8. J. T. McNeill and H. Gamer, trans., *Medieval Handbooks of Penance* (New York: Octagon Books, 1965), pp. 184–197.
9. L. White, "The Life of the Silent Majority," in *Life and Thought in the Early Middle Ages,* ed. R. S. Hoyt (Minneapolis: University of Minnesota Press, 1967), p. 100.
10. Peter 2:11–20.
11. V. L. Bullough, *The Subordinate Sex: A History of Attitudes Toward Women* (Urbana: University of Illinois Press, 1973), pp. 118–119.
12. Ibid.
13. See J. Boswell, *Christianity, Social Tolerance, and Homosexuality: Gay People in Western Europe from the Beginning of the Christian Era to the Fourteenth Century* (Chicago: University of Chicago Press, 1980), chaps. 3 and 5, esp. pp. 87, 127–131.
14. F. J. Sheed, trans., *The Confessions of St. Augustine* (New York: Sheed & Ward, 1953), bk. 1, pt. 3.
15. A. Talbot, "Monasteries," in *The Oxford Dictionary of Byzantium,* ed. A. P. Kazhdan, vol. 2 (New York: Oxford University Press, 1991), p. 1393.
16. See Patrick J. Geary, "Barbarians and Ethnicity," in *Late Antiquity: A Guide to the Postclassical World,* ed. G. W. Bowerstock, Peter Brown, and Oleg Grabar (Cambridge, Mass.: Harvard University Press, 1999), pp. 107–129, esp. pp. 107–113.
17. H. Wolfram, *History of the Goths* (Berkeley: University of California Press, 1988), pp. 6–10.
18. Ibid., p. 7. See also T. Burns, *A History of the Ostrogoths* (Bloomington: University of Indiana Press, 1984), pp. 18, 21.
19. See W. Goffart, *Barbarians and Romans: The Techniques of Accommodation* (Princeton, N.J.: Princeton University Press, 1980), chap. 3 and esp. Conclusion, pp. 211–230.
20. See P. J. Geary, *Before France and Germany: The Creation and Transformation of the Merovingian World* (New York: Oxford University Press, 1988), pp. 18–25.
21. Wolfram, *History of the Goths,* pp. 125–131.
22. E. James, *The Franks* (New York: Basil Blackwell, 1988), pp. 3, 7–10, 58.

23. I. Wood, *The Merovingian Kingdoms, 450–751* (New York: Longman, 1994), pp. 41–45.

24. Geary, *Before France and Germany,* pp. 108–112.

25. E. F. Henderson, ed., *Select Historical Documents of the Middle Ages* (London: G. Bell & Sons, 1912), pp. 176–189.

26. Geary, *Before France and Germany,* p. 46.

27. Ibid., p. 50.

28. See S. F. Wemple, "Sanctity and Power: The Dual Pursuit of Early Medieval Women," in *Becoming Visible: Women in European History,* ed. R. Bridenthal et al., 2d ed. (Boston: Houghton Mifflin, 1987), pp. 133–136.

29. See S. F. Wemple, *Women in Frankish Society: Marriage and the Cloister, 500–900* (Philadelphia: University of Pennsylvania Press, 1981), pp. 28–31, 175–187.

30. Mark Whittow, *The Making of Byzantium, 600–1025* (Berkeley: University of California Press, 1996), p. 99.

31. Ibid., pp. 99–103.

32. See A. Papadakis and A. P. Kazhdan, "Caesaropapism," in *The Oxford Dictionary of Byzantium,* ed. A. P. Kazhdan, vol. 1 (New York: Oxford University Press, 1991), pp. 364–365.

33. Quoted in J. B. Bury, *History of the Latter Roman Empire,* vol. 1 (New York: Dover, 1958), pp. 233–234.

34. R. Atwater, trans., *Procopius: The Secret History* (Ann Arbor: University of Michigan Press, 1963), bk. 8.

35. W. H. McNeill, *Plagues and Peoples* (New York: Doubleday, 1976), pp. 127–128.

36. J. L. Esposito, *Islam: The Straight Path* (New York: Oxford University Press, 1988), p. 15; see also pp. 6–17.

37. F. E. Peters, *A Reader on Classical Islam* (Princeton, N.J.: Princeton University Press, 1994), pp. 208–209.

38. J. O'Faolain and L. Martines, eds., *Not in God's Image: Women in History from the Greeks to the Victorians* (New York: Harper & Row, 1973), pp. 108–114.

39. See Jane I. Smith, "Islam and Christendom: Historical, Cultural, and Religious Interaction from the Seventh to the Fifteenth Centuries," in *The Oxford History of Islam,* ed. John L. Esposito (New York: Oxford University Press, 1999), pp. 317–321.

40. T. F. Glick, *Islamic and Christian Spain in the Early Middle Ages* (Princeton, N.J.: Princeton University Press, 1979), pp. 77–78.

41. See Smith, "Islam and Christendom," pp. 317–321.

42. See R. W. Brauer, *Boundaries and Frontiers in Medieval Muslim Geography* (Philadelphia: American Philosophical Society, 1995), p. 41.

43. Ibid., p. 69.

44. Ibid., pp. 12–13.

45. See Esposito, *Islam: The Straight Path,* p. 40; Peters, *A Reader on Classical Islam,* p. 154.

46. JoAnn Hoeppner Moran Cruz, "Western Views of Islam in Medieval Europe," in *Perceptions of Islam,* ed. D. Blanks and M. Frassetto (New York: St. Martin's Press, 1999), pp. 55–81.

47. See B. Lewis, *The Muslim Discovery of Europe* (New York: W. W. Norton, 1982), pp. 296–297.

48. See J. Herrin, *The Formation of Christendom* (Princeton, N.J.: Princeton University Press, 1987), pp. 7–8, 477, passim.

Suggested Reading

Students seeking information on the early Christian church will find sound material in the following reference works: J. F. Kelly, *The Concise Dictionary of Early Christianity* (1992); J. McManners, ed., *The Oxford Illustrated History of Christianity* (1990); and A. P. Kazhdan, ed., *The Oxford Dictionary of Byzantium* (1991).

J. Herrin, *The Formation of Christendom* (1987), is the best synthesis of the history of the early Middle Ages; it also contains an excellent discussion of Byzantine, Muslim, and Western art. In addition to the other studies listed in the Notes, students may consult the following works for a more detailed treatment of the early Middle Ages. P. Brown, *The World of Late Antiquity, A.D. 150–750,* rev. ed. (1989), stresses social and cultural change, is lavishly illustrated, and has lucidly written introductions to the entire period. J. Pelikan, *The Excellent Empire: The Fall of Rome and the Triumph of the Church* (1987), describes how interpretations of the fall of Rome have influenced our understanding of Western culture.

W. Meeks, *The First Urban Christians: The Social World of the Apostle Paul* (1983), shows that the early Christians came from all social classes. For a solid appreciation of Christian life in a non-Christian society, see M. Mullin, *Called to Be Saints: Christian Living in First Century Rome* (1992). P. Brown, *The Cult of the Saints: Its Rise and Function in Latin Christianity* (1982), describes the significance of the saints in popular religion. Students seeking to understand early Christian attitudes on sexuality and how they replaced Roman ones should consult the magisterial work of P. Brown, *The Body and Society: Men, Women, and Sexual Renunciation in Early Christianity* (1988). R. Macmullen, *Christianity and Paganism in the Fourth to Eighth Centuries* (1998), explores the influences of Christianity and paganism on each other.

The best biography of Saint Augustine is P. Brown, *Augustine of Hippo* (1967), which treats him as a symbol of change. J. B. Russell, *Dissent and Order in the Middle Ages: The Search for Legitimate Authority* (1992), offers a provocative discussion of religious orthodoxy and heresy in the church.

The phenomenon of monasticism has attracted interest throughout the centuries. The best modern edition of the Benedictine *Rule* is T. Fry et al., eds., *RB 1980: The Rule of St. Benedict in Latin and English with Notes* (1981), which contains a history of Western monasticism and a scholarly commentary on the *Rule.* L. Eberle, trans., *The Rule of the Master* (1977), offers the text of and a commentary on Benedict's major source. C. H. Lawrence, *Medieval Monasticism: Forms of Religious Life in Western Europe in the Middle Ages* (1988), provides a good general sketch and a helpful glossary of terms, though it confuses the monastic and the mendicant orders. For women in monastic life, see S. F. Wemple, *Women in Frankish Society: Marriage and the Cloister, 500–900* (1981), an important book with a good bibliography; and the magisterial achievement of J. K. McNamara, *Sisters in Arms: Catholic Nuns Through Two Millennia* (1996).

For the early Germans, see, in addition to the titles by Geary, Goffart, James, Wolfram, and Wood cited in the Notes, B. D. Shaw, "War and Violence," in *Late Antiquity: A Guide to the Postclassical World,* ed. G. W. Bowerstock et al.

(1999), an excellent sketch of the nature of warfare in late antiquity; P. B. Ellis, *Celt and Roman: The Celts in Italy* (1998), a study of the Celtic peoples in preimperial Italy; and the superbly written R. Fletcher, *The Barbarian Conversion: From Paganism to Christianity* (1998).

For Byzantium and the Arabs, see J. J. Norwich, *Byzantium: The Early Centuries* (1989), an elegantly written sketch; E. Patlagean, "Byzantium in the Tenth and Eleventh Centuries," in *A History of Private Life,* vol. 1, *From Pagan Rome to Byzantium* (1987); J. Hussey, *The Byzantine World* (1961); S. Runciman, *Byzantine Civilization* (1956); and A. Bridge, *Theodora: Portrait in a Byzantine Landscape* (1984), a romantic and amusing biography of the courtesan who became empress. A. Harvey, *Economic Expansion in the Byzantine Empire, 900–1200* (1989), should prove useful for research on social and economic change. J. L. Esposito, *Islam: The Straight Path* (1988), is an informed and balanced work based on the best modern scholarship, but the older study of M. Rodinson, *Mohammed* (1974), is still useful.

R. Collins, *The Arab Conquest of Spain, 710–797* (1994), assesses the cultural impact of Arab rule, and D. J. Wasserstein, *The Caliphate in the West: An Islamic Political Institution in the Iberian Peninsula* (1993), studies the major political institution. The articles in B. Lewis, *Islam and the West* (1993), especially "The Encounter of Europe and Islam" and "The Shi'a in Islamic History," offer a provocative treatment of some of the themes of this chapter. L. Ahmed, *Women and Gender in Islam: Historical Roots of a Modern Debate* (1992), is a most important contribution and the starting point for all research on Islam and gender, while N. R. Keddie and B. Brown, eds., *Women in Middle Eastern History: Shifting Boundaries in Sex and Gender* (1992), provides a variety of perspectives on women's roles. R. Fletcher, *The Cross and the Crescent: Christianity and Islam from Muhammad to the Reformation* (2003), provides a highly readable introduction to the intricate and controversial relationships between Christianity and Islam down to the sixteenth century.

Listening to the Past

The Conversion of Clovis

Modern Christian doctrine holds that conversion is a process, the gradual turning toward Jesus and the teachings of the Christian Gospels. But in the early medieval world, conversion was perceived more as a one-time event determined by the tribal chieftain. If he accepted baptism, the mass conversion of his people followed. The selection here about the Frankish king Clovis is from The History of the Franks *by Gregory, bishop of Tours (ca 504–594), written about a century after the events it describes.*

The first child which Clotild bore for Clovis was a son. She wanted to have her baby baptized, and she kept urging her husband to agree to this. "The gods whom you worship are no good," she would say. "They haven't even been able to help themselves, let alone others. . . . Take your Saturn, for example, who ran away from his own son to avoid being exiled from his kingdom, or so they say; and Jupiter, that obscene perpetrator of all sorts of mucky deeds, who couldn't keep his hands off other men, who had his fun with all his female relatives and couldn't even refrain from intercourse with his own sister. . . .

"You ought instead to worship Him who created at a word and out of nothing heaven, and earth, the sea and all that therein is, who made the sun to shine, who lit the sky with stars, who peopled the water with fish, the earth with beasts, the sky with flying creatures, by whose hand the race of man was made, by whose gift all creation is constrained to serve in deference and devotion the man He made." However often the Queen said this, the King came no nearer to belief. . . .

The Queen, who was true to her faith, brought her son to be baptized. . . . The child was

baptized; he was given the name Ingomer; but no sooner had he received baptism than he died in his white robes. Clovis was extremely angry. He began immediately to reproach his Queen. "If he had been dedicated in the name of my gods," he said, "he would have lived without question; but now that he has been baptized in the name of your God he has not been able to live a single day!"

"I give thanks to Almighty God," replied Clotild, "the Creator of all things who has not found me completely unworthy, for He has deigned to welcome into his Kingdom a child conceived in my womb. . . ."

Some time later Clotild bore a second son. He was baptized Chlodomer. He began to ail and Clovis said, "What else do you expect? It will happen to him as it happened to his brother: no sooner is he baptized in the name of your Christ than he will die!" Clotild prayed to the Lord and at His commands the baby recovered.

Queen Clotild continued to pray that her husband might recognize the true God and give up his idol-worship. Nothing could persuade him to accept Christianity. Finally war broke out against the Alamanni and in this conflict he was forced by necessity to accept what he had refused of his own free will. It so turned out that when the two armies met on the battlefield there was a great slaughter and the troops of Clovis were rapidly being annihilated. He raised his eyes to heaven when he saw this, felt compunction in his heart and was moved to tears. "Jesus Christ," he said, "you who Clotild maintains to be the Son of the living God, you who deign to give help to those in travail and victory to those who trust in you, in faith I beg the glory of your help. If you will give me victory over my enemies, and if I may have evidence to that miraculous power which the people dedicated to your name say that they have experienced, then I will believe in you and I will be baptized in your name. I have called upon my own gods, but, as I see only too clearly, they have no intention of helping me. I therefore cannot believe that they possess any power for they do not come to the assistance of those who trust them. I now call upon you. I want to believe in you, but I must first be saved from my enemies." Even as he said this the Alamanni turned their backs and began to run away. As soon as they saw that their King was killed, they submitted to Clovis. "We beg you," they said, "to put an end to this slaughter. We are prepared to obey you." Clovis stopped the war. He made a speech in which he called for peace. Then he went home. He told the Queen how he had won a victory by calling on the name of Christ. This happened in the fifteenth year of his reign (496).

The Queen then ordered Saint Remigius, Bishop of the town of Rheims, to be summoned in secret. She begged him to impart the word of salvation to the King. The Bishop asked Clovis to meet him in private and began to urge him to believe in the true God, Maker of heaven and earth, and to forsake his idols, which were powerless to help him or anyone else. The King replied: "I have listened to you willingly, holy father. There remains one obstacle. The people under my command will not agree to forsake their gods. I will go and put to them what you have just said to me." He arranged a meeting with his people, but God in his power had preceded him, and before he could say a word all those present shouted in unison: "We will give up worshipping our mortal gods, pious King, and we are prepared to follow the immortal God about whom Remigius preaches." This news was reported to the Bishop. He was greatly pleased and he ordered the baptismal pool to be made ready. . . . The baptistry was prepared, sticks of incense gave off clouds of perfume, sweet-smelling candles gleamed bright and the holy place of baptism was filled with divine fragrance. God filled the hearts of all present with such grace that they imagined themselves to have been transported to some perfumed paradise. King Clovis asked that he might be baptized first by the Bishop. Like some new Constantine he stepped forward to the baptismal pool, ready to wash away the sores of

Ninth-century ivory carving showing Clovis being baptized by Saint Remi. *(Musée Condé, Chantilly/Laurie Platt Winfrey, Inc.)*

his old leprosy and to be cleansed in flowing water from the sordid stains which he had borne so long.

King Clovis confessed his belief in God Almighty, three in one. He was baptized in the name of the Father, the Son and the Holy Ghost, and marked in holy chrism [an anointing oil] with the sign of the Cross of Christ. More than three thousand of his army were baptized at the same time.

Questions for Analysis

1. Who took the initiative in urging Clovis's conversion? What can we deduce from that?

2. According to this account, why did Clovis ultimately accept Christianity?

3. For the Salian Franks, what was the best proof of divine power?

4. On the basis of this selection, do you consider *The History of the Franks* reliable history? Why or why not?

Sources: L. Thorpe, trans., *The History of the Franks by Gregory of Tours* (Harmondsworth, England: Penguin, 1974), p. 159; P. J. Geary, ed., *Readings in Medieval History* (Peterborough, Ontario: Broadview Press, 1991), pp. 165–166.

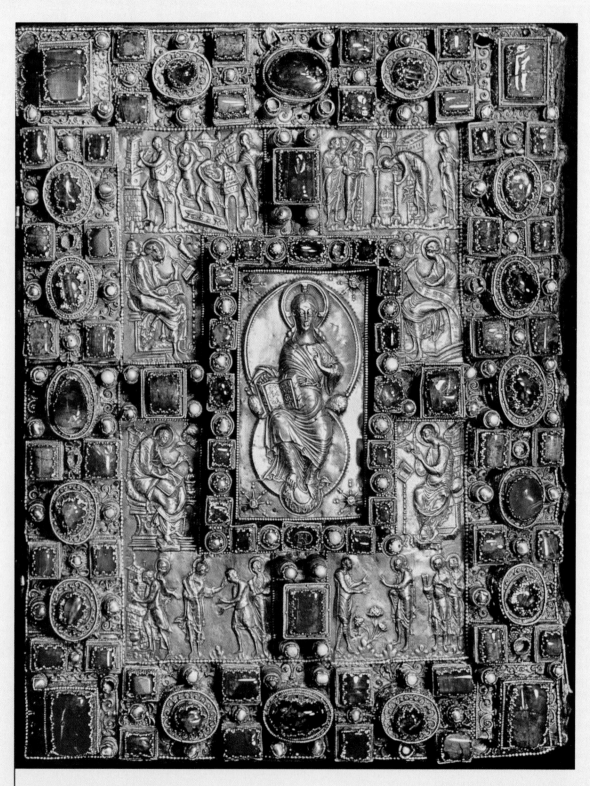

Cover of codex Aureus of Saint Emmeram, ca 870.
(Stadtsbibliothek, Munich)

The Carolingian World: Europe in the Early Middle Ages

*T*he Frankish chieftain Charles Martel defeated Muslim invaders in 732 at the Battle of Poitiers in central France.[1] Muslims and Christians have interpreted the battle differently. To the Muslims, it was a minor skirmish, won by the Franks because of Muslim difficulties in maintaining supply lines over long distances and the distraction of ethnic conflicts and unrest in Islamic Spain. For Christians, the Frankish victory was one of the great battles of history: it halted Muslim expansion in Europe. A century after this victory, in 843, Charles Martel's three great-great-grandsons concluded the Treaty of Verdun, which divided the European continent among them.

Between 732 and 843, a distinctly European society emerged. A new kind of social and political organization, later called "feudalism," appeared. And for the first time since the collapse of the Roman Empire, most of western Europe was united under one government. That government reached the peak of its development under Charles Martel's grandson, Charlemagne. Christian missionary activity among the Germanic peoples continued, and strong ties were forged with the Roman papacy. The heavy trade of European slaves to the Islamic world tied Christian Europe and the Muslim Middle East. A revival of study and learning, sometimes styled the "Carolingian Renaissance," occurred under Charlemagne.

- How did Merovingian and Carolingian rulers govern their kingdoms and empire?

- What was the significance of the relations between Carolingian rulers and the church?

- The culture of the Carolingian Empire has been described as the "first European civilization." What does this mean?

- What factors contributed to the disintegration of the Carolingian Empire?

- In a society wracked with constant war and violence, what medical care was available?

- What are some of the historiographical problems posed by the word *feudalism?*

- How did Viking expansion lead to the establishment of the Kievan principality?

These are among the questions that this chapter will explore.

The Frankish Kingdom and the Emergence of the Carolingians

The success of the Frankish king Clovis (see pages 210–211) rested on three major developments: Clovis's series of military victories over other Germanic tribes; his acquisition of the wealthy provinces of Roman Gaul with their administrative machinery intact; and, after Clovis's conversion to orthodox Christianity, the ideological support of the Roman papacy and of the bishops of Gaul. By selecting as his capital Paris—legendary scene of the martyrdom of Saint Denis, believed to be a disciple of Saint Paul—Clovis identified himself with the cult of Saint Denis and used it to strengthen his rule. The Frankish kingdom included much of what is now France and a large section of southwestern Germany.

When he died, following Frankish custom, Clovis divided his kingdom among his four sons, a partition not according to strict acreage but in portions yielding roughly equal revenues.[2] Historians have long described Merovingian Gaul in the sixth and seventh centuries as wracked by civil wars, chronic violence, and political instability as Clovis's descendants fought among themselves. So brutal and destructive were these wars and so violent the ordinary conditions of life that the term *Dark Ages* came to designate the entire Merovingian period. Recent research has presented a more complex picture. The civil wars were indeed destructive, but they "did not pose a threat to the survival of the kingdom. Indeed, in a sense, they were a unifying part of the structure of the Frankish state in the sixth century and for most of the seventh."[3]

What caused the civil wars? First, the death or even reported death of a king triggered crisis and war. Lacking a clear principle of succession, any male of Merovingian blood could claim the throne, and within the Merovingian family there were often many possibilities. A prince-claimant had to prove himself worthy on the battlefield. Second, the desire for new lands provoked conflict. Royal officials and warriors had a similar desire for new estates, and they sold their support to the prince who would promise them more lands. Royal armies also wanted war because war meant booty and plunder. No one disputed the Merovingian family's right to rule: it alone possessed the blood and charisma. The issue was which member. Thus the royal family and the royal court served as the focus around which conflicts arose, and in this sense the civil wars actually held the kingdom together.[4]

Merovingian politics provided royal women with opportunities, and some queens not only influenced but occasionally dominated events. The theoretical status of a princess or queen rested on her diplomatic importance, with her marriage sealing or divorce breaking an alliance; on her personal relationship with her husband and her ability to give him sons and heirs; on her role as the mother and guardian of princes who had not reached legal adulthood; and on her control of the royal treasury. For example, when King Chilperic I (561–584) was murdered, his wife Fredegunda controlled a large state treasury. The historian Fredegar alleges that Queen Brunhilda (d. 613), wife of King Sigebert of the East Frankish kingdom, killed twelve kings in pursuit of her political goals, including Sigebert, her grandchildren, and their offspring. When her sister Galswintha was found strangled to death in bed shortly after her marriage to Chilperic, ruler of the West Frankish kingdom, Brunhilda suspected Chilperic of the murder—so that he could marry his then mistress, Fredegunda. Brunhilda instigated war between the two kingdoms. After 592 she was the real power behind her sons' and grandsons' shaky thrones, and she also ruled Burgundy, which her maneuvers had united to the East Frankish kingdom. Contemporaries may have exaggerated Brunhilda's murders, but her career reflects both the domestic violence of the Merovingian royal family and the fierce determination of some queens to exercise power.

How did Merovingian rulers govern? What were their sources of income? How did they communicate with their peoples? While local administration probably varied somewhat according to regional tradition, the **civitas**—the city and surrounding territory—served as the basis of the administrative system in the Frankish kingdom. A **comites**—senior official or royal companion, later called a count—presided over the civitas. He collected royal revenue, heard lawsuits, enforced justice, and raised troops. To receive his tax revenues, a Frankish king had to be sure of the comites' loyalty. Rebellion led to confiscation of the comites' lands. A ruler's general sources of income were revenues from the royal estates, especially large in the north; the right to hospitality when he visited an area (with wives, children, servants, court officials, and several hundred warriors, plus all their horses, hospitality could be a severe drain on the resources of a region); the conquest and confiscation of new lands, which replenished lands given as monastic or religious endowments; and the "gifts" of subject peoples, such as plunder and tribute paid by peoples east of the Rhine River. Specific income derived from a land tax paid by all free landowners, originally collected by the Romans and continued by the

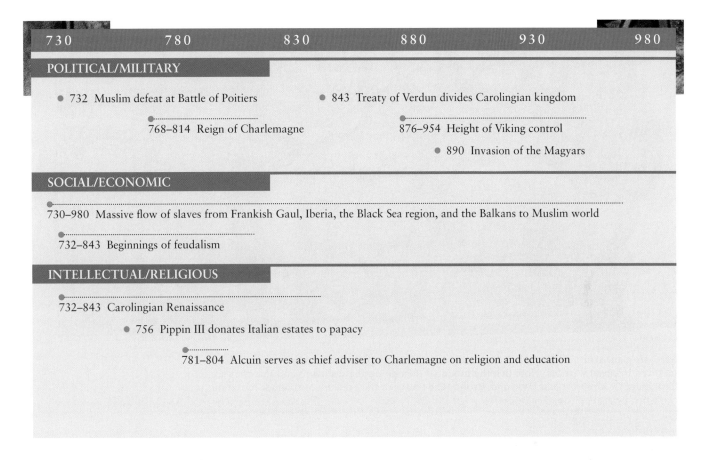

| 730 | 780 | 830 | 880 | 930 | 980 |

POLITICAL/MILITARY

- 732 Muslim defeat at Battle of Poitiers
- 768–814 Reign of Charlemagne
- 843 Treaty of Verdun divides Carolingian kingdom
- 876–954 Height of Viking control
- 890 Invasion of the Magyars

SOCIAL/ECONOMIC

730–980 Massive flow of slaves from Frankish Gaul, Iberia, the Black Sea region, and the Balkans to Muslim world

732–843 Beginnings of feudalism

INTELLECTUAL/RELIGIOUS

732–843 Carolingian Renaissance

- 756 Pippin III donates Italian estates to papacy
- 781–804 Alcuin serves as chief adviser to Charlemagne on religion and education

Franks. In the course of the seventh century, the value of this tax declined as all Franks gradually gained immunity from it. In fact, the term **Frank** began to be associated with freedom from taxation, which may have been an incentive for Gallo-Romans to shift their ethnic allegiance to the Franks. Fines imposed for criminal offenses and tolls and customs duties on roads, bridges, and waterways (and the goods transported over them) also yielded income. As with the Romans, the minting of coins was a royal monopoly, with drastic penalties for counterfeiting. For all this, the comites had responsibility.[5]

Merovingian, Carolingian (see page 238), and later medieval rulers led peripatetic lives, traveling constantly to check up on local administrators and peoples. Merovingian kings also relied on the comites and bishops to gather and send local information to them. Gallo-Roman by descent, bishops and comites were usually native to the regions they administered and knew their areas well. Frankish royal administration involved a third official, the *dux* (duke). He was a military leader, commanding troops in the territory of several civitas, and thus responsible for all defensive and offensive strategies. Kings seem to have appointed only Franks to this position.

Clovis and his descendants in the sixth and seventh centuries also issued **capitularies,** administrative and legislative orders divided into *capitula,* chapters or articles. These laws attempted to regulate a variety of matters: for example, protecting priests, monks, nuns, and church property from violence; defining ownership and inheritance; punishing drunkenness, robbery, arson, rape, and murder. Apart from the violent and crime-ridden realities of Merovingian society, capitularies show the strong influence of Roman law. They also reveal Merovingian kings trying to maintain law and order, holding courts, and being actively involved in exercising judicial authority.

The court or household of Merovingian kings also included scribes who kept records, legal officials who advised the king on matters of law, and treasury agents responsible for aspects of royal finance. These officials could all read and write Latin. Over them all presided the mayor of the palace, the most important secular figure in the kingdom. Usually a leader of one of the great aristocratic families, the mayor governed the palace and the kingdom in the king's absence.[6]

Kings also consulted regularly with the leaders of the aristocracy. This class represented a fusion of Franks and

Merovingian Army   This sixth- or seventh-century ivory depicts a nobleman in civilian dress followed by seven warriors. Note that the mounted men do not have stirrups and that they seem to have fought with spears and bows and arrows. The power of the Frankish aristocracy rested on these private armies. *(Landesmuseum, Trier)*

the old Gallo-Roman leadership. It possessed landed wealth, villas over which it exercised lordship, dispensing local customary, not royal, law; and it often led a rich and lavish lifestyle. Members of this class constituted, when they were with the king, the royal court, those around the king at a given time. If he consulted them and they were in agreement, there was peace. Failure to consult could mean resentment and the potential for civil war.

From this aristocracy there gradually emerged in the eighth century one family that replaced the Merovingian dynasty. The emergence of the Carolingians—whose name comes from the Latin *Carolus,* or Charles—rests on several factors. First, beginning with Pippin I (d. 640), the head of the family acquired and held on to the powerful position of **mayor of the palace**. He served as head of the Frankish bureaucracy, governed in the king's absence, and, after the king, was the most important figure in the Frankish kingdom. Second, a series of advantageous marriage alliances brought the family estates and influence in different parts of the Frankish world. Thus Pippin II (d. 714), through his first marriage, won influence in the territory around Echternach (modern Luxembourg) and, by his second wife, estates in the Meuse Valley. The landed wealth and treasure acquired by Pippin II, Charles

Martel (r. 714–741), and Pippin III (r. 751–768) formed the basis of Carolingian power.[7] Although Pippin II and his son Charles Martel possessed more lands than any other single aristocratic family, and although they held the positions of mayor of the palace and duke, their ultimate supremacy was by no means certain. Other dukes rallied to the support of the Merovingians, and Pippin devoted much energy to fighting these magnates. Only his victory over them and King Theuderich at Tertry in 687 ensured his dominance. Such victories gave the family a reputation for military strength. Charles Martel's successful wars against the Saxons, Frisians, Alamanni, and Bavarians, as well as his defeat of the Arabs near Poitiers in 732, further enhanced the family's prestige, while also adding distinction as defenders of Christendom against the Muslims.

The early Carolingians also acquired the support of the church, perhaps the decisive asset. Irish, Frankish, and Anglo-Saxon missionaries, of whom the Englishman Boniface (680–754) is the most famous, preached Christianity to pagan peoples and worked to reorganize the Frankish church. Boniface's courage in chopping down the oak of Thor at Geismar, near Fritzlar, the center of a large pagan cult, won him many converts. With

Saint Boniface The upper panel of this piece from an early-eleventh-century Fulda Mass book shows the great missionary to Germany baptizing, apparently by full immersion. The lower panel shows his death scene, with the saint protecting himself with a Gospel book. The fluttering draperies suggest contemporary Anglo-Saxon parallels, understandable since Boniface had founded Fulda Abbey, in modern-day Hesse, and secured English books for it. *(Stadtsbibliothek Bamberg)*

close ties to the Roman papacy, Boniface participated in establishing the abbey of Fulda and the archdiocese of Mainz, held church councils, and promoted *The Rule of Saint Benedict* in all monasteries. (In the latter, Boniface was not successful. Many monasteries preferred to be guided by several monastic directives.) The Carolingian mayors of the palace, Charles Martel and Pippin III, fully supported this evangelizing activity, as missionaries also preached obedience to secular authorities as a religious duty.

As mayor of the palace, Charles Martel had exercised the power of king of the Franks. His son Pippin III aspired to the title as well. Against the background of collaboration between missionaries and the Frankish mayors, Pippin sent delegates to Pope Zacharias asking him whether the man who held the power should also have the title of king. Pippin's ambassadors reached Rome at a diplomatically opportune moment. In the eighth century, the Lombards severely threatened the papacy, which, being subject to the Byzantine emperor, looked to Constantinople for support. But Byzantium, pressured from the outside by attacks from the Arabs and the Avars and wracked internally by the dispute over the veneration of icons, known as iconoclasm, was in no position to send help to the West. Pope Zacharias therefore shifted his allegiance from the Greeks to the Franks and told Pippin that "it was better to call him king who had the royal power 'in order to prevent provoking civil war in Francia'" and that Zacharias "by virtue of his apostolic authority commanded that Pippin should be made king."[8] Chilperic, the last Merovingian ruler, was consigned to a monastery. An assembly of Frankish magnates elected Pippin king, and he was anointed by Boniface at Soissons. When, in 754, Lombard expansion again threatened the papacy, Pope Stephen II journeyed to the Frankish kingdom seeking help. On this occasion, he personally anointed Pippin and gave him the title "Patrician of the Romans." Pippin promised restitution of the papal lands.

Thus an important alliance had been struck between the papacy and the Frankish monarchs. On a successful campaign in Italy in 756, Pippin made a large donation to the papacy. The gift consisted of estates in central Italy that technically belonged to the Byzantine emperor. Because of his **anointment,** Pippin's kingship took on a special spiritual and moral character. Before Pippin, only priests and bishops had received anointment. Pippin became the first to be anointed with the sacred oils and acknowledged as *rex et sacerdos* (king and priest). Anointment, rather than royal blood, set the Christian king apart. Pippin also cleverly eliminated possible threats to the Frankish throne, and the pope promised him support in the future. When Pippin died, his son Charles, generally known as Charlemagne, succeeded him.

When Charlemagne went to Rome in 800, Pope Leo III showed him the signs of respect due only to the emperor. The Carolingian family thus received official recognition from the leading spiritual power in Europe, and the papacy gained a military protector. The Greeks regarded the papal acts as rebellious and Charlemagne as a usurper.

From Baghdad, Harun al Rashid, caliph of the Abbasid Empire (786–809), congratulated the Frankish ruler with the gift of an elephant. It was named Abu-l-Abbas after the founder of the Abbasid dynasty and may have served as a symbol of the diplomatic link between the Muslim world and Christian Europe. Having plodded its way to Charlemagne's court at Aachen, the elephant survived for nine years, and its death was considered important enough to be mentioned in the Frankish *Royal Annals* for the year 810.[9] The imperial coronation marks a decisive break between Rome and Constantinople.

The Imperial Coronation of Charlemagne

In the autumn of the year 800, Charlemagne paid a momentous visit to Rome. Charlemagne's secretary and biographer, Einhard, gives this account of what happened:

His last journey there [to Rome] was due to another factor, namely that the Romans, having inflicted many injuries on Pope Leo—plucking out his eyes and tearing out his tongue, he had been compelled to beg the assistance of the king. Accordingly, coming to Rome in order that he might set in order those things which had exceedingly disturbed the condition of the Church, he remained there the whole winter. It was at the time that he accepted the name of Emperor and Augustus. At first he was so much opposed to this that he insisted that although that day was a great [Christian] feast, he would not have entered the Church if he had known beforehand the pope's intention. But he bore very patiently the jealousy of the Roman Emperors [that is, the Byzantine rulers] who were indignant when he received these titles. He overcame their arrogant haughtiness with magnanimity.[10]

For centuries scholars have debated the significance of the imperial coronation of Charlemagne. Did Charlemagne plan the ceremony in Saint Peter's on Christmas Day, or did he merely accept the title of emperor? What did he have to gain from it? If, as Einhard implies, the coronation displeased Charlemagne, did that displeasure rest on Pope Leo's role in the ceremony, which, on the principle that he who gives can also take away, placed the pope in a higher position than the emperor? Did Pope Leo arrange the coronation in order to identify the Frankish monarchy with the papacy and papal policy?

Though final answers will probably never be found, several things seem certain. First, Charlemagne gained the imperial title of Holy Roman emperor and considered himself a Christian king ruling a Christian people. His motto, *Renovatio romani imperi* (Revival of the Roman Empire), "implied a revival of the Western Empire in the image of Augustinian political philosophy."[11] Charlemagne was consciously perpetuating old Roman imperial notions, while at the same time identifying with the new Rome of the Christian church. Charlemagne and his government represented a combination of Frankish practices and Christian ideals, the two basic elements of medieval European society. Second, later German rulers were anxious to gain the imperial title and to associate themselves with the legends of Charlemagne and ancient Rome. They wanted to use the ideology of imperial Rome to strengthen their positions. Finally, ecclesiastical authorities continually cited the event as proof that the dignity of the imperial crown could be granted only by the pope. The imperial coronation of Charlemagne, whether planned by the Carolingian court or by the papacy, was to have a profound effect on the course of German history and on the later history of Europe.

The Empire of Charlemagne

Charles the Great (r. 768–814), known as Charlemagne, built on the military and diplomatic foundations of his ancestors and on the administrative machinery of the Merovingian kings. Einhard wrote a lengthy idealization of this warrior-ruler. It has serious flaws, partly because it is modeled directly on the Roman author Suetonius's *Life of the Emperor Augustus*. Still, it is the earliest medieval biography of a layman, and historians consider it generally accurate:

Charles was large and strong, and of lofty stature, though not disproportionately tall . . . the upper part of his head was round, his eyes very large and animated, nose a little long, hair fair, and face laughing and merry. Thus his appearance was always stately and dignified . . . although his neck was thick and somewhat short, and his belly rather prominent; but the symmetry of the rest of his body concealed these defects. His gait was firm, his whole carriage manly and his voice clear, but not so strong as his size led one to expect. His health was excellent, except during the four years preceding his death. . . .

In accordance with the national custom, he took frequent exercise on horseback and in the chase. . . . He . . . often practiced swimming, in which he was such an adept that none could surpass him. . . . He used not only to invite his sons to his bath, but his nobles and friends.[12]

Though crude and brutal, Charlemagne was a man of enormous intelligence. He appreciated good literature, such as Saint Augustine's *City of God,* and Einhard considered him an unusually effective speaker. Recent scholsons reached adulthood, only one outlived him. Four surviving grandsons ensured perpetuation of the family.[13]

Territorial Expansion

Continuing the expansionist policies of his ancestors, Charlemagne fought more than fifty campaigns and became the greatest warrior of the early Middle Ages. He subdued all of the north of modern France. In the south, the lords of the mountainous ranges of Aquitaine fought off his efforts at total conquest. The Muslims in northeastern Spain were checked by the establishment of strongly fortified areas known as *marches*.

Charlemagne's greatest successes were in today's Germany. In the course of a thirty-year war against the Saxons, he added most of the northwestern German tribes to the Frankish kingdom. Because of their repeated rebellions, Charlemagne ordered, according to Einhard, more than four thousand Saxons slaughtered in one day.

To the south, he also achieved spectacular results. In 773 to 774, the Lombards in northern Italy again threatened the papacy. Charlemagne marched south, overran fortresses at Pavia and Spoleto, and incorporated Lombardy into the Frankish kingdom. To his title king of the Franks he added king of the Lombards. Charlemagne also ended Bavarian independence and defeated the nomadic Avars, opening the Danubian plain for later settlement. He successfully fought the Byzantine Empire for Venetia (excluding the city of Venice itself), Istria, and Dalmatia and temporarily annexed those areas to his kingdom.

Charlemagne also tried to occupy Basque territory in northwestern Spain. When his long siege of Saragossa proved unsuccessful and the Saxons on his northeastern borders rebelled, Charlemagne decided to withdraw, but the Basques annihilated his rear guard under Count Roland at Roncesvalles (778), near Pamplona in the Pyrenees. This attack represented Charlemagne's only defeat, and he forbade people to talk about it. However, the expedition inspired the great medieval epic *The Song of Roland*. Based on legend and written about 1100 at the beginning of the European crusading movement, the poem portrays Roland as the ideal chivalric knight and Charlemagne as exercising a sacred kind of kingship. Although many of the epic's details differ from the historical evidence, *The Song of Roland* is important because it reveals the popular image of Charlemagne in later centuries.

By around 805, the Frankish kingdom included all of northwestern Europe except Scandinavia (see Map 8.1).

Reliquary Bust of Charlemagne This splendid twelfth-century gothic idealization portrays the emperor of legend and myth rather than the squat, potbellied ruler described by his contemporary Einhard. The jeweled helmet or crown is symbolic of Charlemagne's role as defender of church and people. *(Das Dom Kapitel, Aachen)*

arship disputes Einhard's claim that Charlemagne could not write.

The security and continuation of his dynasty and the need for diplomatic alliances governed Charlemagne's complicated marriage pattern. The high rate of infant mortality required many sons. Married first to the daughter of Desiderius, king of the Lombards, Charlemagne divorced her either because she failed to produce a child within a year or for diplomatic reasons. His second wife, Hildegard, produced nine children in twelve years. When she died, Charlemagne married Fastrada, daughter of an East Frankish count whose support he needed in his campaign against the Saxons. Charlemagne had a total of four legal wives and six concubines, and even after the age of sixty-five, he continued to sire children. Though three

242

MAP 8.1 *Charlemagne's Empire* The extent of Charlemagne's nominal jurisdiction was not equaled before the nineteenth century. Trade, especially perhaps in European slaves, linked the empire and the Muslim world. (*Source: Some data from Michael McCormick, Origins of the European Economy: Communications and Commerce, A.D. 300–900 [Cambridge: Cambridge University Press, 2001], p. 762.*)

Not since the third century A.D. had any ruler controlled so much of the Western world.

The Government of the Carolingian Empire

Charlemagne ruled a vast rural world dotted with isolated estates and small villages and characterized by constant warfare. According to the chroniclers of the time, between 714 and 814 only seven years were peaceful. Charlemagne's empire was not a state as people today understand that term; it was a collection of peoples and tribes. Apart from a small class of warrior-aristocrats and clergy, and a very tiny minority of Jews, almost everyone engaged in agriculture. Towns served as the headquarters of bishops, as ecclesiastical centers. The Carolingians inherited the office and the administrative machinery of the Merovingian kings and the functions of the mayor of the palace. The Carolingians relied heavily on the personality and energy of the monarchs. The scholar-adviser Alcuin (see pages 248–249) wrote that "a king should be strong against his enemies, humble to Christians, feared by pagans, loved by the poor and judicious in counsel and maintaining justice."[14] Charlemagne worked to realize that ideal. By military expeditions that brought wealth—lands, booty, slaves, and tribute—and by peaceful travel, personal appearances, and the sheer force of his personality, Charlemagne sought to awe newly conquered peoples and rebellious domestic enemies with his fierce presence and terrible justice. By confiscating the estates of great territorial magnates, he acquired lands and goods with which to gain the support of lesser lords, further expanding the territory under his control.

The political power of the Carolingians rested on the cooperation of the dominant social class, the Frankish aristocracy. By the seventh century, through mutual cooperation and frequent marriage alliances, these families exercised great power that did not derive from the Merovingian kings. The Carolingians themselves had emerged from this aristocracy, and the military and political success that Carolingians such as Pippin II achieved depended on the support of the nobility. The lands and booty with which Charles Martel and Charlemagne rewarded their followers in these families enabled the nobles to improve their economic position, but it was only with noble help that the Carolingians were able to wage wars of expansion and suppress rebellions. In short, Carolingian success was a matter of reciprocal help and reward.[15]

For administrative purposes, Charlemagne divided his entire kingdom into *counties,* based closely on the old Merovingian civitas (see page 236). Each of the approximately six hundred counties was governed by a count (or in his absence, a viscount), who published royal orders, held courts and resolved legal cases, collected taxes and tolls, raised troops for the army, and supervised maintenance of roads and bridges. Counts were at first sent out from the royal court; later someone native to the region was appointed. As a link between local authorities and the central government, Charlemagne appointed officials called **missi dominici,** "agents of the lord king." The empire was divided into visitorial districts. Each year, beginning in 802, two missi, usually a count and a bishop or abbot, visited assigned districts. They held courts and investigated the district's judicial, financial, and clerical activities. They organized commissions to regulate crime, moral conduct, the clergy, education, the poor, and many other matters. The missi checked up on the counts. In the marches, especially in unstable or threatened areas such as along the Spanish or Danish frontiers, officials called *margraves* had extensive powers to govern.

A modern state has institutions of government, such as a civil service, courts of law, financial agencies for collecting and apportioning taxes, and police and military powers with which to maintain order internally and defend against foreign attack. These simply did not exist in Charlemagne's empire. Instead, society was held together by dependent relationships cemented by oaths promising faith and loyalty.

Although the empire lacked viable institutions, some Carolingians involved in governing did have vigorous political ideas. The abbots and bishops who served as Charlemagne's advisers worked out what was for their time a sophisticated political ideology. They wrote that a ruler may hold power from God but is responsible to the law. Just as all subjects of the empire were required to obey him, he, too, was obliged to respect the law. They envisioned a unified Christian society presided over by a king who was responsible for maintaining peace, law, and order and doing justice, without which neither the ruler nor the kingdom had any justification. These views derived largely from Saint Augustine's theories of kingship and have been labeled **political Augustinianism.** Inevitably, they could not be realized in an illiterate, preindustrial society. But they were the seeds from which medieval and even modern ideas of government were to develop.

*T*he Carolingian Slave Trade

Shortly after the death of Belgian historian Henri Pirenne in 1935, his book *Mohammed and Charlemagne* was published. Pirenne held that ancient civilizations had centered around the Mediterranean Sea; in this he

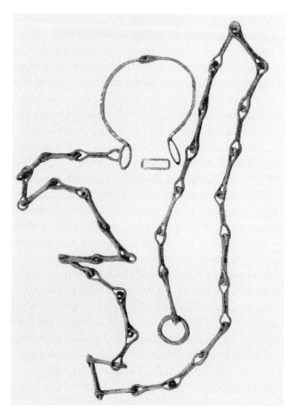

Balkan Neck Shackle (tenth century) The slave trader restrained the captive by slipping the chain through the loops in the neck collar (*top*), fastening it securely, and then attaching the chain to the captive's limbs. Similar devices for controlling slaves while allowing them to walk were later used in other parts of the world. (*Courtesy of the National Museum of History, Sofia*)

echoed the Greek philosopher Socrates (see page 84), who told his Athenian friends, "We live around a sea (the Mediterranean) like frogs around a pond."[16] According to Pirenne, Muslim expansion and control of the Mediterranean pushed the center of political gravity northward to Frankland and led to the beginnings of a new "Western" or European civilization. Islam caused that change; hence Pirenne wrote that "without Mohammed there would be no Charlemagne." Economically, the shift of Europe's core meant the decline of the urban and commercial culture that had characterized the Greco-Roman world and an acceleration of the movement to an agricultural and rural society typical of what came to be called the Middle Ages. Moreover, Pirenne maintained, Muslim expansion, combined with Germanic tribal warfare and generally unstable conditions,

resulted in sharp declines in population, agricultural production, and long-distance trade. The isolated villa and the self-sufficient monastery, rather than the city or town, became the typical unit of economic production. Local communities had little to export; and even if they had export goods, dangerous conditions made trade impossible.[17]

For decades scholars have debated Pirenne's conclusions. His idea that agricultural output and population declined has been largely disproved. Rather, historians have shown, the Carolingian period witnessed moderate population growth, as indicated by the steady reduction of forests and wasteland. Economic historians have nuanced Pirenne's thesis that the isolated monastery or villa was the typical unit of economic production. They acknowledge that craftsmen on manorial estates (see page 255) manufactured textiles, weapons, glass, and pottery primarily for local consumption. But they point out that sometimes abbeys and manors served as markets, that goods were shipped away to towns and fairs for sale, and that a good deal of inter-regional commerce existed.[18]

The theory that long-distance trade came to a halt in the Carolingian era has been completely disproved. From the late seventh century through the tenth, Europeans carried on "international trade" with the Muslim world (see Map 8.1). True, the Arabs had little interest in European pottery and glass, and only a slight interest in swords, weapons, and woolens. But one "product" was much in demand in the Islamic world. From Visigothic Spain during the Muslim conquests, from Frankish Gaul during the reigns of Pippin III, Charlemagne, and Louis the Pious, from the southern coasts of the Black Sea, and from the Balkans, substantial numbers of European slaves poured into the Muslim world. Michael McCormick, a leading student of the Pirenne thesis and of the early medieval economy, emphasizes this flow. Although evidence for the trade in human beings is scattered, fragmentary, and difficult to assess, he argues that "the shadow of slavery hangs over the whole body of written evidence which survives from the Mediterranean Sea."[19] He writes of the "voracious appetite" and the "insatiable demand" for slaves in the Muslim heartland—in Egypt, Syria, Persia, and the Arabian peninsula.

Let us consider three questions about the slave trade between Frankish Europe and the Islamic world. Why was the market for slaves in Muslim territories so large? Why did Europeans sell slaves? Within Europe was there opposition to this commerce in human beings?

Disease helps explain why Arab dealers in Tripoli, Alexandria, Damascus, and Baghdad (see Map 7.5 on page 225) were eager to buy European slaves. The 740s witnessed an extremely virulent outbreak of the bubonic plague (the Black Death). It spread from Sicily and Calabria in southern Italy to Greece, to Constantinople, and across North Africa. Mortality rates in Muslim cities ranged between 25 and 36 percent, creating a severe labor shortage. We know much more about the consequences of this plague in the fourteenth century (see pages 386–387) than about the effects in the eighth century. In the 1300s, the high death rate meant that wealth came to be concentrated in the hands of survivors who had plentiful means to buy replacement labor. This could be what happened in the eighth century.[20] Seizing the opportunity, Venetian slave dealers jumped into this "seller's market" and contracted with Muslim merchants to sell their slaves. Significantly, the first Venetian agreement dates from 748, when the epidemic reached its peak.[21] Demographic historians believe that after 755, the virulence of the disease declined and remained at low levels until the fourteenth century.

A second clue to Arab interest in European slaves may lie in simple proximity: Christian Europe and the Muslim Middle East were geographical neighbors. From the European hinterland, slaves could move easily across the Alps, and they could even carry other wares to the markets at Venice and other Italian and Dalmatian ports.[22] After a millennium of experience, European mariners knew the Mediterranean well, and the transportation of goods by water is always faster and cheaper than overland shipment. The costs of transporting groups of slaves from Carolingian Gaul to North African ports were lower than the costs of marching black slaves from sub-Saharan Africa to markets in Tripoli. Likewise, the European and Mediterranean journeys were far less perilous than the south-to-north expeditions across the Sahara.

A third reason for the "insatiable demand" for European slaves in the Muslim world may have derived from racial or ethnic preferences. Perhaps the appetite for Europeans rested in a predilection among olive-skinned Middle Easterners for fair-skinned Europeans. Perhaps the possession of light-skinned European slaves carried some sort of social prestige in Muslim societies. Perhaps blond Europeans represented the rare and exotic, a kind of "trophy slave" to Arab peoples, as black Africans did to Italian merchant aristocrats during the Renaissance (see page 438). Until more is known about market supplies in Africa, Asia (Muslim dealers also bought Chinese slaves from Central Asia), and Europe, and about the proportion of European slaves to slaves of other racial groups, we cannot reach a definitive understanding of Muslim preferences.

Why did Europeans sell slaves to the Islamic world? As in antiquity (see page 139), so in early medieval Europe, war prisoners were "an utterly commonplace source of merchandise slaves, and profit." For Arabs and Europeans alike, selling captives was standard procedure. Moreover, in a world divided by language, ethnic groups, and religion, Europeans had little sense of unity. People looked upon those from other regions and provinces as aliens and outsiders eligible for enslavement. Thus slaves were usually persons captured in war. Most were young and most were male; female slaves brought higher prices in Middle Eastern markets. The Muslim conquest of Spain produced thousands of prisoner-slaves. So, too, did Charlemagne's long wars against the Lombards, Avars, Saxons, Danes, and Slavic peoples on the frontiers yield *captivi*, prisoner-slaves. When the Frankish conquests declined in the tenth century, the empire's eastern marches opened up a vast new area, the Slavic regions. Slaves sold across the Mediterranean fetched three or four times the amounts brought within the Carolingian Empire.

Were there objections to the European slave trade? Not to slavery itself, and not on humanitarian grounds. Moralists complained not about the sale of slaves but about the sale of *Christians* to *pagans*. Councils of bishops repeated this protest, and the brothers Cyril and Methodius (see page 217) vigorously opposed the seizure and enslavement of Slavs and their sale to the Muslims. But these objections proved to no avail: the profits were too great.[23]

The Carolingian Intellectual Revival

It is perhaps ironic that Charlemagne's most enduring legacy was the stimulus he gave to scholarship and learning. Barely literate himself, preoccupied with the control of vast territories, much more a warrior than an intellectual, he nevertheless set in motion a cultural revival that had widespread and long-lasting consequences. The revival of learning associated with Charlemagne and his court at Aachen drew its greatest inspiration from seventh- and eighth-century intellectual developments in the Anglo-Saxon kingdom of Northumbria, situated at the northernmost tip of the old Roman world.

Northumbrian Culture

Despite the victory of the Roman forms of Christian liturgy at the Synod of Whitby in 664 (see page 247), Irish-Celtic culture permeated the Roman church in Britain and resulted in a flowering of artistic and scholarly activity. Northumbrian creativity owes a great deal to the intellectual curiosity and collecting zeal of Saint Benet Biscop (ca 628–689). The manuscripts and other treasures he brought back from Italy formed the library on which much later study rested.

Northumbrian monasteries produced scores of books: *missals* (used for the celebration of the Mass), *psalters* (which contained the 150 psalms and other prayers used by the monks in their devotions), commentaries on the Scriptures, illuminated manuscripts, law codes, and collections of letters and sermons. The finest product of Northumbrian art is probably the Gospel book produced at Lindisfarne around 700. The incredible expense involved in the publication of such a book—for vellum (calfskin or lambskin specially prepared for writing), coloring, and gold leaf—represents in part an aristocratic display of wealth. The script, *uncial,* is a Celtic version of contemporary Greek and Roman handwriting. The illustrations have a strong Eastern quality, combining the ab-

stract, nonrepresentational style of the Christian Middle East and the narrative (storytelling) approach of classical Roman art. Likewise, the use of geometrical decorative designs shows the influence of Syrian art. Many scribes, artists, and illuminators must have participated in the book's preparation.

In Gaul and Anglo-Saxon England, women shared with men in the work of evangelization and in the new Christian learning. Kings and nobles, seeking suitable occupations for daughters who did not or would not marry, founded monasteries for nuns, some of which were double monasteries. A **double monastery** housed both men and women in two adjoining establishments and was governed by one superior, an *abbess*. Nuns looked after the children given to the monastery as *oblates* (offerings), the elderly who retired at the monastery, and travelers who needed hospitality. Monks provided protection, since in a violent age an isolated house of women invited attack. Monks also did the heavy work on the land. Perhaps

Saint Hilda The superior of a mixed monastery of men and women at Whitby in Northumbria, Saint Hilda (614–680) here receives a copy of the scholar Aldhelm's treatise *In Praise of Holy Virgins*. The simple drapery of the nuns' clothing with its nervous quality is characteristic of the eleventh-century Anglo-Saxon scriptoria. *(His Grace the Archbishop of Canterbury and the Trustees of Lambeth Palace Library)*

the most famous abbess of the Anglo-Saxon period was Saint Hilda (d. 680). A noblewoman of considerable learning and administrative ability, she ruled the double monastery of Whitby on the Northumbrian coast, advised kings and princes, hosted the famous synod of 664, and encouraged scholars and poets. "She compelled those under her direction to devote time to the study of the Holy Scriptures, and to exercise themselves in works of justice," with the result that five monks from Whitby became bishops. Several generations after Hilda, Saint Boniface (see page 239) wrote many letters to Whitby and other houses of nuns, pleading for copies of books; these attest to the nuns' intellectual reputations.[24]

The finest representative of Northumbrian, and indeed all Anglo-Saxon, scholarship is the Venerable Bede (ca 673–735). At the age of seven, he was given by his parents as an oblate to Benet Biscop's monastery at Wearmouth. Later he was sent to the new monastery at Jarrow five miles away. Surrounded by the books Benet Biscop had brought from Italy, Bede spent the rest of his life there.

Modern scholars praise Bede for his *Ecclesiastical History of the English People,* the chief source of information about early Britain. Bede searched far and wide for his information, discussed the validity of his evidence, compared various sources, and exercised a rare critical judgment. For these reasons, he has been called "the first scientific intellect among the Germanic peoples of Europe."[25]

Bede popularized the system of dating events from the birth of Christ, rather than from the foundation of the city of Rome, as the Romans had done, or from the regnal years of kings, as the Germans did. Bede introduced the term *anno Domini,* "in the year of the Lord," abbreviated A.D. He fitted the entire history of the world into this new dating method. (The reverse dating system of B.C., "before Christ," does not seem to have been widely used before 1700.) Saint Boniface introduced this system of reckoning time throughout the Frankish empire of Charlemagne.

Is Bede representative of early medieval monasticism? Aside from brief visits to Lindisfarne and York, Bede passed his long and uneventful life in the quiet of his monastery. Using the two hundred to three hundred volumes on early Christian thought that Benet Biscop had brought back from Rome, Bede made that scholarship accessible to his barbarian present. His commentaries on sections of the biblical books of Genesis, Exodus, Samuel, Kings, Acts, and Revelation survive in hundreds of manuscripts, indicating that they were widely studied throughout the Middle Ages. Although the monk-scholar is a fixture in the modern popular imagination, most monks spent their lives in more active work in fields

King Edwin of Northumbria's Palace Complex   This modern illustration reveals a large barnlike structure protected by wooden defenses along sloped terraces. Edwin reigned from 616 to 632. *(English Heritage Photo Library)*

and farms or in management and administration. In neither the pattern of his life nor his considerable pedagogical achievement can the "Venerable" Bede (the adjective means "marked by holiness in life") be called typical.

At about the time that monks at Lindisfarne were producing their Gospel book and Bede at Jarrow was writing his *History,* another Northumbrian monk was at work on a nonreligious epic poem that provides considerable information about the society that produced it. In contrast to the works of Bede, which were written in Latin, the poem *Beowulf* was written in the vernacular Anglo-Saxon. Although *Beowulf* is the only native English heroic epic, all the events of the tale take place in Denmark and Sweden, suggesting the close relationship between England

and the continent in the eighth century. Scholars have hailed it as a masterpiece of Western literature.

Had they remained entirely insular, Northumbrian cultural achievements would have been of slight significance. But an Englishman from Northumbria played a decisive role in the transmission of English learning to the Carolingian Empire and continental Europe.

The Carolingian Renaissance

In Roman Gaul through the fifth century, the general culture rested on an education that stressed grammar; the works of the Greco-Roman orators, poets, dramatists, and historians; and the legal and medical treatises of the Roman world. Beginning in the seventh and eighth centuries, a new cultural tradition common to Gaul, Italy, the British Isles, and to some extent Spain emerged. This culture was based primarily on Christian sources. Scholars have called this new Christian and ecclesiastical culture, and the educational foundation on which it was based, the "Carolingian Renaissance," because Charlemagne was its major patron.

In a letter addressed to the abbot of Fulda, with copies sent to every monastery and bishopric in his kingdom, Charlemagne directed that the monasteries "should cultivate learning and educate the monks and secular clergy so that they might have a better understanding of the Christian writings." Likewise, in a "General Admonition" to all the leading clergy, Charles urged the establishment of cathedral and monastic schools, where boys might learn to read and to pray properly. Thus the main purpose of this rebirth of learning was to promote an understanding of the Scriptures and of Christian writers, to instruct people to pray and to praise God in the correct manner.[26]

At his court at Aachen, Charlemagne assembled learned men from all over Europe. The most important scholar and the leader of the palace school was the Northumbrian Alcuin (ca 735–804). From 781 until his death, Alcuin was the emperor's chief adviser on religious and educational matters. An unusually prolific writer, Alcuin prepared some of the emperor's official documents and wrote many moral *exempla,* or "models," which set high standards for royal behavior and constitute a treatise on kingship. Alcuin's letters to Charlemagne set forth political theories on the authority, power, and responsibilities of a Christian ruler.

Aside from Alcuin's literary efforts, what did the scholars at Charlemagne's court do? They copied books and manuscripts and built up libraries. They used the beauti-

Saint Luke from the Ada Gospels (late eighth to early ninth century)   After the cross, the most famous early Christian symbols were representations of the four evangelists: Matthew (man), Mark (lion), Luke (a winged ox), and John (eagle), based on the text in Revelation 4:7. The "Ada School" of painting was attached to the court of Charlemagne, and gets its name from Ada, a sister of Charlemagne who commissioned some of the school's work. In this lavishly illuminated painting, a statuesque Saint Luke sits enthroned, his draperies falling in nervous folds reminiscent of Byzantine art, and surrounded by an elaborate architectural framework. A splendid example of Carolingian Renaissance art. *(Municipal Library, Trier)*

fully clear handwriting known as "caroline minuscule," from which modern Roman type is derived. (This script is called **minuscule** because unlike the Merovingian majuscule, which had letters of equal size, minuscule had both upper- and lowercase letters.) Caroline minuscule improved the legibility of texts and meant that a sheet of

Organ Music from the Utrecht Psalter In the Carolingian period, books played a large role in the spread of Christianity and in the promotion of learning. The most famous of all Carolingian manuscripts, the Utrecht Psalter (ca 825–850), contains the Old Testament book of Psalms, illustrated with ink drawings. Here an illustration for Psalm 150— "Praise him with blast of trumpet, praise him with strings and pipe"— shows the organ that Louis the Pious built for the palace chapel at Aachen. *(University Library, Utrecht)*

vellum could contain more words and thus be used more efficiently. With the materials at hand, many more manuscripts could be copied. Book production on this scale represents a major manifestation of the revival of learning. Caroline minuscule illustrates the way a seemingly small technological change has broad cultural consequences.

Although scholars worked with Latin, exchanged books between monasteries, and generally collaborated in book production, the common people spoke their local or vernacular languages. The Bretons, for example, retained their local dialect, and the Saxons and Bavarians could not understand each other. Some scholars believe that Latin words and phrases gradually penetrated the various vernacular languages, facilitating communication among diverse peoples.

Once basic literacy was established, monastic and other scholars went on to more difficult work. By the middle years of the ninth century, there was a great outpouring of more sophisticated books. Ecclesiastical writers, imbued with the legal ideas of ancient Rome and the theocratic ideals of Saint Augustine, instructed the semibarbaric rulers of the West. And it is no accident that medical study in the West began at Salerno in southern Italy in the late ninth century, *after* the Carolingian Renaissance.

Alcuin completed the work of his countryman Boniface—the Christianization of northern Europe. Latin Christian attitudes penetrated deeply into the consciousness of European peoples. By the tenth century, the patterns of thought and lifestyles of educated western Europeans were those of Rome and Latin Christianity.

Health and Medical Care in the Early Middle Ages

A surprising amount of information is known about medical treatment in the early Middle Ages. Medical practice consisted primarily of drug and prescription therapy. Through the monks' efforts and recovery of Greek and Arabic manuscripts, a large body of the ancients' prescriptions was preserved and passed on. Balsam was recommended for coughs. For asthma, an ointment combining chicken, wormwood, laurel berries, and oil of roses was to be rubbed on the chest. The scores of prescriptions to rid the body of lice, fleas, and other filth reflect frightful standards of personal hygiene. The large number of prescriptions for eye troubles suggests that they, too, must have been common.

Poor diet caused frequent stomach disorders and related ailments such as dysentery, constipation, and diarrhea. The value of dieting and avoiding greasy foods was recognized. For poor circulation, a potion of meadow wort, oak rind, and lustmock was recommended. Pregnant women were advised to abstain from eating the flesh of almost all male animals, because such meat might deform the child.

Pregnancy and childbirth posed grave threats of infection for both mother and child. Also, heavy field work could cause miscarriages. Some recent scholars have argued that midwives possessed a store of pharmaceutical information deriving from the Romans about fertility, contraception, pregnancy, and childbirth. The weight of present evidence on pre- and postnatal matters, however, is that midwives and matrons actually knew very little about drugs to increase contractions, episiotomy (surgical incision of the perineum to allow birth), or the use of forceps (a seventeenth-century invention) during childbirth. The result was a staggeringly high death rate for mothers and newborns.

All wounds and open injuries invited infection, and infection invited gangrene. Several remedies were known for wounds. Physicians appreciated the antiseptic properties of honey, and prescriptions recommended that wounds be cleaned with it. When an area or a limb had become gangrenous, the physician was instructed to cut above the diseased flesh in order to hasten a cure. The juice of white poppy plants—the source of heroin—could be added to wine and drunk as an anesthetic. Egg whites, which have a soothing effect, were prescribed for burns.

The spread of Christianity in the Carolingian era had a beneficial effect on medical knowledge and treatment. Several of the church fathers expressed serious interest in medicine. The church was deeply concerned about human suffering, whether physical or mental. Christian teaching vigorously supported concern for the poor, sick, downtrodden, and miserable. Churchmen taught that, while all knowledge came from God, He had supplied it so that people could use it for their own benefit.

The foundation of a school at Salerno in southern Italy sometime in the ninth century gave a tremendous impetus to medical study by laypeople. The school's location attracted Arabic, Greek, and Jewish physicians from all over the Mediterranean region. Students flocked there from northern Europe. The Jewish physician Shabbathai Ben Abraham (931–982) left pharmacological notes that were widely studied in later centuries.

Local folk medicine practiced by nonprofessionals provided such help as people could get. Physicians were few in the early Middle Ages, and only the rich could afford them. Apparently most illnesses simply took their course, and death came early. A person aged forty was considered old. People's vulnerability to ailments for which there was no probable cure contributed to a fatalistic acceptance of death at an early age.

Aristocratic Resurgence

Charlemagne left his vast empire to his sole surviving son, Louis the Pious (r. 814–840). (See the feature "Individuals in Society: Ebo of Reims.") Initially, Louis proved as tough and ruthless as his father. He banished from the court real or potential conspirators, crushed rebellions, and blinded his enemies or consigned them to monaster-

ies. Then, in 821, Louis seems to have undergone some sort of change. He pardoned the conspirators implicated in earlier revolts, allowed some to return from exile, and promoted others to high ecclesiastical positions. Perhaps the emperor felt secure enough that he could now be generous. He was not. In pardoning dissident magnates, Louis showed that he underestimated them; they fomented jealousy among his sons and plotted to augment their wealth and power.

At Aachen in 817, Louis drew up the *Arrangement of the Empire,* in which he divided his territories among his three sons but stressed the importance of the unity of the empire. The eldest son, Lothar, received at once the imperial title as co-ruler with his father and was to be heir to the empire after Louis's death. The younger sons were given vast lands and powers, but they were to be subordinate to Lothar and to meet him annually to resolve mutual problems and to promote friendship. Dissatisfied with their portions, anxious to gain the imperial title, and incited by disaffected magnates, Louis's sons fought bitterly among themselves. Finally, in the Treaty of Verdun of 843, the brothers reached an agreement (see Map 8.2).

Lothar retained the title of emperor and the "middle kingdom," the territories bordered by the Meuse, Saône, and Rhône Rivers in the west and the Rhine River in the east, plus the kingdom of Italy. The eastern and most Germanic part of the Carolingian Empire passed to Louis the German. This "eastern kingdom" achieved the greatest relative level of stability, partly because Louis avoided being dependent on any one aristocratic faction, partly because he successfully focused on expansion against the Slavs to the east. The "western kingdom" went to Charles the Bald (r. 843–877); it included the provinces of Aquitaine and Gascony and later formed the basis of medieval and modern France. Harassed on his northern and western frontiers by the Vikings (see page 255) and continually pressured by his magnates for lands and honors, Charles the Bald spent most of his reign at war.

Older scholarship has stressed the fratricidal wars among Louis the Pious's sons and grandsons as the major cause of the disintegration of the Carolingian Empire. Recent and better-informed research emphasizes the conspiracies and revolts of greedy magnates. Why? Perhaps they had never been fully reconciled to Carolingian rule. Perhaps they harbored personal grudges against Louis the Pious or one of his sons. Perhaps some counts and magnates, having acquired great lands and powers, lusted for more. In any case, from 830 (before the death of Louis the Pious) and extending through the later ninth century, "the growing strength and self-interest of the magnates" was the major cause of civil war and

Individuals in Society

Ebo of Reims

The term *social mobility* came into broad use only in the twentieth century, but what it signifies—having the opportunity for an upward shift in status within society—is probably as old as organized society itself. "In all ages, service to the state and to men of power has raised some individuals and enabled them to share in the social prestige that attaches to power."* In the Christian Middle Ages, the Catholic church provided the widest path for social advancement, and the archbishop symbolized political as well as religious prestige. Ebo of Reims (ca 775–851) represents one such individual.

Ebo's father was a serf freed by Charlemagne; his mother was Himiltruda, the nurse of Louis the Pious. Ebo's mother probably launched his career, for Ebo was brought up with Louis at the "palace school" at Aachen, where nobles and others were trained for administrative and judicial service to the emperor. A bond was forged between Ebo and Louis. When Louis became king of Aquitaine, he made Ebo his librarian; when in 814 Louis succeeded as emperor, he secured for Ebo the important archepiscopal see of Reims.

Ebo proved himself a very competent administrator. He began construction of a new cathedral, gaining imperial permission to use the city walls as building blocks. Ebo organized the cathedral chapter—the local clergy who handled routine business of the diocese under the bishop. He reformed the monasteries in his see, ending the diverse forms of religious life by enforcing the *Rule of Saint Benedict* in all houses. Ebo also patronized learning and the arts. He supported the school long associated with the cathedral, and the production of manuscripts; and he commissioned the production of a book that bears his name, the Ebo Gospels.

Ebo served the emperor as *missus* in his province, where he worked to extend royal authority. Archbishop Ebo served both church and state when, acting on behalf of Pope Pascal I and Louis the Pious, he led a mission to King Harold of Denmark, whose goal was the conversion of the Danes to Christianity and peaceful relations with the Franks. When Harold and a large Danish entourage visited Louis in 826, the Danes were baptized and Harold became Louis's vassal.

In 830 Louis was past fifty, by contemporary standards an old man. Louis had three adult sons. Adult sons often posed a test of medieval kingship. Sons wanted power on their own, resented paternal control, and often rebelled. In 833 Archbishop Ebo served as counselor to the sons of Louis the Pious in their plot to remove Louis and replace him with Lothar. Ebo headed a commission of bishops that drew up charges against the emperor, accusing him of failing in his imperial responsibilities, promoting discord among the Frankish people, and tolerating his (second) wife Judith's adultery, thereby bringing moral scandal to the kingdom. Louis was forced to renounce the throne and to do public penance. The charges proved false, and within months Louis regained his throne. A church council deposed Ebo, and he was consigned to a monastery. When Louis the Pious died, Lothar restored Ebo to Reims, but the pope refused to approve the appointment. Then a dispute with Lothar led Ebo to seek the support of Louis the German, who made him bishop of Hildesheim. Ebo died at Hildesheim.

Emperor Louis the Pious confers with bishops and lay magnates. (Bibliothèque nationale de France)

Why did Ebo betray his boyhood friend and great benefactor? Resentment about some real or perceived slight and the desire for revenge? A willingness to listen to dangerous advice? The wish to show himself the equal of any magnate who opposed the emperor? The *Annals of St.-Bertin,* our chief source for these events and the source that modern historians have echoed, describes Ebo as ungrateful, disobedient, disloyal, and cruel. What do you think?

Questions for Analysis

1. How does the career of Ebo of Reims illustrate social mobility?
2. What do Ebo's church appointments tell us about the Frankish state? What secular functions did bishops perform?

*K. Bosl, "On Social Mobility in Medieval Society," in *Early Medieval Society,* ed. S. L. Thrupp (New York: Appleton-Century-Crofts, 1967).

Sources: R. McKitterick, *The Frankish Kingdoms Under the Carolingians* (New York: Longman, 1983); J. L. Nelson, *Politics and Ritual in Early Medieval Europe* (London: Ronceverte, 1986).

The **history companion** *features additional information and activities related to this topic.* history.college.hmco.com/students

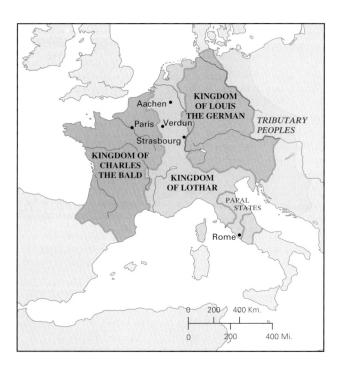

MAP 8.2 Division of the Carolingian Empire, 843
The Treaty of Verdun (843), which divided the empire
among Charlemagne's grandsons, is frequently taken as
the start of the separate development of Germany, France,
and Italy. The "middle kingdom" of Lothar, however,
lacking defensive borders and any political or linguistic
unity, quickly broke up into numerous small territories.

imperial weakness.[27] Nobles frequently worked through
a disaffected member of the royal family, as the case of
Carloman illustrates. Determined to prevent the partition of his kingdom, Charles the Bald used the strategy
of placing his younger sons in the church, thereby removing them from the succession. His youngest boy,
Carloman, was tonsured (crown of the head shaven, symbolic of entry into the clergy) at age five, ordained a dea-
con at eleven, and heaped with abbacies and ecclesiastical
preferments. But Carloman resented being a cleric, and
"gathering around him many accomplices and sons of
Belial [the biblical name of the devil]," as *The Annals of
St-Bertin* describes them,[28] revolted against his father.
Carloman and his noble allies did considerable damage
before he was captured, tried for treason, and blinded.
(Like the Byzantine emperors, a Frankish king had to
possess all his faculties; the loss of sight or reproductive
powers effectively removed candidacy for the monarchy.)
   While Charlemagne had worked to prevent the office
of count from becoming hereditary in one family, in the

ninth century counties passed from father to son in dynastic succession. Some magnates acquired several counties. For example, Robert the Strong held the counties of
Angers, Blois, Tours, Autun, Auxerre, and Nevers, and
Bernard Hairyfeet became count of Toulouse, Narbonne,
Auvergne, and Limousin.[29] In the West Frankish kingdom, Charles the Bald's efforts to gain support with gifts
of lands and comital offices weakened him. Some families
of counts had such conglomerations of lands that they
were able to deny the king's authority and effectively to resist him. The administration system built by Pippin III and
Charlemagne survived, but imperial authority weakened.
Actual power passed into the hands of local magnates.

Feudalism and the Historians

The great English legal historian Frederic William Maitland used to amuse his classes at Cambridge University at
the start of the twentieth century by telling them that
feudalism was introduced into England in the seventeenth century. By that he meant that the word *feudalism*
was not a medieval term. It was invented by scholars in
the seventeenth century and popularized by French political philosophers in the eighteenth century, especially
Montesquieu in *The Spirit of the Laws* (1748). The term
feudalism did not come into general English usage until
1828. Since then, some of the ablest scholars in Europe
and North America have tried to work out an accurate
definition. Those scholars have not been successful, as
confusion and inaccuracy still surround the word.
   Feudalism draws attention to just one aspect of a very
complicated society—the *feud,* or "fief," an estate in land
or money granted by a superior on condition of render-
ing him (or her) services. We have called the person who
grants the fief the "lord" and the recipient of the fief the
vassus (vassal) or *homo* (man) of the lord, but medieval
people used those Latin words in very different contexts
and with different meanings. Therefore, it is not only im-
precise but inaccurate to use the terms *fief* and *vassal* in a
discussion of the entire period we call the Middle Ages.
Likewise, the form and pattern of feudalism changed
considerably between the ninth and fifteenth centuries in
France, Germany, Italy, and England. The feudalism of
Norman England in 1100, for example, differed greatly
from that of Capetian France, scarcely fifty miles away, at
the same time. Modern historians have casually applied
the technical definitions of seventeenth-century lawyers
or nineteenth-century lexicographers to ninth-, eleventh-,
and thirteenth-century circumstances. As an expert recently reminded us,

Fiefs and vassalage are post-medieval constructs, though rather earlier than the construct of feudalism. . . . Even when historians follow the terminology of the documents . . . they tend to fit their findings into a framework of interpretation that was devised in the sixteenth century and elaborated in the seventeenth or eighteenth. We cannot understand medieval society and its property relations if we see it through seventeenth or eighteenth century spectacles.[30]

So much regional variation existed in the practices we call feudal that any broad generalization requires careful qualification, or we introduce error. Then why have historians clung to this terminology? Why have they, in another scholar's words, "been tyrannized by a construct"?[31] The answer is that they have not been able to come up with a better alternative.

Interpretations of Feudalism

Two broad interpretations of feudalism have conditioned medievalists' thinking. In 1940, the great French economic and social historian Marc Bloch published *Feudal Society*. Bloch regarded feudalism as a whole system of life—not only economic but political, cultural, and ecclesiastical—centered on lordship. He saw feudalism as a political system, an economic system, and a system of values. Bloch described a feudal economy, a feudal literature, and a feudalized church in much the way we use the word *capitalistic* to mean not only a certain kind of production and exchange but also government, thought, or capitalistic spirit.

The major alternative interpretation explains feudalism largely in political and legal terms. It holds that the feudalism that emerged in western Europe in the ninth century was a type of government "in which political power was treated as a private possession and was divided among a large number of lords."[32] This kind of government characterized most parts of western Europe from about 900 to 1300. Feudalism actually existed at two social levels: first, at the level of armed retainers who became knights; and second, at the level of royal officials, such as counts, who ruled great feudal principalities. A wide and deep gap in social standing and political function separated these social levels. (See the feature "Listening to the Past: Feudal Homage and Fealty" on pages 262–263.)

While both of these interpretations present defensible explanations for the nature of feudalism, the legal-political version has proven to be more useful, especially for the beginning student. Throughout western Europe, counts

Homage and Fealty Although the rite of entering a feudal relationship varied widely across Europe and sometimes was entirely verbal, we have a few illustrations of it. Here the vassal kneels before the lord, places his clasped hands between those of the lord, and declares, "I become your man." Sometimes the lord handed over a clump of earth, representing the fief, and the ceremony concluded with a kiss, symbolizing peace between them. *(Osterreichische Nationalbibliothek)*

or earls exercised the most effective political power at the local level: they raised armies of fighting men, held courts that dispensed some form of law, coined money used in commercial transactions, and conducted relations with outside or foreign powers. Modern political scientists call these the powers of a sovereign or independent state. In the early Middle Ages, local counts or earls administered these powers, and for their own personal benefit. Beginning in the twelfth and thirteenth centuries, the kings of France and England began to clip and check the powers of local authorities. Until then, counts possessed the actual power; knights did not.

The Origins of Feudalism

Scholars have debated two theories about the origins of feudalism. According to the older explanation, in the early eighth century the Carolingian kings and other powerful men needed bodyguards and retainers, armed men who could fight effectively on horseback. Around this time, the arrival in western Europe of a Chinese technological invention, the stirrup, revolutionized warfare. An unstirruped rider had difficulty impaling an enemy, but a horseman in stirrups could utilize the galloping animal's force to strike and damage his enemy. Charles Martel recognized the potential of an effective cavalry; thus the availability of stirrups increased his need for large numbers of retainers. Horses and armor were terribly expensive, and few could afford them. It also took considerable time to train an experienced cavalryman. As a result, the value of retainers increased. Therefore, Charles and other powerful men bound their retainers by oaths of loyalty and ceremonies of homage.

The other, more recent theory of the origin of feudalism does not give much importance to the stirrup. According to this interpretation, the stirrup did not lead to the wide use of mounted troops, since most warfare in the Carolingian period was siege warfare conducted by infantry. Rather, Charles Martel, using techniques common among his Merovingian predecessors, purchased the support and loyalty of his followers with grants of land or estates taken from churchmen or laymen, or with movable wealth such as weapons or jewelry, captured in battle.[33] Personal ties of loyalty cemented the relationship between lord and retainer; in exchange for the promise of service and loyalty, the lord distributed land or some other means of material support, such as cash.

These retainers became known as **vassals,** from a Celtic term meaning "servant." Since lesser vassals, or knights, were not involved in any governmental activity, and since only men who exercised political power were considered

noble, knights were not part of the noble class. Instead, down to the eleventh century, political power was concentrated in a small group of counts.

Counts, descended from the Frankish aristocracy (see page 236), constituted the second level of feudalism. Under Charles Martel and his heirs, counts monopolized the high offices in the Carolingian Empire. While countships were not at first hereditary in the eighth century, they tended to remain within the same family. In the ninth century, regional concentrations of power depended on family connections and political influence at the king's court. The weakening of the Carolingian Empire, however, served to increase the power of regional authorities. Civil wars weakened the power and prestige of kings, because there was little they could do about domestic violence. Likewise, the great invasions of the ninth century, especially the Viking invasions (see pages 255–257), weakened royal authority. The West Frankish kings could do little to halt the invaders, and the aristocracy had to assume responsibility for defense. Common people turned for protection to the strongest local power, the counts, whom they considered their rightful rulers. Thus, in the ninth and tenth centuries, great aristocratic families increased their authority in the regions of their vested interests. They governed virtually independent territories in which distant and weak kings could not interfere. "Political power had become a private, heritable property for great counts and lords."[34] This is feudalism as a form of government.

Manorialism

Feudalism concerned the rights, powers, and lifestyle of the military elite; *manorialism* involved the services and obligations of the peasant classes. The economic power of the warring class rested on landed estates, which were worked by peasants. Hence feudalism and manorialism were inextricably linked. Peasants needed protection, and lords demanded something in return for that protection. Free peasants surrendered themselves and their lands to the lord's jurisdiction. The land was given back, but the peasants became tied to the land by various kinds of payments and services. In France, England, Germany, and Italy, local custom determined precisely what those services were, but certain practices became common everywhere. The peasant was obliged to turn over to the lord a percentage of the annual harvest, usually in produce, sometimes in cash. The peasant paid a fee to marry someone from outside the lord's estate. To inherit property, the peasant paid a fine, often the best beast the person owned. Above all, the peasant became part of the lord's

Ox Team Plowing   From an eleventh-century calendar showing manorial occupations for each month, this illustration for January—the time for sowing winter wheat—shows two pairs of oxen pulling a wheeled plow, which was designed for deeper tillage. One man directs the oxen, a second prods the animals, and a third drops seeds in the ground. *(British Library Cott. Tib. B.V. 3, Min. Pt 1)*

permanent labor force. With vast stretches of uncultivated virgin land and a tiny labor population, lords encouraged population growth and immigration. The most profitable form of capital was not land but laborers.

In entering into a relationship with a feudal lord, free farmers lost status. Their position became servile, and they became **serfs**. That is, they were bound to the land and could not leave it without the lord's permission. They were also subject to the jurisdiction of the lord's court in any dispute over property and in any case of suspected criminal behavior.

The transition from freedom to serfdom was slow; its speed was closely related to the degree of political order in a given region. In the late eighth century, there were still many free peasants. And within the legal category of serfdom there were many economic levels, ranging from the highly prosperous to the desperately poor. Nevertheless, a social and legal revolution was taking place. By the year 800, perhaps 60 percent of the population of western Europe—completely free a century before—had been reduced to serfdom. The ninth-century Viking assaults on Europe created extremely unstable conditions and individual insecurity, leading to additional loss of personal freedom. (Chapter 10 details the lives of the peasants. As it shows, the later Middle Ages witnessed considerable upward social mobility.)

Great Invasions of the Ninth Century

After the Treaty of Verdun (843), continental Europe presented an easy target for foreign invaders. All three kingdoms controlled by Louis the Pious's sons (see page 250) were torn by domestic dissension and disorder. No European political power was strong enough to put up effective resistance to external attacks. The frontier and coastal defenses erected by Charlemagne and maintained by Louis the Pious were neglected. Three groups attacked Europe: Vikings from Scandinavia, representing the final wave of Germanic migrants; Muslims from the Mediterranean; and Magyars, Asiatic nomads forced westward by other peoples (see Map 8.3). The combination of their assaults hastened the collapse of the Carolingian Empire.

Assaults on Western Europe

From the moors of Scotland to the mountains of Sicily, there arose in the ninth century the prayer, "Save us, O God, from the violence of the Northmen." The Northmen, also known as Normans or Vikings, were Germanic peoples from Norway, Sweden, and Denmark who had remained beyond the sway of the Christianizing and civilizing influences of the Carolingian Empire. Some scholars believe that the name *Viking* derives from the old Norse word *vik,* meaning "creek." A Viking, then, was a pirate who waited in a creek or bay to attack passing vessels.

The Vikings were superb seamen. Their advanced methods of boat building gave them great speed and maneuverability. Propelled either by oars or by sails, deckless, and about sixty-five feet long, a Viking ship could carry between forty and sixty men—quite enough to harass an isolated monastery or village. These ships, navigated by thoroughly experienced and utterly fearless sailors, moved through the most complicated rivers,

MAP 8.3 The Great Invasions of the Ninth Century   Note the Vikings' penetration of eastern Europe and their probable expeditions to North America. What impact did their various invasions have on European society?

estuaries, and waterways in Europe. The Carolingian Empire, with no navy and no notion of the importance of sea power, was helpless. The Vikings moved swiftly, attacked, and escaped to return again.

Scholars disagree about the reasons for Viking attacks and migrations. Recent research asserts that a very unstable Danish kingship and disputes over the succession led to civil war and disorder, which drove warriors abroad in search of booty and supporters. Other writers insist that the Vikings were looking for trade and new commercial contacts. What better targets for plunder than the mercantile centers of Francia and Frisia?

Viking attacks were very savage. The Vikings burned, looted, and did extensive short-term property damage, but there is little evidence that they caused long-term destruction—perhaps because, arriving in small bands, they lacked the manpower to do so. They seized magnates and high churchmen and held them for ransom; they also demanded tribute from kings. In 844–845 Charles the Bald had to raise 7,000 pounds of silver,[35] and across the English Channel Anglo-Saxon rulers collected a land tax, the Danegeld, to buy off the Vikings. The Vikings exploited conflicts among the Carolingians, as in 841, when they sailed up the Seine and sacked Rouen, knowing that Charles the Bald had crushed a revolt of nobles there just a few weeks before and the region was vulnerable. The Carolingians also manipulated the Vikings, as Lothar "used his Viking ally Harald against his brothers in Frisia."[36] In the Seine and Loire Valleys, the frequent presence of Viking war bands seems to have had economic consequences, stimulating the production of food and wine and possibly the manufacture (for sale) of weapons and the breeding of horses. During the tenth century, as the Vikings settled down and adopted Frankish customs and military practices, considerable assimilation occurred among the two peoples.

Between 876 and 954, Viking control extended from Dublin across the Irish Sea to Britain, across northern Britain between the Dee and the Solway Rivers, and then across the North Sea to the Vikings' Scandinavian homelands. These invaders also overran a large part of north-western France and called the territory "Norsemanland," from which the word *Normandy* derives. In the East, they pierced the rivers of Russia as far as the Black Sea (see Map 8.4). In the West, they sailed as far as Iceland, Greenland, and even the coast of North America, perhaps as far south as Long Island Sound (New York).

Scarcely had the savagery of the Viking assaults begun to subside when Europe was hit from the east and south. Beginning about 890, Magyar tribes crossed the Danube and pushed steadily westward. (Since people thought of them as returning Huns, the Magyars came to be known as "Hungarians.") They subdued northern Italy, compelled Bavaria and Saxony to pay tribute, and penetrated even into the Rhineland and Burgundy. These roving bandits attacked isolated villages and monasteries, taking prisoners and selling them in the Eastern slave markets. The Magyars were not colonizers; their sole object was booty and plunder.

The Vikings and Magyars depended on fear. In their initial attacks on isolated settlements, many people were put to the sword. From the British Isles and territories along the Baltic Sea, the Vikings took *thralls* (slaves) for the markets of Magdeburg on the Elbe River and Regensburg in Bavaria on the Danube, for the fairs of Lyons on the Rhône River, and to supply the huge demand for slaves in the Muslim world. The slave trade represented an important part of Viking commerce. The Icelander Hoskuld Dala-Kolsson of Laxardal paid 3 marks of silver, three times the

Animal Headpost from Viking Ship
Skilled woodcarvers produced ornamental headposts for ships, sledges, wagons, and bedsteads; the fearsome quality of many carvings suggests that they were intended to ward off evil spirits and to terrify. (*© University Museum of Cultural Heritage, Oslo. Photographer: Eirik Irgens Johnsen*)

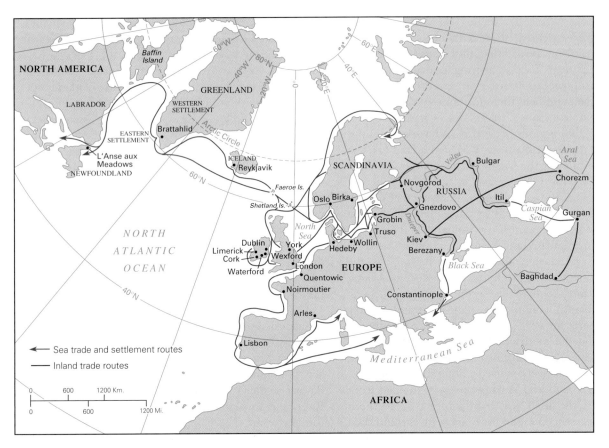

MAP 8.4 Viking Settlement and Trade Routes   Viking trade and settlements extended from Newfoundland and Greenland to deep into Russia.

price of a common concubine, for a pretty Irish girl; she was one of twelve offered by a Viking trader. No wonder many communities bought peace by paying tribute.

From the south, the Muslims also began new encroachments, concentrating on the two southern peninsulas, Italy and Spain. Seventh- and early-eighth-century Islamic movements (see pages 224–225) had been for purposes of conquest and colonization, but the goal of ninth- and tenth-century incursions was plunder; these later raids were essentially piratical attacks. The Muslims drove northward and sacked Rome in 846. Expert seamen, they sailed around the Iberian Peninsula, braved the notoriously dangerous shoals and winds of the Atlantic coast, and attacked the Mediterranean settlements along the coast of Provence. But Muslim attacks on the European continent in the ninth and tenth centuries were less destructive than Viking and Magyar assaults. Compared to the rich, sophisticated culture of the Arab capitals, northern Europe was primitive and backward and offered little.

What was the effect of these invasions on the structure of European society? Viking, Magyar, and Muslim attacks accelerated the fragmentation of political power. Lords capable of rallying fighting men, supporting them, and putting up resistance to the invaders did so. They also assumed political power in their territories. Weak and defenseless people sought the protection of local strongmen. Free peasants sank to the level of serfs.

The ninth-century invaders also left significant traces of their own cultures. The Vikings, for example, made positive contributions to the areas they settled. They carried everywhere their unrivaled knowledge of shipbuilding and seamanship. The northeastern and central parts of England where the Vikings settled became known as the *Danelaw* because Danish law and customs, not English, prevailed there. Scholars believe that some legal institutions, such as the ancestor of the modern grand jury, originated in the Danelaw. York in northern England, once a Roman army camp and then an Anglo-Saxon town, became a thriving center of Viking trade with Scandinavia. At Dublin on the east coast of Ireland, Viking iron- and steelworkers and combmakers established a center for trade with the Hebrides, Iceland, and Norway. The Irish cities of Limerick, Cork, Wexford, and Waterford trace their origins to Viking trading centers.

The Vikings and the Kievan Principality

In antiquity the Slavs lived as a single people in central Europe. With the start of the mass migrations of the late Roman Empire, the Slavs moved in different directions and split into three groups. The group later labeled the West Slavs included the Poles, Czechs, Slovaks, and Wends. The South Slavs, comprising peoples who became the Serbs, Croats, Slovenes, Macedonians, and Bosnians, migrated southward into the Balkans and eventually achieved a relatively high degree of political development before being absorbed by the Ottoman Turks in the fourteenth and fifteenth centuries. Between the fifth and ninth centuries, the eastern Slavs, from whom the Ukrainians, Russians, and White Russians descend, moved into the vast and practically uninhabited area of present-day European Russia and Ukraine.

This enormous area consisted of an immense virgin forest to the north, where most of the eastern Slavs settled, and an endless prairie grassland to the south. Probably organized as tribal communities, the eastern Slavs, like many North American pioneers much later, lived off the great abundance of wild game and a crude "slash and burn" agriculture. After clearing a piece of the forest to build log cabins, they burned the stumps and brush. The ashes left a rich deposit of potash and lime, and the land produced several good crops before it was exhausted. The people then moved on to another, untouched area and repeated the process.

In the ninth century, the Vikings appeared in the lands of the eastern Slavs. Called "Varangians" in the old Russian chronicles, the Vikings were interested primarily in international trade, and the opportunities were good. Moving up and down the rivers, the Vikings soon linked Scandinavia and northern Europe to the Black Sea and to the Byzantine Empire with its capital at Constantinople. They built a few strategic forts along the rivers, from which they raided the neighboring Slavic tribes and collected tribute. **Slaves** were the most important article of tribute, and *Slav* became the word for "slave" in several European languages.

In order to increase and protect their international commerce, the Vikings declared themselves the rulers of the eastern Slavs. According to tradition, the semilegendary chieftain Ruirik founded a princely dynasty about 860. In any event, the Varangian ruler Oleg (r. 878–912) established his residence at Kiev. He and his successors ruled over a loosely united confederation of Slavic territories—the Kievan state—until 1054. The Viking prince and his clansmen quickly became assimilated into the Slavic population, taking local wives and emerging as the noble class.

Assimilation was accelerated by the conversion of the Vikings and local Slavs to Eastern Orthodox Christianity by missionaries of the Byzantine Empire. The written language of these missionaries, an early form of Slavic now known as Old Church Slavonic, was subsequently used in all religious and nonreligious documents in the Kievan principality. Thus the rapidly Slavified Vikings left two important legacies for the future: they created a loose unification of Slavic territories under a single ruling prince and a single ruling dynasty, and they imposed a basic religious unity by accepting Orthodox Christianity, as opposed to Roman Catholicism, for themselves and the eastern Slavs.

Even at its height under Great Prince Iaroslav the Wise (r. 1019–1054), the unity of the Kievan principality was extremely tenuous. Trade, rather than government, was the main concern of the rulers. Moreover, the Slavified Vikings failed to find a way of peacefully transferring power from one generation to the next. In medieval western Europe, this fundamental problem of government was increasingly resolved by resorting to the principle of primogeniture: the king's eldest son received the crown as his rightful inheritance when his father died. Civil war was thus averted; order was preserved. In early Kiev, however, there were apparently no fixed rules, and much strife accompanied each succession.

Possibly to avoid such chaos, Great Prince Iaroslav, before his death in 1054, divided the Kievan principality among his five sons, who in turn divided their properties when they died. Between 1054 and 1237, Kiev disintegrated into more and more competing units, each ruled by a prince claiming to be a descendant of Ruirik. Even when only one prince claimed to be the great prince, the whole situation was very unsettled.

The princes divided their land like private property because they thought of it as private property. A given prince owned a certain number of farms or landed estates and had them worked directly by his people, mainly slaves, called *kholops* in Russian. Outside of these estates, which constituted the princely domain, the prince exercised only very limited authority in his principality. Excluding the clergy, two kinds of people lived there: the noble boyars and the commoner peasants.

The **boyars** were the descendants of the original Viking warriors, and they also held their lands as free and clear private property. Although the boyars normally fought in princely armies, the customary law declared that they could serve any prince they wished. The ordinary peasants were also truly free. They could move at will wherever opportunities were greatest. In the touching phrase of the times, theirs was "a clean road, without boundaries."[37] In short, fragmented princely power, private property, and personal freedom all went together.

Summary

Building on the military and diplomatic foundations of his ancestors, Charlemagne waged constant warfare to expand his kingdom. His wars with the Saxons in northwestern Germany and with the Lombards in northern Italy proved successful, and his kingdom ultimately included most of continental Europe. He governed this vast territory through a military elite, the Frankish counts, who exercised political, economic, and judicial authority at the local level.

The culture that emerged in Europe between 732 and 843 has justifiably been called the "first" European civilization. That civilization had definite characteristics: it was Christian, feudal, and infused with Latin ideas and models. Almost all people were baptized Christians. Latin was the common language—written as well as spoken—of educated people everywhere. This culture resulted from the mutual cooperation of civil and ecclesiastical authorities. Kings and church leaders supported each other's goals and utilized each other's prestige and power. Kings encouraged preaching and publicized church doctrines, such as the stress on monogamous marriage. In return, church officials urged obedience to royal authority. The support that Charlemagne gave to education and learning, the intellectual movement known as the Carolingian Renaissance, proved his most enduring legacy. An overwhelmingly agricultural economy supplied food for local needs, but there was some inter-regional trade in glass, pottery, and woolens and a sizable long-distance trade with the Muslim world in slaves.

The resurgence of an ambitious aristocracy composed of greedy magnates who pressured later Carolingian kings for ever more lands; the growth of hereditary and semi-independent countships; and the invasions of the Vikings, Magyars, and Muslims—these factors all contributed to the empire's disintegration. As the empire broke down, a new form of decentralized government, later known as feudalism, emerged. In a feudal society, public and political power was held by a small group of military leaders. No civil or religious authority could maintain a stable government over a very wide area. Lo-cal strongmen provided what little security existed. Commerce and long-distance trade were drastically reduced. Because of their agricultural and commercial impact, the Viking and Muslim invaders represent the most dynamic and creative forces of the period. By the twelfth century, the Kievan principality—Slavic in ethnicity, Eastern Orthodox in religion, and the center of considerable trade with the Chinese and Muslim worlds—constituted a loose collection of territories without a strong central government.

Key Terms

civitas	political Augustinianism
comites	double monastery
Frank	minuscule
capitularies	vassals
mayor of the palace	serfs
anointment	slaves
missi dominici	boyars

Notes

1. The sources, both Muslim and Christian, dispute both the date (732) and the place of the battle (Poitiers or Tours). I. Wood, *The Merovingian Kingdoms, 450–751* (New York: Longman, 1994), pp. 282–286, provides a careful analysis of all the documentary evidence.
2. Wood, *The Merovingian Kingdoms,* p. 60.
3. Ibid., p. 101.
4. See ibid., chap. 6.
5. Ibid., pp. 60–66; and E. James, *The Franks* (New York: Basil Blackwell, 1988), pp. 191–194.
6. Wood, *The Merovingian Kingdoms,* pp. 102–119.
7. See R. McKitterick, *The Frankish Kingdoms Under the Carolingians, 751–987* (New York: Longman, 1983), pp. 36–37.
8. Quoted ibid., p. 34.
9. R. Fletcher, *The Cross and the Crescent: Christianity and Islam from Muhammad to the Reformation* (New York: Viking, 2004), p. 51.
10. Quoted in B. D. Hill, ed., *Church and State in the Middle Ages* (New York: John Wiley & Sons, 1970), pp. 46–47.
11. P. Geary, "Carolingians and the Carolingian Empire," in *Dictionary of the Middle Ages,* ed. J. R. Strayer, vol. 3 (New York: Charles Scribner's Sons, 1983), p. 110.
12. Einhard, *The Life of Charlemagne,* with a foreword by S. Painter (Ann Arbor: University of Michigan Press, 1960), pp. 50–51.
13. P. Stafford, *Queens, Concubines, and Dowagers: The King's Wife in the Early Middle Ages* (Athens: University of Georgia Press, 1983), pp. 60–62.
14. Quoted in McKitterick, *The Frankish Kingdoms,* p. 77.
15. See K. F. Werner, "Important Noble Families in the Kingdom of Charlemagne," in *The Medieval Nobility: Studies on the Ruling Class of France and Germany from the Sixth to the Twelfth Century,* ed. and trans. T. Reuter (New York: North-Holland, 1978), pp. 174–184.
16. Quoted in P. Brown, *The World of Late Antiquity,* A.D. *150–750* (New York: Harcourt Brace Jovanovich, 1971), p. 11.

17. H. Pirenne, *Mohammed and Charlemagne* (New York: Meridian Books, 1958), *passim,* but esp. pp. 147–186 and pp. 236–285.

18. See A. Verhulst, *The Carolingian Economy* (New York: Cambridge University Press, 2002), for population, pp. 25–26, for local trade, pp. 97–103, and for agricultural growth, pp. 32–43.

19. Michael McCormick, *Origins of the European Economy: Communications and Commerce* (New York: Cambridge University Press, 2001), p. 244.

20. Ibid., p. 753.

21. Ibid.

22. Ibid., p. 758.

23. Ibid., pp. 748–752.

24. J. Nicholson, "Feminae Glorisae: Women in the Age of Bede," in *Medieval Women,* ed. D. Baker (Oxford: Basil Blackwell, 1978), pp. 15–31, esp. p. 19; and C. Fell, *Women in Anglo-Saxon England and the Impact of 1066* (Bloomington: Indiana University Press, 1984), p. 109.

25. R. W. Southern, *Medieval Humanism and Other Studies* (Oxford: Basil Blackwell, 1970), p. 3.

26. McKitterick, *The Frankish Kingdoms,* p. 145.

27. Ibid., pp. 134–136, 169.

28. J. L. Nelson, trans., *The Annals of St-Bertin* (New York: Manchester University Press, 1991); and J. L. Nelson, *Charles the Bald* (New York: Longman, 1992), pp. 225–227.

29. McKitterick, *The Frankish Kingdoms,* pp. 182–183.

30. S. Reynolds, *Fiefs and Vassals: The Medieval Evidence Reconsidered* (Oxford: Clarendon Press, 1996), pp. 2–3.

31. E. A. R. Brown, "The Tyranny of a Construct: Feudalism and Historians of Medieval Europe," *American Historical Review* 79 (1974): 1060–1088.

32. J. R. Strayer, "The Two Levels of Feudalism," in *Medieval Statecraft and the Perspectives of History* (Princeton, N.J.: Princeton University Press, 1971), p. 63.

33. See B. S. Bachrach, "Charles Martel, Mounted Shock Combat, the Stirrup, and Feudalism," *Studies in Medieval and Renaissance History* 7 (1970): 49–75, esp. 66–75.

34. Strayer, "The Two Levels," pp. 66–76, esp. p. 71.

35. Nelson, *Charles the Bald,* p. 151.

36. Ibid., p. 39.

37. Quoted in R. Pipes, *Russia Under the Old Regime* (New York: Charles Scribner's Sons, 1974), p. 48.

Suggested Reading

For the Merovingians, the best general treatment is I. Wood, *The Merovingian Kingdoms, 450–751* (1994). For the Carolingians, see R. McKitterick, *The Frankish Kingdoms Under the Carolingians, 751–987* (1983). The scholarship of these books supersedes all previous work. R. McKitterick, *The Carolingians and the Written Word* (1989), will prove essential for many aspects of the Carolingian Renaissance, as will R. McKitterick, ed., *The Uses of Literacy in Early Medieval Europe* (1990), which includes essays on Ireland, Anglo-Saxon England, Merovingian Gaul, Muslim Spain, and Byzantium. J. L. Nelson, *Charles the Bald* (1992), is broader in scope than the biographical title would imply, since it contains excellent material on the entire late Carolingian period. J. L. Nelson, *The Frankish World, 750–900* (1996), has useful articles on literacy, knighthood, and women.

The best general biography of Charlemagne is D. Bullough, *The Age of Charlemagne* (1965). P. Riche, *Daily Life in the World of Charlemagne,* trans. J. McNamara (1978), is a detailed study of many facets of Carolingian society. P. Riche, *Education and Culture in the Barbarian West: From the Sixth Through the Eighth Century,* trans. J. J. Contreni (1976), provides a good treatment of intellectual activity. For agricultural and economic life, G. Duby, *The Early Growth of the European Economy: Warriors and Peasants from the Seventh to the Twelfth Century* (1978), relates economic behavior to other aspects of human experience in a thoroughly readable style. E. James, *The Origins of France: From Clovis to the Capetians, 500–1000* (1982), is a solid introductory survey of early French history, with an emphasis on family relationships.

Those interested in women and children in early medieval society should see C. Klapisch-Zuber, *A History of Women,* vol. 2, *Silences of the Middle Ages* (1992), which is especially helpful on issues of women's health and birthrates; J. Tibbets-Schulenburg, *Forgetful of Their Sex: Female Sanctity and Society, ca. 500–1100* (1998), which provides insights into society through the lives of medieval women who became saints; D. Herlihy, "Land, Family, and Women in Continental Europe, 701–1200," in *Women in Medieval Society,* ed. S. M. Stuart (1976); and S. F. Wemple, *Women in Frankish Society: Marriage and the Cloister, 500–900* (1981), still a fundamental work.

For the Carolingian economy, see the titles by Pirenne, Verhulst, and McCormick cited in the Notes; McCormick's is a large magisterial work with valuable material on the Slavic, Byzantine, and Iberian worlds. R. Hodges and D. Whitehouse, *Mohammed, Charlemagne and the Origin of Europe: Archeology and the Pirenne Thesis* (1963), is still reliable.

On many issues related to the Muslim conquest of Spain, see O. R. Constable, ed., *Medieval Iberia: Readings from Christian, Muslim, and Jewish Sources* (1997), an exciting collection of source material. H. Kennedy, *Muslim Spain and Portugal: A Political History of al-Andalus* (1996), provides a good chronological narrative of developments in the Iberian Peninsula. The best general background survey of Christian Muslim relations is R. Fletcher, *The Cross and the Crescent: Christianity and Islam from Muhammad to the Reformation* (2004).

For feudalism and manorialism, see, in addition to the references given in the Notes, especially those by Reynolds and Brown, F. L. Ganshof, *Feudalism* (1961), and J. R. Strayer, "Feudalism in Western Europe," in *Feudalism in History,* ed. R. Coulborn (1956). M. Bloch, *Feudal Society,* trans. L. A. Manyon (1961), remains important.

The Oxford Illustrated History of the Vikings (1997), ed. P. Sawyer, provides a sound account of the Vikings by an international team of scholars. J. Brondsted, *The Vikings* (1960), is an excellently illustrated study of many facets of Viking culture. G. Jones, *A History of the Vikings,* rev. ed. (1984), provides a comprehensive survey of the Viking world based on the latest archaeological findings and numismatic evidence, while P. H. Sawyer, *Kings and Vikings: Scandinavia and Europe, A.D. 700–1100* (1983), relies heavily on the literary evidence.

Listening to the Past

Feudal Homage and Fealty

Feudalism provided social and political order held together by bonds of kinship, homage, and fealty and by grants of benefices—lands or estates given by king, lay lord, or ecclesiastical officer (bishop or abbot) to another member of the nobility or to a knight. In return for the benefice, or fief, the recipient became the vassal of the lord and agreed to perform certain services, usually military ones. Feudalism developed in the ninth century during the disintegration of the Carolingian Empire because rulers needed fighting men and officials. In a society that lacked an adequate government bureaucracy, a sophisticated method of taxation, or even the beginnings of national consciousness, personal ties provided some degree of cohesiveness.

In the first document, a charter dated 876, the emperor Charles the Bald (r. 843–877), Charlemagne's grandson, grants a benefice. In the second document, dated 1127, the Flemish notary Galbert of Bruges describes homage and fealty before Count Charles the Good of Flanders (r. 1119–1127). The ceremony consists of three parts: the act of homage; the oath of fealty, intended to reinforce the act; and the investiture (apparently with property). Because all three parts are present, historians consider this evidence of a fully mature feudal system.

In the name of the holy and undivided Trinity. Charles by the mercy of Almighty God august emperor . . . let it be known to all the faithful of the holy church of God and to our now, present and to come, that one of our faithful subjects, by name of Hildebertus, has approached our throne and has beseeched our serenity that through this command of our authority we grant to him for all the days of his life and to his son after him, in right of usufruct and benefice, certain estates which are . . . called Cavaliacus, in the county of Limoges. Giving assent to his prayers for reason of his meritorious service, we have ordered this charter to be written, through which we grant to him the estates already mentioned, in all their entirety, with lands, vineyards, forests, meadows, pastures, and with the men living upon them, so that, without causing any damage through exchanges or diminishing or lessening the land, he for all the days of his life and his son after him, as we have said, may hold and possess them in right of benefice and usufruct. . . .

Done of the sixteenth kalends of August [July 15th] the thirty-seventh year of the reign of Charles most glorious emperor in France . . . at Ponthion in the palace of the emperor. In the name of God, happily. Amen.

On Thursday, the seventh of the ides of April [April 7, 1127], acts of homage were again made to the count, which were brought to a conclusion through this method of giving faith and assurance. First, they performed homage in this fashion: the count inquired if [the prospective vassal] wished completely to become his man. He replied, "I do wish it," and with his hands joined and covered by the hands of the count, the two were united by a kiss. Second, he who had done the homage gave faith to the representative of the count in these words: "I promise in my faith that I shall henceforth be faithful to Count William, and I shall fully observe the homage owed him against all men, in good faith and without deceit." Third, he took an oath on the relics of the saints. Then the count, with the rod which he had in his right

The hand of God blesses Charles the Bald as he receives the Bible, symbolic of his connection with Israelite kings David and Solomon. *(Bibliothèque nationale de France)*

hand, gave investiture to all those who by this promise had given assurance and due homage to the count, and had taken the oath.

Questions for Analysis

1. Why was the charter drawn up? Why did Charles grant the benefice?

2. Who were the "men living on it," and what economic functions did they perform?

3. What did the joined hands of the prospective vassal and the kiss symbolize?

4. In the oath of fealty, what was meant by the phrase "in my faith"? Why did the vassal swear on relics of the saints? What were these, and why were they used?

5. What does this ceremony tell us about the society that used it?

Source: The History of Feudalism by David Herlihy, ed. Copyright © 1970 by David Herlihy. Reprinted by permission of HarperCollins Publishers, Inc.

Pope Urban II, surrounded by mitred bishops, consecrates the new abbey church of Cluny. *(Bibliothèque nationale de France)*

chapter

9

Revival, Recovery, Reform, and Expansion

*B*eginning in the last half of the tenth century, after a long winter of discontent, Latin Christendom—that area of western Europe "that recognized papal authority and celebrated the Latin liturgy"[1]—saw the first hints of spring. The European springtime lasted from the middle of the eleventh century to the end of the thirteenth. This period from about 1050 to 1300 has been called the "High Middle Ages" or the "Central Middle Ages." Either term designates a time of change, growth, and cultural achievement between two eras of economic, political, and social crisis. These centuries also witnessed the expansion of Latin Christian culture into frontier zones, "border regions and regions of warfare"[2]—Ireland, the Baltic, Scandinavia, eastern Europe, and Spain—through conquest and colonization.

• What were the ingredients of revival, and how did they come about?
• How did political revival affect the reform of the church? How, in turn, did religious reform influence secular developments?
• How did the reform of the Christian church come to affect relations between the church and civil authorities?
• What was the impact of Muslim Spain on European culture and civilization?
• What were the Crusades, and how did they manifest the influence of the church and the ideals of medieval society?
• What were the means of Latin Christian penetration into pagan and Muslim regions, and how did that penetration bring about change?

These are the questions that will frame the discussion in this chapter.

*P*olitical Revival

The eleventh century witnessed the beginnings of new political stability. Rulers in France, England, and Germany worked to reduce private warfare and civil anarchy. Domestic disorder subsided, and external invasions from the Vikings, Muslims, and Magyars (see page 255) gradually declined. Political order and stability provided the foundation for economic recovery and contributed to a slow increase in population.

265

In the tenth century, Charlemagne's descendants continued to hold the royal title in the West Frankish kingdom but exercised no effective control over the great feudal lords. Research on medieval France has focused on regions and principalities, emphasizing the diversity of languages and cultures, the differences in social structures, and the division of public authority. Northern French society, for example, had strong feudal elements, but the fief and vassalage were almost unknown in the south. The southern territories used Roman law, while the northern counties and duchies relied on customary law that was not formally codified until the thirteenth century. Thus broad generalizations about France, or indeed any single part of Europe, are very dangerous.[3]

France

Five counties dominated northern France: Anjou, Blois-Champagne, Brittany, Flanders, and Normandy. Normandy gradually emerged as the strongest territory with the greatest relative level of peace.

The territory that we call Normandy takes its name from the Northmen, or Vikings, who settled there in the tenth century. In 911 the West Frankish ruler Charles the Simple, unable to oust the Vikings, officially recognized their leader, Rollo, and later invested him with more lands; in return, Rollo gave allegiance and agreed to hold the region as a barrier against future Viking attacks. Rollo and his men were baptized as Christians and supported the West Frankish ruler when he needed their help. Although additional Northmen arrived, they were easily pacified. The late tenth and early eleventh centuries saw the assimilation of Norman and French, and major assaults on France ended.

During the minority of Rollo's descendant Duke William I (r. 1035–1089), however, rebellious lords ignored ducal authority, built private castles, and engaged in private warfare—with general instability the result. The alliance of Count Geoffrey Martel of Anjou and King Henry I of France posed a dire threat to ducal authority until 1054, when William defeated them. This victory turned the tide. Beginning in 1060, William united the Norman nobility under threat of external aggression from the counts of Blois and Maine and defended his frontier with a circle of castles. William also made feudalism work as a system of government. He insisted on the homage of his vassals, attached specific quotas of knight service to the lands he distributed, swiftly executed vassals who defaulted on their obligations, limited private warfare, and forbade the construction of private castles, always the

symbol of feudal independence. The duke controlled the currency and supervised the church by participating in the selection of all bishops and abbots. By 1066 the Norman frontiers were stable, and the duchy possessed a feudal hierarchy. By the standards of the time, Normandy was an orderly and well-controlled principality.

Following the death of the last Carolingian ruler in 987, an assembly of nobles met to choose a successor. They selected Hugh Capet, head of a powerful clan in the West Frankish kingdom. Soon after his own coronation, Hugh crowned his son Robert to ensure the succession and prevent disputes after his death and to weaken the feudal principle of elective kingship. The Capetian kings (so called from the *cope,* or cloak, Hugh wore as abbot of Saint-Denis) subsequently saved France from further division, but this was hardly apparent in 987. Compared with the duke of Normandy, the first rulers of the **Capetian dynasty** were weak. By hanging on to what they had, however, they laid the foundation for later political stability.

Aquitaine, to the south, was the largest duchy in France geographically, and few lords in the north could match the power of Duke William V (995–1030). His authority extended from the Loire to the Garonne. Although scholars dispute the meaning of the term *vassal* in Aquitaine and whether William's knights actually performed their military service, he seems to have maintained their loyalty.[4] The export of wine and salt brought the duke wealth; the German emperor and the kings of Navarre, Aragon, and England sent him gifts; and William influenced the election of bishops in the duchy. All these suggest a relatively high level of political stability, and a contemporary chronicler said that the duke was thought to be more a king than a duke.[5]

England

Recovery followed a different pattern in Anglo-Saxon England. Before the Viking invasions, England had never been united under a single ruler, and in 877 only parts of the kingdom of Wessex survived. The victory of the remarkable Alfred, king of the West Saxons (or Wessex), over Guthrun the Dane at Edington in 878 inaugurated a great political revival. Alfred and his immediate successors built a system of local defenses and slowly extended royal rule beyond Wessex to other Anglo-Saxon peoples until one law, royal law, took precedence over local custom. Alfred and his successors also laid the foundation for an efficient system of local government responsible directly to the king. Under the pressure of the Vikings, England was gradually united under one ruler.

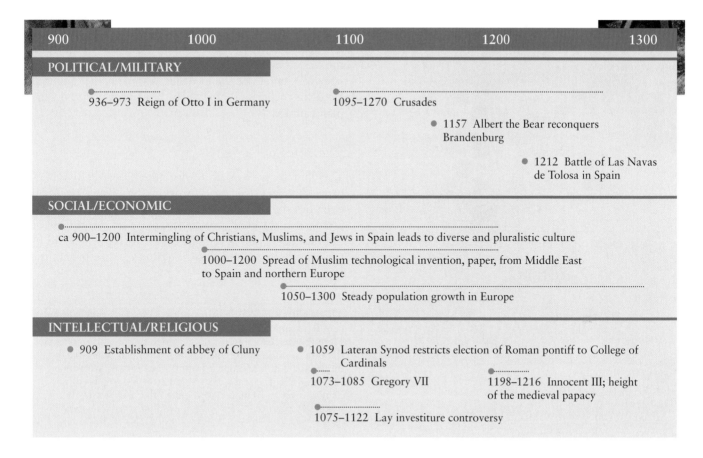

900	1000	1100	1200	1300

POLITICAL/MILITARY

936–973 Reign of Otto I in Germany

1095–1270 Crusades

1157 Albert the Bear reconquers Brandenburg

1212 Battle of Las Navas de Tolosa in Spain

SOCIAL/ECONOMIC

ca 900–1200 Intermingling of Christians, Muslims, and Jews in Spain leads to diverse and pluralistic culture

1000–1200 Spread of Muslim technological invention, paper, from Middle East to Spain and northern Europe

1050–1300 Steady population growth in Europe

INTELLECTUAL/RELIGIOUS

909 Establishment of abbey of Cluny

1059 Lateran Synod restricts election of Roman pontiff to College of Cardinals

1073–1085 Gregory VII

1198–1216 Innocent III; height of the medieval papacy

1075–1122 Lay investiture controversy

In 1013 the Danish ruler Swen Forkbeard invaded England. His son Canute completed the subjugation of the island. King of England (1016–1035) and after 1030 king of Norway as well, Canute made England the center of his empire. He promoted a policy of assimilation and reconciliation between Anglo-Saxons and Vikings. This assimilation was personified by King Edward the Confessor (r. 1042–1066), the son of an Anglo-Saxon father and a Norman mother who had taken Canute as her second husband.

Germany and Italy

In the east, the German king Otto I (r. 936–973) inflicted a crushing defeat on the Hungarians on the banks of the Lech River (Lechfeld) in 955. The **Battle of Lechfeld** halted the Magyars' threat to Germany and made Otto a great hero to the Germans. It also signified the revival of the German monarchy and demonstrated that Otto was a worthy successor to Charlemagne.

When chosen king, Otto had selected Aachen as the site of his coronation to symbolize his intention to continue the tradition of Charlemagne. The basis of his power was alliance with and control of the church. Otto asserted the right to control ecclesiastical appointments. Before receiving religious consecration and being invested with the staff and ring symbolic of their offices, bishops and abbots had to perform feudal homage for the lands that accompanied the church office. (This practice, later known as "lay investiture," was to create a grave crisis in the eleventh century [see pages 274–276].)

To halt anarchy, Otto relied on the church, getting financial support and the bulk of his army from ecclesiastical lands. Between 936 and 955 he broke the territorial power of the great German dukes.

Some of our knowledge of Otto derives from *The Deeds of Otto,* a history of his reign in heroic verse written by a nun, Hroswita of Gandersheim (ca 935–ca 1003). A learned poet, she also produced six verse plays, and she is considered the first dramatist after the fall of the ancient classical theater. Hrotswitha's literary productions give her an important place in the mainstream of tenth-century civilization.

Otto's coronation by the pope in 962 revived the imperial dignity and laid the foundation for what was later called the Holy Roman Empire. Further, the coronation

Christ Enthroned with Saints and the Emperor Otto I (tenth century)   Between 933 and 973, Emperor Otto I founded the church of Saint Mauritius in Magdeburg. As a memorial to the event, Otto commissioned the production of this ivory plaque showing Christ accepting a model of the church from the emperor. Ivory was a favorite medium of Ottonian artists, and squat figures in a simple geometrical pattern characterize their work. *(The Metropolitan Museum of Art, Bequest of George Blumenthal, 1941 [41.100.157]. Photograph © 1986 The Metropolitan Museum of Art)*

Milan and Cremona, with those cities and Sicily supplying Venice with food in exchange for luxury goods from the East. The rising economic importance of Venice and later of Genoa, Pisa, and other cities became a central factor in the struggle between the papacy and the German Empire.

The Peace of God

The church also worked to promote peace. Petty crimes proved most destructive of order and stability. Attacks on churches for the ceremonial vessels and sacred objects; assaults on traveling priests, monks, and merchants for the money or goods they might be carrying; seizure of peasants' livestock and extortion through threats of burn-

Thieves Plunder Saint Edmund's Chapel   In the eleventh century, crime and violence preoccupied religious authorities. Here thieves searching for jewelry, rich burial fabrics, or even the bones of the dead, which could be sold as relics, try to dig up the coffin of Saint Edmund, the king of East Anglia (r. 841–869) who was defeated in battle and executed by Danish invaders. Thieves even pulled the nails out of the wooden structure. *(Pierpont Morgan Library/Art Resource, NY)*

showed that Otto had the support of the church in Germany and Italy. The uniting of the kingship with the imperial crown advanced German interests. Otto filled a power vacuum in northern Italy and brought peace among the great aristocratic families. The level of order there improved for the first time in over a century.

Although plague, climatic deterioration that reduced agricultural productivity, and invasions had reduced the population throughout Italy, most of the northern cities had survived the disorders of the early Middle Ages. By the ninth century, some of these cities showed considerable economic dynamism, in particular Venice, which won privileged access to Byzantine markets and imported silks, textiles, cosmetics, and Crimean slaves to sell to Padua and other cities. By the eleventh century, Venetian commerce had stimulated economic growth in ing their crops and homes; and kidnapping rustics and holding them for ransom—these kinds of violent acts were endemic across western Europe. The church had always preached peace; in the late tenth and early eleventh centuries, it began to do something about it.

At a series of church councils (assemblies of bishops and abbots) in central France, where the violence was the worst, the bishops took action. Councils formed peace associations—groups of men in particular districts who assessed themselves and used the money to provide armed protection against thuggish lords. The councils also published decrees forbidding attacks on peasants, clerics, and merchants and prohibiting the destruction of crops and unfortified places under penalty of total exclusion from the Christian community. These measures had some success in reducing the violence of minor feudal lords, but not in stopping great barons from private warfare. Nevertheless, in central France peace associations continued until the thirteenth century, when they were taken over by the central government of the French monarchy.

Another ecclesiastical effort, the Truce of God, had less impact. In this movement churchmen tried to reduce the amount of warfare by limiting the number of days on which fighting was permitted. Sundays, special feast days, and the seasons of Lent and Advent were to be free of fighting. If all the forbidden days had been observed, fighting would have been permissible on only 80 days of the year. Lay barons did not take the Truce of God very seriously.[6]

Population, Climate, and Mechanization

A steady growth of population also contributed to Europe's general recovery. The decline of foreign invasions and internal civil disorder reduced the number of people killed and maimed. Feudal armies in the eleventh through thirteenth centuries continued their destruction, but they were very small by modern standards and fought few pitched battles. Most medieval conflicts consisted of sieges directed at castles or fortifications. As few as twelve men could defend a castle. With sufficient food and an adequate water supply, they could hold out for a long time. Most conflicts were petty skirmishes with slight loss of life. The survival of more young people—those most often involved in war and usually the most sexually active—meant a population rise.

Nor was there any "natural," or biological, hindrance to population expansion. Between the tenth and four-

teenth centuries, Europe was not hit by any major plague or other medical scourge, though leprosy and malaria did strike down some people. Leprosy, caused by a virus, was not very contagious. Lepers presented a frightful appearance: the victim's arms and legs slowly rotted away, and gangrenous sores emitted a horrible smell. For these reasons, and because of the command in the thirteenth chapter of Leviticus that lepers be isolated, medieval lepers were eventually segregated in hospitals called **leprosaria**.

Crop failure and the ever-present danger of starvation were much more pressing threats. The weather cooperated with the revival. Meteorologists believe that a slow but steady retreat of polar ice occurred between the ninth and eleventh centuries. A significant warming trend continued until about 1200. The century between 1080 and 1180 witnessed exceptionally clement weather in England, France, and Germany, with mild winters and dry summers. Increased agricultural output had a profound impact on society: it improved Europeans' health, commerce, industry, and general lifestyle. A better diet had an enormous impact on women's lives: it meant increased body fat, which increased fertility; also, more iron in the diet meant that women were less anemic and less subject to opportunistic diseases. Some researchers believe that it was in the High Middle Ages that Western women began to outlive men.

The tenth and eleventh centuries also witnessed a remarkable spurt in mechanization, especially in the use of energy. The increase in the number of water mills was spectacular. An ancient water mill unearthed near Monte Cassino could grind about 1.5 tons of grain in 10 hours, a quantity that would formerly have required the exertions of 40 slaves. The abundance of slave labor in the ancient world had retarded the development of mills, but by the mid-ninth century, on the lands of the abbey of Saint-Germaine-des-Prés near Paris, there were 59 water mills. Succeeding generations saw a continued increase. Thus, on the Robec River near Rouen, there were 2 mills in the tenth century, 4 in the eleventh, 10 in the thirteenth, and 12 in the fourteenth. Besides grinding wheat or other grains to produce flour, water mills became essential in *fulling,* the process of scouring, cleansing, and thickening cloth. Rather than men or women trampling cloth in a trough, wooden hammers were raised and dropped on the cloth by means of a revolving drum connected to the spindle of a water wheel. Water mills revolutionized the means of grinding and fulling by using natural, rather than human, energy.

Successful at adapting waterpower to human needs, medieval engineers soon harnessed wind power. They replaced the wheels driven by water with sails. But while

Windmill   The mill was constructed on a pivot, so that it could turn in the direction of the wind. Used primarily to grind grain, as shown here with a man carrying a sack of grain to be ground into flour, windmills were also used to process cloth, brew beer, drive saws, and provide power for iron forges. *(Bodleian Library, Oxford)*

water always flows in the same direction, wind can blow from many directions. Windmill engineers solved this problem very ingeniously by mounting the framed wooden body, which contained the machinery and carried the sails, on a massive upright post free to turn in the wind. After 1180, the construction of water mills accelerated. Many were erected in areas of northern Europe that lacked fast-flowing streams and where they could operate in freezing winter conditions. The early thirteenth century saw the introduction of windmills into Holland.[7]

Revival and Reform in the Christian Church

The eleventh century also witnessed the beginnings of a remarkable religious revival. Monasteries, always the leaders in ecclesiastical reform, remodeled themselves under the leadership of the Burgundian abbey of Cluny. Subsequently, new religious orders were founded and became a broad spiritual movement.

The papacy itself, after a century of corruption and decadence, was cleaned up. The popes worked to clarify church doctrine and codify church law, communicating through a clearly defined, obedient hierarchy of bishops. The popes wanted the basic loyalty of all members of the clergy. Pope Gregory VII's strong assertion of papal power led to profound changes and serious conflict with secular authorities. The revival of the church was manifested in the twelfth and thirteenth centuries by a flowering of popular piety, reflected in the building of magnificent cathedrals.

Monastic Revival

In the early Middle Ages, the best Benedictine monasteries had been citadels of good monastic observance and centers of learning. Between the seventh and ninth centuries, religious houses such as Bobbio in northern Italy, Luxeuil in France, and Jarrow in England copied and preserved manuscripts, maintained schools, and set high standards of monastic observance. Charlemagne had encouraged and supported these monastic activities, and the collapse of the Carolingian Empire had disastrous effects.

The Viking, Magyar, and Muslim invaders attacked and ransacked many monasteries across Europe. Some

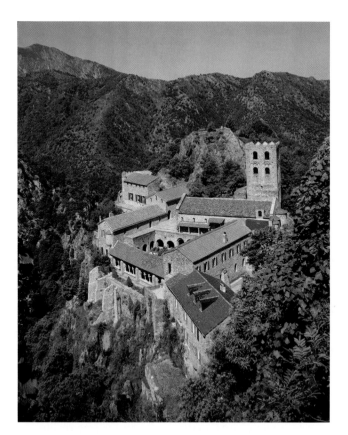

Monastery of Saint Martin de Canigou Located in the eastern Pyrenees, Saint Martin de Canigou was constructed in the early eleventh century in the new Romanesque style. With its thick walls and strategic position, it served as a Christian defensive fortress against the Muslims. *(Edition Gaud)*

communities fled and dispersed. In the period of political disorder that followed the disintegration of the Carolingian Empire, many religious houses fell under the control and domination of local lords. Powerful laymen appointed themselves or their relatives as abbots, took the lands and goods of monasteries, and spent monastic revenues. Temporal powers all over Europe dominated the monasteries. The level of spiritual observance and intellectual activity declined.

Since the time of Charlemagne, secular powers had selected church officials and compelled them to become their vassals. Abbots, bishops, and archbishops thus had military responsibilities that required them to fight with their lords, or at least to send contingents of soldiers when called on to do so. Church law forbade clerics to shed blood, but many prelates found the excitement of battle too great to resist. In the ninth century, Abbot Lupus of Ferrières wrote his friend Abbot Odo of Corbie:

I am often most anxious about you, recalling your habit of heedlessly throwing yourself, all unarmed, into the thick of battle whenever your youthful energy is overcome with the greedy desire to conquer. . . . I, as you know, have never learned how to strike an enemy or to avoid his blows. Nor do I know how to execute all the other obligations of military service on foot or horseback.

Lupus preferred the quiet of his scriptorium to the noise of the battlefield.[8] In the twelfth and thirteenth centuries, ecclesiastical barons owed heavy contingents of knight service; some prelates actually fought with the king. For example, in twelfth-century England, the abbot of Peterborough owed the king the service of sixty knights, the abbot of Bury Saint Edmunds forty knights, and the archbishop of Canterbury the huge service of five hundred knights, though after 1166 the service was usually commuted into a cash payment.[9] As feudal lords, ecclesiastical officials also had judicial authority over the knights, whose cases prelates tried in their feudal courts, and peasants, whose disputes they resolved in the manorial courts. For some prelates, the conflict between their religious duties on the one hand, and their judicial and military obligations on the other, posed a serious dilemma.

In 909 William the Pious, duke of Aquitaine, established the abbey of Cluny near Macon in Burgundy. In his charter of endowment, Duke William declared that Cluny was to enjoy complete independence from all feudal (or secular) and episcopal lordship. The new monastery was to be subordinate only to the authority of Saints Peter and Paul as represented by the pope. The duke then renounced his own possession of and influence over Cluny.

This monastery and its foundation charter came to exert vast religious influence. The first two abbots of Cluny, Berno (910–927) and Odo (927–942), set very high standards of religious behavior. Cluny gradually came to stand for clerical celibacy and the suppression of **simony** (the sale of church offices). In the eleventh century, Cluny was fortunate in having a series of highly able abbots who ruled for a long time. These abbots paid careful attention to sound economic management. In a disorderly world, Cluny gradually came to represent religious and political stability. Therefore, laypersons placed lands under its custody and monastic priories (a priory is a religious house, usually smaller in number than an abbey, governed by a prior) under its jurisdiction for reform. Benefactors wanted to be associated with Cluniac piety. Moreover, properties and monasteries under Cluny's jurisdiction enjoyed special protection, at least theoretically, from violence.[10] In this way, hundreds of monasteries, primarily in France and Spain, came under Cluny's authority.

Deeply impressed laypeople showered gifts on monasteries with good reputations. Jewelry, rich vestments, elaborately carved sacred vessels, even lands and properties poured into some houses. But as the monasteries became richer, the lifestyle of the monks grew increasingly luxurious. Monastic observance and spiritual fervor declined. Soon fresh demands for reform were heard, and the result was the founding of new religious orders in the late eleventh and early twelfth centuries. The Cistercians, because of their phenomenal expansion and the great economic, political, and spiritual influence they exerted, are the best representatives of the new reforming spirit.

In 1098 a group of monks left the rich abbey of Molesmes in Burgundy and founded a new house in the swampy forest of Cîteaux. They planned to avoid all involvement with secular feudal society. They decided to accept only uncultivated lands far from regular habitation. They intended to refuse all gifts of mills, serfs, tithes, and ovens—the traditional manorial sources of income. The early Cistercians determined to avoid elaborate liturgy and ceremony and to keep their chant simple. Finally, they refused to allow the presence of powerful laypeople in their monasteries, because such influence was usually harmful to careful observance.

The first monks at Cîteaux experienced sickness, a dearth of recruits, and terrible privations. But their obvious sincerity and high ideals eventually attracted attention. In 1112 a twenty-three-year-old nobleman called Bernard joined the community at Cîteaux, together with some of his brothers and other noblemen. Three years later, Bernard was appointed founding abbot of Clairvaux in Champagne. From this position, he conducted a vast correspondence, attacked the theological views of Peter Abelard (see page 358), intervened in the disputed papal election of 1130, drafted a constitution for the Knights Templars (see page 280), and preached the Second Crusade. This reforming movement gained impetus. Cîteaux founded 525 new monasteries in the course of the twelfth century, and its influence on European society was profound. Unavoidably, however, Cistercian success brought wealth, and wealth brought power. By the later twelfth century, economic prosperity and political power had begun to compromise the original Cistercian ideals.

Reform of the Papacy

Some scholars believe that the monastic revival spreading from Cluny influenced reform of the Roman papacy and eventually of the entire Christian church. Certainly Abbot Odilo of Cluny (994–1048) was a close friend of the German emperor Henry III, who promoted reform throughout the empire. Pope Gregory VII, who carried the ideals of reform to extreme lengths, had spent some time at Cluny. And the man who consolidated the reform movement and strengthened the medieval papal monarchy, Pope Urban II (1088–1099), had been a monk and prior at Cluny. The precise degree of Cluny's impact on the reform movement cannot be measured, but the broad goals of the Cluniac movement and those of the Roman papacy were the same.

The papacy provided little leadership to the Christian peoples of western Europe in the tenth century. Factions in Rome sought to control the papacy for their own material gain. Popes were appointed to advance the political ambitions of their families—the great aristocratic families of the city—and not because of special spiritual qualifications. A combination of political machinations and sexual immorality damaged the papacy's moral prestige. For example, Pope John XII (955–963) was appointed pope by his powerful father when he was only eighteen, and lacking interest in spiritual matters, he concentrated on expanding papal territories.

At the local parish level, there were many married priests. Taking Christ as the model for the priestly life, the Roman church had always encouraged clerical celibacy, and it had been an obligation for ordination since the fourth century. But in the tenth and eleventh centuries, probably a majority of European priests were married or living with a woman. Such priests were called **Nicolaites** from a reference in the Book of Revelation to early Christians who advocated a return to pagan sexual practices.

Serious efforts at reform began under Pope Leo IX (1049–1054). Not only was Leo related to Emperor Henry III but, as bishop of Toul and a German, he was also an outsider who owed nothing to any Roman faction. Leo traveled widely and held councils at Pavia, Reims, and Mainz that issued decrees against simony, Nicolaitism, and violence. Leo's representatives held church councils across Europe, pressing for moral reform. They urged those who could not secure justice at home to appeal to the pope for ultimate justice.

Papal reform continued after Leo IX. During the short reign of Nicholas II (1058–1061), a council held in the ancient church of Saint John Lateran in 1059 reached a momentous decision. To remove the influence of Roman aristocratic factions and to make papal elections independent of imperial influences, a new method of electing the pope was devised. Since the eighth century, the priests of the major churches in and around Rome had constituted a special group, called a "college," that advised the pope when he summoned them to meetings. These chief priests were called "cardinals," from the Latin *cardo,* meaning "hinge." The cardinals were the hinges on which the church turned. The Lateran Synod of 1059 decreed that the authority and power to elect the pope rested solely in this **college of cardinals.** The college retains that power today. In the Middle Ages, the college of cardinals numbered around twenty-five or thirty, most of them from Italy. In 1586 the figure was set at seventy. When the office of pope was vacant, the cardinals were responsible for governing the church.

By 1073 the progress of reform in the Christian church was well advanced. The election of Cardinal Hildebrand as Pope Gregory VII changed the direction of reform from a moral to a political one.

The Gregorian Revolution

The papal reform movement of the eleventh century is frequently called the Gregorian reform movement, after Pope Gregory VII (1073–1085). While reform began long before Gregory's pontificate and continued after it,

Gregory VII was the first pope to emphasize the *political* authority of the papacy. His belief that kings had failed to promote reform in the church prompted him to claim an active role in the politics of Western Christendom.[11]

Pope Gregory VII's Ideas

Cardinal Hildebrand had received a good education at Rome and had served in the papal secretariat under Leo IX; after 1065 he was probably the chief influence there. Hildebrand was dogmatic, inflexible, and unalterably convinced of the truth of his own views. He believed that the pope, as the successor of Saint Peter, was the vicar of God on earth and that papal orders were the orders of God.

Once Hildebrand became pope, the reform of the papacy took on a new dimension. Its goal was not just the moral regeneration of the clergy and centralization of the church under papal authority. Gregory and his assistants began to insist on the "freedom of the church." By this they meant the freedom of churchmen to obey canon law and freedom from control and interference by laypeople.

"Freedom of the church" pointed to the end of **lay investiture**—the selection and appointment of church officials by secular authority. Bishops and abbots were

Emperor Otto III Handing a Staff to Archbishop Adalbert of Prague (tenth century) The staff, or crozier, symbolized a bishop's spiritual authority. Receiving the staff from the emperor gave the appearance that the bishop gained his spiritual rights from the secular power. To this practice, Pope Gregory VII vigorously objected. *(Bildarchiv Marburg/Art Resource, NY)*

invested with the staff, representing pastoral jurisdiction, and the ring, signifying union with the diocese or monastic community. When laymen gave these symbols, they appeared to be distributing spiritual authority. Ecclesiastical opposition to lay investiture was not new in the eleventh century. It, too, had been part of church theory for centuries. But Gregory's attempt to put theory into practice was a radical departure from tradition. Since feudal monarchs depended on churchmen for the operation of their governments, Gregory's program seemed to spell disaster for stable royal administration. It provoked a terrible crisis.

The Controversy over Lay Investiture

In February 1075, Pope Gregory held a council at Rome. It published decrees not only against Nicolaitism and simony but also against lay investiture:

If anyone henceforth shall receive a bishopric or abbey from the hands of a lay person, he shall not be considered as among the number of bishops and abbots. . . . If any emperor, king . . . or any one at all of the secular powers, shall presume to perform investiture with bishoprics or with any other ecclesiastical dignity . . . he shall feel the divine displeasure as well with regard to his body as to his other belongings.[12]

In short, clerics who accepted investiture from laymen were to be deposed, and laymen who invested clerics were to be *excommunicated* (cut off from the sacraments and all Christian worship).

The church's penalty of **excommunication** relied for its effectiveness on public opinion. Gregory believed that the strong support he enjoyed for his *moral* reforms would carry over to his political ones; he thought that excommunication would compel rulers to abide by his changes. Immediately, however, Henry IV in the empire, William the Conqueror in England (see page 332), and Philip I in France protested.

Why did the issue of lay investiture provoke the wrath of kings? Any institution or organization needs a bureaucracy or administration to function. The most fundamental requirement of any administration is simple literacy, people who can read and write. In the late eleventh century, virtually the only people with these basic skills were monks and priests. Therefore kings appointed monks and clerics as their administrators. How were they to be paid? Rulers used church offices, bishoprics, and abbacies as the financial means with which to support royal governments. The revenues of a diocese or monastery supplied the incomes for royal officials and their staffs. So church officials were paid by the church for the work they did for the state. From the perspective of a king or emperor, this practice had the merit of financial prudence and had long stood the test of time. Thus Gregory VII's condemnation of lay investiture seemed revolutionary.

The strongest reaction came from Germany. Henry IV had supported the moral aspects of church reform within the empire. In fact, most eleventh-century rulers could not survive without the literacy and administrative knowledge of bishops and abbots. Naturally, then, kings selected and invested most of them. In two basic ways, however, the relationship of the German kings to the papacy differed from that of other monarchs: the pope crowned the German emperor, and both the empire and the Papal States claimed northern Italy. Since the time of Charlemagne (see page 240), the emperor had controlled some territory and bishops in Italy.

An increasingly bitter exchange of letters ensued. Gregory accused Henry of lack of respect for the papacy and insisted that disobedience to the pope was disobedience to God. Henry protested in a now-famous letter beginning, "Henry King not by usurpation, but by the pious ordination of God, to Hildebrand, now not Pope, but false monk." Henry went on to argue that Gregory's type of reform undermined royal authority and that the pope "was determined to rob me of my soul and my kingdom or die in the attempt."[13]

Within the empire, those who had the most to gain from the dispute quickly took advantage of it. In January 1076 many of the German bishops who had been invested by Henry withdrew their allegiance from the pope. Gregory replied by excommunicating them and suspending Henry from the kingship. The lay nobility delighted in the bind the emperor had been put in: with Henry IV excommunicated and cast outside the Christian fold, they did not have to obey him and could advance their own interests. Powerful nobles invited the pope to come to Germany to settle their dispute with Henry. Gregory hastened to support them. In the pope's mind, the German nobility "shared his vision of the vicar of St. Peter as an arbiter of secular affairs."[14] The Christmas season of 1076 witnessed an ironic situation in Germany: the clergy supported the emperor, while the great nobility favored the pope.

Henry outwitted the pope. Crossing the Alps in January 1077, he approached the castle of Countess Matilda of Tuscany, where the pope was staying. According to legend, Henry stood for three days in the snow seeking forgiveness. As a priest, Pope Gregory was obliged to grant absolution and to readmit the emperor to the Chris-

Countess Matilda A staunch supporter of the reforming ideals of the papacy, Countess Matilda (ca 1046–1115) planned this dramatic meeting at her castle at Canossa in the Apennines. The arrangement of the figures—King Henry kneeling, Abbot Hugh of Cluny lecturing, and Matilda persuading—suggests contemporary understanding of the scene where Henry received absolution. Matilda's vast estates in northern Italy and her political contacts in Rome made her a person of considerable influence in the late eleventh century *(Biblioteca Apostolica Vaticana)*

tian community. Some historians claim that this marked the peak of papal power because the most powerful ruler in Europe, the emperor, had bowed before the pope. Actually, Henry scored a temporary victory. When the sentence of excommunication was lifted, Henry regained the kingship and authority over his rebellious subjects. But in the long run, in Germany and elsewhere, secular rulers were reluctant to pose a serious challenge to the papacy for the next two hundred years.

In Germany the controversy over lay investiture and the position of the king in Christian society continued. In 1080 Gregory VII again excommunicated and deposed the emperor; in return, Henry invaded Italy, captured Rome, and controlled the city when Gregory died in 1085. But Henry won no lasting victory. Gregory's successors encouraged Henry's sons to revolt against their father. With lay investiture the ostensible issue, the conflict between the papacy and the successor of Henry IV continued into the twelfth century.

Finally, in 1122, at a conference held at **Worms,** the issue was settled by compromise. Bishops were to be chosen according to canon law—that is, by the clergy—in the presence of the emperor or his delegate. The emperor surrendered the right of investing bishops with the ring and staff. But since lay rulers were permitted to be present at ecclesiastical elections and to accept or refuse feudal homage from the new prelates, they still possessed an effective veto over ecclesiastical appointments. Papal power was enhanced, but neither side won a clear victory.

What effect did the reform movement have on houses of religious women? The struggle against lay investiture had the effect of emphasizing the distinction between priests and laypeople. Monasticism had begun, and for many centuries flourished, primarily as a lay movement: most monks were not priests. In the twelfth century, however, increasing numbers of monks were ordained priests. But women could not be ordained. Thus the Gregorian reform movement, in building a strict hierarchical church structure and in subjecting all houses of monks and nuns to the bishop's authority, did not serve as a means for the equality of female monasticism within Christian monasticism.

The long controversy had tremendous social and political consequences in Germany. For half a century, between 1075 and 1125, civil war was chronic in the empire. Preoccupied with Italy and the quarrel with the papacy, emperors could do little about it. The lengthy struggle between papacy and emperor allowed emerging noble dynasties, such as the Zähringer of Swabia, to enhance their position. By the eleventh century, these great German families had achieved a definite sense of themselves as noble.[15] To control their lands, the great lords built castles, symbolizing their increased power and growing independence. (In no European country do more castles survive today.) The castles were both military strongholds and centers of administration for the surrounding territories. The German aristocracy subordinated the knights and reinforced their dependency with strong feudal ties. They reduced free men and serfs to a servile position. Henry IV and Henry V were compelled to surrender rights and privileges to the nobility. When the papal-imperial conflict ended in 1122, the nobility held the balance of power in Germany, and later German kings, such as Frederick Barbarossa (see page 338), would fail in their efforts to strengthen the monarchy against the princely families. For these reasons, particularism, localism, and feudal independence characterized the Holy Roman Empire in the High Middle Ages. The investiture controversy had a catastrophic effect there.

The Papacy in the High Middle Ages

In the late eleventh century and throughout the twelfth, the papacy pressed Gregory's campaign for reform of the church. Pope Urban II laid the foundations for the papal monarchy by reorganizing the central government of the Roman church, the papal writing office (the chancery), and papal finances. He recognized the college of cardinals as a definite consultative body. These agencies, together with the papal chapel, constituted the papal court, or **curia Romana (Roman curia)**—the papacy's administrative bureaucracy and its court of law. The papal curia, although not fully developed until the mid-twelfth century, was the first well-organized institution of monarchical authority in medieval Europe.

The Roman curia had its greatest impact as a court of law. As the highest ecclesiastical tribunal, it formulated canon law for all of Christendom. The curia sent legates to hold councils in various parts of Europe. Councils published decrees and sought to enforce the law. When individuals in any part of Christian Europe felt they were being denied justice in their local church courts, they could appeal to Rome. Slowly but surely, in the High Middle Ages the papal curia developed into the court of final appeal for all of Christian Europe.

What kinds of appeals came to the Roman curia? The majority of cases related to disputes over church property or ecclesiastical elections and above all to questions of marriage and annulment. Since the fourth century, Christian values had influenced the administration of the law, and bishops frequently sat in courts that heard marriage cases. Beginning in the tenth and eleventh centuries, church officials began to claim that they had exclusive jurisdiction over marriage. Appeals to an ecclesiastical tribunal, rather than to a civil court, or appeals from a civil court to a church court implied the acceptance of the latter's jurisdiction. Moreover, most of the popes in the twelfth and thirteenth centuries were canon lawyers who pressed the authority of church courts. The most famous of them, the man whose pontificate represented the height of medieval papal power, was Innocent III (1198–1216).

Innocent judged a vast number of cases. He compelled King Philip Augustus of France to take back his wife, Ingeborg of Denmark. He forced King John of England to accept as archbishop of Canterbury a man John did not want.

By the early thirteenth century, papal efforts at reform begun more than a century before had attained phenomenal success. The frequency of clerical marriage had declined considerably. The practice of simony was much more the exception than the rule. Yet the seeds of future difficulties were being planted. As the volume of appeals to Rome multiplied, so did the size of the papal bureaucracy. As the number of lawyers increased, so did concern for legal niceties and technicalities, fees, and church offices. Nevertheless, the power of the curia continued to grow, as did its bureaucracy.

Thirteenth-century popes devoted their attention to the bureaucracy and their conflicts with the German emperor Frederick II. Some, like Gregory IX (1227–1241), abused their prerogatives to such an extent that their moral impact was seriously weakened. Even worse, Innocent IV (1243–1254) used secular weapons, including military force, to maintain his leadership. These popes badly damaged papal prestige and influence. By the early fourteenth century, the seeds of disorder would grow into a vast and sprawling tree, and once again cries for reform would be heard.

The Crusades

The Crusades of the eleventh and twelfth centuries were the most obvious manifestation of the papal claim to the leadership of Christian society. The enormous popular response to papal calls for crusading reveals the influence of the reformed papacy. The Crusades also reflect the church's new understanding of the noble warrior class. A distinguished scholar of the Crusades wrote:

At around the turn of the millennium [the year 1000], the attitude of the church toward the military class underwent a significant change. The contrast between militia Christi [war for Christ] and militia saecularis [war for worldly purposes] was overcome and just as rulership earlier had been Christianized . . . , so now was the military profession; it acquired a direct ecclesiastical purpose, for war in the service of the church or for the weak came to be regarded as holy and was declared to be a religious duty not only for the king but also for every individual knight.[16]

Crusades in the late eleventh and early twelfth centuries were holy wars sponsored by the papacy for the recovery of the Holy Land from the Muslims. The Crusades grew out of the centuries-long debate among Christian intellectuals over the concept of "the just war" and about the righteousness (determined by the clergy) of conflict between the forces of good and those of evil. Pressure for the liberation of Jerusalem, scene of Christ's death, from Muslim control, was stimulated by pilgrimages from the West to Jerusalem; 7,000 Germans reputedly traveled there in 1064–1065. Europeans regarded the Muslims as pagans (see page 228), and news of Muslim victories over Christians in the Middle East or in Spain provoked smoldering hatred and the desire for revenge in European Christians. For example, in October 1086 Muslims defeated King Alfonso VI of León and Castile at Sagrajas (called Zallaqa by the Arabs) in southwestern Spain, collected the heads of the dead in wagons, and drove the wagons of gruesome trophies through the peninsula and across North Africa.[17] The mid-eleventh-century wars of Christian expansion in Spain (see page 287) did not directly inspire Crusades to the Middle East, but those conflicts did lead church authorities "to see the West as engaged in a single struggle characterized by deep religious feeling."[18] Finally, the violence that pervaded many aspects of life in the eleventh century provides background from which the crusading movement emerged. Knights perpetrated much of that violence (see pages 311–312). Mounted on horseback, encased in armor, and equipped with a lance and sword,

the knight represented the distinctive and dominant figure of broad economic and social status.[19] The Crusades manifested intellectual, religious, and social developments in eleventh-century Europe.

Background

The Roman papacy had been involved in the bitter struggle over church reform and lay investiture with the German emperors. If the pope could muster a large army against the enemies of Christianity, his claim to be leader of Christian society in the West would be strengthened. Moreover, in 1054 a serious theological disagreement had split the Greek church of Byzantium and the Roman church of the West. The pope believed that a crusade would lead to strong Roman influence in Greek territories and eventually the reunion of the two churches.

In 1071 at Manzikert in eastern Anatolia, Turkish soldiers defeated a Greek army and occupied much of Asia Minor (see Map 9.1). The emperor at Constantinople appealed to the West for support. Shortly afterward, the holy city of Jerusalem, the scene of Christ's preaching and burial, fell to the Turks. Pilgrimages to holy places in the Middle East became very dangerous, and the papacy claimed to be outraged that the holy city was in the hands of unbelievers. Since the Muslims had held Palestine since the eighth century, the papacy actually feared that the Seljuk Turks would be less accommodating to Christian pilgrims than the previous Muslim rulers had been.

In 1095 Pope Urban II journeyed to **Clermont** in France and on November 27 called for a great Christian holy war against the infidels. Urban's appeal at Clermont represents his policy of *rapprochement,* or reconciliation, with Byzantium, with church union his ultimate goal. (Mutual ill will, quarrels, and the plundering of Byzantine property by undisciplined westerners were to frustrate this hope.) He urged Christian knights who had been fighting one another to direct their energies against the true enemies of God, the Muslims. Urban proclaimed an *indulgence,* or remission of the temporal penalties imposed by the church for sin, to those who would fight for and regain the holy city of Jerusalem.

Godfrey of Bouillon, Raymond of Toulouse, and other great lords from northern France immediately had the cross of the Crusader sewn on their tunics. Encouraged by popular preachers such as Peter the Hermit and by papal legates in Germany, Italy, and England, thousands of people of all classes joined the crusade. Although most of the Crusaders were French, pilgrims from many regions streamed southward from the Rhineland, through Germany and the Balkans. Of all of the developments of

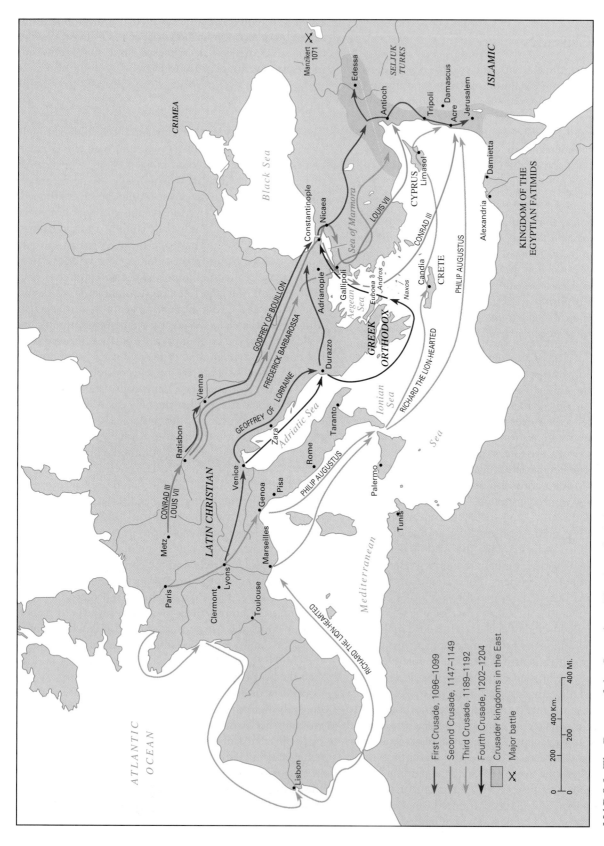

MAP 9.1 The Routes of the Crusades   The Crusades led to a major cultural encounter between Muslim and Christian values. What significant intellectual and economic effects resulted?

the High Middle Ages, none better reveals Europeans' religious and emotional fervor and the influence of the reformed papacy than the extraordinary outpouring of support for the First Crusade. (See the feature "Listening to the Past: An Arab View of the Crusades" on pages 292–293.)

Motives and Course of the Crusades

Religious convictions inspired many Crusaders, but for the curious and the adventurous, the Crusades offered foreign travel and excitement. It provided kings, who were trying to establish order and build states, the perfect opportunity to get rid of troublemaking knights. It gave land-hungry younger sons a chance to acquire fiefs in the Middle East. Even some members of the middle class who stayed at home profited from the Crusades. Nobles often had to borrow money from the burghers to pay for their expeditions, and they put up part of their land as security. If a noble did not return home or could not pay the interest on the loan, the middle-class creditor took over the land.

The Crusades also brought to the surface latent Christian prejudice against the Jews. Between the sixth and tenth centuries, descendants of **Sephardic** (from the modern Hebrew word *Separaddi,* meaning Spanish or Portuguese) **Jews** had settled along the trade routes of western Europe; northern European Jews, those living north of the Alps, later came to be called **Ashkenazi.** In the eleventh century, they played a major role in the international trade between the Muslim Middle East and the West. Jews also lent money to peasants, townspeople, and nobles. When the First Crusade was launched, many poor knights had to borrow from Jews to equip themselves for the expedition. Debt bred resentment. (See the feature "Individuals in Society: The Jews of Speyer: A Collective Biography.")

The First Crusade was successful, mostly because of the dynamic enthusiasm of the participants. The Crusaders had little more than religious zeal. They knew nothing about the geography or climate of the Middle East. Although there were several counts with military experience among the host, the Crusaders could never agree on a leader, and the entire expedition was marked by disputes among the great lords. Lines of supply were never set up. Starvation and disease wracked the army, and the Turks slaughtered hundreds of noncombatants. Nevertheless, convinced that "God wills it," the war cry of the Crusaders, the army pressed on and in 1099 captured Jerusalem. Although the Crusaders fought bravely, Arab disunity was a chief reason for their victory. At Jeru-

salem, Edessa, Tripoli, and Antioch, Crusader kingdoms were founded on the Western feudal model (see Map 9.1).

Between 1096 and 1270, the crusading ideal was expressed in eight papally approved expeditions to the East. Despite the success of the First Crusade, none of the later ones accomplished very much. The Third Crusade (1189–1192) was precipitated by the recapture of Jerusalem by the sultan Saladin in 1187. Frederick Barbarossa of the Holy Roman Empire, Richard the Lion-Hearted of England, and Philip Augustus of France participated, and the Third Crusade was better financed than previous ones. But disputes among the leaders and strategic problems prevented any lasting results.

During the Fourth Crusade (1202–1204), careless preparation and inadequate financing had disastrous consequences for Latin-Byzantine relations. In April 1204, the Crusaders and Venetians stormed Constantinople; sacked the city, destroying its magnificent library; and grabbed thousands of relics, which were later sold in Europe. (See the feature "Individuals in Society: Enrico Dandolo" on page 353.) The Byzantine Empire, as a political unit, never recovered from this destruction. Although the Crusader Baldwin IX of Flanders was chosen emperor, the empire splintered into three parts and soon consisted of little more than the city of Constantinople. Moreover, the assault of one Christian people on another—when one of the goals of the crusade was reunion of the Greek and Latin churches—made the split between the churches permanent. It also helped to discredit the entire crusading movement. In 1208, in one of the most memorable episodes, two expeditions of children set out on a crusade to the Holy Land. One contingent turned back; the other was captured and sold into slavery.

Crusades were also mounted against groups within Europe that were perceived as heretical, political, or pagan threats. In 1208 Pope Innocent III proclaimed a crusade against the **Albigensians,** a heretical sect. The Albigensians, whose name derived from the southern French town of Albi where they were concentrated, rejected orthodox doctrine on the relationship of God and man, the sacraments, and clerical hierarchy. Fearing that religious division would lead to civil disorder, the French monarchy joined the crusade against the Albigensians. Under Count Simon de Montfort, the French inflicted a savage defeat on the Albigensians at Muret in 1213; the county of Toulouse passed to the authority of the French crown. Fearful of encirclement by imperial territories, the popes also promoted crusades against Emperor Frederick II in 1227 and 1239. This use of force backfired, damaging papal credibility as the sponsor of peace.

The Capture of Jerusalem in 1099   As engines hurl stones to breach the walls, Crusaders enter on scaling ladders. Scenes from Christ's passion in the top half of the piece identify the city as Jerusalem. *(Bibliothèque nationale de France)*

The Crusades also inspired the establishment of new religious orders. For example, the Knights Templars, founded in 1118 with the strong backing of Saint Bernard of Clairvaux, combined the monastic ideals of obedience and self-denial with the crusading practice of military aggression. Another order, the Teutonic Knights, waged wars against the pagan Prussians in the Baltic region. After 1230, and from a base in Poland, they established a new territory, Christian Prussia, and gradually the entire eastern shore of the Baltic came under their hegemony. Military orders served to unify Christian Europe.

Women from all walks of life participated in the Crusades. Because of the chroniclers' belief that the *fragilitas sexus* ("weaker sex") was unfit for arms, and the chroniclers' aristocratic bias, we know more about royal and noble women than about others. After her husband

Individuals in Society

The Jews of Speyer: A Collective Biography

In the winter of 1095–1096, news of Pope Urban II's call for a crusade spread. In spring 1096, the Jews of northern France, fearing that a crusade would arouse anti-Semitic hostility, sent a circular letter to the Rhineland Jewry seeking its prayers. Jewish leaders in Mainz responded, "All the (Jewish) communities have decreed a fast. . . . May God save us and save you from all distress and hardship. We are deeply fearful for you. We, however, have less reason to fear (for ourselves), for we have heard not even a rumor of the crusade."* Ironically, French Jewry survived almost unscathed, while the Rhenish Jewry suffered frightfully.

Beginning in the late tenth century Jews trickled into Speyer—partly through Jewish perception of opportunity and partly because of the direct invitation of the bishop of Speyer. The bishop's charter meant that Jews could openly practice their religion, could not be assaulted, and could buy and sell goods. But they could not proselytize their faith, as Christians could. Jews also extended credit on a small scale, and, in an expanding economy with many coins circulating, determined the relative value of currencies. Unlike their Christian counterparts, many Jewish women were literate and acted as moneylenders. Jews also worked as skilled masons, carpenters, and jewelers. As the bishop had promised, the Jews of Speyer lived apart from Christians in a walled enclave where they exercised autonomy: they maintained law and order, raised taxes, and provided religious, social, and educational services for their community. (This organization lasted in Germany until the nineteenth century.) Jewish immigration to Speyer accelerated; everyday relations between Jews and Christians were peaceful.

But Christians resented Jews as newcomers, outsiders, and aliens; for enjoying the special protection of the bishop; and for providing economic competition. Anti-Semitic ideology had received enormous impetus from the virulent anti-Semitic writings of Christian apologists in the first six centuries A.D. Jews, they argued, were *deicides* (Christ-killers); worse, Jews could understand the truth of Christianity but deliberately rejected it; thus, they were inhuman. By the late eleventh century, anti-Semitism was an old and deeply rooted element in Western society.

Late in April 1096, Emich of Leisingen, a petty Rhineland lord who had the reputation of being a lawless thug, approached Speyer with a large band of Crusaders. Joined by a mob of burghers, they planned to surprise the Jews in their synagogue on Saturday morning, May 3, but the Jews prayed early and left before the attackers arrived. Furious, the mob randomly murdered eleven Jews. The bishop took the entire Jewish community into his castle, arrested some of the burghers, and cut off their hands. News of these events raced up the Rhine to Worms, creating confusion in the Jewish community. Some took refuge with Christian friends; others sought the bishop's protection. A combination of Crusaders and burghers killed a large number of Jews, looted and burned synagogues, and desecrated the Torah (see page 41) and other books. Proceeding on to the old and prosperous city of Mainz, Crusaders continued attacking Jews. Facing overwhelming odds, eleven hundred Jews killed their families and themselves. Crusaders and burghers vented their hatred by inflicting barbaric tortures on the wounded and dying. The Jews were never passive; everywhere they put up resistance. If the Crusades had begun as opposition to Islam, after 1096 that hostility extended to those Christians saw as enemies of society—lepers, Jews, and homosexuals (see pages 345–346). But Jews continued to move to the Rhineland and to make important economic and intellectual contributions. Crusader-burgher attacks served as harbingers of events to come in the later Middle Ages and well into modern times.

An engraving (18th century) of the mass suicide of the Jews of Worms in 1096, when they were overwhelmed by Crusaders (with shields). (Bildarchiv Preussischer Kulturbesitz / Art Resource, NY)

Questions for Analysis

1. How do you explain Christian attacks on the Jews of Speyer? Were they defenses of faith?
2. What is meant by the phrase "dehumanization of the enemy" (see page 282)? Can you give other examples?

*Quoted in R. Chazan, *In the Year 1096: The First Crusade and the Jews* (Philadelphia: Jewish Publication Society, 1996), p. 28.

The **history companion** features additional information and activities related to this topic. history.college.hmco.com/students

King Fulk died, Queen Melisande ruled the Latin kingdom of Jerusalem. When King Louis IX of France was
captured on the Seventh Crusade (1248–1254), his wife
Queen Marguerite negotiated the surrender of the Egyptian city of Damietta to the Muslims. In war zones some
women concealed their sex by donning chain mail and
helmets and fought with the knights.

Much of medieval warfare consisted of the besieging
of towns and castles. Help could not enter nor could anyone leave; the larger the number of besiegers, the greater
was the chance the fortification would fall. Women
swelled the numbers of besiegers. Woman assisted in fill-
ing with earth the moats surrounding fortified places so
that ladders and war engines could be brought close.
More typically women provided emotional and other assistance. They offered water to fighting men, a service
not to be underestimated in the hot, dry climate of the
Middle East. If they were old and unattractive and not
likely to arouse the men, officials allowed them to work
as washerwomen. Likewise, women with fingers smaller
than men's assumed the task of removing lice from soldiers' heads. Male Crusaders sought the services of prostitutes, a contribution that raised morale. In crusading
victories, women shared in the booty.[20]

Cultural Consequences

The Crusades introduced some Europeans to Eastern
luxury goods, but their immediate cultural impact on the
West remains debatable. By the late eleventh century,
strong economic and intellectual ties with the East had
already been made. The Crusades testify to the religious
enthusiasm of the High Middle Ages, but Steven Runciman, a distinguished scholar of the Crusades, concludes
in his three-volume history:

*The triumphs of the Crusades were the triumphs of faith. . . .
In the long sequence of interaction and fusion between ori-
ent and occident out of which our civilization has grown, the
Crusades were a tragic and destructive episode. . . . High
ideals were besmirched by cruelty and greed, enterprise and
endurance by a blind and narrow self-righteousness; and
the Holy War itself was nothing more than a long act of in-
tolerance in the name of God, which is the sin against the
Holy Ghost.*[21]

Along the Syrian and Palestinian coasts, the Crusaders
set up a string of feudal states that managed to survive for
about two centuries before the Muslims reconquered
them. The Crusaders left two more permanent legacies
in the Middle East that continue to affect us today. First,
the long struggle between Islam and Christendom, and

the example of persecution set by Christian kings and
prelates, left an inheritance of deep bitterness; relations
between Muslims and their Christian and Jewish subjects
worsened. Second, European merchants, primarily Italians, had established communities in the Crusader states.
After those kingdoms collapsed, Muslim rulers still encouraged trade with European businessmen. Commerce
with the West benefited both Muslims and Europeans,
and it continued to flourish.[22]

The European Crusades had a profound effect in shaping the very identity of the West. They represent the first
great colonizing movement beyond the geographical
boundaries of the European continent. The ideal of a
sacred mission to conquer or convert Muslim peoples
entered Europeans' consciousness and became a continuing goal. When, in 1492, Christopher Columbus sailed
west hoping to reach India, he used the language of the
Crusades in his diaries, which show that he was preoccupied with the conquest of Jerusalem (see Chapter 15).
Columbus wanted to establish a Christian base in India
from which a new crusade could be launched against Islam.

But most medieval and early modern Europeans knew
very little about Islam or its adherents. As the crusading
goal of conquest and conversion persisted through the
centuries, Europeans adopted a strategy that served as a
central feature of Western thought and warfare: the dehumanization of the enemy. They described Muslims as
"filth." In turn, Muslims called Europeans "infidels" (unbelievers) and considered them "barbarians" because of
the unsophisticated level of European medical, philosophical, and mathematical knowledge in comparison to
that of the Islamic world. Whereas Europeans perceived
the Crusades as sacred religious movements, Muslims saw
them as expansionist and imperialistic. Even today, some
Muslims see the conflict between Arab and Jew as just another manifestation of the medieval Crusades. Some Arab
historians interpret the Jews and the state of Israel as new
Crusaders or as tools of Western imperialism.

For Jewish-Christian relations, the Crusades proved to
be a disaster. After the experience of the Rhineland Jews
during the First Crusade (see page 281), any burst of
Christian zeal or enthusiasm evoked in European Jews
suspicion, unease, and fear. From 1095 on, most Christians did not regard Jews (or Muslims) as normal human
beings, viewing them instead as inhuman monsters. According to one scholar, "Every time a crusade was summoned against the Muslims there was a new outbreak of
anti-Semitism in Europe which became an indelible European habit."[23]

Although the legal position of Jews in European society deteriorated after the First Crusade, and despite the

pervasive anti-Semitism of the time, Jewish culture flourished. In the period from about 1000 to 1400, Jews were overwhelmingly an urban people. They worked as tradesmen, craftsmen, moneychangers, and long-distance business people. They established schools for education in the Torah (the body of Hebraic religious law) and the Talmud (rabbinic commentary on the Torah) and produced beautifully illuminated manuscripts. Around 1375 Abraham and Judah Cresques in Majorca drew the famed *Catalan Atlas* (see page 503) showing the world and its navigational routes. Scholars enjoyed great respect in Jewish communities, and Christian and Muslim nobles sought Jewish physicians. Although both Jewish and Christian law banned Jews from the emerging universities, Jews flocked to university towns. In spite of harassment and humiliation—at Pisa on the Feast of Saint Catherine (November 25) students seized the stoutest Jew they could find, put him on scales, and fined the Jewish community his weight in sweets—Jews became students and professors. In 1300 Jacob ben Machir was even appointed dean of the medical school at Montpellier. Andalusian Spain, the safest place for Jews in the Latin West until the fifteenth century, witnessed a "golden age" of Jewish culture in science, music, medicine, philosophy, and especially Hebrew poetry.

The Expansion of Latin Christendom

The period after the millennial year 1000 witnessed great migrations and cross-regional contacts. The movement of peoples and ideas from western France, the heartland of Christendom, and from western Germany into frontier regions—Ireland, Scandinavia, the Baltic lands, eastern Europe, and Spain—had, by about 1300, profound cultural consequences for those fringe territories. Wars of expansion, the establishment of new Christian bishoprics, and the vast migration of colonists, together with the papal emphasis on a unified Christian world, brought about the gradual Europeanization of the frontier (see Map 9.2).

The Crusades provided the means for what a scholar has called "the aristocratic diaspora," the movement of knights from their homes in France to areas then on the frontiers of Christian Europe.[24] Wars of foreign conquest had occurred before the Crusades, as the Norman Conquest of England in 1066 illustrates (see page 332), but for many knights "migration began with the taking of the cross." We have already seen how restless, ambitious knights, many of them younger sons with no prospects, left on crusade to the Holy Land. Some of them were able to

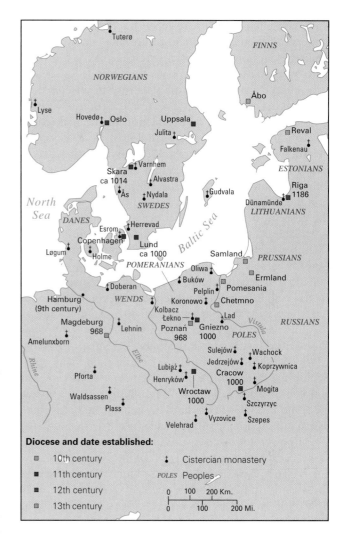

MAP 9.2 Christianization of the Baltic Region Dioceses and monasteries served as the means by which pagan Baltic peoples were Christianized and brought into the framework of Latin Christian culture. *(Source: Some data from R. Bartlett,* The Making of Europe: Conquest, Colonization and Cultural Change, *950–1350 [Princeton, N.J.: Princeton University Press, 1993], pp. 16 and 259.)*

carve out lordships in Palestine, Syria, and Greece. Others went to northwestern, eastern, and southern Europe.

Northern Europe

In 1177 John de Courcy, a Norman with small estates in Somerset (southwestern England), crossed the Irish Sea with his army and raided Ulcad in the province of Ulster. John easily defeated the local ruler, Rory MacDunlevy, seized the town of Downpatrick, and with this foothold built himself a sizable lordship. Other Anglo-Norman settlers followed. Ireland had technically been Christian since the days of Saint Patrick (see page 195), but John de Courcy's intervention led to the remodeling of the Irish church from a monastic structure to an episcopal one with defined territorial dioceses. The Anglo-Norman invasion also meant the introduction of the fief, feudal cavalry, and Anglo-Norman landlords, as well as the beginnings of chartered towns on an English pattern. Similarly, Anglo-Norman, Anglo-French, and Flemish knights poured into Scotland in the twelfth century, bringing the fief and the language of feudalism. In 1286 the descendants of twelfth-century colonists held five of the thirteen Scottish earldoms. Scottish feudalism closely resembled that of western France, and immigrant knights transformed Scottish society.

Latin Christian influences entered Scandinavian and Baltic regions primarily through the erection of dioceses. As an easily identifiable religious figure, as judge, and as the only person who could ordain priests, the bishop was the essential instrument in the spread of Christianity. Otto I (see page 267) established the first Scandinavian sees—Schleswig, Ribe, and Århus in Denmark—between 948 and 965. In 1060 a network of eight bishoprics was organized, and in 1103–1104 the Danish kingdom received its first archbishopric, Lund, in Scania (now part of Sweden). Royal power advanced institutional Christianity in Denmark; because that power was weaker in Sweden, Norway, and Iceland, Christianity progressed much more slowly in those lands. In the 1060s, however, two dioceses were set up in Norway and six in Sweden, and in 1164 Uppsala in Sweden, long a center of the pagan cults of Thor and Odin, became a Catholic archdiocese.

Eastern Europe

In the lands between the Oder River in the east and the Elbe and Saale Rivers in the west lived the Wends, a West Slavic people, and their linguistic cousins, the Balts (Prussians, Lithuanians, Latvians, Livonians, Estonians, and Finns). These peoples clung tenaciously to paganism in spite of extensive Christian missionary activity. Nevertheless, Otto I established a string of dioceses along his northern and eastern frontiers to pacify newly conquered Slavic lands and to Christianize. Among these were the archdiocese of Magdeburg, intended for "all the people of the Slavs beyond the Elbe and Saale, lately converted and to be converted to God,"[25] and the dioceses of Brandenburg, Schwerin, and Lübeck, all filled with German bishops. Repeated Slavic revolts, illustrating ethnic opposition to German lords and German bishops, indicate

Saint Hedwig of Bavaria (1174–1243) Hedwig was married to Henry, duke of Saxony, by whom she had seven children and from whom she suffered great abuse. She ruled Silesia (today partly in the Czech Republic, partly in Poland) when her husband was away at war; conducted diplomatic negotiations; and founded monasteries, including Trebnitz, the first Cistercian house for women. Hedwig and her niece Saint Elizabeth of Hungary (1207–1231) illustrate the powerful influence of women in the spread of Christianity in central and eastern Europe. In a manuscript commissioned by her fourteenth-century descendants (shown in small-scale donor portraits), Hedwig carries a book, rosary, and tiny statue of the Virgin Mary, references to her devout character. *(The John Paul Getty Museum, Los Angeles, Court Atelier of Duke Ludwig I of Liegnitz and Brieg [illuminator], Vita beatae Hedwigis, 1353. Tempera colors, colored washes and ink bound between wood boards covered with red-stained pigskin, 34.1 × 24.8 cm)*

that the new faith did not easily penetrate the Baltic region. Only the ruthless tactics of Albert the Bear (d. 1170) pacified the region and forced the incorporation of the eastern and northern bishoprics into the structure of the Latin church.

A member of the Saxon nobility, with experience in border warfare against the Slavs, Albert the Bear reconquered the town of Brandenburg on June 11, 1157. With this base, and to support his **Ostiedlung** (orientation to the East), Albert proclaimed a German crusade against the Slavs. He invited Dutch, Flemish, and German knights from the Rhineland to colonize conquered territories. To keep the region as far as the Oder pacified, he built castles manned by these newly recruited knights. Slav revolts were ruthlessly crushed. Meantime, Duke Boleslaw I of Silesia (1163–1201) invited German knights and German Cistercian monks to settle in Silesia, thereby contributing to the political stability and agricultural development of his lands.[26]

Along with German knights, German (or Roman) ecclesiastical influences entered other parts of eastern Europe in the tenth and eleventh centuries. Prague in Bohemia became a bishopric in 973; from Prague missionaries set out to convert the Poles. The first diocese in Poland, Poznan, was erected in 968. Likewise in Hungary, Esztergom became a diocese in 1001, and during the eleventh century Hungarian rulers established new ecclesiastical centers along the Danube and eastward into Transylvania (modern central Romania).

In the twelfth and thirteenth centuries, tens of thousands of German settlers poured into eastern Europe, Silesia, Mecklenburg, Bohemia, Poland, Hungary, and Transylvania. Towns there contained the residence of the military leader of the region, the duke, and his servants and knights. The Christian baptism of Duke Mieszko (d. 992) and his court in 966 at Gniezno led to the construction of a cathedral, the arrival of churchmen, and the building of churches and monasteries for monks and nuns. All these people represented a demand for goods and services. Centers such as Gniezno, Cracow, Wroclaw, and Plock attracted craftsmen and merchant immigrants seeking business opportunities.[27]

With urbanization came Germanization. Duke Boleslaw's charter for his new city of Cracow in Poland stated that "the city of Cracow was converted to German law and the site of the market, the houses and the courtyards was changed by the duke's officials."[28] Boleslaw specifically excluded Polish peasants from becoming burgesses, because he feared the depopulation of his estates. New immigrants were German in descent, name, language, and law. Towns such as Cracow and Riga engaged in long-distance trade and gradually grew into large urban centers. But there were also hundreds of small market towns populated by German immigrants, such as Kröpelin in Mecklenburg, which supplied the needs of the rural countryside.

Al-Andalus, or Moorish Spain

The name **al-Andalus** probably derives from the Arabic for "land of the Vandals," the Germanic people who swept across Spain in the fifth century. Throughout the Islamic world, Muslims used the term *al-Andalus* to describe the part of the Iberian Peninsula under Muslim control. In the eighth century that meant the entire peninsula from Gibraltar in the south to the Cantabrian Mountains in the north (see Map 9.3); by the late thirteenth century, al-Andalus consisted of the small principality of Granada. Christians throughout Europe called the peninsula "Moorish Spain," which reminds us that the people who invaded and conquered it were Moors—Berbers from northwest Africa. But the ethnic term *Moorish* can be misleading, because the peninsula was home to sizable numbers of Jews and Christians as well as (Muslim) Moors. In business transactions and in much of daily life, all peoples used the Arabic language. With Muslims, Christians, and Jews trading, intermarrying, and learning from each other, Moorish Spain and Norman Sicily (see Chapter 11) were the only distinctly pluralistic societies in medieval Europe.

Al-Andalus can be analyzed from several perspectives. From the sophisticated centers of Muslim culture in Baghdad, Damascus, and Cairo (founded 969), al-Andalus seemed a provincial backwater, a frontier outpost with little significance in the wide context of Islamic civilization. Even "Northern barbarians," as Muslims everywhere perceived European peoples, acknowledged the urbane splendor of Spanish culture. For example, the Saxon nun and writer Hroswita of Gandersheim called the city of Córdoba "the ornament of the world." With a population of about one million; with well-paved and -lighted streets and an abundance of fresh water; with 1,000 mosques, 900 public baths, 213,177 houses for ordinary people, and 60,000 mansions for officials and the wealthy; with 80,455 shops and 13,000 weavers producing silks, woolens, and brocades; with 27 free schools and a library containing 400,000 volumes (the largest library in northern Europe at the Benedictine abbey of St. Gall in Switzerland had 600 books), Córdoba was indeed an ornament with no comparable urban center in the Western world.

Islamic Spain was to play a profound part in shaping the culture of medieval and early modern Europe. Middle Eastern Arabs translated and codified the scientific and

MAP 9.3 The Reconquista   The Christian conquest of Muslim Spain was followed by ecclesiastical reorganization, with the establishment of dioceses, monasteries, and the Latin liturgy, which gradually tied the peninsula to the heartland of Christian Europe and to the Roman papacy. *(Source: Adapted from David Nicholas,* The Evolution of the Medieval World. *Copyright © 1992. Reprinted by permission of Pearson Education Limited.)*

philosophical learning of Greek and Persian antiquity. In the ninth and tenth centuries that knowledge was brought to Spain, where between 1150 and 1250 it was translated into Latin. Europeans' knowledge of Aristotle changed the entire direction of European philosophy and theology (see page 361). In the seventeenth century, Isaac Newton's discoveries in mathematics rested on ancient Greek theories translated through Spain. Likewise, seventeenth-century medical science advanced because of Muslim observation and practice.[29]

In the transmission of Greek learning, one Muslim technological accomplishment played a most significant role—paper. Second-century Chinese initially used rags to make paper, but they soon shifted to woody fibers from such plants as hemp, jute, and bamboo. The Chinese invented paper not for writing but for wrapping goods. Merchants

and Buddhist missionaries carried the skills of papermaking to Samarkand in Central Asia (see Map 7.5 on page 225). After Arab armies overran Central Asia in the eighth century, Muslim papermakers improved on Chinese techniques: Muslims beat the fibers of rags and then used starch to fill the pores in the surfaces of the sheets. Muslims carried this new method to Baghdad in Iraq, Damascus in Syria, Cairo in Egypt, and the Maghrib (North Africa), from which it entered Spain. Papermaking, even before the invention of printing (see page 429), had a revolutionary impact on the collection and diffusion of knowledge, and thus on the transformation of society.[30]

Al-Andalus, or Moorish Spain, has another, global dimension, extending beyond the history, culture, and time frame of Spain and medieval Europe. As a consequence of the reconquista (see the next page) the Spanish and

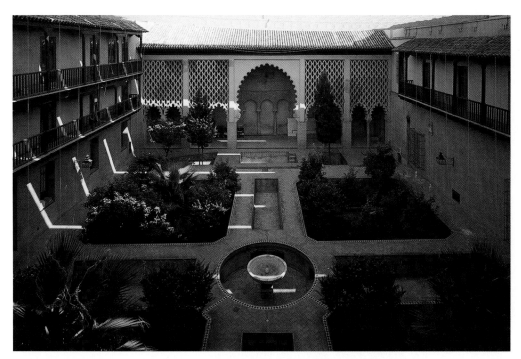

Moorish Garden   In Islamic culture a garden represented paradise (the English word derives from the Persian *paradeisos*). From Persia (modern Iran) gardening spread through the Muslim world. This twelfth-century garden in Seville shows typical Islamic features: raised paths, sunken beds for flowers and shrubs, and fountains. *(Photo Achim Bednorz)*

Portuguese learned how to administer vast tracts of newly acquired territory. When, in the sixteenth and seventeenth centuries, they gained overseas empires in the Americas, Africa, and Asia, medieval models guided them. The precedents of medieval Andalusia were imposed on colonial Mexico, Brazil, Peru, Angola, and the Philippines.[31]

The spirit of al-Andalus lives on. Its loss inspires radical Islamists with desire for revenge: in one of Osama bin Laden's post–September 11 broadcasts, his deputy invoked "the tragedy of al-Andalus."[32]

About 950 Caliph Abd al-Rahman III (912–961) of the Umayyad dynasty of Córdoba ruled most of the Iberian Peninsula from the Mediterranean in the south to the Ebro River in the north. Christian Spain consisted of the kingdoms of Castile, León, Catalonia, Aragon, Navarre, and Portugal; the Almoravid dynasty (successor to the Umayyads) governed through the caliphate of Córdoba (see Map 9.3). The civil wars that erupted among Rahman III's descendants had two important consequences: they divided the peninsula into small Muslim territories, and they made the Christian reconquest easier.

Fourteenth-century clerical propagandists called the movement to expel the Muslims the **reconquista** (reconquest)—a sacred and patriotic crusade to wrest the country from "alien" Muslim hands. This religious myth became part of Spanish political culture and of the national psychology. In 1085 King Alfonso VI of Castile and León captured Toledo on the Tagus River in central Spain, center of the old Visigothic kingdom. He immediately named Bernard, a monk of Cluny in Burgundy, as archbishop of Toledo. Alfonso, who had married a Frenchwoman, invited French knights to settle in the *meseta,* the central plateau of Spain, a region well suited for sheep farming, viticulture, and cereal agriculture. His successor, Alfonso VIII (1158–1214), aided by the kings of Aragon, Navarre, and Portugal, crushed the Muslims at **Las Navas de Tolosa** in 1212, accelerating the Christian push southward. James the Conqueror of Aragon (r. 1213–1276) captured Valencia on the Mediterranean coast in 1233, immediately turning the chief mosque into a cathedral. In 1236 Ferdinand of Castile and León captured the great Muslim industrial and intellectual center of Córdoba in the heart of Andalusia. The city's mosque became a Christian cathedral, and the city itself served thereafter as the main military base against Granada.

Almohad Banner   At Las Navas de Tolosa in 1212, King Alfonso VIII of Castile won a decisive victory over the Almohads, a puritanical Muslim sect from North Africa that had ruled most of Spain in the twelfth century. The Spanish victory marked the beginning of Muslim decline. *(Institut Amatller d'Art Hispanic)*

When Seville fell to Ferdinand's Castilians in 1248 after a long siege, Christians controlled the entire Iberian Peninsula, save for the small state of Granada.

Once in Seville, Ferdinand's heart "was full of joy at the great reward God had given him for his labours. . . . His mother (wanted) to revive the archiepiscopal see which had of old been abandoned, despoiled (by the Muslims) . . . and a worthy foundation was established in honor of Saint Mary."[33] Ferdinand's mother thus inspired the use of the chief mosque as the diocesan cathedral. (Since religious buildings serve as windows into the broader culture, with valuable social, intellectual, and economic information, scholars in many fields have deplored this assimilation of mosques at Córdoba, Valencia, and Seville to Christian religious use, as it involved the destruction of Muslim art. Just as the Muslims, when they conquered Spain in the eighth century, had desecrated ancient pagan shrines for the erection of their mosques, so Christians in the reconquista followed suit on Muslim buildings.)

By the end of the thirteenth century, Spain had fifty-one bishoprics: the reconquista meant the establishment of a Roman ecclesiastical structure. As in eastern Europe, new monasteries aided the growth of Christian culture. As Spanish ruler-kings of the reconquista pushed southward, they established Cistercian monasteries for the military, as well as the religious and cultural, integrity of the conquered areas. As a fortress and base for regional tactical operations, these abbeys served royal needs. Thus

Ramón Berenguer IV, count of Barcelona (1131–1162) and prince of Aragon (1137–1162), founded Poblet in Catalonian Aragon in 1149; Poblet subsequently developed into a great banking center. In 1187 Alfonso VIII and his wife, Eleanor, sponsored the foundation of Los Huelgas in Burgos, the only Cistercian house of women. Its abbess was always a royal princess, and its nuns were recruited from the highest aristocracy. These Iberian houses were all Cistercian, established during the great wave of Cistercian expansion (see page 272). They also were royal monasteries: the inspiration for their foundation came from royal princes who endowed them as religious supports for their political power, resided in them, and were buried in the tombs attached to the abbey churches. Thus these abbeys came to exercise a broad cultural, military, political, and economic influence, as well as a religious one, in the areas where they existed.[34]

In the early years of the reconquista, Spanish princes used the fighting skills of French knights. With Spanish victories, those knights were rewarded with Spanish lands. As the pace of the reconquista quickened in the thirteenth century and the resettlement of gigantic amounts of land acquired from the Muslims (perhaps 150,000 square miles) preoccupied the rulers, a few knights trickled down from north of the Pyrenees, but French aristocratic involvement in Spain declined. Most settlers came from within the peninsula. French feudalism left a small imprint on Spain.

Foreign business people, however, did come to northern Spain in the eleventh century. Muslim Spain had had more cities than any other country in Europe, so Christian Spain became highly urbanized. Towns along the Pyrenees or on the pilgrimage route to the shrine of Santiago de Compostela had received a stream of French immigrants, invited by the kings. One example was the town of Logroño. King Alfonso VI decreed

that a town should be established there, assembling from all parts of the world burgesses of many different trades . . . Gaston, Bretons, English, Burgundians, Normans, Toulousains, Provençals and Lombards, and many other traders of various nations and foreign tongues; and thus he populated a town of no mean size.[35]

After decades of warfare during the reconquista, these towns needed settlers to revive. Moreover, victorious Spanish rulers had expelled the Muslims, leaving the towns with a population shortage. The new lords of Spain recruited immigrants from Old Catalonia, Castile, and León. The thirteenth century thus witnessed a huge migration of peoples from the north to the central and southern parts of the peninsula, into the depopulated cities of the reconquista.

Toward a Christian Society

It was one matter for Western institutions, such as French feudalism and a diocesan pattern of ecclesiastical organization, to penetrate the borderlands of continental Europe, including the Celtic fringe of Wales, Scotland, and Ireland; the Scandinavian fringe of Denmark, Sweden, and Norway; the Baltic fringe of Prussia and Lithuania; the Slavic fringe of Silesia, Bohemia, Poland, and Hungary; and the Iberian fringe of Spain and Portugal. Achieving a cultural unity between these frontier regions and the European heartland, however, presented a more difficult problem. Yet by about 1300, the geographical area that we now call Europe possessed a broad cultural uniformity. How did this unity, or homogeneity, come about?

Papal pressure for uniformity of religious worship and a growing loyalty to the institution of the Roman papacy promoted this homogeneity. Beginning with the reform movement of the eleventh century (see pages 270–273), papal power increased. Reverence in the broad public consciousness for Saint Peter and his successors in Rome meant obedience to the pope. Obedience to the pope meant a local commitment—whether in Scotland, Spain, or Silesia—to the Roman liturgy, the form of worship practiced in Rome. Pope Gregory VII and his successors in the twelfth century, through their letters and their legates, campaigned continually for one religious rite, the Roman rite, in all countries and places.

The period between 1075 and 1125 witnessed the establishment of new and regular contacts between the papacy, eastern Europe, and Celtic and Iberian lands. Gregory denied permission for a vernacular liturgy in Bohemia; he insisted on the Latin rite. He pressed for the abolition of a special rite in Spain, partly because it was believed to contain Arabic elements, partly because it differed from the Roman Latin rite. In 1081, Gregory wrote triumphantly to King Alfonso VI of Castile and León: "Most dearly beloved, know that one thing pleases us greatly . . . namely, that in the churches of your realm, you have caused the order of the Mother of all, the holy Roman church, to be received and celebrated in the ancient way."[36] By the time of Pope Innocent III (see page 276)—when papal directives and papal legates flowed to all parts of Europe; when twelve hundred prelates obediently came to Rome from the borderlands as well as the heartland for the Fourth Lateran Council of 1215; and when the same religious service was celebrated everywhere—the papacy was recognized as the nerve center of a homogeneous Christian society. Europeans identified themselves first and foremost as Christians and even described themselves as belonging to "the Christian race."[37] As in the Islamic world, religion had replaced tribal, political, and ethnic structures as the essence of culture. Whether Europeans were Christian in their observance of the Gospels remains another matter.

▌ Summary

The end of the great invasions signaled the beginning of profound changes in European society—social, political, and ecclesiastical. In the year 1000, having enough to eat was the rare privilege of a few nobles, priests, and monks. By the eleventh century, however, manorial communities were slowly improving their agricultural output through increased mechanization, especially the use of waterpower and wind power; these advances, aided by warmer weather, meant more food and increasing population.

Also in the eleventh century, rulers and local authorities gradually imposed some degree of order within their territories. Peace and domestic security contributed to the rise in population, bringing larger crops for the peasants and improving trading conditions for the townspeople. The church overthrew the domination of lay influences, and the spread of the Cluniac and Cistercian orders marked the ascendancy of monasticism. The Gregorian reform movement led to a grave conflict with kings over lay investiture. The papacy achieved a technical success on the religious issue, but in Germany the greatly increased power of the nobility, at the expense of the emperor, represents the significant social consequence. Having put its own house in order, the Roman papacy in the twelfth and thirteenth centuries built the first strong government bureaucracy. In the High Middle Ages, the church exercised general leadership of European society. The Crusades exhibited that leadership, though their consequences for Byzantine-Western and for Christian-Muslim relations proved disastrous.

These centuries also saw the penetration of Latin Christian culture into frontier regions. Through the spread of Cluniac and Cistercian monasteries; through the use of military force against Muslim and pagan peoples; through the activities of new religious orders, such as the Knights Templars, who combined piety and aggression; and through the immigration of tens of thousands of settlers, border regions became incorporated into the Christian faith and Latin culture of the western European heartland. Christianization was the impulse for this incorporation. The Latin liturgy and loyalty to the Roman pontiff gradually bound all these regions together. Al-Andalus, while retaining powerful Islamic and Jewish influences, was assimilated into Latin Christian culture. The Iberian Peninsula witnessed developments later basic to Spanish and Portuguese colonial societies.

Key Terms

Capetian dynasty	Crusades
Battle of Lechfeld	Clermont
leprosaria	Sephardic Jews
simony	Ashkenazi
Nicolaites	Albigensians
college of cardinals	Ostiedlung
lay investiture	al-Andalus
excommunication	reconquista
Worms	Las Navas de Tolosa
curia Romana (Roman curia)	

Notes

1. R. Bartlett, *The Making of Europe: Conquest, Colonization and Cultural Change, 950–1350* (Princeton, N.J.: Princeton University Press, 1993), p. 6. The last section of this chapter leans on this important and seminal work.
2. See R. I. Burns, "The Significance of the Frontier in the Middle Ages," in *Medieval Frontier Societies,* ed. R. Bartlett and A. MacKay (Oxford: Clarendon Press, 1989), p. 322.
3. See E. M. Hallam, *Capetian France, 987–1328* (New York: Longman, 1980), pp. 12–43.
4. S. Reynolds, *Fiefs and Vassals: The Medieval Evidence Reconsidered* (Oxford: Clarendon Press, 1996), pp. 126–128, 174.
5. E. James, *The Origins of France: From Clovis to the Capetians, 500–1000* (New York: St. Martin's Press, 1982), pp. 190–191.
6. See *The Peace of God: Social Violence and Religious Response Around the Year 1000,* ed. T. Head and R. Landes (Ithaca, N.Y.: Cornell University Press, 1992), passim.
7. J. Gimpel, *The Medieval Machine: The Industrial Revolution of the Middle Ages* (New York: Penguin Books, 1976), pp. 10–25.
8. Quoted in P. Riche, *Daily Life in the World of Charlemagne,* trans. JoAnn McNamara (Philadelphia: University of Pennsylvania Press, 1978), p. 86.
9. See D. Knowles, *The Monastic Order in England,* rev. ed. (Cambridge: Cambridge University Press, 1950), p. 712.
10. See B. Rosenwein, *Rhinoceros Bound: Cluny in the Tenth Century* (Philadelphia: University of Pennsylvania Press, 1982), chap. 2.
11. I. S. Robinson, *The Papacy, 1073–1198: Continuity and Innovation* (New York: Cambridge University Press, 1990), p. 295.
12. B. D. Hill, ed., *Church and State in the Middle Ages* (New York: John Wiley & Sons, 1970), p. 68.
13. Robinson, *The Papacy,* p. 403.
14. Ibid., p. 405.
15. See J. B. Freed, *The Counts of Falkenstein: Noble Self-Consciousness in Twelfth-Century Germany,* Transactions of the American Philosophical Society, vol. 74, pt. 6 (Philadelphia, 1984), pp. 9–11.
16. C. Erdmann, *The Origin of the Idea of the Crusade,* trans. M. Baldwin and W. Goffart (Princeton, N.J.: Princeton University Press, 1977), p. 57.
17. W. C. Jordan, *Europe in the High Middle Ages* (London: Penguin Books, 2001), pp. 100–102.
18. J. Riley-Smith, "The Crusading Movement and Historians," in *The Oxford Illustrated History of the Crusades,* ed. J. Riley-Smith (New York: Oxford University Press, 1997), p. 16.
19. M. Bull, "Origins," in Riley-Smith, ibid., pp. 20–22.
20. See K. Caspi-Reisfeld, "Women Warriors During the Crusades, 1095–1254," in *Gendering the Crusades,* ed. S. B. Edgington and S. Lambert (New York: Columbia University Press, 2002), pp. 94–105.
21. S. Runciman, *A History of the Crusades,* vol. 3: *The Kingdom of Acre* (Cambridge: Cambridge University Press, 1955), p. 480.
22. See B. Lewis, *The Muslim Discovery of Europe* (New York: W. W. Norton, 1982), pp. 23–25.
23. K. Armstrong, *Holy War: The Crusades and Their Impact on Today's World* (New York: Doubleday, 1991), pp. 373–375.
24. Bartlett, *The Making of Europe,* p. 24.
25. Ibid., p. 8.
26. Ibid., pp. 34–35.
27. See P. Knoll, "Economic and Political Institutions on the Polish-German Frontier in the Middle Ages: Action, Reaction, Interaction," in *Medieval Frontier Societies,* ed. R. Bartlett and A. MacKay (Oxford: Clarendon Press, 1989), pp. 151–159.
28. Quoted in Bartlett, *The Making of Europe,* pp. 179–180.
29. See R. Fletcher, *Moorish Spain* (New York: Henry Holt, 1992), pp. 1–8.
30. J. M. Bloom, *Paper Before Print: The History and Impact of Paper in the Islamic World* (New Haven: Yale University Press, 2001), pp. 9–10, 17, 45, 85–89.
31. Fletcher, *Moorish Spain,* p. 7.
32. See Edward Rothstein, "Was the Islam of Old Spain Truly Tolerant," *New York Times,* September 27, 2003, p. B9.
33. Bartlett, *The Making of Europe,* p. 13.
34. B. D. Hill, "Abbey of Poblet," in *Medieval Iberia: An Encyclopedia,* ed. E. Michael Gerli (New York: Routledge, 2003), p. 1.
35. Bartlett, *The Making of Europe,* p. 178.
36. Quoted ibid., p. 249.
37. Ibid., pp. 250–255.

Suggested Reading

For England, R. Bartlett, *England Under the Norman and Angevin Kings, 1075–1225* (2000), offers an excellent synthesis of social, cultural, and political history in highly readable prose. Advanced students will find in M. Strickland, *War and Chivalry: The Conduct and Perception of War in England and Normandy, 1066–1217* (1996), a sophisticated treatment of military history and a detailed study of the aristocracy that fought. Two studies by G. M. Spiegel—"The Cult of Saint-Denis and Capetian Kingship," *Journal of Medieval History* 1 (April 1975), and *The Chronicle Tradition of Saint-Denis* (1978)—treat the close relationship between the Capetian dynasty and the royal abbey of Saint-Denis. For central and eastern Europe, see, in addition to the studies by Burns and Knoll cited in the Notes, J. W. Bernhardt, *Itinerant Kingship and Royal Monasteries in Early Medieval Germany* (1993), which describes how tenth- and eleventh-century German kings founded monasteries and used them for the implementation of royal policy; and P. Gorecki, *Economy, Society, and Lordship in Medieval Poland* (1992), which has articles on aspects of economic and social life. For Spain, R. Fletcher, *The Quest for El Cid* (1990), provides an excellent introduction to Spanish social and political conditions through a study of Rodrigo Dias, the eleventh-century soldier of fortune who became the Spanish national hero. R. Fletcher, *Moorish Spain* (1992), is a highly readable sketch of the history of Islamic Spain from the eighth to the seventeenth century. R. Fletcher, *The Cross and the Crescent: Christianity and Islam from Muhammad to the Reformation* (2003), shows how each religion's perception of the other led to aversion and conflict. O. R. Constable, *Trade and Traders in Muslim Spain: The Commercial Realignment of the Iberian Peninsula, 900–1500* (1996), surveys Iberian "international" trade and treats the impact of Christian conquest on that trade.

For monastic reform, the papacy, and ecclesiastical developments, see B. Rosenwein, *To Be the Neighbor of Saint Peter: The Social Meaning of Cluny's Property, 909–1049* (1989), and the same scholar's earlier study, *Rhinoceros Bound: Cluny in the Tenth Century* (1982), which offer interpretations of Cluny. C. B. Bouchard's *Sword, Miter, and Cloister: Nobility and the Church in Burgundy* (1987) and *Holy Entrepreneurs: Cistercians, Knights, and Economic Exchange in Twelfth-Century Burgundy* (1991) are basic for study of the Cistercian economy. C. H. Berman, *Medieval Agriculture, the Southern French Countryside, and the Early Cistercians: A Study of Forty-three Monasteries* (1986), presents a provocative interpretation of some French Cistercian houses. For the legal, social, and liturgical significance of property gifts to monasteries, see S. D. White, *Custom, Kinship, and Gifts to Saints: The Laudatio Parentum in Western France, 1050–1150* (1988). I. S. Robinson, *The Papacy, 1073–1198: Continuity and Innovation* (1990), explores the changing role of the papacy in the eleventh and twelfth centuries and traces the development of the new model of church government. G. Tellenbach, *The Church in Western Europe from the Tenth to the Twelfth Century* (1993), is a very good survey by an expert on the investiture controversy.

For the Crusades, J. France, *Victory in the East: A Military History of the First Crusade* (1997), offers excellent scholarship, but the title suggests its limited scope. Likewise, J. Riley-Smith, *The First Crusade and the Idea of Crusading* (1986), explores many facets of the First Crusade. Other important recent works include J. Riley-Smith, ed., *The Oxford Illustrated History of the Crusades* (1997), a collection of useful articles, and M. C. Lyons, *Saladin: The Politics of the Holy War* (1997), which treats political issues of the Third Crusade. For the impact of the Crusades on modern times, see P. Partner, *God of Battles: Holy Wars of Islam and Christianity* (1997), and K. Armstrong, *Holy War: The Crusades and Their Impact on Today's World* (1991); both of these books show how the crusading ideal permeated medieval Christendom and affected the modern world. For legal, moral, and sexual issues raised by the Crusades, such as relations between Crusaders and Muslim women, see J. A. Brundage, *Law, Sex, and Christian Society in Medieval Europe* (1987). There are sound articles on many facets of the Crusades in J. R. Strayer, ed., *The Dictionary of the Middle Ages*, vol. 4 (1984). For the relationship of Christian heresy and the Crusades, see S. O'Shea, *The Perfect Heresy: The Revolutionary Life and Death of the Medieval Cathars* (2000), a stimulating journalistic account; and J. Sumption, *The Albigensian Crusade* (2000), a sensitive and nuanced account with more depth than O'Shea's book. The best work on the Fourth Crusade remains D. E. Queller, *The Fourth Crusade: The Capture of Constantinople* (1977), which gives an important revisionist interpretation. H. Kennedy, *Crusader Castles* (1994), studies the evolution of castle styles, siege techniques, and the defensive technologies of castles in the Middle East. For the Crusades and women, S. B. Edgington and S. Lambert, *Gendering the Crusades* (2002), is a pioneering study.

For the Rhineland Jews and many issues related to the Jews and the Crusades, see K. Stow, "Conversion, Apostasy, and Apprehensiveness: Emicho of Flonheim and the Fear of Jews in the Twelfth Century," *Speculum* 76, no. 4 (October 2001): 911–933; R. Chazan, *In the Year 1096: The First Crusade and the Jews* (1996); B. Netanyahu, *The Origins of the Inquisition in Fifteenth Century Spain* (1995), a magisterial work that is much broader in scope than the title would imply; R. Gay, *The Jews of Germany: A Historical Portrait* (1992), a nicely illustrated study; and G. Langmuir, *History, Religion, and Anti-Semitism* (1990), a very sophisticated study with a nuanced distinction drawn between anti-Semitic and anti-Judaic.

For the expansion of Latin Christendom into northern and eastern Europe, see the title by Bartlett cited in the Notes and L. R. Johnson, *Central Europe: Enemies, Neighbors, Friends* (1996). For the Spanish reconquista, see the titles by Fletcher cited above.

Listening to the Past

An Arab View of the Crusades

*T*he Crusades helped shape the *understanding that Arabs and Europeans had of each other and all subsequent relations between the Christian West and the Arab world. To medieval Christians, the Crusades were papally approved military expeditions for the recovery of holy places in Palestine; to the Arabs, these campaigns were "Frankish wars" or "Frankish invasions" for the acquisition of territory.*

Early in the thirteenth century, Ibn Al-Athir (1160–1223), a native of Mosul, an important economic and cultural center in northern Mesopotamia (modern Iraq), wrote a history of the First Crusade. He relied on Arab sources for the events he described. Here is his account of the Crusaders' capture of Antioch.

The power of the Franks first became apparent when in the year 478/1085–86* they invaded the territories of Islam and took Toledo and other parts of Andalusia. Then in 484/1091 they attacked and conquered the island of Sicily and turned their attention to the African coast. Certain of their conquests there were won back again but they had other successes, as you will see.

In 490/1097 the Franks attacked Syria. This is how it all began: Baldwin, their King, a kinsman of Roger the Frank who had conquered Sicily, assembled a great army and sent word to Roger saying: "I have assembled a great army and now I am on my way to you, to use your bases for my conquest of the African coast. Thus you and I shall become neighbors."

Roger called together his companions and consulted them about these proposals. "This will be a fine thing for them and for us!" they declared, "for by this means these lands will be converted to the Faith!" At this Roger raised one leg and farted loudly, and swore that it was of more use than their advice. "Why?" "Because if this army comes here it will need quantities of provisions and fleets of ships to transport it to Africa, as well as reinforcements from my own troops. Then, if the Franks succeed in conquering this territory they will take it over and will need provisioning from Sicily. This will cost me my annual profit from the harvest. If they fail they will return here and be an embarrassment to me here in my own domain." . . .

He summoned Baldwin's messenger and said to him: "If you have decided to make war on the Muslims your best course will be to free Jerusalem from their rule and thereby win great honor. I am bound by certain promises and treaties of allegiance with the ruler of Africa." So the Franks made ready to set out to attack Syria.

Another story is that the Fatimids of Egypt were afraid when they saw the Seljuqids extending their empire through Syria as far as Gaza, until they reached the Egyptian border and Atsiz invaded Egypt itself. They therefore sent to invite the Franks to invade Syria and so protect Egypt from the Muslims.† But God knows best.

When the Franks decided to attack Syria they marched east to Constantinople, so that they could cross the straits and advance into Muslim territory by the easier, land route. When they reached Constantinople, the Emperor of the East refused them permission to pass through his domains. He said: "Unless you first promise me Antioch, I shall not allow you to cross into the

---

*Muslims traditionally date events from Muhammad's hegira, or emigration, to Medina, which occurred in 622 according to the Christian calendar.

† Although Muslims, Fatimids were related doctrinally to the Shi'ites, but the dominant Sunni Muslims considered the Fatimids heretics.

Muslim empire." His real intention was to incite them to attack the Muslims, for he was convinced that the Turks, whose invincible control over Asia Minor he had observed, would exterminate every one of them. They accepted his conditions and in 490/1097 they crossed the Bosphorus at Constantinople. . . . They . . . reached Antioch, which they besieged.

When Yaghi Siyan, the ruler of Antioch, heard of their approach, he was not sure how the Christian people of the city would react, so he made the Muslims go outside the city on their own to dig trenches, and the next day sent the Christians out alone to continue the task. When they were ready to return home at the end of the day he refused to allow them. "Antioch is yours," he said, "but you will have to leave it to me until I see what happens between us and the Franks." "Who will protect our children and our wives?" they said. "I shall look after them for you." So they resigned themselves to their fate, and lived in the Frankish camp for nine months, while the city was under siege.

Yaghi Siyan showed unparalleled courage and wisdom, strength and judgment. If all the Franks who died had survived they would have overrun all the lands of Islam. He protected the families of the Christians in Antioch and would not allow a hair of their heads to be touched.

After the siege had been going on for a long time the Franks made a deal with . . . a cuirass-maker called Ruzbih whom they bribed with a fortune in money and lands. He worked in the tower that stood over the riverbed, where the river flowed out of the city into the valley. The Franks sealed their pact with the cuirass-maker, God damn him! and made their way to the water-gate. They opened it and entered the city. Another gang of them climbed the tower with their ropes. At dawn, when more than 500 of them were in the city and the defenders were worn out after the night watch, they sounded their trumpets. . . . Panic seized Yaghi Siyan and he opened the city gates and fled in terror, with an escort of thirty pages. His army commander arrived, but when he discovered on enquiry that

Miniature showing heavily armored knights fighting Muslims. *(Bibliothèque nationale de France)*

Yaghi Siyan had fled, he made his escape by another gate. This was of great help to the Franks, for if he had stood firm for an hour, they would have been wiped out. They entered the city by the gates and sacked it, slaughtering all the Muslims they found there. This happened in jumada I (491/April/May 1098). . . .

It was the discord between the Muslim princes . . . that enabled the Franks to overrun the country.

Questions for Analysis

1. From the Arab perspective, when did the Crusade begin?

2. How did Ibn Al-Athir explain the Crusaders' expedition to Syria?

3. Why did Antioch fall to the Crusaders?

4. The use of dialogue in historical narrative is a very old device dating from the Greek historian Thucydides (fifth century B.C.). Assess the value of Ibn Al-Athir's dialogues for the modern historian.

Sources: P. J. Geary, ed., *Readings in Medieval History* (Peterborough, Ontario: Broadview Press, 1991), pp. 443–444; E. J. Costello, trans., *Arab Historians of the Crusades* (Berkeley and Los Angeles: University of California Press, 1969).

Allegorical harvesting scenes from a German manuscript,
Speculum Virginum, ca 1190. *(Rheinisches Landesmuseum, Bonn)*

10 Life in Christian Europe in the High Middle Ages

*I*n one of the writings produced at the court of the late-ninth-century Anglo-Saxon king Alfred, Christian society is described as composed of those who pray (the monks), those who fight (the nobles), and those who work (the peasants). Close links existed between educated circles on both sides of the English Channel; in France, Bishop Adalbero of Laon used the same device in a poem written about 1028. This image of the structure of society, in which function determined social classification,[1] gained wide circulation in the High Middle Ages. It explained social organization in terms of mutual recompense, with the relationship among the three orders seen as being beneficial rather than exploitative. The peasants toiled for the other two orders and in return received the prayers of the monks and the physical protection of the nobles. Whereas modern people generally look upon prayer as a private, individual matter, medieval people understood the monks' prayers as an important public and social service for the common good. Just as workers nourished everyone, so noble warriors fought earthly demons and monks battled spiritual enemies. From the perspective of medieval thinkers, the relationship was reciprocal.[2]

These social divisions, however, do not exactly reflect reality. In the eleventh and twelfth centuries, most monks descended from the noble class and as monks retained aristocratic attitudes and values; the lay brothers who did most of the agricultural work on many monastic estates, though legally monks, derived from the peasant classes. Moreover, this tripartite plan entirely omits the parish clergy, who usually were not monks. The division of society into fighters, monks, and peasants also presents too static a view of a world in which there was considerable social mobility. Such a social scheme does not take into consideration townspeople and the emerging commercial classes (see pages 346–351). Traders and other city dwellers were not typical of medieval society, however. Medieval people were usually contemptuous (at least officially) of profit-making activities, and even after the appearance of urban commercial groups, the ideological view of medieval Christian society remained the one formulated in the ninth century. Even more misleading, the tripartite division of medieval society entirely ignores issues of gender: what of women and the significant roles they played? Nevertheless, though artificial and not inclusive, the sociological division of peasants, nobles, and monks provides insight into the medieval mind.

- How did these people actually live?
- What were their preoccupations and lifestyles?
- To what extent was social mobility possible for them?

These are some questions that this chapter will explore.

Those Who Work

The largest and economically most productive group in medieval European society was the peasants. "Peasants were rural dwellers who possess (if they do not own) the means of agricultural production." Some peasants worked continuously on the land; others supplemented their ordinary work as brewers, carpenters, tailors, or housemaids with wage labor in the field. In either case, all peas-

ants supported lords, clergy, and townspeople, as well as themselves.[3] The men and women who worked the land in the twelfth and thirteenth centuries made up the overwhelming majority of the population, probably more than 90 percent. Yet the records that serve as historical sources were written by and for the aristocratic classes. Since peasants did not perform what were considered "noble" deeds, the aristocratic monks and clerics did not waste time or precious writing materials on them. When peasants were mentioned, it was usually with contempt or in terms of the services and obligations they owed.

Usually—but not always. In the early twelfth century, Honorius, a monk and teacher at Autun, wrote: "What do you say about the agricultural classes? Most of them will be saved because they live simply and feed God's people by means of their sweat."[4] This sentiment circulated widely. Honorius's comment suggests that peasant

Man Stomping on Grapes   Before the invention of the winepress in 1526, grapes were crushed by human power—people treading on them in barrels. The French province of Poitou, the region of Bordeaux, and the Rhine and Moselle Valleys supplied wine to an expanding European market. The staple drinks for peasants and monks were ale, beer, and cider; wine was considered an aristocratic drink. *(Glasgow University Library, Department of Special Collections, Ms Hunter 229)*

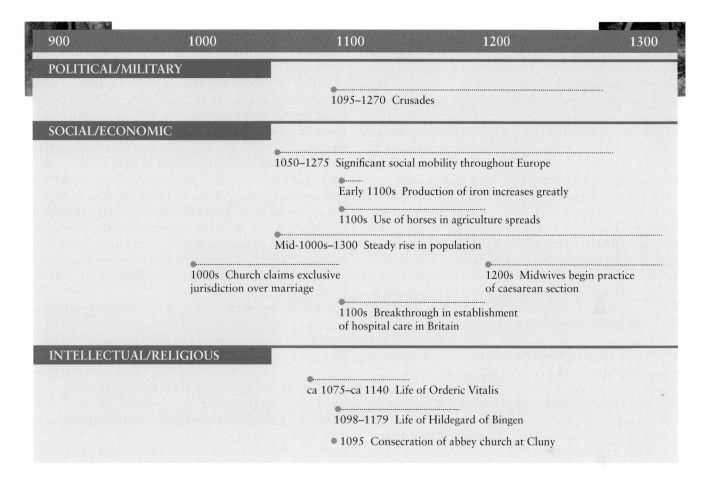

| 900 | 1000 | 1100 | 1200 | 1300 |

POLITICAL/MILITARY

1095–1270 Crusades

SOCIAL/ECONOMIC

1050–1275 Significant social mobility throughout Europe

Early 1100s Production of iron increases greatly

1100s Use of horses in agriculture spreads

Mid-1000s–1300 Steady rise in population

1000s Church claims exclusive jurisdiction over marriage

1200s Midwives begin practice of caesarean section

1100s Breakthrough in establishment of hospital care in Britain

INTELLECTUAL/RELIGIOUS

ca 1075–ca 1140 Life of Orderic Vitalis

1098–1179 Life of Hildegard of Bingen

1095 Consecration of abbey church at Cluny

workers may have been appreciated and respected more than modern students have generally believed.

In 1932 a distinguished economic historian wrote, "The student of medieval social and economic history who commits himself to a generalization is digging a pit into which he will later assuredly fall and nowhere does the pit yawn deeper than in the realm of rural history."[5] Although recent decades have seen an explosion of literature on agrarian change, this statement retains some validity. It is therefore important to remember that peasants' conditions varied widely across Europe, that geographical and climatic features as much as human initiative and local custom determined the peculiar quality of rural life. The problems that faced the farmer in Yorkshire, England, where the soil was rocky and the climate rainy, were very different from those of the Italian peasant in the sun-drenched Po Valley.

Another difficulty has been historians' tendency to group all peasants into one social class. It is true that medieval theologians lumped everyone who worked the land into the category of "those who work." In fact, however, there were many levels of peasants, ranging from complete slaves to free and very rich farmers. The period from 1050 to 1275 was one of considerable fluidity with significant social mobility. The status of the peasantry fluctuated widely all across Europe.

Slavery, Serfdom, and Upward Mobility

Slaves were found in western Europe in the High Middle Ages, but in steadily declining numbers. That the word *slave* derives from *Slav* attests to the widespread trade in men and women from the Slavic areas in the early Middle Ages. Around the year 1200, there were in aristocratic and upper-middle-class households in Provence, Catalonia, Italy, and Germany a few slaves—Slavs from the Baltic, Syrians, and blacks from sub-Saharan Africa. In Scandinavia, the Balkans, and Sicily, also, recent research has demonstrated the persistence of **ancillae**, female chattel slaves whose lifelong legal servitude passed to their descendants, well into early modern times.[6]

Since ancient times, it had been a universally accepted practice to enslave conquered peoples. The Christian Gospels contain no explicit teaching on slavery, but they do stress the spiritual equality of all as children of the same God, the golden rule, and Jesus' affection for the oppressed. Saint Paul did not condemn slavery, but he tried to imbue both masters and slaves with the spirit of charity, which, over many centuries, was to reduce drastically the practice. But since slavery remains widespread in parts of the world today, it has never completely disappeared.

In western Europe during the Middle Ages, the distinction between slave and serf was not always clear. Both lacked freedom—the power to do as they wished—and both were subject to the arbitrary will of one person, the lord. A serf, however, could not be bought and sold like an animal or an inanimate object, as a slave could.

The serf was required to perform labor services on the lord's land, usually three days a week except in the planting or harvest seasons, when it was more. Serfs frequently had to pay arbitrary levies. When a man married, he had to pay his lord a fee. When he died, his son or heir had to pay an inheritance tax to inherit his parcels of land. The precise amounts of tax paid to the lord on these important occasions depended on local custom and tradition. A free person had to pay rent to the lord, and that was often the sole obligation. A free person could move and live as he or she wished.

Serfs were tied to the land, and serfdom was a hereditary condition. A person born a serf was likely to die a serf, though many did secure their freedom. About 1187 Glanvill, an official of King Henry II and an expert on English law, described how **villeins** (literally, "inhabitants of small villages")—as English serfs were called—could be made free:

A person of villein status can be made free in several ways. For example, his lord, wishing him to achieve freedom from the villeinage by which he is subject to him, may quit-claim [release] him from himself and his heirs; or he may give or sell him to another with intent to free him. It should be noted, however, that no person of villein status can seek his freedom with his own money, for in such a case he could, according to the law and custom of the realm, be recalled to villeinage by his lord, because all the chattels of a villein are deemed to such an extent the property of his lord that he cannot redeem himself from villeinage with his own money, as against his lord. If, however, a third party provides the money and buys the villein in order to free him, then he can maintain himself for ever in a state of freedom as against his lord who sold him. . . . If any villein stays peaceably for a year and a day in a privileged town and is admitted as a citizen into their com-mune, that is to say, their gild, he is thereby freed from villeinage.[7]

Thus a serf could not buy his freedom with his own money, since technically all his chattels belonged to his lord. But he could give money to a third party, who could buy him in order to free him. Many energetic and hard-working serfs acquired their freedom through this method of **manumission** in the High Middle Ages. More than anything else, the economic revival that be-gan in the eleventh century (see pages 346–349) advanced the cause of individual liberty. The revival saw the rise of towns, increased land productivity, the growth of long-distance trade, and the development of a money economy. With the advent of a money economy, serfs could save money and, through a third-person interme-diary, buy their freedom.

Another opportunity for increased personal freedom, or at least for a reduction in traditional manorial obliga-tions and dues, was provided by the reclamation of waste-land and forestland in the eleventh and twelfth centuries. Resettlement on newly cleared land offered unusual pos-sibilities for younger sons and for those living in areas of acute land shortage or on overworked, exhausted soil. Historians still do not know much about this movement: how the new frontier territory was advertised, how men were recruited, how they and their households were transported, and how the new lands were distributed. It is certain, however, that there was significant migration and that only a lord with considerable authority over a wide territory could sponsor such a movement. Great lords supported the fight against the marshes of northern and eastern Germany and against the sea in the Low Coun-tries. For example, in the twelfth century the invitation of German rulers led to peasant settlements in "the territory between the Saale and the upper Elbe" Rivers.[8] The thir-teenth century witnessed German peasant migrations into Brandenburg, Pomerania, Prussia, and the Baltic States.

In the thirteenth century, the noble class frequently needed money to finance crusading, building, or other projects. For example, in 1240 when Geoffrey de Mon-tigny became abbot of Saint-Pierre-le-Vif in the Sénonais region of France, he found the abbey church in disrepair. Geoffrey also discovered that the descendants of families who had once owed the abbey servile obligations now re-fused to recognize their bondage. Some of these peasants had grown wealthy. When the abbot determined to re-claim these peasants in order to get the revenues to rebuild his church, a legal struggle ensued. In 1257 a compromise was worked out whereby Geoffrey manu-mitted 366 persons, who in turn agreed to pay him

500 pounds a year over a twelve-year period.[9] (See the feature "Individuals in Society: Jean Mouflet of Sens.")

As land long considered poor was brought under cultivation, there was a steady nibbling away at the wasteland on the edges of old villages. Clearings were made in forests. Marshes and fens were drained and slowly made arable. This type of agricultural advancement frequently improved the peasants' social and legal condition. A serf could clear a patch of fen or forestland, make it productive, and, through prudent saving, buy more land and eventually purchase freedom. In the thirteenth century there were many free tenants on the lands of the bishop of Ely in eastern England, tenants who had moved into the area in the twelfth century and drained the fens. Likewise, settlers on the lowlands of the abbey of Bourbourg in Flanders, who had erected dikes and extended the arable lands, possessed hereditary tenures by 1159. They secured personal liberty and owed their overlord only small payments.

Peasants who remained in the villages of their birth often benefited because landlords, threatened with the loss of serfs, relaxed ancient obligations and duties. While it would be unwise to exaggerate the social impact of the settling of new territories, frontier lands in the Middle Ages did provide opportunities for upward mobility.

The Manor

In the High Middle Ages, most European peasants, free and unfree, lived on estates called **manors.** The word *manor* derives from a Latin term meaning "dwelling," "residence," or "homestead." In the twelfth century it meant the estate of a lord and his dependent tenants.

The manor was the basic unit of medieval rural organization and the center of rural life. All other generalizations about manors and manorial life have to be limited by variations in the quality of the soil, local climatic conditions, and methods of cultivation. Manors varied from several thousand to as little as 120 acres. Recent evidence suggests that a manor might include several villages, a village whose produce was divided among several lords, or an isolated homestead.

The arable land of the manor was divided into two sections. The *demesne,* or home farm, was cultivated for the lord. The other part was held by the peasantry. Usually the peasants' portion was larger, held on condition that they cultivate the lord's demesne. All the arable land, both the lord's and the peasants', was divided into strips that were scattered throughout the manor. If one strip yielded little, other strips (of better soil) might be more bountiful. All peasants cooperated in the cultivation of

The Three Classes of Society (fourteenth century) A business—or "middle"—class had clearly emerged by the twelfth century, so the idea that society was composed of fighters (who defended it), clergy (who prayed for it), and peasants (who nourished it) was anachronistic by then. The theory, however, survived as a useful model. In contrast with most illustrations, this one shows a woman: the veiled nun among the clergy. Nuns ranked as laypeople. *(Courtesy, Royal Library, Brussels, MS RL 11202)*

Boarstall Manor, Buckinghamshire   In 1440 Edmund Rede, lord of this estate, had a map made showing his ancestor receiving the title from King Edward I (*lower field*). Note the manor house, church, and peasants' cottages along the central road. In the common fields, divided by hedges, peasants cultivated on a three-year rotation cycle: winter wheat, spring oats, a year fallow. Peasants' pigs grazed freely in the woods, indicated by trees; we don't know whether they could hunt the deer. (*Buckinghamshire Record Office, Aylesbury*)

tainers. Last but hardly least, the forests were used for feeding pigs, cattle, and domestic animals on nuts, roots, and wild berries. If the manor was intersected by a river, it had a welcome source of fish and eels.

Manors, however, do not represent the only form of medieval rural economy. In Frisia, in parts of Germany, and in much of southern France, free independent farmers held **allodial land**—that is, land that they owned outright, free of rents and services. These farms tended to be small and surrounded by large estates that gradually swallowed them up.

Agricultural Methods

According to the method historians have called the "open-field system," the arable land of a manor was divided into two or three fields without hedges or fences to mark the individual holdings of the lord, serfs, and freemen. Beginning in the eleventh century in those parts of France, England, and Germany where the quality of the soil permitted intensive cultivation, peasants divided all the arable land into three large fields, two of which in any one year were cultivated, while the third lay fallow. One part of the land was sown with winter cereals such as rye and wheat, the other with spring crops such as peas, beans, and barley. What was planted in a particular field varied each year as the crops were rotated.

Local needs, the fertility of the soil, and dietary customs determined what was planted and the method of crop rotation. Where one or several manors belonged to a great aristocratic establishment, such as the abbey of Cluny, which needed large quantities of oats for horses, more of the arable land would be planted in oats than in other cereals. Where the land was extremely fertile, such as in the Alsace region of Germany, a biennial cycle was used: one crop of wheat was sown and harvested every other year, and in alternate years all the land lay fallow.

Farmers knew the value of animal fertilizers such as chicken and sheep manure. Gifts to English Cistercian monasteries (see page 272) were frequently given on condition that the monks' sheep be allowed to graze at certain periods on the benefactor's demesne. Because cattle were fed on the common pasture and were rarely stabled, gathering their manure was laborious and time-consuming. Nevertheless, whenever possible, animal manure was gathered and thinly spread. So also was house garbage—eggshells, fruit cores, onion skins—that had disintegrated in a compost heap.

In the early twelfth century, the production of iron increased greatly. There is considerable evidence for the manufacture of iron plowshares (the part of the plow that

the land, working it as a group. This meant that all shared in any disaster as well as any large harvest.

A manor usually held pasture or meadowland for the grazing of cattle, sheep, and sometimes goats. Often the manor had some forestland as well. Forests were the source of wood for building and resin for lighting; ash for candles, and ash and lime for fertilizers and all sorts of sterilizing products; wood for fuel and bark for the manufacture of rope. From the forests came wood for the construction of barrels, vats, and all sorts of storage con-

Individuals in Society

Jean Mouflet of Sens

Throughout most of Western history, the vast majority of people left little behind that identifies them as individuals. Baptismal, marriage, and death records; wills; grants for memorial masses; and, after the eighteenth century, brief census information collected by governments—these forms of evidence provide exciting information about groups of people but little about individuals. Before the late eighteenth century, most people were illiterate; the relative few who could write, such as business people, used such literary skills as they had in matters connected with their work. The historian, therefore, has great difficulty reconstructing the life of an "ordinary" person. An exception occurs when a person committed a crime in a society that kept judicial records or when he or she made a legal agreement that was preserved. Such is the case of Jean Mouflet of Sens.*

We know little about him except what is revealed in a document granting what was probably the central desire of his life—his personal freedom. His ancestors had been serfs on the lands of the abbey of Saint-Pierre-le-Vif in the Sénonais region of France. There a serf was subject to legal disabilities that debased his dignity and implied inferior status. Work required on the lord's land bred resentment, because work was simultaneously needed on the rustic's own land. At death a peasant gave the lord a token, or not so token, gift—his best beast. Marriage presented another disability, first because one partner had to change dwelling and to do so had to gain the lord's permission; second because it raised the question of children: whose dependents did they become? Special "gifts" to the lord "encouraged" him to resolve these issues. Again, an unfree person, even if he or she possessed the expected dowry, could not become a monk or nun or enter holy orders without the lord's permission, because the lord stood to lose labor services. Finally, residence in a town for a year and a day did not always ensure freedom; years after the person settled there, the lord could claim him or her as a dependent.

In 1249 Jean Mouflet made an agreement with the abbot: in return for an annual payment, the monastery would recognize Jean as a "citizen of Sens." With a stroke of his quill, the abbot manumitted Jean and his heirs, ending centuries of servile obligations.

The agreement describes Jean as a leather merchant. Other evidence reveals that he had a large leather shop in the leather goods section of town† that he leased for the very high rent of fifty shillings a year. If not "rich," Jean was certainly well-to-do. Circumstantial evidence suggests that Jean's father had originally left the land to become a leatherworker and taught his son the trade. The agreement was witnessed by Jean's wife, Douce, daughter of a wealthy and prominent citizen of Sens, Félis Charpentier. To have been a suitable candidate for Douce, Jean would have to have been extremely industrious, very lucky, and accepted as a "rising young man" by the grudging burghers of the town. Such a giant step upward in one generation seems unlikely.

The customary form of manumission, not the manner in which Jean Mouflet gained his freedom. (British Library)

In addition to viticulture (the cultivation of grapes), the Sénonais was well suited for cereal production and for animal grazing. Jean undoubtedly bought hides from local herders and manufactured boots and shoes; saddles, bridles, and reins for horses; and belts and purses. He may also have made wineskins for local vintners or for those of Champagne. It is also fair to assume that the wealthy cathedral clergy, the townspeople, and, if his goods were of sufficiently high quality, the merchants of the nearby fairs of Champagne were his customers.

By private agreements with lords, servile peasants gained the most basic of human rights—freedom.

Questions for Analysis

1. What is human freedom?
2. How did trade and commerce contribute to the development of individual liberty?

*This essay rests on the fine study of W. C. Jordan, *From Servitude to Freedom: Manumission in the Sénonais in the Thirteenth Century* (Philadelphia: University of Pennsylvania Press, 1986).
†As in all medieval towns, merchants in particular trades—butchers, bakers, leatherworkers—had shops in one area. Sens is still a major French leather-tanning center.

The **history companion** *features additional information and activities related to this topic.*
history.college.hmco.com/students

cuts the furrow and grinds up the earth). In the thirteenth century, the wooden plow continued to be the basic instrument of agricultural production, but its edge was strengthened with iron. Only after the start of the fourteenth century, when lists of manorial equipment began to be kept, is there evidence for pitchforks, spades, axes, and harrows. The harrow, a cultivating instrument with heavy teeth, broke up and smoothed the soil. While the modern harrow has steel teeth (or disks), medieval ones were wooden and weighed down with stones to force a deep cut in the earth.

Plow and harrow were increasingly drawn by horses. The development of the padded horse collar, resting on the horse's shoulders and attached to the load by shafts, led to an agricultural revolution. The horse collar meant that the animal could put its entire weight into the task of pulling. The use of horses, rather than oxen, spread in the twelfth century, because horses' greater strength brought greater efficiency to farming and reduced the amount of human labor involved. The quality of the soil and the level of rainfall in the area seem to have determined whether peasants shifted from ox teams to horses. Horses worked best on light, dry, and easily tilled soil, but they had difficulties plowing through clay soils and in places where heavy moisture caused earth to cling to the plow. Oxen, on the other hand, worked well on heavy, muddy, or clay soil, but they slipped and suffered hoof damage on dry, stony land. Thus, in England, horses were employed in the light soils of Norfolk on the northeastern coast and on the stony lands of Yorkshire, while oxen remained common in the Midlands until the late sixteenth century.[10] At the same time, horses were an enormous investment, perhaps comparable to a modern tractor. They had to be shod (another indication of increased iron production), and the oats they ate were costly.

The thirteenth century witnessed a tremendous spurt in the use of horses to haul carts to market. Large and small farmers increasingly relied on horses to pull wagons because they could travel much faster than oxen. Consequently, goods reached market faster, and the number of markets to which the peasant had access increased. The opportunities and temptations for consumer spending on nonagricultural goods multiplied.[11]

Agricultural yields varied widely from place to place and from year to year. Even with good iron tools, horsepower, and careful use of seed and fertilizer, medieval peasants were at the mercy of the weather. Even today lack of rain or too much rain can cause terrible financial loss and extreme hardship. How much more vulnerable was the medieval peasant with his primitive tools! By twenty-first-century standards, medieval agricultural yields were very low. Inadequate soil preparation, poor seed selection, lack of manure—all made this virtually inevitable.

Yet there was striking improvement over time. Between the ninth and early thirteenth centuries, it appears that yields of cereals approximately doubled, and on the best-managed estates, for every bushel of seed planted, the farmer harvested five bushels of grain. This is a tentative conclusion. Because of the scarcity of manorial inventories before the thirteenth century, it is difficult to determine how much the land produced. A thirteenth-century author of a treatise on land husbandry, Walter of Henley, wrote that the land should yield three times its seed; that amount was necessary for sheer survival. The surplus would be sold to grain merchants in the nearest town. Townspeople were wholly dependent on the surrounding countryside for food, which could not be shipped a long distance. A poor harvest meant that both town and rural people suffered.

Grain yields were probably greatest on large manorial estates, where there was more professional management. For example, the estates of Battle Abbey in Sussex, England, enjoyed a very high yield of wheat, rye, and oats between 1350 and 1499. This was due to heavy seeding, good crop rotation, and the use of manure from the monastery's sheep flocks. Battle Abbey's yields seem to have been double those of smaller, less efficiently run farms. A modern Illinois farmer expects to get 40 bushels of soybeans, 150 bushels of corn, and 50 bushels of wheat for every bushel of seed planted. Of course, modern costs of production in labor, seed, and fertilizer are quite high, but this yield is at least ten times that of the farmer's medieval ancestor. While some manors may have achieved a yield of 12 or even 15 to 1, the *average* manor probably got a yield of only 5 to 1 in the thirteenth century.[12] As low as that may seem by current standards, it marked a rise in productivity equal to that of the years just before the start of the great agricultural revolution of the eighteenth century. Most goods produced on manorial estates were for local consumption, but some manors had skilled craftspeople who made textiles, leather goods, glass, and weapons that were shipped away for sale at markets and nearby fairs.

Life on the Manor

Life for most people in medieval Europe meant country life. A person's horizons were largely restricted to the manor on which he or she was born. True, peasants who colonized such sparsely settled regions as eastern Germany must have traveled long distances. But most people rarely traveled more than twenty-five miles beyond their villages. Everyone's world was small, narrow, and provincial in the original sense of the word: limited by the boundaries of the province. This way of life did not have entirely unfortunate results. A farmer had a strong sense of family and the certainty of its support and help in time of trouble. People knew what their life's work would be—the same as their mother's or father's. They had a sense of place, and pride in that place was reflected in adornment of the village church. Religion and the village gave people a sure sense of identity and with it psychological peace. Modern people—urban, isolated, industrialized, rootless, and thoroughly secularized—have lost many of these reinforcements.

On the other hand, even aside from the unending physical labor, life on the manor was dull. Medieval men and women often sought escape in heavy drinking. English judicial records of the thirteenth century reveal a surprisingly large number of "accidental" deaths. Strong, robust, commonsensical farmers do not ordinarily fall on their knives and stab themselves, or slip out of boats and drown, or get lost in the woods on a winter's night, or fall from horses and get trampled. They were probably drunk. Many of these accidents occurred, as the court records say, "coming from an ale." Brawls and violent fights were frequent at taverns.

Scholars have little concrete evidence about the structure of medieval peasant households. It appears, however, that a peasant household consisted of a simple nuclear family: a married couple alone, a couple with children, or widows or widowers with children. Peasant households were *not* extended families containing grandparents or married sons and daughters and their children. The simple family predominated in thirteenth-century England, in northern France in the fourteenth century, and in fifteenth-century Tuscany. Before the first appearance of the Black Death, perhaps 94 percent of peasant farmers married, and bride and groom were both in their early twenties. The typical household numbered about five people, the parents and three children.[13]

Women played a significant role in the agricultural life of medieval Europe. They worked with men in wheat and grain cultivation, in the vineyards, and in the harvest and preparation of crops needed by the textile industry—flax and plants used for dyeing cloth, such as madder (which produces shades of red) and woad (which yields blue dye). Especially at harvest time women shared with their fathers and husbands the backbreaking labor in the fields, work that was probably more difficult for them because of frequent pregnancies. Lords of great estates commonly hired female day laborers as well as men to shear sheep, pick hops (used in the manufacture of beer and ale), tend gardens, and do household chores such as

cleaning, laundry, and baking; servant girls in the country considered their hired status as temporary, until they married. Thrifty farm wives contributed to the family income by selling for cash the produce of their gardens or kitchen: butter, cheese, eggs, fruit, soap, mustard, cucumbers. The adage from the Book of Proverbs—"Houses and riches are the inheritance of fathers; but a prudent wife is from the Lord"—was seldom more true than in an age when careful management was often all that separated a household from starvation in a year of crisis.

Women managed the house. The size and quality of peasants' houses varied according to their relative prosperity, and that prosperity usually depended on the amount of land held. Poorer peasants lived in windowless cottages built of wood and clay or wattle (poles interwoven with branches or reeds) and thatched with straw. These cottages consisted of one large room that served as the kitchen and living quarters for all. The house had an earthen floor and a fireplace. The lack of windows meant that the room was very sooty. A trestle table, several stools, one or two beds, and a chest for storing clothes constituted the furniture. A shed attached to the house provided storage for tools and shelter for animals. Prosperous peasants added rooms and furniture as they could be afforded, and some wealthy peasants in the early fourteenth century had two-story houses with separate bedrooms for parents and children.

Every house had a small garden and an outbuilding. Onions, garlic, turnips, and carrots were grown and stored through the winter in the main room of the dwelling or in the shed attached to it. Cabbage was raised almost everywhere and, after being shredded, salted, and packed in vats of hot water, was turned into kraut. Peasants ate vegetables not because they appreciated their importance for good health but because there was usually little else. Preserving and storing foods were the basic responsibility of the women and children.

Women dominated in the production of ale for the community market. This industry required an initial investment in large vessels and knowledge of the correct proportions of barley, water, yeast, and hops. Women found brewing hard and dangerous work: it involved carrying twelve-gallon vats of hot liquid. Records of the English coroners' courts reveal that 5 percent of women who died lost their lives in brewing accidents, by falling into the vats of boiling liquid.[14] Ale was the universal drink of the common people in northern Europe. By modern American standards the rate of consumption was heroic. Each monk of Abingdon Abbey in twelfth-century England was allotted three gallons a day, and a man working in the fields for ten hours probably drank much more.[15]

Baking Bread Bread and beer or ale were the main manorial products for local consumption. While women dominated the making of ale and beer, men and women cooperated in the making and baking of bread—the staple of the diet. Notice the communal manorial oven, which, like a modern pizza oven, could bake several loaves at once. *(Bibliothèque nationale de France)*

The mainstay of the diet for peasants everywhere—and for all other classes—was bread. It was a hard, black substance made of barley, millet, and oats, rarely of expensive wheat flour. The housewife usually baked the household supply once a week. Where sheep, cows, or goats were raised, she also made cheese. In places like the Bavarian Alps of southern Germany, where hundreds of sheep grazed on the mountainsides,[16] or at Cheddar in southwestern England, cheese was a staple.

The diet of those living in an area with access to a river, lake, or stream would be supplemented with fish, which could be preserved by salting; people living close to the sea could gather shellfish such as oysters, mussels, and whelks. In many places there were severe laws against hunting and trapping in the forests. Deer, wild boars, and other game were strictly reserved for the king and nobility. These laws were flagrantly violated, however, and stolen rabbits and wild game often found their way to the peasants' tables.

Lists of peasant obligations and services to the lord, such as the following from Battle Abbey, commonly included the payment of chickens and eggs: "John of Coyworth holds a house and thirty acres of land, and owes yearly 2 p at Easter and Michaelmas; and he owes a cock and two hens at Christmas, of the value of 4 d."[17] Chickens and eggs must have been highly valued in the prudently managed household. Except for the rare chicken or illegally caught wild game, meat appeared on the table only on the great feast days of the Christian year: Christmas, Easter, and Pentecost. Then the meat was likely to be pork from the pig slaughtered in the fall and salted for the rest of the year. Some scholars believe that, by the mid-thirteenth century, there was an increase in the consumption of meat generally. If so, this improvement in diet is further evidence of an improved standard of living.

Farmers, then as now, ate their main meal around noon. This was often soup—a thick *potage* of boiled cabbage, onions, turnips, and peas, seasoned with a bone or perhaps a sliver of meat. The evening meal, taken at sunset, consisted of leftovers from the noon meal, perhaps with bread, cheese, milk, or ale.

Once children were able to walk, they helped their parents in the hundreds of chores that had to be done. Small children were set to collecting eggs, if the family had chickens, or gathering twigs and sticks for firewood. As they grew older, children had more responsible tasks, such as weeding the family vegetable garden, milking the cows, shearing the sheep, cutting wood for fires, and helping with the planting or harvesting.

Health Care

Scholars are only beginning to explore questions of medieval health care, and there are still many aspects of public health that we know little about. The steady rise in population between the mid-eleventh and fourteenth centuries, usually attributed to the beginnings of political stability and the reduction of violence and to the great expansion of land put under cultivation and thus the increased food supply, may also be ascribed partly to better health care. Survival to adulthood probably meant a tough people. A recent study of skeletal remains in the village of Brandes in Burgundy showed that peasants enjoyed very good health: they were well built, had excellent teeth, and their bones revealed no signs of chronic disease. Obviously we cannot generalize about the health of all people on the basis of evidence from one village, but preliminary research confirms the picture in romantic literature: in the prime of life the average person had a raw vitality that enabled him or her to eat, drink, work, and make love with great gusto.[18]

In recent years scholars have produced some exciting information relating to the natural processes of pregnancy and childbirth. But the acquisition of information has not been easy, because modesty forbade the presence of men at the birth of a child (hence very few men could write about it) and because of the general illiteracy of women. One woman who wrote extensively, the twelfth-century physician Trotula of Salerno, tended to explain gynecological and obstetrical problems in terms of the relative degree of heat and cold, of moisture and dryness within the female body. Thus on the potential difficulty of parturition, she wrote:

There are, however, certain women so narrow in the function of childbearing that scarcely ever or never do they succeed. This is wont to happen for various reasons. Sometimes external heat comes up around the internal organs and they are straightened in the act of giving birth. Sometimes the exit from the womb is too small, the woman is too fat, or the foetus is dead, not helping nature by its own movements. This often happens to a woman giving birth in winter. If she has by nature a tight opening of the womb, the coldness of the season constricts the womb still more. Sometimes the heat all goes out of the woman herself and she is left without strength to help herself in childbearing.

Trotula believed that sneezing, which forced the woman to push her inner organs downward, should be induced.[19]

Midwives learned their work through a practical apprenticeship, not through any sort of professional study. The first pregnancy of many women ended fatally, and thus women of all social classes had a great fear of childbirth. Trotula, Hildegard of Bingen, and other writers on obstetrics urged pregnant women to pray that Christ would grant them a safe childbed.[20]

In the thirteenth century midwives began the practice of delivery by caesarean section, birth by an incision through the abdominal wall and uterus, so called from the traditional belief that the Roman statesman Julius Caesar had been born by this operation. Caesarean sections were performed only if the mother had died in labor; the purpose of the operation was the baptism of the child (the theological premise being that the baptism ensured its salvation). But the caesareans posed serious ethical problems: Who was to decide if the mother was dead? (The stethoscope or instrument for measuring sounds within the body, such as heartbeat, was not invented until 1819.) Who could decide if the fetus was alive after the mother's death? In a very difficult birth, should the life of the mother be sacrificed for the sake of the child? A translation of Trotula's advice to midwives states that "when the woman is feeble and the child may not come out, then it is better that the child is slain than that the mother of the child also die." The greatest theologian of the age, Saint Thomas Aquinas (see page 360) in his treatise on baptism is also explicit: "Evil should not be done that good may come. Therefore one should not kill the mother in order to baptize the child; if, however, the child be still alive in the womb after the mother has died, the mother should be opened in order to baptize the child."[21] About 1400, male surgeons, motivated by professional, scientific, and probably financial interests, began to perform caesarean sections. Thus, through caesarean births, men entered the field of obstetrics.[22]

Childhood diseases, poor hygiene, tooth decay, wounds received in fighting, and the myriad ailments and afflictions for which even modern medical science has no cure, from cancer to the common cold, must have caused considerable suffering. One student of medieval medicine estimates that in the mid-twelfth century one person in two hundred suffered from leprosy.[23]

What care existed for the sick? As in the past, the sick everywhere depended above all on the private nursing care of relatives and friends. In the British Isles, however, the twelfth century witnessed a momentous breakthrough in the establishment of institutional care in "hospitals, that is professional centers with physicians, laboratories, medicines, operations and convalescing patients." In addition to the infirmaries run by monks and nuns, there were at least 113 hospitals in England with possibly as many as 3,494 beds, or one bed for every 600 to 1,000 persons. (In 1982 the ratio in England was 1:108 persons.) The organization of hospitals followed the structure and routine of monastic communities. Patients were segregated according to sex, wore a common uniform, and were required to keep periods of silence and to

A Caesarean Birth   Unlike a normal birth, a caesarean was a surgical procedure; as such, male physicians in the fourteenth century gradually marginalized women in the field of obstetrics, which they had always dominated. Here the midwife (identifiable from her headdress) lifts a male child from the abdominal opening in the mother's dead body. Her helper prepares the tub of water to bathe the child. Since few infants survived the procedure, midwives needed witnesses to assert that they had not bungled the birth or deliberately killed the infant. *(British Library, Roy.16.G.VII, 219)*

attend devotions in the hospital chapel. We have no information about rates of recovery. Medieval hospitals were built by the royal family, the clergy, barons, and ordinary people to alleviate the suffering of the sick, not just to house them. Hospitals attracted considerable popular support, and women played an especially strong role in the endowment of hospitals.[24]

As in the developed modern world, persons living in or near a town or city had a better chance of receiving some form of professional attention than did those in remote rural areas. English documents label at least 90

practitioners as *medicus,* meaning physician, surgeon, or medical man, but that is a pitifully small number in a population of perhaps 2 million people. With so few doctors, only the largest cities, such as London, York, Winchester, and Canterbury, which all catered to pilgrims and travelers, had resident physicians; at other hospitals physician consultants were brought in as the occasion required. Most people, of course, did not live in or near large towns. They relied for assistance on the chance medical lore of local people—a monk or nun with herb and pharmaceutical knowledge who could prescribe therapy for particular ailments, a local person skilled in setting broken bones, the wise woman or man of the village experienced in treating diseases.

The Latin words *matronae* and *obstetrices* appear occasionally to refer to midwives. Since public morality and ancient tradition forbade the examination of female patients by men, obstetrics and gynecology were the only branches of medicine that women could practice.[25] Although women played active roles as healers and in the general care of the sick, male doctors jealously guarded their status and admitted very few women to university medical schools when they were founded. Francesca Romano, who was licensed as a surgeon in 1321 by Duke Carl of Calabria, is the exception that proves the rule. The medical faculty at the University of Paris in the fourteenth century penalized women who practiced medicine because they lacked a degree—which they were not allowed to get.

Popular Religion

Apart from the land, the weather, and the peculiar conditions that existed on each manor, the Christian religion had the greatest impact on the daily lives of ordinary people in the High Middle Ages. Religious practices varied widely from country to country and even from province to province. But nowhere was religion a one-hour-on-Sunday or High Holy Days affair. Christian practices and attitudes permeated virtually all aspects of everyday life.

In the ancient world, participation in religious rituals was a public and social duty. As Germanic, Celtic, Slavic, Baltic, and Magyar peoples were Christianized, their new religion became a fusion of Jewish, pagan, Roman, and Christian practices. By the High Middle Ages, religious rituals and practices represented a synthesis of many elements, and all people shared as a natural and public duty in the religious life of the community.

The village church was the center of community life— social, political, and economic as well as religious. A person was baptized there, within hours of birth. Men and women confessed their sins to the village priest there and received, usually at Easter and Christmas, the sacrament of the Eucharist. In front of the church, the bishop reached down from his horse and confirmed a person as a Christian by placing his hands over the candidate's head and making the sign of the cross on the forehead. (Bishops Thomas Becket of Canterbury and Hugh of Lincoln were considered especially holy men because they got down from their horses to confirm.) Young people courted in the churchyard and, so the sermons of the priests com-

plained, made love in the church cemetery. Priests urged couples to marry publicly in the church, but many married privately, without witnesses (see page 399).

The parish priest had responsibility for all these religious activities. Although church law placed him under the bishop's authority, the manorial lord appointed him and financed such education in Latin, Scripture, and liturgy as he might receive. Far more numerous than the monks, parish priests were peasants and often were poor. They received a tithe of produce from their parishioners, and depending on the spiritual quality of their lives, they enjoyed status and prestige. Since they often worked in the fields with the people, they understood the people's labor, needs, and frustrations. The parish priest was also responsible for the upkeep of the village church and for taking the lead in providing local poor relief.

In the church, women and men could pray to the Virgin and the local **saints.** The stone in the church altar contained **relics** of the saints—bones, articles of clothing, the saint's tears, saliva, even the dust from the saint's tomb. These relics often belonged to a local saint to whom the church itself had been dedicated. The saints had once lived on earth and thus could well understand human problems. They could be helpful intercessors with Christ or God the Father. The cult of the saints had

Pilgrimage to Compostela Like tourists everywhere, the pilgrims to Santiago de Compostela (see pages 328–329) wanted a souvenir. The special mark of this pilgrimage depicted Santiago (Saint James) with pilgrim's staff and scalloped shell, shown above a doorway on the cathedral. *(Institut Amatller d'Art Hispanic)*

begun in the East, spread in the early Middle Ages, and gained enormous popularity in the West in the eleventh and twelfth centuries. People believed that the saints possessed supernatural powers that enabled them to perform miracles, and the saint became the special property of the locality where his or her relics rested. Thus to secure the saint's support and to guarantee the region's prosperity, a busy traffic in relics developed. The understanding that existed between the saint and the peasants rested on the customary medieval relationship of mutual fidelity and aid: peasants would offer the saint prayers, loyalty, and gifts at the shrine or church under his or her patronage, in return for the saint's healing and support. (See the feature "Listening to the Past: The Pilgrim's Guide to Santiago de Compostela" on pages 328–329.)

In the later Middle Ages, popular hagiographies (biographies of saints based on myths, legends, and popular stories) attributed specialized functions to the saints. Saint Elmo (ca 300), who supposedly had preached unharmed during a thunder and lightning storm, became the patron of sailors. Saint Agatha (third century), whose breasts were torn with shears because she rejected the attentions of a powerful suitor, became the patron of wet nurses, women with breast difficulties, and bell ringers (because of the resemblance of breasts to bells). Saint Jude the Apostle, whom no one invoked because his name resembled that of Jesus' betrayer, Judas, became the patron of lost causes; Saint Gertrude was reputed to guard houses against the entry of mice.

How were saints chosen, and what was the official church position on them? What had been their social background when alive? "The initiative in creating a cult (of a saint) always belonged to believers"[26] (ordinary people). Since the early days of Christianity, individuals whose exemplary virtue was proved by miracles at their tomb had been venerated by laypeople. Although, as part of the general centralization of papal power in the twelfth and thirteenth centuries, the Roman authorities insisted that they had the exclusive right to examine the lives and activities of candidates for sainthood in a formal "trial," popular opinion still continued to declare people saints. Between 1185 and 1431, only seventy official investigations were held at Rome, but hundreds of new persons across Europe were venerated as saints. Church officials and educated clergy evaluated candidates according to the "heroic virtue" of their lives, but laypeople judged solely by the saint's miracles. Some clergy preached against the veneration of relics and called it idolatry, but their appeals had little effect.

Current research suggests that a connection exists between the models of holiness and the character of the social structure in different parts of Europe. Northern and south-

ern Europeans chose saints of different social backgrounds or classes. In Italy and Mediterranean lands, saints tended to be **popolani**—non-nobles, non-aristocrats—whereas in France and Germany, primarily men and women of the nobility became saints. The cult of the saints, which developed in a rural and uneducated environment, represents a central feature of popular culture in the Middle Ages.[27]

According to official church doctrine, the center of the Christian religious life was the Mass, the re-enactment of Christ's sacrifice on the cross. Every Sunday and on holy days, the villagers stood at Mass or squatted on the floor (there were no chairs), breaking the painful routine of work. The feasts that accompanied baptisms, weddings, funerals, and other celebrations were commonly held in the churchyard. Medieval drama originated within the church. Mystery plays, based on biblical episodes, were performed first in the sanctuary, then on the church porch, which was often in front of the west door, and then at stations around the town.

From the church porch the priest read to his parishioners orders and messages from royal and ecclesiastical authorities. Royal judges traveling on circuit opened their courts on the church porch. The west front of the church, with its scenes of the Last Judgment, was the background against which the justices disposed of civil and criminal cases. Farmers from outlying districts pushed their carts to the marketplace in the village square near the west front. In busy mercantile centers such as London, business agreements and commercial exchanges were made in the aisles of the church itself, as at Saint Paul's.

Popular religion consisted largely of rituals heavy with symbolism. Before slicing a loaf of bread, the good wife tapped the sign of the cross on it with her knife. Before planting, the village priest customarily went out and sprinkled the fields with water, symbolizing refreshment and life. Shortly after a woman had successfully delivered a child, she was "churched." This was a ceremony of thanksgiving, based on the Jewish rite of purification. When a child was baptized, a few grains of salt were dropped on its tongue. Salt had been the symbol of purity, strength, and incorruptibility for the ancient Hebrews, and the Romans had used it in their sacrifices. It was used in Christian baptism to drive away demons and to strengthen the infant in its new faith.

The entire calendar was designed with reference to Christmas, Easter, and Pentecost. Saints' days were legion. Everyone participated in village processions. The colored vestments the priests wore at Mass gave the villagers a sense of the changing seasons of the church's liturgical year. The signs and symbols of Christianity were visible everywhere.

Was popular religion largely a matter of rituals and ceremonies? What did people actually *believe?* It is difficult to say, partly because medieval peasants left few written records of their thoughts, partly because in any age there is often a great disparity between what people profess to believe and their conduct or the ways they act on their beliefs. Recent research has shown, however, that in the High Middle Ages a new religious understanding emerged. "Whereas early Christians looked to holy men and women and early medieval society turned to saints to effect the connection between God and humankind through prayers of intercession," in the twelfth century theologians developed a sacramental system. They expanded on Saint Augustine's definition (see page 203) and declared a **sacrament** an outward and visible sign instituted by Christ to give grace. Only a priest could dispense a sacrament (except when someone was in danger of death), and the list of seven sacraments, originally compiled by Peter Lombard, was formally accepted by the Fourth Lateran Council (1215).

Baptism is the rite by which a person enters the Christian community. This is signified by sprinkling the person with holy water or fully immersing him or her in water. If the person has reached the age of reason (seven), a profession of faith and repentance for previous sins are required. *Penance* (from the Latin *poena,* meaning "punishment") is the rite by which, through oral confession to a priest, sins committed after baptism are forgiven. The penitent often has to perform some act as compensation, such as paying for stolen goods or apologizing for sins against charity. **Eucharist** is the name given to the central ceremony of Christian worship (also called the Mass, the Lord's Supper, and Holy Communion) as well as to the bread and wine consecrated by the priest and consumed by believers. In *confirmation,* the Christian receives the Holy Spirit through the laying on of the bishop's hands and his anointment of the candidate's forehead with oil. The person is now a full member of the Christian community. Although there are many examples of the administration of this sacrament in the early church, there were

The Eucharist The Fourth Lateran Council of 1215 encouraged all Christians to receive the Eucharist at least once a year, after confession and penance. Here a priest places the consecrated host on people's tongues. *(Biblioteca Apostolica Vaticana)*

also wide differences in the method of its administration. *Matrimony* as a sacrament derives from Jesus' presence at the marriage feast of Cana, the first public appearance of his ministry, which medieval theologians interpreted as proof of his wish to bless marriages. In the eleventh century the church claimed exclusive jurisdiction over marriage, and civil authorities acquiesced. In the sixteenth century the church claimed that for a marriage to be valid, the couple must be blessed by a priest. *Orders* is the rite by which men, through the laying on of the bishop's hands and his anointment of the candidate's hands, enter into the service of the people. Last, *extreme unction* or *anointment of the sick* is usually administered when a person is gravely ill and in danger of death. Anointing was widely practiced in the early church, and Bede (see page 247) represents it as a well-established custom in his time.

Medieval Christians believed that these seven sacraments brought grace, the divine assistance or help needed to lead a good Christian life and to merit salvation. Sermons and homilies taught that at the center of the sacramental system stood the Eucharist, the small piece of bread that through the words of priestly consecration at the Mass became the living body of Christ and, when worthily consumed, became a channel of Christ's grace. The ritual of consecration, repeated at every altar of Christendom, became a unifying symbol in a complex world.[28] The sacramental system, however, did not replace strong devotion to the saints.

The Mass was in Latin, but the priest delivered sermons on the Gospel in the vernacular. Or he was supposed to. An almost universal criticism of the parish clergy in the twelfth and thirteenth centuries was that they were incapable of explaining basic Christian teachings to their parishioners. The growth of the universities (see page 357) did not improve the situation, because few diocesan clerics attended them, and those who did and won degrees secured administrative positions with prelates or lay governments. The only parish priest to be canonized in the entire Middle Ages, the Breton lawyer and priest Saint Yves (d. 1303), had resigned a position as a diocesan judge to serve rural parishioners. At the trial for his canonization, laypeople stressed that not only had he led a simple and frugal life but he had put his forensic skills to the service of preaching the Christian Gospels. He represents a great exception to the prevailing inability of the medieval parish clergy to preach in a rural milieu. Parish priests celebrated the liturgy and administered the sacraments, but they had other shortcomings. A thirteenth-century Alsatian chronicler said that the peasants of the region did not complain that their pastors lived in concubinage, because that made them less fearful for the virtue of their daughters.[29]

Nevertheless, people grasped the meaning of biblical stories and church doctrines from the paintings on the church walls or, in wealthy parishes, the scenes in stained-glass windows. Illiterate and uneducated, they certainly could not reason out the increasingly sophisticated propositions of clever theologians. Still, Scriptural references and proverbs dotted everyone's language. The English "good-bye," the French "adieu," and the Spanish "adios" all derive from words meaning "God be with you." Christianity was the foundation of the common people's culture.

In the eleventh century, theologians began to emphasize the depiction of Mary at the Crucifixion in the Gospel of John: "When Jesus saw his mother and the disciple whom he loved standing near, he said to his mother, 'Woman, behold, your son!' Then he said to the disciple, 'Behold, your mother!'" Medieval scholars interpreted this passage as expressing Christ's compassionate concern for all humanity and Mary's spiritual motherhood of all Christians. The huge outpouring of popular devotions to Mary concentrated on her special relationship to Christ, as all-powerful intercessor with him. The most famous prayer, "Salve Regina," perfectly expresses medieval people's confidence in Mary, their advocate with Christ:

Hail, holy Queen, Mother of Mercy! Our life, our sweetness, and our hope. To thee we cry, poor banished children of Eve; to thee we send up our sighs, mourning and weeping in this valley of tears. Turn, then, most gracious advocate, thy merciful eyes upon us; and after this our exile show us the blessed fruit of thy womb, Jesus. O merciful, O loving, O sweet Virgin Mary!

Peasants had a strong sense of the presence of God. They believed that God rewarded the virtuous with peace, health, and material prosperity and punished sinners with disease, poor harvests, and war. Sin was caused by the Devil, who lurked everywhere. The Devil constantly incited people to evil deeds and sin, especially sins of the flesh. Sin frequently took place in the dark. Thus evil and the Devil were connected in the peasant's mind with darkness or blackness. In some medieval literature the Devil is portrayed as black, an identification that has had a profound and sorry impact on Western racial attitudes.

For peasants life was not only hard but short. Few lived beyond the age of forty. Belief in an afterlife where the dead were rewarded or punished according to how they had lived on earth was a central principle of medieval people's faith. The clergy taught the immortality of the soul after the death of the body. The deceased, however, did not go immediately to Heaven or Hell. Rather, people believed that the recently deceased returned to the places they had frequented during their lives and either sought the prayers of the living or settled accounts with them. Hence the widespread belief in ghosts who haunted their former houses and frightened relatives and friends. Late in the twelfth century, to free houses and people of the haunting presence of the dead, the church affirmed the existence of *purgatory,* a temporary place where distressed souls made amends for their earthly sins before being admitted to Heaven.[30] Prayers and masses helped those in purgatory. So did *indulgences,* documents bearing the pope's name that released the souls from purgatory. (Indulgences, it was believed, also relieved the living of those penalties imposed by the priest in confession for serious sins.) Indulgences could be secured for a small fee. People came to believe that indulgences and pilgrimages to the shrines of saints "promised" salvation. Vast numbers embarked on pilgrimages to the shrines of Saint James at Compostela in Spain, Saint Thomas Becket at Canterbury, Saint-Gilles de Provence, and Saints Peter and Paul at Rome.

Those Who Fight

The **nobility,** though a small fraction of the total population, strongly influenced all aspects of medieval culture—political, economic, religious, educational, and artistic. For that reason, European society in the twelfth and thirteenth centuries may be termed aristocratic. Despite political, scientific, and industrial revolutions, the nobility continued to hold real political and social power in Europe down to the nineteenth century. In order to account for this continuing influence, it is important to understand its development in the High Middle Ages. How did the social status and lifestyle of the nobility in the twelfth and thirteenth centuries differ from their tenth-century forms? What political and economic role did the nobility play?

First, in the tenth and eleventh centuries, the social structure in different parts of Europe varied considerably. Broad generalizations about the legal and social status of the nobility, therefore, are dangerous, because they are not universally applicable. For example, in Germany until about 1200, approximately one thousand families, descended from the Carolingian imperial aristocracy and perhaps from the original German tribal nobility, formed the ruling social group. Its members intermarried and held most of the important positions in church and state.[31] Rigid distinctions existed between free and non-free individuals, preventing the absorption of those of servile birth into the ranks of the nobility. Likewise, in the region around Paris from the tenth century on, a group of great families held public authority, was self-conscious about its ancestry and honorable status, was bound to the royal house, and was closed to the self-made man. From this aristocracy descended the upper nobility of the High Middle Ages.[32] To the west, however, in the provinces of Anjou and Maine, men of fortune became part of the closely related web of noble families by marrying into those families; in these regions, considerable upward mobility existed. Some scholars argue that before the thirteenth century the French nobility was an open caste.[33] Across the English Channel, the English nobility in the High Middle Ages derived from the Norman, Breton, French, and Flemish warriors who helped Duke William of Normandy defeat the Anglo-Saxons at the Battle of Hastings in 1066. In most places, for a son or daughter to be considered a noble, both parents had to be noble. Non-noble women could not usually enter the nobility through marriage, though evidence from Germany shows that some women were ennobled because they had married nobles. There is no evidence of French or English women being raised to the nobility.

Members of the nobility enjoyed a special legal status. A nobleman was free personally and in his possessions. He had immunity from almost all outside authorities. He was limited only by his military obligation to king, duke, or prince. As the result of his liberty, he had certain rights and responsibilities. He raised troops and commanded them in the field. He held courts that dispensed a sort of justice. Sometimes he coined money for use within his territories. He conducted relations with outside powers. He was the political, military, and judicial lord of the people who settled on his lands. He made political decisions affecting them, resolved disputes among them, and protected them in time of attack. The liberty of the noble meant that he possessed special privileges that were inheritable, perpetuated by blood and not by wealth alone.

The nobleman was a professional fighter. He protected the weak, the poor, and the churches by arms. He possessed a horse and a sword. These, and the leisure time in which to learn how to use them in combat, were the visible signs of his nobility. He was encouraged to display chivalric virtues. Chivalry was a code of conduct originally devised by the clergy to transform the crude and brutal behavior of the knightly class. A knight was supposed to be brave, anxious to win praise, courteous, loyal to his commander, generous, and gracious. Above all, he was to be loyal to his lord and brave in battle. In a society lacking strong institutions of government, loyalty was the cement that held aristocratic society together. That is why the greatest crime was called a "felony," which meant treachery to one's lord. The medieval nobility developed independently of knighthood and preceded it; all nobles were knights, but not all knights were noble.[34]

During the eleventh century, the term *chevalier,* meaning "horseman" or "knight," gained wide currency in France. Non-French people gradually adopted it to refer to the nobility, "who sat up high on their warhorses, looking down on the poor masses and terrorizing the monks."[35] In France and England by the twelfth century, the noble frequently used the Latin term *miles,* or "knight." The word connoted moral values, a consciousness of family, and participation in a superior hereditary caste. Those who aspired to the aristocracy desired a castle, the symbol of feudal independence and military lifestyle. Through military valor, a fortunate marriage, or outstanding service to king or lord, poor knights could and did achieve positions in the upper nobility. In Germany there also existed a large class of unfree knights, or **ministerials.** Recruited from the servile dependents of great lords, ministerials fought as warriors or served as stewards who managed nobles' estates or households. In the twelfth century, ministerials sometimes acquired fiefs and wealth. The most important ministerials served the German kings and had significant responsibilities. Legally, however, they remained of servile status: they were not noble.[36] Consequently, in southeastern Germany the term *knight* applied to the servile position of a ministerial.

How did the nobility look on the peasants, who performed all kinds of labor, such as repair of roads, castles, bridges, and other infrastructure? There is no simple answer. Medieval writers often cited the scriptural account of Genesis 9:20–28. When Noah's youngest son, Ham, uncovered his drunken father's nakedness, Noah condemned Ham's son, Canaan, and his descendants to serve the descendants of Noah's other two sons. Why this curse was levied on Canaan rather than Ham Scripture does not make clear. Yet it clearly sets up two classes: servants and masters. Using the evidence of this biblical story; of patristic, philosophical, and theological literature; and of fabliaux (satirical verse tales), a recent study reveals that the European nobility had complex, conflicting, and sometimes contradictory attitudes toward the peasants, also called **rustics.**

On the one hand, elite classes thought the peasantry coarse, ill-dressed, hairy, dark, and dirty, because of their proximity to the earth and their work in the sun. Often they seemed deformed. The upper classes also considered the peasants stupid, boorish, mentally slow, and dull witted. They associated peasants with excrement, because they used animal and human manure to fertilize their fields. On the other hand, nobles acknowledged that some peasants were endowed with a practical cunning and shrewdness, and nobles sometimes recognized peasants as virtuous, pious, and beloved of God. The upper classes also appreciated the rustics' agricultural productivity. Thus the opinion of elite observers vacillated wildly. God, the nobles held, had decreed the peasants to be unfree (because of the story in Genesis), and their entire nature had been debased to the level of brute beasts. Yet they were beloved by God if they kept their place and were productive.[37]

Infancy and Childhood

Very exciting research has been done on childbirth in the upper classes in the Middle Ages. Most of the information comes from manuscript illuminations, which depict the birth process from the moment of coitus through pregnancy to delivery. An interesting thirteenth-century German miniature from Vienna shows a woman in labor. She is sitting on a chair or stool surrounded by four other women, who are present to help her in the delivery.

The rate of infant mortality (the number of babies who would die before their first birthday) in the High Middle Ages must have been staggering. Such practices as jolting the pregnant woman up and down to speed delivery surely contributed to the death rate of both the newborn and the mother. Natural causes—disease and poor or insufficient food—also resulted in many deaths. Infanticide, however, which was common in the ancient world, seems to have declined in the High Middle Ages. Ecclesiastical pressure worked steadily against it.

On the other hand, the abandonment of infant children seems to have been the most favored form of family limitation, widely practiced throughout the Middle Ages. Abandonment was "the voluntary relinquishing of control over children by their natal parents or guardians, whether by leaving them somewhere, selling them, or legally consigning authority to some other person or institution."[38] Why did parents do this? What became of the children? What attitudes did medieval society have toward this practice?

Poverty or local natural disaster led some parents to abandon their children because they could not support them. Before the eleventh century, food was so scarce that few parents could feed themselves, let alone children. Thus Saint Patrick wrote that in times of famine, fathers would sell their sons and daughters so that the children could be fed. Parents sometimes gave children away because they were illegitimate or the result of incestuous unions. An eighth-century penitential collection describes the proper treatment for a woman who exposes her unwanted child—

Monastic Entrance   In a world with few career opportunities for "superfluous children," monasteries served a valuable social function. Because a dowry was expected, monastic life was generally limited to the children of the affluent. Here a father—advising his son to be obedient and holding a bag of money for the monastery—hands his son over to the abbot. The boy does not look enthusiastic. *(The J. Paul Getty Museum, Los Angeles. Unknown illuminator, Initial Q: An Abbot Receiving a Child Decretum, ca 1170–1180 [83.MQ.163.fol.63])*

that is, leaves it in the open to die—because she has been raped by an enemy or is unable to nourish it. She is not to be blamed, but she should do penance.[39]

Sometimes parents believed that someone of greater means or status might find the child and bring it up in better circumstances than the natal parents could provide. Disappointment in the sex of the child, or its physical weakness or deformity, might have also led parents to abandon it. Finally, some parents were indifferent—they "simply could not be bothered" with the responsibilities of parenthood.[40]

The Christian Middle Ages witnessed a significant development in the disposal of superfluous children: they were given to monasteries as **oblates.** The word *oblate* derives from the Latin *oblatio,* meaning "offering." Boys and girls were given to monasteries or convents as permanent gifts. Saint Benedict (see pages 205–206), in the fifty-ninth chapter of his *Rule,* takes oblation as a normal method for entrance into the monastic life. By the seventh century, church councils and civil codes had defined the practice: "Parents of any social status could donate a child, of either sex, at least up to the age of ten." Contemporaries considered oblation a religious act, since the child was offered to God often in recompense for parental sin. But oblation also served social and economic functions. The monastery nurtured and educated the child in a familial atmosphere, and it provided career opportunities for the mature monk or nun whatever his or her origins. Oblation has justifiably been described as "in many ways the most humane form of abandonment ever devised in the West."[41]

Recent research suggests that abandonment was very common among the poor until about the year 1000. The next two hundred years, which saw great agricultural change and relative prosperity, witnessed a low point in the abandonment of poor children. On the other hand, in the twelfth and thirteenth centuries, the incidence of noble parents giving their younger sons and daughters to religious houses increased dramatically; nobles wanted to preserve the estate intact for the eldest son. Consequently, oblates composed a high percentage of monastic populations. At Winchester in England, for example, 85 percent of the new monks between 1030 and 1070 were oblates. In the early thirteenth century, the bishop of Paris observed that children were "cast into the cloister by parents and relatives just as if they were kittens or piglets whom their mothers could not nourish; so that they may die to the world not spiritually but . . . civilly, that is—so that they may be deprived of their hereditary position and that it may devolve on those who remain in the world." The abandonment of children remained a socially acceptable institution. Ecclesiastical and civil authorities never legislated against it.[42]

In addition to abandonment, nobles used other family-planning strategies to preserve family estates, but scholars disagree about the nature of these methods. According to one authority, "The struggle to preserve family holdings intact led them to primogeniture [the exclusive right of the first-born son to inherit]."[43] Another student has argued persuasively that nobles deliberately married late or limited the number of their children who could marry by placing them in the church or forbidding them to marry while still laypersons. Nobles may also have practiced birth control. The counts of Falkenstein, who held lordships in Upper Bavaria and Lower Austria, adopted the strategy of late marriages for men and few children. This custom plus a violent lifestyle ultimately backfired and extinguished the dynasty.[44] Another student, using evidence from tenth-century Saxony, maintains that parents during their lifetimes commonly endowed their sons with estates. This practice allowed sons to marry at a young age and to demonstrate their military prowess.[45] Until we know more, however, we cannot generalize about universal practices.

For children of aristocratic birth, the years from infancy to around the age of seven or eight were primarily years of play. Infants had their rattles, as the twelfth-century monk Guibert of Nogent reports, and young children their special toys. Of course, then as now, children would play with anything handy—balls, rings, pretty stones, horns, any small household object. Gerald of Wales, who later became a courtier of King Henry II, describes how as a child he built monasteries and churches in the sand while his brothers were making castles and palaces. Vincent of Beauvais, who composed a great encyclopedia around 1250, recommended that children be bathed twice a day, fed well, and given ample playtime.

Guibert of Nogent speaks in several places in his autobiography of "the tender years of childhood"—the years from six to twelve. Describing the severity of the tutor whom his mother assigned to him, Guibert wrote:

Placed under him, I was taught with such purity and checked with such honesty from the vices which commonly spring up in youth that I was kept from ordinary games and never allowed to leave my master's company, or to eat anywhere else than at home . . . ; in everything I had to show self-control. . . . While others of my age wandered everywhere at will and were unchecked in the indulgence of such inclinations as were natural at their age, I, hedged in with constant restraints and dressed in my clerical garb, would sit and look at the troops of players like a beast awaiting sacrifice.[46]

Guibert's mother had intended him for the church. Other boys and girls had much more playtime and freedom.

At about the age of seven, a boy of the noble class who was not intended for the church was placed in the household of one of his father's friends or relatives. There he became a servant to the lord and received his formal training in arms. He was expected to serve the lord at the table, to assist him as a private valet when called on to do so, and, as he gained experience, to care for the lord's horses and equipment. The boy might have a great deal of work to do, depending on the size of the household and the personality of the lord. The work children did, medieval people believed, gave them experience and preparation for later life.

Training was in the arts of war. The boy learned to ride and to manage a horse. He had to acquire skill in wielding a sword, which sometimes weighed as much as twenty-five pounds. He had to be able to hurl a lance, shoot with a bow and arrow, and care for armor and other equipment. Increasingly, in the eleventh and twelfth centuries, noble youths learned to read and write some Latin. Still, on thousands of charters from that period, nobles signed with a cross (+) or some other mark. Literacy for the nobility became more common in the thirteenth century. Formal training was concluded around the age of twenty-one with the ceremony of knighthood. The custom of knighting, though never universal, seems to have been widespread in France and England but not in Germany. The ceremony of knighthood was one of the most important in a man's life.

Youth

Knighthood did not necessarily mean adulthood, power, and responsibility. Sons were completely dependent on their fathers for support. A young man remained a youth until he was in a financial position to marry—that is, until his father died. That might not happen until he was in his late thirties, and marriage at forty was not uncommon. A famous English soldier of fortune, William Marshal, had to wait until he was forty-five to take a wife. One factor—the inheritance of land and the division of properties—determined the lifestyle of the aristocratic nobility. The result was tension, frustration, and sometimes violence.

Once knighted, the young man traveled for two to three years. His father selected a group of friends to accompany, guide, and protect him. The band's chief pursuit was fighting. They meddled in local conflicts, sometimes departed on crusade, hunted, and did the tournament circuit. The **tournament,** in which a number of men competed from horseback (in contrast to the **joust,** which involved only two competitors), gave the bachelor knight experience in pitched battle. Since the horses and equipment of the vanquished were forfeited to the victors, the knight could also gain a reputation and a profit. Young knights took great delight in spending money on horses, armor, gambling, drinking, and women. Everywhere they went they stirred up trouble. It is no wonder that kings supported the Crusades to rid their countries of the violence caused by bands of footloose young knights.

Parents often wanted to settle daughters' futures as soon as possible. Men, even older men, tended to prefer young brides. A woman in her late twenties or thirties would have fewer years of married fertility, limiting the number of children she could produce and thus threatening the family's survival. Therefore, aristocratic girls in the High Middle Ages were married at around the age of sixteen.

The future of many young women was not enviable. For a girl of sixteen, marriage to a man in his thirties was not the most attractive prospect, and marriage to a widower in his forties or fifties was even less so. If there were a large number of marriageable young girls in a particular locality, their "market value" was reduced. In the early Middle Ages, it had been the custom for the groom to present a dowry to the bride and her family, but by the late twelfth century the process was reversed. Thereafter, the size of the marriage portions offered by brides and their families rose higher and higher.

Within noble families and medieval society as a whole, paternal control of the family property and wealth led to serious difficulties. Because marriage was long delayed for men, a considerable age difference existed between husbands and wives and between fathers and sons. Because of this generation gap, as one scholar has written, "the father became an older, distant, but still powerful figure. He could do favors for his sons, but his very presence, once his sons had reached maturity, blocked them in the attainment and enjoyment of property and in the possession of a wife."[47] Consequently, disputes between the generations were common in the twelfth and thirteenth centuries. Older men held on to property and power. Younger sons wanted a "piece of the action."

The mother, closer in years to her children than her husband, seemed better able to understand their needs and frustrations. She often served as a mediator between conflicting male generations. One authority on French epic poetry has written, "In extreme need, the heroes betake themselves to their mother, with whom they always find love, counsel and help. She takes them under her protection, even against their father."[48]

When society included so many married young women and unmarried young men, sexual tensions also arose. The young male noble, unable to marry for a long time, could satisfy his lust with peasant girls or prostitutes. But what was a young woman unhappily married to a much older man to do? The literature of courtly love is filled with stories of young bachelors in love with young married women. How hopeless their love was is not known. The cuckolded husband is also a stock figure in such masterpieces as *The Romance of Tristan and Isolde,* the *Lais* of Marie de France, Chaucer's *The Merchant's Tale,* and Boccaccio's *Fiammetta's Tale*.

Power and Responsibility

A male member of the nobility became an adult when he came into the possession of his property. He then acquired vast authority over lands and people. With it went responsibility. In the words of Honorius of Autun:

Soldiers: You are the arm of the Church, because you should defend it against its enemies. Your duty is to aid the oppressed, to restrain yourself from rapine and fornication, to repress those who impugn the Church with evil acts, and to resist those who are rebels against priests. Performing such a service, you will obtain the most splendid of benefices from the greatest of Kings.[49]

Nobles rarely lived up to this ideal, and there are countless examples of nobles attacking the church. In the early thirteenth century, Peter of Dreux, count of Brittany, spent so much of his time attacking the church that he was known as the "Scourge of the Clergy."

The nobles' conception of rewards and gratification did not involve the kind of postponement envisioned by the clergy. They wanted rewards immediately. Since by definition a military class is devoted to war, those rewards came through the pursuit of arms. When nobles were not involved in local squabbles with neighbors—usually disputes over property or over real or imagined slights—they participated in tournaments.

Complete jurisdiction over properties allowed the noble, at long last, to gratify his desire for display and lavish living. Since his status in medieval society depended

Saint Maurice The cult of Saint Maurice (d. 287), a soldier executed by the Romans for refusing to renounce his Christian faith, presents a paradox. Although no solid evidence for him has survived, his cult spread widely in the Carolingian period. Later, he was held up as a model knight and declared a patron of the Holy Roman Empire and protector of the imperial (German) army in wars against the pagan Slavs. His image was used on coins, and his cult was promoted by the archbishops of Magdeburg. Always, until 1240, he was portrayed as a white man. Then, from 1240 to the sixteenth century, he was represented as a black man, as in this sandstone statue from Magdeburg Cathedral (ca 1240–1250). Who commissioned this statue? Who carved it? What black man served as the model? Only further research can answer these questions, as well as the question of his race. *(Image of the Black Project, Harvard University/Hickey-Robertson, Houston)*

on the size of his household, he would be anxious to increase the number of his household retainers. The elegance of his clothes, the variety and richness of his table, the number of his horses and followers, the freedom with which he spent money—all were public indications of his social standing. To maintain this lifestyle, nobles often borrowed from financiers or wealthy monasteries.

At the same time, nobles had a great deal of work to do. The responsibilities of a noble in the High Middle Ages depended on the size and extent of his estates, the number of his dependents, and his position in his territory relative to others of his class and to the king. As a vassal he was required to fight for his lord or for the king when called on to do so. By the mid-twelfth century, this service was limited in most parts of western Europe to forty days a year. The noble might have to perform guard duty at his lord's castle for a certain number of days a year. He was obliged to attend his lord's court on important occasions when the lord wanted to put on great displays, such as at Easter, Pentecost, and Christmas. When the lord knighted his eldest son or married off his eldest daughter, he called his vassals to his court. They were expected to attend and to present a contribution known as a "gracious aid."

Until the late thirteenth century, when royal authority intervened, a noble in France or England had great power over the knights and peasants on his estates. He maintained order among them and dispensed justice to them. Holding the manorial court, which punished criminal acts and settled disputes, was one of his gravest obligations. The quality of justice varied widely: some lords were vicious tyrants who exploited and persecuted their peasants; others were reasonable and evenhanded. In any case, the quality of life on the manor and its productivity were related in no small way to the temperament and decency of the lord—and his lady.

Women played a large and important role in the functioning of the estate. They were responsible for the practical management of the household's "inner economy"—cooking, brewing, spinning, weaving, caring for yard animals. The lifestyle of the medieval warrior-nobles required constant travel, both for purposes of war and for the supervision of distant properties. When the lord was away for long periods, the women frequently managed the herds, barns, granaries, and outlying fields as well.

Frequent pregnancies and the reluctance to expose women to hostile conditions kept the lady at home and therefore able to assume supervision of the family's fixed properties. When a husband went away on crusade—and this could last anywhere from two to five years, if he returned at all—his wife often became the sole manager of the family properties. When her husband went to the Holy Land between 1060 and 1080, the lady Hersendis was the sole manager of her family's properties in northern France.

Nor were women's activities confined to managing households and estates in their husbands' absence. Medieval warfare was largely a matter of brief skirmishes, and few men were killed in any single encounter. But altogether the number slain ran high, and there were many widows. Aristocratic widows frequently controlled family properties and fortunes and exercised great authority. Although the evidence is scattered and sketchy, there are indications that women performed many of the functions of men. In Spain, France, and Germany they bought, sold, and otherwise transferred property. Gertrude, labeled "Saxony's almighty widow" by the chronicler Ekkehard of Aura, took a leading role in conspiracies against the emperor Henry V. And Eilika Billung, widow of Count Otto of Ballenstedt, built a castle at Burgwerben on the Saale

River and, as advocate of the monastery of Goseck, removed one abbot and selected his successor. From her castle at Bernburg, the countess Eilika was also reputed to ravage the countryside.

Throughout the High Middle Ages, fighting remained the dominant feature of the noble lifestyle. The church's preachings and condemnations reduced but did not stop violence. Lateness of inheritance, depriving the nobility of constructive outlets for their energy, together with the military ethos of their culture, encouraged petty warfare and disorder. The nobility thus represented a constant source of trouble for the monarchy. In the thirteenth century, kings drew on the financial support of the middle classes to build the administrative machinery that gradually laid the foundations for strong royal government. The Crusades relieved the rulers of France, England, and the German Empire of some of their most dangerous elements. Complete royal control of the nobility, however, came only in modern times.

Elephant Ivory Mirror Case
The mirror case, forerunner of the modern woman's compact, protected a polished metal disk used by wealthy ladies as a looking glass. In this mid-fourteenth-century case, the French artist created a courtly love/hunting scene. An aristocratic couple on horseback, holding falcons and accompanied by attendants, are portrayed in a forested landscape, held in an eight-lobed frame with lions around the disk. Amazingly, the diameter of the case is less than four inches. Elephant ivory came from sub-Saharan Africa via the Mediterranean trade. *(The Metropolitan Museum of Art, Gift of George M. Blumenthal, 1941 [41.100.160]. Photograph © The Metropolitan Museum of Art)*

Those Who Pray

Medieval people believed that monks performed an important social service, prayer. In the Middle Ages, prayer was looked on as a vital service, one as crucial as the labor of peasants and the military might of nobles. Just as the knights protected and defended society with the sword and the peasants provided sustenance through their toil, so the monks with their prayers and chants worked to secure God's blessing for society.

Monasticism represented some of the finest aspirations of medieval civilization. The monasteries produced the educated elite that was continually drawn into the administrative service of kings and great lords. Monks kept alive the remains of classical culture and experimented with new styles of architecture and art. They introduced new techniques of estate management and land reclamation. Although relatively few in number in the High Middle Ages, the monks played a significant role in medieval society.

Recruitment

Toward the end of his *Ecclesiastical History,* when he was well into his sixties, Orderic Vitalis (ca 1075–ca 1140), a monk of the Norman abbey of Saint Evroul, interrupted his narrative to explain movingly how he happened to become a monk:

And so, O glorious God, you didst inspire my father Odeleric to renounce me utterly and submit me in all things to thy governance. So, weeping, he gave me, a weeping child, into the care of the monk Reginald, and sent me away into exile for love of thee, and never saw me again. And I, a mere boy, did not presume to oppose my father's wishes, but obeyed him in all things, for he promised me for his part that if I became a monk I should taste of the joys of Heaven with the Innocents after my death. . . . And so, a boy of ten, I crossed the English channel and came into Normandy as an exile, unknown to all, knowing no one. . . . But thou didst suffer me through thy grace to find nothing but kindness among strangers. I was received as an oblate in the abbey of St. Evroul by the venerable abbot Mainier in the eleventh year of my life. . . . The name of Vitalis was given me in place of my English name, which sounded harsh to the Normans.[50]

Orderic Vitalis was one of the leading scholars of his time. As such, he is not a representative figure or even a typical monk. In one respect, however, Orderic was quite representative of the monks of the High Middle Ages: although he had no doubt that God wanted him to be a monk, the decision was actually made by his parents, who gave him to a monastery as a child-oblate. Orderic was the son of Odelerius, a Norman priest of the household of Earl Roger of Montgomery and (after the Conquest of 1066) Shrewsbury, and an Englishwoman. The law requiring a celibate priesthood was not yet operative in England, but qualms of conscience may have led him to place his son in a Norman monastery.[51]

Medieval monasteries were religious institutions whose organization and structure fulfilled the social needs of the feudal nobility. The monasteries provided noble children with both an honorable and aristocratic life and opportunities for ecclesiastical careers.[52] Some men did become monks as adults, apparently for a wide variety of reasons: belief in a direct call from God, disgust with the materialism and violence of the secular world, the encouragement and inspiration of others, economic failure or lack of opportunity, poverty, sickness, fear of Hell. However, most men who became monks, until about the early thirteenth century, seem to have been given as child-oblates by their parents.

In the thirteenth century, the older Benedictine and Cistercian orders had to compete with new orders of friars—the Franciscans and Dominicans. More monks had to be recruited from the middle class, that is, from small landholders or traders in the district near the abbey. As medieval society changed economically, and as European society ever so slowly developed middle-class traits, the monasteries almost inevitably drew their manpower, when they were able, from the middle classes. Until that time, they were preserves of the aristocratic nobility.

The Nuns

Throughout the Middle Ages, social class also defined the kinds of religious life open to women. Kings and nobles usually established convents for their daughters, sisters, aunts, or aging mothers. Entrance was restricted to women of the founder's class. Since a wellborn lady could not honorably be apprenticed to a tradesperson, and since her dignity did not permit her to do any kind of manual labor, the sole alternative to life at home was the religious life.

The founder's endowment and support greatly influenced the later social, economic, and political status of the convent. Social and religious bonds between benefactors and communities of nuns frequently continued over many generations. A few convents received large endowments and could accept many women. Amesbury Priory in Wiltshire, England, for example, received a handsome endowment from King Henry II in 1177, and his successors Henry III and Edward I also made lavish gifts. In 1256 Amesbury supported a prioress and 76 nuns, 7 priests, and 16 lay brothers. It owned 200 oxen, 23 horses, 7 cows, 4 calves, 300 pigs, and 4,800 sheep. The convent raised 100 pounds in annual rents and 40 pounds from the wool clip, very large sums at the time. The entrance of such highborn ladies as the dowager queen Eleanor (widow of Henry III), Edward I's daughter Mary, and his niece Isabella of Lancaster stimulated the gift of additional lands and privileges. By 1317 Amesbury had 177 nuns.[53] Most houses of women, however, possessed limited resources and remained small in numbers.

The office of **abbess** or **prioress,** the house's superior, customarily went to a nun of considerable social standing. Thus William the Conqueror's daughter Cecelia became abbess of her mother's foundation, Holy Trinity Abbey in Caen, and Henry II's daughter became abbess of Barking. Since an abbess or prioress had responsibility for governing her community and for representing it in any business with the outside world, she was a woman of local power and importance. Sometimes her position brought national prominence. In 1306 Edward I of England summoned several abbesses to Parliament; he wanted their financial support for the expenses connected with knighting his eldest son.

What kind of life did the nuns lead? Religious duties held prime importance. Then there were business responsibilities connected with lands, properties, and rents that preoccupied those women of administrative ability. Sewing, embroidery, and fine needlework were considered the special pursuits of gentlewomen. Nuns in houses with an intellectual tradition copied manuscripts. Although the level of intellectual life in the women's houses varied widely, the careers of two nuns—Hildegard of Bingen and Isabella of Lancaster—suggest the activities of some nuns in the High Middle Ages.

The tenth child of a lesser noble family, Hildegard (1098–1179) was given when eight years old as an oblate to an abbey in the Rhineland, where she learned Latin and received a good education. Obviously possessed of leadership and administrative talents, Hildegard went in 1147 to found the convent of Rupertsberg near Bingen. There she produced a body of writings including the *Scivias* (Know the Ways), a record of her mystical visions that incorporates vast theological learning (see the illustration at right); the *Physica* (On the Physical Elements), a classification of the natural elements; a mystery play; and a medical work that led a distinguished twentieth-century historian of science to

Hildegard of Bingen's Vision of Synagogue Here Synagogue (personifying the Jewish people commissioned by God to prepare humanity for the Messiah) is portrayed as a very tall woman who holds in her arms Moses with stone tablets of the commandments. In her lap the patriarchs and prophets foretell the birth of Christ. As the headband symbolizes Mary, who gave the world the Messiah, so Synagogue is mother of the Incarnation. Hildegard was the first major German mystic. *(Rheinische Bildarchiv)*

describe Hildegard as "one of the most original writers of the Latin West in the twelfth century." At the same time, she carried on a vast correspondence with scholars, prelates, and ordinary people and had such a reputation for wisdom that a recent writer has called her "the Dear Abby of the twelfth century to whom everyone came or wrote for advice or comfort."[54] An exceptionally gifted person, Hildegard represents the Benedictine ideal of great learning combined with a devoted monastic life.

As with monks, however, intellectual nuns were not typical of the era. The life of the English nun Isabella of Lancaster better exemplifies the careers of highborn women who became nuns. The niece of King Edward I, she was placed at Amesbury Priory in early childhood, grew up there, made her profession of commitment to the convent life, and became abbess in 1343. Isabella seems to have been a conventional but not devout nun. She traveled widely, spent long periods at the royal court, and with the support of her wealthy relations maintained a residence apart from the priory. She was, however, an able administrator who handled the community finances with prudent skill. Amesbury lacked the intellectual and spiritual standards of Bingen. Isabella's interests were secular, and her own literary production was a book of romances.

Prayer and Other Work

In medieval Europe the monasteries of men greatly outnumbered those of women. The pattern of life within individual monasteries varied widely from house to house and from region to region. One central activity, however—the work of God—was performed everywhere. Daily life centered on the liturgy.

Seven times a day and once during the night, the monks went to choir to chant the psalms and other prayers prescribed by Saint Benedict. Prayers were offered for peace, rain, good harvests, the civil authorities, the monks' families, and their benefactors. Monastic patrons in turn lavished gifts on the monasteries, which often became very wealthy.

Prayer justified the monks' spending a large percentage of their income on splendid objects to enhance the liturgy; monks praised God, they believed, not only in prayer but in everything connected with prayer. They sought to accumulate priestly vestments of the finest silks, velvets, and embroideries, as well as sacred vessels of embossed silver and gold. Thuribles containing sweet-smelling incense brought at great expense from the Ori-

ent were used at the altars, following ancient Jewish ritual. The pages of Gospel books were richly decorated with gold leaf, and the books' bindings were ornamented and bejeweled. Every monastery tried to acquire the relics of its patron saint, which necessitated the production of a beautiful reliquary to house them. The liturgy, then, inspired a great deal of art, and the monasteries became the crucibles of art in Western Christendom.

The administration of the abbey's estates and properties consumed considerable time. The operation of a large establishment, such as Cluny in Burgundy or Bury Saint Edmunds in England, which by 1150 had several hundred monks, involved planning, prudence, and wise management. The usual method of economic organization was the manor. Many monastic manors were small enough and close enough to the abbey to be supervised directly by the abbot. But if a monastery held and farmed vast estates, the properties were divided into administrative units under the supervision of one of the monks of the house. The lands of the German abbey of Saint Emmeran at Regensburg, for example, were divided into thirty-three manorial centers.

Because the *choir monks* were aristocrats, they did not till the land themselves. In each house one monk, the *cellarer*, or general financial manager, was responsible for supervising the peasants or lay brothers who did the actual agricultural labor. **Lay brothers** were vowed religious drawn from the servile classes, with simpler religious and intellectual obligations than those of the choir monks. The cellarer had to see to it that the estates of the monastery produced enough income to cover its expenses. Another monk, the *almoner,* was responsible for feeding and caring for the poor of the neighborhood. At the French abbey of Saint-Requier in the eleventh century, 110 persons were fed every day. At Corbie fifty loaves of bread were distributed daily to the poor.

The *novice master* was responsible for the training of recruits, instructing them in the *Rule,* the chant, the Scriptures, and the history and traditions of the house. For some monks work was some form of intellectual activity, such as the copying of books and manuscripts, the preparation of manuals, and the writing of letters. The efficient operation of a monastic house, however, required the services of cooks, launderers, gardeners, tailors, mechanics, blacksmiths, pharmacists, and others whose essential work left, unfortunately, no written trace.

Although several orders forbade monks to study law and medicine, that rule was often ignored. In the twelfth and thirteenth centuries, many monks gained considerable reputations for their knowledge and experience in

Monk and Nun in Stocks   Stocks, heavy wooden frames with holes for restraining the ankles and sometimes the wrists, were used for punishment. A person confined in stocks endured great physical discomfort, as well as the shame of public disgrace. The monk and nun here were being punished for immoral behavior. *(British Library Roy.10.f.IV.187)*

the practice of both the canon law of the church and the civil law of their countries. For example, the Norman monk Lanfranc, because of his legal knowledge and administrative ability, became the chief adviser of William the Conqueror as archbishop of Canterbury.

Although knowledge of medicine was primitive by our standards, monastic practitioners were less ignorant than one would suspect. Long before 1066, a rich medical literature had been produced in England. The most important of these treatises was *The Leech Book of Bald* (*leech* means "medical"). This work exhibits a wide knowledge of herbal prescriptions, ancient authorities, and empirical practice. Bald discusses diseases of the lungs and stomach, together with their remedies, and demonstrates his acquaintance with surgery. Medical knowledge was sometimes rewarded. Henry II made his medical adviser, the monk Robert de Veneys, abbot of Malmesbury.

The religious houses of medieval Europe usually took full advantage of whatever resources and opportunities their location offered. For example, the raising of horses could produce income in a world that depended on horses for travel and for warfare. Some monasteries, such as the Cistercian abbey of Jervaulx in Yorkshire, became famous for and quite wealthy from their production of prime breeds. In the eleventh and twelfth centuries, a period of considerable monastic expansion, large tracts of swamp, fen, forest, and wasteland were brought under cultivation—principally by the Cistercians (see Map 10.1).

The Cistercians, whose rules insisted that they accept lands far from human habitation and forbade them to be involved in the traditional feudal-manorial structure, were ideally suited to the agricultural needs and trends of their times. In the Low Countries (present-day Holland, Belgium, and French Flanders) they built dikes to hold back the sea, and the reclaimed land was put to the production of cereals. In the eastern parts of Germany— Silesia, Mecklenburg, and Pomerania—they took the lead in draining swamps and cultivating wasteland. Because of a labor shortage, they advertised widely across Europe for monks and brothers. As a result of their efforts, the rich, rolling land of French Burgundy was turned into lush vineyards. In northern and central England, the rocky soil and damp downs of Lincolnshire, poorly suited to agriculture, were turned into sheep runs. By the third quarter of the twelfth century, the Cistercians were raising sheep and playing a large role in the production of England's staple crop, wool.

Some monasteries got involved in iron and lead mining. In 1291 the Cistercian abbey of Furness operated at least forty forges. The German abbeys of Königsbronn,

MAP 10.1 Cistercian Expansion   The rapid expansion of the Cistercian order in the twelfth century reflects the spiritual piety of the age and its enormous economic vitality. The White Monks (so called because of their white robes) took advantage of whatever economic opportunities their locales offered: coal, iron, and silver mining, sheep farming, cereal growing, wine producing, and horse breeding.

Waldsassen, and Saabergen also mined iron in the thirteenth century. The monks entered this industry first to fill their own needs, but in an expanding economy they soon discovered a large market. Iron had hundreds of uses. Nails, hammers, plows, armor, spears, axes, stirrups, horseshoes, and many weapons of war were all made from this basic metal. Lead also had a great variety of uses. It could be used for roofing; as an alloy for

strengthening silver coinage; for framing pane-glass windows in parish, monastery, and cathedral churches; even for lavatory drainpipes.

Some monasteries lent their surplus revenues to the local nobility and peasantry. In the twelfth century the abbey of Savigny in Normandy, for example, acted as a banking house, providing loans at interest to noble families of Normandy and Brittany. Although church law opposed usury, or lending at interest, one reliable scholar has written that "it was clerics and ecclesiastical institutions (monasteries and nunneries) that constituted the main providers of credit."[55]

Monks also performed social services. Monasteries often ran schools that gave primary education to young boys. Abbeys like Saint Albans, situated north of London on a busy thoroughfare, served as hotels and resting places for travelers. Monasteries frequently operated "hospitals" and leprosaria, which provided care and attention to the sick, the aged, and the afflicted—primitive care, it is true, but often all that was available. In short, monasteries performed a variety of social services in an age when there was no "state" and no conception of social welfare as a public responsibility.

Economic Difficulties

In the twelfth century, expenses in the older Benedictine monastic houses increased more rapidly than did income, leading to a steadily worsening economic situation. Cluny is a good example. Life at Cluny was lavish and extravagant. The monks dined on rich food and wore habits of the best cloth available. Cluny's abbots and priors traveled with sizable retinues, as great lords were required to do. The abbots worked to make the liturgy

Beekeeping at Monte Cassino Because of the scarcity and expense of sugar, honey was the usual sweetener for pastries and liquids throughout the Middle Ages. This illustrator had never actually seen the process: without veils, nets, and gloves, the beekeepers would be badly stung. *(Biblioteca Apostolica Vaticana)*

ever more magnificent, and large sums were spent on elaborate vestments and jeweled vessels. Hugh, the sixth abbot (1049–1109), embarked on an extraordinarily expensive building program. He rebuilt the abbey church, and when Pope Urban II consecrated it in 1095, it was the largest church in Christendom. The monks lived like lords, which in a sense they were.

Revenue came from the hundreds of monasteries scattered across France, Italy, Spain, and England that Cluny had reformed in the eleventh century; each year they paid Cluny a cash sum. King Ferdinand I of León and Castile (1035–1065) made an agreement with Abbot Hugh: in return for Cluny's prayers for his dynasty, Ferdinand arranged to pay Cluny a large annual assessment, possibly amounting to 2,000 gold dinars. Ferdinand's successors, however, shifted their benefactions to the new Cistercian order, causing a severe financial loss for Cluny.

Novices were expected to make a gift of land or cash when they entered Cluny. For reasons of security, knights departing on crusade often placed their estates under Cluny's authority. Still this income was not enough. The management of Cluny's manors across Europe was entrusted to bailiffs, or wardens, who were not monks and were given lifetime contracts. Frequently these bailiffs were poor managers, but they could not be removed and replaced. In order to meet expenses, Cluny had to rely on cash reserves. For example, Cluny's estates produced only a small percentage of needed food supplies; the rest had to be paid for from cash reserves.

Cluny had two basic alternatives—improve management to cut costs or borrow money. The abbey could have placed the monastic manors under the jurisdiction of monks, rather than hiring bailiffs who would grow rich as middlemen. It could have awarded annual rather than lifetime contracts, supervised all revenues, and tried to cut costs within the monastery. But Cluny chose the second alternative—borrowing. The abbey spent hoarded reserves of cash and fell into debt.

In contrast to the abbot of Cluny, Suger, the superior of the royal abbey of Saint-Denis near Paris from 1122 to 1151, was a shrewd manager. Though he too spared no expense to enhance the beauty of his monastery and church, Suger kept an eye on costs and made sure that his properties were soundly managed. But the management of Saint-Denis was unusual. Far more typical was the economic mismanagement at Cluny. By the early thirteenth century, small and great monasteries were facing comparable financial difficulties.

The agricultural recession of the fourteenth century (see pages 379–380) forced the lay nobility to reduce their endowment of monasteries. This development, combined with internal mismanagement, compelled the older Benedictine houses to restrict the number of recruits so that they could live within their incomes. Since the nobility continued to send their children to monasteries, there was no shortage of applicants for the limited number of places. Widespread relaxation in the observance of the Benedictine *Rule* and the weakening of community life, however, meant that the atmosphere in many monasteries resembled that of a secular college offering comfort and security. Adult candidates with ascetic fervor and those seeking a spiritual challenge turned to the austere Cistercians or the preaching friars serving the needs of the townspeople[56] (see pages 369–370).

Summary

Generalizations about peasant life in the High Middle Ages must always be qualified according to manorial customs, the weather and geography, and the personalities of local lords. Everywhere, however, the performance of agricultural services and the payment of rents preoccupied peasants. Though peasants led hard lives, the reclamation of wastelands and forestlands, migration to frontier territory, or manumission (see the "Individuals in Society" feature on page 301 and Chapter 11) offered means of social mobility. The Christian faith, though perhaps not understood at an intellectual level, provided strong emotional and spiritual solace.

By 1100 the knightly class was united in its ability to fight on horseback, its insistence that each member was descended from a valorous ancestor, its privileges, and its position at the top of the social hierarchy. The nobility possessed a strong class consciousness. Aristocratic values and attitudes shaded all aspects of medieval culture. Trained for war, nobles often devoted considerable time to fighting, and intergenerational squabbles were common. Yet a noble might have shouldered heavy judicial, political, and economic responsibilities, depending on the size of his estates.

The monks and nuns exercised a profound influence on matters of the spirit. In their prayers, monks and nuns battled for the Lord, just as the chivalrous knights did on the battlefield. In their chants and rich ceremonials, in their architecture and literary productions, and in the example of many monks' lives, the monasteries inspired Christian peoples to an incalculable degree. As the crucibles of sacred art, the monasteries became the cultural centers of Christian Europe.

Improved agricultural technology that brought larger crop yields, which in turn led to population growth; the movement from servile to free social status; the use of free, instead of servile, labor; the recruitment of nuns and monks from the upper middle rather than the aristocratic classes—these changes represent the enormous dynamism of the High Middle Ages.

Key Terms

ancillae	Eucharist
villeins	nobility
manumission	ministerials
manors	rustics
allodial land	oblates
saints	tournament
relics	joust
popolani	abbess/prioress
sacrament	lay brothers

Notes

1. G. Duby, *The Chivalrous Society,* trans. C. Postan (Berkeley: University of California Press, 1977), pp. 90–93.

2. See P. Freedman, *Images of the Medieval Peasant* (Stanford, Calif.: Stanford University Press, 1999), pp. 16, 20–24.

3. B. A. Hanawalt, *The Ties That Bound: Peasant Families in Medieval England* (New York: Oxford University Press, 1986), p. 5.

4. Honorius of Autun, "Elucidarium sive Dialogus de Summa Totius Christianae Theologiae," in *Patrologia Latina,* ed. J. P. Migne (Paris: Garnier Brothers, 1854), vol. 172, col. 1149.

5. E. Power, "Peasant Life and Rural Conditions," in J. R. Tanner et al., *The Cambridge Medieval History,* vol. 7 (Cambridge: Cambridge University Press, 1958), p. 716.

6. See S. M. Stuard, "Ancillary Evidence for the Decline of Medieval Slavery," *Past and Present* 149 (November 1995): 1–28.

7. Glanvill, "De Legibus Angliae," bk. 5, chap. 5, in *Social Life in Britain from the Conquest to the Reformation,* ed. G. G. Coulton (London: Cambridge University Press, 1956), pp. 338–339.

8. J. B. Freed, *The Friars and German Society in the Thirteenth Century* (Cambridge, Mass.: Medieval Academy of America, 1977), p. 55.

9. See W. C. Jordan, *From Servitude to Freedom: Manumission in the Sénonais in the Thirteenth Century* (Philadelphia: University of Pennsylvania Press, 1986), esp. chap. 3, pp. 37–58.

10. J. Langdon, *Horses, Oxen, and Technological Innovation: The Use of Draught Animals in English Farming, 1066–1500* (Cambridge: Cambridge University Press, 1986), p. 256.

11. Ibid., pp. 254–270.

12. G. Duby, *The Early Growth of the European Economy: Warriors and Peasants from the Seventh to the Twelfth Century* (Ithaca, N.Y.: Cornell University Press, 1978), pp. 213–219.

13. Hanawalt, *The Ties That Bound,* pp. 90–100.

14. Ibid., p. 149.

15. On this quantity and medieval measurements, see D. Knowles, "The Measures of Monastic Beverages," in *The Monastic Order in England* (Cambridge: Cambridge University Press, 1962), p. 717.

16. G. Duby, *Rural Economy and Country Life in the Medieval West,* trans. C. Postan (London: Edward Arnold, 1968), pp. 146–147.

17. S. R. Scargill-Bird, ed., *Custumals of Battle Abbey in the Reigns of Edward I and Edward II* (London: Camden Society, 1887), pp. 213–219.

18. G. Duby, ed., *A History of Private Life,* vol. 2: *Revelations of the Middle Ages* (Cambridge, Mass.: Harvard University Press, 1988), p. 585.

19. Cited in E. Amt, ed., *Women's Lives in the Middle Ages: A Sourcebook* (New York: Routledge, 1992), pp. 103–104.

20. See C. Klapisch-Zuber, ed., *A History of Women,* vol. 2: *Silences of the Middle Ages* (Cambridge, Mass.: Harvard University Press, 1992), p. 289 et seq.

21. See R. Blumenfeld-Kosinski, *Not of Woman Born: Representations of Caesarian Birth in Medieval and Renaissance Culture* (Ithaca, N.Y.: Cornell University Press, 1990), p. 27.

22. Ibid., p. 47.

23. E. J. Kealey, *Medieval Medicus: A Social History of Anglo-Norman Medicine* (Baltimore: Johns Hopkins University Press, 1981), p. 102.

24. Ibid., pp. 88–97.

25. Klapisch-Zuber, *A History of Women,* vol. 2, p. 299.

26. See A. Gurevich, *Medieval Popular Culture: Problems of Belief and Perception,* trans. J. M. Bak and P. A. Hollingsworth (New York: Cambridge University Press, 1990), chap. 2, pp. 39–77, esp. p. 76.

27. Ibid.

28. See M. Rubin, *Corpus Christi: The Eucharist in Late Medieval Culture* (New York: Cambridge University Press, 1992), p. 13 et seq.

29. A. Vauchez, *The Laity in the Middle Ages: Religious Beliefs and Devotional Practices,* ed. D. E. Bornstein, trans. M. J. Schneider (Notre Dame, Ind.: University of Notre Dame Press, 1993), pp. 99–102.

30. Ibid., pp. 85–87.

31. J. B. Freed, "The Origins of the European Nobility: The Problem of the Ministerials," *Viator* 7 (1976): 213.

32. Duby, *The Chivalrous Society,* pp. 104–105.

33. See C. Bouchard, "The Origins of the French Nobility," *American Historical Review* 86 (1981): 501–532.

34. Duby, *The Chivalrous Society,* p. 98.

35. G. Duby, *The Age of the Cathedrals: Art and Society, 980–1420,* trans. E. Levieux and B. Thompson (Chicago: University of Chicago Press, 1981), p. 38.

36. Freed, "The Origins of the European Nobility," p. 214.

37. P. Freedman, *Images of the Medieval Peasant,* pp. 289–303, passim.

38. J. Boswell, *The Kindness of Strangers: The Abandonment of Children in Western Europe from Late Antiquity to the Renaissance* (New York: Pantheon Books, 1989), p. 24. This section relies heavily on this important work.

39. Ibid., pp. 214, 223.

40. Ibid., pp. 428–429.

41. Ibid., pp. 238–239.

42. Ibid., pp. 297, 299, and Conclusion.

43. J. C. Russell, *Late Ancient and Medieval Population Control* (Philadelphia: American Philosophical Society, 1985), p. 180.

44. See J. B. Freed, *The Counts of Falkenstein: Noble Self-Consciousness in Twelfth-Century Germany,* Transactions of the American Philosophical Society, vol. 74, pt. 6 (Philadelphia, 1984), pp. 163–167.

45. R. J. Leyser, *Rule and Conflict in an Early Medieval Society: Ottonian Saxony* (Bloomington: Indiana University Press, 1979), pp. 49, 59.

46. J. F. Benton, ed. and trans., *Self and Society in Medieval France: The Memoirs of Abbot Guibert of Nogent* (New York: Harper & Row, 1970), p. 46.

47. D. Herlihy, "The Generation Gap in Medieval History," *Viator* 5 (1974): 360.

48. Quoted ibid., p. 361.

49. Honorius of Autun, "Elucidarium sive Dialogus," vol. 172, col. 1148.

50. M. Chibnall, ed. and trans., *The Ecclesiastical History of Ordericus Vitalis* (Oxford: Oxford University Press, 1972), 2.xiii.

51. See M. Chibnall, *The World of Ordericus Vitalis: Norman Monks and Norman Knights* (Woodbridge, England: Boydell Press, 1996), p. 8.

52. R. W. Southern, *Western Society and the Church in the Middle Ages* (Baltimore: Penguin Books, 1970), pp. 224–230, esp. p. 228.

53. See M. W. Labarge, *A Small Sound of the Trumpet: Women in Medieval Life* (Boston: Beacon Press, 1986), pp. 104–105.

54. J. M. Ferrante, "The Education of Women in the Middle Ages in Theory, Fact, and Fantasy," in *Beyond Their Sex: Learned Women of the European Past,* ed. P. H. Labalme (New York: New York University Press, 1980), pp. 22–24.

55. W. C. Jordan, *Women and Credit in Pre-Industrial and Developing Societies* (Philadelphia: University of Pennsylvania Press, 1993), p. 61.

56. See C. H. Lawrence, *Medieval Monasticism: Forms of Religious Life in Western Europe in the Middle Ages* (New York: Longman, 1988), pp. 221–223.

Suggested Reading

Students seeking further elaboration of the material of this chapter will find the titles by Amt, Boswell, Duby, Hanawalt, Jordan, Langdon, and Vauchez cited in the Notes especially valuable. For a broad treatment of frontier regions, see R. Bartlett, *The Making of Europe: Conquest, Colonization and Cultural Change, 950–1350* (1993). For the three orders as a model of medieval society, see, in addition to the title by Freedman and Duby (*The Chivalrous Society,* cited in the Notes), G. Constable, "The Three Orders," in *Three Studies in Medieval Religious and Social Thought* (1995).

For medieval slavery, serfdom, or the peasantry, see M. Bloch, "How Ancient Slavery Came to an End" and "Personal Liberty and Servitude in the Middle Ages, Particularly in France," in *Slavery and Serfdom in the Middle Ages: Selected Essays,* trans. W. R. Beer (1975); and P. Freedman, *The Origins of Peasant Servitude in Medieval Catalonia* (1991). There is a helpful discussion of these problems in the important work of W. C. Jordan, *From Servitude to Freedom: Manumission in the Sénonais in the Thirteenth Century* (1986). G. Duby, *The Early Growth of the European Economy* (1978), is a synthesis by a leading authority.

For the religion of the people, in addition to the works by Vauchez and Gurevich cited in the Notes, two studies are recommended: R. and C. Brooke, *Popular Religion in the Middle Ages* (1984), a readable synthesis; and T. J. Heffernan, *Sacred Biography: Saints and Their Biographers in the Middle Ages* (1992), a study of the goals, assumptions, and audiences of saints' lives.

For the origins and status of the nobility in the High Middle Ages, students are urged to see the studies by Bouchard, Freed, and Duby, cited in the Notes. In addition, see T. N. Bisson, ed., *Cultures of Power: Lordship, Status, and Process in Twelfth Century Europe* (1995), a collection of essays by leading scholars on many areas of northern Europe, including Flanders and Laon; and the articles in F. L. Cheyette, ed., *Lordship and Community in Medieval Europe: Selected Readings* (1968). C. A. Newman, *The Anglo-Norman Nobility in the Reign of Henry I* (1988), examines the economic, political, and religious network of noble relationships in twelfth-century England, while P. R. Coss, *Lordship, Knighthood and Locality: A Study in English Society, c. 1180–1280* (1991), also focuses on English social conditions. Social mobility among both aristocracy and peasantry is discussed in T. Evergates, *Feudal Society in the Bailliage of Troyes Under the Counts of Champagne, 1152–1284* (1976). K. F. Bosl, "Kingdom and Principality in Twelfth-Century France," and the same author's "'Noble Unfreedom': The Rise of the Ministerials in Germany," in T. Reuter, ed., *The Medieval Nobility: Studies on the Ruling Classes of France and Germany from the Sixth to the Twelfth Century* (1978), are also useful. The career of the man described by contemporaries as "the greatest of knights" is celebrated in G. Duby, *William Marshal: The Flowering of Chivalry,* trans. R. Howard (1985), a rags-to-riches story. For noblewomen, see T. Evergates, *Aristocratic Women in Medieval France* (1999). Both S. C. Rowell, *Lithuania Ascending: A Pagan Empire Within East Central Europe, 1295–1345* (1994), and Pál Engel, *The Realm of St. Stephen: A History of Medieval Hungary, 895–1526* (2001), have valuable material on the nobility in eastern Europe.

There is no dearth of good material on the monks in medieval society. The titles listed in the Suggested Reading for Chapter 7 represent a good starting point for study. B. D. Hill's articles "Benedictines" and "Cistercian Order," in *Dictionary of the Middle Ages,* ed. J. R. Strayer, vols. 2 and 3 (1982 and 1983), provide broad surveys of the premier monastic orders and contain useful bibliographies. Students seeking cross-cultural material comparing Christian and Buddhist monasticism should find W. M. Johnston, ed., *Encyclopedia of Monasticism,* 2 vols. (2000), useful. B. Harvey, *Living and Dying in England: The Monastic Experience, 1100–1540* (1993), has valuable material on monastic diet, clothing, routine, sickness, and death. L. J. Lekai, *The Cistercians: Ideals and Reality* (1977), synthesizes research on the white monks and carries their story down to the twentieth century. P. D. Johnson, *Prayer, Patronage, and Power: The Abbey of La Trinité, Vendome, 1032–1187* (1981), examines one important French monastery in its social environment; this book is a valuable contribution to medieval local history. For a sound study of a uniquely English monastic order, see B. Golding, *Gilbert of Sempringham and the*

Gilbertine Order, c. 1130–1300 (1995). J. Burton, *Monastic and Religious Orders in Britain, 1000–1300* (1995), treats many often neglected issues. B. P. McGuire, *Friendship and Community: The Monastic Experience, 350–1250* (1988), explores monastic friendships within the context of religious communities. The best study of medieval English Cistercian architecture is P. Fergusson, *Architecture of Solitude: Cistercian Abbeys in Twelfth Century England* (1984). For the architecture of England's most famous monastic ruins, see the splendidly illustrated work by P. Fergusson and S. Harrison, *Rievaulx Abbey: Community, Architecture, Memory* (1999).

For women and children, in addition to the titles by Labarge and Boswell cited in the Notes, see B. A. Hanawalt, *Growing Up in Medieval London: The Experience of Childhood in History* (1993), which has exciting material on class and gender, apprenticeship, and the culture of matrimony; D. Herlihy, *Medieval Households* (1985), which treats marriage patterns, family size, sexual relations, and emotional life; and C. Brooke, *The Medieval Idea of Marriage* (1991), which draws on a wide variety of evidence to answer his question, "What is marriage and what sets it apart from other human relationships?" J. M. Bennett, *Women in the Medieval English Countryside* (1987), is an important and pioneering study of women in rural, preindustrial society. Also useful are J. McNamara and S. F. Wemple, "Sanctity and Power: The Dual Pursuit of Medieval Women," in *Becoming Visible: Women in European History,* ed. R. Bridenthal and C. Koonz (1987); B. Hanawalt, ed., *Women and Work in Preindustrial Europe* (1986), which describes the activities of women as alewives, midwives, businesswomen, nurses, and servants; and D. Baker, ed., *Medieval Women* (1978), which contains articles on many facets of women's history. For children, see N. Orme, *Medieval Children* (2001).

For further treatment of nuns, see J. K. McNamara, *Sisters in Arms* (1996), a broad survey tracing the lives of religious women from the mothers of the Egyptian desert to the twentieth century; and M. Schmitt and L. Kulzer, eds., *Medieval Women Monastics: Wisdom's Wellsprings* (1996), which focuses on women mystics. In addition to the title by Lekai cited earlier, see B. Newman, *Sister of Wisdom: St. Hildegard's Theology of the Feminine* (1987), a learned and lucidly written study; S. Elkins, *Holy Women in Twelfth-Century England* (1985); C. Bynum, *Jesus as Mother: Studies in the Spirituality of the High Middle Ages* (1984), which contains valuable articles on facets of women's religious history and an excellent contrast of the differing spirituality of monks and nuns; and C. Bynum, *Holy Feast and Holy Fast* (1987), which treats the significance of food for nuns and others in medieval society. For health and medical care, B. Rowland, *Medieval Woman's Guide to Health* (1981), makes very interesting reading.

Listening to the Past

The Pilgrim's Guide to Santiago de Compostela

The practice of making pilgrimages to the shrines of holy persons antedates Christianity, and pilgrimages are common in other religions. A pilgrimage to Mecca, for example, is obligatory for all Muslims (see page 222). A Christian shrine contained a saint's body or objects that had been in physical contact with the saint; thus believers perceived shrines as places where Heaven and earth met. A visit to a shrine and veneration of the saint's relics, Christians believed, would lead to the saint's intercession with God. After Jerusalem and Rome, the shrine of Saint James (Sant'Iago in Spanish) at Compostela in Spain became the most famous in the Christian world.

The apostle James, a fisherman like his brother, the apostle John (Matthew 4:21), is said to have carried Christianity to Spain, then returned to Palestine, where he was beheaded, the first apostle martyred. Somehow James's body was taken back to Compostela, where miracles led to the construction of a great shrine-cathedral at the site of his tomb. In the 1300s, using James's charisma to advance political goals, Catholic propagandists pushed the legend that James had begun the expulsion of Muslims from Spain. This claim was patently false because Muslims arrived on the Iberian Peninsula seven centuries after James's death.

Santiago de Compostela was situated in the kingdom of Navarre, a small polity in the Pyrenees Mountains between (French) Gascony and (Spanish) León. Navarre had been part of the Spanish march (frontier) set up by Charlemagne. Once at the shrine, pilgrims were expected to make as large a contribution as their means allowed, lest the saint be offended and retaliate with some sort of affliction. Pilgrims' donations financed the superb Romanesque sculpture at Santiago. Public demand for information led to advertising literature, such as The Pilgrim's Guide *excerpted here.*

The Names of the Lands and the Characteristics of the Peoples on the Road to Santiago

. . . And also in the Basque country, there is on the way of Saint James a most excellent mountain which is called the Port de Cize, either because the gateway to Spain is there, or because it is by this mountain that necessary things are transported from one country to the other. . . .

In truth, at the summit of this mountain is a place which is called the Cross of Charlemagne because it is here that with axes and picks and spades and other implements Charlemagne, going to Spain with his armies, once made a road, and he raised on it the sign of the cross of the Lord. And then, kneeling facing Galicia, he poured out his prayer to God and Saint James. On account of this, the pilgrims, bending the knee towards the land of Saint James, are accustomed to pray, and each one plants his own standard of the cross of the Lord. About a thousand crosses are to be found there. That is why that place is considered the first station of prayer to Saint James. . . .

Near this mountain, that is, toward the north, is a valley called Valcarlos, in which Charlemagne was encamped with his armies while the warriors were being killed at Roncesvalles. Indeed, through there pass many pilgrims travelling to Santiago who do not wish to climb the mountain.

Finally in truth, on the way down from that same mountain, are found a hospice and the church which contains the rock that Roland, that most powerful hero, split through the middle from top to bottom with a triple blow of his sword. Then comes Roncesvalles, the very place where the great battle was once fought in which King Marsile, and Roland and Oliver and other warriors died, together with forty thousand Christians and Saracens.

After this valley is found the land of Navarre, which abounds in bread and wine, milk and cattle. The Navarrese and Basques are held to be exactly alike in their food, their clothing and their language, but the Basques are held to be of whiter complexion than the Navarrese. The Navarrese wear short black garments extending just down to the knee, like the Scots, and they wear sandals which they call *lavarcas* made of raw hide with the hair on and are bound around the foot with thongs, covering only the soles of the feet and leaving the upper foot bare. In truth, they wear black woollen hooded and fringed capes, reaching to their elbows, which they call *saias*. These people, in truth, are repulsively dressed, and they eat and drink repulsively. For in fact all those who dwell in the household of a Navarrese, servant as well as master, maid as well as mistress, are accustomed to eat all their food mixed together from one pot, not with spoons but with their own hands, and they drink with one cup. If you saw them eat you would think them dogs or pigs. If you heard them speak, you would be reminded of the barking of dogs. For their speech is utterly barbarous. . . .

This is a barbarous race unlike all other races in customs and in character, full of malice, swarthy in color, evil of face, depraved, perverse, perfidious, empty of faith and corrupt, libidinous, drunken, experienced in all violence, ferocious and wild, dishonest and reprobate, impious and harsh, cruel and contentious, unversed in anything good, well-trained in all vices and iniquities, like the Geats and Saracens in malice. . . .

However, they are considered good on the battlefield, bad at assaulting fortresses, regular in giving tithes, accustomed to making offerings for altars. For, each day, when the Navarrese goes to church, he makes God an offering of bread or wine or wheat or some other substance. . . .

Then comes Galicia . . . ; this is wooded and has rivers and is well-provided with meadows and excellent orchards, with equally good fruits and very clear springs; there are few cities, towns or cornfields. It is short of wheaten bread and wine, bountiful in rye bread and cider, well-stocked with cattle and horses, milk and honey, ocean fish both gigantic and small, and wealthy in gold, silver, fabrics, and furs of forest animals and other riches, as well as Saracen treasures. The Galicians, in truth, more than all the other uncultivated Spanish peoples, are those who most closely resemble our French race by their manners, but they are alleged to be irascible and very litigious. . . .

The master stonemasons who first constructed the basilica of the blessed James were called Master Bernard the Elder, a marvellous master, and Robert, who, with about fifty other stonemasons, worked there actively when the most faithful lord Wicart and the lord canon of the

Monasteries in Cluny, Vézelay, Saint-Gilles, and Moissac served as inns for pilgrims.

chapter, Segeredo, and the lord abbot Gundesindo were in office. . . .

The church, however, was begun in the year 1116 of the Spanish era [1078 A.D.]. . . .

From the time when it was begun up to the present day, this church is renewed by the light of the miracles of the blessed James. In it, indeed, health is given to the sick, sight restored to the blind, the tongue of the mute is loosened, hearing is given to the deaf, soundness of limb is granted to cripples, the possessed are delivered, and what is more, the prayers of the faithful are heard, their vows are accepted, the bonds of sin are broken, heaven is opened to those who knock, consolation is given to the grieving, and all the people of foreign nations, flocking from all parts of the world, come together here in crowds bearing with them gifts of praise to the Lord.

Questions for Analysis

1. What historical significance did the region of Santiago de Compostela have?

2. How would you evaluate the *Guide*'s opinion of the people of Navarre?

3. Pilgrimages were precursors of modern tourism. Consider the economic effects of medieval pilgrimages.

Source: The Pilgrim's Guide to Santiago de Compostela, critical edition and annotated translation by Paula Gerson, Jeanne Krochalis, Annie Shaver-Crandell, and Alison Stones. Copyright © 1997. Reprinted by permission of the authors. Data for map from Jonathan Sumption, *Pilgrimage: An Image of Medieval Religion* (Totowa, N.J.: Rowman and Littlefield, 1975).

Because it took Louis VII of France thirty years and three wives to sire a son, the chroniclers joyfully hailed Philip Augustus's birth to Adèle of Champagne in 1165 as Dieudonné (given by God). *(© Bibliothèque Sainte-Geneviève, Paris)*

chapter

11

The Creativity and Vitality of the High Middle Ages

*T*he High Middle Ages witnessed some of the most remarkable achievements in the entire history of Western society. Europeans displayed tremendous creativity and vitality in many facets of culture. Political rulers tried to establish contact with all their peoples, developed new legal and financial institutions, and slowly consolidated power in the hands of the monarchy. The kings of France and England succeeded in laying the foundations of modern national states. The German emperors achieved a reduction of violence and disorder through alliances with the princes. The European economy underwent a remarkable recovery, as evidenced by the growth and development of towns and the revival of long-distance trade. Some towns and urbanized areas saw the growth of heretical movements. The university, a uniquely Western contribution to civilization and a superb expression of medieval creativity, came into being. The Gothic cathedral manifested medieval people's deep Christian faith and their appreciation for the worlds of nature, humanity, and God.

- How did medieval rulers in England, France, and Germany work to solve their problems of government, thereby laying the foundations of the modern state?

- How did medieval towns originate, and how do they reveal the beginnings of radical change in medieval society?

- Why did towns become the center of religious heresy, and what was the church's response?

- How did universities evolve, and what needs of medieval society did they serve?

- What do the Gothic cathedral and troubadour poetry reveal about the ideals, attitudes, and interests of medieval people?

This chapter will focus on these questions.

Medieval Origins of the Modern State

Rome's great legacy to Western civilization had been the concepts of the state and the law, but for almost five hundred years after the disintegration of the Roman Empire in the West, the state as a reality did not exist. Political authority was completely decentralized. Power was spread among many lords, who gave their localities such protection and security as their strength allowed. The fiefdoms, kingdoms, and territories that covered the continent of early medieval Europe did not have the characteristics or provide the services of a modern state. They did not have jurisdiction over many people, and their laws affected a relative few. There existed many frequently overlapping layers of authority—earls, counts, barons, knights—between a king and the ordinary people.

In these circumstances, medieval rulers had common goals. The rulers of England, France, and Germany wanted to strengthen and extend royal authority within their territories. They wanted to establish an effective means of communication with all peoples, in order to increase public order. They wanted more revenue and efficient bureaucracies. The solutions they found to these problems laid the foundations for modern national states.

The modern state is an organized territory with definite geographical boundaries that are recognized by other states. It has a body of law and institutions of government. The modern national state counts on the loyalty of its citizens, or at least of a majority of them. In return, it provides order so that citizens can go about their daily work and other activities. It protects its citizens in their persons and property. The state tries to prevent violence and to apprehend and punish those who commit it. It supplies a currency or medium of exchange that permits financial and commercial transactions. The state conducts relations with foreign governments. In order to accomplish these minimal functions, the state must have officials, bureaucracies, laws, courts of law, soldiers, information, and money. By the twelfth century, medieval kingdoms and some lesser lordships possessed these attributes, at least to the extent that most modern states have them.[1]

Unification and Communication

Political developments in England, France, and Germany provide good examples of the beginnings of the national state in the High Middle Ages. These developments took a different course in southern Europe. In Italy independent city-states evolved. In Spain the reconquest of the peninsula, which was under Muslim control, preoccupied the rulers of the Christian kingdoms. Spain and Italy will be discussed in Chapter 13. England, France, and Germany are discussed here.

England

Under the pressure of the Danish (or Viking) invasions of the ninth and tenth centuries, the seven kingdoms of Anglo-Saxon England united under one king (see page 266). At the same time, England was divided into local units called "shires," or counties, each under the jurisdiction of a sheriff appointed by the king. The Danish king Canute (r. 1016–1035) and his successor, Edward the Confessor (r. 1042–1066), exercised broader authority than any contemporary ruler on the continent. All the English *thegns,* or local chieftains, recognized the central authority of the kingship. The kingdom of England, therefore, had a political head start on the rest of Europe.

When Edward the Confessor died, his cousin Duke William of Normandy—known in English history as William the Conqueror—claimed the English throne and in 1066 defeated the Anglo-Saxon claimant on the battlefield of Hastings. Pre-Conquest Normandy, with clearly defined frontiers marked by rivers, with uniform legal customs, and with strong ducal government, possessed a political coherence and autonomy "unmatched elsewhere in feudal Europe."[2] Normandy already showed attributes of a modern state. As William subdued the rest of England, he distributed lands to his Norman followers and assigned specific military quotas to each estate. He also required all feudal lords to swear an oath of allegiance to him as king.

William the Conqueror (r. 1066–1087) preserved the Anglo-Saxon institution of sheriffs representing the king at the local level but replaced Anglo-Saxon sheriffs with Normans. A sheriff had heavy duties. He maintained order in the shire. He caught criminals and had them tried in the hundred court, over which his deputy, the undersheriff, presided. He collected taxes and, when the king ordered him to do so, raised an army of foot soldiers. For all his efforts, the sheriff received no pay. This system, whereby unpaid officials governed the county, served as the basic pattern of English local government for many centuries. It cost the Crown nothing, but it restricted opportunities for public service to the well-to-do.

William also retained another Anglo-Saxon device, the *writ.* This brief administrative order, written in the vernacular (Anglo-Saxon) by a government clerk, was the means by which the central government communicated with people at the local level.

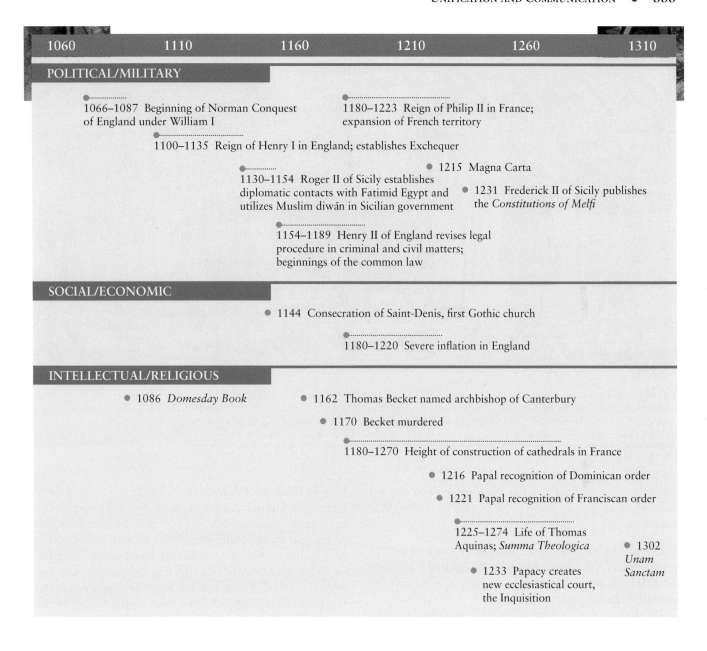

| 1060 | 1110 | 1160 | 1210 | 1260 | 1310 |

POLITICAL/MILITARY

1066–1087 Beginning of Norman Conquest of England under William I

1100–1135 Reign of Henry I in England; establishes Exchequer

1130–1154 Roger II of Sicily establishes diplomatic contacts with Fatimid Egypt and utilizes Muslim diwān in Sicilian government

1154–1189 Henry II of England revises legal procedure in criminal and civil matters; beginnings of the common law

1180–1223 Reign of Philip II in France; expansion of French territory

1215 Magna Carta

1231 Frederick II of Sicily publishes the *Constitutions of Melfi*

SOCIAL/ECONOMIC

1144 Consecration of Saint-Denis, first Gothic church

1180–1220 Severe inflation in England

INTELLECTUAL/RELIGIOUS

1086 *Domesday Book*

1162 Thomas Becket named archbishop of Canterbury

1170 Becket murdered

1180–1270 Height of construction of cathedrals in France

1216 Papal recognition of Dominican order

1221 Papal recognition of Franciscan order

1225–1274 Life of Thomas Aquinas; *Summa Theologica*

1233 Papacy creates new ecclesiastical court, the Inquisition

1302 *Unam Sanctam*

The Conqueror introduced into England a major innovation, the Norman inquest. At his Christmas court in 1085, William discussed the state of the kingdom with his vassals and decided to conduct a systematic investigation of the entire country. The survey was to be made by means of *inquests,* or general inquiries, held throughout England. William wanted to determine how much wealth there was in his new kingdom, who held what land, and what land had been disputed among his vassals since the Conquest of 1066. Groups of royal officials were sent to every part of the country. In every village and farm, the priest and six local people were put under oath to answer the questions of the king's commissioners truthfully. In the words of a contemporary chronicler:

He sent his men over all England into every shire and had them find out how many hundred hides there were in the shire [a hide was a measure of land large enough to support one family], or what land and cattle the king himself had, or what dues he ought to have in twelve months from the shire. Also . . . what or how much everybody had who was occupying land in England, in land or cattle, and how much money it was worth. So very narrowly did he have it investigated, that there was no single hide nor yard of land, nor indeed . . .

The Bayeux Tapestry Measuring 231 feet by 19½ inches, the Bayeux Tapestry gives a narrative description of the events surrounding the Norman Conquest of England. The tapestry provides an important historical source for the clothing, armor, and lifestyles of the Norman and Anglo-Saxon warrior class. *(Tapisserie de Bayeux et avec autorisation spéciale de la Ville de Bayeux)*

one ox nor one cow nor one pig was there left out, and not put down in his record: and all these records were brought to him afterwards.[3]

The resulting record, called **Domesday Book** from the Anglo-Saxon word *doom* meaning "judgment," still survives. It is an invaluable source of social and economic information about medieval England.

The Conqueror's scribes compiled *Domesday Book* in less than a year. It provided William and his descendants with information vital for the exploitation and government of the country. Knowing the amount of wealth every area possessed, the king could tax accordingly. Knowing the amount of land his vassals had, he could allot knight service fairly. The inclusion of material covering England helped English kings to regard their country as one unit.

In 1128 the Conqueror's granddaughter Matilda was married to Geoffrey of Anjou. Their son, who became Henry II of England and inaugurated the Angevin (from Anjou, his father's county) dynasty, inherited the French provinces of Normandy, Anjou, Maine, and Touraine in northwestern France. When Henry married the great heiress Eleanor of Aquitaine in 1152, he claimed lordships over Aquitaine, Poitou, and Gascony in southwestern France (see Map 11.1). Each of these provinces had a separate administration made up of men native to the region; the provinces constituted a loose conglomeration of client territories linked together by dynastic law and personal oaths. There was no unity among them.[4] But the histories of England and France in the High Middle Ages were closely intertwined, leading to disputes and conflicts down to the fifteenth century.

France

In the early twelfth century, France consisted of a number of virtually independent provinces. Each was governed by its local ruler; each had its own laws and customs, coinage, and dialect. Unlike the king of England, the king of France had jurisdiction over a very small area. Chroniclers called King Louis VI (r. 1108–1137) *roi de Saint-Denis,* king of Saint-Denis, because the territory he controlled was limited to Paris and the Saint-Denis area surrounding the city (see Map 11.1). This region, called the *Île-de-France,* or royal domain, became the nucleus of

MAP 11.1 **The Growth of the Kingdom of France** Some scholars believe that Philip II received the title "Augustus" (from a Latin word meaning "to increase") because he vastly expanded the territories of the kingdom of France.

the French state. The clear goal of the medieval French king was to increase the royal domain and extend his authority.

The term *Saint-Denis* had political and religious charisma, which the Crown exploited. Following the precedent of the Frankish chieftain Clovis (see page 210), Louis VI and his Capetian successors supported and identified with the cult of Saint Denis, a deeply revered saint whom the French believed protected the country from danger. Under Saint Denis's banner, the *oriflamme,* French kings fought their battles and claimed their victories. The oriflamme rested in the abbey of Saint-Denis, which served as the burial place of the French kings. The Capetian kings identified themselves with the cult of Saint Denis in order to tap popular devotion to him and tie that devotion and loyalty to the monarchy.[5]

The work of unifying France began under Louis VI's grandson Philip II (r. 1180–1223). Rigord, Philip's biographer, gave him the title "Augustus" (from a Latin word meaning "to increase") because he vastly enlarged

the territory of the kingdom of France. By defeating a baronial plot against the Crown, Philip Augustus acquired the northern counties of Artois and Vermandois. When King John of England, who was Philip's vassal for the rich province of Normandy, defaulted on his feudal obligation to come to the French court, Philip declared Normandy forfeit to the French crown. He enforced his declaration militarily, and in 1204 Normandy fell to the French. Within two years Philip also gained the farmlands of Maine, Touraine, and Anjou. By the end of his reign Philip was effectively master of northern France.

In the thirteenth century, Philip Augustus's descendants acquired important holdings in the south. Louis VIII (r. 1223–1226) added the county of Poitou to the kingdom of France by war. Louis IX (r. 1226–1270) gained a vital interest in the Mediterranean province of Provence through his marriage to Margaret of Provence. Louis's son Philip III (r. 1270–1285) secured Languedoc through inheritance. By the end of the thirteenth century, most of the provinces of modern France had been added to the royal domain through diplomacy, marriage, war, and inheritance. The king of France was stronger than any group of nobles who might try to challenge his authority.

Philip Augustus devised a method of governing the provinces and providing for communication between the central government in Paris and local communities. Philip decided that each province would retain its own institutions and laws. But royal agents, called **baillis** in the north and **seneschals** in the south, were sent from Paris into the provinces as the king's official representatives with authority to act for him. Often middle-class lawyers, these men possessed full judicial, financial, and military jurisdiction in their districts. The baillis and seneschals were appointed by, paid by, and responsible to the king. Unlike the English sheriffs, they were never natives of the provinces to which they were assigned, and they could not own land there. This policy reflected the fundamental principle of French administration that royal interests superseded local interests.

Germany

In the High Middle Ages, the political and institutional history of Germany evolved in a course different from that of France and England. Those western countries witnessed the beginnings of the nation-state, while Germany experienced the development of *territorial lordship.* In the period from about 1050 to about 1400 and down to 1871, German history is regional history. Why did Germany move in the direction of multiple independent principalities? What were the relations between the princes and the German monarchy?

As large entities, the German duchies such as Bavaria, Saxony, Swabia, Thuringia, and Lotharingia emerged from the East Frankish kingdom (see Chapter 8) in the tenth century as defensive units against Magyar and Slavic invaders. The four great archbishoprics—Mainz, Trier, Cologne, and Salzburg—trace their origins to Charlemagne's reign, while Hamburg-Bremen was established for missionary work in Scandinavia, and Magdeburg was set up by Otto I for the Christianization of the Slavs. Although the authority of the imperial crown increased under Otto I, his empire was too vast geographically, and his resources were too limited, to be governable from one center. To hold it together, a kind of confederacy (a weak union of strong states, or principalities) in which the emperor shared power with the princes, dukes, archbishops, margraves, counts, and bishops developed. The investiture controversy between the German emperor and the Roman papacy solidified power in the hands of the territorial lords (see page 276).

Between 1000 and 1300, regionally based princely authority emerged in the duchies as dynasties that had a strong sense of local identity and traced their descent through the paternal line. Newly constructed stone castles bearing the family name symbolized the dynasty's power and served as the center of its lands and rights—that is, its *Landesherrschaft,* or territorial lordship.

The enormous expansion of the German economy in the twelfth and thirteenth centuries supplied the financial basis for the wealth and power of the princes as landowners. The exploitation of vast tracts of forestland, the colonization and settlement of land east of the Elbe River, and the establishment of new markets, towns, manors, and monasteries brought local princes considerable wealth with which to maintain their lordships. The Wittelsbach dynasty in the duchy of Bavaria is a typical example of territorial lordship.[6]

Through most of the first half of the twelfth century, civil war wracked Germany. When Conrad III died in 1152, the resulting anarchy was so terrible that the *electors*—the seven princes responsible for choosing the emperor—decided that the only alternative to continued chaos was the selection of a strong ruler. They chose Frederick Barbarossa of the house of Hohenstaufen.

Frederick Barbarossa (r. 1152–1190) tried valiantly to bring peace to the empire, using his family duchy of Swabia in southwestern Germany as a power base (see Map 11.2). Just as William the Conqueror had done, Frederick required all vassals in Swabia to take an oath of allegiance to him as emperor, no matter who their immediate lord might be. He appointed ministerials (see page 312) to exercise the full imperial authority over the administrative districts of Swabia. Ministerials linked the emperor and local communities.

To promote peace and increase order, the monarchy itself supported princely territorial power and jurisdiction. From Carolingian times, regional wars and feuds among lords represented a traditional feature of German aristocratic society. In 1158 Frederick Barbarossa forbade private warfare and ordered severe penalties for violations of the peace. But imperial orders alone did not bring peace. In 1179 he announced, "Out of duty to the imperial office, we are held of necessity and by the state of the provinces to ordain peace throughout our Empire and to confirm the ordinance by our authority." His solution was **Landfrieden,** sworn peace associations with the princes of various regions. In 1179 Landfrieden were issued for Franconia, and in 1223 Landfrieden were reissued for Saxony. They had already been established in the dioceses of Cologne and Bamberg. These peace associations had the judicial authority to punish breaches of the

MAP 11.2 The Holy Roman Empire, ca 1200 Frederick Barbarossa tried to use the feudal bond to tie the different provinces to the imperial monarchy.

peace and criminals. Penalties for serious crimes, such as incendiary conduct during a conflict, increased from maiming to execution. German kings traveled continually and extensively, and the royal court could mete out justice anywhere. The presence of the royal court in an area temporarily superseded local jurisdiction, but in practice legal jurisdiction in the German Empire "meant the courts of counts, dukes, margraves, bishops and ecclesiastical advocates for serious cases and seigneurial or manorial courts for lesser misdemeanors." German monarchs regarded the local authority of the princes as traditional, legitimate, and essentially to the Crown's own benefit. As the emperor Frederick II put it in 1232,

The sublime throne of our Empire is exalted, and the governing powers of the Empire we dispose in full justice and peace, when we look ahead with due provisions for the rights of our princes and magnates in whom, as the head rests upon honorable limbs, our imperial rule is invigorated and strengthened, for the edifice of Caesar's magnitude so far directs and elevates those upon whose shoulders it is founded and carried.[7]

In the eleventh and twelfth centuries, the northern Italian cities had grown rich on trade. Frederick Barbarossa, considering himself heir to the traditions of Charlemagne and having resumed the title "Holy Roman emperor" (see page 276), surrounded himself with men trained in Roman law. He used Roman law to justify his assertion of imperial rights over the towns of northern Italy. Those towns' wealth did not escape the emperor's notice. Between 1154 and 1188, Frederick made six expeditions into Italy. His scorched-earth policy was successful at first, making for significant conquests in the north. The brutality of his methods, however, provoked revolts, and the Italian cities formed an alliance with the papacy. In 1176 Frederick suffered a defeat at Legnano (see Map 11.2). This battle marked the first time a feudal cavalry of armed knights was decisively defeated by bourgeois infantrymen. Frederick was forced to recognize the municipal autonomy of the northern Italian cities. Germany and Italy remained separate and followed separate courses of development.

Finance

As medieval rulers expanded territories and extended authority, they required more officials, larger armies, and more money with which to pay for them.

England

In England William the Conqueror's son Henry I (r. 1100–1135) established a bureau of finance called the **Exchequer** (for the checkered cloth at which his officials collected and audited royal accounts). Henry's income came from a variety of sources: from taxes paid by peasants living on the king's estates; from the *Danegeld,* an old tax originally levied to pay tribute to the Danes; from the *dona,* an annual gift from the church; from money paid to the Crown for settling disputes; and from fines paid by people found guilty of crimes. Henry also received income because of his position as feudal lord. If, for example, one of his vassals died and the son wished to inherit the father's properties, the heir had to pay Henry a tax called **relief.** From the knights Henry took **scutage,** money paid in lieu of the performance of military service. With the scutage collected, Henry could hire mercenary troops. The sheriff in each county was responsible for collecting all these sums and paying them twice a year to the king's Exchequer. Henry, like other medieval kings, made no distinction between his private income and state revenues.

An accurate record of expenditures and income is needed to ensure a state's solvency. Henry assigned a few of the barons and bishops at his court to keep careful records of the monies paid into and out of the royal treasury. These financial officials, called "barons of the

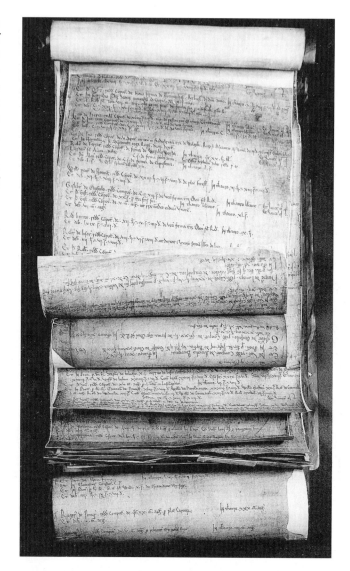

The Pipe Rolls Twice yearly English medieval sheriffs appeared before the Barons of the Exchequer to account for the monies they had collected from the royal estates and from fines for civil and criminal offenses. Clerks recorded these revenues and royal expenditures on the pipe rolls, whose name derives from the pipelike form of the rolled parchments. A roll exists for 1129–1130, then continuously from 1156 to 1832, representing the largest series of English public records. *(Crown copyright material in the Public Record Office is reproduced by permission of the Controller of the Britannic Majesty's Stationery Office [E40 1/1565])*

Exchequer," gradually developed a professional organization with its own rules, procedures, and esprit de corps. The Exchequer, which by 1170 sat at Westminster, became the first institution of the governmental bureaucracy of England.

France

The development of royal financial agencies in most continental countries lagged behind the English Exchequer. Twelfth-century French rulers derived their income from their royal estates in the Île-de-France. As Philip Augustus and his successors added provinces to the royal domain, the need for money became increasingly acute. Philip made the baillis and seneschals responsible for collecting taxes in their districts. This income came primarily from fines and confiscations imposed by the courts. Three times a year the baillis and seneschals reported to the king's court with the money they had collected.

In the thirteenth century, French rulers acquired some income from the church and some from people living in the towns. Townspeople paid **tallage** or the **taille**—a tax arbitrarily laid by the king. In all parts of the country, feudal vassals owed military service to the king when he called for it. Louis IX converted this military obligation into a cash payment, called "host tallage," and thus increased his revenues. Moreover, pervasive anti-Semitism allowed Philip Augustus, Louis VIII, and Louis IX to tax their Jewish subjects mercilessly.

Medieval people believed that a good king lived on the income of his own land and taxed only in time of a grave emergency—that is, a just war. Because the church, and not the state, performed what we call social services, such as education and care of the sick, the aged, and orphaned children, there was no ordinary need for the government to tax. Taxation meant war financing. The French monarchy could not continually justify taxing the people on the grounds of the needs of war. Thus the French kings were slow to develop an efficient bureau of finance. French provincial laws and institutions—in contrast to England's early unification—also retarded the growth of a central financial agency. Not until the fourteenth century, as a result of the Hundred Years' War, did a state financial bureau emerge—the Chamber of Accounts.

Sicily and the German Empire

The one secular government other than England that developed a financial bureaucracy was the kingdom of Sicily. Sicily provides a good example of how strong government could be built on a feudal base by determined rulers. The Sicilian administration came to have a significant Muslim component.

Like England, Sicily had come under Norman domination. Between 1061 and 1091, a bold Norman knight, Roger de Hauteville, with a small band of mercenaries had defeated the Muslims and Greeks who controlled the island. Roger then governed a heterogeneous population of Sicilians, Italians, Greeks, Jews, Arabs, and Normans. Like William the Conqueror in England, Roger introduced Norman institutions in Sicily and made them work as a means of government. Roger distributed scattered fiefs to his followers so no vassal would have a centralized power base. He took an inquest of royal property and rights and forbade private warfare. To these Norman practices, Roger fused Arabic and Greek governmental devices. For example, he retained the Kalbid Muslims' (previous rulers over Sicily) main financial agency, the diwān, a sophisticated bureau for record keeping.

Under his son and heir, Count Roger II (r. 1130–1154), the process of state building continued. Roger II developed diplomatic ties with the Fatimid rulers of Egypt, exchanging letters, gifts, and embassies with the caliph al-Hafid. Through this Fatimid connection, Muslim administrative procedures came to predominate at Palermo, Sicily's capital. Because Sicilians and Muslims usually could not read each other's languages, the chancery kept official documents in Greek, Latin, and Arabic. Roger imported diwāni script used at Cairo; following Muslim custom, Sicilian royal documents opened with the *basmala,* or pious invocation—for example, "the King Roger II . . . may God perpetuate his rule. . . ."[8] Roger also adopted the Muslim custom of using eunuch slaves as administrators in the diwān.[9]

The term *diwān* refers to the entire bureaucratic machinery of Norman Sicily; it was divided into several divisions. It supervised the royal estates in Sicily, collected revenues from rustics living on feudal lands, had jurisdiction over vacant ecclesiastical properties (abbeys and dioceses), preserved records of grants of land and the sales of royal properties, and registered all income to the treasury.[10] The diwān also managed the state monopoly of the sale of salt and lumber. With revenues derived from those products, Roger hired mercenaries. He encouraged appeals from local courts to his court, because such appeals implied respect for the royal court.

Arabic influence in Sicily is also evident in the public presentation, or image, of the king. Following Islamic custom, Roger II became less visible, deliberately secluding himself in his palace at Palermo. Then on special occasions, he rode out in elegant finery surrounded by retinues of guards, household retainers, and "lords of the diwān,"[11] thereby ceremonially displaying himself. Some Christian critics considered this practice evidence of the tyranny of the Norman kings, but an Arabic courtier praised Roger II because "he followed the way of Muslim rulers. . . . He broke with the custom of the Franks who are not acquainted with such things. . . . He treated the Muslims

The Chancellery at Palermo Reflecting the fact that Vandals, Ostrogoths, Greeks, Muslims, and Normans had left their imprint on Sicily, the imperial court bureaucracy kept official records in Greek, Arabic, and Latin, as this manuscript illustration shows. *(Burgerbibliothek Bern Cod. 120 II, fol. 101r)*

with respect, took them as his companions, and kept the Franks off (protected) them."[12] In the multicultural society of medieval Sicily, Muslims and Greeks, as well as Normans, staffed the army, the judiciary, and the diwān.

Frederick II (r. 1212–1250), grandson of Roger II of Sicily through his mother and grandson of Frederick Barbarossa of Germany through his father, was crowned king of the Germans at Aachen (1216) and Holy Roman emperor at Rome (1220). He concentrated his attention on Sicily. Frederick banned private warfare and placed all castles and towers under royal administration. He also replaced town officials with royal governors. In 1231 he published the *Constitutions of Melfi*, a collection of laws that vastly enhanced royal authority. Both feudal and ecclesiastical courts were subordinated to the king's courts. Each year royal judges visited all parts of the kingdom, and the supreme court at Capua heard appeals from all lesser courts. Thus churchmen accused of crimes were tried in the royal courts. Royal control of the nobility, of the towns, and of the judicial system added up to great centralization, which required a professional bureaucracy and sound state financing.

In 1224 Frederick founded the University of Naples to train officials for his bureaucracy. University-educated administrators and lawyers emphasized the stiff principles of Roman law, such as the maxim of the Justinian *Code* that "what pleases the prince has the force of law." Frederick's financial experts regulated agriculture, public works, even business. His customs service supervised all imports and exports, collecting taxes for the Crown on all products and increasing royal revenues. Frederick strictly regulated currency and forbade the export of gold and silver bullion.

Finally, Frederick secured the tacit consent of his people to regular taxation. This was a noteworthy achievement when most people believed that taxes should be levied only in time of grave emergency. Frederick defined emergency broadly. For much of his reign he was involved in a bitter dispute with the papacy. Churchmen hardly considered the emperor's wars with the popes as just, but Frederick's position was so strong that he could ignore criticism and levy taxes. Moreover, he continued the use of Muslim institutions such as the diwān, and he tried to administer justice fairly to all his subjects, declaring, "We cannot in the least permit Jews and Saracens (Muslims) to be defrauded of the power of our protection and to be deprived of all other help, just because the difference of their religious practices makes them hateful to Chris-

Palatine Chapel at Palermo (1132–1140) Muslim craftsmen from Egypt painted the wooden ceiling of the royal chapel for King Roger of Sicily. This section shows the diverse peoples—Jews, Christians, Muslims—who lived in Palermo. Other genre scenes of scarf dancers, banquets, musicians, and drinkers reflect a Fatimid school, perhaps at Cairo, not the biblical motifs usual in a Christian church. *(Burgerbibliothek Bern Cod. 120 II, fol. 98r)*

visited the empire, in the expectation of securing German support for his Italian policy, he made sweeping concessions to the princes, bishops, duchies, and free cities. In 1220, for example, he exempted German churchmen from taxation and from the jurisdiction of imperial authorities. In 1231 he gave lay princes the same exemptions and even threw in the right to coin money. Frederick gave away so much that imperial authority was seriously weakened. In the later Middle Ages, lay and ecclesiastical princes held sway in the Holy Roman Empire.

Law and Justice

Throughout Europe the form and application of laws depended on local and provincial custom and practice. In the twelfth and thirteenth centuries, the law was a hodgepodge of Germanic customs, feudal rights, and provincial practices. Kings in France and England wanted to blend these elements into a uniform system of rules acceptable and applicable to all their peoples. They successfully contributed to the development of national states through the administration of their laws. In the German Empire, regional magistrates with imperial sanction applied local law. Legal developments in continental countries like France were strongly influenced by Roman law, while England slowly built up a unique, unwritten common law.

France

The French king Louis IX (r. 1226–1270) was famous in his time for his concern for justice. Each French province, even after being made part of the kingdom of France, retained its unique laws and procedures, but Louis IX created a royal judicial system. He established the Parlement of Paris, a kind of supreme court that welcomed appeals from local administrators and from the courts of feudal lords throughout France. By the very act of appealing the decisions of feudal courts to the Parlement of Paris, French people in far-flung provinces were recognizing the superiority of royal justice.

Louis sent royal judges to all parts of the country to check up on the work of the baillis and seneschals and to hear complaints of injustice. He was the first French monarch to publish laws for the entire kingdom. The Parlement of Paris registered (or announced) these laws, which forbade private warfare, judicial duels, gambling, blaspheming, and prostitution. Louis sought to identify justice with the kingship, and gradually royal justice touched all parts of the kingdom.

tians,"[13] implying a degree of toleration exceedingly rare at the time.

Frederick's contemporaries called him the "Wonder of the World." He certainly transformed the kingdom of Sicily. But Sicily required constant attention, and Frederick's absences on crusade and on campaigns in mainland Italy took their toll. Shortly after he died, the unsupervised bureaucracy fell to pieces. The pope, as feudal overlord of Sicily, called in a French prince to rule.

Frederick showed little interest in Germany. He concentrated his attention on Sicily rather than on the historic Hohenstaufen stronghold of Swabia. When he

The Customs of Aragon   King James of Aragon (r. 1213–1276), called "the Conqueror" because of his victories over Catalonia, Valencia, and Majorca, ordered several codifications of law. The most important of these, the Customs of Aragon (1247), drew on Roman canonical practice for legal procedures. This illumination, imitating the style of Parisian court art, shows King James presiding over a law court. (© *The J. Paul Getty Museum, Los Angeles*)

English Legal Developments

Under Henry II (r. 1154–1189), England developed and extended a **common law,** a law that originated in, and was applied by, the king's court and in the next two or three centuries became common to the entire country. England was unusual in developing one system of royal courts and one secular law. Henry I had occasionally sent out **circuit judges** (royal officials who traveled a given circuit or district) to hear civil and criminal cases. Henry II made this way of extending royal justice an annual practice. Every year royal judges left London and set up court in the counties. Wherever the king's judges sat, there sat the king's court.

Henry also improved procedure in criminal justice. In 1166 he instructed the sheriffs to summon local juries to conduct inquests and draw up lists of known or suspected criminals. These lists, or indictments, sworn to by the juries, were to be presented to the royal judges when

they arrived in the community. This accusing jury is the ancestor of the modern grand jury.

The method of trial, determining guilt or innocence, posed a problem. In criminal cases, lacking a specific accuser, the court first sought witnesses, then written evidence. If the judges found neither, and if a suspect had a bad public reputation, he or she was sent to trial by ordeal. But ordeal was always a last resort, applied only when other means of finding the truth failed. (Ordeal was widely used on the continent in both criminal and civil disputes, but it was rarely used in civil cases in England.) An accused person could be tried by fire or water. In the latter case, the accused was tied hand and foot and dropped in a lake or river. People believed that water was a pure substance and would reject anything foul or unclean. Thus a person who sank was considered innocent; a person who floated was found guilty. Trial by ordeal was a ritual that appealed to the supernatural for judgment. God determined guilt or innocence, and thus a priest had to be present to bless the water.

Henry II disliked ordeal, partly because the clergy controlled the procedure, partly because many suspicious people seemed to beat the system and escape punishment. But Henry had no alternative. Because trial by ordeal had no basis in Scripture, it was not found in Roman law, and it appeared to challenge or "force" God to perform a miracle, the Fourth Lateran Council of 1215 forbade the presence of priests at the ordeal and thus effectively abolished it. Secular justice was desacralized.[14]

Gradually, in the course of the thirteenth century, the king's judges adopted the practice of calling on twelve people (other than the accusing jury) to consider the question of innocence or guilt. This became the jury of trial, but it was very slowly accepted because medieval people had more confidence in the judgment of God than in that of twelve ordinary people.

One aspect of Henry's judicial reforms encountered stiff resistance from an unexpected source: a friend and former chief adviser whom Henry had made archbishop of Canterbury—Thomas Becket. Henry selected Becket as archbishop in 1162 because he believed he could depend on Becket's support. But when Henry wanted to bring all persons in the kingdom under the jurisdiction of the royal courts, Thomas Becket's opposition led to another dramatic conflict between temporal and spiritual powers.

In the 1160s many literate people accused of crimes claimed "benefit of clergy," even though they were not clerics and often had no intention of being ordained. An accused person proved he was a cleric by his ability to read. (Later, university students and merchants—who had to keep records—could claim it.) After the courts established the practice of opening the Bible to the Fiftieth Psalm and asking the accused to read, they found that criminals had memorized it. Benefit of clergy gave the accused the right to be tried in church courts, which meted out mild punishments. A person found guilty in the king's court might suffer mutilation—loss of a hand or foot, castration—or even death. Ecclesiastical punishments tended to be an obligation to say certain prayers or to make a pilgrimage. In 1164 Henry II insisted that everyone, including clerics, be subject to the royal courts. Becket vigorously protested that church law required clerics to be subject to church courts. When he proceeded to excommunicate one of the king's vassals, the issue became more complicated. Because no one was supposed to have any contact with an excommunicated person, it appeared that the church could arbitrarily deprive the king of necessary military forces. The disagreement between Henry II and Becket dragged on for years. The king grew increasingly bitter that his appointment of Becket had proved to be such a mistake. Late in December 1170, in a fit of rage, Henry expressed the wish that Becket be destroyed. Four knights took the king at his word. They rode to Canter-

bury Cathedral, and, as the archbishop was leaving evening services, slashed off the crown of his head and scattered his brains on the pavement.

What Thomas Becket could not achieve in life, he gained in death. The assassination of an archbishop turned public opinion in England and throughout western Europe against the king. Miracles were recorded at Becket's tomb, and in a short time Canterbury Cathedral became a major pilgrimage and tourist site. Henry had to back down. He did public penance for the murder and gave up his attempts to bring clerics under the authority of the royal court.

Henry II's sons Richard I, known as Lion-Hearted (r. 1189–1199), and John (r. 1199–1216) lacked their father's interest in the work of government. Richard looked on England as a source of revenue for his military enterprises. Soon after his accession, he departed on crusade to the Holy Land. During his reign he spent only six months in England, and the government was run by ministers trained under Henry II.

John's basic problems were financial. King John inherited a heavy debt from his father and brother. The country had paid dearly for Richard's crusading zeal. While

Limoges Casket The principal city of the Limousin in west-central France, Limoges was famous for the superb work of its enamelers and goldsmiths. This casket, or chest, showing Thomas Becket's execution (*lower panel*) and burial (*upper panel*) was used to preserve his relics. The two scenes are done on gilded copper plaques nailed over wood. (*Courtesy of the Trustees of the Victoria and Albert Museum*)

returning from the Holy Land, Richard had been captured, and England had paid an enormous ransom to secure his release. Further, during the entire period 1180–1220, England experienced a severe inflation, which drove prices up. In 1204 John lost the rich province of Normandy to Philip Augustus of France and then spent the rest of his reign trying to get it back. John took scutage, and each time increased the amount due. He forced widows to pay exorbitant fines to avoid unwanted marriages. He sold young girls who were his feudal wards to the highest bidder. These actions antagonized the nobility.

John also alienated the church and the English townspeople. He rejected Pope Innocent III's nominee to the see of Canterbury. And he infuriated the burghers of the towns by extorting money from them and threatening to revoke their charters of self-government.

All the money John raised did not bring him success. In July 1214 John's coalition of Flemish, German, and English cavalry suffered a severe defeat at the hands of Philip Augustus of France at Bouvines in Flanders. This battle ended English hopes for the recovery of territories from France and also strengthened the barons' opposition to John. His ineptitude as a soldier in a society that idealized military glory was the final straw. Rebellion begun by northern barons eventually grew to involve many of the English nobility, including the archbishop of Canterbury and the earl of Pembroke, the leading ecclesiastical and lay peers.[15] After lengthy negotiations, John met the barons at Runnymede, a meadow along the Thames River. There he was forced to approve and to attach his seal to the peace treaty called **Magna Carta,** "Magna" (great or large) because it was so long and detailed.

For contemporaries, Magna Carta was intended to redress the grievances that particular groups—the barons, the clergy, the merchants of London—had against King John. Charters were not unusual: many kings and lords at the time issued them. But because every English king between 1215 and 1485, as evidence of his promise to observe the law, reissued Magna Carta, this charter alone acquired enduring importance. It came to signify the principle that everyone, including the king and the government, must obey the law.

Although legal scholars coined the phrase "rule of law" only in the late nineteenth century, in the later Middle Ages, references to Magna Carta underlined the old Augustinian theory that a government, to be legitimate, must promote law, order, and justice. As the royal justice Henry of Bracton (d. 1268) put it, the English shall be *"Non sub homine sed sub Deo et lege"* (Not under man but under God and the law), a maxim that appears over

the entrance to Harvard Law School. Thus an English king may not disregard or arbitrarily suspend the law to suit his convenience. Drawn up initially to protect baronial interests, Magna Carta was used in later centuries to protect the interests of widows, orphans, townspeople, freemen, and the church. For example, Chapter 39 states, "No freeman shall be captured or imprisoned or disseised (dispossessed) or outlawed or exiled or in any way destroyed, nor will we go against him or send against him, except by the lawful judgment of his peers or by the law of the land." This statement contains the germ of the idea of "due process of law," meaning that any person has the right to be heard and defended in court and is entitled to the protection of the law. Because later generations referred to Magna Carta as a written statement of English liberties, it gradually came to have an almost sacred importance as a guarantee of law and justice.

In the thirteenth century, the judicial precedents set under Henry II slowly evolved into permanent institutions. The king's judges asserted the royal authority and applied the same principles everywhere in the country. English people found the king's justice more rational and evenhanded than the justice meted out in the baronial courts. Respect for the king's law and courts promoted loyalty to the Crown. By the time of Henry's great-grandson Edward I (r. 1272–1307), one law, the common law, operated all over England.

The German Empire

In the German empire of the thirteenth century, justice was administered at two levels. The manorial or seigneurial court, presided over by the lay or ecclesiastical lord, dealt with matters such as damage to crops and fields, trespass, boundary disputes, and debt—common conflicts at a time when princes were expanding their colonial jurisdictions over forestland and wasteland and receiving thousands of new settlers. Dukes, counts, margraves, bishops, and abbots possessed an authority called **Landgericht,** or regional magistracies. With this power, the lord's agents, or representatives, dispensed justice in serious criminal cases involving theft, arson, assault with a weapon, rape, and homicide. Regional magistrates held powers of high justice, that is, the right to execute a criminal; the imposition of the death penalty by hanging was the distinctive feature of this court. In the early Middle Ages, society perceived of major crimes as acts against an individual, and they were settled by the accused making a cash payment to the victim or his or her kindred. In the later Middle Ages, suspects were pursued and punished for acting against the *public* interest. Punishments varied from province to province, but almost everywhere the German ruling aristocracy made a concerted effort to punish violent crimes. One-third of all fines imposed went to the lord.[16]

Common Law and Roman Law

In the later Middle Ages, the English common law developed features that differed strikingly from the system of Roman law operative in continental Europe. The common law relied on **precedent:** a decision in an important case served as an authority for deciding similar cases. By contrast, continental judges, trained in Roman law, used the fixed legal maxims of the Justinian *Code* (see page 217) to decide their cases. Thus the common-law system evolved according to the changing experience of the people, while the Roman-law tradition tended toward a more rigid or static approach. In countries influenced by the common law, such as Canada and the United States, the court is open to the public; in countries with Roman-law traditions, such as France and the Latin American nations, courts need not be public. Under the common law, people accused in criminal cases have the right to access to the evidence against them; under the other system, they need not. The common law urges judges to be impartial; in the Roman-law system, judges interfere freely in activities in their courtrooms.

Finally, whereas torture is foreign to the common-law tradition, it was once widely used in the Roman legal system as a method of securing evidence or proof.

The extension of law and justice led to a phenomenal amount of legal codification all over Europe. For example, the English judge Henry of Bracton wrote *Treatise on the Laws and Customs of England.* Legal texts and encyclopedias exalted royal authority, consolidated royal power, and emphasized political and social uniformity. The pressure for social conformity in turn contributed to a rising hostility toward Jews and homosexuals.

New Legal Restrictions

By the late eleventh century, many towns in western Europe had small Jewish populations. (See the feature "Individuals in Society: The Jews of Speyer" on page 281.) The laws of most countries forbade Jews to own land, though they could hold land pledged to them for debts. Nor could Jews enter many professions and crafts, and thus they could never become fully integrated into their host society. By the twelfth century, many Jews were usurers: they lent to consumers but primarily to new or growing business enterprises. New towns and underdeveloped areas where cash was scarce welcomed Jewish settlers. Like other business people, the Jews preferred to live near their work; they also settled close to their synagogue or school.

Jewish Execution The German law code *Sachsenspiegel* (ca 1220) uses this typical anti-Semitic libel to depict a Jew hung for stealing a Bible and a chalice containing consecrated wine. *(Courtesy, Herzog August Bibliothek Wolfenbüttel. Cod. Guelf. 3. 1 Aug. 2°)*

Thus originated the Jews' street or quarter or ghetto. Such neighborhoods gradually became legally defined sections where Jews were required to live.

Jews had been generally tolerated and had become important parts of the urban economies through trade and finance. Some Jews had risen to positions of power and prominence. Through the twelfth century, for example, Jews managed the papal household. The later twelfth and entire thirteenth centuries, however, witnessed increasingly ugly anti-Semitism. Why? Present scholarship does not provide completely satisfactory answers, but we have some clues. Shifting agricultural and economic patterns aggravated social tensions. The indebtedness of peasants and nobles to Jews in an increasingly cash-based economy; the xenophobia that accompanied and followed the Crusades; Christian merchants' and financiers' resentment of Jewish business competition; the spread of vicious accusations of ritual murders or sacrileges against Christian property and persons; royal and papal legislation aimed at social conformity—these factors all contributed to rising anti-Semitism. Thus, from 1180 to 1182, Philip Augustus of France used hostility to Jews as an excuse to imprison them and then to demand heavy ransom for their release. The Fourth Lateran Council of 1215 forbade Jews to hold public office, restricted their financial activities, and required them to wear distinctive clothing. In 1290 Edward I of England capitalized on mercantile and other resentment of Jews to expel them from the country in return for a large parliamentary grant. In 1306 Philip IV of France followed suit, expelling the Jews from his kingdom and confiscating their property. But in July 1315 the Crown's need for revenue led Louis X (r. 1314–1316), in return for a huge lump sum and for an annual financial subsidy, to readmit the Jews to France. The returnees faced new economic pressures and old hostilities. Jews were allowed to return to England only in the days of Oliver Cromwell in the seventeenth century.

Early Christians displayed no special prejudice against homosexuals (see page 202). While some of the church fathers, such as Saint John Chrysostom (347–407), preached against them, a general indifference to homosexual activity prevailed throughout the early Middle Ages. In the early twelfth century, a large homosexual literature circulated. Publicly known homosexuals such as Ralph, archbishop of Tours (1087–1118), and King Richard I of England held high ecclesiastical and political positions.

Beginning in the late twelfth century, however, a profound change occurred in public attitudes toward homosexual behavior. Scholars have only begun to investigate the reasons. In the thirteenth century, a fear of foreigners, especially Muslims, became associated with the crusading movement. Heretics were the most despised minority in an age that stressed religious and social uniformity. The notion spread that both Muslims and heretics, the great foreign and domestic menaces to the security of Christian Europe, were inclined to homosexual relations. Finally, the systematization of law and the rising strength of the state made any religious or sexual distinctiveness increasingly unacceptable. Whatever the precise cause, by 1300 homosexuality became illegal in most of Europe—and the most common penalty for conviction was death.[17] Most of these laws remained on statute books until the twentieth century. Anti-Semitism and hostility to homosexuals reflect a dark side of high medieval culture, not the general creativity and vitality of the period.

Towns and Economic Revival

A salient manifestation of Europe's recovery after the tenth-century disorders and of the vitality of the High Middle Ages was the rise of towns and the development of a new business and commercial class. This development was to lay the foundations for Europe's transformation, centuries later, from a rural agricultural society into an industrial urban society—a change with global implications.

Why did these developments occur when they did? What is known of town life in the High Middle Ages? What relevance did towns have for medieval culture? Part of the answer to these questions has already been given. Without increased agricultural output, there would not have been an adequate food supply for new town dwellers. Without a rise in population, there would have been no one to people the towns. Without a minimum of peace and political stability, merchants could not have transported and sold goods.

The Rise of Towns

Early medieval society was traditional, agricultural, and rural. The emergence of a new class that was none of these constituted a social revolution. The new class—artisans and merchants—came from the peasantry. They were landless younger sons of large families, driven away by land shortage. Or they were forced by war and famine to seek new possibilities. Or, as in central Europe and Spain after the reconquista (see page 283), they were immigrants colonizing newly conquered lands. Or they were unusually enterprising and adventurous, curious and willing to take a chance.

Carcassonne This town in Languedoc (southern France) originated in pre-Roman times. Its thick double walls provide an excellent example of the fortified medieval town. *(Jonathan Blair/Woodfin Camp & Associates)*

Historians have proposed three basic theories to explain the origins of European towns. Some scholars believe towns began as *boroughs*—that is, as fortifications erected during the ninth-century Viking invasions. According to this view, towns were at first places of defense, into which farmers from the surrounding countryside moved when their area was attacked. Later, merchants were attracted to the fortifications because they had something to sell and wanted to be where customers were. But most residents of early towns made their living by farming outside the towns.

Belgian historian Henri Pirenne maintained that towns sprang up when merchants who engaged in long-distance trade gravitated toward attractive or favorable spots, such as a fort. Usually traders settled just outside the walls, in the *faubourgs* or *suburbs*—both of which mean "outside" or "in the shelter of the walls." As their markets prospered and as their number outside the walls grew, the merchants built a new wall around themselves every century or so.

A third explanation focuses on the great cathedrals and monasteries, which represented a demand for goods and services. Cathedrals such as Notre Dame in Paris conducted schools, which drew students from far and wide. Consequently, traders and merchants settled near religious establishments to cater to the residents' economic needs. Concentrations of people accumulated, and towns came into being.

All three theories have validity, though none of them explains the origins of *all* medieval towns. Few towns of the tenth and eleventh centuries were "new" in the sense that American towns and cities were new in the seventeenth and eighteenth centuries, carved out of forest and wilderness. Some medieval towns that had become flourishing centers of trade by the mid-twelfth century had

MAP 11.3 Population of European Urban Areas, ca Late Thirteenth Century Though there were scores of urban centers in the thirteenth century, the Italian and Flemish towns had the largest concentrations of people. By modern standards, Paris was Europe's only real city.

originally been Roman army camps. York in northern England, Bordeaux in west-central France, and Cologne in west-central Germany are good examples of ancient towns that underwent revitalization in the eleventh century. Some Italian seaport cities, such as Venice, Pisa, and Genoa, had been centers of shipping and commerce in earlier times; trade with Constantinople and the East had never stopped entirely. The restoration of order and political stability promoted rebirth and new development. Pirenne's interpretation accurately describes the Flemish towns of Ghent, Bruges, and Ypres. It does not fit the course of development in the Italian cities or in such centers as London. Nor does the Pirenne thesis take into account the significance of local trade and markets in the growth of towns. Moreover, the twelfth century witnessed the foundation of completely new towns, such as Lübeck, Berlin, and Munich.

Whether evolving from a newly fortified place or an old Roman army camp, from a cathedral site or a river junction or a place where several overland routes met, medieval towns had a few common characteristics. Walls enclosed the town. (The terms *burgher* and *bourgeois* derive from the Old English and Old German words *burg, burgh, borg,* and *borough* for "a walled or fortified place." Thus a burgher or bourgeois was originally a person who lived or worked inside the walls.) The town had a marketplace. It often had a mint for the coining of money and a court to settle disputes.

In each town, many people inhabited a small, cramped area. As population increased, towns rebuilt their walls, expanding the living space to accommodate growing numbers. Through an archaeological investigation of the amount of land gradually enclosed by walls, historians have gained a rough estimate of medieval town populations. For example, the walled area of the German city of Cologne equaled 100 hectares in the tenth century (1 hectare = 2.471 acres), about 185 hectares in 1106, about 320 hectares in 1180, and 397 hectares in the fourteenth century. In 1180 Cologne's population was at least 32,000; in the mid-fourteenth century, perhaps 40,000.[18] The concentration of the textile industry in the Low Countries brought into being the most populous cluster of cities in western Europe: Ghent with about 56,000 people, Bruges with 27,000, Tournai and Brussels with perhaps 20,000 each.[19] Venice, Florence, and Paris, each with about 110,000 people, and Milan with possibly 200,000, led all Europe in population (see Map 11.3).

In their backgrounds and abilities, townspeople represented diversity and change. They constituted an entirely new element in medieval society. They fit into none of the traditional categories. Their occupations, their preoccupations, were different from those of the feudal nobility and the laboring peasantry. How were the new business people perceived? The nobility and clergy looked upon merchants and townspeople with mild contempt; the upper classes had a certain hostility toward both manual labor (see page 212) and commercial activity. Clerical writers—most of the individuals who wrote anything on tradespeople were clerics—were ambivalent: on the one hand, they recognized that businesspersons performed a necessary social function because they handled and transported goods; on the other hand, clerics had an aristocratic bias against merchants, whom they saw as middlemen producing nothing yet profiting from the labor of others. The new commercial class did not fit into the clergy's world-view: the immediate goal of the merchant was not salvation and Heaven but profit. It took a long time before churchmen developed a theological justification for the new class. Though townspeople derived originally from the peasantry, and though rural people gained from the sale of foodstuffs to the towns, farmers resented what they perceived as an easier, more luxurious lifestyle in the towns. Considerable misunderstanding existed.

Town Liberties

In the words of the Greek poet Alcaeus, "Not houses finely roofed or well built walls, nor canals or dockyards make a city, but men able to use their opportunity."[20] People and opportunity: that is fundamentally what medieval towns meant—concentrations of people and varieties of chances. No matter where groups of traders congregated, they settled on someone's land and had to secure from king or count, abbot or bishop, permission to live and trade. Aristocratic nobles and churchmen soon realized that profits and benefits flowed to them and their territories from the markets set up on their land.

The history of towns in the eleventh through thirteenth centuries consists largely of merchants' efforts to acquire liberties. In the Middle Ages, *liberties* meant special privileges. **Town liberties** included the privilege of living and trading on the lord's land. The most important privilege a medieval townsperson could gain was personal freedom. It gradually developed that an individual who lived in a town for a year and a day, and was accepted by the townspeople, was free of servile obligations and status. (Usually, but not always, as we saw in the case of Jean Mouflet on page 301, lords attempted to regain runaway serfs, even after a generation. How widespread this practice was remains to be investigated.) More than anything else, perhaps, the liberty of personal freedom that came with residence in a town contributed to the emancipation of the serfs in the High Middle Ages. Liberty meant citizenship, and citizenship in a town implied the right to buy and sell goods there. Unlike foreigners and outsiders, the full citizen did not have to pay taxes and tolls in the market. Obviously, this increased profits.

In the twelfth and thirteenth centuries, towns slowly gained legal and political rights. Since the tenth century, some English boroughs had held courts with jurisdiction over members of the town in civil and criminal matters. In the twelfth century, such English towns as London and Norwich developed courts that applied a special kind of law, called "law merchant." It dealt with commercial transactions, debt, bankruptcy, proof of sales, and contracts. Gradually, towns across Europe acquired the right to hold municipal courts that alone could judge members of the town. In effect, this right gave them judicial independence.[21]

In the acquisition of full rights of self-government, the **guilds** played a large role. Medieval people were long accustomed to communal enterprises. In the late tenth and early eleventh centuries, those who were engaged in foreign trade joined together in *merchant guilds;* united enterprise provided them greater security and less risk of losses than did individual action. At about the same time, the artisans and craftsmen of particular trades formed their own guilds. Members of the *craft guilds* determined the quality, quantity, and price of the goods that they produced and the number of apprentices and journeymen that could be affiliated with the guild.

Research indicates that, by the fifteenth century, women composed the majority of the adult urban population. Many women were heads of households.[22] In many manufacturing trades women predominated, and in some places women were a large percentage of the labor force. In fourteenth-century Frankfurt, for example, about 33 percent of the crafts and trades were entirely female, about 40 percent wholly male, and the remaining crafts roughly divided between the sexes. Craft guilds provided greater opportunity for women than did merchant guilds. In late-twelfth-century Cologne, women and men had equal rights in the turners guild (the guild for those who made wooden objects on a lathe). Most members of the Paris silk and woolen trades were women, and some achieved the mastership. Widows frequently followed their late husbands' professions, but if they remarried outside the craft, they lost the mastership. Between 1254 and 1271, the chief magistrate of Paris drew up the following regulations for the silk industry. Any woman who wishes to be a silk spinster (woman who spins) on large spindles in the city of Paris must observe the following customs and usages of the crafts:

No spinster on large spindles may have more than three apprentices, unless they be her own or her husband's children born in true wedlock; nor may she contract with them for an apprenticeship of less than seven years or for a fee of less than 20 Parisian sols to be paid to her, their mistress. . . . If a working woman comes from outside Paris and wishes to practice the said craft in the city, she must swear before the guardians of the craft that she will practice it well and loyally and conform to its customs and usages. . . . No man of this craft who is without a wife may have more than one apprentice; . . . if, however, both husband and wife practice the craft, they may have two apprentices and as many journeymen as they wish.[23]

Guild records show that women received lower wages than men for the same work, on the grounds that they needed less income.

Research also demonstrates that women with ready access to cash, such as female innkeepers, alewives, and women in trade, "extended credit on purchases, gave cash advances to good customers or accepted articles on pawn . . . and many widows supplemented their earnings from their late husbands' businesses or homesteads by putting out cash at interest." Likewise, Christian noblewomen,

nuns, and Jewish businesswomen participated in money lending. In every part of Europe where Jews lived, Jewish women were active moneylenders. Loans made by all women tended to be very small (in comparison to those extended by men), for domestic consumption (to "tide over" a household in some emergency, in contrast to productive loans such as those to repair or replace a piece of farm equipment), and for short terms (a few weeks or a month).[24] But most women workers were not in a guild, and they certainly had no money to lend. As in every age before the twentieth century, the great majority of women employed outside their homes worked in domestic service, as household servants (see pages 432, 513).

By the late eleventh century, especially in the towns of the Low Countries and northern Italy, the leaders of the merchant guilds were quite rich and powerful. They constituted an oligarchy in their towns, controlling economic life and bargaining with kings and lords for political independence. Full rights of self-government included the right to hold a town court, the right to select the mayor and other municipal officials, and the right to tax and collect taxes. Kings often levied on their serfs and unfree townspeople the arbitrary tallage. Such a tax (also known as "customs") called attention to the fact that men were not free. Citizens of a town much preferred to levy and collect their own taxes.

A charter that King Henry II of England granted to the merchants of Lincoln around 1157 nicely illustrates the town's rights. The quoted passages clearly suggest that the merchant guild had been the governing body in the city for almost a century and that anyone who lived in Lincoln for a year and a day was considered free:

Henry, by the grace of God, etc. . . . Know that I have granted to my citizens of Lincoln all their liberties and customs and laws which they had in the time of Edward [King Edward the Confessor] and William and Henry, kings of England. And I have granted them their gild-merchant, comprising men of the city and other merchants of the shire, as well and freely as they had it in the time of our aforesaid predecessors. . . . And all the men who live within the four divisions of the city and attend the market, shall stand in relation to gelds [taxes] and customs and the assizes [ordinances or laws] of the city as well as ever they stood in the time of Edward, William and Henry, kings of England. I also confirm to them that if anyone has lived in Lincoln for a year and a day without dispute from any claimant, and has paid the customs, and if the citizens can show by the laws and customs of the city that the claimant has remained in England during that period and has made no claim, then let the defendant remain in peace in my city of Lincoln as my citizen, without [having to defend his] right.[25]

Kings and lords were reluctant to grant towns self-government, fearing loss of authority and revenue if they gave the merchant guilds full independence. But the lords discovered that towns attracted increasing numbers of people to an area—people whom the lords could tax. Moreover, when burghers bargained for a town's political independence, they offered sizable amounts of ready cash. Consequently, feudal lords ultimately agreed to self-government.

Town Life

Walls to protect valuable goods surrounded almost all medieval towns and cities. Gates pierced the walls, and visitors waited at the gates to gain entrance to the town. When the gates were opened early in the morning, guards inspected the quantity and quality of the goods brought in and collected the customary taxes. Part of the taxes went to the lord on whose land the town stood,

part to the town council for civic purposes. Constant repair of the walls was usually the town's greatest expense.

Peasants coming from the countryside and merchants traveling from afar set up their carts as stalls just inside the gates. The result was that the road nearest the gate was the widest thoroughfare. It was the ideal place for a market, because everyone coming in or going out used it. Most streets in a medieval town were marketplaces as much as passages for transit.

In some respects the entire city was a marketplace. The place where a product was made and sold was also typically the merchant's residence. Usually the ground floor was the scene of production. A window or door opened onto the street and displayed the finished product so passersby could look in and see the goods being produced. The merchant's family lived above the business on the second or third floor. As the business and the family expanded, the merchant built additional stories on top of the house.

Spanish Apothecary Town life meant variety—of peoples and products. Within the town walls, a Spanish pharmacist, seated outside his shop, describes the merits of his goods to a crowd of Christians and Muslims. *(From the* Cantigas *of Alfonso X, ca 1283. El Escorial/Laurie Platt Winfrey, Inc.)*

Second and third stories were built jutting out over the ground floor and thus over the street. Since the streets were narrow to begin with, houses lacked fresh air and light. Initially, houses were made of wood and thatched with straw. Fire represented a constant danger, and because houses were built so close together, fires spread rapidly. Municipal governments consequently urged construction in stone or brick.

Most medieval cities developed with little town planning. As the population increased, space became more and more limited. Air and water pollution presented serious problems. Many families raised pigs for household consumption in sties next to the house. Horses and oxen, the chief means of transportation and power, dropped tons of dung on the streets every year. It was universal practice in the early towns to dump household waste, both animal and human, into the road in front of one's house. The stench must have been abominable. In 1298 the burgesses of the town of Boutham in Yorkshire, England, received the following order (one long, vivid sentence):

To the bailiffs of the abbot of St. Mary's York, at Boutham. Whereas it is sufficiently evident that the pavement of the said town of Boutham is so very greatly broken up . . . , and in addition the air is so corrupted and infected by the pigsties situated in the king's highways and in the lanes of that town and by the swine feeding and frequently wandering about . . . and by dung and dunghills and many other foul things placed in the streets and lanes, that great repugnance overtakes the king's ministers staying in that town and also others there dwelling and passing through, the advantage of more wholesome air is impeded, the state of men is grievously injured, and other unbearable inconveniences . . . , to the nuisance of the king's ministers aforesaid and of others there dwelling . . . : the king, being unwilling longer to tolerate such great and unbearable defects there, orders the bailiffs to cause the pavement to be suitably repaired within their liberty before All Saints next, and to cause the pigsties, aforesaid streets and lanes to be cleansed from all dung . . . and to cause them to be kept thus cleansed hereafter.[26]

A great deal of traffic passed through Boutham in 1298 because of the movement of English troops to battle-fronts in Scotland. Conditions there were probably not typical. Still, this document suggests that space, air pollution, and sanitation problems bedeviled urban people in medieval times, as they do today.

The Revival of Long-Distance Trade

The eleventh century witnessed a remarkable revival of trade, as artisans and craftsmen manufactured goods for local and foreign consumption (see Map 11.4). Most trade centered in towns and was controlled by professional traders. Because long-distance trade was risky and required large investments of capital, it could be practiced only by professionals. The transportation of goods involved serious risks. Shipwrecks were common. Pirates infested the sea-lanes, and robbers and thieves roamed virtually all of the land routes. Since the risks were so great, merchants preferred to share them. A group of people would thus pool their capital to finance an expedition to a distant place. When the ship or caravan returned and the goods brought back were sold, the investors would share the profits. If disaster struck the caravan, an investor's loss was limited to the amount of that individual's investment.

What goods were exchanged? What towns took the lead in medieval "international" trade? In the late eleventh century, the Italian cities, especially Venice, led the West in trade in general and completely dominated the oriental market. Ships carried salt from the Venetian lagoon, pepper and other spices from North Africa, and silks and purple textiles from the East to northern and western Europe. In the thirteenth century, Venetian caravans brought slaves from the Crimea and Chinese silks from Mongolia to the West. Lombard and Tuscan merchants exchanged those goods at the town markets and regional fairs of France, Flanders, and England. (Fairs were periodic gatherings that attracted buyers, sellers, and goods from all over Europe.) Flanders controlled the cloth industry. The towns of Bruges, Ghent, and Ypres built up a vast industry in the manufacture of cloth. Italian merchants exchanged their products for Flemish tapestries, fine broadcloth, and various other textiles.

Two circumstances help to explain the lead Venice and the Flemish towns gained in long-distance trade. Both enjoyed a high degree of peace and political stability. Geographical factors were equally, if not more, important. Venice was ideally located at the northwestern end of the Adriatic Sea, with easy access to the transalpine land routes as well as the Adriatic and Mediterranean sea-lanes. The markets of North Africa, Byzantium, and Russia and the great fairs of Ghent in Flanders and Champagne in France provided commercial opportunities that Venice quickly seized. (See the feature "Individuals in Society: Enrico Dandolo.") The geographical situation of Flanders also offered unusual possibilities. Just across the Channel from England, Flanders had easy access to English wool. Indeed, Flanders and England developed a very close economic relationship.

Sheep had been raised for their wool in England since Roman times. Beginning in the early twelfth century, but especially after the arrival of Cistercian monks around

Individuals in Society

Enrico Dandolo

In the first week of Lent,* 1201, six French barons—the diplomatic envoys of a contingent of northern French and Flemish barons who had taken the cross—appeared in Venice. They wanted Venetian help in transporting them to the Holy Land. The lords had selected Venice, at the northwestern edge of the Adriatic Sea, as the port of departure because of the city's vast maritime facilities, which no French or other Italian shipyard (at Genoa or Pisa) could match. The ambassadors were formally received by the head of state, Doge Enrico Dandolo, with great pomp and splendor.

Dandolo was ninety-four years old. Partially blind, and doge since 1192, he had already reformed the Venetian currency, revised the penal code, and published the republic's first collection of civil statutes. A skilled diplomat and strategist and an eloquent speaker, he was above all a passionate patriot.

The Crusaders requested transportation for 33,500 men and 4,500 horses. For a fee of 85,000 marks the Venetians agreed to transport them to Palestine and to provision horses and men for one year; the expedition was to sail in April 1202, its first object Egypt.

From this treaty would stem momentous consequences and ultimately great wealth for Venice. Immediately after the treaty, the city built five hundred ships to carry men and horses. When it became apparent that the Crusaders could produce neither the manpower promised nor about a third of the fee, Doge Enrico Dandolo proposed that the crusading army conquer Zara (modern Zadar in Croatia on the Adriatic coast), a fueling station for Venetian ships and the port through which oak, essential for Venetian shipbuilding, passed; Zara had recently been seized by the king of Hungary. Some Crusaders objected to an attack on a Christian city, but the majority acceded to the doge's request. Zara was assaulted and fell. Then Alexius, son of the deposed Byzantine emperor, arrived at Zara and promised financial support for the crusade and the reunion of the Greek and Latin churches, if the Crusaders would help him regain the Byzantine throne; sharp divisions again arose among the Crusaders. Doge Dandolo, who had recently seen Venetian trading rights in Constantinople rescinded and given to Genoa, eloquently urged support for an attack on Constantinople; the restoration of Alexius would offer a perfect opportunity for the recovery of Venetian privileges. Moreover, he reminded the army, Venice controlled the fleet.

Although a thousand Crusaders defected and went home, Venice and the remaining Crusaders signed the Treaty of Zara, agreeing to assault the Byzantine capital and to restore Alexius. The fleet sailed and, after a long siege, Constantinople was conquered and mercilessly sacked on April 13–15, 1204.

In the division of the Byzantine Empire, Venice got the lion's share: three-eighths of Constantinople, including the harbor area crucial to Venice's commercial interests, plus several strategic islands in the eastern Mediterranean. The conquest of Constantinople, a contradiction of the entire religious enterprise, laid the foundation for Venetian commercial power for the next three centuries.

The Fourth Crusade saw the fusion of many goals—religious, chivalric, economic, and ecumenical (reunion of the two churches). Whereas the Crusaders appeared indecisive and lacked effective leadership, Doge Enrico Dandolo, in spite of his age and handicap, displayed great vitality and willingness to seize opportunities; his policy was consistent and calculating. He used every crisis in this sorry expedition to advance the commercial interests of Venice. Perhaps he represents more the spirit of the modern world than that of the medieval.

Enrico Dandolo (1107?–1205). (Biblioteca Nazionale Marciana, Venice)

Questions for Analysis

1. How did commercial, financial, and political issues determine the course of the Fourth Crusade?
2. What is meant by "secular values"? How did Enrico Dandolo display them?

*In Christian medieval Europe, people dated events by the church year—Advent, Lent, Pentecost, or saints' feast days. Everyone would have known that the first week of Lent came between mid-February and early March.

Sources: D. E. Queller, *The Fourth Crusade: The Conquest of Constantinople, 1201–1204* (Philadelphia: University of Pennsylvania Press, 1977); T. F. Madden, *Enrico Dandolo and the Rise of Venice* (Baltimore: The Johns Hopkins University Press, 2003).

The *features additional information and activities related to this topic.* history.college.hmco.com/students

MAP 11.4 Trade and Manufacturing in Medieval Europe Note the number of cities and the sources of silver, iron, copper, lead, paper, wool, carpets and rugs, and slaves.

Textile and manufacturing areas
Northern sea routes
Venetian sea routes
Genoese sea routes
Overland routes

1130, the size of the English flocks doubled and then tripled. Scholars have estimated that, by the end of the twelfth century, roughly six million sheep grazed on the English moors and downs. They produced fifty thousand sacks of wool a year.[27] Originally, a "sack" of wool was the burden one packhorse could carry, an amount eventually fixed at 364 pounds; fifty thousand sacks, then, represented huge production.

Wool was the cornerstone of the English medieval economy. Population growth in the twelfth century and the success of the Flemish and Italian textile industries created foreign demand for English wool. The production of English wool stimulated Flemish manufacturing, and the expansion of the Flemish cloth industry in turn spurred the production of English wool. The availability of raw wool also encouraged the development of domestic cloth manufacture within England. The towns of Lincoln, York, Leicester, Northampton, Winchester, and Exeter became important cloth-producing towns. The port cities of London, Hull, Boston, and Bristol thrived on the wool trade. In the thirteenth century, commercial families in these towns grew fabulously rich.

The Commercial Revolution

A steadily expanding volume of international trade from the late eleventh through the thirteenth centuries was a sign of the great economic surge, but it was not the only one. Beginning in the 1160s, the opening of new silver mines in Germany, Bohemia, northern Italy, northern France, and western England led to the minting and circulation of vast quantities of silver coins. The widespread use of cash brought about an enormous quantitative change in the volume of international trade. Demand for sugar (to replace honey), pepper, cloves, and Asian spices to season a bland diet; for fine wines from the Rhineland, Burgundy, and Bordeaux; for luxury woolens from Flanders and Tuscany; for furs from Ireland and Russia; for brocades and tapestries from Flanders and silks from Constantinople and even China; for household furnishings such as silver plate—not to mention the desire for products associated with a military aristocracy such as swords and armor—surged phenomenally.

Business procedures changed radically. The individual traveling merchant who alone handled virtually all aspects of exchange evolved into an operation involving three separate types of merchants: the sedentary merchant who ran the "home office" financing and organizing the firm's entire export-import trade; the carriers who transported goods by land and sea; and the company agents resident in cities abroad who, on the advice of the home office, looked after sales and procurements. Commercial correspondence, unnecessary when one businessperson oversaw everything and made direct bargains with buyers and sellers, proliferated. Regular courier service among commercial cities began. Commercial accounting became more complex when firms had to deal with shareholders, manufacturers, customers, branch offices, employees, and competing firms. Tolls on roads became high enough to finance what has been called a "road revolution," involving new surfaces, bridges, new passes through the Alps, and new inns and hospices for travelers. The growth of mutual confidence among merchants facilitated the growth of sales on credit and led to the development of the bill of exchange, which in turn made the long, slow, and very dangerous shipment of coins unnecessary. Begun in the late twelfth century, the bill of exchange was by the early fourteenth century the normal method of making commercial payments among the cities of western Europe. In all these transformations, merchants of the Italian cities led the way.[28]

The ventures of the German Hanseatic League also illustrate these impulses. The **Hanseatic League** was a mercantile association of towns. Though scholars trace the league's origin to the foundation of the city of Lübeck in 1159, the mutual protection treaty later signed by Lübeck and Hamburg marks the league's actual expansion. Lübeck and Hamburg wanted mutual security, exclusive trading rights, and, where possible, a monopoly. During the next century, perhaps two hundred cities from Holland to Poland, including Cologne, Brunswick, Dortmund, Danzig, and Riga, joined the league, but Lübeck always remained the dominant member. From the thirteenth to the sixteenth century, the Hanseatic League controlled trade along the axis of Novgorod-Reval-Lübeck-Hamburg-Bruges-London, that is, the trade of northern Europe (see Map 11.4). In the fourteenth century, the Hanseatics branched out into southern Germany and Italy by land and into French, Spanish, and Portuguese ports by sea.

Across regular, well-defined trade routes along the Baltic and North Seas, the ships of league cities carried furs, wax, copper, fish, grain, timber, and wine. These goods were exchanged for finished products, mainly cloth and salt, from western cities. At cities such as Bruges and London, Hanseatic merchants secured special trading concessions exempting them from all tolls and allowing them to trade at local fairs. Hanseatic merchants established foreign trading centers, called "factories," the most famous of which was the London Steelyard, a walled community with warehouses, offices, a church, and residential quarters for company representatives.[29]

Wismar   Founded in 1229 in Mecklenburg on the Baltic Sea, Wismar won full rights of self-government in 1236 from the dukes of Mecklenburg-Pomerania, who resided there. A fishing and shipbuilding center, Wismar became one of the most powerful members of the Hanseatic League. Warehouses lined the shore, while the town's many church steeples dominated the skyline. *(Biblioteca Civica "Angelo Mai," Bergamo)*

By the late thirteenth century, Hanseatic merchants had developed an important business technique, the business register. Merchants publicly recorded their debts and contracts and received a league guarantee for them. This device proved a decisive factor in the later development of credit and commerce in northern Europe.[30] These activities required capital, risk taking, and aggressive pursuit of opportunities—the essential ingredients of capitalism. They also yielded fat profits.

These developments added up to what one modern scholar has called "a commercial revolution, . . . probably the greatest turning point in the history of our civilization."[31] In the long run, the commercial revolution of the High Middle Ages brought about radical change in European society. One remarkable aspect of this change is that the commercial classes constituted a small part of the total population—never more than 10 percent. They exercised an influence far in excess of their numbers.

The commercial revolution created a great deal of new wealth. Wealth meant a higher standard of living. Contact with Eastern civilizations introduced Europeans to eating utensils, and table manners improved. Nobles learned to eat with forks, as well as knives, instead of tearing the meat from a roast with their hands. They began to use napkins instead of wiping their greasy fingers on the dogs lying under the table.

The existence of wealth did not escape the attention of kings and other rulers. Wealth could be taxed, and through taxation kings could create strong and centralized states. In the years to come, alliances with the middle classes were to enable kings to defeat feudal powers and aristocratic interests and to build the states that came to be called "modern."

The commercial revolution also provided the opportunity for thousands of serfs to improve their social position. The slow but steady transformation of European society from almost completely rural and isolated to relatively more sophisticated constituted the greatest effect of the commercial revolution that began in the eleventh century.

Even so, merchants and business people did not run medieval communities, except in central and northern Italy and in the county of Flanders. Most towns remained small. The castle, the manorial village, and the monastery dominated the landscape. The feudal nobility and churchmen determined the preponderant social attitudes, values, and patterns of thought and behavior. The commercial changes of the eleventh through thirteenth centuries did, however, lay the economic foundations for the development of urban life and culture.

Medieval Universities

Just as the first strong secular states emerged in the thirteenth century, so did the first universities. This was no coincidence. The new bureaucratic states and the church needed educated administrators, and universities were a response to this need. The word *university* derives from the Latin *universitas,* meaning "corporation" or "guild." Medieval universities were educational guilds that produced educated and trained individuals. They were also an expression of the tremendous vitality and creativity of the High Middle Ages. Their organization, methods of instruction, and goals continue to influence institutionalized learning in the Western world.

Origins

In the early Middle Ages, outside of the aristocratic court or the monastery, anyone who received education got it from a priest. Priests instructed the clever boys on the manor in the Latin words of the Mass and taught them the rudiments of reading and writing. Few boys acquired elementary literacy, however, and peasant girls did not obtain even that. The peasant who wished to send his son to school had to secure the permission of his lord, because the result of formal schooling tended to be a career in the church or some trade. If a young man were to pursue either, he would have to leave the manor and gain free status. Because the lord stood to lose the services of educated peasants, he limited the number of serfs sent to school.

Since the time of the Carolingian Empire, monasteries and cathedral schools had offered most of the available formal instruction. The monasteries were geared to religious concerns, and the monastic curriculum consisted of studying the Scriptures and the writings of the church fathers. Monasteries wished to maintain an atmosphere of seclusion and silence and were unwilling to accept large numbers of noisy lay students. In contrast, schools attached to cathedrals and run by the bishop and his clergy were frequently situated in bustling cities, and in the eleventh century in Italian cities like Bologna, wealthy businessmen had established municipal schools. In the course of the twelfth century, cathedral schools in France and municipal schools in Italy developed into universities (see Map 11.5). "The term *studium generale* ('general centre of study'), eventually the most common medieval designation of a university, probably indicated the capacity of certain centres to attract students from beyond their immediate area." Members of the *studium generale* (university) formed professional associations for the protection of their members, the most typical examples being the students university at Bologna and the masters university at Paris.[32] The first European universities appeared in Italy, at Bologna and Salerno.

The growth of the University of Bologna coincided with a revival of interest in Roman law during the investiture controversy. The study of Roman law as embodied in the Justinian *Code* had never completely died out in the West, but this sudden burst of interest seems to have been inspired by Irnerius (d. 1125), a great teacher at Bologna. His fame attracted students from all over Europe. Irnerius not only explained the Roman law of the Justinian *Code,* he applied it to difficult practical situations.

At Salerno interest in medicine had persisted for centuries. Greek and Muslim physicians there had studied the use of herbs as cures and experimented with surgery. The twelfth century ushered in a new interest in Greek medical texts and in the work of Arab and Greek doctors. Students of medicine poured into Salerno and soon attracted royal attention. In 1140, when King Roger II of Sicily took the practice of medicine under royal control, his ordinance stated:

Who, from now on, wishes to practice medicine, has to present himself before our officials and examiners, in order to pass their judgment. Should he be bold enough to disregard this, he will be punished by imprisonment and confiscation of his entire property. In this way we are taking care that our subjects are not endangered by the inexperience of the physicians.[33]

In the first decades of the twelfth century, students converged on Paris. They crowded into the cathedral school of Notre Dame and spilled over into the area later called the "Latin Quarter"—whose name reflects either the Italian origin of many of the students attracted to Paris by the surge of interest in the classics, logic, and theology, or the Latin language spoken in the area. The cathedral school's international reputation had already drawn to Paris scholars from all over Europe, one of whom was Peter Abelard.

The son of a minor Breton knight, Peter Abelard (1079–1142) studied in Paris, quickly absorbed a large amount of material, and set himself up as a teacher. Abelard was fascinated by logic, which he believed could be used to solve most problems. He had a brilliant mind and, though orthodox in his philosophical teaching, appeared to challenge ecclesiastical authorities. His book

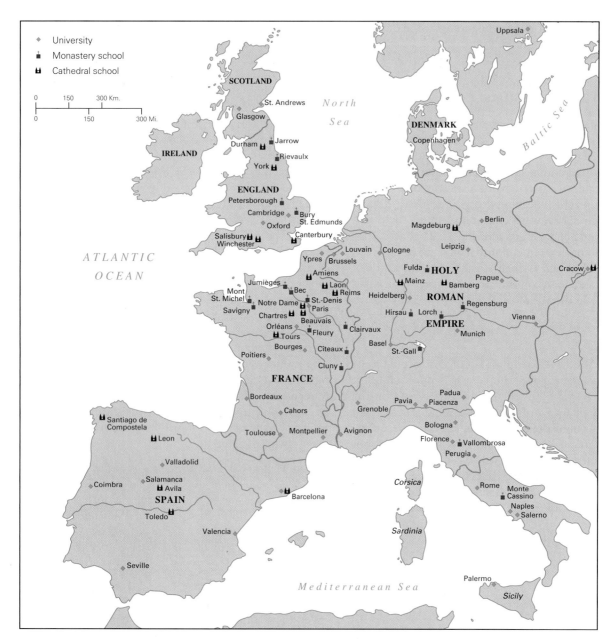

MAP 11.5 Intellectual Centers of Medieval Europe   Universities obviously provided more sophisticated instruction than did monastery and cathedral schools. What other factors distinguished the three kinds of intellectual centers?

Sic et Non (Yes and No) was a list of apparently contradictory propositions drawn from the Bible and the writings of the church fathers. One such proposition, for example, stated that sin is pleasing to God and is not pleasing to God. Abelard used a method of systematic doubting in his writing and teaching. As he put it in the preface to *Sic*

et Non, "By doubting we come to questioning, and by questioning we perceive the truth." While other scholars merely asserted theological principles, Abelard discussed and analyzed them. Through reasoning he even tried to describe the attributes of the three persons of the Trinity, the central mystery of the Christian faith. Abelard was

Law Lecture at Bologna This beautifully carved marble sculpture, with the fluid drapery characteristic of late Gothic style, suggests the students' intellectual intensity. The profusion of books and the presence of a woman (*bottom row, center*) make us wonder whether the artist actually witnessed such a scene. Universities generally did not admit women until the late nineteenth century. *(Museo Civico, Bologna/Scala/Art Resource, NY)*

severely censured by a church council, but his cleverness, boldness, and imagination made him a highly popular figure among students.

In a supposedly autobiographical statement, *A History of My Calamities,* Abelard described his academic career and his private life. His reputation for intellectual brilliance and arrogance drew the attention of one of the cathedral canons, Fulbert, who hired Abelard to tutor his clever niece Heloise. The relationship between teacher and pupil passed beyond the intellectual. Abelard said that he seduced Heloise to learn about sexuality. She became pregnant, and Canon Fulbert pressured the couple to marry. Abelard insisted that the union be kept secret for the sake of his career, an arrangement Heloise much resented. Distrusting Abelard, Canon Fulbert hired men

to castrate him. Wounded in spirit as well as body, Abelard persuaded Heloise to enter a convent; he became a monk of Saint-Denis; their baby, baptized Astrolabe for a recent Muslim navigational invention, was given to her family for adoption. Heloise secured a copy of Abelard's *History* and took great exception to his statement that their relationship had been based solely on physical desire. She considered her religious life hypocritical. Abelard spent his later years as abbot of an obscure monastery in Brittany, where he wrote Heloise letters of spiritual direction. The two unfortunate lovers were united in death and later buried together in a cemetery in Paris. Some scholars consider *A History of My Calamities* the most famous autobiography of the twelfth century, a fine example of the new self-awareness of the period's rebirth of learning. Other scholars believe the entire *History* a forgery, the source of a romantic legend with no basis in historical fact.[34]

The influx of students eager for learning, together with dedicated and imaginative teachers, created the atmosphere in which universities grew. In northern Europe—at Paris and later at Oxford and Cambridge in England—associations or guilds of professors organized universities. They established the curriculum, set the length of time for study, and determined the form and content of examinations.

Instruction and Curriculum

University faculties grouped themselves according to academic disciplines—law, medicine, arts, and theology. The professors (a term first used in the fourteenth century) were known as "schoolmen" or **Scholastics;** they developed a method of thinking, reasoning, and writing in which questions were raised and authorities cited on both sides of the question. The goal of the Scholastic method was to arrive at definitive answers and to provide a rational explanation for what was believed on faith. Schoolmen held that reason and faith constituted two harmonious realms whose truths complemented each other.

The Scholastic approach rested on the recovery of classical philosophical texts. Ancient Greek and Arabic texts had entered Europe in the early twelfth century. Knowledge of Aristotle and other Greek philosophers came to Paris and Oxford by way of Islamic intellectual centers at Baghdad, Córdoba, and Toledo. But these texts, forming the basis of Western philosophical and theological speculation, were not the only Islamic gifts. The major contribution of Arabic culture to the new currents of Western thought rested in the stimulus Arabic philosophers and commentators gave to Europeans' reflection on the Greek texts. For example, in Islam a strong tension exists between faith and reason. Western scholars' understanding of Aristotle's philosophy was closely tied to their discovery of Arabic thought. The tension between reason and faith became a fundamental theme in Christian thought.[35]

Aristotle had stressed the importance of the direct observance of nature, as well as the principles that theory must follow fact and that knowledge of a thing requires an explanation of its causes. The schoolmen reinterpreted Aristotelian texts in a Christian sense. But in their exploration of the natural world, they did not precisely follow Aristotle's axioms. Medieval scientists argued from authority, such as the Bible, the Justinian *Code,* or an ancient scientific treatise, rather than from direct observation and experimentation, as modern scientists do. Thus the conclusions of medieval scientists were often wrong. Nevertheless, natural science gradually emerged as a discipline distinct from philosophy, and Scholastics laid the foundations for later scientific work.

Many of the problems that Scholastic philosophers raised dealt with theological issues. For example, they addressed the question that interested all Christians, educated and uneducated: how is a person saved? Saint Augustine's thesis—that, as a result of Adam's fall, human beings have a propensity to sin—had become a central feature of church doctrine. The church taught that it possessed the means to forgive the sinful: grace conveyed through the sacraments. However, although grace provided a predisposition to salvation, the Scholastics held that one must also *decide* to use the grace received. In other words, a person must use his or her will and reason to advance to God.

Thirteenth-century Scholastics devoted an enormous amount of time to collecting and organizing knowledge on all topics. These collections were published as **summa,** or reference books. There were summa on law, philosophy, vegetation, animal life, and theology. Saint Thomas Aquinas (1225–1274), a professor at Paris, produced the most famous collection, the *Summa Theologica,* which deals with a vast number of theological questions.

Aquinas drew an important distinction between faith and reason. He maintained that, although reason can demonstrate many basic Christian principles such as the existence of God, other fundamental teachings such as the Trinity and original sin cannot be proved by logic. That reason cannot establish them does not, however, mean they are contrary to reason. Rather, people understand such doctrines through revelation embodied in Scripture. Scripture cannot contradict reason, nor reason Scripture:

The light of faith that is freely infused into us does not destroy the light of natural knowledge [reason] implanted in us naturally. For although the natural light of the human mind is insufficient to show us these things made manifest by faith, it is nevertheless impossible that these things which the divine principle gives us by faith are contrary to these implanted in us by nature [reason]. Indeed, were that the case, one or the other would have to be false, and, since both are given to us by God, God would have to be the author of untruth, which is impossible. . . . [I]t is impossible that those things which are of philosophy can be contrary to those things which are of faith.[36]

Aquinas also investigated the branch of philosophy called *epistemology,* which is concerned with how a person knows something. Aquinas stated that one knows, first, through sensory perception of the physical world— seeing, hearing, touching, and so on. He maintained that there can be nothing in the mind that is not first in the senses. Second, knowledge comes through reason, the mind exercising its natural abilities. Aquinas stressed the power of human reason to know, even to know God. Proofs of the existence of God exemplify the Scholastic method of knowing.

Aquinas began with the things of the natural world— earth, air, trees, water, birds. Then he inquired about their original source or cause: the mover, creator, planner who started it all. Everything, Aquinas maintained, has an ultimate and essential explanation, a reason for existing. Here he was following Aristotle. Aquinas went further and identified this reason for existing, or first mover, with God. Aquinas and all medieval intellectuals held that the end of faith and reason was the knowledge of, and union with, God. His work later became the fundamental text of Roman Catholic doctrine.

At all universities, the standard method of teaching was the *lecture*—that is, a reading. The professor read a passage from the Bible, the Justinian *Code,* or one of Aristotle's treatises. He then explained and interpreted the passage; his interpretation was called a *gloss.* Texts and glosses were sometimes collected and reproduced as textbooks. For example, the Italian Peter Lombard (d. 1160), a professor at Paris, wrote what became the standard textbook in theology, *Sententiae* (The Sentences), a compilation of basic theological principles.

Because books had to be copied by hand, they were extremely expensive, and few students could afford them. Students therefore depended for study on their own or friends' notes accumulated over a period of years. The choice of subjects was narrow. The syllabus at all universities consisted of a core of ancient texts that all students studied and, if they wanted to get ahead, mastered.

Examinations were given after three, four, or five years of study, when the student applied for a degree. The professors determined the amount of material students had to know for each degree, and students frequently insisted that the professors specify precisely what that material was. When the candidate for a degree believed himself prepared, he presented himself to a committee of professors for examination.

Examinations were oral and very difficult. If the candidate passed, he was awarded the first, or bachelor's, degree. Further study, about as long, arduous, and expensive as it is today, enabled the graduate to try for the master's and doctor's degrees. All degrees certified competence in a given subject, and degrees were technically licenses to teach. Most students, however, did not become teachers. They staffed the expanding diocesan, royal, and papal administrations.

Gothic Art

Medieval churches stand as the most spectacular manifestations of medieval vitality and creativity. It is difficult for people today to appreciate the extraordinary amounts of energy, imagination, and money involved in building them. Between 1180 and 1270 in France alone, eighty cathedrals, about five hundred abbey churches, and tens of thousands of parish churches were constructed. This construction represents a remarkable investment for a country of scarcely 18 million people. More stone was quarried for churches in medieval France than had been mined in ancient Egypt, where the Great Pyramid alone consumed 40.5 million cubic feet of stone. All these churches displayed a new architectural style, which actually preceded the modern term for it. The Italian Renaissance art historian Giorgio Vasari (1511–1574) first applied the term **Gothic** to the architectural and artistic style that prevailed in Europe (particularly northern Europe) from the mid-twelfth to the sixteenth century. Vasari and other Renaissance artists used *Gothic* as a word of abuse: they condemned medieval architecture as barbaric, implying, wrongly, that it was the style of the Gothic tribes who had destroyed the classical architecture of the Roman Empire. In fact, the Gothic style developed partly in reaction to the earlier Romanesque style, which resembled ancient Roman architecture. (See the feature "Images in Society: From Romanesque to Gothic" on pages 362–363.)

From Romanesque Gloom to "Uninterrupted Light"

In the ninth and tenth centuries, the Vikings and Magyars had burned hundreds of wooden churches. In the eleventh century, the abbots wanted to rebuild in a more permanent fashion, and after the year 1000, church building increased on a wide scale. Because fireproofing was essential, builders replaced wooden roofs with arched stone ceilings called "vaults." The stone ceilings were heavy; only thick walls could support them. Because the walls were so thick, the windows were small, allowing little light into the interior of the church. The basic features of such Romanesque architecture are stone vaults in

Images in Society

From Romanesque to Gothic

The word *church* has several meanings: assembly, congregation, sect. The Greek term from which it is derived means "a thing belonging to the Lord," and this concept was applied to the building where a congregation assembled. In the Middle Ages, people understood the church building to be "the house of God and the gate to heaven"; it served as an image or representation of supernatural reality (heaven). A church symbolized faith. Christians revealed and exercised faith; they communicated with God through prayer, that is, by raising the mind and heart to God. The church building seemed the ideal place for prayer: communal prayer built faith, and faith encouraged prayer.

Architecture became the dominant art form of the Middle Ages. Nineteenth-century architectural historians coined the term *Romanesque,* meaning "in the Roman manner," to describe church architecture in most of Europe between the tenth and twelfth centuries. The main features of the Romanesque style—solid walls, rounded arches, and masonry vaults—had been the characteristics of large Roman buildings. With the massive barrel vaulting of the roof, heavy walls were required to carry the weight (see Image 1). Romanesque churches had a massive quality, reflecting the increasing political and economic stability of the period and suggesting that they were places of refuge and security in times of attack. A Romanesque church was a "fortress of God."

Gothic churches were laid out in a cruciform (shaped like a cross) plan. The pilgrim approached the west end of the building, noticing the carved statues in the *tympanum* (space above the portal, or door), perhaps awestruck by the lancets and rose window over the portal. Inside, a long row of columns directed his gaze down the *nave* (center aisle), and he proceeded to the *transept* (cross aisle), which separated the sanctuary and the choir (reserved for the clergy) from the body of the church (the laypeople's area). See Image 2. So that the flow of pilgrims would not disturb the clergy in their chants, *ambulatories* (walkways) were constructed around the sanctuary. Off the ambulatories, radiating chapels surrounded the *apse,* the semicircular domed

Image 1 Saint-Savin-sur-Gartempe (Romanesque), Early Twelfth Century *(Editions Gaud)*

projection at the east end of the building. Apsidal chapels, each dedicated to and containing the relics of a particular saint, were visible from the exterior, as were the *flying buttresses* that supported the outward thrusts of the interior vaults. Above the apse and the west, south, and north portals, circular windows emerged from the radiating stone tracery in the form of a rose.

Study the model of Chartres Cathedral (Image 3). Cover it with a piece of paper. In the photo of Notre Dame Cathedral on page 365, identify the following parts of a Gothic church: west portal, nave, transept, ambulatory, apse, pointed arch, flying buttress, spire, lancet, rose window. Explain the function of each feature you identify. How do you account for the fact that some churches were never finished?

Compare the interior of the abbey church of Saint-Savin-sur-Gartempe (Image 1), a Romanesque church

Image 2 Amiens Cathedral, Mid-Thirteenth Century
(*Editions Gaud*)

Floor Plan

North portal
Apse
East
Transept
Choir and sanctuary
Ambulatory
Nave
West portal
South portal

Spire

Ribbed vaulting

Rose window

Rose window

Lancets

South portal

Tympanum

West portal

Flying buttress

Pointed arch

Image 3 Elements of a Gothic Church (Chartres Cathedral)

Image 4 Sainte-Chapelle, Paris, Mid-Thirteenth Century
(*Scala/Art Resource, NY*)

built in about 1100 in Poitou, France, and the interior of Amiens Cathedral (Image 2), a Gothic church built from 1220 to 1288. What are the most striking differences? What developments made the changes from Romanesque to Gothic structurally possible?

Architecture reveals the interests and values of a society, its goals and aspirations. What does Sainte-Chapelle (Image 4), built by King Louis IX of France to house relics—the crown of thorns placed on Jesus' head before the Crucifixion, a nail from the Crucifixion, a fragment of Jesus' cross—tell us about the values and aspirations of thirteenth-century French society?

A Gothic church represents more than a house of prayer or worship. Medieval people did not compartmentalize the various aspects of their lives as modern people tend to do. What civic, social, economic, and political functions did a church building serve?

The *history companion* features additional information and activities related to this topic.
history.college.hmco.com/students

the ceiling, a rounded arch over the nave (the central part of the church), and thick, heavy walls. In northern Europe, twin bell towers often crowned Romanesque churches, giving them a powerful, fortresslike appearance. Built primarily by monasteries, Romanesque churches reflect the quasi-military, aristocratic, and pre-urban society that built them.

The inspiration for the Gothic style originated in the brain of one monk, Suger, abbot of Saint-Denis (1122–1151). When Suger became abbot, he decided to reconstruct the old Carolingian abbey church at Saint-Denis. Work began in 1137. On June 11, 1144, King Louis VII and a large crowd of bishops, dignitaries, and common people witnessed the solemn consecration of the first Gothic church in France.

The basic features of Gothic architecture—the pointed arch, the ribbed vault, and the flying buttress—were not unknown before 1137. What was without precedent was the interior lightness they made possible. Since the ceiling of a Gothic church weighed less than that of a Romanesque church, the walls could be thinner. Stained-glass windows were cut into the stone, flooding the church with light. The bright interior was astounding. Suger, describing his achievement, exulted:

Moreover, it was cunningly provided that . . . the central nave of the old nave should be equalized, by means of geometrical and arithmetical instruments, with the central nave of the new addition; and, likewise, that the dimensions of the old side-aisles should be equalized with the new dimensions of the new side-aisles, except for that elegant and praiseworthy extension, in [the form of] a circular string of chapels, by virtue of which the whole [church] would shine with the wonderful and uninterrupted light of most sacred windows, pervading the interior beauty.[37]

Begun in the Île-de-France, Gothic architecture spread throughout France with the expansion of royal power. From France the new style spread to England, Germany, Italy, Spain, and eastern Europe. In those countries, the Gothic style competed with strong indigenous architectural traditions and thus underwent transformations that changed it to fit local usage. French master masons were soon invited to design and supervise the construction of churches in other parts of Europe. For example, William of Sens was commissioned to rebuild Canterbury Cathedral after a disastrous fire in 1174. The distinguished scholar John of Salisbury was then in Canterbury and observed William's work. After John became bishop of Chartres, he wanted William of Sens to assist in the renovation of Chartres Cathedral. Through such contacts the new style traveled rapidly over Europe.

The Creative Outburst

It was the bishop and the clergy of the cathedral who made the decision to build, but they depended on the support of all social classes. Bishops raised revenue from contributions by people in their dioceses, and the clergy appealed to the king and the nobility. Since Suger deliberately utilized the Gothic style to glorify the French monarchy, it was called "French royal style" from its inception. Thus the French kings were generous patrons of many cathedrals. Louis IX endowed churches in the Île-de-France—most notably, Sainte-Chapelle, a small chapel to house relics. Noble families often gave contributions to have their crests in the stained-glass windows. Above all, the church relied on the help of those with the greatest amount of ready cash, the commercial classes.

Money was not the only need. A great number of craftsmen had to be assembled: quarrymen, sculptors, stonecutters, masons, mortar makers, carpenters, blacksmiths, glassmakers, roofers. Each master craftsman had apprentices, and unskilled laborers had to be recruited for the heavy work. The construction of a large cathedral was rarely completed in a lifetime; many were never finished at all. Because generation after generation added to the building, many Gothic churches show the architectural influences of two or even three centuries.

Bishops and abbots sketched out what they wanted and set general guidelines, but they left practical needs and aesthetic considerations to the master mason. He held overall responsibility for supervision of the project. (Medieval chroniclers applied the term *architect* to the abbots and bishops who commissioned the projects or the lay patrons who financed them, not to the draftsmen who designed them.) **Master masons** were paid higher wages than other masons, their contracts usually ran for several years, and great care was taken in their selection. Being neither gentlemen, clerics, nor laborers, master masons fit uneasily into the social hierarchy.[38]

Since cathedrals were symbols of civic pride, towns competed to build the largest and most splendid church. In northern France in the late twelfth and early thirteenth centuries, cathedrals grew progressively taller. In 1163 the citizens of Paris began Notre Dame Cathedral, planning it to reach the height of 114 feet. When reconstruction on Chartres Cathedral was begun in 1194, it was to be 119 feet. The people of Beauvais exceeded everyone: their church, started in 1247, reached 157 feet. Unfortunately, the weight imposed on the vaults was too great, and the building collapsed in 1284. Medieval people built cathedrals to glorify God—and if mortals were impressed, all the better.[39]

Notre Dame Cathedral, Paris (begun 1163), View from the South   This view offers a fine example of the twin towers *(left)*, the spire, the great rose window over the south portal, and the flying buttresses that support the walls and the vaults. Like hundreds of other churches in medieval Europe, it was dedicated to the Virgin. With a nave rising 226 feet, Notre Dame was the tallest building in Europe. *(David R. Frazier/Photo Researchers)*

Cathedrals served secular as well as religious purposes. The sanctuary containing the altar and the bishop's chair belonged to the clergy, but the rest of the church belonged to the people. In addition to marriages, baptisms, and funerals, there were scores of feast days on which the entire town gathered in the cathedral for festivities. Amiens Cathedral could hold the entire town population. Local guilds, which fulfilled the economic, fraternal, and charitable functions of modern labor unions, met in the cathedrals to arrange business deals and plan recreational events and the support of disabled members. Magistrates and municipal officials held political meetings there. Some towns never built town halls, because all civic functions took place in the cathedral. Pilgrims slept there, lovers courted there, traveling actors staged plays there. The cathedral belonged to all.

First and foremost, however, the cathedral was intended to teach the people the doctrines of Christian faith through visual images. Architecture became the servant of theology. The main altar was at the east end, pointing toward Jerusalem, the city of peace. The west front of the cathedral faced the setting sun, and its wall was usually devoted to the scenes of the Last Judgment. The north side, which received the least sunlight, displayed events from the Old Testament. The south side, washed in warm sunshine for much of the day, depicted scenes from the New Testament. This symbolism implied that the Jewish people of the Old Testament lived in

Tree of Jesse   In Christian symbolism, a tree stands for either life or death. Glassmakers depicted the ancestors of Christ as a tree's branches, based on the prophecy of Isaiah (11:1–2)—"a shoot shall sprout from the stump of Jesse, and from his roots a bud shall blossom, the spirit of the Lord shall rest upon him"—and the genealogy of Jesus in Matthew (1:1–16). In this stained glass from the west façade of Chartres Cathedral (ca 1150–1170), Jesse, David, and Solomon are shown from bottom to top, with Mary holding the Christ child (unseen) at the top. The glass is set within a rectilinear framework. *(© Clive Hicks)*

darkness and that the Gospel brought by Christ illuminated the world. Every piece of sculpture, furniture, and stained glass had religious or social significance.

Stained glass beautifully reflects the creative energy of the High Middle Ages. It is both an integral part of Gothic architecture and a distinct form of painting. The ancient Egyptians had invented the process. The designer first sketched a picture on a wooden panel the size of the window opening. He noted the colors of each form or shape in the planned composition. Then glass blowers made sheets of colored glass, adding metallic oxides— cobalt for blue, manganese for red or purple, silver for yellow—to a basic mixture of sand and ash or lime, which was fused at a high temperature. From the large sheets of stained glass, artisans cut small pieces and laid them out on the wooden panel. Details were added with an enamel emulsion, and the glass was reheated to fuse the enamel. Last, the designer assembled the pieces and linked them together with narrow strips of lead, called *cames*. The assembled window was then set into an iron frame prepared to fit the window opening.[40] As Gothic churches became more skeletal and had more windows, stained glass replaced manuscript illumination as the leading form of painting.

Contributors to the cathedral and workers left their imprints on it. Stonecutters cut their individual marks in each block of stone, partly so that they would be paid. At Chartres the craft and merchant guilds—drapers, furriers, haberdashers, tanners, butchers, bakers, fishmongers, and wine merchants—donated money and are memorialized in stained-glass windows. Thousands of scenes in the cathedral celebrate nature, country life, and the activities of ordinary people. All members of medieval society had a place in the City of God, which the Gothic cathedral represented. No one, from king to peasant, was excluded.

Romanesque and Gothic churches housed relics of Jesus, Mary, or the saints. These bones or material objects were believed to have been part of, or in contact with, the bodies of saints. Abbey and cathedral churches at-

Fifteenth-Century Flemish Tapestry
The weavers of Tournai (in present-day Belgium) spent twenty-five years (1450–1475) producing this magnificent tapestry, which is based on the Old Testament story of Jehu, Jezebel, and the sons of Ahab (2 Kings, 9–10). *(Isabella Stewart Gardner Museum, Boston)*

tracted pilgrims from far and near to pray near the relics. Consider the economic opportunities pilgrims afforded to a Gothic cathedral and its locality.

Tapestry making also came into its own in the fourteenth century. Heavy woolen tapestries were first made in the monasteries and convents as wall hangings for churches. Because they could be moved and lent an atmosphere of warmth, they replaced mural paintings. Early tapestries depicted religious scenes, but later hangings produced for the knightly class bore secular designs, especially romantic forests and hunting spectacles.

Drama, derived from the church's liturgy, emerged as a distinct art form during the same period. For centuries skits based on Christ's Nativity and Resurrection had been performed in monasteries and cathedrals. Beginning in the thirteenth century, plays based on these and other biblical themes and on the lives of the saints were performed in the towns. Students of theater history distinguish three kinds of medieval plays: *mystery* plays financed and performed by "misteries," members of the craft guilds; *miracle* plays acted by amateurs or professional actors, not guild members; and *morality* plays in which the characters personified virtues and vices and the actors represented the struggle between good and evil. Performed first at the cathedral altar, then in the church square, later at stations around the town, and finally in the town marketplace, mystery plays enjoyed great popularity. By combining comical farce based on ordinary life with serious religious scenes, they gave ordinary people an opportunity to identify with religious figures and think about the mysteries of their faith.

Troubadour Poetry

In the twelfth and thirteenth centuries, a remarkable literary culture blossomed in southern France. The word *troubadour* comes from the Provençal word *trobar,* which in turn derives from the Arabic *taraba,* meaning "to sing" or "to sing poetry." A troubadour was a poet of Provençal who wrote lyric verse in his or her native language and sang it at one of the noble courts. Troubadour songs had a great variety of themes: "courtly love," the pure love a knight felt for his lady, whom he sought to win by military prowess and patience; or the love he felt for the wife of his feudal lord; or carnal desires seeking satisfaction. Women troubadours (*trobairitz*) focused on their emotions or their experiences with men. Some poems exalt the married state, others idealize adulterous relationships; some are earthy and bawdy, others advise young girls to remain chaste in preparation for marriage. Many poems celebrate the beauties of nature; a few speak of the sexual frustrations of nuns. The married Countess

Beatrice of Dia (1150–1200?) expresses the hurt she feels after being jilted by a young knight:

I've suffered great distress
From a knight whom I once owned.
Now, for all time, be it known:
I loved him—yes, to excess.
  His jilting I've regretted,
Yet his love I never really returned.
Now for my sin I can only burn:
  Dressed, or in my bed.

O if I had that knight to caress
Naked all night in my arms,
He'd be ravished by the charm
Of using, for cushion, my breast.
  His love I more deeply prize
Than Floris did Blancheflor's
Take that love, my core,
  My sense, my life, my eyes!

Lovely lover, gracious, kind,
When will I overcome your fight?
O if I could lie with you one night!
Feel those loving lips on mine!
  Listen, one thing sets me afire:
Here in my husband's place I want you,
If you'll just keep your promise true:
  Give me everything I desire.[41]

Because of its varied and contradictory themes, courtly love has been one of the most hotly debated topics in all medieval studies. One scholar concludes that it was at once "a literary movement, an ideology, an ethical system, an expression of the play element in culture, which arose in an aristocratic Christian environment exposed to Hispano-Arabic influences."[42] Another scholar insists there is no evidence for the practice of courtly love. If, however, the knight's love represented the respect of a vassal for his lady, a respect that inspired him to noble deeds, then perhaps courtly love contributed to an improvement in the status of women.

Hispano-Arabic influences troubadours certainly felt. In the eleventh century Christians of southern France were in intimate contact with the Arabized world of Andalusia, where reverence for the lady in a "courtly" tradition had long existed. In 1064 the Provençal lord Guillaume de Montreuil captured Barbastro and, according to legend, took one thousand slave girls from Andalusia in southern Spain back to Provence. Even if this figure is an exaggeration, those women who came to southern France would have been familiar with the Arabic tradition of sung poetry and continued it in their new

land. Troubadour poetry thus represents another facet of the strong Muslim influence on European culture and life.[43] Troubadour lyric poetry enjoyed the patronage of many of the great lords of southern France, including William IX, duke of Aquitaine, himself a famed author, and Richard the Lion-Hearted of England.

The romantic motifs of the troubadours also influenced the northern French *trouvères,* who wrote adventure-romances in the form of epic poems. Trouvères wrote in their native language, which we call Old French. At the court of his patron, Marie of Champagne, Chrétien de Troyes (ca 1135–ca 1190) used the legends of the fifth-century British king Arthur (see page 214) to discuss contemporary chivalric ideals and their moral implications. Such poems as *Lancelot, Percival and the Holy Grail,* and *Tristan and Isolde* reveal Chrétien as the founding father of the Western romantic genre and as the most innovative figure in the twelfth-century vernacular literature. The theme of these romances centers on the knight-errant seeking adventures, who, when faced with crises usually precipitated by love, acquires new values and grows in stature.

Since the songs of the troubadours and trouvères were widely imitated in Italy, England, and Germany, they spurred the development of the nascent vernacular languages. In the thirteenth century, for example, German Minnesängers (love singers) such as Walther von der Wogelweide (1170–1220) wrote stylized verses on a variety of topics. Most of the troubadours and trouvères came from and wrote for the aristocratic classes, and their poetry suggests the interests and values of noble culture in the High Middle Ages.

Heresy and the Friars

As the commercial revolution of the High Middle Ages fostered urban development, the towns experienced an enormous growth of heresy. In fact, in the twelfth and thirteenth centuries, "the most economically advanced and urbanized areas: northern Italy, southern France, Flanders-Brabant, and the lower Rhine Valley" witnessed the strongest heretical movements.[44] Why did heresy flourish in such places? The bishops, usually drawn from the feudal nobility, did not understand urban culture and were suspicious of it. Christian theology, formulated for an earlier, rural age, did not address the problems of the more sophisticated mercantile society. The new monastic orders of the twelfth century, situated in remote, isolated areas, had little relevance to the towns.[45] Finally, towns-people wanted a pious clergy, capable of preaching the

Gospel in a manner that satisfied their spiritual needs. They disapproved of clerical ignorance and luxurious living. Critical of the clergy, neglected, and spiritually unfulfilled, townspeople turned to heretical sects.

The term *heresy,* which derives from the Greek *hairesis,* meaning "individual choosing," is older than Christianity. At the end of the fourth century, when Christianity became the official religion of the Roman Empire, religious issues took on a legal dimension. Theologians and kings defined the Roman Empire as a Christian society. Since religion was thought to bind society in a fundamental way, religious unity was essential for social cohesion. A heretic, therefore, threatened not only the religious part of the community, but the community itself. As described on page 194, civil authority could (and did) punish heresy. In the early Middle Ages, the term *heresy* came to be applied to the position of a Christian who chose and stubbornly held to doctrinal error in defiance of church authority.[46]

Ironically, the eleventh-century Gregorian reform movement, which had worked to purify the church of disorder, led to some twelfth- and thirteenth-century heretical movements. Papal efforts to improve the sexual morality of the clergy, for example, had largely succeeded. When Gregory VII forbade married priests to celebrate church ceremonies, he expected public opinion to force priests to put aside their wives and concubines. But Gregory did not foresee the consequences of this order. Laypersons assumed they could remove immoral priests. Critics and heretics could accuse clergymen of immorality and thus weaken their influence. Moreover, by forbidding sinful priests to administer the sacraments, Gregory unwittingly revived the old Donatist heresy, which held that sacraments given by an immoral priest were useless; thus Donatist beliefs spread. The clergy's inability to provide adequate instruction weakened its position. In the thirteenth century secular governments, such as that of Frederick II, pressed for social conformity, using ecclesiastical courts of the Inquisition to search out heretics (see page 346).

In northern Italian towns, Arnold of Brescia, a vigorous advocate of strict clerical poverty, denounced clerical wealth. In France Peter Waldo, a rich merchant of Lyons, gave his money to the poor and preached that only prayers, not sacraments, were needed for salvation. The "Waldensians"—as Peter's followers were called—bitterly attacked the sacraments and church hierarchy, and they carried these ideas across Europe. Another group, known either as the Cathars (from the Greek *katharos,* meaning "pure") or as the **Albigensians** (from the town of Albi in southern France), rejected not only the hierarchical organization and the sacraments of the church, but the Roman church itself. The Cathars' primary tenet was the dualist belief that God had created spiritual things and the Devil had created material things; thus the soul was good and the body evil. Forces of good and evil battled constantly, and leading a perfect life meant being stripped of all physical and material things. Thus sexual intercourse was evil because it led to the creation of more physical bodies. To free oneself from the power of evil, a person had to lead a life of extreme asceticism, avoiding all material things. Albigensians were divided into the "perfect," who followed the principles of Catharism, and the "believers," who led ordinary lives until their deaths, when they repented and were saved.

The Albigensian heresy won many adherents in southern France. Townspeople admired the virtuous lives of the "perfect," women were attracted because the Albigensians treated them as men's equals, and nobles were drawn because they coveted the wealth of the clergy. Faced with widespread defection in southern France, Pope Innocent III in 1208 proclaimed a crusade against the Albigensian heretics. When the papal legate was murdered by a follower of Count Raymond of Toulouse, the greatest lord in southern France and a suspected heretic, the crusade took on a political character; heretical beliefs became fused with feudal rebellion against the French crown. Northern French lords joined the crusade and inflicted severe defeats on the towns of the province of Languedoc. The Albigensian crusade, however, was a political rather than a religious success, and the heresy went underground.

In its continuing struggle against heresy, the church gained the support of two remarkable men, Saint Dominic and Saint Francis, and of the orders they founded. Born in Castile, the province of Spain famous for its zealous Christianity and militant opposition to Islam, Domingo de Gúzman (1170?–1221) received a sound education and was ordained a priest. In 1206 he accompanied his bishop on a mission to preach to the Albigensian heretics in Languedoc. Although the austere simplicity in which they traveled contrasted favorably with the pomp and display of the papal legate in the area, Dominic's efforts had little practical success. Determined to win the heretics back with ardent preaching, Dominic subsequently returned to France with a few followers. In 1216 the group—known as the "Preaching Friars"—won papal recognition as a new religious order. Their name indicates their goal; they were to preach, and in order to preach effectively, they had to study. Dominic sent his recruits to the universities for training in theology.

Francesco di Bernardone (1181–1226), son of a wealthy cloth merchant from the northern Italian town of Assisi, was an extravagant wastrel until he had a sudden conversion. Directed by a vision to rebuild the dilapidated chapel of Saint Damiano in Assisi, Francis sold some of his father's cloth to finance the reconstruction. His enraged father insisted that he return the money and enlisted the support of the bishop. When the bishop told Francis to obey his father, Francis took off all his clothes and returned them to his father. Thereafter he promised to obey only his Father in Heaven. Francis was particularly inspired by two biblical texts: "If you seek perfection, go, sell your possessions, and give to the poor. You will have treasure in heaven. Afterward, come back and follow me" (Matthew 19:21); and Jesus' advice to his disciples as they went out to preach, "Take nothing for the journey, neither walking staff nor travelling bag, nor bread, nor money" (Luke 9:3). Over the centuries, these words have stimulated countless young people. With Francis, however, there was a radical difference: he intended to observe them literally and without compromise. He set out to live and preach the Gospel in absolute poverty.

The simplicity, humility, and joyful devotion with which Francis carried out his mission soon attracted companions. Although he resisted pressure to establish an order, his followers became so numerous that he was obliged to develop some formal structure. In 1221 the papacy approved the "Rule of the Little Brothers of Saint Francis," as the Franciscans were known.

The new Dominican and Franciscan orders differed significantly from older monastic orders such as the Benedictines and the Cistercians. (So also did the Beguines, laywomen who wished to live a religious life without becoming cloistered nuns; they lived in or near cities in northwestern Europe, led prayerful lives, and supported themselves through manual labor, teaching, or writing.) First, the Dominicans and Franciscans were friars, not monks. Their lives and work centered on the cities and university towns, the busy centers of commercial and intellectual life, not the secluded and cloistered world of monks. Second, the friars stressed apostolic poverty, a life based on the Gospel's teachings, in which they would own no property and depend on Christian people for their material needs. Hence they were called *mendicants,* begging friars. Benedictine and Cistercian abbeys, on the other hand, held land—not infrequently great tracts of land. Finally, the friars usually drew their members largely from the burgher class, from small property owners and shopkeepers. The monastic orders, by contrast, gathered their members (at least until the thirteenth century) overwhelmingly from the nobility.[47]

The friars represented a response to the spiritual and intellectual needs of the thirteenth century. Research on the German friars has shown that, while the Franciscans initially

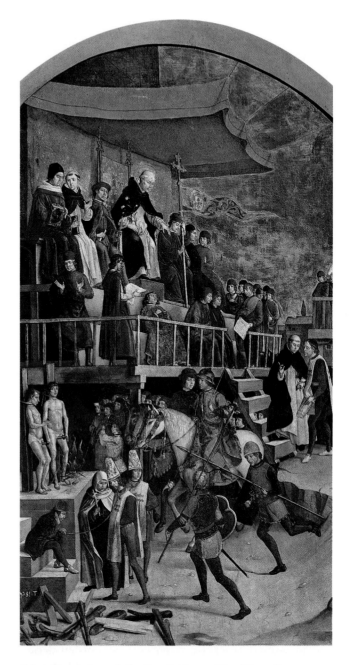

Saint Dominic and the Inquisition The fifteenth-century court painter to the Spanish rulers Ferdinand and Isabella, Pedro Berruguete here portrays an event from the life of Saint Dominic: Dominic presides at the trial of Count Raymond of Toulouse, who had supported the Albigensian heretics. Raymond, helmeted and on horseback, repented and was pardoned; his companions, who would not repent, were burned. Smoke from the fire has put one of the judges to sleep, and other officials, impervious to the human tragedy, chat among themselves. *(Museo del Prado, Madrid/Institut Amatller d'Art Hispanic)*

accepted uneducated men, the Dominicans always showed a marked preference for university graduates.[48] A more urban and sophisticated society required a highly educated clergy. The Dominicans soon held professorial chairs at leading universities, and they count Thomas Aquinas, probably the greatest medieval philosopher in Europe, as their most famous member. But the Franciscans followed suit at the universities and also produced intellectual leaders. The friars interpreted Christian doctrine for the new urban classes. By living Christianity as well as by preaching it, they won the respect of the medieval bourgeoisie.

Beginning in 1233, the papacy used the friars to staff a new ecclesiastical court, the Inquisition. Popes selected the friars to direct the Inquisition because bishops proved unreliable and because special theological training was needed. *Inquisition* means "investigation," and the Franciscans and Dominicans developed expert methods of rooting out unorthodox thought. Modern Americans consider the procedures of the Inquisition exceedingly unjust, and there was substantial criticism of it in the Middle Ages. The accused did not learn the evidence against them or see their accusers; they were subjected to lengthy interrogations often designed to trap them; and torture could be used to extract confessions. Medieval people, however, believed that heretics destroyed the souls of their neighbors. By attacking religion, it was also thought, heretics destroyed the very bonds of society. By the mid-thirteenth century secular governments steadily pressed for social conformity, and they had the resources to search out and to punish heretics. So successful was the Inquisition as a tool of royal power that within a century heresy had been virtually extinguished.

A Challenge to Religious Authority

Societies, like individuals, cannot maintain a high level of energy indefinitely. In the later years of the thirteenth century, Europeans seemed to run out of steam. The crusading movement gradually fizzled out. Few new cathedrals were constructed, and if a cathedral had not been completed by 1300, the chances were high that it never would be. The strong rulers of England and France, building on the foundations of their predecessors, increased their authority and gained the loyalty of all their subjects. The vigor of those kings, however, did not pass to their immediate descendants. Meanwhile, the church, which for two centuries had guided Christian society, began to face grave difficulties. A violent dispute between the papacy and the kings of England and France badly damaged the prestige of the pope.

In 1294 King Edward I of England and Philip the Fair of France declared war on each other. To finance this war, both kings laid taxes on the clergy. Kings had been taxing the church for decades. Pope Boniface VIII (1294–1303), arguing from precedent, insisted that kings gain papal consent for taxation of the clergy and forbade churchmen to pay the taxes. But Edward and Philip refused to accept this decree, partly because it hurt royal finances and partly because the papal order threatened royal authority within their countries. Edward immediately denied the clergy the protection of the law, an action that meant its members could be attacked with impunity. Philip halted the shipment of all ecclesiastical revenue to Rome. Boniface had to back down.

Philip the Fair and his ministers continued their attack on all powers in France outside royal authority. Philip arrested a French bishop who was also the papal legate. When Boniface defended the ecclesiastical status and diplomatic immunity of the bishop, Philip replied with the trumped-up charge that the pope was a heretic. The papacy and the French monarchy waged a bitter war of propaganda. Finally, in 1302, in a letter titled **Unam Sanctam** (because its opening sentence spoke of one holy Catholic church), Boniface insisted that all Christians were subject to the pope. Although the letter made no specific reference to Philip, it held that kings should submit to papal authority. Philip's university-trained advisers responded with an argument drawn from Roman law. They maintained that the king of France was completely sovereign in his kingdom and responsible to God alone. French mercenary troops went to Italy and assaulted and arrested the aged pope at Anagni. Although Boniface was soon freed, he died shortly afterward. The confrontation at Anagni foreshadowed serious difficulties within the Christian church, but religious struggle was only one of the crises that would face Western society in the fourteenth century.

Summary

The High Middle Ages represent one of the most creative periods in the history of Western society. Advances were made in the evolution of strong government and urban life, economic development, architectural design, and education. Through the instruments of justice and finance, the kings of England and France attacked feudal rights and provincial practices, built centralized bureaucracies, and gradually came in contact with all their subjects. In so doing these rulers laid the foundations for modern nation-states. The German emperors, who were preoccupied with Italian affairs and with a quest for the imperial crown, supported feudal and local interests.

Medieval cities—whether beginning around the sites of cathedrals, fortifications, or market towns—recruited people from the countryside and brought into being a new social class, the middle class. Cities provided economic opportunity, which, together with the revival of long-distance trade and a new capitalistic spirit, led to greater wealth, a higher standard of living, and upward social mobility. The soaring Gothic cathedrals that medieval towns erected demonstrate civic pride, deep religious faith, and economic vitality. Universities, institutions of higher learning unique to the West, emerged from cathedral and municipal schools and provided trained officials for the new government bureaucracies. While the church exercised leadership of Christian society in the High Middle Ages, the clash between the papacy and the kings of France and England at the end of the thirteenth century seriously challenged papal power.

Key Terms

Domesday Book	precedent
baillis/seneschals	town liberties
Landfrieden	guilds
Exchequer	Hanseatic League
relief	Scholastics
scutage	summa
tallage/taille	Gothic
common law	master masons
circuit judges	Albigensians
Magna Carta	*Unam Sanctam*
Landgericht	

Notes

1. S. Reynolds, *Fiefs and Vassals: The Medieval Evidence Reconsidered* (Oxford: Clarendon Press, 1996), p. 27.
2. C. W. Hollister, "Normandy, France and the Anglo-Norman Regnum," in *Monarchy, Magnates and Institutions in the Anglo-Norman World* (London: Hambledon Press, 1986), p. 20.
3. D. C. Douglas and G. E. Greenaway, eds., *English Historical Documents,* vol. 2 (London: Eyre & Spottiswoode, 1961), p. 853.
4. W. L. Warren, *Henry II* (Berkeley: University of California Press, 1973), pp. 229–230.
5. See G. E. Spiegel, "The Cult of Saint Denis and Capetian Kingship," *Journal of Medieval History* 1 (April 1975): 43–65, esp. pp. 56–64.
6. B. Arnold, *Princes and Territories in Medieval Germany* (New York: Cambridge University Press, 1991), pp. 65–72.
7. Ibid., pp. 45–52, 73, passim.
8. J. Johns, *Arabic Administration in Norman Sicily: The Royal Dīwān* (New York: Cambridge University Press, 2002), pp. 268–272, esp. p. 271.
9. Ibid., pp. 213, 257–283.
10. Ibid., pp. 200–210.
11. Ibid., pp. 286–289.
12. Ibid., p. 289.
13. Ibid., p. 293.
14. R. Bartlett, *Trial by Fire and Water: The Medieval Judicial Ordeal* (Oxford: Clarendon Press, 1986), pp. 25–27 and chap. 3.
15. For the active role played by William Marshal, earl of Pembroke, in the negotiations leading up to Magna Carta, see D. Crouch, *William Marshal: Court, Career and Chivalry in the Angevin Empire, 1147–1219* (New York: Longman, 1990), pp. 112–113.
16. Arnold, *Princes and Territories,* pp. 186–200.
17. J. Boswell, *Christianity, Social Tolerance, and Homosexuality: Gay People in Western Europe from the Beginning of the Christian Era to the Fourteenth Century* (Chicago: University of Chicago Press, 1980), pp. 270–293; the quotation is from p. 293. For alternative interpretations, see K. Thomas, "Rescuing Homosexual History," *New York Review of Books,* December 4, 1980, 26ff.; and J. DuQ. Adams, *Speculum* 56 (April 1981): 350ff. For the French monarchy's persecution of the Jews, see J. W. Baldwin, *The Government of Philip Augustus: Foundations of French Royal Power in the Middle Ages* (Berkeley: University of California Press, 1986), pp. 51–52; and W. C. Jordan, *The French Monarchy and the Jews* (Philadelphia: University of Pennsylvania Press, 1989).
18. J. C. Russell, *Medieval Regions and Their Cities* (Bloomington: University of Indiana Press, 1972), p. 91.
19. Ibid., pp. 113–117.
20. Quoted in R. S. Lopez, "Of Towns and Trade," in *Life and Thought in the Early Middle Ages,* ed. R. S. Hoyt (Minneapolis: University of Minnesota Press, 1967), p. 33.
21. H. Pirenne, *Economic and Social History of Medieval Europe* (New York: Harcourt Brace, 1956), p. 53.
22. See D. Herlihy, *Medieval and Renaissance Pistoia: The Social History of an Italian Town, 1200–1430* (New Haven, Conn.: Yale University Press, 1967), p. 257.
23. Quoted in J. O'Faolain and L. Martines, eds., *Not in God's Image: Women in History from the Greeks to the Victorians* (New York: Harper & Row, 1973), pp. 155–156.
24. W. C. Jordan, *Women and Credit in Pre-Industrial and Developing Societies* (Philadelphia: University of Pennsylvania Press, 1993), pp. 20 et seq.
25. Douglas and Greenaway, *English Historical Documents,* vol. 2, pp. 969–970.
26. H. Rothwell, ed., *English Historical Documents,* vol. 3 (London: Eyre & Spottiswoode, 1975), p. 854.
27. M. M. Postan, *The Medieval Economy and Society: An Economic History of Britain in the Middle Ages* (Baltimore: Penguin Books, 1975), pp. 213–214.
28. See P. Spufford, *Money and Its Use in Medieval Europe* (Cambridge: Cambridge University Press, 1988), pp. 250–255.
29. See P. Dollinger, *The German Hansa,* trans. and ed. D. S. Ault and S. H. Steinberg (Stanford, Calif.: Stanford University Press, 1970).
30. C. M. Cipolla, *Before the Industrial Revolution: European Society and Economy, 1000–1700,* 2d ed. (New York: W. W. Norton, 1980), p. 197.
31. R. S. Lopez, "The Trade of Medieval Europe: The South," in *The Cambridge Economic History of Europe,* vol. 2, ed. M. M. Postan and E. E. Rich (Cambridge: Cambridge University Press, 1952), p. 289.
32. M. Haren, *Medieval Thought: The Western Intellectual Tradition from Antiquity to the Thirteenth Century,* 2d ed. (Toronto: University of Toronto Press, 1992), pp. 137–138.
33. Quoted in H. E. Sigerist, *Civilization and Disease* (Chicago: University of Chicago Press, 1943), p. 102.
34. See John F. Benton, "Fraud, Fiction and Borrowing in the Corre-

spondence of Abelard and Heloise," in *Culture, Power and Personality in Medieval France,* ed. T. N. Bisson (London and Rio Grande: The Hambledon Press, 1991), pp. 417–449, esp. pp. 430–443, which convincingly demonstrate that "the most personal parts of the correspondence are not genuine" and that the letters were probably written in the later thirteenth century; and the same scholar's "The Correspondence of Abelard and Heloise," in the same volume, pp. 487–512.

35. See Haren, *Medieval Thought,* pp. 117–119.

36. Quoted in J. H. Mundy, *Europe in the High Middle Ages, 1150–1309* (New York: Basic Books, 1973), pp. 474–475.

37. E. Panofsky, trans. and ed., *Abbot Suger on the Abbey Church of St. Denis and Its Art Treasures* (Princeton, N.J.: Princeton University Press, 1946), p. 101.

38. See C. M. Radding and W. W. Clark, *Medieval Architecture, Medieval Learning: Builders and Masters in the Age of Romanesque and Gothic* (New Haven, Conn.: Yale University Press, 1992), pp. 34–36.

39. See J. Gimpel, *The Cathedral Builders* (New York: Grove Press, 1961), pp. 42–49.

40. See "The Technique of Stained Glass Windows," in M. Stokstad, *Art History* (New York: Harry N. Abrams, 1995), p. 559, on which I have leaned.

41. Quoted in J. J. Wilhelm, ed., *Lyrics of the Middle Ages: An Anthology* (New York: Garland Publishers, 1993), pp. 83–84.

42. Quoted in R. Boase, *The Origin and Meaning of Courtly Love* (Manchester: Manchester University Press, 1977), pp. 129–130.

43. I have leaned on the very persuasive interpretation of M. R. Menocal, *The Arabic Role in Medieval Literary History* (Philadelphia: University of Pennsylvania Press, 1990), pp. ix–xv and 27–33.

44. J. B. Freed, *The Friars and German Society in the Thirteenth Century* (Cambridge, Mass.: Medieval Academy of America, 1977), p. 8.

45. Ibid., p. 9.

46. See F. Oakley, *The Western Church in the Later Middle Ages* (Ithaca, N.Y.: Cornell University Press, 1979), p. 175.

47. See Freed, *The Friars and German Society,* pp. 119–128.

48. Ibid., esp. p. 125.

Suggested Reading

Students interested in almost any aspect of English warfare will find M. Prestwich, *Armies and Warfare in the Middle Ages: The English Experience* (1996), exciting and readable. S. Morillo, *Warfare Under the Anglo-Norman Kings, 1066–1135* (1994), is also useful. S. D. Church, ed., *King John: New Interpretations* (1999), contains useful articles on many topics, including John's personality, the English economy, and the English and Norman aristocracies.

Several studies contain helpful perspectives: H. G. Richardson and G. O. Sayles, *The Governance of Medieval England from the Conquest to Magna Carta* (1963), focuses on administrative change. For the Celtic fringe, S. Duffy, *Ireland in the Middle Ages* (1997), incorporates the latest research; M. Richter, *Medieval Ireland: The Enduring Tradition* (1996), concentrates on Irish society; and B. Webster, *Medieval Scotland* (1997), stresses the evolution of a distinctly Scottish identity. Students interested in the evolution of English common law should see the studies by A. Murson and W. M. Ormrod, *The Evolution of English Justice: Law, Politics and Society in the Fourteenth Century* (1999), and J. Hudson, ed., *The History of English Law: Centenary Essays on Pollock and Maitland* (1996). Those interested in crime, society, and legal developments will find the following works useful and sound: J. S. Cockburn and T. A. Green, *Twelve Good Men and True: The Criminal Trial Jury in England, 1200–1800* (1988); J. B. Given, *Society and Homicide in Thirteenth-Century England* (1977); and R. C. Palmer, *The County Courts of Medieval England, 1150–1350* (1982). E. M. Hallam, *Domesday Book Through Nine Centuries* (1986), is an excellent appreciation of that important document, while J. R. Strayer, *On the Medieval Origins of the Modern State* (1970), is a good synthesis of political, legal, and administrative developments. The standard study of Magna Carta is J. C. Holt, *Magna Carta,* 2d ed. (1992). For the Becket controversy, see F. Barlow, *Thomas Becket* (1986), and D. Knowles, *Thomas Becket* (1970). J. Butler, *The Quest for Becket's Bones* (1995), explores the mystery of the location of the relics of England's most famous saint in a gripping and illustrated account.

Biographies often provide valuable insight into the issues of a reign through a focus on the king. For England, see F. Barlow, *Edward the Confessor* (1970); D. C. Douglas, *William the Conqueror* (1964); C. W. Hollister, *Henry I* (2001); W. L. Warren, *Henry II* (1973); J. Gillingham, *Richard I* (1999); and M. Prestwich, *Edward I* (1997).

For France, E. Hallam, *The Capetian Kings of France, 987–1328* (1980) is a readable introduction. Advanced students of medieval French administrative history should see J. Baldwin, *The Government of Philip Augustus: Foundations of French Royal Power in the Middle Ages* (1986); W. C. Jordan, *Louis IX and the Crusade* (1979); and J. R. Strayer, *The Reign of Philip the Fair* (1980).

For important revisionist interpretations of medieval Germany, see, in addition to the title by Arnold cited in the Notes, B. Arnold, *Count and Bishop in Medieval Germany* (1992), which is essential for understanding regional power and diversity; and J. B. Freed, *Noble Bondsmen: Ministerial Marriages in the Archdiocese of Salzburg, 1100–1343* (1995), a fine exploration of the disparity between the social status of the nobility and their legal status in southeastern Germany. P. Gorecki, *Economy, Society and Lordship in Poland, 1100–1250* (1992), contains helpful material on Germany as well as Poland. A. Haverkamp, *Medieval Germany, 1056–1273,* trans. H. Braun and R. Mortimer (1992), gives a comprehensive picture. D. Abulafia, *Frederick II: A Medieval Emperor* (1992), is a beautifully written study, but T. Van Cleve, *The Emperor Frederick II of Hohenstaufen* (1972), remains fundamental. For developments in Sicily, see J. Johns, *Arabic Administration in Norman Sicily* (2002). For Islamic Spain, see H. Kennedy, *Muslim Spain and Portugal: A Political History* (1998); R. Fletcher, *Moorish Spain* (1992); T. F. Ruiz, *Crisis and Continuity: Land and Town in Late Medieval Castile* (1994); and T. N. Bisson, *The Medieval Crown of Aragon* (1991).

(continued on page 376)

Listening to the Past

Early Islamic Views on Trade and Commerce

*T*rade and commerce served as a link between Europe and its geographical neighbors in the Islamic world. The Middle East had spices and many other things that Europeans wanted, but Muslims believed that, except for furs from the Baltic and fine English woolens, Europeans had nothing to trade except their own people: slaves (see page 228). Most Islamic trade involved the sophisticated economies of East Asia, South Asia, and southwestern Asia, and that commerce centered on the Red Sea and the Indian Ocean. European trade, small by Muslim standards, focused on the Mediterranean Sea.

  The Prophet Muhammad had been a merchant (see page 222), and from its beginnings Islam had esteemed business activity. By the thirteenth century the Muslim world had a well-developed mercantile philosophy. Europe did not. In both Muslim and European societies, trade and commerce were concentrated in urban communities, and although European cities were growing and trade was expanding, Europe remained overwhelmingly rural. The businessperson was something of an anomaly. Attitudes about trade and commerce, about the social status of the merchant, tell us a great deal about Christian and Muslim cultures.

Sayings Attributed to the Prophet

The best of gain is from honorable trade and from a man's work with his own hands.

To seek lawful gain is the duty of every Muslim.

To seek lawful gain is Holy War.

The honest, truthful Muslim merchant will stand with the martyrs on the Day of Judgment.

If a man works for his aged parents, that is in the path of God; if he works for his young children, that is in the path of God; if he works for himself, to be free of want, that too, is in the path of God.

I commend the merchants to you, for they are the couriers of the horizons and God's trusted servants on earth.

The devils come to the markets early in the morning with their flags; they arrive with the first to arrive, and they leave with the last to leave.

The most worthy of earnings are those of the merchants who, if they are spoken to, do not lie; if they are trusted, do not betray; if they promise, do not fail; if they buy, do not condemn; if they sell, do not extol; if they owe, do not delay; and if they are owed, do not press.

If God permitted the inhabitants of Paradise to trade, they would deal in cloth and perfume.

If there were trade in Heaven, they would sell cloth, and if there were trade in Hell, they would sell food. Whoever sells for forty days, mercy is plucked out of his heart.

He who brings supplies to our market is like a warrior in the Holy War for God. He who hoards and corners supplies in our market is like a heretic deviating from the Book of God.

It is God who fixes prices.

Dearness and cheapness are two of God's soldiers. One is called greed, and the other is called fear. If God desires dearness, He puts greed in the hearts of the merchants, who become greedy and hoard their wares. If God desires cheapness, He puts fear in the hearts of the merchants, and they release what is in their hands.

أللهم أجرني من لدنك سلطانًا نصيرًا واجعل لي من لدنك سلطانًا نصيرًا سلط على مغير

Because a camel can carry 500 pounds as far as 25 miles a day, camel caravans were the traditional means of transporting goods overland in the Muslim world. *(Bibliothèque nationale de France)*

When God is angry with a people [*umma*], He makes their prices high, their markets sluggish, their misdeeds many, and their rulers very oppressive, whereupon their rich do not thrive, their sultan does not remit, their poor do not pray.

Questions for Analysis

1. Based on the material of this chapter, especially page 349, what was the prevailing European attitude toward trade and commerce? How did Europeans view the merchant?

2. Compare and contrast Christian and Muslim views of trade and business.

3. Do you agree with the exalted *religious* status of the merchant in Islamic society? Why or why not?

Source: Bernard Lewis, *A Middle East Mosaic: Fragments of Life, Letters and History.* Copyright © 2000 by Bernard Lewis. Used by permission of Random House, Inc.

For the economic revival of Europe, see, in addition to the titles by Dollinger, Herlihy, Postan, Russell, and Spufford given in the Notes, D. Nicholas, *Medieval Flanders* (1992), and T. H. Lloyd, *England and the German Hanse, 1157–1611: A Study in Their Trade and Commercial Diplomacy* (1992). For the evolution, power, and activities of one highly important commercial city, see S. A. Epstein, *Genoa and the Genoese, 958–1528* (1996).

For women, see S. Shahar, *The Fourth Estate: Women in the Middle Ages* (1983), a provocative work. J. M. Bennett, *Women in the Medieval English Countryside: Gender and Household in Brigstock Before the Plague* (1987), is a fascinating case study, while E. Amt, ed., *Women's Lives in Medieval Europe: A Sourcebook* (1993), has fresh primary material on many aspects of women's lives. P. J. P. Goldberg, ed., *Women in England, 1275–1525* (1996), is a useful collection of sources. For royal women, M. Howell, *Eleanor of Provence: Queenship in Thirteenth Century England* (1998), shows how Henry III's wife used her diplomatic and managerial skills to attain considerable power, while P. Stafford, *Queen Emma and Queen Edith: Queenship and Women's Power in Eleventh-Century England* (1997), treats the earlier period. J. C. Parsons, *Eleanor of Castile* (1995), is probably the best study of Edward I's wife.

Students interested in the origins of medieval towns and cities should see S. Reynolds, *An Introduction to the History of English Medieval Towns* (1982), and R. H. Hilton, *English and French Towns in Feudal Society* (1992). C. Tilly and W. P. Blockmans, eds., *Cities and the Rise of States in Europe, A.D. 1000–1800* (1994), contains valuable articles on cities in Italy, Spain, the German Empire, Scandinavia, and the Low Countries.

For the new currents of thought in the High Middle Ages, see, in addition to the title by Haren cited in the Notes, the provocative J. Marenbon, *The Philosophy of Peter Abelard* (1997), which includes an excellent treatment of Abelard's ethics; D. W. Robertson, Jr., *Abélard and Héloïse* (1972), which is highly readable and commonsensical; and M. T. Clanchy, *Abelard: A Medieval Life* (1997), which incorporates the most recent international research. N. Orme, *Education and Society in Medieval and Renaissance England* (1989), focuses on early education, schools, and literacy in English medieval society. For the development of literacy among laypeople and the formation of a literate mentality, the advanced student should see M. T. Clanchy, *From Memory to Written Record: England, 1066–1307,* 2d ed. (1992). Written by outstanding scholars in a variety of fields, R. L. Benson and G. Constable with C. D. Lanham, eds., *Renaissance and Renewal in the Twelfth Century* (1982), contains an invaluable collection of articles.

On the medieval universities, H. De Ridder-Symoens, ed., *A History of the University in Europe,* vol. 1: *Universities in the Middle Ages* (1991), offers up-to-date interpretations by leading scholars. For the beginnings of Scholasticism and humanism, see the essential R. W. Southern, *Scholastic Humanism and the Unification of Western Europe,* vol. 1 (1994). W. J. Courtenay, *Parisian Scholars in the Early Fourteenth Century* (1999), contains a wealth of information on students and professors, including biographies of many students and material on the university's benefactors. Students interested in the relevance of Scholasticism to capitalism might consult O. Langholm, *The Legacy of Scholasticism in Economic Thought: Antecedents of Choice and Power* (1998).

The following studies are all valuable for the evolution and development of the Gothic style: J. Harvey, *The Gothic World* (1969) and *The Master Builders* (1971); P. Frankl, *The Gothic* (1960); and J. Bony, *French Gothic Architecture of the Twelfth and Thirteenth Centuries* (1983). D. Grivot and G. Zarnecki, *Gislebertus, Sculptor of Autun* (1961), is the finest appreciation of Romanesque architecture written in English. For the most important cathedrals in France, architecturally and politically, see A. Temko, *Notre Dame of Paris: The Biography of a Cathedral* (1968); G. Henderson, *Chartres* (1968); and A. Katzenellengoben, *The Sculptural Programs of Chartres Cathedral* (1959). C. A. Bruzelius, *The Thirteenth-Century Church at St. Denis* (1985), traces later reconstruction. J. Gimpel, *The Medieval Machine: The Industrial Revolution of the Middle Ages* (1977), discusses the mechanical and scientific problems involved in early industrialization. Based on the fragmentary architectural plans and careful archaeological reconstruction, P. Fergusson and S. Harrison, *Rievaulx Abbey: Community, Architecture, Memory* (1999), provides an elegantly written and splendidly illustrated study of England's most famous Cistercian house.

On troubadour poetry, see, in addition to the titles by Boase and Wilhelm cited in the Notes, M. Bogin, *The Women Troubadours* (1980).

For the Jews, see N. Golb, *The Jews of Medieval Normandy: A Social and Intellectual History* (1998); W. C. Jordan, *The French Monarchy and the Jews: From Philip Augustus to the Last Capetians* (1989); and H. Richardson, *English Jewry Under the Angevin Kings* (1960). Modern knowledge about homosexuality in the Middle Ages has been advanced by M. D. Jordan, *The Invention of Sodomy in Christian Theology* (1997); G. Woods, *A History of Gay Literature: The Male Tradition* (1998), especially chap. 4, "The Christian Middle Ages"; and L. Crompton, *Homosexuality and Civilization* (2003), chaps. 6 and 7.

For what the friars actually preached, see the important and provocative study of J. Hanska, *"And the Rich Man Died; and He Was Buried in Hell"* (1997). The following works are helpful in understanding the Inquisition and medieval heresy: J. B. Given, *Inquisition and Medieval Society: Power, Discipline and Resistance* (1997); E. Peters, *Heresy and Authority in Medieval Europe* (1980), *Inquisition* (1989), and *Torture* (1985); and R. Kieckhefer, *Magic in the Middle Ages* (1990).

The conflict between Pope Boniface VIII and the kings of France and England is well treated in J. R. Strayer, *The Reign of Philip the Fair* (1980), and M. Prestwich, *Edward I* (1988), both sound and important biographies.

Procession of the Magi. Having bankrolled the entire Council of Florence (1439), including the presence of the Byzantine emperor John VIII Paleologus, who came seeking Western support against the Ottoman Turks, Cosimo de' Medici immortalized the event in the Medici chapel with Benozzo Gozzoli's frescoes. *(Scala/Art Resource, NY)*

chapter

12 The Crisis of the Later Middle Ages

During the later Middle Ages, the last book of the New Testament, the Book of Revelation, inspired thousands of sermons and hundreds of religious tracts. The Book of Revelation deals with visions of the end of the world, with disease, war, famine, and death. It is no wonder this part of the Bible was so popular. Between 1300 and 1450, Europeans experienced a frightful series of shocks: economic dislocation, plague, war, social upheaval, and increased crime and violence. Death and preoccupation with death make the fourteenth century one of the most wrenching periods of Western civilization. Yet, in spite of the pessimism and crises, important institutions and ideas, such as representative assemblies and national literatures, emerged.

The miseries and disasters of the later Middle Ages bring to mind a number of questions.

- What economic difficulties did Europe experience?
- What were the social and psychological effects of repeated attacks of plague and disease?
- Some scholars maintain that war is often the catalyst for political, economic, and social change. Does this theory have validity for the fourteenth century?
- What provoked schism in the church, and what impact did it have on the lives of ordinary people?
- How did new national literatures reflect political and social developments?
- How and why did the laws of settlers in frontier regions reveal a strong racial or ethnic discrimination?

This chapter will focus on these questions.

Prelude to Disaster

In the first decade of the fourteenth century, the countries of northern Europe experienced a considerable price inflation. The cost of grain, livestock, and dairy products rose sharply. Severe weather, which historical geographers label the "Little Ice Age," made a serious situation frightful. An unusual

379

number of storms brought torrential rains, ruining the wheat, oat, and hay crops on which people and animals almost everywhere depended. Since long-distance transportation of food was expensive and difficult, most urban areas depended for bread and meat on areas no more than a day's journey away. Poor harvests—and one in four was likely to be poor—led to scarcity and starvation. Almost all of northern Europe suffered a **"Great Famine"** in the years 1315–1322, which contemporaries interpreted as a recurrence of the biblical "seven lean years" (Genesis 42).

Reduced caloric intake meant increased susceptibility to disease, especially for infants, children, and the elderly. Workingmen and workingwomen on a reduced diet had less energy, which in turn meant lower productivity, lower output, and higher grain prices. The great famine proved a demographic disaster in France; in Burgundy perhaps one-third of the population died. The many religious houses of Flanders experienced a high loss of monks, nuns, and priests.

Hardly had western Europe begun to recover from this disaster when another struck. An epidemic of typhoid fever carried away thousands. In 1316, 10 percent of the population of the city of Ypres may have died between May and October alone. Then in 1318 disease hit cattle and sheep, drastically reducing the herds and flocks. Another bad harvest in 1321 brought famine and death.

The province of Languedoc in France presents a classic example of agrarian crisis. For over 150 years, Languedoc had enjoyed continual land reclamation, steady agricultural expansion, and enormous population growth. Then the fourteenth century opened with four years of bad harvests. Torrential rains in 1310 ruined the harvest and brought on terrible famine. Harvests failed again in 1322 and 1329. In 1332 desperate peasants survived the winter on raw herbs. In the half century from 1302 to 1348, poor harvests occurred twenty times. The undernourished population was ripe for the Grim Reaper, who appeared in 1348 in the form of the Black Death.

These catastrophes had grave social consequences. Poor harvests and famine led to the abandonment of homesteads. In parts of the Low Countries and in the Scottish-English borderlands, entire villages were abandoned. This meant a great increase in the number of vagabonds, what we call "homeless people." In Flanders and East Anglia (eastern England), where aspects of the famine have been carefully analyzed, some rustics were forced to mortgage, sublease, or sell their holdings to get money to buy food. Rich farmers bought out their poorer neighbors. When conditions improved, debtors tried to get their lands back, leading to a very volatile land mar-

ket. To reduce the labor supply and the mouths to feed in the countryside, young males sought work in the towns.[1] Poor harvests probably meant that marriage had to be postponed. Later marriages and the deaths caused by famine and disease meant a reduction in population. Meanwhile, the international character of trade and commerce meant that a disaster in one country had serious implications elsewhere. For example, the infection that attacked English sheep in 1318 caused a sharp decline in wool exports in the following years. Without wool, Flemish weavers could not work, and thousands were laid off. Without woolen cloth, the businesses of Flemish, Hanseatic, and Italian merchants suffered. Unemployment encouraged people to turn to crime.

To none of these problems did governments have effective solutions. The three sons of Philip the Fair who sat on the French throne between 1314 and 1328 condemned speculators, who held stocks of grain back until conditions were desperate and prices high, forbade the sale of grain abroad, and published legislation prohibiting fishing with traps that took large catches. These measures had few positive results. As the subsistence crisis deepened, popular discontent and paranoia increased. Starving people focused their anger on the rich, speculators, and the Jews, who were targeted as creditors fleecing the poor through pawnbroking. (Expelled from France in 1306, Jews were readmitted in 1315 and granted the privilege of lending at high interest rates.) Rumors spread of a plot by Jews and their agents, the lepers, to kill Christians by poisoning the wells. With "evidence" collected by torture, many lepers and Jews were killed, beaten, or hit with heavy fines.

In England Edward I's incompetent son, Edward II (r. 1307–1327), used Parliament to set price controls, first on the sale of livestock after disease and poor lambing had driven prices up, and then on ale, which was made from barley (the severe rains of 1315 had contributed to molds and mildews, sharply reducing the crop). Baronial conflicts and wars with the Scots dominated Edward II's reign. Fearing food riots and violence, Edward condemned speculators, which proved easier than enforcing price controls. He did try to buy grain abroad, but yields in the Baltic were low; the French crown, as we have seen, forbade exports; and the grain shipped from Castile in northern Spain was grabbed by Scottish, English, and rogue Hanseatic pirates on the high seas. Such grain as reached southern English ports was stolen by looters and sold on the black market. The Crown's efforts at famine relief failed.

In Scandinavia and the Baltic countries, low cereal harvests, declines in meat and dairy production, economic

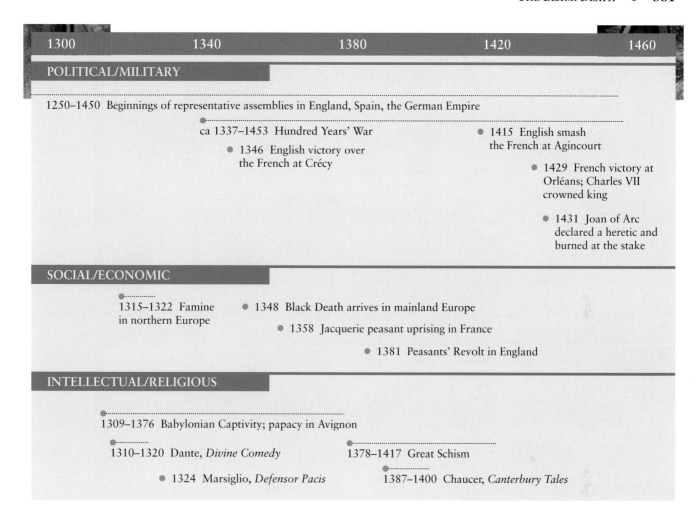

1300	1340	1380	1420	1460

POLITICAL/MILITARY

1250–1450 Beginnings of representative assemblies in England, Spain, the German Empire

ca 1337–1453 Hundred Years' War

1346 English victory over the French at Crécy

1415 English smash the French at Agincourt

1429 French victory at Orléans; Charles VII crowned king

1431 Joan of Arc declared a heretic and burned at the stake

SOCIAL/ECONOMIC

1315–1322 Famine in northern Europe

1348 Black Death arrives in mainland Europe

1358 Jacquerie peasant uprising in France

1381 Peasants' Revolt in England

INTELLECTUAL/RELIGIOUS

1309–1376 Babylonian Captivity; papacy in Avignon

1310–1320 Dante, *Divine Comedy*

1324 Marsiglio, *Defensor Pacis*

1378–1417 Great Schism

1387–1400 Chaucer, *Canterbury Tales*

recessions, and the lack of salt, used for preserving herring, resulted in terrible food shortages. One scholar describes conditions there as "catastrophic."[2] Economic and social problems were aggravated by the appearance of a frightful disease.

The Black Death

In 1291 Genoese sailors had opened the Strait of Gibraltar to Italian shipping by defeating the Moroccans. Then, shortly after 1300, important advances were made in the design of Italian merchant ships. A square rig was added to the mainmast, and ships began to carry three masts instead of just one. Additional sails better utilized wind power to propel the ship. The improved design permitted year-round shipping for the first time, and Venetian and Genoese merchant ships could sail the dangerous Atlantic coast even in the winter months. With ships con-

tinually at sea, shipboard rats were constantly on the move, and thus any rat-transmitted disease could spread rapidly.

Scholars dispute the origins of the bubonic plague, often known as the **Black Death.** One legend holds that the plague broke out in the Tartar (or Tatar) army under Khan Djani-Beg that was besieging the city of Caffa (modern Feodosiya) in the Crimea, in southern Russia. The Khan ordered the heads of Tartar victims hurled into Caffa to infect the defenders.[3] Some scholars hold that the plague broke out in China or Central Asia around 1331, and during the next fifteen years merchants and soldiers carried it over the caravan routes until in 1346 it reached the Crimea. Other scholars believe the plague was endemic in southern Russia. In either case, from the Crimea the plague had easy access to Mediterranean lands and western Europe.

In October 1347, Genoese ships brought the plague to Messina, from which it spread across Sicily. Venice and

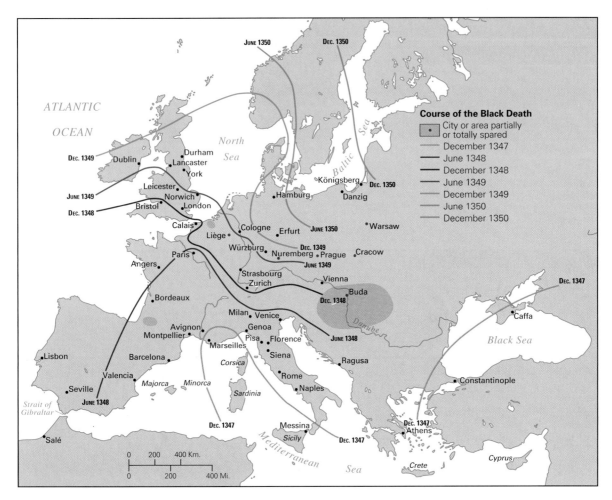

MAP 12.1   The Course of the Black Death in Fourteenth-Century Europe   Note the routes that the bubonic plague took across Europe. How do you account for the fact that several regions were spared the "dreadful death"?

Genoa were hit in January 1348, and from the port of Pisa the disease spread south to Rome and east to Florence and all of Tuscany. By late spring, southern Germany was attacked. Frightened French authorities chased a galley bearing the disease from the port of Marseilles, but not before plague had infected the city, from which it spread to Languedoc and Spain. In June 1348, two ships entered the Bristol Channel and introduced it into England. All Europe felt the scourge of this horrible disease (see Map 12.1).

Pathology and Care

Modern understanding of the bubonic plague rests on the research of two bacteriologists, one French and one

Japanese, who in 1894 independently identified the bacillus that causes the plague, *Pasteurella pestis* (so labeled after the French scientist's teacher, Louis Pasteur). The bacillus liked to live in the bloodstream of an animal or, ideally, in the stomach of a flea. The flea in turn resided in the hair of a rodent, sometimes a squirrel but preferably the hardy, nimble, and vagabond black rat. Why the host black rat moved so much, scientists still do not know, but it often traveled by ship. There the black rat could feast for months on a cargo of grain or live snugly among bales of cloth. Fleas bearing the bacillus also had no trouble nesting in saddlebags.[4] Comfortable, well-fed, and having greatly multiplied, the black rats ended their ocean voyage and descended on the great cities of Europe.

Procession of Saint Gregory   According to the *Golden Legend,* a thirteenth-century collection of saints' lives, the bubonic plague ravaged Rome when Gregory I was elected pope (590–604). He immediately ordered special prayers and processions around the city. Here, as people circle the walls, new victims fall (*center*). The architecture, the cardinals, and the friars all indicate that this painting dates from the fourteenth, not the sixth, century. *(Musée Condé, Chantilly/Art Resource, NY)*

The plague took two forms—bubonic and pneumonic. In the bubonic form, the flea was the vector, or transmitter, of the disease. In the pneumonic form, the plague was communicated directly from one person to another.

Although by the fourteenth century urban authorities from London to Paris to Rome had begun to try to achieve a primitive level of sanitation, urban conditions remained ideal for the spread of disease. Narrow streets filled with refuse and human excrement were as much cesspools as thoroughfares. Dead animals and sore-covered beggars greeted the traveler. Houses whose upper stories projected over the lower ones blocked light and air. And extreme overcrowding was commonplace. When all members of an aristocratic family lived and slept in one room, it should not be surprising that six or eight persons in a middle-class or poor household slept in one bed— if they had one. Closeness, after all, provided warmth. Houses were beginning to be constructed of brick, but many remained of wood, clay, and mud. A determined rat had little trouble entering such a house.

Standards of personal hygiene remained frightfully low. True, most large cities had public bathhouses, but we have no way of knowing how frequently ordinary people used them. Lack of personal cleanliness, combined with any number of temporary ailments such as diarrhea and the common cold, weakened the body's resistance to serious disease. Fleas and body lice were universal afflictions: everyone from peasants to archbishops had them. One more bite did not cause much alarm. But if that nibble came from a bacillus-bearing flea, an entire household or area was doomed.

The classic symptom of the bubonic plague was a growth the size of a nut or an apple in the armpit, in the groin, or on the neck. This was the boil, or **buba,** that gave the disease its name and caused agonizing pain. If the buba was lanced and the pus thoroughly drained, the victim had a chance of recovery. The next stage was the appearance of black spots or blotches caused by bleeding under the skin. (This syndrome did not give the disease its common name; contemporaries did not call the plague the Black Death. Sometime in the fifteenth century, the Latin phrase *atra mors,* meaning "dreadful death," was translated "black death," and the phrase stuck.) Finally, the victim began to cough violently and spit blood. This stage, indicating the presence of millions of bacilli in the bloodstream, signaled the end, and death followed in two or three days. Rather than evoking compassion for the victim, a French scientist has written, everything about the bubonic plague provoked horror and disgust: "All the matter which exuded from their bodies let off an unbearable stench; sweat, excrement, spittle, breath, so fetid as to be overpowering; urine turbid, thick, black or red."[5]

Fourteenth-century medical literature indicates that physicians could sometimes ease the pain, but they had no cure. Most people—lay, scholarly, and medical—believed that the Black Death was caused by some "vicious property in the air" that carried the disease from place to place. When ignorance was joined to fear and ancient bigotry, savage cruelty sometimes resulted. Many people believed that the Jews had poisoned the wells of Christian communities and thereby infected the drinking water. This charge led to the murder of thousands of Jews across Europe. According to one chronicler, sixteen thousand were killed at the imperial city of Strasbourg alone in 1349. Though sixteen thousand is probably a typical medieval numerical exaggeration, the horror of the massacre is not lessened. Scholars have yet to explain the economic impact that the loss of such a productive people had on Strasbourg and other cities.

The Italian writer Giovanni Boccaccio (1313–1375), describing the course of the disease in Florence in the preface to his book of tales *The Decameron,* pinpointed the cause of the spread:

Moreover, the virulence of the pest was the greater by reason that intercourse was apt to convey it from the sick to the whole, just as fire devours things dry or greasy when they are brought close to it. Nay, the evil went yet further, for not merely by speech or association with the sick was the malady communicated to the healthy with consequent peril of common death, but any that touched the clothes of the sick or aught else that had been touched or used by them, seemed thereby to contract the disease.[6]

The highly infectious nature of the plague, especially in areas of high population density, was recognized by a few sophisticated Muslims. When the disease struck the town of Salé in Morocco, Ibu Abu Madyan shut in his household with sufficient food and water and allowed no one to enter or leave until the plague had passed. Abu Madyan was entirely successful. The rat that carried the disease-bearing flea avoided travel outside the cities. Thus the countryside was relatively safe. City dwellers who could afford to move fled to the country.

If medical science had no effective treatment, could victims' suffering be eased? Perhaps in hospitals. What was the geographical distribution of hospitals, and, although our estimates of medieval populations remain rough, what was the hospital-to-population ratio? How many patients could a hospital serve? Whereas earlier the feudal lord had made philanthropic foundations, beginning in the thirteenth century individual merchants—out of compassion, generosity, and the custom of giving to parish collections, and in the belief that the sick would be prayerful intercessors with God for the donors' sins—endowed hospitals. Business people established hospitals in the towns of northern France and Flanders; Milan, Genoa, and Venice were well served, and the 30 hospitals in Florence provided 1,000 beds in 1339. Sixty hospitals served Paris in 1328—but probably not enough for its population of 200,000. The many hospitals in the Iberian Peninsula continued the Muslim tradition of care for the poor and ill. Merchants in the larger towns of the German Empire, in Poland, and in Hungary also founded hospitals in the fourteenth century, generally later than those in western Europe. Sailors, long viewed as potential carriers of disease, benefited from hospitals reserved for them; in 1300 the Venetian government paid a surgeon to care for sick sailors. At the time the plague erupted, therefore, most towns and cities had hospital facilities.

When trying to determine the number of people a hospital could accommodate, the modern researcher considers the number of beds, the size of the staff, and the building's physical layout. Since each medieval hospital bed might serve two or more patients, we cannot calculate the number of patients on the basis of the beds alone. We do know that rural hospices usually had twelve to fifteen beds, and city hospitals, as at Lisbon, Narbonne,

Patients in a Hospital Ward, Fifteenth Century In many cities hospitals could not cope with the large numbers of plague victims. The practice of putting two or more adults in the same bed, as shown here, contributed to the spread of the disease. At the Hôtel-Dieu in Paris, nurses complained of being forced to put eight to ten children in a single bed in which a patient had recently died. *(Giraudon/The Bridgeman Art Library)*

and Genoa, had on average twenty-five to thirty beds, but these figures do not tell us how many patients were accommodated. Only the very rare document listing the number of wrapping sheets and coffins for the dead purchased in a given period provides the modern scholar with information on the number of patients a hospital had. Hospitals could offer only shelter, compassion, and care for the dying.[7]

Mortality rates cannot be specified, because population figures for the period before the arrival of the plague do not exist for most countries and cities. The largest amount of material survives for England, but it is difficult to use; after enormous scholarly controversy, only educated guesses can be made. Of a total English population of perhaps 4.2 million, probably 1.4 million died of the Black Death in its several visits.[8] Densely populated Italian cities endured incredible losses. Florence lost between one-half and two-thirds of its 1347 population of 85,000 when the plague visited in 1348.

Nor did central and eastern Europe escape the ravages of the disease. Moving northward from the Balkans, eastward from France, and southward from the Baltic, the plague swept through the German Empire. In the Rhineland in 1349, Cologne and Mainz endured heavy losses. In 1348 it swept through Bavaria, entered the Moselle Valley, and pushed into northern Germany. One chronicler records that in the summer and autumn of 1349, between five hundred and six hundred died every day in Vienna. Styria, in what today is central Austria, was very hard hit, with cattle straying unattended in the fields.

As the Black Death took its toll on the German Empire, waves of emigrants fled to Poland, Bohemia, and Hungary. The situation there was better, though not completely absent of disease. The plague seems to have entered Poland through the Baltic seaports and spread from there. Still, population losses were lower than elsewhere in Europe. The plague spread from Poland to Russia, reaching Pskov, Novgorod, and Moscow, where it felled Grand Duke Simeon.[9] No estimates have been made of population losses there or in the Balkans. In Serbia, though, the plague left vast tracts of land unattended, which prompted an increase in Albanian immigration to meet the labor shortage.

Across Europe the Black Death recurred intermittently from the 1360s to 1400. It reappeared many times with reduced virulence, making its last appearance in the French port city of Marseilles in 1721. Survivors became more prudent. Because periods of famine had caused malnutrition, making people vulnerable to disease, Europeans controlled population growth so that population did not outstrip food supply. Western Europeans improved navigation techniques and increased long-distance trade, which permitted the importation of grain from sparsely populated Baltic regions (see page 381). They strictly enforced quarantine measures.[10] They worked on the development of vaccines. But it was only in 1947, six centuries after the arrival of the plague in the West, that the American microbiologist Selman Waksman discovered an effective vaccine, streptomycin.

Social, Economic, and Cultural Consequences

It is noteworthy that, in an age of mounting criticism of clerical wealth (see page 394), the behavior of the clergy during the plague was often exemplary. Priests, monks, and nuns cared for the sick and buried the dead. In places like Venice, from which even physicians fled, priests remained to give what ministrations they could. Consequently, their mortality rate was phenomenally high. The German clergy especially suffered a severe decline in personnel in the years after 1350. With the ablest killed off, the wealth of the German church fell into the hands of the incompetent and weak. The situation was ripe for reform (see Chapter 14).

In taking their pastoral responsibilities seriously, some clergy did things that the church in a later age would vigorously condemn. The institutional church has traditionally opposed laymen, and especially laywomen, administering the sacraments. But the shortage of priests was so great that in 1349 Ralph, bishop of Bath and Wells in England (1329–1363), advised his people that "if they are on the point of death and cannot secure the services of a priest, then they should make confession to each other, as is permitted in the teaching of the Apostles, whether to a layman or, if no man is present, even to a woman."[11]

Economic historians and demographers sharply dispute the impact of the plague on the economy in the late fourteenth century. The traditional view that the plague had a disastrous effect has been greatly modified. The clearest evidence comes from England, where the agrarian economy showed remarkable resilience. While the severity of the disease varied from region to region, it appears that by about 1375 most landlords enjoyed revenues near those of the pre-plague years. By the early fifteenth century, seigneurial prosperity reached a medieval peak. Why? The answer appears to lie in the fact that England and many parts of Europe suffered from overpopulation in the early fourteenth century. Population losses caused by the Black Death "led to increased productivity by restoring a more efficient balance between labour, land, and capital."[12]

What impact did visits of the plague have on urban populations? The rich evidence from a census of the city of Florence and its surrounding territory taken between 1427 and 1430 is fascinating. The region had suffered repeated epidemics since 1347. In a total population of 260,000 persons, 15 percent were age sixty or over (a very high proportion), suggesting that the plague took the young rather than the mature. Children and youths up to age nineteen constituted 44 percent of the people. Adults between the ages of twenty and fifty-nine, the most economically productive group, represented 41 percent of Florentine society.

The high mortality rate of craftsmen led Florentine guilds to recruit many new members. For example, between 1328 and 1347 the silk merchants guild accepted 730 members, and between 1408 and 1427 it admitted 784. It appears that economic organizations tried to keep their numbers constant, even though the size of the population and its pool of potential guild members was shrinking. Moreover, in contrast to the pre-1348 period, many new members of the guilds were not related to existing members. Thus the post-plague years represent an age of "new men."[13]

The Black Death brought on a general European inflation. High mortality produced a fall in production, shortages of goods, and a general rise in prices. The shortage of labor and workers' demands for higher wages put guild masters on the defensive. They retaliated with measures such as the Statute of Laborers (1351), an attempt by the English Parliament to freeze the wages of English workers at pre-1347 levels. Such statutes could not be enforced and thus were unsuccessful. The price of wheat in most of Europe increased, as did the costs of meat, sausage, and cheese. This inflation continued to the end of the fourteenth century. But wages in the towns rose faster, and the broad mass of people enjoyed a higher standard of living. "A more efficient balance between labour, land, and capital" brought increased productivity.[14] Population decline meant a sharp increase in per capita wealth. The greater demand for labor meant greater mobility for peasants in rural areas and for industrial workers in the towns and cities.

Labor shortages caused by the Black Death throughout the Mediterranean region, from Constantinople to Spain, presented aggressive businessmen with a golden opportunity. The price of slaves rose sharply. Venetian slavers from their colony at Tana on the Sea of Azov in the Crimea took advantage of the boom in demand as prices soared between 1350 and 1410. "By about 1408, no less than 78 per cent of Tana's export earnings came from slaves. Out of their misery, and out of the profits born of the Black Death, one palace after another was raised along the (Venetian) Rialto."[15]

Even more significant than the social effects were the psychological consequences. The knowledge that the disease meant almost certain death provoked the most profound pessimism. Imagine an entire society in the grip of the belief that it was at the mercy of a frightful affliction about which nothing could be done, a disgusting disease from which family and friends would flee, leaving one to die alone and in agony. It is not surprising that some sought release in orgies and gross sensuality, while others turned to the severest forms of asceticism and frenzied religious fervor. Some extremists joined groups of **flagellants,** who whipped and scourged themselves as penance for their and society's sins, in the belief that the Black Death was God's punishment for humanity's wickedness.

Plague ripped apart the social fabric. In the thirteenth century, funerals, traditionally occasions for the mutual consolation of the living as much as memorial services for the dead, grew increasingly elaborate, with large corteges and many mourners. In the fourteenth century, public horror at the suffering of the afflicted and at the dead reduced the size of mourning processions and eventually resulted in failure even to perform the customary death rites. Fear of infection led to the dead being buried hastily, sometimes in mass graves.

People often used pilgrimages to holy places as justification for their flight from cities. Suspected of being carriers of plague, travelers, pilgrims, and the homeless aroused deep hostility. All European port cities followed the example of Ragusa (modern Dubrovnik in southwestern Croatia on the Dalmatian coast) and quarantined arriving ships, crews, passengers, and cargoes to determine whether they brought the plague. Deriving from a Venetian word, the English term *quarantine* originally meant forty days' isolation.

Popular endowments of educational institutions multiplied. The years of the Black Death witnessed the foundation of new colleges at old universities, such as Corpus Christi and Clare Colleges at Cambridge and New College at Oxford, and of entirely new universities. The beginnings of Charles University in Prague (1348) and the Universities of Florence (1350), Vienna (1364), Cracow (1364), and Heidelberg (1385) were all associated with the plague: their foundation charters specifically mention the shortage of priests and the decay of learning. Whereas universities such as those at Bologna and Paris had an international student body, new institutions established in the wake of the Black Death had more national or local constituencies. Thus the international character of medieval culture weakened. The decline of cultural cohesion paved the way for schism in the Catholic church even before the Reformation.[16]

The literature and art of the fourteenth century reveal a terribly morbid concern with death. One highly popular artistic motif, the Dance of Death, depicted a dancing skeleton leading away a living person. A long international war added further misery to the frightful disasters of the plague.

The Hundred Years' War (ca 1337–1453)

In January 1327, Queen Isabella of England, her lover Mortimer, and a group of barons, having deposed and murdered Isabella's incompetent husband, King Edward II, proclaimed his fifteen-year-old son king as Edward III. Isabella and Mortimer, however, held real power until 1330, when Edward seized the reins of government. In 1328 Charles IV of France, the last surviving son of Philip the Fair, died childless. With him ended the Capetian dynasty. An assembly of French barons, meaning to exclude Isabella—who was Charles's sister and the daughter of Philip the Fair—and her son Edward III from the French throne, proclaimed that "no woman nor her son could succeed to the [French] monarchy." French lawyers defended this position—that no woman or her descendant could rule France—with the claim that the Salic Law, a long-obsolete sixth-century Germanic law code (see page 210), was part of the fundamental law of France. The barons passed the crown to Philip VI of Valois (r. 1328–1350), a nephew of Philip the Fair. In these actions lie the origins of another phase of the centuries-old struggle between the English and French monarchies, one that was fought intermittently from 1337 to 1453.

Causes

The Hundred Years' War had both distant and immediate causes. In 1259 France and England signed the Treaty of Paris, in which the English king agreed to become—for himself and his successors—vassal of the French crown for the duchy of Aquitaine. The English claimed Aquitaine as an ancient inheritance. French policy, however, was strongly expansionist, and the French kings resolved to absorb the duchy into the kingdom of France. In 1329 Edward III paid homage to Philip VI for Aquitaine. In 1337 Philip, eager to exercise full French jurisdiction in Aquitaine, confiscated the duchy. Edward III interpreted this action as a gross violation of the treaty of 1259 and as a cause for war. Moreover, Edward argued, as the eldest directly surviving male descendant of Philip the Fair, he must assume the title of king of France in order to wield his rightful authority in Aquitaine.[17] In short, Edward rejected the decision of the French barons excluding him from the throne. Edward III's dynastic argument upset the feudal order in France: to increase their independent power, French vassals of Philip VI used the excuse that they had to transfer

their loyalty to a more legitimate overlord, Edward III. One reason the war lasted so long was that it became a French civil war, with some French barons supporting English monarchs in order to thwart the centralizing goals of the French crown.

Economic factors involving the wool trade and the control of Flemish towns had served as justifications for war between France and England for centuries. The wool trade between England and Flanders served as the cornerstone of both countries' economies; they were closely interdependent. Flanders was a fief of the French crown, and the Flemish aristocracy was highly sympathetic to the monarchy in Paris. But the wealth of Flemish merchants and cloth manufacturers depended on English wool, and Flemish burghers strongly supported the claims of Edward III. The disruption of commerce with England threatened their prosperity.

The Popular Response

The governments of both England and France manipulated public opinion to support the war. Whatever significance modern scholars ascribe to the economic factor, public opinion in fourteenth-century England held that the war was waged for one reason: to secure for King Edward the French crown he had been unjustly denied.[18]

Flanders and the English Merchant Staplers Flanders was officially on the French side during the Hundred Years' War, but Flemish cities depended heavily on English wool for their textile manufacturing. Hence the Merchant Staplers, the English trading company with a monopoly on trade in wool, sought concessions. In this 1387 illustration, the master of the staple and his fellow merchants plead their case to the count of Flanders. *(British Library)*

Edward III issued letters to the sheriffs describing in graphic terms the evil deeds of the French and listing royal needs. Kings in both countries instructed the clergy to deliver sermons filled with patriotic sentiment. The royal courts sensationalized the wickedness of the other side and stressed the great fortunes to be made from the war. Philip VI sent agents to warn communities about the dangers of invasion and to stress the French crown's revenue needs to meet the attack.

The royal campaign to rally public opinion was highly successful, at least in the early stage of the war. Edward III gained widespread support in the 1340s and 1350s. The English developed a deep hatred of the French and feared that King Philip intended "to have seized and slaughtered the entire realm of England." When England was successful in the field, pride in the country's military proficiency increased.

Most important of all, the Hundred Years' War was popular because it presented unusual opportunities for wealth and advancement. Poor knights and knights who were unemployed were promised regular wages. Criminals who enlisted were granted pardons. The great nobles expected to be rewarded with estates. Royal exhortations to the troops before battles repeatedly stressed that, if victorious, the men might keep whatever they seized. The French chronicler Jean Froissart wrote that, at the time of Edward III's expedition of 1359, men of all ranks flocked to the English king's banner. Some came to acquire honor, but many came "to loot and pillage the fair and plenteous land of France."[19]

The Course of the War to 1419

The war was fought almost entirely in France and the Low Countries (see Map 12.2). It consisted mainly of a series of random sieges and cavalry raids. In 1335 the French began supporting Scottish incursions into northern England, ravaging the countryside in Aquitaine, and

Siege of the Castle of Mortagne Near Bordeaux (1377) Medieval warfare usually consisted of small skirmishes and attacks on castles. This miniature shows the French besieging an English-held castle. Most of the soldiers use longbows, although at the left two men shoot primitive muskets above a pair of cannon. The castle held out for six months. Painted in the late fifteenth century, the scene reflects contemporary developments rather than fourteenth-century events. *(British Library)*

sacking and burning English coastal towns, such as Southampton. Such tactics lent weight to Edward III's propaganda campaign. In fact, royal propaganda on both sides fostered a kind of early nationalism.

During the war's early stages, England was highly successful. At **Crécy** in northern France in 1346, English longbowmen scored a great victory over French knights and crossbowmen. Although the aim of the longbow was not very accurate, it allowed for rapid reloading, and English archers could send off three arrows to the French crossbowmen's one. The result was a blinding shower of arrows that unhorsed the French knights and caused mass confusion. The firing of cannon—probably the first use of artillery in the West—created further panic. Thereupon the English horsemen charged and butchered the French.

This was not war according to the chivalric rules that Edward III would have preferred. Nevertheless, his son Edward the Black Prince used the same tactics ten years later to smash the French at Poitiers, where he captured the French king and held him for ransom. Again, at **Agincourt** near Arras in 1415, the chivalric English soldier-king Henry V (r. 1413–1422) gained the field over vastly superior numbers. Henry followed up his triumph at Agincourt with the reconquest of Normandy. By 1419 the English had advanced to the walls of Paris (see Map 12.2). But the French cause was not lost. Though England had scored the initial victories, France won the war.

Joan of Arc and France's Victory

The ultimate French success rests heavily on the actions of an obscure French peasant girl, **Joan of Arc,** whose vision and work revived French fortunes and led to victory. A great deal of pious and popular legend surrounds Joan the Maid, because of her peculiar appearance on the scene, her astonishing success, her martyrdom, and her canonization by the Catholic church. The historical fact is that she saved the French monarchy, which was the embodiment of France.

Born in 1412 to well-to-do peasants in the village of Domrémy in Champagne, Joan of Arc grew up in a religious household. During adolescence she began to hear voices, which she later said belonged to Saint Michael, Saint Catherine, and Saint Margaret. In 1428 these voices spoke to her with great urgency, telling her that the dauphin (the uncrowned King Charles VII) had to be crowned and the English expelled from France. Joan went to the French court, persuaded the king to reject the rumor that he was illegitimate, and secured his support for her relief of the besieged city of Orléans.

The astonishing thing is not that Joan the Maid overcame serious obstacles to see the dauphin, not even that Charles and his advisers listened to her. What is amazing is the swiftness with which they were convinced. French fortunes had been so low for so long that the court believed only a miracle could save the country. Because Joan cut her hair short and dressed like a man, she scandalized the court. But hoping she would provide the miracle, Charles allowed her to accompany the army that was preparing to raise the English siege of Orléans.

In the meantime Joan, herself illiterate, dictated this letter calling on the English to withdraw:

King of England . . . , do right in the King of Heaven's sight. Surrender to The Maid *sent hither by God the King of Heaven, the keys of all the good towns you have taken and laid waste in France. She comes in God's name to establish the Blood Royal, ready to make peace if you agree to abandon France and repay what you have taken. And you, archers, comrades in arms, gentles and others, who are before the town of Orléans, retire in God's name to your own country.*[20]

Joan arrived before Orléans on April 28, 1429. Seventeen years old, she knew little of warfare and believed that if she could keep the French troops from swearing and frequenting brothels, victory would be theirs. On May 8 the English, weakened by disease and lack of supplies, withdrew from Orléans. Ten days later, Charles VII was crowned king at Reims. These two events marked the turning point in the war.

Joan's presence at Orléans, her strong belief in her mission, and the fact that she was wounded enhanced her reputation and strengthened the morale of the army. In 1430 England's allies, the Burgundians, captured Joan and sold her to the English. When the English handed her over to the ecclesiastical authorities for trial, the French court did not intervene. While the English wanted Joan eliminated for obvious political reasons, sorcery (witchcraft) was the ostensible charge at her trial. Witch persecution was increasing in the fifteenth century, and Joan's wearing of men's clothes appeared not only aberrant but indicative of contact with the Devil. In 1431 the court condemned her as a heretic—her claim of direct inspiration from God, thereby denying the authority of church officials, constituted heresy—and burned her at the stake in the marketplace at Rouen. A new trial in 1456 rehabilitated her name. In 1920 she was canonized and declared a holy maiden, and today she is revered as the second patron saint of France. The nineteenth-

1337
(before the Battle of Crécy)

- English holdings
- French holdings
- Extent of English holdings after Treaty of Paris, 1259

1360
(after the Battle of Poitiers)

- English holdings
- French holdings
- ✕ Major battles

ca 1429
(after the siege of Orléans)

- English holdings
- French holdings
- Burgundian lands allied with England to 1435
- ✕ Major battle

1453
(end of war)

- English holdings
- French holdings
- Burgundian lands reconciled with France after 1435
- ✕ Last battle

MAP 12.2 English Holdings in France During the Hundred Years' War The year 1429 marked the greatest extent of English holdings in France. Why is it unlikely that England could have held these territories permanently?

century French historian Jules Michelet extolled Joan of Arc as a symbol of the vitality and strength of the French peasant classes.

The relief of Orléans stimulated French pride and rallied French resources. As the war dragged on, loss of life mounted, and money appeared to be flowing into a bottomless pit, demands for an end increased in England. The clergy and intellectuals pressed for peace. Parliamentary opposition to additional war grants stiffened. Slowly the French reconquered Normandy and, finally, ejected the English from Aquitaine. At the war's end in 1453, only the town of Calais remained in English hands.

Costs and Consequences

In France the English had slaughtered thousands of soldiers and civilians. In the years after the sweep of the Black Death, this additional killing meant a grave loss of population. The English had laid waste to hundreds of thousands of acres of rich farmland, leaving the rural economy of many parts of France a shambles. The war had disrupted trade and the great fairs, resulting in the drastic reduction of French participation in international commerce. Defeat in battle and heavy taxation contributed to widespread dissatisfaction and aggravated peasant grievances.

In England only the southern coastal ports experienced much destruction, and the demographic effects of the Black Death actually worked to restore the land-labor balance (see page 386). The costs of the war, however, were tremendous. England spent over £5 million on the war effort, a huge sum at the time. Manpower losses had greater social consequences. The knights who ordinarily handled the work of local government as sheriffs, coroners, jurymen, and justices of the peace were abroad, and their absence contributed to the breakdown of order at the local level. The English government attempted to finance the war effort by raising taxes on the wool crop. Because of steadily increasing costs, the Flemish and Italian buyers could not afford English wool. Consequently, raw wool exports slumped drastically between 1350 and 1450.

Many men of all social classes had volunteered for service in France in the hope of acquiring booty and becoming rich. The chronicler Walsingham, describing the period of Crécy, wrote: "For the woman was of no account who did not possess something from the spoils of . . . cities overseas in clothing, furs, quilts, and utensils . . . tablecloths and jewels, bowls of murra [semi-precious stone] and silver, linen and linen cloths."[21] Walsingham is referring to 1348, in the first generation of war. As time went on, most fortunes seem to have been squandered as fast as they were made.

If English troops returned with cash, they did not invest it in land. In the fifteenth century, returning soldiers were commonly described as beggars and vagabonds, roaming about making mischief. Even the large sums of money received from the ransom of the great—such as the £250,000 paid to Edward III for the freedom of King John of France—and the money paid as indemnities by captured towns and castles did not begin to equal the more than £5 million spent. England suffered a serious net loss.[22]

The long war also had a profound impact on the political and cultural lives of the two countries. Most notably, it stimulated the development of the English Parliament. Between 1250 and 1450, **representative assemblies** flourished in many European countries. In the English Parliament, German diets, and Spanish cortes, deliberative practices developed that laid the foundations for the representative institutions of modern liberal-democratic nations. While representative assemblies declined in most countries after the fifteenth century, the English Parliament endured. Edward III's constant need for money to pay for the war compelled him to summon not only the great barons and bishops, but knights of the shires and burgesses from the towns as well. Parliament met in thirty-seven of the fifty years of Edward's reign.[23]

The frequency of the meetings is significant. Representative assemblies were becoming a habit. Knights and burgesses—or the "Commons," as they came to be called—recognized their mutual interests and began to meet apart from the great lords. The Commons gradually realized that they held the country's purse strings, and a parliamentary statute of 1341 required that all nonfeudal levies have parliamentary approval. When Edward III signed the law, he acknowledged that the king of England could not tax without Parliament's consent. Increasingly, during the course of the war, money grants were tied to royal redress of grievances: if the government was to raise money, it had to correct the wrongs its subjects protested.

In England theoretical consent to taxation and legislation was given in one assembly for the entire country. France had no such single assembly; instead, there were many regional or provincial assemblies. Why did a national representative assembly fail to develop in France? The initiative for convening assemblies rested with the king, who needed revenue almost as much as the English ruler. But the French monarchy found the idea of representative assemblies thoroughly distasteful. Large gatherings of the nobility potentially or actually threatened the king's power. The advice of a counselor to King Charles VI (r. 1380–1422), "above all things be sure that no great assemblies of nobles or of *communes* take place in your kingdom," was accepted.[24] Charles VII (r. 1422–1461) even threatened to punish those proposing a national assembly.

No one in France wanted a national assembly. Linguistic, geographical, economic, legal, and political differences were very strong. People tended to think of themselves as Breton, Norman, Burgundian, or whatever, rather than French. Through much of the fourteenth and early fifteenth centuries, weak monarchs lacked the power to call a national assembly. Provincial assemblies, highly jealous of their independence, did not want a national assembly. The costs of sending delegates to it would be high, and the result was likely to be increased taxation.

In both countries, however, the war did promote the growth of **nationalism**—the feeling of unity and identity that binds together a people. After victories, each country experienced a surge of pride in its military strength. Just as English patriotism ran strong after Crécy and Poitiers, so French national confidence rose after Orléans. French national feeling demanded the expulsion of the enemy not merely from Normandy and Aquitaine but from French soil. Perhaps no one expressed this national consciousness better than Joan of Arc, when she exulted that the enemy had been "driven out of *France.*"

The Decline of the Church's Prestige

In times of crisis or disaster, people of all faiths have sought the consolation of religion. In the fourteenth century, however, the official Christian church offered little solace. In fact, the leaders of the church added to the sorrow and misery of the times.

The Babylonian Captivity

From 1309 to 1376, the popes lived in Avignon in southeastern France. In order to control the church and its policies, Philip the Fair of France pressured Pope Clement V to settle in Avignon (see Map 11.5 on page 358). Clement, critically ill with cancer, lacked the will to resist Philip. This period in church history is often called the **Babylonian Captivity** (referring to the seventy years the ancient Hebrews were held captive in Mesopotamian Babylon).

The Babylonian Captivity badly damaged papal prestige. The Avignon papacy reformed its financial administration and centralized its government. But the seven popes at Avignon concentrated on bureaucratic matters to the exclusion of spiritual objectives. Though some of the popes led austere lives, the general atmosphere was one of luxury and extravagance. The leadership of the church was cut off from its historic roots and the source of its ancient authority, the city of Rome. In the absence of the papacy, the Papal States in Italy lacked stability and good government. The economy of Rome had been based on the presence of the papal court and the rich tourist trade the papacy attracted. The Babylonian Captivity left Rome poverty-stricken.

In 1377 Pope Gregory XI brought the papal court back to Rome. Unfortunately, he died shortly after the return. At Gregory's death, Roman citizens demanded an Italian pope who would remain in Rome. Between the time of Gregory's death and the opening of the conclave, great pressure was put on the cardinals to elect an Italian. At the time, none of them protested this pressure.

Sixteen cardinals—eleven Frenchmen, four Italians, and one Spaniard—entered the conclave on April 7, 1378. After two ballots, they unanimously chose a distinguished administrator, the archbishop of Bari, Bartolomeo Prignano, who took the name Urban VI. Each of the cardinals swore that Urban had been elected "sincerely, freely, genuinely, and canonically."

Urban VI (1378–1389) had excellent intentions for church reform. He wanted to abolish simony, *pluralism* (holding several church offices at the same time), absenteeism, and clerical extravagance. These were the very abuses being increasingly criticized by Christian people across Europe. Unfortunately, Pope Urban went about the work of reform in a tactless and bullheaded manner. The day after his coronation, he delivered a blistering attack on cardinals who lived in Rome while drawing their income from benefices elsewhere. His criticism was well-founded but ill-timed and provoked opposition before Urban had consolidated his authority.

In the weeks that followed, Urban stepped up attacks on clerical luxury, denouncing individual cardinals by name. He threatened to strike the cardinal archbishop of Amiens. Urban even threatened to excommunicate certain cardinals, and when he was advised that such excommunications would not be lawful unless the guilty had been warned three times, he shouted, "I can do anything, if it be my will and judgment."[25] Urban's quick temper and irrational behavior have led scholars to question his sanity. Whether he was medically insane or just drunk with power is a moot point. In any case, Urban's actions brought on disaster.

In groups of two and three, the cardinals slipped away from Rome and met at Anagni. They declared Urban's election invalid because it had come about under threats from the Roman mob, and they asserted that Urban himself was excommunicated. The cardinals then proceeded to the city of Fondi between Rome and Naples and elected Cardinal Robert of Geneva, the cousin of King Charles V of France, as pope. Cardinal Robert took the name Clement VII. There were thus two popes—Urban at Rome and the antipope Clement VII (1378–1394), who set himself up at Avignon in opposition to the legally elected Urban. So began the Great Schism, which divided Western Christendom until 1417.

The Great Schism

The powers of Europe aligned themselves with Urban or Clement along strictly political lines. France naturally recognized the French antipope, Clement. England, France's historic enemy, recognized Pope Urban. Scotland, whose attacks on England were subsidized by France, followed the French and supported Clement. Aragon, Castile, and Portugal hesitated before deciding for Clement at Avignon. The emperor, who bore ancient hostility to France, recognized Urban VI. At first the Italian city-states recognized Urban; when he alienated them, they opted for Clement.

John of Spoleto, a professor at the law school at Bologna, eloquently summed up intellectual opinion of the **schism,** or division: "The longer this schism lasts, the more it appears to be costing, and the more harm it does; scandal, massacres, ruination, agitations, troubles and disturbances."[26] The common people, wracked by inflation, wars, and plague, were thoroughly confused about which pope was legitimate. The schism weakened the religious faith of many Christians and gave rise to instability and religious excesses. It brought the church leadership into serious disrepute. The schism also brought to the fore conciliar ideas about church government.

The Conciliar Movement

Theories about the nature of the Christian church and its government originated in the very early church, but the years of the Great Schism witnessed their maturity. **Conciliarists** believed that reform of the church could best be achieved through periodic assemblies, or general councils, representing all the Christian people. While acknowledging that the pope was head of the church, conciliarists, such as the French theologian Pierre d'Ailly and the German Conrad of Gelnhausen, held that the pope derived his authority from the entire Christian community, whose well-being he existed to promote. Conciliarists favored a balanced or constitutional form of church government, with papal authority shared with a general council, in contrast to the monarchical one that prevailed.

A half century before the Great Schism, in 1324, Marsiglio of Padua, then rector of the University of Paris, had published *Defensor Pacis* (The Defender of the Peace). Marsiglio argued that the state was the great unifying power in society and that the church was subordinate to the state. He put forth the revolutionary ideas that the church had no inherent jurisdiction and should own no property. Authority in the Christian church, according to Marsiglio, should rest in a general council, made up of laymen as well as priests and superior to the pope. These ideas directly contradicted the medieval notion of a society governed by the church and the state, with the church supreme. *Defensor Pacis* was condemned by the pope, and Marsiglio was excommunicated.

Even more earthshaking than the theories of Marsiglio of Padua were the ideas of the English scholar and theologian John Wyclif (ca 1330–1384). Wyclif wrote that papal claims of temporal power had no foundation in the Scriptures and that the Scriptures alone should be the standard of Christian belief and practice. He urged the abolition of such practices as the veneration of saints, pilgrimages, pluralism, and absenteeism. Sincere Christians, according to Wyclif, should read the Bible for themselves. In response to that idea, the first English translation of the Bible was produced and circulated. Wyclif's views had broad social and economic significance. He urged that the church be stripped of its property. His idea that every Christian free of mortal sin possessed lordship was seized on by peasants in England during a revolt in 1381 and used to justify their goals.

In advancing these views, Wyclif struck at the roots of medieval church structure. Consequently, he has been hailed as the precursor of the Reformation of the sixteenth century. Although Wyclif's ideas were vigorously condemned by ecclesiastical authorities, they were widely disseminated by humble clerics and enjoyed great popularity in the early fifteenth century. Wyclif's followers were called "Lollards." The term, which means "mumblers of prayers and psalms," refers to what they criticized. Lollard teaching allowed women to preach. Women, some well educated, played a significant role in the movement. After Anne, sister of Wenceslaus, king of Germany and Bohemia, married Richard II of England, members of her household carried Lollard books back to Bohemia.

In response to continued calls throughout Europe for a council, the two colleges of cardinals—one at Rome, the other at Avignon—summoned a council at Pisa in 1409.

Spoon with Fox Preaching to Geese (southern Nether-lands, ca 1430) Taking as his text a contemporary proverb, "When the fox preaches, beware your geese," the artist shows, in the bowl of a spoon, a fox dressed as a monk or friar, preaching with three dead geese in his hood, while another fox grabs one of the congregation. The preaching fox reads from a scroll bearing the word *pax* (peace), implying the perceived hypocrisy of the clergy. The object suggests the widespread criticism of churchmen in the later Middle Ages. *(Painted enamel and gilding on silver; 17.6 cm [6⅞ in]. Museum of Fine Arts, Boston, Helen and Alice Coburn Fund, 51.2472)*

That gathering of prelates and theologians deposed both popes and selected another. Neither the Avignon pope nor the Roman pope would resign, however, and the appalling result was the creation of a threefold schism.

Finally, because of the pressure of the German emperor Sigismund, a great council met at the imperial city of Constance (1414–1418). It had three objectives: to end the schism, to reform the church "in head and members" (from top to bottom), and to wipe out heresy. The council condemned the Czech reformer Jan Hus (see the feature "Individuals in Society: Jan Hus"), and he was burned at the stake. The council eventually deposed both the Roman pope and the successor of the pope chosen at Pisa, and it isolated the Avignon antipope. A conclave elected a new leader, the Roman cardinal Colonna, who took the name Martin V (1417–1431).

Martin proceeded to dissolve the council. Nothing was done about reform. The schism was over, and though councils subsequently met at Basel and at Ferrara-Florence, in 1450 the papacy held a jubilee, celebrating its triumph over the conciliar movement. In the later fifteenth century, the papacy concentrated on Italian problems to the exclusion of universal Christian interests. But the schism and the conciliar movement had exposed the crying need for ecclesiastical reform, thus laying the foundations for the great reform efforts of the sixteenth century.

The Life of the People

In the fourteenth century, economic and political difficulties, disease, and war profoundly affected the lives of European peoples. Decades of slaughter and destruction, punctuated by the decimating visits of the Black Death, made a grave economic situation virtually disastrous. In many parts of France and the Low Countries, fields lay in ruin or untilled for lack of labor power. In England, as taxes increased, criticisms of government policy and mismanagement multiplied. Crime, aggravated economic troubles, and throughout Europe the frustrations of the common people erupted into widespread revolts. But for most people, marriage and the local parish church continued to be the center of their lives.

Marriage

Marriage and the family provided such peace and satisfaction as most people attained. Scholars long believed that because peasants were illiterate and left very few statements about their marriages, generalizations could not be made about them. Recent research in English manorial, ecclesiastical, and coroners' records, however, has uncovered fascinating material. Evidence abounds of teenage flirtations, and many young people had sexual contacts—some leading to conception. Premarital pregnancy may have been deliberate: because children were economically important, the couple wanted to be sure of fertility before entering marriage.

"Whether rich or poor, male or female, the most important rite de passage for peasant youth was marriage."[27] Did they select their own spouses or accept parents' choices? Church law stressed that for a marriage to be valid, both partners must freely consent to it. The evidence overwhelmingly shows, above all where land or property accompanied the union, that parents took the lead in arranging their children's marriages; if the parents were dead, the responsibility fell to the inheriting son. Marriage determined not only the life partner and the economic circumstances in which the couple would live, but also the son-in-law who might take over the family land or the daughter-in-law who might care for her elderly in-laws. These kinds of interests required careful planning.

Most marriages were between men and women of the same village; where the name and residence of a husband is known, perhaps 41 percent were outsiders. Once the prospective bride or groom had been decided on, parents paid the **merchet** (fine to the lord for a woman's marriage—since he stood to lose a worker). Parents saw that the parish priest published on three successive Sundays the **banns,** public announcements that the couple planned to marry, to allow for objections to the union. And parents made the financial settlement. The couple then proceeded to the church door, where they made the vows, rings were blessed and exchanged, and the ceremony concluded with some kind of festivity.[28]

Although most peasants were illiterate, the gentry could write. The letters exchanged between Margaret and John Paston, who lived in Norfolk, England, in the fifteenth century, provide evidence for the experience of one couple. John and Margaret Paston were married about 1439, after an arrangement concluded entirely by their parents. John spent most of his time in London fighting through the law courts to increase his family properties and business interests; Margaret remained in Norfolk to supervise the family lands. Her enormous responsibilities involved managing the Paston estates, hiring workers, collecting rents, ordering supplies for the large household, hearing complaints and settling disputes among tenants, and marketing her crops. In these duties, she proved herself a remarkably shrewd businessperson. Moreover, when an army of over a thousand men led by the aristocratic thug Lord Moleyns attacked her house, she successfully withstood the siege. When the Black Death entered her area, Margaret moved her family to safety.

Margaret Paston did all this on top of raising eight children (there were probably other children who did not survive childhood). Her husband died before she was forty-three, and she later conducted the negotiations for the children's marriages. Her children's futures, like her estate management, were planned with an eye toward economic and social advancement. When one daughter secretly married the estate bailiff, an alliance considered beneath her, the girl was cut off from the family as if she were dead.[29]

The many letters surviving between Margaret and John reveal slight tenderness toward their children. They seem to have reserved their love for each other, and during many of his frequent absences they wrote to express mutual affection and devotion. How typical the Paston relationship was modern historians cannot say, but the marriage of John and Margaret, although completely arranged by their parents, was based on respect, responsibility, and love.[30]

At what age did people usually marry? The largest amount of evidence on age at first marriage survives from Italy. For girls, population surveys at Prato place the age at 16.3 years in 1372 and 21.1 in 1470. Chaucer's Wife of Bath (in England) says that she married first in her twelfth year. Among the German nobility, research has indicated that in the Hohenzollern family in the late Middle Ages, "five brides were between 12 and 13; five about 14, and five about 15." Generally in northern Europe, however, the evidence suggests that rural and urban women married in their twenties.

Men were older when they married. An Italian chronicler writing about 1354 says that men did not marry before the age of 30. At Prato in 1371, the average age of men at first marriage was 24 years, very young for Italian men, but these data may signal an attempt to regain population losses due to the recent attack of the plague. In England Chaucer's Wife of Bath describes her first three husbands as "goode men, and rich, and old." Among seventeen males in the noble Hohenzollern family, eleven were over 20 years when married, five between 18 and 19, one 16. The general pattern in late medieval Europe was marriage between men in their middle or late twenties and women under 20.[31] Poor peasants and wage laborers did not marry until their mid- or late twenties.

With marriage for men postponed, was there any socially accepted sexual outlet? Research on the southern French province of Languedoc in the fourteenth and fifteenth centuries has revealed the establishment of legal houses of prostitution. Prostitution involves "a socially definable group of women [who] earn their living primarily or exclusively from the [sexual] commerce of their bodies."[32] Municipal authorities in Toulouse, Montpellier, Albi, and other towns set up houses or red-light

Individuals in Society

Jan Hus

In May 1990, the Czech Republic's parliament declared July 6, the date of Jan Hus's execution in 1415, a Czech national holiday. The son of free farmers, Hus (ca 1369–1415) was born in Husinec in southern Bohemia, an area of heavy German settlement, and grew up conscious of the ethnic differences between Czechs and Germans. Most of his professors at Charles University in Prague were Germans. In 1396 he received a master's degree, and just before his ordination as a priest in 1400, he wrote that he would not be a "clerical careerist," implying that ambition for church offices motivated many of his peers.

The young priest lectured at the university and preached at the private Bethlehem Chapel. During his twelve years there, Hus preached only in Czech. He denounced superstition, the sale of indulgences, and other abuses, but his remarks were thoroughly orthodox. He attracted attention among artisans, the small Czech middle class, but not Germans. His austere life and lack of ambition enhanced his reputation.

Around 1400, Czech students returning from study at Oxford introduced into Bohemia the reforming ideas of the English theologian John Wyclif. When German professors condemned Wyclif's ideas as heretical, Hus and the Czechs argued "academic freedom," the right to read and teach Wyclif's works regardless of their particular merits. When popular demonstrations against ecclesiastical abuses and German influence at the university erupted, King Vaclav IV (1378–1419) placed control of the university in Czech hands. Hus was elected rector, the top administrative official.

The people of Prague, with perhaps the largest urban population in central Europe, 40 percent of it living below the poverty line and entirely dependent on casual labor, found Hus's denunciations of an overendowed church appealing. Hus considered the issues theological; his listeners saw them as socioeconomic.

Hus went into exile, where he wrote *On the Church*. He disputed papal authority, denounced abuses, and approved *utraquism*, the reception of the Eucharist under both species, bread and wine. Hus also defended transubstantiation (see page 460); insisted that church authority rested on Scripture, conscience, and tradition (in contrast to sixteenth-century Protestant reformers, who placed authority in Scripture alone); and made it clear that he had no intention of leaving the church or inciting a popular movement.

In 1413 the emperor Sigismund urged the calling of a general council to end the schism. Hus was invited, and, given the emperor's safe conduct (protection from attack or arrest), agreed to go. What he found was an atmosphere of inquisition. The safe conduct was disregarded, and Hus was arrested. Under questioning about his acceptance of Wyclif's ideas, Hus repeatedly replied, "I have not held; I do not hold." Council members were more interested in proving Hus a Wyclifite than in his responses. They took away his priesthood, banned his teachings, burned his books, and burned Hus himself at the stake. He then belonged to the ages.

The execution of Jan Hus. (University Library, Prague)

The ages have made good use of him. His death aggravated the divisions between the bishops at Constance and the Czech clerics and people. In September 1415, 452 nobles from all parts of Bohemia signed a letter saying that Hus had been unjustly executed and rejecting council rulings. This event marks the first time that an ecclesiastical decision was publicly defied. Revolution swept through Bohemia, with Hussites—Czech nobles and people—insisting on clerical poverty and Communion under both species, and German citizens remaining loyal to the Roman church. In the sixteenth century, reformers hailed Hus as the forerunner of Protestantism. In the eighteenth century, Enlightenment philosophes evoked Hus as a defender of freedom of expression. In the nineteenth century, central European nationalists used Hus's name to defend national sentiment against Habsburg rule. And in the twentieth century, Hus's name was used against German fascist and Russian communist tyranny.

Questions for Analysis

1. Since Jan Hus lived and died insisting that his religious teaching was thoroughly orthodox, why has he been hailed as a reformer?
2. What political and cultural interests did the martyred Hus serve?

The **history companion** *features additional information and activities related to this topic.* history.college.hmco.com/students

Prostitute Invites a Traveling Merchant   Poverty and male violence drove women into prostitution, which, though denounced by moralists, was accepted as a normal part of the medieval social fabric. In the cities and larger towns where prostitution flourished, public officials passed laws requiring prostitutes to wear a special mark on their clothing, regulated hours of business, forbade women to drag men into their houses, and denied business to women with the "burning sickness," gonorrhea. *(Bodleian Library, MS. Bodl. 264, fol. 245V)*

districts either outside the city walls or away from respectable neighborhoods. For example, authorities in Montpellier set aside Hot Street for prostitution, required public women to live there, and forbade anyone to molest them. Prostitution thus passed from being a private concern to a social matter requiring public supervision.[33] Publicly owned brothels were more easily policed and supervised than privately run ones. Prostitution was an urban phenomenon, because only populous towns had large numbers of unmarried young men, communities of transient merchants, and a culture accustomed to a cash exchange. Although the risk of disease limited the number of years a woman could practice this profession, many women prospered. Some acquired sizable incomes. In 1361 Françoise of Florence, a prostitute working in a brothel in Marseilles, made a will in which she made legacies to various charities and left a large sum as a dowry for a poor girl to marry. Archives in several cities show expensive properties bought by women who named their occupation as prostitution.

The towns of Languedoc were not unique. Public authorities in Amiens, Dijon, Paris, Venice, Genoa, London, Florence, Rome, most of the larger German towns, and the English port of Sandwich set up brothels. Legalized prostitution suggests that public officials believed the prostitute could make a positive contribution to society; it does not mean the prostitute was respected. Rather, she was scorned and distrusted. Legalized broth-

els also reflect a greater tolerance for male than for female sexuality.[34]

In the later Middle Ages, as earlier—indeed, until the late nineteenth century—economic factors, rather than romantic love or physical attraction, determined whom and when a person married. The young agricultural laborer on the manor had to wait until he had sufficient land. Thus most men had to wait until their fathers died or yielded the holding. Late marriage affected the number of children a couple had. The journeyman craftsman in the urban guild faced the same material difficulties. Once a couple married, the union ended only with the death of one partner.

Deep emotional bonds knit members of medieval families. Most parents delighted in their children, and the church encouraged a cult of paternal care. The church stressed its right to govern and sanctify marriage, and it emphasized monogamy. Tighter moral and emotional unity within marriages resulted.

Divorce did not exist in the Middle Ages. The church held that a marriage validly entered into could not be dissolved. A valid marriage consisted of the mutual oral consent or promise of two parties. Church theologians of the day urged that the couple's union be celebrated and witnessed in a church ceremony and blessed by a priest.

Many couples did not observe the church's regulations. Some treated marriage as a private act—they made the promise and spoke the words of marriage to each other without witnesses and then proceeded to enjoy the sexual pleasures of marriage. This practice led to a great number of disputes, because one of the two parties could later deny having made a marriage agreement. The records of the ecclesiastical courts reveal many cases arising from privately made contracts. Evidence survives of marriages contracted in a garden, in a blacksmith's shop, at a tavern, and, predictably, in a bed. The records of church courts that relate to marriage reveal that, rather than suing for divorce, the great majority of petitions asked the court to enforce the marriage contract that one of the parties believed she or he had validly made. Annulments were granted in extraordinary circumstances, such as male impotence, on the grounds that a lawful marriage had never existed.[35]

Life in the Parish

In the later Middle Ages, the land and the parish remained the focus of life for the European peasantry. Work on the land continued to be performed collectively. Both men and women cooperated in the annual tasks of planting and harvesting. The close association of the cycle of agriculture and the liturgy of the Christian calendar endured. The parish priest blessed the fields before the annual planting, offering prayers on behalf of the people for a good crop. If the harvest was rich, the priest led the processions and celebrations of thanksgiving.

How did the common people feel about their work? Since the vast majority were illiterate, it is difficult to say. Certainly the peasants hated the ancient services and obligations on the lords' lands and tried to get them commuted for money rents. When lords attempted to reimpose service duties, the peasants revolted.

In the thirteenth century, the craft guilds provided the small minority of men and women living in towns and cities with the psychological satisfaction of involvement in the manufacture of a superior product. The guild member also had economic security. The craft guilds set high standards for their merchandise. The guilds looked after the sick, the poor, the widowed, and the orphaned. Masters and employees worked side by side.

In the fourteenth century, those conditions began to change. The fundamental objective of the craft guild was to maintain a monopoly on its product, and to do so recruitment and promotion were carefully restricted. Some guilds required a high entrance fee for apprentices; others admitted only relatives of members. Apprenticeship increasingly lasted a long time, seven years. Even after a young man had satisfied all the tests for full membership in the guild and had attained the rank of master, other hurdles had to be passed, such as finding the funds to open his own business or special connections just to get into a guild. Restrictions limited the number of apprentices and journeymen to match the anticipated openings for masters.

Women experienced the same exclusion. A careful study of the records of forty-two craft guilds in Cologne shows that in the fifteenth century all but six had become male preserves, either greatly restricting women's participation or allowing so few female members that they cannot be considered mixed guilds.[36] Popular and educated culture, supporting a patriarchal system that held women to be biologically and intellectually inferior, consigned them to low-status and low-paying jobs.

The larger a particular business was, the greater was the likelihood that the master did not know his employees. The separation of master and journeyman and the decreasing number of openings for master craftsmen created serious frustrations. Strikes and riots occurred in the Flemish towns, in France, and in England.

The recreation of all classes reflected the fact that late medieval society was organized for war and that violence was common. The aristocracy engaged in tournaments or jousts; archery and wrestling had great popularity among ordinary people. Everyone enjoyed the cruel sports of bullbaiting and bearbaiting. The hangings and mutilations of criminals were exciting and well-attended events, with all the festivity of a university town before a Saturday football game. Chroniclers exulted in describing executions, murders, and massacres. Here a monk gleefully describes the gory execution of William Wallace (ca 1270–1305), the Scottish hero who led a revolt against Edward I of England and retains importance as a symbol of resistance to English rule and of Scottish nationalism:

Wilielmus Waleis, a robber given to sacrilege, arson and homicide . . . was condemned to most cruel but justly deserved death. He was drawn through the streets of London at the tails of horses, until he reached a gallows of unusual height, there he was suspended by a halter; but taken down while yet alive, he was mutilated, his bowels torn out and burned in a fire, his head then cut off, his body divided into four, and his quarters transmitted to four principal parts of Scotland.[37]

Violence was as English as roast beef and plum pudding, as French as bread, cheese, and *potage*.

If violent entertainment was not enough to dispel life's cares, alcohol was also available. Beer or ale commonly provided solace to the poor, and the frequency of drunkenness reflects their terrible frustrations.

Spanish Bullfight   The Romans may have introduced bullfighting in Spain but the Muslims popularized it. The sport takes place in a large outdoor arena, the object being for the bullfighter or matador (*torero*) to kill a wild bull (*toro*) with a sword. Here unsporting spectators goad the bull with whips. *(From the* Cantigas *of Alfonso X, ca 1283. El Escorial/Laurie Platt Winfrey, Inc.)*

During the fourteenth and fifteenth centuries, the laity began to exercise increasing control over parish affairs. The constant quarrels of the mendicant orders (the Franciscans and Dominicans), the mercenary and grasping attitude of the parish clergy, the scandal of the Great Schism and a divided Christendom—all these did much to weaken the spiritual mystique of the clergy in the popular mind. The laity steadily took responsibility for the management of parish lands. Laypeople organized associations to vote on and purchase furnishings for the church. And ordinary laypeople secured jurisdiction over the structure of the church building and its vestments, books, and furnishings. These new responsibilities of the laity reflect the increased dignity of parishioners in the late Middle Ages.[38]

Fur-Collar Crime

The Hundred Years' War had provided employment and opportunity for thousands of idle and fortune-seeking knights. But during periods of truce and after the war finally ended, many nobles once again had little to do. Inflation hurt them. Although many were living on fixed incomes, their chivalric code demanded lavish generosity and an aristocratic lifestyle. Many nobles turned to crime as a way of raising money. The fourteenth and fifteenth centuries witnessed a great deal of "fur-collar crime," so called for the miniver fur the nobility alone were allowed to wear on their collars.

Fur-collar crime rarely involved such felonies as homicide, robbery, rape, and arson. Instead, nobles used their superior social status to rob and extort from the weak and then to corrupt the judicial process. Groups of noble brigands roamed the English countryside stealing from both rich and poor. Sir John de Colseby and Sir William Bussy led a gang of thirty-eight knights who stole goods worth £3,000 in various robberies. Operating like modern urban racketeers, knightly gangs demanded that peasants pay "protection money" or else have their hovels burned and their fields destroyed.

Attacks on the rich often took the form of kidnapping and extortion. Wealthy travelers were seized on the highways and held for ransom. In northern England a gang of gentry led by Sir Gilbert de Middleton abducted Sir Henry Beaumont; his brother, the bishop-elect of Durham; and two Roman cardinals in England on a peacemaking visit. Only after a ransom was paid were the victims released.[39]

Fur-collar criminals were terrorists, but like some modern-day white-collar criminals who commit nonviolent crimes, medieval aristocratic criminals got away with their outrages. When accused of wrongdoing, fur-collar criminals intimidated witnesses. They threatened jurors. They used "pull" or cash to bribe judges. As a fourteenth-century English judge wrote to a young nobleman, "For the love of your father I have hindered charges being brought against you and have prevented execution of indictment actually made."[40]

The ballads of Robin Hood, a collection of folk legends from late medieval England, describe the adventures of the outlaw hero and his band of followers, who lived in Sherwood Forest and attacked and punished those who violated the social system and the law. Most of the villains in these simple tales are fur-collar criminals—grasping landlords, wicked sheriffs such as the famous sheriff of Nottingham, and mercenary churchmen. Robin and his merry men performed a sort of retributive justice. Robin Hood was a popular figure because he symbolized the deep resentment of aristocratic corruption and abuse; he represented the struggle against tyranny and oppression.

Criminal activity by nobles continued decade after decade because governments were too weak to stop it. Persecution by lords, on top of war, disease, and natural disaster, eventually drove long-suffering and oppressed peasants all across Europe to revolt.

Peasant Revolts

Nobles, clergy, and city dwellers lived on the produce of peasant labor. Early in the thirteenth century, the French preacher Jacques de Vitry asked rhetorically, "How many serfs have killed their lords or burnt their castles?"[41] And in the fourteenth and fifteenth centuries, social and economic conditions caused a great increase in peasant uprisings (see Map 12.3). They were very common and provide most of the evidence of peasants' long-suffering and exploitation.

We will never be able fully to answer Jacques de Vitry's questions, for rustics were not literate and, apart from their explosive uprisings, left no record of their aspirations. The clerical writers who mentioned the rebellions viewed the peasants with aristocratic disdain and hostility. Recent research provides some insight into **peasant revolts** in Flanders in the 1320s. Although the vast majority of people engaged in agriculture, Flanders was the most highly urbanized region in northern Europe. The commercial cities of Ghent, Bruges, and Ypres were huge

textile centers and the hearts of networks of smaller towns such as Arras, Lille, and Douai. Uprisings in Flanders were the first mass movements of the fourteenth century, perhaps unequaled anywhere in Europe before the German Peasants' Revolt of 1525 (see page 461). The English Peasants' Revolt of 1381 lasted five weeks, but the Flemish uprising extended over five years.[42]

Long-existing conflicts along the Flemish-French border came to a head at Courtrai in July 1302 when Flemish infantry smashed a French army, killing many knights and nobles (their golden spurs retrieved from the battlefield gave the battle its name, the Battle of the Spurs). The Flemish victory failed to resolve disputes over the French crown's claim to fiscal rights over the county of Flanders. Moreover, the peace agreements imposed heavy indemnities on Flemish peasants, who in 1323 began to revolt in protest of officials' demands for taxes and the misappropriation of the money collected. Also, monasteries pressed peasants for fees higher than the customary tithes. In retaliation, peasants subjected castles and aristocratic country houses to arson and pillage. At the same time, in Bruges and other Flemish cities, low- and middle-class workers deeply resented the widening social gap separating them from mercantile elites and the aristocracy. Eventually, rural and urban movements coalesced: peasants wanted "a world without corruption," and urban workers sought "a world without privilege." This amounted to revolutionary class warfare. A French army intervened and on August 23, 1328, near the town of Cassel in southwestern Flanders, crushed peasant forces. Savage repression and the confiscation of rustic property followed in the 1330s. In the towns, however, leaders of cloth guilds gained access to seats in town governments and used their influence to improve guild members' economic and political positions.[43]

In 1358, when French taxation for the Hundred Years' War fell heavily on the poor, the frustrations of the French peasantry exploded in a massive uprising called the **Jacquerie,** after a mythical agricultural laborer, Jacques Bonhomme (Good Fellow). Two years earlier, the English had captured the French king John and many nobles and held them for ransom. The peasants resented paying for their lords' release. Recently hit by plague, experiencing famine in some areas, and harassed by fur-collar criminals, peasants in Picardy, Champagne, and the Île-de-France erupted in anger and frustration. Crowds swept through the countryside slashing the throats of nobles, burning their castles, raping their wives and daughters, killing or maiming their horses and cattle. Peasants blamed the nobility for oppressive taxes, for the criminal brigandage of the countryside, for defeat in war, and for the general

MAP 12.3 Fourteenth-Century Peasant Revolts In the later Middle Ages and early modern times, peasant and urban uprisings were endemic, as common as factory strikes in the industrial world. The threat of insurrection served to check unlimited exploitation.

misery. Artisans, small merchants, and parish priests joined the peasants. Urban and rural groups committed terrible destruction, and for several weeks the nobles were on the defensive. Then the upper class united to repress the revolt with merciless ferocity. Thousands of the "Jacques," innocent as well as guilty, were cut down.

That forcible suppression of social rebellion, without some effort to alleviate its underlying causes, served to drive protest underground. Between 1363 and 1484, serious peasant revolts swept the Auvergne; in 1380 uprisings occurred in the Midi; and in 1420 they erupted in the Lyonnais region of France.

The Peasants' Revolt in England in 1381 involved thousands of people (see Map 12.3). Its causes were complex and varied from place to place. In general, though, the thirteenth century had witnessed the steady commutation of labor services for cash rents, and the Black Death had drastically cut the labor supply. As a result, peasants demanded higher wages and fewer manorial obligations. The parliamentary Statute of Laborers of 1351 (see page 386) had declared:

Whereas to curb the malice of servants who after the pestilence were idle and unwilling to serve without securing excessive wages, it was recently ordained . . . that such servants, both men and women, shall be bound to serve in return for salaries and wages that were customary . . . five or six years earlier.[44]

But this attempt to freeze wages and social mobility could not be enforced. Some scholars believe that the peasantry in most places was better off in the period 1350 to 1450 than it had been for centuries before or was to be for four centuries after.

Why then was the outburst in England in 1381 so serious? It was provoked by a crisis of rising expectations. The relative prosperity of the laboring classes led to demands that the upper classes were unwilling to grant. Unable to climb higher, the peasants sought release for their economic frustrations in revolt. But economic grievances combined with other factors. The south of England, where the revolt broke out, had been subjected to destructive French raids. The English government did little to protect the south, and villagers grew increasingly scared and insecure. Moreover, decades of aristocratic violence against the weak peasantry had bred hostility and bitterness. Social and religious agitation by the popular preacher John Ball fanned the embers of discontent. Ball's famous couplet "When Adam delved and Eve span; Who was then the gentleman?" reflected real revolutionary sentiment.

The straw that broke the camel's back in England was the reimposition of a head tax on all adult males. Despite widespread opposition to the tax in 1380, the royal council ordered the sheriffs to collect it again in 1381 on penalty of a huge fine. Beginning with assaults on the tax collectors, the uprising in England followed a course similar to that of the Jacquerie in France. Castles and manors were sacked. Manorial records were destroyed. Many nobles, including the archbishop of Canterbury, who had ordered the collection of the tax, were murdered.

The center of the revolt lay in the highly populated and economically advanced south and east, but sections of the north and the Midlands also witnessed rebellions. Violence took different forms in different places. Urban discontent merged with rural violence. In English towns where skilled Flemish craftsmen were employed, fear of competition led to their being attacked and murdered. Apprentices and journeymen, frustrated because the highest positions in the guilds were closed to them, rioted.

The boy-king Richard II (r. 1377–1399) met the leaders of the revolt, agreed to charters ensuring peasants' freedom, tricked them with false promises, and then crushed the uprising with terrible ferocity. The nobility tried to restore ancient duties of serfdom, but nearly a century of freedom had elapsed and the commutation of manorial services continued. Rural serfdom disappeared in England by 1550.

Conditions in Flanders, England, and France were not unique. In Florence in 1378, the *ciompi,* the poor propertyless workers, revolted. Serious social trouble occurred in Lübeck, Brunswick, and other German cities. In Spain in 1391, aristocratic attempts to impose new forms of serfdom, combined with demands for tax relief, led to massive working-class and peasant uprisings in Seville and Barcelona. These took the form of vicious attacks on Jewish communities. Rebellions and uprisings everywhere reveal deep peasant and working-class frustration and the general socioeconomic crisis of the time.

Race and Ethnicity on the Frontiers

Large numbers of people in the twelfth and thirteenth centuries migrated from one part of Europe to another: the English into Scotland and Ireland; Germans, French,

and Flemings into Poland, Bohemia, and Hungary; the French into Spain. In the fourteenth century, many Germans moved into eastern Europe, fleeing the Black Death. The colonization of frontier regions meant that peoples of different ethnic or racial backgrounds lived side by side. Race relations became a basic factor in the lives of peoples living in those frontier areas.

Racial categories rest on socially constructed beliefs and customs, not on any biological or anthropological classification. When late medieval chroniclers used the language of race—words such as *gens* (race or clan) and *natio* (species, stock, or kind)—they meant cultural differences. Medieval scholars held that peoples differed according to descent, language, customs, and laws. Descent or blood, basic to the color racism of the United States, played an insignificant part in eleventh- and twelfth-century ideas about race and ethnicity. Rather, the chief marks of an ethnic group were language (which could be learned), customs (for example, dietary practices, dance, marriage and death rituals, clothing, and hairstyles, all of which could be adopted), and laws (which could be changed or modified). How did the law reflect attitudes and race relations in the Middle Ages?

In the early periods of conquest and colonization, and in all frontier regions, a legal dualism existed: native peoples remained subject to their traditional laws; newcomers brought and were subject to the laws of the countries from which they came. On the Prussian and Polish frontier, for example, the law was that "men who come there . . . should be judged on account of any crime or contract engaged in there according to Polish custom if they are Poles and according to German custom if they are Germans."[45] Likewise, in Spain Mudéjars, Muslim subjects of Christian kings, received guarantees of separate but equal judicial rights. King Alfonso I of Aragon's charter to the Muslims of Toledo states, "They shall be in lawsuits and pleas under their (Muslim) qadi (judges) . . . as it was in the times of the Moors."[46] Thus conquered peoples, whether Muslims in Spain, or minority immigrant groups, such as Germans in eastern Europe, had legal protection and lived in their own juridical enclaves. Subject peoples experienced some disabilities, but the broad trend was toward a legal pluralism.

The great exception to this broad pattern was Ireland. From the start, the English practiced an extreme form of racial discrimination toward the native Irish. The English distinguished between the free and the unfree, and the entire Irish population, simply by the fact of Irish birth, was unfree. In 1210 King John declared that "English law and custom be established there (in Ireland)." Accordingly, a legal structure modeled on that of England, with county courts, itinerant justices, and the common law (see pages 342–344), was set up. But the Irish had no access to the common-law courts. In civil (property) disputes, an English defendant need not respond to his Irish plaintiff; no Irish person could make a will. In criminal procedures, the murder of an Irishman was not considered a felony. In 1317–1318, Irish princes sent a Remonstrance to the pope complaining that "any non-Irishman is allowed to bring legal action against an Irishman, but an Irishman . . . except any prelate (bishop or abbot) is barred from every action by that fact alone." An English defendant in the criminal matter would claim "that he is not held to answer . . . since he [the plaintiff] is Irish and not of free blood."[47] This emphasis on blood descent naturally provoked bitterness.

The later Middle Ages witnessed a movement away from legal pluralism or dualism and toward a legal homogeneity and an emphasis on blood descent. Competition for ecclesiastical offices and the cultural divisions between town and country people became arenas for ethnic tension and racial conflict. Since bishoprics and abbacies carried religious authority, spiritual charisma, and often rights of appointment to subordinate positions, they were natural objects of ambition. When prelates of a language or "nationality" different from those of the local people gained church positions, the latter felt a loss of influence. Bishops were supposed to be pastors. Their pastoral work involved preaching, teaching, and comforting, duties that could be performed effectively only when the bishop (or priest) could communicate with the people. Ideally in a pluralistic society, he should be bilingual; often he was not.

In the late thirteenth century, as waves of Germans migrated into Danzig on the Baltic, into Silesia, and into the Polish countryside and towns, they encountered Jakub Swinka, archbishop of Gniezno (1283–1314), whose jurisdiction included these areas of settlement. The bishop hated Germans and referred to them as "dog heads." His German contemporary, Bishop John of Cracow, detested the Poles, wanted to expel all Polish people, and refused to appoint Poles to any church office. In Ireland, English colonists and the native Irish competed for ecclesiastical offices until 1217, when the English government in London decreed:

Since the election of Irishmen in our land of Ireland has often disturbed the peace of that land, we command you . . . that henceforth you allow no Irishman to be elected . . . or preferred in any cathedral . . . (and) you should seek by all means to procure election and promotion to vacant bishoprics of . . . honest Englishmen.[48]

Although criticized by the pope and not totally enforceable, this law remained in effect in many dioceses for centuries.

Likewise, the arrival of Cistercians and mendicants (Franciscans and Dominicans) from France and Germany in Baltic and Slavic lands provoked racial and "national" hostilities. In the fourteenth and fifteenth centuries, in contrast to earlier centuries, racial or ethnic prejudices became conspicuous. Slavic prelates and princes saw the German mendicants as "instruments of cultural colonization," and Slavs were strongly discouraged from becoming friars. In 1333, when John of Drazic, bishop of Prague, founded a friary at Roudnice (Raudnitz), he specified that "we shall admit no one to this convent or monastery of any nation except a Bohemian [Czech], born of two Czech-speaking parents."[49]

Everywhere in Europe, towns recruited people from the countryside (see pages 346–347). In frontier regions, townspeople were usually long-distance immigrants and, in eastern Europe, Ireland, and Scotland, ethnically different from the surrounding rural population. In eastern Europe, German was the language of the towns; in Ireland, French, the tongue of Norman or English settlers, predominated. In fourteenth-century Prague, between 63 percent and 80 percent of new burgesses bore identifiable German names, as did almost all city council members. Towns in eastern Europe "had the character of German islands in Slav, Baltic, Estonian, or Magyar seas."[50] Although native peoples commonly held humbler positions, both immigrant and native townspeople prospered during the expanding economy of the thirteenth century. When economic recession hit during the fourteenth century, ethnic tensions multiplied.

On the frontiers of Latin Europe discrimination, ghettoization, and **racism**—now based on blood descent—characterized the attitudes of colonists toward native peoples. But the latter also could express racial savagery. In the ***Dalimil Chronicle,*** a survey of Bohemian history pervaded with Czech hostility toward Germans, one anti-German prince offered 100 marks of silver "to anyone who brought him one hundred noses cut off from the Germans."[51] Regulations drawn up by various guilds were explicitly racist, with protectionist bars for some groups and exclusionist laws for others. The Deutschtum paragraph of the *Chronicle,* applicable to parts of eastern Europe, required that applicants for guild membership be of German descent. Cobblers in fourteenth-century Beeskow, a town close to the large Slavic population of Lausitz in Silesia, required that "an apprentice who comes to learn his craft should be brought before the master and guild members. . . . We forbid the sons of barbers, linen workers, shepherds, Slavs." The bakers of the same town decreed:

Whoever wishes to be a member must bring proof to the councillors and guildsmen that he is born of legitimate, upright, German folk. . . . No one of Wendish (Slavic) race may be in the guild. In Limerick and Dublin in Ireland, guild masters agreed to accept "noo apprentice but that he be of English berthe."[52]

Intermarriage was forbidden in many places, such as Riga on the Baltic (now the capital of Latvia), where legislation for the bakers guild stipulated that "whoever wishes to have the privilege of membership in our company shall not take as a wife any woman who is ill-famed . . . or non-German; if he does marry such a woman, he must leave the company and office." Not only the guilds but eligibility for public office depended on racial purity, as at the German burgher settlement of Pest in Hungary, where a town judge had to have four German grandparents. The most extensive attempt to prevent intermarriage and protect racial purity is embodied in Ireland's **Statute of Kilkenny** (1366), which states that "there were to be no marriages between those of immigrant and native stock; that the English inhabitants of Ireland must employ the English language and bear English names; that they must ride in the English way (i.e., with saddles) and have English apparel; that no Irishmen were to be granted ecclesiastical benefices or admitted to monasteries in the English parts of Ireland. . . ."[53] Rulers of the Christian kingdoms of Spain drew up comparable legislation discriminating against the Mudéjars.

All these laws had an economic basis: to protect the financial interests of the privileged German, English, or Spanish colonial minorities. The laws also reflect a racism that not only pervaded the lives of frontier peoples at the end of the Middle Ages but also sowed the seeds of difficulties still unresolved today.

Vernacular Literature

Across Europe people spoke the language and dialect of their particular locality and class. In England, for example, the common people spoke regional English dialects, while the upper classes conversed in French. Official documents and works of literature were written in Latin or French. Beginning in the fourteenth century, however, national languages—the vernacular—came into widespread use not only in verbal communication but in literature as well. Three masterpieces of European culture, Dante's *Divine Comedy* (1310–1320), Chaucer's *Canter-*

bury Tales (1387–1400), and Villon's *Grand Testament* (1461), brilliantly manifest this new national pride.

Dante Alighieri (1265–1321) descended from a landowning family in Florence, where he held several positions in the city government. Dante called his work a "comedy" because he wrote it in Italian and in a different style from the "tragic" Latin; a later generation added the adjective *divine,* referring both to its sacred subject and to Dante's artistry. The *Divine Comedy* is an allegorical trilogy of one hundred cantos (verses) whose three equal parts (1 + 33 + 33 + 33) each describe one of the realms of the next world: Hell, Purgatory, and Paradise. The Roman poet Virgil, representing reason, leads Dante through Hell, where he observes the torments of the damned and denounces the disorders of his own time, especially ecclesiastical ambition and corruption. Passing up into Purgatory, Virgil shows the poet how souls are purified of their disordered inclinations. From Purgatory, Beatrice, a woman Dante once loved and the symbol of divine revelation in the poem, leads him to Paradise. In Paradise, home of the angels and saints, Saint Bernard—representing mystic contemplation—leads Dante to the Virgin Mary. Through her intercession, he at last attains a vision of God.

The *Divine Comedy* portrays contemporary and historical figures, comments on secular and ecclesiastical affairs, and draws on Scholastic philosophy. Within the framework of a symbolic pilgrimage to the City of God, the *Divine Comedy* embodies the psychological tensions of the age. A profoundly Christian poem, it also contains bitter criticism of some church authorities. In its symmetrical structure and use of figures from the ancient world, such as Virgil, the poem perpetuates the classical tradition, but as the first major work of literature in the Italian vernacular, it is distinctly modern.

Geoffrey Chaucer (1342–1400), the son of a London wine merchant, was an official in the administrations of the English kings Edward III and Richard II and wrote poetry as an avocation. Chaucer's *Canterbury Tales* is a collection of stories in lengthy, rhymed narrative. On a pilgrimage to the shrine of Saint Thomas Becket at Canterbury (see page 343), thirty people of various social backgrounds each tell a tale. The Prologue sets the scene and describes the pilgrims, whose characters are further revealed in the story each one tells. For example, the gross Miller tells a vulgar story about a deceived husband; the earthy Wife of Bath, who has buried five husbands, sketches a fable about the selection of a spouse; and the elegant Prioress, who violates her vows by wearing jewelry, delivers a homily on the Virgin. In depicting the interests and behavior of all types of people, Chaucer fellen konwen vnd junckkouwen wer fin bedarff der kum har jn wir wirt drüwlich gelert vm em zimlichen lon · Aber die junge knabe vnd meitlin noch den kronualten · wie gewonheit ist · 1 5 1 6 ·

Schoolmaster and His Wife Teaching   Ambrosius Holbein, elder brother of the more famous Hans Holbein, produced this signboard for the Swiss educator Myconius; it is an excellent example of what we would call commercial art—art used to advertise, in this case Myconius's profession. The German script above promised that all who enrolled would learn to read and write. By modern standards the classroom seems bleak: the windows have glass panes but they don't admit much light, and the schoolmaster is prepared to use the sticks if the boy makes a mistake. *(Kunstmuseum Basel/Martin Bühler, photographer)*

presents a rich panorama of English social life in the fourteenth century. Like the *Divine Comedy, Canterbury Tales* reflects the cultural tensions of the times. Ostensibly Christian, many of the pilgrims are also materialistic, sensual, and worldly, suggesting the ambivalence of the broader society's concern for the next world and frank enjoyment of this one.

Our knowledge of François Villon (1431–1463), probably the greatest poet of late medieval France, derives from Paris police records and his own poetry. Born to poor parents in the year of Joan of Arc's execution, Villon was sent by his guardian to the University of Paris, where he earned the master of arts degree. A rowdy and free-spirited student, he disliked the stuffiness of academic life. In 1455 Villon killed a man in a street brawl; banished from Paris, he joined one of the bands of wandering thieves that harassed the countryside after the Hundred Years' War. For his fellow bandits, he composed ballads in thieves' jargon.

Villon's *Lais* (1456) is a series of farcical bequests to friends and enemies. The word *lais* refers to short rhymed tales but is also a pun on the French word *legs,* meaning "legacy." Villon's greatest and most self-revealing work, the *Grand Testament,* contains another string of bequests, including a legacy to a prostitute, and describes his unshakable faith in the beauty of life on earth. The *Grand Testament* possesses elements of social rebellion, bawdy humor, and rare emotional depth. While the themes of Dante's and Chaucer's poetry are distinctly medieval, Villon's celebration of the human condition brands him as definitely modern. Although he used medieval forms of versification, Villon's language was the despised vernacular of the poor and the criminal.

Perhaps the most versatile and prolific French writer of the later Middle Ages was Christine de Pisan (1363?–1434?). The daughter of a professor of astrology at Bologna and then a prominent member of the French court, Christine had a broad knowledge of Greek, Latin, French, and Italian literature. The deaths of her father and husband left her with three small children and her mother to support; she had to earn her living with her pen. In addition to poems and books on love, religion, and morality, Christine produced the *Livre de la mutacion de fortune,* a major historical work; a biography of King Charles V; the *Ditié,* celebrating Joan of Arc's victory; and many letters. *The City of Ladies* lists the great women of history and their contributions to society, and *The Book of Three Virtues* provides practical advice on household management for women of all social classes. Christine de Pisan's wisdom and wit are illustrated in her autobiographical *Avison-Christine.* She records that a man told her an educated woman is unattractive, since there are so few, to which she responded that an ignorant man was even less attractive, since there are so many. (See the feature "Listening to the Past: Christine de Pisan" on pages 410–411.)

Beginning in the fourteenth century, a variety of evidence attests to the increasing literacy of laypeople. Wills and inventories reveal that many people, not just nobles, possessed books, mainly devotional, but also romances, manuals on manners and etiquette, histories, and sometimes legal and philosophical texts. In England the number of schools in the diocese of York quadrupled between 1350 and 1500. Information from Flemish and German towns is similar: children were sent to schools and received the fundamentals of reading, writing, and arithmetic. Laymen increasingly served as managers or stewards of estates and as clerks to guilds and town governments; such positions obviously required that they be able to keep administrative and financial records.

The penetration of laymen into the higher positions of governmental administration, long the preserve of clerics, also illustrates rising lay literacy. For example, in 1400 beneficed clerics held most of the posts in the English Exchequer; by 1430 clerics were the exception. With growing frequency, the upper classes sent their daughters to convent schools, where, in addition to instruction in singing, religion, needlework, deportment, and household management, girls gained the rudiments of reading and sometimes writing. Reading and writing represent two kinds of literacy. Scholars estimate that many more people, especially women, possessed the first literacy, but not the second. The spread of literacy represents a response to the needs of an increasingly complex society. Trade, commerce, and expanding governmental bureaucracies required more and more literate people. Late medieval culture remained an oral culture in which most people received information by word of mouth. But by the mid-fifteenth century, even before the printing press was turning out large quantities of reading materials, the evolution toward a literary culture was already perceptible.[54]

Summary

The crises of the fourteenth and fifteenth centuries were acids that burned deeply into the fabric of traditional medieval society. Bad weather brought poor harvests, which contributed to the international economic depression. Disease, over which people also had little control, fostered widespread depression. Population losses caused by the Black Death and the Hundred Years' War encouraged the working classes to try to profit from the labor shortage by selling their services higher: they wanted to move up the economic ladder. The theological ideas of thinkers like John Wyclif, John Hus, and John Ball fanned the flames of social discontent. When peasant frustrations exploded in uprisings, the frightened nobility and upper middle class joined to crush the revolts and condemn heretical preachers as agitators of social rebellion.

The Hundred Years' War served as a catalyst for the development of representative government in England. In France, on the other hand, the war stiffened opposition to national assemblies.

The war also stimulated technological experimentation, especially with artillery. Cannon revolutionized warfare, because the stone castle was no longer impregnable. Because only central governments, and not private nobles, could afford cannon, they strengthened the military power of national states.

The migration of peoples from the European heartland to the frontier regions of Ireland, the Baltic, eastern Europe, and Spain led to ethnic frictions between native peoples and new settlers. Economic difficulties heightened ethnic consciousness and spawned a vicious racism.

Religion held society together. European culture was a Christian culture. But the Great Schism weakened the prestige of the church and people's faith in papal authority. The conciliar movement, by denying the church's universal sovereignty, strengthened the claims of secular government to jurisdiction over all their peoples. The later Middle Ages witnessed a steady shift of basic loyalty from the church to the emerging national states.

The increasing number of schools leading to the growth of lay literacy represents another positive achievement of the later Middle Ages. So also does the development of national literatures. The first signs of a literary culture appeared.

Key Terms

Great Famine
Black Death
buba
flagellants
Crécy
Agincourt
Joan of Arc
representative
 assemblies
nationalism

Babylonian Captivity
schism
conciliarists
merchet
banns
peasant revolts
Jacquerie
racism
Dalimil Chronicle
Statute of Kilkenny

Notes

1. W. C. Jordan, *The Great Famine: Northern Europe in the Early Fourteenth Century* (Princeton, N.J.: Princeton University Press, 1996), pp. 97–102.
2. Ibid., pp. 167–179.
3. N. Ascherson, *Black Sea* (New York: Hill & Wang, 1996), pp. 95–96.
4. W. H. McNeill, *Plagues and Peoples* (New York: Doubleday, 1976), pp. 151–168.
5. Quoted in P. Ziegler, *The Black Death* (Harmondsworth, England: Pelican Books, 1969), p. 20.
6. J. M. Rigg, trans., *The Decameron of Giovanni Boccaccio* (London: J. M. Dent & Sons, 1903), p. 6.
7. M. Mollatt, *The Poor in the Middle Ages: An Essay in Social History,* trans. A. Goldhammer (New Haven, Conn.: Yale University Press, 1986), pp. 146–153, 193–197.
8. Ziegler, *The Black Death*, pp. 232–239.
9. Ibid., p. 84.
10. G. Huppert, *After the Black Death: A Social History of Early Modern Europe* (Bloomington, Ind.: Indiana University Press, 1986), p. ix.
11. Quoted in D. Herlihy, *The Black Death and the Transformation of the West* (Cambridge, Mass.: Harvard University Press, 1997), p. 42.
12. J. Hatcher, *Plague, Population, and the English Economy, 1348–1530* (London: Macmillan Education, 1986), p. 33.
13. See Herlihy, *The Black Death*, pp. 43–45.
14. Ibid., pp. 46–47; Hatcher, *Plague,* p. 33. The quotation is from Hatcher.
15. Ascherson, *Black Sea*, p. 96.
16. See Herlihy, *The Black Death*, pp. 59–81.
17. See P. Cuttino, "Historical Revision: The Causes of the Hundred Years' War," *Speculum* 31 (July 1956): 463–472.
18. J. Barnie, *War in Medieval English Society: Social Values and the Hundred Years' War* (Ithaca, N.Y.: Cornell University Press, 1974), p. 6.
19. Quoted ibid., p. 34.
20. W. P. Barrett, trans., *The Trial of Jeanne d'Arc* (London: George Routledge, 1931), pp. 165–166.
21. Quoted in Barnie, *War in Medieval English Society*, pp. 36–37.
22. M. M. Postan, "The Costs of the Hundred Years' War," *Past and Present* 27 (April 1964): 34–53.

23. See G. O. Sayles, *The King's Parliament of England* (New York: W. W. Norton, 1974), app., pp. 137–141.
24. Quoted in P. S. Lewis, "The Failure of the Medieval French Estates," *Past and Present* 23 (November 1962): 6.
25. Quoted in J. H. Smith, *The Great Schism, 1378: The Disintegration of the Medieval Papacy* (New York: Weybright & Talley, 1970), p. 141.
26. Ibid., p. 15.
27. B. A. Hanawalt, *The Ties That Bound: Peasant Families in Medieval England* (New York: Oxford University Press, 1986), p. 197. This section leans heavily on Hanawalt's work.
28. Ibid., pp. 194–204.
29. A. S. Haskell, "The Paston Women on Marriage in Fifteenth Century England," *Viator* 4 (1973): 459–469.
30. Ibid., p. 471.
31. See D. Herlihy, *Medieval Households* (Cambridge, Mass.: Harvard University Press, 1985), pp. 103–111.
32. L. L. Otis, *Prostitution in Medieval Society: The History of an Urban Institution in Languedoc* (Chicago: University of Chicago Press, 1987), p. 2.
33. Ibid., pp. 25–27, 64–66, 100–106.
34. Ibid., pp. 118–130.
35. See R. H. Helmholz, *Marriage Litigation in Medieval England* (Cambridge: Cambridge University Press, 1974), pp. 28–29, et passim.
36. See M. C. Howell, *Women, Production, and Patriarchy in Late Medieval Cities* (Chicago: University of Chicago Press, 1986), pp. 134–135.
37. A. F. Scott, ed., *Everyone a Witness: The Plantagenet Age* (New York: Thomas Y. Crowell, 1976), p. 263.
38. See E. Mason, "The Role of the English Parishioner, 1000–1500," *Journal of Ecclesiastical History* 27 (January 1976): 17–29.
39. B. A. Hanawalt, "Fur Collar Crime: The Pattern of Crime Among the Fourteenth-Century English Nobility," *Journal of Social History* 8 (Spring 1975): 1–14.
40. Quoted ibid., p. 7.
41. Quoted in M. Bloch, *French Rural History,* trans. J. Sondeimer (Berkeley: University of California Press, 1966), p. 169.
42. W. H. TeBrake, *A Plague of Insurrection: Popular Politics and Peasant Revolt in Flanders, 1323–1328* (Philadelphia: University of Pennsylvania Press, 1993), pp. 1–9.
43. Ibid., pp. 15–99.
44. C. Stephenson and G. Marcham, eds., *Sources of English Constitutional History,* rev. ed. (New York: Harper & Row, 1972), p. 225.
45. Quoted in R. Bartlett, *The Making of Europe: Conquest, Colonization and Cultural Change, 950–1350* (Princeton, N.J.: Princeton University Press, 1993), p. 205. For an alternative, if abstract, discussion of medieval racism, see I. Hannaford, *Race: The History of an Idea in the West* (Baltimore: Johns Hopkins University Press, 1995), pp. 87–146.
46. Quoted in Bartlett, *The Making of Europe,* p. 208.
47. Quoted ibid., p. 215.
48. Quoted ibid., p. 224.
49. Quoted ibid., p. 228.
50. Quoted ibid., p. 233.
51. Quoted ibid., p. 236.
52. Quoted ibid., p. 238.
53. Quoted ibid., p. 239.
54. See M. Keen, *English Society in the Later Middle Ages, 1348–1500* (New York: Penguin Books, 1990), pp. 219–239.

Suggested Reading

The best starting point for study of the great epidemic that swept the European continent is D. Herlihy, *The Black Death and the Transformation of the West* (1997), a fine treatment of the causes and cultural consequences of the disease. P. Binski, *Medieval Death: Ritual and Representation* (1995), discusses the impact of the Black Death on medieval art and literature. For the social implications of the Black Death, see L. Poos, *A Rural Society After the Black Death: Essex, 1350–1525* (1991), and G. Huppert, *After the Black Death: A Social History of Early Modern Europe* (1986). For the economic effects of the plague, see J. Hatcher, *Plague, Population, and the English Economy, ca. 1300–1450* (1977). The older study of P. Ziegler, *The Black Death* (1969), remains important.

For the background and early part of the long military conflicts of the fourteenth and fifteenth centuries, see the provocative M. M. Vale, *The Origins of the Hundred Years War: The Angevin Legacy, 1250–1340* (1996). See also C. Allmand, *The Hundred Years War: England and France at War, ca 1300–1450* (1988). The broad survey of J. Keegan, *A History of Warfare* (1993), contains a useful summary of significant changes in military technology during the war. The main ruler of the age has found his biographer in W. M. Ormrod, *The Reign of Edward III: Crown and Political Society in England, 1327–1377* (1990). J. Keegan, *The Face of Battle* (1977), chap. 2, "Agincourt," describes what war meant to the ordinary soldier. For strategy, tactics, armaments, and costumes of war, see H. W. Koch, *Medieval Warfare* (1978), a beautifully illustrated book. R. Barber, *The Knight and Chivalry* (1982), and M. Keen, *Chivalry* (1984), give interpretations of the cultural importance of chivalry.

For political and social conditions in the fourteenth and fifteenth centuries, see the works by Lewis, Sayles, Bloch, TeBrake, and especially Hanawalt and Helmholz cited in the Notes. C. Dyer, *Standards of Living in the Later Middle Ages* (1989), contains much valuable social history. The papers in R. H. Hilton and T. H. Aston, eds., *The English Rising of 1381* (1984), stress the importance of urban, as well as rural, participation in the movement, but see also R. Hilton, *Bond Men Made Free: Medieval Peasant Movements and the English Rising of 1381* (1973), a comparative study. T. F. Glick, *From Muslim Fortress to Christian Castle: Social and Cultural Change in Medieval Spain* (1995), is based in part on rare archaeological information and explores the reorganization of Spanish society after the reconquest. J. S. Gerber, *The Jews of Spain: A History of the Sephardic Experience* (1992), treats growing anti-Jewish sentiment in the wake of the Black Death. P. C. Maddern, *Violence and Social Order: East Anglia, 1422–1442* (1991), deals with social disorder in eastern England. I. M. W. Harvey, *Jack Cade's Rebellion of 1450* (1991), is an important work in local history. J. C. Holt, *Robin Hood* (1982), is a soundly researched and highly readable study of the famous outlaw. For the Pastons, see R. Barber, ed., *The Pastons: Letters of a Family in the Wars of the Roses* (1984). The starting point for study of the widespread starvation of the early fourteenth century is the prizewinning work by Jordan cited in the Notes. For social attacks on various ethnic and religious minorities, see D. Nirenberg, *Communities of Violence: Persecution of Minorities in the Middle Ages* (1996).

D. Herlihy, *Women, Family and Society in Medieval Europe: Historical Essays, 1978–1991* (1995), contains valuable articles dealing with the later Middle Ages, while the exciting study by B. Gottlieb, *The Family in the Western World from the Black Death to the Industrial Age* (1993), explores the family's political, emotional, and cultural roles. For prostitution, see, in addition to the title by Otis cited in the Notes, J. Rossiaud, *Medieval Prostitution* (1995), a very good treatment of prostitution's social and cultural significance.

For women's economic status in the late medieval period, see the titles by Howell and Hanawalt cited in the Notes. J. S. Bennett, *Ale, Beer, and Brewsters in England: Women's Work in a Changing World, 1300–1600* (1996), stresses the persistence of patriarchal attitudes. P. J. P. Goldberg, *Women, Work, and Life Cycle in a Medieval Economy: Women in York and Yorkshire, c 1300–1520* (1992), explores the relationship between economic opportunity and marriage.

The poetry of Dante, Chaucer, and Villon may be read in the following editions: D. Sayers, trans., *Dante: The Divine Comedy*, 3 vols. (1963); N. Coghill, trans., *Chaucer's Canterbury Tales* (1977); P. Dale, trans., *The Poems of Villon* (1973). The social setting of *Canterbury Tales* is brilliantly evoked in D. W. Robertson, Jr., *Chaucer's London* (1968). Students interested in further study of Christine de Pisan should consult A. J. Kennedy, *Christine de Pisan: A Bibliographical Guide* (1984), and C. C. Willard, *Christine de Pisan: Her Life and Works* (1984).

For religion and lay piety, A. D. Brown, *Popular Piety in Late Medieval England: The Diocese of Salisbury, 1250–1550* (1995), is a good case study showing the importance of guilds, charity, and heresy and how they affected parish life. F. Oakley, *The Western Church in the Later Middle Ages* (1979), is an excellent broad survey, while R. N. Swanson, *Church and Society in Late Medieval England* (1989), provides a good synthesis of English conditions. The important achievement of A. Vauchez, *The Laity in the Middle Ages: Religious Beliefs and Devotional Practices,* ed. D. E. Bornstein and trans. M. J. Schneider (1993), explores many aspects of popular piety and contains considerable material on women.

Listening to the Past

Christine de Pisan

The passage below is taken from The Book of the City of Ladies, *one of the many writings of Christine de Pisan (1363?–1434?). Christine was a highly educated woman who wrote prolifically in French, her native tongue. Her patron was the queen of France. Christine wrote amid the chaos of the Hundred Years' War about a wide range of topics. The excerpt below is not reflective of all French women. Rather, it focuses on the behavior of courtly women only. And it expresses Christine's and her patron's views about women's role in the creation and stabilization of an elite court culture during a time of political and social upheaval.*

Just as the good shepherd takes care that his lambs are maintained in health, and if any of them becomes mangy, separates it from the flock for fear that it may infect the others, so the princess will take upon herself the responsibility for the care of her women servants and companions, who she will ensure are all good and chaste, for she will not want to have any other sort of person around her. Since it is the established custom that knights and squires and all men (especially certain men) who associate with women have a habit of pleading for love tokens from them and trying to seduce them, the wise princess will so enforce her regulations that there will be no visitor to her court so foolhardy as to dare to whisper privately with any of her women or give the appearance of seduction. If he does it or if he is noticed giving any sign of it, immediately she should take such an attitude towards him that he will not dare to importune them any more. The lady who is chaste will want all her women to be so too, on pain of being banished from her company.

She will want them to amuse themselves with decent games, such that men cannot mock, as they do the games of some women, though at the time the men laugh and join in. The women should restrain themselves with seemly conduct among knights and squires and all men. They should speak demurely and sweetly and, whether in dances or other amusements, divert and enjoy themselves decorously and without wantonness. They must not be frolicsome, forward, or boisterous in speech, expression, bearing or laughter. They must not go about with their heads raised like wild deer. This kind of behaviour would be very unseemly and greatly derisory in a woman of the court, in whom there should be more modesty, good manners and courteous behaviour than in any others, for where there is most honour there ought to be the most perfect manners and behaviour. Women of the court in any country would be deceiving themselves very much if they imagined that it was more appropriate for them to be frolicsome and saucy than for other women. For this reason we hope that in time to come our doctrine in this book may be carried into many kingdoms, so that it may be valuable in all places where there might be any shortcoming.

We say generally to all women of all countries that it is the duty of every lady and maiden of the court, whether she be young or old, to be more prudent, more decorous, and better schooled in all things than other women. The ladies of the court ought to be models of all good things and all honour to other women, and if they do otherwise they will do no honour to their mistress nor to themselves. In addition, so that everything may be consistent in modesty, the wise princess will wish that the clothing and the ornaments of her women, though they be appropriately beautiful and rich, be of a modest fashion, well fitting and seemly, neat and properly cared for. There should be no deviation from this modesty

Christine de Pisan, shown here producing her *Collected Works,* was devoted to scholarship. *(British Library)*

nor any immodesty in the matter of plunging necklines or other excesses.

In all things the wise princess will keep her women in order just as the good and prudent abbess does her convent, so that bad reports about it may not circulate in the town, in distant regions or anywhere else. This princess will be so feared and respected because of the wise management that she will be seen to practise that no man or woman will be so foolhardy as to disobey her commands in any respect or to question her will, for there is no doubt that a lady is more feared and respected and held in greater reverence when she is seen to be wise and chaste and of firm behaviour. But there is nothing wrong or inconsistent in her being kind and gentle, for

the mere look of the wise lady and her subdued reception is enough of a sign to correct those men and women who err and to inspire them with fear.

Questions for Analysis

1. How did Christine think courtly women should behave around men?

2. How did women fit into the larger picture of court culture? What was their role at court?

Source: Christine de Pisan, "The Book of the City of Ladies," in *Treasures of the City of Ladies,* translated with an introduction by Sarah Lawson. Translation copyright © 1985 by Sarah Lawson. Reprinted by permission of Penguin Group UK.

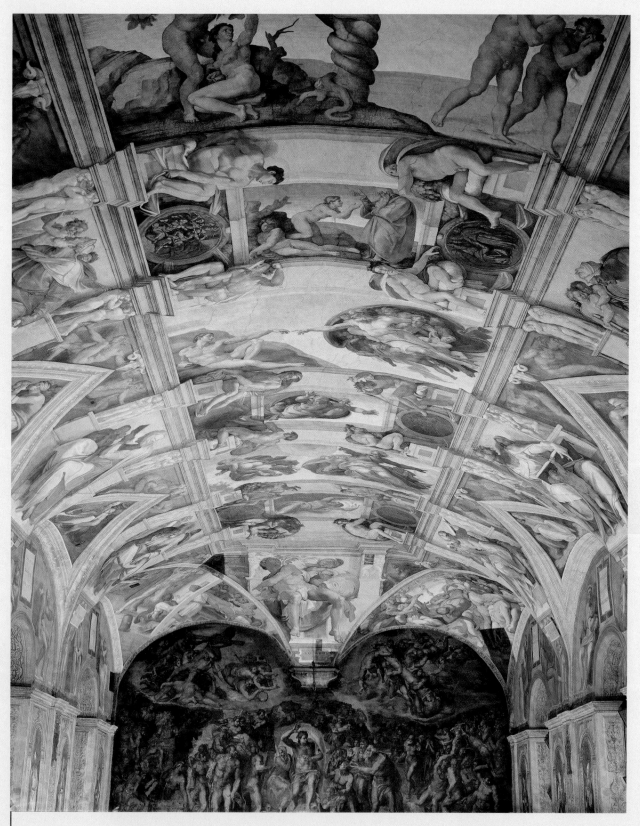

Michelangelo painted the entire Sistine Chapel ceiling
by himself, in 1508–1512. *(Vatican Museum)*

European Society in the Age of the Renaissance

*W*hile the Four Horsemen of the Apocalypse seemed to be carrying war, plague, famine, and death across northern Europe, a new culture was emerging in southern Europe. The fourteenth century witnessed the beginnings of remarkable changes in many aspects of Italian society. In the fifteenth century, these phenomena spread beyond Italy and gradually influenced society in northern Europe. These cultural changes have been collectively labeled the "Renaissance."

- What does the term *Renaissance* mean?
- How was the Renaissance manifested in politics, government, and social organization?
- What were the intellectual and artistic hallmarks of the Renaissance?
- Did the Renaissance involve shifts in religious attitudes?
- What developments occurred in the evolution of the nation-state?

This chapter will concentrate on these questions.

*T*he Evolution of the Italian Renaissance

Economic growth laid the material basis for the Italian Renaissance. The period extending roughly from 1050 to 1300 witnessed phenomenal commercial and financial development, the growing political power of self-governing cities, and great population expansion. Then the period from the late thirteenth to the late sixteenth century was characterized by an incredible efflorescence of artistic energies.[1] Scholars commonly use the term **Renaissance** to describe the cultural achievements of the fourteenth through sixteenth centuries; those achievements rest on the economic and political developments of earlier centuries.

In the great commercial revival of the eleventh century, northern Italian cities led the way. By the middle of the twelfth century, Venice, supported by a huge merchant marine, had grown enormously rich through overseas trade. It profited tremendously from the diversion of the Fourth Crusade to Constantinople (see page 353). Genoa and Milan also enjoyed the benefits of a

A Bank Scene, Florence Originally a "bank" was just a counter; if covered with a carpet like this Ottoman geometric rug with a kufic border, it became a bank of distinction. Money-changers who sat behind the counter became "bankers," exchanging different currencies and holding deposits for merchants and business people. *(Prato, San Francesco/Scala/Art Resource, NY)*

large volume of trade with the Middle East and northern Europe. These cities fully exploited their geographical positions as natural crossroads for mercantile exchange between the East and West. Furthermore, in the early fourteenth century, Genoa and Venice made important strides in shipbuilding that allowed their ships for the first time to sail all year long. Advances in ship construction greatly increased the volume of goods that could be transported; improvements in the mechanics of sailing accelerated speed. Most goods were purchased directly from the producers and sold a good distance away. For example, Italian merchants bought fine English wool directly from the Cistercian abbeys of Yorkshire in northern England. The wool was transported to the bazaars of North Africa either overland or by ship through the Strait of Gibraltar. The risks in such an operation were great, but the profits were enormous. These profits were continually reinvested to earn more. The Florentine wool industry was the major factor in that city's financial expansion and population increase.

Scholars tend to agree that the first artistic and literary manifestations of the Italian Renaissance appeared in Florence, which possessed enormous wealth despite geographical constraints: it was an inland city without easy access to sea transportation. But toward the end of the thirteenth century, Florentine merchants and bankers acquired control of papal banking. From their position as tax collectors for the papacy, Florentine mercantile families began to dominate European banking on both sides of the Alps. These families had offices in Paris, London, Bruges, Barcelona, Marseilles, Tunis and other North African ports, and, of course, Naples and Rome. The profits from loans, investments, and money exchanges that poured back to Florence were pumped into urban industries. Such profits contributed to the city's economic vitality. Banking families, such as the Medici in Florence, controlled the politics and culture of their cities.

By the first quarter of the fourteenth century, the economic foundations of Florence were so strong that even severe crises could not destroy the city. In 1344 King Edward III of England repudiated his huge debts to Florentine bankers and forced some of them into bankruptcy. Florence suffered frightfully from the Black Death, losing at least half of its population. Serious labor unrest, such as the *ciompi* revolts of 1378 (see page 403), shook the political establishment. Nevertheless, the basic Florentine economic structure remained stable. Driving enterprise, technical know-how, and competitive spirit saw Florence through the difficult economic period of the late fourteenth century.

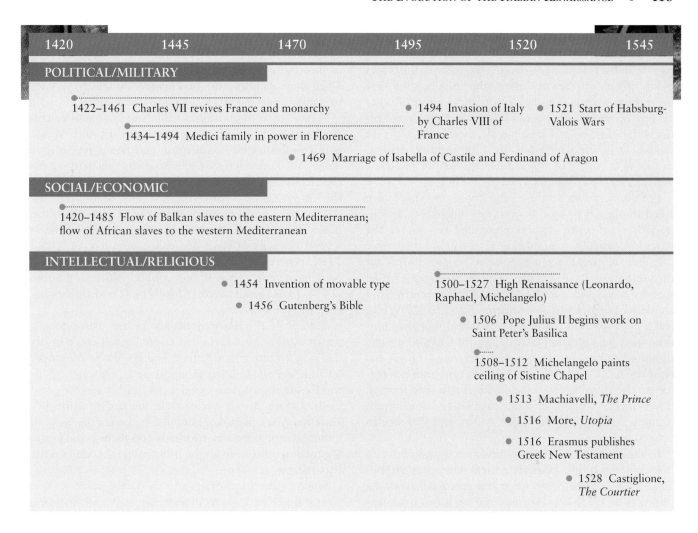

1420	1445	1470	1495	1520	1545

POLITICAL/MILITARY

1422–1461 Charles VII revives France and monarchy

1434–1494 Medici family in power in Florence

● 1494 Invasion of Italy by Charles VIII of France

● 1521 Start of Habsburg-Valois Wars

● 1469 Marriage of Isabella of Castile and Ferdinand of Aragon

SOCIAL/ECONOMIC

1420–1485 Flow of Balkan slaves to the eastern Mediterranean; flow of African slaves to the western Mediterranean

INTELLECTUAL/RELIGIOUS

● 1454 Invention of movable type

● 1456 Gutenberg's Bible

1500–1527 High Renaissance (Leonardo, Raphael, Michelangelo)

● 1506 Pope Julius II begins work on Saint Peter's Basilica

1508–1512 Michelangelo paints ceiling of Sistine Chapel

● 1513 Machiavelli, *The Prince*

● 1516 More, *Utopia*

● 1516 Erasmus publishes Greek New Testament

● 1528 Castiglione, *The Courtier*

Communes and Republics

The northern Italian cities were **communes,** sworn associations of free men seeking complete political and economic independence from local nobles. The merchant guilds that formed the communes built and maintained the city walls, regulated trade, raised taxes, and kept civil order. In the course of the twelfth century, communes at Milan, Florence, Genoa, Siena, and Pisa fought for and won their independence from surrounding feudal nobles. The nobles, attracted by the opportunities of long-distance and maritime trade, the rising value of urban real estate, the new public offices available in the expanding communes, and the chances for advantageous marriages into rich commercial families, frequently settled within the cities. Marriage vows often sealed business contracts between the rural nobility and the mercantile aristocracy. This merger of the northern Italian feudal nobility and the commercial aristocracy constituted the formation of a

new social class, an urban nobility. Within this nobility, groups tied by blood, economic interests, and social connections formed tightly knit alliances to defend and expand their rights.

This new class made citizenship in the communes dependent on a property qualification, years of residence within the city, and social connections. Only a tiny percentage of the male population possessed these qualifications and thus could hold office in the commune's political councils. A new force, called the **popolo,** disenfranchised and heavily taxed, bitterly resented their exclusion from power. The popolo wanted places in the communal government and equality of taxation. Throughout most of the thirteenth century, in city after city, the popolo used armed force and violence to take over the city governments. Republican governments—in which political power theoretically resides in the people and is exercised by their chosen representatives—were established in Bologna, Siena, Parma, Florence, Genoa, and other cities. The victory of the popolo, however, proved temporary. Because they practiced the same sort of political exclusivity as had the noble communes—denying influence to the classes below them, whether the poor, the unskilled, or new immigrants—the popolo never won the support of other groups. Moreover, the popolo could not establish civil order within their cities. Consequently, these movements for republican government failed. By 1300 **signori** (despots, or one-man rulers) or **oligarchies** (the rule of merchant aristocracies) had triumphed everywhere in Italy.[2]

For the next two centuries, the Italian city-states were ruled by signori or by constitutional oligarchies. In signorial governments, despots pretended to observe the law while actually manipulating it to conceal their basic illegality. Oligarchic regimes possessed constitutions, but through a variety of schemes a small, restricted class of wealthy merchants exercised the judicial, executive, and legislative functions of government. Thus in 1422 Venice had a population of eighty-four thousand, but two hundred men held all the power; Florence had about forty thousand people, but six hundred men ruled. Oligarchic regimes maintained only a façade of republican government. The Renaissance nostalgia for the Roman form of government, combined with calculating shrewdness, prompted the leaders of Venice, Milan, and Florence to use the old forms.

In the fifteenth century, political power and elite culture centered on the **princely courts** of despots and oligarchs. "A court was the space and personnel around a prince as he made laws, received ambassadors, made appointments, took his meals, and proceeded through the streets."[3] The princely court afforded the despot or oligarch the opportunity to display and assert his wealth and power. He flaunted his patronage of learning and the arts by munificent gifts to writers, philosophers, and artists. He used ceremonies connected with family births, baptisms, marriages, funerals, or triumphant entrances into the city as occasions for magnificent pageantry and elaborate ritual.

The Balance of Power Among the Italian City-States

Renaissance Italians had a passionate attachment to their individual city-states: political loyalty and feeling centered on the local city. This intensity of local feeling perpetuated the dozens of small states and hindered the development of one unified state.

In the fifteenth century, five powers dominated the Italian peninsula: Venice, Milan, Florence, the Papal States, and the kingdom of Naples (see Map 13.1). The rulers of the city-states—whether despots in Milan, patrician elitists in Florence, or oligarchs in Venice—governed as monarchs. They crushed urban revolts, levied taxes, killed their enemies, and used massive building programs to employ, and the arts to overawe, the masses.

Venice, with its enormous trade and vast colonial empire, ranked as an international power. Though Venice had a sophisticated constitution and was a **republic** in name, an oligarchy of merchant aristocrats actually ran the city. Milan was also called a republic, but despots of the Sforza family ruled harshly and dominated the smaller cities of the north. Likewise in Florence the form of government was republican, with authority vested in several councils of state. In reality, between 1434 and 1494, power in Florence was held by the great Medici banking family. Though not public officers, Cosimo (1434–1464) and Lorenzo (1469–1492) ruled from behind the scenes.

Central Italy consisted mainly of the Papal States, which during the Babylonian Captivity had come under the sway of important Roman families. Pope Alexander VI (1492–1503), aided militarily and politically by his son Cesare Borgia, reasserted papal authority in the papal lands. Cesare Borgia became the hero of Machiavelli's *The Prince* (see page 429) because he began the work of uniting the peninsula by ruthlessly conquering and exacting total obedience from the principalities making up the Papal States.

South of the Papal States was the kingdom of Naples, consisting of virtually all of southern Italy and, at times, Sicily. The kingdom of Naples had long been disputed by the Aragonese and by the French. In 1435 it passed to Aragon.

The major Italian city-states controlled the smaller ones, such as Siena, Mantua, Ferrara, and Modena, and competed furiously among themselves for territory. The large cities used diplomacy, spies, paid informers, and any other available means to get information that could be used to advance their ambitions. While the states of northern Europe were moving toward centralization and consolidation, the world of Italian politics resembled a jungle where the powerful dominated the weak.

In one significant respect, however, the Italian city-states anticipated future relations among competing European states after 1500. Whenever one Italian state appeared to gain a predominant position within the peninsula, other states combined to establish a *balance of power* against the major threat. In 1450, for example, Venice went to war against Milan in protest against Francesco Sforza's acquisition of the title of duke of Milan. Cosimo de' Medici of Florence, a long-time sup-

MAP 13.1 The Italian City-States, ca 1494   In the fifteenth century, the Italian city-states represented great wealth and cultural sophistication. The political divisions of the peninsula invited foreign intervention.

porter of a Florentine-Venetian alliance, switched his position and aided Milan. Florence and Naples combined with Milan against powerful Venice and the papacy. In the peace treaty signed at Lodi in 1454, Venice received territories in return for recognizing Sforza's right to the duchy. This pattern of shifting alliances continued until

1494. In the formation of these alliances, Renaissance Italians invented the machinery of modern diplomacy: permanent embassies with resident ambassadors in capitals where political relations and commercial ties needed continual monitoring. The resident ambassador was one of the great achievements of the Italian Renaissance.

Uccello: Battle of San Romano Fascinated by perspective—the representation of spatial depth or distance on a flat surface—the Florentine artist Paolo Uccello (1397–1475) celebrated the Florentine victory over Siena (1432) in a painting with three scenes. Though a minor battle, it started Florence on the road to domination over smaller nearby states. The painting hung in Lorenzo de' Medici's bedroom. *(National Gallery, London/Erich Lessing/Art Resource, NY)*

At the end of the fifteenth century, Venice, Florence, Milan, and the papacy possessed great wealth and represented high cultural achievement. However, their imperialistic ambitions at one another's expense and their resulting inability to form a common alliance against potential foreign enemies made Italy an inviting target for invasion. When Florence and Naples entered into an agreement to acquire Milanese territories, Milan called on France for support.

At Florence the French invasion had been predicted by Dominican friar Girolamo Savonarola (1452–1498). In a number of fiery sermons between 1491 and 1494, Savonarola attacked what he called the paganism and moral vice of the city, the undemocratic government of Lorenzo de' Medici, and the corruption of Pope Alexander VI. For a time, Savonarola enjoyed popular support among the ordinary people; he became the religious leader of Florence and as such contributed to the fall of the Medici dynasty. Eventually, however, people tired of

his moral denunciations, and he was excommunicated by the pope and executed. Savonarola stands as proof that the common people did not share the worldly outlook of the commercial and intellectual elite. His career also illustrates the internal instability of Italian cities such as Florence, an instability that invited foreign invasion.

The invasion of Italy in 1494 by the French king Charles VIII (r. 1483–1498) inaugurated a new period in Italian and European power politics. Italy became the focus of international ambitions and the battleground of foreign armies. Charles swept down the peninsula with little opposition, and Florence, Rome, and Naples soon bowed before him. When Piero de' Medici, Lorenzo's son, went to the French camp seeking peace, the Florentines exiled the Medici and restored republican government.

Charles's success simply whetted French appetites. In 1508 his cousin and heir, Louis XII, formed the League of Cambrai with the pope and the German emperor Maximilian for the purpose of stripping rich Venice of its mainland possessions. Pope Leo X (1513–1521) soon found France a dangerous friend and in a new alliance called on the Spanish and Germans to expel the French from Italy. This anti-French combination was temporarily successful. In 1519 Charles V succeeded his grandfather Maximilian (1493–1519) as Holy Roman emperor. When the French returned to Italy in 1521, a series of conflicts called the Habsburg-Valois Wars (named for the German and French dynasties) began. The battlefield was often Italy.

In the sixteenth century, the political and social life of Italy was upset by the relentless competition for dominance between France and the empire. The Italian cities suffered severely from continual warfare, especially in the frightful sack of Rome in 1527 by imperial forces under Charles V. Thus the failure of the city-states to form some federal system, consolidate, or at least establish a common foreign policy led to the continuation of the centuries-old subjection of the peninsula by outside invaders. Italy was not to achieve unification until 1870.

Intellectual Hallmarks of the Renaissance

The Renaissance was characterized by self-conscious awareness among fourteenth- and fifteenth-century Italians that they were living in a new era. The realization that something new and unique was happening first came to men of letters in the fourteenth century, especially to the poet and humanist Francesco Petrarch (1304–1374). Petrarch thought that he was living at the start of a new age, a period of light following a long night of Gothic gloom. He considered the first two centuries of the Roman Empire to represent the peak in the development of human civilization. Medieval people had believed that they were continuing the glories that had been ancient Rome and had recognized no cultural division between the world of the emperors and their own times. But for Petrarch, the Germanic migrations had caused a sharp cultural break with the glories of Rome and inaugurated what he called the "Dark Ages." He believed, with many of his contemporaries, that the thousand-year period between the fourth and the fourteenth centuries constituted a barbarian, Gothic, or "middle" age. The sculptors, painters, and writers of the Renaissance spoke contemptuously of their medieval predecessors and identified themselves with the thinkers and artists of Greco-Roman civilization. Petrarch believed that he was witnessing a new golden age of intellectual achievement—a rebirth or, to use the French word that came into Eng-

lish, a renaissance. The division of historical time into periods is often arbitrary and done for the convenience of historians. In terms of the way most people lived and thought, no sharp division exists between the Middle Ages and the Renaissance. Some important poets, writers, and artists, however, believed they were living in a new golden age.

The Renaissance also manifested itself in a new attitude toward men, women, and the world—an attitude that may be described as individualism. A humanism characterized by a deep interest in the Latin classics and a deliberate attempt to revive antique lifestyles emerged, as did a bold new secular spirit.

Individualism

Though the Middle Ages had seen the appearance of remarkable individuals, recognition of such persons was limited. The examples of Saint Augustine in the fifth century and Peter Abelard and Guibert of Nogent in the twelfth—men who perceived themselves as unique and produced autobiographical statements—stand out for that very reason: Christian humility discouraged self-absorption. In the fourteenth and fifteenth centuries, moreover, such characteristically medieval and corporate attachments as the guild and the parish continued to provide strong support for the individual and to exercise great social influence. Yet in the Renaissance, intellectuals, unlike their counterparts in the Middle Ages, developed a new sense of historical distance from earlier periods. A large literature specifically concerned with the nature of individuality emerged. This literature represented the flowering of a distinctly Renaissance individualism.

The Renaissance witnessed the emergence of many distinctive personalities who gloried in their uniqueness. Italians of unusual abilities were self-consciously aware of their singularity and unafraid to be unlike their neighbors; they had enormous confidence in their ability to achieve great things. Leon Battista Alberti (1404–1474), a writer, architect, and mathematician, remarked, "Men can do all things if they will."[4] Florentine goldsmith and sculptor Benvenuto Cellini (1500–1574) prefaced his *Autobiography* with a declaration:

My cruel fate hath warr'd with me in vain:
Life, glory, worth, and all unmeasur'd skill,
Beauty and grace, themselves in me fulfill
That many I surpass, and to the best attain.[5]

Cellini, certain of his genius, wrote so that the whole world might appreciate it.

Benvenuto Cellini: Saltcellar of Francis I (ca 1539–1543)
In gold and enamel, Cellini depicts the Roman sea god,
Neptune (with trident, or three-pronged spear), sitting beside
a small boat-shaped container holding salt from the sea. Opposite him, a female figure personifying Earth guards pepper,
which derives from a plant. Portrayed on the base are the four
seasons and the times of day, symbolizing seasonal festivities
and daily meal schedules. The grace, poise, and elegance of
the figures reflect Mannerism, an artistic style popular during
the Italian High Renaissance (1520–1600). *(Kunsthistorisches
Museum, Vienna/The Bridgeman Art Library)*

Individualism stressed personality, uniqueness, genius,
and full development of one's capabilities and talents.
Artist, athlete, painter, scholar, sculptor, whatever—a person's abilities should be stretched until fully realized.
Thirst for fame, a driving ambition, and a burning desire
for success drove such people to the complete achievement of their potential. The quest for glory was a central
component of Renaissance individualism.

Humanism

In the cities of Italy, especially Rome, civic leaders and
the wealthy populace showed phenomenal archaeological zeal for the recovery of manuscripts, statues, and
monuments. Pope Nicholas V (1447–1455), a distinguished scholar, planned the Vatican Library for the nine
thousand manuscripts he had collected. Pope Sixtus IV
(1471–1484) built that library, which remains one of the
richest repositories of ancient and medieval documents.

The revival of antiquity also took the form of profound
interest in and study of the Latin classics. This feature of
the Renaissance became known as the "new learning," or
simply **humanism,** the term of Florentine rhetorician
and historian Leonardo Bruni (1370–1444). The words
humanism and *humanist* derive ultimately from the Latin
humanitas, which Cicero used to mean the literary culture needed by anyone who would be considered educated and civilized. Humanists studied the Latin classics
to learn what they reveal about human nature. Humanism emphasized human beings, their achievements, interests, and capabilities. Although churchmen supported
the new learning, by the later fifteenth century Italian
humanism was increasingly a lay phenomenon.

Appreciation for the literary culture of the Romans
had never died in the West. Bede and John of Salisbury,
for example, had studied and imitated the writings of the
ancients. Medieval writers, however, had studied the
ancients in order to come to know God. Medieval scholars had interpreted the classics in a Christian sense and
had invested the ancients' poems and histories with
Christian meaning.

Renaissance humanists, although deeply Christian, approached the classics differently. Whereas medieval writers accepted pagan and classical authors uncritically,
Renaissance humanists were skeptical of their authority,
conscious of the historical distance separating themselves
from the ancients, and fully aware that classical writers often disagreed among themselves. Whereas medieval writers looked to the classics to reveal God, Renaissance
humanists studied the classics to understand human nature, and while they fully grasped the moral thought of
pagan antiquity, Renaissance humanists viewed humanity
from a strongly Christian perspective: men and women
were made in the image and likeness of God. For example, in a remarkable essay, *On the Dignity of Man,* the
Florentine writer Pico della Mirandola stressed that man
possesses great dignity because he was made as Adam in
the image of God before the Fall and as Christ after the
Resurrection. According to Pico, man's place in the universe is somewhere between the beasts and the angels,
but because of the divine image planted in him, there are
no limits to what he can accomplish. Humanists rejected
classical ideas that were opposed to Christianity. Or they
sought through reinterpretation an underlying harmony
between the pagan and secular and the Christian faith.
The fundamental difference between Renaissance humanists and medieval ones is that the former were more
self-conscious about what they were doing, and they
stressed the realization of human potential.[6]

The fourteenth- and fifteenth-century humanists loved the language of the classics and considered it superior to the corrupt Latin of the medieval schoolmen. They eventually became concerned more about form than about content, more about the way an idea was expressed than about the significance and validity of the idea. Literary humanists of the fourteenth century wrote each other highly stylized letters imitating ancient authors, and they held witty philosophical dialogues in conscious imitation of the Platonic Academy of the fourth century B.C. Renaissance humanists heaped scorn on the "barbaric" Latin style of the medievalists. The leading humanists of the early Renaissance were rhetoricians, seeking effective and eloquent communication, both oral and written.

Secular Spirit

Secularism involves a basic concern with the material world instead of with the eternal world of spirit. A secular way of thinking tends to find the ultimate explanation of everything and the final end of human beings within the limits of what the senses can discover. Even though medieval business people ruthlessly pursued profits and medieval monks fought fiercely over property, the dominant ideals focused on the otherworldly, on life after death. Renaissance people often held strong and deep spiritual interests, but in their increasingly secular society, attention was concentrated on the here and now, often on the acquisition of material things. Church doctrine, relying on Scripture (Leviticus 25:36–37, Psalms 37:26, Luke 11:15), frowned on usury (lending money at interest), but the law had always been difficult to enforce. In the twelfth century, Cistercian monks had been severely criticized for practicing usury. During the Renaissance, the practice became widespread, even acceptable. Considerable wealth derived from interest on loans. The fourteenth and fifteenth centuries witnessed the slow but steady growth of such secularism in Italy.

The economic changes and rising prosperity of the Italian cities in the thirteenth century worked a fundamental change in social and intellectual attitudes and values. Worries about shifting rates of interest, shipping routes, personnel costs, and employee relations did not leave much time for thoughts about penance and purgatory. The busy bankers and merchants of the Italian cities calculated ways of making and increasing their money. Such wealth allowed greater material pleasures, a more comfortable life, the leisure time to appreciate and patronize the arts. Money could buy many sensual gratifications, and the rich, social-climbing patricians of Venice,

Florence, Genoa, and Rome came to see life more as an opportunity to be enjoyed than as a painful pilgrimage to the City of God.

In *On Pleasure,* humanist Lorenzo Valla (1406–1457) defends the pleasures of the senses as the highest good. Scholars praise Valla as a father of modern historical criticism. His study *On the False Donation of Constantine* (1444) demonstrates by careful textual examination that an anonymous eighth-century document supposedly giving the papacy jurisdiction over vast territories in western Europe was a forgery. Medieval people had accepted the Donation of Constantine as a reality, and the proof that it was an invention weakened the foundations of papal claims to temporal authority. Lorenzo Valla's work exemplifies the application of critical scholarship to old and almost-sacred writings as well as the new secular spirit of the Renaissance.

The tales in *The Decameron* by the Florentine Giovanni Boccaccio (1313–1375), which describe ambitious merchants, lecherous friars, and cuckolded husbands, portray a frankly acquisitive, sensual, and worldly society. Although Boccaccio's figures were stock literary characters, *The Decameron* contains none of the "contempt of the world" theme so pervasive in medieval literature. Renaissance writers justified the accumulation and enjoyment of wealth with references to ancient authors.

Nor did church leaders do much to combat the new secular spirit. In the fifteenth and early sixteenth centuries, the papal court and the households of the cardinals were just as worldly as those of great urban patricians. Of course, most of the popes and higher church officials had come from the bourgeois aristocracy. Renaissance popes beautified the city of Rome, patronized artists and men of letters, and expended enormous enthusiasm and huge sums of money. A new papal chancellery, begun in 1483 and finished in 1511, stands as one of the architectural masterpieces of the High Renaissance. Pope Julius II (1503–1513) tore down the old Saint Peter's Basilica and began work on the present structure in 1506. Michelangelo's dome for Saint Peter's is still considered his greatest work. Papal interests, which were far removed from spiritual concerns, fostered, rather than discouraged, the new worldly attitude.

The broad mass of the people and the intellectuals and leaders of society remained faithful to the Christian church. Few people questioned the basic tenets of the Christian religion. Italian humanists and their aristocratic patrons were anti-ascetic, anti-Scholastic, and ambivalent, but they were not agnostics or skeptics. The thousands of pious paintings, sculptures, processions, and pilgrimages of the Renaissance period prove that strong religious feeling persisted.

Art and the Artist

No feature of the Renaissance evokes greater admiration than its artistic masterpieces. The 1400s (*quattrocento*) and 1500s (*cinquecento*) bore witness to a dazzling creativity in painting, architecture, and sculpture. In all the arts, the city of Florence led the way. According to Renaissance art historian Giorgio Vasari (1511–1574), the painter Perugino once asked why it was in Florence and not elsewhere that men achieved perfection in the arts. The first answer he received was, "There were so many good critics there, for the air of the city makes men quick and perceptive and impatient of mediocrity."[7] But Florence was not the only artistic center. In the period art historians describe as the "High Renaissance" (1500–1527), Rome took the lead. The main characteristics of High Renaissance art—classical balance, harmony, and restraint—are revealed in the masterpieces of Leonardo da Vinci (1452–1519), Raphael (1483–1520), and Michelangelo (1475–1564), all of whom worked in Rome.

Art and Power

In early Renaissance Italy, art manifested corporate power. Powerful urban groups such as guilds or religious confraternities commissioned works of art. The Florentine cloth merchants, for example, delegated Filippo Brunelleschi to build the magnificent dome on the cathedral of Florence and selected Lorenzo Ghiberti to design the bronze doors of the Baptistry. These works represented the merchants' dominant influence in the community. Corporate patronage was also reflected in the Florentine government's decision to hire Michelangelo to create the sculpture of David, the great Hebrew hero and king. The subject matter of art through the early fifteenth century, as in the Middle Ages, remained overwhelmingly religious. Religious themes appeared in all media—woodcarvings, painted frescoes, stone sculptures, paintings. As in the Middle Ages, art served an educational purpose. A religious picture or statue was intended to spread a particular doctrine, act as a profession of faith, or recall sinners to a moral way of living.

Increasingly in the later fifteenth century, individuals and oligarchs, rather than corporate groups, sponsored works of art. Patrician merchants and bankers, popes and princes, supported the arts as a means of glorifying themselves and their families. Vast sums were spent on family chapels, frescoes, religious panels, and tombs. Writing about 1470, Florentine oligarch Lorenzo de' Medici declared that over the previous thirty-five years his family had spent the astronomical sum of 663,755 gold florins for artistic and architectural commissions. Yet "I think it casts a brilliant light on our estate [public reputation] and it seems to me that the monies were well spent and I am very pleased with this." Powerful men wanted to exalt themselves, their families, and their offices. A magnificent style of living, enriched by works of art, served to prove the greatness and the power of the despot or oligarch.[8]

In addition to power, art reveals changing patterns of consumption in Renaissance Italy. "Consumer habits introduced into economic life a creative and dynamic process for growth and change that was fundamental to the development of the West."[9] If modern consumerism has its roots in the eighteenth century, the latter period's consumer practices can be traced to the Italian Renaissance.

In the rural world of the Middle Ages, society had been organized for war. Men of wealth spent their money on military gear—swords, armor, horses, crenelated castles, towers, family compounds—all of which represent offensive or defensive warfare. As Italian nobles settled in towns (see page 415), they adjusted to an urban culture. Rather than employing knights for warfare, cities hired mercenaries. Expenditure on military hardware declined. For the rich merchant or the noble recently arrived from the countryside, the urban palace represented the greatest outlay of cash. It was his chief luxury, and although a private dwelling, the palace implied grandeur.[10] Within the palace, the merchant-prince's chamber, or bedroom, where he slept and received his intimate guests, was the most important room. In the fourteenth and fifteenth centuries, a large, intricately carved wooden bed, a chest, and perhaps a bench served as its sole decorations. The chest held the master's most precious goods—silver, tapestries, jewelry, clothing. Other rooms, even in palaces of fifteen to twenty rooms, were very sparsely furnished. As the fifteenth century advanced and wealth increased, other rooms were gradually furnished with carved chests, tables, benches, chairs, tapestries for the walls, paintings (an innovation), and sculptural decorations, and a private chapel was added. By the late sixteenth century, the Strozzi banking family of Florence spent more on household goods than on anything else except food; the value of those furnishings was three times that of their silver and jewelry.[11]

After the palace itself, the private chapel within the palace symbolized the largest expenditure. Equipped with

Botticelli: Primavera, or Spring (ca 1482)   Framed by a grove of orange trees, Venus, goddess of love, is flanked on her left by Flora, goddess of flowers and fertility, and on her right by the Three Graces, goddesses of banquets, dance, and social occasions. Above, Venus's son Cupid, the god of love, shoots darts of desire, while at the far right the wind-god Zephyrus chases the nymph Chloris. The entire scene rests on classical mythology, though some art historians claim that Venus is an allegory for the Virgin Mary. *(Digital image © The Museum of Modern Art/Licensed by Scala/Art Resource, NY)*

the ecclesiastical furniture—tabernacles, chalices, thuribles, and other liturgical utensils—and decorated with religious scenes, the chapel served as the center of the household's religious life and its cult of remembrance of the dead. In fifteenth-century Florence, only the Medici had a private chapel, but by the late sixteenth century, most wealthy Florentine families had private chapels. Since the merchant banker or prince appointed the chaplain, usually a younger son of the family, religious power passed into private hands.[12]

As the fifteenth century advanced, the subject matter of art became steadily more secular. The study of classical texts brought deeper understanding of ancient ideas.

Classical themes and motifs, such as the lives and loves of pagan gods and goddesses, figured increasingly in painting and sculpture. Religious topics, such as the Annunciation of the Virgin and the Nativity, remained popular among both patrons and artists, but frequently the patron had himself and his family portrayed. People were conscious of their physical uniqueness and wanted their individuality immortalized. Paintings were also means of displaying wealth.

The content and style of Renaissance art were decidedly different from those of the Middle Ages. The individual portrait emerged as a distinct artistic genre. In the fifteenth century, members of the newly rich middle

Andrea Mantegna: Adoration of the Magi (ca 1495–1505) Applying his study of ancient Roman relief sculpture, and elaborating on a famous scriptural text (Matthew 2:1), Mantegna painted for the private devotion of the Gonzaga family of Mantua this scene of the Three Kings coming to recognize the divinity of Christ. The Three Kings represent the entire world—that is, the three continents known to medieval Europeans: Europe, Asia, and Africa. They also symbolize the three stages of life: youth, maturity, and old age. Here Melchior, the oldest, his large cranium symbolizing wisdom, personifies Europe. He offers gold in a Chinese porcelain cup from the Ming Dynasty. Balthazar, with an olive complexion and dark beard, stands for Asia and maturity. He presents frankincense in a stunning vessel of Turkish tombac ware. Caspar, representing Africa and youth, gives myrrh in an urn of striped marble. The child responds with a blessing. The black background brings out the rich colors. (© *The J. Paul Getty Museum, Los Angeles. Mantegna, Andrea,* Adoration of the Magi, *ca 1495–1505, distemper on linen, 54.6 × 70.7 cm [85.PA.417]*)

class often had themselves painted in a scene of romantic chivalry or courtly society. Rather than reflecting a spiritual ideal, as medieval painting and sculpture tended to do, Renaissance portraits mirrored reality. The Florentine painter Giotto (1276–1337) led the way in the use of realism; his treatment of the human body and face replaced the formal stiffness and artificiality that had for so long characterized representation of the human body. The sculptor Donatello (1386–1466) probably exerted the greatest influence of any Florentine artist before

Michelangelo. His many statues express an appreciation of the incredible variety of human nature. Whereas medieval artists had depicted the nude human body only in a spiritualized and moralizing context, Donatello revived the classical figure, with its balance and self-awareness. The short-lived Florentine Masaccio (1401–1428), sometimes called the father of modern painting, inspired a new style characterized by great realism, narrative power, and remarkably effective use of light and dark. As important as realism was the new "international style," so called be-

Renaissance Wedding Chest (Tuscany, late fifteenth century) A wedding chest was a gift from the groom's family to the bride. Appreciated more for their decorative value than for practical storage purposes, these chests were prominently displayed in people's homes. This 37" × 47" × 28" chest is carved with scenes from classical mythology. *(Marriage chest with Ceres, Goddess of Agriculture searching for her abducted daughter, Prosperpina. Philadelphia Museum of Art. Purchased with the Joseph E. Temple Fund)*

cause of the wandering careers of influential artists, the close communications and rivalry of princely courts, and the increased trade in works of art. Rich color, decorative detail, curvilinear rhythms, and swaying forms characterized the international style. As the term *international* implies, this style was European, not merely Italian.

Narrative artists depicted the body in a more scientific and natural manner. The female figure is voluptuous and sensual. The male body, as in Michelangelo's *David* and *The Last Judgment,* is strong and heroic. Renaissance glorification of the human body revealed the secular spirit of the age. Filippo Brunelleschi (1377–1446) and Piero della Francesca (1420–1492) seem to have pioneered *perspective* in painting, the linear representation of distance and space on a flat surface. *The Last Supper* by Leonardo da Vinci, with its stress on the tension between Christ and the disciples, is an incredibly subtle psychological interpretation.

The Status of the Artist

In the Renaissance, the social status of the artist improved. Whereas the lower-middle-class medieval master mason had been viewed in the same light as a mechanic, the Renaissance artist was considered a free intellectual

worker. Artists did not produce unsolicited pictures or statues for the general public; that could mean loss of status. They usually worked on commission from a powerful prince. The artist's reputation depended on the support of powerful patrons, and through them some artists and architects achieved not only economic security but also very great wealth.

Lorenzo Ghiberti's salary of 200 florins a year compared very favorably with that of the head of the city government, who earned 500 florins. Moreover, at a time when a person could live in a princely fashion on 300 ducats a year, Leonardo da Vinci was making 2,000 annually.[13]

Renaissance society respected and rewarded the distinguished artist. In 1537 the prolific letter writer, humanist, and satirizer of princes Pietro Aretino (1492–1556) wrote to Michelangelo while he was painting *The Last Judgment* behind the altar in the Sistine Chapel:

To the Divine Michelangelo:
Sir, just as it is disgraceful and sinful to be unmindful of God so it is reprehensible and dishonourable for any man of discerning judgment not to honour you as a brilliant and venerable artist whom the very stars use as a target at which to shoot the rival arrows of their favour. . . . It is surely my duty to honour you with this salutation, since the world has many kings but only one Michelangelo.[14]

Gentile and Giovanni Bellini: Saint Mark Preaching in Alexandria (1504–1507)   Reliable evidence does not support the tradition that Saint Mark preached and died in Alexandria, nor did either of the Bellinis ever visit there. Rather, they confected this painting from Gentile's stay in Constantinople, general information derived from Venice's long commercial contacts with Egypt, and their imagination. With a group of Venetians behind him, Saint Mark on a platform preaches to a group of heavily veiled Muslim women, behind whom stand Asian figures mingling with Europeans. A domed basilica reminiscent of Saint Mark's in Venice and of Sancta Sophia with minarets in Constantinople forms the background. The painting glorifies cosmopolitan Venice's patron saint, but the artists also wanted to acknowledge that Islamic society possessed not only commodities but scientific knowledge and business techniques more sophisticated than those in the West. *(Scala/Art Resource, NY)*

When Holy Roman Emperor Charles V (r. 1519–1556) visited the workshop of the great Titian (1477–1576) and stooped to pick up the artist's dropped paintbrush, the emperor was demonstrating that the patron himself was honored in the act of honoring the artist.

Renaissance artists were not only aware of their creative power; they also boasted about it. Describing his victory over five others, including Brunelleschi, in the competition to design the bronze doors of Florence's Baptistry, Ghiberti exulted, "The palm of victory was conceded to me by all the experts and by all my fellow-competitors. By universal consent and without a single exception the glory was conceded to me."[15] Some medieval painters and sculptors had signed their works; Renaissance artists almost universally did so, and many of them incorporated self-portraits, usually as bystanders, in their paintings.

The Renaissance, in fact, witnessed the birth of the concept of the artist as genius. In the Middle Ages, people believed that only God created, albeit through individuals; the medieval conception recognized no particular value in artistic originality. Renaissance artists and humanists came to think that a work of art was the deliberate creation of a unique personality who transcended traditions, rules, and theories. A genius had a peculiar gift, which ordinary laws should not inhibit. Cosimo de' Medici described a painter, because of his genius, as "divine," implying that the artist shared in the powers of God. The word *divine* was widely applied to Michelangelo. (See the feature "Individuals in Society: Leonardo da Vinci.")

But students must guard against interpreting Italian Renaissance culture in twenty-first-century democratic terms. The culture of the Renaissance was that of a small mercantile elite, a business patriciate with aristocratic pretensions. Renaissance culture did not directly affect the broad middle classes, let alone the vast urban proletariat. A small, highly educated minority of literary humanists and artists created the culture of and for an exclusive elite. The Renaissance maintained a gulf between

Individuals in Society

Leonardo da Vinci

What makes a genius? An infinite capacity for taking pains? A deep curiosity about an extensive variety of subjects? A divine spark as manifested by talents that far exceed the norm? Or is it just "one percent inspiration and ninety-nine percent perspiration," as Thomas Edison said? By whatever criteria, Leonardo da Vinci was one of the greatest geniuses in the history of the Western world.

He was born in Vinci, near Florence, the illegitimate son of Caterina, a local peasant girl, and Ser Piero da Vinci, a notary public. Caterina later married another native of Vinci. When Ser Piero's marriage to Donna Albrussia produced no children, they took in Leonardo, who remained with them until Ser Piero secured Leonardo's apprenticeship with the painter and sculptor Andrea del Verrocchio. In 1472, when Leonardo was just twenty years old, he was listed as a master in Florence's "Company of Artists."

Leonardo contributed to the modern concept of the artist as an original thinker and as a special kind of human being: an isolated figure with exceptional creative powers. Leonardo's portrait *Ginevra de' Benci* anticipates his most famous portrait, *Mona Lisa,* with the enigmatic smile that Giorgio Vasari described as "so pleasing that it seemed divine rather than human." Leonardo's experimental method of fresco painting of *The Last Supper* caused the picture to deteriorate rapidly, but it has been called "the most revered painting in the world." To the annoyance of his patrons, none of these paintings was ever completed to Leonardo's satisfaction. For example, *The Last Supper* was left unfinished because he could not find a model for the face of Christ that would evoke the spiritual depth he felt it deserved.

Leonardo once said that "a painter is not admirable unless he is universal." He left notes and plans on drawing, painting, sculpture, music, architecture, town planning, optics, astronomy, biology, zoology, mathematics, and various branches of engineering, such as a model for a submarine, designs for tank warfare, and cranes for dredging. These drafts suggest the astonishing versatility of his mind. One authority has said that Leonardo "saw art from the scientific point of view and science from the artist's point of view."

Vasari described Leonardo as a handsome man with a large body and physical grace, a "sparkling conversationalist" talented at singing while accompanying himself on the lyre. According to Vasari, "his genius was so wonderfully inspired by God, his powers of expression so powerfully fed by a willing memory and intellect . . . that his arguments confounded the most formidable critics."

In a famous essay, the Viennese psychiatrist Sigmund Freud argued that Leonardo was a homosexual who sublimated, pouring his sexual energy into his art. Freud wrote that it is doubtful that Leonardo ever touched a woman or even had an intimate spiritual relationship with one. Although as a master artist he surrounded himself with handsome young men and even had a long emotional relationship with one, Francesco Melzi, the evidence suggests that his male relationships never resulted in sexual activity. On a page of his *Codex Atlanticus,* which includes his sketch of the Florentine navigator Amerigo Vespucci, Leonardo wrote, "Intellectual passion drives out sensuality." For Freud, Leonardo transferred his psychic energy into artistic and scientific study. This thesis has attracted much attention, but no one has refuted it.

Leonardo worked in Milan for the despot Ludovico Sforza, planning a gigantic equestrian statue in honor of Ludovico's father, Duke Francesco Sforza. The clay model collapsed, and only notes survived. Leonardo also worked as a military engineer for Cesare Borgia (see page 416). In 1516 he accepted King Francis I's invitation to France. At the French court and in the presence of his faithful companion Francesco Melzi, Leonardo died in the arms of the king.

Leonardo da Vinci, Lady with an Ermine. *The whiteness of the ermine's fur symbolizes purity.* (Czartoryski Museum, Krakow/ The Bridgeman Art Library)

Questions for Analysis

1. How would you explain Leonardo's genius?
2. Consider sublimation as a source of artistic and scientific creativity.

Sources: Giorgio Vasari, *Lives of the Artists,* vol. 1, trans. G. Bull (London: Penguin Books, 1965); S. B. Nuland, *Leonardo da Vinci* (New York: Lipper/Viking, 2000); Sigmund Freud, *Leonardo da Vinci: A Study in Psychosexuality* (New York: Random House, 1947).

The **history Companion** *features additional information and activities related to this topic.* history.college.hmco.com/students

the learned minority and the uneducated multitude that has survived for many centuries.

Social Change

Renaissance ideals permeated educational theory and practice and political thought. The era's most stunning technological invention, printing, affected many forms of social life. Renaissance culture witnessed a shift in the status and experience of women. Slaves also played a role in Renaissance society.

Education and Political Thought

One of the central preoccupations of the humanists was education and moral behavior. Humanists poured out treatises, often in the form of letters, on the structure and goals of education and the training of rulers. In one of the earliest systematic programs for the young, Peter Paul Vergerio (1370–1444) wrote Ubertinus, the ruler of Carrara:

For the education of children is a matter of more than private interest; it concerns the State, which indeed regards the right training of the young as, in certain aspects, within its proper sphere. . . . Tutors and comrades alike should be chosen from amongst those likely to bring out the best qualities, to attract by good example, and to repress the first signs of evil. . . . Above all, respect for Divine ordinances is of the deepest importance; it should be inculcated from the earliest years. Reverence towards elders and parents is an obligation closely akin.

We call those studies liberal which are worthy of a free man; those studies by which we attain and practice virtue and wisdom.[16]

Part of Vergerio's treatise specifies subjects for the instruction of young men in public life: history teaches virtue by examples from the past, ethics focuses on virtue itself, and rhetoric or public speaking trains for eloquence.

No book on education had broader influence than Baldassare Castiglione's *The Courtier* (1528). This treatise sought to train, discipline, and fashion the young man into the courtly ideal, the gentleman. According to Castiglione, the educated man of the upper class should have a broad background in many academic subjects, and his spiritual and physical as well as intellectual capabilities should be trained. The courtier should have easy familiarity with dance, music, and the arts. Castiglione envisioned a man who could compose a sonnet, wrestle, sing a song and accompany himself on an instrument, ride expertly, solve difficult mathematical problems, and, above all, speak and write eloquently.

In the sixteenth and seventeenth centuries, *The Courtier* was widely read. It influenced the social mores and patterns of conduct of elite groups in Renaissance and early modern Europe. The courtier became the model of the European gentleman.

In the cities of Renaissance Italy, well-to-do girls received an education similar to boys'. Young ladies learned their letters and studied the classics. Many read Greek as well as Latin, knew the poetry of Ovid and Virgil, and could speak one or two "modern" languages, such as French or Spanish. In this respect, Renaissance humanism represented a real educational advance for women. Some women, though a small minority among humanists, acquired great learning and fame. (See the feature "Listening to the Past: Christine de Pisan" on pages 410–411.) In the later sixteenth century, at least twenty-five women published books in Italy, Sofonisba Anguissola (1530–1625) and Artemisia Gentileschi (1593–1653) achieved international renown for their paintings, and Isabella Andreini (1562–1604) enjoyed a reputation as the greatest actress of her day.

Humanist Laura Cereta (1469–1499) illustrates the successes and failures of educated Renaissance women. Educated by her father, who was a member of the governing elite of Brescia in Lombardy, she learned languages, philosophy, theology, and mathematics. She also gained self-confidence and a healthy respect for her own potential. By the age of fifteen, when she married, her literary career was already launched, as her letters to several cardinals attest. For Laura Cereta, however, as for all educated women of the period, the question of marriage forced the issue: she could choose a husband, family, and full participation in social life or study and withdrawal from the world. Marriage brought domestic responsibilities and usually prevented women from fulfilling their scholarly potential. Although Cereta chose marriage, she was widowed at eighteen, and she spent the remaining twelve years of her life in study. But she had to bear the envy of other women and the hostility of men who felt threatened. In response, Cereta condemned "empty women, who strive for no good but exist to adorn themselves. . . . These women of majestic pride, fantastic coiffures, outlandish ornament, and necks bound with gold or pearls bear the glittering symbols of their captivity to men." For Laura Cereta, women's inferiority was derived not from the divine order of things but from women themselves: "For knowledge is not given as a gift, but through study. . . . The free mind, not afraid of labor, presses on to attain the good."[17] Despite Cereta's faith in women's potential, men frequently believed that in becoming learned, a woman violated nature and thus ceased to be a woman.

Laura Cereta was a prodigy. Ordinary girls of the urban upper middle class, in addition to a classical education, received some training in painting, music, and dance. What were they to do with this training? They were to be gracious, affable, charming—in short, decorative. So although Renaissance women were better educated than their medieval counterparts, their education prepared them for the social functions of the home. An educated woman was supposed to know how to attract artists and literati to her husband's court and how to grace her husband's household, whereas an educated man was supposed to know how to rule and participate in public affairs.

No Renaissance book on any topic, however, has been more widely read and studied in all the centuries since its publication (1513) than the short political treatise **The Prince,** by Niccolò Machiavelli (1469–1527). The subject of *The Prince* is political power: how the ruler should gain, maintain, and increase it. Machiavelli implicitly addresses the question of the citizen's relationship to the state. As a good humanist, he explores the problems of human nature and concludes that human beings are selfish and out to advance their own interests. This pessimistic view of humanity led him to maintain that the prince may have to manipulate the people in any way he finds necessary:

For a man who, in all respects, will carry out only his professions of good, will be apt to be ruined amongst so many who are evil. A prince therefore who desires to maintain himself must learn to be not always good, but to be so or not as necessity may require.[18]

The prince should combine the cunning of a fox with the ferocity of a lion to achieve his goals. Asking rhetorically whether it is better for a ruler to be loved or feared, Machiavelli writes: "It will naturally be answered that it would be desirable to be both the one and the other; but as it is difficult to be both at the same time, it is much more safe to be feared than to be loved, when you have to choose between the two."[19]

Medieval political theory had derived ultimately from Saint Augustine's view that the state arose as a consequence of Adam's fall and people's propensity to sin. The test of good government was whether it provided justice, law, and order. Political theorists and theologians from Alcuin to Marsiglio of Padua had stressed the way government *ought* to be; they had set high moral and Christian standards for the ruler's conduct.

Machiavelli maintained that the ruler should be concerned not with the way things ought to be but with the way things actually are. The sole test of a "good" government is whether it is effective, whether the ruler increases his power. Machiavelli did not advocate amoral behavior, but he believed that political action cannot be restricted by moral considerations. While amoral action might be the most effective approach in a given situation, he did not argue for generally amoral, rather than moral, behavior. Nevertheless, on the basis of a crude interpretation of *The Prince,* the word *Machiavellian* entered the language as a synonym for the politically devious, corrupt, and crafty, indicating actions in which the end justifies the means. The ultimate significance of Machiavelli rests on two ideas: first, that one permanent social order reflecting God's will cannot be established, and second, that politics has its own laws and ought to be a science.[20]

The Printed Word

Sometime in the thirteenth century, paper money and playing cards from China reached the West. They were *block-printed*—that is, Chinese characters or pictures were carved into a wooden block, the block was inked, and the words or illustrations were transferred to paper. Since each word, phrase, or picture was on a separate block, this method of reproduction was extraordinarily expensive and time-consuming.

Around 1454, probably through the combined efforts of three men—Johann Gutenberg, Johann Fust, and Peter Schöffer, all experimenting at Mainz—movable type came into being. The mirror image of each letter (rather than entire words or phrases) was carved in relief on a small block. Individual letters, easily movable, were put together to form words; words separated by blank spaces formed lines of type; and lines of type were brought together to make up a page. Since letters could be arranged into any format, an infinite variety of texts could be printed by reusing and rearranging pieces of type.

By the middle of the fifteenth century, acquiring paper was no problem. The knowledge of paper manufacture had originated in China, and the Arabs introduced it to the West in the twelfth century (see page 286). Europeans quickly learned that durable paper was far less expensive than the vellum (calfskin) and parchment (sheepskin) on which medieval scribes had relied for centuries.

The effects of the invention of movable-type printing were not felt overnight. Nevertheless, within a half century of the publication of Gutenberg's Bible of 1456,

The Print Shop   Sixteenth-century printing involved a division of labor. Two persons (*left*) at separate benches set the pieces of type. Another (*center, rear*) inks the chase (or locked plate containing the set type). Yet another (*right*) operates the press, which prints the sheets. The boy removes the printed pages and sets them to dry. Meanwhile, a man carries in fresh paper on his head. *(Giraudon/Art Resource, NY)*

movable type had brought about radical changes. Printing transformed both the private and the public lives of Europeans (see Map 13.2). Governments that "had employed the cumbersome methods of manuscripts to communicate with their subjects switched quickly to print to announce declarations of war, publish battle accounts, promulgate treaties or argue disputed points in pamphlet form. Theirs was an effort 'to win the psychological war.'" Printing made propaganda possible, emphasizing differences between opposing groups, such as Crown and nobility, church and state. These differences laid the basis for the formation of distinct political parties. Printed materials reached an invisible public, allowing silent individuals to join causes and groups of individuals widely separated by geography to form a common identity; this new group consciousness could compete with older, localized loyalties.[21]

Printing also stimulated the literacy of laypeople and eventually came to have a deep effect on their private lives. Although most of the earliest books and pamphlets dealt with religious subjects, students, housewives, businessmen, and upper- and middle-class people sought books on all subjects. Printers responded with moralizing, medical, practical, and travel manuals. Pornography as well as piety assumed new forms. For example, satirist Pietro Aretino (1492–1556) used the shock of sex in pornography as a vehicle to criticize: his *Sonnetti Lussuriosi* (1527) and *Ra-*gionamenti* (1534–1536), sonnets accompanying sixteen engravings of as many sexual positions, attacked princely court life, humanist education, and false clerical piety.[22] Broadsides and flysheets allowed great public festivals, religious ceremonies, and political events to be experienced vicariously by the stay-at-home. Since books and other printed materials were read aloud to illiterate listeners, print bridged the gap between written and oral cultures.

Clocks

The English word *quantification* was first used in 1840, but five centuries earlier, before the invention of movable type, Europeans learned how to quantify, or measure, time with the mechanical clock. Who invented the clock remains a subject of scientific debate. Between A.D. 700 and 1000, Arabs relied on the sundial, using their knowledge of astronomy to correct for the varying motion of the sun during the course of the year. The Arabs knew that the length of daylight, caused by the changing distance between the earth and the sun as the earth moves in elliptical orbit, varies with the seasons. Chinese knowledge of mechanical clocks may have allowed Gerbert, later Pope Sylvester II (999–1003), to build the first mechanical clock in the West.

The English word *clock* resembles the French *cloche* and the German *Glocke,* all meaning "bells." In monastic

MAP 13.2 The Growth of Printing in Europe Although many commercial and academic centers developed printing technology, the press at Venice, employing between four hundred and five hundred people and producing one-eighth of all printed books, was by far the largest in Europe.

houses, bells determined the times for the recitation of the Hours, the Work of God. Bells also paced the life of the rural world nearby, but country people needed only approximate times—dawn, noon, sunset—for their work. The measurement of time played a much more urgent role for *city* people.

Buying and selling goods had initiated city people into the practice of quantification: they needed precise measurement of the day's hours. City people's time was what the American polymath Benjamin Franklin later called it: money. In the Italian cities, clocks must have been wide-

spread, since the poet Dante, writing about 1320, took them for granted. Mechanical clocks, usually installed on the cathedral or town church, were in general use in Germany by the 1330s, in England by the 1370s, and in France by the 1380s.[23]

Clocks contributed to the development of a mentality that conceived of the universe in visual and quantitative terms. Measuring the world brought not only understanding of it but the urge to control it. The mechanical clock enabled Europeans to divide time into equal hours, allowing the working day to be fixed in both winter and

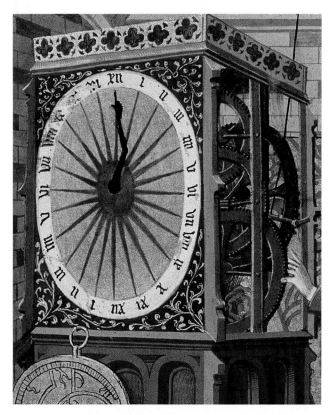

Mechanical Clock   Slowly falling weights provide the force that pushes the figures' arms to strike the bells on the quarter-hour in this sixteenth-century German clock. The sound of a machine now marked time. *(Bibliothèque royale Albert 1er, Brussels)*

summer. The Maya in Central America and the Chinese had theoretical knowledge of time, but Europeans put that knowledge to practical use. Along with cannon and printing, clocks gave Europeans technological advantages over other peoples.[24]

Women and Work

Early modern cultural values identified women with marriage and the domestic activities of the home. Revisionist scholarship today stresses that women's economic roles must include reproduction—defined not only as childbearing but as everything connected with the care and nurturing of family members. In preindustrial societies, the production of goods often took place in the home in the intervals when women were not engaged in specific domestic chores; all family members benefited from that work. Women also worked outside the household. In

whatever economic activity they engaged in, women were considered as "married or to be married." Their work was valued less than men's, and they earned half of what men did even for the same work.[25]

In the Venetian Arsenal, the state-controlled dock and shipbuilding area (the largest single industrial plant in Europe and the builder of the biggest fleet) women made the ships' sails. Women were heavily involved in the Florentine textile industry, weaving cloth and reeling and winding silk. In the 1560s, a woman named Suzanne Erkur managed the imperial silver mint at Kutná Hora in Bohemia. Women conducted the ferry service across the Rhône River at Lyons. Throughout Europe rural women assisted fathers and husbands in the many agricultural tasks, and urban women helped in shops and businesses. Widows often ran their husbands' establishments. Tens of thousands of women worked as midwives, maids, cooks, laundresses, and household servants. From the port city of Dubrovnik (formerly Ragusa) on the Dalmatian coast came tens of thousands of female slaves to enter domestic service in upper-class households throughout Italy[26] (see page 436).

What of women of the upper classes? During the Renaissance, the status of upper-class women declined. In terms of the kind of work they performed, their access to property and political power, and their role in shaping the outlook of their society, women in the Renaissance ruling classes generally had less power than comparable women in the feudal age. As mentioned earlier (see page 429), well-to-do girls generally received an education, but even so, men everywhere held the conviction that a woman's attention should be focused on the domestic affairs of family life. The Italian humanist and polymath Leon Battista Alberti (1404–1472), discussing morality in his *On the Family*, stressed that a wife's role should be restricted to the orderliness of the household, food and the serving of meals, the education of children, and the supervision of servants. The Spanish humanist Juan Luis Vives (1492–1540), in his *Instruction of the Christian Woman*, held that a woman's sphere should be the home, not the public arena, where she might compete with men. The English statesman Sir Thomas Smith (1513–1577) wrote in *The English Commonwealth* that women were "those whom nature hath made to keepe home and to nourish the familie and children, and not to meddle with affairs abroad."[27] Wealthy women might support charitable organizations, but men denied them any sort of political or legal activity.

Excluded from the public arena, the noblewoman or spouse of a rich merchant managed the household where

Working Women Women did virtually every kind of work in Renaissance Europe. They often sold food, cloth, hand-made jewelry, trinkets, and other merchandise in the town marketplace, just as many women in developing countries do today. *(Scala/Art Resource, NY)*

the husband displayed his wealth and power (the larger the number of servants and retainers, the greater his prestige). Households depended on domestic servants, and the lady of the house had to have the shrewdness and managerial prudence to employ capable cooks, maids, tailors and seamstresses, laundresses, gardeners, coachmen, stable hands, nurses, and handymen. If a prosperous Florentine or Venetian merchant's household had fifteen to twenty servants, a great lord or a Medici banker could easily employ four times that number. The lady of the house had to make sure that all these people were adequately fed and clothed; to maintain harmony among them; to tend anyone who fell ill, meaning that she must have at least a rudimentary knowledge of medications; and to look after the girl who "accidentally" became pregnant and then her child. Custom also laid on the lady the responsibility for providing the servants with religious instruction. Then there was the education of her own children and possibly the care of aged or infirm in-laws. Her husband expected her to entertain (which, depending on his position, could be an elaborate and complicated undertaking) and preside over each occasion

with grace and, if possible, charm. All of these burdens, in addition to her own pregnancies, added up to an enormous responsibility.

Culture and Sexuality

With respect to love and sex, the Renaissance witnessed a downward shift in women's status. In contrast to the medieval tradition of relative sexual equality, Renaissance humanists laid the foundations for the bourgeois double standard. Castiglione, the foremost spokesman of Renaissance love and manners, completely separated love from sexuality. For women, sex was restricted entirely to marriage. Women were bound to chastity and then to the roles of wife and mother in a politically arranged marriage. Men, however, could pursue sensual indulgence outside marriage.[28]

Official attitudes toward rape provide an index of the status of women in the Renaissance. According to a study of the legal evidence from Venice in the years 1338 to 1358, rape was not considered a particularly serious crime against either the victim or society. Noble youths

Artemesia Gentileschi: Judith Slaying Holofernes The Old Testament Book of Judith tells the tale of the beautiful widow Judith, who first charms and then decapitates the Assyrian general Holofernes, thus saving Israel. The message is that trust in God will bring deliverance. The talented Roman artist Artemesia Gentileschi (1593–1652/3), elected to the Florentine Academy of Design at age twenty-three, rendered the story in this dramatic and gruesome painting, whose light and gushing blood give it great power. Some scholars hold that the painting is Gentileschi's pictorial revenge for her alleged rape by the decorative artist Agostino Tassi. *(Uffizi, Florence/Alinari/Art Resource, NY)*

committed a higher percentage of rapes than their small numbers in Venetian society would imply. The rape of a young girl of marriageable age or a child under twelve was considered a graver crime than the rape of a married woman. Nevertheless, the punishment for rape of a noble, marriageable girl was only a fine or about six months' imprisonment. In an age when theft and robbery were punished by mutilation, and forgery and sodomy by burning, this penalty was very mild indeed. When a youth of the upper class was convicted of the rape of a non-noble girl, his punishment was even lighter. By contrast, the sexual assault of a noblewoman by a working-class man, which was extraordinarily rare, re-

sulted in severe penalization because the crime had social and political overtones.[29]

A new study of country women based on fifteenth-century Florentine court records raises interesting questions but provides inconclusive evidence about women's condition. These records read like twenty-first-century tabloids, with virtually every sensational criminal activity: incest, wife beatings, sexual assaults on children and nuns, murders provoked by adulterous relationships. For instance, one priest had a long love affair with a married woman and hired a "hit man" to kill the husband. Indicted for homicide and adultery, the priest was decapitated. In another case, while his wife was out shopping, middle-aged Muccino raped his eleven-year-old niece. The court ordered Muccino whipped with branches to the place of justice, where his penis was mutilated. The courts saw sexual crimes as "originating in bodily parts that had to be punished or removed."[30] But sexual crimes, however broadly defined, never constituted more than 5 percent of the courts' annual caseload. Fewer women appear in these fifteenth-century records than had appeared in similar records a century earlier. Why? We do not know.[31]

The term *homosexuality* was coined only in 1892, but erotic activity with a person of the same sex goes back very far in human history (see pages 79, 200–202). Medieval and Renaissance people used two terms concerning such activity: *sodomy,* meaning all sexual acts between persons of the same sex, whether male with male or female with female, and *sexual acts against nature,* meaning any act that did not lead to conception.[32] When early modern Italians used the term *sodomite,* they usually had males in mind, partly because those acts were most conspicuous, partly because theological and "scientific" teaching held that women could not have erotic pleasure without a man. While we tend to classify people according to the gender of their sexual partners, Renaissance people did not frame their understanding and representation of sexuality on this basis.

In the cities of Renaissance Italy, the sermons of the Franciscan Bernardino of Siena (1380–1444) and the Dominican Savonarola (1452–1498) severely condemned sodomitical activities, and civil authorities seem to have been preoccupied with it: Siena passed legislation against it in 1425, Venice in 1496, Florence in 1415, 1418, 1432, 1494, and 1542.[33] When a law is repeatedly put on the statute books, it is not observed or cannot be enforced. How prevalent was homosexuality? Florence provides a provocative case study.

On April 17, 1432, the Florentine government set up a special magistracy, the Office of the Night, to "root out . . . the abominable vice of sodomy." This board of professional men at least forty-five years of age and married was elected annually and charged with pursuing and punishing sodomitical activity between males.[34] The name of the magistracy derived from the nocturnal activities of most male encounters, especially in the spring and summer months, and on feast days and Sundays. Between 1432 and the abolition of the magistracy in 1502, about seventeen thousand men came to its attention, which, even over a seventy-year period, represents a great number in a population of about forty thousand. Sodomy was not a marginal practice.

Thirteenth-Century Moral Code This illustration, from a French book of morals, interprets female and male homosexuality as the work of devils; modern science offers other explanations. *(Österreichische Nationalbibliothek)*

Moreover, careful and statistical analysis of judicial records shows that all classes of society engaged in it—those in the textile trade, in commerce, in education, and in the food industry, especially butchers, as well as construction workers, tavern keepers, and innkeepers. Evidence also reveals that adult males rarely had sex together, or if they did, it did not come to the Office of the Night's attention. Rather, boys were the objects of desire. These roles carried cultural values. Florentines believed in a generational model in which different roles were appropriate to different stages in life. In a socially and sexually hierarchical world, the boy in the passive role was identified as subordinate, dependent, and mercenary, words usually applied to women. Florentines, however, never described the dominant partner in feminine terms, for he had not compromised his masculine identity or violated a gender ideal. Only if an adult male assumed the passive role was his masculinity jeopardized. Such cases were extremely rare.[35]

Why was this kind of sexual activity so common? The evidence offers a variety of explanations. First among these is the general seclusion of "respectable" women and the late marriages of men. Perhaps 30 percent of the adult male population never married because many men were clerics, and three-fourths of the men who eventually wed postponed marriage, largely for economic reasons, until about age thirty-two. An occasional sexual experience with a boy did not preclude sex with women. Other explanations include the construction of male identity and of forms of male sociability.

In 1476 an informer denounced the carpenter Piero di Bartolomeo for sexual relations with Bartolomeo di Jacopo, son of a grocer. When interrogated, fifteen-year-old Bartolomeo di Jacopo confessed that Piero "did [this] out of great love and good brotherhood, because they are in a confraternity together, and he did as good neighbors do." Bartolomeo di Jacopo understood their relationship as being based on the traditional emotional bonds between members of their confraternity and neighborhood associations.[36]

Other explanations for youthful homoerotic activity include the desire for gifts, money, or some material reward from the adult partner; parental complicity in urging attractive teenage sons to accept the attentions of wealthy suitors; the need for companionship and same-age cohorts—that is, peer pressure; gang rapes; and soldiers' demands that youthful servants satisfy their sexual needs. Sex among males—kinsmen, neighbors, coworkers, and groups of friends—fashioned the collective male experience. Homoerotic relationships played important roles in defining stages of life, expressing distinctions of status, and shaping masculine gender identity.[37]

Slavery and Ethnicity

The French historian Marc Bloch once observed that "Western and Central Europe, taken as a whole, were never free of slaves during the High Middle Ages."[38] In central and eastern Europe, where political conditions were very unstable and permitted the enslavement of pagans, slavery allowed strong lords to satisfy cheaply the needs of their estates; slaves also offered merchants a commodity for profitable exchange with foreigners. Thus, in the period of eastward expansion (see Chapter 12), German lords seized Polish and Bohemian peoples; used them as agricultural laborers, domestics, and concubines; and sold the rest. In the thirteenth century, Prague was a large slave market. The word *slave* always carried a definite ethnic connotation: it meant an unfree person of Slavic background.[39]

In the fourteenth century, Genoa and Venice dominated the Mediterranean slave trade. The labor shortage caused by the Black Death led to the flow of Russians, Tartars, and Circassian slaves from Azov in the Crimea

and of Serbs, Albanians, Greeks, and Hungarians from the Balkans. Venetian control of the northern regions of the Dalmatian coast enabled Venetian slavers to import large numbers of female slaves from the port city of Dubrovnik.[40] All of these people, Slavic but of different ethnic backgrounds, gradually intermingled with the native Italian population.

Ever since the time of the Roman republic, a few black people had lived in western Europe. They had come, along with white slaves, as the spoils of war. Even after the collapse of the Roman Empire, Muslim and Christian merchants continued to import them. The evidence of medieval art attests to the presence of Africans in Europe and to Europeans' awareness of them.

As in Slavic regions, unstable political conditions in many parts of Africa enabled enterprising merchants to seize people and sell them into slavery. Local authorities afforded them no protection. Long tradition, moreover, sanctioned the practice of slavery. Beginning in the fifteenth century, sizable numbers of black slaves entered Europe. Portuguese explorers imported perhaps a thousand a year and sold them at the markets of Seville, Barcelona, Marseilles, and Genoa. By the mid-sixteenth century, blacks, slave and free, constituted about 10 percent of the populations of the Portuguese cities of Lisbon and Évora; other cities had smaller percentages. In all, blacks made up roughly 3 percent of the Portuguese population. The Venetians specialized in the importation of white slaves, but blacks were so greatly in demand at the Renaissance courts of northern Italy that the Venetians defied papal threats of excommunication to secure them. Although blacks were concentrated in the Iberian Peninsula, there must have been some Africans in northern Europe as well. In the 1580s, for example, Queen Elizabeth I of England complained that there were too many "blackamoores" competing with needy English people for places as domestic servants.[41]

What roles did blacks play in Renaissance society? Although few written records survive, obviously black slaves in Europe hated the loss of their freedom, separation from their societal roots, and forced labor without compensation. No doubt, too, they disliked the alien culture, the cold climate, and the strange foods. But so far as we know, few who managed to secure their freedom through manumission or escape chose to return to Africa. The lack of black slave revolts in Europe, so common in South and North America and in Africa under colonial rule, attests to the small numbers and wide dispersion of blacks and to a relatively benign pattern of slavery. Moreover, the legal definition of *slave* never took on the rigid character in Europe that it did in the United States.

Carpaccio: Black Laborers on the Venetian Docks (detail) Enslaved and free blacks, besides working as gondoliers on the Venetian canals, served on the docks: here seven black men careen— clean, caulk, and repair—a ship. Carpaccio's reputation as one of Venice's outstanding painters rests on his eye for details of everyday life. *(Gallerie dell'Accademia, Venice/Scala/Art Resource, NY)*

Within Africa, the economic goals of rulers and merchants took priority over any cultural, ethnic, or racial hostilities they may have felt toward Europeans. For example, in 1492 the king of the Congo learned of the arrival of Portuguese ships off the Congo estuary. He needed support in a local war and new resources; his biggest asset was a large concentration of slaves near his capital. So he accepted Christian baptism and began to exchange slaves for weapons and other Portuguese goods. His son Alfonso Mbemba Nzinga adopted a European lifestyle: he renamed his capital São Salvador; took on Portuguese dress, etiquette, and literacy; and assigned Portuguese titles to his officials and courtiers. Meanwhile, the flow of slaves from the region accelerated. Between 1500 and 1525, about seventeen hundred slaves a year were traded to the Portuguese. By 1530 between four thousand and five thousand were being sold to the Portuguese each year.[42] What does this tell us about Africans'

attitudes toward white Europeans? First, obviously, the interests of African rulers and those of their peoples diverged considerably. Second, African rulers' and merchants' desire for revenue and goods was the driving force in the sale of black people to white Europeans.

Westerners tend to lump all sub-Saharan Africans into one category: black. However, Africans, like Europeans and Asians, belonged to and identified themselves by ethnic groups. In Africa, the world's second-largest continent, there were (and are) more than six hundred distinct ethnic groups. In addition, African slaves in the Iberian Peninsula (and elsewhere in Europe), like Slavic ones in Italy, intermingled with the people they lived among, and their offspring were, in fact, biracial.

However Africans may have been defined in Europe, black servants were much sought after, as the medieval interest in curiosities, the exotic, and the marvelous continued into the Renaissance. In the late fifteenth century, Isabella, the wife of Gian Galazzo Sforza, took pride in the fact that she owned ten blacks, seven of them females. A black lady's maid was both a curiosity and a symbol of wealth. In 1491 Isabella of Este, duchess of Mantua, instructed her agent to secure a black girl between four and eight years old, "shapely and as black as possible." The duchess saw the child as a source of entertainment: "We shall make her very happy and shall have great fun with her." She hoped the girl would become "the best buffoon in the world,"[43] as the cruel ancient practice of a noble household retaining a professional "fool" for the family's amusement persisted through the Renaissance—and down to the twentieth century.

Adult black slaves served as maids, valets, and domestic servants. Italian aristocrats such as Marchesa Elena Grimaldi had their portraits painted with their black pageboys to indicate their wealth. The Venetians employed blacks—slave and free—as gondoliers and stevedores on the docks. In Portugal kings, nobles, laborers, monasteries and convents, and prostitutes owned slaves. They supplemented the labor force in virtually all occupations—as agricultural laborers, craftsmen, and seamen on ships going to Lisbon and Africa.[44] Tradition, stretching back at least as far as the thirteenth century, connected blacks with music and dance. In Renaissance Spain and Italy, blacks performed as dancers, as actors and actresses in courtly dramas, and as musicians, sometimes making up full orchestras.[45] Slavery during the Renaissance foreshadowed the American, especially the later Brazilian, pattern.

Before the sixteenth-century "discoveries" of the non-European world, Europeans had little concrete knowledge of Africans and their cultures. What Europeans did know was based on biblical accounts. The European attitude toward Africans was ambivalent. On the one hand, Europeans perceived Africa as a remote place, the home of strange people isolated by heresy and Islam from superior European civilization. Africans' contact, even as slaves, with Christian Europeans could only "improve" the blacks. Most Europeans' knowledge of the black as a racial type was based entirely on theological speculation. Theologians taught that God was light. Blackness, the opposite of light, therefore represented the hostile forces of the underworld: evil, sin, and the Devil. Thus the Devil was commonly represented as a black man in medieval and early Renaissance art (see the illustration on page 435). On the other hand, blackness possessed certain positive qualities. It symbolized the emptiness of worldly goods, the humility of the monastic way of life. Black clothes permitted a conservative and discreet display of wealth. Black vestments and funeral trappings indicated grief, and Christ had said that those who mourn are blessed. Until the exploration and observation of the sixteenth, seventeenth, and nineteenth centuries allowed, ever so slowly, for the development of more scientific knowledge, the Western conception of black people remained bound up with religious notions.[46] As for the sterile and meaningless concept of race, recent scholarship stresses that it emerged only in the late seventeenth century.[47] In Renaissance society, blacks, like women, were signs of wealth; both were used for display.

The Renaissance in the North

In the last quarter of the fifteenth century, students from the Low Countries, France, Germany, and England flocked to Italy, imbibed the "new learning," and carried it back to their countries. Northern humanists interpreted Italian ideas about and attitudes toward classical antiquity, individualism, and humanism in terms of their own traditions. The cultural traditions of northern Europe tended to remain more distinctly Christian, or at least pietistic, than those of Italy. But in Italy, secular and pagan themes and Greco-Roman motifs received more humanistic attention. North of the Alps, the Renaissance had a distinctly religious character, and humanists stressed biblical and early Christian themes. What fundamentally distinguished Italian humanists from northern ones is that the latter had a program for broad social reform based on Christian ideals.

Christian humanists were interested in the development of an ethical way of life. To achieve it, they believed that the best elements of classical and Christian cultures should be combined. For example, the classical ideals of calmness, stoical patience, and broad-mindedness should be joined in human conduct with the Christian virtues of love, faith, and hope. Northern humanists also stressed the use of reason, rather than acceptance of dogma, as the foundation for an ethical way of life. Like the Italians, they were impatient with Scholastic philosophy. Christian humanists had a profound faith in the power of human intellect to bring about moral and institutional reform. They believed that, although human nature had been corrupted by sin, it was fundamentally good and capable of improvement through education.

The Englishman Thomas More (1478–1535) towered above other figures in sixteenth-century English social and intellectual history. Trained as a lawyer, More lived as a student in the London Charterhouse, a Carthusian monastery.

He subsequently married and practiced law but became deeply interested in the classics; his household served as a model of warm Christian family life and as a mecca for foreign and English humanists. In the career pattern of such Italian humanists as Petrarch, More entered government service under Henry VIII and was sent as ambassador to Flanders. There More found the time to write *Utopia* (1516), which presents a revolutionary view of society.

Utopia, which means "nowhere," describes an ideal socialistic community on an island somewhere off the mainland of the New World. All children receive a good education, primarily in the Greco-Roman classics, and learning does not cease with maturity, for the goal of all education is to develop rational faculties. Adults divide their days between manual labor or business pursuits and intellectual activities.

Because profits from business and property are held in common, there is absolute social equality. The Utopians use gold and silver to make chamber pots and to prevent wars by buying off their enemies. By this casual use of precious metals, More meant to suggest that the basic problems in society are caused by greed. Citizens of Utopia lead an ideal, nearly perfect existence because they live by reason; their institutions are perfect. More punned on the word *utopia*, which he termed "a good place. A good place which is no place."

More's ideas were profoundly original in the sixteenth century. Contrary to the long-prevailing view that vice and violence existed because women and men were basically corrupt, More maintained that acquisitiveness and private property promoted all sorts of vices and civil disorders. Since society protected private property, society's flawed institutions were responsible for corruption and war. According to More, the key to improvement and reform of the individual was reform of the social institutions that molded the individual. Today this view is so much taken for granted that it is difficult to appreciate how radical More's approach was in the sixteenth century.

Better known by contemporaries than Thomas More was the Dutch humanist Desiderius Erasmus (1466?–1536) of Rotterdam. Orphaned as a small boy, Erasmus was forced to enter a monastery. Although he hated the monastic life, he developed there an excellent knowledge of the Latin language and a deep appreciation for the Latin classics. During a visit to England in 1499, Erasmus met the scholar John Colet, who decisively influenced his life's work: the application of the best humanistic learning to the study and explanation of the Bible. As a mature scholar with an international reputation stretching from Cracow to London, a fame that rested largely on his ex-

ceptional knowledge of Greek, Erasmus could boast with truth, "I brought it about that humanism, which among the Italians . . . savored of nothing but pure paganism, began nobly to celebrate Christ."[48]

Erasmus's long list of publications includes *The Education of a Christian Prince* (1504), a book combining idealistic and practical suggestions for the formation of a ruler's character through the careful study of Plutarch, Aristotle, Cicero, and Plato; *The Praise of Folly* (1509), a satire of worldly wisdom and a plea for the simple and spontaneous Christian faith of children; and, most important, a critical edition of the Greek New Testament (1516). In the preface to the New Testament, Erasmus explained the purpose of his great work:

For I utterly dissent from those who are unwilling that the sacred Scriptures should be read by the unlearned translated into their vulgar tongue, as though Christ had taught such subtleties that they can scarcely be understood even by a few theologians. . . . Christ wished his mysteries to be published as openly as possible. I wish that even the weakest woman should read the Gospel—should read the epistles of Paul. And I wish these were translated into all languages, so that they might be read and understood, not only by Scots and Irishmen, but also by Turks and Saracens.[49]

Two fundamental themes run through all of Erasmus's work. First, education is the means to reform, the key to moral and intellectual improvement. The core of education ought to be study of the Bible and the classics. (See the feature "Listening to the Past: An Age of Gold" on pages 450–451.) Second, the essence of Erasmus's thought is, in his own phrase, "the philosophy of Christ." By this Erasmus meant that Christianity is an inner attitude of the heart or spirit. Christianity is not formalism, special ceremonies, or law; Christianity is Christ—his life and what he said and did, not what theologians have written. The Sermon on the Mount, for Erasmus, expresses the heart of the Christian message.

Whereas the writings of Erasmus and More have strong Christian themes and have drawn the attention primarily of scholars, the stories of French humanist François Rabelais (1490?–1553) possess a distinctly secular flavor and have attracted broad readership among the literate public. Rabelais's *Gargantua* and *Pantagruel* (serialized between 1532 and 1552) belong among the great comic masterpieces of world literature. These stories' gross and robust humor introduced the adjective *Rabelaisian* into the language.

Gargantua and *Pantagruel* can be read on several levels: as a comic romance about the adventures of the giant

Rogier van der Weyden: Deposition   Taking as his subject the suffering and death of Jesus, a popular theme of Netherlandish piety, van der Weyden describes (in an inverted **T**) Christ's descent from the cross, surrounded by nine sorrowing figures. An appreciation of the human anatomy, the rich fabrics of the clothes, and the pierced and bloody hands of Jesus were all intended to touch the viewers' emotions. *(Museo del Prado/Scala/Art Resource, NY)*

Gargantua and his son, Pantagruel; as a spoof on contemporary French society; as a program for educational reform; or as an illustration of Rabelais's prodigious learning. The reader enters a world of Renaissance vitality, ribald joviality, and intellectual curiosity. In his travels, Gargantua meets various absurd characters, and within their hilarious exchanges occur serious discussions of religion, politics, philosophy, and education. Like More and Erasmus, Rabelais did not denounce institutions directly. Like Erasmus, Rabelais satirized hypocritical monks, pedantic academics, and pompous lawyers. But whereas Erasmus employed intellectual cleverness and sophisticated wit, Rabelais applied wild and gross humor. Like Thomas More, Rabelais believed that institutions molded individuals and that education was the key to a moral and healthy life. Whereas the middle-class inhabitants of More's Utopia lived lives of restrained moderation, the aristocratic residents of Rabelais's Thélèma lived for the gratification of their physical instincts and rational curiosity.

The distinctly religious orientation of the literary works of the Renaissance in the north also characterized northern art and architecture. Some Flemish painters, notably Rogier van der Weyden (1399/1400–1464) and Jan van

Eyck (1366–1441), were considered the artistic equals of Italian painters, were much admired in Italy, and worked a generation before Leonardo and Michelangelo. Van Eyck, one of the earliest artists to use oil-based paints successfully, shows the Flemish love for detail in paintings such as *Ghent Altarpiece* and the portrait *Giovanni Arnolfini and His Bride;* the effect is great realism and remarkable attention to human personality.

A quasi-spiritual aura infuses architectural monuments in the north. The city halls of wealthy Flemish towns such as Bruges, Brussels, Louvain, and Ghent strike the viewer more as shrines to house the bones of saints than as settings for the mundane decisions of politicians and business people. Northern architecture was little influenced by the classical revival so obvious in Renaissance Rome and Florence.

Politics and the State in the Renaissance (ca 1450–1521)

The High Middle Ages had witnessed the origins of many of the basic institutions of the modern state. Sheriffs, inquests, juries, circuit judges, professional bureaucracies, and representative assemblies all trace their origins to the twelfth and thirteenth centuries (see pages 342–344). The linchpin for the development of states, however, was strong monarchy, and during the period of the Hundred Years' War, no ruler in western Europe was able to provide effective leadership. The resurgent power of feudal nobilities weakened the centralizing work begun earlier.

Beginning in the fifteenth century, rulers utilized the aggressive methods implied by Renaissance political ideas to rebuild their governments. First in Italy, then in France, England, and Spain, rulers began the work of reducing violence, curbing unruly nobles, and establishing domestic order. Divided into scores of independent principalities, Germany could not deal with the Roman church as an equal.

The dictators and oligarchs of the Italian city-states, together with Louis XI of France, Henry VII of England, and Ferdinand of Aragon, were tough, cynical, calculating rulers. In their ruthless push for power and strong governments, they subordinated morality to hard results. They preferred to be secure, if feared, rather than loved. They could not have read Machiavelli's *The Prince,* but they acted as though they understood its ideas.

Some historians have called Louis XI, Henry VII, and Ferdinand and Isabella in Spain "new monarchs." The term is only partly appropriate. These monarchs were new in that they invested kingship with a strong sense of royal authority and national purpose. They stressed that monarchy was the one institution that linked all classes and peoples within definite territorial boundaries. These rulers emphasized royal majesty and royal sovereignty and insisted on the respect and loyalty of all subjects. These monarchs ruthlessly suppressed opposition and rebellion, especially from the nobility. They loved the business of kingship and worked hard at it.

In other respects, however, the methods of these rulers, which varied from country to country, were not so new. They reasserted long-standing ideas and practices of strong monarchs in the Middle Ages. They seized on the maxim of the Justinian *Code,* "What pleases the prince has the force of law," to advance their authority. Some medieval rulers, such as Henry I of England, had depended heavily on middle-class officials. Renaissance rulers, too, tended to rely on middle-class civil servants. With tax revenues, medieval rulers had built armies to crush feudal anarchy. Renaissance townspeople with commercial and business interests naturally wanted a reduction of violence, and usually they were willing to pay taxes in order to achieve it.

France

The Hundred Years' War left France drastically depopulated, commercially ruined, and agriculturally weak. Nonetheless, the ruler whom Joan of Arc had seen crowned at Reims, Charles VII (r. 1422–1461), revived the monarchy and France. He seemed an unlikely person to do so. Frail, indecisive, and burdened with questions about his paternity (his father had been deranged; his mother, notoriously promiscuous), Charles VII nevertheless began France's long recovery.

Charles reconciled the Burgundians and Armagnacs, who had been waging civil war for thirty years. By 1453 French armies had expelled the English from French soil except in Calais. Charles reorganized the royal council, giving increased influence to middle-class men, and strengthened royal finances through such taxes as the **gabelle** (on salt) and the *taille* (land tax). These taxes remained the Crown's chief sources of income until the Revolution of 1789.

By establishing regular companies of cavalry and archers—recruited, paid, and inspected by the state—Charles created the first permanent royal army. In 1438 Charles published the **Pragmatic Sanction of Bourges,** asserting the superiority of a general council over the papacy, giving the French crown major control over the appointment of bishops, and depriving the pope of

French ecclesiastical revenues. The Pragmatic Sanction established Gallican (or French) liberties because it affirmed the special rights of the French crown over the French church. Greater control over the church and the army helped to consolidate the authority of the French crown.

Charles's son Louis XI (r. 1461–1483), called the "Spider King" because of his treacherous character, was very much a Renaissance prince. Facing the perpetual French problem of reduction of feudal disorder, he saw money as the answer. Louis promoted new industries, such as silk weaving at Lyons and Tours. He welcomed foreign craftsmen and entered into commercial treaties with England, Portugal, and the towns of the Hanseatic League (see page 355). He used the revenues raised through these economic activities and severe taxation to improve the army. With the army, Louis stopped aristocratic brigandage and slowly cut into urban independence.

Luck favored his goal of expanding royal authority and unifying the kingdom. On the timely death of Charles the Bold, duke of Burgundy, in 1477, Louis invaded Burgundy and gained some territories. Three years later, the extinction of the house of Anjou brought Louis the counties of Anjou, Bar, Maine, and Provence.

Two further developments strengthened the French monarchy. The marriage of Louis XII (r. 1498–1515) and Anne of Brittany added the large western duchy of Brittany to the state. Then the French king Francis I and Pope Leo X reached a mutually satisfactory agreement in 1516. The new treaty, the Concordat of Bologna, rescinded the Pragmatic Sanction's assertion of the superiority of a general council over the papacy and approved the pope's right to receive the first year's income of new bishops and abbots. In return, Leo X recognized the French ruler's right to select French bishops and abbots. French kings thereafter effectively controlled the appointment and thus the policies of church officials within the kingdom.

England

English society suffered severely from the disorders of the fifteenth century. The aristocracy dominated the government of Henry IV (r. 1399–1413) and indulged in mischievous violence at the local level. Population, decimated by the Black Death, continued to decline. Between 1455 and 1471, adherents of the ducal houses of York and Lancaster waged civil war, commonly called the Wars of the Roses because the symbol of the Yorkists was a white rose and that of the Lancastrians a red one. The chronic disorder hurt trade, agriculture, and domestic industry. Under the pious but mentally disturbed Henry

VI, the authority of the monarchy sank lower than it had been in centuries.

The Yorkist Edward IV (r. 1461–1483) began establishing domestic tranquillity. He succeeded in defeating the Lancastrian forces and after 1471 began to reconstruct the monarchy. Edward, his brother Richard III (r. 1483–1485), and Henry VII (r. 1485–1509) of the Welsh house of Tudor worked to restore royal prestige, to crush the power of the nobility, and to establish order and law at the local level. All three rulers used methods that Machiavelli himself would have praised—ruthlessness, efficiency, and secrecy.

The Hundred Years' War had been financed by Parliament. Dominated by baronial factions, Parliament had been the arena where the nobility exerted its power. As long as the monarchy was dependent on the Lords and the Commons for revenue, the king had to call Parliament. Edward IV and subsequently the Tudors, excepting Henry VIII, conducted foreign policy on the basis of diplomacy, avoiding expensive wars. Thus the English monarchy did not depend on Parliament for money, and the Crown undercut that source of aristocratic influence.

Henry VII did summon several meetings of Parliament in the early years of his reign primarily to confirm laws, but the center of royal authority was the **royal council,** which governed at the national level. There Henry VII revealed his distrust of the nobility: though not completely excluded, very few great lords were among the king's closest advisers. Regular representatives on the council numbered between twelve and fifteen men, and while many gained high ecclesiastical rank (the means, as it happened, by which the Crown paid them), their origins were in the lesser landowning class, and their education was in law. They were, in a sense, middle-class.

The royal council handled any business the king put before it—executive, legislative, and judicial. For example, the council conducted negotiations with foreign governments and secured international recognition of the Tudor dynasty through the marriage in 1501 of Henry VII's eldest son, Arthur, to Catherine of Aragon, the daughter of Ferdinand and Isabella of Spain. The council dealt with real or potential aristocratic threats through a judicial offshoot, the **court of Star Chamber,** so called because of the stars painted on the ceiling of the room. The court applied principles of Roman law, and its methods were sometimes terrifying: accused persons were not entitled to see evidence against them, sessions were secret, torture could be applied to extract confessions, and juries were not called. These procedures ran directly counter to English common-law precedents, but they effectively reduced aristocratic troublemaking.

Unlike the continental countries of Spain and France, England had no standing army or professional civil service bureaucracy. The Tudors relied on the support of unpaid local officials, the **justices of the peace.** These influential landowners in the shires handled all the work of local government. They apprehended and punished criminals, enforced parliamentary statutes, fixed wages and prices, maintained proper standards of weights and measures, and even checked up on moral behavior.

The Tudors won the support of the influential upper middle class because the Crown linked government policy with the interests of that class. A commercial or agricultural upper class fears and dislikes few things more than disorder and violence. The Tudors promoted peace and social order, and the gentry did not object to arbitrary methods, like those of the court of Star Chamber, because the government had halted the long period of anarchy.

Secretive, cautious, and thrifty, Henry VII rebuilt the monarchy. He encouraged the cloth industry and built up the English merchant marine. English exports of wool and the royal export tax on that wool steadily increased. Henry crushed an invasion from Ireland and secured peace with Scotland through the marriage of his daughter Margaret to the Scottish king. When Henry VII died in 1509, he left a country at peace both domestically and internationally, a substantially augmented treasury, and the dignity and role of the royal majesty much enhanced.

Spain

While England and France laid the foundations of unified nation-states during the Renaissance, Spain remained a conglomerate of independent kingdoms. Castile and León formed a single political organization, but Aragon consisted of the principalities of Aragon, Valencia, Majorca, Sicily, Cardeña, and Naples, each tied to the crown of Aragon in a different way. On the one hand, the legacy of Hispanic, Roman, Visigothic, Jewish, and Muslim peoples made for rich cultural diversity; on the other hand, the Iberian Peninsula lacked a common cultural tradition.

The centuries-long reconquista—the wars of the northern Christian kingdoms to control the entire peninsula (see pages 287–288)—had military and religious objectives: conversion or expulsion of the Muslims and Jews and political control of the south. By the middle of the fifteenth century, the kingdoms of Castile and Aragon dominated the weaker Navarre, Portugal, and Granada, and the Iberian Peninsula, with the exception of Granada, had been won for Christianity. But even the wedding in 1469 of the dynamic and aggressive Isabella of Castile and the crafty and persistent Ferdinand of Aragon did not bring about administrative unity. Rather, their marriage constituted a dynastic union of two royal houses, not the political union of two peoples. Although Ferdinand and Isabella (r. 1474–1516) pursued a common foreign policy, Spain existed until about 1700 as a loose confederation of separate kingdoms (see Map 13.3), each maintaining its own *cortes* (parliament), laws, courts, and systems of coinage and taxation.

To curb the rebellious and warring aristocracy, Ferdinand and Isabella revived an old medieval institution: the **hermandades,** or "brotherhoods," which were popular groups in the towns given authority to act as local police forces and as judicial tribunals. The hermandades repressed violence with such savage punishments that by 1498 they could be disbanded.

The decisive step Ferdinand and Isabella took to curb aristocratic power was the restructuring of the royal council. Aristocrats and great territorial magnates were rigorously excluded; thus the influence of the nobility on state policy was greatly reduced. Ferdinand and Isabella intended the council to be the cornerstone of their government system, with full executive, judicial, and legislative powers under the monarchy. The council was also to be responsible for the supervision of local authorities. The king and queen therefore appointed to the council only people of middle-class background. The council and various government boards recruited men trained in Roman law, which exalted the power of the Crown as the embodiment of the state.

In the extension of royal authority and the consolidation of the territories of Spain, the church was the linchpin. If the Spanish crown could select the higher clergy, then the monarchy could influence ecclesiastical policy, wealth, and military resources. Through a diplomatic alliance with the Spanish pope Alexander VI, the Spanish monarchs secured the right to appoint bishops in Spain and in the Hispanic territories in America. This power enabled the "Catholic Kings of Spain," a title granted Ferdinand and Isabella by the papacy, to establish, in effect, a national church.[50]

Revenues from ecclesiastical estates provided the means to raise an army to continue the reconquista. The victorious entry of Ferdinand and Isabella into Granada on January 6, 1492, signaled the culmination of eight centuries of Spanish struggle against the Arabs in southern Spain and the conclusion of the reconquista (see Map 9.3 on page 286). Granada in the south was incorporated into the Spanish kingdom, and in 1512 Ferdinand conquered Navarre in the north.

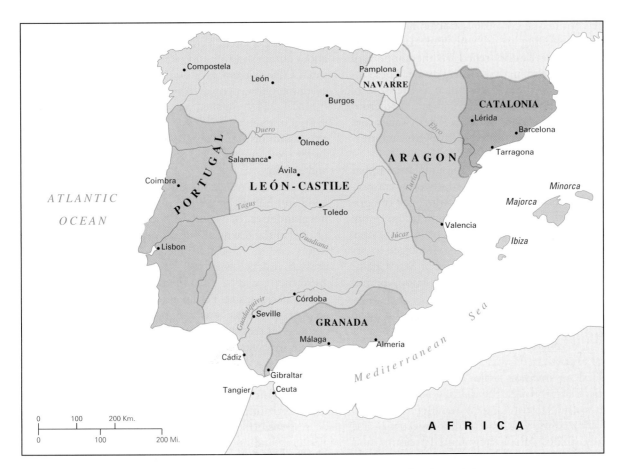

MAP 13.3 Spain in 1492   The marriage of Ferdinand of Aragon and Isabella of Castile in 1469 represented a dynastic union of two houses, not a political union of two peoples. Some principalities, such as León (part of Castile) and Catalonia (part of Aragon), had their own cultures, languages, and legal systems. Barcelona, the port city of Catalonia, controlled a commercial empire throughout the Mediterranean. The culture of Granada was heavily Muslim.

There still remained a sizable and, in the view of the majority of the Spanish people, potentially dangerous minority, the Jews. During the long centuries of the reconquista, Christian kings had renewed Jewish rights and privileges; in fact, Jewish industry, intelligence, and money had supported royal power. While Christians of all classes borrowed from Jewish moneylenders, and while all who could afford them sought Jewish physicians, a strong undercurrent of resentment of Jewish influence and wealth festered. When the kings of France and England had expelled the Jews from their kingdoms (see pages 345–346), many had sought refuge in Spain. In the fourteenth century, Jews formed an integral and indispensable part of Spanish life. With vast numbers of Muslims, Jews, and Moorish Christians, medieval Spain represented the most diverse and cosmopolitan country in Europe. Diversity and cosmopolitanism, however, were not medieval social ideals.

Since ancient times, governments had seldom tolerated religious pluralism; religious faiths that differed from the official state religion were considered politically dangerous. But in the fourteenth century, anti-Semitism in Spain rose more from popular sentiment than from royal policies. Aggravated by fiery anti-Jewish preaching, by economic dislocation, and by the search for a scapegoat during the Black Death, the fourteenth century witnessed rising anti-Semitic feeling. In 1331 a mob attacked the Jewish community of Gerona in Catalonia. In 1355 royal troops massacred Jews in Toledo. On June 4, 1391, inflamed by "religious" preaching, mobs sacked and burned the Jewish community in Seville and compelled such Jews as survived to accept baptism. From Seville anti-Semitic pogroms swept the towns of Valencia, Barcelona, Burgos, Madrid, and Segovia. One scholar estimates that 40 percent of the Jewish population of Spain was killed or forced to convert.[51] Those converted were called *conversos, Marranos,* or **New Christians,** the three terms here used interchangeably.

King Ferdinand was not a religious fanatic. He was a Renaissance prince who wanted to *appear* as a moral and devout Christian, respectful of public opinion. He feared urban rioting and disorder, but he knew that the vast majority of the Spanish people hated the conversos. If the Crown protected them, it would lose popular support. Ferdinand resolved the dilemma by seeking papal permission to set up the Inquisition in Spain; if the actions of the Inquisition provoked public criticism, the papacy could be blamed. Pope Sixtus IV's bull authorizing the Inquisition reached Spain in November 1478, and on September 28, 1480, Ferdinand and Isabella ordered the establishment of tribunals to "search out and punish converts from Judaism who had transgressed against Christianity by secretly adhering to Jewish beliefs and performing rites of the Jews."[52]

What do we know of these New Christians? Why did they inspire such hostility? How did they view their

Felipe Bigarny: Ferdinand the Catholic and Isabella the Catholic All governments try to cultivate a popular image. For Ferdinand and Isabella, it was the appearance of piety. Contemporaries, such as the Burgundian sculptor Bigarny, portrayed them as paragons of Christian piety, as shown in these polychrome wooden statues. If Isabella's piety was perhaps more genuine, she used it—together with rich ceremony, elaborate dress, and a fierce determination—to assert royal authority. *(Capilla Real, Granada/Laurie Platt Winfrey, Inc.)*

religious position? In the administration of Castile, New Christians held the royal secretaryship, controlled the royal treasury, and composed a third of the royal council. In the church, they held high positions as archbishops, bishops, and abbots. In the administration of the towns, conversos often held the highest public offices; in Toledo they controlled the collection of royal revenues. They included some of the leading merchants and business people. They also served great magnates, and by intermarrying with the nobility, they gained political leverage. In the professions of medicine and law, New Christians held the most prominent positions. Numbering perhaps 200,000 in a total Spanish population of about 7.5 million, New Christians and Jews exercised influence disproportionate to their numbers. Aristocratic grandees resented their financial dependence, the poor hated the converso tax collectors, and churchmen doubted the sincerity of their conversions.

Recent scholarship has carefully analyzed documents written by New Christians for their reactions to the rising anti-Semitism. They identified themselves as Christians. In the 1480s, they unanimously insisted that they were happy to be Christians and failed to see why they should be labeled New Christians: many came from families that had received baptism generations before. They argued that just as Christ had never abandoned the ancient (Hebrew) Law, so they had not abandoned it; in fact, they had a better understanding of the Christian faith. For the New Christians, the issue was not that they had relinquished the faith of the Jews (and secretly reconverted); rather, in accepting Christianity, they had become real Jews and, in following Jesus, real Christians.[53]

This argument satisfied neither the Jews nor the conversos' enemies. The Jewish reaction to persecution of the conversos was, bluntly put, "Well, we told you so; it's just what you get."[54] Searching for a viable principle to use against both New Christians and Jews, their detractors hit not on what conversos believed, not on what they did, but on what they *were* as human beings. Hence arose the following racial theory: "Since race, they maintained, formed man's qualities and indeed his entire mental constitution, the Marranos, who were all offspring of Jews, retained the racial makeup of their forebears. . . . [E]thnically they were what they (or their ancestors) had been before their conversion to Christianity; in other words, they were Jews."[55] This absurd racist theory, which violated scriptural teaching, maintained that all conversos were malicious, immoral, and criminally inclined by their nature, and thus they could not be truly converted to Christianity.

Fifteenth-century Spanish anti-Semitism emerged at the very time a Spanish national feeling was emerging, a national sentiment that looked to the building of a single nation. Whereas earlier anti-Semitism, such as that during the time of the Black Death, alleged Jewish schemes to kill off entire Christian populations—by poisoning the wells, for example, from which Jews derived no profit—fifteenth-century theories held that Jews or New Christians planned to take over all public offices in Spain. Jews, therefore, represented a grave threat to national unity.[56]

Although the Inquisition was a religious institution established to ensure the Catholic faith, it was controlled by the Crown and served primarily as a politically unifying tool. Because the Spanish Inquisition commonly applied torture to extract confessions, first from lapsed conversos, then from Muslims, and later from Protestants, it gained a notorious reputation. Thus the word *inquisition,* meaning "any judicial inquiry conducted with ruthless severity," came into the English language. The methods of the Spanish Inquisition were cruel, though not as cruel as the investigative methods of some twentieth-century governments. Shortly after the reduction of the Moorish stronghold at Granada in 1492, Isabella and Ferdinand issued an edict expelling all practicing Jews from Spain. Of the community of perhaps 200,000 Jews, 150,000 fled. (Efforts were made, through last-minute conversions, to retain good Jewish physicians.) Absolute religious orthodoxy and purity of blood (untainted by Jews or Muslims) served as the theoretical foundation of the Spanish national state.

The diplomacy of the Catholic rulers of Spain achieved a success they never anticipated. Partly out of hatred for the French and partly out of a desire to gain international recognition for their new dynasty, Ferdinand and Isabella in 1496 married their second daughter, Joanna, heiress to Castile, to the archduke Philip, heir through his mother to the Burgundian Netherlands and through his father to the Holy Roman Empire. Philip and Joanna's son, Charles V (r. 1519–1556), thus succeeded to a vast patrimony. When Charles's son Philip II joined Portugal to the Spanish crown in 1580, the Iberian Peninsula was at last politically united. The various kingdoms, however, were administered separately.

Summary

The Italian Renaissance rested on the phenomenal economic growth of the High Middle Ages. In the period from about 1050 to 1300, a new economy emerged based on Venetian and Genoese shipping and long-distance trade and on Florentine banking and cloth manufacture. These commercial activities, combined with the struggle of urban communes for political independence from surrounding feudal lords, led to the appearance of a new aristocratic class. The centuries extending roughly from 1300 to 1600 witnessed a remarkable intellectual flowering. Based on a strong interest in the ancient world, the Renaissance had a classicizing influence on many facets of culture: law, literature, government, education, religion, and art. In the city-states of fifteenth- and sixteenth-century Italy, oligarchic or despotic powers governed; Renaissance culture was manipulated to enhance the power of those rulers.

Expanding outside Italy, the intellectual features of this movement affected the culture of all Europe. The intellectual characteristics of the Renaissance were a secular attitude toward life, a belief in individual potential, and a serious interest in the Latin classics. The printing press revolutionized communication. Meanwhile, the status of women in society declined, and black people entered Europe in sizable numbers for the first time since the collapse of the Roman Empire. Male culture in Italian cities had a strongly homoerotic character, reflecting a significant contrast between Renaissance attitudes toward male sexuality and attitudes today. In northern Europe, city merchants and rural gentry allied with rising monarchies. With taxes provided by business people, kings established greater peace and order, both essential for trade. Northern humanism had a more pietistic strain than did the Italian. In Spain, France, and England, rulers also emphasized royal dignity and authority, and they utilized Machiavellian ideas to ensure the preservation and continuation of their governments. Feudal monarchies gradually evolved in the direction of nation-states.

Key Terms

Renaissance	The Prince
communes	gabelle
popolo	Pragmatic Sanction of
signori	Bourges
oligarchies	royal council
princely courts	court of Star Chamber
republic	justices of the peace
individualism	hermandades
humanism	New Christians
secularism	

Notes

1. See L. Martines, *Power and Imagination: City-States in Renaissance Italy* (New York: Vintage Books, 1980), esp. pp. 332–333.
2. Ibid., pp. 22–61.
3. Ibid., p. 221.
4. Quoted in J. Burckhardt, *The Civilization of the Renaissance in Italy* (London: Phaidon Books, 1951), p. 89.
5. *Memoirs of Benvenuto Cellini; A Florentine Artist; Written by Himself* (London: J. M. Dent & Sons, 1927), p. 2.
6. See C. Trinkaus, *In Our Image and Likeness: Humanity and Divinity in Italian Humanist Thought,* vol. 2 (London: Constable, 1970), pp. 505–529.
7. B. Burroughs, ed., *Vasari's Lives of the Artists* (New York: Simon & Schuster, 1946), pp. 164–165.
8. See Martines, *Power and Imagination,* chap. 13, esp. pp. 241, 243.
9. R. A. Goldthwaite, *Wealth and the Demand for Art in Italy, 1300–1600* (Baltimore: Johns Hopkins University Press, 1993), p. 5.
10. Ibid., p. 213.
11. Ibid., pp. 224–229.
12. Ibid., pp. 121–129.
13. See A. Hauser, *The Social History of Art,* vol. 2 (New York: Vintage Books, 1959), chap. 3, esp. pp. 60, 68.
14. G. Bull, trans., *Aretino: Selected Letters* (Baltimore: Penguin Books, 1976), p. 109.
15. Quoted in P. and L. Murray, *A Dictionary of Art and Artists* (Baltimore: Penguin Books, 1963), p. 125.
16. Quoted in W. H. Woodward, *Vittorino da Feltre and Other Humanist Educators* (Cambridge: Cambridge University Press, 1897), pp. 96–97.
17. M. L. King, "Book-Lined Cells: Women and Humanism in the Early Italian Renaissance," in *Beyond Their Sex: Learned Women of the European Past,* ed. P. H. Labalme (New York: New York University Press, 1980), pp. 66–81, esp. p. 73.
18. C. E. Detmold, trans., *The Historical, Political and Diplomatic Writings of Niccolò Machiavelli* (Boston: J. R. Osgood, 1882), pp. 51–52.
19. Ibid., pp. 54–55.
20. See F. Gilbert, *Machiavelli and Guicciardini: Politics and History in Sixteenth Century Florence* (New York: W. W. Norton, 1984), pp. 197–200.
21. E. L. Eisenstein, *The Printing Press as an Agent of Change: Communications and Cultural Transformations in Early Modern Europe,* vol. 1 (New York: Cambridge University Press, 1979), p. 135. For an overall discussion, see pp. 126–159.
22. See L. Hunt, *The Invention of Pornography: Obscenity and the Origins of Modernity, 1500–1800* (New York: Zone Books, 1993), pp. 10, 93–95.
23. See A. W. Crosby, *The Measure of Reality: Quantification and Western Society* (New York: Cambridge University Press, 1997), pp. 76–78.
24. Ibid., pp. 49–74.
25. See M. E. Wiesner, *Women and Gender in Early Modern Europe* (New York: Cambridge University Press, 1994), pp. 85–86 passim.
26. See Susan Mosher Stuard, "Ancillary Evidence for the Decline of Medieval Slavery," *Past and Present* 149 (November 1995): 3–28.
27. Quoted in J. Hale, *The Civilization of Europe in the Renaissance* (New York: Atheneum, 1994), p. 270.
28. This account rests on J. Kelly-Gadol, "Did Women Have a Renaissance?" in *Becoming Visible: Women in European History,* ed. R. Bridenthal and C. Koonz (Boston: Houghton Mifflin, 1977), pp. 137–161, esp. p. 161.
29. G. Ruggerio, "Sexual Criminality in Early Renaissance Venice, 1338–1358," *Journal of Social History* 8 (Spring 1975): 18–31.
30. For these and a variety of other remarkable court cases, see S. K. Cohn, Jr., *Women in the Streets: Essays on Sex and Power in*

Renaissance Italy (Baltimore: Johns Hopkins University Press, 1996), pp. 103–121.

31. Ibid., pp. 30–35, 105–115.

32. M. Rocke, *Forbidden Friendships: Homosexuality and Male Culture in Renaissance Florence* (New York: Oxford University Press, 1996), pp. 10–11.

33. Ibid.

34. Ibid., p. 45.

35. See ibid., chap. 3, "Age and Gender in the Social Organization of Sodomy," and chap. 4, "Social Profiles."

36. Ibid., p. 148.

37. Ibid., pp. 190–191.

38. Marc Bloch, *Slavery and Serfdom in the Middle Ages,* trans. William R. Beer (Berkeley: University of California Press, 1975), p. 30.

39. Ibid., p. 28.

40. See Stuard, "Ancillary Evidence for the Decline of Medieval Slavery."

41. Hale, *The Civilization of Europe,* p. 44.

42. J. Iliffe, *Africans: The History of a Continent* (Cambridge: Cambridge University Press, 1995), p. 130; H. Thomas, *The Slave Trade: The Story of the Atlantic Slave Trade, 1440–1870* (New York: Simon & Schuster, 1997), pp. 109–110.

43. Quoted in J. Devisse and M. Mollat, *The Image of the Black in Western Art,* vol. 2, trans. W. G. Ryan (New York: William Morrow, 1979), pt. 2, pp. 187–188.

44. See A. C. de C. M. Saunders, *A Social History of Black Slaves and Freedmen in Portugal, 1441–1555* (New York: Cambridge University Press, 1982), pp. 59, 62–88, 176–179.

45. Ibid., pp. 190–194.

46. Ibid., pp. 255–258.

47. See I. Hannaford, *Race: The History of an Idea in the West* (Washington, D.C.: Woodrow Wilson Center Press, 1996), pp. 3–182 passim, 182–187.

48. Quoted in E. H. Harbison, *The Christian Scholar and His Calling in the Age of the Reformation* (New York: Charles Scribner's Sons, 1956), p. 109.

49. Quoted in F. Seebohm, *The Oxford Reformers* (London: J. M. Dent & Sons, 1867), p. 256.

50. See J. H. Elliott, *Imperial Spain, 1469–1716* (New York: Mentor Books, 1963), esp. pp. 75, 97–108.

51. See B. F. Reilly, *The Medieval Spains* (New York: Cambridge University Press, 1993), pp. 198–203.

52. B. Netanyahu, *The Origins of the Inquisition in Fifteenth Century Spain* (New York: Random House, 1995), p. 921.

53. Ibid., pp. 934–935.

54. Ibid., p. 930.

55. Ibid., p. 982.

56. Ibid., pp. 996–1005.

▌Suggested Reading

A comprehensive treatment of the period is J. Hale, *The Civilization of Europe in the Renaissance* (1994), a magisterial achievement, while G. Holmes, ed., *The Oxford History of Italy* (1997), contains valuable articles on politics, society, and culture. P. Burke, *The Historical Anthropology of Early Modern Italy* (1987), contains useful essays on Italian cultural history in a European framework. G. Holmes, ed., *Art and Politics in Renaissance Italy* (1993), treats the art of Florence and Rome against a political background. For an explanation of why Italy lagged in developing a national state, see G. Chittolini, "Cities, 'City-States,' and Regional States in North-Central Italy," in *Cities and the Rise of States in Europe, A.D. 1000 to 1800,* ed. C. Tilly and W. P. Blockmans (1994). For the Renaissance court, see the splendid work of G. Lubkin, *A Renaissance Court: Milan Under Galeazzo Maria Sforza* (1994), as well as the title by Martines cited in the Notes.

For Renaissance humanism and education, see D. R. Kelley, *Renaissance Humanism* (1991), a good survey of humanism as a cultural movement; A. Grafton and L. Jardine, *From Humanism to the Humanities: Education and the Liberal Arts in Fifteenth and Sixteenth Century Europe* (1986), a sophisticated study; P. F. Grendler, *Schooling in Renaissance Italy: Literacy and Learning, 1300–1600* (1989); and J. F. D'Amico, *Renaissance Humanism in Papal Rome: Humanists and Churchmen on the Eve of the Reformation* (1983), another work of outstanding scholarship.

J. R. Hale, *Machiavelli and Renaissance Italy* (1966), is a sound short biography, but advanced students may want to consult the intellectual biography S. de Grazia, *Machiavelli in Hell* (1989), which is based on Machiavelli's literary as well as political writing. C. Singleton, trans., *The Courtier* (1959), presents an excellent picture of Renaissance court life.

The best introduction to the Renaissance in northern Europe and a book that has greatly influenced modern scholarship is J. Huizinga, *The Waning of the Middle Ages: A Study of the Forms of Life, Thought, and Art in France and the Netherlands in the Dawn of the Renaissance* (1954): it challenges the whole idea of the Renaissance. R. J. Knecht, *Renaissance Warrior and Patron: The Reign of Francis I* (1994), is the standard study of that important French ruler. The leading northern humanist is sensitively treated in J. McConica, *Erasmus* (1991). Advanced students interested in his program for the reform of Christian society should see J. D. Tracy, *Erasmus of the Low Countries* (1996). R. Marius, *Thomas More: A Biography* (1984), is a useful study of the English humanist and statesman, while the works of Rabelais, the French humanist and wit, are available in J. Leclercq, trans., *The Complete Works of Rabelais* (1963).

For the experiences of women as wives, mothers, slaves, servants, and workers in the crafts, see B. Hanawalt, ed., *Women and Work in Pre-industrial Europe* (1986), and M. L. King, *Women of the Renaissance* (1991). For the status of women, see C. Klapisch-Zuper, ed., *A History of Women,* vol. 3 (1994); R. Chartier, ed., *A History of Private Life,* vol. 3: *Passions of the Renaissance* (1990); and I. Maclean, *The Renaissance Notion of Women* (1980). J. C. Brown, *The Life of a Lesbian Nun in Renaissance Italy* (1985), and J. M. Saslow, *Ganymede in the Renaissance* (1986), both treat sexual issues, as do the titles by Rocke and Cohn cited in the Notes.

Renaissance art has understandably inspired vast research. In addition to Burroughs's edited version of Vasari's volume of biographical sketches on the masters referred to in the Notes, see, for Vasari's aims and methods of interpretation, P. L. Rubin, *Giorgio Vasari: Art and History* (1995). For Venice, see the highly readable and beautifully illustrated G. Wills, *Venice, Lion City: The Religion of Empire* (2001), which tells the story of the republic through an appreciation of its art and architecture; P. F. Brown, *Venice and Antiquity: The Venetian Sense of the Past* (1997), which treats the ways Venice invented its past to celebrate the city and its people; P. F. Brown, *Venetian Narrative Painting in the Age of Carpaccio* (1989); P. Humfrey, *Painting in Renaissance Venice* (1995), a useful survey for the beginning student; and P. Humfrey, *Lorenzo Lotto* (1997), a fine study of a distinctive Venetian painter. For artist families, see P. Burke, *The Italian Renaissance: Culture and Society in Italy* (1986). For the city of Milan, see E. S. Welch, *Art and Authority in Milan* (1996); and for Rome, see C. Hibbert, *Rome: The Biography of a City* (1985), an elegantly illustrated work, and P. Partner, *Renaissance Rome, 1500–1559: A Portrait of a Society* (1979). For Florence, see R. W. B. Lewis, *The City of Florence: Historical Vistas and Personal Sightings* (1995), an evocative appreciation of the city with a good study of the Medici achievement; and D. C. Ahl, *Benozzo Gozzoli* (1996), which places Gozzoli's art in its social context. M. Baxandall, *Painting and Experience in Fifteenth Century Italy* (1988), has important material on Florentine art. The magisterial achievement of J. Pope-Hennessy, *Cellini* (1985), is a superb evocation of that artist's life and work, while R. Jones and N. Penny, *Raphael* (1983), celebrates the work of that master. Leonardo's scientific and naturalistic ideas and drawings are available in I. A. Richter, ed., *The Notebooks of Leonardo da Vinci* (1985). The best introduction to the art of northern Europe is C. Harbison, *The Mirror of the Artist: Northern Renaissance Art in Its Historical Context* (1995).

The following studies should be helpful to students interested in issues relating to the political and religious history of Spain: N. Rubin, *Isabella of Castile: The First Renaissance Queen* (1991); P. Lis, *Isabel the Queen: Life and Times* (1992); J. S. Gerber, *The Jews of Spain: A History of the Sephardic Experience* (1992); H. Kamen, *Inquisition and Society in Spain in the Sixteenth and Seventeenth Centuries* (1985); P. F. Albaladejo, "Cities and the State in Spain," in *Cities and the Rise of States in Europe, A.D. 1000 to 1800,* eds. C. Tilly and W. M. Blockmans (1994); and B. Netanyahu, *The Origins of the Inquisition in Fifteenth Century Spain* (1995).

Listening to the Past

An Age of Gold

As the foremost scholar of the early sixteenth century and a writer with international contacts, Desiderius Erasmus (1466?–1536) maintained a vast correspondence. In the letters here, he explains his belief that Europe was entering a golden age. The letters also reflect the spiritual ideals of northern European humanists. Wolfgang Capito (1478?–1541), a German scholar, was professor of theology at the University of Basel. Pope Leo X (1513–1521), second son of Lorenzo de' Medici, extended the hospitality of the papal court to men of letters, sought to rebuild Rome as a Renaissance capital, and pushed the building of the new Saint Peter's Basilica by licensing the sale of indulgences (see pages 457–458).

To Capito

It is no part of my nature, most learned Wolfgang, to be excessively fond of life; whether it is that I have, to my own mind, lived nearly long enough, having entered my fifty-first year, or that I see nothing in this life so splendid or delightful that it should be desired by one who is convinced by the Christian faith that a happier life awaits those who in this world earnestly attach themselves to piety. But at the present moment I could almost wish to be young again, for no other reason but this, that I anticipate the near approach of a golden age, so clearly do we see the minds of princes, as if changed by inspiration, devoting all their energies to the pursuit of peace. The chief movers in this matter are Pope Leo and Francis, King of France.

There is nothing this king does not do or does not suffer in his desire to avert war and consolidate peace . . . and exhibiting in this, as in everything else, a magnanimous and truly royal character. Therefore, when I see that the highest sovereigns of Europe—Francis of France, Charles the King Catholic, Henry of England, and the Emperor

Maximilian—have set all their warlike preparations aside and established peace upon solid and, as I trust, adamantine foundations, I am led to a confident hope that not only morality and Christian piety, but also a genuine and purer literature, may come to renewed life or greater splendour; especially as this object is pursued with equal zeal in various regions of the world—at Rome by Pope Leo, in Spain by the Cardinal of Toledo,* in England by Henry, eighth of the name, himself not unskilled in letters, and among ourselves by our young King Charles.† In France, King Francis, who seems as it were born for this object, invites and entices from all countries men that excel in merit or in learning. Among the Germans the same object is pursued by many of their excellent princes and bishops, and especially by Maximilian Caesar,‡ whose old age, weary of so many wars, has determined to seek rest in the employments of peace, a resolution more becoming to his own years, while it is fortunate for the Christian world. To the piety of these princes it is due, that we see everywhere, as if upon a given signal, men of genius are arising and conspiring together to restore the best literature.

Polite letters, which were almost extinct, are now cultivated and embraced by Scots, by Danes, and by Irishmen. Medicine has a host of champions. . . . The Imperial Law is restored at Paris by William Budé, in Germany by Udalric Zasy; and mathematics at Basel by Henry of Glaris. In the theological sphere there was no little to be done,

---

*Francisco Jiménez de Cisneros (1436–1517), Spanish statesman and adviser to Queen Isabella who gained renown for his reform of the monasteries and the Spanish church.

†After 1516 king of Spain and much of the Netherlands; after 1519 Holy Roman emperor.

‡Holy Roman emperor (1493–1519), he was succeeded by his grandson Charles (above).

because this science has been hitherto mainly professed by those who are most pertinacious in their abhorrence of the better literature,§ and are the more successful in defending their own ignorance as they do it under pretext of piety, the unlearned vulgar being induced to believe that violence is offered to religion if anyone begins an assault upon their barbarism. . . . But even here I am confident of success if the knowledge of the three languages continues to be received in schools, as it has now begun. . . .

The humblest part of the work has naturally fallen to my lot. Whether my contribution has been worth anything I cannot say; . . . although the work was not undertaken by me with any confidence that I could myself teach anything magnificent, but I wanted to construct a road for other persons of higher aims, so that they might be less impeded by pools and stumbling blocks in carrying home those fair and glorious treasures.

Why should I say more? Everything promises me the happiest success. But one doubt still possesses my mind. I am afraid that, under cover of a revival of ancient literature, paganism may attempt to rear its head—as there are some among Christians that acknowledge Christ in name but breathe inwardly a heathen spirit—or, on the other hand, that the restoration of Hebrew learning may give occasion to a revival of Judaism. This would be a plague as much opposed to the doctrine of Christ as anything that could happen. . . . Some books have lately come out with a strong flavour of Judaism. I see how Paul exerted himself to defend Christ against Judaism, and I am aware that some persons are secretly sliding in that direction. . . . So much the more do I wish you to undertake this province; I know that your sincere piety will have regard to nothing but Christ, to whom all your studies are devoted. . . .

To Pope Leo X

While on the one hand, as a private matter, I acknowledge my own felicity in obtaining the approbation not only of the Supreme Pontiff but of Leo, by his own endowments supreme among the supreme, so on the other hand, as a matter of public concern, I congratulate this our age—which bids fair to be an age of gold, if ever such there was—wherein I see, under your happy auspices and by your holy counsels, three of the chief blessings of humanity are about to be restored to her. I mean, first, that truly Christian piety, which has in

§Latin, Greek, and Hebrew.

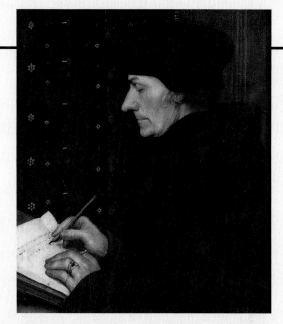

Hans Holbein the Younger, *Erasmus* (ca 1521). Holbein persuaded his close friend Erasmus to sit for this portrait and portrayed him at his characteristic work, writing. *(Louvre/Scala/Art Resource, NY)*

many ways fallen into decay; secondly, learning of the best sort, hitherto partly neglected and partly corrupted; and thirdly, the public and lasting concord of Christendom, the source and parent of piety and erudition. These will be the undying trophies of the tenth Leo, which, consecrated to eternal memory by the writings of learned men, will forever render your pontificate and your family‖ illustrious. I pray God that he may be pleased to confirm this purpose in you, and so protract your life, that after the affairs of mankind have been ordered according to your designs, Leo may make a long-delayed return to the skies.

Questions for Analysis

1. What does Erasmus mean by a "golden age"? What are its characteristics?

2. Do education and learning ensure improvement in the human condition?

3. What would you say are the essential differences between Erasmus's educational goals and those of modern society?

‖The Florentine House of Medici, whose interests Leo X, himself a Medici, was known always to support.

Source: Epistles 522 and 530, from *The Epistles of Erasmus,* trans. F. M. Nichols (London: Longmans, Green & Co. 1901).

Josse Lieferinxe, *Pilgrims in a Sanctuary.* Christians, especially those who were ill or handicapped, flocked to the shrines of saints in hopes of a cure. *(Scala/Art Resource, NY)*

chapter 14

Reform and Renewal in the Christian Church

*T*he idea of reform is as old as Christianity itself. In his letter to the Christians at Rome, Saint Paul exhorted, "Do not model yourselves on the behavior of the world around you, but let your behavior change, reformed by your new mind. That is the only way to discover the will of God." In the early fifth century, Saint Augustine of Hippo, describing the final stage of world history, wrote, "In the sixth age of the world our reformation becomes manifest, in newness of mind, according to the image of Him who created us." In the middle of the twelfth century, Saint Bernard of Clairvaux complained about the church of his day: "There is as much difference between us and the men of the primitive Church as there is between muck and gold." The Christian humanists of the late fifteenth and early sixteenth centuries—More, Erasmus, and Colet—urged reform of the church on the pattern of the early church, primarily through educational and social change.

Men and women of every period believed the early Christian church represented a golden age, and critics in every period called for reform. Thus sixteenth-century cries for reformation were hardly new. What was new, however, were the criticisms of educated laypeople whose religious needs were not being met. Many scholars interpret the sixteenth-century Reformation against the background of reforming trends begun in the fourteenth century. Unlike any other period, the sixteenth century experienced religious changes that had profound social, political, and cultural consequences.

- What late medieval religious developments paved the way for the adoption and spread of Protestant thought?
- Why did the strictly theological ideas of Martin Luther trigger political, social, and economic reactions?
- What were the consequences of religious schism?
- Do the various reform movements represent revolution or continuity? How?

These are some of the questions that this chapter will explore.

The Condition of the Church (ca 1400–1517)

The papal conflict with the German emperor Frederick II in the thirteenth century, followed by the Babylonian Captivity and then the Great Schism, badly damaged the prestige of church leaders. In the fourteenth and fifteenth centuries, leaders of the conciliar movement reflected educated public opinion when they called for the reform of the church "in head and members." Humanists denounced corruption in the church. As Machiavelli put it, "We Italians are irreligious and corrupt above others, because the Church and her representatives set us the worst example."[1] In *The Praise of Folly,* Erasmus condemned the superstitions of the parish clergy and the excessive rituals of the monks. The records of episcopal visitations of parishes, civil court records, and even such literary masterpieces as Chaucer's *Canterbury Tales* and Boccaccio's *Decameron* tended to confirm the sarcasm of the humanists.

Signs of Disorder

The religious life of most people in early-sixteenth-century Europe took place at the village or local level. At this parish level, priests were peasants, and they were poor. All too frequently, the spiritual quality of their lives was not much better than that of the people to whom they ministered.

In the early sixteenth century, critics of the church concentrated their attacks on three disorders: clerical immorality, clerical ignorance, and clerical pluralism, with the related problem of absenteeism. There was little pressure for doctrinal change; the emphasis was on moral and administrative reform.

Since the fourth century, church law had required that candidates for the priesthood accept absolute celibacy. That requirement had always been difficult to enforce. Many priests, especially those ministering to country people, had concubines, and reports of neglect of the rule of celibacy were common. Immorality, of course, included more than sexual transgressions. Clerical drunkenness, gambling, and indulgence in fancy dress were frequent charges. Because such conduct was so much at odds with the church's rules and moral standards, it scandalized the educated faithful.

The bishops only casually enforced regulations regarding the education of priests. As a result, standards for ordination were shockingly low. When Saint Antonio, archbishop of Florence, conducted a visitation of his metropolitan see in the late fifteenth century, he found churches and service books in a deplorable state and many priests barely able to read and write. The evidence points consistently to the low quality of the Italian clergy, although in northern Europe—in England, for example—recent research shows an improvement in clerical educational standards in the early sixteenth century. Nevertheless, parish priests throughout Europe were not as educated as the educated laity. Predictably, Christian humanists, with their concern for learning, condemned the ignorance or low educational level of the clergy. Many priests could barely read and write, and critics laughed at the illiterate priest mumbling Latin words of the Mass that he could not understand.

In regard to absenteeism and **pluralism,** many clerics, especially higher ecclesiastics, held several *benefices* (or offices) simultaneously but seldom visited their benefices, let alone performed the spiritual responsibilities those offices entailed. Instead, they collected revenues from all of them and hired a poor priest, paying him just a fraction of the income to fulfill the spiritual duties of a particular local church. King Henry VIII's chancellor Thomas Wolsey was archbishop of York for fifteen years before he set foot in his diocese. The French king Louis XII's famous diplomat Antoine du Prat was perhaps the most notorious example of absenteeism: as archbishop of Sens, he entered his cathedral for the first time in his own funeral procession.

Many Italian officials in the papal curia held benefices in England, Spain, and Germany. Revenues from those countries paid the Italian priests' salaries, provoking not only charges of absenteeism but also nationalistic resentment. Critics condemned pluralism, absenteeism, and the way money seemed to change hands when a bishop entered into his office.

Although royal governments strengthened their positions and consolidated their territories in the fifteenth and sixteenth centuries, rulers lacked sufficient revenues to pay and reward able civil servants. The Christian church, with its dioceses and abbeys, possessed a large proportion of the wealth of the countries of Europe. What better way to reward government officials, who were usually clerics, than with high church offices? After all, the practice was sanctioned by centuries of tradition. Thus all over Europe—because church officials served their monarchs, those officials were allowed to govern the church. Churchmen served as royal councilors, diplomats, treasury officials, chancellors, viceroys, and judges. These positions had nothing whatsoever to do with spiritual matters. Bishops worked for their respective states as

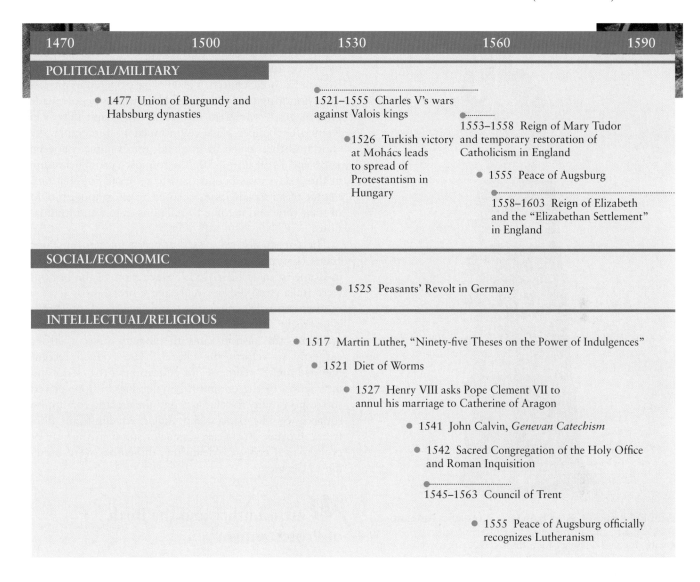

1470	1500	1530	1560	1590

POLITICAL/MILITARY

● 1477 Union of Burgundy and Habsburg dynasties

1521–1555 Charles V's wars against Valois kings

● 1526 Turkish victory at Mohács leads to spread of Protestantism in Hungary

1553–1558 Reign of Mary Tudor and temporary restoration of Catholicism in England

● 1555 Peace of Augsburg

1558–1603 Reign of Elizabeth and the "Elizabethan Settlement" in England

SOCIAL/ECONOMIC

● 1525 Peasants' Revolt in Germany

INTELLECTUAL/RELIGIOUS

● 1517 Martin Luther, "Ninety-five Theses on the Power of Indulgences"

● 1521 Diet of Worms

● 1527 Henry VIII asks Pope Clement VII to annul his marriage to Catherine of Aragon

● 1541 John Calvin, *Genevan Catechism*

● 1542 Sacred Congregation of the Holy Office and Roman Inquisition

1545–1563 Council of Trent

● 1555 Peace of Augsburg officially recognizes Lutheranism

---

well as for the church, and they were paid by the church for their services to the state. It is astonishing that so many conscientiously tried to carry out their religious duties on top of their public burdens.

In most countries except England, members of the nobility occupied the highest church positions. The spectacle of proud, aristocratic prelates living in magnificent splendor contrasted very unfavorably with the simple fishermen who had been Christ's disciples.

Signs of Vitality

Calls for reform testify to the spiritual vitality of the church as well as to its numerous problems. In the late fifteenth and early sixteenth centuries, both individuals and

groups within the church were working actively for reform. In Spain, for example, Cardinal Francisco Jiménez de Cisneros (1436–1517) visited religious houses, encouraged the monks and friars to uphold their rules and constitutions, and set high standards for the training of the diocesan clergy.

In Holland beginning in the late fourteenth century, a group of pious laypeople called the "Brethren of the Common Life" lived in stark simplicity while daily carrying out the Gospel teaching of feeding the hungry, clothing the naked, and visiting the sick. The Brethren also taught in local schools with the goal of preparing devout candidates for the priesthood. The Brethren sought to make religion a personal, inner experience. The spirituality of the Brethren of the Common Life found its

Arm Reliquary of Saint Babylas   Silver, glass paste, stones, rock crystals, and an amethyst were attached to an oak base to create this arm reliquary for a third-century martyred bishop of Antioch. Containers for relics were designed in forms related to the objects they held; here the bishop's hand is raised in blessing. Shrines possessing saints' relics drew pilgrims, who represented a demand for food, shelter, and souvenirs. *(Germany, Brunswick, 1467. Philadelphia Museum of Art, purchased with Museum funds. 1951-12-1)*

finest expression in the classic ***The Imitation of Christ*** by Thomas à Kempis, which gained wide appeal among laypeople. It urges Christians to take Christ as their model and seek perfection in a simple way of life. Like the later Protestants, the Brethren stressed the centrality of the Scriptures in spiritual life.[2] In the mid-fifteenth century, the movement had founded houses in the Netherlands, in central Germany, and in the Rhineland; it was a true religious revival.

If external religious observances are a measure of depth of heartfelt conviction, Europeans in the early sixteenth century remained deeply pious and loyal to the Roman Catholic church. Villagers participated in processions honoring the local saints. Middle-class people made pilgrimages to the great shrines, such as Saint Peter's in Rome. The upper classes continued to remember the church in their wills. In England, for example, between 1480 and 1490 almost 30,000 pounds, a prodigious sum in those days, was bequeathed to religious foundations. People of all social classes devoted an enormous amount of their time and income to religious causes and foundations.

The papacy also expressed concern for reform. Pope Julius II summoned an **ecumenical council,** which met in Rome from 1512 to 1517. Since most of the bishops were Italian and did not represent a broad cross section of international opinion, the term *ecumenical* (universal) is not really appropriate to describe their meetings. Nevertheless, the bishops and theologians present strove earnestly to reform the church. The council recommended higher standards for education of the clergy and instruction of the common people. The bishops placed the responsibility for eliminating bureaucratic corruption squarely on the papacy and suggested significant doctrinal reforms. But many obstacles stood in the way of ecclesiastical change. Meantime, difficulties were brewing in Germany.

Martin Luther and the Birth of Protestantism

As the result of a personal religious struggle, a German Augustinian friar, Martin Luther (1483–1546), launched the Protestant Reformation of the sixteenth century. Luther was not a typical person of his time; miners' sons who become professors of theology are never typical. But Luther was representative of his time in the sense that he articulated the widespread desire for reform of the Christian church and a deep yearning for salvation. In the sense that concern for salvation was an important motivating force for Luther and other reformers, the sixteenth-century Reformation was in part a continuation of the medieval religious search.

Luther's Early Years

Martin Luther was born at Eisleben in Saxony, the second son of a copper miner and, later, mine owner. At considerable sacrifice, his father sent him to school and then to the University of Erfurt, where he earned a master's degree with distinction at the young age of twenty-one. Hans Luther intended his son to proceed to the study of law and a legal career, which for centuries had been the steppingstone to public office and material success. Badly frightened during a thunderstorm, however, Martin Luther vowed to become a friar. Without consulting his father, he entered the monastery of the Augustinian friars at Erfurt in 1505. Luther was ordained a priest in 1507 and after additional study earned a doctorate of theology. From 1512 until his death in 1546, he served as professor of the Scriptures at the new University of Wittenberg. Luther was deadly serious when he said, years later, "I would not take all the world's goods for my doctorate." His doctorate led to his professorship, and his professorship conferred on him the *authority* to teach: throughout his life, he frequently cited his professorship as justification for his reforming work.

Martin Luther was a very conscientious friar. His scrupulous observance of the religious routine, frequent confessions, and fasting, however, gave him only temporary relief from anxieties about sin and his ability to meet God's demands. These apprehensions in turn led him to doubt the value of the monastic life itself. Since the medieval church had long held that the monastic life was a sure and certain road to salvation, Luther's confusion and anxieties increased.

Luther's wise and kindly confessor, John Staupitz, directed him to the study of Saint Paul's letters. Gradually, Luther arrived at a new understanding of the Pauline letters and of all Christian doctrine. He came to believe that salvation comes not through external observances and penance but through a simple faith in Christ. Faith is the means by which God sends humanity his grace, and faith is a free gift that cannot be earned. Thus Martin Luther discovered himself, God's work for him, and the centrality of faith in the Christian life.

The Ninety-five Theses

An incident illustrative of the condition of the church in the early sixteenth century propelled Martin Luther onto the stage of history and brought about the Reformation. The University of Wittenberg lay within the ecclesiastical jurisdiction of the archdiocese of Magdeburg. The twenty-seven-year-old archbishop of Magdeburg, Albert, was also administrator of the see of Halberstadt and had been appointed archbishop of Mainz. To hold all three offices simultaneously—blatant pluralism—required papal dispensation. At that moment, Pope Leo X was eager to continue the construction of Saint Peter's Basilica

The Folly of Indulgences   In this woodcut the church's sale of indulgences is viciously satirized. With one claw in the holy water symbolizing the rite of purification (Psalm 50), and the other claw resting on the coins paid for indulgences, the church, in the form of a rapacious eagle with its right hand stretched out for offerings, writes out an indulgence with excrement—which represents its worth. Fools, in a false security, sit in the animal's gaping mouth, representing Hell, to which a devil delivers the pope in a three-tiered crown and holding the keys to Heaven originally given to Saint Peter. *(Kunstsammlungen der Veste Coburg)*

but was hard-pressed for funds. Archbishop Albert borrowed money from the Fuggers, a wealthy banking family of Augsburg, to pay for the papal dispensation allowing him to hold the several episcopal benefices. Only a few powerful financiers and churchmen knew the details of the arrangement, but Leo X authorized Archbishop Albert to sell indulgences in Germany to repay the Fuggers.

Wittenberg was in the political jurisdiction of Frederick of Saxony, one of the seven electors of the Holy Roman Empire. When Frederick forbade the preaching and sale of indulgences within his duchy, the people of Wittenberg, including some of Professor Luther's students, streamed across the border from Saxony into Jütenborg in Thuringia to buy indulgences.

What exactly was an **indulgence?** According to Catholic theology, individuals who sin alienate themselves from God and his love. In order to be reconciled to God, the sinner must confess his or her sins to a priest and do the penance assigned. For example, a person who steals must first return the stolen goods and then perform the penance given by the priest, usually certain prayers or good works. This is known as the temporal (or earthly) penance since no one knows what penance God will ultimately require.

The doctrine of indulgence rested on three principles. First, God is merciful, but he is also just. Second, Christ and the saints, through their infinite virtue, established a "treasury of merits" on which the church, through its special relationship with Christ and the saints, can draw. Third, the church has the authority to grant sinners the spiritual benefits of those merits. Originally an indulgence was a remission of the temporal (priest-imposed) penalties for sin. Beginning in the twelfth century, the papacy and bishops had given Crusaders such indulgences. By the later Middle Ages, people widely believed that an indulgence secured total remission of penalties for sin—on earth or in purgatory—and ensured swift entry into Heaven.

Archbishop Albert hired Dominican friar John Tetzel to sell the indulgences. Tetzel mounted an advertising blitz. One of his slogans—"As soon as coin in coffer rings, the soul from purgatory springs"—brought phenomenal success. Men and women could buy indulgences not only for themselves but also for deceased parents, relatives, or friends. Tetzel even drew up a chart with specific prices for the forgiveness of particular sins.

Luther was severely troubled that ignorant people believed they had no further need for repentance once they had purchased an indulgence. He wrote a letter to Archbishop Albert on the subject and enclosed in Latin "Ninety-five Theses on the Power of Indulgences." His argument was that indulgences undermined the seriousness of the sacrament of penance, competed with the preaching of the Gospel, and downplayed the importance of charity in Christian life. After Luther's death, his disciple Philipp Melanchthon reported that the theses were also posted on the door of the church at Wittenberg Castle on October 31, 1517. Some modern scholars believe that event never happened, meaning all the subsequent dramatic and artistic renderings of it rest on myth.

In any case, Luther intended the theses for academic debate. By December 1517, they had been translated into German and were read throughout the empire.

Luther firmly rejected the notion that salvation could be achieved by good works, such as indulgences. Some of his theses challenged the pope's power to grant indulgences, and others criticized papal wealth. When questioned, Luther rested his fundamental argument on the principle that there was no biblical basis for indulgences. But, replied Luther's opponents, to deny the legality of indulgences was to deny the authority of the pope who had authorized them. The issue was drawn: where did authority lie in the Christian church?

Through 1518 and 1519, Luther studied the history of the papacy. In 1519 in a large public disputation with Catholic debater John Eck at Leipzig, Luther denied both the authority of the pope and the infallibility of a general council. The Council of Constance, he said, had erred when it had condemned Jan Hus (see page 397).

The papacy responded with a letter condemning some of Luther's propositions, ordering that his books be burned, and giving him two months to recant or be excommunicated. Luther retaliated by publicly burning the letter. By January 3, 1521, when the excommunication was supposed to become final, the controversy involved more than theological issues. The papal legate wrote, "All Germany is in revolution. Nine-tenths shout 'Luther' as their war cry; and the other tenth cares nothing about Luther, and cries 'Death to the court of Rome.'"[3]

In this highly charged atmosphere, the twenty-one-year-old emperor Charles V held his first diet (assembly of the Estates of the empire). Charles summoned Luther to appear before the **Diet of Worms.** When ordered to recant, Luther replied in language that rang all over Europe:

Unless I am convinced by the evidence of Scripture or by plain reason—for I do not accept the authority of the Pope or the councils alone, since it is established that they have often erred and contradicted themselves—I am bound by the Scriptures I have cited and my conscience is captive to the Word of God. I cannot and will not recant anything, for it is neither safe nor right to go against conscience. God help me. Amen.[4]

When Charles V declared Luther an outlaw, meaning he was denied legal protection, Duke Frederick of Saxony protected him.

Meanwhile, the Swiss humanist and admirer of Erasmus, Ulrich Zwingli (1484–1531), introduced the reformation in Switzerland. Elected People's Priest at the New Minster in Zurich, Zwingli first mounted the pulpit on January 1, 1519, and announced that he would preach not from the church's prescribed readings but, relying on Erasmus's New Testament, go right through the

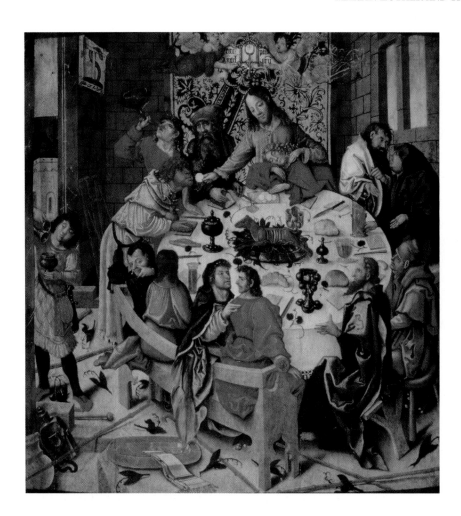

Jörg Ratgeb: The Last Supper A painter in Heilbronn (modern Baden-Württemberg), Ratgeb (ca 1480–1526) moved his wife and children to that town but could not gain citizenship for them because they were serfs of the duke of Württemberg, who would not free them. This early work shows Ratgeb's innovative style: the disciples are grouped in pairs, wear lavish shimmering costumes, and seem engaged in private conversation as Jesus distributes the Eucharist. A roasted pascal lamb rests in the middle of the table, but a knife is the only eating utensil. *(Loan: The Netherlands Institute of Cultural Heritage. Museum Boijmans Van Beuningen, Rotterdam)*

New Testament "from A to Z," that is, from Matthew to Revelation. Zwingli was convinced that Christian life rested on the Scriptures, which were the pure words of God and the sole basis of religious truth. He went on to attack indulgences, the Mass, the institution of monasticism, and clerical celibacy. In his gradual reform of the church in Zurich, where he remained the rest of his life, he had the strong support of the town's civil authorities. He disagreed, however, with Luther on various theological issues, notably the nature of the Eucharist. The Colloquy of Marburg, summoned in 1529 to unite Protestant opinion, failed to resolve those differences.

Protestant Thought

Between 1520 and 1530, Luther worked out the basic theological tenets that became the articles of faith for his new church and subsequently for all Protestant groups. The word **Protestant** derives from the protest drawn up by a small group of reforming German princes at the Diet of Speyer in 1529. The princes "protested" the decisions of the Catholic majority. At first Protestant meant "Lutheran," but with the appearance of many protesting sects, it became a general term applied to all non-Catholic Christians. Lutheran Protestant thought was officially formulated in the Confession of Augsburg in 1530.

Ernst Troeltsch, a German student of the sociology of religion, has defined Protestantism as a "modification of Catholicism, in which the Catholic formulation of questions was retained, while a different answer was given to them." Luther provided new answers to four old, basic theological issues.

First, how is a person to be saved? Traditional Catholic teaching held that salvation is achieved by both faith and good works. Luther held that salvation comes by faith alone. Women and men are saved, said Luther, by the arbitrary decision of God, irrespective of good works or the sacraments. God, not people, initiates salvation.

Lucas Cranach the Elder: The Ten Commandments (early sixteenth century) Protestants condemned images of all kinds but recognized their value for instructional purposes. Here Cranach, an early adherent of Luther's Reformation, illustrates the Ten Commandments. Can you name the commandments? Is it unfair to say that the painting has a misogynistic tinge, given the female devil in number 5 and the wife in number 9? The semicircular rainbow running through the ten scenes symbolizes the covenant between God and humankind. *(Lutherhalle, Wittenberg/The Bridgeman Art Library)*

Second, where does religious authority reside? Christian doctrine had long maintained that authority rests both in the Bible and in the traditional teaching of the church. Luther maintained that authority rests in the Word of God as revealed in the Bible alone and as interpreted by an individual's conscience. He used the Latin phrase *sola scriptura,* "scripture alone," to mean that authority in the church rested only on the Scriptures: for a doctrine or issue to be valid, it had to have a scriptural basis. (Luther, of course, did not have the advantage of modern biblical research, which has demonstrated that tradition *preceded* the writing of the New Testament—that is, the New Testament is not exactly contemporaneous with Jesus but is based on the traditional understanding of his life and teachings current in first-century Christian communities.) He urged that each person read and reflect on the Scriptures.

Third, what is the church? Luther re-emphasized the Catholic teaching that the church consists of the entire community of Christian believers. Medieval churchmen, in contrast, had tended to identify the church with the clergy.

Fourth, what is the highest form of Christian life? The medieval church had stressed the superiority of the monastic and religious life over the secular. Luther argued that all vocations have equal merit, whether ecclesiastical or secular, and that every person should serve God in his or her individual calling.[5]

As Protestant thought developed, it differed from Roman Catholic teaching on several other fundamental issues. Luther's idea of the church as a spiritual *priesthood of all believers,* an invisible fellowship not fixed in any place or person, differed markedly from the Roman Catholic practice of a clerical, hierarchical institution headed by the pope in Rome. Because faith required no institutional structure, Luther stressed the invisibility of the church. Whereas Catholic doctrine holds that there are seven sacraments, Luther believed that the Scriptures support only three sacraments—baptism, penance, and the Eucharist, or Lord's Supper. Protestant sects, as they emerged, developed a theology of the Eucharist. Catholics hold the dogma of **transubstantiation:** by the consecrating words of the priest during the Mass, the bread and wine become the actual body and blood of Christ, who is then fully present in the bread and wine. In opposition, Luther defined **consubstantiation,** the belief that after consecration the bread and wine undergo a spiritual change whereby Christ is really present (the Real Presence) but the bread and wine are not transformed. Swiss reformer Ulrich Zwingli affirmed that the **Lord's Supper** is a *memorial* of the Last Supper and that no change whatever occurs in the elements. John Calvin believed that the body and blood of Christ are spiritually but not physically present in the bread and wine and are consumed spiritually. Catholics and Protestants agreed that the sacrament must be received worthily and that it is a source of grace.

The Social Impact of Luther's Beliefs

Every encounter Luther had with ecclesiastical or political authorities attracted attention. Pulpits and printing presses spread his message all over Germany. By the time of his death, people of all social classes had become Lutheran. What was the immense appeal of Luther's religious ideas?

Historical research on the German towns has shown that two significant late medieval developments prepared the way for Luther's ideas. First, since the fifteenth century, city governments had expressed resentment of clerical privileges and immunities. Priests, monks, and nuns paid no taxes and were exempt from civic responsibilities, such as defending the city. Yet religious orders frequently held large amounts of urban property. At Zurich in 1467, for example, religious orders held one-third of the city's taxable property. City governments were determined to integrate the clergy into civic life by reducing their privileges and giving them public responsibilities. Accordingly, the Zurich magistracy subjected the religious to taxes, inspected wills so that legacies to the church and legacies left by churchmen could be controlled, and placed priests under the jurisdiction of the civil courts.

Second, critics of the late medieval church, especially educated townspeople, condemned the irregularity and poor quality of sermons. As a result, prosperous burghers in many towns established **preacherships.** Preachers were men of superior education who were required to deliver about a hundred sermons a year, each lasting about forty-five minutes. Endowed preacherships had important consequences after 1517. Luther's ideas attracted many preachers, and in such towns as Stuttgart, Reutlingen, Eisenach, and Jena, preachers became Protestant leaders. Preacherships also encouraged the Protestant form of worship, in which the sermon, not the Eucharist, was the central part of the service.[6]

In the countryside, the attraction of German peasants to Lutheran beliefs was predictable. Luther himself came from a peasant background, and he admired the peasants' ceaseless toil. They thrilled to the words of Luther used in his treatise *On Christian Liberty* (1520)—"A Christian man is the most free lord of all and subject to none"—choosing to ignore the second clause of Luther's statement: "A Christian man is the most dutiful servant of all, and subject to everyone." (See the feature "Listening to the Past: Martin Luther, *On Christian Liberty*" on pages 486–487.) Taken by itself, the first clause contributed to social unrest.

Fifteenth-century Germany had witnessed several **peasant revolts**. In the early sixteenth century, the economic condition of the peasantry varied from place to place but was generally worse than it had been in the fifteenth century and was deteriorating. Crop failures in 1523 and 1524 aggravated an explosive situation. In 1525 representatives of the Swabian peasants met at the city of Memmingen and drew up the Twelve Articles, which expressed their grievances. The Twelve Articles condemned lay and ecclesiastical lords and summarized the agrarian crisis of the early sixteenth century. The articles complained that nobles had seized village common lands, which traditionally had been used by all; that they had imposed new rents on manorial properties and new services on the peasants working those properties; and that they had forced the poor to pay unjust death duties in the form of the peasants' best horses or cows. Wealthy, socially mobile peasants especially resented these burdens, which they emphasized as new.[7] The peasants believed their demands conformed to the Scriptures and cited Luther as a theologian who could prove that they did.

Luther wanted to prevent rebellion. Initially he sided with the peasants, and in his tract *An Admonition to Peace* (1525) he blasted the lords:

We have no one on earth to thank for this mischievous rebellion, except you lords and princes, especially you blind bishops and mad priests and monks. . . . In your government you do nothing but flay and rob your subjects in order that you may lead a life of splendor and pride, until the poor common folk can bear it no longer.[8]

But, he warned, nothing justified the use of armed force: "The fact that rulers are unjust and wicked does not excuse tumult and rebellion; to punish wickedness does not belong to everybody, but to the worldly rulers who bear the sword." As for biblical support for the peasants' demands, he maintained that Scripture had nothing to do with earthly justice or material gain.[9]

Massive revolts first broke out near the Swiss frontier and then swept through Swabia, Thuringia, the Rhineland,

German Burgher Domestic Scene   With what Jesus called the greatest commandment ("You shall love the Lord your God with all your heart and all your soul and your neighbor as yourself" [Deut. 6, Matt. 22]) inscribed on tablets over the room, a German family begins a meal. The father listens as his son says grace, the mother passes bread, the older daughters seem to have begun eating, and a small child biting a chicken drumstick seems dangerously close to the fire. The little dog begs for food; the cat laps milk. *(Mary Evans Picture Library)*

and Saxony. The crowds' slogans came directly from Luther's writings. "God's righteousness" and the "Word of God" were invoked in an effort to secure social and economic justice. The peasants who expected Luther's support were soon disillusioned. Freedom for Luther meant independence from the authority of the Roman church; it did *not* mean opposition to legally established secular powers. Firmly convinced that rebellion would hasten the end of civilized society, he wrote the tract *Against the Murderous, Thieving Hordes of the Peasants:* "Let everyone who can smite, slay, and stab [the peasants], secretly and openly, remembering that nothing can be more poisonous, hurtful or devilish than a rebel."[10] The nobility ferociously crushed the revolt. Historians estimate that over seventy-five thousand peasants were killed in 1525.

Luther took literally these words of Saint Paul's Letter to the Romans: "Let every soul be subject to the higher powers. For there is no power but of God: the powers that be are established by God. Whosoever resists the power, resists the ordinance of God: and they that resist shall receive to themselves damnation."[11] As Lutheran theology developed, it exalted the state, subordinated the church to the state, and everywhere championed

"the powers that be." The German Peasants' Revolt of 1525 greatly strengthened the authority of lay rulers. Peasant economic conditions, however, moderately improved. For example, in many parts of Germany, enclosed fields, meadows, and forests were returned to common use.

Scholars in many disciplines have attributed Luther's fame and success to the invention of the printing press, which rapidly reproduced and made known his ideas. (See the feature "Images in Society: From Reformation to Baroque" on pages 464–465.) Equally important was Luther's incredible skill with language. Some thinkers have lavished praise on the Wittenberg reformer; others have bitterly condemned him. But in the words of psychologist Erik Erikson:

The one matter on which professor and priest, psychiatrist and sociologist, agree is Luther's immense gift for language: his receptivity for the written word; his memory for the significant phrase; and his range of verbal expression (lyrical, biblical, satirical, and vulgar) which in English is paralleled only by Shakespeare.[12]

Language proved to be the weapon with which this peasant's son changed the European world.

Like the peasants, educated people and humanists were much attracted by Luther's words. He advocated a simpler, personal religion based on faith, a return to the spirit of the early church, the centrality of the Scriptures in the liturgy and in Christian life, and the abolition of elaborate ceremonies—precisely the reforms the northern humanists had been calling for.

Luther's linguistic skill, together with his translation of the New Testament into German in 1523, led to the acceptance of his dialect of German as the standard version of German. His insistence that everyone should read and reflect on the Scriptures attracted the literate and thoughtful middle classes partly because Luther appealed to their intelligence. Moreover, the business classes envied the church's wealth, disapproved of the luxurious lifestyle of some churchmen, and resented tithes and ecclesiastical taxation. Luther's doctrines of salvation by faith and the priesthood of all believers not only raised the religious status of the commercial classes but also protected their pocketbooks.

Hymns, psalms, and Luther's two catechisms (1529), compendiums of basic religious knowledge, also show the power of language in spreading the ideals of the Reformation. The reformers knew "that rhyme, meter, and melodies could forcefully impress minds and affect sensibilities." Such hymns as the famous "A Mighty Fortress Is Our God" expressed deep human feelings, were easily remembered, and imprinted on the mind central points of doctrine. Luther's *Larger Catechism* contained brief sermons on the main articles of faith, whereas the *Shorter Catechism* gave concise explanations of doctrine in question-and-answer form. Both catechisms stressed the importance of the Ten Commandments, the Lord's Prayer, the Apostle's Creed, and the sacraments for the believing Christian. Although originally intended for the instruction of pastors, these catechisms became powerful techniques for the indoctrination of men and women of all ages, especially the young.[13]

What appeal did Luther's message have for women? Luther's argument that all vocations have equal merit in the sight of God gave dignity to those who performed ordinary, routine, domestic tasks. The abolition of monasticism in Protestant territories led to the exaltation of the home, which Luther and other reformers stressed as the special domain of the wife. The Christian home, in contrast to the place of business, became the place for the exercise of the gentler virtues—love, tenderness, reconciliation, the carrying of one another's burdens. The Protestant abolition of private confession to a priest freed women from possibly embarrassing explorations of their sexual lives. Protestants established schools where girls as well as boys became literate in the catechism and the

Martin Luther and Katharina von Bora   The couple married on June 13, 1525, when Katharina was twenty-six and Luther forty-two. His parents were present for the ceremony. She brewed beer; managed the house, garden, and accounts; and produced six children. She also gave her husband her complete devotion, but having a no-nonsense character, she scolded him for what she perceived as his excessive generosity. For Luther, it was an exceptionally happy union. (*Uffizi, Florence/Scala/Art Resource, NY*)

Images in Society

From Reformation to Baroque

In the Reformation era, controversy raged over the purpose and function of art. Protestants and Catholics disagreed, and Protestant sects disagreed with one another. The Latin phrase *sola scriptura* ("scripture alone") summarizes the fundamentalist Protestant position. The Bible specifically prohibits the making of images of anything "in the heavens above or the earth below or the waters beneath the earth" (Exodus 20:4–6 and Deuteronomy 5:8–10), so some Protestant leaders stressed that "the Word of God" should be the only instrument used in the work of evangelization. Martin Luther disagreed, saying he was not "of the opinion that the Gospel should blight and destroy all the arts." Luther believed that painting and sculpture had value in spreading the Gospel message because "children and simple folk are more apt to retain the divine stories when taught by pictures and parables than merely by words or instruction." For John Calvin (see pages 470–472), the utter transcendence of God made impossible any attempt to bring God down to human level through visual portraiture; to domesticate or to humanize God would deprive him of his glory. In houses of worship Calvin emphasized the centrality of the divine word, allowing wall inscriptions from the Bible. In later life, Calvin tolerated narrative biblical scenes, as long as they did not include pictures of God or Jesus Christ, his son.

Many of the formerly Catholic churches in the Netherlands were redesigned with a stark, bare simplicity that mirrored the ideal of Protestant architecture. Notice the interior of the church of Saint Bavo in Haarlem (Image 1). The medieval Gothic structure was stripped of all statues, images, and decoration.

Lucas Cranach the Elder (1472–1553), a close friend of Luther's, is the finest representative of Protestant Reformation artists. He and Luther collaborated on the production of woodcuts and paintings, such as *The Ten Commandments* (see page 460), that spread the new evangelical theology. Protestants condemned images of all kinds but recognized their value for instructional purposes. Each square in the elder Cranach's painting represents one of the Ten Commandments. How many of the commandments can you name? Notice the female devil figure in number 5 and the portrayal of the wife in number 9. What conclusions can you draw from these representations of women? The semicircular rainbow running through the ten scenes symbolizes the covenant between God and humankind.

Lucas Cranach the Younger (1515–1586) continued his father's work. His wood engraving *The True and False Churches* (Image 2) shows the "true church" listening as Luther (gesturing from the pulpit) preaches the word of God from an open Bible. The engraving reveals a sacramental piety through Christ's presence on the altar as shown in the lamb of God and crucified Savior distributed to all in both bread and wine (left). An open mouth (right) symbolizing the jaws of Hell engulfs the pope, cardinals, and friars—the "false church."

The Catholic church officially addressed the subject of art at the Council of Trent in December 1563. The church declared that honor and veneration should be given to likenesses of Christ, the Virgin Mary, and the saints; that images would remind people of the saints' virtues, which should be imitated; and that pictorial art would promote piety and the love of God. Examine the

Image 1 Church of Saint Bavo, Haarlem *(Pieter Jansz. Saenredam,* S. Bavo in Haarlem. *John G. Johnson Collection, Philadelphia Museum of Art)*

Image 2 Lucas Cranach the Younger: The True and False Churches *(Staatliche Kunstsammlungen Dresden)*

Image 3 Jesuit Priest Distributing Holy Pictures *(From Pierre Chenu,* The Reformation *[New York: St. Martin's Press, 1986])*

Image 4 Ceiling of the Gésu *(Scala/Art Resource, NY)*

painting *Jesuit Priest Distributing Holy Pictures* (Image 3). Such pictures and images of saints were often given to children to help educate them on matters of doctrine. How do these pictures serve the same function as the Protestant *Ten Commandments*?

Both Protestants and Catholics used religious art for propaganda purposes, to oppose religious heterodoxy, and to arouse piety in laypeople. Catholic Reformation art came into full flowering with the style later known as baroque (see page 582). Baroque art originated in Rome and reflected the dynamic and proselytizing spirit of the Counter-Reformation. The church encouraged artists to appeal to the senses, to touch the souls and kindle the faith of ordinary people while proclaiming the power and confidence of the reformed Catholic church.

In addition to this underlying religious emotionalism, the baroque drew from the Catholic Reformation its sense of drama, motion, and ceaseless striving. The interior of the Jesuit church of Jesus—the Gésu—combined all these characteristics in its lavish, shimmering, wildly active decorations and frescoes (Image 4). This triumphant, elaborate, and flamboyant church celebrates both the Catholic baroque and Rome as the artistic capital of Europe. What is the purpose of the ornate gilded ceiling and three-dimensional painting? How would you compare the Gésu with the Saint Bavo church (Image 1)?

The **history companion** *features additional information and activities related to this topic.* **history.college.hmco.com/students**

Bible. Finally, the reformers stressed marriage as the cure for clerical concupiscence. Protestantism thus proved attractive to the many women who had been priests' concubines and mistresses: now they became legal and honorable wives.[14]

For his time, Luther held enlightened views on matters of sexuality and marriage. He wrote a letter to a young man, "Dear lad, be not ashamed that you desire a girl, nor you my maid, the boy. Just let it lead you into matrimony and not into promiscuity, and it is no more cause for shame than eating and drinking."[15] Luther was confident that God took delight in the sexual act and denied that original sin affected the goodness of creation. He believed, however, that marriage was a woman's career. A student recorded Luther as saying early in his public ministry, "Let them bear children until they are dead of it; that is what they are for." A happy marriage to ex-nun Katharina von Bora mellowed him, and another student later quoted him as saying, "Next to God's Word there is no more precious treasure than holy matrimony. God's highest gift on earth is a pious, cheerful, God-fearing, home-keeping wife, with whom you may live peacefully, to whom you may entrust your goods, and body and life."[16] With many relatives and constant visitors, Luther's home was a large and happy household, a model for Protestants but an abomination for Catholics. The wives of other reformers, though they exercised no leadership role in the reform, shared their husbands' work and concerns.

Germany and the Protestant Reformation

Unlike Spain, France, and England, the German Empire lacked a strong central power. The Golden Bull of 1356 legalized what had long existed—government by an aristocratic federation. Each of seven electors—the archbishops of Mainz, Trier, and Cologne, the margrave of Brandenburg, the duke of Saxony, the count palatine of the Rhine, and the king of Bohemia—gained virtual sovereignty in his own territory. The agreement ended disputed elections in the empire; it also reduced the central authority of the emperor. Germany was characterized by weak borders, localism, and chronic disorder. The nobility strengthened its hold on its territories, while imperial power declined.

Against this background of decentralization and strong local power, Martin Luther had launched a movement to reform the church. Two years after Luther pub-

lished the Ninety-five Theses, the electors chose as emperor a nineteen-year-old Habsburg prince who ruled as Charles V. Luther's interests and motives were primarily religious, but many people responded to his teachings for political, social, or economic reasons.

The Rise of the Habsburg Dynasty

The marriage in 1477 of Maximilian I of the house of Habsburg and Mary of Burgundy was a decisive event in early modern European history. Burgundy consisted of two parts: the French duchy, with its capital at Dijon, and the Burgundian Netherlands, with its capital at Brussels. Through this union with the rich and powerful duchy of Burgundy, the Austrian house of Habsburg, already the strongest ruling family in the empire, became an international power.

In the fifteenth and sixteenth centuries, as in the Middle Ages, relations among states continued to be greatly affected by the connections of royal families. Marriage often determined the diplomatic status of states. The Habsburg-Burgundian marriage angered the French, who considered Burgundy French territory and had lusted after the Burgundian Netherlands (Flanders) for centuries. Louis XI of France repeatedly ravaged parts of the Burgundian Netherlands until he was able to force Maximilian to accept French terms: the Treaty of Arras (1482) declared French Burgundy a part of the kingdom of France. The Habsburgs, however, never really renounced their claim to Burgundy, and intermittent warfare over it continued between France and Maximilian. But Louis could not conquer it. It remained outside French control. Within the empire, German principalities that resented Austria's preeminence began to see that they shared interests with France. The marriage of Maximilian and Mary inaugurated centuries of conflict between the Austrian house of Habsburg and the kings of France. And Germany was to be the chief arena of the struggle.

"Other nations wage war; you, Austria, marry." Historians dispute the origins of this adage, but no one questions its accuracy. The heir of Mary and Maximilian, Philip of Burgundy, married Joanna of Castile, daughter of Ferdinand and Isabella of Spain. Philip and Joanna's son Charles V (1500–1558) fell heir to a vast conglomeration of territories. Through a series of accidents and unexpected deaths, Charles inherited Spain from his mother, her New World possessions, and the Spanish dominions in Italy, Sicily, and Sardinia. From his father he inherited the Habsburg lands in Austria, southern Germany, the Low Countries, and Franche-Comté in east-central France.

The Heritage of Charles V

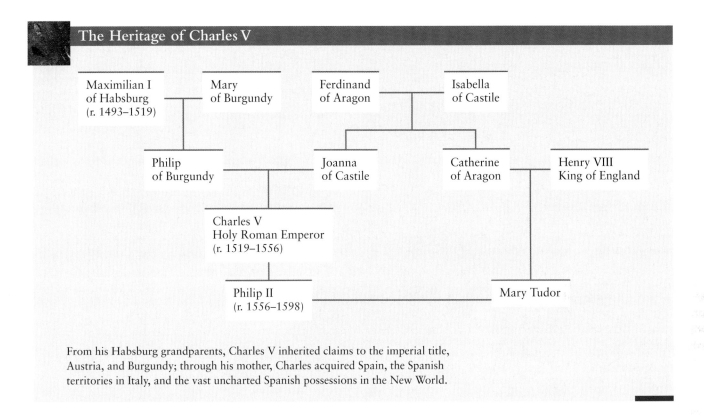

From his Habsburg grandparents, Charles V inherited claims to the imperial title, Austria, and Burgundy; through his mother, Charles acquired Spain, the Spanish territories in Italy, and the vast uncharted Spanish possessions in the New World.

Charles's inheritance was an incredibly diverse collection of states and peoples, each governed in a different manner and held together only by the person of the emperor (see Map 14.1). Charles's Italian adviser, the grand chancellor Gattinara, told the young ruler, "God has set you on the path toward world monarchy." Charles not only believed this, but also was convinced that it was his duty to maintain the political and religious unity of Western Christendom. In this respect, Charles V was the last medieval emperor.

Charles needed and in 1519 secured the imperial title. Forward-thinking Germans proposed placing the administration in the hands of an imperial council whose president, the emperor's appointee, would have ultimate executive power. Reforms of the imperial finances, the army, and the judiciary were also recommended. Such ideas did not interest the young emperor at all. When he finally arrived in Germany from Spain and opened his first diet at Worms in January 1521, he naively announced that "the empire from of old has had not many masters, but one, and it is our intention to be that one." In view of the long history of aristocratic power, Charles's notions were pure fantasy. He continued the Burgundian policy of his grandfather Maximilian. That is, German revenues and German troops were subordinated to the needs of other parts of the empire, first Burgundy and then Spain. Habsburg international interests came before the need for reform in Germany.

The Political Impact of Luther's Beliefs

In the sixteenth century, the practice of religion remained a public matter. Everyone participated in the religious life of the community, just as almost everyone shared in the local agricultural work. Whatever spiritual convictions individuals held in the privacy of their consciences, the emperor, king, prince, magistrate, or other civil authority determined the official form of religious practice within his jurisdiction. Almost everyone believed that the presence of a faith different from that of the majority represented a political threat to the security of the state. Only a tiny minority, and certainly none of the princes, believed in religious liberty.

Against this background, the religious storm launched by Martin Luther swept across Germany. Elements in his religious reformation stirred patriotic feelings. Anti-Roman sentiment ran high. Humanists lent eloquent intellectual support. And Luther's translation of the New Testament evoked national pride.

MAP 14.1 The Global Empire of Charles V Charles V exercised theoretical jurisdiction over more European territory than anyone since Charlemagne. He also claimed authority over large parts of North and South America.

For decades devout laypeople and churchmen had called on the German princes to reform the church. In 1520 Luther took up the cry in his *Appeal to the Christian Nobility of the German Nation*. Unless the princes destroyed papal power in Germany, Luther argued, reform was impossible. He urged the princes to confiscate ecclesiastical wealth and to abolish indulgences, dispensations, pardons, and clerical celibacy. He told them that it was their public duty to bring about the moral reform of the church. Luther based his argument in part on the papacy's financial exploitation of Germany:

How comes it that we Germans must put up with such robbery and such extortion of our property at the hands of the pope? If the Kingdom of France has prevented it, why do we Germans let them make such fools and apes of us? It would all be more bearable if in this way they only stole our property; but they lay waste the churches and rob Christ's sheep of their pious shepherds, and destroy the worship and the Word of God. As it is they do nothing for the good of Christendom; they only wrangle about the incomes of bishoprics and prelacies, and that any robber could do.[17]

These words fell on welcome ears and itchy fingers. Luther's appeal to German patriotism gained him strong support, and national feeling influenced many princes otherwise confused by or indifferent to the complexities of the religious issues.

The rejection of Roman Catholicism and adoption of Protestantism would mean the legal confiscation of lush farmlands, rich monasteries, and wealthy shrines.

Some German princes, such as the prince-archbishop of Cologne, Hermann von Wied, were sincerely attracted to Lutheranism, but material considerations swayed many others to embrace the new faith. A steady stream of duchies, margraviates, free cities, and bishoprics secularized church property, accepted Lutheran theological doctrines, and adopted simpler services conducted in German. The decision reached at Worms in 1521 to condemn Luther and his teaching was not enforced because the German princes did not want to enforce it.

Charles V was a vigorous defender of Catholicism, and contemporary social and political theory denied the possibility of two religions coexisting peacefully in one territory. Thus many princes used the religious issue to extend their financial and political independence. When doctrinal differences became linked to political ambitions and financial receipts, the results were unfortunate for the improvement of German government. The Protestant movement ultimately proved a political disaster for Germany.

Charles V must share blame with the German princes for the disintegration of imperial authority in the empire. He neither understood nor took an interest in the constitutional problems of Germany, and he lacked the material resources to oppose Protestantism effectively there. Throughout his reign, he was preoccupied with his Flemish, Spanish, Italian, and American territories. Moreover, the Turkish threat prevented him from acting effectively against the Protestants; Charles's brother, Ferdinand, needed Protestant support against the Turks who besieged Vienna in 1529.

Fresco of Pope Clement VII and the Emperor Charles V by Giorgio Vasari Since Vasari's *Lives of the Most Eminent Italian Painters, Sculptors, and Architects* (rev. ed. 1568), still the basic historical source for Renaissance art and culture, held that "art is the imitation of nature," we may assume that these are faithful likenesses of the Medici pope and the Holy Roman emperor. *(Palazzo Vecchio, Florence/ Scala/Art Resource, NY)*

Five times between 1521 and 1555, Charles V went to war with the Valois kings of France. The issue each time was the Habsburg lands acquired by the marriage of Maximilian and Mary of Burgundy. Much of the fighting occurred in Germany. The cornerstone of French foreign policy in the sixteenth and seventeenth centuries was the desire to keep the German states divided. Thus Europe witnessed the paradox of the Catholic king of France supporting the Lutheran princes in their challenge to his fellow Catholic, Charles V. French foreign policy contributed to the continuing division of Germany. The long dynastic struggle commonly called the Habsburg-Valois Wars advanced the cause of Protestantism and promoted the political fragmentation of the German Empire.

Finally, in 1555 Charles agreed to the Peace of Augsburg, which, in accepting the status quo, officially recognized Lutheranism. Each prince was permitted to determine his territory's religion. Most of northern and central Germany became Lutheran, while the south remained Roman Catholic. There was no freedom of religion, however. Princes or town councils established state churches to which all subjects of the area had to belong. Dissidents, whether Lutheran or Catholic, had to convert or leave. The political difficulties Germany inherited from the Middle Ages had been compounded by the religious crisis of the sixteenth century.

$\mathcal{T}$ he Growth of the Protestant Reformation

By 1555 much of northern Europe had broken with the Roman Catholic church. All of Scandinavia, England (except under Mary Tudor), Scotland, and such self-governing cities as Geneva and Zurich in Switzerland and Strasbourg in Germany had rejected the religious authority of Rome and adopted new faiths. Because a common religious faith had been the one element uniting all of Europe for almost a thousand years, the fragmentation of belief led to profound changes in European life and society. The most significant new form of Protestantism was Calvinism, of which the Peace of Augsburg had made no mention at all.

Calvinism

In 1509 while Luther was studying for a doctorate at Wittenberg, John Calvin (1509–1564) was born in Noyon in northwestern France. Luther inadvertently launched the Protestant Reformation. Calvin, however, had the greater impact on future generations. His theological writings pro-

foundly influenced the social thought and attitudes of Europeans and English-speaking peoples all over the world, especially in Canada and the United States. Although he had originally intended to have an ecclesiastical career, Calvin studied law, which had a decisive impact on his mind and later thought. In 1533 he experienced a religious crisis, as a result of which he converted to Protestantism.

Convinced that God selects certain people to do his work, Calvin believed that God had specifically called him to reform the church. Accordingly, he accepted an invitation to assist in the reformation of the city of Geneva. There, beginning in 1541, Calvin worked assiduously to establish a Christian society ruled by God through civil magistrates and reformed ministers. Geneva, "a city that was a Church," became the model of a Christian community for sixteenth-century Protestant reformers.

To understand Calvin's Geneva, it is necessary to understand Calvin's ideas. These he embodied in **The Institutes of the Christian Religion,** first published in 1536 and definitively issued in 1559. The cornerstone of Calvin's theology was his belief in the absolute sovereignty and omnipotence of God and the total weakness of humanity. Before the infinite power of God, he asserted, men and women are as insignificant as grains of sand.

Calvin did not ascribe free will to human beings because that would detract from the sovereignty of God. Men and women cannot actively work to achieve salvation; rather, God in his infinite wisdom decided at the beginning of time who would be saved and who damned. This viewpoint constitutes the theological principle called **predestination:**

Predestination we call the eternal decree of God, by which he has determined in himself, what he would have become of every individual. . . . For they are not all created with a similar destiny; but eternal life is foreordained for some, and eternal damnation for others. . . . In conformity, therefore, to the clear doctrine of the Scripture, we assert, that by an eternal and immutable counsel, God has once for all determined, both whom he would admit to salvation, and whom he would condemn to destruction. . . . To those whom he devotes to condemnation, the gate of life is closed by a just and irreprehensible, but incomprehensible, judgment. How exceedingly presumptuous it is only to inquire into the causes of the Divine will; which is in fact, and is justly entitled to be, the cause of everything that exists. . . . For the will of God is the highest justice; so that what he wills must be considered just, for this very reason, because he wills it.[18]

Many people have found the doctrine of predestination, which dates back to Saint Augustine and Saint Paul, a pessimistic view of the nature of God, who, they feel, revealed himself in the Old and New Testaments as merciful as well as just. But "this terrible decree," as even Calvin called it, did not lead to pessimism or fatalism. Rather, the Calvinist believed in the redemptive work of Christ and was confident that God had elected (saved) him or her. Predestination served as an energizing dynamic, forcing a person to undergo hardships in the constant struggle against evil.

Calvin aroused Genevans to a high standard of morality. He had two remarkable assets: complete mastery of the Scriptures and exceptional eloquence. Through his sermons and a program of religious education, God's laws and man's were enforced in Geneva. Calvin's powerful sermons delivered the Word of God and thereby monopolized the strongest contemporary means of communication: preaching. Through his *Genevan Catechism,* published in 1541, children and adults memorized set questions and answers and acquired a summary of their faith and a guide for daily living. Calvin's sermons and his *Catechism* gave a whole generation of Genevans thorough instruction in the reformed religion.[19]

In the reformation of the city, the Genevan Consistory also exercised a powerful role. This body consisted of twelve laymen plus the Company of Pastors, of which Calvin was the permanent moderator (presider). The duties of the Consistory were "to keep watch over every man's life [and] to admonish amiably those whom they see leading a disorderly life." Even though Calvin emphasized that the Consistory's activities should be thorough and "its eyes may be everywhere," corrections were considered only "medicine to turn sinners to the Lord."[20]

Although all municipal governments in early modern Europe regulated citizens' conduct, none did so with the severity of Geneva's Consistory under Calvin's leadership. Nor did it make any distinction between what we would consider crimes against society and simple un-Christian conduct. Absence from sermons, criticism of ministers, dancing, card playing, family quarrels, and heavy drinking were all investigated and punished by the Consistory. Serious crimes and heresy were handled by the civil authorities, which, with the Consistory's approval, sometimes used torture to extract confessions. Between 1542 and 1546 alone, seventy-six persons were banished from Geneva and fifty-eight executed for heresy, adultery, blasphemy, and witchcraft.

Calvin reserved his harshest condemnation for religious dissenters, declaring them "dogs and swine":

God makes plain that the false prophet is to be stoned without mercy. We are to crush beneath our heel all affections of nature when His honor is concerned. The father should not

Young John Calvin Even in youth, Calvin's face showed the strength and determination that was later to characterize his religious zeal. *(Geneva, CIG, coll. Bibliothèque publique et universitaire)*

spare his child, . . . nor husband his own wife or the friend who is dearer to him than life. No human relationship is more than animal unless it be grounded in God.[21]

In the 1550s, Spanish humanist Michael Servetus had gained international notoriety for his publications denying the Christian dogma of the Trinity. Servetus had been arrested by the Inquisition but escaped to Geneva, where he was promptly rearrested. At his trial, he not only held to his belief that there is no scriptural basis for the Trinity but also rejected child baptism and insisted that a person under twenty cannot commit a mortal sin. The city fathers considered this last idea dangerous to public morality, "especially in these days when the young are so corrupted." Though Servetus begged that he be punished by banishment, Calvin and the town council maintained that the denial of child baptism and the Trinity amounted to a threat to all society. Servetus was burned at the stake.

To many sixteenth-century Europeans, Calvin's Geneva seemed "the most perfect school of Christ since the days of the Apostles." Religious refugees from France, England, Spain, Scotland, and Italy visited the city. Subsequently, the Reformed church of Calvin served as the model for the Presbyterian church in Scotland, the Huguenot church in France, and the Puritan churches in England and New England. For women, the Calvinist provision for congregational participation and vernacular liturgy helped satisfy their desire to belong to and participate in a meaningful church organization.

On women the views of reformers such as Calvin did not differ much from those of medieval Scholastic theologians. Protestants exalted marriage, stressing the husband's authority over his family and the wife's duty of obedience to her husband. Marriage provided the outlet for women's sexual urges, which reformers believed were stronger than men's. Calvin and other reformers did not distinguish between noblewomen and commoners, but they recognized that noblewomen had influence and power. Thus Calvin maintained a large correspondence with them and worked hard to persuade Marguerite d'Angoulême and her daughter Jeanne of Navarre to support the Calvinist cause. Most women expressed their religious feelings in a domestic setting—praying, reciting the catechism, and reading the Bible with their children and servants. As public welfare, long the responsibility of local Catholic institutions, became secularized, well-to-do Protestant women aided the poor on a case-by-case basis; some wealthy women founded and endowed schools, orphanages, and dowries for girls and provided funds for poor widows. Women's charitable interests focused specifically on other women.[22]

Calvinism became the compelling force in international Protestantism. The Calvinist ethic of the "calling" dignified all work with a religious aspect. Hard work, well done, was pleasing to God. This doctrine encouraged an aggressive, vigorous activism. These factors, together with the social and economic applications of Calvin's theology, made Calvinism the most dynamic force in sixteenth- and seventeenth-century Protestantism.

The Anabaptists

The name *Anabaptist* derives from a Greek word meaning "to baptize again." The **Anabaptists** believed that only adults could make a free choice about religious faith, baptism, and entry into the Christian community. Thus they considered the practice of baptizing infants and children preposterous and claimed there was no scriptural basis for it. They wanted to rebaptize believers who had been baptized as children. Anabaptists took the Gospel and, at first, Luther's teachings absolutely literally and favored a return to the kind of church that they thought had existed among the earliest Christians—a voluntary association of believers who had experienced an inner light.

Anabaptists maintained that only a few people would receive the inner light. This position meant that the Christian community and the Christian state were not identical. In other words, Anabaptists believed in religious toleration. They almost never tried to force their values on others. In an age that believed in the necessity of state-established churches, Anabaptist views on religious liberty were thought to undermine that concept. Each Anabaptist community or church was entirely independent; it selected its own ministers and ran its own affairs.

Anabaptists admitted women to the ministry. They shared goods as the early Christians had done, refused all public offices, and would not serve in the armed forces. In fact, they laid great stress on pacifism. A favorite Anabaptist scriptural quotation was "By their fruits you shall know them," suggesting that if Christianity was a religion of peace, then the Christian should not fight. Good deeds were the sign of Christian faith, and to be a Christian meant to imitate the meekness and mercy of Christ. With such beliefs Anabaptists were inevitably a minority. Anabaptism later attracted the poor, the unemployed, and the uneducated. Geographically, Anabaptists drew their members from depressed urban areas—from among the followers of Zwingli in Zurich and from Basel, Augsburg, and Nuremberg.

Ideas such as absolute pacifism and the distinction between the Christian community and the state brought down on these unfortunate people fanatical hatred and bitter persecution. Zwingli, Luther, Calvin, and Catholics all saw—quite correctly—the separation of church and state as leading ultimately to the complete secularization of society. The powerful rulers of Swiss and German society immediately saw the connection between religious heresy and economic dislocation. Civil authorities feared that the combination of religious differences and economic grievances would lead to civil disturbances. In Saxony, in Strasbourg, and in the Swiss cities, Anabaptists were either banished or cruelly executed by burning, beating, or drowning. Their community spirit and the edifying example of their lives, however, contributed to the survival of Anabaptist ideas. Later, the Quakers, with their gentle pacifism; the Baptists, with their emphasis on an inner spiritual light; the Congregationalists, with their democratic church organization; and, in 1787, the authors of the U.S. Constitution, with their opposition to the "establishment of religion" (state churches), would all trace their origins, in part, to the Anabaptists of the sixteenth century.

The English Reformation

As on the continent, the Reformation in England had economic causes as well as religious ones. When the personal matter of the divorce of King Henry VIII (r. 1509–1547) became enmeshed with political issues, a complete break with Rome resulted.

Demands for ecclesiastical reform dated back at least to the fourteenth century. The Lollards (see page 394) had been driven underground in the fifteenth century but survived in parts of southern England and the Midlands. Working-class people, especially cloth workers, were attracted to their ideas. The Lollards stressed the individual's reading and interpretation of the Bible, which they considered the only standard of Christian faith and holiness. Consequently, they put no stock in the value of the sacraments and were vigorously anticlerical. Lollards opposed ecclesiastical wealth, the veneration of the saints, prayers for the dead, and all war. Although they had no notion of justification by faith, like Luther they insisted on the individual soul's direct responsibility to God.

Recent scholarship indicates that the English church was in a very healthy condition in the early sixteenth century. Traditional Catholicism exerted an enormously strong and vigorous hold over the imagination and loyalty of the people. The teachings of Christianity were graphically represented in the liturgy, reiterated in sermons, enacted in plays, carved and printed on walls, screens, and the windows of churches. A zealous clergy, increasingly better educated, engaged in a "massive catechetical enterprise." No substantial gulf existed between the religion of the clergy and educated elite and the broad mass of the English people.[23] The Reformation in England was an act of state initiated by the king's emotional life.

In 1527, having fallen in love with Anne Boleyn, Henry wanted his marriage to Catherine of Aragon annulled. When Henry had married Catherine, he had secured a dispensation from Pope Julius II eliminating all legal technicalities about Catherine's previous union with Henry's late brother, Arthur. Henry claimed that a disputed succession and the anarchy of the Wars of the Roses would be repeated if a woman, the princess Mary, sole surviving child of his marriage to Catherine, inher-

ited the throne. Accordingly, Henry petitioned Pope Clement VII for an annulment, stating that a valid marriage to Catherine had never existed. The pope was an indecisive man whose attention at the time was focused on the Lutheran revolt in Germany and the Habsburg-Valois struggle for control of Italy. But there is a stronger reason Clement could not grant Henry's petition. Henry argued that Pope Julius's dispensation had contradicted the law of God—that a man may not marry his brother's widow. The English king's request reached Rome at the very time that Luther was publishing tracts condemning the papacy as the core of wickedness. Had Clement granted Henry's annulment and thereby admitted that his recent predecessor, Julius II, had erred, Clement would have given support to the Lutheran assertion that popes substituted their own evil judgments for the law of God. This Clement could not do, so he delayed acting on Henry's request.[24] The capture and sack of Rome in 1527 by the emperor Charles V (see the chart on page 467), Queen Catherine's nephew, thoroughly tied the pope's hands.

Since Rome appeared to be thwarting Henry's matrimonial plans, he decided to remove the English church from papal jurisdiction. Henry used Parliament to legalize the Reformation in England. The Act in Restraint of Appeals (1533) declared the king to be the supreme sovereign in England and forbade judicial appeals to the papacy, thus establishing the Crown as the highest legal authority in the land. The Supremacy Act (1534) declared the king the supreme head of the Church of England. Both the Act in Restraint of Appeals and the Supremacy Act led to heated debate in the House of Commons. An authority on the Reformation Parliament has written that probably only a small number of those who voted for the Restraint of Appeals actually knew they were voting for a permanent break with Rome.[25] Some opposed the king. John Fisher, the bishop of Rochester, a distinguished scholar and a humanist, lashed the clergy with scorn for its cowardice in abjectly bending to the king's will. Another humanist, Thomas More, resigned the chancellorship: he could not take the oath required by the Supremacy Act because it rejected papal authority and made the king head of the English church. Fisher, More, and other dissenters were beheaded.

When Anne Boleyn failed twice to produce a male child, Henry VIII charged her with adulterous incest and in 1536 had her beheaded. Parliament promptly proclaimed Anne's daughter, the princess Elizabeth, illegitimate and, with the royal succession thoroughly confused, left the throne to whomever Henry chose. His third wife, Jane Seymour, gave Henry the desired son, Edward, but died in childbirth. Henry went on to three more wives. Before he passed to his reward in 1547, he got Parliament to reverse the decision of 1536, relegitimating Mary and Elizabeth and fixing the succession first in his son and then in his daughters.

Between 1535 and 1539, under the influence of his chief minister, Thomas Cromwell, Henry decided to dissolve the English monasteries because he wanted their wealth. The king ended nine hundred years of English monastic life, dispersed the monks and nuns, and confiscated their lands. Hundreds of properties were sold to the middle and upper classes and the proceeds spent on war. The dissolution of the monasteries did not achieve a more equitable distribution of land and wealth. Rather, the "bare ruined choirs where late the sweet birds sang"—as Shakespeare described in Sonnet 73 the desolate religious houses—testified to the loss of a valuable cultural force in English life. The redistribution of land strengthened the upper classes and tied them to the Tudor dynasty.

Did the religious changes accompanying this political upheaval have broad popular support? The surviving evidence does not allow us to gauge the degree of opposition to (or support for) Henry's break with Rome. Certainly, many laypeople wrote to the king begging him to spare the monasteries. "Most laypeople acquiesced in the Reformation because they hardly knew what was going on, were understandably reluctant to jeopardise life or limb, a career or the family's good name."[26] But all did not quietly acquiesce. In 1536 popular opposition in the north to the religious changes led to the Pilgrimage of Grace, a massive multiclass rebellion that proved the largest in English history. The "pilgrims" accepted a truce, and their leaders were arrested, tried, and executed. In 1546 serious rebellions in East Anglia and in the west, despite possessing economic and Protestant components, reflected considerable public opposition to the state-ordered religious changes.[27]

Henry's motives combined personal, political, social, and economic elements. Theologically he retained such traditional Catholic practices and doctrines as auricular confession, clerical celibacy, and transubstantiation. Meanwhile, Protestant literature circulated, and Henry approved the selection of men of Protestant sympathies as tutors for his son.

The nationalization of the church and the dissolution of the monasteries led to important changes in government administration. Vast tracts of formerly monastic land came temporarily under the Crown's jurisdiction, and new bureaucratic machinery had to be developed to manage those properties. Cromwell reformed and centralized the king's household, the council, the secretariats, and the Exchequer. New departments of state were set up. Surplus funds from all of the departments went into a liquid fund to be applied to areas where there were deficits. This balancing resulted in greater efficiency and economy. Henry VIII's reign saw the growth of the modern centralized bureaucratic state.

In the short reign of Henry's sickly son, Edward VI (r. 1547–1553), strongly Protestant ideas exerted a significant influence on the religious life of the country. Archbishop Thomas Cranmer simplified the liturgy, invited Protestant theologians to England, and prepared the first **Book of Common Prayer** (1549). In stately and dignified English, the *Book of Common Prayer* included, together with the Psalter, the order for all services of the Church of England.

The equally brief reign of Mary Tudor (r. 1553–1558) witnessed a sharp move back to Catholicism. The devoutly Catholic daughter of Catherine of Aragon, Mary rescinded the Reformation legislation of her father's reign and restored Roman Catholicism. Mary's marriage to her cousin Philip of Spain, son of the emperor Charles V, proved highly unpopular in England, and her execution of several hundred Protestants further alienated her subjects. During her reign, many Protestants fled to the continent. Mary's death raised to the throne her sister, Elizabeth (r. 1558–1603), and inaugurated the beginnings of religious stability.

Elizabeth had been raised a Protestant, but at the start of her reign sharp differences existed in England. On the one hand, Catholics wanted a Roman Catholic ruler. On the other hand, a vocal number of returning exiles wanted all Catholic elements in the Church of England eliminated. The latter, because they wanted to "purify" the church, were called "Puritans." Probably one of the shrewdest politicians in English history, Elizabeth chose a middle course between Catholic and Puritan extremes. She insisted on dignity in church services and political order in the land. She did not care what people believed as long as they kept quiet about it. Avoiding precise doctrinal definitions, Elizabeth had herself styled "Supreme Governor of the Church of England, Etc.," and left it to her subjects to decide what the "Etc." meant.

The parliamentary legislation of the early years of Elizabeth's reign—laws sometimes labeled the **Elizabethan Settlement**—required outward conformity to the Church of England and uniformity in all ceremonies. Everyone had to attend Church of England services; those who refused were fined. In 1563 a convocation of bishops approved the Thirty-nine Articles, a summary in thirty-nine

Allegory of the Tudor Dynasty The unknown creator of this work intended to glorify the virtues of the Protestant succession; the painting has no historical reality. Enthroned Henry VIII (r. 1509–1547) hands the sword of justice to his Protestant son Edward VI (r. 1547–1553). The Catholic Queen Mary (r. 1553–1558) and her husband Philip of Spain are followed by Mars, god of war, signifying violence and civil disorder. At right the figures of Peace and Plenty accompany the Protestant Elizabeth I (r. 1558–1603), symbolizing England's happy fate under her rule. *(Yale Center for British Art, Paul Mellon Collection/The Bridgeman Art Library)*

short statements of the basic tenets of the Church of England. During Elizabeth's reign, the Anglican church (from the Latin *Ecclesia Anglicana*), as the Church of England was called, moved in a moderately Protestant direction. Services were conducted in English, monasteries were not re-established, and clergymen were allowed to marry. But the episcopate was not abolished and the bishops remained as church officials; apart from language, the services were quite traditional.

The Establishment of the Church of Scotland

In Scotland as elsewhere, political authority was the decisive influence in reform. The monarchy was weak, and factions of virtually independent nobles competed for power. King James V and his daughter, Mary, Queen of Scots (r. 1560–1567), staunch Catholics and close allies of Catholic France, opposed reform. The Scottish nobles supported it. One man, John Knox (1505?–1572), dominated the movement for reform in Scotland.

In 1559 Knox, a dour, single-minded, and fearless man with a reputation as a passionate preacher, set to work reforming the church. He had studied and worked with Calvin in Geneva and was determined to structure the Scottish church after the model of Calvin's Geneva. In 1560 Knox persuaded the Scottish parliament, which was dominated by reform-minded barons, to enact legislation ending papal authority. The Mass was abolished. Knox then established the Presbyterian Church of Scotland, so named because *presbyters,* or ministers, not bishops, governed it. The Church of Scotland was strictly Calvinist in doctrine, adopted a simple and dignified service of worship, and laid great emphasis on preaching. Knox's *Book of Common Order* (1564) became the liturgical directory for the church. The Presbyterian Church of Scotland was a national, or state, church, and many of its members maintained close relations with English Puritans.

Protestantism in Ireland

To the ancient Irish hatred of English political and commercial exploitation, the Reformation added the bitter antagonism of religion. Henry VIII wanted to "reduce that realm to the knowledge of God and obedience to us." English rulers in the sixteenth century regarded the Irish as barbarians, and a policy of complete extermination was rejected only because "to enterprise [attempt] the whole extirpation and total destruction of all the Irishmen in the land would be a marvelous sumptious charge and great difficulty."[28] In other words, it would have cost too much.

In 1536 on orders from London, the Irish parliament, which represented only the English landlords and the people of the Pale (the area around Dublin), approved the English laws severing the church from Rome and making the English king sovereign over ecclesiastical organization and practice. The Church of Ireland was established on the English pattern, and the (English) ruling class adopted the new reformed faith. Most of the Irish, probably for political reasons, defiantly remained Roman Catholic. Monasteries were secularized. Catholic property was confiscated and sold and the profits were shipped to England. With the Roman church driven underground, Catholic churchmen acted as national as well as religious leaders.

Lutheranism in Sweden, Norway, and Denmark

In Sweden, Norway, and Denmark, the monarchy took the initiative in the religious Reformation. The resulting institutions were Lutheran state churches. Since the late fourteenth century, the Danish kings had ruled Sweden and Norway as well as Denmark. In 1520 Swedish nobleman Gustavus Vasa (r. 1523–1560) led a successful revolt against Denmark, and Sweden became independent. As king, Gustavus Vasa seized church lands and required the bishops' loyalty to the Swedish crown. Wittenberg-educated Swedish reformer Olaus Petri (1493–1552) translated the New Testament into Swedish and, with the full support of Gustavus Vasa, organized the church along strict Lutheran lines. This consolidation of the Swedish monarchy in the sixteenth century was to profoundly affect the development of Germany in the seventeenth century.

Christian III, king of Denmark (r. 1503–1559) and of Norway (r. 1534–1559), secularized church property and set up a Lutheran church. Norway, which was governed by Denmark until 1814, adopted Lutheranism as its state religion under Danish influence.

The Reformation in Eastern Europe

While political and economic issues determined the course of the Reformation in western and northern Europe, ethnic factors often proved decisive in eastern Europe. In the later Middle Ages, the migration of diverse peoples into Bohemia, Poland, and Hungary meant that in the sixteenth century those countries had heterogeneous populations. Ethnic background tended to resolve religious matters.

In Bohemia in the fifteenth century, the ethnic grievances of the Czech majority against German economic and ecclesiastical domination (see page 404) fused with Czech resentment at the corruption of the Roman church. By 1500, most Czechs had adopted Jan Hus's utraquist position (communion in both bread and wine). Germans adhered to the Roman Catholic tenet. Martin Luther's approval of utraquism led to the rapid spread of Lutheranism among Germans in Bohemia in the 1520s and 1530s; many Germans lived near the border of Luther's Saxony. Though a practicing Catholic and brother of the Habsburg emperor Charles V, King Ferdinand I of Bohemia had to acquiesce in the establishment of utraquism to become king, thereby aiding the spread of Lutheranism. Moreover, the nobility's identification of Lutheranism with opposition to the Habsburgs contributed, as in Germany, to the growth of Protestantism. Ferdinand's successors Maximilian II and Rudolf II had more tolerant religious policies, but the forces of Counter-Reformation spearheaded by the Council of Trent (see pages 479–480) promoted a Catholic spiritual revival in Bohemia. The contest between the ruler and the nobility would be resolved only in the Thirty Years' War (see pages 497–501).

By 1500 Poland and the Grand Duchy of Lithuania were united in a dynastic union. A king, senate, and diet (parliament) governed, but the two territories retained separate officials, judicial systems, armies, and forms of citizenship. In the fifteenth century, rulers had granted the Polish *szlachta* (nobility) extensive rights; though hereditary, the monarchy was weak and had to cooperate with the szlachta. The combined realms covered about 440,150 square miles, making Poland-Lithuania the largest European polity. A population of only about 7.5 million people was very thinly scattered over that land.

In comparison with western Europe, Poland-Lithuania was overwhelmingly rural, its largest cities Gdansk (30,000) and Cracow (15,000) very small in population by Italian or French standards. Yet with Germans, Italians, Tartars, and Jews, Poland-Lithuania represented great diversity. Such peoples had come as merchants, invited by medieval rulers because of their wealth or to make agricultural improvements. Each group spoke its native language, though all educated people spoke Latin. In the late fifteenth century, Italian Renaissance humanism influenced Polish art, architecture, literature, and historical writing.

Luther's ideas spread first to the German-speaking Baltic towns, then to the University of Cracow, where his works were translated. His ideas met two major obstacles: King Sigismund I (r. 1506–1548) banned Luther's teachings in Poland, and strong anti-German feeling among Poles meant that Lutheranism would have limited success outside Germanized towns.

The Reformed tradition of John Calvin, with its stress on the power of church elders, appealed to the Polish szlachta, however. The fact that Calvinism originated in France, not in Germany, also made it more attractive than Lutheranism. Several Polish magnates, including Jan Laski (1499–1560), converted to Calvinism, and Calvinist nobles dominated the important diet of 1555. But doctrinal differences among Calvinists, Lutherans, and other sects prevented united opposition to Catholicism.

Under Stanislaus Hosius (1505–1579), who attended the Council of Trent, a systematic Counter-Reformation gained momentum. Hosius pressed for reform within the Catholic church, held provincial synods, and published a comprehensive and clear statement of Roman Catholic faith and morals. The Jesuits (see page 483) complemented his work by establishing schools for the sons of the szlachta. By 1650, the identification of Poland and Roman Catholicism was well established.

Merchants from Poland carried the first news about Martin Luther to Hungary in 1521. Hungarian students flocked to Wittenberg; they became the major agents for the spread of Lutheranism in Hungary, and sympathy for it developed at the royal court at Buda. But concern about "the German heresy" in the Catholic hierarchy and among the magnates found expression in a decree of the Hungarian diet in 1523 that "all Lutherans and those favoring them . . . should have their property confiscated and themselves punished with death as heretics."[29]

A military event on August 26, 1526, had profound consequences for both the Hungarian state and the Protestant Reformation there. On the plain of Mohács in southern Hungary, the Ottoman sultan Suleiman the Magnificent (see page 570) inflicted a crushing defeat on the Hungarians, killing King Louis II, many of the magnates, and over sixteen thousand ordinary soldiers. Rival factions elected different kings, and the Hungarian kingdom was divided into three parts: the Ottoman Turks absorbed the great plains, including the capital, Buda; the Habsburgs ruled the north and west; Ottoman-supported Janos Zapolya held eastern Hungary and Transylvania. The Turks were indifferent to the religious conflicts of the infidels.

Mohács led to a great advance of Protestantism. Many Magyar (Hungarian) magnates accepted Lutheranism; Lutheran schools and parishes headed by men educated at Wittenberg multiplied; peasants welcomed the new faith. In spite of the foundation of Jesuit colleges, in 1585 the papal nuncio noted that 85 percent of the population was Protestant, 10 percent remained Greek Orthodox, and just 5 percent (concentrated in Croatia) stayed Catholic. Hungary seemed lost to Catholicism. Then in the late seventeenth century, Hungarian nobles' recognition of Habsburg (Catholic) rule, and Ottoman Turkish withdrawal in 1699, led to Catholic restoration.

The Catholic Reformation and the Counter-Reformation

Between 1517 and 1547, the reformed versions of Christianity known as Protestantism made remarkable advances. Nevertheless, the Roman Catholic church made a significant comeback. After about 1540, no new large areas of Europe, except for the Netherlands, accepted Protestant beliefs (see Map 14.2).

Historians distinguish between two types of reform within the Catholic church in the sixteenth and seventeenth centuries. The Catholic Reformation began before 1517 and sought renewal basically through the stimulation of a new spiritual fervor. The Counter-Reformation started in the 1540s as a reaction to the rise and spread of Protestantism. The Counter-Reformation involved Catholic efforts to convince or coerce dissidents or heretics to return to the church lest they corrupt the entire community of Catholic believers. Fear of the "infection" of all Christian society by the religious dissident was a standard sixteenth-century attitude. If the heretic could not be persuaded to reconvert, counter-reformers believed it necessary to call on temporal authorities to defend Christian society by expelling or eliminating the dissident. The Catholic Reformation and the Counter-Reformation were not mutually exclusive; in fact, after about 1540 they progressed simultaneously.

The Slowness of Institutional Reform

The Renaissance princes who sat on the throne of Saint Peter were not blind to the evils that existed. Modest reform efforts had begun with the Lateran Council called in 1512 by Pope Julius II. The Dutch pope Adrian VI

MAP 14.2 The Protestant and the Catholic Reformations The Reformations shattered the religious unity of Western Christendom. What common cultural traits predominated in regions where a particular branch of the Christian faith was maintained or took root?

(1522–1523) instructed his legate in Germany to "say that we frankly confess that God permits this [Lutheran] persecution of his church on account of the sins of men, especially those of the priests and prelates. . . . We know that in this Holy See now for some years there have been many abominations."[30] Adrian VI tried desperately to reform the church and to check the spread of Protestantism. His reign lasted only thirteen months, however, and the austerity of his life and his Dutch nationality provoked the hostility of pleasure-loving Italian curial bureaucrats.

Overall, why did the popes, spiritual leaders of the Western church, move so slowly? The answers lie in the personalities of the popes themselves, their preoccupation with political affairs in Italy, and the awesome difficulty of reforming so complicated a bureaucracy as the Roman curia.

Clement VII (r. 1523–1534), a true Medici, was far more interested in elegant tapestries and Michelangelo's painting of the Last Judgment than in theological disputes in barbaric Germany. Indecisive and vacillating, Pope Clement must bear much of the responsibility for the great spread of Protestantism. While Emperor Charles V and the French king Francis I competed for the domination of divided Italy, the papacy worried about the security of the Papal States. Clement tried to follow a middle course, backing first the emperor and then the French ruler. At the Battle of Pavia in 1525, Francis I suffered a severe defeat and was captured. In a reshuffling of diplomatic alliances, the pope switched from Charles and the Spanish to Francis I. In retaliation for Clement's diplomatic shift, and to pay his near mutinous soldiers, Charles allowed his German and Spanish troops to sack Rome (May 1527) and to capture the pope. With the city destroyed, its art treasures stolen, and its population decimated, a contemporary reported that "hell itself must have been a prettier sight." The event marked the end of the High Renaissance in Rome.

The idea of reform was closely linked to the idea of a general council representing the entire church. A strong contingent of countries beyond the Alps—Spain, Germany, and France—wanted to reform the vast bureaucracy of Latin officials, reducing offices, men, and revenues. Popes from Julius II to Clement VII, remembering fifteenth-century conciliar attempts to limit papal authority, resisted calls for a council. The papal bureaucrats who were the popes' intimates warned the popes against a council, fearing loss of power, revenue, and prestige.

The Council of Trent

In the papal conclave that followed the death of Clement VII, Cardinal Alexander Farnese promised two German cardinals that if he was elected pope, he would summon a council. He won the election and ruled as Pope Paul III (1534–1549). This Roman aristocrat, humanist, and astrologer, who immediately made his teenage grandsons cardinals, seemed an unlikely person to undertake serious reform. Yet Paul III appointed as cardinals several reform-minded men, such as Gian Pietro Caraffa (later Pope Paul IV); established the Inquisition in the Papal States; and—true to his word—called a council, which finally met at Trent, an imperial city close to Italy.

The Council of Trent met intermittently from 1545 to 1563. It was called not only to reform the church but also to secure reconciliation with the Protestants. Lutherans and Calvinists were invited to participate, but their insistence that the Scriptures be the sole basis for discussion made reconciliation impossible. International politics repeatedly cast a shadow over the theological debates. Charles V opposed discussions on any matter that might further alienate his Lutheran subjects, fearing the loss of additional imperial territory to Lutheran princes. Meanwhile, the French kings worked against the reconciliation of Roman Catholicism and Lutheranism. As long as religious issues divided the German states, the empire would be weakened, and a weak and divided empire meant a stronger France. Portugal, Poland, Hungary, and Ireland sent representatives, but very few German bishops attended.

Another problem was the persistence of the conciliar theory of church government (see page 394). Some bishops wanted a concrete statement asserting the supremacy of a church council over the papacy, but the centralizing tenet was established that all acts of the council required papal approval.

In spite of the obstacles, the achievements of the Council of Trent were impressive. It dealt with both doctrinal and disciplinary matters. The council gave equal validity to the Scriptures and to tradition as sources of religious truth and authority. It reaffirmed the seven sacraments and the traditional Catholic teaching on transubstantiation. Thus it rejected Lutheran and Calvinist positions.

The council tackled the problems arising from ancient abuses by strengthening ecclesiastical discipline. Tridentine (from *Tridentum,* the Latin word for Trent) decrees required bishops to reside in their own dioceses, suppressed pluralism and simony, and forbade the sale of indulgences. Clerics who kept concubines were to give them up. The jurisdiction of bishops over all the clergy of their dioceses was made almost absolute, and bishops were ordered to visit every religious house within the diocese at least once every two years. In a highly original canon, the council required every diocese to establish a seminary for the education and training of the clergy; the council even

School of Titian: The Council of Trent   Since the early sessions were sparsely attended, this well-attended meeting seems to be a later session. Few bishops from northern Europe, however, ever attended. The Swiss guards (*forefront*) of the Vatican were founded by Pope Julius II in 1505 to defend the papacy. (*Louvre/Réunion des Musées Nationaux/Art Resource, NY*)

prescribed the curriculum and insisted that preference for admission be given to sons of the poor. Seminary professors were to determine if candidates for ordination had *vocations,* genuine callings as determined by purity of life, detachment from the broader secular culture, and a steady inclination toward the priesthood. This was a novel idea since from the time of the early church, parents had determined their sons' (and daughters') religious careers (see page 205). Finally, great emphasis was laid on preaching and instructing the laity, especially the uneducated.

One decision had especially important social consequences for laypeople. Since the time of the Roman Empire, many couples had treated marriage as a completely personal matter, exchanged vows privately without witnesses, and thus formed what were called clandestine (secret) unions. This widespread practice frequently led later to denials by one party, conflicts over property, and disputes in the ecclesiastical courts that had jurisdiction over marriage once it became a sacrament (which occurred in the twelfth century). The Tridentine decree Tametsi (November 1563) stipulated that for a marriage

to be valid, consent (the essence of marriage) as given in the vows had to be made publicly before witnesses, one of whom had to be the parish priest. Trent thereby ended secret marriages in Catholic countries. (They remained a problem for civil and church courts in England until the Hardwicke Act of 1753 abolished them.)

The Council of Trent did not meet everyone's expectations. Reconciliation with Protestantism was not achieved, nor was reform brought about immediately. Nevertheless, the Tridentine decrees laid a solid basis for the spiritual renewal of the church and for the enforcement of correction. For four centuries, the doctrinal and disciplinary legislation of Trent served as the basis for Roman Catholic faith, organization, and practice.

New Religious Orders

The establishment of new religious orders within the church reveals a central feature of the Catholic Reformation. Most of these new orders developed in response to one crying need: to raise the moral and intellectual level

Individuals in Society

Teresa of Ávila

Her family derived from Toledo, center of the Moorish, Jewish, and Christian cultures in medieval Spain. Her grandfather, Juan Sanchez, made a fortune in the cloth trade. A "New Christian" (see pages 445–446), he was accused of secretly practicing Judaism. Although he endured the humiliation of a public repentance, he moved his family south to Ávila. Beginning again, he recouped his wealth and, aspiring to the prestige of an "Old Christian," bought noble status. Juan's son Alzonzo Sanchez de Cepeda married a woman of thoroughly Christian background, giving his family an aura of impeccable orthodoxy. The third of their nine children, Teresa, became a saint and the first woman declared a Doctor of the Church—a theologian of outstanding merit and saintliness (1970).

At age twenty, inspired more by the fear of Hell than the love of God, Teresa (1515–1582) entered the Carmelite Convent of the Incarnation in Ávila. The 140 nuns there were supported by rents from their lands; they did not practice poverty. Nor did they observe enclosure, as guests were frequently entertained. The nuns, privileged daughters of Ávila's leading citizens, were obsessed with status and social prestige.

For twenty years Teresa remained in this worldly atmosphere that contradicted the convent's religious ideals. Francesco de Osuna's book *The Third Spiritual Alphabet* introduced Teresa to a more meaningful spiritual life, and she began to devour devotional literature. In her late thirties, she had profound mystical experiences—visions and voices in which Christ chastised her for her frivolous life and friends. She described one such experience in 1560:

It pleased the Lord that I should see an angel. . . . Short, and very beautiful, his face was so aflame that he appeared to be one of the highest types of angels. . . . In his hands I saw a long golden spear and at the end of an iron tip I seemed to see a point of fire. With this he seemed to pierce my heart several times so that it penetrated to my entrails. When he drew it out . . . he left me completely afire with the great love of God.*

Teresa responded with a new sense of purpose: although she encountered stiff opposition, she resolved to found a reformed house. Four basic principles were to guide the new convent. First, poverty was to be fully observed, symbolized by the nuns being barefoot, hence *discalced*. Ending a long-established monastic practice, Teresa rejected rents: charity and the nuns' own work must support the community. Second, the convent must keep strict enclosure; the visits of powerful benefactors with material demands were forbidden. Third, Teresa intended an egalitarian atmosphere where class distinctions were forbidden. She had always rejected the emphasis on "purity of blood," a distinctive and racist feature of Spanish society especially out of place in the cloister. All sisters, including those of aristocratic background, must share the manual chores. Finally, like Ignatius Loyola and the Jesuits, Teresa placed great emphasis on obedience, especially to one's confessor.

Seventeenth-century cloisonné enamelwork illustrating Teresa of Ávila's famous vision. (By gracious permission of Catherine Hamilton Kappauf)

Between 1562 and Teresa's death in 1582, she founded or reformed fourteen other houses of nuns, no small feat for a woman in a very sexist society. She was the first spiritual author to provide a scientific description of the life of prayer from simple meditation to mystical union with God. Her books, along with her five hundred extant letters, show her as capable of great discernment of individual character. But for all her mystical experiences, Teresa was a motherly, practical, and down-to-earth woman with a strong sense of humor. From her brother who had obtained wealth in the Spanish colonies, Teresa learned about conditions in Peru and instructed her nuns "to pray unceasingly for the missionaries working among the heathens." In this way, they shared in evangelization.

Teresa of Ávila responded to change not with doubt, but with deeper belief.

Questions for Analysis

1. How did sixteenth-century convent life reflect the values of Spanish society?
2. How does Teresa of Ávila represent the spirit of the Catholic Reformation?

**The Autobiography of St. Teresa of Ávila,* trans. and ed. E. A. Peers (New York: Doubleday, 1960), pp. 273–274.

The **history companion** *features additional information and activities related to this topic.* history.college.hmco.com/students

Juan de Valdes Leal: Pope Paul III Approves the Jesuit Constitutions   Although Paul III devoted considerable energy to advancing the interests of his (Farnese) family, he also tried to meet the challenge of Protestantism—through the Council of Trent and new religious orders. When the Jesuit constitutions were read to him, Paul III supposedly murmured, "There is the finger of God." The portrait of Ignatius Loyola is a reasonable likeness, that of the pope an idealization: in 1540 he was a very old man. *(Institut Amatller d'Art Hispanic)*

of the clergy and people. (See the feature "Individuals in Society: Teresa of Ávila.") Education was a major goal of the two most famous orders.

The Ursuline order of nuns, founded by Angela Merici (1474–1540), attained enormous prestige for the education of women. The daughter of a country gentleman, Angela Merici worked for many years among the poor, sick, and uneducated around her native Brescia in northern Italy. In 1535 she established the Ursuline order to combat heresy through Christian education. The first women's religious order concentrating exclusively on teaching young girls, the Ursulines sought to re-Christianize society by training future wives and mothers. Because the Council of Trent placed great stress on the *claustration* (strict enclosure) of religious women and called for the end of all active ministries for women, Angela had great difficulty gaining papal approval. Official recognition finally came in 1565, and the Ursulines rapidly spread to France and the New World. Their schools in North America, stretching from Quebec to New Orleans, provided superior education for young women and inculcated the spiritual ideals of the Catholic Reformation.

The Society of Jesus, founded by Ignatius Loyola (1491–1556), a former Spanish soldier, played a powerful international role in resisting the spread of Protestantism, converting Asians and Latin American Indians to Catholicism, and spreading Christian education all over Europe. While recuperating from a severe battle wound in his legs, Loyola studied a life of Christ and other religious books and decided to give up his military career and become a soldier of Christ. During a year spent in seclusion, prayer, and personal mortification, he gained insights that went into his great classic, *Spiritual Exercises* (1548). This work, intended for study during a four-week period of retreat, directed the individual imagination and will to the reform of life and a new spiritual piety.

Loyola was a man of considerable personal magnetism. After study at universities in Salamanca and Paris, he gathered a group of six companions and in 1540 secured papal approval of the new Society of Jesus, whose members were called **Jesuits.** The first Jesuits, recruited primarily from the wealthy merchant and professional classes, saw the Reformation as a pastoral problem, its causes and cures related not to doctrinal issues but to people's spiritual condition. Reform of the church, as Luther and Calvin understood that term, played no role in the future the Jesuits planned for themselves. Their goal was "to help souls." Loyola also possessed a gift for leadership that consisted in spotting talent and in seeing "how at a given juncture change is more consistent with one's scope than staying the course."[31]

The Society of Jesus developed into a highly centralized, tightly knit organization. Candidates underwent a two-year novitiate, in contrast to the usual one-year probation. In addition to the traditional vows of poverty, chastity, and obedience, professed members vowed "special obedience to the sovereign pontiff regarding missions."[32] Thus as stability—the promise to live his life in the monastery—was what made a monk, so mobility—the commitment to go anywhere for the help of souls—was the defining characteristic of a Jesuit. Flexibility and the willingness to respond to the needs of time and circumstance formed the Jesuit tradition. In this respect, Jesuits were very modern, and they attracted many recruits.

They achieved phenomenal success for the papacy and the reformed Catholic church. Jesuit schools adopted the modern humanist curricula and methods, and though they first concentrated on the children of the poor, they were soon educating the sons of the nobility. As confessors and spiritual directors to kings, Jesuits exerted great political influence. Operating on the principle that the end sometimes justifies the means, they were not above spying. Indifferent to physical comfort and personal safety, they carried Christianity to India and Japan before 1550, to Brazil, North America, and the Congo in the seventeenth century. Within Europe the Jesuits brought southern Germany and much of eastern Europe back to Catholicism.

The Congregation of the Holy Office

In 1542 Pope Paul III established the Sacred Congregation of the **Holy Office,** with jurisdiction over the Roman Inquisition, a powerful instrument of the Counter-Reformation. The Inquisition was a committee of six cardinals with judicial authority over all Catholics and the power to arrest, imprison, and execute. Under the fanatical Cardinal Caraffa, it vigorously attacked heresy.

The Roman Inquisition operated under the principles of Roman law. It accepted hearsay evidence, was not obliged to inform the accused of charges against them, and sometimes applied torture. Echoing one of Calvin's remarks about heresy, Cardinal Caraffa wrote, "No man is to lower himself by showing toleration towards any sort of heretic, least of all a Calvinist."[33] The Holy Office published the *Index of Prohibited Books,* a catalogue of forbidden reading.

Within the Papal States, the Inquisition effectively destroyed heresy (and some heretics). Outside the papal territories, however, its influence was slight. In Venice, a major publishing center, the *Index* had no influence on scholarly research in nonreligious areas such as law, classical literature, and mathematics. As a result of the Inquisition, Venetians and Italians were *not* cut off from the main currents of European learning.

The Reformations: Revolution or Continuity?

The introduction to this chapter casts reformation in general in terms of the individual Christian's and the institutional church's continual need and search for reform. Indeed, the first critical moment came with one man, Martin Luther, whose inner questioning about his own salvation led to his criticism of the Roman papacy. Historians ask a central question: do the sixteenth-century religious movements represent continuity—a constant feature of the institutional faith—or do those movements demonstrate revolution and radical discontinuity? Recent scholarly research argues that the Reformations constituted both.

Revolution, by definition, rejects the status quo. Protestantism rejected the authority of the Roman papacy. The appearance and growth of new churches—such as Lutheran, Calvinist, Anabaptist, and Anglican in the sixteenth century and Baptist, Quaker, and Methodist, among others, in the seventeenth and eighteenth centuries—represent revolution and a radical discontinuity from the religious situation in Europe over the previous thousand years. Whereas previously there had been one Christian church to which all Christians at least nominally belonged, after 1555 there were many. Protestantism meant fragmentation.

Moreover, some historians, mainly Protestant ones, have identified Protestantism with "modernity," by which they mean not only rejection of the Middle Ages and that period's main symbol, the Roman church, but also the embrace of light and genius. By contrast, students of the Catholic church have seen the Reformations in terms of continuity. While acknowledging that there were grave abuses in the institutional church, these scholars stress that serious movements for reform began in the fifteenth century. The Brethren of the Common Life in the Low Countries, the reforming efforts of Francisco Jiménez de Cisneros in Spain, the preaching programs of the friars, and the Lateran Council of 1512 all antedate Martin Luther. Within the Roman church, there was a great deal of spiritual vitality and many serious attempts to spread the Gospel message (see pages 455–456). After about 1550, the focus shifted from an emphasis on the church as an institution—its powers and prerogatives—to what both the Council of Trent and the Jesuits called "what's good for souls." The Catholic church became a pastoral and a missionary church.[34]

Summary

Martin Luther's strictly religious call for reform, rapidly spread by preaching, hymns, and the printing press, soon became enmeshed in social, economic, and political issues. The German peasants interpreted Luther's ideas in an economic sense: Christian liberty for them meant the end of harsh manorial burdens. Princes used the cloak of the new religious ideas to acquire the material wealth of the church and to thwart the centralizing goals of the emperor. In England the political issue of the royal succession triggered that country's break with Rome, and in

Switzerland and France the political and social ethos of Calvinism attracted many people. The Protestant doctrine that all callings have equal merit in God's sight and its stress on the home as the special domain of women drew women to Protestantism. The reformulation of Roman Catholic doctrine at the Council of Trent and the new religious orders such as the Jesuits and the Ursulines represented the Catholic response to the demands for reform.

Religious belief remained tremendously strong. In fact, the strength of religious convictions caused political fragmentation. In the later sixteenth century and through most of the seventeenth, religion and religious issues continued to play a major role in the lives of individuals and in the policies and actions of governments. Religion, whether Protestant or Catholic, decisively influenced the growth of national states.

Although most of the church reformers rejected the idea of religious toleration, they helped pave the way for it. They also paved the way for the eighteenth-century revolt against the Christian God, one of the strongest supports of life in Western culture. In this respect, the Reformation marked the beginning of the modern world, with its secularism and rootlessness. At the same time, it can equally be argued that the sixteenth century represented the culmination of the Middle Ages. Martin Luther's anxieties about salvation showed him to be very much a medieval man. His concerns had deeply troubled serious individuals since the time of Saint Augustine. In modern times, such concerns have tended to take different forms.

Key Terms

pluralism

The Imitation of Christ

ecumenical council

indulgence

Diet of Worms

Protestant

sola scriptura

transubstantiation

consubstantiation

Lord's Supper

preacherships

peasant revolts

The Institutes of the Christian Religion

predestination

Anabaptists

Book of Common Prayer

Elizabethan Settlement

Jesuits

Holy Office

Notes

1. Quoted in J. Burckhardt, *The Civilization of the Renaissance in Italy* (London: Phaidon Books, 1951), p. 262.
2. See R. R. Post, *The Modern Devotion: Confrontation with Reformation and Humanism* (Leiden: E. J. Brill, 1968), esp. pp. 237–238, 255, 323–348.
3. Quoted in O. Chadwick, *The Reformation* (Baltimore: Penguin Books, 1976), p. 55.
4. Quoted in E. H. Harbison, *The Age of Reformation* (Ithaca, N.Y.: Cornell University Press, 1963), p. 52.
5. This passage leans on ibid., pp. 52–55.
6. See S. E. Ozment, *The Reformation in the Cities: The Appeal of Protestantism to Sixteenth-Century Germany and Switzerland* (New Haven, Conn.: Yale University Press, 1975), pp. 32–45.
7. See S. E. Ozment, *The Age of Reform, 1250–1550: An Intellectual and Religious History of Late Medieval and Reformation Europe* (New Haven, Conn.: Yale University Press, 1980), pp. 273–279.
8. Quoted ibid., p. 280.
9. Ibid., p. 281.
10. Quoted ibid., p. 284.
11. Romans 13:1–2.
12. E. Erikson, *Young Man Luther: A Study in Psychoanalysis and History* (New York: W. W. Norton, 1962), p. 47.
13. G. Strauss, *Luther's House of Learning: Indoctrination of the Young in the German Reformation* (Baltimore: Johns Hopkins University Press, 1978), esp. pp. 159–162, 231–233.
14. See R. H. Bainton, *Women of the Reformation in Germany and Italy* (Minneapolis: Augsburg, 1971), pp. 9–10; and Ozment, *The Reformation in the Cities,* pp. 53–54, 171–172.
15. Quoted in H. G. Haile, *Luther: An Experiment in Biography* (Garden City, N.Y.: Doubleday, 1980), p. 272.
16. Quoted in J. Atkinson, *Martin Luther and the Birth of Protestantism* (Baltimore: Penguin Books, 1968), pp. 247–248.
17. *Martin Luther: Three Treatises* (Philadelphia: Muhlenberg Press, 1947), pp. 28–31.
18. J. Allen, trans., *John Calvin: The Institutes of the Christian Religion* (Philadelphia: Westminster Press, 1930), bk. 3, chap. 21, paras. 5, 7.
19. E. W. Monter, *Calvin's Geneva* (New York: John Wiley & Sons, 1967), pp. 98–108.
20. Ibid., p. 137.
21. Quoted in Bainton, *Women of the Reformation,* pp. 69–70.
22. See M. E. Wiesner-Hanks, "Women," in *The Oxford Encyclopedia of the Reformation,* ed. H. J. Hillerbrand, vol. 4 (New York: Oxford University Press, 1996), pp. 290–298.
23. E. Duffy, *The Stripping of the Altars: Traditional Religion in England, 1400–1580* (New Haven, Conn.: Yale University Press, 1992), pp. 2–6.
24. See R. Marius, *Thomas More: A Biography* (New York: Alfred A. Knopf, 1984), pp. 215–216.
25. See S. E. Lehmberg, *The Reformation Parliament, 1529–1536* (Cambridge: Cambridge University Press, 1970), pp. 174–176, 204–205.
26. J. J. Scarisbrick, *The Reformation and the English People* (Oxford: Basil Blackwell, 1984), p. 81.
27. Ibid.
28. Quoted in P. Smith, *The Age of the Reformation,* rev. ed. (New York: Henry Holt, 1951), p. 346.
29. Quoted in D. P. Daniel, "Hungary," in *The Oxford Encyclopedia of the Reformation,* vol. 2, ed. H. J. Hillerbrand (New York: Oxford University Press, 1996), p. 273.
30. Quoted in Smith, *Age of the Reformation,* p. 84.
31. See J. W. O'Malley, *The First Jesuits* (Cambridge, Mass.: Harvard University Press, 1993), p. 376.
32. Ibid., p. 298.
33. Quoted in Chadwick, *The Reformation,* p. 270.
34. See J. W. O'Malley, *Trent and All That: Renaming Catholicism in the Early Modern Era* (Cambridge, Mass.: Harvard University Press, 2000), chap. 2, et passim.

Suggested Reading

A. Levi, *Renaissance and Reformation: The Intellectual Genesis* (2002), surveys the ideas of major Reformation figures against the background of important political issues. The best reference work is H. J. Hillerbrand, ed., *The Oxford Encyclopedia of the Reformation,* 4 vols. (New York: Oxford University Press, 1996). E. Cameron, *The European Reformation* (1991), provides a comprehensive survey based on recent research; A. Pettegree, ed., *The Early Reformation in Europe* (1992), compares developments in different parts of Europe; and the books by Chadwick and Harbison listed in the Notes are good general introductions. L. W. Spitz, *The Protestant Reformation, 1517–1559* (1985), provides a comprehensive survey that incorporates sound scholarly research. For the trend in scholarship interpreting the Reformation against the background of fifteenth-century reforming developments, see the excellent study of J. F. D'Amico, *Renaissance Humanism in Papal Rome: Humanists and Churchmen on the Eve of the Reformation* (1983); and J. H. Overfield, *Humanism and Scholasticism in Late Medieval Germany* (1984), which portrays the intellectual life of the German universities, the milieu from which the Protestant Reformation emerged.

For the central figure of the early Reformation, Martin Luther, students should see the works by Atkinson, Erikson, and Haile mentioned in the Notes; and G. Brendler, *Martin Luther: Theology and Revolution* (1991), a response to the Marxist interpretation of Luther as a tool of the aristocracy who sold out the peasantry. Beginning as well as advanced students will find a vividly written interpretation of Luther's writings in the recent work by R. Marius, *Martin Luther: The Christian Between God and Death* (1999), which also contains a considerable amount of new information.

The scope of P. Benedict, *Christ's Churches Purely Reformed: A Social History of Calvinism* (2002), is indicated by its title; this is a most important work. The best study of John Calvin is W. J. Bouwsma, *John Calvin: A Sixteenth-Century Portrait* (1988), an authoritative study that situates Calvin within Renaissance culture. D. C. Steinmetz, *Calvin in Context* (1995), treats Calvin as an interpreter of the Bible. W. E. Monter, *Calvin's Geneva* (1967), shows the effect of Calvin's reforms on the social life of that Swiss city. R. T. Kendall, *Calvinism and English Calvinism to 1649* (1981), presents English conditions. Students interested in the left wing of the Reformation should see the profound, though difficult, work of G. H. Williams, *The Radical Reformers* (1962).

For various aspects of the social history of the period, see S. Ozment, *Magdalena and Balthasar* (1987), which reveals many features of social life through the letters of a Nuremberg couple. For women, see M. E. Wiesner, *Women and Gender in Early Modern Europe* (1993); L. Roper, *The Holy Household: Women and Morals in Reformation Augsburg* (1991), an important study in local religious history as well as the history of gender; and M. Wiesner, *Women in the Sixteenth Century: A Bibliography* (1983), a useful reference tool. The best recent treatment of marriage and the family is S. Ozment, *When Fathers Ruled: Family Life in Reformation Europe* (1983). Ozment's edition of *Reformation Europe: A Guide to Research* (1982), contains helpful references.

For England, in addition to the fundamental work by Duffy cited in the Notes, K. Thomas, *Religion and the Decline of Magic* (1971), provides a useful treatment of pre-Reformation popular religion. S. J. Gunn and P. G. Lindley, eds., *Cardinal Wolsey: Church, State and Art* (1991), is a useful study of that important prelate. The marital trials of Henry VIII are treated in both the sympathetic study by G. Mattingly, *Catherine of Aragon* (1949), and A. Fraser, *The Wives of Henry VIII* (1992). The legal implications of Henry VIII's divorces have been thoroughly analyzed in J. J. Scarisbrick, *Henry VIII* (1968), an almost definitive biography. On the dissolution of the English monasteries, see D. Knowles, *The Religious Orders in England,* vol. 3 (1959), one of the finest examples of historical prose in English written in the twentieth century. G. R. Elton, *The Tudor Revolution in Government* (1959), discusses the modernization of English government under Thomas Cromwell, whereas the same author's *Reform and Reformation: England, 1509–1558* (1977), combines political and social history in a broad study.

The definitive study of the Council of Trent was written by H. Jedin, *A History of the Council of Trent,* 3 vols. (1957–1961). For the Jesuits, see W. W. Meissner, *Ignatius of Loyola: The Psychology of a Saint* (1993), and J. W. O'Malley, *The First Jesuits* (1993). These books are basic not only for the beginnings of the Society of Jesus but also for the refutation of many myths. Perhaps the best recent work on the Spanish Inquisition is W. Monter, *Frontiers of Heresy: The Spanish Inquisition from the Basque Lands to Sicily* (1990). For the impact of the Counter-Reformation on ordinary Spanish people, see H. Kamen, *The Phoenix and the Flame: Catalonia and the Counter Reformation* (1993). In exceptionally lucid prose, J. W. O'Malley, *Trent and All That: Renaming Catholicism in the Early Modern Era* (2000), provides an excellent historiographical review of the literature and explains why and how early modern Catholicism influenced early modern European history.

Listening to the Past

Martin Luther, *On Christian Liberty*

*T*he idea of liberty has played a powerful role in the history of Western society and culture; that idea is unique to the European world. But the meaning and understanding of liberty has undergone continual change and interpretation. In the Roman world, where slavery was a basic institution, liberty meant the condition of being a free person, independent of obligations to a master. In the Middle Ages, possessing liberty meant having special privileges or rights that other persons or institutions did not have. A lord or a monastery, for example, might speak of his or its liberties. Likewise, the first chapter of Magna Carta (1215), often called the "Charter of Liberties," states: "Holy Church shall be free and have its rights entire and its liberties inviolate," meaning that the English church was independent of the authority of the king.

The idea of liberty also has a religious dimension, and the reformer Martin Luther formulated a classic interpretation of liberty in his treatise On Christian Liberty, *arguably his finest piece. It contains the main themes of Luther's theology: the importance of faith, the relationship of Christian faith and good works, the dual nature of human beings, and the fundamental importance of Scripture in Christian life.*

Christian faith has appeared to many an easy thing; nay, not a few even reckon it among the social virtues, as it were; and this they do because they have not made proof of it experimentally, and have never tasted of what efficacy it is. For it is not possible for any man to write well about it, or to understand well what is rightly written, who has not at some time tasted of its spirit, under the pressure of tribulation; while he who has tasted of it, even to a very small extent, can never write, speak, think, or hear about it sufficiently. . . .

I hope that . . . I have attained some little drop of faith, and that I can speak of this matter, if not with more elegance, certainly with more solidity. . . .

A Christian man is the most free lord of all, and subject to none; a Christian man is the most dutiful servant of all, and subject to everyone.

Although these statements appear contradictory, yet, when they are found to agree together, they will do excellently for my purpose. They are both the statements of Paul himself, who says, "Though I be free from all men, yet have I made myself a servant unto all" (I Cor. 9:19), and "Owe no man anything but to love one another" (Rom. 13:8). Now love is by its own nature dutiful and obedient to the beloved object. Thus even Christ, though Lord of all things, was yet made of a woman; made under the law; at once free and a servant; at once in the form of God and in the form of a servant.

Let us examine the subject on a deeper and less simple principle. Man is composed of a twofold nature, a spiritual and a bodily. As regards the spiritual nature, which they name the soul, he is called the spiritual, inward, new man; as regards the bodily nature, which they name the flesh, he is called the fleshly, outward, old man. The Apostle speaks of this: "Though our outward man perish, yet the inward man is renewed day by day" (II Cor. 4:16). The result of this diversity is that in the Scriptures opposing statements are made concerning the same man, the fact being that in the same man these two men are opposed to one another; the flesh lusting against the spirit, and the spirit against the flesh (Gal. 5:17).

We first approach the subject of the inward man, that we may see by what means a man becomes justified, free, and a true Christian; that is, a spiritual, new, and inward man. It is certain that absolutely none among outward things, under whatever name they may be reckoned, has any influence in producing Christian righteousness or liberty, nor, on the other hand, unrighteousness or slavery. This can be shown by an easy argument.

What can it profit to the soul that the body should be in good condition, free, and full of life, that it should eat, drink, and act according to its pleasure, when even the most impious slaves of every kind of vice are prosperous in these matters? Again, what harm can ill health, bondage, hunger, thirst, or any other outward evil, do to the soul, when even the most pious of men, and the freest in the purity of their conscience, are harassed by these things? Neither of these states of things has to do with the liberty or the slavery of the soul.

And so it will profit nothing that the body should be adorned with sacred vestment, or dwell in holy places, or be occupied in sacred offices, or pray, fast, and abstain from certain meats, or do whatever works can be done through the body and in the body. Something widely different will be necessary for the justification and liberty of the soul, since the things I have spoken of can be done by an impious person, and only hypocrites are produced by devotion to these things. On the other hand, it will not at all injure the soul that the body should be clothed in profane raiment, should dwell in profane places, should eat and drink in the ordinary fashion, should not pray aloud, and should leave undone all the things above mentioned, which may be done by hypocrites.

. . . One thing, and one alone, is necessary for life, justification, and Christian liberty; and that is the most Holy Word of God, the Gospel of Christ, as He says, "I am the resurrection and the life; he that believeth in me shall not die eternally" (John 9:25), and also, "If the Son shall make you free, ye shall be free indeed" (John 8:36), and "Man shall not live by bread alone, but by every word that proceedeth out of the mouth of God" (Matt. 4:4).

Let us therefore hold it for certain and firmly established that the soul can do without everything except the Word of God, without which none at all of its wants is provided for. But, having the Word, it is rich and wants for nothing, since that is the Word of life, of truth, of light, of peace, of justification, of salvation, of joy, of liberty, of wisdom, of virtue, of grace, of glory, and of every good thing. . . .

But you will ask, "What is this Word, and by what means is it to be used, since there are so many words of God?" I answer, "The Apostle Paul (Rom. 1) explains what it is, namely the Gospel of God, concerning His Son, incarnate, suffering, risen, and glorified through the Spirit, the Sanctifier." To preach Christ is to feed the soul, to justify it, to set it free, and to save it, if it believes the preaching. For faith alone, and the efficacious use of the Word of God, bring salvation. "If thou shalt confess with thy mouth the Lord Jesus, and shalt believe in thine heart that God hath raised Him from the dead, thou

On effective preaching, especially to the uneducated, Luther urged the minister "to keep it simple for the simple." *(Church of St. Marien, Wittenberg/The Bridgeman Art Library)*

shalt be saved" (Rom. 9:9); . . . and "The just shall live by faith" (Rom. 1:17). . . .

But this faith cannot consist of all with works; that is, if you imagine that you can be justified by those works, whatever they are, along with it. . . . Therefore, when you begin to believe, you learn at the same time that all that is in you is utterly guilty, sinful, and damnable, according to that saying, "All have sinned, and come short of the glory of God" (Rom. 3:23). . . . When you have learned this, you will know that Christ is necessary for you, since He has suffered and risen again for you, that, believing on Him, you might by this faith become another man, all your sins being remitted, and you being justified by the merits of another, namely Christ alone.

. . . [A]nd since it [faith] alone justifies, it is evident that by no outward work or labour can the inward man be at all justified, made free, and saved; and that no works whatever have any relation to him. . . . Therefore the first care of every Christian ought to be to lay aside all reliance on works, and strengthen his faith alone more and more, and by it grow in knowledge, not of works, but of Christ Jesus, who has suffered and risen again for him, as Peter teaches (I Peter 5).

Questions for Analysis

1. What did Luther mean by liberty?

2. Why, for Luther, was Scripture basic to Christian life?

Source: Luther's Primary Works, ed. H. Wace and C. A. Buchheim (London: Holder and Stoughton, 1896). Reprinted in *The Portable Renaissance Reader,* ed. James Bruce Ross and Mary Martin McLaughlin (New York: Penguin Books, 1981), pp. 721–726.

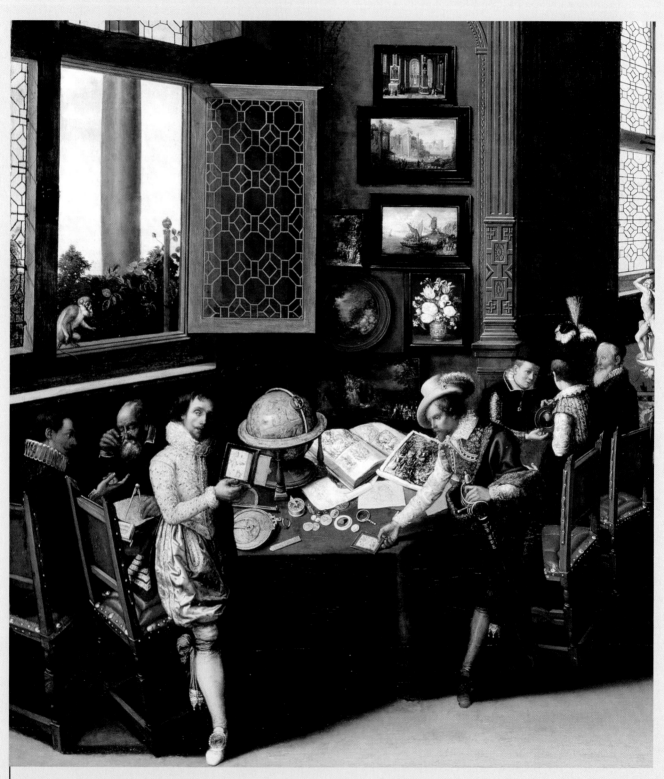

A detail from an early-seventeenth-century Flemish painting depicting
maps, illustrated travel books, a globe, a compass, and an astrolabe.
(Reproduced by courtesy of the Trustees, The National Gallery, London)

chapter
15

The Age of Religious Wars and Overseas Expansion

*B*etween 1560 and 1648, two developments dramatically altered the world in which Europeans lived: the Reformations of the Christian churches and overseas expansion. The Renaissance and the Reformations drastically changed cultural, political, religious, and social life in Europe and inspired magnificent literary, artistic, and musical achievements. Overseas expansion broadened the geographical horizons of Europeans and brought them into confrontation with ancient civilizations in Africa, Asia, and the Americas. These confrontations led first to conquest, then to exploitation, and finally to profound social changes in both Europe and the conquered territories. War and religious issues dominated politics and were intertwined: religion was commonly used to rationalize wars, which were often fought for power and territorial expansion. Meanwhile, Europeans carried their political, religious, and social attitudes to their newly acquired territories.

- What were the causes and consequences of the religious wars in France, the Netherlands, and Germany?

- How and why, in the sixteenth and seventeenth centuries, did a relatively small group living on the edge of the Eurasian landmass gain control of the major sea-lanes of the world and establish political and economic influence on distant continents?

- What immediate effect did overseas expansion have on Europe and on the conquered societies?

- How and why did slave labor become the dominant form of labor organization in the New World?

- How did the religious crises of this period affect religious faith, literary and artistic developments, and the status of women?

This chapter will address these questions.

Politics, Religion, and War

In 1559 France and Spain signed the **Treaty of Cateau-Cambrésis,** which ended the long conflict known as the Habsburg-Valois Wars. Spain was the victor. France, exhausted by the struggle, had to acknowledge Spanish dominance in Italy, where much of the wars had been fought. Spanish governors ruled in Sicily, Naples, and Milan, and Spanish influence was strong in the Papal States and Tuscany. The Treaty of Cateau-Cambrésis ended an era of dynastic wars and initiated a period of conflicts in which politics and religion played the dominant roles. Governments used religious faiths to persuade people to acquiesce to heavier taxation. Religious differences served as the motivating force for ordinary people to participate in wars. Religious passions conditioned the mindsets of all elements of European society.

Wars of the late sixteenth century differed considerably from earlier wars. Sixteenth- and seventeenth-century armies were bigger than medieval ones; some forces numbered as many as fifty thousand men. Because large armies were expensive, governments had to reorganize their administrations to finance these armies. The high cost of maintaining fortresses, such as those Philip II erected in Italy—at Milan, Sicily, Naples, and Sardinia—contributed heavily to state indebtedness.[1] The use of gunpowder altered the nature of war and popular attitudes toward it. Guns and cannon killed and wounded from a distance, indiscriminately. Writers scorned gunpowder as a coward's weapon that allowed a common soldier to kill a gentleman. Gunpowder weakened the notion, common during the Hundred Years' War, that warfare was an ennobling experience. At the same time, governments utilized propaganda, pulpits, and the printing press to arouse public opinion to support war.[2]

Late-sixteenth-century conflicts fundamentally tested the medieval ideal of a unified Christian society governed by one political ruler, the emperor, and one church to which all people belonged. The Protestant Reformation had killed this ideal, but few people recognized it as dead. Catholics continued to believe that Calvinists and Lutherans could be reconverted; Protestants persisted in thinking that the Roman church should be destroyed. Most people believed that a state could survive only if its members shared the same faith. Catholics and Protestants alike feared people of the other faith living in their midst. The settlement finally achieved in 1648, known as the Peace of Westphalia, signaled the end of the medieval ideal.

The Origins of Difficulties in France (1515–1559)

In the first half of the sixteenth century, France continued the recovery begun under Louis XI (see page 442). The population losses caused by the plague and the disorders accompanying the Hundred Years' War had created such a labor shortage that serfdom almost disappeared. Cash rents replaced feudal rents and servile obligations. This development clearly benefited the peasantry. Meanwhile, the declining buying power of money hurt the nobility. The increase in France's population in the late fifteenth and sixteenth centuries brought new lands under cultivation, but the division of property among sons meant that most peasant holdings were very small. Domestic and foreign trade picked up, mercantile centers such as Rouen and Lyons expanded, and in 1517 a new port city was founded at Le Havre.

The charming and cultivated Francis I (r. 1515–1547) and his athletic, emotional son Henry II (r. 1547–1559) governed through a small, efficient council. Great nobles held titular authority in the provinces as governors, but Paris-appointed baillis and seneschals continued to exercise actual fiscal and judicial responsibility (see page 336). In 1539 Francis issued an ordinance that placed the whole of France under the jurisdiction of the royal law courts and made French the language of those courts. This act had a powerful centralizing impact. The taille, a tax on land, provided what strength the monarchy had and supported a strong standing army. Unfortunately, the tax base was too narrow for Francis's extravagant promotion of the arts and ambitious foreign policy.

The Habsburg-Valois Wars, waged intermittently through the first half of the sixteenth century, also cost more than the government could afford. Financing the wars posed problems. In addition to the time-honored practices of increasing taxes and engaging in heavy borrowing, Francis I tried two new devices to raise revenue: the sale of public offices and a treaty with the papacy. The former proved to be only a temporary source of money. The offices sold tended to become hereditary within a family, and once a man bought an office, he and his heirs were tax-exempt.

The treaty with the papacy was the Concordat of Bologna (see page 442), in which Francis agreed to recognize the supremacy of the papacy over a universal council. In return, the French crown gained the right to appoint all French bishops and abbots. This understanding gave the monarchy a rich supplement of money and offices and a power over the church that lasted until the Revolution of 1789. The Concordat of Bologna helps

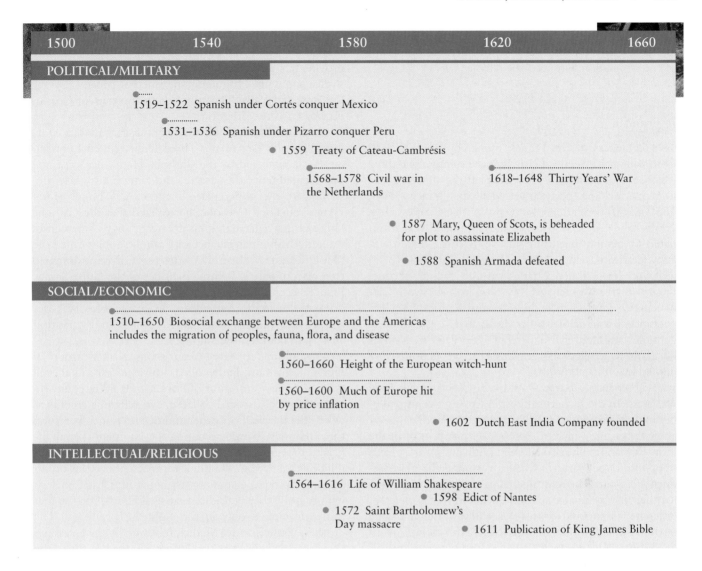

| 1500 | 1540 | 1580 | 1620 | 1660 |

POLITICAL/MILITARY

1519–1522 Spanish under Cortés conquer Mexico

1531–1536 Spanish under Pizarro conquer Peru

1559 Treaty of Cateau-Cambrésis

1568–1578 Civil war in the Netherlands

1618–1648 Thirty Years' War

1587 Mary, Queen of Scots, is beheaded for plot to assassinate Elizabeth

1588 Spanish Armada defeated

SOCIAL/ECONOMIC

1510–1650 Biosocial exchange between Europe and the Americas includes the migration of peoples, fauna, flora, and disease

1560–1660 Height of the European witch-hunt

1560–1600 Much of Europe hit by price inflation

1602 Dutch East India Company founded

INTELLECTUAL/RELIGIOUS

1564–1616 Life of William Shakespeare

1598 Edict of Nantes

1572 Saint Bartholomew's Day massacre

1611 Publication of King James Bible

explain why France did not later become Protestant: in effect, it established Catholicism as the state religion. Because French rulers possessed control over appointments and had a vested financial interest in Catholicism, they had no need to revolt against Rome.

However, the Concordat of Bologna perpetuated disorders within the French church. Ecclesiastical offices were used primarily to pay and reward civil servants. Churchmen in France, as elsewhere, were promoted to the hierarchy not because they possessed any special spiritual qualifications but because they had rendered services to the state. Such bishops were unlikely to work to elevate the intellectual and moral standards of the parish clergy. Few priests devoted scrupulous attention to the needs of their parishioners. Thus the teachings of Luther

and Calvin, as the presses disseminated them, found a receptive audience.

Luther's tracts first appeared in France in 1518, and his ideas attracted some attention. After the publication of Calvin's *Institutes* in 1536, sizable numbers of French people were attracted to the "reformed religion," as Calvinism was called. Because Calvin wrote in French rather than Latin, his ideas gained wide circulation. Initially, Calvinism drew converts from among reform-minded members of the Catholic clergy, the industrious middle classes, and artisan groups. Most Calvinists lived in major cities, such as Paris, Lyons, and Rouen.

In spite of condemnation by the universities, government bans, and massive burnings at the stake, the numbers of Protestants grew steadily. When Henry II died in

1559, there were 40 well-organized Calvinist churches and 2,150 mission stations in France. Perhaps one-tenth of the population had become Calvinist.

Religious Riots and Civil War in France (1559–1598)

The feebleness of the French monarchy was the seed from which the weeds of civil violence sprang. The three weak sons of Henry II who occupied the throne could not provide the necessary leadership. Francis II (r. 1559–1560) died after seventeen months. Charles IX (r. 1560–1574) succeeded at the age of ten and was dominated by his mother, Catherine de' Medici. The intelligent, cultivated, and erratic Henry III (r. 1574–1589) followed his brother Charles on the French throne; Henry divided much of his attention between debaucheries with his male favorites and frantic acts of repentance. From 1560 to her death in 1589, Catherine genuinely wanted civil and religious peace—so long as her sons controlled the government; her actions were guided by political motives.

The French nobility took advantage of this monarchical weakness. In the second half of the sixteenth century, between two-fifths and one-half of the nobility at one time or another became Calvinist. Just as German princes in the Holy Roman Empire had adopted Lutheranism as a means of opposition to Emperor Charles V, so French nobles frequently adopted the reformed religion as a religious cloak for their independence. No one believed that peoples of different faiths could coexist peacefully within the same territory. The Reformation thus led to a resurgence of feudal disorder. Armed clashes between Catholic royalist lords and Calvinist antimonarchical lords occurred in many parts of France. Both Calvinists and Catholics believed that the others' books, services, and ministers polluted the community. Preachers incited violence, and ceremonies such as baptisms, marriages, and funerals triggered it.

A savage Catholic attack on Calvinists in Paris on August 24, 1572 (Saint Bartholomew's Day), followed the usual pattern. The occasion was a religious ceremony, the marriage of the king's sister Margaret of Valois to the Protestant Henry of Navarre, which was intended to help reconcile Catholics and **Huguenots,** as French Calvinists were called. Among the many Calvinists present for the wedding festivities was Admiral Gaspard de Coligny, head of one of the great noble families of France and leader of the Huguenot party. When, the night before the wedding, the leader of the Catholic aristocracy, Henry of Guise, had Coligny attacked, rioting and

slaughter followed. The Huguenot gentry in Paris was massacred, and religious violence spread to the provinces. Between August 25 and October 3, perhaps twelve thousand Huguenots perished at Meaux, Lyons, Orléans, and Paris. The contradictory orders of Charles IX worsened the situation.

The **Saint Bartholomew's Day massacre** led to fighting called the War of the Three Henrys, a civil conflict among factions led by the Catholic Henry of Guise, the Protestant Henry of Navarre, and King Henry III, who succeeded the tubercular Charles IX. Though King Henry remained Catholic, he realized that the Catholic Guise group represented his greatest danger. The Guises wanted, through an alliance of Catholic nobles called the "Holy League," not only to destroy Calvinism but also to replace Henry III with a member of the Guise family. France suffered fifteen more years of religious rioting and domestic anarchy. Agriculture in many areas was destroyed, commercial life declined severely, and starvation and death haunted the land.

What ultimately saved France was a small group of moderates of both faiths called **politiques**, who believed that only the restoration of strong monarchy could reverse the trend toward collapse. No religious creed was worth the incessant disorder and destruction. Therefore, the politiques favored accepting the Huguenots as an officially recognized and organized pressure group. (But religious toleration, the full acceptance of peoples of different religious persuasions within a pluralistic society, with minorities having the same civil liberties as the majority, developed only in the eighteenth century.) The death of Catherine de' Medici, followed by the assassinations of Henry of Guise and King Henry III, paved the way for the accession of Henry of Navarre, a politique who became Henry IV (r. 1589–1610).

This glamorous prince, "who knew how to fight, to make love, and to drink," as a contemporary remarked, wanted above all a strong and united France. He knew, too, that the majority of the French were Roman Catholics. Allegedly saying "Paris is worth a Mass," Henry knelt before the archbishop of Bourges and was received into the Roman Catholic church. Henry's willingness to sacrifice religious principles to political necessity saved France. The **Edict of Nantes,** which Henry published in 1598, granted to Huguenots liberty of conscience and liberty of public worship in 150 fortified towns, such as La Rochelle. The reign of Henry IV and the Edict of Nantes prepared the way for French absolutism in the seventeenth century by helping restore internal peace in France.

Giorgio Vasari: Massacre of Coligny and the Huguenots (1573) Commissioned by Pope Gregory XIII to decorate a hall in the Vatican with frescoes asserting the church's struggle against "unbelief," Vasari here depicts the Saint Bartholomew's Day massacre in Paris: the Huguenot Admiral Coligny is hurled from a window while his followers are slaughtered. In another fresco Vasari glorified the Catholic victory over the Ottoman Turkish fleet at Lepanto. *(Vatican Palace/Scala/Art Resource, NY)*

The Netherlands Under Charles V

In the last quarter of the sixteenth century, the political stability of England, the international prestige of Spain, and the moral influence of the Roman papacy all became mixed up with the religious crisis in the Low Countries. The Netherlands was the pivot around which European money, diplomacy, and war revolved. What began as a movement for the reformation of the church developed into a struggle for Dutch independence.

Emperor Charles V (r. 1519–1556) had inherited the seventeen provinces that compose present-day Belgium and Holland (see page 466). Since the time of the great medieval fairs, cities of the Low Countries (so called because much of the land lies below sea level) had been important sites for the exchange of products from the Baltic and Italy. Antwerp, ideally situated on the Scheldt River at the intersection of many trading routes, steadily expanded as the chief intermediary for international commerce and finance. English woolens; Baltic wheat, fur, and timber; Portuguese spices; German iron and copper; Spanish fruit; French wines and dyestuffs; Italian silks, marble, and mirrors; and vast amounts of cash—all were exchanged at Antwerp. The city's harbor could dock twenty-five hundred vessels at once, and five thousand merchants from many nations gathered daily in the **bourse** (or exchange). Other great towns—Bruges, Ghent, Brussels, Arras, and Amsterdam—made their living by trade and industry as well. The French-speaking southern towns produced fine linens and woolens, while the wealth of the Dutch-speaking northern cities rested on fishing, shipping, and international banking. In these cities, trade and commerce had produced a vibrant atmosphere, as personified in the urbane Erasmus of Rotterdam (see page 439).

Each of the seventeen provinces of the Netherlands possessed historical liberties: each was self-governing and enjoyed the right to make its own laws and collect its own taxes. In addition to important economic connections, only the recognition of a common ruler in the person of Emperor Charles V united the provinces. Delegates from the various provinces met together in the States General, but important decisions had to be referred back to each province for approval. In the middle of the sixteenth century, the provinces of the Netherlands had a limited sense of federation.

In the Low Countries as elsewhere, corruption in the Roman church and the critical spirit of the Renaissance provoked pressure for reform. Lutheran tracts and Dutch translations of the Bible flooded the seventeen provinces in the 1520s and 1530s, attracting many people to Protestantism. Charles V's government responded with condemnation and mild repression. This policy was not effective, however, because ideas circulated freely in the

The Spanish and Habsburg Successions, 1493–1637

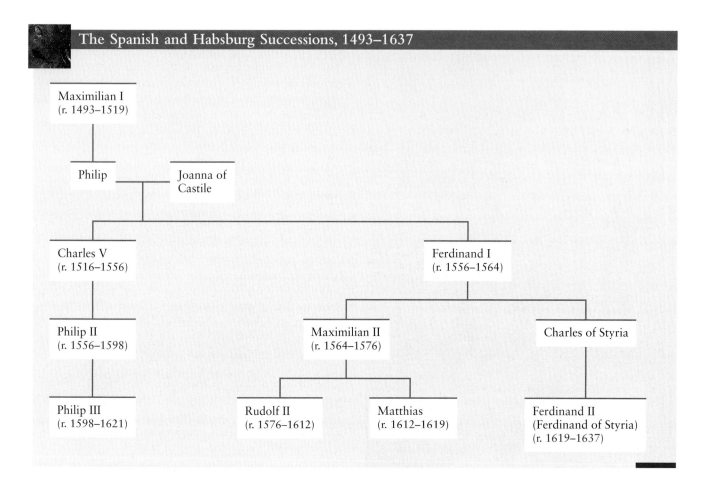

cosmopolitan atmosphere of the commercial centers. But Charles's loyalty to the Flemings checked the spread of Lutheranism. Charles had been born in Ghent and raised in the Netherlands; he was Flemish in language and culture. He identified with the Flemish and they with him.

In 1556, however, Charles V abdicated, dividing his territories between his brother Ferdinand, who received Austria and the Holy Roman Empire, and his son Philip, who inherited Spain, the Low Countries, Milan and the kingdom of Sicily, and the Spanish possessions in the Americas. Charles delivered his abdication speech before the States General at Brussels. The emperor was then fifty-five years old, white-haired, and so crippled in the legs that he had to lean for support on the young Prince William of Orange. According to one contemporary account of the emperor's appearance, "His under lip . . . was heavy and hanging, the lower jaw protruding so far beyond the upper that it was impossible for him to . . . speak a whole sentence in an intelligible voice."[3] Charles spoke in Flemish. Philip responded in Spanish; he could speak neither French nor Flemish. Netherlanders had al-

ways felt that Charles was one of their own. They were never to forget that Philip was Spanish.

The Revolt of the Netherlands (1566–1587)

Lutheranism had posed no serious threat to Spanish rule; it was the spread of Calvinism that upset the apple cart. By the 1560s, there was a strong, militant minority of Calvinists in most of the cities of the Netherlands. The seventeen provinces possessed a large middle-class population, and the reformed religion, as a contemporary remarked, had a powerful appeal "to those who had grown rich by trade and were therefore ready for revolution."[4] Calvinism appealed to the middle classes because of its intellectual seriousness, moral gravity, and emphasis on any form of labor well done. It took deep root among the merchants and financiers in Amsterdam and the northern provinces. Working-class people were also converted, partly because their employers would hire only other Calvinists. Well organized and backed by rich merchants, Calvinists quickly gained a wide following. Whereas Lutherans taught respect for the powers that be, Calvinist reformed religion in the 1570s tended to encourage opposition to "illegal" civil authorities.

In August 1566, a year of very high grain prices, fanatical Calvinists, primarily of the poorest classes, embarked on a rampage of frightful destruction. As in France, Calvinist destruction in the Low Countries was incited by popular preaching, and attacks were aimed at religious images as symbols of false doctrines, not at people. The cathedral of Notre Dame at Antwerp was the first target.

Begun in 1124 and finished only in 1518, this church stood as a monument to the commercial prosperity of Flanders, the piety of the business classes, and the artistic genius of centuries. On six successive summer evenings, crowds embarked on a rampage of destruction. Before the havoc was over, thirty more churches had been sacked and irreplaceable libraries burned. From Antwerp the destruction spread to Brussels and Ghent and north to the provinces of Holland and Zeeland.

From Madrid Philip II sent twenty thousand Spanish troops under the duke of Alva to pacify the Low Countries. Alva interpreted "pacification" to mean the ruthless extermination of religious and political dissidents. On top of the Inquisition, he opened his own tribunal, soon called the "Council of Blood." On March 3, 1568, fifteen hundred men were executed.

For ten years, between 1568 and 1578, civil war raged in the Netherlands between Catholics and Protestants and between the seventeen provinces and Spain. Spanish generals could not halt the fighting. In 1576 the seventeen provinces united under the leadership of Prince William of Orange, called "the Silent" because of his remarkable discretion. In 1578 Philip II sent his nephew Alexander Farnese, duke of Parma, to crush the revolt once and for all. Farnese arrived with an army of German mercenaries. Avoiding pitched battles, he fought by patient sieges. One by one, the cities of the south fell—Maastricht, Tournai, Bruges, Ghent, and, finally, the financial capital of northern Europe, Antwerp (see Map 15.1). Calvinism was forbidden in these territories, and Protestants were compelled to convert or leave. The collapse of Antwerp marked the farthest extent of Spanish jurisdiction and ultimately the religious division of the Netherlands.

The ten southern provinces, the Spanish Netherlands (the future Belgium), remained under the control of the Spanish Habsburgs. The seven northern provinces, led by Holland, formed the **Union of Utrecht** and in 1581 declared their independence from Spain. The Dutch struggle for independence continued because it became inextricably tied up with English affairs.

Geography and sociopolitical structure differentiated the two countries. The northern provinces were ribboned

To Purify the Church   The destruction of pictures and statues representing biblical events, Christian doctrine, or sacred figures was a central feature of the Protestant Reformation. Here Dutch Protestant soldiers destroy what they consider idols in the belief that they are purifying the church. *(The Fotomas Index, U.K.)*

with sluices and canals and therefore were highly defensible. Several times the Dutch had broken the dikes and flooded the countryside to halt the advancing Farnese. In the southern provinces, the Ardennes mountains interrupted the otherwise flat terrain. In the north, the commercial aristocracy possessed the predominant power; in the south, the landed nobility had the greater influence. The north was Protestant; the south remained Catholic. Philip II and Alexander Farnese did not accept this geographical division, and the struggle continued after 1581. The United Provinces repeatedly asked the Protestant queen of England, Elizabeth, for assistance.

Three developments forced Elizabeth's hand. First, the wars in the Low Countries—the chief market for English

MAP 15.1 The Netherlands, 1559–1609   Some provinces were overwhelmingly agricultural, some involved in manufacturing, others heavily commercial. Each of the seventeen was tied to the Spanish crown in a different way.

woolens—badly hurt the English economy. When wool was not exported, the Crown lost valuable customs revenues. Second, the murder of William the Silent in July 1584 eliminated not only a great Protestant leader but also the chief military check on the Farnese advance. Third, the collapse of Antwerp appeared to signal a Catholic sweep through the Netherlands. The next step, the English feared, would be a Spanish invasion of their island. For these reasons, Elizabeth pumped 250,000 pounds and two thousand troops into the Protestant cause in the Low Countries between 1585 and 1587.

Philip II and the Spanish Armada

Philip pondered the Dutch and English developments at the **Escorial,** northwest of Madrid. The monastery of Saint Lawrence of the Escorial served as a residence for Jeromite monks, a tomb for the king's Habsburg ances-

tors, and a royal palace for Philip and his family. The vast buildings resemble a gridiron, the instrument on which Saint Lawrence (d. 258) had supposedly been roasted alive. The royal apartments were in the center of the Italian Renaissance building complex. King Philip's tiny bedchamber possessed a concealed sliding window that opened directly onto the high altar of the monastery church so that he could watch the services and pray along with the monks. In this somber atmosphere, surrounded by a community of monks and close to the bones of his ancestors, the Catholic ruler of Spain and much of the globe passed his days.

In 1587 Philip turned sixty, by the standards of his day an old man. Traditional scholarship, shaped largely by his Protestant enemies, has depicted Philip as morose and melancholic, a religious bigot determined to reimpose Roman Catholicism on northern Europe. Recent research portrays him as a more complicated, even paradoxical, figure. In his youth, "he had visited northern Italy, the Alps, southern Germany, the Rhineland, the Netherlands, parts of France, and southern England." He had walked the streets of Antwerp, Augsburg, Brussels, Cologne, London, and Trent. With the exception of his father, Charles V, no other European ruler of the time had traveled or seen so much, or accumulated so much political experience in international relations. Philip impressed ambassadors as formal, tight-lipped, and forbidding; he spoke only his native Castilian and Latin. He was deeply pious: he attended daily Mass, and every year he retired to a monastery during Holy Week. On the other hand, in his younger days, he was much given to pleasure, and a critical contemporary wrote, "He is dissipated with women, likes to go in disguise at night, and enjoys all types of gaming (gambling)." He also liked jokes and had a good sense of humor.[5]

After Philip buried his fourth wife (enough to make any man "melancholic"), Anna of Austria, to whom he had been deeply devoted, contemporaries noticed a more marked devotion to religion. He relied more and more on God for political help. On the issues of the Inquisition and religious toleration, Philip was completely inflexible. He identified toleration with the growth of heresy, civil disorder, violence, and bloodshed: "Had there been no inquisition (in Spain) there would have been more heretics, and the country would be in a lamentable state like others (the Netherlands) where there is no inquisition as we have in Spain."[6] In this respect, Philip II differed little from the Protestant reformers Luther and Calvin, who initially called for individual liberty of conscience and then insisted on the right of church and civil powers to extirpate heresy within their jurisdictions.

Philip was a man of his times, and the times did not favor religious toleration. And just as the Protestant princes of northern Europe governed religious life within their states, so Philip II controlled ecclesiastical appointments and revenues in Spain.

With his determination to crush heresy in the Low Countries, and with the enormous wealth of American silver enabling him to hire the mercenary armies he needed, why did Philip II have such trouble achieving his goal? Philip ruled the first global empire in history. He was preoccupied with other parts of that empire, especially the advance of the Ottoman Turks into the western Mediterranean. This issue, combined with the death of his son and heir, Don Carlos; the death of his third wife, Elizabeth of Valois; and then a revolt of the Moriscos (Muslims) in Granada, made it impossible to concentrate on the Netherlands. At one point in 1566 he complained, "I have so much on my mind that I rarely know what I am doing or saying." Only after Philip learned that Suleiman the Magnificent had led a Turkish army into Hungary, ordered his fleet from the Mediterranean to the Adriatic, and died, did Philip feel able to focus on the Netherlands.[7]

But the Netherlands could not be separated in Philip's mind from what he perceived as the "British problem." In 1586, Mary, Queen of Scots, cousin and heir of Elizabeth of England, became implicated in a plot to assassinate Elizabeth. Philip, hoping to reunite England with Catholic Europe through Mary, gave the conspiracy his full backing. Mary was discovered and beheaded on February 18, 1587. News of her execution reached Philip in mid-April. When Pope Sixtus V (1585–1590) learned of Mary's death on March 24 (the dates suggest the slowness of communication in the late sixteenth century), the pope promised to pay Philip 1 million gold ducats the moment Spanish troops landed in England. Alexander Farnese had repeatedly warned that to subdue the Dutch, he would have to conquer England and cut off the source of Dutch support. Two plans for an expedition were considered. Philip's naval adviser recommended that a fleet of 150 ships sail from Lisbon, attack the English navy in the Channel, and invade England. Another proposal was to assemble a collection of barges and troops in Flanders to stage a cross-Channel assault. With the expected support of English Catholics, Spain would achieve a great victory. Farnese opposed this plan as militarily unsound.

As plans for an armada proceeded in 1587, two serious difficulties burdened the king. First, he was so badly crippled by gout that he could not sign documents and could walk, painfully, only with a cane. Second, official reports indicated that the Ottoman Turks might seize the mo-ment of preoccupation with the Netherlands and England to attack Spain from the Mediterranean. Philip prepared a vast fleet to sail from Lisbon to Flanders, fight off Elizabeth's navy if it attacked, rendezvous with Farnese, and escort his barges across the English Channel. The expedition's purpose was to transport the Flemish army.

On May 9, 1588, *la felícissima armada*—"the most fortunate fleet," as it was ironically called in official documents—sailed from Lisbon harbor. The **Spanish Armada** of 130 vessels met an English fleet of about 150 ships in the Channel. The English fleet was composed of smaller, faster, more maneuverable ships, many of which had greater firing power than their Spanish counterparts. A combination of storms and squalls, spoiled food and rank water, inadequate Spanish ammunition, and, to a lesser extent, English fire ships that caused the Spanish to scatter gave England the victory. Many Spanish ships went down on the journey home around Ireland; perhaps 65 managed to reach home ports.

The battle in the Channel has frequently been described as one of the decisive battles in the history of the world. In fact, it had mixed consequences. Spain soon rebuilt its navy, and after 1588 the quality of the Spanish fleet improved. The destruction of the Spanish Armada did not halt the flow of silver from the New World. More silver reached Spain between 1588 and 1603 than in any other fifteen-year period. The war between England and Spain dragged on for years.

The defeat of the Spanish Armada was decisive, however, in the sense that it prevented Philip II from reimposing religious unity on western Europe by force. He did not conquer England, and Elizabeth continued her financial and military support of the Dutch. In the Netherlands, neither side gained significant territory. The borders of 1581 tended to become permanent. In 1609 Philip III of Spain (r. 1598–1621) agreed to a truce, in effect recognizing the independence of the United Provinces. In seventeenth-century Spain, memory of the loss of the Spanish Armada contributed to a spirit of defeatism. In England the victory contributed to a David and Goliath legend that enhanced English national sentiment.

The Thirty Years' War (1618–1648)

While Philip II dreamed of building a second armada and Henry IV began the reconstruction of France, the political-religious situation in central Europe deteriorated. An uneasy truce had prevailed in the Holy Roman Empire since the Peace of Augsburg of 1555 (see page 470). According to the Augsburg settlement, the faith of the prince determined the religion of his subjects. Later in the century, however, Catholics grew alarmed because Lutherans, in violation of the Peace of Augsburg, were steadily acquiring German bishoprics. The spread of Calvinism further confused the issue. The Augsburg settlement had pertained only to Lutheranism and Catholicism, so Calvinists ignored it and converted several princes. Lutherans feared that the Augsburg principles would be totally undermined by Catholic and Calvinist gains. Also, the militantly active Jesuits had reconverted several Lutheran princes to Catholicism. In an increasingly tense situation, Lutheran princes formed the **Protestant Union** (1608), and Catholics retaliated with the Catholic League (1609). Each alliance was determined that the other should make no religious (that is, territorial) advance. The empire was composed of two armed camps.

Dynastic interests were also involved in the German situation. The Spanish Habsburgs strongly supported the goals of their Austrian relatives: the unity of the empire and the preservation of Catholicism within it.

Violence erupted first in Bohemia (see Map 15.2), where in 1617 Ferdinand of Styria, the new Catholic king of Bohemia, closed some Protestant churches. On May 23, 1618, Protestants hurled two of Ferdinand's officials from a castle window in Prague. They fell seventy feet but survived: Catholics claimed that angels had caught them; Protestants said that the officials had fallen on a heap of soft horse manure. Called the "defenestration of Prague," this event marked the beginning of the Thirty Years' War (1618–1648).

Historians traditionally divide the war into four phases. The first, or Bohemian, phase (1618–1625) was characterized by civil war in Bohemia between the Catholic League, led by Ferdinand, and the Protestant Union, headed by Frederick, the elector of the Palatinate. The Bohemians fought for religious liberty and independence from Habsburg rule. In 1620 Frederick was defeated by Catholic forces at the Battle of the White Mountain. Ferdinand, recently elected Holy Roman emperor as Ferdinand II, followed up his victories by wiping out Protestantism in Bohemia through forcible conversions and the activities of militant Jesuit missionaries. Within ten years, Bohemia was completely Catholic.

The second, or Danish, phase of the war (1625–1629)—so called because of the participation of King Christian IV of Denmark (r. 1588–1648), the ineffective leader of the Protestant cause—witnessed additional Catholic victories. The Catholic imperial army led by Albert of Wallenstein scored smashing victories. It swept through Silesia, north through Schleswig and Jutland to the Baltic, and east into Pomerania. Wallenstein, who had made himself indispensable to the emperor Ferdinand, was an unscrupulous opportunist who used his vast riches to build an army loyal only to himself. The general seemed interested more in carving out an empire for himself than in aiding the Catholic cause. He quarreled with the Catholic League, and soon the Catholic forces were divided. Religion was eclipsed as a basic issue of the war.

The year 1629 marked the peak of Habsburg power. The Jesuits persuaded the emperor to issue the Edict of Restitution, whereby all Catholic properties lost to Protestantism since 1552 were to be restored and only Catholics and Lutherans (not Calvinists, Hussites, or other sects) were to be allowed to practice their faiths. When Wallenstein began ruthless enforcement of the edict, Protestants throughout Europe feared collapse of the balance of power in north-central Europe.

The third, or Swedish, phase of the war (1630–1635) began with the arrival in Germany of the Swedish king Gustavus Adolphus (r. 1594–1632). The ablest administrator of his day and a devout Lutheran, Gustavus Adolphus intervened to support the oppressed Protestants within the empire. Cardinal Richelieu, the chief minister of King Louis XIII of France (r. 1610–1643), subsidized the Swedes, hoping to weaken Habsburg power in Europe. In 1631, with a small but well-disciplined army equipped with superior muskets, Gustavus Adolphus won a brilliant victory at Breitenfeld. Again in 1632 he was victorious at Lützen, though he was fatally wounded in the battle.

The participation of the Swedes in the Thirty Years' War proved decisive for the future of Protestantism and later German history. When Gustavus Adolphus landed on German soil, he headed a Baltic empire under Swedish influence. The Swedish victories ended the Habsburg ambition of uniting all the German states under imperial authority.

The death of Gustavus Adolphus in 1632, followed by the defeat of the Swedes at the Battle of Nördlingen in 1634, prompted the French to enter the war on the side of the Protestants. Thus began the French, or international, phase of the Thirty Years' War (1635–1648). For almost a century, French foreign policy had been based on opposition to the Habsburgs because a weak empire divided into scores of independent principalities enhanced France's international stature. In 1635 Cardinal Richelieu declared war on Spain and again sent financial and military assistance to the Swedes and the German Protestant princes. The war dragged on. French, Dutch, and Swedes, supported by Scots, Finns, and German mercenaries,

Soldiers Pillage a Farmhouse   Billeting troops among civilian populations caused untold hardships. In this late-seventeenth-century Dutch illustration, brawling soldiers take over a peasant's home, eat his food, steal his possessions, and insult his family. Peasant retaliation sometimes proved swift and bloody. *(Rijksmuseum-Stichting Amsterdam)*

burned, looted, and destroyed German agriculture and commerce. The Thirty Years' War lasted so long because neither side had the resources to win a quick, decisive victory. Finally, in October 1648, peace was achieved.

The treaties signed at Münster and Osnabrück, commonly called the **Peace of Westphalia,** marked a turning point in European political, religious, and social history. Conflicts fought over religious faiths ended. The treaties recognized the sovereign, independent authority of more than three hundred German princes; each would govern his territory and make war and peace. Since the time of Frederick II Hohenstaufen (see pages 340–341), Germany had followed a pattern of state building different from that of France and England: the imperial power (the emperor) had shared authority with the princes. After the Peace of Westphalia, the Habsburg emperors'

power was severely limited, but the Holy Roman Empire continued to function as a federation.

The independence of the United Provinces of the Netherlands was acknowledged. Political divisions within the empire, Germany's weak frontiers, and the acquisition of the province of Alsace increased France's size and prestige. Sweden received a large cash indemnity and jurisdiction over German territories along the Baltic Sea. The powerful Swedish presence in northeastern Germany subsequently posed a major threat to the future kingdom of Brandenburg-Prussia. The treaties also denied the papacy the right to participate in German religious affairs—a restriction symbolizing the reduced role of the church in European politics.

In religion, the Westphalian treaties stipulated that the Augsburg agreement of 1555 should stand permanently.

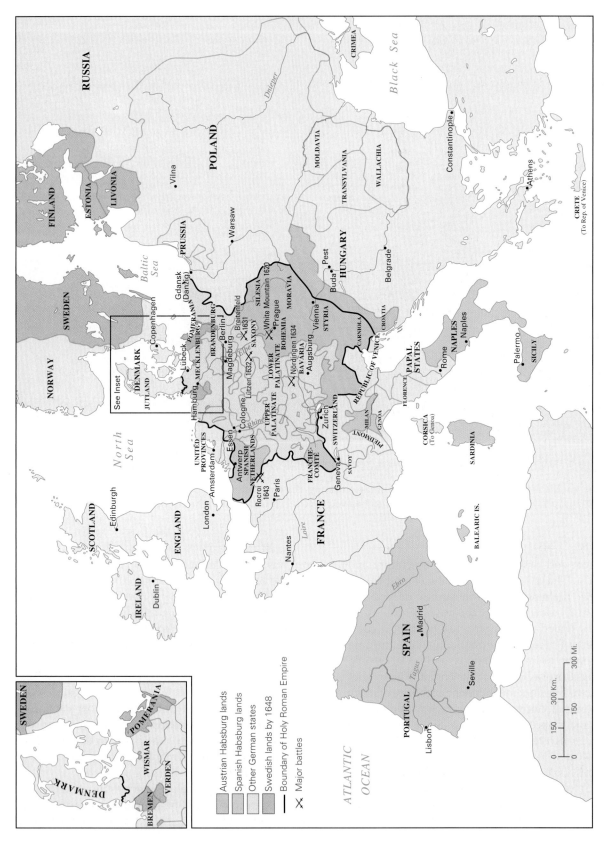

MAP 15.2 Europe in 1648 Which country emerged from the Thirty Years' War as the strongest European power? What dynastic house was that country's major rival in the early modern period?

Laplandter. Liff Ländter. Schotländter.

Abbildung der wunderselgamen Völcker so sich under der Schwödischen Armada befinden.

Dehumanization of the Enemy During the Thirty Years' War, Protestants viewed Gustavus Adolphus as the savior of Protestantism, the leader of a "godly army." The Catholic Habsburgs saw him differently. To them, he was the Antichrist, and his soldiers were grotesque monsters. In this broadsheet, Lapps, Livonians (riding reindeer), and Scots in the Protestant Swedish army are portrayed as superhuman, brutal, and barbaric. *(Anon, Picture of the supernatural people to be found in the Swedish army, ca 1630)*

The sole modification was that Calvinism, along with Catholicism and Lutheranism, would become a legally permissible creed. The north German states remained Protestant; the south German states, Catholic.

Germany After the Thirty Years' War

The Thirty Years' War was a disaster for the German economy and society, probably the most destructive event in German history before the twentieth century. Perhaps one-third of the urban residents and two-fifths of the inhabitants of rural areas died. Entire areas of Germany were depopulated, partly by military actions, partly by disease—typhus, dysentery, bubonic plague, and syphilis accompanied the movements of armies—and partly by the thousands of refugees who fled to safer areas.

In the late sixteenth and early seventeenth centuries, all Europe experienced an economic crisis primarily caused by the influx of silver from South America. Because the Thirty Years' War was fought on German soil, these economic difficulties were badly aggravated in the empire. Scholars still cannot estimate the value of losses in agricultural land and livestock, in trade and commerce. The trade of southern cities such as Augsburg, already hard hit by the shift in transportation routes from the Mediterranean to the Atlantic, was virtually destroyed by the fighting in the south. Meanwhile, towns such as Lübeck, Hamburg, and Bremen in the north and Essen in the Ruhr area actually prospered because of the many refugees they attracted. The destruction of land and foodstuffs, compounded by the flood of Spanish silver, brought on a severe price rise. During and after the war, inflation was worse in Germany than anywhere else in Europe.

Agricultural areas suffered catastrophically. The population decline caused a rise in the value of labor, and owners of great estates had to pay more for agricultural workers.

Farmers who needed only small amounts of capital to restore their lands started over again. Many small farmers, however, lacked the revenue to rework their holdings and had to become day laborers. Nobles and landlords bought up many small holdings and acquired great estates. In parts of Germany, especially in areas east of the Elbe River such as Mecklenburg and Pomerania, peasants' loss of land led to the rise of a new serfdom.[8] Thus the Thirty Years' War contributed to the legal and economic decline of the largest segment of German society.

Discovery, Reconnaissance, and Expansion

Historians have variously called the period from 1450 to 1650 the "Age of Discovery," the "Age of Reconnaissance," and the "Age of Expansion." All three labels are appropriate. The Age of Discovery refers to the era's phenomenal advances in geographical knowledge and technology. In 1350 it took as long to sail from the eastern end of the Mediterranean to the western end as it had taken a thousand years earlier. Even in the fifteenth century, Europeans knew little more about the earth's surface than the Romans had. By 1650, however, Europeans had made an extensive reconnaissance—or preliminary exploration—and had sketched fairly accurately the physical outline of the whole earth. Much of the geographical information they had gathered was tentative and not fully understood—hence the appropriateness of the term the Age of Reconnaissance.

The designation of the era as the Age of Expansion refers to the migration of Europeans to other parts of the world. This colonization resulted in political control of much of South and North America; coastal regions of Africa, India, China, and Japan; and many Pacific islands. This political hegemony was accompanied by economic exploitation, religious domination, and the introduction of European patterns of social and intellectual life. Indeed, the sixteenth-century expansion of European society launched a new age in world history.

Overseas Exploration and Conquest

The outward expansion of Europe began with the Viking voyages across the Atlantic in the ninth and tenth centuries. Under Eric the Red and Leif Ericson, the Vikings discovered Greenland and the eastern coast of North America. The Vikings also made permanent settlements in, and a legal imprint on, Iceland, Ireland, England, Normandy, and Sicily (see pages 256–257). The Cru-

sades of the eleventh through thirteenth centuries were another phase in Europe's attempt to explore and exploit peoples on the periphery of the continent. But the lack of a strong territorial base, superior Muslim military strength, and sheer misrule combined to make the Crusader kingdoms short-lived. In the mid-fifteenth century, Europe seemed ill-prepared for further international ventures, and by 1450 a grave new threat had appeared in the East—the Ottoman Turks.

Combining excellent military strategy with efficient administration of their conquered territories, the Turks had subdued most of Asia Minor and begun to settle on the western side of the Bosporus. The Muslim Ottoman Turks under Sultan Mohammed II (r. 1451–1481) captured Constantinople in 1453, pressed northwest into the Balkans, and by the early sixteenth century controlled the eastern Mediterranean. The Turkish menace badly frightened Europeans. In France in the fifteenth and sixteenth centuries, twice as many books were printed about the Turkish threat as about the American discoveries. Yet these centuries witnessed a fantastic continuation, on a global scale, of European expansion.

Political centralization in Spain, France, and England helps explain those countries' outward push. In the fifteenth century, Isabella and Ferdinand had consolidated their several kingdoms to achieve a more united Spain and revamped the Spanish bureaucracy. The Spanish monarchy was stronger than before and in a position to support foreign ventures; it could bear the costs and dangers of exploration. But Portugal, situated on the extreme southwestern edge of the European continent, got a head start on the rest of Europe. Still insignificant as a European land power despite its recently secured frontiers, Portugal sought greatness in the unknown world overseas.

Portugal's taking of Ceuta, an Arab city in northern Morocco, in 1415 marked the beginning of European exploration and control of overseas territory. The objectives of Portuguese policy included the historic Iberian crusade to Christianize Muslims and to find gold, an overseas route to the spice markets of India, and the mythical Christian ruler of Ethiopia, Prester John.

In the early phases of Portuguese exploration, Prince Henry (1394–1460), called "the Navigator" because of the school he established for the study of geography and navigation and for the annual expeditions he sent down the western coast of Africa, played the leading role. In the fifteenth century, most of the gold that reached Europe came from the Sudan in West Africa and from the Akan peoples living near the area of present-day Ghana. Muslim caravans brought the gold from the African cities

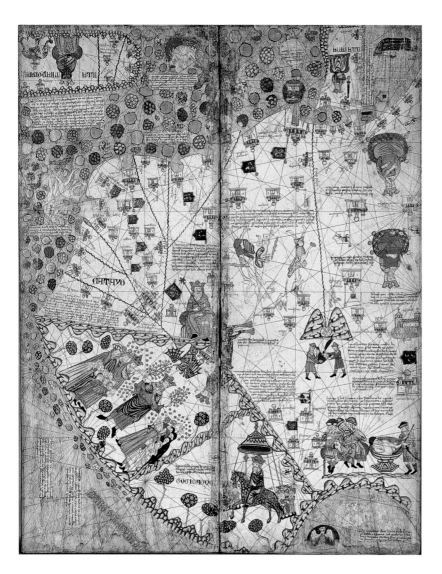

Catalan Atlas, 1375 Abraham Cresques and his son Yehuda, Jews living in Palma on the island of Majorca (at the time, almost all the best mapmakers were Jewish), produced this atlas for Peter IV of Aragon. Consulting Marco Polo's manuscripts and interviewing Arabic seamen and European travelers, the Cresques aimed to produce a world map showing the various peoples inhabiting it. The atlas consists of twelve leaves mounted on boards to be folded like a screen. Primitive by modern standards, the atlas was at the time a masterpiece of empirical evidence. *(Bibliothèque nationale de France)*

of Niani and Timbuktu and carried it north across the Sahara to Mediterranean ports. Then the Portuguese muscled in on this commerce in gold. Prince Henry's carefully planned expeditions succeeded in reaching Guinea, and under King John II (r. 1481–1495) the Portuguese established trading posts and forts on the Guinea coast and penetrated into the continent all the way to Timbuktu (see Map 15.3). Portuguese ships transported gold to Lisbon, and by 1500 Portugal controlled the flow of gold to Europe. The golden century of Portuguese prosperity had begun.

Still the Portuguese pushed farther south down the west coast of Africa. In 1487 Bartholomew Diaz rounded the Cape of Good Hope at the southern tip, but storms and a threatened mutiny forced him to turn back. On a later ex-

pedition (1497–1499), the Portuguese mariner Vasco da Gama reached India and returned to Lisbon loaded with spices and samples of Indian cloth. King Manuel (r. 1495–1521) promptly dispatched thirteen ships under the command of Pedro Alvares Cabral, assisted by Diaz, to set up trading posts in India. On April 22, 1500, the coast of Brazil in South America was sighted and claimed for the Crown of Portugal. Cabral then proceeded south and east around the Cape of Good Hope and reached India. Half the fleet was lost on the return voyage, but the six spice-laden vessels that dropped anchor in Lisbon harbor in July 1501 more than paid for the entire expedition. Thereafter, convoys were sent out every March. Lisbon became the entrance port for Asian goods into Europe—but this was not accomplished without a fight.

MAP 15.3 Overseas Exploration and Conquest, Fifteenth and Sixteenth Centuries The voyages of discovery marked another phase in the centuries-old migrations of European peoples. Consider the major contemporary significance of each of the three voyages depicted on the map.

For centuries the Muslims had controlled the rich spice trade of the Indian Ocean, and they did not surrender it willingly. Portuguese commercial activities were accompanied by the destruction or seizure of strategic Muslim coastal forts, which later served Portugal as both trading posts and military bases. Alfonso de Albuquerque, whom the Portuguese crown appointed as governor of India (1509–1515), decided that these bases, not inland territories, should control the Indian Ocean. Accordingly, his cannon blasted open the ports of Calicut, Ormuz, Goa, and Malacca, the vital centers of Arab domination of South Asian trade. This bombardment laid the foundation for Portuguese imperialism in the sixteenth and seventeenth centuries: a strange way to bring Christianity to "those who were in darkness." As one scholar wrote about the opening of China to the West, "while Buddha came to China on white elephants, Christ was borne on cannon balls."[9]

In March 1493, between the voyages of Diaz and da Gama, Spanish ships under a triumphant Genoese mariner named Christopher Columbus (1451–1506), in the service of the Spanish crown, entered Lisbon harbor. Spain also had begun the quest for an empire.

Technological Stimuli to Exploration

Technological developments were the key to Europe's remarkable outreach. By 1350 *cannon*—iron or bronze guns that fired iron or stone balls—had been fully developed in western Europe. These pieces of artillery emitted frightening noises and great flashes of fire and could batter down fortresses and even city walls. Sultan Mohammed II's siege of Constantinople in 1453 provides a classic illustration of the effectiveness of cannon fire.

Constantinople had very strong walled fortifications. The sultan secured the services of a Western technician, who built fifty-six small cannon and a gigantic gun that could hurl stone balls weighing about eight hundred pounds. The gun could be moved only by several hundred oxen and loaded and fired only by about a hundred men working together. This awkward but powerful weapon breached the walls of Constantinople, which cracked on the second day of the bombardment. Lesser cannon finished the job.

Early cannon posed serious technical difficulties. Iron cannon were cheaper than bronze to construct, but they were difficult to cast effectively and were liable to crack and injure artillerymen. Bronze guns, made of copper and tin, were less subject than iron to corrosion, but they were very expensive. All cannon were extraordinarily difficult to move, required considerable time for reloading, and were highly inaccurate. They thus proved inefficient for land warfare. However, they could be used at sea.

The mounting of cannon on ships and improved techniques of shipbuilding gave impetus to European expansion. Since ancient times, most seagoing vessels had been narrow, open boats called *galleys,* propelled largely by manpower. Slaves or convicts who had been sentenced to the galleys manned the oars of the ships that sailed the Mediterranean, and both cargo ships and warships carried soldiers for defense. Though well suited to the placid and thoroughly explored waters of the Mediterranean, galleys could not withstand the rough winds and uncharted shoals of the Atlantic. The need for sturdier craft, as well as population losses caused by the Black Death, forced the development of a new style of ship that would not require soldiers for defense or much manpower to sail.

In the course of the fifteenth century, the Portuguese developed the *caravel,* a small, light, three-masted sailing ship. Though somewhat slower than the galley, the caravel held more cargo and was highly maneuverable. When fitted with cannon, it could dominate larger vessels, such as the round ships commonly used as merchantmen. The substitution of wind power for manpower and artillery fire for soldiers signaled a great technological advance and gave Europeans navigational and fighting ascendancy over the rest of the world.[10]

Other fifteenth-century developments in navigation helped make possible the conquest of the Atlantic. The

Nocturnal An instrument for determining the hour of night at sea by finding the progress of certain stars around the polestar (center aperture). *(National Maritime Museum, London)*

magnetic compass enabled sailors to determine their direction and position at sea. The **astrolabe,** an instrument developed by Muslim navigators in the twelfth century and used to determine the altitude of the sun and other celestial bodies, permitted mariners to plot their *latitude,* or position north or south of the equator. Steadily improved maps and sea charts gave information about distance, sea depths, and general geography.

The Explorers' Motives

The expansion of Europe was not motivated by demographic pressures. The Black Death had caused serious population losses from which Europe had not recovered in 1500. Few Europeans immigrated to North or South America in the sixteenth century. Half of those who did sail to America died en route; half of those who reached the New World eventually returned to their homeland. Why, then, did explorers brave the Atlantic and Pacific Oceans, risking their lives to discover new continents and spread European culture?

The reasons are varied and complex. People of the sixteenth century were still basically medieval in the sense that their attitudes and values were shaped by religion and expressed in religious terms. In the late fifteenth century, crusading fervor remained a basic part of the Portuguese and Spanish national ideal. Queen Isabella of Spain, for example, showed a fanatical zeal for converting the Muslims to Christianity, and she concentrated her efforts on the Muslims in Granada. After the abortive crusading attempts of the thirteenth century, rulers realized full well that they lacked the material resources to mount the full-scale assault on Islam necessary for victory. Crusading impulses thus shifted from the Muslims to the pagan peoples of Africa and the Americas.

Moreover, after the reconquista, enterprising young men of the Spanish upper classes found their economic and political opportunities severely limited. As a study of the Castilian city of Ciudad Real shows, the ancient aristocracy controlled the best agricultural land and monopolized urban administrative posts. Great merchants and a few nobles (surprisingly, since Spanish law forbade participation by nobles in commercial ventures) dominated the textile and leather-glove manufacturing industries. Consequently, many ambitious men immigrated to the Americas to seek their fortunes.[11]

Government sponsorship and encouragement of exploration also accounted for the results of the various voyages. Mariners and explorers could not as private individuals afford the massive sums needed to explore mysterious oceans and control remote continents. The strong financial support of Prince Henry the Navigator led to Portugal's phenomenal success in the spice trade. Even the grudging and modest assistance of Isabella and Ferdinand eventually brought untold riches—and complicated problems—to Spain. The Dutch in the seventeenth century, through such government-sponsored trading companies as the Dutch East India Company, reaped enormous wealth, and although the Netherlands was a small country in size, it dominated the European economy in 1650.

Scholars have frequently described the European discoveries as a manifestation of Renaissance curiosity about the physical universe—the desire to know more about the geography and peoples of the world. Cosmography, natural history, and geography aroused enormous interest among educated people in the fifteenth and sixteenth centuries. Just as science fiction and speculation about life on other planets excite readers today, quasi-scientific literature about Africa, Asia, and the Americas captured the imaginations of literate Europeans. Fernández de Oviedo's *General History of the Indies* (1547), a detailed eyewitness account of plants, animals, and peoples, was widely read.

Spices were another important incentive for voyages of discovery. Introduced into western Europe by the Crusaders in the twelfth century, nutmeg, mace, ginger, cinnamon, and pepper added flavor and variety to the monotonous diet of Europeans. Spices were also used in the preparation of medicinal drugs and incense for religious ceremonies. In the late thirteenth century, Venetian Marco Polo (1254?–1324?), the greatest of medieval travelers, had visited the court of the Chinese emperor. The widely publicized account of his experiences in *Travels* (ca 1298) stimulated the trade in spices between Asia and Italy. The Venetians came to hold a monopoly of that trade in western Europe.

Spices were grown in India and China, shipped across the Indian Ocean to ports on the Persian Gulf, and then transported by Arabs across the Arabian Desert to Mediterranean ports. But the rise of the Ming Dynasty in China in the late fourteenth century resulted in the expulsion of foreigners. And the steady penetration of the Ottoman Turks into the eastern Mediterranean forced Europeans to seek a new route to the Asian spice markets.

The basic reason for European exploration and expansion, however, was the quest for material profit. Mariners and explorers frankly admitted this. As Bartholomew Diaz put the matter, his motives were "to serve God and His Majesty, to give light to those who were in darkness and to grow rich as all men desire to do." When Vasco da

Pepper Harvest To break the monotony of a bland diet, Europeans had a passion for pepper, which—along with cinnamon, cloves, nutmeg, and ginger—was the main object of the Asian trade. Since one kilo of pepper cost 2 grams of silver at the place of production in the East Indies, 10 to 14 grams of silver in Alexandria, Egypt, 14 to 18 grams in Venice, and 20 to 30 grams at the markets of northern Europe, we can appreciate the fifteenth-century expression "as dear as pepper." Here natives fill vats, while the dealer tastes a peppercorn for pungency. *(Bibliothèque nationale de France)*

Gama reached the port of Calicut, India, in 1498, a native asked what the Portuguese wanted. Da Gama replied, "Christians and spices."[12] The bluntest of the Spanish conquistadors, Hernando Cortés announced as he prepared to conquer Mexico, "I have come to win gold, not to plow the fields like a peasant."[13] A sixteenth-century diplomat, Ogier Gheselin de Busbecq, summed up this paradoxical attitude well: in expeditions to the Indies and the Antipodes, he said, "religion supplies the pretext and gold the motive."[14]

Spanish and Portuguese explorers carried the fervent Catholicism and missionary zeal of the Iberian Peninsula to the New World, and once in America they urged home governments to send clerics. At bottom, however, wealth was the driving motivation.

The Problem of Christopher Columbus

The year 1992, which marked the quincentenary of Columbus's first voyages to the Americas, spawned an enormous amount of discussion about the significance of his voyages. Journalists, scholars, amateurs, and polemicists debated Columbus's accomplishments and failures. Until the 1980s, however, most writers would have generally agreed with Harvard historian Samuel Eliot Morison in his 1942 biography of the explorer:

The whole history of the Americas stems from the Four Voyages of Columbus; today a score of independent nations and dominions unite in homage to Columbus, the stout-hearted son of Genoa, who carried Christian civilization across the Ocean Sea.[15]

In 1942, the Western Powers believed they were engaged in a life-and-death struggle to defend "Christian civilization" against the evil of fascism.

In contrast to this lavish praise, Columbus has recently undergone severe criticism. He enslaved and sometimes killed the Indians he encountered. He was a cruel and ineffective governor of Spain's Caribbean colony. Moreover, he did not discover the continents: others—Africans and Europeans—had been there before him. And not only did he not discover the continents; he also misunderstood what he had found. In short, he was a fool who did not know what was going on around him. Some have criticized him because he abandoned the mother of his illegitimate son. Other writers have faulted Columbus as an opportunistic adventurer who loved the trappings of grand titles. Some claim he was the originator of European exploitation of the non-European world; he destroyed the paradise that had been the New World.[16] Because these judgments rest on social and ethical standards that did not exist in Columbus's world, responsible scholars consider them ahistorical.

Using the evidence of his journal (sea log) and letters, let us ask three basic questions. First, what kind of man was Columbus, and what forces or influences shaped him? Second, in sailing westward from Europe, what were his goals? Third, did he achieve his goals, and what did he make of his discoveries?

The central feature in the character of Christopher Columbus is that he was a deeply religious man. He began the *Journal* of his voyage to the Americas in the form of a letter to Ferdinand and Isabella of Spain:

On 2 January in the year 1492, when your Highnesses had concluded their war with the Moors who reigned in Europe, I saw your Highnesses banners victoriously raised on the towers of the Alhambra, the citadel of the city, and the Moorish king come out of the city gates and kiss the hands of your Highnesses and the prince, My Lord. And later in that same month, on the grounds of information I had given your Highnesses concerning the lands of India . . . your Highnesses decided to send me, Christopher Columbus, to see these parts of India and the princes and peoples of those lands and consider the best means for their conversion.[17]

Thus he had witnessed the Spanish reconquest of Granada and shared fully in the religious and nationalistic fervor surrounding that event. Just seven months separated Isabella and Ferdinand's entry into Granada on January 2 and Columbus's departure westward on August 3, 1492. In his mind, the two events were clearly linked. Long after Europeans knew something of Columbus's discoveries in the Caribbean, they nevertheless considered the restoration of Muslim Granada to Christian hands as Ferdinand and Isabella's greatest achievement; for the reconquest the Spanish pope Alexander VI rewarded them in 1494 with the title "Most Catholic Kings." Like the Spanish rulers and most Europeans of his age, Columbus understood Christianity as a missionary religion that should be carried to places and peoples where it did not exist. Although Columbus certainly had material and secular goals, first and foremost, as he wrote in 1498, he believed he was a divine agent: "God made me the messenger of the new heaven and the new earth of which he spoke in the Apocalypse of St. John . . . and he showed me the post where to find it."[18]

Columbus was also very knowledgeable about the sea. He was familiar with such fifteenth-century Portuguese navigational developments as *portolans*—written descriptions of the courses along which ships sailed, showing bays, coves, capes, ports, and the distances between these places—and the use of the magnetic needle as a nautical instrument. And, as he implied in his *Journal,* he had acquired not only theoretical but also practical experience: "I have spent twenty-three years at sea and have not left it for any length of time worth mentioning, and I have seen everything from east to west [meaning he had been to England] and I have been to Guinea [north and west Africa]."[19] Although some of Columbus's geographical theories, such as his measurement of the distance from Portugal to Japan at 2,760 miles, when it is actually 12,000, proved inaccurate, his successful thirty-three-day voyage to the Caribbean owed a great deal to his seamanship and his knowledge of the accurate use of instruments.

What was the object of this first voyage? He gave the answer in the very title of the expedition, "The Enterprise of the Indies." He wanted to find a direct ocean route to Asia that would provide the opportunity for a greatly expanded trade in which Spain would participate. Two recent scholars have written, "If Columbus had not sailed westward in search of Asia, someone else would have done so. The time was right for such a bold undertaking." Someone else might have done so, but the fact remains that Columbus, displaying a characteristic Renaissance curiosity and restless drive, actually did it.

How did Columbus interpret what he had found, and in his mind did he achieve what he had set out to do? His mind had been formed by the Bible and the geographical writings of classical authors, as had the minds of most educated people of his times. Thus as people have often done in every age, Columbus ignored the evidence of his eyes and described what he wanted to see in the Caribbean as an idyllic paradise, a peaceful garden of

Eden. (See the feature "Listening to the Past: Columbus Describes His First Voyage" on pages 526–527.) When accounts of his travels were published, Europeans' immediate fascination with this image of the New World meant that Columbus's propaganda created an instant myth. But having sensed that he had not found the spice markets and bazaars of Asia, Columbus shifted his goal from establishing trade with the (East) Indians and Chinese to establishing the kind of trade the Portuguese then conducted with Africa and with the Atlantic islands. That meant setting up some form of government in the islands, and Columbus had little interest in or capacity for governing. In 1496 he had forcibly subjugated the island of Hispaniola, enslaved the Indians, and laid the basis for a system of land grants tied to the Indians' labor service. Borrowing practices and institutions from reconquest Spain and the Canary Islands, Columbus laid the foundation for Spanish imperial administration. In all of this, Columbus was very much a man of his times. He never understood, however, that the scale of his discoveries created problems of trade, settlers, governmental bureaucracy, and, from a twenty-first-century perspective, the rights of native peoples.[20]

Later Explorers

News of Columbus's first voyage rapidly spread across Europe. On April 1, 1493, a printer in Barcelona published in Spanish Columbus's letter describing what he believed he had found. By the end of that month, the letter had been translated into Latin and published in Rome as *De Insulis Inventis* (On the Discoveries of the Islands). Within a year, printers in Paris, Basel, Antwerp, and Venice had brought out six more Latin editions, which were soon followed by translations in German and Tuscan, the dialect of the Florentines. In a 1503 letter, Florentine navigator Amerigo Vespucci (1454–1512), in whose honor America was named, wrote, "Those new regions which we found and explored with the fleet . . . we may rightly call a New World." This letter, titled *Mundus Novus* (The New World), was the first document to describe America as a continent separate from Asia. Some scholars today try to avoid the terms *discovery* and *New World,* lest they be considered Eurocentric, but the use of those words rests on a tradition begun by the early explorers themselves.

The search for precious metals determined the direction of Spanish exploration and expansion into South America. When it became apparent that placer mining (in which ore is separated from soil by panning) in the Caribbean islands was slow and the rewards were slim, new routes to the East and new sources of gold and silver were sought.

In 1519 Spanish ruler Charles V commissioned Ferdinand Magellan (1480–1521) to find a direct route to the spices of the Moluccas off the southeast coast of Asia. Magellan sailed southwest across the Atlantic to Brazil and proceeded south around Cape Horn into the Pacific Ocean (see Map 15.3). He crossed the Pacific, sailing west, to the Malay Archipelago, which he called the "Western Isles." (Some of these islands were conquered in the 1560s and named the "Philippines" for Philip II of Spain.)

Though Magellan was killed, the expedition continued, returning to Spain in 1522 from the east by way of the Indian Ocean, the Cape of Good Hope, and the Atlantic. Terrible storms, mutiny, starvation, and disease haunted this voyage. Nevertheless, it verified the theory that the earth was round and brought information about the vastness of the Pacific. Magellan also proved that the earth was much larger than Columbus had estimated.

Ecclesiastical Wealth (Yanhuitian Codex) Through their control of tithes—taxes on agricultural production and livestock—the rulers of Spain and Portugal supported the colonial church and promoted the conversion of Amerindians. By 1600, the church was the largest property owner in the Americas and had vast agricultural, commercial, and mining interests. Here noble and commoner deliver payments to the bishop. (*Couresty, M. E. Grenander Department of Special Collections and Archives, University of Albany, SUNY*)

In the West Indies, the slow recovery of gold, the shortage of a healthy labor force, and sheer restlessness speeded up Spain's search for wealth. In 1519, the year Magellan departed on his worldwide expedition, a brash and determined Spanish adventurer named Hernando Cortés (1485–1547) crossed from Hispaniola to mainland Mexico with six hundred men, seventeen horses, and ten cannon. Within three years, Cortés had taken captive the Aztec emperor Montezuma, conquered the fabulously rich Aztec Empire, and founded Mexico City as the capital of New Spain. The subjugation of northern Mexico took longer, but between 1531 and 1550 the Spanish gained control of Zacatecas and Guanajuato, where rich silver veins were soon tapped.

Another Spanish conquistador, Francisco Pizarro (1470–1541), repeated Cortés's feat in Peru. Between 1531 and 1536, with even fewer resources, Pizarro crushed the Inca Empire in western South America and established the Spanish viceroyalty of Peru, with its center at Lima. In 1545 the Spanish opened at Potosí in the Peruvian highlands what became the richest silver mines in the New World.

Between 1525 and 1575, the riches of the Americas poured into the Spanish port of Seville and the Portuguese capital of Lisbon. For all their new wealth, however, Lisbon and Seville did not become important trading centers. It was the Flemish city of Antwerp, controlled by the Spanish Habsburgs, that developed into the great entrepôt for overseas bullion and Portuguese spices and served as the commercial and financial capital of the entire European world (see page 493).

By the end of the sixteenth century, Amsterdam had overtaken Antwerp as the financial capital of Europe. The Dutch had also embarked on foreign exploration and conquest. The Dutch East India Company, founded in 1602, became the major organ of Dutch imperialism and within a few decades expelled the Portuguese from Ceylon and other East Indian islands. By 1650 the Dutch West India Company had successfully intruded on the Spanish possessions in the Americas, in the process gaining control of much of the African and American trade.

English and French explorations lacked the immediate, sensational results of those of the Spanish and Portuguese. In 1497 John Cabot, a Genoese merchant living in London, sailed for Brazil but discovered Newfoundland. The next year he returned and explored the New England coast and perhaps as far south as Delaware. Since these expeditions found no spices or gold, King Henry VII lost interest in exploration. Between 1534 and 1541, Frenchman Jacques Cartier made several voyages and explored the St. Lawrence region of Canada, but the first permanent French settlement, at Quebec, was not founded until 1608.

The Economic Effects of Spain's Discoveries in the New World

The sixteenth century has been called the **Golden Century of Spain.** The influence of Spanish armies, Spanish Catholicism, and Spanish wealth was felt all over Europe. This greatness rested largely on the influx of precious metals from the New World. The mines at Zacatecas and Guanajuato in Mexico and Potosí in Peru poured out huge quantities of precious metals. To protect this treasure from French and English pirates, armed convoys transported it each year to Spain. Between 1503 and 1650, 16 million kilograms of silver and 185,000 kilograms of gold entered the port of Seville.

Meanwhile, Spain was experiencing a steady population increase, creating a sharp rise in the demand for food and goods. Spanish colonies in the Americas also represented a demand for products. Because Spain had expelled some of its best farmers and business people, the Jews in 1492 and the Muslims in the sixteenth and seventeenth centuries, the Spanish economy suffered and could not meet the new demands. Prices rose and with them the costs of manufacturing cloth and other goods. As a result, Spanish products could not compete in the international market with cheaper products made elsewhere. The textile industry was badly hurt. Prices spiraled upward faster than the government could levy taxes to dampen the economy. (Higher taxes would have cut the public's buying power; with fewer goods sold, prices would have come down.)

Did the flood of American silver bullion cause the inflation? Scholars have long debated this question. Prices rose most steeply before 1565, but bullion imports reached their peak between 1580 and 1620. Thus there is no direct correlation between silver imports and the inflation rate. Did the substantial population growth accelerate the inflation rate? Perhaps: when the population pressure declined after 1600, prices gradually stabilized. One fact is certain: the **price revolution** severely strained government budgets. Several times between 1557 and 1647, Philip II and his successors were forced to repudiate the state debt, which in turn undermined confidence in the government. By the seventeenth century, the economy was a shambles, and Spanish predominance was over.

As Philip II paid his armies and foreign debts with silver bullion, the Spanish inflation was transmitted to the rest of Europe. Between 1560 and 1600, much of Europe experienced large price increases. Prices doubled and in some cases quadrupled, and wages did not keep pace with prices. Spain suffered most severely, but all European countries were affected. People who lived on fixed incomes, such as the continental nobles, were badly hurt because their money bought less. Those who owed fixed sums of money, such as the middle class, prospered: in a time of rising prices, debts had less value each year. Food costs rose most sharply, and the poor fared worst of all.

The Columbian Exchange

Besides the consequences of American silver and gold, what impact did contacts with the Americas have on Europeans? Europeans had had commercial relations with Asia and sub-Saharan Africa since Roman times. In the Carolingian era the slave trade had linked northern Europe and the Islamic Middle East. The High Middle Ages had witnessed a great expansion of trade between Europe and Africa and Asia (see pages 352, 356, and 437). But with the American discoveries, commercial and other relations for the first time became worldwide, involving all the continents except Australia. European involvement in the Americas led to the acceleration of global contacts. In time, these contacts had a profound influence on Europeans.

An important historical study asserts that the most significant changes brought about by the Columbian voyages were biosocial. The Age of Discovery led to the migration of peoples, which in turn led to an exchange of fauna and flora, of animals, plants, and disease. Spanish and Portuguese immigrants to the Americas wanted the foods with which they were familiar—wheat for bread, grapes for wine, olive oil for culinary and sacramental purposes. By 1535, Mexico was exporting wheat to Spain, and shortly after, wine and olive oil went to Spain from Chile and Peru. The Spanish and Portuguese also took back to Europe maize (corn) from Mexico (the main American cereal), white potatoes from Peru, and many varieties of beans, squash, pumpkins, and tomatoes (Europeans distrusted tomatoes, fearing they were sexually stimulating). Although they were initially contemptuous of white potatoes, once Europeans discovered their nutritional value, cultivation spread from Ireland and England in the seventeenth century to Germany, Poland, and Russia in the eighteenth. But maize—which grows in climates too dry for rice and too wet for wheat, has a short growing season, and gives a high yield per unit of land—proved to be the great Amerindian gift to Europe and the rest of the world.

Because Native Americans had only wild game for food and no large beasts of burden, on his second voyage to America Columbus brought horses, cattle, sheep, pigs, and chickens. The rapid multiplication of these animals allowed the Spaniards to take herds of swine on exploring expeditions; horses enabled them to move faster and farther. Columbus also introduced sugar cane into the Caribbean, Cortés took it to Mexico, and the European demand for sugar began to be satisfied.[21]

Europeans also brought something that had a devastating effect on the Amerindian population: disease.

Physician Scraping Sores In five years, syphilis spread across Europe, reaching Russia in 1499. The running sores, boils, and aches in the joints caused agonizing pain. European physicians first followed the treatment described by Arab doctors, scraping sores from the skin and rubbing the skin with mercury (shown here). Later, Europeans adopted a remedy common in Espaniola (Haiti, where syphilis was thought to have originated)—brewing a concoction made from shavings of the guaiacum tree and water, which the patient drank for thirty days. This treatment proved amazingly effective. The Fugger banking family of Augsburg gained a monopoly on the import of guaiacum, but because of its high cost only the rich could afford the remedy from the New World. *(Anon, from B. Steber,* A Mala Franzos Morbo Gallorum, Praeservatio ac Cura *[Venice, 1498])*

Long isolated from other peoples, Amerindians had no resistance to European diseases, especially smallpox. Students of the history of medicine estimate that the population of central Mexico fell from 25.3 million people in 1519 to 1 million in 1605 and the Andean population of Peru went from 1.3 million in 1570 to 600,000 in 1620. Some demographers dispute these figures, but all agree the decline of the native peoples was catastrophic.

In return, Amerindians gave the Spaniards the venereal disease syphilis. Sailors and settlers carried it back to Europe in 1493. Transmitted by sailors and armies to Europe after 1493, syphilis raced across the continent in the sixteenth century. Its precise origin is disputed, but no evidence for the disease in Europe exists before 1493.[22]

Colonial Administration

Columbus, Cortés, and Pizarro claimed the lands they had "discovered" for the Crown of Spain. How were these lands to be governed? According to the Spanish theory of absolutism, the Crown was entitled to exercise full authority over all imperial lands. In the sixteenth century, the Crown divided its New World territories into four **viceroyalties,** or administrative divisions: New Spain, which consisted of Mexico, Central America, and present-day California, Arizona, New Mexico, and Texas, with the capital at Mexico City; Peru, originally all the lands in continental South America, later reduced to the territory of modern Peru, Chile, Bolivia, and Ecuador, with the viceregal seat at Lima; New Granada, including present-day Venezuela, Colombia, Panama, and, after 1739, Ecuador, with Bogotá as its administrative center; and La Plata, consisting of Argentina, Uruguay, and Paraguay, with Buenos Aires as the capital. Within each territory, the viceroy, or imperial governor, exercised broad military and civil authority as the direct representative of the sovereign in Madrid. The viceroy presided over the *audiencia,* a board of twelve to fifteen judges that served as his advisory council and the highest judicial body. The enlightened Spanish king Charles III (r. 1759–1788) introduced the system of *intendants.* These royal officials possessed broad military, administrative, and financial authority within their intendancy and were responsible not to the viceroy but to the monarchy in Madrid.

From the early sixteenth century to the beginning of the nineteenth, the Spanish monarchy acted on the mercantilist principle that the colonies existed for the financial benefit of the home country. The mining of gold and silver was always the most important industry in the colonies. The Crown claimed the **quinto,** one-fifth of all precious metals mined in South America. Gold and silver yielded the Spanish monarchy 25 percent of its total income. In return, it shipped manufactured goods to the Americas and discouraged the development of native industries.

The Portuguese governed their colony of Brazil in a similar manner. After the union of the Crowns of Portugal and Spain in 1580, Spanish administrative forms were introduced. Local officials called *corregidores* held judicial and military powers. Mercantilist policies placed severe restrictions on Brazilian industries that might compete with those of Portugal. In the seventeenth century, the use of black slave labor made possible the cultivation of coffee and cotton, and in the eighteenth century Brazil led the world in the production of sugar. The unique feature of colonial Brazil's culture and society was its thoroughgoing intermixture of Indians, whites, and blacks.

Changing Attitudes

What were the cultural consequences of the religious wars and of the worldwide discoveries? What impact did the discoveries and wars have on Europeans' attitudes? The clash of traditional religious and geographical beliefs with the new knowledge provided by explorers—combined with decades of devastation and disorder within Europe—bred confusion, uncertainty, and insecurity. Geographical evidence based on verifiably scientific proofs contradicted the evidence of the Scriptures and of the classical authors.

The age of religious wars was one of extreme and violent contrasts. It was a deeply religious period in which people fought passionately for their beliefs; 70 percent of the books printed dealt with religious subjects. Yet the times saw the beginnings of religious skepticism. Europeans explored new continents, partly with the missionary aim of Christianizing the peoples they encountered. Yet the Spanish, Portuguese, Dutch, and English proceeded to dominate and enslave the Indians and blacks they found. While Europeans indulged in gross sensuality, the social status of women declined. The exploration of new continents reflected deep curiosity and broad intelligence, yet Europeans believed in witches and burned thousands at the stake. Sexism, racism, and skepticism had all originated in ancient times. But late in the sixteenth century, they began to take on their familiar modern forms.

The Status of Women

Religious writers of the Reformation and early modern period did not express consistent views on women. Sometimes they were terribly negative, at other times very positive (see, for example, Luther's opinions on page 466). Some Reformation leaders, such as Calvin, addressed the subject of women only obliquely, in the context of some other topic; thus, interpretation of their views is difficult.

Although Protestant reformers rejected medieval Scholastic ideas on celibacy and marriage and broke with the institutional Catholic church, Protestants scarcely differed with Scholastics' notions about women. Luther, Calvin, Zwingli, and the English Puritans all held that women could merit salvation and that men and women were spiritually equal, but they also insisted that women were subordinate to men. Protestant reformers stressed the value of marriage. Marriage had three purposes: the procreation of children, the avoidance of sin, and mutual help and companionship. By "mutual help and companionship," however, they did not mean equality of husband and wife. Reformers urged everyone to marry. One Lutheran pastor held that "A man without a wife is only half a person and has only half a body and is a needy and miserable man who lacks help and assistance."[23] It was even more incumbent on women to marry. Reformers saw marriage as a woman's highest calling and believed that it freed women from sexual urges. They scorned unmarried women for upsetting the divine order, which they thought made women subject to men. While the reformers elevated marriage over celibacy, they did not elevate women as women. Sermons (in most parts of Europe people were required to go to church), pamphlets, and engravings reiterated these views, so women could not fail to know them.

Catholic thinkers upheld the traditional teaching that the celibate life was the highest form of Christian life. The institutional church vigorously enforced the Council of Trent's doctrine on a celibate clergy and removed candidates deemed unworthy. Church authorities recognized that most women would marry, and Catholic writings described the ideal wife in the same terms as Protestant manuals: she was obedient, silent, and pious.[24]

As for same-sex marriages, Protestants and Catholics would have agreed that lacking a scriptural basis such unions could not occur. When Maria of Antwerp (1719–1781) was arrested twice for marrying a woman, she claimed that she was a man in a woman's body. Perhaps we may infer she had no words to describe sexual love between two women. Male bias and general ignorance of the female anatomy led even educated people to insist that a woman could not achieve sexual satisfaction without a man.

Manuals emphasized the qualities expected of each partner. A husband was obliged to provide for the mate-rial welfare of his wife and children. He was directed to protect his family while remaining steady and self-controlled. Especially was a husband and father to rule his household firmly but justly. But he was not to behave as a tyrant, a guideline counselors repeated frequently. A wife should be a mature person, a good household manager, and a subservient and faithful spouse. The husband also owed fidelity, and both Protestant and Catholic moralists rejected the double standard of sexual morality as a threat to family unity. Counselors believed that marriage should be based on mutual respect and trust. While they discouraged impersonal unions arranged by parents, they did not think romantic attachments—based on physical attraction and emotional love—a sound basis for an enduring relationship.

Moralists held that the household was a woman's first priority. She might assist in her own or her husband's business and do charitable work. Involvement in social or public activities, however, was inappropriate because it distracted the wife from her primary responsibility, her household. If women suffered under their husbands' yokes, writers explained that submission was the punishment they had inherited from Eve, penance for man's fall, like the pain of childbearing. Moreover, they said, a woman's lot was no worse than a man's: he had to earn the family's bread by the sweat of his brow.[25]

Catholics viewed marriage as a sacramental union that, if validly entered into, could not be dissolved. Protestants saw marriage as a contract in which each partner promised the other support, companionship, and the sharing of mutual goods. Protestants recognized a mutual right to divorce and remarriage for various reasons, including adultery and irreparable breakdown.[26] Society in the early modern period was patriarchal. While women neither lost their identity nor lacked meaningful work, the pervasive assumption was that men ruled.

There were some remarkable success stories, however. Elizabeth Hardwick, the orphaned daughter of an obscure English country squire, made four careful marriages, each of which brought her more property and carried her higher up the social ladder. She managed her estates, amounting to more than 100,000 acres, with a degree of business sense rare in any age. The two great mansions she built, Chatsworth and Hardwick, stand today as monuments to her acumen. Having established several aristocratic dynasties, she died in 1608, past her eightieth year, one of the richest people in England.[27]

Artists' drawings of plump, voluptuous women and massive, muscular men revealed the contemporary standards of physical beauty. It was a sensual age that gloried in the delights of the flesh. Some people, such as humanist poet Aretino, found sexual satisfaction with both sexes. Reformers and public officials simultaneously condemned and condoned sexual "sins." The oldest profession had many practitioners, and when in 1566 Pope Pius IV expelled all the prostitutes from Rome, so many people left and the city suffered such a loss of revenue that in less than a month the pope was forced to rescind the order. Scholars debated Saint Augustine's notion that whores served a useful social function by preventing worse sins. Prostitution was common because poverty forced women and young men into it. Since the later Middle Ages, licensed houses of prostitution had been common in urban centers (see page 398). The general public took the matter for granted. Consequently, civil authorities in both Catholic and Protestant countries licensed houses of public prostitution. These establishments were intended, however, for the convenience of single men, and some Protestant cities, such as Geneva and Zurich, installed officials in the brothels with the express purpose of preventing married men from patronizing them.

Moralists naturally railed against prostitution. For example, Melchior Ambach, the Lutheran editor of many tracts against adultery and whoring, wrote in 1543 that if "houses of women" for single and married men were allowed, why not provide a "house of boys" for women who lacked husbands to service them? "Would whoring be any worse for the poor, needy female sex?"[28] Ambach, of course, was not being serious: by treating infidelity from the perspective of female, rather than male, customers, he was still insisting that prostitution destroyed the family and society.

Single women of the middle and working classes in the sixteenth and seventeenth centuries worked in many occupations and professions—as domestic servants, butchers, shopkeepers, nurses, goldsmiths, midwives, and workers in the weaving and printing industries. Married women normally assisted in their husbands' businesses. What became of the thousands of women who left convents and nunneries during the Reformation? Luther and the Protestant reformers believed that celibacy had no scriptural basis; they favored the suppression of women's religious houses and encouraged ex-nuns to marry. Marriage, the reformers maintained, freed women from clerical domination, cultural deprivation, and sexual repression.[29] Consequently, these women apparently passed from clerical domination to subservience to husbands.

If some nuns in the Middle Ages lacked a genuine religious vocation and if some religious houses witnessed financial mismanagement and moral laxness, convents nevertheless provided women of the upper classes with scope for their literary, artistic, medical, or administrative talents if they could not or would not marry. With the closing of convents, marriage became virtually the only occupation for upper-class Protestant women. This helps explain why Anglicans, Calvinists, and Lutherans established communities of religious women, such as the Lutheran one at Kaiserwerth in the Rhineland, in the eighteenth and nineteenth centuries.[30]

The Great European Witch-hunt

The great European witch scare reveals something about contemporary attitudes toward women. The period of the religious wars witnessed a startling increase in the phenomenon of witch-hunting, whose prior history was long but sporadic. "A **witch,**" according to Chief Justice Coke of England, "was a person who hath conference with the Devil to consult with him or to do some act." This definition by the highest legal authority in England demonstrates that educated as well as ignorant people believed in witches. Witches were thought to be individuals who could mysteriously injure other people or animals—by causing a person to become blind or impotent, for instance, or by preventing a cow from giving milk. Belief in witches predated Christianity. For centuries, tales had circulated about old women who made nocturnal travels on greased broomsticks to *sabbats,* or assemblies of witches, where they participated in sexual orgies and feasted on the flesh of infants. In the popular imagination, witches had definite characteristics. The vast majority were married women or widows between fifty and seventy years old, crippled or bent with age, with pockmarked skin. They often practiced midwifery or folk medicine, and most had sharp tongues and were quick to scold.

Religious reformers' extreme notions of the Devil's powers and the insecurity created by the religious wars contributed to the growth of belief in witches. The idea developed that witches made pacts with the Devil in return for the power to work mischief on their enemies. Since pacts with the Devil meant the renunciation of God, witchcraft was considered heresy. Persecution for witchcraft had actually begun in the later fourteenth century, when witchcraft was declared heresy. The century between 1560 and 1660, when mainstream Protestantism and Tridentine Catholicism had begun to settle into definite confessional blocs, saw witch-hunting on an unprecedented and virulent scale, touching every part of Europe from Iceland to Russia. Scholars currently estimate that during the sixteenth and seventeenth centuries between 100,000 and 200,000 people were officially tried for witchcraft, and between 50,000 and 100,000 were executed.

Witches' Sabbat (1510) Trained by the great German graphic artist and painter Albrecht Dürer at Nuremberg, Hans Baldung Grien (1484/5–1545) in this woodcut combines learned and stereotypical beliefs about witches: they traveled at night on broomsticks, met at sabbats (or assemblies), feasted on infants (in dish held high), concocted strange potions, and possessed an aged and debauched sensuality. *(Germanisches Nationalmuseum Nürnberg)*

Historians, sociologists, and anthropologists have presented a variety of explanations. Some scholars see witch-hunts as a consequence of the Reformation: rulers proved their piety and religious commitment either by religious wars or by cracking down on heretics or persons considered socially marginal. Some scholars attribute witch-hunts to socioeconomic factors: severe inflation; periodic famines due to poor harvests; wars; the enclosure of land, leading to the movement of the dispossessed and an increase in vagrants (beggars and homeless people)—all creating an atmosphere of instability and uncertainty in values. Still other writers blame demo-

graphic changes caused by late marriages and the increasing number of women who never married at all, women who were not under a man's supervision and thus highly suspect. Perhaps a number of causes—religious, intellectual, social, and economic—created the atmosphere that led to the deaths of so many.[31] Given the broad strand of misogyny (hatred of women) in Western religion, the long-held belief in the susceptibility of women (so-called weaker vessels) to the Devil's allurements, and the pervasive seventeenth-century belief about women's multiple and demanding orgasms and thus their sexual insatiability, it is not difficult to understand why women were accused of all sorts of mischief and witchcraft. As the most important capital crime for women in early modern times, witchcraft has considerable significance for the history and status of women.[32] Witch-hunting declined only in the eighteenth century, as fear of the Devil and his powers of malevolent sorcery waned among the educated ruling classes.

European Slavery and the Origins of American Racism

Since ancient times, victors in battle have enslaved conquered peoples. Throughout the Middle Ages, slavery was deeply entrenched in southern Italy, Sicily, Crete, Iberia, and the Balkans. The bubonic plague, famines, and other epidemics created a severe shortage of agricultural and domestic workers throughout Europe, encouraging Italian merchants to buy slaves from the Balkans, Thrace, southern Russia, and central Anatolia for sale in the West. In 1364 the Florentine government allowed the unlimited importation of slaves so long as they were not Christians. Between 1414 and 1423, at least ten thousand slaves were sold in Venice alone. The slave trade represented one aspect of Italian business enterprise during the Renaissance: where profits were lucrative, papal threats of excommunication failed to stop Genoese slave traders (see page 436). The Genoese set up colonial stations in the Crimea and along the Black Sea, and according to an international authority on slavery, these outposts were "virtual laboratories" for the development of slave plantation agriculture in the New World.[33] This form of slavery had nothing to do with race; almost all slaves were white. How, then, did black African slavery enter the European picture and take root in South and then North America?

In 1453 the Ottoman capture of Constantinople halted the flow of white slaves from the Black Sea region and the Balkans. Mediterranean Europe, cut off from its traditional source of slaves, had no alternative source for

African Slave and Indian Woman A black slave approaches an Indian prostitute. Unable to explain what he wants, he points with his finger; she eagerly grasps for the coin. The Spanish caption above moralizes on the black man using stolen money—yet the Spaniards ruthlessly expropriated all South American mineral wealth. *(New York Public Library/Art Resource, NY)*

Henry the Navigator's sailors (see page 502) discovered the Madeira Islands and made settlements there. In this stage of European expansion, "the history of slavery became inextricably tied up with the history of sugar." Though it was an expensive luxury that only the affluent could afford, population increases and monetary expansion in the fifteenth century led to an increasing demand for sugar. Resourceful Italians provided the capital, cane, and technology for sugar cultivation on plantations in southern Portugal, Madeira, and the Canary Islands. Meanwhile, in the period 1490 to 1530, the port of Lisbon saw between three hundred and two thousand black slaves arrive annually (see Map 15.4). From Lisbon, where African slaves performed most of the manual labor and constituted 10 percent of the city's population, slaves were transported to the sugar plantations of Madeira, the Azores, and the Cape Verde Islands. Sugar and the small Atlantic islands gave New World slavery its distinctive shape. Columbus himself, who spent a decade in Madeira, brought sugar plants on his voyages to "the Indies."[34]

As already discussed, European expansion across the Atlantic led to the economic exploitation of the Americas. In the New World, the major problem settlers faced was a shortage of labor. As early as 1495, the Spanish solved the problem by enslaving the native Indians. In the next two centuries, the Portuguese, Dutch, and English followed suit.

Although the Aztecs of Mexico and the Incas of Peru had various forms of servile labor, including domestic, agricultural, and industrial slavery, before European intrusion, Native American peoples were not accustomed to the harshness of Spanish exploitation. They could not endure panning for gold for twelve hours a day in the broiling sun. The Indians died "like fish in a bucket," one Spanish settler reported.[35] In 1515 a Spanish missionary, Bartolomé de las Casas (1474–1566), who had seen the evils of Indian slavery, urged the future emperor Charles V to end Indian slavery and to import blacks from Africa. Church law did not strictly forbid slavery, and Las Casas thought blacks could better survive under South American conditions. Charles agreed, and in 1518 the African slave trade began. (When the blacks arrived, Las Casas immediately regretted his suggestion.)

In Africa, where slavery was entrenched (as it was in the Islamic world, southern Europe, and China), African kings and dealers sold black slaves to European merchants who participated in the transatlantic trade. The Portuguese brought the first slaves to Brazil; by 1600, 4,000 were being imported annually. After its founding in 1621, the Dutch West India Company, with the full support of the government of the United Provinces,

slave labor but sub-Saharan Africa. The centuries-old trans-Saharan trade was greatly stimulated by the existence of a ready market in the vineyards and sugar plantations of Sicily and Majorca. By the later fifteenth century, the Mediterranean had developed an "American" form of slavery before the discovery of America. (See the feature "Individuals in Society: Juan de Pareja.") Because slavery was sanctioned by the Bible and the ancient philosophers, few people thought it morally wrong.

Meanwhile, the Genoese and other Italians had colonized the Canary Islands in the eastern Atlantic. Prince

Individuals in Society

Juan de Pareja

A marginal person is one who lives outside the mainstream of the dominant society, who is not fully assimilated into or accepted by that society, but from whose life and experience we learn about the values and ideals of the dominant group. Such a person was the Spanish religious and portrait painter Juan de Pareja.

Pareja was born in Antequera, an agricultural region and the old center of Muslim culture near Seville in southern Spain. Of his parents we know nothing. Because a rare surviving document calls him a "mulatto," one of his parents must have been white and the other must have had some African blood. The Spanish word *mulatto* derives from the Arabic *muwallad,* a person of mixed race, and some scholars, using religion to describe ethnic category, speak of Pareja's "Muslim descent." The region from which he came makes that possible, but we do not know whether he actually believed in or practiced Islam.

In 1630 Pareja applied to the mayor of Seville for permission to travel to Madrid to visit his brother and "to perfect his art." The document lists his occupation as "a painter in Seville." Since it mentions no other name, it is reasonable to assume that Pareja arrived in Madrid a free man. Sometime between 1630 and 1648, however, he came into the possession of the artist Diego Velázquez (1599–1660); Pareja became a slave.

In the twelfth century, Muslim slaves helped build the cathedral of Saint James at Santiago de Compostela, one of the great shrines of medieval Christendom. During the long wars of the reconquista, Muslims and Christians captured each other in battle and used the defeated as slaves. The fifteenth and sixteenth centuries had seen a steady flow of sub-Saharan Africans into the Iberian Peninsula. Thus early modern Spain was a slave-holding society.

How did Velázquez acquire Pareja? By purchase? As a gift? Had Pareja fallen into debt, or committed some crime, and thereby lost his freedom? We do not know. Velázquez, the greatest Spanish painter of the seventeenth century, had a large studio with many assistants. Pareja was set to grinding powders to make colors and to preparing canvases. He must have demonstrated ability because, when Velázquez went to Rome in 1648, he chose Pareja to accompany him.

In 1650, as practice for a portrait of Pope Innocent X, Velázquez painted Pareja. That same year, Velázquez signed the document that gave Pareja his freedom, to become effective in 1654. From 1654 until his death, Pareja worked in Madrid as an independent painter.

Although he received recognition for his work, only one painting survives: *The Calling of Saint Matthew,* signed and dated 1661 (see page 522). Modern art historians dispute its merit. Some believe it shows a forceful baroque energy and considerable originality; others consider it derivative of Velázquez.

What does the public career of this seventeenth-century marginal person tell us about the man and his world? After living in Seville and Madrid, he traveled widely, visiting Genoa, Venice, Rome, and Naples. Travel may have broadened him, producing a cosmopolitan man. Pareja's career suggests that a person of talent and ability could rise in Spanish society, despite the social and religious barriers that existed at the time. Jonathan Brown, the leading authority on Velázquez, describes Pareja's appearance in Velázquez's portrait as "self-confident." A more enthusiastic student writes, "The Metropolitan is probably the greatest museum in the world . . . and this [Velázquez's portrait of Pareja] is its greatest painting. . . . The man was technically a slave. . . . However, we can see from Velázquez's painting that the two were undeniably equals. That steady look of self-controlled power can even make us wonder which of the two had a higher opinion of himself."

Velázquez, Juan de Pareja *(1650).* (The Metropolitan Museum of Art, Fletcher Fund, Rogers Fund, and Bequest of Miss Adelaide Milton de Groot (1876–1967), by exchange, supplemented by gifts from friends of the Museum, 1971. [1971.86]. Photograph © 1986 The Metropolitan Museum of Art)

Questions for Analysis

1. Since slavery was an established institution in Spain, speculate on Velázquez's possible reasons for giving Pareja his freedom.
2. What issues of cultural diversity might Pareja have faced in seventeenth-century Spain?

Sources: Jonathan Brown, *Velázquez: Painter and Courtier* (New Haven, Conn.: Yale University Press, 1986); *Grove Dictionary of Art* (New York: Macmillan, 2000); *Sister Wendy Beckett's 1000 Masterpieces* (New York: Dorling Kindersley Inc., 1999).

The **history companion** *features additional information and activities related to this topic.* **history.college.hmco.com/students**

MAP 15.4 The Worldwide Slave Trade By the mid-seventeenth century, trade in spices, silk, sugar, and slaves linked all parts of the globe. The trans-Atlantic trade in African peoples was one facet of worldwide slavery.

transported thousands of Africans to Brazil and the Caribbean. In the late seventeenth century, with the chartering of the Royal African Company, the English got involved. Thereafter, large numbers of African blacks poured into the West Indies and North America. In 1790 there were 757,181 blacks in a total U.S. population of 3,929,625. When the first census was taken in Brazil in 1798, blacks numbered about 2 million in a total population of 3.25 million.

Settlers brought to the Americas the racial attitudes they had absorbed in Europe. Settlers' beliefs and attitudes toward blacks derived from two basic sources: Christian theological speculation (see page 438) and Arab ideas. In the sixteenth and seventeenth centuries, the English, for example, were extremely curious about Africans' lives and customs, and slavers' accounts were extraordinarily popular. Travel literature depicted Africans as savages because of their eating habits, morals, clothing, and social customs; as barbarians because of their language and methods of war; and as heathens because they were not Christian (nearly the identical language with which the English described the Irish—see page 404). Africans were believed to possess a potent sexuality. One seventeenth-century observer considered Africans "very lustful and impudent, . . . (for a Negroes hiding his members, their extraordinary greatness) is a token of their lust." African women were considered sexually aggressive, with a "temper hot and lascivious."[36]

"At the time when Columbus sailed to the New World, Islam was the largest world religion, and the only world religion that showed itself capable of expanding rapidly in areas as far apart and as different from each other as Senegal [in northwest Africa], Bosnia [in the Balkans], Java, and the Philippines."[37] Medieval Arabic literature spoke of blacks' physical repulsiveness, mental inferiority, and primitivism. In contrast to civilized peoples from the Mediterranean to China, some Arab writers absurdly claimed, sub-Saharan blacks were the only peoples who had produced no sciences or stable states. Though black kings, the Muslim historian Khaldun alleged, sold their subjects without even a pretext of crime or war, the victims bore no resentment because they gave no thought to the future and had "by nature few cares and worries; dancing and rhythm are for them inborn."[38] It is easy to see how such ridiculous myths developed into the stereotypes used to justify black slavery in South and North America in the seventeenth, eighteenth, and nineteenth centuries. Medieval Christians and Arabs had similar notions of blacks as primitive people ideally suited to enslavement. Perhaps centuries of commercial contacts between Middle Eastern and Mediterranean peoples had familiarized the latter with Arab racial attitudes. The racial beliefs that the Portuguese, Spanish, Dutch, and English brought to the New World, however, derived primarily from Christian theological speculation.

Literature and Art

The age of religious wars and overseas expansion also witnessed an extraordinary degree of intellectual and artistic ferment. This effervescence can be seen in the development of the essay as a distinct literary genre; in other prose, poetry, and drama; in art; and in music. In many ways, literature, the visual arts, music, and the drama of the period mirrored the social and cultural conditions that gave rise to them.

The Essay: Michel de Montaigne

Decades of religious fanaticism, bringing famine, civil anarchy, and death, led both Catholics and Protestants to doubt that any one faith contained absolute truth. The late sixteenth and seventeenth centuries witnessed the beginning of modern skepticism. Skepticism is a school of thought founded on doubt that total certainty or definitive knowledge is ever attainable. The skeptic is cautious and critical and suspends judgment. Perhaps the finest representative of early modern skepticism is Frenchman Michel de Montaigne (1533–1592).

Montaigne descended from a bourgeois family that had made a fortune selling salted herring and wine and in 1477 had purchased the title and property of Montaigne in Gascony; his mother came from a Jewish family that had been forced to flee Spain. Montaigne received a classical education, studied law, and secured a judicial appointment in 1554. He condemned the ancient nobility for being more concerned with war and sports than with the cultivation of the mind.

At the age of thirty-eight, Montaigne resigned his judicial post, retired to his estate, and devoted the rest of his life to study, contemplation, and an effort to understand himself. His wealth provided him with the leisure time to do so. A humanist, he believed that the object of life was to "know thyself," for self-knowledge teaches men and women how to live in accordance with nature and God. Montaigne developed a new literary genre, the essay—from the French *essayer,* meaning "to test or try"—to express his thoughts and ideas.

Montaigne's *Essays* provides insight into the mind of a remarkably civilized man. From the ancient authors, especially the Roman Stoic Seneca, Montaigne acquired a sense of calm, patience, tolerance, and broad-mindedness. Montaigne had grown up during the French civil wars, perhaps the worst kind of war. Religious ideology had set family against family, even brother against brother. He wrote:

In this controversy . . . France is at present agitated by civil wars, the best and soundest side is undoubtedly that which maintains both the old religion and the old government of the country. However, among the good men who follow that side . . . we see many whom passion drives outside the bounds of reason, and makes them sometimes adopt unjust, violent, and even reckless courses.[39]

Though he remained a Catholic, Montaigne possessed a detachment, an independence, an openness of mind, and a willingness to look at all sides of a question. As he wrote, "I listen with attention to the judgment of all men; but so far as I can remember, I have followed none but my own. Though I set little value upon my own opinion, I set no more on the opinions of others."

Montaigne's essay "On Cannibals" reflects the impact of overseas discoveries on Europeans' consciousness. His tolerant mind rejected the notion that one culture is superior to another:

I long had a man in my house that lived ten or twelve years in the New World, discovered in these latter days, and in that part of it where Villegaignon landed [Brazil]. . . .

I find that there is nothing barbarous and savage in [that] nation, . . . excepting, that every one gives the title of barbarism to everything that is not in use in his own country. As, indeed, we have no other level of truth and reason, than the example and idea of the opinions and customs of the place wherein we live.[40]

Montaigne's rejection of dogmatism, his secularism, and his skepticism thus represented a basic change. In his own time and throughout the seventeenth century, few would have agreed with him. The publication of his ideas, however, anticipated a basic shift in attitudes. Montaigne inaugurated an era of doubt. "Wonder," he said, "is the foundation of all philosophy, research is the means of all learning, and ignorance is the end."[41]

Elizabethan and Jacobean Literature

In addition to the essay as a literary genre, the period fostered remarkable creativity in other branches of literature. England, especially in the latter part of Elizabeth's reign and in the first years of her successor, James I (r. 1603–1625), witnessed remarkable literary expression. The terms *Elizabethan* and *Jacobean* (referring to the reign of James) are used to designate the English music, poetry, prose, and drama of this period. The poetry of Sir Philip Sidney (1554–1586), such as *Astrophel* and *Stella*, strongly influenced later poetic writing. The *Faerie Queene* of Edmund Spenser (1552–1599) endures as one of the greatest moral epics in any language. The rare poetic beauty of the plays of Christopher Marlowe (1564–1593), such as *Tamburlaine* and *The Jew of Malta*, paved the way for the work of Shakespeare. Above all, the immortal dramas of William Shakespeare (1564–1616) and the stately prose of the Authorized, or King James, Bible marked the Elizabethan and Jacobean periods as the golden age of English literature.

William Shakespeare, the son of a successful glove manufacturer in Stratford-on-Avon, chose a career on the London stage. By 1592 he had gained recognition as an actor and playwright. He performed in Lord Chamberlain's Company and became co-owner of the Globe Theatre, which after 1603 presented his plays.

Shakespeare's genius lay in the originality of his characterizations, the diversity of his plots, his understanding of human psychology, and his unexcelled gift for language. Shakespeare was a Renaissance man in his deep appreciation for classical culture, individualism, and humanism. Such plays as *Julius Caesar, Pericles,* and *Antony and Cleopatra* deal with classical subjects and figures. Several of his comedies have Italian Renaissance settings. The nine history plays, including *Richard II, Richard III*, and *Henry IV*, enjoyed the greatest popularity among Shakespeare's contemporaries. Written during the decade after the defeat of the Spanish Armada, the history plays express English national consciousness. Lines such as these from *Richard II* reflect this sense of national greatness with unparalleled eloquence:

This royal Throne of Kings, this sceptre'd Isle,
This earth of Majesty, this seat of Mars,
This other Eden, demi-paradise,
This fortress built by Nature for herself,
Against infection and the hand of war:
This happy breed of men, this little world,
This precious stone, set in the silver sea,
Which serves it in the office of a wall,
Or as a moat defensive to a house,
Against the envy of less happier Lands,
This blessed plot, this earth, this Realm, this England.

Shakespeare's later plays, above all the tragedies *Hamlet, Othello,* and *Macbeth,* explore an enormous range of human problems and are open to an almost infinite variety of interpretations. *Othello* portrays an honorable man destroyed by a flaw in his own character and the satanic

Titus Andronicus With classical allusions, fifteen murders and executions, a Gothic queen who takes a black lover, and incredible violence, this early Shakespearean tragedy (1594) was a melodramatic thriller that enjoyed enormous popularity with the London audience. Modern critics believe that it foreshadowed *King Lear* with its emphasis on suffering and madness. *(Reproduced by permission of the Marquess of Bath, Longleat House, Warminster, Wilts)*

evil of his supposed friend Iago. *Macbeth*'s central theme is exorbitant ambition. Shakespeare analyzes the psychology of sin in the figures of Macbeth and Lady Macbeth, whose mutual love under the pressure of ambition leads to their destruction. The central figure in *Hamlet,* a play suffused with individuality, wrestles with moral problems connected with revenge and with the human being's relationship to life and death. The soliloquy in which Hamlet debates suicide is perhaps the most widely quoted passage in English literature:

To be, or not to be: that is the question:
Whether 'tis nobler in the mind to suffer
The slings and arrows of outrageous fortune,
Or to take arms against a sea of troubles,
And by opposing end them?

Hamlet's sad cry "There is nothing either good or bad but thinking makes it so" expresses the anguish and uncertainty of modern life. *Hamlet* has always enjoyed great

popularity because in the title character's many-faceted personality people have seen an aspect of themselves.

Another great masterpiece of the Jacobean period was the Authorized Bible. At a theological conference in 1604, a group of Puritans urged James I to support a new translation of the Bible. The king in turn assigned the task to a committee of scholars, who published their efforts in 1611. Divided into chapters and verses, the Authorized Version is actually a revision of earlier Bibles more than an original work. Yet it provides a superb expression of the mature English vernacular in the early seventeenth century. Consider Psalm 37:

Fret not thy selfe because of evill doers, neither bee thou
*   envious against the workers of iniquitie.*
For they shall soone be cut downe like the grasse; and
*   wither as the greene herbe.*
Trust in the Lord, and do good, so shalt thou dwell in the
*   land, and verely thou shalt be fed.*

The Authorized Version, so called because it was produced under royal sponsorship—it had no official ecclesiastical endorsement—represented the Anglican and Puritan desire to encourage laypeople to read the Scriptures. It quickly achieved great popularity and displaced all earlier versions. British settlers carried this Bible to the North American colonies, where it became known as the King James Bible. For centuries the King James Bible has had a profound influence on the language and lives of English-speaking peoples.

Baroque Art and Music

Throughout European history, the cultural tastes of one age have often seemed quite unsatisfactory to the next. So it was with the baroque. The term **baroque** itself may have come from the Portuguese word for an "odd-shaped, imperfect pearl" and was commonly used by late-eighteenth-century art critics as an expression of scorn for what they considered an overblown, unbalanced style. The hostility of these critics, who also scorned the Gothic style of medieval cathedrals in favor of a classicism inspired by antiquity and the Renaissance, has long since passed. Specialists now agree that the triumphs of the baroque marked one of the high points in the history of Western culture.

In the early development of the baroque, scholars stress the influence of Rome and the revitalized Catholic church of the later sixteenth century. The papacy and the Jesuits encouraged the growth of an intensely emotional,

Juan de Pareja: The Calling of Saint Matthew   Using rich but subdued colors, Pareja depicts the biblical text (Mark 2:13–17), with Jesus in traditional first-century dress and the other figures, arranged around a table covered with an oriental carpet, in seventeenth-century apparel. Matthew, at Jesus' right hand, seems surprised by the "call." Pareja, following a long tradition, includes himself (*standing, rear center*). (*Museo Nacional del Prado, Madrid/The Bridgeman Art Library*)

Rubens: The Horrors of War With enormous intellectual and physical energy, as well as a large studio of assistants, Peter Paul Rubens was incredibly productive, the most influential figure in baroque art in northern Europe. In this dynamic allegory from 1638, Venus tries to restrain Mars (holding the torch); he is followed by disease and famine. The shrieking lady at left, clad in black, represents miserable Europe. *(Palazzo Pitti/The Bridgeman Art Library)*

exuberant art. These patrons wanted artists to go beyond the Renaissance focus on pleasing a small, wealthy, cultural elite. They wanted artists to appeal to the senses and thereby touch the souls and kindle the faith of ordinary churchgoers while proclaiming the power and confidence of the reformed Catholic church. In addition to this underlying religious emotionalism, the baroque drew its sense of drama, motion, and ceaseless striving from the Catholic Reformation. The interior of the famous Jesuit Church of Jesus in Rome—the Gesù—combined all these characteristics in its lavish, shimmering, wildly active decorations and frescoes.

Taking definite shape in Italy after 1600, the baroque style in the visual arts developed with exceptional vigor in Catholic countries—in Spain and Latin America, Austria, southern Germany, and Poland. Yet baroque art was more than just "Catholic art" in the seventeenth century and the first half of the eighteenth. True, neither Protes-

tant England nor the Netherlands ever came fully under the spell of the baroque, but neither did Catholic France. And Protestants accounted for some of the finest examples of baroque style, especially in music. The baroque style spread partly because its tension and bombast spoke to an agitated age, which was experiencing great violence and controversy in politics and religion.

In painting, the baroque reached maturity early with Peter Paul Rubens (1577–1640), the most outstanding and representative of baroque painters. Studying in his native Flanders and in Italy, where he was influenced by masters of the High Renaissance such as Michelangelo, Rubens developed his own rich, sensuous, colorful style, which was characterized by animated figures, melodramatic contrasts, and monumental size. Rubens excelled in glorifying monarchs such as Queen Mother Marie de' Medici of France. He was also a devout Catholic; nearly half of his pictures treat Christian subjects. Yet one of

Rubens's trademarks was fleshy, sensual nudes, who populate his canvases as Roman goddesses, water nymphs, and remarkably voluptuous saints and angels.

Rubens was enormously successful. To meet the demand for his work, he established a large studio and hired many assistants to execute his rough sketches and gigantic murals. Sometimes the master artist added only the finishing touches. Rubens's wealth and position—on occasion he was given special diplomatic assignments by the Habsburgs—affirmed that distinguished artists continued to enjoy the high social status they had won in the Renaissance.

In music, the baroque style reached its culmination almost a century later in the dynamic, soaring lines of the endlessly inventive Johann Sebastian Bach (1685–1750), one of the greatest composers the Western world has ever produced. Organist and choirmaster of several Lutheran churches across Germany, Bach was equally at home writing secular concertos and sublime religious cantatas. Bach's organ music, the greatest ever written, combined the baroque spirit of invention, tension, and emotion in an unforgettable striving toward the infinite. Unlike Rubens, Bach was not fully appreciated in his lifetime, but since the early nineteenth century his reputation has grown steadily.

Summary

European expansion and colonization took place against a background of religious conflict and rising national consciousness. Though the medieval religious framework had broken down, people still thought largely in religious terms. Europeans explained what they did politically and economically in terms of religious doctrine. Religious ideology served as a justification for a variety of goals, such as the French nobles' opposition to the Crown and the Dutch struggle for political and economic independence from Spain. In Germany, religious hatred and foreign ambition led to the Thirty Years' War. After 1648 the divisions between Protestant and Catholic tended to become permanent. Religious skepticism and racial attitudes were harbingers of developments to come. The essays of Montaigne, the plays of Marlowe and Shakespeare, the King James Bible, and the splendors of baroque art remain classic achievements of the Western cultural heritage.

In the sixteenth and seventeenth centuries, Europeans for the first time gained access to large parts of the globe. European peoples had the intellectual curiosity, driving ambition, and scientific technology to attempt feats that

were as difficult and expensive then as going to the moon is today. Exploration and exploitation contributed to a more sophisticated standard of living, in the form of spices and Asian luxury goods, and to a terrible international inflation resulting from the influx of South American silver and gold. Governments, the upper classes, and the peasantry were badly hurt by the resulting inflation. Meanwhile, the middle class of bankers, shippers, financiers, and manufacturers prospered for much of the seventeenth century.

Key Terms

Treaty of Cateau-Cambrésis
Huguenots
Saint Bartholomew's Day massacre
politiques
Edict of Nantes
bourse
Union of Utrecht
Escorial
Spanish Armada
Protestant Union
Peace of Westphalia
magnetic compass
astrolabe
General History of the Indies
Golden Century of Spain
price revolution
viceroyalties
quinto
witch
baroque

Notes

1. G. Parker, *The Grand Strategy of Philip II* (New Haven, Conn.: Yale University Press, 2000), pp. 83–84.
2. J. H. Hale, "War and Public Opinion in the Fifteenth and Sixteenth Centuries," *Past and Present* 22 (July 1962): 18–32.
3. Quoted in J. L. Motley, *The Rise of the Dutch Republic* (Philadelphia: David McKay, 1898), 1.109.
4. Quoted in P. Smith, *The Age of the Reformation* (New York: Henry Holt, 1951), p. 248.
5. H. Kamen, *Philip of Spain* (New Haven, Conn.: Yale University Press, 1997), pp. 76–78; the quotations are on pp. 77 and 76, respectively.
6. Quoted ibid., p. 235.
7. Parker, *Grand Strategy of Philip II,* pp. 115–122; the quotation is on p. 119.
8. H. Kamen, "The Economic and Social Consequences of the Thirty Years' War," *Past and Present* 39 (April 1968): 44–61.
9. Quoted in C. M. Cipolla, *Guns, Sails, and Empires: Technological Innovation and the Early Phases of European Expansion, 1400–1700* (New York: Minerva Press, 1965), pp. 115–116.
10. J. H. Parry, *The Age of Reconnaissance* (New York: Mentor Books, 1963), chaps. 3 and 5.
11. See C. R. Phillips, *Ciudad Real, 1500–1750: Growth, Crisis, and Readjustment in the Spanish Economy* (Cambridge, Mass.: Harvard University Press, 1979), pp. 103–104, 115.

12. Quoted in Cipolla, *Guns, Sails, and Empires,* p. 132.

13. Quoted in F. H. Littell, *The Macmillan Atlas: History of Christianity* (New York: Macmillan, 1976), p. 75.

14. Quoted in Cipolla, *Guns, Sails, and Empires,* p. 133.

15. S. E. Morison, *Admiral of the Ocean Sea: A Life of Christopher Columbus* (Boston: Little, Brown, 1942), p. 339.

16. T. K. Rabb, "Columbus: Villain or Hero," *The Princeton Alumni Weekly,* October 14, 1992, p. 13.

17. J. M. Cohen, ed. and trans., *The Four Voyages of Christopher Columbus* (New York: Penguin Books, 1969), p. 37.

18. Quoted in R. L. Kagan, "The Spain of Ferdinand and Isabella," in *Circa 1492: Art in the Age of Exploration,* ed. J. A. Levenson (Washington, D.C.: National Gallery of Art, 1991), p. 60.

19. Quoted in F. Maddison, "Tradition and Innovation: Columbus' First Voyage and Portuguese Navigation in the Fifteenth Century," ibid., p. 69.

20. See W. D. Phillips and C. R. Phillips, *The Worlds of Christopher Columbus* (Cambridge: Cambridge University Press, 1992), p. 273.

21. A. W. Crosby, Jr., *The Columbian Exchange: Biological and Cultural Consequences of 1492* (Westport, Conn.: Greenwood, 1972), pp. 64–121.

22. Ibid., pp. 122–163.

23. See M. E. Wiesner, *Women and Gender in Early Modern Europe* (New York: Cambridge University Press, 1994), pp. 21–25; the quotation is on p. 22.

24. Ibid., pp. 23–24.

25. This passage is based heavily on S. Ozment, *When Fathers Ruled: Family Life in Reformation Europe* (Cambridge, Mass.: Harvard University Press, 1983), pp. 50–99.

26. Ibid., pp. 85–92.

27. See D. Durant, *Bess of Hardwick: Portrait of an Elizabethan Dynasty* (London: Weidenfeld & Nicolson, 1977).

28. Quoted in Ozment, *When Fathers Ruled,* p. 56.

29. Ibid., pp. 9–14.

30. See F. Biot, *The Rise of Protestant Monasticism* (Baltimore: Helicon Press, 1968), pp. 74–78.

31. Wiesner, *Women and Gender in Early Modern Europe,* pp. 220–223.

32. See E. W. Monter, "The Pedestal and the Stake: Courtly Love and Witchcraft," in *Becoming Visible: Women in European History,* ed. R. Bridenthal and C. Koonz (Boston: Houghton Mifflin, 1977), pp. 132–135; and A. Fraser, *The Weaker Vessel* (New York: Random House, 1985), pp. 100–103.

33. C. Verlinden, *The Beginnings of Modern Colonization,* trans. Y. Freccero (Ithaca, N.Y.: Cornell University Press, 1970), pp. 5–6, 80–97.

34. This section leans heavily on D. B. Davis, *Slavery and Human Progress* (New York: Oxford University Press, 1984), pp. 54–62; the quotation is on p. 58.

35. Quoted in D. P. Mannix, with M. Cowley, *Black Cargoes: A History of the Atlantic Slave Trade* (New York: Viking Press, 1968), p. 5.

36. Quoted ibid., p. 19.

37. See P. Brown, "Understanding Islam," *New York Review of Books,* February 22, 1979, pp. 30–33.

38. Quoted in Davis, *Slavery and Human Progress,* pp. 43–44.

39. D. M. Frame, trans., *The Complete Works of Montaigne* (Stanford, Calif.: Stanford University Press, 1958), pp. 175–176.

40. C. Cotton, trans., *The Essays of Michel de Montaigne* (New York: A. L. Burt, 1893), pp. 207, 210.

41. Ibid., p. 523.

Suggested Reading

For the religious wars, in addition to the references in the Suggested Reading for Chapter 14 and the Notes to this chapter, see H. Kamen, *The Iron Century: Social Change in Europe, 1550–1660* (1971), a fundamental work; and G. Huppert, *After the Black Death: A Social History of Early Modern Europe* (1986), a lucidly written and highly recommended work for students. P. Roberts, *A City in Conflict: Troyes During the French Wars of Religion* (1996), provides a fascinating account of the bitter divisions the religious conflicts created among neighbors in one important French city. A. N. Galpern, *The Religions of the People in Sixteenth-Century Champagne* (1976), is a useful case study in religious anthropology, and W. A. Christian, Jr., *Local Religion in Sixteenth-Century Spain* (1981), traces the attitudes and practices of ordinary Spanish people. A. Cunningham and O. P. Grell, *The Four Horsemen of the Apocalypse: Religion, War, Famine and Death in Reformation Europe* (2000), explores the period 1490–1648 in terms of crises and the popular belief in the approaching Last Judgment.

For Spanish military operations in the Low Countries, see R. A. Stradling, *The Armada of Flanders: Spanish Maritime Policy and European War, 1568–1668* (1992). For the later phases of the Dutch-Spanish conflict, see J. I. Israel, *The Dutch Republic and the Hispanic World, 1606–1661* (1982), which treats the struggle in global perspective. Similarly, Geoffrey Parker, *The Grand Strategy of Philip II* (2000), treats Philip's attempts to rule a global empire.

The starting point for the study of England's great ruler is W. MacCaffrey, *Elizabeth I* (1993). N. Jones, *The Birth of the Elizabethan Age* (1993), brings to life the concerns of the English people. S. Frye, *Elizabeth I: The Competition for Representation* (1996), uses feminist analysis to describe the way Elizabeth built her public image and used her authority. C. Erickson, *The First Elizabeth* (1983), gives a psychologically resonant portrait, and C. Haight, *Elizabeth I* (1988), and J. E. Neale, *Queen Elizabeth I* (1957), remain helpful.

Nineteenth- and early-twentieth-century historians described the defeat of the Spanish Armada as a great victory for Protestantism, democracy, and capitalism, which those scholars tended to link together. More recent historians have treated the event in terms of its contemporary significance. H. Kamen, *Philip of Spain* (1971), offers a fine revisionist portrait of the ruler at the center of late-sixteenth-century international affairs. A. W. Lovett, *Early Habsburg Spain, 1517–1598* (1986), discusses many facets of Spanish culture. G. Mattingly, *The Armada* (1959), remains the most exciting and readable account of that event, but G. Parker and C. Martin, *The Spanish Armada* (1988), incorporates later literature.

R. G. Asch, *The Thirty Years War: The Holy Roman Empire and Europe* (1997), is an important revisionist study with

(continued on page 528)

Listening to the Past

Columbus Describes His First Voyage

*O*n his return voyage to Spain in January 1493, Christopher Columbus composed a letter intended for wide circulation and had copies of it sent ahead to Isabella and Ferdinand and others when the ship docked at Lisbon. Because the letter sums up Columbus's understanding of his achievements, it is considered the most important document of his first voyage. Remember that his knowledge of Asia rested heavily on Marco Polo's Travels, *published around 1298.*

Since I know that you will be pleased at the great success with which the Lord has crowned my voyage, I write to inform you how in thirty-three days I crossed from the Canary Islands to the Indies, with the fleet which our most illustrious sovereigns gave me. I found very many islands with large populations and took possession of them all for their Highnesses; this I did by proclamation and unfurled the royal standard. No opposition was offered.

I named the first island that I found "San Salvador," in honour of our Lord and Saviour who has granted me this miracle. . . . When I reached Cuba, I followed its north coast westwards, and found it so extensive that I thought this must be the mainland, the province of Cathay.* . . . From there I saw another island eighteen leagues eastwards which I then named "Hispaniola."† . . .

Hispaniola is a wonder. The mountains and hills, the plains and meadow lands are both fertile and beautiful. They are most suitable for planting crops and for raising cattle of all kinds, and there are good sites for building towns and villages. The harbours are incredibly fine and there are many great rivers with broad channels and the majority contain gold.‡ The trees, fruits and plants are very different from those of Cuba. In Hispaniola there are many spices and large mines of gold and other metals. . . .§

The inhabitants of this island, and all the rest that I discovered or heard of, go naked, as their mothers bore them, men and women alike. A few of the women, however, cover a single place with a leaf of a plant or piece of cotton which they weave for the purpose. They have no iron or steel or arms and are not capable of using them, not because they are not strong and well built but because they are amazingly timid. All the weapons they have are canes cut at seeding time, at the end of which they fix a sharpened stick, but they have not the courage to make use of these, for very often when I have sent two or three men to a village to have conversation with them a great number of them have come out. But as soon as they saw my men all fled immediately, a father not even waiting for his son. And this is not because we have harmed any of them; on the contrary, wherever I have gone and been able to have conversation with them, I have given them some of the various things I had, a cloth and other articles, and received nothing in exchange. But they have still remained incurably timid. True, when they have been reassured and lost their fear, they are so ingenuous and so liberal with all their possessions that no one who has not seen them would believe it. If one asks for anything they have they never say no. On the contrary, they offer a share to anyone with demonstrations of

---

*Cathay is the old name for China. In the log-book and later in this letter Columbus accepts the native story that Cuba is an island which they can circumnavigate in something more than twenty-one days, yet he insists here and later, during the second voyage, that it is in fact part of the Asiatic mainland.
†Hispaniola is the second largest island of the West Indies; Haiti occupies the western third of the island, the Dominican Republic the rest.

‡This did not prove to be true.
§These statements are also inaccurate.

heartfelt affection, and they are immediately content with any small thing, valuable or valueless, that is given them. I forbade the men to give them bits of broken crockery, fragments of glass or tags of laces, though if they could get them they fancied them the finest jewels in the world.

I hoped to win them to the love and service of their Highnesses and of the whole Spanish nation and to persuade them to collect and give us of the things which they possessed in abundance and which we needed. They have no religion and are not idolaters; but all believe that power and goodness dwell in the sky and they are firmly convinced that I have come from the sky with these ships and people. In this belief they gave me a good reception everywhere, once they had overcome their fear; and this is not because they are stupid—far from it, they are men of great intelligence, for they navigate all those seas, and give a marvellously good account of everything—but because they have never before seen men clothed or ships like these. . . .

In all these islands the men are seemingly content with one woman, but their chief or king is allowed more than twenty. The women appear to work more than the men and I have not been able to find out if they have private property. As far as I could see whatever a man had was shared among all the rest and this particularly applies to food. . . . In another island, which I am told is larger than Hispaniola, the people have no hair. Here there is a vast quantity of gold, and from here and the other islands I bring Indians as evidence.

In conclusion, to speak only of the results of this very hasty voyage, their Highnesses can see that I will give them as much gold as they require, if they will render me some very slight assistance; also I will give them all the spices and cotton they want. . . . I will also bring them as much aloes as they ask and as many slaves, who will be taken from the idolaters. I believe also that I have found rhubarb and cinnamon and there will be countless other things in addition. . . .

So all Christendom will be delighted that our Redeemer has given victory to our most illustrious King and Queen and their renowned kingdoms, in this great matter. They should hold great celebrations and render solemn thanks to the Holy Trinity with many solemn prayers, for the great triumph which they will have, by the

Christopher Columbus, by Ridolpho Ghirlandio. Friend of Raphael and teacher of Michelangelo, Ghirlandio (1483–1561) enjoyed distinction as a portrait painter, and so we can assume this is a good likeness of the older Columbus. *(Scala/Art Resource, NY)*

conversion of so many peoples to our holy faith and for the temporal benefits which will follow, for not only Spain, but all Christendom will receive encouragement and profit.

This is a brief account of the facts. Written in the caravel off the Canary Islands.[||]
15 February 1493

At your orders
THE ADMIRAL

Questions for Analysis

1. How did Columbus explain the success of his voyage?

2. What was Columbus's view of the Native Americans he met?

3. Evaluate his statements that the Caribbean islands possessed gold, cotton, and spices.

4. Why did Columbus cling to the idea that he had reached Asia?

[||]Actually, Columbus was off Santa Maria in the Azores.

Source: J. M. Cohen, ed. and trans., *The Four Voyages of Christopher Columbus* (Penguin Classics, 1958), pp. 115–123. Copyright © J. M. Cohen, 1958. Reproduced by permission of Penguin Books, Ltd.

valuable material on the role of war finance in domestic and international aspects of the conflict. G. Parker, *The Thirty Years' War* (1984), is important but densely written. A variety of opinions on the causes and results of the war are given in T. K. Rabb's anthology, *The Thirty Years' War* (1981).

A good starting point for the study of European society in the age of exploration is J. A. Levenson's anthology *Circa 1492: Art in the Age of Exploration* (1991), which treats geographical, nautical, political, and humanistic developments in a worldwide context. Parry, cited in the Notes, which addresses the causes and consequences of the voyage of discovery, and J. H. Parry, *The Discovery of South America* (1979), which examines Europeans' reactions to the maritime discoveries and the whole concept of discovery, are still valuable. The urbane studies of C. M. Cipolla, including the one cited in the Notes, *Clocks and Culture, 1300–1700* (1967), *Cristofano and the Plague: A Study in the History of Public Health in the Age of Galileo* (1973), and *Public Health and the Medical Profession in the Renaissance* (1976), present fascinating material on technological and sociological developments in a lucid style. The work of W. D. Phillips and C. R. Phillips, cited in the Notes, is strongly recommended. The advanced student should consult F. Braudel, *Civilization and Capitalism, 15th–18th Century*, vol. 1: *The Structures of Everyday Life* (1981); vol. 2: *The Wheels of Commerce* (1982); and vol. 3: *The Perspective of the World* (1984). These fat volumes combine vast erudition, a global perspective, and remarkable illustrations.

On witches and witchcraft, M. E. Wiesner, *Women and Gender in Early Modern Europe* (1994), contains sound material as well as an extensive bibliography. For women, marriage, and the family, see in addition to the title by Wiesner, L. Stone, *The Family, Sex, and Marriage in England, 1500–1800* (1977), a controversial work; D. Underdown, "The Taming of the Scold," and S. Amussen, "Gender, Family, and the Social Order," in *Order and Disorder in Early Modern England*, ed. A. Fletcher and J. Stevenson (1985); A. Macfarlane, *Marriage and Love in England: Modes of Reproduction, 1300–1848* (1986); C. R. Boxer, *Women in Iber-*ian *Expansion Overseas, 1415–1815* (1975), a helpful study of women's role in overseas migration; S. M. Wyntjes, "Women in the Reformation Era," in *Becoming Visible: Women in European History,* ed. R. Bridenthal and C. Koonz (1977), a quick survey of conditions in different countries; A. Clark, *The Working Life of Women in the Seventeenth Century* (1968); K. M. Wilson, ed., *Women Writers of the Renaissance and Reformation* (1987); M. J. M. Ezell, *The Patriarch's Wife: Literary Evidence and the History of the Family* (1987); and L. Pollock, *A Lasting Relationship: Parents and Children over Three Centuries* (1987). Ozment's work listed in the Notes is a seminal study concentrating on Germany and Switzerland.

As background to slavery and racism in North and South America, students should see J. L. Watson, ed., *Asian and African Systems of Slavery* (1980), a valuable collection of essays, as well as the works by Davis and by Mannix and Cowley mentioned in the Notes: Davis shows how slavery was viewed as a progressive force in the expansion of the Western world, and Mannix and Cowley provide a hideously fascinating account of the slave trade. For North American conditions, interested students should consult W. D. Jordan, *The White Man's Burden: Historical Origins of Racism in the United States* (1974). The excellent essays in G. M. Frederickson, *The Arrogance of Race: Historical Perspectives on Slavery, Racism, and Social Inequality* (1988), stress the social and economic circumstances associated with the rise of plantation slavery. For Caribbean and South American developments, see F. P. Bowser, *The African Slave in Colonial Peru* (1974); J. S. Handler and F. W. Lange, *Plantation Slavery in Barbados: An Archeological and Historical Investigation* (1978); and R. E. Conrad, *Children of God's Fire: A Documentary History of Black Slavery in Brazil* (1983).

The leading authority on Montaigne is D. M. Frame; see his *Montaigne's Discovery of Man* (1955) and his translation listed in the Notes. For baroque art, see V. L. Tapié, *The Age of Grandeur: Baroque Art and Architecture* (1961), and J. Montague, *Roman Baroque Sculpture: The Industry of Art* (1985), an original and entertaining study.

Pierre-Denis Martin, *View of the Chateau de Versailles,* 1722. With their classically harmonious, symmetrical, and geometric design, Versailles and its gardens nevertheless seem baroque in their vast size and extension. *(Châteaux de Versailles et de Trianon, Versailles/Réunion des Musées Nationaux/Art Resource, NY)*

chapter

16

Absolutism and Constitutionalism in Western Europe (ca 1589–1715)

chapter outline

- Absolutism

- Constitutionalism

*T*he seventeenth century was a period of revolutionary transformation. That century witnessed agricultural and manufacturing crises that had profound political consequences. A colder and wetter climate throughout most of the period meant a shorter farming season. Grain yields declined. In an age when cereals constituted the bulk of the diet for most people everywhere, smaller harvests led to food shortages and starvation. Food shortages in turn meant population decline or stagnation. Industry also suffered. While the evidence does not permit broad generalizations, it appears that the output of woolen textiles, one of the most important manufactures, declined sharply in the first half of the century. This economic crisis was not universal: it struck various sections of Europe at different times and to different degrees. In the middle decades of the century, Spain, France, Germany, and England all experienced great economic difficulties; but these years saw the golden age of the Netherlands.

Meanwhile, governments increased their spending, primarily for state armies; in the seventeenth century, armies grew larger than they had been since the time of the Roman Empire. To pay for these armies, governments taxed. The greatly increased burden of taxation, falling on a population already existing at a subsistence level, triggered revolts. Peasant revolts were extremely common;[1] in France, urban disorders were so frequent an aspect of the social and political landscape as to be "a distinctive feature of life."[2]

Princes struggled to free themselves from the restrictions of powerful social groups or competing institutions. Spanish and French monarchs gained control of the major institution in their domains, the Roman Catholic church. Rulers of England and some of the German principalities set up national churches. In the German Empire, the Peace of Westphalia placed territorial sovereignty in the princes' hands. The kings of France, England, and Spain claimed the basic loyalty of their subjects. Monarchs made and enforced public laws, such as criminal law, which concerned the state and its rights and powers; but private or customary law, such as property law, which concerned relations between citizens, continued in the control of local elites, the nobility.

Monarchical power added up to something close to **sovereignty**. A state may be termed *sovereign* when it possesses a monopoly over the instruments of justice and the use of force within clearly defined boundaries. In a sovereign

531

state, no system of courts, such as ecclesiastical tribunals, competes with state courts in the dispensation of justice; and private armies, such as those of feudal lords, present no threat to royal authority because the state's army is stronger. Royal law touches all persons within the country.

Sovereignty had been evolving during the late sixteenth century. Most seventeenth-century governments now needed to address the problem of *which* authority within the state would possess sovereignty—the Crown or privileged groups. In the period between roughly 1589 and 1715, two basic patterns of government emerged in Europe: absolute monarchy and the constitutional state. Almost all subsequent European governments have been modeled on one of these patterns.

- How did these forms of government differ from the feudal and dynastic monarchies of earlier centuries?
- In what sense were these forms "modern"?
- What social and economic factors limited absolute monarchs?
- Which Western countries most clearly illustrate the new patterns of political organization?
- Why is the seventeenth century considered the "golden age of the Netherlands"?

This chapter will explore these questions.

Absolutism

In the Middle Ages, jurists held that as a consequence of kings' coronation and anointment with sacred oil, they ruled "by the grace of God." Law was given by God, kings discovered or "found" the law, and kings acknowledged that they must respect and obey the law. In contrast, in the *absolutist* state, kings claimed to rule "by divine right," meaning that they were responsible to God alone. In the seventeenth and eighteenth centuries, kings became legislators: they made law. Because they made the law, sovereignty was embodied in the person of the king. The seal of the king of France, showing him sitting in judgment, was intended to reveal his full power (the physical means to do something) and his authority (the legal right to do something).

Absolute rulers tried to control competing jurisdictions, institutions, or interest groups in their territories. They regulated religious sects. They abolished the liberties long held by certain areas, groups, or provinces. Absolute kings also secured the cooperation of the one class that historically had posed the greatest threat to monarchy, the nobility. Medieval governments, restrained

by the church, the feudal nobility, and their own financial limitations, had been able to exert none of these controls.

In some respects, the key to the power and success of absolute monarchs lay in how they solved their financial problems. Medieval kings frequently had found temporary financial support through bargains with the nobility: the nobility agreed to an ad hoc grant of money in return for freedom from future taxation. In contrast, the absolutist solution was the creation of new state bureaucracies that directed the economic life of the country in the interests of the king, either forcing taxes ever higher or devising alternative methods of raising revenue.

Bureaucracies were composed of career officials appointed by and solely accountable to the king. The backgrounds of these civil servants varied. Absolute monarchs sometimes drew on the middle class, as in France, or utilized members of the nobility, as in Spain and eastern Europe. Where there was no middle class or an insignificant one, as in Austria, Prussia, Spain, and Russia, the government of the absolutist state consisted of an interlocking elite of monarchy, aristocracy, and bureaucracy.

Royal agents in medieval and Renaissance kingdoms had used their public offices and positions to benefit themselves and their families. In England, for example, Crown servants from Thomas Becket to Thomas Wolsey had treated their high offices as their private property and reaped considerable profit from them. Early modern bureaucrats continued to use their offices to enrich themselves.[3] The striking difference between seventeenth-century bureaucracies and their predecessors was that seventeenth-century civil servants served the state as represented by the king. Bureaucrats recognized that the offices they held were public, or state, positions. The state paid them salaries to handle revenues that belonged to the Crown. Bureaucrats gradually came to distinguish between public duties and private property.

Absolute monarchs also maintained permanent standing armies. Medieval armies had been raised by feudal lords for particular wars or campaigns, after which the troops were disbanded. In the seventeenth century, monarchs alone recruited and maintained armies—in peacetime as well as wartime. Kings deployed their troops both inside and outside the country in the interests of the monarchy. Armies became basic features of absolutist, and modern, states. Absolute rulers also invented new methods of compulsion. They concerned themselves with the private lives of potentially troublesome subjects, often through the use of secret police.

The word **absolutism** was coined in 1830, two centuries after the developments it attempts to classify occurred. Some scholars today deny that absolute monarchy

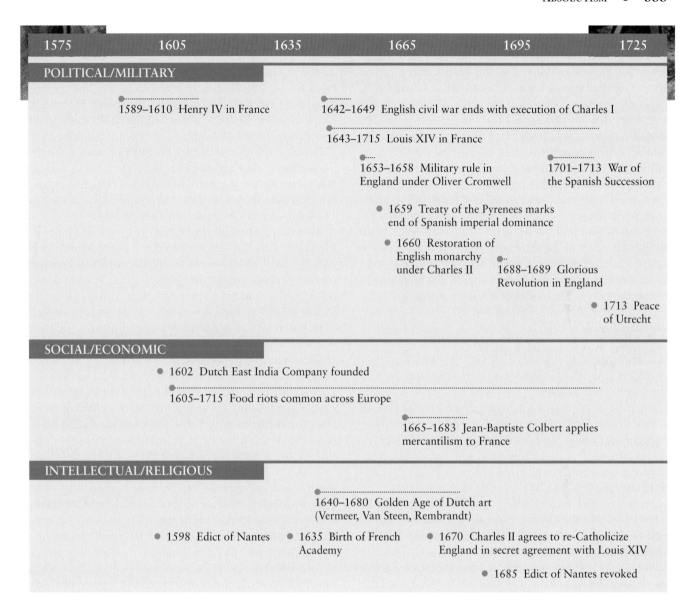

1575	1605	1635	1665	1695	1725

POLITICAL/MILITARY

1589–1610 Henry IV in France

1642–1649 English civil war ends with execution of Charles I

1643–1715 Louis XIV in France

1653–1658 Military rule in England under Oliver Cromwell

1701–1713 War of the Spanish Succession

1659 Treaty of the Pyrenees marks end of Spanish imperial dominance

1660 Restoration of English monarchy under Charles II

1688–1689 Glorious Revolution in England

1713 Peace of Utrecht

SOCIAL/ECONOMIC

1602 Dutch East India Company founded

1605–1715 Food riots common across Europe

1665–1683 Jean-Baptiste Colbert applies mercantilism to France

INTELLECTUAL/RELIGIOUS

1640–1680 Golden Age of Dutch art (Vermeer, Van Steen, Rembrandt)

1598 Edict of Nantes

1635 Birth of French Academy

1670 Charles II agrees to re-Catholicize England in secret agreement with Louis XIV

1685 Edict of Nantes revoked

was a stage in the evolution of the modern state between medieval feudal monarchies and the constitutional governments of recent centuries. As one student of early modern France writes, "I believe the prevailing historiographical concept of 'absolute monarchy' is a myth promulgated by the royal government and legitimized by historians."[4] Such historians prefer the term *administrative monarchy,* by which they mean that the French state in the seventeenth century became stronger in that it could achieve more of its goals, it was centralized from Paris, and its administrative bureaucracy greatly expanded. Although the administrative monarchy interfered in many aspects of the private individual's daily life, it did not have

the consent of the governed, and it especially lacked the idea of the rule of law—law made by a representative body—the administrative monarchy was actually limited, or checked, in ways that traditional interpretations of absolute monarchy did not consider.[5]

The rule of absolute monarchs was not all-embracing because they lacked the financial and military resources and the technology to make it so. Thus the absolutist state was not the same as a totalitarian state. **Totalitarianism** was a twentieth-century phenomenon; it sought to direct all facets of a state's culture—art, education, religion, the economy, and politics—in the interests of the state. By definition, totalitarian rule is *total* regulation. By twentieth-century standards, the ambitions of absolute monarchs were quite limited: each ruler sought the exaltation of himself or herself as the embodiment of the state. Whether or not Louis XIV of France actually said, *"L'état, c'est moi!"* (I am the state!), the remark expresses his belief that he personified the French state. Perhaps over the course of his long life, however, he changed his mind. Louis is reputed to have said on his deathbed, "I am going, but the state remains," a remark suggesting that at the end of his life he drew a distinction between himself and the state. Scholars debate this issue but agree that absolutist states such as France did foreshadow recent totalitarian regimes in two fundamental respects: in the glorification of the state over all other aspects of the culture and in the use of war and an expansionist foreign policy to divert attention from domestic ills. France itself is aptly known as the model of absolute monarchy.

The Foundations of French Absolutism: Henry IV, Sully, and Richelieu

In 1589 Henry IV (r. 1589–1610) inherited an enormous mess (see pages 490–492). Civil wars had wracked France since 1561. Catastrophically poor harvests meant that all across France peasants lived on the verge of starvation, fighting off wolves and bands of demobilized soldiers. Some provinces, such as Burgundy, suffered almost complete depopulation. Commercial activity had fallen to one-third its 1580 level. Nobles, officials, merchants, and peasants wanted peace, order, and stability. "Henri le Grand" (Henry the Great), as the king was called, promised "a chicken in every pot" and inaugurated a remarkable recovery. Henry may have been the first French ruler since Louis IX, in the thirteenth century, genuinely to care about his people, and he was the only king whose statue the Paris crowd did not tear down in the Revolution of 1789.

Henry converted to Catholicism and sought better relations with the pope. He tried to gain Protestant confidence by issuing the Edict of Nantes in 1598 (see page 492) and by appointing the devout Protestant Maximilien de Béthune, duke of Sully, as his chief minister. Aside from a short, successful war with Savoy in 1601, Henry kept France at peace. Maintaining that "if we are without compassion for the people, they must succumb and we all perish with them," Henry sharply lowered taxes on the overburdened peasants. In compensation for the lost revenues, in 1602–1604 he introduced the *paulette,* an annual fee paid by royal officials to guarantee heredity in their offices.

Sully proved to be an effective administrator. He combined the indirect taxes on salt, sales, and transit and leased their collection to financiers. Although the number of taxes declined, revenues increased because of the revival of trade.[6] One of the first French officials to appreciate the possibilities of overseas trade, Sully subsidized the Company for Trade with the Indies. He started a country-wide highway system and even dreamed of an international organization for the maintenance of peace.

In only twelve years, Henry IV and Sully restored public order in France and laid the foundations for economic prosperity. By the standards of the time, Henry IV's government was progressive and promising. His murder in 1610 by a crazed fanatic led to a severe crisis.

After the death of Henry IV, the queen-regent Marie de' Medici headed the government for the child-king Louis XIII (r. 1610–1643), but in fact feudal nobles and princes of the blood dominated the political scene. In 1624 Marie de' Medici secured the appointment of Armand Jean du Plessis—Cardinal Richelieu (1585–1642)—to the council of ministers. It was a remarkable appointment. The next year, Richelieu became president of the council, and after 1628 he was first minister of the French crown. Richelieu used his strong influence over King Louis XIII to exalt the French monarchy as the embodiment of the French state. One of the greatest servants of that state, Richelieu set in place the cornerstone of French absolutism, and his work served as the basis for France's cultural hegemony of Europe in the later seventeenth century.

Richelieu's policy was the total subordination of all groups and institutions to the French monarchy. The French nobility, with its selfish and independent interests, had long constituted the foremost threat to the centralizing goals of the Crown and to a strong national state. Therefore, Richelieu sought to curb the power of the nobility. In 1624 he succeeded in reshuffling the royal council, eliminating potential power brokers. Thereafter Richelieu dominated the council in an unprecedented way. He leveled castles, long the symbol of feudal independence, and crushed aristocratic conspiracies with quick executions. For example, when the duke of Montmorency, the first peer of France and godson of Henry IV, became involved in a revolt, he was summarily beheaded.

The constructive genius of Cardinal Richelieu is best reflected in the administrative system he established. He extended the use of the royal commissioners called intendants. France was divided into thirty-two *généralités* (districts), in each of which after 1634 a royal intendant held a commission to perform specific tasks, often financial but also judicial and policing. Intendants transmitted information from local communities to Paris and delivered

Louis de Caulery: Ball in the Reign of Henry IV (detail) Children dressed as adults imitate the courtly manners and aristocratic behavior of their parents. The vastness of space, the rich clothes, and the columns in the rear suggest the elegance and wealth of the French court. *(Musée de Beaux-Arts, Rennes/Giraudon/The Bridgeman Art Library)*

royal orders from the capital to their généralités. Almost always recruited from the newer judicial nobility, the *noblesse de robe,* intendants were appointed directly by the monarch, to whom they were solely responsible. They could not be natives of the districts where they held authority; thus they had no vested interest in their localities. The intendants recruited men for the army, supervised the collection of taxes, presided over the administration of local law, checked up on the local nobility, and regulated economic activities—commerce, trade, the guilds, marketplaces—in their districts. They were to use their power for two related purposes: to enforce royal orders in the généralités of their jurisdiction and to weaken the power and influence of the regional nobility. As the intendants' power increased under Richelieu, so did the power of the centralized French state.

In 1598 Henry IV's lawyers had drawn up the "Law of Concord." It had been published as the Edict of Nantes to create a temporary and provisional situation of religious toleration in order to promote *temporary* religious and civil concord between the Calvinist, Reformed, or Huguenot faith and Roman Catholicism. Full religious toleration of peoples of differing faiths in a pluralistic society developed only in the eighteenth century (see page 484). Meantime, all French people were theoretically reunited under the king's religion, Roman Catholicism. The Edict of Nantes named 150 towns throughout France; the king granted Protestants the right to practice their faith in those towns, and he gave the towns 180,000 écus to support the maintenance of their military garrisons. Huguenots numbered perhaps 10 percent of the total French population, most of them concentrated in the southwest. In 1627 Louis XIII, with the unanimous consent of the royal council, decided to end Protestant military and political independence, because, he said, it constituted "a state within a state." According to Louis, Huguenots demanded freedom of conscience but did not allow Catholics to worship in their cities. He interpreted this inequity as *political* disobedience.[7]

Attention focused on La Rochelle, fourth largest of the French Atlantic ports and a major commercial center with strong ties to the northern Protestant states of Holland and England. Louis intended to cut off English aid, and he personally supervised the siege of La Rochelle. The city fell in October 1628. Its municipal government was suppressed, and its walled fortifications were destroyed. Although Protestants retained the right of public worship, the king reinstated the Catholic liturgy, and Cardinal Richelieu himself celebrated the first Mass. The military fall of La Rochelle weakened the influence of aristocratic adherents of Calvinism and was one step in the evolution of a unified French state.

Louis XIII, Richelieu, and later Louis XIV also faced serious urban protests. Real or feared unemployment, high food prices, grain shortages, new taxes, and what ordinary townspeople perceived as oppressive taxation all triggered domestic violence. Major insurrections occurred at Dijon in 1630 and 1668, at Bordeaux in 1635 and 1675, at Montpellier in 1645, at Lyons in 1667–1668 and 1692, and at Amiens in 1685, 1695, 1704, and 1711. Sometimes rumor and misinformation sparked these riots. In any case, they were all characterized by deep popular anger, a vocabulary of violence, and what a recent historian calls "the culture of retribution"—that is, the punishment of royal "outsiders," officials who attempted to announce or to collect taxes. These officials often were seized, beaten, and hacked to death. For example, in 1673 Louis XIV's imposition of new taxes on legal transactions, tobacco, and pewterware provoked a major uprising in Bordeaux.

Municipal and royal authorities responded feebly. They lacked the means of strong action. They feared that stern repressive measures, such as sending in troops to fire on crowds, would create martyrs and further inflame the situation, while forcible full-scale military occupation of a city would be very expensive. Thus authorities allowed the crowds to "burn themselves out," as long as they did not do too much damage. Royal edicts were suspended, prisoners were released, and discussions were initiated. By the end of the century, municipal governments were better integrated into the national structure, and local authorities had the prompt military support of the Paris government. Those who publicly opposed government policies and taxes received swift and severe punishment.[8]

French foreign policy under Richelieu was aimed at the destruction of the fence of Habsburg territories that surrounded France. Consequently, Richelieu supported the Habsburgs' enemies. In 1631 he signed a treaty with the Lutheran king Gustavus Adolphus promising French support against the Catholic Habsburgs in what has been called the Swedish phase of the Thirty Years' War (see page 498). French influence became an important factor in the political future of the German Empire. Richelieu acquired for France extensive rights in Alsace in the east and Arras in the north.

Richelieu's efforts at centralization extended even to literature. In 1635 he gave official recognition to a group of philologists who were interested in grammar and rhetoric. Thus was born the French Academy. With Richelieu's encouragement, the French Academy began the preparation of a dictionary to standardize the French language; it was completed in 1694. The French Academy survives as a prestigious society, and its membership now includes people outside the field of literature.

All of these new policies, especially war, cost money. In his *Political Testament,* Richelieu wrote, "I have always said that finances are the sinews of the state." He meant that revenues determine a government's ability to inaugurate and enforce policies and programs. A state secures its revenues through taxation. But the political and economic structure of France greatly limited the government's ability to tax. Seventeenth-century France remained "a collection of local economies and local societies dominated by local elites." The rights of some as-

semblies in some provinces, such as Brittany, to vote their own taxes; the hereditary exemption from taxation of many wealthy members of the nobility and the middle class; and the royal pension system drastically limited the government's power to tax.

Richelieu and, later, Louis XIV temporarily solved their financial problems by securing the cooperation of local elites. The central government shared the proceeds of tax revenue with local powers. It never gained all the income it needed. Because the French monarchy could not tax at will, it never completely controlled the financial system. In practice, therefore, French absolutism was limited.[9]

In building the French state, Richelieu believed he had to resort to drastic measures against persons and groups within France and to conduct a tough anti-Habsburg foreign policy. He knew also that his approach sometimes seemed to contradict traditional Christian teaching. As a priest and bishop, how did he justify his policies? He developed his own **raison d'état** (reason of state): "Where the interests of the state are concerned, God absolves actions which, if privately committed, would be a crime."[10]

Richelieu's successor as chief minister and then regent for the boy-king Louis XIV was Cardinal Jules Mazarin (1602–1661). He continued Richelieu's centralizing policies, but his attempts to increase royal revenues led to the civil wars of 1648–1653 known as the **Fronde.**

The word *fronde* means "slingshot" or "catapult," and a *frondeur* was originally a street urchin who threw mud at the passing carriages of the rich. But the Fronde originated in the provinces, not Paris, and the term *frondeur* came to be applied to anyone who opposed the policies of the government. Many individuals and groups did so. Influential segments of the nobility resented the increased power of the monarchy under Louis XIII and what they perceived as their diminished role in government. Mazarin could not control them as Richelieu had done. Royal bureaucrats, judges in the parlements, and intendants who considered their positions the means to social and economic advancement felt that they were being manipulated by the Crown and their interests ignored.[11] The state's financial situation steadily weakened because entire regions of France refused to pay taxes. The French defeat of Spanish armies at Rocroi in 1643 marked the final collapse of Spanish military power in Europe; the victory also led the French people to believe that because peace was at hand, taxes were unnecessary. When a desperate government devised new taxes, the Parlement of Paris rejected them. Popular rebellions led by aristocratic factions broke out in the provinces and spread to Paris.[12] As rebellion continued, civil order broke down completely. A vast increase in the state bureaucracy, representing an expansion of royal power, and new means of extracting money from working people incurred the bitter opposition of peasants and urban artisans. Violence continued intermittently for the next twelve years.

The conflicts of the Fronde had three significant results for the future. First, it became apparent that the government would have to compromise with the bureaucrats and social elites that controlled local institutions and constituted the state bureaucracy. These groups were already largely exempt from taxation, and Louis XIV confirmed their privileged social status. Second, the French economy was badly disrupted and would take years to rebuild. Third, the Fronde had a traumatic effect on the young Louis XIV. The king and his mother were frequently threatened and sometimes treated as prisoners by aristocratic factions. On one occasion, a mob broke into the royal bedchamber to make sure the king was actually there; it succeeded in giving him a bad fright. Louis never forgot such humiliations. The period of the Fronde formed the cornerstone of his political education and of his conviction that the sole alternative to anarchy was absolute monarchy. The personal rule of Louis XIV represented the culmination of the process of centralization, but it also witnessed the institutionalization of procedures that would ultimately undermine the absolute monarchy.

The Absolute Monarchy of Louis XIV

According to the court theologian Bossuet, the clergy at the coronation of Louis XIV in Reims Cathedral asked God to cause the splendors of the French court to fill all who beheld it with awe. God subsequently granted that prayer. In the reign of Louis XIV (r. 1643–1715), the longest in European history, the French monarchy reached the peak of absolutist development. In the magnificence of his court, in the brilliance of the culture that he presided over and that permeated all of Europe, and in his remarkably long life, the "Sun King" dominated his age. No wonder scholars have characterized the second half of the seventeenth century as the "Grand Century," the "Age of Magnificence," and, echoing the eighteenth-century philosopher Voltaire, the "Age of Louis XIV."

In old age, Louis claimed that he had grown up learning very little, but recent historians think he was being modest. True, he knew little Latin and only the rudiments of arithmetic and thus by Renaissance standards was not well educated. Nevertheless, he learned to speak Italian and Spanish fluently, he spoke and wrote elegant French, and he knew some French history and more European geography than the ambassadors accredited to his court. He imbibed the devout Catholicism of his mother, Anne of Austria, and throughout his long life scrupu-

lously performed his religious duties. (Beginning in 1661, Louis attended Mass daily, but rather than paying attention to the liturgy, he said his rosary—to the scorn of his courtiers, who considered this practice "rustic.") Religion, Anne, and Mazarin all taught Louis that God had established kings as his rulers on earth. The royal coronation consecrated Louis to God's service, and he was certain—to use Shakespeare's phrase—that there was a divinity that doth hedge a king. Though kings were a race apart, they could not do as they pleased: they had to obey God's laws and rule for the good of the people.

Louis's education was more practical than formal. Under Mazarin's instruction, he studied state papers as they arrived, and he attended council meetings and sessions at which French ambassadors were dispatched abroad and foreign ambassadors received. He learned by direct experience and gained professional training in the work of government. Above all, the misery he suffered during the Fronde gave him an eternal distrust of the nobility and a profound sense of his own isolation. Accordingly, silence, caution, and secrecy became political tools for the achievement of his goals. His characteristic answer to requests of all kinds became the enigmatic *"Je verrai"* (I shall see).

Louis grew up with an absolute sense of his royal dignity. Contemporaries considered him tall (he was actually five feet five inches) and distinguished in appearance but inclined to heaviness because of the gargantuan meals in which he indulged. Louis XIV was a consummate actor, and his "terrifying majesty" awed all who saw him. He worked extremely hard and succeeded in being "every moment and every inch a king." Because he so relished the role of monarch, historians have had difficulty distinguishing the man from the monarch.

Historians have often said that Louis XIV introduced significant government innovations, the greatest of which was "the complete domestication of the nobility." By this phrase scholars mean that he exercised complete control over the powerful social class that historically had opposed the centralizing goals of the French monarchy. Recent research has suggested that notions of "domestication" represent an exaggeration. What Louis XIV actually achieved was the cooperation of the nobility. Throughout France the nobility agreed to participate in projects that both exalted the monarchy and reinforced the aristocrats' ancient prestige. Thus the relationship between the Crown and the nobility constituted collaboration rather than absolute control.

In the province of Languedoc, for example, Louis and his agents persuaded the notables to support the construction of the Canal des Deux Mers, a waterway linking the Mediterranean Sea and the Atlantic Ocean. Royal

Luca Giordano: The Pasta Eater   In the seventeenth century, rich people carried a fork when they dined out, but its use spread very slowly from Italy and came into common use only about 1750. A German preacher damned the fork as a diabolical luxury: "God would not have given us fingers if he wanted us to use forks." So, if King Louis XIV could eat chicken stew with his fingers without spilling it, how can we fault this Neapolitan workingman for enjoying his pasta without a fork? *(The Art Museum, Princeton University Museum purchase, John Maclean Magie and Gertrude Magie Fund. Photo: Bruce White)*

encouragement for the manufacture of luxury draperies in Languedocian towns likewise tied provincial business people to national goals, although French cloths subsequently proved unable to compete with cheaper Dutch ones. Above all, in the campaign for the repression of the Huguenots, the interests of the monarchy and nobility coincided (see page 541). Through mutual collaboration, the nobility and the king achieved goals that neither could have won without the other. For his part, Louis won increased military taxation from the Estates of Languedoc. In return, Louis graciously granted the nobility and dignitaries privileged social status and increased access to his person, which meant access to the enormous patronage the king had to dispense. French

government rested on the social and political structure of seventeenth-century France, a structure in which the nobility historically exercised great influence. In this respect, therefore, French absolutism was not so much modern as the last phase of a historical feudal society.[13]

Louis XIV installed his royal court at Versailles, a small town ten miles from Paris. He required all the great nobility of France, at the peril of social, political, and sometimes economic disaster, to come live at Versailles for at least part of the year. Today Versailles stands as the best surviving museum of a vanished society on earth. In the seventeenth century, it became a model of rational order, the center of France, and the perfect symbol of the king's power. (See the feature "Listening to the Past: The Court at Versailles" on pages 562–563.)

Louis XIII had begun Versailles as a hunting lodge, a retreat from a queen he did not like. His son's architects, Le Nôtre and Le Vau, turned what the duke of Saint-Simon called "the most dismal and thankless of sights" into a veritable paradise. Wings were added to the original building to make the palace U-shaped. Everywhere at Versailles the viewer had a sense of grandeur, vastness, and elegance. Enormous staterooms became display galleries for inlaid tables, Italian marble statuary, Gobelin tapestries woven at the state factory in Paris, silver ewers, and beautiful (if uncomfortable) furniture. If genius means attention to detail, Louis XIV and his designers had it: the decor was perfected down to the last doorknob and keyhole. In the gigantic Hall of Mirrors, later to reflect so much of German as well as French history, hundreds of candles illuminated the domed ceiling, where allegorical paintings celebrated the king's victories.

The art and architecture of Versailles served as fundamental tools of state policy under Louis XIV. The king used architecture to overawe his subjects and foreign visitors. Versailles was seen as a reflection of French genius. Thus the Russian tsar Peter the Great imitated Versailles in the construction of his palace, Peterhof, as did the Prussian emperor Frederick the Great in his palace at Potsdam outside Berlin.

As in architecture, so too in language. Beginning in the reign of Louis XIV, French became the language of polite society and the vehicle of diplomatic exchange. French also gradually replaced Latin as the language of international scholarship and learning. The wish of other kings to ape the courtly style of Louis XIV and the imitation of French intellectuals and artists spread the language all over Europe. The royal courts of Sweden, Russia, Poland, and Germany all spoke French. In the eighteenth century, the great Russian aristocrats were more fluent in French than in Russian. In England the first Hanoverian king, George I, spoke fluent French and only halting English. France inspired a cosmopolitan European culture in the late seventeenth century, and that culture was inspired by the king. The French today revere Louis XIV as one of their greatest national heroes because of the culture that he inspired and symbolized.

Against this background of magnificent splendor, Saint-Simon writes, Louis XIV

reduced everyone to subjection, and brought to his court those very persons he cared least about. Whoever was old enough to serve did not dare demur. It was still another device to ruin the nobles by accustoming them to equality and forcing them to mingle with everyone indiscriminately. . . .

Louis XIV took great pains to inform himself on what was happening everywhere, in public places, private homes, and even on the international scene. . . . Spies and informers of all kinds were numberless.[14]

Though this passage was written by one of Louis's severest critics, all agree that the king used court ceremonials to undermine the power of the great nobility. By excluding the highest nobles from his councils, he weakened their ancient right to advise the king and to participate in government; they became mere instruments of royal policy. Operas, fetes, balls, gossip, and trivia occupied the nobles' time and attention. Through painstaking attention to detail and precisely calculated showmanship, Louis XIV reduced the major threat to his power. He separated power from status and grandeur: he secured the nobles' cooperation, and the nobles enjoyed the status and grandeur in which they lived.

In government Louis utilized several councils of state, which he personally attended, and the intendants, who acted for the councils throughout France. A stream of questions and instructions flowed between local districts and Versailles, and under Louis XIV a uniform and centralized administration was imposed on the country. In 1685 France was the strongest and most highly centralized state in Europe.

Councilors of state came from the recently ennobled or the upper middle class. Royal service provided a means of social mobility. These professional bureaucrats served the state in the person of the king, but they did not share power with him. Louis stated that he chose bourgeois officials because he wanted "people to know by the rank of the men who served him that he had no intention of sharing power with them."[15] If great ones were the king's advisers, they would seem to share the royal authority; professional administrators from the middle class would not.

Throughout his long reign and despite increasing financial problems, he never called a meeting of the Es-

The Spider and the Fly In reference to the insect symbolism (*upper left*), the caption on the lower left side of this illustration states, "The noble is the spider, the peasant the fly." The other caption (*upper right*) notes, "The more people have, the more they want. The poor man brings everything— wheat, fruit, money, vegetables. The greedy lord sitting there ready to take everything will not even give him the favor of a glance." This satirical print summarizes peasant grievances. *(The New York Public Library, Art Resource, NY)*

tates General. The nobility therefore had no means of united expression or action. Nor did Louis have a first minister; he kept himself free from worry about the inordinate power of a Richelieu. Louis's use of spying and terror—a secret police force, a system of informers, and the practice of opening private letters—foreshadowed some of the devices of the modern state. French government remained highly structured, bureaucratic, centered at Versailles, and responsible to Louis XIV.

Financial and Economic Management Under Louis XIV: Colbert

Finance proved the grave weakness in Louis XIV's administration. An expanding professional bureaucracy, the court at Versailles, extensive military reform (see page 542), and war cost a great deal of money. English kings relied on one national assembly, Parliament, for consent to taxation for the entire country. French rulers had to consult local or provincial Estates for approval of taxes for particular regions. The reactions of the Estates of Burgundy to Louis's requests for revenue illustrate the king's relationship with the provincial Estates and his financial difficulties. That reaction also shows the limitations of royal absolutism. In 1658, 1662, 1665, and 1668, Louis called assemblies of deputies of Burgundy: the Estates legally consisted of the clergy, the nobility (the First and Second Estates), and representatives of all other people—merchants, artisans, and peasants (the Third Estate). Since the clergy and the nobility had many exemptions, the great burden of taxation fell on the Third Estate. At each of the assemblies, deputies pleaded their poverty, citing the crop failures of recent years; or they bargained for lower sums than the king asked for; or they asked that the taxes be postponed for a year or two; or if an assessment was grudgingly approved, they put off collecting it. Louis was never able to secure from the Estates of Burgundy all that he requested.[16]

In many parts of France the method of collecting taxes consistently failed to produce enough revenue. Tax farmers, agents who purchased from the Crown the right to collect taxes in a particular district, pocketed the difference between what they raked in and what they handed over to the state. Consequently, the tax farmers profited, while the government got far less than the people paid. In addition, by an old agreement between the Crown and the nobility, the king could freely tax the common people provided he did not tax the nobles. The nobility thereby relinquished a role in government: since nobles did not pay taxes, they could not legitimately claim a say in how taxes were spent. Louis, however, lost enormous potential revenue. The middle classes, moreover, secured many tax exemptions. With the rich and prosperous classes exempt, the tax burden fell heavily on those least able to pay, the poor peasants.

The king named Jean-Baptiste Colbert (1619–1683), the son of a wealthy merchant-financier of Reims, as controller general of finances. Colbert came to manage the entire royal administration and proved himself a financial genius. Colbert's central principle was that the wealth and the economy of France should serve the state. He did not invent the system called "mercantilism," but he rigorously applied it to France.

Mercantilism is a collection of governmental policies for the regulation of economic activities, especially commercial activities, by and for the state. In seventeenth- and eighteenth-century economic theory, a nation's international power was thought to be based on its wealth, specifically its gold supply. Because, mercantilist theory held, resources were limited, state intervention was needed to secure the largest part of a limited resource. To accumulate gold, a country always had to sell more goods abroad than it bought. Colbert believed that a successful economic policy meant more than a favorable balance of trade, however. He insisted that the French sell abroad and buy *nothing* back. France should be self-sufficient, able to produce within its borders everything the subjects of the French king needed. Consequently, the outflow of gold would be halted, debtor states would pay in bullion, and with the wealth of the nation increased, its power and prestige would be enhanced.

Colbert attempted to accomplish self-sufficiency through state support for both old industries and newly created ones. He subsidized the established cloth industries at Abbeville, Saint-Quentin, and Carcassonne. He granted special royal privileges to the rug and tapestry industries at Paris, Gobelin, and Beauvais. New factories at Saint-Antoine in Paris manufactured mirrors to replace Venetian imports. Looms at Chantilly and Alençon competed with lacemaking at Bruges in the Spanish Netherlands, and foundries at Saint-Étienne made steel and firearms that reduced Swedish imports. To ensure a high-quality finished product, Colbert set up a system of state inspection and regulation. To ensure order within every industry, he compelled all craftsmen to organize into guilds, and within every guild he gave the masters absolute power over their workers. Colbert encouraged skilled foreign craftsmen and manufacturers to immigrate to France, and he gave them special privileges. To improve communications, he built roads and canals, the most famous, the Canal des Deux Mers. To protect French goods, he abolished many domestic tariffs and enacted high foreign tariffs, which prevented foreign products from competing with French ones.

Colbert's most important work was the creation of a powerful merchant marine to transport French goods. He gave bonuses to French shipowners and shipbuilders and established a method of maritime conscription, arsenals, and academies for the training of sailors. In 1661 France possessed 18 unseaworthy vessels; by 1681 it had 276 frigates, galleys, and ships of the line.

Colbert hoped to make Canada—rich in untapped minerals and some of the best agricultural land in the world—part of a vast French empire. He gathered four thousand peasants from western France and shipped them to Canada, where they peopled the province of Quebec. (In 1608, one year after the English arrived at Jamestown, Virginia, Sully had established the city of Quebec, which became the capital of French Canada.) Subsequently, the Jesuit Jacques Marquette and the merchant Louis Joliet sailed down the Mississippi River and took possession of the land on both sides as far south as present-day Arkansas. In 1684 the French explorer Robert La Salle continued down the Mississippi to its mouth and claimed vast territories and the rich delta for Louis XIV. The area was called, naturally, "Louisiana."

How successful were Colbert's policies? His achievement in the development of manufacturing was prodigious. The textile industry, especially in woolens, expanded enormously, and "France . . . had become in 1683 the leading nation of the world in industrial productivity."[17] The commercial classes prospered, and between 1660 and 1700 their position steadily improved. The national economy, however, rested on agriculture. Although French peasants did not become serfs, as did the peasants of eastern Europe, they were mercilessly taxed. After 1685 other hardships afflicted them: poor harvests, continuing deflation of the currency, and fluctuation in the price of grain. Many peasants emigrated. With the decline in population and thus in the number of taxable people (the poorest), the state's resources fell. A totally inadequate tax base and heavy expenditure for war in the later years of Louis's reign made Colbert's goals unattainable.

The Revocation of the Edict of Nantes

The absolutist state also attempted to control religion.

We now see with the proper gratitude what we owe to God . . . for the best and largest part of our subjects of the so-called reformed religion have embraced Catholicism, and now that, to the extent that the execution of the Edict of Nantes remains useless, we have judged that we can do nothing better to wipe out the memory of the troubles, of the confusion, of the evils that the progress of this false religion has caused our kingdom . . . than to revoke entirely the said Edict.[18]

With those words, in 1685 Louis XIV revoked the Edict of Nantes, by which his grandfather Henry IV had granted liberty of conscience to French Huguenots. The new law ordered the destruction of churches, the closing of schools, the Catholic baptism of Huguenots, and the exile of Huguenot pastors who refused to renounce their faith. Why? There had been so many mass conversions during previous years (many of them forced) that Madame de Maintenon, Louis's second wife, could say that "nearly all the Huguenots were converted." Some Huguenots had emigrated. Richelieu had already deprived French Calvinists of political rights. Why, then, did Louis, by revoking the edict, persecute some of his most loyal and industrially skilled subjects, force others to flee abroad, and provoke the outrage of Protestant Europe?

First, the French monarchy had never intended religious toleration to be permanent (see page 535); religious pluralism was not a seventeenth-century ideal. Although recent scholarship has convincingly shown that Louis XIV was basically tolerant, he considered religious unity politically necessary to realize his goal of "one king, one law, one faith." He hated division within the realm and insisted that religious unity was essential to his royal dignity and to the security of the state.

Second, while France in the early years of Louis's reign permitted religious liberty, it was not a popular policy. Aristocrats had long petitioned Louis to crack down on Protestants. But the revocation was solely the king's decision, and it won him enormous praise. "If the flood of congratulation means anything, it . . . was probably the one act of his reign that, at the time, was popular with the majority of his subjects."[19]

Although contemporaries applauded Louis XIV, later scholars damned him for the adverse impact that revocation of the Edict of Nantes had on the economy and foreign affairs. Tens of thousands of Huguenot craftsmen, soldiers, and business people emigrated, depriving France of their skills and tax revenues and carrying their bitterness to Holland, England, Prussia, and Cape Town in southern Africa. Modern scholarship, however, has greatly modified this picture: Huguenot settlers in northern Europe aggravated Protestant hatred for Louis, but revocation of the Edict of Nantes had only minor and scattered effects on French economic development.[20]

French Classicism

Scholars characterize the art and literature of the age of Louis XIV as **French classicism.** By this they mean that the artists and writers of the late seventeenth century imitated the subject matter and style of classical antiquity, that their work resembled that of Renaissance Italy, and that French art possessed the classical qualities of discipline, balance, and restraint. Classicism was the official style of Louis's court. In painting, however, French classicism had already reached its peak before 1661, the beginning of the king's personal government.

Contemporaries said that Louis XIV never ceased playing the role of grand monarch on the stage of his court. If the king never fully relaxed from the pressures and intrigues of government, he did enjoy music and theater and used them as a backdrop for court ceremonials. Louis favored Jean-Baptiste Lully (1632–1687), whose orchestral works combined lively animation with the restrained austerity typical of French classicism. Lully also composed court ballets, and his operatic productions achieved a powerful influence throughout Europe. Louis supported François Couperin (1668–1733), whose harpsichord and organ works possessed the regal grandeur the king loved, and Marc-Antoine Charpentier (1634–1704), whose solemn religious music entertained him at meals. Charpentier received a pension for the *Te Deums,* hymns of thanksgiving, he composed to celebrate French military victories.

Louis XIV loved the stage, and in the plays of Molière and Racine his court witnessed the finest achievements in the history of the French theater. When Jean-Baptiste Poquelin (1622–1673), the son of a prosperous tapestry maker, refused to join his father's business and entered the theater, he took the stage name "Molière." As playwright, stage manager, director, and actor, Molière produced comedies that exposed the hypocrisies and follies of society through brilliant caricature. *Tartuffe* satirized the religious hypocrite, *Le Bourgeois Gentilhomme* (The Bourgeois Gentleman) attacked the social parvenu, and *Les Femmes Savantes* (The Learned Women) mocked the fashionable pseudo-intellectuals of the day. In structure Molière's plays followed classical models, but they were based on careful social observation. Molière made the bourgeoisie the butt of his ridicule; he stopped short of criticizing the nobility, reflecting the policy of his royal patron.

While Molière dissected social mores, his contemporary Jean Racine (1639–1699) analyzed the power of love. Racine based his tragic dramas on Greek and Roman legends, and his persistent theme was the conflict of good and evil. Several plays—*Andromaque, Bérénice, Iphigénie,* and *Phèdre*—bear the names of women and deal with the power of passion in women. Louis preferred *Mithridate* and *Britannicus* because of the "grandeur" of their themes. For simplicity of language, symmetrical structure, and calm restraint, the plays of Racine represent the finest examples of French classicism. His tragedies and Molière's comedies are still produced today.

Louis XIV's Wars

On his deathbed, Louis XIV is reputed to have said, "I have gone to war too lightly and pursued it for vanity's sake." Perhaps he never actually said this. If he did, perhaps it was part of the confessional style of the time, which required that a penitent exaggerate his sins.[21] In any case, the course of Louis's reign suggests that he acted according to his observation that "the character of a conqueror is regarded as the noblest and highest of titles." In pursuit of the title of "conqueror," he kept France at war for thirty-three of the fifty-four years of his personal rule.

It is an axiom of history that war or the preparation for war is always a government's greatest expense. In 1635, when Richelieu became first minister of Louis XIII, the French army consisted of 25,000 men. In 1659, at the time of the Treaty of the Pyrenees, which ended the war with Spain, the army theoretically was composed of 250,000 men. In 1666 Louis appointed François le Tellier (later marquis de Louvois) secretary of state for war. Under the king's watchful eye, Louvois created a professional army that was modern in the sense that the French state, rather than private nobles, employed the soldiers. The king himself took command and directly supervised all aspects and details of military affairs.

Louvois utilized several methods in recruiting troops: dragooning, in which press gangs seized men off the streets, often drunks, bums, and criminals (this method was not popular); conscription; and, after 1688, lottery. Louvois also recruited regiments of foreign mercenaries. Under the strict direction of Jean Martinet (d. 1672), whose name became a byword in the French and English languages for absolute adherence to the rules, the foreign and native-born soldiers were turned into a tough, obedient military machine. A commissariat was established to feed the troops, taking the place of the ancient method of living off the countryside. An ambulance corps was designed to look after the wounded. Uniforms and weapons were standardized. A rational system of training and promotion was imposed. All this added up to a military revolution. A new military machine now existed that gave one national state, France, the potential to dominate the affairs of the continent for the first time in European history.

Louis continued on a broader scale the expansionist policy begun by Cardinal Richelieu. In 1667, using a dynastic excuse, he invaded Flanders, part of the Spanish Netherlands, and Franche-Comté in the east. In consequence, he acquired twelve towns, including the important commercial centers of Lille and Tournai (see Map 16.1). Five years later, Louis personally led an army of over 100,000 men into Holland, and the Dutch ultimately saved themselves only by opening the dikes and flooding the countryside. This war, which lasted six years and eventually involved the Holy Roman Empire and Spain, was concluded by the Treaty of Nijmegen (1678). Louis gained additional Flemish towns and all of Franche-Comté.

Encouraged by his successes, by the weakness of the German Empire, and by divisions among the other European powers, Louis continued his aggression. In 1681 he seized the city of Strasbourg, and three years later he sent his armies into the province of Lorraine. At that moment, the king seemed invincible. In fact, Louis had reached the limit of his expansion. The wars of the 1680s and 1690s brought him no additional territories.

Louis attempted to support an army of 200,000 men in several different theaters of war against the great nations of

MAP 16.1 The Acquisitions of Louis XIV, 1668–1713 The desire for glory and the weakness of his German neighbors encouraged Louis's expansionist policy, but he paid a high price for his acquisitions.

Europe, the powerful Bank of Amsterdam, and (after 1694) the Bank of England. This task far exceeded French resources, given the very inequitable system of taxation. The military revolution involving the reform and great expansion of the army required funding that the state could not meet. Claude Le Peletier, Colbert's successor as minister of finance, resorted to the devaluation of the currency (which hurt those who hoarded coins) and the old device of selling offices, tax exemptions, and titles of nobility. To raise revenue for the war effort, on December 14, 1689, Louis published a declaration ordering that all the nation's silverware be handed over to the mint. Setting an example, Louis sent off the silver furniture of Versailles. The royal apartments and the Hall of Mirrors looked like a house repossessed by sheriffs.[22] This action did little good. None of these measures produced enough revenue. So the weight of taxation fell on the already-overburdened peasants. They expressed their frustrations in widespread revolts that hit all parts of France in the 1690s.

A series of bad harvests between 1688 and 1694 brought catastrophe. Cold, wet summers reduced the harvests by an estimated one-third to two-thirds. The price of wheat skyrocketed. The result was widespread starvation, and in many provinces the death rate rose to several times the normal figure. Parish registers reveal that France buried at least one-tenth of its population in

those years, perhaps 2 million in 1693 to 1694 alone. Rising grain prices, new taxes for war on top of old ones, a slump in manufacturing and thus in exports, and the constant nuisance of pillaging troops—all these meant great suffering for the French people. France wanted peace at any price. Louis XIV granted a respite for five years while he prepared for the conflict later known as the War of the Spanish Succession (1701–1713).

This war, provoked by the territorial disputes of the previous century, also involved the dynastic question of the succession to the Spanish throne. It was an open secret in Europe that the king of Spain, Charles II (r. 1665–1700), was mentally defective and sexually impotent. In 1698 the European powers, including France, agreed by treaty to partition, or divide, the vast Spanish possessions between the king of France and the Holy Roman emperor, who were Charles II's brothers-in-law. When Charles died in 1700, however, his will left the Spanish crown and the worldwide Spanish Empire to Philip of Anjou, Louis XIV's grandson. While the will specifically rejected union of the French and Spanish crowns, Louis was obviously the power in France, not his seventeen-year-old grandson. Louis reneged on the treaty and accepted the will.

The Dutch and the English would not accept French acquisition of the Spanish Netherlands and of the rich trade with the Spanish colonies. The union of the Spanish and French crowns, moreover, would have totally upset the European balance of power. Claiming that he was following both Spanish national interests and French dynastic and national interests, Louis presented Philip of Anjou to the Spanish ambassador saying, "You may salute him as your king." After a Mass of thanksgiving, the Spanish ambassador was heard to say, "What rapture! The Pyrenees no longer exist."[23] The possibility of achieving this goal provoked the long-anticipated crisis.

In 1701 the English, Dutch, Austrians, and Prussians formed the Grand Alliance against Louis XIV. They claimed that they were fighting to prevent France from becoming too strong in Europe, but during the previous half century, overseas maritime rivalry among France, Holland, and England had created serious international tension. The secondary motive of the allied powers was to check France's expanding commercial power in North America, Asia, and Africa. In the ensuing series of conflicts, two great soldiers dominated the alliance against France: Eugene, prince of Savoy, representing the Holy Roman Empire, and Englishman John Churchill, subsequently duke of Marlborough. Eugene and Churchill inflicted a severe defeat on Louis in 1704 at Blenheim in Bavaria. Marlborough followed with another victory at Ramillies near Namur in Brabant.

The war was finally concluded at Utrecht in 1713, where the principle of partition was applied. Louis's grandson, Philip, remained the first Bourbon king of Spain on the understanding that the French and Spanish crowns would never be united. France surrendered Newfoundland, Nova Scotia, and the Hudson Bay territory to England, which also acquired Gibraltar, Minorca, and control of the African slave trade from Spain. The Dutch gained little because Austria received the former Spanish Netherlands (see Map 16.2).

The **Peace of Utrecht** had important international consequences. It represented the balance-of-power principle in operation, setting limits on the extent to which any one power—in this case, France—could expand. The treaty completed the decline of Spain as a great power. It vastly expanded the British Empire. And it gave European powers experience in international cooperation.

The Peace of Utrecht marked the end of French expansionist policy. Louis's thirty-five-year quest for military glory had brought rights to all of Alsace, the gain of important cities in the north such as Lille, as well as Strasbourg. But at what price? Even revisionist historians, who portray the aging monarch as responsible in negotiation and moderate in his demands, acknowledge "that the widespread misery in France during the period was in part

due to royal policies, especially the incessant wars."[24] To raise revenue for the wars, forty thousand additional offices had been sold, thus increasing the number of families exempt from future taxation. In 1714 France hovered on the brink of financial bankruptcy. Louis had exhausted the country without much compensation. It is no wonder that when he died on September 1, 1715, Saint-Simon wrote, "Those . . . wearied by the heavy and oppressive rule of the King and his ministers, felt a delighted freedom. . . . Paris . . . found relief in the hope of liberation. . . . The provinces . . . quivered with delight . . . [and] the people, ruined, abused, despairing, now thanked God for a deliverance which answered their most ardent desires."[25]

The Decline of Absolutist Spain in the Seventeenth Century

Spanish absolutism and greatness had preceded those of the French. In the sixteenth century, Spain (or, more precisely, the kingdom of Castile) had developed the standard features of absolute monarchy: a permanent bureaucracy staffed by professionals employed in the various councils of state, a standing army, and national taxes, the *servicios,* which fell most heavily on the poor.

France depended on financial and administrative unification within its borders; Spain had developed an international absolutism on the basis of silver bullion from Peru. Spanish gold and silver, armies, and glory had dominated the continent for most of the sixteenth century, but by the 1590s the seeds of disaster were sprouting. The lack of a strong middle class, largely the result of the expulsion of the Jews and Moors (see page 510), the agricultural crisis and population decline, the failure to invest in productive enterprises, the intellectual isolation and psychological malaise—all combined to reduce Spain, by 1715, to a second-rate power.

The fabulous and seemingly inexhaustible flow of silver from Mexico and Peru, together with the sale of cloth, grain, oil, and wine to the colonies, greatly enriched Spain. In the early seventeenth century, however, the Dutch and English began to trade with the Spanish colonies, cutting into the revenues that had gone to Spain. Mexico and Peru themselves developed local industries, further lessening their need to buy from Spain. Between 1610 and 1650, Spanish trade with the colonies fell 60 percent.

At the same time, the native Indians and African slaves who worked the South American silver mines, under conditions that would have shamed the ancient Egyptian pharaohs, suffered frightful epidemics of disease. Moreover, the lodes started to run dry. Consequently, the quantity of metal produced for Spain steadily declined.

Tiepolo: The Triumph of Spain   This painting is from the ceiling of the Royal Palace in Madrid. Arguably the greatest Italian painter of the eighteenth century, Giovanni Tiepolo depicted the Spanish Empire as the self-assured champion of Christian cultural values in Europe and America. Completed in 1764, a century after the empire had gone into irrevocable decline, this piece represents only an illusion of grandeur. *(Palacio Real de Madrid/The Bridgeman Art Library)*

But in Madrid royal expenditures constantly exceeded income. The remedies applied in the face of a mountainous state debt and declining revenues were devaluation of the coinage and declarations of bankruptcy. In 1596, 1607, 1627, 1647, and 1680, Spanish kings found no solution to the problem of an empty treasury other than to cancel the national debt. Given the frequency of cancellation, public confidence in the state deteriorated.

Spain, in contrast to the other countries of western Europe, had only a tiny middle class. Public opinion, taking its cue from the aristocracy, condemned moneymaking as vulgar and undignified. Those with influence or connections sought titles of nobility and social prestige. Thousands entered economically unproductive professions or became priests, monks, and nuns: there were said to be nine thousand monasteries in the province of Castile alone. The flood of gold and silver had produced severe inflation, pushing the costs of production in the textile industry higher and higher to the point that Castilian cloth could not compete in colonial and international markets. Many businessmen found so many obstacles in the way of profitable enterprise that they simply gave up.[26]

Spanish aristocrats, attempting to maintain an extravagant lifestyle they could no longer afford, increased the rents on their estates. High rents and heavy taxes in turn drove the peasants from the land. Agricultural production suffered, and the peasants departed for the large cities, where they swelled the ranks of unemployed beggars.

MAP 16.2 Europe in 1715   The series of treaties commonly called the Peace of Utrecht (April 1713–November 1715) ended the War of the Spanish Succession and redrew the map of Europe. A French Bourbon king succeeded to the Spanish throne on the understanding that the French not attempt to unite the French and Spanish crowns. France surrendered to Austria the Spanish Netherlands (later Belgium), then in French hands, and France recognized the Hohenzollern rulers of Prussia. Spain ceded Gibraltar to Great Britain, for which it has been a strategic naval station ever since. Spain also granted to Britain the *asiento*, the contract for supplying African slaves to America.

Their most Catholic majesties, the kings of Spain, had no solutions to these dire problems. If one can discern personality from pictures, the portraits of Philip III (r. 1598–1622), Philip IV (r. 1622–1665), and Charles II (r. 1665–1700) hanging in the Prado, the Spanish national museum in Madrid, reflect the increasing weakness of the dynasty. Their faces—the small, beady eyes; the long noses; the jutting Habsburg jaws; the pathetically stupid expressions—tell a story of excessive inbreeding and decaying monarchy. The Spanish kings all lacked force of character. Philip III, a pallid, melancholy, and deeply pious man "whose only virtue appeared to reside in a total absence of vice," handed the government over to the lazy duke of Lerma, who used it to advance his personal and familial wealth. Philip IV left the management of his several kingdoms to Gaspar de Guzmán, count-duke of Olivares.

Olivares was an able administrator. He did not lack energy and ideas; he devised new sources of revenue. But he clung to the grandiose belief that the solution to Spain's difficulties rested in a return to the imperial tradition. Unfortunately, the imperial tradition demanded the revival of war with the Dutch at the expiration of a twelve-year truce in 1622 and a long war with France over Mantua (1628–1659). Spain thus became embroiled in the Thirty Years' War. These conflicts, on top of an empty treasury, brought disaster.

In 1640 Spain faced serious revolts in Catalonia and Portugal; in 1643 the French inflicted a crushing defeat on a Spanish army at Rocroi in what is now Belgium. By the Treaty of the Pyrenees of 1659, which ended the French-Spanish wars, Spain was compelled to surrender extensive territories to France. This treaty marked the end of Spain as a great power.

Seventeenth-century Spain was the victim of its past. It could not forget the grandeur of the sixteenth century and look to the future. The bureaucratic councils of state continued to function as symbols of the absolute Spanish monarchy. But because those councils were staffed by aristocrats, it was the aristocracy that held the real power. Spanish absolutism had been built largely on slave-produced gold and silver. When the supply of bullion decreased, the power and standing of the Spanish state declined.

The most cherished Spanish ideals were military glory and strong Roman Catholic faith. In the seventeenth century, Spain lacked the finances and the manpower to fight the expensive wars in which it got involved. Spain also ignored the new mercantile ideas and scientific methods because they came from heretical nations, Holland and England. The incredible wealth of South America destroyed what remained of the Spanish middle class and created contempt for business and manual labor.

The decadence of the Habsburg dynasty and the lack of effective royal councilors also contributed to Spanish failure. Spanish leaders seemed to lack the will to reform. Pessimism and fatalism permeated national life. In the reign of Philip IV, a royal council was appointed to plan

Peeter Snayers: Spanish Troops (detail)   The long wars that Spain fought over Dutch independence, in support of Habsburg interests in Germany, and against France left the country militarily exhausted and financially drained by the mid-1600s. Here Spanish troops—thin, emaciated, and probably unpaid— straggle away from battle. *(Museo Nacional del Prado, Madrid. Photo: José Baztan y Alberto Otero)*

the construction of a canal linking the Tagus and Man-zanares Rivers in Spain. After interminable debate, the committee decided that "if God had intended the rivers to be navigable, He would have made them so."

In the brilliant novel **Don Quixote,** Spanish writer Miguel de Cervantes (1547–1616) produced one of the great masterpieces of world literature. *Don Quixote* delineates the whole fabric of sixteenth-century Spanish society. The main character, Don Quixote, lives in a world of dreams, traveling about the countryside seeking military glory. From the title of the book, the English language has borrowed the word *quixotic*. Meaning "idealistic but impractical," the term characterizes seventeenth-century Spain. As a leading scholar has written, "The Spaniard convinced himself that reality was what he felt, believed, imagined. He filled the world with heroic reverberations. Don Quixote was born and grew."[27]

Constitutionalism

The seventeenth century saw the appearance of the constitutional state. While France and, later, Prussia, Russia, and Austria solved the question of sovereignty with the absolutist state, England and Holland evolved toward the constitutional state. What is constitutionalism? Is it identical to democracy?

Constitutionalism is the limitation of government by law. Constitutionalism also implies a balance between the authority and power of the government, on the one hand, and the rights and liberties of the subjects, on the other.

A nation's constitution may be written or unwritten. It may be embodied in one basic document, occasionally revised by amendment or judicial decision, like the Constitution of the United States. Or it may be partly written and partly unwritten and include parliamentary statutes, judicial decisions, and a body of traditional procedures and practices, like the English, Canadian, and Dutch constitutions. Whether written or unwritten, a constitution gets its binding force from the government's acknowledgment that it must respect that constitution—that is, that the state must govern according to the laws. Likewise, in a constitutional state, the people look on the laws and the constitution as the protectors of their rights, liberties, and property.

Modern constitutional governments may take either a republican or a monarchical form. In a constitutional republic, the sovereign power resides in the electorate and is exercised by the electorate's representatives. In a constitutional monarchy, a king or queen serves as the head of state and possesses some residual political authority, but again the ultimate, or sovereign, power rests in the electorate.

A constitutional government is not, however, quite the same as a democratic government. In a complete democracy, *all* the people have the right to participate either directly or indirectly (through their elected representatives) in the government of the state. Democratic government, therefore, is intimately tied up with the *franchise* (the vote). Most men could not vote until the late nineteenth century. Even then, women—probably the majority in Western societies—lacked the franchise; they gained the right to vote only in the twentieth century. Consequently, although constitutionalism developed in the seventeenth century, full democracy was achieved only in recent times.

The Decline of Royal Absolutism in England (1603–1649)

In 1588 Queen Elizabeth I of England exercised very great personal power; by 1689 the English monarchy was severely circumscribed. Change in England was anything but orderly. Seventeenth-century England displayed little political stability. It executed one king and experienced a bloody civil war; experimented with military dictatorship, then restored the son of the murdered king; and finally, after a bloodless revolution, established constitutional monarchy. Political stability came only in the 1690s. How do we account for the fact that after such a violent and tumultuous century, England laid the foundations for constitutional monarchy? What combination of political, socioeconomic, and religious factors brought on a civil war in 1642–1649 and then the constitutional settlement of 1688–1689?

The extraordinary success of Elizabeth I had rested on her political shrewdness and flexibility, her careful management of finances, her wise selection of ministers, her clever manipulation of Parliament, and her sense of royal dignity and devotion to hard work. The aging queen had always refused to discuss the succession. After her Scottish cousin James Stuart succeeded her as James I (r. 1603–1625), Elizabeth's strengths seemed even greater than they actually had been.

King James was well educated, learned, and, with thirty-five years' experience as king of Scotland, politically shrewd. But he was not as interested in displaying the majesty and mystique of monarchy as Elizabeth had been. He also lacked the common touch. Urged to wave at the crowds who waited to greet their new ruler, James complained that he was tired and threatened to drop his breeches "so they can cheer at my arse." The new king failed to live up to the role expected of him in England. Moreover, James, in contrast to Elizabeth, was a poor judge of character, and in a society already hostile to the

Scots and concerned about proper spoken English, James's Scottish accent was a disadvantage.[28]

James was devoted to the theory of the divine right of kings. He expressed his ideas about divine right in his essay "The Trew Law of Free Monarchy." According to James I, a monarch has a divine (or God-given) right to his authority and is responsible only to God. Rebellion is the worst of political crimes. If a king orders something evil, the subject should respond with passive disobedience but should be prepared to accept any penalty for noncompliance.

He went so far as to lecture the House of Commons: "There are no privileges and immunities which can stand against a divinely appointed King." This notion, implying total royal jurisdiction over the liberties, persons, and properties of English men and women, formed the basis of the Stuart concept of absolutism. Such a view ran directly counter to the long-standing English idea that a person's property could not be taken away without due process of law. James's expression of such views before the English House of Commons constituted a grave political mistake.

The House of Commons guarded the state's pocketbook, and James and later Stuart kings badly needed to open that pocketbook. Elizabeth had left James a sizable royal debt. Through prudent management, the debt could have been gradually reduced. Revisionist historians maintained that political calculations led James to lavish money on court favorites in the hope of building support. More recent scholars have reverted to the traditional view that James was adept at neither finances nor politics.[29]

Elizabeth had also left her Stuart successors a House of Commons that appreciated its own financial strength and intended to use that strength to acquire a greater say in the government of the state. The knights and burgesses who sat at Westminster in the late sixteenth and early seventeenth centuries wanted a voice in royal expenditures, religious reform, and foreign affairs. Essentially, the Commons wanted sovereignty.

Profound social changes had occurred since the sixteenth century. The English House of Commons during the reigns of James I and his son Charles I (r. 1625–1649) was very different from the assembly Henry VIII had manipulated into passing his Reformation legislation. The dissolution of the monasteries and the sale of monastic land had enriched many people. Agricultural techniques such as the draining of wasteland and the application of fertilizers had improved the land and its yield. In the seventeenth century, old manorial common land was enclosed and turned into sheep runs, breeding was carefully supervised, and the size of the flocks increased. In these activities, as well as in the renting and leasing of parcels of land, precise accounts were kept.

Rubens: Ceiling of the Banqueting House, Whitehall Palace, London (1635) King James I is raised by the allegorical figures of Justice, Religion, and Truth into the dazzling light of Heaven, perhaps a fitting memorial for the advocate of the divine right of kings. *(Whitehall, London/The Bridgeman Art Library)*

Many people invested in commercial ventures at home, such as the expanding cloth industry, and through partnerships and joint stock companies engaged in foreign enterprises. Many also made prudent marriages. These developments led to a great deal of social mobility. Both in commerce and in agriculture, the English in the late sixteenth and early seventeenth centuries were capitalists, investing their profits to make more money. Though the international inflation of the period hit everywhere, in England commercial and agricultural income rose faster than prices. Wealthy country gentry, rich city merchants, and financiers invested abroad.

The typical pattern was for the commercially successful to set themselves up as country gentry, thus creating an elite group that possessed a far greater proportion of land and of the national wealth in 1640 than had been the case in 1540. Small wonder that in 1640 someone could declare in the House of Commons, probably accurately, "We could buy the House of Lords three times over." Increased wealth had also produced a better-educated and more articulate House of Commons. Many members had acquired at least a smattering of legal knowledge, which they used to search for medieval precedents from which to argue against the king. The class that dominated the Commons wanted political power corresponding to its economic strength.

In England, unlike France, there was no social stigma attached to paying taxes. Members of the House of Commons were willing to tax themselves provided they had some say in the expenditure of those taxes and in the formulation of state policies. The Stuart kings, however, considered such ambitions intolerable presumption and a threat to their divine-right prerogative. Consequently, at every Parliament between 1603 and 1640, bitter squabbles erupted between the Crown and the wealthy, articulate, and legally minded Commons. Charles I's attempt to govern without Parliament (1629–1640) and to finance his government by arbitrary nonparliamentary levies, brought the country to a crisis.

Religious Issues

An issue graver than royal extravagance and Parliament's desire to make law also disturbed the English and embittered relations between the king and the House of Commons. That problem was religion. In the early seventeenth century, increasing numbers of English people felt dissatisfied with the Church of England established by Henry VIII and reformed by Elizabeth. Many **Puritans** (see page 474) believed that the Reformation had not gone far enough. They wanted to "purify" the Anglican church of Roman Catholic elements—elaborate vestments and ceremonials, bishops, the position of the altar in the church, even the giving and wearing of wedding rings.

It is very difficult to establish what proportion of the English population was Puritan. According to the present scholarly consensus, the dominant religious groups in the early seventeenth century were Calvinist; their more zealous members were Puritans. It also seems clear that many English people were attracted by the socioeconomic implications of John Calvin's theology. Calvinism emphasized hard work, sobriety, thrift, competition, and postponement of pleasure, and it tended to link sin and poverty with weakness and moral corruption. These attitudes fit in precisely with the economic approaches and practices of many (successful) business people and farmers. These values have frequently been called the "Protestant ethic," "middle-class ethic," or "capitalist ethic." While it is hazardous to identify capitalism with Protestantism—there were many successful Catholic capitalists, for example—the "Protestant virtues" represented the prevailing values of members of the House of Commons.

Puritans wanted to abolish bishops in the Church of England, and when James I said, "No bishop, no king," he meant that the bishops were among the chief supporters of the throne. He was no Puritan, but he was Calvinist (see page 470) in doctrine. Yet James and his son Charles I both gave the impression of being sympathetic to Roman Catholicism. Charles supported the policies of William Laud (1573–1645), archbishop of Canterbury, who tried to impose elaborate ritual and rich ceremonials on all churches. Laud insisted on complete uniformity of church services and enforced that uniformity through an ecclesiastical court called the "Court of High Commission." People believed the country was being led back to Roman Catholicism. In 1637 Laud attempted to impose two new elements on church organization in Scotland: a new prayer book, modeled on the Anglican *Book of Common Prayer,* and bishoprics, which the Presbyterian Scots firmly rejected. The Scots therefore revolted. To finance an army to put down the Scots, King Charles was compelled to summon Parliament in November 1640.

Charles I was an intelligent man, but contemporaries found him deceitful, dishonest, and treacherous, and they did not trust him. After quarreling with Parliament over his right to collect customs duties on wine (tonnage) and wool (poundage), and over what the Commons perceived as religious innovations, Charles dissolved Parliament in 1629. From 1629 to 1640, he ruled without Parliament, financing his government through extraordinary stopgap levies considered illegal by most English people. For example, the king revived a medieval law requiring coastal districts to help pay the cost of ships for defense, but he levied the tax, called "ship money," on inland as well as coastal counties. When the issue was tested in the courts, the judges, having been suborned, decided in the king's favor.

Most members of Parliament believed that such taxation without consent amounted to arbitrary and absolute despotism. Consequently, they were not willing to trust the king with an army. Accordingly, this Parliament, called the "Long Parliament" because it sat from 1640 to 1660, proceeded to enact legislation that limited the power of the monarch and made arbitrary government impossible.

In 1641 the Commons passed the Triennial Act, which compelled the king to summon Parliament every three

Puritan Occupations These twelve engravings depict typical Puritan occupations and show that the Puritans came primarily from the artisan and lower middle classes. The governing classes and peasants adhered to the traditions of the Church of England.

years. The Commons impeached Archbishop Laud and abolished the Court of High Commission. It went further and threatened to abolish the institution of episcopacy. King Charles, fearful of a Scottish invasion—the original reason for summoning Parliament—accepted these measures. Understanding and peace were not achieved, however, partly because radical members of the Commons pushed increasingly revolutionary propositions, partly because Charles maneuvered to rescind those he had already approved. An uprising in Ireland precipitated civil war.

Ever since Henry II had conquered Ireland in 1171, English governors had mercilessly ruled the land, and English landlords had ruthlessly exploited the Irish people. The English Reformation had made a bad situation worse: because the Irish remained Catholic, religious differences became united with economic and political oppression. Without an army, Charles I could neither come to terms with the Scots nor put down the Irish rebellion, and the Long Parliament remained unwilling to place an army under a king it did not trust. Charles thus instigated military action against parliamentary forces. He recruited an army drawn from the nobility and its cavalry staff, the rural gentry, and mercenaries. The parliamentary army was composed of the militia of the city of London, country squires with business connections, and men with a firm belief in the spiritual duty of serving.

The English civil war (1642–1649) tested whether sovereignty in England was to reside in the king or in Parliament. The civil war did not resolve that problem, however, although it ended in 1649 with the execution of King Charles on the charge of high treason—a severe blow to the theory of divine-right monarchy. The period between 1649 and 1660, called the "Interregnum" because it separated two monarchical periods, witnessed England's solitary experience of military dictatorship.

Puritanical Absolutism in England: Cromwell and the Protectorate

The problem of sovereignty was vigorously debated in the middle years of the seventeenth century. In *Leviathan,* English philosopher and political theorist Thomas Hobbes (1588–1679) maintains that sovereignty is ultimately derived from the people, who transfer it to the monarchy by implicit contract. The power of the ruler is absolute, but kings do not hold their power by divine right. This view pleased no one.

When Charles I was beheaded on January 30, 1649, the kingship was abolished. A *commonwealth,* or **republican government,** was proclaimed. Theoretically, legislative power rested in the surviving members of Parliament, and executive power was lodged in a council of state. In fact, the army that had defeated the royal forces controlled the government, and Oliver Cromwell controlled the army. Though called the "Protectorate," the rule of Cromwell (1653–1658) constituted military dictatorship.

The army had prepared a constitution, the Instrument of Government (1653), that invested executive power in a lord protector (Cromwell) and a council of state. The instrument provided for triennial parliaments and gave Parliament the sole power to raise taxes. But after repeated disputes, Cromwell tore the document up. He continued the standing army and proclaimed quasi-martial law. He divided England into twelve military districts, each governed by a major general. The major generals acted through the justices of the peace though sometimes overrode them. On the issue of religion, Cromwell favored toleration, and the Instrument of Government gave all Christians, except Roman Catholics, the right to practice their faith. Toleration meant state protection of many different Protestant sects, however, and most English people had no enthusiasm for such a notion; the idea was far ahead of its time. As for Irish Catholicism, Cromwell identified it with sedition. In 1649 he crushed a rebellion at Drogheda in Ireland with merciless savagery, leaving a

Cartoon of 1649: "The Royall Oake of Brittayne"   Chopping down this tree signifies the end of royal authority, stability, Magna Carta (see page 344), and the rule of law. As pigs graze (representing the unconcerned common people), being fattened for slaughter, Oliver Cromwell, with his feet in Hell, quotes Scripture. This is a royalist view of the collapse of Charles I's government and the rule of Cromwell. *(Courtesy of the Trustees of the British Museum)*

legacy of Irish hatred for England that has not yet subsided. The state rigorously censored the press, forbade sports, and kept the theaters closed in England.

Cromwell's regulation of the nation's economy had features typical of seventeenth-century absolutism. The lord protector's policies were mercantilist, similar to those Colbert established in France. Cromwell enforced a Navigation Act (1651) requiring that English goods be transported on English ships. The navigation act was a great boost to the development of an English merchant marine and brought about a short but successful war with the commercially threatened Dutch. Cromwell also welcomed the immigration of Jews because of their skills, and they began to return to England after four centuries of absence.

Military government collapsed when Cromwell died in 1658. Fed up with military rule, the English longed for a return to civilian government, restoration of the common law, and social stability. Moreover, the strain of creating a

community of puritanical saints proved too psychologically exhausting. Government by military dictatorship was an unfortunate experiment that the English never forgot or repeated. By 1660 they were ready to restore the monarchy.

The Restoration of the English Monarchy

The Restoration of 1660 re-established the monarchy in the person of Charles II (r. 1660–1685), eldest son of Charles I. At the same time, both houses of Parliament were restored, together with the established Anglican church, the courts of law, and the system of local government through justices of the peace. The Restoration failed to resolve two serious problems, however. What was to be the attitude of the state toward Puritans, Catholics, and dissenters from the established church? And what was to be the constitutional position of the king—that is, what was to be the relationship between the king and Parliament?

About the first of these issues, Charles II, a relaxed, easygoing, and sensual man, was basically indifferent. He was not interested in doctrinal issues. Members of Parliament were, and they enacted a body of laws that sought to compel religious uniformity. Those who refused to receive the Eucharist of the Church of England could not vote, hold public office, preach, teach, attend the universities, or even assemble for meetings, according to the Test Act of 1673. But these restrictions could not be enforced. When the Quaker William Penn held a meeting of his Friends and was arrested, the jury refused to convict him.

In politics Charles II was determined "not to set out in his travels again," which meant that he intended to get along with Parliament. Charles II's solution to the problem of the relationship between the king and the House of Commons had profound importance for later constitutional development. Generally good rapport existed between the king and the strongly royalist Parliament that had restored him. This rapport was due largely to the king's appointment of a council of five men who served both as his major advisers and as members of Parliament, thus acting as liaison agents between the executive and the legislature. This body—known as the "Cabal" from the names of its five members (Clifford, Arlington, Buckingham, Ashley-Cooper, and Lauderdale)—was an ancestor of the later cabinet system (see page 555). Although its members sometimes disagreed and intrigued among themselves, it gradually came to be accepted that the Cabal was answerable in Parliament for the decisions of the king. This development gave rise to the concept of ministerial responsibility: royal ministers must answer to the Commons.

Harmony between the Crown and Parliament rested on the understanding that Charles would summon frequent parliaments and that Parliament would vote him sufficient revenues. But Parliament did not grant him an adequate income. Accordingly, in 1670 Charles entered into a secret agreement with Louis XIV. The French king would give Charles 200,000 pounds annually, and in return Charles would relax the laws against Catholics, gradually re-Catholicize England, support French policy against the Dutch, and convert to Catholicism himself.

When the details of this secret treaty leaked out, a great wave of anti-Catholic fear swept England. This fear was compounded by a crucial fact: although Charles had produced several bastards, he had no legitimate children. It therefore appeared that his brother and heir, James, duke of York, who had publicly acknowledged his Catholicism, would inaugurate a Catholic dynasty. A combination of hatred for the French absolutism embodied in Louis XIV, hostility to Roman Catholicism, and fear of a permanent Catholic dynasty produced virtual

hysteria. The Commons passed an exclusion bill denying the succession to a Roman Catholic, but Charles quickly dissolved Parliament, and the bill never became law.

James II (r. 1685–1688) did succeed his brother. Almost at once the worst English anti-Catholic fears, already aroused by Louis XIV's revocation of the Edict of Nantes, were realized. In direct violation of the Test Act, James appointed Roman Catholics to positions in the army, the universities, and local government. When these actions were tested in the courts, the judges, whom James had appointed, decided for the king. The king was suspending the law at will and appeared to be reviving the absolutism of his father and grandfather. He went further. Attempting to broaden his base of support with Protestant dissenters and nonconformists, James issued a declaration of indulgence granting religious freedom to all.

Two events gave the signals for revolution. First, seven bishops of the Church of England petitioned the king that they not be forced to read the declaration of indulgence because of their belief that it was an illegal act. They were imprisoned in the Tower of London but subsequently acquitted amid great public enthusiasm. Second, in June 1688 James's second wife produced a male heir. A Catholic dynasty seemed ensured. The fear of a Roman Catholic monarchy supported by France and ruling outside the law prompted a group of eminent persons to offer the English throne to James's Protestant daughter, Mary, and her Dutch husband, Prince William of Orange. In December 1688 James II, his queen, and their infant son fled to France and became pensioners of Louis XIV. Early in 1689, William and Mary were crowned king and queen of England.

The Triumph of England's Parliament: Constitutional Monarchy and Cabinet Government

The English call the events of 1688 to 1689 the "Glorious Revolution." The revolution was indeed glorious in the sense that it replaced one king with another with a minimum of bloodshed. It also represented the destruction, once and for all, of the idea of divine-right monarchy. William and Mary accepted the English throne from Parliament and in so doing explicitly recognized the supremacy of Parliament. The revolution of 1688 established the principle that sovereignty, the ultimate power in the state, was divided between king and Parliament and that the king ruled with the consent of the governed.

The men who brought about the revolution quickly framed their intentions in the Bill of Rights, the cornerstone of the modern British constitution. The basic

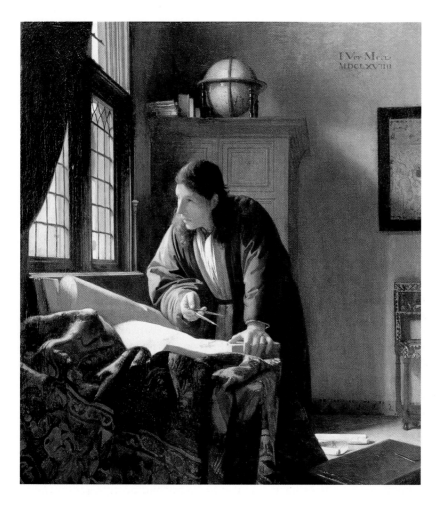

Jan Vermeer: The Geographer (1668)
Vermeer is best known today for his quiet, contemplative scenes of women. The central figure here—surrounded by charts, maps, and atlases, and holding a pair of dividers—conveys the energetic curiosity of the Age of Discovery. *(Stadelsches Kunstinstitut, Frankfurt/akg-images)*

principles of the Bill of Rights were formulated in direct response to Stuart absolutism. Law was to be made in Parliament; once made, it could not be suspended by the Crown. Parliament had to be called at least every three years. Both elections to and debate in Parliament were to be free in the sense that the Crown was not to interfere in them (this aspect of the bill was widely disregarded in the eighteenth century). Judges would hold their offices "during good behavior," a provision that ensured the independence of the judiciary. No longer could the Crown get the judicial decisions it wanted by threats of removal. There was to be no standing army in peacetime—a limitation designed to prevent the repetition of Cromwellian military government. The Bill of Rights granted "that the subjects which are Protestants may have arms for their defense suitable to their conditions and as allowed by law,"[30] meaning that Catholics could not possess firearms because the Protestant majority feared them. Additional legislation granted freedom of worship to Protestant dissenters and noncon-

formists and required that the English monarch always be Protestant.

The Glorious Revolution found its best defense in political philosopher John Locke's **Second Treatise of Civil Government** (1690). Locke (1632–1704) maintained that people set up civil governments to protect life, liberty, and property. A government that oversteps its proper function—protecting the natural rights of life, liberty, and property—becomes a tyranny. (By "natural" rights, Locke meant rights basic to all men because all have the ability to reason.) Under a tyrannical government, the people have the natural right to rebellion. Such rebellion can be avoided if the government carefully respects the rights of citizens and if people zealously defend their liberty. Recognizing the close relationship between economic and political freedom, Locke linked economic liberty and private property with political freedom; his defense of property included a justification for a narrow franchise. Locke served as the great spokesman for the liberal English revolution of 1688 to 1689 and for representative government. His idea that there are natural or universal rights equally valid for all peoples and societies was especially popular in colonial America.

The events of 1688 to 1689 did not constitute a *democratic* revolution. The revolution placed sovereignty in Parliament, and Parliament represented the upper classes. The great majority of English people acquired no say in their government. The English revolution established a constitutional monarchy; it also inaugurated an age of aristocratic government, which lasted at least until 1832 and in many ways until 1928, when women received full voting rights.

In the course of the eighteenth century, the **cabinet system** of government evolved. The term *cabinet* derives from the small private room in which English rulers consulted their chief ministers. In a cabinet system, the leading ministers, who must have seats in and the support of a majority of the House of Commons, formulate common policy and conduct the business of the country. During the administration of one royal minister, Sir Robert Walpole, who led the cabinet from 1721 to 1742, the idea developed that the cabinet was responsible to the House of Commons. The Hanoverian king George I (r. 1714–1727) normally presided at cabinet meetings throughout his reign, but his son and heir,

George II (r. 1727–1760), discontinued the practice. The influence of the Crown in decision making accordingly declined. Walpole enjoyed the favor of the monarchy and of the House of Commons and came to be called the king's first, or "prime," minister. In the English cabinet system, both legislative power and executive power are held by the leading ministers, who form the Government.

The Dutch Republic in the Seventeenth Century

In the late sixteenth century, the seven northern provinces of the Netherlands fought for and won their independence from Spain as the Republic of United Provinces of the Netherlands—an independence that was confirmed by the Peace of Westphalia ending the Thirty Years' War in 1648 (see pages 498–499). The seventeenth century witnessed an unparalleled flowering of Dutch scientific, artistic, and literary achievement. In this period, often called the "golden age of the Netherlands," Dutch ideas and attitudes played a profound role in shaping a new and modern world-view. At the same time, the United Provinces was another model of the development of the modern constitutional state.

Jan Steen: The Christening Feast As the mother, surrounded by midwives, rests in bed (*rear left*) and the father proudly displays the swaddled child, thirteen other people, united by gestures and gazes, prepare the celebratory meal. Very prolific, Steen was a master of warm-hearted domestic scenes. In contrast to the order and cleanliness of many seventeenth-century Dutch genre paintings, Steen's more disorderly portrayals gave rise to the epithet "a Jan Steen household," meaning an untidy house. *(Wallace Collection, London/ The Bridgeman Art Library)*

Room from Het Scheepje (The Little Ship) A retired sea captain who became a successful brewer in Haarlem owned the house (adjacent to his brewery) that included this room. The brass chandelier, plates, tiles, Turkish rug on the table (probably from Transylvania in the Ottoman Empire), oak mantelpiece, and paneling make this a superb example of a Dutch domestic interior during the Golden Age. A bed, built into the wall paneling, was warmed at night by coals in the pan hanging by the fireplace. *(Room from Het Scheepje, Haarlem, The Netherlands, early 17th century. Philadelphia Museum of Art, Gift of Edward W. Bok. 1928-66-1)*

Within each province, an oligarchy of wealthy merchants called "regents" handled domestic affairs in the local Estates. The provincial Estates held virtually all the power. A federal assembly, or **States General,** handled matters of foreign affairs, such as war. But the States General did not possess sovereign authority since all issues had to be referred back to the local Estates for approval. The States General appointed a representative, the **stadholder,** in each province. As the highest executive there, the stadholder carried out ceremonial functions and was responsible for defense and good order. The sons of William the Silent, Maurice and William Louis, held the office of stadholder in all seven provinces. As members of the House of Orange, they were closely identified with Dutch patriotism. The regents in each province jealously guarded local independence and resisted efforts at centralization. Nevertheless, Holland, which had the largest navy and the most wealth, dominated the republic and the States General. Significantly, the Estates assembled at Holland's capital, The Hague.

The government of the United Provinces fit none of the standard categories of seventeenth-century political organization. The Dutch were not monarchical but fiercely republican. The government was controlled by wealthy merchants and financiers. Though rich, their values were not aristocratic but strongly middle-class. The Dutch republic was not a strong federation but a confederation—that is, a weak union of strong provinces. The provinces were a temptation to powerful neighbors, yet the Dutch resisted the long Spanish effort at reconquest and withstood both French and English attacks in the second half of the century.

The political success of the Dutch rested on the phenomenal commercial prosperity of the Netherlands. The moral and ethical bases of that commercial wealth were thrift, frugality, and religious toleration. John Calvin had written, "From where do the merchant's profits come except from his own diligence and industry?" This attitude encouraged a sturdy people who had waged a centuries-old struggle against the sea.

Alone of all European peoples in the seventeenth century, the Dutch practiced religious toleration. Peoples of all faiths were welcome within their borders. Although there is scattered evidence of anti-Semitism, Jews enjoyed a level of acceptance and assimilation in Dutch business and general culture unique in early modern Europe. (See the feature "Individuals in Society: Glückel of Hameln.") For example, Benedict Spinoza (1632–1677), a descendant of Spanish Jews who fled the Inquisition, passed his entire life in Amsterdam, supporting himself as a lens grinder while producing important philosophical treatises. The urbanity of Dutch society allowed a rare degree of religious

Individuals in Society

Glückel of Hameln

In 1690 a Jewish widow in the small German town of Hameln* in Lower Saxony sat down to write her autobiography. She wanted to distract her mind from the terrible grief she felt over the death of her husband and to provide her twelve children with a record "so you will know from what sort of people you have sprung, lest today or tomorrow your beloved children or grand-children came and know naught of their family." Out of her pain and heightened consciousness, Glückel (1646–1724) produced an invaluable source for scholars.

She was born in Hamburg two years before the end of the Thirty Years' War. In 1649 the merchants of Hamburg expelled the Jews, who moved to nearby Altona, then under Danish rule. When the Swedes overran Altona in 1657–1658, the Jews returned to Hamburg "purely at the mercy of the Town Council." Glückel's narrative proceeds against a background of the constant difficulties (harassment) to which Jews were subjected—special papers, permits, bribes—and in Hameln she wrote, "And so it has been to this day and, I fear, will continue in like fashion."

When Glückel was "barely twelve," her father betrothed her to Chayim Hameln. She married at age fourteen. She describes him as "the perfect pattern of the pious Jew," a man who stopped his work every day for study and prayer, fasted, and was scrupulously honest in his business dealings. Only a few years older than Glückel, Chayim earned his living dealing in precious metals and in making small loans on pledges (articles held on security). This work required his constant travel to larger cities, markets, and fairs, often in bad weather, always over dangerous roads. Chayim consulted his wife about all his business dealings. As he lay dying, a friend asked if he had any last wishes. "None," he replied. "My wife knows everything. She shall do as she has always done." For thirty years, Glückel had been his friend, full business partner, and wife. They had thirteen children, twelve of whom survived their father, eight then unmarried. As Chayim had foretold, Glückel succeeded in launching the boys in careers and in providing dowries for the girls.

Glückel's world was her family, the Jewish community of Hameln, and the Jewish communities into which her children married. Social and business activities took her to Amsterdam, Baiersdorf, Bamberg, Berlin, Cleves, Danzig, Metz, and Vienna, so her world was not a narrow or provincial one. She took great pride that Prince Frederick of Cleves, later king of Prussia, danced at the wedding of her eldest daughter. The rising prosperity of Chayim's businesses allowed the couple to maintain up to six servants. Jews, however, lived on the margins of Christian society, and traditional sociological categories cannot be applied to them.

Glückel was deeply religious, and her culture was steeped in Jewish literature, legends, and mystical and secular works. Above all, she relied on the Bible. Her language, heavily sprinkled with scriptural references, testifies to a rare familiarity with the basic book of Western civilization. The Scriptures were her consolation, the source of her great strength in a hostile world.

Students who would learn about business practices, the importance of the dowry in marriage, childbirth, the ceremony of bris, birthrates, family celebrations, even the meaning of life can gain a good deal from the memoirs of this extraordinary woman, who was, in the words of one of her descendants, the poet Heinrich Heine, "the gift of a world to me."

Gentleness and deep mutual devotion seem to pervade Rembrandt's The Jewish Bride. *(Rijksmuseum-Stichting Amsterdam)*

Questions for Analysis

1. Consider the ways in which Glückel of Hameln was an ordinary woman of her times.
2. How was Glückel's life affected by the broad events and issues of the seventeenth century?

*Town immortalized by the Brothers Grimm. In 1284 the town contracted with the Pied Piper to rid it of rats and mice; he lured them away by playing his flute. When the citizens refused to pay, he charmed away their children in revenge.

Source: The Memoirs of Glückel of Hameln, trans. M. Lowenthal (New York: Schocken Books, 1977).

The **History Companion** *features additional information and activities related to this topic.* **history.college.hmco.com/students**

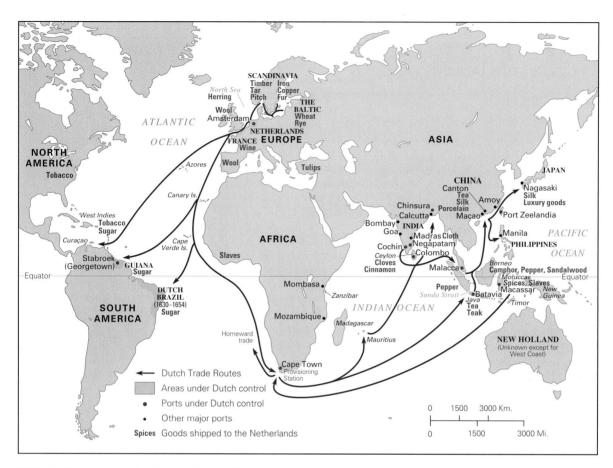

MAP 16.3 Seventeenth-Century Dutch Commerce   Dutch wealth rested on commerce, and commerce depended on the huge Dutch merchant marine, manned by perhaps forty-eight thousand sailors. The fleet carried goods from all parts of the globe to the port of Amsterdam.

freedom. As long as business people conducted their religion in private, the government did not interfere with them.

In the Dutch Republic, toleration paid off: it attracted a great deal of foreign capital and investment. Deposits at the Bank of Amsterdam were guaranteed by the city council, and in the middle years of the century, the bank became Europe's best source of cheap credit and commercial intelligence and the main clearing-house for bills of exchange. People of all races and creeds traded in Amsterdam, at whose docks on the Amstel River five thousand ships were berthed. Joost van den Vondel, the poet of Dutch imperialism, exulted:

God, God, the Lord of Amstel cried, hold every conscience
*   free;*
And Liberty ride, on Holland's tide, with billowing sails
*   to sea,*

And run our Amstel out and in; let freedom gird the bold,
And merchant in his counting house stand elbow deep
*   in gold.*[31]

The fishing industry was the cornerstone of the Dutch economy. For half the year, from June to December, fishing fleets combed the dangerous English coast and the North Sea and raked in tiny herring. Profits from herring stimulated shipbuilding, and even before 1600 the Dutch were offering the lowest shipping rates in Europe. The Dutch merchant marine was the largest in Europe. In 1650 contemporaries estimated that the Dutch had sixteen thousand merchant ships, half the European total. All the wood for these ships had to be imported: the Dutch bought whole forests from Norway. They also bought entire vineyards from French growers before the grapes were harvested. They controlled the Baltic grain trade, buying entire wheat and rye crops in Poland, east

Prussia, and Swedish Pomerania. Because the Dutch dealt in bulk, nobody could undersell them. Foreign merchants coming to Amsterdam could buy anything from precision lenses for the microscope (recently invented by Dutchman Anton van Leeuwenhoek) to muskets for an army of five thousand. Although Dutch cities became famous for their exports—diamonds and linens from Haarlem, pottery from Delft—Dutch wealth depended less on exports than on transport.

In 1602 a group of the regents of Holland formed the **Dutch East India Company,** a joint stock company. The investors each received a percentage of the profits proportional to the amount of money they had put in. Within half a century, the Dutch East India Company had cut heavily into Portuguese trading in East Asia. The Dutch seized the Cape of Good Hope, Ceylon, and Malacca and established trading posts in each place. In the 1630s, the Dutch East India Company was paying its investors about a 35 percent annual return on their investments. The Dutch West India Company, founded in 1621, traded extensively with Latin America and Africa (see Map 16.3).

Trade and commerce brought the Dutch prodigious wealth. In the seventeenth century, the Dutch enjoyed the highest standard of living in Europe, perhaps in the world. Amsterdam and Rotterdam built massive granaries where the surplus of one year could be stored against possible shortages the next. Thus, excepting the 1650s, when bad harvests reduced supplies, food prices fluctuated very little. By the standards of Cologne, Paris, or London, salaries were high for all workers—except women, but even women's wages were high when compared with those of women in other parts of Europe. All classes of society, including unskilled laborers, ate well. The low price of bread meant that, compared to other places in Europe, a higher percentage of the worker's income could be spent on fish, cheese, butter, vegetables, even meat. A scholar has described the Netherlands as "an island of plenty in a sea of want." Consequently, the Netherlands experienced very few of the food riots that characterized the rest of Europe.[32]

Although the initial purpose of the Dutch East and West India Companies was commercial—the import of spices and silks to Europe—the Dutch found themselves involved in the imperialist exploitation of parts of East Asia and Latin America, with great success. In 1652 the Dutch founded Cape Town on the southern tip of Africa as a fueling station for ships planning to cross the Pacific. But war with France and England in the 1670s hurt the United Provinces. The long War of the Spanish Succession—in which the Dutch prince William of Orange utilized, as King William III of England, English wealth in the Dutch

fight against Louis XIV—was a costly drain on Dutch labor and financial resources. The peace signed in 1713 to end the war marked the beginning of Dutch economic decline.

Summary

According to Thomas Hobbes, the central drive in every human is "a perpetual and restless desire of Power, after Power, that ceaseth only in Death." The seventeenth century solved the problem of sovereign power in two fundamental ways: absolutism and constitutionalism. The France of Louis XIV witnessed the emergence of the fully absolutist state. The king commanded all the powers of the state: judicial, military, political, and, to a great extent, ecclesiastical. France developed a centralized bureaucracy, a professional army, and a state-directed economy, all of which Louis personally supervised. For the first time in history, all the institutions and powers of the national state were effectively controlled by a single person. The king saw himself as the representative of God on earth, and it has been said that "to the seventeenth century imagination God was a sort of image of Louis XIV."[33]

As Louis XIV personifies absolutism, so Stuart England exemplifies the evolution of the first modern constitutional state. The conflicts between Parliament and the first two Stuart rulers, James I and Charles I, tested where sovereign power would rest in the state. The resulting civil war did not solve the problem. The Instrument of Government provided for a balance of government authority and recognition of popular rights; as such, the Instrument has been called the first modern constitution. Unfortunately, it lacked public support. James II's absolutist tendencies brought on the Glorious Revolution of 1688 to 1689, and the people who made that revolution settled three basic issues. Sovereign power was divided between king and Parliament, with Parliament enjoying the greater share. Government was to be based on the rule of law. And the liberties of English people were made explicit in written form in the Bill of Rights.

The models of governmental power established by seventeenth-century England and France strongly influenced other states then and ever since. As American novelist William Faulkner wrote, "The past isn't dead; it's not even past."

Key Terms

sovereignty	Fronde
absolutism	mercantilism
totalitarianism	French classicism
raison d'état	Peace of Utrecht

Don Quixote
constitutionalism
Puritans
republican government
Second Treatise of Civil Government

cabinet system
States General
stadholder
Dutch East India Company

Notes

1. G. Parker and L. M. Smith, "Introduction," and N. Steensgaard, "The Seventeenth Century Crisis," in *The General Crisis of the Seventeenth Century,* ed. G. Parker and L. M. Smith (London: Routledge & Kegan Paul, 1985), pp. 1–53, esp. p. 12.

2. See W. Beik, *Urban Protest in Seventeenth-Century France: The Culture of Retribution* (New York: Cambridge University Press, 1997), p. 1.

3. See J. Bergin, *Cardinal Richelieu: Power and the Pursuit of Wealth* (New Haven, Conn.: Yale University Press, 1985), which describes how Richelieu made his vast wealth through his royal and ecclesiastical offices.

4. J. B. Collins, *The State in Early Modern France* (Cambridge: Cambridge University Press, 1995), p. 1.

5. Ibid., p. 3.

6. Ibid., pp. 22–26.

7. See M. Turchetti, "The Edict of Nantes," in *The Oxford Encyclopedia of the Reformation,* ed. H. J. Hillerbrand, vol. 3 (New York: Oxford University Press, 1996), pp. 126–128.

8. See Beik, *Urban Protest,* chaps. 1, 2, 3, and 11.

9. J. B. Collins, *Fiscal Limits of Absolutism: Direct Taxation in Early Seventeenth-Century France* (Berkeley: University of California Press, 1988), pp. 1, 3–4, 215–222.

10. Quoted in J. H. Elliott, *Richelieu and Olivares* (Cambridge: Cambridge University Press, 1984), p. 135; and in W. F. Church, *Richelieu and Reason of State* (Princeton, N.J.: Princeton University Press, 1972), p. 507.

11. D. Parker, *The Making of French Absolutism* (New York: St. Martin's Press, 1983), pp. 146–148.

12. Collins, *The State in Early Modern France,* pp. 65–78.

13. See W. Beik, *Absolutism and Society in Seventeenth-Century France: State Power and Provincial Aristocracy in Languedoc* (Cambridge: Cambridge University Press, 1985), pp. 279–302.

14. S. de Gramont, ed., *The Age of Magnificence: Memoirs of the Court of Louis XIV by the Duc de Saint Simon* (New York: Capricorn Books, 1964), pp. 141–145.

15. Quoted in J. Wolf, *Louis XIV* (New York: W. W. Norton, 1968), p. 146.

16. See J. Swann, *Provincial Power and Absolute Monarchy: The Estates General of Burgundy, 1661–1790* (New York: Cambridge University Press, 2003), pp. 154–162.

17. Quoted in A. Trout, *Jean-Baptiste Colbert* (Boston: Twayne, 1978), p. 128.

18. Quoted in Wolf, *Louis XIV,* p. 394.

19. Ibid.

20. See W. C. Scoville, *The Persecution of the Huguenots and French Economic Development: 1680–1720* (Berkeley: University of California Press, 1960).

21. F. Bluche, *Louis XIV,* trans. M. Greengrass (Oxford: Basil Blackwell, 1990), p. 607.

22. Ibid., p. 458.

23. Quoted ibid., p. 519.

24. W. F. Church, *Louis XIV in Historical Thought: From Voltaire to the Annales School* (New York: W. W. Norton, 1976), p. 92.

25. Quoted in Gramont, *The Age of Magnificence,* p. 183.

26. J. H. Elliott, *Imperial Spain, 1469–1716* (New York: Mentor Books, 1963), pp. 306–308.

27. B. Bennassar, *The Spanish Character: Attitudes and Mentalities from the Sixteenth to the Nineteenth Century,* trans. B. Keen (Berkeley: University of California Press, 1979), p. 125.

28. For a revisionist interpretation, see J. Wormald, "James VI and I: Two Kings or One?" *History* 62 (June 1983): 187–209.

29. See J. P. Sommerville's review of J. Cramsie, "Kingship and Crown Finance Under James VI and I, 1603–1625," *The American Historical Review* 109 (April 2004): 607–608.

30. C. Stephenson and G. F. Marcham, *Sources of English Constitutional History* (New York: Harper & Row, 1937), p. 601.

31. Quoted in D. Maland, *Europe in the Seventeenth Century* (New York: Macmillan, 1967), pp. 198–199.

32. S. Schama, *The Embarrassment of Riches: An Interpretation of Dutch Culture in the Golden Age* (New York: Alfred A. Knopf, 1987), pp. 165–170; quotation is on p. 167.

33. C. J. Friedrich and C. Blitzer, *The Age of Power* (Ithaca, N.Y.: Cornell University Press, 1957), p. 112.

Suggested Reading

Students who wish to explore the problems presented in this chapter in greater depth will easily find a rich and exciting literature. The following surveys all provide good background material: H. Kamen, *The Iron Century: Social Change in Europe, 1550–1660* (1971); G. Parker, *Europe in Crisis, 1598–1618* (1980), a sound introduction to the social, economic, and religious tensions of the period; and R. S. Dunn, *The Age of Religious Wars, 1559–1715* (1979), which examines the period from the perspective of the confessional strife between Protestants and Catholics but contains material on absolutism and constitutionalism.

For the period of Louis XIII, Richelieu, and the Fronde, see L. Moote, *Louis XIII: The Just* (1989), an important biography; J. Bergin, *Richelieu: Power and the Pursuit of Wealth* (1989), a detailed study of how Richelieu used his various offices to acquire great wealth for himself and his family; and O. Ranum, *The Fronde* (1994), probably the best work in English on the Fronde. Two important studies of French local administration are J. B. Collins, *Classes, Estates, and Order in Early Modern Brittany* (1994), and R. Schneider, *Public Life in Toulouse, 1463–1789* (1989). K. Norberg, *Rich and Poor in Grenoble, 1600–1815* (1985), provides an interesting case study of the wretched conditions of the poor, while W. Beik, *Urban Protest in Seventeenth-Century France* (1997), explores the cultural significance of the widespread incidence of urban violence.

For the relationship between the army, finances, and state power, see J. B. Wood, *The King's Army: Warfare, Soldiers, and Society During the Wars of Religion in France, 1562–1576* (1996); J. Lynn, *Giant of the Grand Siècle: The French Army, 1610–1715* (1997); D. Parrott, *Richelieu's Army: War, Government and Society in France, 1624–1642* (2001); and G.

Rowlands, *The Dynastic State and the Army Under Louis XIV: Royal Service and Private Interest, 1661–1701* (2002).

The important work of P. K. Monod, *The Power of Kings: Monarchy and Religion in Europe, 1589–1715* (1999), provides a broad comparative study of the changes in monarchical authority and power and of the shift from medieval ideas of sacred kingship to "modern" ideas of the rational state.

Louis XIV and his age have predictably attracted the attention of many scholars. Bluche, although hagiographical, is an almost definitive study, and Wolf remains valuable; both are cited in the Notes. The excellent work of P. Burke, *The Fabrication of Louis XIV* (1992), explores the images or representations of the king in stone, bronze, paint, plays, operas, and rituals. For the court of Louis XIV, see also K. A. Hoffmann, *Society of Pleasures: Interdisciplinary Readings in Pleasure and Power During the Reign of Louis XIV* (1997), a sophisticated study of the uses of pleasure as a political tool; R. Chartier, *The Cultural Origins of the French Revolution* (1991); and J. F. Solnon, *La Cour de France* (1987). For Louis XIV's foreign policy and wars, see P. Sonnino, *Louis XIV and the Origins of the Dutch Wars* (1988), and H. Kamen, *The War of Succession in Spain, 1700–1715* (1969). R. Hatton, *Europe in the Age of Louis XIV* (1979), is a well-illustrated survey of many aspects of seventeenth-century European culture. O. Ranum, *Paris in the Age of Absolutism* (1968), describes the geographical, political, economic, and architectural significance of the cultural capital of Europe.

For Spain and Portugal, in addition to the works in the Notes, see H. Kamen, *Spain in the Later Seventeenth Century, 1665–1700* (1980); M. Defourneaux, *Daily Life in Spain in the Golden Age* (1976), highly useful for an understanding of ordinary people and of Spanish society; and C. R. Phillips, *Ciudad Real, 1500–1750: Growth, Crisis, and Readjustment in the Spanish Economy* (1979), a significant case study. A. Pagden, *Spanish Imperialism and the Political Imagination* (1990), explores Spanish ideas of empire, primarily in Italy and the Americas, and shows that the failure to revise ideas to meet changing circumstances led to the empire's decline.

The following works offer solid material on English political and social issues of the seventeenth century: J. P. Kenyon, *Stuart England* (1978), and K. Wrightson, *English Society, 1580–1680* (1982). Perhaps the most comprehensive treatments of Parliament are C. Russell, *Crisis of Parliaments, 1509–1660* (1971), and *Parliaments and English Politics, 1621–1629* (1979). On the background of the English civil war, L. Stone's *The Crisis of the Aristocracy* (1965) and *The Causes of the English Revolution* (1972) are standard works; both B. Manning, *The English People and the English Revolution* (1976), and D. Underdown, *Revel, Riot, and Rebellion* (1985), discuss the extent of popular involvement. For English intellectual currents, see J. O. Appleby, *Economic Thought and Ideology in Seventeenth-Century England* (1978). M. J. Braddick, *The Nerves of State: Taxation and the Financing of the English State, 1558–1714* (1996), surveys the evolution of parliamentary taxation as the means of financing state expenses, especially military ones. S. Porter, ed., *London and the Civil War* (1996), treats the city's choice of allegiance and contribution to the war effort.

C. Durston and J. Eales, eds., *The Culture of English Puritanism, 1560–1700* (1996), provides a revisionist definition of the term *Puritan* and explores topics such as Sabbatarianism and iconoclasm.

The excellent achievement of A. Woolrych, *Britain in Revolution, 1625–1660* (rev. ed. 2004), explores Scottish and Irish dynamics in the period in a lucid narrative.

For women, see R. Thompson, *Women in Stuart England and America* (1974), and A. Fraser, *The Weaker Vessel* (1985). For Cromwell and the Interregnum, see C. Firth, *Oliver Cromwell and the Rule of the Puritans in England* (1956); C. Hill, *God's Englishman* (1972); and A. Fraser, *Cromwell, the Lord Protector* (1973).

For the Restoration and the Glorious Revolution, see R. Hutton, *Charles II: King of England, Scotland and Ireland* (1989), and A. Fraser, *Royal Charles: Charles II and the Restoration* (1979), two highly readable biographies; R. Ollard, *The Image of the King: Charles I and Charles II* (1980), which examines the nature of monarchy; J. Miller, *James II: A Study in Kingship* (1977); J. Childs, *The Army, James II, and the Glorious Revolution* (1980); J. R. Jones, *The Revolution of 1688 in England* (1972); and L. G. Schwoerer, *The Declaration of Rights, 1689* (1981), a fine assessment of that fundamental document. For the continuation of an older system during the rise of the Whigs and Tories, see B. Hill, *The Early Parties and Politics in Britain, 1688–1832* (1996).

On Holland, the starting point for serious study is Schama, mentioned in the Notes, a brilliant and beautifully illustrated achievement. J. L. Price, *Culture and Society in the Dutch Republic During the Seventeenth Century* (1974), is a sound scholarly work. R. Boxer, *The Dutch Seaborne Empire* (1980), and the appropriate chapters of the Maland work cited in the Notes are useful for Dutch overseas expansion and the reasons for Dutch prosperity. The following works focus on the economic and cultural life of the leading Dutch city: V. Barbour, *Capitalism in Amsterdam in the Seventeenth Century* (1950), and D. Regin, *Traders, Artists, Burghers: A Cultural History of Amsterdam in the Seventeenth Century* (1977). J. M. Montias, *Artists and Artisans in Delft: A Socio-economic Study of the Seventeenth Century* (1982), examines another major city. The leading statesmen of the period may be studied in these biographies: H. H. Rowen, *John de Witt, Grand Pensionary of Holland, 1625–1672* (1978); S. B. Baxter, *William the III and the Defense of European Liberty, 1650–1702* (1966); and J. den Tex, *Oldenbarnevelt*, 2 vols. (1973).

Many facets of the lives of ordinary French, Spanish, English, and Dutch people are discussed in P. Burke, *Popular Culture in Early Modern Europe* (1978), a provocative study.

Listening to the Past

The Court at Versailles

*A*lthough the Duc de Saint-Simon (1675–1755) was a soldier, courtier, and diplomat, his enduring reputation rests on his Memoirs (1788), an eyewitness account of the personality and court of Louis XIV. A nobleman of ancient lineage, Saint-Simon resented Louis's "domestication" of the nobility and his promotion of the bourgeoisie. The Memoirs, excerpted here, remains a monument of French literature and an indispensable historical source, partly for its portrait of the court at Versailles.

Very early in the reign of Louis XIV the Court was removed from Paris, never to return. The troubles of the minority had given him a dislike to that city; his enforced and surreptitious flight from it still rankled in his memory; he did not consider himself safe there, and thought cabals would be more easily detected if the Court was in the country, where the movements and temporary absences of any of its members would be more easily noticed. . . . No doubt that he was also influenced by the feeling that he would be regarded with greater awe and veneration when no longer exposed every day to the gaze of the multitude.

His love-affair with Mademoiselle de la Vallière, which at first was covered as far as possible with a veil of mystery, was the cause of frequent excursions to Versailles. . . . The visits of Louis XIV becoming more frequent, he enlarged the *château* by degrees till its immense buildings afforded better accommodation for the Court than was to be found at St. Germain, where most of the courtiers had to put up with uncomfortable lodgings in the town. The Court was therefore removed to Versailles in 1682, not long before the Queen's death. The new building contained an infinite number of rooms for courtiers, and the

King liked the grant of these rooms to be regarded as a coveted privilege.

He availed himself of the frequent festivities at Versailles, and his excursions to other places, as a means of making the courtiers assiduous in their attendance and anxious to please him; for he nominated beforehand those who were to take part in them, and could thus gratify some and inflict a snub on others. He was conscious that the substantial favours he had to bestow were not nearly sufficient to produce a continual effect; he had therefore to invent imaginary ones, and no one was so clever in devising petty distinctions and preferences which aroused jealousy and emulation. The visits to Marly later on were very useful to him in this way; also those to Trianon [Marly and Trianon were small country houses], where certain ladies, chosen beforehand, were admitted to his table. It was another distinction to hold his candlestick at his *coucher;* as soon as he had finished his prayers he used to name the courtier to whom it was to be handed, always choosing one of the highest rank among those present. . . .

Not only did he expect all persons of distinction to be in continual attendance at Court, but he was quick to notice the absence of those of inferior degree; at his *lever* [formal rising from bed in the morning], his *coucher* [preparations for going to bed], his meals, in the gardens of Versailles (the only place where the courtiers in general were allowed to follow him), he used to cast his eyes to right and left; nothing escaped him, he saw everybody. If any one habitually living at Court absented himself he insisted on knowing the reason; those who came there only for flying visits had also to give a satisfactory explanation; any one who seldom or never appeared there was certain to incur his displeasure. If asked to bestow a favour on such persons he would reply haughtily: "I do not know him";

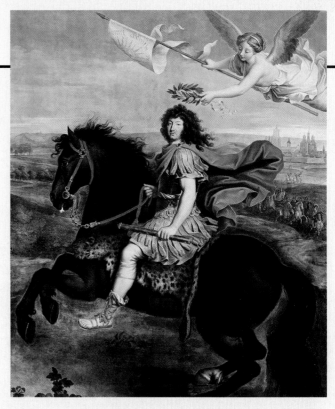

Painting of Louis XIV by Mignard Pierre (1612–1695). *(Galleria Sabauda, Turin/Scala/Art Resource, NY)*

of such as rarely presented themselves he would say, "He is a man I never see"; and from these judgements there was no appeal.

He always took great pains to find out what was going on in public places, in society, in private houses, even family secrets, and maintained an immense number of spies and tale-bearers. These were of all sorts; some did not know that their reports were carried to him; others did know it; there were others, again, who used to write to him directly, through channels which he prescribed; others who were admitted by the backstairs and saw him in his private room. Many a man in all ranks of life was ruined by these methods, often very unjustly, without ever being able to discover the reason; and when the King had once taken a prejudice against a man, he hardly ever got over it. . . .

No one understood better than Louis XIV the art of enhancing the value of a favour by his manner of bestowing it; he knew how to make the most of a word, a smile, even of a glance. If he addressed any one, were it but to ask a trifling question or make some commonplace remark, all eyes were turned on the person so honored; it was a mark of favour which always gave rise to comment. . . .

He loved splendour, magnificence, and profusion in all things, and encouraged similar tastes in his Court; to spend money freely on equipages [the king's horse carriages] and buildings, on feasting and at cards, was a sure way to gain his favour, perhaps to obtain the honour of a word from him. Motives of policy had something to do with this; by making expensive habits the fashion, and, for people in a certain position, a necessity, he compelled his courtiers to live beyond their income, and gradually reduced them to depend on his bounty for the means of subsistence. This was a plague which, once introduced, became a scourge to the whole

country, for it did not take long to spread to Paris, and thence to the armies and the provinces; so that a man of any position is now estimated entirely according to his expenditure on his table and other luxuries. This folly, sustained by pride and ostentation, has already produced widespread confusion; it threatens to end in nothing short of ruin and a general overthrow.

Questions for Analysis

1. How would you define the French court? Why did Louis XIV move it to Versailles?

2. By what means did Louis control the nobility at Versailles? Why did he use those particular means?

3. Consider the role of ritual and ceremony in some modern governments, such as the U.S. government. How does it compare to Louis XIV's use of ceremony, as portrayed by Saint-Simon?

4. Saint-Simon faulted Louis for encouraging the nobles' extravagance. Is that a justifiable criticism?

Source: F. Arkwright, ed., *The Memoirs of the Duke de Saint-Simon,* vol. 5 (New York: Brentano's, n.d.), pp. 271–274, 276–278.

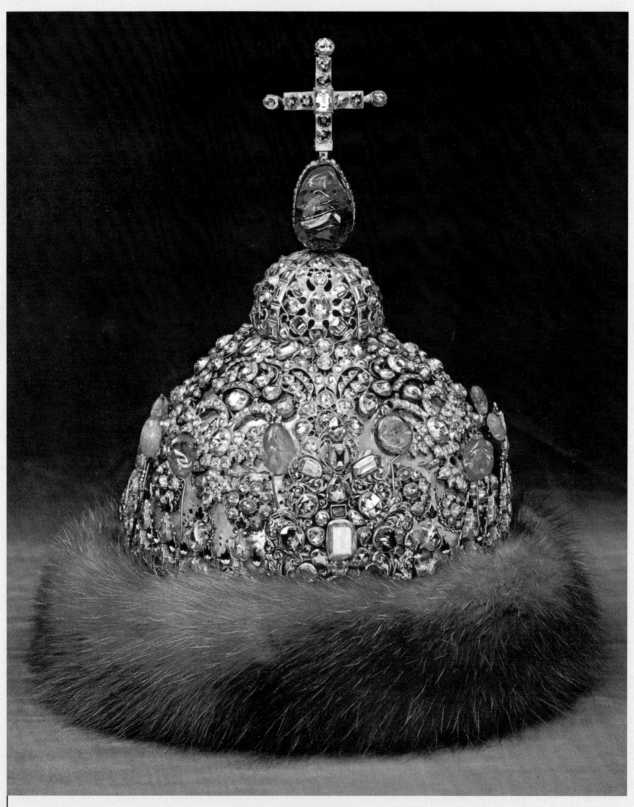

Peter the Great's magnificent new crown, created for his coronation in 1682 with his half-brother Ivan. *(State Museum of the Kremlin, Moscow)*

chapter

17 Absolutism in Eastern Europe to 1740

*T*he seventeenth century witnessed a struggle between constitutionalism and absolutism in eastern Europe, as it did in western Europe (see Chapter 16). But with the notable exception of the kingdom of Poland, monarchical absolutism was triumphant in eastern Europe; constitutionalism was decisively defeated. Absolute monarchies emerged in Austria, Prussia, and Russia. This development had significance for at least two reasons. First, these three monarchies exercised enormous influence until 1918, and they created an authoritarian tradition that lasted into the late twentieth century in eastern Europe. Second, the absolute monarchs of eastern Europe had a powerful impact on culture, encouraging a flowering of the baroque style in architecture and the arts.

Although the monarchs of eastern Europe were greatly impressed by Louis XIV and his model of royal absolutism, their states differed in several important ways from that of their French counterpart. Louis XIV built French absolutism on the foundation of a well-developed medieval monarchy and a strong royal bureaucracy. And when Louis XIV came to the throne, the powers of the nobility were already somewhat limited, the French middle class was relatively strong, and the peasants were generally free from serfdom. Eastern absolutism rested on a very different social reality: a powerful nobility, a weak middle class, and an oppressed peasantry composed of serfs.

These different conditions raise three questions:

- Why did the basic structure of society in eastern Europe move away from that of western Europe in the early modern period?
- How and why did the rulers of Austria, Prussia, and Russia, each in a different social environment, manage to build powerful absolute monarchies that proved more durable than that of Louis XIV?
- How did the absolute monarchs' interaction with artists and architects contribute to the splendid achievements of baroque culture?

These are the questions that this chapter will explore.

Lords and Peasants in Eastern Europe

When absolute monarchy took shape in eastern Europe in the seventeenth century, it built on social and economic foundations laid between roughly 1400 and 1650. In those years, the princes and the landed nobility of eastern Europe—with the major exception of the Ottoman rulers in the Balkans—rolled back the gains made by the peasantry during the High Middle Ages and reimposed a harsh serfdom on the rural masses. The nobility also reduced the importance of the towns and the middle classes. This process differed profoundly from developments in western Europe, where peasants won greater freedom and the urban capitalistic middle class continued its rise.

The Medieval Background

Between roughly 1400 and 1650, nobles and rulers re-established **serfdom** in the eastern lands of Bohemia, Silesia, Hungary, eastern Germany, Poland, Lithuania, and Russia. The east—the land east of the Elbe River in Germany, which historians often call "East Elbia"—gained a certain social and economic unity in the process. But eastern peasants lost their rights and freedoms. They became bound first to the land they worked and then, by degrading obligations, to the lords they served.

This development was a tragic reversal of trends in the High Middle Ages. The period from roughly 1050 to 1300 had been a time of general economic expansion characterized by the growth of trade, towns, and population. Expansion also meant clearing the forests and colonizing the frontier beyond the Elbe River. Anxious to attract German settlers to sparsely populated lands, the rulers and nobles of eastern Europe had offered potential newcomers economic and legal incentives. Large numbers of incoming settlers obtained land on excellent terms and gained much greater personal freedom. These benefits were also gradually extended to the local Slavic populations, even those of central Russia. Thus by 1300 a very general improvement in peasant conditions had occurred in eastern Europe; serfdom had all but disappeared. Peasants bargained freely with their landlords and moved about as they pleased. Opportunities and improvements east of the Elbe had a positive impact on western Europe, where the weight of serfdom was also reduced between 1100 and 1300. Thus fundamental social and economic developments moved in the same direction throughout Europe in the High Middle Ages, reinforcing a cultural and religious unity stretching all across Europe.

After about 1300, however, as Europe's population and economy both declined grievously, mainly because of the Black Death, the east and the west went in different directions. In both east and west, a many-sided land-lord reaction occurred as lords sought to solve their tough economic problems by more heavily exploiting the peasantry. Yet this reaction generally failed in the west. In many western areas by 1500, almost all of the peasants were free, and in the rest of western Europe serf obligations had declined greatly. East of the Elbe, however, the landlords won. By 1500 eastern peasants were well on their way to becoming serfs again.

Throughout eastern Europe, as in western Europe, the drop in population and prices in the fourteenth and fifteenth centuries caused severe labor shortages and hard times for the nobles. Yet rather than offer better economic and legal terms to keep old peasants and attract new ones, eastern landlords used political and police power to turn the tables on peasants. They did this in two ways.

First, the lords made their kings and princes issue laws that restricted or eliminated the peasants' precious, time-honored right of free movement. Thus a peasant could no longer leave to take advantage of better opportunities elsewhere without the lord's permission, and the lord had no reason to make such concessions. In Prussian territories by 1500, the law required that runaway peasants be hunted down and returned to their lords; a runaway servant was to be nailed to a post by one ear and given a knife to cut himself loose. Until the middle of the fifteenth century, medieval Russian peasants had been free to move wherever they wished and seek the best landlord. Thereafter this freedom was gradually curtailed, so that by 1497 a Russian peasant had the right to move only during a two-week period after the fall harvest. Eastern peasants were losing their status as free and independent men and women.

Second, lords steadily took more and more of their peasants' land and imposed heavier and heavier labor obligations. Instead of being independent farmers paying reasonable, freely negotiated rents, peasants tended to become forced laborers on the lords' estates. By the early 1500s, lords in many territories could command their peasants to work for them without pay as many as six days a week.

The gradual erosion of the peasantry's economic position was bound up with manipulation of the legal system. The local lord was also the local prosecutor, judge, and jailer. As a matter of course, he ruled in his own favor in disputes with his peasants. There were no independent royal officials to provide justice or uphold the common law.

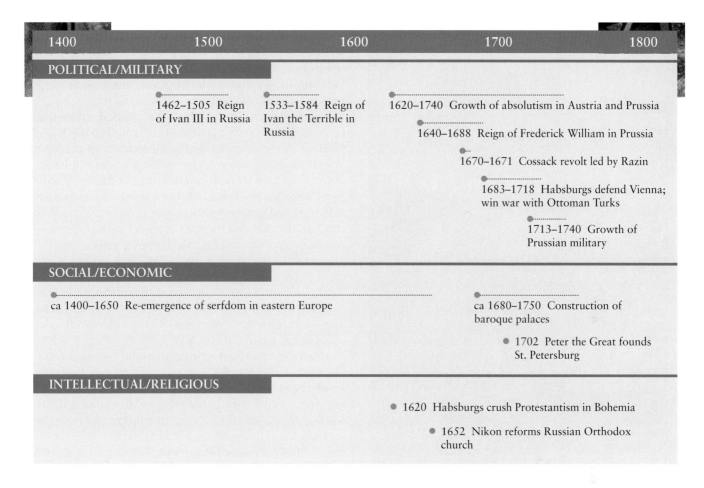

1400	1500	1600	1700	1800

POLITICAL/MILITARY

1462–1505 Reign of Ivan III in Russia

1533–1584 Reign of Ivan the Terrible in Russia

1620–1740 Growth of absolutism in Austria and Prussia

1640–1688 Reign of Frederick William in Prussia

1670–1671 Cossack revolt led by Razin

1683–1718 Habsburgs defend Vienna; win war with Ottoman Turks

1713–1740 Growth of Prussian military

SOCIAL/ECONOMIC

ca 1400–1650 Re-emergence of serfdom in eastern Europe

ca 1680–1750 Construction of baroque palaces

1702 Peter the Great founds St. Petersburg

INTELLECTUAL/RELIGIOUS

1620 Habsburgs crush Protestantism in Bohemia

1652 Nikon reforms Russian Orthodox church

The Consolidation of Serfdom

Between 1500 and 1650, the social, legal, and economic conditions of peasants in eastern Europe continued to decline. Free peasants lost their freedom and became serfs. In Poland, for example, nobles gained complete control over their peasants in 1574, after which they could legally inflict the death penalty on their serfs whenever they wished. In Prussia in 1653, peasants were assumed to be tied to their lords in **hereditary subjugation**—bound to their lords from one generation to the next as well as to the land.

In Russia the right of peasants to move from a given estate was "temporarily" suspended in the 1590s and permanently abolished in 1603. In 1649 a new law code completed the process. The Russian tsar lifted the nine-year time limit on the recovery of runaways, who were to be returned to their lords whenever they were caught. Moreover, the new law code set no limits on the lords' authority over their peasants. Although the political development of the various eastern states differed, the legal re-establishment of permanent hereditary serfdom had become the common fate of peasants in the east by the middle of the seventeenth century.

This consolidation of serfdom was accompanied by the growth of estate agriculture, particularly in Poland and eastern Germany. In the sixteenth century, European economic expansion and population growth resumed after the great declines of the late Middle Ages. Prices for agricultural commodities also rose sharply as gold and silver flowed in from the New World. Thus Polish and German lords had powerful economic incentives to increase the production of their estates. And they did.

Lords seized more and more peasant land for their own estates and then demanded and received ever more unpaid serf labor on those enlarged estates. Even when the estates were inefficient and technically backward, as they generally were, the great Polish nobles and middle-rank German lords squeezed sizable, cheap, and thus very profitable surpluses out of their impoverished

Estonia in the 1660s The Estonians were conquered by German military nobility in the Middle Ages and reduced to serfdom. The German-speaking nobles ruled the Estonian peasants with an iron hand, and Peter the Great reaffirmed their domination when Russia annexed Estonia (see Map 17.3 on page 578). *(Mansell Collection/TimePix/Getty Images)*

peasants. Surpluses in wheat and timber were easily sold to big foreign merchants, who exported them to the growing cities of the west. Thus the poor east helped feed the wealthier west.

The re-emergence of serfdom in eastern Europe in the early modern period was clearly a momentous human development, and historians have advanced a variety of explanations for it. Some scholars have stressed the economic interpretation. Agricultural depression and population decline in the fourteenth and fifteenth centuries led to a severe labor shortage, they have argued, and thus eastern landlords naturally tied their precious peasants to the land. With the return of prosperity and the development of export markets in the sixteenth century, the landlords finished the job, grabbing the peasants' land and making them work as unpaid serfs within the framework of estate agriculture. This argument by itself is not very convincing, for almost identical economic developments "caused" the opposite result in the west.

It seems fairly clear, therefore, that political, rather than economic, factors were crucial in the simultaneous rise of serfdom in the east and decline of serfdom in the west. Specifically, eastern lords enjoyed much greater political power than their western counterparts. In the late Middle Ages, when much of eastern Europe experienced innumerable wars and general political chaos, the noble landlord class greatly increased its political power at the expense of the ruling monarchs. There were, for example, many disputed royal successions, so that weak kings were forced to grant political favors to win the support of the nobility. Thus while strong monarchs were rising in Spain, France, and England and providing effective central government, kings were generally losing power in the east. Such kings could not resist the demands of lords regarding peasants.

Moreover, most eastern monarchs did not want to resist even if they could. The typical king was only first among equals in the noble class. He, too, thought mainly in private, rather than public, terms. He, too, wanted to squeeze his peasants. The western concept and reality of sovereignty, as embodied in a king who protected the interests of all his people, was not well developed in eastern Europe before 1650.

The political power of the peasants was also weaker in eastern Europe and declined steadily after about 1400. Although there were occasional bloody peasant uprisings against the oppression of the landlords, they never succeeded. Nor did eastern peasants effectively resist day-by-day infringements on their liberties by their landlords. Part of the reason was that the lords, rather than the kings, ran the courts—one of the important concessions nobles extorted from weak monarchs.

Similarly, with the approval of weak kings, the landlords systematically undermined the medieval privileges of the towns and the power of the urban classes. Instead of selling products to local merchants in the towns, as required in the Middle Ages, the landlords sold directly to big foreign capitalists. For example, Dutch ships sailed up the rivers of Poland and eastern Germany to the loading docks of the great estates, completely short-circuiting the local towns. Moreover, "town air" no longer "made people free," for the eastern towns had lost their medieval right of refuge and were now compelled to return runaways to their lords. The population of the towns and the importance of the urban middle classes declined greatly. These developments both reflected and promoted the supremacy of noble landlords in most of eastern Europe in the sixteenth century.

Subsequently, in the eighteenth century, travelers and writers from western Europe became increasingly aware of real and even imagined differences that they observed in eastern Europe. Developing their ideas of refined society and gradual progress (see Chapter 18), westerners portrayed eastern Europe as being more "barbaric" and less "civilized" than their homelands.[1] Thus they expanded eastern Europe's undeniably harsher social and economic conditions to encompass a very debatable cultural and moral inferiority.

The Rise of Austria and Prussia

Despite the strength of the nobility and the weakness of many monarchs before 1600, strong kings did begin to emerge in many lands in the course of the seventeenth century. War and the threat of war aided rulers greatly in their attempts to build absolute monarchies. There was also an endless struggle for power, as eastern rulers not only fought one another but also battled with armies of invaders from Asia. In this atmosphere of continual wartime emergency, monarchs reduced the political power of the landlord nobility. Cautiously leaving the nobles the unchallenged masters of their peasants, the would-be absolutist monarchs of eastern Europe gradually gained and monopolized political power in three key areas. First, they imposed and collected permanent taxes without consent. Second, they maintained permanent standing armies, which policed the country in addition to fighting abroad. Third, they conducted relations with other states as they pleased.

As with all general historical developments, there were important variations on the absolutist theme in eastern Europe. The royal **absolutism** created in Prussia was stronger and more effective than that established in Austria. This advantage gave Prussia a thin edge over Austria in the struggle for power in east-central Europe in the eighteenth century. That edge had great long-term political significance, for it was a rising Prussia that unified the German people in the nineteenth century and imposed on them a militaristic Prussian stamp.

Austria and the Ottoman Turks

Like all the other peoples and rulers of central Europe, the Habsburgs of Austria emerged from the brutal Thirty Years' War, which lasted from 1618 to 1648, impoverished and exhausted. Their efforts to root out Protestantism in the German lands and to turn the weak Holy Roman Empire into a real state had failed utterly. The Habsburgs did remain the hereditary emperors of the ancient Holy Roman Empire, which was inhabited mainly by German-speakers and was more accurately called the German Empire. Real power in the German Empire lay in the hands of a bewildering variety of three hundred separate political jurisdictions, which included independent cities, small principalities, medium-size states such as Bavaria and Saxony, and some (but not all) of the territories of Prussia and the Habsburgs.

Defeat in central Europe opened new vistas for the Habsburgs. They were forced to turn inward and eastward in an attempt to fuse their diverse holdings into a strong unified state. An important step in this direction had actually been taken in Bohemia during the Thirty Years' War. Protestantism had been strong among the Czechs, a Slavic people concentrated in Bohemia. Indeed, the lesser Czech nobility was largely Protestant in 1600 and had considerable political power because it dominated the **Bohemian Estates**—the representative body of the different estates, or legal orders, in Bohemia. In 1618 the Bohemian Estates had risen up in defense of Protestant rights. This revolt was crushed in 1620 at the Battle of the White Mountain, a momentous turning point in Czech history. The victorious Habsburg king, Ferdinand II (r. 1619–1637), drastically reduced the power of the Bohemian Estates. Ferdinand also confiscated the landholdings of many Protestant nobles and gave them to a few great Catholic nobles who had remained loyal and to a motley band of aristocratic soldiers of fortune who had nothing in common with the Czech-speaking peasants. After 1650 a large portion of the Bohemian nobility was of recent foreign origin and owed everything to the Habsburgs.

With the help of this new nobility, the Habsburgs established strong direct rule over reconquered Bohemia. The condition of the enserfed peasantry worsened substantially: three days per week of unpaid labor—the *robot*—became the norm, and a quarter of the serfs worked for their lords every day but Sundays and religious holidays. Protestantism was also stamped out, in the course of which a growing unity of religion was brought about. The reorganization of Bohemia was a giant step toward absolutism.

After the Thirty Years' War, Ferdinand III (r. 1637–1657) centralized the government in the hereditary German-speaking provinces, most notably Austria, Styria, and the Tyrol, which formed the core area of the Habsburg holdings. For the first time, Ferdinand III's reign

The Battle of Mohács, 1526   The *Süleymanname* (Book of Suleiman), a biography, contains these fascinating illustrations of the great Ottoman victory at Mohács, which enabled the Turks to add Hungary to their expanding empire. In the right panel, Suleiman in a white turban sits on a black horse surrounded by his personal guard, while his janissary soldiers fire their muskets and cannon at the enemy. In the left panel, the Europeans are in disarray, in contrast to the Turks' discipline and order. *(Topkapi Saray Museum)*

saw the creation of a permanent standing army ready to put down any internal opposition. The Habsburg monarchy was then ready to turn toward the plains of Hungary, which had long been divided and fought over by the Habsburgs and the Ottoman Turks.

The Ottomans had come out of Central Asia as conquering warriors, settled in Anatolia, in present-day Turkey, and created one of history's greatest military empires. At their peak in the middle of the sixteenth century under Sultan Suleiman the Magnificent (r. 1520–1566), they ruled the most powerful empire in the world. Their possessions stretched from western Persia across North Africa and up into the heart of central Europe (see Map 17.1). Followers of Islam, the Ottoman Turks were old and determined foes of the Catholic Habsburgs. Their armies had almost captured Vienna in 1529, and for more than 150 years thereafter the Ottomans ruled the many different ethnic groups living in the Balkans, almost all of Hungary, and part of southern Russia.

The Ottoman Empire was originally built on a fascinating and very non-European conception of state and society. There was an almost complete absence of private landed property. All the agricultural land of the empire was the personal hereditary property of the **sultan,** who exploited the land as he saw fit according to Ottoman political theory. There was therefore no security of land-

MAP 17.1 The Ottoman Empire at Its Height, 1566 The Ottomans, like their great rivals the Habsburgs, rose to rule a vast dynastic empire encompassing many different peoples and ethnic groups. The army and the bureaucracy served to unite the disparate territories into a single state under an absolutist ruler.

holding and no hereditary nobility. The sultan also defended peasant communities from greedy officials, so that peasants could afford to pay their taxes and support the state.

The top ranks of the bureaucracy were staffed by the sultan's slave corps. Every year the sultan levied a "tax" of one to three thousand male children on the conquered Christian populations in the Balkans. These and other slaves were raised in Turkey as Muslims and trained to fight and to administer. The most talented slaves rose to the top of the bureaucracy; the less fortunate formed the brave and skillful core of the sultan's army, the so-called janissary corps. Lurid accounts of weeping Christian boys being carried off into Ottoman slavery did much to foster the idea of the brutal, fanatical Turk in the European mind.

In fact, the Ottomans were much more tolerant of religious differences than Europeans were. Building on the practices of the great Middle Eastern empires, the Ottomans divided their subjects into religious communities, whereby each *millet*—each "nation"—enjoyed autonomous self-government under its religious leaders. (The Ottoman Empire recognized separate millets for Orthodox Christians, Jews, and Armenian Christians, in addition to the Muslim millet for Muslims.) The **millet system** created a powerful stabilizing bond between the Ottoman ruling class and the different religious leaders, who supported the sultan's rule in return for extensive authority over the members of their communities. Each millet collected taxes for the state, regulated group behavior, and maintained law courts, schools, synagogues, and hospitals for its people. Individuals outside the ruling elite had status only through their millet membership.

Supported and reassured by religious toleration and cultural autonomy, non-Muslim minorities coexisted and commingled with the Muslim majority in the Ottoman Empire. Greek, Jewish, and Armenian merchants also moved easily to and from Europe, drawing Ottomans and Europeans closer together despite recurring war and conflict. Armenian merchants excelled as international silk merchants, Jews as textile manufacturers, and Greeks as mariners and shipowners, although all three groups participated in all Ottoman occupations in the sixteenth and seventeenth centuries.[2]

Following the death of Suleiman the Magnificent in 1566, monarchical absolutism and strong centralized rule gave way to palace intrigue, weak sultans, and the emergence of a powerful oligarchy of top officials. Temporary Muslim landowners became hard-to-control permanent oppressors, and the army lost its dedication and lagged behind its European foes in military innovation. The Ottoman Empire practically ceased to expand. Yet in the late seventeenth century, under vigorous reforming leadership, the Ottoman Empire succeeded in marshaling its forces for

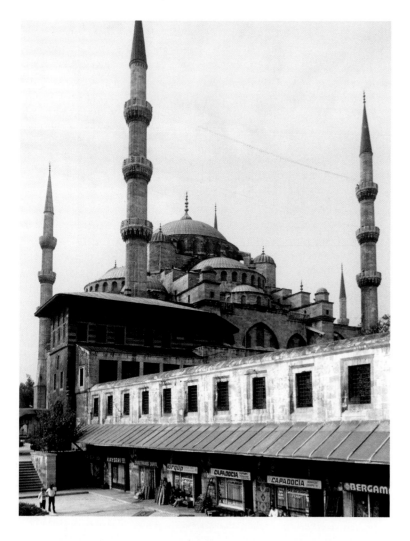

The Sultan Ahmet Mosque, Istanbul Completed in 1614, the mosque of Sultan Ahmet I was built in the heart of the city and gracefully accommodated existing rug merchants, who still operate today. With six soaring minarets to call the faithful to prayer and semi-domes cascading on four axes from the vast central dome, the Sultan Ahmet mosque was intended to outshine Hagia Sophia, the renowned Greek Orthodox cathedral located nearby that the Ottomans had converted to a mosque. This beautiful edifice, also known as the Blue Mosque for its interior Iznik tiles, represents the culmination of Ottoman mosque development. *(Robert Frerck/Woodfin Camp & Associates)*

one last mighty attack on the Habsburgs. A huge Turkish army surrounded Vienna and laid siege to it in 1683. After holding out against great odds for two months, the city was relieved at the last minute by a mixed force of Habsburg, Saxon, Bavarian, and Polish troops, and the Ottomans were forced to retreat. Soon the retreat became a rout. As Russian and Venetian allies attacked on other fronts, the Habsburgs conquered almost all of Hungary and Transylvania (part of present-day Romania) by 1699 (see Map 17.2).

The Turkish wars and this great expansion strengthened the Habsburg army and promoted some sense of unity in the Habsburg lands. But Habsburg efforts to create a fully developed, highly centralized, absolutist state were only partly successful.

The Habsburg state was composed of three separate and distinct territories—the old "hereditary provinces" of Austria, the kingdom of Bohemia, and the kingdom of Hungary. These three parts were tied together primarily by their common ruler, the Habsburg monarch. Each part had its own laws and political life, for the noble-dominated Estates continued to exist in each territory, though with reduced powers. The Habsburgs themselves were well aware of the fragility of the union they had forged. In 1713 Charles VI (r. 1711–1740) proclaimed the so-called **Pragmatic Sanction,** which stated that the Habsburg possessions were never to be divided and were always to be passed intact to a single heir, who might be female since Charles was the last of all Habsburg males. Charles spent much of his reign trying to get this principle accepted by the various branches of the Habsburg family, by the three different Estates of the realm, and by the states of Europe. His fears turned out to be well founded.

The Hungarian nobility, despite its reduced strength, effectively thwarted the full development of Habsburg absolutism. Time and again throughout the seventeenth century, Hungarian nobles—the most numerous in Europe, making up 5 to 7 percent of the Hungarian population—rose in revolt against Vienna's attempts to impose absolute rule. They never triumphed decisively, but neither were they ever crushed, as the Czech nobility had been in 1620.

The Hungarians resisted because many of them remained Protestants, especially in the area long ruled by the more tolerant Turks, and hated the heavy-handed attempts of the conquering Habsburgs to re-Catholicize everyone. Moreover, until 1683 the lords of Hungary had a powerful military ally in Turkey. Finally, the Hungarian nobility, and even part of the Hungarian peasantry, had become attached to a national ideal long before most of the other peoples of eastern Europe did so. Hungarian nobles were determined to maintain as much independence and local control as possible. Thus when the Habsburgs were bogged down in the War of the Spanish Succession (see page 543), the Hungarians rose in one last patriotic rebellion under Prince Francis Rákóczy in 1703. Rákóczy and his forces were eventually defeated, but this time the Habsburgs had to accept a definitive compromise. Charles VI restored many of the traditional privileges of the Hungarian aristocracy in return for Hungarian acceptance of hereditary Habsburg rule. Thus Hungary, unlike Austria or Bohemia, never came close to being fully integrated into a centralized, absolute Habsburg state.

Prussia in the Seventeenth Century

After 1400 the eastern German princes lost political power and influence, while a revitalized landed nobility became the undisputed ruling class. The Hohenzollern family, which ruled through its senior and junior branches as the imperial electors of Brandenburg and the dukes of Prussia, had little real princely power.

Nothing suggested that the Hohenzollern family and its princely territories would ever play an important role in European or even German affairs. The **elector of Brandenburg**'s right to help choose the Holy Roman emperor with six other electors bestowed prestige, but the elector had no military strength whatsoever. Moreover, Brandenburg, the area around Berlin and the elector's power base, was completely cut off from the sea (see Map 17.2). Brandenburg lacked defensible natural frontiers, and the land was poor, a combination of sand and swamp. Contemporaries contemptuously called Brandenburg the "sand-box of the Holy Roman Empire."[3]

Moreover, the territory of the elector's cousin, the duke of Prussia, was totally separated from Brandenburg and was part of Poland. Prussia had originally been conquered in the thirteenth century by the Germanic order of Teutonic Knights as part of a larger struggle between German conquerors and the indigenous Slavic populations. However, by 1600 Prussia's German-speaking peasants had much in common with Polish peasants in other provinces, for both ethnic groups had seen most of their freedoms reduced or revoked by their noble landlords. (Poland's numerous lesser nobility also dominated the Polish state, which was actually a constitutional republic headed by an elected king who had little real power.) In 1618 the junior branch of the Hohenzollern family died out, and Prussia reverted to the elector of Brandenburg.

The elector of Brandenburg was a helpless spectator in the Thirty Years' War, his territories alternately ravaged by Swedish and Habsburg armies. Population fell drastically, and many villages disappeared. Yet the devastation

MAP 17.2 The Growth of Austria and Brandenburg-Prussia to 1748   Austria expanded to the southwest into Hungary and Transylvania at the expense of the Ottoman Empire. It was unable to hold the rich German province of Silesia, however, which was conquered by Brandenburg-Prussia.

of Brandenburg and Prussia prepared the way for Hohenzollern absolutism because foreign armies dramatically weakened the political power of the Estates—the representative assemblies of the realm. This weakening of the Estates helped the very talented young elector Frederick William (r. 1640–1688), later known as the "Great Elector," to ride roughshod over traditional representative rights and to take a giant step toward royal absolutism. This constitutional struggle, often unjustly neglected by historians, was the most crucial in Prussian history for hundreds of years, until that of the 1860s.

When he came to power in 1640, the twenty-year-old Great Elector was determined to unify his three quite separate provinces and add to them by diplomacy and war. These provinces were Brandenburg itself; Prussia, inherited in 1618; and completely separate, scattered holdings along the Rhine in western Germany, inherited in 1614 (see Map 17.2). Each of the three provinces was inhabited by Germans, but each had its own Estates, whose power had increased until about 1600 as the power of the rulers declined. Although the Estates had not met regularly during the chaotic Thirty Years' War, they still had the power of the purse in their respective provinces. Taxes could not be levied without their consent. The Estates of Brandenburg and Prussia were dominated by the nobility and the landowning classes, known as the **Junkers.** But this was also the case in most European countries that had representative bodies, including the English Parliament before and after the civil war. Had the Estates successfully resisted the absolutist demands of the Great Elector, they, too, might have evolved toward more broadly based constitutionalism.

The struggle between the Great Elector and the provincial Estates was long, complicated, and intense. After the Thirty Years' War, representatives of the nobility zealously reasserted the right of the Estates to vote taxes, a right the Swedish armies of occupation had simply ignored. Yet first in Brandenburg in 1653 and then in Prussia between 1661 and 1663, the Great Elector eventually had his way.

To pay for the permanent standing army he first established in 1660, Frederick William forced the Estates to accept the introduction of permanent taxation without consent. The power of the Estates declined rapidly thereafter, for the Great Elector had both financial independence and superior force. The state's total revenue tripled during his reign. The size of the army leaped about tenfold. In 1688 a population of one million was supporting a peacetime standing army of thirty thousand.

In accounting for the Great Elector's fateful triumph, two factors appear central. First, as in the formation of every absolutist state, war was a decisive factor. The ongoing struggle between Sweden and Poland for control of the Baltic after 1648 and the wars of Louis XIV in western Europe created an atmosphere of permanent crisis. The wild Tartars of the Crimea in southern Russia swept through Prussia in the winter of 1656 to 1657, killing and carrying off as slaves more than fifty thousand people, according to an old estimate. This invasion softened up the Estates and strengthened the urgency of the Great Elector's demands for more money for more soldiers.

Second, the nobility had long dominated the government through the Estates, but it was unwilling to join the representatives of the towns in a consistent common front and was focused on its own rights and privileges. When, therefore, the Great Elector reconfirmed these privileges in 1653 and after, even while reducing the political power of the Estates, the nobility growled but did not bite. It accepted a compromise whereby the bulk of the new taxes fell on towns and royal authority stopped at the landlords' gates. The elector could and did use naked force to break the liberties of the towns. The main leader of the urban opposition in the key city of Königsberg, for example, was simply arrested and imprisoned for life without trial.

The Consolidation of Prussian Absolutism

By the time of his death in 1688, the Great Elector had created a single state out of scattered principalities. But his new creation was still small and fragile. All the leading states of Europe had many more people, and strong monarchy was still a novelty. Moreover, the Great Elector's successor, Elector Frederick III, "the Ostentatious" (r. 1688–1713), was weak of body and mind, and he focused on imitating the style of Louis XIV, building an expensive palace and cultivating the arts. His main political accomplishment was winning a prestigious royal title and being crowned King Frederick I in 1701 as a reward for aiding the Holy Roman emperor in the War of the Spanish Succession.

This tendency toward luxury-loving, petty tyranny was completely reversed by Frederick William I, "the Soldiers' King" (r. 1713–1740). A crude, dangerous psychoneurotic, Frederick William I was nevertheless the most talented reformer ever produced by the Hohenzollern family. It was he who truly established Prussian absolutism and gave it a unique character. It was he who created the best army in Europe, for its size, and it was he who infused strict military values into a whole society. In the words of a famous historian of Prussia:

For a whole generation, the Hohenzollern subjects were victimized by a royal bully, imbued with an obsessive bent for military organization and military scales of value. This left a deep mark upon the institutions of Prussiandom and upon the molding of the "Prussian spirit."[4]

Frederick William's attachment to the army and military life was intensely emotional. He had, for example, a bizarre, almost pathological love for tall soldiers, whom he credited with superior strength and endurance. Like some fanatical modern-day basketball coach in search of a championship team, he sent his agents throughout Prussia and all of Europe to trick, buy, and kidnap top recruits. Neighboring princes sent him their giants as gifts to win his gratitude. Prussian mothers told their sons, "Stop growing or the recruiting agents will get you."[5]

Profoundly militaristic in temperament, Frederick William always wore an army uniform, and he lived the highly disciplined life of the professional soldier. He began his work by five or six in the morning; at ten he almost always went to the parade ground to drill or inspect his troops. A man of violent temper, Frederick William personally punished the most minor infractions on the spot: a missing button off a soldier's coat quickly provoked a savage beating with a heavy walking stick.

Frederick William's love of the army was also based on a hardheaded conception of the struggle for power and a dog-eat-dog view of international politics. Years later he summed up his life's philosophy in his instructions to his son: "A formidable army and a war chest large enough to make this army mobile in times of need can create great respect for you in the world, so that you can speak a word like the other powers."[6] This unshakable belief that the

A Prussian Giant Grenadier   Frederick William I wanted tall, handsome soldiers. He dressed them in tight bright uniforms to distinguish them from the peasant population from which most soldiers came. He also ordered several portraits of his favorites from his court painter, J. C. Merk. Grenadiers wore the miter cap instead of an ordinary hat so that they could hurl their heavy grenades unimpeded by a broad brim. *(The Royal Collection © 2004, Her Majesty Queen Elizabeth II)*

welfare of king and state depended on the army above all else reinforced Frederick William's passion for the soldier's life.

The cult of military power provided the rationale for a great expansion of royal absolutism in Prussia. As the ruthless king himself put it: "I must be served with life and limb, with house and wealth, with honour and conscience, everything must be committed except eternal salvation—that belongs to God, but all else is mine."[7] To make good these extraordinary demands, Frederick William created a strong centralized bureaucracy. Meanwhile the last traces of the parliamentary Estates and local self-government vanished.

The king's grab for power brought him into considerable conflict with the noble landowners, the Junkers. In his early years, he even threatened to destroy them; yet, in the end, the Prussian nobility was not destroyed but enlisted—into the army. Responding to a combination of threats and opportunities, the Junkers became the officer caste. A new compromise had been worked out whereby the proud nobility imperiously commanded the peasantry in the army as well as on the estates.

Coarse and crude, penny-pinching and hard-working, Frederick William achieved results. Above all, he built a first-rate army, although he had only third-rate resources. The standing army increased from thirty-eight thousand to eighty-three thousand during his reign. Prussia, twelfth in Europe in population, had the fourth largest army by 1740. Moreover, soldier for soldier, the Prussian army became the best in Europe, astonishing foreign observers with its precision, skill, and discipline. For the next two hundred years, Prussia and then Prussianized Germany would usually win the crucial military battles.

Frederick William and his ministers also built an exceptionally honest and conscientious bureaucracy, which not only administered the country but also tried with some success to develop the country economically. Finally, like the miser he was known to be, living very frugally off the income of his own landholdings, the king loved his "blue boys" so much that he hated to "spend" them. This most militaristic of kings was, paradoxically, almost always at peace.

Nevertheless, the Prussian people paid a heavy and lasting price for the obsessions of their royal drillmaster. Civil society became rigid and highly disciplined. Prussia became the "Sparta of the North"; unquestioning obedience was the highest virtue. As a Prussian minister later summed up, "To keep quiet is the first civic duty."[8] Thus the policies of Frederick William I combined with harsh peasant bondage and Junker tyranny to lay the foundations for probably the most militaristic country of modern times.

The Development of Russia

One of the favorite parlor games of nineteenth-century Russian (and non-Russian) intellectuals was debating whether Russia was a Western, European or a non-Western, Asiatic society. This question was particularly fascinating because it was unanswerable. To this day Russia differs fundamentally from the West in some basic ways, though Russian history has paralleled that of the West in other aspects.

Certainly Russian developments in the early medieval period had important parallels with those in the West. The eastern Slavs were converted by missionaries from the Byzantine Empire to Orthodox Christianity, which became the state religion of the powerful Kievan principality, in the territory of present-day Ukraine. **Eastern Orthodoxy** rejects the authority of the pope, but this is the main difference in religious and moral beliefs dividing it from Roman Catholicism. Also in the mainstream of European medieval civilization was the loose but real political unification of the eastern Slavic territories under a single prince and a single dynasty in the eleventh century. So, too, was the typical feudal division of the land-based society into a **boyard nobility** and a commoner peasantry. After the death of Great Prince Iaroslav the Wise (r. 1019–1054), the Kievan principality disintegrated into competing political units. But similar fragmentations of central authority occurred in many European kingdoms at various points in the Middle Ages, and a strong native ruler might have emerged in Russia eventually to resume the centralizing work of earlier Kievan monarchs.

Such was not the case, however. Brutally conquered and subjugated by a foreign invader, Russia created a system of rule that was nearly unknown in the West between about 1250 and 1690. Thus when absolute monarchy triumphed under the rough guidance of Peter the Great in the early eighteenth century, it was a quite different type of absolute monarchy from that of France or even Prussia.

The Mongol Yoke and the Rise of Moscow

Like the Germans and the Italians, the eastern Slavs might have emerged from the Middle Ages weak and politically divided had it not been for the Mongol conquest of the Kievan principality. Nomadic tribes from present-day Mongolia, the Mongols were temporarily unified in the thirteenth century by Chinggis Khan (1162–1227), one of history's greatest conquerors. In five years his armies subdued all of China. His successors then turned westward, smashing everything in their path and reaching the plains of Hungary victorious before they pulled back in 1242. The Mongol army—the Golden Horde—was savage in the extreme, often slaughtering entire populations of cities before burning them to the ground. En route to Mongolia in 1245, Archbishop John of Plano Carpini, the papal ambassador to Mongolia, passed through Kiev, which the Mongols had sacked in 1242, and wrote an unforgettable eyewitness account:

The Mongols went against Russia and enacted a great massacre in the Russian land. They destroyed towns and fortresses and killed people. They besieged Kiev, which had been the capital of Russia, and after a long siege they took it and killed the inhabitants of the city. For this reason, when we passed through that land, we found lying in the field countless heads and bones of dead people; for this city had been extremely large and very populous, whereas now it has been reduced to nothing: barely two hundred houses stand there, and those people are held in the harshest slavery.[9]

Having devastated and conquered, the Mongols ruled the eastern Slavs for more than two hundred years, the so-called **Mongol Yoke.** They built their capital of Saray on the lower Volga (see Map 17.3). They forced all the bickering Slavic princes to submit to their rule and to give them tribute and slaves. If the conquered peoples rebelled, the Mongols were quick to punish with death and destruction. Thus the Mongols unified the eastern Slavs, for the Mongol khan was acknowledged by all as the supreme ruler.

The Mongol unification completely changed the internal political situation. Although the Mongols conquered, they were quite willing to use local princes as obedient servants and tax collectors. Therefore, they did not abolish the title of "great prince," bestowing it instead on the prince who served them best and paid them most handsomely.

Beginning with Alexander Nevsky in 1252, the previously insignificant princes of Moscow became particularly adept at serving the Mongols. They loyally put down popular uprisings and collected the khan's harsh taxes. By way of reward, the princes of Moscow emerged as hereditary great princes. Eventually the Muscovite princes were able to destroy their princely rivals and even replace the khan as supreme ruler. Ivan III (r. 1462–1505) completed this process of consolidating power around Moscow and won Novgorod, thereby almost reaching the Baltic Sea (see Map 17.3). The prince of Moscow had defeated all rivals to win complete princely authority.

Not only was the prince of Moscow the *unique* ruler, he was the *absolute* ruler, the autocrat, the *tsar*—the

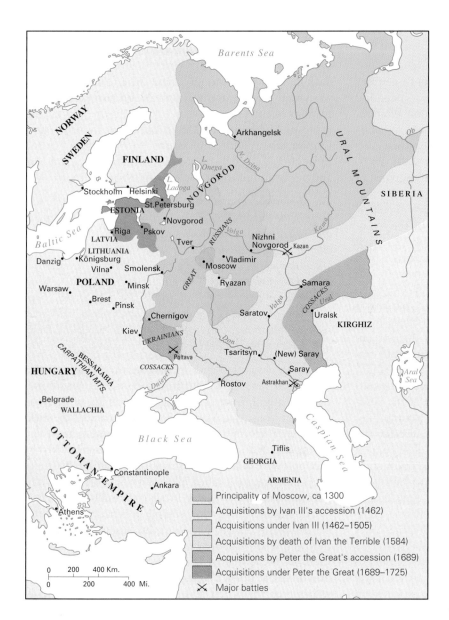

MAP 17.3 The Expansion of Russia to 1725   After the disintegration of the Kievan state and the Mongol conquest, the princes of Moscow and their descendants gradually extended their rule over an enormous territory. Ivan the Terrible acquired more territory than Peter the Great.

Map legend:
- Principality of Moscow, ca 1300
- Acquisitions by Ivan III's accession (1462)
- Acquisitions under Ivan III (1462–1505)
- Acquisitions by death of Ivan the Terrible (1584)
- Acquisitions by Peter the Great's accession (1689)
- Acquisitions under Peter the Great (1689–1725)
- ✕ Major battles

Slavic contraction for "caesar," with all its connotations. This imperious conception of absolute power and **autocracy** was powerfully reinforced by two developments. First, about 1480 Ivan III felt strong enough to stop acknowledging the khan as his supreme ruler. There is good evidence to suggest that Ivan and his successor saw themselves as khans, exercising unrestrained and unpredictable power.

Second, after the fall of Constantinople to the Turks in 1453, the tsars saw themselves as the heirs of both the caesars and Orthodox Christianity, the one true faith. All the other kings of Europe were heretics; only the tsars were rightful and holy rulers. The idea was promoted by Orthodox churchmen, who spoke of "holy Russia" as the "Third Rome." As the monk Pilotheus stated, "Two Romes have fallen, but the third stands, and a fourth there will not be."[10] Ivan's marriage to the daughter of the last Byzantine emperor further enhanced the aura of an imperial inheritance of Moscow.

As peasants had begun losing their freedom of movement in the fifteenth century, so had the noble boyars begun losing power and influence. For example, when

Ivan III conquered the principality of Novgorod in the 1480s, he confiscated fully 80 percent of the land, executing the previous owners or resettling them nearer Moscow. He then kept more than half of the confiscated land for himself and distributed the remainder to members of a newly emerging **service nobility,** who held the tsar's land on the explicit condition that they serve in the tsar's army.

Tsar and People to 1689

The rise of the new service nobility accelerated under Ivan IV (r. 1533–1584), the famous "Ivan the Terrible." Having ascended the throne at age three, Ivan suffered insults and neglect at the hands of the haughty boyars after his mother mysteriously died, possibly poisoned, when he was just eight. At age sixteen he suddenly pushed aside his hated boyar advisers. In an awe-inspiring ceremony complete with gold coins pouring down on his head, he majestically crowned himself and officially took the august title of tsar for the first time.

Selecting the beautiful and kind Anastasia of the popular Romanov family for his wife and queen, the young tsar soon declared war on the remnants of Mongol power. He defeated the faltering khanates of Kazan and Astrakhan between 1552 and 1556, adding vast new territories to Russia. In the course of these wars, Ivan virtually abolished the old distinction between hereditary boyar private property and land granted temporarily for service. All nobles, old and new, had to serve the tsar in order to hold any land.

The process of transforming the entire nobility into a service nobility was completed in the second part of Ivan the Terrible's reign. In 1557 Ivan turned westward, and for the next twenty-five years Muscovy waged an exhausting, unsuccessful war primarily against the large Polish-Lithuanian state, which joined Poland with much of Ukraine in the sixteenth century. Quarreling with the boyars over the war and blaming them for the sudden death of his beloved Anastasia in 1560, the increasingly cruel and demented Ivan turned to strike down all who stood in his way.

Above all, he struck down the ancient Muscovite boyars with a reign of terror. Leading boyars, their relatives, and even their peasants and servants were executed en masse by a special corps of unquestioning servants. Dressed in black and riding black horses, they were forerunners of the modern dictator's secret police. Large estates were confiscated, broken up, and reapportioned to the lower service nobility. The great boyar families were

Ivan the Terrible   Ivan IV, the first to take the title Tsar of Russia, executed many Muscovite boyars and their peasants and servants. His ownership of all the land, trade, and industry restricted economic development. *(National Museum, Copenhagen, Denmark)*

severely reduced. The newer, poorer, more nearly equal service nobility, still less than 0.5 percent of the total population, was totally dependent on the autocrat.

Ivan also took giant strides toward making all commoners servants of the tsar. His endless wars and demonic purges left much of central Russia depopulated. As the service nobles demanded more from the remaining peasants, more and more peasants fled toward the wild, recently conquered territories to the east and south. There they formed free groups and outlaw armies known as **Cossacks,** who maintained a precarious independence beyond the tsar's reach. The solution to the problem of peasant flight was to complete the tying of the peasants to the land and to the noble landholders, who were bound in turn to serve the tsar.

In the time of Ivan the Terrible, urban traders and artisans were also bound to their towns and jobs so that the tsar could tax them more heavily. Ivan assumed that the tsar owned Russia's trade and industry, just as he owned all the land. The urban classes had no security in their

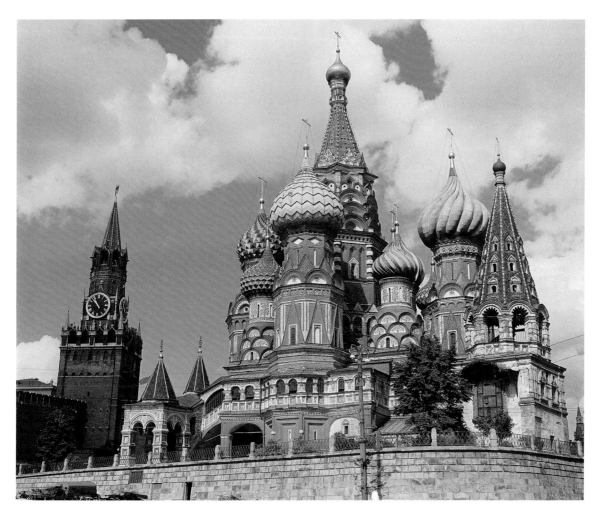

Saint Basil's Cathedral, Moscow With its sloping roofs and colorful onion-shaped domes, Saint Basil's is a striking example of powerful Byzantine influences on Russian culture. According to tradition, an enchanted Ivan the Terrible blinded the cathedral's architects to ensure that they would never duplicate their fantastic achievement, which still dazzles the beholder in today's Red Square. *(George Holton/Photo Researchers)*

work or property, and even the wealthiest merchants were basically dependent agents of the tsar. If a new commercial activity became important and profitable, it was often taken over by the tsar and made a royal monopoly. Royal monopolization and service obligations checked the growth of the Russian middle classes and stood in sharp contrast to developments in western Europe, where the capitalist middle classes were gaining strength and security in their private property.

Ivan the Terrible's system of autocracy and compulsory service struck foreign observers forcibly. Sigismund Herberstein, a German traveler to Russia, wrote in 1571: "All the people consider themselves to be *kholops,* that is,

slaves of their Prince." At the same time, Jean Bodin, the French thinker who did so much to develop the modern concept of sovereignty, concluded that Russia's political system was fundamentally different from those of all other European monarchies and comparable only to that of the Ottoman Empire. In both the Ottoman Empire and Russia, "the prince is become lord of the goods and persons of his subjects . . . governing them as a master of a family does his slaves."[11] The Mongol inheritance weighed heavily on Russia.

As has so often occurred in Russia, the death of an iron-fisted tyrant—in this case, Ivan the Terrible in 1584—ushered in an era of confusion and violent struggles for power. Events were particularly chaotic after Ivan's son, Theodore, died in 1598 without an heir. The years 1598 to 1613 were aptly called the "Time of Troubles."

The close relatives of the deceased tsar intrigued against and murdered one another, alternately fighting and welcoming the invading Swedes and Poles, who even occupied Moscow. Most serious for the cause of autocracy, there was a great social upheaval. Cossack bands, led by a former slave named Ivan Bolotnikov, marched northward, rallying peasants and slaughtering nobles and officials. The mass of Cossacks and peasants called for the "true tsar," who would restore their freedom of movement, reduce their heavy taxes, and lighten the yoke imposed by the landlords.

This social explosion from below brought the nobles, big and small, to their senses. They put aside their quarrels and finally crushed the Cossack rebellion at the gates of Moscow. In 1613 the nobles elected Ivan the Terrible's sixteen-year-old grandnephew, Michael Romanov, the new hereditary tsar. Then they rallied around him in the face of common internal and external threats. Michael's election was a real restoration, and his reign saw the gradual re-establishment of tsarist autocracy. (See the feature "Listening to the Past: A Foreign Traveler in Russia" on pages 590–591.) Thus while peasants were completely enserfed in 1649, Ivan's heavy military obligations on the nobility were relaxed considerably. In the long reign of Michael's successor, the pious Alexis (r. 1645–1676), this asymmetry of obligations was accentuated.

The result was a second round of mass upheaval and protest. In the later seventeenth century, the unity of the Russian Orthodox church was torn apart by a great split. The initiating event was the religious reforms introduced in 1652 by the patriarch Nikon, a dogmatic purist who wished to bring "corrupted" Russian practices of worship into line with the Greek Orthodox model. The self-serving church hierarchy quickly went along, but the intensely religious common people resisted. They saw Nikon as the Antichrist, who was stripping them of the only thing they had—the true religion of "holy Russia."

Great numbers left the church and formed illegal communities of "Old Believers," who were hunted down and persecuted. As many as twenty thousand people burned themselves alive, singing the "hallelujah" in their chants three times rather than twice, as Nikon had demanded. After the great split, the Russian masses were alienated from the established church, which became dependent on the state for its authority.

Again the Cossacks revolted against the state, which was doggedly trying to catch up with them on the frontiers and reduce them to serfdom. Under Stenka Razin they moved up the Volga River in 1670 and 1671, attracting a great army of urban poor and peasants, killing landlords and government officials, and proclaiming freedom from oppression. This rebellion to overthrow the established order was finally defeated by the government. (See the feature "Individuals in Society: Stenka Razin, Russian Rebel.") In response, the thoroughly scared upper classes tightened the screws of serfdom even further. Holding down the peasants, and thereby maintaining the tsar, became almost the principal obligation of the nobility until 1689.

The Reforms of Peter the Great

It is now possible to understand the reforms of Peter the Great (r. 1682–1725) and his kind of monarchical absolutism. Contrary to some historians' assertions, Peter was interested primarily in military power, not in some grandiose westernization plan. A giant for his time, at six feet seven inches, and possessing enormous energy and willpower, Peter was determined to redress the defeats the tsar's armies had occasionally suffered in their wars with Poland and Sweden since the time of Ivan the Terrible.

Peter was equally determined to continue the tsarist tradition of territorial expansion. After a long war, Russia had gained a large mass of Ukraine from weak and decentralized Poland in 1667 (see Map 17.3), and it completed the conquest of Siberia in the seventeenth century. After the seventeen-year-old Peter overturned the regency in 1689, the thirty-six years of his personal rule knew only one year of peace.

When Peter took control in 1689, the heart of his army still consisted of cavalry made up of boyars and service nobility. Foot soldiers played a secondary role, and the whole army served on a part-time basis. The Russian army was lagging behind the professional standing armies being formed in Europe in the seventeenth century. The core of such armies was a highly disciplined infantry that fired and refired muskets as it fearlessly advanced, until it charged with bayonets fixed. Such a large, permanent army would be enormously expensive, and thus Peter's military moves were cautious in the 1690s.

Maintaining an existing Russian alliance with Austria and Poland against the Ottoman Empire, Peter campaigned first against Turkish forts and Tartar vassals on the Black Sea. Learning from early mistakes, he conquered Azov in 1696. Fascinated by weapons and foreign technology, the confident tsar then led a group of 250 Russian officials and young nobles on an eighteen-month tour of western European capitals. Traveling unofficially as an ordinary Russian to avoid formal ceremonies, Peter

Gustaf Cederstrom: The Swedish Victory at Narva (1701)   This poignant re-creation focuses on the contrast between the Swedish officers in handsome dress uniforms and the battered Russian soldiers laying down their standards in surrender. Charles XII of Sweden scored brilliant, rapid-fire victories over Denmark, Saxony, and Russia, but he failed to make peace with Peter while he was ahead and eventually lost Sweden's holdings on the Baltic coast. *(The National Museum of Fine Arts, Stockholm)*

worked with his hands at various crafts and met with foreign kings and experts. He was particularly impressed with the growing power of the Dutch and the English and considered how Russia could profit from their example.

Returning to Russia, Peter entered into a secret alliance with Denmark and the elector of Saxony, who was also the elected king of Poland, to wage a sudden war of aggression against Sweden. Sweden was then a leading power in northern Europe. Despite the country's small population and limited agricultural resources, Swedish rulers in the seventeenth century had developed a strong absolutist state and built an excellent standing army. Expanding beyond Sweden, they held substantial terri-

tory in northern Germany, Finland, and Estonia. Yet these possessions were scattered and appeared vulnerable. Above all, Peter and his allies believed that their combined forces could win easy victories because Sweden was in the hands of a new and inexperienced king. They were mistaken.

Eighteen-year-old Charles XII (1697–1718) surprised Peter when he showed daring military genius. Defeating Denmark quickly in 1700, Charles turned on Russia. In a blinding snowstorm, his well-trained professional army attacked and routed unsuspecting Russians besieging the Swedish fortress of Narva on the Baltic coast. Peter and the survivors fled in panic to Moscow. It was, for the

Individuals in Society

Stenka Razin, Russian Rebel

Stenka Razin in Cossack dress, from a contemporary engraving. (Novosti)

The Don Cossack Stenka Razin led the largest peasant rebellion in Europe in the seventeenth century, a century rich in peasant revolt. Who was this Cossack leader who challenged Moscow, this outlaw who grew into a social revolutionary?

Descended from fugitives who fled to the turbulent southern frontier in search of freedom, Razin epitomized the old Cossack spirit of liberty and self-rule. Sharing the Cossack love of fighting and adventure, Razin also felt great sympathy for northern "have-nots" who had lost out and could not escape their fate. Why this was so remains a mystery. His family belonged to the Cossack establishment, which had settled the lower Don Valley long ago and received annual payments from the tsar in return for friendship and defense. One folk story tells of a hatred kindled by a Russian prince who unjustly hanged an older brother leading a Cossack detachment in Poland. True or not, rebel leaders like Razin have often come from comfortable backgrounds. As Paul Avrich notes, "Seldom have the oppressed themselves led the way, but rather those who have been aroused by their suffering and degradation."*

Whatever his motivation, Stenka Razin was a born leader. A striking personality with violent emotions, he was also shrewd and generous. He understood the lower classes and how to move them. The crowds called him a magician—a magician who hated the privileged and whom they felt compelled to follow.

Razin was a seasoned warrior of about forty years of age when in 1667 he led his first campaign. With an armed band of poor and rootless Cossacks, recent fugitives living upstream from the well-settled Cossacks, Razin sailed down the Volga River and seized a rich convoy of Russian merchant ships. He reportedly told survivors they were free to go or join him as free Cossacks. "I have come to fight only the boyars and the wealthy lords. As for the poor and the plain folk, I shall treat them as brothers."† Moving on to plunder Persian commerce on the Caspian Sea, Razin's forces returned home loaded with booty, which they divided equally according to Cossack custom. Gaining immense popularity and responding to threats from Moscow, Razin and his movement changed. The gang of outlaws became a rebel army.

In early 1670, Razin marched north with seven thousand Don Cossacks. His leaflets proclaimed that he was entering Russia "to establish the Cossack way, so that all men will be equal." Shrewdly blaming treacherous nobles and officials, and not the divinely appointed tsar, for the exploitation of the people, Razin's agents infiltrated the fortified towns along the Volga. Some towns resisted, but many threw open their gates, as the urban poor rose up against the "traitors and bloodsuckers." Peasants joined the revolt, killing lords and burning manor houses.

Frightened but unified, Russia's tiny elite mobilized all its strength. In late 1670, crack cavalry units of service nobility finally repulsed the swollen, ill-equipped army of the poor at Simbirsk on the upper Volga. The insurgents had to retreat. Fighting until the end, Razin was captured, hideously tortured, and chopped into pieces on the execution block. His followers and sympathizers were slaughtered with ferocious cruelty.

A fearless leader in the struggle against tsarist absolutism, Stenka Razin nurtured a myth of rebellion that would inspire future generations with dreams of freedom. He became Russia's most celebrated folk hero. He lived in story and song, an immortal superman who would someday ride out of the forest and deliver the people from oppression.

Questions for Analysis

1. What did Stenka Razin do? Why did his rebellion inspire future generations?
2. How would you interpret Razin? Was he a great hero, a common criminal, or something else?

*Paul Avrich, *Russian Rebels, 1600–1800* (New York: Schocken Books, 1972), p. 67. This account is based on Avrich's masterful study.
†Quoted ibid., p. 70.

The *features additional information and activities related to this topic.* history.college.hmco.com/students

Peter the Great in 1723   This compelling portrait by Grigory Musikiysky captures the strength and determination of the warrior tsar after more than three decades of personal rule. In his hand Peter holds the scepter, symbol of royal sovereignty, and across his breastplate is draped an ermine fur, a mark of honor. In the background are the battleships of Russia's new Baltic fleet and the famous St. Peter and St. Paul Fortress that Peter built in St. Petersburg. *(The Bridgeman Art Library)*

Russians, a grim beginning to the long and brutal Great Northern War, which lasted from 1700 to 1721.

Suffering defeat and faced with a military crisis, the energetic Peter responded with a long series of practical but far-reaching measures designed to increase state power, strengthen his armies, and gain victory. In essence, Peter's solution was to tighten up Muscovy's old service system and really make it work. Every nobleman, great or small, was once again required to serve in the army or in the civil administration—for life. Since a more modern army and government required skilled technicians and experts, Peter created schools and even universities to produce them. One of his most hated reforms required five years of compulsory education away from home for every young nobleman. Peter established an interlocking military-civilian bureaucracy with fourteen ranks, and he decreed that all had to start at the bottom and work toward the top. Some people of non-noble origins rose to high positions in this embryonic meritocracy. Drawing on his experience abroad, Peter searched out talented foreigners and placed them in his service. These measures gradually combined to make the army and government more powerful and efficient.

Peter also greatly increased the service requirements of the commoners. In the wake of the disaster at Narva, he established a regular standing army of more than 200,000 soldiers, made up mainly of peasants commanded by officers from the nobility. In addition, special forces of Cossacks and foreigners numbered more than 100,000. The departure of a drafted peasant boy was celebrated by his family and village almost like a funeral, as indeed it was, since the recruit was drafted for life. The peasantry also served with its taxes, which increased threefold during Peter's reign. Serfs were arbitrarily assigned to work in the growing number of factories and mines. Most of these industrial enterprises were directly or indirectly owned by the state, and they were worked almost exclusively for the military. In general, Russian serfdom became more oppressive under the reforming tsar.

The constant warfare of Peter's reign consumed 80 to 85 percent of all revenues and brought only modest territorial expansion. Yet the Great Northern War with Sweden was crowned in the end by Russian victory. Mobilizing superior resources and a much larger population, Peter's new war machine crushed the smaller army of Sweden's Charles XII in Ukraine at Poltava in 1709, one of the most significant battles in Russian history. The war dragged on until 1721, but Sweden never really regained the offensive, and Russia eventually annexed Estonia and much of present-day Latvia (see Map 17.3), lands that had never before been under Russian rule. Russia became the dominant power on the Baltic Sea and very much a European Great Power. If victory or defeat is the ultimate historical criterion, Peter's reforms were a success.

There were other important consequences of Peter's reign. Because of his feverish desire to use modern technology to strengthen the army, many Westerners and Western ideas flowed into Russia for the first time. A new class of educated Russians began to emerge. At the same time, vast numbers of Russians, especially among the poor and weak, hated Peter's massive changes. The split between the enserfed peasantry and the educated nobility thus widened, even though all were caught up in the demands of the sovereign.

A new idea of state interest, as distinct from the tsar's personal interests, began to take hold. Peter himself claimed time and again to be serving the common good. For the first time, a Russian tsar attached explanations to his decrees in an attempt to gain the confidence and support of the populace. Yet as before, the tsar alone decided what the common good was. Here was a source of future tension between tsar and people.

Thus Peter built on the service obligations of old Muscovy. His monarchical absolutism was truly the culmination of the long development of a unique Russian civilization. Yet the creation of a more modern army and state introduced much that was new and Western to that civilization. This development paved the way for Russia to move much closer to the European mainstream in its thought and institutions during the Enlightenment, especially under Catherine the Great.

Absolutism and Baroque Architecture

The rise of royal absolutism in eastern Europe had many consequences. Nobles served their powerful rulers in new ways, while the great inferiority of the urban middle classes and the peasants was reconfirmed. Armies became larger and more professional, while taxes rose and authoritarian traditions were strengthened. Nor was this all. Royal absolutism also interacted with baroque culture and art, baroque music and literature. Inspired in part by Louis XIV of France, the great and not-so-great rulers called on the artistic talent of the age to glorify their power and magnificence. This exaltation of despotic rule was particularly striking in the lavish masterpieces of architecture.

Palaces and Power

Baroque culture and art grew out of the revitalized Catholic church of the later sixteenth century. The papacy and the Jesuits especially encouraged an emotional, exuberant art, which appealed to the senses of churchgoers and proclaimed the confidence and power of the Catholic Reformation. The baroque style then spread throughout Europe in the seventeenth century, for dramatic baroque palaces symbolized the age of absolutist power, as soaring Gothic cathedrals had expressed the idealized spirit of the High Middle Ages.

By 1700 palace building had become a veritable obsession for the rulers of central and eastern Europe. Their baroque palaces were clearly intended to overawe the people with the monarch's strength. The great palaces were also visual declarations of equality with Louis XIV and were therefore modeled after Versailles to a greater or lesser extent. One such palace was Schönbrunn, an enormous Viennese Versailles begun in 1695 by Emperor Leopold to celebrate Austrian military victories and Habsburg might. Charles XI of Sweden, having reduced the power of the aristocracy, ordered the construction in 1693 of his Royal Palace, which dominates the center of Stockholm to this day.

Petty princes in the German lands also contributed mightily to the palace-building mania. Frederick the Great of Prussia noted that every descendant of a princely family "imagines himself to be something like Louis XIV. He builds his Versailles, has his mistresses, and maintains his army."[12] The not-very-important elector-archbishop of Mainz, the ruling prince of that city, confessed apologetically that "building is a craze which costs much, but every fool likes his own hat."[13]

In central and eastern Europe, the favorite noble servants of royalty became extremely rich and powerful, and they, too, built grandiose palaces in the capital cities. These palaces were in part an extension of the monarch, for they surpassed the buildings of less favored nobles and showed all the high road to fame and fortune. Take, for example, the palaces of Prince Eugene of Savoy, a French nobleman who became Austria's most famous military hero. It was Eugene who led the Austrian army, smashed the Turks, fought Louis XIV to a standstill, and

generally guided the triumph of absolutism in Austria. Rewarded with great wealth by his grateful royal employer, Eugene called on the leading architects of the day, J. B. Fischer von Erlach and Johann Lukas von Hildebrandt, to consecrate his glory in stone and fresco. Fischer built Eugene's Winter (or Town) Palace in Vienna, and he and Hildebrandt collaborated on the prince's Summer Palace on the city's outskirts (see accompanying illustration).

Palaces like those of Prince Eugene were magnificent examples of the baroque style. They expressed the baroque delight in bold, sweeping statements, which

Prince Eugene's Summer Palace, Vienna   The prince's summer residence featured two baroque gems, the Lower Belvedere and the lovely Upper Belvedere, completed in 1722 and shown here. The building's interior is equally stunning, with crouching giants serving as pillars and a magnificent great staircase. Art and beauty convey a feeling of immense prestige and power. *(Erich Lessing/Art Resource, NY)*

were intended to provide a dramatic emotional experience. To create this experience, baroque masters dissolved the traditional artistic frontiers: the architect permitted the painter and the artisan to cover a building's undulating surfaces with wildly colorful paintings, graceful sculptures, and fanciful carvings. Space was used in a highly original way to blend everything together in a total environment. These techniques shone in all their glory in the churches of southern Germany and in the colossal halls of royal palaces. Artistic achievement and political statement reinforced each other.

Royal Cities

Absolute monarchs and baroque architects were not content with fashioning ostentatious palaces. They remodeled existing capital cities, or even built new ones, to reflect royal magnificence and the centralization of political power. Karlsruhe, founded in 1715 as the capital city of a small German principality, is one extreme example. There broad, straight avenues radiated out from the palace so that all roads—like all power—were focused on the ruler. More typically, the monarch's architects added new urban areas alongside the old city; these areas then became the real heart of the expanding capital.

The distinctive features of these new additions were their broad avenues, their imposing government buildings, and their rigorous mathematical layout. Along these major thoroughfares nobles built elaborate baroque townhouses; stables and servants' quarters were built on the alleys behind. Wide avenues also facilitated the rapid movement of soldiers through the city to quell any disturbance (the king's planners had the needs of the military constantly in mind). Under the arcades along the avenues appeared smart and very expensive shops, the first department stores, with plate-glass windows and fancy displays.

The new avenues brought reckless speed to European cities all across the continent. Whereas everyone had walked through the narrow, twisting streets of the medieval town, the high and mighty now raced down the broad boulevards in their elegant carriages. A social gap opened between the wealthy riders and the gaping, dodging pedestrians. "Mind the carriages!" wrote one eighteenth-century observer in Paris:

Here comes the black-coated physician in his chariot, the dancing master in his coach, the fencing master in his surrey—and the Prince behind six horses at the gallop as if he were in the open country. . . . The threatening wheels of the overbearing rich drive as rapidly as ever over stones stained with the blood of their unhappy victims.[14]

Speeding carriages on broad avenues, an endless parade of power and position: here were the symbols and substance of the baroque city.

The Growth of St. Petersburg

No city illustrates better than St. Petersburg the close ties among politics, architecture, and urban development in this period. In 1700, when the Great Northern War between Russia and Sweden began, the city did not exist. There was only a small Swedish fortress on one of the waterlogged islands at the mouth of the Neva River, where it flows into the Baltic Sea. In 1702 Peter the Great's armies seized this desolate outpost. Within a year the reforming tsar had decided to build a new city there and to make it, rather than ancient Moscow, his capital.

Since the first step was to secure the Baltic coast, military construction was the main concern for the next eight years. A mighty fortress was built on Peter Island, and a port and shipyards were built across the river on the mainland as a Russian navy came into being. The land was swampy and uninhabited, the climate damp and unpleasant. But Peter cared not at all: for him the inhospitable northern marshland was a future metropolis, gloriously bearing his name.

After the decisive Russian victory at Poltava in 1709 greatly reduced the threat of Swedish armies, Peter moved into high gear. In one imperious decree after another, he ordered his people to build a city that would equal any in the world. Such a city had to be Western and baroque, just as Peter's army had to be Western and permanent. From such a new city, his "window on Europe," Peter also believed it would be easier to reform the country militarily and administratively.

These general political goals matched Peter's architectural ideas, which had been influenced by his travels in western Europe. First, Peter wanted a comfortable, "modern" city. Modernity meant broad, straight, stone-paved avenues; houses built in a uniform line and not haphazardly set back from the street; large parks; canals for drainage; stone bridges; and street lighting. Second, all building had to conform strictly to detailed architectural regulations set down by the government. Finally, each social group—the nobility, the merchants, the artisans, and so on—was to live in a certain section of town. In short, the city and its population were to conform to a carefully defined urban plan of the baroque type.

St. Petersburg, ca 1760   Rastrelli's remodeled Winter Palace, which housed the royal family until the Russian Revolution of 1917, stands on the left along the Neva River. The Navy Office with its famous golden spire and other government office buildings are nearby and across the river. Russia became a naval power and St. Petersburg a great port. *(Michael Holford)*

Peter used the traditional but reinforced methods of Russian autocracy to build his modern capital. The creation of St. Petersburg was just one of the heavy obligations he dictatorially imposed on all social groups in Russia. The peasants bore the heaviest burdens. Just as the government drafted peasants for the army, it also drafted twenty-five thousand to forty thousand men each summer to labor in St. Petersburg for three months without pay. Every ten to fifteen peasant households had to furnish one such worker each summer and then pay a special tax in order to feed that worker in St. Petersburg.

Peasants hated this forced labor in the capital, and each year one-fourth to one-third of those sent risked brutal punishment and ran away. Many peasant construction workers died each summer from hunger, sickness, and accidents. Thus beautiful St. Petersburg was built on the shoveling, carting, and paving of a mass of conscripted serfs.

Peter also drafted more privileged groups to his city, but on a permanent basis. Nobles were summarily ordered to build costly stone houses and palaces in St. Petersburg and to live in them most of the year. The more serfs a noble possessed, the bigger his dwelling had to be. Merchants and artisans were also commanded to settle and build in St. Petersburg. These nobles and merchants were then required to pay for the city's avenues, parks, canals, embankments, pilings, and bridges, all of which were very costly in terms of both money and lives because they were built on a swamp. The building of St. Petersburg was, in truth, an enormous direct tax levied on the wealthy, which in turn forced the peasantry to do most of the work. No wonder so many Russians hated Peter's new city.

Yet the tsar had his way. By the time of his death in 1725, there were at least six thousand houses and numerous impressive government buildings in St. Petersburg.

Under the remarkable women who ruled Russia throughout most of the eighteenth century, St. Petersburg blossomed fully as a majestic and well-organized city, at least in its wealthy showpiece sections. Peter's youngest daughter, the quick-witted Elizabeth (r. 1741–1762), named as her chief architect Bartolomeo Rastrelli, who had come to Russia from Italy as a boy of fifteen in 1715. Combining Italian and Russian traditions into a unique, wildly colorful St. Petersburg style, Rastrelli built many palaces for the nobility and all the larger government buildings erected during Elizabeth's reign. He also rebuilt the Winter Palace as an enormous, aqua-colored royal residence, now the Hermitage Museum. There Elizabeth established a flashy, luxury-loving, and slightly crude court, which Catherine the Great in turn made truly imperial. All the while St. Petersburg grew rapidly, and its almost 300,000 inhabitants in 1782 made it one of the world's largest cities. Peter and his successors had created out of nothing a magnificent and harmonious royal city, which unmistakably proclaimed the power of Russia's rulers and the creative potential of the absolutist state.

Triumphant absolutism interacted spectacularly with the arts. Baroque art, which had grown out of the Catholic Reformation's desire to move the faithful and exalt the true faith, admirably suited the secular aspirations of eastern European rulers. They built grandiose baroque palaces, monumental public squares, and even whole cities to glorify their power and majesty. Thus baroque art attained magnificent heights in eastern Europe, symbolizing the ideal and harmonizing with the reality of imperious royal absolutism.

Key Terms

serfdom	Junkers
hereditary subjugation	Eastern Orthodoxy
absolutism	boyard nobility
Bohemian Estates	Mongol Yoke
sultan	autocracy
millet system	service nobility
Pragmatic Sanction	Cossacks
elector of Brandenburg	baroque

Summary

From about 1400 to 1650, social and economic developments in eastern Europe increasingly diverged from those in western Europe. In the east, peasants and townspeople lost precious freedoms, while the nobility increased its power and prestige. It was within this framework of resurgent serfdom and entrenched nobility that Austrian and Prussian monarchs fashioned absolutist states in the seventeenth and early eighteenth centuries. These monarchs won absolutist control over standing armies, permanent taxes, and legislative bodies. But they did not question underlying social and economic relationships. Indeed, they enhanced the privileges of the nobility, which furnished the leading servitors for enlarged armies and growing state bureaucracies.

In Russia the social and economic trends were similar, but the timing of political absolutism was different. Mongol conquest and rule were a crucial experience, and a harsh, indigenous tsarist autocracy was firmly in place by the reign of Ivan the Terrible in the sixteenth century. More than a century later, Peter the Great succeeded in tightening up Russia's traditional absolutism and modernizing it by reforming the army, the bureaucracy, and the defense industry. In Russia and throughout eastern Europe, war and the needs of the state in time of war weighed heavily in the triumph of absolutism.

Notes

1. See L. Wolff, *Inventing Eastern Europe: The Map of Civilization on the Mind of the Enlightenment* (Stanford, Calif.: Stanford University Press, 1994).
2. D. Goffman, *The Ottoman Empire and Early Modern Europe* (Cambridge: Cambridge University Press, 2002), pp. 9–18, 83–91.
3. Quoted in F. L. Carsten, *The Origins of Prussia* (Oxford: Clarendon Press, 1954), p. 175.
4. H. Rosenberg, *Bureaucracy, Aristocracy, and Autocracy: The Prussian Experience, 1660–1815* (Boston: Beacon Press, 1966), p. 38.
5. Quoted in R. Ergang, *The Potsdam Fuhrer: Frederick William I, Father of Prussian Militarism* (New York: Octagon Books, 1972), pp. 85, 87.
6. Ibid., p. 43.
7. Quoted in R. A. Dorwart, *The Administrative Reforms of Frederick William I of Prussia* (Cambridge, Mass.: Harvard University Press, 1953), p. 226.
8. Quoted in Rosenberg, *Bureaucracy, Aristocracy, and Autocracy,* p. 40.
9. Quoted in N. V. Riasanovsky, *A History of Russia* (New York: Oxford University Press, 1963), p. 79.
10. Quoted in I. Grey, *Ivan III and the Unification of Russia* (New York: Collier Books, 1967), p. 42.
11. Both quoted in R. Pipes, *Russia Under the Old Regime* (New York: Charles Scribner's Sons, 1974), pp. 65, 85.
12. Quoted in Ergang, *The Potsdam Fuhrer,* p. 13.
13. Quoted in J. Summerson, in *The Eighteenth Century: Europe in the Age of Enlightenment,* ed. A. Cobban (New York: McGraw-Hill, 1969), p. 80.
14. Quoted in L. Mumford, *The Culture of Cities* (New York: Harcourt Brace Jovanovich, 1938), p. 97.

(continued on page 592)

Listening to the Past

A Foreign Traveler in Russia

Russia in the seventeenth century remained a remote and mysterious land for western and even central Europeans, who had few direct contacts with the tsar's dominion. Knowledge of Russia came mainly from occasional travelers who had visited Muscovy and sometimes wrote accounts of what they had seen.

The most famous of these accounts was by the German Adam Olearius (ca 1599–1671), who was sent to Moscow by the duke of Holstein on three diplomatic missions in the 1630s. These missions ultimately proved unsuccessful, but they provided Olearius with a rich store of information for his Travels in Muscovy, *from which the following excerpts are taken. Published in German in 1647 and soon translated into several languages (but not Russian), Olearius's unflattering but well-informed study played a major role in shaping European ideas about Russia.*

The government of the Russians is what political theorists call a "dominating and despotic monarchy," where the sovereign, that is, the tsar or the grand prince who has obtained the crown by right of succession, rules the entire land alone, and all the people are his subjects, and where the nobles and princes no less than the common folk—townspeople and peasants—are his serfs and slaves, whom he rules and treats as a master treats his servants. . . .

If the Russians be considered in respect to their character, customs, and way of life, they are justly to be counted among the barbarians. . . . The vice of drunkenness is so common in this nation, among people of every station, clergy and laity, high and low, men and women, old and young, that when they are seen now and then lying about in the streets, wallowing in the mud, no attention is paid to it, as something habitual. If a cart driver comes upon such a drunken pig whom he

happens to know, he shoves him onto his cart and drives him home, where he is paid his fare. No one ever refuses an opportunity to drink and to get drunk, at any time and in any place, and usually it is done with vodka. . . .

The Russians being naturally tough and born, as it were, for slavery, they must be kept under a harsh and strict yoke and must be driven to do their work with clubs and whips, which they suffer without impatience, because such is their station, and they are accustomed to it. Young and half-grown fellows sometimes come together on certain days and train themselves in fisticuffs, to accustom themselves to receiving blows, and, since habit is second nature, this makes blows given as punishment easier to bear. Each and all, they are slaves and serfs. . . .

Because of slavery and their rough and hard life, the Russians accept war readily and are well suited to it. On certain occasions, if need be, they reveal themselves as courageous and daring soldiers. . . .

Although the Russians, especially the common populace, living as slaves under a harsh yoke, can bear and endure a great deal out of love for their masters, yet if the pressure is beyond measure, then it can be said of them: "Patience, often wounded, finally turned into fury." A dangerous indignation results, turned not so much against their sovereign as against the lower authorities, especially if the people have been much oppressed by them and by their supporters and have not been protected by the higher authorities. And once they are aroused and enraged, it is not easy to appease them. Then, disregarding all dangers that may ensue, they resort to every kind of violence and behave like madmen. . . . They own little; most of them have no feather beds; they lie on cushions, straw, mats, or their clothes; they sleep on benches and, in winter, like the non-Germans [i.e., natives] in Livonia, upon the oven,

The brutality of serfdom is shown in this illustration from Olearius's *Travels in Muscovy*. *(University of Illinois Library, Champaign)*

which serves them for cooking and is flat on the top; here husband, wife, children, servants, and maids huddle together. In some houses in the countryside we saw chickens and pigs under the benches and the ovens. . . .

Russians are not used to delicate food and dainties; their daily food consists of porridge, turnips, cabbage, and cucumbers, fresh and pickled, and in Moscow mostly of big salt fish which stink badly, because of the thrifty use of salt, yet are eaten with relish. . . .

The Russians can endure extreme heat. In the bathhouse they stretch out on benches and let themselves be beaten and rubbed with bunches of birch twigs and wisps of bast (which I could not stand); and when they are hot and red all over and so exhausted that they can bear it no longer in the bathhouse, men and women rush outdoors naked and pour cold water over their bodies; in winter they even wallow in the snow and rub their skin with it as if it were soap; then they go back into the hot bathhouse. And since bathhouses are usually near rivers and brooks, they can throw themselves straight from the hot into the cold bath. . . .

Generally noble families, even the small nobility, rear their daughters in secluded chambers, keeping them hidden from outsiders; and a bridegroom is not allowed to have a look at his bride until he receives her in the bridal chamber. Therefore some happen to be deceived, being given a misshapen and sickly one instead of a fair one, and sometimes a kinswoman or even a maidservant instead of a daughter; of which there have been examples even among the highborn. No wonder therefore that often they live together like cats and dogs and that wife-beating is so common among Russians. . . .

In the Kremlin and in the city there are a great many churches, chapels, and monasteries, both within and without the city walls, over two thousand in all. This is so because every nobleman who has some fortune has a chapel built for himself, and most of them are of stone. The stone churches are round and vaulted inside. . . . They allow neither organs nor any other musical instruments in their churches, saying: Instruments that have neither souls nor life cannot praise God. . . .

In their churches there hang many bells, sometimes five or six, the largest not over two hundredweights. They ring these bells to summon people to church, and also when the priest during mass raises the chalice. In Moscow, because of the multitude of churches and chapels, there are several thousand bells, which during the divine service create such a clang and din that one unaccustomed to it listens in amazement.

Questions for Analysis

1. In what ways were all social groups in Russia similar, according to Olearius?

2. How did Olearius characterize the Russians in general? What supporting evidence did he offer for his judgment?

3. Does Olearius's account help explain Stenka Razin's rebellion? In what ways?

4. On the basis of these representative passages, why do you think Olearius's book was so popular and influential in central and western Europe?

Source: G. Vernadsky and R. T. Fisher, Jr., eds., *A Source Book for Russian History from Early Times to 1917*, vol. 1 (New Haven: Yale University Press, 1972), pp. 249–251. Copyright © 1972 by Yale University Press. Reprinted by permission.

Suggested Reading

All of the books cited in the Notes are recommended. Rosenberg remains the classic analysis of the social context of Prussian absolutism. In addition to Ergang's work, an exciting and critical biography of ramrod Frederick William I, D. McKay, *The Great Elector: Frederick William of Brandenburg-Prussia* (2001), examines the formative years of Prussian power. G. Craig, *The Politics of the Prussian Army, 1640–1945* (1964), expertly traces the great influence of the military on the Prussian state over three hundred years. A. Corvisier, *Armies and Societies in Europe, 1494–1789* (1979), places military organization in a broad social framework. A good general account is provided in D. McKay and H. Scott, *The Rise of the Great Powers, 1648–1815* (1983). J. Gagliardo, *Germany Under the Old Regime, 1600–1790* (1991), is an impressive survey of developments in all the German states and provides an excellent bibliography. M. Hughes, *Early Modern Germany, 1477–1802* (1992), is also recommended. R. J. Evans, *The Making of the Habsburg Empire, 1550–1700* (1979), is an impressive achievement. C. Ingrao, *The Habsburg Monarchy, 1618–1815* (1994), is a superior synthesis with an up-to-date bibliography. J. Stoye, *The Siege of Vienna* (1964), is a fascinating account of the last great Ottoman offensive. D. Goffman, cited in the Notes, is a superb reinterpretation of the Ottoman Empire. M. Greene, *A Shared World: Christians and Muslims in the Early Mediterranean* (2000), is a pioneering study of the two communities living together on the island of Crete. H. Inalcik and D. Quartaert, *Economic and Social History of the Ottoman Empire, 1300–1914* (1994), is an invaluable synthesis. On the Balkans, see T. Stoianovich, *Balkan Worlds: The First and Last Europe* (1994), and the innovative M. Todorova, *Imaging the Balkans* (1997). M. Pinson, ed., *The Muslims of Bosnia-Herzegovina: Their Historic Development from the Middle Ages to the Dissolution of Yugoslavia* (1993), is a good introduction.

On eastern European peasants and serfdom, D. Chirot, ed., *The Origins of Backwardness in Eastern Europe: Economics and Politics from the Middle Ages Until the Twentieth Century* (1989), is a wide-ranging introduction. W. Hagen, *Ordinary Prussians: Brandenburg Junkers and Villagers, 1500–1840* (2002), provides a fascinating and significant encounter with the people of a Prussian estate. S. Ogilve and B. Scribner, eds., *Germany: A New Economic and Social History, 1450–1800*, 2 vols. (1996), presents the fresh findings of today's scholars. T. Scott, ed., *The Peasants of Europe from the Fourteenth to the Eighteenth Centuries* (1998), examines a wide variety of regions and countries. Wolfe, cited in the Notes, argues provocatively that the French philosophes of the eighteenth century were the first to divide Europe into a backward east and a more advanced west. E. Levin, *Sex and Society in the World of the Orthodox Slavs, 900–1700* (1989), examines family history in eastern Europe. R. Mousnier, *Peasant Uprisings in Seventeenth-Century France, Russia, and China* (1970), is a classic comparative study. Another valuable comparative study, analyzing the political struggle between rulers and nobles in Poland, Hungary, Latvia, Moldavia, and Ukraine, is O. Subtelny, *Domination in Eastern Europe* (1986). Also see L. and M. Frey, *Societies in Upheaval: Insurrections in France, Hungary and Spain in the Early Eighteenth Century* (1989). J. Blum, *Lord and Peasant in Russia from the Ninth to the Nineteenth Century* (1961), provides a good look at conditions in rural Russia, and P. Avrich, *Russian Rebels, 1600–1800* (1972), treats some of the violent peasant upheavals those conditions produced. R. Hellie, *Enserfment and Military Change in Muscovy* (1971), is outstanding, as is A. Yanov's provocative *Origins of Autocracy: Ivan the Terrible in Russian History* (1981). In addition to the fine surveys by Pipes and Riasanovsky cited in the Notes, J. Billington, *The Icon and the Axe* (1970), is a stimulating history of early Russian intellectual and cultural developments, such as the great split in the church. M. Raeff, *Origins of the Russian Intelligentsia* (1966), skillfully probes the mind of the Russian nobility in the eighteenth century. James Cracraft, ed., *Peter the Great Transforms Russia,* 3d ed. (1991), groups interpretive essays by leading scholars, and B. Lincoln, *Sunlight at Midnight: St. Petersburg and the Rise of Modern Russia* (2001), captures the spirit of Peter's new northern capital. P. Buskovitch, *Peter the Great: The Struggle for Power, 1671–1725* (2001), is an outstanding, detailed biography, while B. H. Sumner, *Peter the Great and the Emergence of Russia* (1962), is still a useful brief introduction. N. Riasanovsky, *The Image of Peter the Great in Russian History and Thought* (1985), examines the tsar's place in the Russian imagination. G. Vernadsky and R. Fisher, eds., *A Source Book of Russian History from Early Times to 1917,* 3 vols. (1972), is an invaluable, highly recommended collection of documents and contemporary writings. S. Baron, ed., *The Travels of Olearius in Seventeenth-Century Russia* (1967), is also highly recommended. B. Engel, *Women in Russia, 1700–2000* (2004), is outstanding.

R. Harbison, *Reflections on the Baroque* (2001), is a well-illustrated and imaginative integration of ideas and the arts, while G. Hersey, *Architecture and Geometry in the Age of the Baroque* (2001), explores the link between architecture and scientific thinking. Also recommended on art and architecture are E. Hempel, *Baroque Art and Architecture in Central Europe* (1965), and N. Pevsner, *An Outline of European Architecture,* 6th ed. (1960). J. Cracraft has written an impressive two-volume study of the artistic and cultural transformation associated with Peter the Great, *The Petrine Revolution in Russian Architecture* (1988) and *The Petrine Revolution in Russian Imagery* (1997).

Index

Timeline   A History of Western Society: A Brief Overview

	Government	Society and Economy
3200 B.C.	Dominance of Sumerian cities in Mesopotamia, ca 3200–2340 Unification of Egypt; Archaic Period, ca 3100–2660 Old Kingdom of Egypt, ca 2660–2180 Dominance of Akkadian empire in Mesopotamia, ca 2331–2200 Middle Kingdom in Egypt, ca 2080–1640	Neolithic peoples rely on settled agriculture, while others pursue nomadic life, ca 7000–ca 3000 Development of wheeled transport in Mesopotamia, by ca 3200 Expansion of Mesopotamian trade and culture into modern Turkey, the Middle East, and Iran, ca 2600
2000 B.C.	Babylonian empire, ca 2000–1595 Hyksos invade Egypt, ca 1640–1570 Hittite Empire, ca 1600–1200 New Kingdom in Egypt, ca 1570–1075	First wave of Indo-European migrants, by 2000 Extended commerce in Egypt, by ca 2000 Horses introduced into western Asia, by ca 2000
1500 B.C.	Third Intermediate Period in Egypt, ca 1100–700 Unified Hebrew Kingdom under Saul, David, and Solomon, ca 1025–925	Use of iron increases in western Asia, by ca 1300–1100 Second wave of Indo-European migrants, by ca 1200
1000 B.C.	Hebrew Kingdom divided into Israel and Judah, 925 Assyrian Empire, ca 900–612 Phoenicians found Carthage, 813 Kingdom of Kush conquers and reunifies Egypt, 8th c. Medes conquers Persia, 710 Babylon wins independence from Assyria, 626 Dracon issues law code at Athens, 621 Cyrus the Great conquers Medes, founds Persian Empire, 550 Solon's reforms at Athens, ca 549 Persians complete conquest of ancient Near East, 521–464 Reforms of Cleisthenes in Athens, 508	Concentration of landed wealth in Greece, ca 750–600 Greek overseas expansion, ca 750–550 Beginning of coinage in western Asia, ca 640
500 B.C.	Battle of Marathon, 490 Xerxes' invasion of Greece, 480–479 Delian Confederacy, 478/7 Twelve Tables in Rome, 451/0 Valerio-Horatian laws in Rome, 449 Peloponnesian War, 431–404 Rome captures Veii, 396 Gauls sack Rome, 390 Roman expansion in Italy, 390–290 Conquests of Alexander the Great, 334–323 Punic Wars, 264–146 Reforms of the Gracchi, 133–121	Building of the Via Appia begins, 312 Growth of Hellenistic trade and cities, ca 300–100 Beginning of Roman silver coinage, 269 Growth of slavery, decline of small farmers in Rome, ca 250–100 Agrarian reforms of the Gracchi, 133–121